OXFORD HISTORY OF
MODERN EUROPE

General Editors
LORD BULLOCK *and* SIR WILLIAM DEAKIN

Oxford History of Modern Europe

THE STRUGGLE FOR MASTERY
IN EUROPE 1845–1918

By A. J. P. TAYLOR

SPAIN 1808–1939

By RAYMOND CARR

THE RUSSIAN EMPIRE 1801–1917

By HUGH SETON-WATSON

FRANCE 1849–1945

By THEODORE ZELDIN

Vol. 1: Ambition, Love and Politics
Vol. 2: Intellect, Taste and Anxiety

GERMANY
1866–1945

BY

GORDON A. CRAIG

New York
OXFORD UNIVERSITY PRESS
1978

PREFACE

Deutschland ist Hamlet! Ernst und stumm
in seinen Toren jede Nacht
geht die begrabne Freiheit um,
und winkt den Männern auf der Wacht.

FERDINAND FREILIGRATH[1]

FREILIGRATH'S poem was written in 1844, at a time when all of the expectations of political reform and constitutional progress that had been stimulated by the accession of Frederick William IV had come to nothing. It was at once an exhortation and a warning. The poet urged his people to cast a critical eye upon its own failings, to admit that the pale cast of thought had too often lamed its resolution—

Er spann zuviel gelehrten Werg,
sein bestes Tun ist eben Denken;
er stak zu lang in Wittenberg,
im Hörsaal oder in den Schenken.

Drum fehlt ihm die Entschlossenheit—

and to rouse itself for action in freedom's behalf before it was too late. But he did not seem to be very confident that his advice would be followed or that the fifth act of the play could be avoided, and his doubts were justified. While the bulk of the German people stood uncomprehending by, those who championed the cause of political liberty gave themselves over alternatively to prolonged and bootless disquisition and action that was generally ill timed and ill considered and always unsuccessful. In the end, they were powerless to avert the consequence of these delinquencies

und Fortinbras
rückt klirrend ein, das Reich zu erben.

This book tells of the reign of Fortinbras and his successors, and it is a tragic story. For that vigorous prince, who took possession of a stage that was littered with the corpses of liberal hopes, showed no inclination to revive lost causes. He soon revealed himself to be an

---

[1] 'Hamlet', in *Freiligraths Werke in einem Band*, selected and with introduction by Werner Ilberg (Berlin and Weimar, 1967), pp. 73–5. For translations of the epigraphs and other quotations in the text see Appendix.

uncompromising conservative, intent upon preserving the structures of ancient authority against all the forces of change, increasingly jealous of his own prerogatives, and, when the rights of others
appeared to threaten them, ever more willing to deny the validity of
those rights. His ascendancy in the council of nations doubtless
enhanced the self-esteem of his people, but his domestic governance
robbed it of opportunities to grow in self-reliance and to acquire the
rudiments of political education. As a result, when his immediate
successors, ill trained by their self-centred master, proved to be
irresponsible stewards of their inheritance, and when, by a combination of arrogance and lack of perspective, they brought the
anachronistic imperial structure crashing down upon their heads,
there were, to take their places, too few people who combined the
willingness to assume responsibility for building a new realm of
freedom with the practical arts necessary to solve the problems that
stood in the way of its realization. The valiant efforts of those who
tried to establish a stable republic were, to be sure, hampered by the
recurrence of old habits of vacillation and self-doubt, but their
ultimate failure was due less to these weaknesses than to their lack of
numerical strength and to the clamorous demand raised by their
fellow citizens for a new hero who could clear the proscenium of
confusion and bring back the kind of authoritative leadership that
they admired.

The new Fortinbras was waiting in the wings. But this time he was
no respecter of the past and its institutions and values, nor was he
interested in leading a troubled people back to older sureties. Driven
by demons of which those who acclaimed his accession had no
comprehension and prone to a ruthless unconditionality that would
terrify many of his subjects when it was revealed to them, the new
leader was to be the destroyer of the united nation that had been the
goal of generations of German patriots, and he was to accomplish his
work amid scenes of unimaginable carnage and bestiality in which
millions of his own people, and millions of non-Germans who had
had no part in his elevation to power, were the victims of his
grandiose ambitions.

The darkest pages in history are often the most instructive. The
brief history of united Germany, which lasted only seventy-five
years and died in the rubble of Berlin in 1945, demands the attention
of reflective men, not only for what it has to teach about the role of
fear and cupidity and obtuseness in human affairs, about the seductions of power and the consequences of political irresponsibility, and
about the apparently limitless inhumanity that man is capable of

inflicting upon his fellows, but because it also has much to say about courage and steadfastness, about devotion to the cause of liberty, and about resistance to the evils of tyranny. It is important to recall that Fortinbras never lacked for opponents, and that there were always men and women who shared the belief expressed in another of Freiligrath's poems—

> Trotz alledem und alledem,
> trotz Dummheit, List und alledem,
> wir wissen doch: die Menschlichkeit
> behält den Sieg trotz alledem[2]—

and who risked their careers and their lives to create the kind of Germany in which this could come true. What is recounted here is as much their story as that of the powers that triumphed over them.

---

[2] 'Trotz alledem', ibid., pp. 127–8. This poem, based on Burns's 'For a' that and a' that', was quoted by Karl Liebknecht on the day before he was murdered in January 1919. See ibid., p. 18.

CONTENTS

I. THE UNIFICATION OF GERMANY, 1866–1871   1

    I. Ending the War with Austria   3

    II. The Indemnity Law and the Settlement of the Prussian Constitutional Conflict   7

    III. The North German Confederation, the Problem of the Southern States, and Relations with France, 1866–1869   11

    IV. The Hohenzollern Candidacy in Spain and the Onset of War with France   22

    V. Politics and War, 1870–1871: Civil–Military Relations, War Aims, and the Proclamation of the Empire   27

    VI. Reactions to Victory   34

II. THE INSTITUTIONAL STRUCTURE OF THE EMPIRE   38

    I. The National Executive and the Rights of the Separate States   39

    II. Limitations on Popular and Parliamentary Power   43

    III. Crown, Army, and Parliament   49

    IV. The Powers and Weaknesses of the Reich Chancellor   54

    V. Symbols of Nationhood and the Problems of National Identity   55

III. THE CONSOLIDATION OF THE EMPIRE: POLITICS AND ECONOMICS, 1871–1879   61

    I. The Ascendancy of the National Liberals, 1871–1873   62

    II. Bismarck, the National Liberals, and the Attack upon Roman Catholicism   69

    III. The Gründerzeit, the Crash of 1873, and the Revival of Anti-Semitism   78

    IV. Pressure Groups, Tariffs, and Political Realignment, 1873–1879   85

    V. Economic and Political Results   98

IV. IDEOLOGY AND INTEREST: THE LIMITATIONS OF DIPLOMACY, 1871–1890   101

    I. Conservative Solidarity and the War Scare of 1875   103

    II. Near Eastern Crisis, Congress of Berlin, and the Origins of Bismarck's System of Alliances, 1875–1882   110

III. Colonial Agitation and the Foundation of the
       Overseas Empire   116

IV. Strains in the Alliance System: Bulgarian Affairs
       and Army Interference, 1885–1888   124

V. The Foreign Ministry and the Diplomatic Service
       under Bismarck   134

V. THE CAMPAIGN AGAINST SOCIAL DEMOCRACY
   AND BISMARCK'S FALL, 1879–1890   140

   I. The Law of 1878 and Socialist Tactics of Resistance   144

   II. Social Insurance Legislation, Christian Socialism,
        Anti-Semitism, and the Elections of 1881   150

   III. The Puttkamer Era in Prussia: Changes in
         Bureaucracy and Army   157

   IV. The Succession Question and the Kartell, 1884–1887   164

   V. Socialist Law, *Coup d'État* Politics, and the
        Dismissal of the Chancellor   171

   VI. Reactions   178

VI. RELIGION, EDUCATION, AND THE ARTS   180

   I. The Established Churches   181

   II. Elementary and Secondary Education   186

   III. The Universities   192

   IV. Professors, Students, and Academic Freedom   198

   V. Women   207

   VI. The Artist and Society: Inwardness, Alienation,
         and the Apocalyptic Vision   213

VII. THE NEW COURSE AND THE DETERIORATION
     OF GERMANY'S FOREIGN POSITION, 1890–1897   224

   I. William II   225

   II. The Break with Russia and its Consequences   230

   III. Meddle and Muddle: Congo, Samoa, Shimoneseki,
         Transvaal   239

   IV. Public Opinion and Foreign Policy   247

VIII. POLITICAL PARTIES, INTEREST GROUPS, AND
      THE FAILURE OF THE REICHSTAG, 1890–1914   251

   I. Caprivi and the Decline of Governmental Authority   252

   II. Hohenlohe and the Working Class: The Subversion
        and Penitentiary Bills, 1894–1900   261

   III. The Social Democratic Party: Trade-Unionism and
         Revisionism   266

IV. Bülow and the Reichstag: Sammlungspolitik, Financial Problems, and the *Daily Telegraph* Affair, 1900–1909   272

V. Bethmann Hollweg and the Stalemate of the Party System, 1909–1914   286

IX. WELTPOLITIK, NAVALISM, AND THE COMING OF THE WAR, 1897–1914   302

    I. Tirpitz's Naval Programme and Relations with Great Britain   303

    II. Schlieffen and Moltke: Strategy and Decision-Making   314

    III. Bethmann Hollweg, the Arms Race, and the Crisis of 1914   324

    IV. Responsibility   337

X. THE GREAT WAR, 1914–1918   339

    I. Operations, Diplomacy, Economy, 1914–1915   342

    II. War Aims: the Expansionist Groups and Bethmann Hollweg   358

    III. The Ascendancy of Hindenburg and Ludendorff and Bethmann's Dismissal, 1916–1917   368

    IV. The Last Phase   386

    V. Responsibility for the Defeat   395

XI. FROM KIEL TO KAPP: THE ABORTED REVOLUTION, 1918–1920   396

    I. The End of the Monarchy   396

    II. The Suppression of the Extreme Left   402

    III. The Constitution, the Civil Service, the Judiciary, and the Educational System   415

    IV. The Versailles Treaty and the Kapp Putsch   424

    V. The Elections of June 1920   432

XII. REPARATIONS, INFLATION, AND THE CRISIS OF 1923   434

    I. From the Spa Conference to the French Occupation of the Ruhr   435

    II. Inflation Days: Economic and Social Consequences   448

    III. Stresemann as Chancellor and the Crises in Dresden, Hamburg, and Munich   456

    IV. Stabilization   467

XIII. WEIMAR CULTURE   469

    I. The Modern Spirit: the Experimental Theatre, the Bauhaus, and the New Music   470

II. Manners and Morals 476

III. Intellectuals and the Republic: Expressionists and
New Objectivists 479

IV. Right-Wing Intellectuals 486

V. Popular Entertainment: Film, Radio, Sport 495

XIV. PARTY POLITICS AND FOREIGN POLICY, 1924–1930 498

I. Parties, Coalitions, and Cabinet-Making 499

II. Stresemann's Foreign Successes and their Cost 511

III. The Müller Cabinet and the Crisis of Parliamentary
Democracy 524

XV. THE END OF WEIMAR 534

I. The Brüning Government and the Elections of
September 1930 534

II. National Socialism: the Leader and the Party 543

III. The Search for Diplomatic Success and
Brüning's Fall 553

IV. The Papen Government 560

V. The Failure of Schleicher's Grand Design 565

XVI. THE NAZI DICTATORSHIP: THE INSTRUMENTS
OF POWER 569

I. Consolidation: Reichstag Fire and Enabling Act 571

II. *Gleichschaltung* 578

III. Party and State: Duplication, Disharmony, and the SS 590

XVII. THE NAZI REVOLUTION: ECONOMIC AND
SOCIAL DEVELOPMENTS 602

I. Restoring the Economy: Achievements and Problems,
1933–1936 603

II. The Four Year Plan, 1936–1939 612

III. National Socialism and the Working Class 618

IV. Women and National Socialism 627

V. The Expropriation of the Jews 631

VI. Towards the Final Solution 636

XVIII. CULTURAL DECLINE AND POLITICAL
RESISTANCE 638

I. Intellectuals and National Socialism 639

II. Cultural Purges, Official Art, and the Film 645

III. The Press, the Universities, and the Schools 657

IV. The Resistance Movement 663

XIX. HITLER AND EUROPE: FOREIGN POLICY,
1933–1939 673

    I. The Vulnerable Years, 1933–1934 678

    II. Saturday Surprises, the Rhineland *Coup*, the Axis,
and the Anti-Comintern Pact, 1935–1937 684

    III. The Offensive: Austria and Czechoslovakia, 1938–1939 697

    IV. The Nazi–Soviet Pact and the Coming of the War 708

XX. HITLER'S WAR, 1939–1945 714

    I. The Years of Victory, 1939–1941 715

    II. The Home Front: Economic Mobilization, Public
Opinion, Propaganda 732

    III. The New Order in Europe: Occupation, Exploitation,
Resettlement, and the Final Solution 740

    IV. El Alamein, Stalingrad, Normandy 751

    V. The Destruction of the Third Reich 758

    VI. Hitler's Revolution and the German Future 762

APPENDIX: TRANSLATIONS OF THE EPIGRAPHS AND OTHER
QUOTATIONS IN THE TEXT 765

LIST OF BOOKS AND ARTICLES CITED 774

INDEX 811

I
The Unification of Germany
1866–1871

> Ei, das klang wie Donner.
> Und war's nicht Donner, waren es Kanonen.
> Missunde, Düppel. Hurra, weiter, weiter:
> Nußschalen schwimmen auf dem Alsensunde,
> Hin über Lipa stürmen die Geschwader,
> Ein Knäul von Freund und Feind. Da seht ihn selber,
> Der mit dem Helm ist's und dem Schwefelkragen.
> Und Spichern, Wörth und Sedan. Weiter, weiter,
> Und durch Triumphstor triumphierend führt er
> All Deutschland in das knirschende Paris. . .
>
> THEODOR FONTANE (1885)[1]

> Schwarz, weiß und rot! um *ein* Panier
> vereinigt stehen Süd und Norden;
> du bist im ruhmgekrönten Morden
> das erste Land der Welt geworden:
> Germania, mir graut vor dir!
>
> GEORG HERWEGH (1871)[2]

Is it a mistake to begin with Bismarck? So much is written these days, and so insistently, about the primary importance of economic and social forces in history[3] that one runs the risk of being considered old-fashioned if one gives too much prominence to personality. Yet it is certainly unnecessary to apologize for introducing Bismarck's name at the outset. If he had never risen to the top in Prussian politics, the unification of Germany would probably have taken place anyway, but surely not at the same time or in quite the same way as it did. Whatever may be said about the movement of economic forces, there is no burking the fact that the decision concerning the form unification would take was made, not in the area of

---

[1] 'Zeus in Mission', in Theodor Fontane, *Sämtliche Werke* (Munich, 1959 ff.), xx. 271–2.

[2] 'Epilog zum Kriege', in Georg Herwegh, *Morgenruf: Ausgewählte Gedichte* (Leipzig, 1969), p. 130.

[3] See e.g. the important book by Helmut Böhme, *Deutschlands Weg zur Großmacht: Studien zum Verhältnis von Wirtschaft und Staat während der Reichsgründungszeit 1848–81* (Cologne, 1966).

economic and commercial policy, but on the battlefield of König-grätz on 3 July 1866;[4] and it would be idle to deny that when the broken fragments of Benedek's army retreated under the cover of their artillery to the banks of the Elbe on that dark afternoon, they were registering the triumph of Bismarck's policy. It had been he who had possessed the temerity to break with the traditions of Prussian diplomacy and to choose an anti-Austrian policy as the means of dividing the parliamentary opposition that was threatening to paralyse the Prussian Government when he came to power in September 1862; and he had charted the strategy that had jockeyed the Austrian Government into straits in which it felt compelled to assume the responsibility for beginning the war despite the fact that its political and military resources made its chances of winning doubtful. Had the Prussian army not been as good as Bismarck believed it to be, he would have been a dead man before the day of battle was over—at least, he had told the British ambassador that this would be so.[5] But he had not been mistaken in this fundamental judgement, and the victory of the army was therefore also his.

As the Minister President rode through the fields of dead and wounded at the end of the day's fighting, however, he felt depressed rather than elated; and his mood was not lightened by discovering, when he reached Horitz, where the Prussian staff was bivouacked, that no quarters had been prepared for him and that he would have to fend for himself. After a series of misadventures, he took shelter under the colonnade of the market-place, where he dozed fitfully on a carriage cushion until the Duke of Mecklenburg took pity on him and invited him to share his quarters.[6] It was a miserable ending to a day of triumph, and it is not unlikely that, as he shivered in the rain, he ruminated over what lay ahead and reflected unhappily that in politics success creates almost as many problems as failure.

He knew all too well that, as soon as the new day dawned, he would have more than enough tangled matters to deal with. There was, first, the problem of liquidating the war, that is of persuading his own soldiers that, since the political objective of the conflict had been gained, there was no point in continuing their operations and that peace must be made with Austria and its German allies. Given

---

[4] Lothar Gall, 'Staat und Wirtschaft in der Reichsgründungszeit', *Historische Zeitschrift*, 209 (1969), 621–2.

[5] Lord Augustus Loftus, *Diplomatic Reminiscences*, 2nd Ser. (2 vols., London, 1894), i. 60. See also R. von Keudell, *Fürst und Fürstin Bismarck* (Leipzig, 1901), pp. 292 f.

[6] Moritz Busch, *Tagebuchblätter* (2 vols., Leipzig, 1899), ii. 80; Werner Richter, *Bismarck* (Frankfurt-on-Main, 1962), p. 470.

the present mood of the army commanders, this did not promise to be easy, the more so because of the exaggerated view that some of the soldiers took of the territorial demands that Prussia was now entitled to make, a matter in which Bismarck knew foreign Powers could not be expected to be disinterested. Second, there was the necessity of using the military victory to terminate the dispute with the liberal opposition in the Prussian Chamber, which had since the beginning of the decade opposed the policy of the Crown and sought to enhance the power of Parliament at the expense of the royal prerogative.[7] The liberals would have to be persuaded, gently but firmly, that a settlement now would have mutual advantages, and—what might prove to be more difficult—the King would have to be persuaded to accept something short of an abject liberal surrender. Third, and most complicated, was the problem of the future shape of Germany. In the weeks leading up to the outbreak of the war, Bismarck had identified the Prussian cause with that of German unity, and on 10 June he had seemed to make it clear that he defined this as meaning the union of all Germany except Austria.[8] He could not back away from that position now without sacrificing the support of those liberals and nationalists who had been attracted by it. If, therefore, as turned out to be true, the realities of German and international politics made it necessary to postpone the immediate satisfaction of national hopes, the post-war reorganization of Germany must nevertheless contain within itself the promise of satisfaction in a reasonable time. This meant that Bismarck would have to devise a strategical plan for removing the remaining obstacles to German unification, the chief of which were south German particularism and the not unnatural opposition of France.

I

The most pressing of these questions, and the one upon which the solution of all the others depended, was the military one. Inflamed by their triumph on the heights of Chlum, the gallopers in the armies of Frederick Charles and the Crown Prince panted after new laurels and wanted to press on across the Elbe to the gates of Vienna. The thought of a triumphal entrance into the Austrian capital was not the only motivation at work among those who felt this way. Moltke's staff had been impressed by Benedek's success in saving 180,000 of

[7] On the origins and development of this conflict, see Gordon A. Craig, *The Politics of the Prussian Army, 1640–1945* (Oxford, 1955), Ch. 4.

[8] Otto Pflanze, *Bismarck and the Development of Germany: The Period of Unification, 1815–71* (Princeton, 1963), pp. 298, 324–5, 367–9.

his troops from the stricken field and thought it not unlikely that the Austrians would regroup and try again.[9] Others at royal headquarters had more materialistic reasons for pressing on, believing that Austria had to be smashed flat so that Prussia could exact extensive annexations that might include areas like Reichenberg, Karlsbad, and the Egertal.

All of this appalled Bismarck, who knew that needless prolongation of the operations or excessive war claims would jeopardize what had been won at Königgrätz. On 9 July he wrote to his wife:

If we are not excessive in our demands and do not believe that we have conquered the world, we will attain a peace that is worth our effort. But we are just as quickly intoxicated as we are plunged into dejection, and I have the thankless task of pouring water into the bubbling wine and making it clear that we do not live alone in Europe but with three other Powers that hate and envy us.[10]

Trying to persuade the soldiers of this was a wearying business, for even such a normally sensible person as Moltke, the Chief of the General Staff, seemed quite ready to run the risk of a war with France in order to pursue his plan for crossing the river.[11] The vigour and sarcasm with which the Minister President pressed his case[12] merely aroused a resentment of what the soldiers regarded as civilian meddling in the military sphere that persisted for years and caused Bismarck many difficulties during the war of 1870. Nevertheless, he stuck to his guns. The debate reached its critical point at Czernahora in mid-July when the French envoy at royal headquarters informed Bismarck that Napoleon III, who had earlier in the month proposed an armistice and peace talks, had now persuaded the Austrian Government to accept the outlines of a settlement that would provide for the exclusion of Austria from Germany, the formation of a north German federation under Prussian leadership, and the continued independence of the states of southern Germany. The French representative made it clear that the Emperor expected Prussia to accept these terms and to agree to an immediate cessation of hostilities for a period of five days.

[9] Anneliese Klein-Wuttig, *Politik und Kriegführung in den deutschen Einigungskriegen* (Berlin, 1934), pp. 74–6.

[10] Otto von Bismarck, *Briefe an seine Braut und Gattin*, ed. Fürst Herbert Bismarck (Stuttgart, 1900), p. 572.

[11] Generalfeldmarschall Helmuth J. L. Graf von Moltke, *Militärische Werke* (Berlin, 1892–1912), Gruppe 1: *Militärische Korrespondenz*, Teil 2 (1866), no. 329; Max Jähns, *Feldmarschall Moltke* (new edn., Berlin, 1894), pp. 437 ff.

[12] See e.g. Keudell, *Fürst und Fürstin Bismarck*, p. 297; and, in general, Hermann Gackenholz, 'Der Kriegsrat von Czernahora', *Historische Vierteljahrsschrift,* xxvi (1931).

For Bismarck this intelligence was embarrassing because it included no mention of annexations, an omission which he angrily and unjustly blamed upon faulty negotiation on the part of his ambassador in Paris, Robert von der Goltz. The risk of French military intervention if he refused, however, seemed to him greater than the risk of winning nothing if he accepted, and, instructing Goltz to clarify the territorial question as quickly as possible, he urged the King to accept the armistice proposal. The sovereign and his staff were outraged, and it seems likely that it was only the argument of von Roon, the War Minister, that there were not enough supplies on hand to support the projected river crossing that persuaded them grudgingly to give way.[13]

The Prussian acceptance of the armistice and of the outlines of the peace settlement did not, however, end the civil–military dispute, nor did the fact that Napoleon III proved to be generous in the matter of Prussian annexations. On 22 July Goltz telegraphed that the Emperor would not object to Prussia's acquiring as many as four million new subjects in northern Germany, provided the King of Saxony, whose army had fought valiantly on the Austrian side in the war, should not lose his possessions. To Bismarck this seemed reasonable. He had no hankering after acquisitions in Bohemia or other gains at Austria's expense that would leave a desire for revenge in the Hofburg. Who could say, after all, when Prussia might wish to renew the Austrian alliance? He had already agreed not to make territorial demands of the south German states, and he was not sorry to have an excuse for sparing Saxony as well. He had a private list of preferred annexations, which included Electoral Hesse, the duchy of Nassau, the free city of Frankfurt, the duchies of Schleswig and Holstein, and the Kingdom of Hanover, and he felt that the absorption of these would cause enough problems for Prussia without asking for more.

The King had a different view. He believed that Powers that lose wars should suffer in tangible ways, and he saw no reason why this rule should be relaxed for the sake of Emperor Francis Joseph and King John of Saxony. Bismarck's offerings, he thought, would leave the soldiers feeling that they had not been sufficiently rewarded for their sacrifices, and he put up such formidable resistance to them that

---

[13] On all this, see Bismarck, *Die gesammelten Werke* (1st edn., 15 vols., Berlin, 1924 ff.), xv. 271 ff. (hereafter cited as *G.W.*); Hermann Oncken, *Die Rheinpolitik Kaiser Napoleons III von 1863 bis 1870 und der Ursprung des Krieges von 1870–71* (3 vols., Stuttgart, 1926), i. 351 ff.; Herbert Rothfritz, *Die Politik des preußischen Botschafters Grafen Robert von der Goltz in Paris 1863–9* (Berlin, 1934), pp. 89 ff.

his Minister President, emotionally exhausted by the strain of keeping a highly volatile situation under control, was driven to breaking-point and, according to his memoirs, to the thought of suicide.[14] The fact that the Crown Prince came down on Bismarck's side finally brought the King round, but he gave in with bad grace. 'If what the army and the country are justified in expecting,' he wrote angrily on the margin of a memorandum from the Minister President, 'that is, a heavy war indemnity from Austria or an acquisition of land sufficient to impress the eye—cannot be obtained from the vanquished without endangering our principal objective, then the victor at the gates of Vienna must bite into this sour apple and leave to posterity the judgement of its behaviour.'[15]

Graceful or not, this cleared the way for the settlement. On 26 July the preliminary terms, embodying the agreements reached in the secret negotiations between the Prussian and Austrian governments and Napoleon III, were initialled at Nikolsburg, and on 23 August, at Prague, they became final.

Although all of the defeated Powers had to pay indemnities to Prussia, Austria lost no territory, and of the states allied with her in the recent war Baden, Württemberg, Bavaria, and Saxony were also left intact.[16] Electoral Hesse and Hanover were annexed outright—an action that affronted conservative opinion and led Tsar Alexander of Russia to complain to King William that 'the monarchical principle [had] suffered a severe shock'[17]—and so was a small part of Hesse-Darmstadt. While ostensibly yielding to Napoleon's wishes with respect to the states south of the River Main, and leaving them their independence, Bismarck had no intention of permitting that independence to be used against Prussia or allowing the three southern states to become satellites of France or of a resurgent Austria. During the peace negotiations with the governments of Baden, Württemberg, and Bavaria, he insisted, therefore, on inserting into the treaties a clause providing that, in time of war, their railway systems and military establishments should pass under Prussian control. The Badenese and the Württemberger raised no objections, but the Bavarians were more resistant, and Bismarck had to threaten them with punitive financial and territorial exactions before

---

[14] See Bismarck, G.W. xv. 277–9; Kaiser Friedrich III, *Tagebücher von 1848–66*, ed. H. O. Meisner (Leipzig, 1929), pp. 470–5.

[15] Bismarck, G.W. vi. 81.

[16] Bavaria lost a small strip of land that Prussia desired for a railway connection.

[17] Bismarck, G.W. xv, 278–9; vii. 147.

they gave way.[18] As a result, Prussia and the southern states were bound together by formal offensive–defensive alliances that provided for mutual assistance in the case of external attack upon any one of them. Before the constitution of the North German Confederation had been drafted and accepted, Bismarck had taken steps to support it with bridges to the south.[19]

II

On the day after Königgrätz the Crown Prince of Prussia, whose relations with Bismarck had often been troubled, had a long talk with the Minister President at royal headquarters in Horitz and was relieved to learn that Bismarck agreed with his view that the time was now ripe for a settlement of the constitutional crisis in Prussia.[20] Like his liberal friends, Frederick William had feared that the self-willed minister, who was wont to jeer at what he called the Chamber-celebrities in Berlin, might decide in the flush of victory to complete their discomfiture by tearing up the constitution of 1850 and instituting a regime of naked absolutism.

The liberals always had difficulty in understanding the working of Bismarck's mind, but there was little excuse for their persisting in regarding him as a primitive *Krautjunker* whose views were indistinguishable from those of Edwin von Manteuffel. He had, after all, begun his term as Minister President in September 1862 by specifically repudiating Manteuffel's belief that the only way to deal with the recalcitrant Chamber was to turn guns upon it. He had tried instead to reach a compromise with the opposition,[21] and only when it failed had he embarked upon the policy of defying the budgetary restrictions with which the parliamentary majority sought to hamper royal policy. That defiance had been effective, and the success of Bismarck's foreign policy had discomfited and dismayed the liberals. But he was too much of a realist to believe that rubbing in their defeat would be a profitable procedure. There was, on the other hand, every reason to investigate the possibility of a working arrangement with his opponents.

This was all the more so because many of them could hardly be described as opponents any longer. As early as the first Prussian

---

[18] Gustav Roloff, 'Bismarcks Friedensschlüsse mit den Süddeutschen 1866', *Historische Zeitschrift*, 146 (1932), 1–70.

[19] Pflanze, *Bismarck*, p. 371.

[20] *Denkwürdigkeiten des Generals und Admirals Albrecht von Stosch*, ed. Ulrich von Stosch (Stuttgart, 1904), p. 94.

[21] Friedrich III, *Tagebücher*, p. 505; F. Löwenthal, *Der preußische Verfassungsstreit 1862–6* (Altenburg, 1914), pp. 116–21.

military victories at Düppel and Alsen in 1864, there were signs that Bismarck had been correct in believing that a vigorous foreign policy that promised to solve the national question would appeal even to many of those who had been most vehement in their opposition to the reform and expansion of the army; and by the spring of 1866 the strength of this appeal was perceptible in the gradual swing of liberal journals like the *Preußische Jahrbücher*, the *Grenzboten*, and the *Kölnische Zeitung* to support of the government's policy.[22] After the victory in Bohemia the conversions became legion, although some of those who changed their colours were honest enough to admit that they did so almost against their will. Viewing the victory parade of the first units to return to Berlin, Gustav Mevissen wrote:

I cannot recover from the impression of this hour. I am in truth no devotee of Mars; the goddess of beauty and the mother of the graces appeal more to my understanding than the powerful god of war, but the trophies of war exercise a magic spell even upon the child of peace. Involuntarily the look is fettered, and the spirit dwells with those countless masses who are hailing the god of the moment, Success.[23]

In any case, politicians dare not be indifferent to popular currents, and the liberals were given good reason to adjust their views by the results of the elections of 3 July 1866. Although the ballots were cast before the news of the victory at Königgrätz had been received, the count showed a pronounced swing to the right, the conservatives winning 142 seats in the Chamber, a gain of 114, the left centre winning 65 for a loss of 45, and the Fortschrittspartei, which had carried the fight against the Crown since 1860, falling from 143 seats to 83.[24] In the wake of these disastrous results, the bandwagon effect became apparent in liberal ranks, and Bismarck was shrewd enough to detect and to wish to exploit it. This desire was doubtless animated by the belief that a conciliatory attitude towards liberal opinion might help to alleviate feelings of resentment held by people who, in accordance with the provisions of the Peace of Prague, were now becoming Prussian subjects against their will, or at least without being consulted about the matter; and it was certainly influenced by his awareness that, if Prussia was now to pursue a policy that aimed at completing the unification of Germany, the support of the liberals would be more reliable than that of the conservatives, among whom Prussian particularism was still strong.

---

[22] H. Ritter von Srbik, *Deutsche Einheit* (4 vols., Munich, 1935–42), iv. 347 ff., 429.

[23] Johannes Ziekursch, *Politische Geschichte des neuen deutschen Kaiserreiches* (3 vols., Frankfurt-on-Main, 1925 ff.), i. 189.

[24] Ibid. i. 192.

Bismarck had told the Crown Prince that he would propose a settlement at the opening of the new Landtag,[25] and he was as good as his word. The address from the throne extended an olive branch to the parliamentary opposition by admitting, in effect, that during the years of the budgetless regime since 1862 the government had been acting unconstitutionally, although its actions had been in accordance with the precepts of duty and conscience and had been necessary for the security of the state. It requested an indemnity in the form of a retroactive grant of the funds expended.

The admission of constitutional impropriety, even although it was unaccompanied by any assurances with respect to the future, had outraged conservative opinion when it first became known that Bismarck intended to make it. In Berlin members of the Ministry of State were shocked and argued strenuously against the proposal;[26] the *Kreuzzeitung* trumpeted rage and despair; and the reactionary Hans von Kleist-Retzow tried desperately to organize a campaign among his fellows to baulk the Minister President's designs, eliciting from that statesman the disgusted comment that it was easier to cope with enemies than with friends, particularly with those 'who don't have enough to do [and] see no further than their own noses'.[27] Had the King been in the capital rather than in the theatre of war, he might have been influenced by this Tory clamour. As it was, he played his role in Bismarck's scenario, stepping out of character only once, when, after the Chamber's reply to the address from the throne, he grumbled that he had had to act as he had done and would do so again if the occasion arose. His ministers hastily declared that this was off the record and had no significance.[28]

The debate over the Indemnity Bill was protracted because the liberals of the left, led by Max von Forckenbeck and Johann Jacoby and Rudolf Virchow and Rudolf von Gneist, fought a last-ditch battle in behalf of the ideals that had inspired the Progressive party (Fortschrittspartei) since 1860, parliamentary responsibility and the rule of law. What had happened in the plains of Bohemia, they insisted, had not altered the issues at stake, and to vote the indemnity without an assurance that ministers would in the future be responsible to Parliament would be a palpable capitulation. The argument

[25] Stosch, *Denkwürdigkeiten*, p. 94.

[26] Gerhard Ritter, 'Die Entstehung der Indemnitätsvorlage von 1866', *Historische Zeitschrift*, 114 (1915), 17 ff.

[27] Bismarck, *G.W.* xiv. 720, cited in Pflanze, *Bismarck*, p. 333. See also Löwenthal, *Verfassungsstreit*, pp. 292–3.

[28] Kurt Kaminski, *Verfassung und Verfassungskonflikt in Preußen 1862–66* (Königsberg and Berlin, 1938), p. 110.

was unanswerable, but it had little effect upon the result of the debate, which ended on 3 September with a resounding approval of the bill by a vote of 230 to 75. Wilhelm Liebknecht, who was to prove himself a stauncher opponent of the Minister President than those liberals who swelled the majority, wrote that the result was a personal triumph for Bismarck and added sardonically that 'the angel of darkness has become the angel of light, before whom the people lie in the dust and adore. The stigma of violation of the constitution has been washed from his brow and in its place the halo of glory rings his laureled head.'[29]

Apart from liquidating the constitutional struggle and thus ending the stalemate in Prussian politics to the advantage of the Crown, the indemnity debate precipitated changes in the balance of political forces that were important for the evolution of Prussia's policy in the subsequent period. Both liberalism and conservatism were profoundly affected by the issues posed by the bill. The bulk of the liberal party now gave up the attempt to reconcile the demands of freedom and the requirements of power. Speaking for the moderates, Karl Twesten made no bones about the matter. 'No one may be criticized', he said, 'for giving precedence to the issue of power at this time and maintaining that the issues of freedom can wait, provided that nothing happens that can permanently prejudice them.'[30] When the left pointed out that this was a proviso too big for easy swallowing, the moderates were undeterred in their course, which, in fact, became a secession from the Progressive party. After the creation of the North German Confederation, the secessionists were to join with the liberals of the non-Prussian lands to form, under the leadership of the Hanoverians Rudolf von Bennigsen and Johannes Miquel, the National Liberal party that was to provide Bismarck with reliable and enthusiastic backing for his German policy. What was left of the Progressive party carried on the fight for democratic government but with greatly diminished hope of significant success.

The Indemnity Bill also brought to the surface the latent division in the conservative camp. The unorthodox ways of their fellow *Junker* had long worried the more reactionary members of the party (as early as 1855 Leopold von Gerlach found it a suspicious circumstance that the young diplomat should visit Paris and have an interview with Louis Napoleon), and his decision to go to war with Austria had seemed to many of them a flagrant betrayal of ideological principle. The indemnity rubbed salt in the wounds inflicted by

[29] Rudolf Olden, *History of Liberty in Germany* (London, 1946), p. 106.
[30] Pflanze, *Bismarck*, p. 330.

this, for not only did it deprive them of their hope of finally humiliating the liberals and abolishing western constitutional forms but it amounted to a confession that there were limits to the royal prerogative. In consequence, the feudal gentry of East Prussia, Pomerania, and Brandenburg became increasingly critical of Bismarck's policy and increasingly fearful lest it injure Prussian interest, which they defined in the most parochial terms.

But not all conservatives had their eyes turned to the past and their horizons limited by the blinkers of specific Prussianism. In the Rhineland and Silesia, and in some of the annexed areas as well, there were people of conservative views who nevertheless thought in terms of progress and expansion and of the needs and opportunities of industry and commerce. By temperament and interest, these people, among whom were a high percentage of state officials, soldiers, professors, and business men, were enthusiastic supporters of Bismarck's kind of conservatism, which seemed to them to combine authoritarianism and modernity. Under the leadership of Eduard Count von Bethusy-Huc, the Free Conservative party was organized in the autumn of 1866 to represent the views of those who felt this way; and in the subsequent period, although it was never a party that commanded much popular strength, it gave Bismarck undeviating support and provided some of his most dedicated officials and associates.[31]

III

As a result of the annexations, Prussia after 1866 comprised four-fifths of the population and the greater part of the territory north of the River Main. But northern Germany included other sovereignties besides the great northern Power: Saxony and Hesse-Darmstadt, Braunschweig, Oldenburg, Saxe-Weimar and Coburg, the free cities of Hamburg, Lübeck, and Bremen, the feudal and backward Mecklenburgs, and the tiny princedoms of Thuringia and Meiningen. After the settlement of the constitutional question in Prussia, Bismarck's next order of business was to weld these disparate territories into the federation that was provided for in the post-war discussions with the Austrian and French governments and the terms of the Peace of Prague.

The process had indeed begun even before the war was over, for in June those of the lesser states that had not opted for Austria were

---

[31] On the origins of the Free Conservative party, see the unpublished doctoral dissertation of Fredric Aandahl, 'The Rise of German Free Conservatism' (Princeton Univ. 1955).

compelled to place their military forces at Prussia's disposal and to agree, in effect, to join a political union with that Power. After the cessation of hostilities, under veiled threat of annexation, they were pressured into agreeing to co-operate with a popularly elected Parliament in the establishment of a federal constitution. Their assent in effect created the North German Confederation, into which Saxony and Hesse-Darmstadt, which narrowly escaped annexation because of their association with Austria in the war, were incorporated by the peace treaties that the Prussian Government imposed on them in September and October.

The drafting of the constitution had meanwhile begun, and after six months of work by various hands it eventuated in December 1866 in a document that was first submitted to the various governments for their acceptance and then, in amended form, to a constituent Reichstag that was elected in February 1867. Debate over its provisions lasted for five weeks, and on 16 April 1867 the constitution was accepted by a vote of 230 to 53, the negative votes being recorded by the Progressives, the Polish and Catholic factions, and the Socialist August Bebel, who was beginning a parliamentary career that was to extend almost to the eve of the First World War. On 31 May the Prussian Landtag also accepted the document, over the votes of the same minority, and it was promulgated as law.

For the successful completion of this lengthy and complicated task many persons could claim a share of the credit, notably Max Duncker, one-time professor at Halle and adviser of the Prussian Crown Prince but since June 1866 an official in Bismarck's service, Hermann Wagener, the conservative leader of the Prussian Volksverein, and Karl Friedrich von Savigny, the diplomat who had been Prussia's last representative at the Diet of the German Confederation.[32] But the driving and directing force was Bismarck, who supplied the basic structure of the December draft, who persuaded the separate governments, including his own, to accept it without imposing amendments that would impair its delicate balances, and who devised the strategy that carried it safely through the debates of the constituent Reichstag.

As a demonstration of his diplomatic virtuosity this performance was no less impressive than his adroit manœuvring on the European stage during the tangled dispute over the duchies of Schleswig and Holstein. Now as then he proved ever fertile in expedients and masterful in playing potentially hostile forces off against each other.

---

[32] Otto Becker, *Bismarcks Ringen um Deutschlands Gestaltung*, ed. and rev. Alexander Scharff (Heidelberg, 1958), pp. 211 ff., 225–30, 257 ff.

The attempts of the governments of the lesser states to unite on a demand for an increase of princely power that might have been used to limit Prussia's influence he countered on the one hand by divisive tactics in the form of promises and bribes and on the other by suggesting that Prussia might respond to recalcitrance with prescriptions drawn from the doctrines of radical liberal nationalism. He pointed out to the Saxon Government at one tense moment that Prussia always had 'alternatives: either to count completely and forever upon the governments now temporarily allied with us or to face the necessity of seeking our centre of gravity in parliament'.[33] When his own government baulked and sought what he considered to be unreasonable safeguards for its sovereignty, his arguments tended to be different, emphasizing the political price of losing momentum in the campaign for unity or of alienating the other governments. Finally, in April, when it seemed possible that the constituent Reichstag might try to change fundamental features of his constitutional draft, he persuaded the governments of Saxony, Hesse-Darmstadt, Saxe-Weimar, and the Mecklenburgs to join Prussia in a treaty that provided for the dissolution of the Reichstag and the promulgation of the constitution by decree if worse came to worst.[34] The treaty defused the threat, but in the process of negotiating it he used the threat to persuade the co-signatories to accept liberal amendments that he had come to regard as desirable.[35]

Since the main features of the constitution of the North German Confederation were carried over into the imperial constitution of 1871, discussion of the document and the awkward compromises that it embodied can be postponed until a later chapter. It is nevertheless important to note here that the creation of the new confederation was never an end in itself to Bismarck. An agent of the Duke of Saxe-Coburg-Gotha reported in January that the Prussian Crown Prince had told him of a conversation with the Minister President in which Bismarck had made it clear that 'the North German Bund was only a *Provisorium*, that his real energies were directed toward the unification of the whole of Germany, and that this objective would be gained in the not too distant future. In order to attain it, however, it was above all essential that the north come together in a firmer whole. . . .'[36] The skilful fusing of nationalism and states' rights in the

---

[33] Pflanze, *Bismarck*, p. 355.

[34] Egmont Zechlin, *Staatsstreichpläne Bismarcks und Wilhelms II 1890–94* (Stuttgart, 1929), pp. 175–6.

[35] Pflanze, *Bismarck*, p. 356.

[36] Herzog Ernst II von Sachsen-Koburg-Gotha, *Aus meinem Leben und aus meiner Zeit*, iii (Stuttgart, 1889), pp. 634 ff.

new constitution was admirably designed to serve this ultimate purpose by appealing to national patriots in the south, while at the same time demonstrating to their governments and ruling dynasties that the terms for joining the federation were tolerable. It should also be clear, however, that in both his creation of the North German Confederation and his subsequent efforts to make it the basis of a wider union, Bismarck was in no way departing from the principles that had animated his policy during the constitutional conflict. Despite the fears of his old friends in the Mark, he was determined to conserve the feudal-absolutist basis of the Prussian state and to maintain its ascendancy in the new Germany.

It is time now to sort out his views with respect to the question of bringing the southern states into the federal structure, and perhaps the place to start is with his statement in his memoirs that he had always believed 'that a Franco-German war must take place before the construction of a united Germany could be realized'.[37] Like many things in that brilliant but wilful volume, this need not be taken at face value, and it was not Bismarck's way, in any case, to believe in inevitability. That there was always a danger of war with France after July 1866 was, of course, clear to him, for he read the newspapers and was aware that among the literate public in France and in the Corps législatif the Battle of Königgrätz was regarded as a French, as well as an Austrian, defeat.[38] There was no doubt in his mind that a flagrant violation of the terms of the Peace of Prague by Prussia would exacerbate French opinion to the point where an armed clash would be difficult to avoid, and he was therefore determined to prevent such violation from taking place and to discourage overtures from the south that he considered premature (like the expressed interest of the Grand Duke of Baden in joining the Bund in March 1867).[39] On the other hand, he did not believe that Napoleon III, whom he had known since 1855, wanted a war, and he seems to have believed that if the Emperor became convinced that unification was strongly desired by the peoples of southern Germany, he would reconcile himself to this fact and persuade his own people that the restrictive terms of the Peace of Prague were unrealistic.

To mount such a demonstration would take time. It was clear in the wake of the Austrian war that Prussia was even more unpopular in the south than it had been earlier and that pro-union forces were weak and disorganized, particularly in Bavaria, but scarcely less so in

[37] Bismarck, *G.W.* xv. 282.
[38] Ernst II, *Aus meinem Leben*, p. 634.
[39] Hermann Oncken, *Rudolf von Bennigsen* (2 vols., Stuttgart, 1910), ii. 30.

Württemberg. But the Prussian Minister President counted upon three things to change this: the collaboration in security arrangements made possible by the offensive–defensive treaties, which he hoped would kindle a desire for other joint undertakings; the attractions of the constitution of the North German Confederation, which offered its members the advantages of sharing in a wider community without having to give up their uniqueness; and the pressure of economic interest.

The last of these was particularly promising. One of the effects of the war had been to destroy the ascendancy of the Austrian gulden and the virtual control of the Rothschild banking firm of Frankfurt over Germany's commercial life. The Prussian taler was king now, and Berlin the hub of German finance, where both the defeated and the associated states had to negotiate loans before they could pay their indemnities and contributions to Prussia. With this access of influence over the rest of Germany, Bismarck was emboldened to press in June 1867 for a fundamental reorganization of the Customs Union (Zollverein) so as to provide it with a bicameral legislature (a Zollparlament and a Zollbundesrat) with competence for tariff legislation, commercial and navigational negotiation, and the regulation of certain kinds of indirect taxes and excises.[40] Bismarck's calculation was that the Zollparlament, which would include representatives elected in both the northern and the southern states by universal and equal manhood suffrage, would dissolve old prejudices in a community of interest that would be so impressive to the onlooker that no one could rationally object to its translation into political form at the appropriate moment.

This strategy required patience and restraint. Until positive results began to be evident, it was important, in the conduct of Prussia's foreign relations, to do nothing that would jeopardize the chances of success and particularly to refrain from behaviour that would indicate that Prussia wanted to change the situation created by the war. An appearance of satisfaction with the gains made would have the double advantage of reassuring Powers like Great Britain and Russia, which were disturbed by Prussia's new strength and apprehensive about its intentions, and of forcing the French, who *were* interested in territorial change, to assume the responsibility and pay the political price of raising the question.

The point here was that the French continued to believe that they were entitled to compensation for the attitude of neutrality they had

[40] Böhme, *Deutschlands Weg*, pp. 213–21, 249–51.

assumed during the Austrian war. It was, to be sure, rather late in the day for such ambitions. If they had made a determined effort to force the issue before peace was concluded between the German Powers, they might have had some success; but the Emperor and his Foreign Minister Drouyn de Lhuys had not been of one mind, and the French *démarche* had in the end been both belated and so clumsy that it attracted unfavourable attention in other capitals and had to be explained away.[41] The French might have been well advised to drop the whole matter at that point, but public opinion in Paris was in a state of high irritation, 'profoundly wounded', as a member of the Emperor's Privy Council told him, by the fact that 'France had gained nothing from its intervention to save the attachments to its two flanks of neighbours whose power has been immeasurably increased'.[42] Napoleon III felt it wise to attempt to appease the angry patriots, and he instructed his ambassador in Berlin to raise the question of compensation again, but in a somewhat different form.

Bismarck did not discourage this—to have the French appear to be greedy might at some point have its advantages—but he made it clear that Prussia could not countenance the surrender of any German territory to France and that he was not interested in discussing other forms of compensation except in conditional terms and in a context in which some regard was paid to Prussian interest.[43] Undeterred by this, the French drifted with a singular lack of caution into a series of ambiguous discussions about the possibility of a Franco-Prussian alliance that would provide for the French acquisition of the Grand Duchy of Luxemburg and Belgium and for the relaxation of France's views about Prussian expansion to the south. The French ambassador, the impulsive and luckless Benedetti, at one point scribbled this all down on a piece of paper that he was unwise enough to leave with Bismarck, who preserved it carefully until 1870, when he produced it like a rabbit out of a hat to confound the friends of France.[44] Nothing came of the alliance idea (from the beginning Bismarck probably agreed with the King's tart comment in September: 'If Germany should ever learn that I had signed a French

---

[41] On this matter, see, *inter alia*, Herbert Geuss, *Bismarck und Napoleon III: Ein Beitrag zur Geschichte der preußisch-französischen Beziehungen 1851–72* (Cologne, 1959), pp. 172–95; Willard Allen Fletcher, *The Mission of Vincent Benedetti to Berlin, 1864–70* (The Hague, 1965), pp. 80–124; and, on the British reaction, Richard Millman, *British Foreign Policy and the Coming of the Franco-Prussian War* (Oxford, 1965), pp. 39–40.

[42] *Les Origines diplomatiques de la guerre de 1870–1.* Recueil de documents publié par le Ministère des affaires étrangères (29 vols., Paris, 1910–32), xi.123 ff.

[43] Allan Mitchell, *Bismarck and the French Nation, 1848–90* (New York, 1971), p. 40.

[44] Fletcher, *Benedetti*, pp. 135–6.

alliance for the destruction of Belgium in order thus to become ruler of Germany, German sympathies for Prussia would disappear immediately');[45] and the Emperor's decision to concentrate his hopes of compensation upon Luxemburg ended in a fiasco.

This was almost inevitable given the complicated legal situation of the Grand Duchy. It was a personal possession of the King of Holland, and he was presumably free to dispose of it as he wished; but it was also a member of the Zollverein, and, even more important, it had one of the strongest fortresses in Europe, which had been built by the great Vauban, and from 1815 to 1866 this had been part of the German Confederation's security system and was still garrisoned by Prussian troops.[46] It was these national associations that frustrated Napoleon's hopes in April 1867, when the Dutch King first advised the French Government that he was prepared to sell the Grand Duchy but then, when Napoleon had committed himself to the enterprise, decided to protect himself by asking the Prussian King whether he had any objections. The pending exchange became a subject of heated public discussion; the National Liberals (not without Bismarck's collusion) interpellated the government in the constituent Reichstag of the nascent Bund, asking whether it was prepared to defend German rights in Luxemburg; the Minister President replied ambiguously ('The royal government, in agreement with its allies, would watch over the interest of the nation') but with a clear implication of Prussia's opposition to the cession;[47] and the King of Holland took fright and withdrew his offer to sell. The French Government responded with menaces and measures that seemed to forecast mobilization, and of a sudden Europe was faced with a real possibility of war.

It did not come to that. The other Powers intervened, and the affair was adjudicated at an international conference in London in May 1867, which made the Grand Duchy a neutral and demilitarized state under the protection of a collective guarantee of the Powers.[48] For Bismarck, the results of the affair were, on the whole, positive. There was a strong suspicion in Paris that he had deliberately duped the Emperor and his agents, but there had been enough maladroitness on the French side to make this difficult to prove, and in any

[45] *Die auswärtige Politik Preußeus 1858–71: Diplomatische Akten,* hrsg. von der Historischen Reichskommission, viii (Oldenburg, 1934), 76.

[46] G. Wampach, *Le Luxembourg neutre. Étude d'histoire diplomatique* (Paris, 1900), p. 26; L. Gélinet, *Le Grand-Duché de Luxembourg vis-à-vis de la France et de l'Allemagne. Étude militaire* (Paris, 1887), pp. 15 ff.

[47] Fletcher, *Benedetti*, pp. 167–9.

[48] Millman, *British Policy*, pp. 87–96; Geuss, *Bismarck und Napoleon III*, pp. 210–16.

case the mood of indignation might well, Bismarck felt, be followed by one of resignation. On the other hand, the excitement caused by the revelation of French designs on Luxemburg had sensibly accelerated the work of the constituent Reichstag and, by encouraging the liberals to modify their demands for effective control over the army and the military budget, had helped bring it to a happy conclusion.[49] Moreover, there seemed to be some reason for believing that the affair had advanced the cause of unity in southern Germany. At the height of the crisis, the Minister President had received assurances of support from Baden and Hesse-Darmstadt and, although accompanied by an expressed hope that peace would be preserved, from the governments of Bavaria and Württemberg as well; and it seemed to him that popular indignation against the French was as lively in the south as it was in the states of the Bund.

But these appearances were misleading, and before long there was unmistakable evidence that the unity movement was badly stalled in the lands south of the Main, and that anti-Prussian feeling was, if anything, increasing.

For one thing, the military collaboration provided for by the offensive–defensive treaties proved to be more half-hearted than Bismarck had hoped, and the implementation of the treaties was accompanied by bickering and foot-dragging on the part of the southern governments. Since the eighteenth century, the image of Prussia as a gigantic barracks had been a southern stereotype, and a particularist like the Bavarian Edmund Jörg spoke to the converted when he described the victor of 1866 as 'a power which does not hesitate, in the nineteenth century and on German soil, to keep five million German souls under its sway with Russian brutality . . . [with] every sort of centralism, rule by saber, and Caesarism'.[50] Prussian efforts to establish uniformity of military practice, in accordance with the treaties, were regarded as attempts to foist militarism on the south, and, although progress was made slowly, there were complaints about the increased costs, the more rigid disciplinary codes, and the longer term of service that uniformity seemed to require. Indeed, the sacrifices required by the military association made Prussia more unpopular in the eyes of many southerners and, by extension, reduced the attractiveness of the North German Confederation as well. A Prussian agent in Württemberg reported to Berlin that people were saying that the constitution of the Bund

---

[49] Pflanze, *Bismarck*, p. 380, and below, Ch. II, p. 51.

[50] Cited in Theodore S. Hamerow, *The Social Foundations of German Unification, 1858–71: Struggles and Accomplishments* (Princeton, 1972), p. 377.

contained 'only three articles: 1. pay, 2. be a soldier, 3. keep your mouth shut'.[51]

The most striking evidence of this southern temper was provided by the elections for the new Zollparlament in the first months of 1868. Indications that these would disappoint Bismarck's expectations were seen ahead of time, in the demand made at a conference of the Democratic People's party in Württemberg for a boycott of the elections, and in the resolution passed by the Lower House of the Württemberg Parliament which insisted that cases in which newspapers were charged with libel against foreign rulers or governments must be tried by juries. The actual results confirmed these evidences of resentment. The elections in Bavaria on 10 February were an unmistakable victory for the clerical-particularist opponents of union, who elected 26 out of the 48 delegates to the Zollparlament, while the Progressives, who favoured fusion with the north, won only 12 places and the Mittelpartei, which, as its name implied, had no firm policy on any issue, won 9. In Baden, where the elections were held two weeks later, the pro-union forces were successful, as had been predicted, but narrowly so, the clericals showing surprising strength in this stronghold of Prussian sympathizers. As for Württemberg, the pro-union forces polled only 45,787 votes against the opposition's 129,725 and won none of the places in the seventeen-man delegation. The only place in which the National party won a clear victory was in that part of Hesse-Darmstadt that lay south of the Main.

All told, the southern states sent 57 oppositional delegates to the Zollparlament, all determined to oppose any widening of the competence of that body and any extension of Prussian influence in the south. Together with the Old Conservatives of Prussia, the resentful Guelfs of Hanover, the northern Catholics, and the Poles, they had the strength to prevent the parliament from accomplishing anything of significance in relation to the national question and, on 7 May 1868, they roundly defeated the draft of an address to the King of Prussia which had been prepared by the delegates of Baden and Hesse and which expressed support for a policy of economic freedom and 'complete unification of the whole German fatherland in a peaceful and salutary manner'.[52]

This set-back Bismarck took as philosophically as possible. It was

[51] Ibid., p. 379.

[52] Adam Wandruszka, 'Zwischen Nikolsburg und Bad Ems', in Ernst Deuerlein and Theodor Schieder (eds.), *Reichsgründung 1870/71: Tatsachen, Kontroversen, Interpretationen* (Stuttgart, 1970), pp. 51–2; Böhme, *Deutschlands Weg*, pp. 270–7.

clear that he had overestimated the political gains that could be derived from the economic attractions of unification. It was true that manufacturers and merchants, trade associations and chambers of commerce, and the liberal bourgeoisie in general were the most enthusiastic supporters of national unity after 1866, as well they might be in view of the way in which the North German Confederation worked on their behalf, removing restrictions on manufactures and on the proliferation of the joint stock principle and encouraging such things as common codes of commercial law and uniform regulation of bills of exchange.[53] But it appeared that these people were less influential in the south than in the north. Bismarck complained about 'the heterogeneous elements' in the south and said that it would be difficult to determine 'whether the democrats or the clericals are our worst enemies'.[54]

Still, he was not inclined to change prevailing opinion in the south by artificial means or the application of pressure. In February 1869, at a time when some of his southern supporters had become critical of his inactivity and were expressing the view that the cause of unity would be lost for ever unless something was done to reverse current tendencies, he wrote a dispatch to his envoy in Munich, Georg Freiherr von Werthern, which has often been cited, and deservedly, since it tells much about the principles that guided his statecraft. 'That German unity could be promoted by actions involving force,' he wrote,

I think is self-evident. But there is a quite different question, and that has to do with the precipitation of a powerful catastrophe and the responsibility of choosing the time for it. A voluntary intervention in the evolution of history, which is determined by purely subjective factors, results only in the shaking down of unripe fruit, and that German unity is no ripe fruit at this time leaps, in my opinion, to the eye. If the time that lies ahead works in the interest of unity as much as the period since the accession of Frederick the Great has done, and particularly the period since 1840, the year in which a national movement was perceptible for the first time since the war of liberation, then we can look to the future calmly and leave the rest to our successors. Behind the wordy restlessness with which people who do not know the trade search after the talisman that will supposedly produce German unity in a trice, there is generally hidden a superficial and, in any case, impotent lack of knowledge of real things and their consequences.

The true wisdom was to recognize that 'we can set our watches, but the time passes no more quickly because of that, and the

---

[53] Hamerow, *Struggles and Accomplishments*, pp. 337–47.
[54] Bismarck, *G.W.* vii. 258 f.

ability to wait while conditions develop is a requisite of practical policy'.[55]

Despite other political disappointments in the south, Bismarck followed his own advice. His most notable set-back in the months that followed his letter to Werthern was the waning of the fortunes of his loyal supporter Prince Chlodwig zu Hohenlohe-Schillingsfürst. Hohenlohe had been Minister President of Bavaria since December 1866 and, in the spring of 1867, had been the author of an abortive plan whereby Austria would give its assent to the fusion of the southern states with the North German Confederation and would enter into permanent alliance with the resultant union. He fell in January 1870 as a result of an onslaught by conservatives and clericals under the leadership of Edmund Jörg, a reversal that left the unionists in despair and disarray. Yet a month later, when the Grand Duke and the Landtag of Baden petitioned for admission to the northern Bund and when Eduard Lasker of the National Liberal party advocated this partial solution to the southern problem, Bismarck flatly refused, declaring in a speech in the Reichstag that to separate Baden, the force most favourable to the cause of fusion, from its neighbours would be like 'taking the cream off the milk crock and leaving the rest to go sour'.[56] To go on waiting was infinitely preferable to a half-way resolution of the southern problem.

Seen in retrospect, Bismarck's patience during this period of frustration was remarkable. But this was not the quality that had made him a virtuoso on the diplomatic stage. Much as they admired his ability to wait, Bismarck's closest associates in the Foreign Ministry—Bülow the elder, Lothar Bucher, and, later, Radowitz, Brauer, Holstein, and Hatzfeldt—reserved their greatest admiration for his decisiveness, his sureness of touch, and his infinite resourcefulness. Bismarck believed that there were moments in foreign policy which, as he said in 1866, 'never come again' and that it was the statesman's duty to fasten upon them and make the most of the opportunities they presented to him. When his inner clock told him that the time was ripe, he was capable of acting with a speed, an authority, and, if it was needed, a brutality that never failed to impress his subordinates.[57]

[55] Bismarck, *G.W.* vib. 1 ff. See also Hajo Holborn, 'Bismarck und Werthern', *Archiv für Politik und Geschichte*, v (1925–6).

[56] Wandruszka, 'Zwischen Nikolsburg und Bad Ems', p. 56.

[57] Gordon A. Craig, *From Bismarck to Adenauer: Aspects of German Statecraft* (rev. edn., New York, 1965), pp. 8–9.

Such a moment arrived in February 1870, when Eusebio Salazar, a member of the Spanish Cortes, acting on instructions of the provisional government in Madrid, approached the Prussian Government with a request for talks concerning the succession to the vacant Spanish throne.

IV

'What do I care', Metternich is reported to have said once, 'what happens in the courts of Cetinje and Belgrade?' Bismarck had probably been asking the same question about the court of Madrid ever since Queen Isabella II had been deposed in September 1868, although hardly in Metternich's contemptuous and dismissive manner. Among the persons whom Marshal Prim, the head of the provisional government in Madrid, was considering as possible successors to the vacant throne was Leopold of Hohenzollern-Sigmaringen, the son of Prince Charles Anthony, head of the Catholic branch of the ruling house, former Prussian Minister President, and personal friend of the King. Bismarck never for a moment doubted that Leopold's succession to the throne would present him with dangers and opportunities. The question was always whether the possibility of exploiting the latter successfully justified accepting the former.

Throughout 1869 he was inclined to doubt it; when asked questions about the matter, he dismissed it as a private affair that did not concern the Prussian Government; and when Prim actually offered the throne to Leopold in September and the young man turned it down, he seemed satisfied with the result. Yet in February, when the Spanish statesman renewed the offer and this time formally asked the Prussian Government to induce Leopold to reconsider, Bismarck threw off his pose of indifference and, on 9 March, sent a memorandum to the King urging the positive advantages to be gained if Leopold accepted.

How are we to account for this change of front? Bismarck's memorandum to his sovereign is not adequate to answer this question, for its arguments were obviously carefully chosen to appeal to the military and dynastic cast of William's mind. Thus Bismarck pointed out that in the event of a war with France, which was always possible, a Hohenzollern on the Spanish throne would be enough to compel the French to divert one or two army corps to protect their southern frontier. Apart from this, it would be well to bear in mind, he pointed out, that if Leopold did not assume the crown, it might fall to the Wittelsbach dynasty, which would raise the danger of a future Catholic league against Prussia and, even failing that, would have unhappy political repercussions. Pulling out all of the stops, Bismarck wrote:

> The repute of the Hohenzollern dynasty, the justifiable pride with which not only Prussia regards its royal house but Germany too tends more and more to glory in that name as a common national possession, all this forms an important element in political self-confidence, the fostering and strengthening of which would be of benefit to national feeling in general and to monarchist sentiment in particular.[58]

The most interesting aspect of this curious document—whose arguments the King refuted energetically and effectively—was what it did not say. It made virtually no reference to the effect that Leopold's accession would have upon the French Government. Yet there is good reason to believe that Bismarck's real motivation was rooted in his view of the state of French politics and, particularly, of the contest between the hawks and the doves in Paris. He knew that there was, both at the imperial court and in the Foreign Service, an influential anti-Prussian party—including the Empress herself, Eugène Rouher, the 'vice-emperor', and ambassadors like La Guéronnière in Brussels and Gramont in Vienna—who hoped that circumstances would arise that would permit a war of revenge for Königgrätz. He was not greatly worried by their attempts to create such an opportunity by diplomatic means. The possibility of a Franco-Austrian alliance (the ambition of his old enemy Beust in Vienna) was blocked by the opposition of both the Austrian liberals and the Déak party to another German war;[59] the continued occupation of Rome by French troops was an insurmountable obstacle to an alliance with Italy;[60] France's clumsy and unsuccessful attempt to acquire strategic railway lines in Luxemburg and Belgium in 1869 had aroused the liveliest suspicions of the British;[61] and French hopes in Petersburg were foreclosed by the fact that Bismarck had himself effected a working entente with the Russian Government in 1868 which, in view of his intimations of support if the Russians should repudiate the Black Sea clauses of the Paris Treaty of 1856, it was not

---

[58] Georges Bonnin (ed.), *Bismarck and the Hohenzollern Candidature for the Spanish Throne* (London, 1957), pp. 68–73; Keudell, *Fürst und Fürstin Bismarck*, pp. 430 ff.

[59] István Diószegi, *Österreich-Ungarn und der französisch-preußische Krieg 1870–1* (Budapest, 1974), pp. 13–22.

[60] The best book is still Émile Bourgeois, *Rome et Napoléon III, 1849–1870* (Paris, 1907).

[61] See Gordon A. Craig, 'Great Britain and the Belgian Railways Dispute of 1869', *American Historical Review*, l, no. 4 (July 1945), reprinted in *War, Politics and Diplomacy: Selected Essays* (New York, 1966), pp. 153 ff.

in the Russian interest to abandon for anything that France could offer.[62] The war party concerned him, therefore, not because its foreign plans were dangerous but because its influence in Paris was still strong enough to prevent Napoleon III from adopting a conciliatory policy towards the German national movement.

Not all French politicians were hawks, however. In January 1870 Napoleon III crowned his recent experiments in liberalizing the government by installing Émile Ollivier as the head of a new ministry. Bismarck believed, with good reason, that Ollivier was inclined to the view that it was too late to block German unification and that, as long as Prussia did not try to achieve it by force, France should concede the issue gracefully, getting as much incidental benefit from doing so as it could.[63] He wanted to strengthen Ollivier's hand as far as possible, and his speech of 24 February rejecting the Badenese application for admission to the Bund was in part motivated by that desire. So was his advice to the King in the matter of the Hohenzollern candidacy. He fully expected the French to be outraged if Leopold accepted, but as long as Prussian complicity remained secret and the Spanish remained firm, there would be little they could do. The louder the outcry, the more discredit would ultimately fall on those making it, namely the hawks. To protect his own position, Napoleon would have to commit himself whole-heartedly to the liberals, and the hopes of a peaceful resolution of the unification issue would be increased.[64] While it lasted, the excitement would have the effect of stimulating nationalism in southern Germany. If the hawks proved more successful than Bismarck believed they would be and led France into war against Prussia, Bismarck was confident that the Prussian army would be the master of the situation.

It is always dangerous to speak with too great assurance of Bismarck's intentions, but the explanation given here is certainly more reasonable than the argument, often made, that he was seeking war with France from the beginning of the Spanish question. Throughout his life, Bismarck was an opponent of preventive war, main-

[62] Pflanze, *Bismarck*, pp. 419–24.

[63] On Ollivier's views, see Pierre Renouvin, *Histoire des relations internationales*, v: *Le XIXe siècle*, 1:*De 1815 à 1871* (Paris, 1954), pp. 378–9.

[64] Geuss, *Bismarck und Napoleon III*, p. 266. Cf. Jochen Dittrich, 'Ursachen und Ausbruch des Krieges 1870–1', in Deuerlein and Schieder, *Reichsgründung*, p. 75; Lawrence D. Steefel, *Bismarck, the Hohenzollern Candidacy, and the Origins of the Franco-German War of 1870* (Cambridge, Mass., 1962), p. 243, who seems to believe there is no reason for believing that Bismarck 'had any specific single result in mind'; and Eberhard Kolb, *Der Kriegsausbruch 1870: Politische Entscheidungsprozesse und Verantwortlichkeiten in der Julikrise 1870* (Göttingen, 1970), who is too intent on proving French guilt to analyse Bismarck's motives carefully.

taining that it represented an unwarranted interference with the ways of providence and was in any case as irrational as committing suicide because one was afraid to die.[65] If the trumpets of war were to sound in the spring of 1870, the initiative in his view would have to be France's, and he was confident that in the prevailing circumstances Napoleon would not give the necessary command.

None of these calculations could be tested immediately. King William left it to Prince Leopold to decide whether he was to go to Spain or not, but his own attitude was so critical that it dampened any enthusiasm the candidate might have felt, and he was so negative that, by the beginning of May, Bismarck, ill with jaundice at his estate in Varzin, had almost given up the Spanish enterprise for lost. He was prevented from resigning himself to this, however, by what appeared to be a significant change in the political situation in France. On 8 May a plebiscite was held in which the electorate was asked whether it approved of 'the liberal reforms introduced by the Emperor since 1860'. Frenchmen knew that the real question was whether they wanted Napoleon to remain on the throne, and they voted overwhelmingly in the affirmative, 7,336,000 votes to 1,572,000. When the returns were tabulated, one of Napoleon's opponents said morosely that they meant that his contract had been renewed for another twenty years.[66] Bismarck's own view was that, despite the wording of the plebiscite, its result could only mean an end to liberal inclinations in foreign policy, and this interpretation seemed to be borne out almost immediately, when Daru, the French Foreign Minister, resigned and was replaced by the duc de Gramont, well known as a hard-liner and an advocate of a military alliance with Austria. To the Prussian Minister President it seemed a matter of urgency now to create a crisis that would challenge and discredit the new tendency in French policy before it gathered momentum.

With rather less regard for his King's views than perfect loyalty would have seemed to require, Bismarck and his agents Lothar Bucher and Major von Versen therefore talked Prince Leopold round, making it appear that acceptance of the Spanish offer was a patriotic duty. Leopold gave way and so did the irritated monarch, and on 21 June the fateful telegram went off to Madrid. It is remarkable that the explosive news remained a secret for ten days. But by 2 July it had reached Paris and, on the following day, the new Foreign Minister was faced with the necessity of deciding how to respond to it.

[65] See Bismarck, *G.W.* vic. 63.
[66] Renouvin, *Histoire des relations internationales*, v, 1, p. 379.

Gramont has been harshly judged by historians, but certainly not unjustly. Where reflection was needed, he was impulsive; where deliberation of utterance was advisable, he was violent; and where a sense of measure might have crowned his career with a brilliant success, he overreached and tumbled his nation into disaster. On receiving the news from Madrid, he had an excellent opportunity to embarrass Bismarck by making a public request for his assistance in terminating a matter that threatened the peace of Europe, a ploy that would have been all the more effective in view of Bismarck's elaborate pretence that the Prussian Government had not been involved in the negotiations between Leopold and the provisional government in Madrid. Instead, Gramont began by asking the Prussian Government in peremptory tones if it was involved, and then, without waiting for a reply, delivered an inflammatory speech in the Corps législatif on 6 July, in which he flatly accused Prussia of threatening the balance of power and the vital interest and honour of France and intimated plainly that his government was prepared to use force if the Prussian and Spanish governments did not abandon their project at once. The speech in itself created difficulties for the French Government, because it alarmed and excited public opinion, which had reacted calmly to the news from Madrid, and let loose the flood of chauvinism which in the end the government was powerless to withstand.

Worse than this was Gramont's failure to heed Talleyrand's advice to diplomats, '*Pas trop de zèle!*' Although the rapidly mounting excitement in Paris did not shake Bismarck's determination to remain firm in face of the challenge that came from that quarter, his sovereign, taking the waters at Bad Ems far from his ailing minister's influence, had a bad conscience and was less intransigent. Pressed by the French ambassador on 9 July, William was too honest to deny that he had approved Leopold's candidacy and discussed it with Bismarck and, while insisting that he had no authority to force Prince Leopold to renounce the Spanish crown, he admitted that he was carrying on discussions about the matter with his relatives.[67] These admissions were followed on 12 July by Prince Charles Anthony's determined and final withdrawal of his son's candidacy. With that, Gramont had within his grasp a success greater than any won by French statecraft since the days of the first Napoleon. In Berlin, Bismarck was for once in his life bereft of expedients; shaken and humiliated, he wondered whether he ought not resign.

[67] Robert H. Lord, *The Origins of the War of 1870* (Cambridge, 1924), pp. 49 ff.; Fletcher, *Benedetti*, pp. 245 f.; Pflanze, *Bismarck*, pp. 452 f.

But Gramont threw it all away. Either because he did not trust his good fortune or because he wished to make sure that no one failed to appreciate its true magnitude, he sent the hapless Benedetti back to the Prussian King on 13 July with a request for assurance that he would not renew the candidacy. The King refused, politely but firmly, to give any such thing.[68] He then had his aide Abeken telegraph a description of the conversation to Bismarck, who released it to the Press, after abbreviating its wording in such a way as to make the King's language much curter and the rebuff to Benedetti much sharper than they had been in fact. The publication of the Ems dispatch ánd the resultant elaboration of it in sensational newspapers on both sides of the Rhine created an atmosphere in which reason and compromise were impossible. Bismarck had always believed that Napoleon III and Ollivier would be opposed to war, and he was right in this judgement. But even Ollivier felt that to retreat now would represent an intolerable loss of honour, and, as the British ambassador noted, the Emperor believed that, for the sake of the imperial succession, he could not afford the appearance of truckling to Prussia.[69] It cannot be said that Bismarck wanted a war in 1870, but, thanks to the crisis that he had encouraged, to Gramont's maladroitness in handling it, and to the passions it released in French public opinion, that was what he got.[70]

V

But he also received a gratifying demonstration of support for the national cause from southern Germany. Temporarily at least, particularism and distrust of Prussia were swept away on the flood of patriotic exaltation that welled up in all parts of the nation in July 1870. In face of what was universally believed to be a premeditated French assault motivated by arrogance and envy, who could stand idly by? 'Any German,' Arnold Ruge wrote, 'whoever he may be, who is not now on the side of his people, is a traitor!'[71] There was no hesitation about carrying out the terms of the military treaties concluded with Prussia in 1866, and army reserves rallied to their units with enthusiasm. Bavaria and Baden began to mobilize on 16 July, and Württemberg a day later, and their contingents were joined

---

[68] Fletcher, Benedetti, pp. 252–9.

[69] Roger L. Williams, The Mortal Napoleon III (Princeton, 1971), pp. 146 f.

[70] A balanced discussion of the question of responsibility is to be found in S. William Halperin, 'The Origins of the Franco-Prussian War Re-Visited: Bismarck and the Hohenzollern Candidature for the Spanish Crown', Journal of Modern History, xlv, no. 1 (1973), 83 ff.

[71] Hamerow, Struggles and Accomplishments, p. 392.

together in the Third Army, the command of which was assumed by the Prussian Crown Prince. The hero of Chlum had some initial doubts about the spirit and training of the southern troops;[72] they were not borne out when action began.

Thanks to the promptness of the southern response and the efficiency of the mobilization process in general, 1,830,000 regulars and reservists passed through German barracks within a period of eighteen days, and 462,000 were transported to the western frontier. This was almost twice the size of the force mustered in France, where, twenty-three days after the beginning of mobilization, reservists were still straggling into their regimental headquarters, often without the most essential items of uniform and equipment. The French army had relied too long on what was called 'le système D: on se débrouillera toujours' ('we'll muddle through somehow').[73] Against a well-armed and numerically stronger opponent, who also had an efficient supply system, a high command and General Staff that had proved themselves in the wars of 1864 and 1866, and a war plan that had been long in readiness, that was not good enough.

In the last days before the onset of hostilities, Napoleon had improvised a plan for a diversionary amphibious operation in the Baltic area and a massive offensive thrust into southern Germany that would bring Austria and Italy into the war as allies after the first successes had been won. There was something to be said for this, for it was true that both Emperor Francis Joseph and King Victor Emmanuel II were inclined to rally to Napoleon's side.[74] But before the widely dispersed French reserves could be concentrated for the implementation of these operations, the Prussians had rammed their way through the Lorraine gap and, after hard-fought battles at Vionville–Mars-la-Tour, Saint-Privat, and Gravelotte, in which they suffered greater casualties than the enemy, got between Paris and the two main French armies, those of Marshals Bazaine and MacMahon. Bazaine was forced back eastwards and bottled up in the fortress of Metz. When MacMahon's army, which had now been joined by the Emperor, tried to come to his aid, its southern flank was chewed up by units of the Prussian IV Corps, the Royal Saxon XII Army Corps, and the I Bavarian Corps at Beaumont, and the rest of his forces were pinned against the Belgian frontier at Sedan and

---

[72] Michael Howard, *The Franco-Prussian War* (New York, 1961), p. 60.

[73] Ibid., p. 17.

[74] See Diószegi, *Österreich-Ungarn und der französisch-preußische Krieg*, pp. 40 ff.; Federico Chabod, *Storia della politica estera italiana dal 1870 al 1896*, i: *Le premesse* (Bari, 1951), pp. 28, 32, 113, 115, 120.

hammered by continuous fire from the formidable Krupp steel breech-loading field-pieces deployed by Bavarian, Silesian, Hessian, and Saxon units until they surrendered.

This stunning German victory did not end the war, but it brought down the Napoleonic regime. The news that the Emperor and 100,000 troops were in Prussian hands reached Paris on 3 September, and on the following morning, not for the first time in French history, the Republic was proclaimed at the Hotel de Ville. Despite his sympathy for the Emperor, Bismarck received the news with satisfaction since, for the time being, it obviated the possibility of neutral intervention on the Emperor's behalf. It also gave him a plausible rationale for the war aims that he now revealed. The palpable threat of revolutionary contagion spreading outwards from France made it necessary, he informed Vienna and St. Petersburg, for the three eastern monarchies to stand together and for Germany, the Power that was most exposed, to protect itself by annexing Alsace and Lorraine.[75]

The unhappy effects that the acquisition of these provinces were to have in Germany's external and internal affairs after 1871 have made it a subject of uncommon interest for historians, who are still sharply divided with respect to the reasons that made it the principal objective of German policy in 1870.[76] Some of them have found the explanation in the theory that public opinion forced Bismarck against his will to demand Alsace and Lorraine; others have argued that the Minister President was himself the creator of the public agitation, using a skilful Press campaign to arouse expansionist ardour where it had not existed before. An objective view of the evidence would seem to indicate that neither public opinion nor Bismarck needed inducement.

Within a few days of the outbreak of war, annexation was being widely discussed in the country, particularly in southern Germany, where what appeared to be an imminent threat of French invasion recalled the history of French aggression since the days of Louis XIV and encouraged determination to end it once and for all by acquiring a protective glacis. There was no need for an official Press campaign when local newspapers were voluntarily calling for annexation and men of stature and known independence, like the historian of medieval Rome, Ferdinand Gregorovius, were insisting that a pre-

[75] Pflanze, *Bismarck*, p. 465.
[76] See e.g. the controversy in *Historische Zeitschrift*, 199 (1964), 31–112; 206 (1968), 265–386, 586–617; and 209 (1969), 318–56, in which W. Lipgens, Lothar Gall, R. Buchner, and Eberhard Kolb argued the issues.

datory France could be checked definitively only by the acquisition of Germany's natural frontier, the Vosges. Although a few lonely voices were raised—notably that of the writer and later diplomat Julius von Eckhardt—to say that the acquisition of Alsace and Lorraine would cast doubt upon the purity of Germany's motives, would violate the principle of nationality, and would saddle Germany with the lasting enmity of France and a dissident minority, they elicited little apparent support. The argument that a referendum might be used to determine the wishes of the population was rejected scornfully by the *Augsburger Allgemeine Zeitung* which held that what the Alsatians felt was unimportant. 'We must begin with the rod. The alienated children must feel our fist. Love will follow the disciplining, and it will make them Germans again.' The leader of the Liberal party of Württemberg warned that Germans must not be sentimental politicians or doctrinaire fools. In time nationality would triumph; meanwhile military control would suffice.[77] Heinrich von Treitschke, enraptured by the triumph of Prussian arms, wrote an essay entitled 'What We Demand from France' which combined contempt for the beaten foe with an unabashed imperialism.[78]

Bismarck could not ignore this clamour, but it did not determine his policy, which had been bent on annexation from the first. He had been willing to forgo territorial demands on Austria in 1866 because he felt that, in the long run, Austria and Germany were natural allies and that irredentism should not be permitted to trouble that relationship. But he saw no reason to be so modest on this occasion. Quite apart from the fact that to do so would create difficulties with the King and the soldiers, who were annexationists for reasons of military security and from ideological conviction as well, he was convinced that forbearance would have no political point. No Great Power, least of all one as proud as France, would suffer the destruction of its primacy in Europe without resolving to do everything it could to get revenge. 'They did not forgive us for Sadowa', Bismarck said to Keudell on 6 September, 'and they will be even less forgiving with respect to our present victory, no matter how generous we are when it comes to the peace.'[79] It was a simple dictate of prudence, therefore, to seize upon the strong points that would help deny the gratification of French resentment.

[77] Lothar Gall, 'Das Problem Elsaß-Lothringen', in Deuerlein and Schieder, *Reichsgründung*, pp. 373–5.

[78] *Preußische Jahrbücher*, xxvi (1870), 367–409.

[79] Bismarck, *G.W.* vii. 339.

The announcement of the war aims complicated the problem of bringing the war to a speedy conclusion. It certainly made impossible serious negotiation with the provisional government of General Trochu that had replaced the Bonapartist regime on 4 September, for the new Foreign Minister, Jules Favre, had announced bravely on taking office that France would yield 'neither an inch of its territory nor a stone of its fortresses'.[80] But Bismarck had little faith in the staying-power of the provisional government, whose authority did not appear to extend beyond Paris. His problem was to find a government with legitimacy and authority that could speak for the country as a whole and to conclude a peace with it on favourable terms before the neutral Powers began to consider the question of intervention again. The chances of such intervention were, to be sure, not great, and they became slimmer in view of the difficulties caused by Russia's abrogation of the Black Sea clauses in November.[81] Still, Bismarck was a great believer in the *imponderabilia*, the unforeseen factors that can defeat the best-laid plans, and he was intent upon concluding the war as quickly as possible.[82] His efforts to do so were handicapped, however, not only by the complications of French politics but also by the behaviour of the Prussian military.

The soldiers had not forgiven Bismarck for his interference with their plans after Königgrätz, and, from the very beginning of the war with France, they tried to keep him as much as possible in the dark, excluding him from the daily military conferences in which the King and the commanding generals discussed the strategical situation with Moltke and his aides. This did not particularly worry the Chancellor during the first stage of the war. It was only after Sedan, when he began an earnest search for peace, that ignorance of exact military plans promised to hamper him, and he was soon given additional reasons for complaining about the attitude of Moltke and his demigods.

In October, when Bismarck was toying with the idea of helping Napoleon III or his son regain power and was investigating the possibility of combining a capitulation of Bazaine's forces in Metz with a peace treaty that would satisfy Prussian interest and free Bazaine's army to support the Emperor, Prince Frederick Charles,

---

[80] Jules Favre, *Gouvernement de la défense nationale* (3 vols., Paris, 1871–5), i. 383–6.

[81] See e.g. Millman, *British Policy*, pp. 209–18.

[82] On his fears that a conference to regulate the Black Sea question might encourage intervention by the neutrals in the settlement of the French war, see Craig, *Prussian Army*, p. 210 and the authorities cited.

commanding the Prussian forces investing Metz, objected to his policy and foiled his efforts to use the French General Bourbaki as a go-between in negotiations with Bazaine and the Empress. Again, when the capitulation of Metz at the end of October destroyed the last hope of a Napoleonic restoration, and when Bismarck decided that it was necessary to try to break French resistance by bombarding and forcing the surrender of Paris, Moltke and his advisers raised a host of technical objections and refused to bring up the guns until ordered to do so by the King in late December, after the Chancellor had mounted a Press campaign in support of the operation. Finally, when the capitulation of the capital became imminent a month later, Moltke insisted, in a memorandum to his sovereign, that the details should be left in his hands, that the city should be occupied by German troops and ruled by martial law, administered by a military governor, that line troops and Mobile Guards should be disarmed and sent as prisoners to Germany, and that all eagles and flags should be given up to the victors.

Had this prescription been followed, the hope of peace might have been indefinitely postponed. But the fact of the matter was that Moltke was not particularly interested in peace, at least not before the power of France was utterly destroyed. The Chief of Staff was driven by ideological passions that were completely alien to Bismarck's thinking; indeed, as the Crown Prince noted, he really wanted a war of extermination.[83] His deep hatred of the French made him averse to any interruption of operations against them for political reasons that he was incapable of appreciating.

When the Chancellor became fully aware of how directly his policy was threatened by the man whom he described sardonically as a 'verknöcherter Generalstabsmensch', he decided that he must ask the King for an unambiguous declaration of his own primary responsibility for the determination of policy. He was spurred on by the fact that in January French resistance in the south began to falter and there were signs of a growing war-weariness—in February this was to result in the election of a conservative National Assembly that chose Adolphe Thiers as chief of the executive power and authorized him to treat for peace—and he wished to be sure that Moltke had no opportunity to reverse these tendencies by wilfulness or political maladroitness. He was so insistent that the King gave way completely and ended the worrisome civil–military dispute—which was to be contested again with a fatally different result during the First

[83] Kaiser Friedrich III, *Das Kriegstagebuch von 1870–71*, ed. H. O. Meisner (Berlin, 1926), p. 325.

World War—as Bismarck desired it to be ended. On 25 January two royal orders stipulated that Moltke was to engage in no correspondence with French authorities without first learning from the King whether Bismarck should be consulted and that the Chancellor was to be informed about the future course of military operations and given the opportunity to express his views concerning them.[84]

To the indignation of the soldiers, therefore, Bismarck was in complete control of the armistice talks that began on 26 January, even taking responsibility for deciding which of the Parisian forts would have to be surrendered and which army would have the honour of firing the last shot. And a month later, when he sat down with Thiers and Favre to talk about peace terms, the military played no significant part in the negotiations. The peace that resulted was made on the Chancellor's terms, with which, to be sure, the military had no reason to be dissatisfied, since they brought Germany Alsace and Lorraine and the right to keep an army of occupation in France until the French Government had paid a war indemnity of five billion francs.

Even before Thiers had accepted the terms that were to be embodied in the Treaty of Frankfurt of May 1871, the victory of the national cause in Germany had been celebrated in an elaborate ceremony in the Galerie des Glaces in Versailles, in which a rather sulky King William, wearing all his Prussian prejudices on the outside, was hailed as ruler of a united German Reich. The proclamation of 18 January 1871 was almost a foregone conclusion for, although there had, in the course of the last six months, been some abatement of the national enthusiasm that had reigned in July, no responsible politician in southern Germany believed that there was now any alternative to fusion with the north. Dynastic particularism, clericalism, and democracy proved no basis for a viable Third Germany in the new Europe that had been created by the victory over France. It was recognized by all but the most xenophobic Prussian-haters that the price of independence would be political isolation, economic decline, and mounting security costs.[85]

Bismarck was clever enough to play upon this awareness without being too insistent and to make concessions to local sensibilities when this seemed necessary. He had no difficulties in Hesse-Darmstadt and Baden where parliamentary support for union was virtually unanimous and where the governments and the ruling houses were acquiescent. But in the case of Württemberg and

[84] On all this, see Craig, *Prussian Army*, pp. 204–16.
[85] See esp. Hamerow, *Struggles and Accomplishments*, pp. 416–27.

Bavaria the rulers were jealous of their privileges and unwilling to give way to parliamentary or public pressure until they had preserved as many of them as possible. It is interesting to note that Bismarck's delicacy in dealing with their claims annoyed the Prussian Crown Prince and led him to say things that indicate the lack of restraint that was already inherent in the new nationalism. Impatient over the delay in completing the union, Frederick William asked Bismarck why Prussia did not simply compel the southern states to come in. Bismarck answered, 'We guaranteed their rights at the beginning of the war. They are our allies. They achieved the victory in collaboration with us. We cannot use any compulsion against them.' This did not satisfy the man who was later to be described by historians as the liberal Emperor. 'If the army calls King William to be Emperor,' he said angrily, 'what can the south Germans do about it? We have their troops in our power.' The Chancellor replied coldly that the Crown Prince might like to begin by disarming the Bavarian troops in his command. 'Perhaps a prince can do that sort of thing,' he added. 'A nobleman like myself cannot.'[86]

The price that the Chancellor had to pay for union was not in the end exorbitant. The two southern monarchs retained their command over their military establishments and their privilege of appointing and promoting officers, while agreeing that their forces would pass under Prussian command in time of war. Together with the King of Saxony, they also received representational and ceremonial rights in the realm of foreign affairs and the management of the business of the Federal Council. Finally, they were permitted to reserve certain rights in the areas of transportation, taxation, and other local affairs. Bismarck was entirely agreeable to these concessions. Whether particularism was to be a problem in the future would not be determined in his opinion by these trifling reservations but by the advantages or disadvantages that the federal states would derive from membership in the Empire that was proclaimed in Versailles in January 1871.

VI

In 1871, when victory over France was assured, the novelist Gustav Freytag wrote,

There never was a struggle fought for a greater ideal than this; never perhaps did Nemesis strike down the guilty so violently; never perhaps did any army

---

[86] Arnold Oskar Meyer, *Bismarck, der Mensch und der Staatsmann* (Stuttgart, 1949), p. 424; Becker, *Bismarcks Ringen*, p. 748.

have such warmth, such inspiration, and such a deep poetic sense of the fact that the dreadful work of the battlefields served a higher ethical purpose; never perhaps did the working of divine providence in the apportionment of rewards and punishments seem, in human terms, to be so just and logical as on this occasion. Hundreds of thousands perceived this as the poetry of the historical process. . . .[87]

This rhapsodic outburst was not unique. Dozens of similar ones can be found in the letters of politicians and scholars in 1871 and in the columns of German newspapers. Reading them leaves one with the impression that a fair percentage of Germans were not content with the victory that had just been won, at least not as a mere feat of arms; they were intent on proving to themselves and others that it had been preordained, that it was a natural reward for German moral and cultural excellences, and that it was an earnest of other triumphs to come. Gustav Rümelin had said as much on the hundredth anniversary of Hegel's birth, which was celebrated in Tübingen while the fighting was still going on:

Before our astonished eyes, this year has become one of the great landmarks, one of the guiding lights of humanity, which in a trice illumines the dark and twisted pathways of the past and opens before our eyes a broad highway leading clearly into the distant future. If Hegel's view of history is correct—namely, that the leading state-personalities take their turn in being the embodiment of the dominant philosophy of the time and in making their characteristic and essential mark upon their age—then history hardly provides us with a more impressive event than this change of scene in the world theatre, as the hitherto dominant people steps behind the curtain and another, long kept standing in the wings, steps to the centre of the stage. And the effect is doubly sublime, since the change is effected so dramatically, and with such powerful blows, as punishment for unparalleled arrogance and blindness, as a victory for the silent and misunderstood power, as a divine judgement such as the world has never seen, inscribed in letters of fire upon the tablets of history.[88]

The hubris is apparent even through the mixed metaphors, and it was recognized as such, here and in other expressions of the mood of the time, by at least one sober observer. In the first of his *Thoughts out of Season*, written in 1873, Friedrich Nietzsche reminded his fellow countrymen that a victory can sometimes be more dangerous than a defeat and that no victory can be more ruinous than one that is misconstrued by those who win it.

[87] Cited in Karl Heinrich Hoefele, *Geist und Gesellschaft der Bismarckszeit 1870–1890* (Göttingen, 1967), p. 449.
[88] Walter Bußmann, *Treitschke, sein Welt- und Geschichtsbild* (Göttingen, 1952), p. 337.

Of all the evil consequences following in the wake of the recent war against France, the worst perhaps is a . . . general error: the error of public opinion and of all those who air their opinions in public, to the effect that German culture also won a victory in that conflict and therefore deserves to be decorated with the laurels appropriate to such extraordinary events and successes. This delusion is highly pernicious, not at all because it is a delusion—for some errors are most salutary and beneficial—but rather because it is capable of converting our victory into a complete defeat: the defeat, even the death, of German culture for the benefit of the 'German Empire'.[89]

What, after all, Nietzsche asked, were the real reasons for the victory over France? They consisted largely of certain technological advantages enjoyed by the Prussian army, a more scientific conduct of operations, superior knowledge and qualities of leadership at all levels of command, and better discipline in the ranks. None of this deserved any description more dignified than proficiency; its connection with education was remote and with culture (to say nothing of moral superiority) non-existent. 'Culture is, above all, unity of artistic style in all the manifestations of a people's life. But to have learned and to know a great deal is neither a means to culture nor a sign of it and, when necessary, is perfectly compatible with the opposite of culture, barbarism: that is, absence of style or chaotic mixture of all styles.'[90]

This argument persuaded few people in 1873, and Freytag's *Grenzboten* rejected it contemptuously (and with a sovereign disregard for logic) with the words: 'When has Germany ever been greater, sounder, and more worthy of the name of a people of culture than today?'[91] It is much easier for us to appreciate the shrewdness, and the prophetic power, of Nietzsche's criticism. No one was ever to have reason to doubt German proficiency. It was demonstrated repeatedly in many fields of endeavour in the seventy-five years that followed the war with France. But the tendency to invest it with an ideal meaning, to confuse it with virtue and morality, and to make it the basis of claims of superiority, continued to be its concomitant.

This kind of confusion of values was not, of course, confined to Germans, and it would be a mistake to make too much of it or to suggest that it was the sole or chief cause of the dark passages in Germany's brief history as a united national state. It is enough to note

[89] Friedrich Nietzsche, *Unzeitgemäße Betrachtungen*, *Sämtliche Werke*, Kröner edn. (Stuttgart, 1964), p. 3.

[90] Ibid., p. 7.

[91] *Die Grenzboten*, xxxii, no. 4 (1873), 104 ff.

that at the very outset of that tragic history a great German writer warned of the possible consequences of failure to fit all of the vital elements of national life into a coherent style and that he did not hesitate to mention barbarism as one of them.

II
The Institutional Structure of the Empire

'Konschtitution, des is Teilung
der Gewalt. Der König dut, wat
er will, un dajejen das Volk, des
dut, wat der König will. — Die
Minister sind dafür verantwortlich,
deß nischt jeschieht.'

ADOLF GLASSBRENNER (1848)[1]

A MONG the many messages sent to Berlin by friendly governments after the formal proclamation of the new Empire was one from the government of the United States of America. In it President Ulysses S. Grant congratulated the German Government in the name of the American people for having completed the long-desired unification of its territory and for its decision to embark on its new career as a federal union like the United States itself, a decision, the President indicated none too delicately, that showed a desire for speedy progress towards the blessings of democracy.[2]

This engaging exercise in self-satisfaction must have amused its recipient, Prince Bismarck, and he subsequently made a point of assuring American visitors gravely that he had been much influenced by the United States constitution when making his own plans for Germany. It is quite possible that he had gone so far as to read that document, but it would be difficult to demonstrate that he borrowed anything from it. The similarities that President Grant found between the two constitutions were as superficial as his prophecy concerning Germany's future political course was erroneous.

One should not, of course, be too hard on the President. He was not alone in failing to understand the constitution of the German Empire. Indeed, in 1867, when it was being considered in its original form, as the constitution of the North German Confederation, a fair

---

[1] 'Aus Herrn Buffeys Tagebuch' (1848), in Adolf Glassbrenner, *Der politisierende Eckensteher*, ed. Jost Hermand (Stuttgart, 1969), p. 100.

[2] Jeanette Keim, *Forty Years of German-American Political Relations* (Philadelphia, 1919), p. 32.

number of German politicians, charged with protecting the interests of their states, had also failed to understand it until after they had accepted it and had learned belatedly that they had misinterpreted clauses that were to affect them very nearly. In its original form and in the somewhat amended one it assumed when it was adapted in 1871 to the needs of the imperial federation, the constitution was a complicated instrument. This was necessarily so, because its author set out deliberately to draft a document that would provide the legal basis for the kind of national union desired by public opinion and by German economic interests, while at the same time preventing the resultant state from entering upon the road that President Grant believed it was destined to travel. The basic purpose of the constitution, in short, was to create the institutions for a national state that would be able to compete effectively with the most powerful of its neighbours, without, however, sacrificing, or even limiting, the aristocratic-monarchical order of the pre-national period. This task invited complication, and it was in fact achieved at the price of ambiguities and contradictions that were always awkward and, as the years passed, invested German parliamentary life, and politics in general, with an increasing amount of friction and frustration.

I

The Empire was a union of eighteen German states of various sizes and forms of government,[3] and one administrative territory, the so-called Reichsland, which comprised the conquered provinces of Alsace and Lorraine and was administered by an imperial governor-general.[4] The federal government consisted of an executive, in the persons of the Emperor and his Chancellor and their staffs, a Federal Council (Bundesrat), composed of delegations from the separate states, and a National Parliament (Reichstag), which was elected by universal manhood suffrage and secret ballot.

The federal executive possessed important powers, particularly in areas that could affect the life and death of citizens. The Emperor exercised control over the whole area of foreign policy, with the right to make treaties and conclude alliances, as well as to declare war and conclude peace. By virtue of the royal power of command

---

[3] The kingdoms of Prussia, Bavaria, Württemberg, and Saxony, the Grand Duchy of Baden, the free cities of Hamburg, Bremen, and Lübeck, and Oldenburg, Lauenburg, Mecklenburg, Lippe, Brunswick, Anhalt, Waldeck, Hesse-Darmstadt, Reuß, and Thuringia.

[4] See Hans Herzfeld, *Deutschland und das verschlagene Frankreich* (Berlin, 1924), pp. 218 ff.

(*Kommandogewalt*), a constitutional concept which jurists found it difficult to explain or define,[5] he commanded the forces of all of the German states in time of war and most of them in time of peace (although, when doing so, it was in his capacity as King of Prussia rather than Emperor, a point to which we shall return); and he had appointive and administrative powers of remarkable breadth and importance, such as the right to declare martial law in case of civil disorder and, in emergency, to declare federal execution against dissident member states and to sequester their territory and their rights of sovereignty. In addition, he was empowered to appoint and dismiss the Chancellor and all other officials of the federal government, to summon, prorogue, and close the Reichstag, to publish and supervise the execution of all federal laws. Finally, he possessed the right to interpret the constitution, a privilege whose importance cannot be overestimated. Bismarck sometimes claimed in his last years, when he had become impatient with restrictions on his own authority, that he was the only interpreter of the constitution, for he was its author. But the Chancellor was only the agent of the Emperor, as Bismarck's own case proved, and Laband, an authority on this ambiguous document, claimed that the monarch was 'the guardian of the constitution'.[6]

Acting through the Reichstag and the Bundesvat, the federal government had legislative authority in the field of commercial and tariff policy, matters of transportation and communications, control of the banking system, coinage and international exchange, weights and measures, patents, consular rights, and other matters of importance to Germany's economic well-being.

It had the right to collect tolls and sales taxes on certain articles like sugar, salt, tobacco, beer, and spirits, and received the income of the postal and telegraph systems.

It will be apparent from this that quite considerable powers were left to the individual states. In all matters that affected the citizen's daily life and the safety and well-being of his family, they possessed jurisdiction. Thus such important areas of public life as education, health services, and police were within the purview of the separate states rather than the federal government, and so were civil liberties, for it must be noted in passing, as one more curiosity of the imperial system, that, unlike the constitutions of other nations, and unlike the

---

[5] See Paul Laband, *Das Staatsrecht des Deutschen Reiches* (3rd rev. edn., 2 vols., Freiburg im Breisgau and Leipzig, 1895), ii. 511–24; E. R. Huber, *Heer und Staat in der deutschen Geschichte* (Hamburg, 1938), pp. 260–1 and the authorities cited.

[6] Laband, *Staatsrecht* i. 182–203.

German constitution of 1849, Bismarck's included no bill of rights or declaration of fundamental liberties. In addition, the execution of most of the laws that were passed by the federal government was left to the governments of the individual states, the federal government merely reserving the right of supervising the administrative arrangements made for this purpose. Tolls and postage due to the federal government were collected by local authorities and then transferred, a system that subtly underlined the states' disinclination to tolerate federal intervention in local matters. In another respect, the states had financial prerogatives denied to the central government, for they alone had the right to collect direct taxes, a privilege that the federal government tried vainly to have modified as financial difficulties mounted in the Wilhelmine period.

In the rights they enjoyed the member states were not equal, the larger ones having exacted certain privileges from Bismarck as their price for joining the union. All of the states of southern Germany which had not been members of the North German Confederation were exempted from the taxes upon beer and spirits, which gave them a preferred position in the national tax structure. The kingdoms of Bavaria and Württemberg were allowed to retain their own railway, postal, and telegraph systems, and were permitted military privileges not extended to other states. Württemberg administered the affairs of its own army and appointed most of its officers, despite the fact that its contingent became a part of the Prussian army. Bavaria retained full command of its armed forces in peacetime, and continued to have a separate War Ministry and General Staff, although their activities were closely supervised by the Prussian military. As a matter of prestige, the Bavarian Government insisted also on the retention of certain rights of diplomatic representation, and to satisfy its desire for an influence on policy-formulation a foreign affairs committee was established within the Bundesrat under Bavarian presidency and with two other permanent members (Saxony and Württemberg) and two elected ones. This gratification was all but meaningless, since Bismarck was no believer in foreign policy by committee and consulted the committee only once in the course of his twenty years as Imperial Chancellor.[7]

---

[7] In 1875 the Bavarian Government tried to win some authority for this committee, but Bismarck took the line that foreign affairs was a 'monopoly' of the Reich and that the southern kingdoms would have to be content with seeing the dispatches that he considered appropriate for them. See his conversations with the Württemberg Minister of State, Freiherr von Mittnacht, in Mittnacht, *Erinnerungen an Bismarck* (Leipzig, 1904), pp. 52 f.

All of the individual states sent delegations to the Bundesrat, and it was theoretically possible for them to use that body as a means of changing the constitution in their interest whenever they cared to do so. But the most striking feature of the Federal Council was the strong position occupied by Prussia, which, by virtue of its size and influence in Germany as a whole, possessed 17 of the 58 votes cast in that body. This was more than enough to enable it to block constitutional amendments that were not to its own interest, and Bismarck at the outset was always confident that in basic matters Prussia would stand on the side of the federal government and would veto any proposed constitutional change that would subvert the Reich it had founded.

Nevertheless, the states retained very extensive powers, a fact that caused much agonizing on the part of advocates of a high degree of centralization. The historian Heinrich von Treitschke, an ardent battler for the concept of a Prussian-controlled unitary state, was appalled by the reserve clauses in the treaties between the North German Confederation and the south German governments and felt that this would mean that the Empire would be hobbled from the beginning by those forces of particularism which had, for so long, stood in the way of effective unification. As a practical politician, Bismarck knew that the concessions he had made, while offensive to some, were the most effective way of breaking down the resistance of the southern governments ('The maiden is ugly,' as someone said at the time, 'but she has got to be married'), and he could take comfort in the fact that, apart from the financial exemptions, the privileges would not amount to much. One distinguished Bavarian politician agreed with him. Prince Hohenlohe-Schillingsfürst said that it would have been wiser of his government to have been concerned less with the retention, for sentimental reasons, of specific Bavarian institutions and more with enhancing Bavarian influence in all federal matters that would affect the kingdom.[8]

Apart from his concern over the practical problems that had to be dealt with promptly in the last months of 1870, Bismarck had other reasons for the attitude he adopted towards states' rights. The south German states were not the only ones that viewed the elaboration of federal institutions with distrust and had a jealous regard for their own privileges and traditional ways. In a sense, the Prussians were as particularistic as the Bavarians, and they had no more desire to

[8] Speech in a cabinet discussion of the constitutional conventions on 30 December 1870, in *Memoirs of Prince Chlodwig of Hohenlohe-Schillingsfürst*, trans. from the German (2 vols., London, 1906), ii. 37.

merge with the Reich (*in das Reich aufzugehen*) than they had shown in 1849. Bismarck agreed with this attitude, although for reasons of his own. The continued existence within the Reich of an enlarged Prussian state with a virtual monopoly of military power, with a position in the Bundesrat superior to that of the other states, and with a parliamentary system of its own, based on a form of suffrage which was not democratic but favoured the propertied classes,[9] was the best possible assurance against any possibility of the federal government succumbing to the forces of liberalism and democracy. In Bismarck's constitutional system, the federal government was given enough influence (particularly with Prussian backing) to keep the particularism of the south within safe bounds, while Prussia was allowed to retain sufficient power to protect the aristocratic-monarchical system by discouraging dangerous experiments on the part of the federal government. The provisions of the constitution, and the omissions from the constitution, that favoured states' rights were inspired by Bismarck's attitude towards the theory of checks and balances, although the elaborateness of his application of that theory might have bewildered its author Montesquieu. In Bismarck's system, as Otto Pflanze has written,[10] every pressure was neutralized by a counter-pressure—the principle of centralization by that of states' rights, the separate states by the federal government, the federal government by Prussia, the nation by the dynasties, and the Reichstag by various legal and psychological factors built into the imperial system.

II

One could, without insuperable difficulty, compose a reasonably plausible argument to the effect that the German Empire of 1871 was the creation of the German people, or, at least, that the Reich would never have come into being if it had not been for the persistent and growing popular desire for unification.[11] Certainly, the German

[9] By royal order of 30 May 1849, universal equal and secret suffrage, which had prevailed in Prussia since April 1848, was replaced by a system that favoured the propertied classes. It divided voters into three classes, according to the amount of taxes they paid, and gave a third of the suffrages to each class. See Fritz Hartung, *Deutsche Verfassungsgeschichte* (2nd rev. edn., Leipzig and Berlin, 1922), p. 154.

[10] Pflanze, *Bismarck*, p. 47. For a summary, see E. R. Huber, 'Die Bismarcksche Reichsverfassung im Zusammenhang der deutschen Verfassungsgeschichte', in Deuerlein and Schieder, *Reichsgründung*, pp. 164–96.

[11] Theodor Hamerow has pointed out that the argument has to be made with discrimination, since significant elements in the national population were either indifferent or hostile to unification, and attitudes were influenced by religious, social, and ethnic factors. Hamerow, *Struggles and Accomplishments*, pp. 337 ff.

people had a better claim to authorship than the German princes, whose selfishness and narrowness of view had been notorious over the centuries and whose lack of national sense had been demonstrated by their perpetual internecine quarrels and their not infrequent alliances with foreign Powers. Yet Bismarck was little interested in their actual historical role in the process of unification when he stage-managed the proclamation of the Reich at Versailles. He not only gave the princes the privilege of offering the imperial crown to William I of Prussia (who showed little gratitude for this generosity but, at least, unlike his brother in 1849, did not refuse the gift) but also built upon this contrived gesture a constitutional theory that held that the Reich was the creation of Germany's dynastic houses.[12]

There was, in short, to be no nonsense about popular sovereignty in the new Empire. The German people were not to be allowed to claim the dangerous powers that the American people, for example, could demand on the basis of their Declaration of Independence and the preamble of their constitution. On the contrary, it was to be clear from the outset that the Reich was a gift that had been presented to them and that, if it were not properly appreciated, it might be withdrawn. The unspoken corollary to Bismarck's constitutional theory—which was to obsess him during his last year in office—was that, if the situation warranted it, if the German people did not in fact show the loyalty and gratitude that their leaders had a right to expect, then the princes could unmake their own creation and refashion it in any way they saw fit.

In the years of constitution-making, Bismarck was still reasonably confident with respect to the loyalty of the broad masses of the German people, and, while setting his face against theories of popular sovereignty, he did not hesitate to give them the weapon that has always been the principal instrument of such sovereignty, namely the ballot. When he had first announced his support of the idea of giving the vote to the people, it had been during the last stages of the political duel with Austria, and he had been principally interested in taking a position in national affairs that would embarrass his antagonist and bring public opinion to the support of the Prussian cause. But when the necessity of outmanœuvring the Austrians had passed, he did not change his mind, presumably because he believed that the common people could be counted upon to respond instinctively to appeals to their loyalty. He wrote in 1866:

[12] The basis for this can be found in the chapter 'Dynasties and Stems' in his memoirs. See Bismarck, G.W. xv. 197 ff.

At the moment of decision the masses will stand on the side of kingship, regardless of whether the latter happens to follow a liberal or a conservative tendency. . . . May I indeed express it as a conviction based on long experience that the artificial system of indirect and class elections is much more dangerous than that of direct and general suffrage, because it prevents contact between the highest authority and the healthy elements that constitute the core and the mass of the people. In a country with monarchical traditions and loyal sentiments the general suffrage, by eliminating the influences of the liberal bourgeois classes, will also lead to monarchical elections.[13]

Because he felt this way, he saw to it that both the constitution of the North German Confederation and that of the Reich that succeeded it provided that elections to Parliament should be by vote of all male citizens who had reached the age of twenty-five and that this vote should be held by secret ballot.

This was less revolutionary than William I had thought when Bismarck first proposed it to him. Bismarck had no intention of allowing the National Parliament to be filled with genuine members of the lower classes, who might be too conscious of the condition of their fellows and too intent upon correcting it. He prevented this possibility by the simple expedient of stipulating that Reichstag members would receive no salaries. He also seriously restricted parliamentary power. The Reichstag's assent was required for all legislation, but it had few powers of initiative and for the most part merely acted upon matters brought before it by the Chancellor and the Federal Council. Draft legislation that it disliked it might amend or delay or even defeat, although in the last case, if the matter was considered important by the government, it could do so only at the cost of a dissolution of the Reichstag, followed by new elections, a prospect which parliamentarians did not ordinarily relish. It had no legal control over the Chancellor, for although the constitution declared that official to be the 'responsible' minister, this did not mean that he was responsible to the Reichstag or that a defeat of his policies would necessarily lead to his retirement, as it would in English constitutional practice. Nor did the Reichstag possess the kind of right of interpellation that would have forced the Chancellor to explain and defend policies in which its members had an interest at a time of their own choosing. Indeed, some important areas of policy were virtually closed to them. While Bismarck was Chancellor, he encouraged the Reichstag to interest itself in all aspects of the nation's economic policy, but he set his face firmly against debates

[13] *G.W.* v. 429, 457.

about the extension of parliamentary powers or excursions by the Reichstag into the fields of foreign affairs and military policy, which he regarded as lying within the competence of the Chancellor's Office and the Crown. In the case of the military, indeed, even the Reichstag's power of the purse was meaningless during most of the Bismarck period.

Despite the limitations that he placed upon it, there is no doubt that Bismarck regarded the Reichstag as an important part of his constitutional system. At a time when the forces of particularism had not been fully subdued, it was a living symbol of the nation's hard-won unity and, as such, a control over divisive forces. In the management of Germany's foreign relations, it was a convenient and effective sounding-board, by means of which German attitudes and objectives could be given resonant expression. Bismarck had already demonstrated, at the height of the dispute over the Grand Duchy of Luxemburg in 1867, the way in which a parliamentary debate could be used to impress foreign opinion, and on frequent occasions during his chancellorship he was to resort to the same technique. Finally, as long as he could manage the Reichstag better than anyone else and secure its backing for government policy, the Reichstag provided Bismarck with a means of demonstrating to the Emperor, upon whose continued favour his own retention of office depended, that he was indispensable. For Bismarck, a well-behaved and co-operative Reichstag was a kind of insurance policy, and this was no less true in the case of his successors in office.

This being so, it is necessary to ask why the parliamentarians did not realize that the Chancellor was more dependent upon them than it might appear from the text of the constitution, and why they did not use the tactic of stubborn resistance, if not obstreperousness, to increase the Reichstag's influence in the state. The rights of debate and assent were, after all, not negligible powers, and they were protected by the legal stipulation that the Reichstag could not be prorogued indefinitely and that new elections must follow promptly upon dissolution.

That there was not more resort to obstructionism and that it was ineffective when tried is to be explained in large part by the nature of the Reichstag's membership and its attitude toward the role of the Parliament in the state. German parliamentarians as a group never acquired the self-confidence and sense of collegial solidarity that were enjoyed by members of Parliament in England or congressmen in the United States or that was common, in Germany, to bureau-crats and army officers. Although many gifted men sat on its benches, they were exceptions among a membership of mediocre minds. The Reichstag did not attract the best in the nation, and those who came to it did not seem to grow in its service. In its early days the percentage of notables and wealthy amateurs among its ranks was high; later these were replaced by an increasing number of full-time professional politicians, often serving particular economic interests.[14] Except for a progressive narrowing of view, the change was not particularly significant. Common to both the Reichstags of Bismarck's years and those of the period before the First World War was a notable lack of enthusiasm about the prospect of challenging the political establishment—that is, the Crown and its agencies—in matters of political importance. This reluctance to seek and fight for widened influence is perhaps understandable in the Reichstag of the 1870s, for the memory of the Prussian constitutional conflict of the 1860s was still green, and few of the deputies who had been a part of that relished the thought of its repetition. This, as much as anything, explains the cave-in of the National Liberals in 1874 over the question (in itself a memory of the 1860s) of the military budget. But it is striking that in the subsequent period there was no diminution of the Reichstag's reluctance to demand a role in determining the requirements of national interest, and it is clear that many parliamentarians were uncertain about the legitimacy of such a demand. Because of this the Reichstag remained a body that reacted more than it acted, a legislative body which, because its members had no faith in their own ability to assume responsibility, contributed to the general lack of direction that characterized German politics after Bismarck's strong hand was removed.

It is tempting, since Hegel has already been mentioned in these pages, to attribute the excessive modesty with which members of the Reichstag regarded their role to the success that that philosopher had had in persuading Germans that the institutions and forms of civilian life had no essential importance except in their relation to the State. This Hegel defined in a highly involved argument in his *Grundlinien der Philosophie des Rechts* (1821) as the highest form of freedom, which was attainable by the individual only when he had realized and transcended the limitations of the family on the one hand and civil society on the other. In Hegel's formulation, the State has at times an almost comically abstract quality, as when he describes it, in terms that tickled the fancy of the young Lassalle,[15] as 'the reality of the

---

[14] On this development, see James J. Sheehan, 'Leadership in the German Reichstag, 1871–1918', *American Historical Review*, lxxiv (1968), 511–28.

[15] Lassalle's conception of the State was, in fact, closer to this definition than to

substantial will which it has in its generalized self-awareness, the reasonable in and for itself'. But this description is followed by a passage that is, politically, both suggestive and ominous, as Hegel distinguishes between the State and civil society as such.

If the State is confused with civil society, and is defined by security, the protection of property, and personal liberty, the interest of individuals as such becomes the ultimate purpose for which they are united, and it would follow that it is something arbitrary to be a member of the State. But the State has a very different relation to the individual; the State is objective spirit itself, and the individual has objectivity, truth, and morality only insofar as he is a member of it. The union as such is true substance and purpose, and what defines individuals is the fact that they lead a general life; their further specific satisfaction, activity, mode of behaviour has this substance and general validity as its starting-point and result.[16]

Ralf Dahrendorf has pointed out that the decisive implication of these lines is that civil society—because it is constructed out of many individuals with contrary interests and passions and numerous parties and groupings that are competing for advantage—is incapable of bringing about a satisfactory constitution of human society. For this something else is needed—something that rises above the structures of civil society entirely—and that something is the State.[17]

There can be no doubt that the long-delayed attainment of German unity was bound to give new weight to this theory, and we have already seen how Gustav Rumelin in 1870 could claim that Hegel's theory of history had now been confirmed. In these circumstances it was easy to identify the State with the Prussian Crown and its instrumentalities, the bureaucracy and the army above all, and to regard all agencies that sought to dispute their authority as mere manifestations of that divisiveness that characterized Hegel's civil society and had characterized Germany in its pre-national stage. No one was more effective in giving wide currency to the political implications of this identification than Heinrich von Treitschke, whose *German History*, an elaborate and eloquent tribute to the Prussian Crown, was perhaps the work that was most representative of the new national spirit,[18] and whose enormously popular lectures

---

Marx's more pragmatic view of the State as the instrument of a dominating class. See Edmund Wilson, *To the Finland Station* (New York, 1948), p. 246.

[16] G. F. Hegel, *Grundlinien der Philosophie des Rechts*, 95, §258.

[17] Ralf Dahrendorf, *Society and Democracy in Germany*, trans. from the German (New York, 1967), pp. 199–202.

[18] His declared purpose, he said in the dedicatory preface to the first volume of the *Deutsche Geschichte* (1879), was to bring 'vigorously forward the men and the institutions, the ideas and the changes of destiny, that . . . created the new nationality'. See

on politics at the University of Berlin had deep and continuing influence on the generation that was to come to political responsibility after 1890. Although Treitschke distanced himself from the philosophical premisses of Hegel's argument, he repeated its substance in his own rejection of the pluralistic society. Thus, in his lectures, he had no hesitation in declaring:

Law and peace and order cannot come to the multiplicity of eternally struggling interests from inside themselves but only from that power that stands above society, armed with a force that is capable of taming wild social passion. Here one begins to get a clear conception of what can be called the moral sanctity of the State. It is the State that brings justice and reciprocal tolerance into the world of social conflict.[19]

Here Hegel's abstraction has been transformed into the ultimate reality and, as Dahrendorf rightly says, the logical constitutional consequences were inescapable. To the neo-Hegelians and to Treitschke's auditors the Imperial Reichstag symbolized the conflict of interests and the mutual antagonism of parties that were destructive of true unity and that had to be resolved by the only authority that was in its essence non-partisan, the Crown. Whatever claims jurists like Paul Laband might make for its competence,[20] the authority of the Reichstag was fatally compromised from the outset in the minds of those who, for emotional or intellectual reasons, accepted the new national conservatism that Treitschke preached. Unfortunately, until after the turn of the century, when the authority of the Crown was diminished by the behaviour of William II, the great majority of Germany's parliamentarians, if we leave the Socialists apart, did accept that philosophy.

III

In the proceedings in the Galerie des Glaces in Versailles on 18 January 1871, the delegation of deputies from the Bundestag of the North German Confederation played, as has already been indicated, a negligible role. They were, however, although somewhat grudgingly, allowed to observe what went on, and some of them were appalled by what they saw. They had reason to be, for the ceremony resembled nothing more or less than a military review, a kind of

Heinrich von Treitschke, *History of Germany in the Nineteenth Century*, sel. and ed. Gordon A. Craig (Chicago, 1975), editor's introduction, pp. xi–xxix.

[19] Heinrich von Treitschke, *Politik. Vorlesungen gehalten an der Universität zu Berlin*, ed. Max Cornicelius (2nd edn., 2 vols., Leipzig, 1899), i. 56.

[20] Laband, *Staatsrecht* i. 260 ff. But note also pp. 271, 301–4, which emphasize the restrictions on its power and its dependence on the Crown.

Großer Zapfenstreich, with Psalms 66 and 21 intoned by a soldiers' chorus, prayers at command ('Helm ab zum Gebet!'), the liturgy according to the *Militär-Kirchenbuch*, and, after the Emperor's proclamation, a thunderous playing of 'Heil Dir im Siegerkranz' and Frederich the Great's 'Hohenfriedburg' March by a military band. Except for the parliamentarians, nearly everyone was in uniform, with side-arms and decorations. Bismarck was no exception. Although he was at this time involved in a bitter dispute with Helmuth von Moltke, the Chief of the General Staff, in which the principle of civil supremacy was at stake,[21] he did not allow this to affect his sartorial taste. He wore the blue coat of the Magdeburger Kürassiere with the insignia of a lieutenant-general, the orange ribbon of the Order of the Black Eagle, and high riding-boots, and carried a pointed helmet in his hand.

All in all, it was a brave show, but one need only look at Anton von Werner's painting of it to understand the better remark of the Catholic politician Ludwig Windthorst, who said, 'Versailles is the birthplace of a military absolutism like that brought to bloom by Louis XIV.' How were these arrogant warriors, whom Werner shows clustered around the war-lord, to be kept under restraint?

Anyone who studied the constitution with this question in mind would have received little reassurance. Apart from the articles which placed the command of all federal forces in the hands of the Emperor, the most important provisions were to be found in Articles 60 and 63. The second of these stipulated that 'the Emperor determines the peacetime strength, the structure, and the distribution (*Einteilung*) of the army', and it was doubtless intended by its author to avoid the kind of parliamentary disputes about army organization that had produced the constitutional crisis of the 1860s. As it stood, it seemed to give the Emperor a kind of blank cheque for anything he might wish to do with his army. On the other hand, he was bound by the provisions of Article 60 of the constitution, which declared that the size of the armed establishment in peacetime must be determined by law;[22] and there was no doubt that this gave the Reichstag an opportunity to exercise considerable control over the armed forces, particularly if its members insisted that the law determining the strength

---

[21] The issues at stake and the settlement of the dispute in Bismarck's favour by a royal order of 25 January 1871 are described in the last chapters of the first volume of Gerhard Ritter's *Staatskunst und Kriegshandwerk: Das Problem des 'Militarismus' in Deutschland* (4 vols., Munich, 1954 ff.); and in Craig, *Prussian Army*, pp. 213 f.

[22] See Huber, *Heer und Staat*, pp. 260–1.

of the armed forces and its accompanying budget be periodically reviewed.

Such implementation of Article 60 the government was determined to prevent. In the debates of the constituent assembly of the North German Confederation in the spring of 1867 Bismarck had worked strenuously to establish the principle that the strength of the army and the funds provided should be automatically calculated on the basis of the size of the population, a system which, if accepted, would have effectively removed military affairs once and for all from the competence of the Reichstag. The liberal deputies had fought back so strenuously that Bismarck, not wishing to jeopardize the constitution as a whole, had agreed to a compromise, the so-called 'iron budget', which stipulated that the size of the army would, until 31 December 1871, be set at 1 per cent of the population and that the government, for its support, should be granted 225 talers for each man under arms. In 1871 this law was prolonged for another three years, but this was not enough for the army chiefs, who had set their hearts on financial security and complete freedom from parliamentary interference, and, in 1874, with the full support of the Emperor, they sought to settle the issue once and for all. At their urging, the government submitted to the Reichstag a draft law setting the size of the army at 401,659 men, a figure that was to be considered permanent in peacetime until such time as the government should announce a modification. This law was introduced by Moltke, doubtless in the hope that deputies would be too impressed by the victor of Königgrätz and Sedan to oppose his desires.

This tactic did not work, strong resistance to a permanent law manifesting itself in all parties except that of the conservatives, and a situation arose that resembled in some particulars the conflict between Crown and Parliament that had reached its height in 1862. It proved easier to solve, however. Bismarck, in ill health at this time and distracted by foreign affairs, had had, if we can believe what he told the British ambassador, no part in drafting the law, which had been largely the work of Roon, the War Minister, and the Emperor himself. Nor was he much enamoured of it. He had, during the constitutional crises, been the doughtiest defender of the army against parliamentary pretensions, but he was not enthusiastic over the prospect of an expansion of the army's role in the state. In both 1866 and 1870 he had had serious disputes with Moltke, whom he accused of poaching in his own preserve, and he suspected Edwin von Manteuffel, formerly Chief of the Military Cabinet and now one of the strongest supporters of the draft law, of intriguing against him in the hope of succeeding him as Chancellor. Leaving these personal factors aside, Bismarck did not enjoy the thought of having a law enacted that would not only free the army from parliamentary restraints but would make it independent of the civilian authority, which resided in his own person. So he rather relished the discomfiture of the soldiers when their plans went awry, and he resolved to use their difficulties to demonstrate how much they needed him.

He accomplished this by playing upon that essential weakness of the Reichstag members that has been commented on above: their dislike of finding themselves in opposition to the authority of the state. In a series of conversations with key parliamentarians, Bismarck said that it was becoming clear that, in a time of national insecurity, the Reichstag was resolved to render the country powerless. This was being done, moreover, by men who had been elected by patriotic electoral districts after they had posed as supporters of his own policies. If they thought that they could with impunity abandon the duty of supporting the best interests of the Reich, a dissolution of the Reichstag and new elections would prove them wrong. This hint was enough to throw the opponents of the draft law into disarray; they were soon accusing each other of having, by doctrinaire politics, caused what the distinguished Heidelberg jurist Bluntschli called a 'childish conflict between the Reichstag and the Emperor'; and before long there was a manifest desire for a compromise. Bismarck provided it. The strength of the army was established at the figure called for in the original draft law, but it was to stand for only seven years, after which time it had to be renewed.[23]

The Septennial Law did not please the leaders of the army, and the Emperor himself seems initially to have resented Bismarck's willingness to compromise with people whom the monarch had, in a speech delivered after his bill had run into trouble, described as 'internal enemies' who were attempting to shackle 'the leadership of their imperial war-lord'. Upon reflection, however, William came to a more philosophical view. After all, he wrote to the War Minister, 'really in our time seven years are almost half a century when one thinks of the seven years from 1863 to 1870! In this way, we have the army organization intact for seven years and, after seven years, we will perhaps find ourselves *before*, or even *after*, another war; if not, then the population will have grown and we will have to increase the recruits . . .'[24]

[23] On the crisis of 1874, see Craig, *Prussian Army*, pp. 220–2 and the authorities cited.

[24] Albrecht Graf von Roon, *Denkwürdigkeiten* (5th edn., 3 vols., Berlin, 1905), iii. 409.

The military chiefs had, in fact, every reason to be satisfied. They had secured themselves against tight budget control, and they were protected against other forms of parliamentary interference by Article 63 of the constitution and by certain special circumstances arising from the curious relationship between the army and the Empire. The salient fact was that, in the strictest legal sense, there was no imperial army; the national force was an army made up of contingents from the separate states, under Prussian command. This being so, there was no imperial War Minister, unless Bismarck was to be regarded as such. The Chancellor did bear ultimate responsibility for military affairs before the Reichstag, but this did not mean a great deal, since he had no control over the internal affairs of the army. They lay within the competence of the Prussian War Minister, whose authority extended to all of the armed forces of the Empire and who supervised the General Staff, the Academy of War and other military schools, and the logistics, supply, and personnel departments. In the Reichstag, it was this official, rather than the Chancellor, who generally answered questions that might be raised by deputies curious about military developments; but trying to elicit information from him was always a frustrating experience, since he was empowered to answer points raised about imperial forces, if he wished, but not about the Prussian army, and was permitted to discuss administrative matters, but nothing that related to the command of the army (which the Emperor regarded as nobody's business but his own).[25]

The military chiefs were not, however, content with the advantages that this situation gave them. In their eyes, the army was a church that needed worshippers and expected them to bring gifts but had no intention of giving them vestry privileges. To the high priests in the Military Cabinet and the General Staff, the War Minister's parliamentary function was a potential threat to the inviolability of their office, and they sought, therefore, if not to eliminate it, then to render it innocuous. In 1883, for reasons that will be described below,[26] they succeeded, with Bismarck's assistance; and from that success can be dated the growing irresponsibility of the military establishment, which was to bear such tragic fruit in 1914.

---

[25] On the powers and paradoxical position of the War Minister, see esp. H. O. Meisner, *Der Kriegsminister 1814–1914, ein Beitrag zur militärischen Verfassungsgeschichte* (Berlin, 1940).

[26] See below, Ch. V, p. 163.

IV

It will have become apparent from what has been said so far that the constitutional structure of the new German Empire was so clumsy and so full of contradictions and ambiguities that it would not be easy to run the Reich efficiently. Bismarck's system of checks and balances was so elaborate that even its author was uncertain at the outset about how it was to be managed. With his jealous regard for his own authority, he intended as far as possible to keep power in his own hands, but how was that to be done, and from what office? In the days when he was drafting the constitution of the North German Confederation, Bismarck apparently intended the office of Chancellor to be a relatively modest one; the Chancellor was to be little more than the presiding officer of the Bundesrat and would, like the other Prussian delegates to that body, receive his instructions from the Prussian Foreign Minister, that is from Bismarck himself. When the Reich was founded in 1871, Bismarck had long since given up that view and, indeed, the rather excessive emphasis upon Prussian supremacy implied by it. Indeed, he apparently intended to shift the balance the other way, for he assumed the position of Federal Chancellor and began to build up a strong Chancellor's Office (Reichskanzlei) under Rudolf Delbrück, while giving up the position of Minister President of Prussia (although not that of Foreign Minister). This did not work, and there was so much friction between the Prussian and federal governments that, after five months, Bismarck resumed the Prussian premiership. Without his roots in Prussian soil, he said, he was incapable of directing imperial affairs. 'If you make me only a minister of the Reich,' he said later, 'then I am sure that I will be just as bereft of influence as any other minister.'[27]

Yet even with the three key positions in his strong hand, Bismarck found it difficult to run the affairs of the Empire without constantly having to deal with conflicts of competence between its component parts and to wrestle with problems that were the result of compromises written into the charter. He was never free of the irritation caused by indifferent execution of federal laws by local agencies or of the fear that privileges accorded to the Crown and the army might by misused by irresponsible advisers or ambitious brass-hats. At the same time, the constitutional system provided so many opportunities for obstructionism and even for defiance of federal authority that the most expeditious way of solving crises often seemed to be to

[27] On Bismarck's changing views about the appropriate power of the Reich Chancellor's Office, see Böhme, *Deutschlands Weg*, pp. 257 f., 475 ff.

threaten to resort to constitutional revision, or, in plainer words, to the correction of the situation by force rather than existing law. Between 1867 and 1871 various state governments had been bullied into co-operation by these means, and on frequent later occasions the fear of a *coup d'état* persuaded other groups to be co-operative. Early in his official life Bismarck had explained the technique to his friend Roon. 'Once there has been some rattling about with references to proclamations and the making of *coups*, my old reputation of being given to the frivolous application of force stands me in good stead, for people say, "*Nanu, geht's los!*". Then all the people in the middle and all the half-hearted moderates are ready to negotiate.' He never abandoned his belief in the efficacy of the method and he was not alone in believing in its legitimacy. In a sense, as Michael Stürmer has written, the threat of destroying the constitution was a constitutional factor of major importance in Imperial Germany.[28]

V

These constitutional problems were not the only ones that the young Reich faced. It also had what in modern parlance is called a *Bewußtseinsproblem*, a problem of identity. It was neither a new creation nor a product of the past. Its title evoked the memory of the medieval Empire while its structure excluded some of that Empire's most illustrious provinces. In form and structure it was a repudiation of the old German Confederation, but it allowed some of its members privileges similar to those that they had enjoyed in that organization. It looked, at least superficially, like an actualization of the plan of unity devised by the men of the Frankfurt Parliament of 1848–9, but its leaders specifically denied any connection of that kind, as Bismarck did in discussions concerning a national flag when he said, 'The Prussian trooper does not want to hear anything about Black–Red–Gold.'

The uneasy relationship with the past worried some Germans. The political publicist Konstantin Frantz went so far as to argue that the disregard shown for history during the making of the constitution would deprive Germany of the psychological conditions of healthy development.

It is clear that a country containing as many different elements as Germany does, a country entwined with its neighbours on all sides and bordering on six different nationalities, a country, moreover, that has experienced a history comparable to no other in respect both of the variety of political

[28] Michael Stürmer, 'Staatsstreichgedanken im Bismarckreich', *Historische Zeitschrift*, 209 (1969), 566–615.

forms created and the intrinsic importance of its events—that such a country must necessarily have achieved a constitution peculiar to itself. If this constitution was to be amended or improved, how could the appropriate forms be found except by deriving them from existing conditions? Instead an attempt was made to borrow these forms from various foreign constitutions and by means of such a compounded copy to produce a German national constitution, while at the same time proclaiming the principle of nationality which ought rather to have excluded anything foreign. What a strange contradiction!

What had been forgotten in this process, Frantz continued, was the uniqueness of Germany's historical development. Its heritage was imperial, coming from a community that was superior to mere states and had permitted national differences to exist within an international system. 'It was Germany's special privilege and special calling', he insisted, 'to constitute this living connection between state law and international law in the development of Europe.' But that tradition had been sacrificed, impatiently and fecklessly, for the sake of novelty.[29]

The uneasiness that rings in these words was not felt by all, or even most, Germans in 1871. There were many who were fascinated by a sense of release from the past, by an exhilarating feeling that doors had suddenly been flung open to reveal enchanting vistas of the future. The editor of the journal *Historisch-politische Blätter* expressed this feeling in 1871 by writing, 'We all breathe a quite different air than before the great events', and the memory of the excitement of this sensation remained so clear and undimmed in the mind of the Naturalist and theatre director Heinrich Hart that he could still write years later that 1870 had seemed to him, in the little town of Münster in Westphalia, like a spring wind that blew away the stale and airless winter of the Biedermeier period; it has been 'the end of the Middle Ages, the beginning of the modern era'.[30] Nor were these single voices. There were many who felt that German unification would open opportunities in all fields of human endeavour and encourage new triumphs in science and technology, in art and literature, in education, and in politics.

Most entranced by this last possibility were those Germans who had always felt a secret shame over the negligible role played by their

[29] Ellinor von Puttkammer (ed.), *Föderative Elemente im deutschen Staatsrecht seit 1648* (Göttingen, 1955), cited in W. M. Simon, *Germany in the Age of Bismarck* (London, 1968), p. 154. See also K. Frantz, *Der Föderalismus als das leitende Prinzip für die soziale, staatliche und internationale Organisation unter besonderer Bezugnahme auf Deutschland* (Mainz, 1879), esp. pp. 220 ff., 299 ff.

[30] Hoefele, *Geist und Gesellschaft*, pp. 15–16.

country in world affairs and over the tolerant but faintly contemptuous remarks that foreigners made about 'the land of writers and thinkers'. The hero of Friedrich Spielhagen's novel, *Sturmflut* (1877), is a young man of lower-middle-class origin who has earned a master's certificate in the merchant marine and, in consequence, seen much. He explains to an audience critical of the new Germany why he left his ship in order to fight for his country in 1870 and what the victory has meant to him and to all of those

who like me have experienced what it means to belong to a country that is not a nation and, because it isn't, is not regarded as complete by the other nations with whom we trade, yes is really scorned by them . . . And so I thank God with a full heart because we have an Emperor, a German Emperor, for it could be no less than a German Emperor if we were to demonstrate to the English, the Americans, the Chinese, and the Japanese *ad oculos* that they were no longer conducting commerce and concluding treaties with Hamburgers and Bremeners, with Oldenburgers and Mecklenburgers, or even with Prussians, but with Germans who sail under one and the same flag, a flag which has the will and the power to guard and protect the last and most humble of those who have any share in the honour and good fortune of being a German.[31]

Since Spielhagen is not ordinarily inclined to outbursts of patriotism, this passage must be given a certain weight and probably indicates his sense of how widespread these feelings were in Germany in the 1870s. As a progressive, Spielhagen may also have been remembering, and agreeing with, the words that the political historian F. C. Dahlmann had uttered in the Paulskirche in January 1849: 'The road of power is the only one that will satisfy and appease our yearning for freedom. . . . Germany as such must finally step forward into the ranks of the great political Powers of the world.'[32] Certainly there were others who remembered that speech and felt a sense of fulfilment and expectation; and Dahlmann's student and lifelong admirer, Heinrich von Treitschke, spoke to the last feeling when he wrote: 'When the twentieth century rises, the transatlantic world will know that the Germans are no longer, as in Schiller's days, fleeing from life's challenges into the quiet recesses of the soul.'[33]

But was this new-found national pride, and the promise of future gratifications in the transatlantic world, enough to solve the problem of self-recognition? To many Germans it was not, and Theodor

---

[31] Friedrich Spielhagen, *Sturmflut* (1877), Bk.1, Ch. 9.
[32] Friedrich Meinecke, *Die Idee der Staatsraison* (3rd edn., Munich, 1963), p. 464.
[33] Andreas Dorpalen, *Heinrich von Treitschke* (New Haven, 1957), pp. 253 f.

Schieder has described the difficulties that important groups had in making a positive identification with the new national state.[34] Their number included a not inconsiderable number of liberals, who continued to waver between a hope that the Reich would turn out to be the realization of their aspirations and a growing realization that all evidence spoke to the contrary. It included conservative groups who had resisted membership in the Reich in 1870 and who were unreconciled, as well as the bulk of the politically organized working class, who felt that unification had in no wise improved their lot and that the federal system was deliberately designed to thwart their interests. And, finally, it included, and would continue to include, the majority of Germany's writers, painters, and musicians, who, after the heroic Reichsgründungszeit had passed, were, with very few exceptions, critical of the new Germany (if, indeed, they took the trouble to comment on it at all, for in these circles *Innerlichkeit*, the tendency to withdraw from, or be indifferent to, politics was not nearly as dead as Treitschke wanted to believe).[35]

Symptomatic of these signs of the continued incompleteness of Germany was the difficulty of finding any agreement on the question of national symbols. This seems to have been a matter of complete indifference to Bismarck, who once expressed himself on the subject of a national flag by saying, 'For all I care green and yellow and party favours, or even the flag of Mecklenburg-Strelitz'. But even those who regarded such things as being important found it hard to make proposals that were generally satisfactory. Germany had no national flag until 1892, and no national hymn until after the First World War; and the choice of the day of the victory at Sedan as the national holiday was widely opposed. Even in the matter of national monuments, the Germans had their troubles. The Teutoburger Wald monument (1875) and the Niederwald 'Germania' monument (1885) celebrated events so remote in time as to have little sentimental importance for the new Reich. The tendency of artists who received a commission to design a national monument was, *faute de mieux*, to fall back on a statue of Bismarck, like the one by Begas at the Großer Stern in Berlin (1901), showing him in Kürassier uniform, as he used to appear in the Reichstag, with Atlas, Siegfried, and personifications of power and reason of state at his feet, or the one by Lederer and Schaudt at the head of the Reeperbahn

---

[34] Theodor Schieder, *Das deutsche Kaiserreich von 1871 als Nationalstaat* (Cologne, 1961).

[35] See Heinrich von Treitschke, *Aufsätze, Reden, Briefe* (4 vols., Berlin, 1929), i. 78.

in Hamburg (1906), portraying the Chancellor as Roland, the symbol of the indomitability and unshakable unity of his people.[36]

Bismarck, in fact, became not only the political symbol of the Reich but the culture hero as well. It is his figure that we sense behind Treitschke's persistent personification of the state in the *German History*, as well as in his prescriptions for effective statecraft in the lectures on politics. It was fascination with him that was ultimately responsible for the cult of personality that dominated German painting in the 1870s and revealed itself in the heroic figures of Böcklin and Lenbach and Feuerbach, and the same thing may be said of the preoccupation with force and unconditionality that we find in the stories of Paul Heyse and Conrad Ferdinand Meyer, who, after living for years in Switzerland, became a German patriot again as a result of the victory over France and tried in his *Jürg Jenatsch* (1876) to draw a flattering portrait of his hero.[37] The Chancellor's presence was so obsessive that Friedrich Nietzsche (whose own work was not untouched by his influence) wrote wryly in *Götzendämmerung* (1888): ' "Are there German philosophers? Are there German writers? Are there good German books?" people ask me when I am abroad. I blush; but, with that gallantry of which I am capable in hopeless situations, I answer, "Yes! Bismarck!" '[38]

Nietzsche was not alone in sensing that new growth might be difficult under Bismarck's shadow. The novelist Gustav Freytag had long been fascinated with the personality of the Chancellor and had, in 1868, in a letter to Albrecht von Stosch, written a highly original analysis. 'You ask me', he wrote,

in what category of statesmen Bismarck should be placed and whether he will leave a school behind him. Between the romantics and the aesthetes of the aristocracy, the Humboldts, Bunsen, and Usedom, on the one hand, and the constitutional present, on the other, lies a thin cultural layer of undomiciled (*touristischen*) dilettantes. Young German and the *Junker* class in its elegant types—Freiligrath, Lenau, Fürst Pückler, Lichnowsky—insolent, taking pleasure in risks, without firm principles, without a school, chiefly dependent upon French education. The greatest late fruit of this growing

---

[36] See, *inter alia*, Thomas Nipperdey, 'Nationalidee und Nationaldenkmal in Deutschland', *Historische Zeitschrift*, 206 (1968), esp. 542 f.; Hans-Ernst Mittig, Zu Joseph Ernst von Bandels Hermannsdenkmal im Teutoburger Wald', *Lippische Mittelungen aus Geschichte und Landeskunde*, xxvii (1968), 200–23; Rudolf Walter Leonhardt, 'Deutsche Denkmäler', *Die Zeit*, 3 (10 Oct. 1975); German Werth, ' "Mögen sie nur kommen!"': Zur Hunderjahrfeier des Hermannsdenkmals im Teutoburger Wald', *Tagesspiegel* (Berlin) (16 Aug. 1975).

[37] See Richard Hamann and Jost Hermand, *Gründerzeit* (Munich, 1971), pp. 45 ff., 118 f., 156 ff.

[38] Nietzsche, *Götzendämmerung*, Kröner edn., pp. 122 f.

period, which in literature stretches from 1830 to 1840, is, or so it seems to me, Bismarck. The salient feature is lack of reverence, a tendency to regard everything capriciously and from a personal point of view, and, at the same time . . . a vital energy that is fresh and impudent. For that reason, he will not have a following either. . . .[39]

This little-quoted passage is suggestive, on the one hand, because of Freytag's recognition of the fact that Bismarck was not just another *Junker* but precisely the kind of original who would cause the gravest suspicion among his agrarian peers, and on the other, because of his shrewd guess that the Chancellor's style received its imprint from Young Germany, a movement of brilliant prose (but little poetry), slashing political polemics, and total disrespect for the classical past (notably demonstrated by Börne's campaign against Goethe). In our own context, however, Freytag's judgement is interesting principally because of his concern about Bismarck's wilfulness and selfishness. This did not abate with the passage of time. In 1879 the novelist wrote to his publisher: 'We are still going to suffer a long time from the circumstance that the political strength of the nation has, for one and a half decades, been personified in one man. And, along with all of the good fortune and progress of this age, we are going to have to bear the damage that attaches itself to this kind of domination by a single individual.'[40]

---

[39] *Gustav Freytags Briefe an Albrecht von Stosch* (Leipzig, 1913), 24 Sept. 1868.
[40] He repeated these views to Stosch. Ibid., p. 137.

III
The Consolidation of the Empire:
Politics and Economics
1871–1879

Ich bin ein Gründer froh und frisch,
schon heute setz ich mich zu Tisch,
als dürft ich weiter mich nicht quälen,
als meine Zinsen nur zu zählen.

Gottlob, ich weiß mir selber Rat,
nichts soll mich kümmern Stadt noch Staat:
Dem Gründerleben treu ergeben,
verschaff' ich mir ein würdig Leben.
HEINRICH HOFFMANN VON FALLERSLEBEN (1872)[1]

Im schwarzen Frack und weißer Weste
hat Krautz den Hödel amputiert—
auch du, o Reichstag, kommst in Gala
zum Werk, das man im Schilde führt.

Das Beil, vom Bundesrat geschliffen,
wird dir gar sauber vorgelegt,
und das Schafott ist aufgeschlagen
der Block steht fest und unbewegt.

. . .
Die Freiheit aber, die du tötest,
wird nicht beenden ihren Lauf.
Schon morgen, spottend ihrer Henker,
steht sie aus Gräbern siegend auf.
MAX KEGEL (1878)[2]

O UR discussion of the constitution has anticipated events and
consequences that could not have been foreseen by Germans
in 1871 and has reached conclusions that few of them would
have regarded as inevitable. A German admirer of William Ewart

[1] Heinrich Hoffman von Fallersleben, *Gesammelte Werke*, ed. Heinrich Gerstenberg
(8 vols., Berlin, 1890–3), v. 198.
[2] *Deutschland, Deutschland. Politische Gedichte vom Vormärz bis zur Gegenwart*, ed.
Helmut Lamprecht (Bremen, 1969), p. 242.

Gladstone might, indeed, have had some reason for believing that that statesman's principles, or something like them, were beginning to triumph in his own country. He could have pointed to the fact that, at a time when middle-class liberalism was in the political ascendancy throughout Western Europe, the forces of movement in Germany bore a strong resemblance to the parties in office in England, Belgium, and France, shared their philosophy and their vision of the future, and were transforming Germany in accordance with it.

This was, of course, only superficially true, but almost a decade passed before the political and social realities that lay below the surface of German parliamentary life became discernible. The first shock to liberal self-confidence came with the financial crash of 1873; the final dissipation of their political dreams came in 1879 when basic political and economic changes confirmed and consolidated the conservative–feudal social order and the authoritarianism of the political system.

I

The first session of the Imperial Reichstag was formally opened in the White Gallery of the Royal Palace in Berlin on 21 March 1871. In the presence of the Queen-Empress, the Crown Prince and his consort, and other princes of the realm, Emperor William solemnly informed the assembled deputies that

the honourable calling of the first German Reichstag is, first of all, to do everything to heal the wounds caused by the war and to bestow the gratitude of the fatherland upon those who paid for the victory with their blood or with their lives. At the same time, gentlemen, you will begin the work by means of which the organs of the Reich will be created for the fulfilment of the task posed for you by the constitution, namely 'the protection of Germany's existing law and the cultivation of the well-being of the German people'.[3]

The parliamentarians who received this charge were divided into six main party groupings, plus a number of splinter groups representing the Poles of Posen, the Danes of North Schleswig, and the conquered provinces of Alsace and Lorraine. On the extreme right was the German Conservative party, the party of Prussianism, aristocracy, and landed property, with its main support in the districts east of the Elbe. Disorganized and without effective leaders at this time, it had little strength in the Reichstag in 1871, although this appearance of weakness was illusory, since its true seat of power was

---

[3] Ernst Deuerlein, *Der Reichstag: Aufsätze, Protokolle und Darstellungen zur Geschichte der parlamentarischen Vertretung des deutschen Volkes 1871–1933 (Bonn, 1963), p. 160.*

always in the Prussian House of Deputies. An offshoot of this party was the so-called Reichspartei (in Prussia called the Free Conservatives) which was less exclusively agrarian in its point of view, combining both landlords and industrialists in its membership, and less critical of Bismarck than the Conservatives were in the first years of peace. The Free Conservatives were, indeed, called the party of Bismarck *sans phrase*, giving undeviating support to his national policies and providing many officials for his ministries.

Larger than either of these, and more broad-gauged in its appeal, was the Catholic Centre party, an avowedly confessional party that had been founded in 1870 to protect the rights of Roman Catholics in a predominantly Protestant country. Despite this fact, it always embraced individuals and groups of varied political and social views, with the consequence that—unless the autonomy of the Catholic Church, or the freedom of religious education, or the defence of states' rights was at stake—it was likely to show a greater freedom of action than other parties, and was often accused of opportunism. But there was an inner consistency to its policy. For the most part, it was conservative in defence of tradition, of the prerogatives of the Crown, and of the hierarchical structure of society, as well as in all matters affecting the morals of society. On the other hand, it was open-minded about political reform as long as it did not contribute to centralization and, in matters of social reform, it tended to be progressive, in accordance with the tradition of Social Catholicism established by Adolf Kolping in the 1840s and reaffirmed by Bishop Wilhelm Emmanuel von Ketteler, who, from 1850 until his death in 1877, preached the necessity of combating the evils of capitalism by establishing workers' co-operatives, organizing Christian trade unions, and otherwise helping the poor to raise their standard of living.[4] The party's greatest electoral strength lay in southern Germany, the Rhineland, Silesia, and the Polish provinces of Prussia.

There were two liberal parties. The National Liberals represented a fusion of the bulk of the Prussian Progressive party that had fought Bismarck during the constitutional conflict but thrown their support behind his foreign policy in 1866 and a National Liberal party founded in Hanover by Rudolf von Bennigsen in the same year. Representing the educated and wealthy middle class and the upper bureaucrats, they shared, as has already been indicated, many of the characteristics of liberal parties in other countries, being supporters

---

[4] See e.g. Bischof Ketteler, *Die Arbeiterfrage und das Christentum* (1864) and the standard biography, Fritz Vigener, *Ketteler: Ein deutsches Bischofsleben im 19. Jahrhundert* (Munich and Berlin, 1924).

of centralization, *laissez-faire* economics, secularization of national life, constitutional government, and material progress. Their strongholds were in Saxony, Hanover, Baden, and the industrial areas of the Rhineland. The unregenerate left liberals of 1866 formed the bulk of the Progressive party, which shared most of the economic views of the National Liberals but was much more pronouncedly in favour of the extension of parliamentary rights, more critical of government policy in general, and—true to the tradition of the *Konfliktszeit*—suspicious of military expenditure and the army's personnel policies.

Finally, just beginning the remarkable growth that was to make it the largest single party in Germany in 1914, there was the Social Democratic party which will be considered in greater detail below.

In the Reichstag of 1871 the National Liberal party held a commanding position, with 155 seats out of a total of 399. Since it could count on the support of the Progressives and the Free Conservatives for most of its projects, it was assured of a majority. All three of these parties were filled with men who had long regarded German unity as not only politically desirable but economically necessary, and they were intent now upon removing the remaining obstacles to the development of trade and manufacturing and upon doing their utmost to create the kind of economic infrastructure that would enable Germany to compete in the markets of the world. It is unlikely that Bismarck had a very deep understanding of these economic objectives[5]—he accepted the National Liberals as a kind of governmental party because they could bring him the support necessary to strengthen the federal government against the remaining divisive forces in the country—but the head of the Chancellor's Office, Rudolf von Delbrück, understood them very well and thoroughly approved of them.

To the casual observer, Delbrück was a typical Prussian bureaucrat of the old school, competent, reliable, and completely colourless, but this was a misleading impression; he was as passionate in his own way as Bismarck was in his and, late in his life, said that he had always been driven by Lutheran tradition and Hegelian *Staatsethik* 'to devote my person to the generality incorporated in the State'. He

---

[5] He was a good husbandman and watched carefully over the state of his private fortune. He saw Prussian prosperity as an instrument of power and, in general, valued the political aspects of economic policy. Thus he tended to have no fixed economic principles and to be opportunistic. On the other hand, he was not impulsive in this respect and allowed himself to be guided by experts in technical matters. See Fritz Stern, *Gold and Iron: Bismarck, Bleichröder and the Building of the German Empire* (New York, 1977), pp. 34, 97, 177, 179–81.

had found his opportunity in long years of service in the Prussian Zollverein, that remarkable organization that widened the intellectual horizons of dozens of young men who might never otherwise have lifted their eyes above the boundary markers of East Elbia, and there—in the opinion of the great Socialist publicist, Franz Mehring—he had done more to advance the unification of Germany than a dozen generals and diplomats.[6] In the 1850s he had worked effectively to repair the injuries inflicted on the state by the Punctation of Olmütz and had not only fended off Austrian attacks upon the Zollverein but had strengthened the organization by skilful fence-mending with the member states; and in the early sixties he had continued, with a stubbornness that sometimes made Bismarck complain that he was restricting his freedom of diplomatic action, to resist any concessions to Austria that might weaken that organization.[7] When the North German Confederation was established Bismarck made him head of the Bundeskanzleramt, which was tantamount to placing the economic direction of the Confederation in his hands; and in this position he had entered into a fruitful collaboration with the National Liberals and the Free Conservatives that resulted in the passage of eighty-four separate laws and forty new commercial treaties, a remarkable legislative achievement that included the standardization of weights and measures, the establishment of a superior commercial court in Leipzig, a new labour law that gave workers freedom of organization and bargaining, and a law giving joint stock companies freedom to extend their operations throughout the whole are of the federation without having to satisfy special regulations imposed by local authorities.[8]

With the founding of the Empire, the Bundeskanzleramt became the Reichskanzleramt and formed the centre of the federal administrative system, with the function of a combined Ministry of Commerce and Ministry of Finance. For the next five years, Delbrück continued to be the source of inspiration for most of the basic economic legislation that the National Liberal votes turned into law—the legislation that established a uniform coinage for the Empire, for example, a new commercial code for trade and industry, and an Imperial bank (1875)—and his strong influence not only maintained the emphasis on free trade that had long characterized

[6] Franz Mehring, *Gesammelte Schriften*, ed. Thomas Höhle, Hans Koch, and Josef Schleifstein (15 vols., Berlin, 1960–7), vii. 324.

[7] See e.g. Böhme, *Deutschlands Weg*, pp. 175–8.

[8] See Adalbert Wahl, *Deutsche Geschichte von der Reichsgründung bis zum Ausbruch des Weltkrieges* (4 vols., Stuttgart, 1926–36), i. 61 ff.

Prussian commercial policy but encouraged his parliamentary allies to push it further by demanding a scaling-down of existing duties on imports of iron manufactures.[9]

All of the initiative in these earlier years did not, of course, come from Delbrück. The National Liberal leadership had legislative ideas of its own, some of which the Chancellor encouraged, and many of the more than one hundred laws passed by the Reichstag in its first session reflected their common desire to promote centralized government in Germany at the expense of the prerogatives of the separate states. Thus, at the initiative of the National Liberal deputy Eduard Lasker, the legislative competence of the federal government in the field of civil and criminal law was extended, and a far-reaching overhauling of court procedures began that eventuated, in 1877, in a law making rules of procedure identical in local, district, state, and provincial courts. In 1879 the reform of the judicial system was capped by the establishment at Leipzig of a supreme court of appeal, and a codification of the civil law was begun, which was not, however, completed until the turn of the century.

When they departed from the purely administrative sphere and entered that of politics, the liberals found that the federal government was not always as accommodating and that Bismarck was not always as sympathetic to their passion for uniformity and centralization. Their attempts to bring their reforming zeal to the separate states he received coolly, refusing, for instance, any efforts by the Reichstag to correct the situation in Mecklenburg, where unrelieved absolutism still prevailed and where there was no representative parliamentary body of any kind, a situation unique in Germany. Heinrich von Treitschke described conditions in Mecklenburg as being of a kind that 'no civilized nation could regard without a blush of shame',[10] and the overwhelming majority of liberals felt the same way. But, although the Reichstag repeatedly proposed a constitutional amendment stipulating that each federal state must have an elected representative assembly, Bismarck allowed the Bundesrat to defeat this on every occasion.

He was not much more co-operative when the liberals turned their attention to the problem of local self-government in Prussia, and, if he finally tolerated the efforts that led to the reform of the administrative organization of rural counties—the so-called Kreisordnung

[9] Böhme calls the second part of his book 'Das "Delbrücksche Deutschland": Freihandelsautonomie und gouvernementaler Liberalismus (1867–1876)'. *Deutschlands Weg*, pp. 209–416.

[10] Erich Eyck, *Bismarck: Leben und Werk* (3 vols., Zurich, 1941–4), iii. 55.

of 1872—it was probably due to his political differences with the feudal nobility in the early seventies. In any event, it was the feudal class that was affected by the new law, which abolished the hereditary representation of noble families on the county diets as well as their monopoly over the post of county councillor (Landrat). This official, who presided over the county council and the committee it selected to run the county's affairs, was henceforth a state official with legal training, whose ambitions generally lay beyond the district he administered. In the county diet, half the seats were controlled by the landowners, but the others were filled by elected representatives of the towns and the peasantry, a change that could be regarded as only a modest victory for liberalism. Nor was the fact that estate owners were deprived of police power over their holdings a much more impressive one; this represented a formal rather than a real change, since the provincial presidents usually selected the honorary officials charged with administering the newly created police districts from among the local *Junker*. To put an end to feudalism, which was the liberals' objective, proved indeed to be a difficult business, the slightest change in the old order meeting the concerted opposition of the entrenched landowners; and even when they were forced into line—as they were in this instance, when the King created twenty-four new peers to assure final passage of the law in the Prussian Chamber—they remained entrenched. The new Kreisordnung did not substantially alter the dominant position of the *Junker* in the county diets, and did not affect their economic power at all.[11]

Liberal attempts to accomplish something on the city and provincial level made little headway. A law drafted by the Prussian Minister of the Interior, Count Friedrich Eulenburg, for an extension of self-government in the cities, failed in its passage in the Chamber of Peers because of amendments injudiciously tacked on it by liberals in the Lower House; and there were no further attempts to change municipal government before the First World War. Liberal pressure was successful in some broadening of the functions of provincial government, particularly in the area of social welfare and agricultural administration, but all efforts to make the provincial councils truly representative bodies with advisory functions and

[11] See Hans Herzfeld, *Johannes von Miquel* (2 vols., Detmold, 1938), i. 313; Oncken, *Bennigsen* ii. 237; S. von Kardorff, *Wilhelm von Kardorff* (Berlin, 1936), pp. 76, 80 f.; Ziekursch, *Politische Geschichte* ii. 264 ff.; Robert M. Berdahl, 'Conservative Politics and Aristocratic Landholders in Bismarckian Germany', *Journal of Modern History*, xliv (1972), 1–20.

some rights of initiative came to nothing. The new Provinzialordnung of 1875 did not change the authoritarian nature of the provincial government, and the provincial presidents were never much more than agents of the central government.[12]

In areas closer to the heart of governmental power, Bismarck was willing to make even fewer concessions to liberal principles. As we have seen, the debate over the military budget in 1874 was the first real confrontation between the liberal philosophy and that of absolutism since the end of the constitutional crisis in Prussia, but it was also one in which, essentially, the earlier result was confirmed. A similar defeat was suffered by the liberals in the debate over the uniform Press Law in the spring of the same year. Bismarck never had much respect for the people who worked on newspapers, but he did not underestimate the potential effect of what they wrote. During the constitutional conflict he had, in a sense, entered the newspaper business himself, selecting certain newspapers for special favours, in the form of news releases and postal advantages denied to other journals, and after 1868–9 part of the so-called Guelf fund, the sequestered fortune of the royal Hanoverian family, was used to influence the policies of these newspapers. About 700,000 R.M. a year were set aside for the Foreign Office and a smaller amount for the Ministry of the Interior, and both ministries seem to have passed a part of this on to such papers as the *Norddeutsche Allgemeine Zeitung* and the *Post*, both of Berlin, and the *Kölnische Zeitung*. These papers generally supported government policy and were frequently used by the Chancellor to float *ballons d'essai* or give intimations of government intention, and, at least until 1876, when Bismarck began to curtail his Press activities, government control over the first two of these journals extended even to the choice of their editors. Over the great majority of Germany's newspapers, however, the government had no control, except in the laws governing such matters as libel, slander, and treason.[13]

It was the ambition of Eduard Lasker, in the eyes of some the outstanding parliamentarian of the Empire's first decade, to lay the foundations for a truly independent German Press by means of a law

[12] Ziekursch, *Politische Geschichte* ii. 272–5.

[13] On this, see esp. Irene Fischer-Frauendienst, *Bismarcks Pressepolitik* (Münster, 1963) and E. Naujoks, 'Bismarck und die Organisation der Regierungspresse', *Historische Zeitschrift*, 205 (1967). Hans Philippi, in 'Zur Geschichte des Welfenfonds', *Niedersächsische Jahrbücher für Landesgeschichte*, xxi (1959), 190–254, argues that the fund was not big enough to allow Bismarck to do all the things he is supposed to have done with it. But see Stern, *Gold and Iron*, pp. 262 ff. on this, on the government's control of the Wolff Telegraph Bureau, and on Bleichröder's extensive Press contacts.

that would bind all parts of the Empire and free the newspapers from the kind of restrictions which, in Prussia, for example, had shackled them since Bismarck's ordinances in 1863. The crux of the matter was the right of editors to protect their sources, and it was for this that Lasker fought most earnestly in 1874. Even if he had found the National Liberal deputy a more sympathetic person, instead of a constant thorn in his side,[14] Bismarck could not have reached agreement with Lasker on this point. To have done so would, in his opinion, have allowed wholly irresponsible people to speculate about the government's intentions, to spread distorted information about its most intimate concerns, and—here Bismarck's sensitivity to personal criticism, which involved him in dozens of libel suits, betrays itself—to weaken confidence in servants of the Crown. Security of the state denied the possibility of what in western countries was called privileged information, and an editor who allowed his newspaper to reveal what the government felt should be kept secret must be prepared to atone for this with a term in prison. On this point Bismarck was unmovable, and, when the Press Law of 1874 was passed, it was without the kind of guarantees that journalists in the west had come to take for granted.[15]

If measured in terms of legislative success, therefore, the liberal record in the Empire's first years was a mixed one, most impressive in the economic and purely administrative spheres, much less so in matters that touched upon government prerogatives, the powers of the Crown, or even long-established social privilege. In one additional field, that of religion, the liberals' influence upon government policy was impressive but unfortunate in its results.

II

The most sensational new dramatic production of the year 1871 was a play called *Der Pfarrer von Kirchfeld* by an unknown playwright called Ludwig Anzengruber. After its première in the Theater an der Wien in Vienna, Heinrich Laube, the leading critic of the day, described it as 'aesthetically remarkable and politically remarkable',

---

[14] In January 1875, in conversation with Heinrich von Sybel and Christoph von Tiedemann, Bismarck said that Lasker was a 'national disease' and 'even more of a vine-louse than Windthorst'. *Bismarck Gespräche*, ed. Willi Andreas and K. F. Reinking (3 vols., Bremen, 1965), ii. 125. This was after Lasker's revelations in 1873 and at a time when Bismarck was beginning to be uncomfortable in his collaboration with the National Liberals. The Socialists regarded Lasker as a trimmer, and Bebel referred to him as the 'parliamentary chaperone (*Anstandsdame*)'. See August Bebel, *Aus meinem Leben* (5th edn., 3 vols., Stuttgart, 1920), ii. 146.

[15] Ziekursch, *Politische Geschichte* ii. 297–9.

a judgement that a modern reader might be disposed to contest, at least with respect to its literary qualities. Its political thrust, however, is still discernible. Anzengruber's play, a bitter attack upon the inhumanity of the hierarchy of the Roman Church, tells the story of a simple village priest, who places his sense of responsibility to God and his fellow man higher than his duty to the regulations of his Church and who, because he tolerates a mixed marriage and gives Christian burial to a mother who has committed suicide in anguish over her son's atheism, is deprived of his post on orders from Rome.

It is not difficult to see why this play, which marked the beginning of Anzengruber's long and successful career, played for years in Austrian and German theatres, before enthusiastic audiences of all classes. It appealed to both the anticlericalism that is always strong in Catholic countries and the fear of Rome that was, during the nineteenth century, to be found in most Protestant ones, emotional attitudes that had been heightened by the decrees of the Vatican Council of 1869–70, and particularly by the new doctrine of papal infallibility in matters of faith and morals. Anzengruber was not the only artist to respond to the widespread unease which this caused. Such diverse works at Conrad Ferdinand Meyer's *Huttens letzte Tage*, with its powerful evocation of the Reformation hero, Eduard Griesbach's *Tannhäuser in Rom*, Paul Heyse's story *Der letzte Zentaur*, Arnold Böcklin's painting *St. Francis's Sermon to the Fish*, and Wilhelm Busch's masterful combinations of malicious verse and drawing, *Heiliger Antonius*, *Fromme Helene*, and *Pater Filucius*—all products of the years 1870–2—were reflections of a strong anti-papal feeling with deep roots in both the middle and the working classes.

It was inevitable that the German liberal parties should make this feeling their own and give it an aggressive form. As representatives of a philosophy which opposed all institutions that placed restraints upon the freedom of the individual, the liberals saw Rome as a natural enemy, which had, moreover, declared its hostility to the liberal spirit and all forms of progress in Pius IX's *Syllabus Errorum* in 1864. The doctrine of papal infallibility they saw as an aggressive act and they invented the theory that the victory in the war against France was the answer to it. This was the view of Treitschke, who always saw the Church of Rome as a vampire draining the vital energies of *Deutschtum*, and it was the opinion of other National Liberal chiefs, like Johannes Miquel, who said contemptuously of the members of Centre party: 'Germany came into existence against the will of these gentlemen. They are now the vanquished!' Indeed, the very existence of the new Catholic party, and its efforts during the debates on the constitution to win some written assurance that the Roman Catholic Church would be allowed to order its own affairs without interference, appeared to the liberals to be flagrantly provocative and aroused in them the desire to strike back at the party, and at Rome, by attacking it in the field which liberals always regarded as particularly their own, that of education.[16]

They would not have been able to fulfil this desire if Bismarck had not encouraged them to do so, and it is still not easy to explain why he proved to be so co-operative. Certainly, it was not out of doctrinal zeal. In his own way, Bismarck was a religious man who sought the guidance of God in his administration of state affairs (and usually, Ludwig Bamberger jeered, found the Deity agreeing with him), but he was singularly unmoved by confessional differences, and not at all by the somewhat superstitious abhorrence of Rome felt by people like Treitschke. During the recent war he had maintained cordial diplomatic relations with the Vatican and had actually given serious consideration to the advisability of offering an asylum to the pontiff in case he should feel compelled, in consequence of the Italian Government's occupation of Rome, to flee abroad.[17] The Chancellor's fertile mind saw any number of political advantages to be gained from this plan but he also saw that, even if the King could be persuaded to accept it, public opinion never would, and he soon put it aside.

There would have been no reason, however, for him to authorize an anti-papal campaign had it not been for the Centre party. He objected to the existence of a confessional party because it seemed to stand for allegiance to an authority other than the national state; and his worst suspicions were confirmed when a letter of Bishop Wilhelm von Ketteler of Mainz to the Vatican in the spring of 1871 elicited a statement from the papal secretary Antonelli declaring the *Curia*'s solidarity with the party. From that moment on, Bismarck seems to have been prepared to launch an anti-Church campaign on the broadest possible front, justifying it as necessary to the security of the state. Perhaps his most extensive elaboration of this theory came in a speech to the Prussian Chamber of Peers in March 1873, after the campaign was well under way.

The question that confronts us becomes in my opinion distorted and the light in which we regard it falsified if it is looked on as a confessional or

---

[16] See Fritz Fischer, 'Der deutsche Protestantismus und die Politik im 19. Jahrhundert', in *Probleme der Reichsgründungszeit 1848–79*, ed. Helmut Böhme (Cologne and Berlin, 1968), pp. 64–6.

[17] Busch, *Tagebuchblätter*, i. 371.

religious one. It is essentially political. It is not a matter of an attack by a Protestant dynasty upon the Catholic Church, as our Catholic fellow-citizens are being told; it is not a matter of a struggle between faith and unbelief. What we have here is the age-old struggle for power, as old as the human race itself, between kingship and the priestly caste, a struggle for power that goes back far beyond the coming of our Saviour to this world, the struggle for power that Agamemnon fought with his seers at Aulis and which cost him his daughter and prevented the Greeks from putting to sea, the struggle for power that filled German history from the Middle Ages until the destruction of the German Empire . . . and which found its terminus in the medieval period when the last representative of the illustrious Schwabian imperial dynasty died on the scaffold by the axe of a French conqueror who was allied with the Pope of that day. We were close to an analogous solution of the problem, translated of course into terms of our day. If the French war of conquest, whose outbreak coincided with the publication of the Vatican decrees, had been successful, I do not know what things one would have to tell, even in the Catholic parts of Germany, about the *gestis Dei per Francos*.[18]

This curiously unsystematic excursion into history is interesting, not only because of its virtual acceptance of Treitschke's view of the war of 1870 as a victory for Protestantism, but also for its studied reference to France. With that sovereign disregard for fact that he was apt to show when engaged in combat, Bismarck had forgotten how desperately preoccupied the Vatican had been in 1870 with its own problems in Italy and had convinced himself, without much evidence to support his view, that it had been working in the French interest. On other occasions, he was to accuse it of having worked through local priests to arouse disaffection in Prussia's Polish provinces, and he often hinted darkly at an enormous foreign conspiracy of Catholic Powers that would seek to destroy the Empire unless Germans took the proper defensive steps.

The first of those steps had been taken on his own initiative in July 1871 when, after openly declaring war upon the Centre party and the Roman *Curia* in an inspired article in the *Kreuzzeitung*, Bismarck dissolved the Catholic Section of the Prussian Ministry of Culture, because, as he later explained, its chief, a Dr. Kratzig, formerly in the service of the Catholic Radziwill family, had systematically encouraged the Polish language at the expense of German in Posen, so that in many villages young people could speak no German at all. Shortly after that, in a conversation with Beust, the Austrian minister, he intimated that it was his intention to go much further, in fact to remove all priests from the state service, to separate Church and

[18] Bismarck, *G.W.* xi. 289 f.

State, to move against Catholic educational institutions, and to institute civil marriage in Prussia. He was as good as his word.[19]

In January 1871 the office of Minister of Culture in Prussia fell vacant, and, following a suggestion of Delbrück, Bismarck persuaded the King to give the post to a counsellor in the Justice Ministry named Adalbert Falk.[20] The new minister was a gifted and energetic man who deserved more from history than he has received, for he is remembered chiefly for his role in the fight against the Catholic Church, and his important contributions to the Prussian school system, which authorities have ranked second only to those of Altenstein, are largely forgotten. He was Bismarck's chosen instrument for pressing the fight against the Church on the Prussian level (although the Chancellor, characteristically, was given to elaborate disavowals of his measures when these seemed advantageous to him). It was Falk, for instance, who drafted the new law on supervision of schools, which came before the Prussian Parliament in February and touched off acrimonious debates in both Chambers, Bismarck's own interventions—a slashing attack on the Centre leader Windthorst as a supporter of the Guelf dynasty and a scarcely disguised accusation of lack of patriotism against the Conservatives—being so intemperate as to give some weight to the theory that he was still suffering from the strain of the years of unification and was close to a nervous breakdown. The law that occasioned these rhetorical pyrotechnics called for the abolition of all Church supervision of schools, thus outlawing Protestant as well as Catholic influence on school curricula, which explains the lack of enthusiasm that Bismarck complained of among the *Junker*.[21]

The acceptance of the principle of state schools free of clerical influence was hailed by the liberals as a victory for their principles, and their satisfaction increased when, during the summer of 1872, Bismarck authorized the Bundesrat to bring in a law directed at their almost traditional enemy, the Jesuits. As Ludwig Windthorst said in the Reichstag, it was difficult to see what a government that had at its disposal all of the resources of the army, the police, the bureaucracy, the universities, the public schools, and the vast majority of the country's newspapers had to fear from the Society of Jesus, but

---

[19] Friedrich Ferdinand Count von Beust, *Memoirs* (2nd edn., 2 vols., London, 1887), ii. 261 f. Accounts of the Kulturkampf are to be found in Ziekursch, *Politische Geschichte* ii. 220–56; Wahl, *Deutsche Geschichte* i, 136, 139 f., 142 f., 176 ff.; and Kardorff, *Wilhelm von Kardorff*, pp. 68–73.

[20] On Falk, see Eyck, *Bismarck* iii. 93 ff., and the biography by Erich Förster (1927).

[21] See e.g. Wahl, *Deutsche Geschichte* i. 160, 181 f., 202 ff., 204–7.

rational arguments were powerless against a feeling that had been nurtured for decades by novels like Eugène Sue's *The Wandering Jew* and had, more recently, been reinforced by Wilhelm Busch's warnings against

> Pater Luzi, finster blickend,
> Heimlich schleichend um das Haus.

The law passed. It forbade the establishment of Jesuit institutions of any kind in Germany, dissolving those that already existed, and gave the government the right to forbid individual members of the order to reside in defined localities, as well as the right to expel them from the country at will. One might have thought that this glaring example of discriminatory legislation would have moved even the most ardent anti-Jesuits to reflection, for it set an ominous precedent. It did not have this effect, and the law was greeted nationally with enthusiasm bordering on rapture. It was in the wake of this legislation the famous physician and left liberal deputy Rudolf Virchow coined the term Kulturkampf in a speech in which he said that the struggle against the Roman Church was, with every day that passed, assuming more and more 'the character of a great struggle for civilization in the interest of humanity', a formulation that was accepted and repeated from one end of the country to the other.

This enthusiasm was not to last and, indeed, had begun to turn even before the crusade had reached its height. The year 1873 was a difficult one economically, and this had its effect upon public confidence in both the government and the parties that were the loudest in their anticlericalism. Apart from that, the nature of the laws passed in Prussia in May 1873 and the measures used subsequently by the government in its attempt to enforce them could not help but arouse doubts concerning the course the government was following. These laws made attendance in a Gymnasium and a university and successful performance in an examination in philosophy, history, and German literature requirements for ordination as priest or minister and transferred all disciplinary authority over the Church to state agencies. When the church hierarchy, understandably, refused to admit the validity of these laws, the government responded with stringent penalties against the violators and even more extreme legal restrictions on church freedom. A law of May 1874 gave the Prussian Government the power to expel all clerics who persisted in practising their religious functions without having satisfied state requirements, and others authorized the state to take measures to fill sees and churches left vacant by failure of chapters to replace deposed ecclesiastics. In 1875, when a papal encyclical declared all of the measures passed by the government invalid and compliance with them punishable by excommunication, the government responded on the one hand by cutting off financial support until the laws had been recognized by local bishops and on the other by banning from Prussia all monastic orders, except those engaged in medical service. Meanwhile the most extreme measures had been taken against individuals whose conscience would not permit them to obey the new laws. Bishops and priests were imprisoned and expelled in numbers that astonished foreign observers, and by 1876 a total of 1,400 parishes—almost a third of those in Prussia—were without incumbents.

The disruption that was caused in the lives of German Catholics by this circumstance, and by such consequences of it as the deprivation of the sacraments, was profound, but no more so than pangs of conscience felt by many non-Catholics as Falk's laws became increasingly severe. Some years later the Protestant theologian Christian Ernst Luthardt described some of the psychological effects of the Kulturkampf:

It is a bad thing when the state punishes actions that are considered as purely religious ones and as matters of conscience, and when, in consequence, the punishment loses the character of punishment in the eyes of the people and becomes its opposite. It hardly promotes the authority of the state and its sanctions when, in the eyes of many of the better class, even imprisonment begins to be regarded merely as a title to greater respect. In short, the state cannot conduct a war against a large part of its own population without causing, on all sides, profound injury to the moral consciousness.[22]

By the mid-seventies many Germans were concerned about the long-term effects of the anti-Church crusade upon the moral fabric of the nation, already affected by the corrosive materialism of the times, and others were beginning to wonder what the new Empire's chances of survival would be if its Catholic population were permanently alienated by the repression practised against its religious leaders. Bismarck might stoke the anti-Catholic fires with new rhetorical outbursts, as he did following the attempts made on his life in Kissingen in July 1874 by a young and unbalanced Catholic cooper's apprentice, but the unease concerning the effects of his programme continued to spread among all but the most bigoted priest-haters and the most doctrinaire liberals.

But by this time Bismarck himself was uneasy. He could not pretend that his campaign against the Centre party had been suc-

<hr>

[22] Hoefele, *Geist und Gesellschaft*, p. 382.

cessful or promised ever to be so. As the legislative measures drafted by Falk became increasingly severe, so did the solidarity of Catholic believers become increasingly impressive, and this was reflected in election results. In the Reichstag elections of 1874 the Centre party doubled its popular vote and won so many new seats that, with the reliable support of the Danes, the Poles, and the Alsatians, it could now count on 95 votes in parliamentary divisions. Its gains in the Prussian Chamber of Deputies were almost as big. The Chancellor was never one who was given to protracted self-delusion, and he decided to cut his losses.

The first sign of this came in a speech in the Reichstag on 16 April 1875 in which he surprised his auditors by saying that, throughout history, there had been militant popes and peace-loving ones and that he hoped that one day there would again be one of the latter sort with whom it would be possible to make an accommodation. This clear intimation that he was ready to consider an offer had no immediate results, for Pope Pius IX, who was considerably more stubborn about standing by his principles than the Chancellor, lived for almost another three years. But when he died and was succeeded by Leo XIII, the first action of the new pontiff was to dispatch a letter to the German Emperor, expressing the hope that friendly relations might be restored. Leo made it clear, however, that the price would be high and would involve the revocation of the May Laws and the dismissal of their author, Adalbert Falk.

Bismarck could hardly meet these conditions and expect to retain the support of his customary allies in Parliament. But his long association with the National Liberal party had, on the other hand, begun to seem onerous to him, and the party overweening in its demands for a greater share in political power, in the form of ministerial appointments; and he was willing to pay a price for reliable new partners in the Reichstag and in the Prussian Chamber. The religious issue, therefore, like the issue of commercial policy that will be discussed below, was subsumed in the intricate play of Bismarck's domestic politics. An unprecedented visit of Ludwig Windthorst to Bismarck on 31 March 1879, and his appearance at one of the Chancellor's evening receptions for parliamentarians in May indicated that a successful *revirement des alliances* had been achieved. Falk was dismissed in June—not without some hesitation on the Chancellor's part, for he admired the minister's great abilities and his political courage—and from that time onwards the battle for civilization was systematically dismantled, until all that was left of it was the laws on school supervision and civil marriage.

Erich Eyck, in his biography of Bismarck, has described the way in which the Chancellor, during this process, made speech after speech in which he blandly contradicted everything he had said earlier in defence of the laws that were now being repealed.[23] It is doubtful whether any other European statesman of his age could have carried this off without suffering so much in reputation that he would have been forced to resign. But Bismarck never lacked self-assurance, and he was too pleased by the success of his political manœuvre to be concerned over the other effects of his religious policy. One is tempted to compare him with that Earl of Cardigan who led the Light Brigade into the Russian guns at Balaclava and then retired in good order himself, leaving ruin and destruction behind him. However much the Chancellor might seek to gloss it over, the damage wrought by the Kulturkampf was great. Much that had been won for the cause of national unity during the war against France had been trifled away during the years in which Germans had deliberately been set against Germans on confessional grounds. The hierarchy of the Catholic Church in Germany had been made more ultramontane than it ever had been during the days of the Vatican Council, and the great mass of Roman Catholic believers had been imbued with a distrust of their government that was to last for years. The state bureaucracy and the courts had acted in ways —or had been made to act in ways—that could only damage their reputation for strict impartiality in the eyes of German citizens of all faiths, and that was a serious loss indeed. The Protestant Churches suffered a similar loss, for, although their leaders protested bitterly, for selfish reasons, against the institution of civil marriage, they were silent in the face of the repression of their fellow Christians and confirmed the already prevalent impression that the Protestant establishment was merely an instrument of the authoritarian state. Finally, the cause of German liberalism received another and, in this case, an almost irreparable blow.

This last result can, of course, hardly be blamed on Bismarck, for the liberals, in a kind of doctrinaire besottedness, went their way eagerly, and with scant regard for their own principles. Eduard Lasker was one of the few who recognized this, and during the debate on the law against the Jesuits—which the Centre deputy August Reichensperger rightly called 'a declaration of modern liberalism's bankruptcy in the field of the spirit'—he sought to stay his colleagues' heedless course. His efforts were in vain. His colleagues

---

[23] Eyck, *Bismarck* iii. 131 f.

cheered Bismarck's speeches to the echo, even when they violated both parliamentary principle and the laws of evidence, as when he charged the Centre party with responsibility for Kullman's attempt on his life; they blindly approved the same kind of persecution of individuals that they had fought, honourably if vainly, during the constitutional crisis in Prussia. In the name of freedom they under- wrote laws that denied it, and placed their party, which pretended to maintain the cause of the individual against arbitrary authority, squarely behind a state that recognized no limits to its power. Even if Bismarck had not abandoned and broken them in 1879, it is doubtful whether they could have survived this betrayal of their own philos- ophy.

This was all the more so because, once the first popular enthusiasm for the attack on the Church had begun to wane, people began to question the motives of those who had been most eager to launch it, and the doctrinaire anticlericalism that inspired many of them became particularly suspect. Ludwig Windthorst once said that the real cause of the Kulturkampf was the growing lack of religious faith, and he equated this with materialism, 'the materialism that rules the world and fights against everything that is religious'.[24] One did not have to look far to see other signs of this pervasive mat- erialism, for some of its ugliest manifestations were evident in the period of economic boom and speculative frenzy that was called the Gründerzeit, in which it was noticeable that prominent liberals were as active as they were in the fight against Rome. When the economic crash came in 1873, this circumstance was not forgotten, and it was easy for people to draw the kind of conclusion drawn later by Franz Mehring, when he wrote: 'For the wily tribe of Gründer, this 'Kul- turkampf' was only play-acting, which was designed to make it easier to plunder the masses. One can count upon it, with deadly assurance, that whoever thundered loudest in Press and Parliament 'against Rome', whoever most solemnly summoned up the shade of poor old Ulrich Hutten were the ones most deeply stuck in the Gründer swamp.'[25]

III

One of the most interesting, although certainly not one of the most read, of Wilhelm Raabe's novels is *Pfisters Mühle*, written in 1884. A rueful comment on the passing of the pre-industrial age, it is a story

[24] Ludwig Windthorst, *Ausgewählte Reden* (Osnabrück, 1903), i, pt. 2, pp. 132 ff.
[25] Franz Mehring, *Aufsätze zur deutschen Literaturgeschichte*, ed. Hans Koch (2nd edn., Leipzig, 1961), p. 313.

of the Reich's first decade and tells of the way in which an old mill, which houses a restaurant and has for generations been a meeting and drinking place, a centre for picnics and concerts, for local students and townspeople, is destroyed by the establishment of a sugar factory upstream, which pollutes the water, kills the fish and the vegetation, and makes the air unbreathable. Pfister finally hires a lawyer to prosecute the factory owner Krickerode and wins his case, without, however, being able to save his mill. When the lawyer takes up his brief, he looks at Pfister with wondering eyes and asks, 'For God's sake! Why didn't you put some of your money in Krickerode?' ('Weshalb haben Sie eigentlich Krickerode nicht mitgegründet?').

The confusion of values that is suggested by these words was not uncommon in Germany in the first three years of the Empire's existence, during which a great number of people from all classes proved to be so intent upon the accumulation of wealth and the enjoyment of it that they were oblivious to the forms of social pollution that accompanied them. This was the Gründerzeit, named after the great manipulators who 'founded' gigantic enterprises on the basis of paper and little else and who led millions of Germans in a frenzied dance around the statue of Mammon that ended in exhaustion and, for many, financial ruin.

The essential reasons for this are to be found in the victory over France and the resultant unification, which filled the minds of many producers and speculators with excessively great expectations, and, more particularly, in certain features of the settlement made with the defeated foe. The French Government was compelled to cede to Germany the provinces of Alsace and Lorraine—which, with their rich deposits of minette ore and potash, and their well-developed textile industry, greatly contributed to the subsequent economic growth of Germany, although this was not immediately felt—and to pay an indemnity of 5 billion francs plus interest. Bismarck had thought of this as an intolerable burden that would make a speedy military recovery impossible for France, and he had consulted his banker Gerson Bleichröder and Count Henckel-Donnersmarck with respect to the figure that should be demanded. He may subsequently have regretted following their advice, for the French met the terms with inconvenient speed.[26] By means of an international

---

[26] Bleichröder had, in fact, thought 5 billion too high. For his role in the negotiations, see Stern, *Gold and Iron*, pp. 150–5, 320–7. He was surprised by the speed with which the French met the payments.

loan that was greatly over-subscribed, they were able to start payments almost immediately and to pay off the whole sum by May 1873, the transfers being made through the Rothschild banking house to the firm of Bleichröder and Hansemann, who acted for the German Government. Out of the money paid, the Imperial Government retained less than half, and a good part of that went into building projects and military expansion which in themselves stimulated the economy. The rest went to the individual states and from them, by means of local building programmes, railway construction, the repayment of war loans, and the payment of pensions to widows, orphans, and invalids, into private hands. The impact of this significant expansion of the amount of free capital in circulation was made even greater by the currency reform of 1871 which added another 762 million mark to it. This marked increase could not help but cause an overheating of the economy.

The speculative boom that followed was probably inevitable, given this condition of excessive liquidity, but it was encouraged by some special circumstances. The recent war had put a heavy strain on Germany's railway network and used up equipment at a much faster rate than normal. There was now so great a need for repair, re-equipment, and extension of lines in both northern and southern Germany, as well as in the lands annexed from France, that machine and tool works, and other establishments upon which railway construction depended, were swamped with orders.

The expansion needed to meet this demand benefited heavy industry in general, while calling people's attention to the growth potential of railway stock. This explains the success with which the greatest entrepreneur of the boom years, Baron Bethel Strousberg, persuaded investors to support his grandiose schemes for the construction of new lines in Poland and Romania and Eastern Europe. Moreover, the profits that accrued from expansion in one field seemed to prove that expansion in any field would bring profits, that bigness in itself was the key to success. Here is where the Gründer played their part. Aided by the liberalization of the laws governing the establishment of joint stock companies, they would take a modest establishment, a shoe factory perhaps, or a brewery, and incorporate it. Their technique was usually to provide it with a distinguished board of directors, preferably headed by a member of the aristocracy ('We absolutely need a high aristocratic name,' says the Gründer in Spielhagen's *Sturmflut*, the best of the novels dealing with this period. 'You don't understand our insular patriotism. A judas goat must go ahead, but then, I tell you, the whole herd will follow. Therefore, a kingdom for a judas goat!'[27]); this body would issue a glowing prospectus concerning the unlimited profits that would be realized from the investment in what, on paper, was a rapidly expanding enterprise; and then unlimited quantities of shares would be sold, which usually, given the psychological mood of the time, went up. Between 1871 and 1873, 726 such new companies were founded, compared with only 276 in the period 1790 to 1870; and their apparent success encouraged new investment and ever more doubtful expansion. The latter was true, for instance, of the construction industry, which in Berlin, for example, lent itself to plans for the establishment of whole new suburbs, and not only laid out streets and delineated lots, but cut down groves of trees in the Grunewald for the houses that were to stand on them, a process that still lives in the music-hall song

Im Grunewald, im Grunewald, ist Holzauktion!

This kind of optimistic expansion was the order of the day; it affected all branches of production, the proprietors of which comforted themselves, when they had doubts about the financial underpinning of their enterprises, with the thought they would always get support, when it was needed, from banks, which were also proliferating to an astonishing extent (41 new ones since 1871) and were playing a major role in the stock market and the securities exchange.[28]

It is doubtful whether the rage for speculation was ever again as comprehensive and democratic until the days of the big bull market in New York in 1928. Felix Philippi wrote in his memoirs of his youth:

Everyone, everyone flew into the flame: the shrewd capitalist and the inexperienced petty bourgeois, the general and the waiter, the woman of the world, the poor piano teacher and the market woman; people speculated in porter's lodges and theatre cloakrooms, in the studio of the artist and the quiet home of the scholar; the *Droschke* driver on his bench and Aujuste in the kitchen followed the rapid rise of the market with expertise and feverish interest. The market had bullish orgies; millions, coined right out of the ground, were won; national prosperity rose to apparently unimagined heights. A shower of gold rained down on the drunken city.[29]

The country responded by giving itself over to a frenzy of luxury and sensation during which the money that came so easily was spent

[27] *Sturmflut*, Bk. I, Chs. 13–15.
[28] On the growth of German banking, particularly in Berlin, see Annemarie Lange, *Berlin zur Zeit Bebels und Bismarcks* (Berlin, 1972), pp. 203–6, and *idem*, *Das Wilhelminische Berlin* (Berlin, 1967), pp. 225–35. See also Böhme, *Deutschlands Weg*, pp. 320 ff.
[29] Quoted in Hoefele, *Geist und Gesellschaft*, p. 101.

as ostentatiously as possible, in order to prove that one had it. *Gründerprunk* was a term that applied equally to the small tradesman swilling champagne in Poppenberg and Langlet's luxurious restaurant on Unter den Linden, Bavarian farmers buying stables of racehorses, and stock-jobbers building ornate *Paläste* and filling them with overblown paintings by Hans Makart. It had other, more disturbing aspects, for it was accompanied by a relaxation in public morals that was reflected in an increase in the number of drinking places in the big cities, and in the incidence of public drunkenness, in a massive preoccupation with sex on the part of theatre producers, who filled their stages with the crudest kind of bedroom farces, in the growth of prostitution in all large urban centres, and in the sharp increase of crime, particularly sex crimes, the number of rape cases in Berlin, for instance, doubling between 1872 and 1878. There was good reason for church leaders, educators, and officers of the law to be concerned, and the leading philosopher of the day, Eduard von Hartmann, spoke darkly of the manic search for pleasure as a disease that was consuming his country.

But the fevered patient now received a purge. On 7 February 1873 Eduard Lasker rose in the Reichstag and in a three-hour speech laid bare the realities of what he called 'the Strousberg system', demonstrating that it was intended to swindle the small investor in the interest of unscrupulous operators. In convincing detail, Lasker also showed how high-placed politicians and civil servants, including Hermann Wagener, a long-time adviser of Bismarck, had condoned legal irregularities in granting railway concessions from which they profited.[30] These charges fatally weakened public confidence and precipitated a wave of selling in the Bourse; and the boom dissolved into total collapse. Just as the process of enrichment had been democratic so was that of ruin, making no distinction between dignitaries like Field-Marshal Ludwig von der Gablenz, the only Austrian commander to win an engagement against the Prussians in 1866, and humble people like the music teacher Kreisel in Spielhagen's novel about the débâcle. On the balance, it was probably people of moderate means who had entrusted their life savings to the speculators who suffered most, but Gablenz was only one of many distinguished men who committed suicide because their involvement had led to ruin and disgrace.

It has often been pointed out that the stormy figure of Hauke Haien in Theodor Storm's famous story *Der Schimmelreiter* (1888)

---

[30] See Gordon R. Mork, 'The Prussian Railway Scandal of 1873: Economics and Politics in the German Empire', *European Studies Review*, i, no. 1 (1971), 35–48.

may be taken as a symbol of the Gründerzeit, for Hauke fought against the force of the sea to win new land and was in the end swept away to his death by his implacable foe. It should be remembered, however, that his work survived, for the dykes were rebuilt according to his design and accomplished his purpose. This was, to a large extent, true also of the work of the Gründer. It was not all swept away in the financial ruin of 1873. The joint stock company remained the dominant form of business after 1873, and banks played an increasingly important role in the economy, ushering in the age of financial capitalism. The phenomenon of bigness did not disappear. Among the hundreds of new enterprises founded during the Gründerzeit it was the big ones that survived, absorbing those that failed in the process. This was notably true in the world of banking, where the Deutsche Bank and the Dresdener Bank, in particular, greatly improved their position relative to their competitors as a result of the crash, and where one can note the beginning of that process of concentration which, by 1914, was to lead to the domination of German finance by four banks, including the two just mentioned. Much the same tendency was to be seen in the metal trades, the construction industry, and other branches of the economy. At the same time, the process of urbanization, which had been stimulated by railway building and industrial location in urban centres, continued; the age of the big city had come to Germany, with all the problems inherent in metropolitan life.

More negative and, in the long run, more serious, were other consequences of the crash of 1873. As was only natural, given the number of individuals who suffered serious loss, there was a demand for the identification of those responsible, and, as has already been indicated, fingers were pointed immediately at the National Liberals. Had they not, after all, been the authors of the liberties that had been given to joint stock companies and then been so grievously abused? The party gained no credit from the fact that it had been one of their leaders, Eduard Lasker, who had exposed the fraudulent nature of the boom. Those who had lost money were not grateful for Lasker's revelations, and, noting the business connections of many of his colleagues, found it easy to believe that the liberals had been part of a grand design to defraud them. There can be little doubt that the party suffered from this charge, which was elaborated in a widely read series of articles by Otto Glagau that appeared in *Die Gartenlaube* between 1874 and 1876, and that this weakened its position when it came to the clash with Bismarck.

The crash also had the ominous effect of bringing into the open an anti-Semitic feeling that had long existed in Germany but had been quiescent since the 1820s. George Mosse has pointed out that the stereotype of the Jew as rapacious and unprincipled was well established in popular literature;[31] and one need go no further than Gustav Freytag's *Soll und Haben* (1855), Wilhelm Raabe's *Der Hungerpastor* (1864), and Felix Dahn's enormously successful *Ein Kampf um Rom* (1867) to see how true this was.[32] The crash added a dimension to the stereotype by identifying the Jew with the stock market and the domination of unearned capital. It was easy now for a credulous public, which had believed firmly in a Jesuit conspiracy, to believe just as fervently in a Jewish one, and as usual there were lots of people to encourage them to do so. In June 1875 the *Kreuzzeitung*, whose readers hated Jews and liberals equally, made things easy for them by equating the two. In an article that became famous, a writer named Perrot stated:

The financial and economic policy of the newly founded German Empire gives many observers the impression of being purely the policy of the banker. It is no wonder, for Herr von Bleichröder is himself a banker, Herr Delbrück is related to a banking house . . . and Herr Camphausen the Prussian Finance Minister is the brother of a banker. If, on the other hand, the fiscal and economic policy of the German Empire gives one the impression of a Jewish policy, that too is explicable, since Herr von Bleichröder is himself a Jew, . . . Messrs. Lasker, Bamberger, and H. B. Oppenheimer, who are also Jews, are the actual leaders of the so-called National Liberal majority in the Reichstag and in the Prussian parliament. Jewish banking houses influence the nomination of ministers, and try to make the states and statesmen dependent upon them.[33]

The revival of anti-Semitism was perhaps the most important

---

[31] George L. Mosse, *Jews and Germans* (New York, 1970), pp. 61–76.

[32] In the first two of these novels, the German heroes, Anton Wohlfarth and Hans Unwirrsch, who are honourable, idealistic, and dedicated to the service of others, have Jewish counterparts, Veitel Itzig and Moses Freudenstein, who are self-centred, ambitious, materialistic, and without scruples. Itzig, after committing a murder, drowns; Freudenstein becomes a Hofrat, but one who is universally detested, *'burgerlich tot im furchtbarsten Sinne des Wortes'* (*Der Hungerpastor*, Ch. 36). In general, Raabe's view is sympathetic, and it is interesting to note that he talks of anti-Semitism as something that is dying. 'In those vanished days [1819–40] there prevailed, particularly in the smaller towns and villages, a distrust of the Jews, which, happily, one does not find so strongly emphasized today' (Ch. 3). In Dahn's book, the Jew Jochem, whose face bears 'all the calculated cunning of his race', betrays Naples to Byzantium. He is, however, killed himself by Isaak, the good Jew, for his treachery.

[33] Quoted in Ivor N. Lambi, *Free Trade and Protection in Germany, 1868–1879* (Wiesbaden, 1963), pp. 84 f. See also Kardorff, *Wilhelm von Kardorff*, pp. 97 f., and Stern, *Gold and Iron*, pp. 187, 502. The Glagau articles in *Die Gartenlaube* had also attacked Jewish influence in politics and business.

result of the Gründerzeit, and the myth of the Jewish conspiracy was to recur periodically in German politics from this time onwards.[34]

IV

The six years after 1873 saw a fundamental change in Germany's commercial policy, which was accomplished, and in a sense made possible, by a shift in the balance of political forces in the country. In both the economic and the political sphere the philosophy of liberalism was repudiated by the government, its main article of faith, free trade, being abandoned at the same time that the National Liberal partnership with the Chancellor was dissolved.

The commercial change was prompted by the general depression that followed the crash and by the vulnerability of German industry and agriculture in the new conditions prevailing on the world market. Hardest hit was the iron industry, for the crash put an end to the railway construction that had been consuming its products since the end of the war. Some of the newer mills and foundries, with insufficient capital basis, were forced to close their doors almost immediately; those that survived suffered serious reductions in profits, a situation that was aggravated by foreign competition within the domestic as well as the international market. The more highly developed English iron industry still operated at lower cost because of greater volume and low shipping rates, and could afford to cut prices below the German level, while French exporters of finished ironware actually received export premiums (*titres d'acquit à caution*), which gave them an advantage in the German market. Internationally, German exporters of raw iron and ironware were handicapped by high freight rates, and, as the world depression continued, by the rising tariffs they encountered abroad. Finally, the German producers were, competitively, in no position to cope with the shift that was taking place at this time from forged iron to steel. It was only after the Thomas–Gilchrist method of extracting phosphorus from ore was introduced at the end of the decade that the rich deposits of Alsatian minette ore would correct this situation and enable German blast-furnaces to double their steel production within a decade and to surpass British production by the century's end. All that lay in the future; in the present many firms were being forced to operate practically at cost, and industry in general was in deep depression.

The ironmongers found the root of much of their trouble in the

[34] See Hans-Günter Zmarzlik, 'Der Antisemitismus im zweiten Reich', *Geschichte in Wissenschaft und Unterricht*, xiv (1963), 273–86.

doctrine of free trade, which had been the basis of government policy since the 1860s, and the imminent extension of which now threatened to increase their plight. In June 1873 in the Reichstag a coalition of doctrinaire free traders and representatives of commercial and agrarian interests had pushed through a law calling for the elimination of remaining duties on pig-iron and ironware by 1877.[35] The iron interests were determined to block the implementation of this law and, recognizing the strength of the free trade cause, decided that this could only be effected by organization and propaganda.

Their subsequent campaign, both in method and result, greatly resembled that of the English Anti-Corn Law League, which under the leadership of Richard Cobden and John Bright had succeeded in persuading the British Parliament to adopt free trade in 1846; but the organizations that German industry formed to achieve their purpose lasted longer and had more enduring political importance than their English counterpart. The first of what came to be called the Interessenverbände was the Verein zur Wahrung der gemeinsamen wirtschaftlichen Interessen für Rheinland und Westfalen—generally called 'The Long-Name Society'—an association of west German textile and iron industrialists which had been established in 1871 after the annexation of Alsace and Lorraine had increased competition in the textile industry and made the south German spinners more vulnerable to tariff reductions. Initially, its propaganda in favour of retention of existing duties had no effect on government policy, but it was soon receiving the support of other and more effective interest groups. In November 1873 the Verein deutscher Eisen- und Stahl-Industrieller was formed on a national basis and, in a little more than two years, had built a carefully articulated network of regional groupings that represented 214 separate iron and steel concerns. More comprehensive in its membership and, in the long run, more influential was the Centralverband deutscher Industrieller, which was founded in January 1876. Heavy industry had a preponderant influence in this organization too, but it eventually embraced leading cotton, woollen, and linen manufacturers, as well as important paper, leather, and soda interests. Its first secretary-general was H. A. Bueck, who was also a leading figure in the Verein and in the Long-Name Society.

Against the prevailing free trade doctrine, these organizations

---

[35] See Lambi, *Free Trade and Protection*, pp. 56–71. There were also duties on textiles, soda, and some other products.

raised arguments that were not only based upon self-interest but appealed to the mixture of national pride and national insecurity that prevailed in years that were marked by danger in the field of foreign policy as well as by economic depression. Among their prominent propagandists were Wilhelm von Kardoff, one of the founders of the Königs- und Laura-Hütte in Silesia, and Friedrich Stöpel, a leading cotton-spinner from south Germany. In their works—Kardorff's widely read book *Against the Current* and Stöpel's *Commercial Crises in Germany*—they not only attributed the present condition of German industry to free trade—a theory of causality that was scornfully rejected by convinced free traders like the Prussian Finance Minister Ludwig Camphausen—but argued that tariff protection was an element of national security, since without it a nation became dependent upon others and vulnerable to their pressures. 'Let us', Stöpel wrote, 'show that Germany is no longer the step-child of foreign interests and that she can stand economically on her own feet, just as she has become independent in political matters.'[36]

This translation of the theories of the American economist Henry C. Carey to German soil engaged the attention and eventually the support of a group of German economists who came to be called the National School—Wilhelm Roscher, Karl Knies, Gustav Schmoller, and Adolf Wagner—who accepted the strategical argument that a nation should as far as possible possess in itself all the elements of national supply, but who also added a new dimension to the propaganda of the Interessenverbände that, in the long run, proved not to be to the liking of the iron magnates. Wagner, who came to Berlin in 1870 as an ardent free trader, and almost immediately became a critic of Manchester economics, was also a member of the Social Policy Association (Verein für Sozialpolitik), a group of academicians, government officials, journalists, business men, and parliamentarians that was founded in 1872 to investigate ways in which the government might promote the solution of social problems. His opposition to free trade—and this was true also of Gustav Schmoller—was based in part on the fact that it was advocated by, and served the interests of, precisely those people whose liberal philosophy of self-help led them to oppose government intervention in the private life of its citizens and government regulation of its economic aspects. Wagner believed that the revenues produced by a return to protectionism would make possible a more positive social

---

[36] Ibid., pp. 91–5, 98–127; Kardorff, *Wilhelm von Kardorff*, pp. 116–27; Böhme, *Deutschlands Weg*, pp. 354 ff., 359 ff.

policy, an argument, interestingly enough, that had been made in the Reichstag tariff debate of 1873 by Ludwig Windthorst, under the influence of the social ideas of Bishop von Ketteler.[37]

Even with the support of these theorists of change, the Interessenverbände could not hope to reverse the tide of commercial policy, let alone prevent the disappearance in 1877 of the last iron duties, unless they could detach the agricultural interest from the free trade cause. As late as September 1875, if one can judge from statements by agrarian spokesmen at a free trade convocation in Danzig in that month, there was little hope of this. But this was misleading, for German agriculture was beginning to suffer now from the revolution caused by the simultaneous improvement of long-haul shipping facilities and new agricultural machinery, which opened up vast new grain fields in the new world while at the same time making it possible to transport the yield to Central Europe cheaply. American grain had already taken over the English market, formerly a German preserve, during the Danish war of 1864 when German ports were blockaded. Now it began to compete successfully in the German market, almost doubling its sales between 1870 and 1879. Australian wool imports had become a source of concern to German sheepherders as early as 1872; now—as a result of improvements in refrigeration—the meat industry was becoming affected too.

All of this offered opportunities for the propagandists of the industrial associations, and they made the most of them. The first sign of a breakthrough came when the Westphalian agrarian leader Schorlemer Alst supported a bill for the retention of iron tariffs that was introduced in the Reichstag by the Centre party in December 1876 and called upon the East Elbian producers to stop serving commercial interests and think about their own. The appeal was ineffective, and the bill failed, a sensible defeat for the industrial cause. But they persisted. At the beginning of the following year the Long-Name Society arranged a meeting with agriculturists which had no positive results but showed a growing interest on the part of the farmers in protectionism. Finally, at the initiative of the Centralverband deutscher Industrieller a joint meeting was held in October 1877 with representatives of the new Vereinigung der Steuer- und Wirtschaftsreformer, an agricultural association founded in 1876 which had not yet taken a firm position on commercial policy but was apparently drifting towards tariff protection.

---

[37] See Kenneth Barkin, 'Adolf Wagner and German Industrial Development', *Journal of Modern History*, xli (1969), 144 ff.; and Adolf M. Birke, *Bischof Ketteler und der deutsche Liberalismus* (Mainz, 1971), pp. 28–42, 78 ff.

The meeting was successful and was the basis for what was to become a permanent link between the industrial and the agricultural interests. Some indication of what might become the wider significance of that connection is to be found in the fact that the Vereinigung was, according to its founding charter, dedicated to the promotion of a 'national economy beneficial to the whole community and based upon Christian principles' and that, after the *rapprochement* of the two associations, the textile manufacturer Lehmann felt called upon to announce that the time had come 'to restore respect for divine and human authority'. These windy blasts, and Adolf Wagner's accompanying eulogies of the Christian state, were intimations that the attack on the liberal philosophy might have more than economic repercussions.[38]

But that, of course, would depend upon Bismarck, and, although, by the end of 1877, there were plenty of rumours to the effect that the Chancellor was sympathetic to their views and was actually looking for an opportunity to break with the National Liberals, there was little hard evidence that either of these things was so. He had, in a sense, reaffirmed his alliance with the National Liberals in February 1876 when, in a somewhat belated response to Perrot's attacks upon them in *Kreuzzeitung*, he had delivered a scathing attack upon the conservative journal for spreading libellous allegations about responsible and patriotic men. Later in the year, when Rudolf Delbrück suddenly resigned from his post as head of the Chancellor's Office, the hopes of the protectionists arose again. But the reason for Delbrück's going seems to have been a personal one, the growing incompatibility of two strong-minded men. Whatever Bismarck may have said to individuals about it—and he was reported to have told certain members of the Interessenverbände that he was 'sacrificing' Delbrück in their interest—he did nothing in the months that followed to substantiate the theory that it signalled a change in economic policy.[39] During the important debate of December 1876, when Windthorst's proposal for a suspension of the law for the abolition of iron duties was at stake, the government took a neutral position; and after the defeat of the Centre proposal the

[38] Lambi, *Free Trade and Protection*, pp. 131 ff., 137; Böhme, *Deutschlands Weg*, pp. 398–404.

[39] Over the years, Bismarck gave various explanations for Delbrück's resignation, ranging from illness to overweening ambition that made his continued presence in the government intolerable. See *Bismarck Gespräche*, ii. 132, 137, 162, 227, 314. Ludwig Bamberger believed the cause to be the clash of temperament. See *Bismarcks großes Spiel. Die geheimen Tagebücher Ludwig Bambergers*, ed. Ernst Feder (Frankfurt on Main, 1932), p. 317.

most that Bismarck had to offer was a proposal for retaliatory tariffs against nations, like France, that gave their exporters special advantages; and this scheme was defeated too.

The truth of the matter seems to have been that the Chancellor had no real convictions about the difficult tariff problem and that, although he made intermittent attempts to inform himself about it (he read Kardorff's *Against the Current* closely enough to be able to repeat its arguments in the Reichstag at the end of 1878), he was always distracted by other matters. These included the difficulties growing out of the Kulturkampf, the ugly crisis with France that the religious struggle helped precipitate in 1875, the dangerous complications of the Balkan question that followed and extended throughout 1876, and, finally, the major international crisis caused by the war between Russia and Turkey in 1877. On the other hand, these very distractions helped to lead Bismarck towards a position on tariff policy that, in the end, satisfied the industrial and agricultural interests. His concern over the deteriorating international situation in general certainly influenced his desire to strengthen the finances of the Reich by finding new sources of revenue, while the Near Eastern troubles, which divided Germany's allies Russia and Austria and gradually forced Bismarck, despite his efforts to avoid a choice, on to the side of the latter, led the Chancellor, on the one hand, to oppose those people, like Camphausen, the Prussian Finance Minister, who wanted to take a hard line against tariffs in the negotiations which were underway for a new commercial treaty with Austria, and, on the other, to become more responsive to the agrarians' appeal for protection against Russian grain.

Bismarck's interest in financial reform went back as far as 1875. In one of those meetings with friendly parliamentarians in which he was given to lamenting the boredom of life and his own wasting powers, he said in that year: 'To give the German Empire a solid unshakeable financial basis which will give it a dominant position and yet bring it into an organic relationship with all public interests in state, province, county, and community, that would be a great and worthy task, which could stimulate me to devote the last breath of my failing strength to it. But the task is difficult. I am no real expert in these fields and my present advisers'—he presumably meant Delbrück and Camphausen—'however qualified they may be when it comes to current business, have no creative ideas. I have to count upon myself to think up plans for reform and to take the tools for their execution whenever I can find them.'[40]

[40] See Hans Rothfels, *Bismarck und der Staat: Ausgewählte Dokumente* (2nd edn.,

The Chancellor's objective was to free the federal government from its dependence upon the financial contributions of the separate states (the *Matrikularbeiträge*), while at the same time easing the burden of the separate states themselves, which was particularly onerous in times of depression. As a free trader by tradition if not by conviction, he did not originally think of tariffs as a way of achieving this; his mind turned instead to the possibility of increasing indirect taxes upon certain non-essential articles, such as petroleum, tobacco, sugar, beer, and brandy. These increases, apart from their general unpopularity, were opposed by the liberal parties on grounds of principle. Since indirect taxes, once voted, became automatic, any increase would represent some diminution of the Parliament's fiscal powers. There appeared to be no likelihood of winning acceptance for the reform, and Bismarck left it in abeyance.[41] By the middle of 1877, however, while those who advocated tariffs were increasing their propaganda and coming closer to a united front, there were indications that the National Liberals were having second thoughts about Bismarck's scheme, and this led the Chancellor to take a surprising step.

In July 1877 Bismarck had a long discussion with Rudolf von Bennigsen, the Hanoverian co-founder of the party, and offered him the post of Prussian Minister of the Interior, which had been left vacant by the resignation of Count Friedrich Eulenburg after the failure of his plan for the liberalization of city government. The Chancellor further suggested that Bennigsen should serve as his deputy in both Prussia and the Reich. How sincere he was in this we do not know. As General Löe once said, 'Like the ways of God so are those of the Chancellor inscrutable.' If one looks at the offer from the vantage-point of the great change in politics that was imminent, it is possible to see it as an elaborate manœuvre intended to increase the anxieties of the Conservatives and make them more anxious to make peace with the Chancellor. But perhaps the simplest explanation is that Bismarck still regarded the National Liberal party as the most reliable of available partners and the one best suited to support his own policies and strengthen his personal position in Prussia and the Reich.

At the same time, he was now aware of other options and was therefore willing to pay only a moderate price for continued alliance

Stuttgart, 1954), p. 62. As time passed, Bismarck convinced himself that all of the constructive ideas of the Reich's first decade came from his own mind. See e.g. Busch, *Tagebuchblätter*, ii. 587.

[41] Lambi, *Free Trade and Protection*, pp. 169–70.

with the National Liberals. It proved to be not high enough for Bennigsen. Quite properly, he consulted the leading men of his party with respect to the position he should take in his negotiations with Bismarck, and they all agreed that he would be able to wield little influence in policy matters if he entered the Ministry alone. In a second meeting with the Chancellor at Varzin in December, Bennigsen therefore asked for the admission of two additional National Liberals to the Prussian Ministry, Max von Forckenbeck, President of the Reichstag and Lord Mayor of Cologne, and Freiherr von Stauffenberg, President of the Bavarian Chamber of Deputies. Bismarck, apart from intimating that it would be difficult to get the Emperor to agree to this—which was true enough, for the old gentleman was so infuriated by what he learned of the negotiations that he wrote an uncommonly sharp letter to his Chancellor—did not give any indication to the National Liberal leader that the proposal was personally unacceptable to him. There is no doubt, however, that this was so. Bismarck was always jealous of his authority and unwilling to give away power, and that is what the National Liberals were asking for. Bennigsen's counter-proposal, therefore, marked the effective end of the prospect of continued partnership with the Chancellor.[42]

This became clear on 22 February 1878 in the Reichstag. During a debate on new tax legislation Bismarck declared, in flat contradiction to a statement just made by Otto Camphausen, that the government intended to ask for a monopoly of the tobacco industry. The speech was at one and the same time a malicious, and successful, attempt to destroy Camphausen—with whom the Chancellor had had a long series of differences, most recently with respect to the Austrian commercial treaty—and a declaration of war against the liberals whose opposition to a tobacco monopoly was well known. Bennigsen immediately went to Bismarck and informed him that his party had no intention of changing its position on the issue, and thus formally ended the negotiations.[43]

It is no mere coincidence that Bismarck's challenge to the liberals came two days after the receipt of Pope Leo XIII's letter to the Emperor, expressing a desire for an accommodation of the religious feud. The possibility of converting the Centre party from opposition to government policy to support of it now became real, provided the right kind of concessions were made. Apart from religious ones,

[42] Eyck, *Bismarck* iii. 203–16; Wahl, *Deutsche Geschichte* i. 468–74.

[43] R. S. Lucius von Ballhausen, *Bismarck-Erinnerungen* (Stuttgart and Berlin, 1921), p. 131.

these would have to include a sympathetic attitude toward the party's economic views, and the Centre was strongly protectionist. In view of the fact that the National Conservative party, since its reorganization in 1876 much less ideological and much more economic in its thinking, was also rapidly veering in that direction, the Chancellor could see the outlines of a new parliamentary coalition held together by a coherent economic philosophy. It is significant that he now not only adopted protectionism as his policy but began to talk of the necessity of making an end of a situation in which the Reichstag was filled with *Honoratioren*—that is, as he said in a speech in 1879, men who had 'no property, no trade, no industry to occupy them or upon which they were dependent . . . who live off their pay, their salary, off the Press, off the law, to be blunt, the learned estate, with no connection to the productive class'[44]—and of making Parliament a body that would represent occupational and economic interests.

This was another way of saying that he intended to smash the strong parliamentary position of the liberal parties. The year 1878 was given over, not only to negotiations with Centre and Conservative politicians that were intended to make a reality out of the still tentative new government coalition, but also to a search for the issue that would encompass the liberals' ruin. Bismarck did not have to look far. What he needed came to him when two attempts upon the Emperor's life enabled him to revive his old design for a law against socialism.

It would be a mistake to exaggerate the element of opportunism in Bismarck's attack on socialism at this time. If he portrayed the red menace in inflated terms in 1878, this does not mean that he did not believe in its reality. He always recognized in the Socialist movement a fundamental threat, not only to the social and political order that he was establishing in Germany, but to the established order in Europe as a whole. This explains why, as Otto Vossler once pointed out,[45] he was accustomed to attack German Socialists with a virulence that he never used against his country's external adversaries, even in wartime. The Chancellor was not groping for an argument when he claimed that his anti-socialist legislation would strengthen the hand of the Russian Emperor in dealing with his domestic opponents; he was entirely serious.

It is true that in 1878 the Social Democratic party (SPD) was not

[44] Bismarck, *G.W.* xii. 71 f.
[45] Otto Vossler, 'Bismarcks Ethos', *Historische Zeitschrift*, 171 (1951).

very strong. The development of a united working-class movement had been long delayed by doctrinal and sectional differences and by the divisive effects of two wars. The early possibility that the General German Workers' Union (Allgemeiner deutscher Arbeiterverein), founded by Ferdinand Lassalle in 1863, might become the nucleus of a national party was defeated by the abrasive temperament of Lassalle's most gifted successor, the aristocratic lawyer J. B. Schweitzer, and particularly by his admiration of Bismarck and support of his policy in 1866 and 1870. This made impossible any accommodation between the Lassalleans and the liberal-democratic League of Workers' Clubs (Verband deutscher Arbeitervereine) in which Wilhelm Liebknecht, an old associate of Karl Marx in London, and a young lathe-operator named August Bebel were the leading spirits. Their movement was based in Saxony, south-west Germany, and parts of Bavaria, where the Great-German tradition of 1848 was still alive. Their anti-Prussianism was stronger than their socialism, to which, indeed, their organizations did not commit themselves until 1868–9. There was in consequence no basis for a fusion of the northern and southern parties until the last stages of the Franco-Prussian War, when they united in opposing the forcible annexation of Alsace and Lorraine and in supporting the Paris Commune.[46] The deluge of patriotic abuse that this brought down upon their heads and the persecution that followed in some states[47] persuaded the two parties that co-operation was in their best interest. Schweitzer's withdrawal from politics in 1872 facilitated this; his party made a pact of mutual support with Liebknecht and Bebel before the Reichstag elections of January 1874; and a year later, in a conference in Gotha in May, the two parties resolved their differences and united as the German Social Democratic party.[48]

[46] During the debate on the Socialist Law in 1878 Bismarck said that it was Bebel's speech of 25 May 1871 in the Reichstag, in support of the Commune, that first opened his eyes to the dangers of socialism. If so, he did not show it at the time. He spoke immediately after Bebel and made no reference to the speech, except to say that it did not deserve an answer. Bebel, *Aus meinem Leben*, ii. 223. On the Bebel speech, see Pierre-Paul Sagave, *1871: Berlin—Paris, Reichshauptstadt und Hauptstadt der Welt* (Frankfurt-on-Main, 1971), pp. 118–20.

[47] The persecution in Bavaria started with the appointment of Freiherr von Feilitzsch as Director of Police in Munich and the application, in 1874, of the Bavarian Vereinsgesetz against the Social Democratic organizations. See August Kuhn, *Zeit zum Aufstehen: Eine Familienchronik* (Frankfurt-on-Main, 1975), p. 27 and, for the application of the law, pp. 46, 81.

[48] On the early history of the party, see Bebel, *Aus meinem Leben*, i and ii; Mehring, *Gesammelte Schriften*, ii. 159–453 (*Geschichte der deutschen Sozialdemokratie*, pt. 2); and R. F. Morgan, *The German Social Democrats and the First International, 1864–1872* (Cambridge, 1965), esp. Chs. 1, 4, 5.

If he had thought only in terms of present voting and parliamentary strength, Bismarck's concern would not have been great in 1878. In the Reichstag elections of the previous year the new party polled only 500,000 votes (a fivefold increase, however, of the vote of the two workers' parties in 1871) and won only 12 seats. But Bismarck always had an eye to the future. He was disturbed by socialist strength in the cities and industrial areas; he was aware of the financial strength and growing circulation of journals like *Vorwärts* and, recently founded, *Die neue Welt* and *Die Zukunft*; and he had for some time been anxious to find a way of stopping further growth of the movement. He had been disappointed in 1875 when the Reichstag refused to accept his first essay in this direction, a law aimed at increasing the penalties for attacks upon marriage, the family, and private property, and for behaviour calculated to promote class antagonism; but that failure had not changed his view that action against socialism was necessary.

The attempts upon the Emperor's life provided the opportunity for this and, as a by-product, gave Bismarck his chance to break the power of the National Liberals. Only eight days after Hödel, the half-crazed plumber's apprentice, had fired two shots at William's carriage, the Chancellor had a draft law before the Reichstag calling for the banning of the Social Democratic party. It was a botched performance which, by the looseness of its language, was a potential threat to any party that might seek to preserve its independence of the government. This was eloquently stated by Rudolf von Bennigsen in a speech which Franz Mehring, no admirer of his, still remembered with admiration twenty years later;[49] and Bennigsen's words convinced the House, despite the government's attempt to save the bill by having Field-Marshal Moltke speak on its behalf. On this occasion, unlike the debate on the Jesuit law, the National Liberal party stood unanimously by its principles, although Bennigsen had had some trouble in drumming Heinrich von Treitschke into line, for the professor was rabid on the subject of socialism, as on some others, and regarded it as 'an invitation to barbarism'. This moral victory, however, was soon turned into a political disaster, for on 2 June, about a week after the vote in the Reichstag, a Dr. Karl Nobiling shot at the Emperor as he was driving down Unter den Linden and severely wounded him. It proved later to be as difficult to establish a connection between Nobiling and the Socialist party as it had been in the case of Hödel, but such fine distinctions did not bulk

---

[49] Mehring, *Gesammelte Schriften*, vii. 330.

large in Bismarck's mind. He immediately dissolved the Reichstag and, in the subsequent electoral campaign, used all of the resources at his disposal to inflame the public mind against the Socialists and their late defenders, the liberals. The Socialists did not have much to lose and managed to save 9 out of their 12 seats. But the National Liberals sank from 128 to 99 and their Progressive allies from 35 to 26, whereas the Conservatives increased their seats from 40 to 59 and the Free Conservatives from 38 to 57. The Centre, with a delegation of 94 members, gained one seat.

The first result of this swing of parliamentary power to the right was the passage of the law that deprived socialist organizations of the right of assembly and publication and gave the government the power to expel from their place of residence persons whose public activities could be described as agitation for the socialist cause. The way in which the law was administered and the fortunes of socialism during the twelve years in which it stood on the statute books will engage our attention at a later point.[50] It should be noted here, however, that the earlier National Liberal opposition to this kind of legislation did not survive the election campaign, and that the bulk of the party, after Bennigsen and Lasker had secured some minor modifications in the law, voted for it, a sign of the demoralization that was going to increase with the passage of the years. To many men who had prided themselves on being members of *the* national party, the thought of being separated from the state and of being forced into the unenviable position of being regarded as *Reichsfeinde* was intolerable. This influenced their position on the Socialist Law and on the new economic and fiscal policy that was announced at the end of the year, which many of them were now willing to accept although it contravened economic principles for which they had fought since the 1860s.

There were men of liberal conviction who were appalled by this policy of scuttle. The noted economist Lujo Brentano complained that a combination of enhanced state financial power and anti-socialism was a long step toward 'organized brutality', to which his sometime colleague Gustav Schmoller answered sardonically 'Without tombs of victims there is no progress,' adding the comforting thought, 'The principle of the present is the growth of state power.'[51] Academic intellectuals who could take this kind of

---

[50] See below, Ch. V.

[51] See Lujo Brentano, *Mein Leben im Kampf um die soziale Entwicklung Deutschlands* (Jena, 1931), pp. 96 ff., 114, 122; W. Goetz (ed.), 'Der Briefwechsel Gustav Schmollers mit Lujo Brentano', *Archiv für Kulturgeschichte*, xxx, 197–8. On the other hand,

detached view helped reassure their National Liberal colleagues as they swallowed Bismarck's programme. Schmoller's studies of the administration of Frederick William I and Frederick II gave a respectability to neo-mercantilism that they had not appreciated before, while Treitschke's *German History*, the first volume of which appeared in 1879, provided them with any number of proofs that undeviating support of the state was the only right German way in politics.

Not that it did them any good. The programme that was laid before the Reichstag in the spring of 1879 was no surprise to the deputies. On 15 December, after 204 deputies representing agriculture and industry had called for a protectionist policy, Bismarck had publicly announced his personal acceptance of the idea and his intention of combining tariffs with an increase in indirect taxes. The detailed programme called for moderate tariffs on iron and iron goods and grain and increases in the indirect taxes bearing upon tobacco, salt, coffee, and other luxury items. The National Liberals were willing to accept the bundle although they were worried about the way in which the projected increase in the federal government's income would free it from the Reichstag's financial leading-strings. Bennigsen therefore offered the Chancellor party support for his programme provided he would give the Reichstag the right to review the salt tax and the duty on coffee annually. Bismarck was not interested. To assure passage of his programme he preferred to accept the proposal of the Centre party, which was more concerned to preserve the rights of the separate states than the budgetary powers of the Reichstag. The so-called Clausula Franckenstein provided that only a portion of new tax yield and income from duties should go to the federal government—the amount agreed upon eventually was 130 million R.M.—and that the rest be distributed among the states. Since the amount reserved for the Reich could not be expected to cover all of its needs, the system of *Matrikularbeiträge*, which Bennigsen had now been willing to let go, was continued, and this, in the eyes of the Centrists, preserved the federal principle. Bismarck's acceptance of the Centre formula cleared away the last obstacles to the passage of his programme; it also served as a last dramatic demonstration of his break with the National Liberal Party.[52]

Schmoller thought the liberal vote on the Socialist Law a betrayal. Brentano, *Mein Leben*, p. 111.

[52] Ziekursch, *Politische Geschichte* ii. 336–51.

V

It is difficult to assess the economic effects of the shift to protectionism in 1879. That there was an immediate drop in the value of
imports and a conversion from a negative to a positive balance of
trade is true but may be superficial. The gains made by German
industrialists, particularly in the heavy industries, may have been
prompted by the new tariffs, but certainly the introduction of the
Thomas–Gilchrist method of smelting, which enabled steel-makers
to compete on favourable terms with their English counterparts, was
fully as important, and possibly more so. That the grain producers,
particularly those east of the Elbe, profited is also undeniable, for
they received what were in effect subsidies that shielded them from
the rigours of the continuing agricultural depression. Their private
gains, however, were paid for by the ordinary German citizen and
were made at the cost of technical progress. What happened in effect
was that land remained in grain production (as late as 1902, 60 per
cent of cultivated land was used for this purpose) that might more
profitably have been converted to cattle raising, dairy farming, and
specialized production. Such conversion would probably have made
Germany more vulnerable to blockade during the First World War,
but that is hardly a good argument in favour of the grain tariff,
particularly when one remembers its political and social significance.[53]

The grain tariff and Bismarck's break with the National Liberals
assured the great landowners—a group of about 25,000 men and
their dependents, half of whom owned Prussian estates—of an all but
dominant position in the Reich after 1879. Hans Rosenberg has
written that henceforth the opinions of these landed proprietors of
the *Junker* class, who were connected by many intimate bonds with
the Prussian officer corps, determined the social and political
attitudes of the higher bureaucracy and a significant part of the
industrialists and the educated middle class, to say nothing of the
smaller farmers and business men, particularly of eastern Germany.[54] Their influence throughout the administrative structure can
be explained by the fact that Bismarck accompanied the commercial
and financial changes of 1879 with a significant remodelling of the
governmental structure of the Reich. Federal agencies, like the
Chancellor's Office and the Imperial Railway Office, were

---

[53] Lambi, *Free Trade and Protection*, pp. 231–40.
[54] Hans Rosenberg, *Große Depression und Bismarckzeit* (Berlin, 1967), pp. 183–7.

diminished in authority and saw some of their most important functions transferred to Prussian ministers. In Prussia itself, Bismarck—working through the person of Robert von Puttkamer, who became Prussian Minister of the Interior in 1881—carried out a reform of the Civil Service which effectively purged it of liberal elements.[55] The state administration came thus to be dominated by officials with conservative social and political views, and during the 1880s the Chancellor saw to it that an increasing number of these reliable Prussian bureaucrats received important posts in federal agencies as well. In short, Bismarck reversed the administrative course that he had followed in the early 1870s, and the result was a heightening of the control over the Empire that was exercised by Prussia with its conservative franchise, its virtual monopoly of military power, concentrated in the hands of an aristocratic monarchical officer corps, and its feudal social and economic structure.

In 1901 Georg von Siemens, the son of the founder of Germany's electrical industry and a man of progressive views, wrote:

That the government would go so far to accommodate the agrarians was not expected on our side. But for twenty-five years now these people have occupied all official positions and, by means of the bureaucracy, have secured the domination of the parliamentary bodies. If a government has a choice, it always goes along with the powerful ones, and right now the powerful ones are the excellently organized conservative agrarians, while the liberals feud with each other, like the Jews at the time of the siege of Jerusalem by Titus.[56]

This is at once a comment on the political results of the changes of 1879 and on the continued and fateful demoralization of German liberalism after that date. The fragmentation of the liberal political parties was serious enough, as we shall see, and always prevented an effective consolidation of the forces for progress in Germany. Worse was the growing social insecurity of a once proud and self-reliant liberal middle class. It was not only the governments that went along with the powerful ones; the wealthier sections of the middle class did also. The tolerant bourgeois contempt for the aristocracy that one finds in Karl Immermann's stories *Die Epigonen* and *Münchhausen* and in Gustav Freytag's *Soll und Haben* now gave way to the slavish aping of feudal style that is described so well in Ompteda's novel

[55] See Eckart Kehr, *Economic Interest, Militarism and Foreign Policy: Essays*, trans. from the German, ed. Gordon A. Craig (Berkeley, 1977), pp. 109–31 ('The Social System of Reaction under the Puttkamer Ministry'); Rosenberg, *Große Depression*, pp. 180 f.

[56] Rosenberg, *Große Depression*, p. 150 n.

Deutsche Adel and, later, in the works of Heinrich Mann, particularly *Im Schlaraffenland* and *Der Untertan*. Social aspiration assumed ludicrous forms, and wealthy parvenus were willing to pay for a counterfeit acceptance by the nobility with financial collaboration and political subservience.[57]

The resultant feudalization of an important part of the middle class brought significant advantages to the ruling powers, and these, and the other political and social effects of the restructuring of the Empire in 1879, were more important than the economic effects. The rise of Germany to the position of the world's third industrial Power by 1914 would almost certainly have taken place even if the protectionists had not had their way in 1879. But it is unlikely that Germany's subsequent domestic history, or, for that matter, its course in foreign policy, would have been the same if Bismarck had decided to frustrate their desires.

[57] See Kehr, *Economic Interest*, pp. 97–108 ('The Genesis of the Prussian Reserve Officer'); and Ernst Kohn-Bramstedt, *Aristocracy and the Middle Classes in Germany: Social Types in German Literature, 1830–1900* (London, 1937), esp. Ch. 7.

IV
Ideology and Interest:
the Limitations of Diplomacy
1871–1890

> An ancient philosopher once said that friendship between men is
> nothing but a commerce in which each seeks his own interest. The
> same is true or even truer of the liaisons and treaties which bind one
> sovereign to another, for there is no durable treaty which is not
> founded on reciprocal advantage, and indeed a treaty which does
> not satisfy this condition is no treaty at all, and is apt to contain the
> seeds of its own dissolution.
>
> FRANÇOIS DE CALLIÈRES (1716)[1]

FOREIGN policy after 1871 reflected the events described in the
last chapter. Until the tasks of internal organization and
appeasement were accomplished, domestic policy necessarily
assumed a primacy that it had not had in recent years, and the
government had neither the desire nor the energy to pursue the kind
of aggressive policy abroad that some foreign statesmen seemed to
expect.[2] The economic troubles and social unrest that followed the
crash of 1873 militated against the kind of adventurism that had been
so triumphantly successful between 1864 and 1871, and this helps
explain why the man who had been the greatest enemy of the public
order in those years now became its staunchest and most effective
defender. War or the threat of war could only make the depression
worse, Bismarck wrote in 1879. 'Uncertainty about the peace of
Europe [would] be reflected in a continuation of the lack of confidence', whereas a consolidation of the international system would
'recreate a sound basis for commerce and trade'.[3] It would also
prevent the possibility of a European-wide social revolution, which
was inherent in the economic *malaise* and would be encouraged if

---

[1] François de Callières, *On the Manner of Negotiating with Princes*, trans. A. F. Whyte
(Notre Dame, 1963), pp. 109–10.
[2] Rosenberg, *Große Depression*, pp. 263 f.
[3] *Die Große Politik der Europäischen Kabinette 1871–1914: Sammlung der diplomatischen
Akten des Auswärtigen Amtes* (40 vols., Berlin, 1921 ff.), iii. 58 (Bismarck to the
Emperor, 7 Sept. 1879) (hereafter cited as *G.P.*).

governments were distracted by international conflict. 'Any war that breaks out', the Chancellor wrote to his ambassador in Vienna in November 1883, 'must place the survival of the European order in jeopardy.'[4]

On the domestic front, Bismarck found the kind of stability that he desired in a conservative alliance against liberalism and socialism. In a parallel action, he sought international stability in a union of the conservative monarchs against the forces of subversion. The same year that witnessed the passage of the Tariff Law that symbolized the consolidation of the domestic system on the basis of an alliance between the feudal and the producing classes saw the foundations laid for his new international system. The Dual Alliance of 1879 was intended by its author to make possible an effective collaboration between its signatories and Russia. This would not only stabilize conditions in South-Eastern Europe, where war was always imminent, but have the additional advantage of restoring the centre of gravity in the Russian Empire to the conservative and propertied classes, thus erecting a barrier against revolutionary Pan-Slavism and the possibility of its allying with French republicanism in a general assault upon the European system.[5]

Bismarck's success in effecting this union and his virtuosity in patching it up on the frequent occasions when it threatened to dissolve into war have won the admiration of generations of historians. This feeling should be tempered with the reflection that, in the last stage of his career, Bismarck's statecraft was characterized by expediency rather than creativity and that it removed none of the causes of the recurring crises. Even before his successors abandoned it, his alliance system was on the point of collapse because of the irreconcilable conflict of interest between Austria and Russia in the Balkan peninsula. The erosion of the effectiveness of monarchical solidarity was accelerated, moreover, by the growing ambitions of the conservative forces whom Bismarck had taken as his partners in Germany. The industrialists, the great merchants, the agrarians, and the soldiers all developed appetites and fears that threatened the cohesiveness of the alliance system, and the Chancellor's concessions to them contributed to the process of dissolution and the coming of a new period of tension and threat of war.

---

[4] Ibid. 305 ff.

[5] See *Bismarck Gespräche*, ii. 282 (conversation with Freiherr von Mittnacht, the Württemberg Minister of State, 11 Sept. 1879); 297–9 (conversation with Kálnoky, the Austrian ambassador to St. Petersburg, 9 Feb. 1880).

I

Bismarck had been in politics long enough to know that conspicuous success invites suspicion and hostility, and he was well aware of the fact that Germany's victory over France had been so shattering that it left all of its neighbours apprehensive. Even in England's Conservative party, for which Bismarck always had a certain *tendresse* (in contrast to his contempt for the Gladstonian Liberals), there were doubts about Germany's intentions, and in a speech in the House of Commons in February 1871 Disraeli actually suggested that the revolutionary change in the balance of power might pose a threat to British security. Given the fact that the French were unreconciled and the Italians unreliable, that influential circles in Vienna still wanted revenge for Königgrätz, and that the emerging Pan-Slav party in Russia opposed the pro-German tendencies of Tsarist policy, the outlook was hardly encouraging.[6] To speak of German isolation would have been to take an exaggerated view, although there were moments when Bismarck talked as if that danger was not remote; but certainly the situation called for circumspection and for fence-mending, particularly in Vienna and Petersburg.

In approaching this task, Bismarck showed a regard for ideological affinity that had been markedly absent from his policy before 1870. As early as September 1870, while the war was still being fought, he had sent a telegram to St. Petersburg in which he spoke of the desirability of a 'firm closing of the ranks of the monarchical-conservative elements of Europe' in opposition to 'those not merely republican but strongly socialistic forces that are now assuming dominance in France', and he had followed this up with similar approaches to Vienna in which he had argued that, in order to protect themselves against the tide of revolution, the conservative governments must have a co-ordinated policy.[7] When the war was over and the Treaty of Frankfurt signed, he pursued his purpose, inspired by a new sense of urgency caused by the growth of Pan-Slavism in Russia and by the argument of its spokesmen—in Danilevski's *Russia and Europe* (1871), for example—that an alliance with France was to be preferred to continued association with Germany, but encour-

---

[6] William L. Langer, *European Alliances and Alignments* (rev. edn., New York, 1950), pp. 13 f. As late as the beginning of December 1870, Kuhn, the Austrian War Minister, was urging a declaration of war on Prussia and an offensive into Silesia. See Diószegi, *Österreich-Ungarn*, p. 222.

[7] Bismarck, *G.W.* vib. 631, 689; *Schulthess Geschichtskalendar* (1870), p. 306; Beust, *Memoirs* ii. 267; Eyck, *Bismarck* iii. 35; Diószegi, *Österreich-Ungarn*, p. 219.

aged at the same time by the replacement of his old enemy Beust by Count Julius Andrássy in the Austro-Hungarian Foreign Office. When both Tsar Alexander and Emperor Francis Joseph invited themselves to the army manœuvres of 1872, he took advantage of the occasion to arrange a general discussion of a possible tripartite agreement. This came to nothing, the participants finding it difficult to discover what they were supposed to agree about and being loath to sign anything that might lead to derisive comment about a return to the time of the Carlsbad Decrees. At the same time, the Austrians and Russians were not forgetful of the diplomatic truism that every agreement gives a measure of control and doubtless felt that, given Bismarck's incalculability, a modicum of this was desirable. They persisted in their efforts in the months that followed and finally devised a political formula that also met the approval of the German Emperor and was signed on 22 October 1873.[8]

The Three Emperors' League (Dreikaiserabkommen), apart from its inclusion of some cautious statements about the spread of revolutionary socialism in Europe, was essentially nothing but a declaration on the part of its signatories of their belief in the importance of maintaining a close association so that 'the maintenance of the peace of Europe [might] be secured, and if necessary enforced, against attacks from any quarter'. Despite its vagueness and its lack of any provision for specific sanctions against an aggressor, it was regarded with satisfaction by Bismarck. He had never been favourably disposed to engagements with binding stipulations, preferring to retain his freedom of action; it was only with reluctance that he turned, six years after this, to the negotiation of a more formal agreement. The Three Emperors' League seemed to him to have the advantage of protecting Germany against potential isolation at little cost.

These gains, however, he now trifled away by precipitating a crisis with France.

Bismarck had thought that he was protected against trouble from this quarter, not only by the deprivations forced on France by the Treaty of Frankfurt,[9] but by the state of French politics after 1871, which seemed admirably designed to prevent either a military or a diplomatic recovery. His gratification over the apparent lack of political stability in France and his desire that nothing should be done from the German side to relieve it brought the Chancellor into bruising conflict with his ambassador in Paris, Count Harry

[8] Langer, *European Alliances*, p. 24.   [9] See above, Ch. I, p. 33.

Arnim.[10] A vain and ambitious man, who dreamed of replacing Bismarck as Chancellor, Arnim argued, in both his dispatches to the Foreign Ministry and private letters for the Emperor's eyes, that Germany's object should be to restore the monarchy in France. William was not unimpressed and communicated his concern to Bismarck. Was it not folly, he asked, for Germany to stand by while republicanism took firm root in France? What if it degenerated into anarchy or inspired imitation in other lands, including Germany? Bismarck reacted with scarcely concealed impatience. Surely it should be clear that French weakness was synonymous with European peace. 'Our chief danger in the future', he wrote to the Emperor in December 1872,

> begins at the moment when France once more appears to the royal courts of Europe as a possible and appropriate ally, which is not true in its present uncertain and disunited situation and will be even less true under Gambetta or any regime inspired by him. For allied monarchical Europe, the volcano in Paris is not in the least dangerous; it will burn out by itself, and for the rest of Europe it will at least perform the service of giving another frightening example of what happens to France under popular republican rule.

He reasoned with Arnim too, pointing out that, even if conditions should degenerate in Paris to the point where there was 'another act in the uninterrupted drama of the Commune, which, for humane reasons, I would not wish', this would serve as a persuasive argument in favour of monarchical institutions and might have favourable results in Germany. He also warned the ambassador against pursuing a policy that was contrary to that of the Foreign Ministry, and, when the headstrong diplomat disregarded that advice and persisted in his intrigues, persuaded the Emperor to agree to his replacement and then—with the brutality that he often employed against those who crossed him—hounded him out of the service and brought criminal charges against him for the misuse and private retention of state papers.[11]

---

[10] The most complete account of this famous case is George O. Kent, *Arnim and Bismarck* (Oxford, 1968), but see also E. von Wertheimer, 'Der Prozeß Arnim', *Preußische Jahrbücher*, ccxxii (1930); Fritz Hartung, Bismarck und Arnim', *Historische Zeitschrift*, 171 (1951); and Norman Rich, 'Holstein and the Arnim Affair', *Journal of Modern History*, xxviii (1956).

[11] Bismarck did not get rid of Arnim easily. The ambassador hung on in Paris throughout 1873, while the Chancellor sought to persuade the Emperor to transfer him; and the competition between his banking friends and Bleichröder and his associates for the major share of the loans floated by the French Government in order to facilitate payment of the war indemnity was one of the least edifying aspects of the Arnim affair. See Stern, *Gold and Iron*, pp. 319–26.

It is clear that Bismarck allowed the Arnim case—the conclusion of which was hardly designed to inspire Germany's diplomatic corps with a spirit of independence—to get out of perspective. If he really supposed that the disgrace of Arnim would have a significant effect upon the course of French politics, he was wrong. The French refused to play in accordance with the script he had written for them. They were supposed to be confused and weak, but there was no compelling evidence that they were any more confused than any one else in the early 1870s (one could hardly claim that the Kulturkampf was proof of a German capacity for clear thinking) and with every day that passed it became increasingly difficult to believe in their weakness. They paid off the war indemnity with disconcerting promptitude, helping, as a result, to cause serious inflation in the creditor nation and contributing to the coming of the crash of 1873. In August of that year the German army of occupation had, in accordance with the stipulations of the Treaty of Frankfurt, to be marched home, to Bismarck's dissatisfaction.[12] Even more troubling to the Chancellor was the fact that the government of Marshal MacMahon, which had replaced that of Adolphe Thiers in March 1873, was rapidly developing into precisely the sort of regime that he did not want to see in France, one that was royalist, clerical, and bent upon military recovery. The possibility of that government's being able to restore the French monarchy evaporated, to be sure, even before the end of 1873, thanks to the unparalleled ineptitude of the Bourbon pretender, the comte de Chambord, but this did not alleviate Bismarck's concern over other aspects of its policy.

The fact, for instance, that the MacMahon government made no attempt to restrain French bishops from publishing pastoral letters in which they attacked anti-Church legislation in Germany made him so indignant that, in the spring of 1874, he authorized the German Foreign Ministry to let it be known in Paris that it had informed the other Powers that the peace of Europe would be threatened if the French Government made the interests of the Vatican and of the ultramontane party its own, and his semi-official newspaper, the *Norddeutsche Allgemeine Zeitung*, repeated the warning in even blunter language. The French Government was, not unnaturally, alarmed by these ominous rumblings from Berlin, and the Foreign Minister, the duc de Decazes, made energetic and generally successful efforts to persuade French churchmen to moderate their rhetoric. It soon transpired that this was not enough. The German soldiers entered the picture.

---

[12] This withdrawal was eighteen months ahead of schedule.

The victory over the French in 1870 had given the military establishment so enhanced a position in the state that it was perhaps inevitable that its influence would be felt with increasing weight in political matters. This was particularly true in questions of national security, which, in a technological age, seemed more and more to depend upon an expert knowledge of weaponry, logistics, relative national capacities for mobilization, and other arcane matters that lay beyond the full comprehension of civilian statesmen. The advice of the soldiers was therefore solicited whenever the nation's security seemed to be at stake, and, even when it was not solicited, it was tendered anyway.

Which of these alternatives was the case in 1875, we do not know. But there is no doubt that the soldiers expressed grave concern over the military recovery of France and that they discussed the reasons for this with Bismarck. We have become sophisticated enough in these matters to realize that military cries of alarm are sometimes bogus, being designed to increase army appropriations by frightening the public, and that, when they are sincere, they are often mistaken (which is, among other things, why Georges Clemenceau said that war was too serious a business to be left to soldiers). Since the German generals had just been made the beneficiaries of a new Army Law that was largely to their liking, they can be absolved of the suspicion of being activated by economic motives. The truth seems to be that their intelligence broke down, and they misread the situation completely. Rumours that were implausible on their face were accepted as accurate, and the French Assembly's passage in March 1873 of an Army Organization Law that increased the number of battalions in an infantry regiment from three to four seemed to convince the German General Staff that this routine administrative change had altered the relationship between the strength of the two armies to Germany's grave disadvantage. Moltke himself was persuaded that 144 new battalions would mean 144,000 new men in the French order of battle, and was so impressed by this groundless conclusion that he began immediately to think in terms of a preventive war. In April he asked Johannes Miquel, the National Liberal deputy, how the country would react if the army launched an offensive war before the year was out, adding with a gloomy relish that it would cost 100,000 men less this year than two years hence.[13]

[13] Moltke's views are discussed in Jähns, *Moltke*, pp. 572, 600; Heinrich von Treitschke, *Briefe*, ed. Max Cornicelius (3 vols., Leipzig, 1913–20), iii. 414; Winifred Taffs, *Lord Odo Russell* (London, 1938), p. 89; and at length in W. Kloster, *Der deutsche*

Although Bismarck's behaviour in the subsequent crisis poses many questions to which there are no completely satisfactory answers, one is reasonably safe in saying that he never contemplated accepting the Chief of Staff's recommendation of prophylactic action. As we have seen,[14] the Chancellor had never believed in preventive war, but, as he told the Emperor in 1875, it was not his view that 'one should give an antagonist the assurance that whatever happens one will wait for *his* attack'.[15] In his mind, the growth of the French army was dangerous and must be stopped, and he set out to accomplish this by means of direct and indirect pressure on Paris. Unfortunately, once he got started, he seemed incapable of restraining the violence of his language and his gestures; all his accustomed diplomatic finesse seemed to desert him, and what adroitness might have accomplished was ruined by the crudest kind of sabre-rattling. It may be that he had persuaded himself that an anti-German ultramontane conspiracy was hatching and could only be defeated by the tactics of terror. It is more likely that Prince Gorchakov, the Russian Chancellor, had the right answer when he said, after the affair was over, 'Bismarck is sick, because he eats too much, drinks too much, and works too much.'[16] In any case, his judgement of the international climate was as faulty as Moltke's of the French army, and he paid for this with a serious diplomatic defeat.

His principal mistake was to believe that, because of the Three Emperors' League, he could count on the sympathetic support of the Austrian and Russian governments and that his menaces would alarm the British to the point of making them urge the French to decelerate their military buildup. He was wrong on both counts. When he inspired an article in the *Kölnische Zeitung* of 5 April, which drew a fearsome picture of the putative Catholic conspiracy (and which did not hesitate to suggest that important people in Vienna were participating in it); when another of his *Tintenkulis*, Constantin Rößler, wrote a leading article in the *Berliner Post* of 9 April, entitling it 'Is War in Sight?' and making it clear that people in high places believed it was; when in mid-April an alarmist report on the French army by Moltke was dispatched to the London Embassy for communication to the British Government; and, finally, when one of Bismarck's diplomatic stars, J. M. von Radowitz, who had been serving as chargé d'affaires in St. Petersburg, blandly informed the

---

Generalstab und der Präventivkriegsgedanke (Stuttgart, 1932), pp. 6–19. See also Ritter, *Kriegshandwerk* i. 288 ff. and notes.

[14] See above, Ch. I, p. 24.   [15] Bismarck, *G.W.* vic. 63.
[16] Eyck, *Bismarck* iii. 181.

French ambassador in Berlin, Gontaut-Biron, that many German parliamentarians were beginning to think in terms of a preventive war, which he added was defensible on political, philosophical, and Christian grounds, the reaction, in all capitals, was one of shock and, in two of them, London and St. Petersburg, of resistance. In Paris, Decazes played to the latter mood by circulating Gontaut-Biron's account of his talk with Radowitz, by sending a special envoy to St. Petersburg to solicit Russian support, and by borrowing a leaf from Bismarck's book and persuading the Paris correspondent of *The Times*, Henri de Blowitz, to write an article about Bismarck's apparent acceptance of the theory of preventive war, which appeared in London on 6 May. The result of all this was a good deal of excitement and a hastily concerted *démarche* by the Russians and the English. With the personal encouragement of Queen Victoria and a promise of full support from the British Embassy in Berlin, Tsar Alexander, accompanied by Gorchakov, paid a visit to that capital. He had private talks with the German Emperor and then went on his way to the waters at Bad Ems, authorizing Gorchakov to inform the Press that he was 'leaving Berlin completely convinced of the conciliatory disposition that reigns there and that assures the maintenance of peace'. This effectively ended the war scare of 1875, a curious episode in the diplomatic history of the nineteenth century but one that has some instructive features, illustrating as it does the growing importance of military factors in decision-making, the mischief that can be caused by a manipulated Press, and the continued importance, even in an age that was rapidly becoming one of mass politics, of personal relationships between the reigning sovereigns of Europe.[17]

As far as Bismarck was concerned, the affair was a chastening experience. He raged at Gorchakov, whom he accused, not unjustly, of having organized a cheap triumph, and he was no less furious at the British, whom he had, not for the last time, underestimated. But he stopped talking publicly about anti-German Catholic conspiracies, an indication, perhaps, of a feeling that it was time to concern himself with real dangers, rather than fictional ones. The fact of the matter was that, because of his reversion to the farouche tactics of the 1860s, he had reinforced the general suspicion of Germany, while demonstrating that the Three Emperors' League had neither cohesion nor weight. The latter was a serious loss, for, despite all its fragility, the combination had seemed to give the

---

[17] There is a detailed discussion of the crisis of 1875 in Langer, *European Alliances*, pp. 43–55.

Chancellor some measure of control over an international situation that, uncontrolled, would pose the most serious of dangers to Germany.

II

How true this was became clear in the course of the next three years when risings against Turkish rule in Bosnia and Bulgaria and armed intervention in these troubles by the Serbs and the Montenegrins threatened to embroil all of the Great Powers. Russia was the first to be drawn into this labyrinth, for the plight of its co-religionists under Turkish rule made abstention all but impossible, but the Austrians and the British were not far behind, the former motivated by suspicion of the Russians and interest in acquiring Bosnia, the latter by concern over the future of the Straits if Russian influence grew in the Balkans. For a time there seemed to be some possibility of concerted action; as late as July 1876 the Austrians and Russians were able at Reichstadt to submerge their mutual suspicions in a plan for partitioning Turkey's European holdings in the event of that Empire's collapse. But the Turks did not collapse, and, in defence of the hard-pressed Serbs and Bulgarians, the Russian Government opened hostilities in April 1877. After that, a gulf rapidly developed between it and the governments in Vienna and London.

One suspects that Bismarck was not unhappy to see the attention of the Powers diverted to the Near East or to observe the development of serious differences among them. These circumstances relieved him of the fear of new combinations against his own country. Throughout 1875 and 1876 the Chancellor played a singularly negative role in Balkan affairs. In conversations with representatives of other governments he was affable, superficially co-operative, but essentially non-committal, showing some moderate interest in plans of partition (which might perpetuate differences among the Powers to Germany's advantage) but generally holding to the position defined by his famous statement, 'The whole of the Balkans is not worth the healthy bones of a single Pomeranian musketeer.' When other governments became too pressing with questions about what Germany's role might be in the case of this or that unpleasant contingency, he resorted to evasive action and hid behind the gloomy trees of his estate at Varzin. These tactics irritated the other Powers and moved Disraeli to say, in words whose bitterness was exceeded only by their orotundity, 'When I hear that the German chancellor is unavailable and that Her Majesty's ambassador is here because he can do no useful business in his proper position, then I listen to eccentricities that should not be permitted to affect the destinies of great nations.'[18]

Once Russia had intervened in the war, and Pan-Slav agitation in Moscow was being answered by jingoism in London and pro-Turkish speeches in Budapest by Magyar patriots who remembered 1849, evasiveness was not enough. The Chancellor knew perfectly well that he would be in an awkward, indeed dangerous, position if other Powers resorted to hostilities, and particularly if the Austro-Hungarian Government felt compelled to send troops south to oppose Russian expansion in the Balkans. Both Vienna and St. Petersburg would expect German support—the Russians had made it clear that this would be a fair return for their neutrality in 1870—and neither would forgive either a neutral stance or assistance to its adversary. Apart from this, any major war would have incalculable results in the present state of Europe. Bismarck was forced, therefore, to intervene whether he liked it or not, and he did so by stepping forward as a mediator and offering the hospitality of Berlin for a congress that might draw up a general settlement for Eastern affairs.

The speech in which he made this offer, in the course of it comparing himself to an honest broker stepping between disputatious clients, was delivered in the Reichstag in February 1878;[19] there was continued doubt about its being accepted until the beginning of June. The British Government, shocked by the nature of the terms of peace which the Russians sought to impose after the collapse of Turkish resistance at the beginning of the year, at first wanted no conference and later refused to consider participation until preliminary talks had assured them of acceptable provisions, meanwhile pushing their own and encouraging Austrian military preparations. The government of the Tsar, torn and distracted by revolutionary disorders that reached new heights of violence in the spring of 1878, vacillated between discouragement and defiance. In March Gorchakov wrote to Shuvalov, the Russian ambassador in London, 'It is no longer a question of interests being at stake here, but rather amour-propre and prestige. That can take us a long way. . . . At this moment, after a bloody and victorious war, we cannot conceive of abasing the dignity of Russia before the prestige of England, even as a matter of form.'[20] As late as 12 May, when Shuvalov returned to St.

[18] Raymond J. Sontag, *Germany and England: The Background of Conflict, 1848–1894* (New York, 1939), p. 151.

[19] Bismarck, *G.W.* xi. 520–9.

[20] B. H. Sumner, *Russia and the Balkans, 1870–1880* (Oxford, 1937), p. 437.

Petersburg to fight Pan-Slav intrigues against his policy of accommodation, he found appeals in the newspapers for subscriptions, to
be sent to the Tsarevich, for the fitting-out of cruisers to destroy
British commerce. Had the Russians not feared Austrian partnership
with Britain, they might very well have risked war; and, this being
so, Bismarck's great service, in this dangerous period—apart from
his invitation to the conference—was his steadfast refusal to yield to
Russian pleas for pressure upon Austria and his repeated reminders
that Russia's best interest lay in remaining true to the principles of
the Three Emperors' League, which would have prevented its present plight and made possible an earlier settlement on the basis of
something like the Reichstadt terms.

Once the Russians had caved in, his relatively modest role became
a dominant one. There was no question in the minds of the participants in the congress in Berlin, the greatest assembly of diplomatic talent since the great meeting in Vienna in 1814, that he was
in command, physically and intellectually. He impressed the other
participants equally by his strange appetites (they were unused to
seeing cherries and shrimps eaten alternately), his elaborate snubs to
the nominal head of the Russian delegation, Prince Gorchakov (he
had told Shuvalov, its real motor, before the congress assembled that
he would not allow Gorchakov, 'to climb a second time upon my
shoulders in order to make a pedestal for himself'),[21] and his control of
the direction and the pace of the negotiations. He knew the perils that
lurked just below the surface of the congress and recognized how
easily they might be released if momentum were lost. He continually
warned the representatives of the Great Powers that their principal
business was to reach a settlement among themselves and not to
worry unduly about the happiness of lesser breeds without the law.
As one delegate put it, 'Prince Bismarck never misses an opportunity
to make it known that, in his view, the eastern question, in so far as it
concerns peoples and forms of government situated, so to speak,
outside the circle of European civilization and having no future,
ought to have no interest for Europe apart from the consequences
that it can have on the relations of the great European powers with
each other.'[22] When the other delegations forgot this or became
entangled in matters that he considered of secondary importance, he
threatened to withdraw unless they moved faster towards a settlement, reminding them that he had other important matters to deal
with, as indeed he had, for he had arranged for talks with the papal

---

[21] Ibid., p. 489.   [22] Ibid., p. 511.

representative, Cardinal Marsella, at Bad Kissingen, he was in the middle of an important election campaign, and he was preparing the anti-socialist legislation which was to be submitted to the Reichstag in October.

These hectoring tactics helped to produce a settlement of the Balkan troubles, at least for the time being, but they were unsuccesful in reconciling the interests of the Eastern courts or in effecting a revitalization of the Three Emperors' League. Even if the Russian delegation had not been handicapped by Gorchakov's senile vanity and his sedulous intrigues against Shuvalov, it could not have avoided abandoning the dominant position in the Balkans which the Pan-Slavs had thought was achieved by victory over Turkey; to have done otherwise would have been to invite war with Britain and Austria, which Disraeli and Salisbury made clear enough during the territorial discussions. The Russians did not, to be sure, do badly at Berlin. The Bessarabian lands taken from them in 1856 were restored; the important strong points Kars and Batum in Asiatic Turkey passed into their possession; they could claim to have won full independence for the Serbs, the Montenegrins, and the Romanians and to have laid the basis of national life for the Bulgars; and they had forced the Turks to promise far-reaching concessions to their remaining Christian subjects and to pay a heavy indemnity. But this was not enough for the Tsar, whose armies had fought and died for months before Plevna, and his chagrin was increased by the gains made by states whose armies had not fought at all—Austria, which was given administrative control over Bosnia, and Great Britain, which acquired the island of Cyprus. Prompted by Gorchakov, he concluded that the congress had been a 'European coalition against Russia under the leadership of Prince Bismarck', and he withdrew his favour from Shuvalov, who he came to believe had been duped by the German Chancellor, and whose diplomatic career was ruined in consequence.[23]

In the first months of 1879 the Russians had additional reasons for rancour against Germany— the new tariff duties against their corn, timber, and cattle, for example, and quarantine measures against an outbreak of the plague in Russia—and they vented their feelings in the nationalist Press in Moscow and the semi-official Press in St. Petersburg, which Gorchakov saw was kept well supplied with material for attacks upon his adversary in Berlin. The Press offensive

[23] The best account of the Berlin Congress is Sumner's, but see also Sontag, *Germany and England*, pp. 155 ff.; Langer, *European Alliances*, pp. 150–66; and W. N. Medlicott, *The Congress of Berlin and After* (London, 1938).

became so ugly that Bismarck seems to have convinced himself that relations might rapidly get worse rather than better; he was unhappy about Russian troop movements in Poland in the spring of 1879, and by what appeared to be the growing strength of the Pan-Slav party. All things considered, it appeared advisable to take out an insurance policy, 'The alliance of the three emperors', he told the French ambassador Saint-Vallier in June, 'has, unfortunately, ceased to exist. I regret this, and I should like to revive it, but I see that that is impossible.'[24] He decided to demonstrate to the Russians that he could do without them and began the negotiations that eventuated in the Dual Alliance.

Because of his Emperor's strong predilection for Russia, he would have preferred to keep the terms of his treaty fairly general. Andrássy, the Austro-Hungarian Foreign Minister, jibbed at this, pointing out that it would then be interpreted as anti-French, an impression that he wished to avoid in view of his own good relations with Paris, and he insisted that Russia be mentioned explicitly. It is a measure of Bismarck's uneasiness about the international situation that he gave way, agreeing to a treaty that called for mutual assistance if either signatory were attacked by Russia and benevolent neutrality if either were attacked by another Power. The completed treaty, which Bismarck persuaded his sovereign to ratify only by threatening to resign if he refused to do so, was a landmark in European history. While previous treaties had usually been concluded during or on the eve of wars, or for specific purposes and restricted duration, this peacetime engagement turned out to be a permanent one, lapsing only when both of the empires bound by it collapsed in 1918. It was, moreover, the first of the secret treaties, whose contents were never fully known but always suspected, and which encouraged other Powers to negotiate similar treaties in self-defence, until all Europe was divided into league and counter-league.

But that lay in the future, and Bismarck was not looking that far ahead. He was seeking a greater measure of security in an uncertain international climate, and the new alliance enabled him to attain it. It put an end, for a time at least, to the hopes of the Pan-Slavs and strengthened the conservative tendencies in St. Petersburg in a way that made possible a renewal of the Three Emperors' League, which

---

[24] *Documents diplomatiques français, 1932–1939* (Paris, 1949 ff.), 1st Ser. ii. 459–60 (hereafter cited as *DDF*). See the interesting letter of 12 November 1878 from Holstein in the Foreign Ministry to the ambassador Paul von Hatzfeldt about the mood after the Berlin Congress. Botschafter Paul Graf von Hatzfeldt, *Nachgelassene Papiere 1838–1901*, ed. Gerhard Ebel and Michael Behnen (2 vols., Boppard, 1976), i. 323–5.

is what Bismarck had been driving at all along, despite what he had said to the French ambassador. When, as a result of patient collaboration with Saburov, the Russian ambassador in Berlin, Bismarck achieved a new tripartite alliance in June 1881, which pledged the three partners to neutrality in the event of war between one of their number and a fourth European Power and to mutual consultation in Balkan affairs, he had reason to hope that he could avoid new Austro-Russian confrontations. From a more general point of view, the renewal of the Three Emperors' League gratified him because it gave him a measure of control over all European politics. He told Saburov in January 1880 that one must not lose sight of 'the importance of being one of three on the European chess-board. That is the invariable objective of all cabinets and of mine above all others. Nobody wishes to be in a minority. All politics reduce themselves to this formula: to try to be one of three, as long as the world is governed by an unstable equilibrium of five Powers.'[25] Bismarck's grouping of three, like the conservative alliance which he had just finished constructing inside Germany, appeared to isolate the forces of subversion in international affairs, Russian Pan-Slavism on the one hand and French *revanchisme* on the other.

As far as France was concerned, the possibility that it might be able to escape this quarantine by seeking alliance with Italy or Great Britain was rendered negligible by developments outside of Europe. The French seizure of Tunis in 1881—a belated consequence of certain conversations between Bismarck and French representatives at the Berlin Congress—aroused indignation and apprehension in Italy, which had North African ambitions of its own. To secure some assurance of support against future French attempts to exclude them from an area in which their economic interests were growing, the Italian Government consulted Bismarck about the possibility of an alliance, and were told by him that they must reach an accommodation with Austria as a first step. The Italians recognized that this meant an end to any immediate hope of winning the Trentino or Trieste, but the French danger bulked too large in their minds to allow them to hesitate. In May 1882 they joined with Germany and Austria in the so-called Triple Alliance, which assured them of aid in the event of a French attack on Italy but obliged them to go to war if Germany were attacked by France or if either Germany or Austria were attacked by two or more Powers.

The Italian gains from this were illusory, and some years later

French resentment over Rome's continued adhesion to the engagement took the form of a tariff war that had ruinous effects upon the
Italian economy. For Bismarck, on the other hand, the Triple
Alliance provided insurance against an Italian assault on Austria's
southern flank in time of an Austro-Russian conflict, while at the
same time depriving France of a potential ally. He did not have to
worry about France's allying itself with Great Britain, because in
July 1882 the Gladstone government became heavily involved in
Egyptian affairs, ultimately sending forces to occupy the country,
and this action, in a country in which France had been active for
almost a century, aroused a hostility against Britain that kept the two
Western nations apart until the beginning of the new century.

Throughout these complications Bismarck had shown none of the
faults of judgement or lack of perspective that had marked his
conduct in 1875. Since 1879, when he had turned to Austria, he had
moved with assurance and aplomb, taking advantage of the
apprehensions of other governments, making the most of
unforeseen opportunities, always retaining the initiative, and by
1882 he had so enhanced Germany's position that Berlin was now
regarded as the diplomatic capital of Europe. But even by that date
the system that he had elaborated to give Germany security was a
very complicated one, and in its complications were the germs of
future trouble. [26]

III

Before there was any intimation of that, however, a new dimension
was added to Germany's foreign policy, as the government
embarked upon a policy of colonial acquisition.

It is a measure of the fascination that Bismarck has exercised over
historians that his motives for taking this step have been the subject
of endless investigation and speculation, some of it so laborious that
one is inclined to wonder why the question seems so difficult. The
Chancellor was always a pragmatist, who adopted policies that
promised to be advantageous. He was not himself much interested in
overseas activity, for the focus of his policy had always been continental and he was too old now to change in any essential way. Thus
he was speaking from the heart when he grumbled to one colonial
enthusiast, 'Your map of Africa is very fine, but my map of Africa is

---

[26] For the evolution of the Bismarck alliance system, see W. Windelband, *Bismarck
und die europäischen Großmächte 1879–85* (2nd edn., Essen, 1942) and A. J. P. Taylor,
The Struggle for Mastery in Europe, 1848–1918 (Oxford, 1954), Ch. XII. See also
Langer, *European Alliances*, Chs. VI, VII.

here in Europe. Here is Russia and here is France and here we are in the middle. That is my map of Africa.'[27] Instinctively he regarded colonialism as an activity for other nations, and one that would, he hoped, absorb their energies sufficiently to keep them from disturbing the European peace.

On the other hand, he was not so set in his ways as to close his ears to those who thought differently, particularly when they were people on whom he depended for political support. By the beginning of the 1880s some influential members of his conservative coalition were convinced that the acquisition of colonies was an economic necessity for Germany, while at the same time the vision of a German overseas empire was arousing enthusiasm among large numbers of people who were moved more by patriotism than the hope of gain. In view of these circumstances, the Chancellor seems to have concluded, in 1884, that the political capital that might be derived from a colonial policy outweighed the risks involved, that such a policy, if properly directed, might indeed even serve to strengthen the system of alliances that he had elaborated since 1879 in his search for national security, and that it might have some incidental domestic advantages. Hence the leap outwards into the world in 1884.[28]

The idea of building a German overseas empire was not new. It predated the establishment of the Reich itself, and the petition sent to the North German Confederation in November 1870 by 35 Bremen and three Berlin commercial firms asking that the French surrender of Cochin-China be made part of the peace terms, was only the last in a long series of proposals of this nature from traders and missionaries that stretched back to the 1850s.[29] This scheme for acquiring the

[27] Eugen Wolf, *Vom Fürsten Bismarck* (Leipzig, 1904), p. 16.

[28] Henry Turner argues that Bismarck saw a number of advantages to be gained from a vigorous colonial policy at this time and believes that the Chancellor was not immune to the feeling that it would not be advisable for Germany to exclude itself from what might well be the last great sharing-out of colonial territory. Henry Ashby Turner, jun., 'Bismarck's Imperialist Venture: Anti-British in Origin?', in *Britain and Germany in Africa: Imperial Rivalry and Colonial Rule*, ed. Prosser Gifford and William Roger Lewis (New Haven, 1967), pp. 47 ff. In a book that is impressive in both substance and method, Hans-Ulrich Wehler takes the position that Bismarck's main motive was the desire to use colonial acquisition to solve the internal stresses within the Reich: *Bismarck und der Imperialismus* (Cologne and Berlin, 1969). Paul M. Kennedy has disagreed strongly in 'German Colonial Expansion: Has the "Manipulated Social Imperialism" been Ante-Dated?', *Past and Present*, 54 (1972), 134–41.

[29] Wehler, *Bismarck und der Imperialismus*, pp. 201 ff. This elicited from Bismarck the remark that for 'Germans, colonies would be exactly like the silks and sables of the Polish nobleman who had no shirt to wear under them'. Busch, *Tagebuchblätter*, i. 552.

southern part of Vietnam Bismarck refused to pursue—it is intriguing to speculate about what the future history of South-East Asia
might have been if his decision had been different—and, in the
decade that followed, the Imperial Government showed no inclination to change the European orientation of its policy. This is not to
say that it was indifferent to the activities of its subjects overseas.
German missionary societies received diplomatic support when they
needed it; the government looked favourably on the extension of
German commercial interests in Zanzibar and the west coast of
Africa; and in 1889 Bismarck tried, although without success, to
persuade the Reichstag to give a subvention to the Hamburg firm of
Godeffroy, which was having financial difficulties in Samoa, where
it had been active since 1860.[30]

After the passage of the tariff legislation of 1879, demands for a
positive colonial policy became more insistent, and the government's resistance to them weaker. The return to protectionism
had brought some improvement in economic conditions but not
enough to satisfy the great expectations of its advocates. By 1882
things had taken a turn for the worse again, and Bismarck's financial
adviser, the banker Gerson Bleichröder, was predicting continued
depression for German industry unless commercial policy were
changed. Others agreed, even the Deutscher Handelstag, formerly a
preserve of free traders, calling for more government support for the
export trade and an all-out effort to acquire new markets. Trade
journals advanced the argument that, since the domestic market
could not keep up with the increase in production, present conditions could only deteriorate further unless new outlets were found,
and respected publications like the *Preußische Jahrbücher* referred with
alarm to the crisis of over-production and predicted that failure to
cope with it would result in domestic misery and possibly social
disorder. The rapid growth of Social Democracy, despite the operation of the Socialist Law, was cited to support this view.

It did not take long for the argument in favour of new markets to
be transformed into a call for the actual acquisition of colonies. The
international scramble for overseas possessions was well under way
by the beginning of the 1880s, and the spectacle of the French and the
Italians and the British vying for tracts of territory in Africa and
islands in the Pacific naturally aroused fear lest Germany be excluded
from the new markets that it needed unless it too became a colonial
Power. In making this case, writers like Ernst von Weber (who had

---

[30] Wehler, *Bismarck und der Imperialismus*, pp. 215–25.

urged the acquisition of Saigon in 1870), Wilhelm Hubbe-Schleiden, and Friedrich Fabri played the same role that was played in England by Sir John Seeley and in France by Leroy-Beaulieu, propagating the view that colonies were not only an economic necessity but, in an age dominated by considerations of power, a form of insurance against a loss of standing among the nations of the world. These arguments became the stock-in-trade also of the Kolonialverein (Colonial Union), which was founded in 1882 and two years later had 9,000 members organized into 43 local unions. Liberally supplied with funds by banks and various special interest groups in heavy industry, and with articles and speeches by leading members of the academic community like Adolf Wagner, Gustav Schmoller, Heinrich von Sybel, and Heinrich von Treitschke, who had concluded by 1884 that 'colonization was a matter of life and death (*eine Daseinsfrage*)', the Union had an influence out of proportion to its size. Also important in making propaganda for the imperial idea was the Gesellschaft für deutsche Kolonisation, founded in 1884 by a curious mixture of mountebank, patriot, and Jew-baiter named Carl Peters who was inspired by a desire to emulate British triumphs in the world overseas.[31]

Already persuaded of the necessity of doing what he could for German trade, Bismarck was so impressed by the popular enthusiasm for colonialism that he resolved to exploit it. He decided further that, in order to derive the greatest possible political advantage from doing so, Germany's début as a colonial Power should be dramatic and combative in style and, in the main, anti-English. From the standpoint of foreign politics, this would have the advantage of further improving Germany's relations with the government of Jules Ferry in France, which Bismarck had been cultivating in large part because it was more interested in Africa and Asia than it was in Alsace-Lorraine. From a domestic point of view, it would inject the issue of nationalism into the elections of 1884, in which Bismarck wished to improve his support in the Reichstag, and it might also help isolate the Crown Prince and his wife, whose pro-English sympathies were well known and whose presumably imminent accession to the throne Bismarck feared for personal and political reasons. According to Holstein, Bismarck told Tsar Alexander III that this was the sole aim of his colonial policy, which moved the Tsar, who was concerned about the course German policy might take after the death of William I, to comment, 'Voilà qui est intel-

[31] Ibid., pp. 142 ff., 158 ff., 163–8.

ligent!'[32] Bismarck's son Herbert also emphasized this motive, telling Lothar von Schweinitz in 1890 that '. . . we had to count on a
long period of government by the Crown Prince during which
English influence would dominate. In order to avoid this, we had to
inaugurate the policy of colonialism, which is popular and can bring
on a conflict with England at any moment.'[33]

This issue that signalized the new policy and gave it its tone was
that of Angra-Pequeña, although this was largely accidental. In this
now forgotten harbour, which lies on the west coast of Africa about
a hundred and sixty miles north of the mouth of the Orange river,
the Bremen merchant Lüderitz had built a trading station and had, in
1883, begun to buy land from native chiefs. Lüderitz was a man of
some influence, having contacts with, among others, the
Diskonto-Gesellschaft, one of the most powerful of German banks,
and these connections were used to interest Bismarck in his undertaking. In February 1883—that is, more than a year before he had
decided to found a colony—Bismarck had asked the Foreign Office
in London what its attitude would be toward the extension of
Lüderitz's enterprise and whether it would be willing to extend its
protection to German traders. In dealing with this query, and a
second one later in the year asking for a definition of British legal
claims along the coast of South West Africa, the British were
remarkably dilatory, partly because these were questions on which
the Colonial Office and the government of Cape Colony had a right
to be heard, and more so perhaps because the Foreign Offfice,
believing, on the strength of earlier statements by Bismarck to the
British ambassador, that the Chancellor was opposed to colonial
acquisitions, saw no reason to hurry. This irritated Bismarck, and led
him to react abruptly and violently. On 24 April 1884 he telegraphed
his consul in South Africa and instructed him to inform the Cape
Government that Germany had taken Lüderitz's holdings under its
protection.

Neither the extent of the holdings nor the precise meaning of the
concept of protection was made clear in this communication, nor
was the German ambassador in London, Count Münster, able to
enlighten the British Foreign Office with respect to these matters,
for Bismarck had left the Embassy completely uninformed, an
unfortunate habit of his whenever he wished to confuse antagonists
or—and this was probably true in this case—whenever he had not

---

[32] Norman Rich, *Friedrich von Holstein: Politics and Diplomacy in the Era of Bismarck
and William II* (2 vols., Cambridge, 1965), i. 145.

[33] H. L. von Schweinitz, *Briefwechsel*, ed. W. von Schweinitz (Berlin, 1928), p. 193.

fully made up his mind concerning which way he was going to jump.[34] Without waiting for clarification, the British Government, on the advice of the Colonial Office and authorities at the Cape, made preparations to annex the whole of the coast of South West Africa from the Orange river northwards to Walfisch Bay, including the area in which Lüderitz had interested himself. Bismarck immediately plunged into an acrimonious dispute with London, refusing to recognize British claims in the area, accusing the British of trying to establish a new Monroe Doctrine in Africa, and claiming that German national feeling was outraged. Since Münster was, in his opinion, too much of a gentleman to bully the English effectively, he sent his son Herbert to London on 14 June as special envoy. A skilled diplomat, who unfortunately mirrored some of his father's worst traits, Herbert, by dint of a good bit of unnecessary table-thumping and some painful reminders to his hosts of their awkward position in Egypt, where they needed all the diplomatic support they could find, won a British recognition of the German protectorate over Angra-Pequeña and also of certain German claims in the Fiji Islands which had been a source of mutual difficulty.[35]

These British concessions, of which Bismarck made good use in the elections at home, did not ease Anglo-German relations, which the Chancellor preferred to keep in a state of high tension. There were new quarrels and sharp diplomatic exchanges when the Cape Government renewed its interest in the South West African coast but found itself anticipated by the arrival of a German warship and the announcement that the Imperial Government was extending its protectorate over the whole stretch between the Cape Colony and Angola. Further to the north, the German explorer and sometime consul in Tunisia, Gustav Nachtigal, raised the flag over Togo and the Cameroons in May, an action that threatened British interests in the Niger delta and, later in the year, touched off tribal risings which,

---

[34] On this practice, see H. L. von Schweinitz, *Denkwürdigkeiten des Botschafters H. L. von Schweinitz*, ed. W. von Schweinitz (2 vols., Berlin, 1927), i. 200. William O. Aydelotte, 'The First German Colony and its Diplomatic Consequences', *Cambridge Historical Journal*, v (1937), 302, 312 makes Münster's dilemma clear. See also Stern, *Gold and Iron*, p. 411 on Münster's view of 'this colonial nonsense'. He wrote to Bleichröder in December 1890: 'If we had stayed away from [Africa] and if the stupid German *Michel* had not stuck his finger in the dark mush, we could now peacefully look on as the English, French, Italians, Portuguese . . . quarrel over it. A role we left to the Russkii! ! ! It was not my fault; you know that.'

[35] On Herbert von Bismarck, see Graf Herbert von Bismarck, *Aus seiner politischen Privatkorrespondenz*, ed. Walter Bußmann (Göttingen, 1964), editor's introduction and, on the London mission, pp. 239 ff. See also *G.P.* iv. 63 ff.; and Windelband, *Bismarck und die Großmächte*, pp. 551 ff.

the Germans said, were inspired by British agents. In East Africa the 28-year-old Carl Peters, acting on his own initiative, negotiated treaties with native chiefs which brought under the protection of his Society for German Colonization enormous tracts of territory that lay athwart the north–south Cape-to-Cairo route that already existed in the imagination of British imperialists.[36] On the other side of the world, the German announcement in December 1884 of a protectorate over New Britain and the north-eastern part of New Guinea startled the British Government and laid it open to bitter reproaches from the Australians, who had had plans for those areas. Involved as they were in growing difficulties in Egypt and the Sudan, the Gladstone government had to put the best face possible on all of this, and Lord Granville, the Foreign Secretary, kept repeating with a hollow cheerfulness that Britain welcomed Germany as a colonial neighbour. But the competition was a little too obvious to be comfortable.

Even more disturbing was Bismarck's deliberate policy of playing French interests off against British, which assumed its most offensive form in German objections to the Anglo-Portuguese Congo Treaty of 1884 and proposals to Paris in August for an agreement for mutual support in West Africa, the Congo, and Egypt. Under this pressure, the British found it expedient to agree to attend a conference on Congolese affairs which was assembled in Berlin in December 1885. The negotiations there, which organized the enormously expansive and rich Congo Basin as a free state under the administration of King Leopold II of Belgium and opened it to traders of all nations, and which further laid down regulations concerning the navigation of the Niger and the slave trade and commerce in firearms in Africa, doubtless flattered the *armour propre* of the Germans, but they did not hurt the British in any material sense, for they had never intended to annex the Congo and benefited from the new regulations as much as anyone else.[37]

To Bismarck, the creation of the free trade zone in the Congo may well have been, in retrospect, the most gratifying of the German colonial achievements, for all of the others, one way or another, were

---

[36] On Peters, see Henry M. Baer, 'Carl Peters and German Colonialism: A Study in the Ideas and Actions of Imperialism', Dissertation, Stanford Univ. 1968. Peters was inspired during a visit to England to make his own country a world Power. He said: 'I got tired of being accounted among the pariahs and wished to belong to the master race.'

[37] On the Berlin Congo Conference, see Howard E. Yarnell, *The Great Powers and the Congo Conference* (Göttingen, 1934); and S. E Crowe, *The Berlin West African Conference 1884–85* (New York, 1942).

disappointing or too expensive. The Chancellor had really hoped to support the economic interests of his most powerful friends without having to assume government responsibility for the areas penetrated. His preference was for an 'informal empire' in which the commercial interests that benefited from imperial protection would pay the costs of administration and maintenance of peaceful relations with local tribes. But the consortium of banks that moved in to support Lüderitz's faltering enterprise in South West Africa—the Diskonto-Gesellschaft, the Deutsche Bank, the Dresdener Bank, and enterprises in which the bankers Bleichröder, Oppenheimer, Warschau, Hammacher, and Schwabach were active—had no desire to act like chartered companies and to take the risks that this involved; nor did the syndicate that was put together under a certain amount of government pressure for West Africa (under the presidency of the Hamburg merchant Adolf Woermann); and nor did the agriculturists engaged in the export of spirits, which comprised three-fifths of German exports to West Africa.[38] In both cases, the protectorates became colonies in which the costs of empire were borne by the state, and in the case of South West Africa these exceeded returns until 1906, when the discovery of rich diamond and copper deposits began to redress an unhappy balance. In East Africa, all of Bismarck's original distrust of Peters was more than substantiated. The financial backers of that erratic freebooter formed a German East Africa Company, but it developed more obligations than financial strength; and in 1888, when government pressure upon the Sultan of Zanzibar procured for them coastal territories that they had sought for three years, a rising of the natives caused so much damage to their holdings that they threw up their hands and announced that they would have to pull out unless the government annexed the area. Bismarck was by that time heartily sick of East Africa—he once said that his consul at Zanzibar sent more reports and raised more problems than all the rest of the Foreign Service combined—but he had no choice. The subsequent campaign to pacify East Africa took almost two years and cost 9 million R.M.

Bismarck had reason, therefore, for disenchantment with the economic results of his colonial adventure, and he was not entirely joking when, during a visit of the Italian Prime Minister to Fried-

---

[38] Wehler, *Bismarck und der Imperialismus*, pp. 298 ff., 317 f., 320 f., 325–8. The increase in the trade in spirits was to the advantage of the East Elbian grain producers, who were suffering from falling prices which they hoped exports would relieve. Wehler points out that Bismarck, who owned four distilleries, was not indifferent to this.

richsruh in May 1889, he offered to sell his guest all of his African holdings.[39] As for the political advantages, they were more modest than he had hoped. The colonial *Rausch* had certainly contributed to the Chancellor's success in smashing the Progressive Union in the elections of 1884 and in strengthening his position in the Reichstag. On the other hand, the anti-English tone that he adopted in his efforts to ingratiate himself with the French puzzled rather than gratified them and certainly did not persuade them, in Bismarck's words to Courcel in December 1884, 'to turn away from their painful memories . . . to forgive Sedan, as after 1815 [they had learned] to forgive Waterloo'.[40] Indeed, when the Tonkin disaster of 1885 brought the imperialist government of Ferry down, the French seemed to conclude that they had been too absent-minded of late about things that really mattered. General Boulanger now came to the fore, and the ominous word *revanche* was heard once more. When that happened and when, simultaneously, a new wave of Pan-Slavism began to colour Russian policy in Eastern Europe, Bismarck rapidly developed an interest in effecting a collaboration between the British Government and the Triple Alliance. It would have been easier to achieve this if his policy in 1884 had been less truculent.

IV

In the mid-1880s Bismarck's security system was strained to the utmost by new Balkan complications, this time in the state of Bulgaria. These arose from the fact that Russia, having fought for Bulgarian freedom and, in the first years after the Congress of Berlin, helped the fledgeling state organize its political and military institutions, expected Bulgaria to repay these services, not only with gratitude but with deference to Russian advice. The majority of literate Bulgarians, however, were imbued with national pride and had no desire to be particularly deferential to anyone. This difference of view was given specific point by the politics of Prince Alexander of Battenberg, a nephew of the Tsar who had been elected to the Bulgarian throne in 1879 with Russian approval. An energetic but ambitious ruler, without judgement or balance, Alexander first annoyed the Russians by becoming involved in disputes with Russian officials who occupied high positions in his administration; he then infuriated them by giving preference to Austrian groups who

---

[39] Francesco Crispi, *Questioni internationali* (Milan, 1913), p. 219. For expressions of Bismarck's exasperation over colonial questions, see also Lucius von Ballhausen, *Bismarck-Erinnerungen*, pp. 500 f. and Schweinitz, *Denkwürdigkeiten*, ii. 374.
[40] *DDF* 1st Ser. v, nos. 468, 469, 471.

wished to construct a Bulgarian link that would complete the projected Orient Railways, designed to run from Austria across Serbia and Bulgaria to Adrianople and Constantinople. To the Russians, already alarmed by Austrian political and commercial treaties with Serbia (1881) and Romania (1883), it seemed essential to block the construction of the Bulgarian part of this rail system; Alexander's refusal to fall in with their plans was intolerable.

The Prince's open brushes with the Russians nevertheless made him popular with the Bulgarian Assembly and with those sections of the population who had learned to hate the high-handedness of Russian officials; and this made it impossible for him to change his course. His self-assurance was increased, moreover, by two events in 1885: his successful annexation of the Turkish province of Eastern Rumelia, after a revolution in its capital Philippopolis; and a brilliant military campaign against the Serbs, who were ill advised enough to seek compensation for the Rumelian annexation by military means and were soundly beaten within four weeks.

After this had happened, the Russians were afraid that they might lose all control over the Bulgarian state, and their overbearing attempts in subsequent months to reduce it to the position of a satellite embroiled all the Great Powers and came close to destroying Bismarck's alliance system.

Certainly the reconstituted Three Emperors' League of 1881 was brought to the verge of collapse, for the Russians, as early as 1886, seemed to be approaching willingness to use force to subdue Bulgaria, and the Austrians were making preparations to counter Russian moves. The thought of an Austro-Russian war filled the Chancellor with foreboding, for he had little faith in Austria's military efficiency and was aware that Germany would have to come to its support. He once made this point crystal clear to his son Herbert, who had, after a rapid but not undistinguished diplomatic career, assumed the position of Secretary of State for Foreign Affairs in 1885. Herbert had no confidence in, or sympathy for, the Austrians, whom he regarded as an effete people whose moral fibre had been sapped by Catholicism and whose policy was secretly directed by the Jesuits; and he often speculated upon the advisability of abandoning Vienna and forming a new diplomatic system based upon alliances with Great Britain and Russia, which, he was fond of pointing out, had been the dream of Lord Odo Russell. His father had no patience with this kind of fantasy. If war should come between Austria and Russia, he wrote to Herbert in October 1886, 'we could certainly tolerate Austria's losing a battle but not that it should be destroyed or fatally wounded or made a dependency of Russia. The Russians do not possess the kind of self-restraint that would make it possible for us to live alone with them and France on the Continent. If they had eliminated Austria or brought it to their heels, we know from experience that they would become so domineering towards us that peace with them would be untenable.' Austria, therefore, must be protected. On the other hand, Germany's position on this point must not be made too explicit, for 'we would then have no guarantee against Austrian provocations' against Russia. Indeed, the best assurance against the latter was a clear statement of Germany's support of 'Russian rights' in Bulgaria.[41]

This letter provides not only the key to Bismarck's policy during the Bulgarian affair but the best explanation for the devious course that he followed in implementing it. This has won the uncritical praise of those historians who admire what they consider to be Bismarck's 'Machiavellism', and the reprobation of others who consider its complications a mark of weakness and—as one distinguished British scholar has written—a sign 'that the old gentleman had slightly lost his head'.[42] It is possible that both judgements are wrong. If there had been a simpler way to attain his objectives, the Chancellor would certainly have taken it, for he was no admirer of complexity for its own sake. But all the simple routes were dangerous and self-defeating, and Bismarck found it necessary to go the twisted way at the cost of bewildering not only posterity but even some of his closest collaborators—his son, the political counsellor Holstein, and such leading members of his Diplomatic Service as Reuß in Vienna and Radowitz in Constantinople.

It was the attitude that Bismarck adopted towards Russian claims in Bulgaria that misled most of his associates, and it is instructive, in this regard, to consider the position taken by Friedrich von Holstein. This skilled and conscientious official had been intimately connected with Bismarck's policy since the 1860s, when he had served under him in the St. Petersburg Embassy, and since 1875 he had sat at the centre of power in the Foreign Ministry. One might have supposed that, after all that time, he would have understood what his chief was driving at. But the very qualities that made Holstein so useful a subaltern made it impossible for him to do so. His severely analytical and logical mind was offended by what appeared to him to be the inherent inconsistencies of the Chancellor's diplomatic system,

---

[41] Herbert von Bismarck, *Privatkorrespondenz*, p. 393.
[42] W. N. Medlicott, *Bismarck and Modern Germany* (London, 1965), p. 163.

while Bismarck's penchant for ambiguity struck him as being both negligent and irresponsible. The fact of the matter was that Holstein suffered from what Bismarck once called the characteristic failing of his countrymen—the inability to wait upon events and the insistence upon prejudging situations. Bitterly hostile towards Russia, for reasons that are obscure and probably personal, Holstein was eager to sever ties with St. Petersburg, and was oblivious to the advantages that the Russian connection possessed, not only as a means of control over Austria and France, but also—at least potentially—as an instrument for bringing pressure to bear upon Great Britain.

Increasingly, Holstein inclined to the view that retention of the Russian connection was dangerous, since Russia was bent upon using it to isolate and crush Austria. Bismarck's attitude toward Russian claims in Bulgaria, and particularly Herbert von Bismarck's intimations to the Russians that they could count on German support, confirmed Holstein's worst suspicions. In November 1885, as the Russian campaign against Alexander of Battenberg began to take shape, Holstein, a strong supporter of that wilful ruler, convinced himself that the younger Bismarck was a tool in the Russian hands. 'Herbert is completely taken in by the Russians', he wrote in his diary. 'He dines with Shuvalov two or three times a week, is served (as he says himself) seven different kinds of wine and is grossly flattered. But on the diplomatic level Shuvalov treats him as a callow youth, as can be seen from his demands.'[43] Two months later, his fears were more explicit.

Herbert's behaviour is such that not only I, but Brauer [the Near Eastern expert] and Berchem [the Under-Secretary] too, have the feeling that he wants his own little war too, so as to become a famous man. That would be the war of the Bismarck succession. Herbert hates the Prince of Bulgaria and hates the Austrians. He would prefer anything to Battenberg's remaining in Bulgaria, if only because he, Herbert, told Prince Wilhelm that Battenberg would be driven out. As a first step toward this goal, Austria is to be urged to have a demarcation line drawn between herself and Russia in the Balkan Peninsula, i.e., she is to recognize that Bulgaria belongs to the Russian sphere of interest, and that Russia may do what she wishes there. When I told Herbert today I did not think the Austrians were disposed to accept this view, he replied in his usual way: 'In that case it's all up with Austria.' I should not attach any importance to such childish behaviour if I did not see more clearly every day *how* weak the old man is in the face of his son. . . . For the first time in twenty-five years I mistrust Bismarck's foreign policy. The

[43] *The Holstein Papers. The Memoirs, Diaries, and Correspondence of Friedrich von Holstein, 1837–1909*, ed. Norman Rich and M. H. Fisher (4 vols., Cambridge, 1955–63), ii. 266.

old man is led by his son, and the son is led by vanity and the Russian Embassy.[44]

All of this was exaggerated to the point of fantasy. If it is true that Herbert von Bismarck found the Russians more sympathetic than the Austrians, he made no concessions to them and loyally reported their requests for support to his father, who—whenever they took specific forms, as they did in February 1886 when the Russian ambassador asked for assistance in getting rid of Alexander of Battenberg—evaded them. Whatever Holstein might think, it was the old man who was in control, and he was playing an infinitely more complicated game than the counsellor realized. In the first months of 1886 there was a sharp increase in anti-German sentiment in France, inspired by disappointments in the colonial field and symbolized by the elevation of General Georges Boulanger to the post of Minister of War. With the boulevard Press once more beating the drums for the liberation of the lost provinces of Alsace and Lorraine, there was no assurance that the French Government might not succumb to public pressure and adopt a militant stance; and, if this were true, Bismarck could not ignore the possibility that the Russians might become discontented with expressions of good will from Berlin and seek an alliance in Paris. To discourage any movement in this direction, he felt compelled, while continuing to assure the Russian Government of his sympathetic understanding of their Balkan interests, to mobilize new diplomatic resources to contain their ambitions. And, at the same time, he had to discourage French adventurism by demonstrating how dangerous its indulgence might be.

He undertook to achieve this second objective by countering recent French military reforms by impressive additions to German military strength. In November 1886, at a time when the sensationalist Press in France was becoming increasingly chauvinistic and when Boulanger was alarming even his own colleagues by ordering the construction of new barracks and the concentration of army units in the eastern districts, Bismarck introduced a new military bill in the Reichstag, although normally new appropriations would not have been expected until the spring of 1888. The increase in troop strength requested—from 427,000 to 468,000 men—was not in itself alarming, leaving France, at least in proportion to population, with the larger force. More sobering to the French was the speech with which Bismarck supported it in the final debate in the

[44] Ibid. 276.

Reichstag in January 1887.[45] In what is generally considered by historians to be one of his oratorical masterpieces, and which deserves equal praise for its psychological acuity, the Chancellor pointed out that his demand for army increases was due solely to the possibility of a war with France, a war that was not, in his opinion, desired by the present French Government but which might, nevertheless, be forced upon it by an inflamed public opinion that had been misled by ambitious men. The French people could be assured, he said, that Germany would never resort to a preventive war against them, but who could assure Germany that the French would not attack out of a mistaken belief in their military superiority, or as a means of escaping from domestic perplexities, or because military men, who believed that bayonets could solve all problems, were allowed to come to power. The implicit warning to the French Government that *boulangisme*, unless controlled, might cause a bloodier repetition of the events of 1870 was repeated in somewhat more menacing tones in the months that followed, for the Reichstag, largely because Bismarck would not agree to limit the appropriations to a term of three years, rejected the bill, and the Chancellor made it the subject of a national referendum by dissolving Parliament and going to the people. As he did so, his rhetoric became less restrained, while those newspapers which followed his lead showed no restraint whatsoever. On 31 January 1887 the Berlin *Post*, which, in 1875, had asked whether war was in sight, repeated the question in a leading article entitled 'The Razor's Edge', which took the view that Boulanger could no longer be checked and that war was all but inevitable. Reactions of this sort, and Bismarck's decision in February to have the army call up 72,000 reservists for training in Alsace and Lorraine, had the expected effect upon the electorate, which returned a large government majority and assured the passage of the Appropriations Bill.[46]

Bismarck's tactics were not without effect in France either, where enthusiasm for *boulangisme* began to wane rapidly and where circumspection became the rule on the part of the government. In the last months of 1886 there had been a lot of talk in Paris about the possibility of a Franco-Russian alliance, and some tentative overtures had been made to St. Petersburg; by January 1887 a leading French statesman was expressing the view that, 'if Germany suspected that we were trying to estrange it from Russia and take its place in the alliances of the future, I have reason to fear that this

---

[45] Bismarck, *G.W.* xiii. 207–33 (speech in the Reichstag, 11 Jan. 1887).
[46] See Langer, *European Alliances*, pp. 382 ff.; Eyck, *Bismarck* iii. 458 ff.

attitude would be of the very nature to bring about the dangers it is our object to avoid'. The renewal of the Triple Alliance in February 1887 also gave the French something to think about, for there seemed to be some evidence that the Chancellor had strengthened the likelihood of Italy fighting on Germany's side in a French war by making new political concessions to the Italian Government.[47]

If Bismarck had succeeded in alleviating tension in the West by these manœuvres, he had not been so successful in Eastern Europe, where the situation was complicated by the abdication of Prince Alexander under Russian pressure in September 1886 and then, as the Bulgarian Government proved as obdurate as their former ruler, by Russia's breaking off diplomatic relations with Bulgaria in November. There seemed to be good reason to fear a Russian push that would invite Austrian retaliation, with both Powers appealing for German aid, unless some means were found to persuade the Tzar that this would be unwise. After all of his assurances to that sovereign in recent months, Bismarck had no desire to assume open responsibility for disappointing Russian hopes in Bulgaria. He preferred to leave this to others, and specifically to the British.

It seems clear that the Chancellor's frequent and elaborate disclaimers of any German interest in the Balkans and the Mediterranean were designed not only to hold the Austrians in check but also to shake the British out of their isolation, by intimating that, if they had any concern about the tendencies of Russian policy, they had better be prepared to participate in their containment. The chances of this signal eliciting the right kind of response were enhanced when the Conservatives took over the reins of government in England in November 1886, for Salisbury could be expected to take a stronger line in the Near East than Gladstone. Bismarck took advantage of this shift in two ways. He encouraged the Italian Government, which had intimated during the negotiations for the renewal of the Triple Alliance that it would not welcome Russian domination of the Balkans, to seek an agreement with the British to prevent this.[48] And he persuaded the Crown Princess to write a letter to Queen Victoria—at least we must assume that his was the mind behind the

---

[47] See *DDF* 1st Ser. vi, nos. 408, 416, 418, 433, 452 f.

[48] On the negotiations for the renewal of the Triple Alliance, see *G.P.* iv. 190, 196, 237–43, 248. As renewed, the Alliance included an agreement whereby Austria recognized Italy's right to be consulted on projected changes in the Balkans and Italy promised to help defend the interests of the other signatories in that area, and a second agreement between Italy and Germany, promising German support of Italian interests in North Africa in return for Italian support of the *status quo* in the lands bordering on the Adriatic and Aegean seas.

pen—in which she described Bismarck's fear that there would be a general deterioration of the situation in the Near East unless Great Britain re-established its influence in Turkey, a move that would be supported by Austria and Italy and would surely succeed in bringing the Russians to reason. If Russia reacted by seeking an alliance with France for aggressive purposes, Germany would then be in a better position to meet that threat. In any case, the Near Eastern problem would be solved.[49]

To this approach the British reacted positively; in January 1887 Salisbury suggested to the Italian ambassador in London that conversations with respect to the common interests of the two Powers were desirable and a month later an exchange of notes between them provided for co-operation in Mediterranean affairs. The orientation of this informal arrangement was anti-French, but Salisbury soon made it evident that he was interested in extending it to the Near East by inviting Austrian adherence; and when he began to approach Vienna Bismark urged the Austrians to be receptive, and in March they followed his advice and became a party to the Anglo-Italian agreement. The result—the so-called First Mediterranean Agreement—was clearly aimed at the preservation of the *status quo* in both the eastern and western Mediterranean and, by implication, in the Balkans as well. By making England an associate of the Triple Alliance, it promised to be a deterrent to both French and Russian adventurism.[50]

Bismarck had every reason to be gratified by this result, the more so because, not being a signatory, he could disclaim responsibility for it. Moreover, it enabled him to repair the weakening of the German tie to Russia which had resulted from the collapse of the Three Emperors' League under the pressure of events in Bulgaria. In June 1887, after two months of negotiation, the Russian and German governments signed what came to be called the Reinsurance Treaty, which bound each of the signatories to neutrality in a war waged by the other, with two exceptions: the treaty would not apply in wars caused by a German attack on France or a Russian attack on Austria. The advantage of this for Bismarck was that it seemed to remove the possibility of Franco-Russian collaboration in an aggressive war against Germany; its dangerous feature was that its terms, and the renewed assurances which Bismarck made in its secret articles of

[49] *Letters of Queen Victoria*, 3rd Ser., ed. George Earle Buckle (London, 1930–2), i. 246.
[50] On the convergence of British and German policy, see Sontag, *Germany and England*, pp. 234–44; and Taylor, *Struggle for Mastery*, pp. 310–14.

German support of Russia's rights of predominant influence in Bulgaria and at the Straits, might persuade the Russians to adopt a policy in Bulgaria that was designed to provoke a violent Austrian rejoinder, which they would then expect Germany to help them counter. Indeed, in the summer and autumn of 1887, after the Bulgarian Assembly had elected Ferdinand of Coburg as their new prince, the Russians, who disapproved of the choice, seemed clearly bent upon this course; and their manoeuvring to unseat Ferdinand aroused general fear that war was not far off. Bismarck answered this threat by encouraging the signatories of the Mediterranean Agreement to strengthen and broaden their previous undertaking, advice that they followed in December, by reaffirming their support of the *status quo* and making specific reference to Bulgaria and the Straits. In the face of this clear warning the Russian Government was forced to abandon its intention of asserting its control over Bulgaria, probably not without some bitter reflections about the disadvantage of having an ally who took away with his left hand what he had given with his right.[51]

Russian disappointment with respect to the Reinsurance Treaty was certainly increased by the so-called Lombardverbot of 10 November 1887, by which the German Government forbade the Reichsbank to accept Russian securities as collateral for loans. This move was regarded by investors as a sign of lack of confidence in Russian credit, and the resultant sales of Russian holdings led to a precipitous fall in prices and seriously handicapped Russia's financial operations. Ostensibly, the action was in retaliation for discriminatory practices against German landholders in Poland, but there is little doubt that Bismarck's primary motive was to create one more obstacle to effective Russian military action in the Balkans. His stroke doubtless had some effect on the solution of the crisis. It also had a more far-reaching result. It induced the Russian Government in subsequent years to turn to the French financial market and thus helped pave the way for the very Franco-Russian political *rapprochement* that Bismarck feared.[52]

If the Chancellor's tactics left the Russians feeling aggrieved, there were other people closer to home who felt the same way. Holstein's anti-Russian feelings had become steadily more inflamed as the Bulgarian crisis deepened, and he persistently misread the true purpose of Bismarck's policy. Whereas the Chancellor encouraged the

---

[51] See Langer, *European Alliances*, pp. 434–41.

[52] For years, Bleichröder had warned of this possibility. On Russian policy, he and Bismarck parted ways in 1887–8. Stern, *Gold and Iron*, pp. 440 ff.

conclusion of the Mediterranean Agreement in order to check the drift to war, Holstein welcomed it as a means of facilitating a reckoning with the Tsar's government. In May 1887 he wrote in his diary, 'Now that the Austria–Italy–England bloc has been welded together, the sooner this group comes to blows with Russia the better.'[53] Through his network of contacts Holstein did his best to encourage the Austrian Government to adopt a militant stance in everything that concerned Bulgaria,[54] and his efforts were seconded with dangerous persistence by the Germany military. The *spiritus rector* here was General Alfred von Waldersee, who had in 1882 been appointed to the post of Quartermaster General in the General Staff. An ambitious man who aspired to the chancellorship, Waldersee was one of the prime movers of that administrative organization of 1883 which had freed the General Staff from control by the Ministry of War and which subsequently enabled him, as Moltke's deputy, not only to present his views at court but to deal independently with, and meddle in the affairs of, other governmental departments. He used this power to dabble in foreign politics, for which, he fancied, he had a special talent; and his activity in this sphere reached its height during the last phase of the protracted Bulgarian affair. His view of the future of Russian–German relations was as apocalyptic as that of Holstein, with whom he was in contact; and, feeling that war was inevitable, he believed that Germany and Austria must anticipate the action of their antagonist by launching a preventive war at a time of their own choosing. 'A good many men will be killed,' he wrote in November 1887. 'However, as long as no man can prove to me that a man can die more than once, I am not inclined to regard death for the individual as a misfortune.' Fortified with this cheerful philosophy, Waldersee, like Holstein, did his best to egg the Austrians on to a clash with Russia.[55]

As the Bulgarian affair reached its most dangerous state, Bismarck discovered the extent to which his policy was being crossed by the military. In Berlin, Waldersee was trying to use Moltke's influence

---

[53] *Holstein Papers* ii. 342. Holstein was sure that Bismarck had 'lost his nerve'. He said: 'In addition, he is suffering from a positive mania for secret treaties. For instance, after concluding treaties with Austria and Italy, which are directed against Russia and France, he now wants to conclude a treaty *with* Russia.' Ibid. 337 (29 Apr. 1887).

[54] On his activities, see Helmut Krausnick, 'Holsteins großes Spiel im Frühjahr 1887', in *Geschichte und Gegenwartsbewußtsein: Festschrift für Hans Rothfels*, ed. W. Besson and F. Freiherr Hiller von Gärtringen (Göttingen, 1963), pp. 357–427; Rich, *Holstein* i. 204 ff., 212 ff.

[55] On Waldersee's role in 1887, see Craig, *Prussian Army*, pp. 266 ff. For a perceptive judgement see Hans Herzfeld, *Ausgewählte Aufsätze* (Berlin, 1962), p. 73.

with the Emperor to convince William of the necessity of immediate war against Russia; in Vienna, the German military attaché, Major von Deines, in a series of confidential talks with the Austrian Chief of Staff and the Emperor, was doing the same thing and giving the impression that Austrian initiative was desired in Berlin and would be supported. The Chancellor reacted swiftly to this recurrence of the preventive-war psychology of 1875. In a masterly instruction to his ambassador in Vienna he pointed out that, according to the Dual Alliance of 1879, Germany was obliged to support its ally only if it were attacked by Russia, and he urged him to remind the Emperor of this. 'I cannot avoid the impression', he wrote, 'that it is the aim of certain military circles in Vienna to distort our alliance. . . . We must both take care that the privilege of giving political advice to our monarchs does not in fact slip out of our hands and pass over to the General Staffs.'[56]

At the same time, Bismarck spoke some plain truths to the military chiefs in Berlin, pointing out that war would be foolhardy in view of Germany's internal situation (Parliament was increasingly unmanageable, and the country was faced with an impending change of ruler) and threatening to wash his hands of responsibility for policy if there were further interference. By the end of December, Moltke and Albedyll, the Chief of the Military Cabinet, were assuring Bismarck that they had no intention of meddling in his sphere of activity, the military campaign to take over the direction of policy was in incomplete disarray, and the Bulgarian affair had passed the critical stage.

This did not please Holstein and Waldersee and others who felt as they did, but they were vastly outnumbered by the people in all countries who noted, and were relieved by, the sensible relaxation of international tension. As for Bismarck, he could take satisfaction in the fact that his network of alliances was still in good repair and, indeed, had been strengthened by Great Britain's association with the junior members of the Triple Alliance. There was no immediate prospect of new troubles in Europe. The warmongers in France and the Pan-Slavs in Russia were in eclipse, and the attention of all Powers was becoming increasingly absorbed by problems of territorial expansion and colonial exploitation in areas far from the European centre.

V

Judged by the talent and general competence of their members, the

[56] *G.P.* vi. 67, 69.

German Foreign Ministry and the Diplomatic Service during the Bismarck period were probably the equal of any in Europe.[57] From 1879 until 1885 Bismarck's Secretary of State for Foreign Affairs was Paul Hatzfeldt, a man who was generally respected and liked by his juniors and whose only failings were ill health and a personal life complicated by debts and an unfortunate marriage. (Holstein, one of Hatzfeldt's strongest supporters, did not hesitate to describe his wife as having 'the strong nerves and brazen character of a concierge's prostitute daughter'.[58]) In 1885 Hatzfeldt was succeeded by Herbert von Bismarck, whose bluff manner and rather excessive pride in calling a spade a spade was offensive to some of those who had to work with him, but whose competence was never questioned, even by Holstein, who distrusted the direction of his policy. Since the Secretary of State's time was generally devoted to political affairs, the Under-Secretary was chosen on the basis of his administrative talent or his competence in non-political fields. Hatzfeldt's Under-Secretary was Clemens Busch, who busied himself mostly with matters of personnel; Herbert von Bismarck's was Graf von Berchem, who was an expert on economic matters.

The heart of the Foreign Ministry was the Political Division, generally known simply as 'A'. Ludwig von Raschdau, who served in it in the late 1880s, wrote later that 'the distance that existed between the officers of a Guard Cavalry Regiment and those of a transport battalion could hardly be greater than that between the counsellors of the so-called Political Division and those of the other parts of the Ministry',[59] like the Second Division, which took care of economic and legal matters, the Central Bureau, which distributed incoming correspondence and kept the archives, the Chiffrierbureau, which did the coding and ciphering, and the other sections. The members of the Political Division, in contrast with those in other divisions, were generally people who had distinguished themselves in the Diplomatic Service, to which they frequently returned after a period of years in Berlin. In the 1880s the most important members were Lothar Bucher, Fritz von Holstein, Arthur von Brauer, and Kuno von Rantzau. Bucher was an old Forty-eighter who had been forced to flee the country as a result of his revolutionary activities and had remained abroad until he was

[57] On the Foreign Ministry under Bismarck, see esp. Arthur von Brauer, *Im Dienste Bismarcks: Persönliche Erinnerungen*, ed. H. Rogge (Berlin, 1936).

[58] *Holstein Papers* ii. 89 f. On Hatzfeldt's financial problems and Bleichröder's attempts to alleviate them, see Stern, *Gold and Iron*, pp. 243–8.

[59] Ludwig von Raschdau, *Wie ich Diplomat wurde* (Berlin, 1938), p. 43.

amnestied in 1861, earning his living by his pen. Bismarck, who brought him into the Foreign Ministry in 1864, valued him for his literary gifts (he was to lean on him heavily during the composition of his memoirs) and for his knowledge of England, which, with the Americas and Southern Europe, was considered Bucher's private sphere in the Ministry. Holstein, who joined the Political Division in 1876 after a varied diplomatic career, had a general responsibility for the affairs of France, Belgium, Holland, Spain, and Switzerland. Near Eastern affairs were Brauer's province, while Rantzau, who owed his position to the fact that he had married Bismarck's only daughter but who was also a clever and energetic man, oversaw relations with the German confederate states and took care of Bismarck's personal correspondence. At the end of the decade there was an infusion of new blood, with the addition of Paul Kayser, first as a legal expert, later as head of the new Colonial Division, Rudolf Lindau, to handle relations with the Press, Ludwig von Raschdau, promoted from the Second Division and charged with miscellaneous duties, including the task of accompanying the young Emperor William II when he travelled, and Alfred von Kiderlen-Wächter, a future Secretary of State, whose speciality was Eastern Europe. The high premium that Bismarck placed upon talent and his indifference to other characteristics is shown by the fact that both Kayser and Lindau, whom he appointed and advanced, were Jews.[60]

The Diplomatic Service was not inferior in quality to the Ministry.[61] Within ten years of his coming to power in 1862 Bismarck had corrected the disorder and lack of system that had characterized the old Prussian service and made his own corps of envoys as effective an instrument of state policy as any in Europe. Certainly any of the major Powers would have been glad to be served by the Bismarckian diplomatists of the 1870s and 1880s: Hohenlohe, a delicate and ingratiating talent who succeeded in making the best of a difficult position in republican France; Prince Henry VII of Reuß, member of an ancient Thuringian family, who received his training in the lesser German courts and rose to full stature in St. Petersburg and Vienna; Lothar von Schweinitz, 'the mighty Magus of the North', who succeeded Reuß in St. Petersburg and, in his blunt soldierly way,

---

[60] Ludwig von Raschdau, *Unter Bismarck und Caprivi* (2nd edn., Berlin, 1939), pp. 35 ff., 58 f., 64; Brauer, *Im Dienste Bismarcks*, pp. 95, 118–23.

[61] Lamar Cecil, *The German Diplomatic Service, 1871–1914* (Princeton, 1976); and Gordon A. Craig, 'Bismarck and his Ambassadors: The Problem of Discipline', *Foreign Service Journal* (Washington, D.C.), xxxiii (June 1956) upon which the following pages are based.

quickly won the confidence of the Russian court; Radowitz, an energetic representative and a skilled negotiator who proved his abilities at the Congress of Berlin, served later in Constantinople, and ended his career at the Algeciras Conference of 1906; Münster, a Hanoverian nobleman, placid, easygoing, and with a strong sense of humour, a brilliant conversationalist who served long years in London and Paris; and Hatzfeldt, who, after resigning as Secretary of State in 1885, went as ambassador to London, where he showed great skill in handling political questions and an almost intuitive ability to establish rapport with those with whom he had to deal. And, in addition to these 'great prophets', as they were called by Werthern, the witty and discerning envoy to Munich, there were scores of less distinguished but nevertheless competent and dedicated representatives in other embassies and legations.

Even so, the German Diplomatic Service, and the Foreign Ministry as well, had grave weaknesses, and the responsibility for them lay with the Chancellor himself. Bismarck chose his aides with care and with an eye to their intelligence, their technical skills, and their judgement; he protected their rights against attacks from outsiders and always sought to improve the material conditions in which they had to work; and he always regarded them as the principal instruments by which his foreign policy was executed. But it was always *his* policy, and they were always *only* instruments; and he placed so much emphasis on this that, in the long run, he stunted initiative and judgement in his Foreign Service.

The fault was perhaps the emphasis which he placed upon discipline. This is understandable for, in his early days, Bismarck had found it necessary to correct practices in the Foreign Service that were easygoing to the point of anarchy, and he had also had to cope with envoys, who, presuming upon the fact that ambassadors are personal representatives of the sovereign, had on occasion sought to substitute their own foreign policies for that which had been formulated in Berlin. The rigour with which Bismarck corrected these delinquencies and, particularly, the ruthless brutality which he had employed against the ambassador to Paris, Harry Arnim, in 1873, put an end to insubordination. Attempts to circumvent the Chancellor became unthinkable, and the efficiency with which policy was executed increased.

Yet the cost was great. After the Arnim case there were many members of the Foreign Service who were terrified at the thought of Bismarck's displeasure. Radowitz, an ordinarily courageous and independent man, wrote in his memoirs, 'To oppose the Bismarck of the seventies and eighties in any matter would have been unthinkable!'; and Arthur von Brauer wrote feelingly of the near terror that overcame even experienced counsellors in the Political Division when they had to make a presentation before the Chancellor. It is not too much to say that the atmosphere in the Foreign Ministry came to resemble that of an oriental court ruled by a cruel and capricious tyrant, and, as in such courts, terror was accompanied by intrigue. There surely can have been no Foreign Office in Europe in which jealousy, tale-bearing, and conspiracy were more rampant than in the German Foreign Ministry of the 1880s.[62] In the first half of the decade Holstein spun endless plots against Bucher and also worked with Hohenlohe to bring Busch down, because he was reported to have diminished the influence of Philippsborn, chief of the Second Division, and to be trying to undermine Hatzfeldt's position. In the second half the intrigues were so complicated as to defy description. A feud between Holstein and Rantzau, which almost led to a duel between them, split the Political Division, and Holstein, by means of his correspondence with the missions abroad and his influence over the new recruits to the Division, began to form an anti-Bismarck Fronde, in which he was abetted by Kiderlen-Wächter and by Paul Kayser, always a man with an eye to the main chance. What all this meant to the general efficiency of the service can be imagined.

More serious, perhaps, was the general shrivelling of initiative that fear of Bismarck caused in the Diplomatic Service. The Chancellor's shadow hung over even the ablest of his ambassadors; their subordination to him drained them of independence; and they were never quite the same after 1890, when they could no longer feel him standing behind him. Kurd von Schlözer, who had begun his career under Bismarck in the St. Petersburg mission of the 1860s and had later served with distinction in Rome, where he penned the charming letters for which he is generally remembered, wrote after Bismarck's dismissal: 'We German diplomats, who were merely modest executors of Bismarck's will at foreign courts, grew with him and felt ourselves strong in the service we performed for this greatest of statesmen and for our fatherland. It is different now that he is gone. We . . . can no longer speak in the name of an overwhelming personality. . . .'[63]

[62] See e.g. Schweinitz, *Denkwürdigkeiten*, ii. 211, 271; Helmuth Rogge, *Holstein und Hohenlohe* (Stuttgart, 1957), p. 183; *Holstein Papers* ii. 129 f.

[63] Kurd von Schlözer, *Letzte römische Briefe*, ed. L. von Schlözer (Stuttgart, 1924), pp. 149 f. So also Hatzfeldt, in a *Memoirenfragment* written in 1892: '. . . each of us lived in the unshakeable conviction that the Prince must know and understand everything far better than we'. Hatzfeldt, *Nachgelassene Papiere* i. 29.

It is worth adding that Bismarck often made it dangerous for his envoys to strike out on their own by keeping them in the dark concerning his intentions and then venting his wrath upon them if they did anything of which he later disapproved. Chiefs of mission sometimes received reprimands for failure to carry out instructions that were, in fact, so cryptic as to be misleading, as Münster discovered in 1884, or were deliberately phrased in order to be misleading, which was the experience of Robert von der Goltz in Paris in 1867. When Hatzfeldt was ambassador in London in 1886, he wrote home to find out what line he should take if Lord Salisbury should make direct advances to him with respect to Anglo-German diplomatic collaboration. He later complained to Holstein that Bismarck's rejoinder was the reverse of enlightening. 'I can only understand the comments in this way. Do not compromise me but keep the door open.'[64]

In such circumstances it was easy for envoys to make mistakes. Even so experienced a hand as Reuß, the ambassador in Vienna, proved capable in 1887 of flying in the face of one of the fundamental axioms of Bismarck's diplomacy: his insistence that the alliance with Austria was strictly defensive in nature. Inadequately informed and bewildered by Bismarck's tactics, Reuß intimated to the Austrians that they could expect German support even if they took the initiative in precipitating a war, an interpretation which he had subsequently to correct.

There is no more striking proof of the ill effects of Bismarck's refusal to open his mind to his ambassadors than the result of the debate over the renewal of the Reinsurance Treaty in 1890, after his fall from office. One might have supposed that the leading lights of his diplomatic corps would have tried to defend the tie with Russia, upon which he had always put such store. They neither did so nor seemed even to appreciate what was at stake. Familiar only with the problems of their own posts, they were incompetent to make judgements about greater issues of policy. At the moment of crisis, Bismarck's methods of dealing with his Foreign Service helped destroy the foundations of his diplomatic system.

[64] *Holstein Papers* iii. 167 n.

V
The Campaign against Social Democracy and Bismarck's Fall
1879–1890

Wenn ich nicht staatsstreichere, setze
ich nichts durch.

OTTO VON BISMARCK (1878)[1]

Wenn wir dereinst sein Leben buchen,
nachdem er sank in letzten Schlaf,
nicht segnen werden wir, nicht fluchen,
wir schreiben ihm das Epitaph:
'Dem großen Ganzen stellt vermessen
entgegen er sein trotzig Ich.
Nicht Idealen, nur Int'ressen
dient' er, ein andrer Metternich.

Die Freiheit leichter zu besiegen,
hat er im Dienst der Reaktion
der Freiheit eigen Roß bestiegen,
wie vordem Klein-Napoleon.
Doch dies Roß ist keine Rosinante,
es ist ein feur'ger Buzephal;
es warf ihn ab, er lag im Sande:
das allgemeine Recht der Wahl!'

JAKOB STERN (1890)[2]

BETWEEN 1879 and 1890 Bismarck created a system of foreign politics that gave his country both security and dominant influence in European affairs, and he proved capable of maintaining it in time of crisis, although not, to be sure, without employing diplomatic means that were so complex as to invite the charge of duplicity. At times his tactics recalled the story of Field-Marshal Blücher's complaint that no one would play cards with him. 'But,

[1] Bismarck, *G.W.* viii. 261.
[2] 'Bismarcks Sturz', in *Deutschland, Deutschland. Politische Gedichte*, ed. Lamprecht, p. 250.

my dear Blücher,' the King replied, 'they say that you always cheat.' 'Yes, Majesty,' Blücher said shamefacedly, 'it always goes better if you cheat a little.'[3] During the Bulgarian crisis of 1887 Bismarck appears to have operated on the same principle and, although he swept the board in the end, he left at least one of his partners permanently distrustful.

Even so, he succeeded in preserving the elaborate structure of alliances that he had taken such pains to erect. This was an achievement that was in marked contrast to his performance in internal affairs in these same years. For there his political virtuosity was not enough to maintain his system of domestic politics and, as problems multiplied, he felt compelled to resort to increasingly desperate means, until he had finally jettisoned the principles that had guided him during his early career in office and was actually advocating the destruction of the edifice he had built between 1866 and 1871. By 1890 he seemed to be undergoing a metamorphosis in reverse and to be on the point of emerging as 'the red reactionary [who] smells of blood' of the 1850s. When this became too painfully apparent, his monarch hastened to get rid of him.

There can be no doubt that the circumstances of Bismarck's fall in 1890 were profoundly influenced by his own personal failings: a capriciousness that seemed to grow in inverse proportion to his dwindling physical powers and a brutality in personal and official relations that became increasingly palpable. As the Chancellor grew older, he became increasingly self-centred—'It was always Me! Me! Me!' Fontane wrote after his dismissal, 'and, when that did not work, complaints about ingratitude and tears of North German sentimentality'[4]—and more and more convinced that everyone beyond the limits of his own family circle was conspiring against him. He reacted savagely, and the Wilhelmstraße was littered with the corpses of his real and fancied rivals. This did not really strengthen his position. On the contrary, as that shrewd observer Fontane noted as early as 1881:

Gradually a storm is brewing in the people against Bismarck. In the upper strata of society it has, of course, been perceptible for a long time. It is not what he does that is ruining him as much as his accusations. . . . For his genius everyone still has tremendous respect, even his enemies, indeed, perhaps his enemies most of all. But the respect for his character is in a marked decline. What once made him so popular was the feeling that everyone had: 'Ah, a

---

[3] *Fontanes Briefe in zwei Bänden*, ed. Gotthard Erler (Berlin and Weimar, 1968), ii. 324.

[4] Ibid. 325.

great man.' But there is not much left of that now, and people say, 'He is a great genius, but a petty man.'[5]

One can doubtless find all the elements of classical tragedy in Bismarck's last years, the hero being brought low by his own weaknesses. But it would be a mistake to allow reflection upon the dangers of hubris to obscure the fact that Bismarck's defeat was more the result of the frailties of his politics than of those of his character. The fact was that the methods of political management that had worked in the 1860s and 1870s proved incapable of meeting the problems of the 1880s.

When Bismarck became Minister President of Prussia in 1862, the struggle over William I's proposed military reform had brought government to a standstill, and most political observers believed that, unless he wished to abdicate, the King had only two choices, either to accept the victory of the parliamentary principle or to destroy the constitution of 1850 by a *coup d'état* and to try to rule the country by force. Bismarck's great achievement was to contain the parliamentary threat to the prerogatives of the Crown without accepting the prescriptions of the reactionary military party led by Edwin von Manteuffel, who believed that 'only soldiers are effective against democrats'. Bismarck had distrusted Manteuffel ever since the days of 1848, and he was sure that, even if the kind of power-play advocated by the 'fanatical corporal' was immediately successful, it would in the long run impose an intolerable burden of unpopularity upon the Crown, while at the same time requiring the diversion of the army's strength, for an indefinite period, to tasks of internal repression and control. This would make impossible the attainment of objectives in foreign policy which Bismarck regarded as indispensable and would also make the new Minister President a prisoner of the reactionary party, which was not, in any case, interested in his foreign plans.[6]

Rejecting the extremist position, Bismarck privately defined his goal—and the definition is valid, *mutatis mutandis*, for his policy after 1866 as well as before that date—as 'an understanding with the majority of the deputies that will not at the same time prejudice the future authority and governmental powers of the Crown or endanger the proficiency of the army'.[7] When he discovered that the

---

[5] Ibid. 32 f.

[6] For a fuller discussion of Bismarck's thinking in 1862, see Egmont Zechlin, *Bismarck und die Grundlegung der deutschen Großmacht* (Stuttgart, 1930), pp. 324–5; Craig, *Prussian Army*, pp. 160 ff.; Pflanze, *Bismarck*, pp. 171 ff.

[7] Friedrich III, *Tagebücher von 1848–66*, p. 505.

liberal majority in the Chamber of Deputies was not prepared to accept this implied limitation upon their parliamentary ambitions voluntarily, he set out to force their acquiescence by treating them as enemies of the state, by employing every legal expedient to harass them, and by using the threat, if not the reality, of a *coup d'état* in order to arouse fears that continued resistance to his wishes might cost them whatever rights and liberties were still assured by the constitution of 1850.[8] These tactics worked, thanks in large part, of course, to the success of Bismarck's anti-Austrian foreign policy, which made opposition to the Crown seem unpatriotic, if not treasonable; and with the Indemnity Act of September 1866 the parliamentary liberals indirectly recognized that the prerogatives of the Crown lay beyond their competence and accepted the restricted role in the governance of the state that Bismarck had delineated for them.

Bismarck's success in the constitutional conflict of the 1860s had a permanent effect upon his parliamentary practice. In later years, whenever the monarchical-conservative principle was threatened by a renewal of parliamentary ambitions, he tended to revert to the methods that had been effective in that earlier time: the violent posturing, the identification of political opposition with lack of patriotism and subversion, the ruthless employment of calumny and harassment against individuals and parties labelled as *Reichsfeinde*,[9] the menacing references to worse things to come, the attempt to go over the heads of the Reichstag and to appeal to the German people in campaigns in which the issues were over-simplified or distorted,[10] and the use of foreign policy to distract and divide his antagonists.

This kind of politics was reasonably effective during the 1870s and, in the course of 1878, the Chancellor showed a tactical virtuosity in using it that was as dazzling as his performance in the 1860s. But, even so, the fundamental weakness of the system was already manifesting itself. As Wolfgang Sauer has written, its salient characteristic was its social immobility. Bismarck seemed to assume that the relationship between the democratic-constitutional and the con-

---

[8] See esp. Eugene N. Anderson, *The Social and Political Conflict in Prussia, 1858–64* (Berkeley, 1954).

[9] Wolfgang Sauer, 'Das Problem des deutschen Nationalstaates', in *Moderne deutsche Sozialgeschichte*, ed. Hans-Ulrich Wehler (Cologne and Berlin, 1966), p. 431.

[10] On these and other Bonapartist aspects of Bismarck's policy, see H. Gollwitzer, 'Der Cäsarismus Napoleons III. im Widerhall der öffentlichen Meinung Deutschlands', *Historische Zeitschrift*, 173 (1952), 23–75; G. A. Rein, *Die Revolution in der Politik Bismarcks* (Göttingen, 1957), pp. 81–132; Wehler, *Bismarck und der Imperialismus*, pp. 455–504.

servative forces would remain basically unchanged and that he would be able to continue standing between the two camps, making the adjustments necessary to keep the system working. This was an impossibility, given the dynamic social development that was generated by the process of industrialism in Germany after 1871, one of the fruits of which was Germany's first mass party, the Social Democrats.

The growth of Social Democracy greatly exacerbated the basic conflict that was inherent in the Bismarck constitution, that between monarchical power and parliamentary pretension; and this made the Reichstag, where the conflict centred, more and more unmanageable. Bismarck's apprehension of this is shown by his growing preoccupation in the years after 1878 with the idea of a *coup d'état* against Parliament and the number of references, often remarkably frank, to a *Staatsstreich* in his private and parliamentary utterances.[11] There is no doubt that as in the 1860s many of his implied threats were bluffs. But, as all of his measures against socialism failed, some kind of a real *coup* began to seem to be the only alternative to a surrender to the parliamentary principle. As the tide of Social Democracy remorselessly eroded the middle ground upon which he had chosen to stand, he did what he had refused to do in 1862 and adopted the policy of Edwin von Manteuffel.

I

Bismarck's motives in launching his attack upon the Social Democratic party have been discussed above.[12] Within the broader context of Bismarck's concerns, the assault was designed to promote a regrouping of parliamentary forces in the interest of conservatism and to facilitate fundamental changes in parliamentary practice.[13] But it also had a more specific justification. The Chancellor was determined to eliminate what now seemed to him to be the most

[11] See esp. Stürmer, 'Staatsstreichgedanken', who demonstrates how threats of a *Staatsstreich* became a 'ritual of constitutional life' after 1878. In June 1878, when the south German states showed some reluctance about supporting the dissolution of the Reichstag, Bismarck, who wanted unanimous support from the Bundesrat, was almost brutal in suggesting that foot-dragging on their part would lead to fundamental constitutional change. This would be a *Staatsstreich* by Prussia, he admitted to the Badenese minister in Berlin, adding, 'If I don't *putsch*, I get nothing done.' Bismarck, *G.W.* viii. 261

[12] See above, Ch. III, p. 93.

[13] Stürmer, 'Staatsstreichgedanken' 611. Bismarck considered for a time the feasibility of replacing the Reichstag with an Economic Chamber, a Volkswirtschaftsrat. See H. Goldschmidt, *Das Reich und Preußen* (Berlin, 1931), pp. 76 f. and Böhme, *Deutschlands Weg*, pp. 575 f.

serious ideological threat to the unity of the new Reich, and for a time it appeared that he would be able to do so without serious difficulty.

For one thing, popular feeling seemed to be on his side. In the weeks following Nobiling's attempt to kill the Emperor, the country fell into a state of hysteria, in which sympathy for the wounded monarch took ugly forms. Scores of people were reported to the police for harmless remarks that were interpreted as amounting to lese-majesty, and the courts viewed these charges with complete seriousness and handed down savage sentences, eighteen months in prison, for example, to a woman in Brandenburg who had been heard to say, 'At least, the Emperor is not poor; he can have himself cared for.' On a single day in June 1878 a Berlin court sentenced seven persons to a total of 22 years and six months for *Majestätsbeleidigung* on evidence no more substantial than this, a circumstance that prompted a journalist to say, 'The Emperor has the wounds, the nation the fever.'[14]

One symptom of this was the general assumption that Nobiling's deed was inspired by the Socialists. It was not considered necessary to prove this; it was simply accepted as true: by Heinrich von Treitschke, for instance, who immediately called upon employers to dismiss all workers with socialist inclinations,[15] by the newspapers which reported attacks upon Socialist party headquarters with barely concealed satisfaction, by the Reichstag deputies, who now let Bismarck know that they were ready to vote for emergency legislation, and by the ordinary man in the street, who simply parroted what all the important people around him were saying. In the period between the dissolution of the Reichstag on 11 June and the elections of 30 July, the national government found that it was speaking to the converted when it used its Press connections to inflame anti-Socialist feelings with dark hints of conspiracies hatching and with chilling revelations of what the godless revolutionaries intended to make out of Germany if they were not stopped in time. All of this contributed to Bismarck's electoral success,[16] and, three months later, to the passage of the Socialist Law.

The law gave local police authorities the right to forbid the exis-

---

[14] Mehring, *Geschichte der deutschen Sozialdemokratie*, ii. 499.

[15] On the question of socialism, Treitschke again has a good claim to be the quintessential German of his times. As early as 1874 he believed that any sympathy for socialism was 'an incitation to bestiality'. He described socialism to Gustav Freytag as 'an un-German madness'. Hamann and Hermand, *Gründerzeit*, p. 190.

[16] See above, Ch. III, p. 96.

tence of clubs and organizations of any kind, including co-operative funds and publications that supported 'social democratic, socialist, or communist activities designed to subvert the existing political and social order in ways that threaten the public order and particularly the harmony of the social classes'. Assemblies serving the same purpose were also forbidden, as was the collection of contributions for social democratic causes. Offences against these prohibitions, membership of illegal organizations, and the publication and distribution of forbidden journals were punishable by heavy fines and prison sentences. Local courts had the right to expel professional agitators or persons convicted under the provisions of the law from certain districts and localities and could withdraw licences from bookbinders, booksellers, lending libraries, and public houses for offences against the law. Finally, in districts and localities where public order was threatened by social democratic activities, the federated governments could impose a minor state of siege for periods not to exceed a year, during which police permission would be required for publication, assembly, and the bearing of weapons, and persons endangering the peace could be expelled summarily by police order.[17]

The law received the approval of the Reichstag on 19 October 1878 and went into effect immediately, with devastating results. Of the 47 leading party newspapers, 45 were suppressed immediately, including *Vorwärts*, *Die neue Rundschau*, *Die Zukunft*, the *Berliner Freie Presse*, and the *Hamburg-Altonaer Volksblatt*, as well as a large number of periodical publications of no political consequence, which were snuffed out at the same time. The police came down upon every kind of workers' club and, not content with that, extended their attack to include the trade unions as well. Trade-unionism was still a tender plant in Germany, because big industry and large-scale manufacturing were still relatively new. In the mid-seventies only about 50,000 workers were enrolled in unions of various kinds. But now all unions that had had any association with Social Democracy in the past, and some that had now, were crushed, and this virtually ended trade-unionism in Germany until the late 1880s. From organizations the authorities moved on implacably to individuals. In late November the Prussian Government imposed

---

[17] If Bismarck had had his way, the law would have deprived Social Democrats of the right to vote or to be elected to the Reichstag and would have threatened civil servants who adopted Social Democratic views with dismissal without a pension. These were after-thoughts, however, which came to him when the Reichstag was already considering the bill. On the debate on the law, see Mehring, *Geschichte* ii. 506 ff.

the minor state of siege on Berlin, and the police immediately rounded up 67 of the city's leading Socialists, including Ignaz Auer, Friedrich Wilhelm Fritzsche, and Heinrich Rackow, and ordered them to leave the city. In subsequent months this treatment was to be accorded to other large Prussian cities, like Hamburg and Breslau, and other state governments were to follow the Prussian example.[18]

During the debate in the Reichstag one Socialist deputy had shouted defiantly, 'We don't care a rap for the law!'[19] Once it had been put into effect, the party's mood was less confident, for it had not expected the government to be so ruthless, and it reacted with confusion and, in some cases, with panic. Among the rank and file, many simply capitulated when the police appeared, giving up their membership of the party in the hope of saving their jobs and avoiding legal difficulties. Among the party leaders, the atmosphere was one of bewilderment; and, with respect to the tactics that should be followed in face of the government persecution, there was no common agreement. As was perhaps natural, there were some who were so impressed by the government's determination that they counselled a policy of appeasement, arguing that the abandonment of opposition to the government on political issues might at least enable the party to work for economic gains. At the other end of the scale were people like Johannes Most, who, from a safe refuge in London, where he published a paper called *Freiheit*, called for a programme of defiance and revolutionary action. Between the extremes, Liebknecht and Bebel, and gifted younger men like Paul Singer and Eduard Bernstein, tried to find a policy that would rally the shaken party and encourage it to fight back in a disciplined way.

They were aided by the fact that Bismarck's use of the state of siege opened the eyes of many of those who had hoped to reach an accommodation with the government by making concessions and made them aware that the Chancellor was not engaged in a policy of petty harassment but was bent on the complete destruction of the party organization and the personal ruin of its members. Many

[18] The so-called Hirsch-Duncker unions, which were closely associated with the liberal parties and were benevolent associations rather than organizations seeking to improve the working conditions and wages of their members, were untouched by the application of the law. See Vernon L. Lidtke, *The Outlawed Party: Social Democracy in Germany, 1878–1890* (Princeton, 1966), pp. 80 ff. On expulsions, see Julius Bruhns, *Es klingt im Sturm ein altes Lied: Aus der Jugendzeit der Sozialdemokratie* (Stuttgart and Berlin, 1921), pp. 45 ff.

[19] His shout electrified the Reichstag, and the President felt called upon to send a messenger to the Press to make clear that the verb used was not stronger. Mehring, *Geschichte* ii. 507.

Socialists admitted later that it was the spectacle of the police uproot-
ing people from homes in which they had lived for thirty years,
destroying their livelihood, and sending them out on the roads to
beg that convinced them that they must fight back. As that determination grew, the party found the weapons that would reintegrate
its membership and give them direction.

The most effective of these was a new party newspaper that was
founded in Zurich in September 1879 and called the *Sozialdemokrat*.
Edited by the Bavarian Socialist George Vollmar, and later by
Eduard Bernstein, and following a policy laid down by Bebel,
Liebknecht, and Fritzsche, this paper restored the tie between the
leaders and the local organizations that the police had broken in the
first days of the law's implementation and made it possible for the
party leaders to pass down news about foreign reaction to Bismarck's persecution and about the growing resistance in all parts of
Germany, as well as warnings against the kind of unstructured
anarchism preached by Most and his associates, and information
concerning the party's attitude towards current issues and pending
legislation. To do all this the paper had, of course, to reach Socialists
inside Germany, but the outlawed party soon developed a postal
service of its own that was so effective that it won the grudging
admiration of the Prussian Minister of the Interior, Robert von
Puttkamer, whose agents tried in vain to penetrate and destroy it.[20]
Before the end of 1879, 3,600 copies of the *Sozialdemokrat* were being
printed and distributed, and this figure increased rapidly in the years
that followed.[21]

The printed word was not, of course, enough to co-ordinate the
thinking and activities of the party. It was necessary for the party
directorate—that is, the Reichstag delegation, upon whom the duties
of an executive necessarily devolved since they were the only Social
Democrats whose public activities were legal—to establish some
kind of contact with local leaders and, whenever they existed, organizations. It was not easy to do this, for the deputies were under
constant surveillance and had to school themselves in the arts of

---

[20] The director of this elaborate operation and of the party's intelligence service
which proved very efficient in uncovering police spies and *agents provocateurs* was
Julius Motteler. On his activities see Lidtke, *The Outlawed Party*, pp. 93 f. The most
informative work on police activities is Dieter Fricke, *Bismarcks Praetorianer. Die
Berliner politische Polizei gegen die deutsche Arbeiterbewegung 1871–1898* (Berlin, 1962).
See also the last chapter of *Denkwürdigkeiten des Geheimen Regierungsrathes Dr. Stieber*,
ed. L. Auerbach (Berlin, 1884); and Lange, *Berlin zur Zeit Bebels und Bismarcks*, pp. 25,
257–60.

[21] Bebel, *Aus meinem Leben*, iii. 97.

evasion. Bebel, a spare and athletic man, resorted to direct methods ('Many a peaceful citizen watched me with some astonishment as my quick stride gradually changed to a smooth trot, and, some distance behind me, there appeared, panting and dripping with sweat, an individual about whose character he was not quite clear.'[22]); but often elaborate deceptions were necessary, particularly when the meetings involved numbers of people, and, when they succeeded, they were celebrated with delight and became part of the growing legend of the heroic time. Often they did not succeed, for the police were adroit in the use of spies and bribes, and there were many people whose sympathy for the party was not as strong as their need of money. For any thorough discussion of issues or tactics, meetings that had to be disguised as musical concerts or held on the decks of Rhine steamers could not be effective.

The party leaders therefore felt it necessary periodically to organize secret conferences on foreign soil. During the years of persecution there were three of these, the first at Schloß Wyden in Switzerland in August 1880, the second in Copenhagen in 1883, and the third near St. Gall, Switzerland, in 1887. The Wyden Conference was probably the most important of these, for, at a time when the future still seemed black, the reunion of all the party's leading lights was psychologically heartening in itself, while at the same time providing them with an opportunity to reach agreement concerning their methods of resisting the persecution of the government. Of great significance for the party's future was the conference's decisive repudiation of the counter-tactics of anarchism and terrorism, a decision capped by the expulsion from the party of Johannes Most and Wilhelm Hasselmann, a former Lassallean who, in the Reichstag session of 1880, to the discomfiture of his Socialist colleagues, had declared his sympathy for those Russian anarchists who had now begun the programme of direct action that was to eventuate in the assassination of Alexander II in March 1881. Hasselmann had announced to a Reichstag moved equally by indignation and hilarity that 'the time for parliamentary chatter is past and the time for deeds begins'.[23] The conferees at Wyden decided that they could not afford further embarrassment of this kind and cast their uncomfortable brother into the outer darkness. For the rest, they reconfirmed the blend of Lassallean and Marxist principles that they had taken for their programme at the Gotha Conference of 1875, although they amended their statement of purpose—'the Social Democratic Party

[22] Ibid. 109.
[23] Reichstag, *Stenographische Berichte* (1880), ii. 1168.

endeavors to obtain the free state and the Socialist society—by all legal means'—by striking out the final adjective, an entirely appropriate thing to do since all of their activities had been defined by German law as illegal.[24]

If the Socialist leaders were heartened by their three days at Schloß Wyden, their mood quickly darkened after they got home. The new year was to confront them for the first time with the problem of trying to win Reichstag seats in an election for which they could not properly campaign. Moreover, as they prepared for it, they had to meet two new challenges: one posed by Bismarck's projected programme of social insurance, the other by Adolf Stoecker's combination of state socialism and anti-Semitism.

II

Erich Eyck has written that the fact that Bismarck never mentioned his social insurance legislation in his memoirs proves that it was something in which he had no serious interest and which he had taken up only for the political advantage he might gain from doing so.[25] This is not a compelling argument. The *Erinnerungen und Gedanken* are not, and were not intended to be, a complete record of their author's policies, and they are very far from being a reliable record of his private thoughts about the duties imposed upon him by his office. It would be a mistake to conclude from what is or is not said there that Bismarck was insincere in his repeated assertions that the state had a responsibility for the welfare of its more deprived and handicapped subjects.[26] In his first years as Minister President of Prussia, in 1862 and 1863, he had begun to think of the possibility of state-supported insurance plans for the benefit of the working class,[27] and his plans for accident, sickness, and old age insurance in the 1880s were rooted in the same concern that had motivated the abortive plans of the earlier period.[28]

[24] See Peter Gay, *The Dilemma of Democratic Socialism: Eduard Bernstein's Challenge to Marx* (rev. edn., New York, 1962) p. 49.

[25] Eyck, *Bismarck* iii. 368.

[26] See e.g. his notes of January 1881 in *G.W.* vic. 205, and, more generally, Karl Griewank, *Das Problem des christlichen Staatsmannes bei Bismarck* (Berlin, 1953) and Leonhard von Muralt, *Bismarcks Verantwortlichkeit* (Göttingen, 1955).

[27] See, *inter alia*, Otto Vossler, 'Bismarcks Sozialpolitik', *Historische Zeitschrift*, 167 (1953), 339.

[28] Bismarck's motives in this matter have been debated for years. A brief listing of the most important works on the subject is to be found in Hartmut Lehmann, 'Bodelschwingh und Bismarck: Christlichkonservative Sozialpolitik im Kaiserreich', *Historische Zeitschrift*, 208 (1969), 611 n. 10.

The political was never, of course, far from the centre of Bismarck's thinking, and there can be little doubt that he was aware of the advantage that might be derived from an insurance programme in his campaign against socialism. Much has been written about his cunning in offering a *Zuckerbrot* to seduce those who could be presumed to have been softened up by the *Peitsche*. It would be fairer to say that he wished to demonstrate that the state had more to offer to the working class than the Social Democrats—something that he believed deeply himself—and that he expected the beneficiaries of his policy to see the light and to abandon their false friends.

The announcement of Bismarck's plans in the spring of 1881 placed the Socialists in a dilemma. If they rejected what bourgeois society seemed to be offering, they could be accused of sacrificing the needs of their followers to tactical considerations; if they accepted it, they would be suspected of abandoning socialist principle for material advantage. In the first debate over accident insurance in April, the party leaders chose the second course. Taking some comfort from the consternation caused in liberal ranks by the project and seizing upon Bismarck's lame answer when Ludwig Bamberger said that the bill might properly have been introduced by Bebel, the Saxon Socialist leader ironically offered the Chancellor the assistance that he could not expect from his usual allies, provided that he amend the legislation so as to place the costs of the insurance solely on the shoulders of the capitalist employers, where they belonged. It was a source of some satisfaction to note, he added, that, since the bill would never have come before the Reichstag except as a disguised weapon with which to combat Social Democracy, his party could, in a real sense, claim to be its author.[29]

The party took its cue from Bebel in the months and years that followed, as Bismarck persisted with the programme that eventuated in the passing of a Sickness Insurance Law in 1883, an amended Accident Insurance Law in the following year, and Old Age and Disability Insurance in 1889.[30] The Socialists accepted the government's initiative but not its drafts, always seeking either to substitute bills of their own or to amend proposed legislation in the interest of the working class. As Liebknecht said on one occasion, 'Prince Bismarck may move further toward our goals—on this

---

[29] Reichstag, *Stenographische Berichte* (1881), i. 746; Bebel, *Aus meinem Leben*, iii. 174.

[30] In the end, the costs of accident insurance devolved upon the employers. Sickness insurance was financed by contributions from employees and employers on a ratio of 2 to 1. In the case of old age insurance, the costs were shared by the employer, the employees, and the state.

course we march together, and we do not hang on his coat-tails.'[31]

Even so, there were some doubts among at least the left-wing leaders of the party. Although Marx and Engels had sent praise from London for Bebel's April speech and had thus, by implication, given their approval of the course being followed, was there not a danger that this flirting with the government would strengthen the latent influence of Lassallean thinking in the party, encouraging the unwary to believe that state socialism had more to offer than revolutionary Marxism? In a letter to Friedrich Engels in September 1882, Eduard Bernstein spoke of 'the colossal State Cult [that] haunts our ranks';[32] and he was not alone in fearing that Bismarck's insurance schemes, if followed by other social legislation, might decisively weaken the militancy of the party.

In addition to this troubling but still remote problem, the party had to concern itself in 1881 with a threat to its position in Berlin, for that was the centre of the activities of Adolf Stoecker.[33]

This remarkable man, certainly one of the most interesting political personalities of the 1880s, was an Evangelical pastor, who in October 1874 was appointed fourth Court and Cathedral Preacher and, three years later, given responsibility for the direction of the City Mission. Stoecker performed the charitable labours involved in this post with enthusiasm and efficiency, inspired in part perhaps by a desire to outdo the achievements of Bishop Wilhelm Emmanuel von Ketteler in Mainz. There is no doubt that he had a compassionate understanding of the needs of the masses, but from the beginning he was equally impressed by their vulnerability to the arguments of Social Democracy. Like many Germans, he had acquired an almost neurotic fear and hatred of socialism during the bloody days of the Paris Commune in 1871, and in 1877 his feelings were reinforced by his reading of Rudolf Todt's *Der radikale deutsche Sozialismus und die christliche Gesellschaft* which gloomily predicted a future of republicanism and communism.[34] Stoecker's restless and ambitious temperament rose to the challenge; he resolved to save the masses for Christianity, not by charity but by political action.

Stoecker was a superb orator—Theodor Heuß was to call him 'the

---

[31] Cited in Lidtke, *The Outlawed Party*, p. 160.

[32] Ibid., p. 166.

[33] The most complete accounts of Stoecker's career are Walter Frank, *Hofprediger Adolf Stoecker und die christlichsoziale Bewegung* (2nd edn., Hamburg, 1935) and the first chapters of Theodor Heuß, *Friedrich Naumann, der Mann, das Werk, die Zeit* (Stuttgart and Berlin, 1937).

[34] On the effect of this, see Frank, *Stoecker*, pp. 38 f.

greatest popular missionary of Germany'[35]—but an indifferent organizer, and his demagogic talents were further compromised by his position as court chaplain, which hardly commended him to working-class audiences. His attempt to form a Christian and patriotic workers' party ran into difficulties from the beginning. His slashing attack upon the Social Democrats in the so-called *Eiskellerversammlung* of 3 January 1878—'They hate their fatherland ... and that is bad. To hate one's fatherland is like hating one's mother'—did not impress his largely working-class audience; and his subsequent attempt to persuade them, in the July elections, to support a programme that proclaimed that only the state could improve the lot of the worker and that authority and piety were the medicines for the present was a fiasco, his Christian Social Workers' party receiving only 1,421 votes in all Berlin. But Stoecker did not admit defeat. Not only did he go on preaching his particular brand of state socialism (he enthusiastically accepted Bismarck's insurance schemes, and had more radical plans for social reform than any that Bismarck would have countenanced), but he now reinforced his appeal to audiences by taking up anti-Semitism.

Something has been said above about the roots of anti-Jewish feeling in Germany.[36] It was particularly strong in Berlin which, by 1880, had 45,000 Jewish residents, at a time when in all of England there were only 46,000 and in all of France only 51,000.[37] Konstantin Frantz, who hated Berlin, wrote in 1879 that it was better suited to be the capital of a Jewish Reich than of a Germanic one,

because one meets here in all areas of public life the arrogant Jew ... the flea-market and marts-of-trade and stock-market Jew, the Press and literature Jew, the parliamentary Jew, the theatre and music Jew, the culture and humanity Jew, and—what is unique to Berlin—the city-government Jew. Almost half of Berlin's city councillors ... are Jews ... and, hand in hand with their kept Press and stock-market, they actually control the whole city government.

With somewhat more restraint, Franz Mehring tried to explain the animus against the Jews:

In Berlin, the Jewish element between 1780 and 1880 became an important and inseparable part of the population, just as the French colony had become between 1680 and 1780. As long as a hundred years ago, the good and bad elements of Jewry formed a sharp contrast. On the one side were ranged Lessing's friends Herz and Mendelssohn; on the other, the money-changer Jews, Ephraim and Itzig. ... But throughout this long period the alien,

[35] Heuß, *Naumann*, p. 58.   [36] See above, Ch. III.
[37] Frank, *Stoecker*, pp. 73 f.

unpleasant, or at least unaccustomed features of the Jewish character never impressed themselves so painfully on the great majority of Berlin's population as during the last ten years. . . . At the beginning of the 1870's victory, so long hoped for and finally won, intoxicated the Jews; and, when in full flush, one is anything but modest and sensible, thoughtful and cautious. In those days, the more mischievous elements among Berlin's Jews participated, in an abnormally high proportion, in bogus stock and stock-company swindles. Jewish writers and speakers delighted in criticizing the internal affairs of our Christian churches, and frequently with an effrontery that was in inverse proportion to the understanding their criticism revealed. Each day produced new evidence of that strange lack of *verecundia* which Schopenhauer rightly or wrongly imputes to the Jewish people. As a result, there arose among the cultured groups of Berlin society, irrespective of political, religious and social beliefs, a deep animosity against the Jewish character. Whoever denies this has either not spent the last ten years in Berlin or disputes the truth.[38]

It was to this mood that Stoecker was responding when, in September 1879, he addressed himself to the Jewish problem in a lecture entitled 'Our Demands on Modern Jewry', just as it was in the case of Heinrich von Treitschke who, in November 1879, wrote the notorious article in the *Preußische Jahrbücher* in which he declared, 'The Jews are our national misfortune.'[39] It should be stated that neither Stoecker nor Treitschke had any racial animus against the Jews. Their arguments were essentially religious and nationalistic; the Jews to them were an alien force in society, whose only temple was the stock exchange, and whose influence, exerted through the Jewish-controlled Press, was subversive of the foundations of the Reich. Provided that they embraced Christianity, took up an honest trade, and became good German patriots, Stoecker and Treitschke were willing to accept them without prejudice. The fine distinctions involved in this kind of reasoning were probably lost on most of their auditors. By virtue of their prominence, Stoecker and Treitschke made anti-Semitism respectable, and this opened the door to every variant of the disease.[40]

As far as the working class was concerned, it was no more immune to anti-Semitism than other sections of society, and when Stoecker

[38] Franz, *Der Föderalismus*, p. 268. The Mehring passage is cited in Paul W. Massing, *Rehearsal for Destruction: A Study of Political Anti-Semitism in Imperial Germany* (New York, 1949), pp. 313 f.

[39] See below, Ch. VI, p. 204.

[40] Treitschke was perhaps the most influential force in the founding of the Verein deutscher Studenten in the early eighties, a society that was violently anti-Semitic almost from the beginning. See below, Ch. VI, p. 206 and Hellmuth von Gerlach, *Von rechts nach links*, ed. Emil Ludwig (Zurich, 1937), p. 108.

made attacks upon the Jews part of his political box of tricks, he became a more formidable factor in Berlin politics than he had been in 1878. This may have been one of the reasons why Bismarck tolerated the Court Preacher's activities. When he framed the Socialist Law, the Chancellor had considered including Stoecker's Christian Social movement among its targets, and, in 1880, after Stoecker had attacked his banker and economic adviser, Gerson Bleichröder, he said that he regretted not having done so.[41] But there was always the chance that Stoecker's appeal to anti-Jewish feeling would be attractive, not only to the lower-middle-class voters, with a resultant drain on the strength of the liberal parties, but to working men as well. So the Chancellor held his hand.[42]

All things considered, the Social Democrats were confronted with formidable difficulties as they approached the Reichstag elections, and the government did its best to increase them. On 28 October 1880 the minor state of siege had been declared in Hamburg-Altona and in the months that followed it was extended to Harburg. Over a hundred active Socialists were expelled from these places, and the majority of these, in disgust, emigrated to America. This vindictive attack upon individuals was repeated when the state of siege was imposed in Leipzig in June 1881. In all parts of Germany the police also redoubled their efforts to apprehend persons distributing socialist literature and election appeals, and the courts handed out stiff sentences even when the evidence of law-breaking was not compelling. In the last weeks before the election, some 600 Socialists were behind bars, at a time when their services were badly needed.[43] Moreover, the party had a dearth of candidates with national or even local visibility. Some of the best-known fighters for the cause were dead, many had gone abroad, others could not run for office because their services were indispensable in the party's organization in Switzerland. To contest all constituencies, many of the Socialist candidates had to run in more than one place. Bebel, indeed, stood in 35 constituencies, and Liebknecht and Hasenclever in 16.[44]

[41] See Frank, *Stoecker*, p. 85. A factor in Bismarck's decision was William I's sympathy for Stoecker's views about the Jews. Ibid., p. 92.

[42] The threat was real enough to make Socialist leaders issue warnings to their followers about being taken in by the anti-Semitic movement. See Mehring, *Geschichte* ii. 546. Bismarck's attitude toward anti-Semitism was always ambivalent. His son Herbert once explained that the Chancellor opposed Stoecker because of his radical social views and because he was attacking the *wrong* Jews, the rich ones, who were committed to the *status quo*, rather than the propertyless Jews in the Parliament and the Press, who had nothing to lose and therefore joined every opposition movement. Frank, *Stoecker*, pp. 91–5.

[43] See Mehring, *Geschichte* ii. 541–9.   [44] Bebel, *Aus meinem Leben*, iii. 189.

Despite these handicaps, the Social Democratic party did not suffer the disaster that its enemies were predicting and some of its friends expecting. Its popular vote was, to be sure, cut by a third, from the 437,158 gained in 1878 to 311,961, and in Berlin it suffered a sharp decline, from 56,147 votes in 1878 to a mere 20,168, which was due primarily to the vigour of Stoecker's campaign. But there are always two ways of reading election figures, and, although the losses were substantial, the fact that two-thirds of the party's followers had remained loyal despite all the exertions of the police and the government Press was an impressive fact. Moreover, although the party won only one Reichstag seat in the initial balloting, it ended up with 12 after the run-off elections, an increase of three in its parliamentary strength, and it might have done even better if it had been willing to enter into electoral deals with Stoecker and the Conservatives before the final balloting in Berlin.[45] Bebel was to write in his memoirs that the Socialist Law was defeated on 27 October 1881.[46] It is doubtful whether many in the party felt that way at the time, but certainly they had every reason for satisfaction.

This was all the more true because of the obvious discomfiture of their great adversary. No matter how he read the election figures, there was little in them to please the Chancellor. He had managed neither to smash socialism nor to build an effective pro-government coalition of non-Socialist forces. The National Liberal party, which he imagined he had bent to his will, had fractured in the summer of 1880, the most independent-minded of its members—Forckenbeck, Bamberger, Stauffenberg, Bunsen, Rickert—forming a party of their own. In the elections of 1881 these Secessionists did as well as the party they left, winning 47 Reichstag seats, and, heartened by this, they began almost immediately to make overtures to the Progressive party of Eugen Richter, a man whom Bismarck detested, with reason, for he opposed the Chancellor on nearly all issues. The Centre party had won 90 seats, a source of no satisfaction to Bismarck, since his relations with the Catholics were always at a word and a blow; and, if they supported him on social insurance, they always voted against proposals that seemed to threaten the rights of the separate states or to limit the functions of the Reichstag. On the

---

[45] The Conservative and Christian Social leaders in Berlin were intent on destroying the Progressive party's position in the city and, probably not without Bismarck's knowledge, offered the Socialists support in two run-off elections and eventual help in removing the Socialist Law in return for an acceptance of the government's brand of social reform. The party executive rejected this with scorn. Ibid. 192–5.

[46] Ibid. 190.

balance, he regarded the Centre as an opposition party.[47] The Conservatives and Free Conservatives, upon whose votes he could generally rely, had lost a total of 30 seats in the elections and, with a joint Fraktion that numbered only 85, were far from being able to give Bismarck the kind of strength he needed to control the Reichstag. Indeed, lack of control was to be the salient characteristic of the Reichstag for the next five years, and frequently, on issues that he considered of vital importance—the establishment of an Economic Council (Volkswirtschaftsrat), which he hoped might in time replace the Reichstag, and the assumption by the federal government of all taxes on tobacco, a measure designed to relieve the government's financial dependence upon the separate states—Bismarck found the majority of the Reichstag in solid opposition.[48] It is understandable that he cursed and grumbled and talked about retirement, and predicted a bad end for a Reichstag that seemed headed for the oppositional stance of the Prussian Parliament of 1862. In a conversation with Mittnacht, the Württemberg minister, a month after the elections, Bismarck said that 'it was quite possible that the day would come when the German princes would have to decide whether the present state of parliamentarianism was compatible with the best interests of the Empire'.[49]

III

But the backbone of the Reich was Prussia, and, provided the sources of Prussian strength—the bureaucracy and the army—were protected from infection, the interests of the state would be protected even if a real flare-up came with the Reichstag. In the period that followed his set-back in the elections of 1881, the Chancellor was particularly attentive to the problem of innoculating or immunizing these bodies.

The executor of Bismarck's plans for the Civil Service was Robert von Puttkamer, a rather colourless and uninventive bureaucrat, whose strongest qualities were complete loyalty to Bismarck's wishes and a profound conviction that Prussian greatness was part of the divine plan. He had been appointed as Kultusminister in 1879 and

---

[47] In May 1880, after the Centre had opposed his plans for the incorporation of Hamburg in the Zollverein, Bismarck spoke of it as 'the crystallization point for every kind of hankering after opposition'. Eyck, *Bismarck* iii. 362.

[48] Funds for the establishment of a Volkswirtschaftsrat were denied by the Reichstag on 2 December 1881, and the Tabakmonopol was defeated on 14 June 1882. On both occasions, the Centre voted in opposition.

[49] Freiherr von Mittnacht, *Erinnerungen an Bismarck. Neue Folge* (Berlin, 1905), pp. 29 f.

Minister of the Interior two years later, succeeding Adalbert Falk, who had played so prominent a part in the Kulturkampf. Puttkamer's influence was felt almost immediately in the Prussian educational system, manifesting itself in an increase of religious instruction in the elementary schools and the encouragement of already pronounced conservative tendencies in the universities.[50] But the work for which he has been remembered was his house-cleaning of the Prussian administration. His sternest critic has described his objective as being a social conformism (*Alexandrinismus*) in which all branches of the state service and the classes from which those active in them were drawn were rendered inimical to the proletariat and all elements in the country that were sympathetic to the working class were excluded from influence upon the machinery of state and were denied standing in polite society.[51] To accomplish this, Puttkamer saw to it that advancement in the Civil Service was denied to anyone whose views smacked of liberalism, and, at the same time, shook up the whole Department of Justice, by reducing the number of courts and eliminating judges and prosecutors in the upper age bracket, the generation whose thinking had been moulded by the progressive tendencies of the 1860s. The billets that were freed by this procedure were filled a decade later by officials with impeccably conservative views.

The spirit of these reforms received its most explicit expression in the royal decree of 4 January 1882, which announced that the King-Emperor was personally responsible for the direction of his government's policy—in a speech of 24 January 1882 Bismarck said: 'In fact, the real Minister President of Prussia is and remains His Majesty the King'[52]—and that civil servants were bound by their oath of office to support that policy. In issuing this startling reassertion of the monarchical principle, the Chancellor was giving hostages to fortune, and in the end he was to be the victim of the personal government of the sovereign that he announced in 1882. But the Beamtenerlass was intended to discipline, if not to intimidate, the Prussian bureaucracy and to remind the oppositional Reichstag that emerged from the elections of 1881 that parliaments were transitory but the power of the monarch a permanent political reality.[53]

[50] On the state of the universities, see below, Ch. VI, pp. 192 ff.

[51] Kehr, *Economic Interest*, pp. 109–31 ('The Social System of Reaction under the Puttkamer Ministry').

[52] *Die politischen Reden des Fürsten Bismarcks*, ed. Horst Kohl (12 vols., Stuttgart, 1892–4), ix. 232.

[53] J. M. von Radowitz, *Aufzeichnungen und Erinnerungen aus dem Leben des Botschafters J. M. von Radowitz*, ed. Hajo Holborn (2 vols., Stuttgart, 1925), ii. 198.

Even before the decree had been issued, the results of the Bismarck–Puttkamer policy were a matter of concern to reflective men. The Crown Prince told General von Schweinitz in November 1880 that Bismarck was destroying the independence and initiative of the higher civil servants and that the result would be that, when he became emperor himself, he would not know where to turn for reliable aides.[54] There was a sad clairvoyance about this remark. The Chancellor and his chosen instrument succeeded all too well in their procustean tactics, and the Prussian bureaucracy, forced into their cruel mould, completely lost that progressive spirit for which in an earlier age it had been famous.

It was a sign of the growing seriousness with which the governing class viewed the political tendencies of the day that it was considered necessary to subject the officer corps of the army to something of the same kind of treatment that was experienced by the bureaucracy. In an older day this would have been thought an idle exercise, for before 1870 the Prussian officer corps had been almost completely homogeneous as far as politics was concerned, and progressive ideas were virtually non-existent. But the rapid expansion of the army after unification widened the social base from which officers were recruited; the old aristocratic monopoly was broken, and an increasing number of middle-class candidates had to be commissioned. Because their political orthodoxy could not simply be taken for granted, a mixture of indoctrination and coercion was employed to assure it. Throughout the 1880s official directives and semi-official military journals pointed to the forces of subversion in society and emphasized the role of the army as 'the only fixed point in the whirlpool, the rock in the sea of revolution that threatens us on all sides, the talisman of loyalty, and the palladium of the prince'.[55] In a kind of echo of the Beamtenerlass, they insisted that the officer's personal oath of allegiance to the monarch required that he subordinate his political convictions to those of his *Kriegsherr* and give undeviating support to his policies.

This applied not only to regular officers but to those in the reserve as well, who were mainly of middle-class origin and, unlike regular officers, were allowed to participate in politics and to stand for public office. One manual for reserve officers made it clear that

the officer in reserve status must never, while an officer, belong to a party which places itself in opposition to the government of our Emperor or of his local ruler (*Landesherr*). If he feels conscientiously restricted by this, then he

[54] Schweinitz, *Denkwürdigkeiten*, ii. 134.
[55] 'Offizier als Erzieher des Volkes', *Militärwochenblatt* (Beihefte, 1882, Heft 2), 73.

must request his dismissal. As an officer, he is his imperial master's 'man' in the old German sense of the word. Under no circumstances must he place himself in opposition to him. On the other hand, however, he is fully justified in making use of his political rights and intervening in the political struggle in behalf of the objectives which the government of the *Landesherr* and the Emperor pursue.[56]

There were some hardy types who were outraged by this infringement of their political rights. When their resistance was too blatant—as in the cases of a reserve major who joined the Progressive party and a cavalry captain who voted with the left on a matter involving the prerogatives of the Crown[57]—they lost their commissions. But such cases were few. Mention has been made above of the growing social aspirations of the wealthier middle class after 1870 and of their desire to be accepted by the aristocracy.[58] It came to be widely believed that a reserve lieutenancy in a good regiment was an essential step in the achievement of that goal,[59] and those who acquired such commissions were not in general willing to risk losing them by adopting extreme political views. They were, on the contrary, only too willing to be feudalized, to join that 'nobility of temperament' (*Adel der Gesinnung*) which Emperor William II appealed for in March 1890 to supplement the 'nobility of birth' that had traditionally officered the army.[60]

And since this was true, the army could expand while remaining a reliable bulwark of the existing order. But this advantage was gained at a cost. The eagerness with which bourgeois youths sought commissions and, once they were won, the zeal with which they imitated and exaggerated the thinking, the manners, and the vices of their aristocratic fellows, made a strong contribution to the latent antimilitarism in the country, if only because it had the effect, in Eckart Kehr's words, of converting 'the Prussian lieutenant, who up to this time had been on the average relatively modest, into the unbearable prig of the Wilhelmine era'.[61]

In 1883 Bismarck took another important step to protect the army from the possibility of external attack, when he tolerated far-

---

[56] Quoted by Josef Wirth in a Reichstag debate in 1926. *Stenographische Berichte* (1926–7), 8591.

[57] Craig, *Prussian Army*, p. 237.

[58] See above, pp. 99–100.

[59] Some expressions of this belief are provided in Carl Zuckmayer's play *Der Hauptmann von Köpenick* (1931).

[60] Karl Demeter, *Das deutsche Heer und seine Offiziere* (Berlin, 1930), pp. 28–9.

[61] Kehr, *Economic Interest*, pp. 97–108 ('The Genesis of the Prussian Reserve Officer').

reaching administrative changes in the structure of the military establishment. Specifically, he authorized the diminution of the powers of the War Minister, to whom, since Scharnhorst's time, all branches of the military administration had been subordinate, and the elevation of the Military Cabinet and the General Staff to the status of independent agencies responsible only to the King-Emperor.

This change was rooted in part in intramural jealousy. Ever since Edwin von Manteuffel had been Chief of the Military Cabinet in the days of the constitutional conflict, that agency, which handled the King's correspondence on military subjects and his relations with his commanding generals but also had the duty of administering all personnel matters in the army, including appointments and promotions, had felt that its connection with the War Ministry was a false one; and Manteuffel's successor, E. L. Albedyll, worked persistently after 1871 to win a position of independence. The General Staff took the same line. The victories of 1866 and 1870 had made the name of Helmuth von Moltke a household word, and his juniors in the General Staff, the so-called 'demigods', felt it demeaning that, once peacetime conditions were restored, their revered chief should have access to his sovereign only through, and with the permission of, the War Minister. Moltke himself was too modest a man to raise difficulties about this, but, when Alfred von Waldersee became Quartermaster General in 1882, that ambitious officer decided that the situation must be corrected and was soon working in tether with Albedyll to promote their common interests.

The parliamentary situation aided them by providing new arguments and bringing a powerful ally to their side in the person of the Chancellor. In January 1883 Eugen Richter, an inveterate critic of the army, whose attacks upon it were all the more formidable because of the expert and detailed knowledge with which they were informed,[62] began a systematic critique of military expenditures, criticizing the excessive outlay on the Guards and cavalry regiments, which he described as parade troops, and military bands, which he considered a luxury, and then widening his attack by demanding a review of promotion policy and a shortening of the term of service. Richter's campaign was supported by the Centre, the Secessionists,

---

[62] Richter's admirers included Waldersee who once called him the only parliamentarian whose views deserved attention. *Denkwürdigkeiten des Generalfeldmarschalls Alfred Grafen von Waldersee*, ed. H. O. Meisner (3 vols., Stuttgart, 1923–5), ii. 286. For a modern view, see Moritz J. Bonn, *Wandering Scholar* (New York, 1948), p. 47.

and the Socialists,[63] an alliance that was formidable enough to throw the government forces into temporary disarray. The War Minister, General A. K. G. von Kameke, protested that the debate was improper, since the opposition was touching upon matters of command that were reserved for royal decision; but he proved incapable of stemming the wave of anti-militarism that beat against the government benches.

The debate infuriated the Emperor, an old soldier who was jealous of his prerogatives and to whom the opposition speeches were an unpleasant reminder of the parliamentary difficulties of the 1860s. William's indignation played into the hands of Albedyll and Waldersee, who now intimated that Kameke's inadequate performance in the Reichstag demonstrated the dangers of giving the War Minister any authority over sensitive subjects like command and staff matters, since the mere fact of his appearing in Parliament invited opposition questions and criticism. The two military chiefs found a strong supporter in Bismarck, to whom the debate in the Reichstag was one more proof of the necessity of curbing the pretensions of that body before it was too late. As usual, the Chancellor was motivated in part by personal factors. He disliked Kameke, a soldier who strongly believed that it was to the army's interest to appease its parliamentary critics. To Bismarck this smacked of flabbiness and of the kind of liberalism which he associated with the Crown Prince, to whose circle, indeed, Kameke was reputed to belong. 'A parliamentary general on active service is always a disagreeable phenomenon,' the Chancellor wrote to his sovereign, 'but one as War Minister is dangerous.'[64] He was quite ready, therefore, not only to purge the War Minister, but to arrange things so that future Kamekes would be able to do no harm.

In February it became clear to the unhappy War Minister that he had lost the Emperor's favour and had no supporters in either the Bendlerstraße or the Chancellor's Office, and that there was no point in trying to hold on to office. He therefore resigned and, to Bismarck's satisfaction, was followed in that course by his friend the Chief of the Admirality, Albrecht von Stosch, another liberal-minded officer with whom Bismarck had had many differences and

---

[63] This was a marriage of convenience, for Richter was anti-Socialist and disliked by the Socialists. Mehring was critical even of his anti-militarism, saying that he criticized the army as an auditor of books would. *Gesammelte Schriften*, xi. 351.

[64] Bismarck, *G. W.* vic. 264. See also H. O. Meisner, 'Militärkabinett, Kriegsminister und Reichskanzler zur Zeit Wilhelms I', *Forschungen zur brandenburgischen und preußischen Geschichte*, 1 (1935), 95.

who he suspected was also a member of the Crown Prince's entourage.[65] To succeed Kameke, Albedyll, who seems to have been the chief architect of the change-over,[66] chose Paul Bronsart von Schellendorf, who had served on Moltke's staff during the French war. Bronsart's appointment was made conditional upon his agreeing, first, that the Chief of the General Staff would be granted direct access to the Emperor without the War Minister's mediation and, second, that all army personnel matters should be removed from the purview of the War Ministry and lodged in the Military Cabinet. In short, Bronsart was asked to agree to the emasculation of the office before it was offered to him. He did not complain. He approved of the purpose behind the change and admitted this by saying, 'In the political realm I will oppose with severity and determination any attempt to endanger the rights of the Crown, as well as any pretension on the part of the political parties to win any influence whatsoever over the power of command.'[67]

The administrative reorganization of 1883 was a constitutional change of major importance, for it not only weakened the authority of the Reichstag in military affairs but that of the Chancellor himself. That Bismarck should have condoned this, after having fought so stoutly during the wars of unification and in 1874[68] to maintain his position of primacy, is to be explained by his growing disenchantment with the results of universal manhood suffrage and his increasing concern over attacks in the Reichstag upon the feudal-military foundations of the Reich. To the Chancellor the change was a necessary defensive move, but he was to have occasion before his retirement to regret the new latitude that he had given the soldiers, particularly when the General Staff began to use its new independence to dabble in international politics, as it did during the Bulgarian crisis of 1887.[69] Bismarck's successors were to suffer even more than he did from the political irresponsibility which the change of 1883 encouraged.

Nor can it be said that the new arrangement did anything to improve Bismarck's position *vis-à-vis* Parliament. The method he had chosen to avert parliamentary criticism of the army was a

---

[65] On Kameke's fall, see Bismarck, *G.W.* vic. 274; Meisner, *Kriegsminister*, pp. 33–4; R. Schmidt-Bückeburg, *Das Militärkabinett der preußischen Könige und deutschen Kaiser* (Berlin, 1933), pp. 140–3. On Stosch, see Frederick B. M. Hollyday, *Bismarck's Rival: A Political Biography of General and Admiral Albrecht von Stosch* (Durham, N.C., 1960), esp. Chs. 5 and 6.

[66] See Waldersee, *Denkwürdigkeiten* i. 225.

[67] Meisner, *Kriegsminister*, p. 37.

[68] See above, p. 52 and Craig, *Prussian Army*, Ch. V.   [69] See above, pp. 133 f.

clumsy one, and it could hardly be expected that the opposition would be content, during future debates on military subjects, to be fobbed off with declarations of ignorance or lack of jurisdiction by the War Minister. If anything, the fact that that official had been rendered impotent goaded the opposition on to new attacks upon the military establishment, which became particularly vehement whenever its budget came up for review. This became a problem of increasing gravity because the most anti-militarist of the political parties continued, despite Bismarck's efforts, to grow in strength.

IV

The story of the Reichstag elections of 1884, which once more demonstrated the Chancellor's failure to stem the tide of socialism, is interesting for the light it throws upon another of Bismarck's principal preoccupations in this period, his concern over what would happen when William I died. Although the Emperor had recovered completely from the wounds inflicted by Nobiling, and although he was still clear of mind and vigorous in the expression of his political prejudices, he was well advanced in years and could not be expected to live much longer. Throughout the 1880s—particularly after 1885, when the Emperor had a mild stroke—Bismarck was always aware that he could, with very little warning, be forced to deal with a new ruler, in the person of the Crown Prince, Frederick William. This was not a prospect that he relished. Frederick William was the very model of a model emperor—a handsome, bearded man with a soldierly bearing and a reputation for enlightened views—but the appearance belied the reality. If life were like romantic fiction, he would have ascended to the throne immediately after his military successes at Königgrätz and Gravelotte, when he was at the height of his physical powers and was a popular hero. But his father lived on for another eighteen years and the long wait for power frustrated the Prince, blunted his energies, and made him prey to alternating fits of irritation and melancholy. His self-confidence was eroded by inactivity as well as by his awareness of the superior intellectual capacity of his wife, the daughter of Queen Victoria of Great Britain. Bismarck did not believe that he possessed either the will or the political judgement needed in a sovereign. He remembered the Crown Prince's impatience over the protracted negotiations with the south German princes in 1870 and his expressed willingness to use force to compel them to join the Empire,[70] and his opinion that Frederick

---

[70] See e.g. Bismarck's remarks to Waldersee on 25 December 1870. Waldersee, *Denkwürdigkeiten* i. 116.

William had no sense of political realities must have been confirmed when he learned that the Prince desired to revive the tradition of the Holy Roman Empire by assuming the title of Frederick IV upon his accession.[71] The Crown Prince, he told Busch in 1885, had little knowledge of affairs and little interest in studying them seriously, and he had no courage.[72]

In saying this, Bismarck may have been thinking of the way in which the Prince deferred to the political opinions of his wife, who was certainly a stronger and more determined person than he. It was to Crown Princess Victoria that Frederick William owed his reputation as a liberal, and it was due to her influence that his entourage included politicians and officials like Franz von Roggenbach, Albrecht von Stosch, Max von Forckenbeck, and Ludwig Bamberger, as well as publicists like Heinrich Geffcken and representatives of literature and the fine arts. It was no accident that most of these persons were deeply critical of Bismarck's policies, for the Crown Princess had had a deep personal animus against the Chancellor since the 1860s, a feeling that was reciprocated.[73] Roggenbach, a former Badenese Minister of State, who had worked faithfully for the creation of a united and liberal Germany and had broken with the Chancellor in 1865, was convinced that Bismarck's long tenure of office had been a misfortune for his country (he spoke of '*das Fatum, das Kismet in Gestalt des Reichskanzlers*'[74]) and that it was due to him that unification had brought only 'absolutism, tricked out with parliamentary decoration and naïve trifling with pseudoconstitutionalism'.[75] He hoped that a change of throne would lead, under a new Chancellor, to a change of direction, and this hope was shared by all members of the Crown Prince's circle of confidants and advisers.

Although he was always well informed about what went on inside this Fronde,[76] and although he never missed an opportunity to damage or discredit its members, Bismarck did not take the fact of its existence too seriously, believing apparently that it would remain

---

[71] This idea horrified the Crown Prince's liberal advisers. See Roggenbach to Stosch, 18 August 1885, in *Im Ring der Gegner Bismarcks: Politische Briefe Franz von Roggenbachs 1865–1896*, ed. Julius Heyderhoff (2nd edn., Leipzig, 1943), p. 229.

[72] Busch, *Tagebuchblätter*, iii. 192.

[73] See, *inter alia*, *Bismarck Gespräche*, ii. 44.

[74] *Im Ring der Gegner Bismarcks*, p. 22.

[75] Ibid., p. 223.

[76] Albedyll, the Chief of the Military Cabinet, who had entrée to the Crown Prince's circle, seems to have kept Bismarck informed in the early eighties, although his position was ambivalent and he manœuvred between the two camps.

relatively harmless, even in the event of a change of throne, as long as it had no real political base in the country at large. But in 1884 it appeared that there might be some possibility of its acquiring such strength, and his appreciation of this determined the Chancellor's tactics in the elections of that year.

On the eve of the elections, the Secessionists, who had broken away from the National Liberal party in 1881, decided to unite formally with the Progressive party. The new combination took the name Deutsche Freisinnige Partei (German Free Thought party) but was widely known as the Crown Prince's party, because he was among the first to congratulate its founders on their action, which created a bloc of over a hundred deputies, including some of the most brilliant and experienced members of the Reichstag. However much Bismarck might sneer at the new party's hope of forming 'a Gladstone ministry', he could not take this threat lightly. If the Freisinnige could attract what was left of the National Liberal party to their side, German liberalism would have recovered from the blow it had suffered in 1878–9 and might, with a liberal Emperor's encouragement, transform the political system.[77] The fury that the very thought of this possibility aroused in Bismarck's breast was shown by his behaviour when Eduard Lasker, a doughty fighter for the liberal cause, died in January 1884 during a visit to the United States. When Lasker's body was returned to Germany for burial, the Chancellor saw to it that there was no government representative at his funeral service and, when the United States House of Representatives sent an official message of sympathy to the Reichstag, Bismarck refused, on a pretext, to transmit it, and in a debate in the Reichstag some days later bitterly attacked the dead parliamentarian.[78]

As for Lasker's living colleagues in the Freisinnige party, the Chancellor, in the last days of the Reichstag session and in the electoral campaign that followed, turned all his batteries against the weaknesses in their lines. These were serious, for the new partners were not fundamentally united on such important issues as state-supported insurance schemes, tariff policy, or the attitude to be adopted toward socialism. During the debate on the renewal of the Socialist Law and the legality of the state of siege currently imposed on Berlin, Leipzig, and Hamburg, which took place in the last days

---

[77] This was the hope of liberals like the historian Mommsen. See Alfred Heuß, *Theodor Mommsen und das 19. Jahrhundert* (Kiel, 1956), p. 204.

[78] Louis L. Snyder, 'Bismarck and the Lasker Resolution, 1884', *Review of Politics*, xxix, no. 1 (Jan. 1967), 41–64.

of the 1884 session of the Reichstag, it soon became apparent that the new party's programme, which called for equality before the law regardless of person or party, was not firmly enough held to withstand Bismarck's attacks. The Chancellor's revival of the so-called anarchist threat to the public order and his cavalier identification of left liberals as men who encouraged subversion by their softness toward socialism frightened an appreciable number of members of the new party, first, into seeking a compromise solution that would lighten the rigours of the law and then, when that failed, into giving the votes necessary to assure its extension. Franz Mehring jeered later at the liberal attempts to excuse their breach of principle and compared their protestations to those of a girl claiming virginity on the grounds that the baby she had produced was very small and that she would not do it again.[79] All in all, the renewal of the Socialist Law did little to support the idea that a new and militant liberalism was in the making.

During the electoral campaign the Chancellor continued his tactics of intimidation while at the same time exploiting the social insurance legislation as proof that all social progress came from the state. Finally, like a magician producing a rabbit from a hat, he held up before the eyes of the electorate the vision of a new colonial empire that would not only enhance Germany's position in the world but would increase the prosperity of the country. Both issues confused the Freisinnige, the latter because Germany's first venture into colonial politics was accompanied by a worsening of relations with Great Britain which, given the Anglophile sympathies of the Crown Prince's circle, put them in the position of seeming to oppose a policy in which the electorate was deeply interested. As the campaign progressed, hopes of accomplishing a comprehensive union of liberals disappeared, their demise becoming official when the National Liberal party made a decisive shift to the right at its conference at Heidelberg in March and, under the new leadership of Johannes Miquel,[80] made it clear that, on all decisive contemporary issues—social and colonial policy and the military question—it was closer to the Conservative than to the opposition parties. The election returns showed the cumulative results of these blows. The united party of Progressives and Secessionists, which had for a brief period claimed 106 Reichstag seats, was able to hold only 67 of them, a defeat for political liberalism that proved to be both decisive and permanent.

[79] Mehring, *Gesammelte Schriften*, ii. 593.
[80] Rudolf von Bennigsen, the former party leader, retired from politics in 1883.

For Bismarck, this result, accompanied as it was by the shift of the National Liberals, who won 50 seats, and the Conservative gain of 28 for 78 seats, was gratifying, or would have been if it had not been for the success won by the Social Democrats. Despite the handicaps under which they had to operate, the Socialists polled a quarter of a million votes and doubled their representation in the Reichstag. With 24 seats they were now big enough to have the right of representation on all major Reichstag committees, which meant that their potential for disruption was greatly enhanced.[81] Since the Centre party, which as often as not opposed the Chancellor's policies, had won 99 seats, the new Reichstag was as unmanageable as the old.

This became apparent as soon as it assembled, for it administered two stinging rebuffs to the Chancellor, by rejecting a request for new positions in the Foreign Ministry and by defeating his proposal for a new federal tax on spirits, and in the course of the next two years it proved highly refractory, particularly so during the debate on renewal of the Socialist Law in 1886, which passed with some difficulty.[82] As early as December 1884 Bismarck was raging against the unmanageability of the Reichstag, telling the members of the Ministry of State that one could get nowhere with the present electoral law and that the logical thing to do was to conclude, as Prince Felix zu Schwarzenberg had concluded with respect to the Kremsier constitution of 1848, that 'this arrangement has not worked out'. He wished, he added, that the Social Democrats would try a putsch, for that might solve a lot of problems. Failing that, there was always the possibility of a budgetless regime, like that of 1862–6 in Prussia. That would be an ironical end to his career, and perhaps not feasible, for, he added significantly, whereas William I had allowed him to defy Chamber majorities for four years, 'the Crown Prince believed in majorities'.[83]

Bismarck was saved from extreme solutions to his parliamentary problem by the deterioration of Germany's international position as a result of the series of Bulgarian crises that filled the years 1885–7.

---

[81] On the other hand, 15 of the 24 seats had been won in the run-off elections, some by private bargains with other parties. Both Bebel and Engels scented in these results a revival of Lassalleanism, and, indeed, the success did encourage a new tendency to moderation in the party. It is perhaps not an exaggeration to say that revisionism had its roots in the party's first real success. See Lidtke, *The Outlawed Party*, pp. 188–91.

[82] Ibid., pp. 242–4. If Bebel had not been so intransigent in his opposition to compromise, the Reichstag would probably have eliminated the harshest aspects of the law.

[83] Ballhausen, *Bismarck-Erinnerungen*, pp. 306.

These destroyed the viability of the Three Emperors' League and raised the possibility that Germany, in defence of its ally Austria-Hungary, might find itself engaged in a two-front war against Russia and France. The elaborate diplomatic game that Bismarck played in order to avert this possibility has been described above,[84] and it has been noted that this turned upon an increase in Germany's armaments sufficiently large to impress both potential antagonists. In the process of carrying this Armament Bill through Parliament, Bismarck won control of the Reichstag for the first time in seven years.

There is no better illustration of the intimate connection between foreign and domestic factors in Bismarck's statecraft than this incident.[85] The Chancellor was convinced that increased armaments were necessary and that they might be the key to the solution of the foreign situation,[86] but he refused to choose a way of getting them that would not bring him domestic advantages as well. The idea of asking the Reichstag for a supplement to the Septennat Law of 1881 he rejected in the spring of 1886 specifically because such a procedure would not be likely to lead to 'a blow against the Reichstag majority'.[87] Instead he asked for a new Septennat a full year before the old one was due to expire. The Reichstag was perfectly willing to grant the increases asked for and the funds to pay for them but insisted that the increased budget be for a term of three, rather than seven, years. Bismarck then did what he had intended to do all along; he dissolved the Reichstag, counting upon the war scare that had been created by government-inspired articles in the Press and by the calling-up of reserves and the announcement of a war loan to rally patriotic voters to the parties that supported the government. His calculation was shrewd. In the elections of 1887 the Conservatives, the Free Conservatives, and the National Liberals, forming the so-called Kartell,[88] won 220 of the 375 Reichstag seats, thanks in part to the preference given to rural areas in the apportionment of seats, and more to their co-operation in the run-off elections. Of the opposition parties, the Centre held its own, but the Freisinnige lost more than half of their seats, and the Socialist delegation was reduced from 24 to 11.

Bismarck could now, for the first time, await the change of monarch with confidence. Thanks to his masterful handling of the

[84] See above, Ch. IV.
[85] See Michael Stürmer's remarks on this in *Bismarck und die preußisch-deutsche Politik* (Munich, 1970), p. 227.
[86] See e.g. his letter of 24 December 1886 to Bronsart von Schellendorf. Bismarck, *G.W.* vic. 346.
[87] *Bismarck und die preußisch-deutsche Politik*, p. 230.
[88] On the formation of the Kartell, see Kardorff, *Wilhelm von Kardorff*, pp. 191 f.

international crisis, his reputation was at its height and he now had the kind of commanding position in the Reichstag that could frustrate any liberal experiments that the Crown Prince might try to make. It cannot be said that he took his triumph gracefully. On the contrary, when the Emperor died in March 1888 and the Crown Prince, at long last, ascended the throne as Frederick III, Bismarck seemed to delight in baulking every desire of the new imperial couple. They were hardly in a position to fight back, for Frederick was suffering from a disease that was diagnosed, belatedly, as cancer of the throat. But this did not prevent the Chancellor from interfering with appointments to the imperial household, objecting to the Emperor's desire to bestow decorations on certain old friends, and intervening to block the projected wedding of the Emperor's daughter Victoria to Prince Alexander of Battenberg. This last he did in the most blatant way possible, letting it be known that he was resigning because the Emperor and his wife wished to embroil Germany with the Russian Government (which had, after a long series of differences with Alexander, forced him from the throne of Bulgaria) and to turn Germany into a kind of British satellite (for it was well known that Queen Victoria favoured the match). As a result of the Chancellor's gesture, the Press of the Kartell parties conducted a malicious and mendacious campaign against the Empress and her daughter which darkened the last days of Frederick III.

It is difficult to see what Bismarck hoped to gain from this, or from his subsequent attacks upon the editor of the Emperor Frederick's diary of 1866–70[89] and upon the British diplomat, Sir Robert Morier, who was a friend of the imperial couple.[90] The vindictiveness that characterized his conduct during the three months of Frederick's reign was perhaps a revelation of the true Bismarck who was disguised by the external trappings of the statesman—the man who could never forgive an enemy or forget a slight. It was certainly a sign of the growing unconditionality of the Chancellor's temperament as he grew old, a tendency that manifested itself with increasing frequency in the two years that followed Frederick's death in June 1888.

---

[89] Erich Eyck argues sensibly that the diary, among other things, showed the weakness of Bismarck's theory that the Empire was the creation of the princes. Eyck, *Bismarck* iii. 539. For details of the case brought against the editor, Heinrich Geffcken, see Raschdau, *Unter Bismarck und Caprivi*, p. 53.

[90] On this case, see Frederic B. M. Hollyday, ' "Love Your Enemies! Otherwise Bite Them!" Bismarck, Herbert, and the Morier Affair, 1888–9', *Central European History* (Mar. 1968), 56.

V

Four years after Bismarck's departure from the centre of the political stage, Theodor Fontane wrote: 'Bismarck is the greatest scorner of principle who has ever existed and a "principle" finally brought him down, the same principle that he carried written on his banner all his life and in accordance with which he *never* acted. The power of the Hohenzollern monarchy . . . was stronger than his genius and his falsehoods.'[91]

There was a good deal of truth in this. Throughout his career Bismarck had exalted the monarchical principle, generally as a means of defeating opposition to his policies or of justifying courses of action that could not otherwise be justified. The speech of January 1882, in which he said that the Emperor was the real Minister President of Prussia, was one example of this;[92] his speech defending his refusal to send the Lasker resolution to the Reichstag in 1884—in which he said, *'As Chancellor I can, of course do nothing without the Emperor's approval,* and I could not be expected to ask his permission to present such a resolution to the Reichstag'[93]—was an even more incautious one. It was the constitutional theory implicit in these utterances that was turned against him after 1888, when a young ruler who took it seriously used it to drive the Chancellor from power, essentially on the grounds of disobedience to the royal will.

William II came to throne when he was barely thirty years of age and the Chancellor was seventy-three. Adolf Stoecker, who was still active in politics, claimed that, immediately after his accession, William had said of Bismarck: 'I will let the old man snuffle on for six months, and then I will rule myself.'[94] It seems unlikely that this was true. William was still awed by Bismarck's authority and flattered by the attention paid to him by the Chancellor and his son in the days when his grandfather and his father were still alive. But he was, nevertheless, young and impressionable, and there was no shortage of people who were ready to flatter him and to urge him to stand on his own feet and go his own way. Waldersee, now Chief of the General Staff, Stoecker, Johannes Miquel of the National Liberty party, and William's old teacher Hinzpeter were particularly zealous in this respect and artful in the praise of William's own talents, and their influence was not countered effectively by the Chancellor, who at this time of his life preferred to live as much as possible in Varzin and Friedrichsruh and who left attendance upon the Emperor to his

[91] Fontane, *Briefe* ii. 324.   [92] See above, p. 158.
[93] Bismarck, *Politische Reden*, x. 16. My italics.   [94] Frank, *Stoecker*, p. 183.

son Herbert, a man not particularly noted for his social graces.[95] In these circumstances, differences were bound to develop.

Significantly, it was the sensitive issue of German politics in the 1880s that encouraged this, the social question. William had become aware of the problems of poverty and want during his grandfather's reign, when Waldersee and Stoecker had awakened his interest in the work of the Inner Mission. In November 1887 the Prince had in fact been patron of a gathering of notables in Waldersee's house that was convened to discuss financial support for the Berlin City Mission, and he had made a widely reported speech about the necessity of propagating Christian Social principles.[96] The publicity occasioned by this affair had led Bismarck to write a masterly letter to the young Prince, which was designed to warn him about falling under the influence of priests and evangelists and, more important, to suggest that a mistaken humanitarianism would only increase subversion in the country, which was already being encouraged by 'social and other democrats'. 'The strongest kind of monarchy', Bismarck wrote, 'I look for in a . . . monarch who is determined not only to co-operate industriously in the business of governing the country but who in critical times would rather fall with sword in hand on the steps of his throne, fighting for his right, than surrender. No German soldier would abandon such a ruler, and the old motto of 1848 is still true: *"Gegen Demokraten helfen nur Soldaten."* '[97]

William does not seem to have been persuaded, and out of his lack of conviction grew the breach with the Chancellor. The first indication that there might be a parting of the ways came in May 1889 when there was a massive strike in the Ruhr coalfields. The Emperor broke all precedent by receiving a delegation of miners in the Berlin Schloß, and he became so agitated by what they told him that he burst into a meeting of the Prussian Ministry of State and, in the presence of the Chancellor, delivered an excited speech, attacking the Westphalian coal producers and ordering that they be forced to end the strike on the miners' terms. Bismarck was rather startled by this but seems to have thought the Emperor's mood represented a passing whim. However, he was mistaken.

It took him some time to discover that this was so. He was, perhaps because of age, less attentive than usual to political developments in the country and imperfectly informed even of the

[95] For a balanced and sympathetic portrait of Herbert von Bismarck, see Bußmann's introduction to the *Privatkorrespondenz*.

[96] Frank, *Stoecker*, p. 166; Kardorff, *Wilhelm von Kardorff*, p. 201.

[97] Bismarck, *G.W.* xv. 455.

divisiveness that was beginning to affect his Reichstag majority. The Kartell had proved to be an efficient instrument as far as he was concerned. He was not aware that its achievements—another renewal of the Socialist Law, the passing of the Septennat, new taxes on liquor and sugar, an increase of the tariff on grains, and the lengthening of the legislative period from three to five years, with a consequent diminution of the electorate's influence on the political process—were not widely popular; nor did he appreciate the fact that a considerable number of National Liberal deputies were finding it increasingly uncongenial to have to work in tether with the *Kreuzzeitung* reactionaries who formed the right wing of the Conservative party. His lack of perception proved damaging when he decided in October 1889 that the time had come to complete the destruction of the Social Democratic party by passing a new Socialist Law that would not have a limited term, as in the past, but would be permanent. The National Liberals reacted by intimating that they would support such legislation only if the provisions that authorized the police to expel persons from their homes on suspicion of subversion were deleted. This was countered by Conservative insistence that the power of expulsion was a *sine qua non*.

On this question the Chancellor and his sovereign came down on opposite sides, Bismarck being opposed to any concession while William instinctively adopted the position of the National Liberals. The Emperor had, in fact, decided that the Socialist Law was less important than a project of his own, a plan for legislation that would improve working conditions and regulate working hours for all German labourers. More and more, he was talking himself into the idea that he could be a *roi des gueux* and that his personal initiative would inspire the working classes with loyalty and fealty and thus destroy the sinister attractions of Social Democracy. Bismarck, who took an old-fashioned Manchesterian view of restrictions upon the right to work, dismissed all of this as *Humanitätsdusel*[98] and resolved to sabotage the Emperor's project, while going ahead with his own plans.

That William and his chief minister were on a collision course became evident at a Crown Council held on 24 January 1890. Here the monarch presented a draft of legislation for regulating Sunday work and shortening working hours for women and children labourers and argued that the rise of socialism was to be attributed directly to the government's failure to control the rapacity of the

[98] Eyck, *Bismarck* iii. 565.

employer class. The discussion then turned to the Socialist Law, which had passed its second reading in the Reichstag the day before, but only after the expulsion clauses had been voted down. After that vote, the Conservative delegation leader Helldorf had informed Bismarck's Minister of the Interior and floor-manager, Heinrich von Boetticher, that the Conservatives would vote against the law on the third reading unless the government gave its explicit approval of the deletion. During the discussion in council, the Emperor made it clear that he wanted such a declaration to be made. Bismarck, however, not only opposed this, but, losing his composure, said that if the law failed the government should take advantage of the situation to push matters to a real confrontation. This startled the Emperor, and he appealed to the other ministers to support the conciliatory approach. Under Bismarck's cold eye, however, no one had the heart for that. The ministers supported their chief's decision to sacrifice the law, which was duly defeated on 25 January by the votes of the Centre, the Freisinnige, the Social Democrats, and the Conservatives.[99]

There is every evidence that William was shocked by Bismarck's grim inflexibility and what it portended, and well he might have been. Throughout the 1880s, as his parliamentary troubles increased, the Chancellor's mind had turned more and more frequently to the idea of cutting the Gordian knot by means of a radical revision of the constitution. As in the 1860s, when he invented the ingenious *Lückentheorie* to give a spurious legal justification to his defiance of the constitutional powers of the Prussian Chamber of Deputies, he had now elaborated a theory to serve his purposes, one that held that the Reich, being the creation of its princes, could be dissolved by them and reconstituted on a different basis.[100] 'It can very well happen', he said to the ambassador Schweinitz in April 1886, 'that I will have to destroy what I made. People forget that the same thing can happen to the existing federation that happened to the Frankfurt Bundestag in 1866; the princes can withdraw from it and form a new one without the Reichstag.'[101] That this might involve civil violence he knew and accepted. After the elections of 1887 he said, 'If the campaign had failed, it would have led to a *Staatsstreich* and perhaps

---

[99] On the Crown Council, see Waldersee's remarks in *Denkwürdigkeiten* ii. 96.

[100] The *Lückentheorie*, or 'Theory of the Gap', claimed that, since the constitution of 1850 did not provide a procedure to be followed when there was a failure of agreement between the Upper and Lower Houses, the residual powers of the sovereign must be used to continue the business of state, even if this meant collecting taxes that had not been authorized by the Lower House. On Bismarck's constitutional theory in 1890, see esp. Zechlin, *Staatsstreichpläne*, pp. 43–7, 58–9.

[101] Schweinitz, *Denkwürdigkeiten*, ii. 317.

to uprisings';[102] two years later, speaking to his ambassador Reuß in December 1889, he had not changed his mind: 'With the eventuality of a hostile majority we must always reckon. You can dissolve three or four times, but in the end you have to smash the crockery. These questions—like that of Social Democracy and that of the relationship between Parliament and the separate states—will not be solved without a blood-bath, just as the question of German unity was not.'[103]

It may be that, as late as the Crown Council of 24 January 1890, Bismarck was still not sure that the time had come to implement these ideas and that his allusions to them, and his suggestion that it might be wise to increase the size of the Berlin garrison, were intended only to wean the Emperor away from his ideas about appeasing the left.[104] But his hesitations were removed by the disastrous results of the elections of 20 February, which smashed the Kartell, cost the National Liberals 57 seats and the two Conservative parties 28, restored to the Freisinnige what they had lost in 1887, increased the Centre delegation to 106, and brought the Social Democrats, who polled an astonishing 1,427,298 votes, 35 Reichstag seats.

These results, Franz von Roggenbach wrote two weeks later, marked the end of any possibility of Bismarck's controlling the Reichstag and left him only the option of illegality. 'There is not the slightest prospect', he said,

that future elections will ever again produce a majority as accommodating as the Kartell majority. The appeal to the services performed in founding the Reich, the arousing of the dark emotions of the Kulturkampf, the log-rolling of the protectionist phase, and finally the goose-pimples raised by the supposed danger of war—these tactics will not work any more. There remains only, as the last means, the social danger—Will an attempt to use that succeed against universal suffrage? I believe only if the diabolical means is used of terrifying petty bourgeois and rural circles by contrived putsches.[105]

Bismarck seems to have reached the same conclusion. The time

[102] Zechlin, *Staatsstreichpläne*, p. 26.
[103] Ibid., p. 8.
[104] According to Waldersee, Bismarck was warning the Emperor about possible Socialist risings in mid-December. *Denkwürdigkeiten* ii. 88. Regarding Bismarck's intentions, Ludwig Raschdau, on the basis of personal acquaintance, denied that he ever contemplated a *Staatsstreich* that would have involved the use of force. This is the position adopted by Werner Pöls, *Sozialistenfrage und Revolutionsfurcht in ihrem Zusammenhang mit den angeblichen Staatsstreichplänen Bismarcks* (Lübeck and Hamburg, 1960).
[105] *Im Ring der Gegner Bismarcks*, pp. 345–7.

had now come to smash the crockery. It was, he told himself, the only way of assuring the continuation of his system of policy and, for that matter, his personal position. He was aware that the election results had given additional ammunition to those in the Emperor's entourage who were plotting his fall and who were, in fact, already eagerly discussing who his successor should be.[106] If there was a major constitutional crisis, he was confident that his rivals would prove to be as lacking in resource as their predecessors had been in 1874,[107] and that the Emperor would be forced to turn to him as the only one with the combination of imagination and ruthlessness necessary to weather the storm. He was perfectly willing to confront the possibility that such a crisis would eventuate in violence.

There was no doubt in the minds of politicians close to him that he was deadly serious now. The Bavarian delegate to the Bundesrat reported that the Chancellor was sure that the best way of confronting the threatening revolution was by force of arms and that he planned to goad the Reichstag into a position in which it could be destroyed.[108] The lengths to which he was prepared to go were reflected in instructions sent by the War Ministry to the Commanding Generals in mid-March, alerting them to the possibility of risings and indicating that the use of force might be necessary.[109]

In the first days after the elections the Emperor was so alarmed by socialist gains that he seemed almost inclined to go along with Bismarck,[110] but this mood did not last. The Grand Duke of Baden, whose judgement he trusted, intimated that Bismarck was not right in the head. Other confidants encouraged him to believe that his own ideas of social reform might provide a basis for effective co-operation with the new Reichstag. Thus, when the Chancellor revealed that he intended to defy that body in the new session by presenting both a new Socialist Law and a new Military Bill that it could not possibly be expected to pass, both Miquel of the National

[106] See esp. Zechlin, *Staatsstreichpläne*, p. 72; Waldersee, *Denkwürdigkeiten* ii. 102 n.; and *Aus dem Briefwechsel des Generalfeldmarschalls Alfred Grafen von Waldersee 1886–91*, ed. H. O. Meisner (Berlin, 1928), p. xiv and no. 214.

[107] See above, Ch. II, pp. 51–2.

[108] Hugo Graf Lerchenfeld-Koefering, *Erinnerungen und Denkwürdigkeiten* (2nd edn., Berlin, 1935), p. 365.

[109] See John C. G. Röhl, 'Staatsstreichplan oder Staatsstreichbereitschaft? Bismarcks Politik in der Entlassungskrise', *Historische Zeitschrift*, 203 (1966), 623.

[110] Zechlin, *Staatsstreichpläne*, p. 32. Some of the Emperor's confidants were talking openly of the necessity of a *coup*. Philipp Eulenburg talked of 'a *Staatsstreich* in which shooting can hardly be avoided' (Röhl, 'Staatsstreichplan', p. 613); Waldersee wrote in his diary: 'There is nothing left but to do away with universal suffrage. I will be glad to co-operate in that' (*Denkwürdigkeiten* ii. 106).

Liberals and Helldorf of the Conservatives urged that this must not be permitted and suggested that imperial initiative could create new party alignments.[111] These arguments flattered and impressed the Emperor. Ever since the January Crown Council he had been chafing at Bismarck's apparent assumption that Ministers of State were his own rather than the Emperor's creatures, and he was irritated by repeated references in the official Press to 'the Chancellor's policy'. He did not relish the prospect of Bismarck's solving the present crisis if he could do so himself.

It was his failure to appreciate the intensity of William's desire to be recognized as the real director of German policy—to play the role, indeed, that Bismarck had always claimed, rather disingenuously, was the Emperor's rightful one—that proved to be the Chancellor's undoing, for it led him to make mistakes that played into the hands of his enemies. For one thing, with a clumsiness extraordinary for one who was usually so adroit in foreign affairs, he tried to persuade the French Government to torpedo the Emperor's plans for an international labour conference by declining to attend. At the same time, he had become inordinately suspicious of Boetticher[112] and other members of the Prussian Ministry of State, who were, he was convinced, secretly encouraging the Emperor to hold to policies that he found offensive; and this led him to invoke a long-forgotten cabinet order of 1852 which forbade ministers to have access to the sovereign except with the permission, and in the presence, of the Prime Minister. Finally, in a last attempt to assess the possibility of creating a viable new parliamentary combination before pursuing his more violent plans, he had a long discussion with his old enemy Ludwig Windthorst of the Centre party, without having informed the Emperor that he was going to do so.

These last indiscretions relieved the Emperor of the necessity of taking an unambiguous position with respect to Bismarck's desire for a major confrontation with the Reichstag. Instead, in an agitated conversation with the Chancellor on 15 March 1890, William reproached him for seeking to keep his monarch in the dark by putting barriers between him and his ministers, demanded the abrogation of the order of 1852, and bitterly reproached him for discussing parliamentary arrangements with the Centre without his knowledge and assent.[113] Nor did he stop there. It was his im-

---

[111] Zechlin, *Staatsstreichpläne*, pp. 73–8.

[112] This suspicion of Boetticher seemed to him to be confirmed when the Emperor conferred the Order of the Red Eagle upon that industrious official.

[113] The fact that the meeting with Windthorst had been arranged by Gerson

pression, he added, that Bismarck's failure to keep him informed was not restricted to matters like the meeting with Windthorst but extended to the sphere of foreign policy as well, where Bismarck had been less than candid in informing him about the perilous state of Russo-German relations.

After that interview, Bismarck was aware that his plans to solve the domestic crisis had been rejected and that his own position could no longer be saved. If he had any doubts on the latter score, they were relieved on the morning of 16 March when the Chief of the Military Cabinet, General von Hahnke, appeared at the Reich Chancellery to remind him that the Emperor expected an immediate announcement with respect to the order of 1852. In effect, this was a request for his resignation, and it was ironical that it should have been transmitted by a representative of an agency that owed Bismarck gratitude for his services to it in 1883. Not the least interesting aspect of the crisis of 1890 was that both the Military Cabinet and the General Staff abandoned Bismarck, and that their chiefs urged the Emperor to dismiss him.[114] The argument that he had failed to keep William informed about the Russian danger merely reflected the General Staff's phobia on this score, which was as rabid as it had been in 1887[115] and was now, as then, supported by highly coloured information supplied by Holstein in the Foreign Ministry.[116] Bismarck did not yield to Hahnke's implied request. He delayed his resignation for another four days, spending the time in devising an ingenious apologia for his own policy that appeared in print after his death and charged the Emperor with a serious lack of understanding of the true state of relations with Russia and a dangerous tendency to take precipitate action on insufficient knowledge. When that was done, he retired to his estates.

VI

When the great star fell, many Germans had a chilling presentiment that their country had suffered an irreparable loss and that it would not soon again be governed with such intelligence and assurance. Time was to prove them correct, although it must be said that the

---

Bleichröder made it doubly offensive to the Emperor, who talked rather wildly to one of his friends about a Jewish–Jesuit conspiracy.

[114] Waldersee, *Denkwürdigkeiten* ii. 114.

[115] See above, Ch. IV.

[116] Graf von Wedel, *Zwischen Kaiser und Kanzler* (Leipzig, 1943), pp. 32–52. Holstein had become convinced as early as 1885 that Bismarck's powers were waning. See above, pp. 127–8 and *Holstein Papers* ii. 306.

mistakes of Bismarck's successors might have been less disastrous if he had not contributed to the difficulties of their task by leaving them an anachronistic political system in which he had sought—in the case of liberalism with success—to stifle every progressive tendency.

There were other Germans whose reaction to the Chancellor's dismissal was one of relief, for they perceived that his undoubted political talents had been blunted increasingly in his last years by defects of character and that his behaviour had tarnished his earlier triumphs. Theodor Fontane wrote on 1 May 1890:

Bismarck had no greater admirer than I; my wife never read me one of his speeches or letters or sayings without my feeling a real enchantment. The world has seldom seen a greater genius, seldom a man with greater spirit, seldom a greater humorist. But one thing he always lacked: nobility. Its opposite, which finally took the hateful form of petty spite, ran through his life (without the infernal humour that accompanied it, it would have become intolerable much earlier) and because of this lack of nobility, he finally came to ruin, and in this lack of nobility is to be found the explanation of the relative indifference with which even his admirers watched him being forced to leave. . . . It is fortunate that we are rid of him, and many, many questions will now be handled better, more honourably, more clearly than before.[117]

There was more hope than expectation in these last words, and it was to be disappointed. At the end of his career, Bismarck had no other answer for the problems of his society but violence. His successors proved to be no more fertile in expedients than he.

[117] Fontane, *Briefe* ii. 272.

VI
Religion, Education, and the Arts

Bemooster Bursche zieh ich aus, ade!
behüt' dich Gott, Philisterhaus, ade!
Zur alten Heimat geh ich ein,
muß selber nun Philister sein.
Ade! ade! ade!
Ja, Scheiden und Meiden tut weh!

G. SCHWAB (1815)[1]

Und wir: Zuschauer, immer, überall,
dem allen zugewandt und nie hinaus!
Uns überfüllts. Wir ordnens. Es zerfällt.
Wir ordnens wieder und zerfallen selbst.

RAINER MARIA RILKE (1923)[2]

IN his memoirs the historian Friedrich Meinecke made a sharp
distinction between what was happening in politics in the last
years of the nineteenth century and the intellectual currents of the
time, suggesting that, while things were going downhill politically,
the life of the spirit was characterized by energy and health.[3] It is
difficult to support this hypothesis. Whatever may be said in praise
of individual scholarly, scientific, and artistic achievements in the
Bismarckian and Wilhelmine periods, it is difficult to deny that the
intellectual life of the country and such manifestations of its spirit as
its Churches and universities reflected all too faithfully the weaknesses of the political and social system that supported them. Indeed,
as the years passed, the energies of Germany's religious and educational institutions seemed to be diverted increasingly from their
true functions and used instead to buttress the *status quo*. Simultaneously, in the world of the arts, talents that might have been
employed for constructive social criticism were used timidly, if at all,
and the majority of writers and artists either tacitly accepted the
system or professed a spiritless and ineffective alienation.

---

[1] 'Komitat', in *Neues deutsches Kommersbuch* (3rd edn., Frankfurt-on-Main, 1928), pp.
303 f.
[2] *Duineser Elegien* (eighth elegy). On this, see Georg Lukács, *Skizze einer Geschichte
der neuen deutschen Literatur* (Berlin, 1953), pp. 119–20.
[3] Friedrich Meinecke, *Erlebtes 1862–1901* (Leipzig, 1941), pp. 167–8.

I

Like the established Churches in other countries of Western Europe, those in Germany were subject to the strains caused by industrialization on the one hand and the scientific revolution on the other. Although figures for church membership remained high—in 1890, out of a population of 49,428,470, there were 31,026,810 members of the Evangelical Church, 17,674,921 Catholics, 145,540 members of other Christian sects, and 567,884 orthodox Jews—they were decreasing year by year, for the movement of urbanization that was encouraged by industrial growth broke normal congregational ties irreparably, the workers who migrated to the cities often leaving their religion behind them. In any case, the statistics were an imperfect measurement of religious faith. Many who maintained their church membership did so from custom rather than from conviction, which was apt to be susceptible anyway to the challenge of science and the tendency toward modernism that had resulted from textual criticism of the sacred writings.

These last tendencies the Roman Catholic Church was able to resist more effectively than the other churches. This was due partly to the new fervour imparted to the Catholic faith by the government's attack upon it in the mid-seventies, partly to the enlightened leadership given to the Church by Pope Leo XIII in the 1880s, and doubtless partly to the fact that the individual believer was given less latitude to impose his own interpretation upon doctrine than was granted members of the Evangelical Church. Certainly, the winds of fashionable doctrine blew strong in the world of Protestantism. On the one hand, church leaders had to contend with the Darwinian assault, and, in Ernst Haeckel, the famous Jena zoologist, they had an opponent more combative and certainly more presumptuous than Darwin, since he did not scruple to offer them a surrogate faith, a monistic religion which, free of all transcendental elements, was a blend of positivism and ethical culture. At the same time, David Friedrich Strauß, whose *Life of Jesus* (1835–6) had represented the first strong blow against the pillars of fundamentalism, argued in a new work, *The Old Faith and the New* (1872), that Christianity should properly be considered as part of the cultural legacy of the past, and that the new German should place his faith in the miracles that had been demonstrated in the field in 1870 and were being revealed daily in the laboratories and the factories of the Reich. 'During the last years', Strauß wrote, 'we have taken an active part and each of us has co-operated in his own way in the great national war and the establishment of the German state, and we find ourselves inwardly exalted by this unexpected and glorious turn in the fortunes of our much tried nation. For reflection over what determines the salvation or destruction of peoples and individuals, that war offers inexhaustible material; in moral lessons there was never a time richer than these last years.' Instead of going to church, which was mere habit, one could reflect upon these, aided by the reading of history, the appreciation of nature, and the inspiration that could be derived 'for spirit and temperament, fantasy and humour' from 'the writings of our great poets and the performance of the works of our great musicians. . . . *So leben wir, so wandeln wir beglückt!'*[4]

It was a sign of the times that Nietzsche's devastating attack, in *Thoughts out of Season*, on this vulgar paean to nationalism and materialism should have hurt its author rather than the *Bildungsphilister* Strauß, as Nietzsche aptly labelled him;[5] and it was also significant that Haeckel's monism enjoyed, in the 1890s, the kind of popularity that the Saint-Simonian *cénacles* had had in the 1840s, congregations being formed for its elucidation and celebration. Given the influence exerted by these substitutes for religion, it was only natural that Protestant leaders would bend to the storm. The most distinguished theologians of the age had long since abandoned the dogmatic rigour of an earlier age. Julius Wellhausen, Professor of Theology at Marburg from 1885 to 1892 and at Göttingen after that date, produced a virtual revolution in Old Testament scholarship by upsetting received ideas about the chronology of the Pentateuch; Albrecht Ritschl, professor at Göttingen from 1864 to 1889, rejected all of the mystical and intuitive elements in New Testament history and called for a practical everyday religion;[6] and his follower Adolf von Harnack, in his *History of Dogma* (1885–90), stressed the evolutionary and syncretic nature of the Christian faith in such a way as to make it difficult to maintain that it was either unique or divinely revealed. These adjustments of creed to the discoveries of scholarship encouraged less learned churchmen to give themselves over to an incautious eagerness to adapt the beliefs of the Church to the latest fashions in scientific speculation. In the long run, the result was a watering-down of dogma and theology to a point where the Protestant religion threatened to become nothing but a bundle of ethical

---

[4] D. F. Strauß, *Der alte und der neue Glaube* (5th edn., 1873, p. 297

[5] Nietzsche, *Unzeitgemäße Betrachtungen*, p. 9.

[6] On Ritschl, with special emphasis on his contributions to the growing conservatism of the Protestant Church, see esp. Fischer, in *Probleme der Reichsgründungszeit*, pp. 63–70.

rules, inspired not by divine authority but by social utility. To the extent that this happened, the Church's ability to withstand the competition of secular religions was gravely weakened.

In one sphere of activity the Christian sects showed great vigour in the years after 1871, although here too the Evangelical Church showed a waning of energy and will as the century drew to its close. Both the Catholic and the Protestant churches had a long and honourable record of ameliorative work among the underprivileged, which they pursued with the same zeal that inspired their overseas missionary activities. The Catholic doctrine of social reform had its modern origins in the work of Adolf Kolping, who in the 1840s had founded Catholic journeymen's associations to give free vocational training to working men; and his ideas were given new life and vigour by Wilhelm Emmanuel von Ketteler, Bishop of Mainz, who argued that the Church had a duty to help the working class withstand the demoralizing effects of capitalism by organizing co-operative societies, Christian trade unions, and recreational clubs, and that such efforts would be repaid with renewed religious faith. Ketteler, whose works had a profound influence upon Pope Leo XIII and served as a basis for his encyclical *Rerum novarum* (1891), established a tradition of German Social Catholicism that was to remain a constant feature of the programme of the Centre party. Indeed, that party not only supported and expanded the programme of vocational instruction that Kopling had started and encouraged the growth of a Catholic trade union movement that was to remain vigorous until 1933, but also used its influence on behalf of legislation for the improvement of working conditions, the reduction of the working day, factory inspection, child-labour laws, and arbitration between labour and management.[7]

The activities of the Evangelical Church in this area were in the long run less impressive, partly because of the methods used to promote them but more, perhaps, because of the inherent conservatism of the Church as a whole. The first notable Evangelical preachers of the social gospel were V. A. Huber, whose *Die Selbsthilfe der arbeitenden Klassen durch Wirtschaftsvereine und innere Ansiedlung* (1848) advanced the idea of Christian workers' associations or co-operatives as a means of combating poverty, and J. H. Wichern, who in the 1850s gave practical form to the concept of 'inner mission' by instituting a programme (*Das rauhe Haus*) for the building of

---

[7] On the tradition of social service in the Catholic Church and the work of Kolping and Ketteler, see Vigner, *Ketteler* and Birke, *Ketteler und Liberalismus, passim.*

homes for the indigent.[8] This pioneer work was continued and given a dramatic new dimension by Adolf Stoeker,[9] whose activities were in the long run, however, self-defeating, since they frightened his superiors in the Church and made them anxious to withdraw from a sphere that seemed to encourage controversy.

As *summus episcopus* of the Evangelical Church, William I had long been uneasy about the Church's social activities, and when Stoecker gave these a political dimension, he reacted with distaste. Taking their key from their sovereign, the Evangelical Church Council (Evangelischer Oberkirchenrat), a strongly conservative body, declared in October 1878 that the Church should remain clear of politics and be cautious about taking positions on social questions and, three months later, it reinforced this stand by warning pastors that it was not their duty to address social demands to the government in the name of, and with the authority of, the Gospel. The Church, it added, must stand in a mediatorial position among the parties, showing no partiality except in the case of those that departed from the ground of legality and patriotism.

This was to remain the position of the Oberkirchenrat until the war, with one brief exception. In 1890, when Emperor William II was passing through his liberal phase and was convinced that he would be able to do what neither Bismarck nor Stoecker had succeeded in doing—namely, inspire the working class with patriotism and devotion to the state—the Oberkirchenrat relaxed its view to the point of admitting that social concern was one of the duties of the Church. But as soon as the Emperor's private social schemes had fallen flat, and he had reacted by concluding that the working classes were an ungrateful, if not a treasonable, horde, the Council swung back again and in December 1895 issued a decree against 'social parsons' and their 'thoughtless advocacy of the demands of a single class'. 'Against these obtrusive and mistaken views', it said sternly, 'it cannot be emphasized too much that all attempts to turn the Evangelical Church into an active agent in the political and social disputes of the day must divert the Church from the goal set for it by its Maker: namely, the creation of blessedness for the soul.'

This was, of course, an attack upon Stoecker, who had by this time lost his position as Court Preacher[10] but was still actively interested

[8] See Frank, *Stoecker*, p. 17.

[9] See above, Ch. V.

[10] He was dismissed in November 1891 after the Grand Duke of Baden had complained to the Emperor about a speech he had made to a Conservative party conference in Karlsruhe in which he had violently attacked the Jews. See Frank, *Stoecker*, p. 217 and Heuß, *Naumann*, p. 92.

in social work, as his prominent role in the Evangelical Social Congress of 1890 had shown. But it was also aimed at all of those churchmen who continued to believe that social activism was a Christian duty—men like Theodor Lohmann, who wrote the report of the General Committee of the Inner Mission in 1885, a document which was entitled *Die Aufgabe der Kirche und ihrer inneren Mission gegenüber den wirtschaftlichen und gesellschaftlichen Kämpfen der Gegenwart* and anticipated much that was to be said six years later in Leo XIII's *Rerum novarum*, and the outstanding Christian Social reformer of the next generation, Friedrich Naumann.

Like Stoecker, Naumann had begun his work in the Inner Mission movement, and in the 1880s he had been a frequent contributor to Pastor Martin Rade's *Evangelisch-Lutherisches Gemeindeblatt* (later called *Die Christliche Welt*), a paper that gave prominence to the discussion of controversial social questions. Like Stoecker, he too came to doubt the efficacy of voluntary private charitable work and, as early as 1890, when he became Stoecker's successor as head of the Christian Social movement, was beginning to think of the solution that he was to advance in his widely read book *Demokratie und Kaisertum* (1902)—the reconciliation of the working class to the state by an enlightened use of government power and private enterprise that would bring tangible benefits to the masses. Meanwhile he insisted in all of his writings upon the necessity of reducing the gulf that existed between the working classes and bourgeois society, but he was soon aware that he had become a thorn in the flesh of the governing bodies of his Church. In 1893 the consistory of the Frankfurt Lutheran Church openly criticized him for participating in a meeting organized by the Social Democrat Theodor von Wächter, and in 1896 it was clear that he was the principal target of a telegraphic statement that the industrialist Stumm-Halberg had elicited from the Emperor, which read: '*Politische Pastoren sind ein Un-Ding*. Anyone who is a Christian is social too, but Christian-Social is nonsense.'[11]

Despite this opposition, Naumann continued to urge better understanding between the classes, in the columns of *Die Hilfe* which he founded in 1890; but there can be little doubt that others of his persuasion were intimidated into silence. Indeed, the majority of Protestant churchmen seemed perfectly willing to conclude, with Albrecht Ritschl, that the Christian's principal duty was to believe in God and remain true to the demands of his calling (*Beruf*), without

[11] Heuß, *Naumann*, p. 134.

believing that he had any responsibility for the good of the whole. In any case, to attempt to assume such responsibility was presumptuous, since it might easily contravene state policy and weaken the basis of social authority. Again it was Ritschl, whom Harnack called 'the last Church Father', who laid down the official line when, in his speech as Prorektor during the 150th anniversary of the University of Göttingen in 1887, he attacked the coalition of Centre, Progressive, and Socialist parties that had just defeated the government's Military Appropriations Bill, as an alliance based on Aquinian and Jesuitical principles of natural law, which represented a dangerous assault upon rights of the state that had received their legitimacy from history.[12] This evocation of the *Staatslehre* of Hegel and Julius Stahl was an apt summary of the political and social position of the Evangelical hierarchy and explains why the government could count on the uncritical support of the Church for its policies.

II

One of the things that always impressed foreign visitors to the German states in the last third of the nineteenth century was what appeared to them to be the excellence of their institutions of elementary education, and it is understandable why this was so. If one took as one's standard the effectiveness of the elementary school system in reducing illiteracy, there was no doubt that Germany's record was the best in Europe. Even so politically progressive a country as Great Britain had nothing resembling a comprehensive elementary educational system until the Forster Education Act of 1871, and English children were not compelled to go to school until 1880. Other countries were even more dilatory, France, for instance, only beginning to elaborate a system of primary schools in the 1880s. As a result of this neglect, almost a third of the male population and almost half of the female population in Great Britain in the 1860s could neither read nor write; over half of the population in France and Belgium were in the same condition in the 1870s; and in Italy and Spain the figure was closer to 75 per cent.

In contrast, the German states had established elementary schools and passed laws requiring attendance by most children as early as the eighteenth century. German rulers considered it a duty to see that their subjects acquired the elements of literacy, and in some states children who did not attend church schools were required to attend

---

[12] See Fischer, in *Probleme der Reichsgründungszeit*, p. 68.

state Elementarschulen until they were in their teens. In Prussia, which even in the eighteenth century had been notable for the attention paid to popular education, the defeat suffered at the hands of Napoleon in 1806 was a goad to redoubled effort. The Prussian reform party of that period regarded the education of the masses as the key to the moral and physical recovery of their country, and they were supported by their sovereign Frederick William III, who said: 'We have indeed lost territory and it is true that the state has declined in outward splendour and power, and for that very reason it is my solemn desire that the greatest attention be paid to the education of the people.' In the years that followed, the Prussian elementary schools, renamed Volksschulen, were expanded and their curriculum reformed, and after the expulsion of the French they became a model for schools in the neighbouring states. The zeal with which basic skills were taught in these institutions was responsible for the fact that by 1830 almost all Germans could read and write; and by the end of the century the rate of illiteracy in Germany was only 0·05 per cent.[13]

There was doubtless a connection between this high level of literacy and the remarkable growth of German industry after 1871, for modern industry depended to a large extent upon operatives and clerks who could read; and it is ironical that, as the years passed, many of the mill-owners who profited from that skill came to fear it, since it could be applied as easily to the perusal of socialist literature as to time-sheets and company directives. Nor were these timorous entrepreneurs the only critics of the development of elementary education. The landed proprietors of the east complained that education tempted agricultural workers to leave the soil and seek more lucrative jobs in the towns; middle-class liberals who had formerly paid lip-service to the social utility of a broadening educational base began now to fear that its results might be a subversion of the existing order; and some widely read publicists expressed the view that the emphasis placed on the education of the masses was dangerous because it could not avoid diluting the quality of German education in general. This was the view of Friedrich Nietzsche, who in a remarkable series of lectures, 'On the Future of our Educational Institutions', delivered in Basle in 1872, stated that 'not the education

[13] The comparable rates for Great Britain and France by that time were 1 per cent and 4 per cent. Official statistics must, of course, be taken with a grain of salt. Ralf Dahrendorf has pointed out (*Society and Democracy*, p. 76) that, even in the second half of the twentieth century, it is impossible, because of exceptions to compulsory schooling, to say how high the proportion of real illiterates is in Germany and that there are wide discrepancies between rural and urban areas.

of the masses can be our goal but the education of individually selected people, armed for great and permanent achievements' and went on to charge that those who argued for a further extension of *Volksbildung* were seeking to destroy 'the natural order of rank in the kingdom of the intellect'.[14] Nietzsche's views were repeated with variations by Paul de Lagarde, an embittered eccentric who saw German culture imperilled by the advance of barbarism and blamed this on the educational system, and Julius Langbehn, the author of the enormously popular *Rembrandt als Erzieher* (1890), whose insistence upon the necessity of training a racially pure élite was later to take more extreme forms in the educational practices of Heinrich Himmler.[15]

Whatever may be said of the concerns of the capitalists and the *Junker*, there can be no doubt that the idea that the elementary educational system represented a potential threat to Germany's hierarchical social and intellectual structure was exaggerated to the point of fantasy. In reality, that system was one of the principal supports of the existing order. Ever since 1815 the Prussian schools (and what is said of Prussia in this respect was generally true of the other German states) had been administered by men with rigidly conservative views concerning the educational needs and rights of the masses. In the 1820s and 1830s Altenstein, the Prussian Minister of Education, made no secret of his determination that the education in the Volksschulen must not be allowed to 'raise the common people out of the sphere designated for them by God and human society'; and the vigilance he showed in this respect was more insistently observed by his successors after the Revolution of 1848. King Frederick William IV placed the responsibility for this catastrophe at the door of the Volksschule instructors, and once order was restored corrective measures were taken. In 1854 the Minister of Education, von Raumer, issued directives which were to remain in force until 1872 and which made it clear to all teachers that their function was to impress upon their charges discipline, order, and

[14] *Unzeitgemäße Betrachtungen*, pp. 451–2.

[15] Both Langbehn and de Lagarde felt that the German spirit was being smothered by over-learning, that mass education should be restricted to elementary skills, and that a chosen Christian élite should be specially trained, by a Spartan education that emphasized physical skills and Germanness (*Volkstümlichkeit*) rather than book-learning, to rule the nation. See Fritz Stern, *The Politics of Cultural Despair: A Study in the Rise of the Germanic Ideology* (Berkeley, 1961), pp. 102 ff., 164 ff., and the somewhat too respectful treatment of de Lagarde's theories in Robert W. Lougee, *Paul de Lagarde, 1827–1891: A Study of Radical Conservatism in Germany* (Cambridge, Mass., 1962), pp. 203–10.

obedience to authority. This command was apparently obeyed (the supposedly revolutionary teachers of 1848 were, a generation later, being given credit for winning the Battle of Königgrätz) with the aid of a curriculum that was restricted to religion (with which the school-day began), reading, writing, arithmetic, and singing.[16]

During the ascendancy of the National Liberals in the 1870s the Prussian Kultusminister, Adalbert Falk, sought to widen the curriculum, by introducing history, geography, natural science, and geometry and by reducing the emphasis on rote learning. These reforms were commendable, but it is ironical, considering their liberal origin, that they gave the government new opportunities to reinforce loyalty to the *status quo*. In 1889 William II said, 'For some time now, I have been occupied with the idea of making the school in its various grades useful in combating the spread of socialistic and communistic ideas. In the first place, it will fall upon the school to lay the foundation for a healthy conception of political and social relations, through the cultivation of God and love of country.' Historical instruction, he believed, would be particularly useful in this regard. 'Historical instruction', the Emperor said in 1890, 'must strive to give our youth the impression that the teachings of Social Democracy not only contradict the divine commandments and Christian morals, but that they are in reality impossible of achievement and, in their consequences, dangerous for the individual and society.' Apart from this, the Emperor pointed out, 'We must bring up nationalistic young Germans, and not young Greeks and Romans . . . More than ever, the instruction in history must provide an instruction of the present, and especially an understanding of our country's position in the present. To this purpose, German history, particularly that of modern and contemporary times, must be stressed more, whereas ancient and medieval history is to be taught primarily to prepare the pupils for heroic and historic greatness.' These imperial prescriptions were not without effect.[17]

Even more important was the fact that the very organization of the German school system served as a brake upon social mobility and tended to freeze the existing social system. Throughout the

[16] On all this and on much of what follows, the most informative brief account is that of Richard Samuel and R. H. Thomas, *German Education*.

[17] Walter Consuelo Langsam in *Nationalism and Internationalism: Essays Inscribed to Carleton J. H. Hayes*, ed. Edward Mead Earle (New York, 1950), pp. 242–5. Bismarck was not free from similar views about the duty of schools to combat Social Democracy. See *Klassenbuch 2: Ein Lesebuch zu den Klassenkämpfen in Deutschland 1850–1919*, ed. Hans Magnus Enzensberger, Rainer Nitsche, Klaus Roehler, and Winfried Schafhausen (Darmstadt, 1972), pp. 116 f.

nineteenth century the great majority of German children went to school for only eight years and spent all of them in the Volksschulen. They were not expected to seek higher education, and it was made difficult for them to do so. The road to higher education, and the more lucrative forms of employment and the attendant social benefits that it brought, was through one of the secondary schools—the Gymnasium, which offered a humanistic education with a heavy emphasis upon the classics, the Oberrealschule, which concentrated on modern languages, mathematics, and the natural sciences, and the Realgymnasium, whose curriculum was a compromise between those of the other two. These schools took their students from private preparatory schools or, in lesser numbers, from the Volksschulen, at the age of ten, after they had completed four years of school. Their course of instruction lasted another nine years, at the end of which time they took examinations for the Abitur or certificate of graduation. The Abitur gave its possessor the right to enrol in a university, which was not, until 1900, true of the graduates of the other secondary schools, who generally, if they went further, enrolled in one of the technical institutions (Technische Hochschulen).[18]

The mass of the school population was deterred from entering upon this course of study by a number of factors. Unless Volksschule students transferred to a secondary school at the end of their fourth year, it was practically impossible for them ever to acquire a university or a higher technical education; once this moment had passed they were so quickly outdistanced by the secondary school students in knowledge of languages and other skills not provided in the Volksschule curriculum that later transfer, even if permitted, was bound to be unavailing. Yet transfer at the right time was made difficult for most children. It was rarely encouraged by teachers, for Volksschule instructors were graduates of normal or vocational schools rather than of institutions of higher learning and were not given to nurturing ambition in their students, or by local pastors or

---

[18] Graduates of Oberrealschulen and Realgymnasien could apply for admission to a university but had no assurance that it would be granted. Even when admitted, they were not until 1900 allowed to take state examinations for any posts except as secondary school teachers of mathematics, natural sciences, and modern languages. The 'monopoly of the Gymnasium' was finally broken as the result of a long campaign waged against 'the humanists' by 'the realists', details of which are described in the autobiography of Friedrich Paulsen, a doughty warrior on the 'realist' side. The technical institutions also had to fight for equality with the universities and, until late in the nineteenth century, they were not permitted to grant doctoral degrees.

priests, whose sense of social hierarchy tended to make their advice, when solicited, negative. In addition, the financial requirements were daunting. The cost of a complete higher education, according to Fritz Ringer, was between 4,000 and 8,000 R.M., a sum beyond the means of most working-class and lower-middle-class families, and a chancy speculation even for those of them who could afford it, since they had no reliable way of calculating whether their children had the talent to succeed in higher schools. The fact that German secondary schools were designed in such a way as to place a heavy emphasis upon learning with the help of one's parents, and that the drop-out rate, which amounted to about two-thirds of those who began secondary school, was highest among children whose parents had not gone to upper-schools, made the investment seem even more of a risk.[19] Finally, probably the strongest deterrent was social diffidence or fear—the feeling that the world of higher education was for 'the rich' or for their 'betters' and that no good would come from venturing into it. Ralf Dahrendorf has pointed out that, even in the second half of the twentieth century, this mental set is one of the main causes of educational inequality in Germany—'an attitude of traditionalism that prevents [people] from perceiving the chance to shorten and simplify the mountain hike to the peaks of stratification by using the funicular of educational institutions'.[20] In the nineteenth century it was infinitely stronger and was one of the principal reasons why, of the students in Prussian universities between 1887 and 1890, barely one in a thousand were the sons of workers. By 1900 that figure had increased to one in a hundred, while the sons of white-collar workers amounted to only 2·3 per cent and the sons of independent merchants, innkeepers, tradesmen, and artisans to only 26·3 per cent. In contrast, 22·6 per cent of the students were sons of middle and lower officials and teachers and 23·3 per cent sons of military and high government officials, teachers with university education, clergymen or theologians, and doctors, veterinarians, and apothecaries. The fathers of 35·1 per cent of the total either held government positions or were teachers in government-controlled schools.[21]

It is clear from these figures that, far from encouraging social mobility, the German educational system—like that of England, France, and other countries, for it should not be thought that Ger-

---

[19] On this see Fritz Ringer, 'Higher Education in Germany in the Nineteenth Century', *Journal of Contemporary History*, ii (1967), 123–38.

[20] *Society and Democracy*, p. 111.

[21] Ringer, 'Higher Education' 136–7.

many was unique in this respect—was structured in a way that effectively kept the masses in their place. This is underlined by the circumstance that preferment in the government service was reserved for those with higher education. Students who completed six years of secondary school were absolved from the duty of serving as conscripts in the army, being allowed instead to enlist as *Einjährig-Freiwillige* (one-year volunteers) which assured them later on of reserve officers' commissions. Attendance in the secondary schools was also a necessary prerequisite for the taking of the various state examinations for admission to the middle ranks of the Civil Service, while examinations for the higher branches of the Service, as well as for the preferred secondary teaching positions, were reserved for those who went to university. Since 85 per cent of the students in Prussian universities were, as late as 1890, graduates of humanistic Gymnasien, there was good reason for Nietzsche to speak mockingly in his Basle lectures of the Gymnasium bestowing 'honour by graduation' and of the Prussian state as a 'mystagogue of culture', which required its servants to appear before it bearing the torch of general education, 'in whose uncertain light they will acknowledge it as the highest goal and the reward for all their educational exertions'. He continued, 'It would not be exaggerated to maintain that, in the subordination of all educational objectives to the state-objectives of Prussia, the practical and convertible legacy of the Hegelian philosophy has been realized, and its apotheosis of the State has reached its height in this subordination.'[22]

III

At the beginning of the nineteenth century Germany had more and better universities that most of its neighbours, for one of the good aspects of German particularism was the pride that the separate states took in their higher educational institutions and the eagerness with which they competed for great scholars. This pre-eminence was threatened during the period of Napoleon's domination of German life, not only because of the repressive measures taken by his officials against individual universities—as in the case of Halle, which was closed by Jerome Bonaparte in 1807 and never completely recovered its position—but also because the Emperor's establishment of the Université impériale in 1808 supplied a model of educational centralization that was dangerously attractive to some German rulers. The failure of its principles to spread in Germany can be attributed in

---

[22] *Unzeitgemäße Betrachtungen*, p. 461.

large part to Wilhelm von Humboldt's work as Minister of Education in Prussia and his founding of the University of Berlin in 1809. As Friedrich Paulsen wrote in 1906, the new university 'was expressly organized in direct contrast to the higher schools of the military dictator. Its principle was to be not unity and subordination, but freedom and independence. The professors were to be not teaching and examining state-officials but independent scholars. Instruction was to be carried on not according to a prescribed order, but with a view to liberty of teaching and learning. The aim was not encyclopaedic information, but genuine scientific culture.'[23] It was in accordance with these ideals that the German universities developed after the French had been expelled, and the reputation that they gained as the nineteenth century wore on eclipsed that of the earlier period.

Their growth in distinction was particularly notable in the natural and experimental sciences, in which such pioneers as the mathematician Gauss, the physicist Weber, the great chemist Justus Liebig, and the Berlin physiologist Johann Müller were succeeded by a long line of distinguished scientists among whom need be mentioned only Schönlein, Dubois-Reymond, Helmholtz, Langenbeck, Rudolf Virchow, and Robert Koch. Under their influence, specialization, rigid objectivity, and scrupulous attention to the laws of evidence became hallmarks of German scholarship. Yet the sciences were not allowed to dominate the universities. Even in the age of empiricism and materialism, the humanistic tradition remained strong, and leaders like the famous historian, Theodor Mommsen, stoutly resisted any tendency that appeared to threaten the university's role as an institution whose primary function was to give its students, not useful knowledge or special skills, but *Bildung*—that is, that cultivation of the whole person which the Greeks called παιδεία and which Wilhelm von Humboldt had declared, at the time of his reform of the Prussian educational system, to be the true end of education.[24]

To serve this ideal was the duty of the Philosophische Fakultät, which, unlike the more specialized faculties of law and theology,

---

[23] Friedrich Paulsen, *The German Universities and University Study* (New York, 1906), p. 52.

[24] See esp. Wilhelm von Humboldt, 'Ueber die innere and äussere Organisation der höheren wissenschaftlichen Anstalten in Berlin' (1810), in *Werke in fünf Bänden* (Darmstadt, 1960–4), iv. 255–66. See also Friedrich Paulsen's definition in *Enzyklopädisches Handbuch der Pädagogik* (1895) in which he said: 'Nicht der Stoff entscheidet über die Bildung sondern die Form'. Cited in Harry Pross, *Jugend, Eros, Politik: Die Geschichte der deutschen Jugendverbände* (Berne, 1964), p. 47.

embraced the whole range of historical and aesthetic studies. Throughout the nineteenth century—indeed, until well into the second half of the twentieth[25]—this remained the heart of the German university, and in the years before the First World War a university was more often judged by the distinction of its humanists than by any other standard.

In later days, people were to look upon the late nineteenth century as a golden age of humanistic scholarship, and they were not unjustified in doing so, as even a short list of university professors will indicate. In philosophy, the great names after 1871 were Eduard von Hartmann, whose 'philosophy of the unconscious' appealed to an age that had turned away from Hegelian rationalism and from system-building of any kind;[26] Kuno Fischer, who, with Hermann Cohen and H. Rickert, revived Kantianism in the 1870s and whose lectures on logic in the following decade made him one of the sights that visitors to Heidelberg were supposed to see; Wilhelm Windelband, whose rectoral address at Strasburg in 1894 marked a decisive breaking-away from the materialism, mechanism, and naturalism that had resulted from the influence of Darwin and Comte; and, at the end of the century, Edmund Husserl at Göttingen, who discovered the phenomenological method as a new approach to the description of the essence of conscious data, and Cohen's student, Ernst Cassirer, whose work on symbolic forms and the analysis of cultural values had international influence. In philological studies, the classical tradition that had begun with Heyne and F. A. Wolff was continued in the work of Gottfried Hermann at Leipzig, Otfried Müller, Ulrich Wilamovitz, and E. R. Curtius at Göttingen, and Friedrich Thiersch at Munich; but new branches of the subject also found a place at the universities—romance studies at Bonn, oriental languages and literature in Berlin and elsewhere. At the same time, Germanistik, established as a major field by the work of the brothers Jakob and Wilhelm Grimm early in the century, seemed to be transformed by the unification of the country from a course of study to a form of patriotism—in the words Rudolf Hildebrand in 1869, 'not merely a science but a handmaid for the salvation of the nation'. The man who exemplified this view, certainly the most famous of

[25] The decline, if not demise, of the faculty was celebrated by Walther Killy in a 'Leichenrede auf eine Fakultät', *Die Zeit* (Hamburg), 28 June 1970.

[26] In Spielhagen's *Sturmflut* a young woman says: 'At this moment there are only three men whom one must study carefully: Bismarck, Hartmann, and Wagner: the politics of the present, the music of the future, reconciled by the philosophy of the unconscious—there you have the signature of the century!' (bk. II, Ch. 12).

the great teachers of German language and literature in his time, was Wilhelm Scherer, who fascinated audiences in Berlin in the 1880s with lectures on poetry that were the reverse of exegetical, going beyond form to social content and always emphasizing the importance of literature as a source of national pride and strength.

In the historical sciences, the critical method had become firmly established, thanks to the influence of Leopold von Ranke, who had taught at the University of Berlin since 1825,[27] who was seventy-five years old in the year of unification, and who was to live and work for another sixteen years.[28] Careful study of the documents and monuments of the past was the approved criterion of excellence, and a work like Jakob Burckhardt's *Cultural History of Greece*, which appeared in 1872, was regarded with suspicion in academic circles because the author had done no original research, as he gaily admitted. The period after 1871 saw the publication of such monuments of historical scholarship as Wilhelm Hauck's *German Church History*, Adolf von Harnack's *History of Dogma*, Eduard Meyer's *History of Antiquity*, the last volume of Theodor Mommsen's *History of Rome*, and Ranke's sadly unfinished *Universal History*, all works of great erudition which were, even so, not lacking in literary grace.

In Ranke's view of history—as in that of such historians of the first part of the century as Niebuhr, Dahlmann, and Droysen—power and the state played a major role. The unification movement strengthened this tendency, and research and teaching in the history of the modern period particularly was dominated by political historians. Foremost among them in the early years of the Empire were Heinrich von Sybel, Professor of History at Bonn since 1861 and after 1875 Director of the Prussian State Archives, whose multivolume *Founding of the German Empire by William I* was the first documented study of its subject,[29] and Heinrich von Treitschke,

---

[27] Hoefele, *Geist und Gesellschaft*, p. 308.

[28] There were differences of opinion as to his ability as a teacher. Heinrich von Sybel once called him 'ein Lehrer von Gottes Gnaden', But Andrew D. White, who heard him in 1855–6, described him as 'mumbling through a kind of rhapsody, which most of my German fellow-students confessed they could not understand' and added: 'It was a comical sight: half a dozen students crowding around his desk listening to the professor as priests might listen to the Sybil on her tripod, the other students being scattered through the room in various stages of discouragement.' *The Autobiography of Andrew D. White* (2 vols., New York, 1905), i. 39. For a recent assessment, see Gunter Berg, *Leopold von Ranke als akademischer Lehrer* (Göttingen, 1968).

[29] This achievement does not seem to have impressed Bismarck, who said in 1884: 'There are two kinds of historians, the first of whom make the water of the past clear so that you can see right to the bottom, while the second make this water murky.

Professor of History at Berlin from 1874 to 1896, whose *German History* was an extended tribute to the qualities that had enabled Prussia to win the hegemony of Germany. They were followed by a long line of gifted scholars—Max Lenz, Max Lehmann, Walter Goetz, Hermann Oncken, Erich Marcks, Hans Delbrück among them—who were equally fascinated by the problems of national history and interstate relations.

The historians who followed the traditional paths of political history were generally unmoved by critics who charged that the scope of their work was too narrow or its emphasis false. In his *Introduction to the Cultural Sciences* (1883) the Berlin philosopher Wilhelm Dilthey challenged historians to develop analytical tools that would enable them to investigate the world of ideas, which, he suggested, should be regarded not abstractly but in their societal context, as expressions of human experience in history. Dilthey was later to be considered as the father of a new kind of intellectual history; in his own lifetime his importance was recognized only by a few gifted younger historians. These included Ernst Troeltsch, Professor of Theology at Heidelberg, who, in the decade before the war, began to make the studies that were to eventuate in the monumental *Social Teaching of the Christian Churches*, and Friedrich Meinecke, whose early work was no less political than Treitschke's but who turned increasingly to the problems posed by Dilthey and, in 1908, gave a triumphant demonstration of the possibilities of Geistesgeschichte with the publication of his *Cosmopolitanism and the National State*.[30] Another pioneer, Karl Lamprecht, had less success when he tried to stimulate an interest in social and economic history. The first volumes of his *German History* (1891–3) were subjected to a massive barrage of criticism from political historians like Georg von Below, Max Lenz, and Max Lehmann, and some sniping from Meinecke, whose receptivity to new ideas was not so great as to welcome this departure from orthodoxy. Although some talented scholars, like Otto Hintze and Kurt Breysig, followed Lamprecht's lead, with greater methodological rigour than was characteristic of his work, their accomplishments were little regarded by their professional colleagues, who looked on social history as a form of local

Taine belongs to the first group, Sybel to the second!' *Bismarck Gespräche*, ii. 408 (to Julius von Eckardt).

[30] H. Stuart Hughes has pointed out that Meinecke's interest in history as idea and problem was inherited from Droysen rather than from Dilthey, with whom he became acquainted later in his course of study. *Consciousness and Society: The Reorientation of European Social Thought, 1890–1930* (New York, 1958), p. 232.

history that was not worthy of the attention of great scholars, and who were blind to the significance of Hintze's pioneering work in institutional and comparative history. In 1908, when Breysig addressed the International Historical Congress in Berlin and suggested a new scheme of universal history that would integrate intellectual, economic, and political developments, he was advised that he should be 'very careful that his imagination does not dominate his scholarship and become a substitute for research'.[31]

While the universities maintained the tradition of the humanistic disciplines, they also opened their doors increasingly after 1871 to the social or behavioural sciences. Economic studies had been firmly established before that time, with the work of Wilhelm Roscher, Bruno Hildebrand, and Karl Knies, but new vitality was injected into the field by their successors, Gustav Schmoller and Adolf Wagner, who began to lecture at Berlin in the seventies, and Lujo Brentano, who was Roscher's successor at Leipzig and later went on to Munich. These scholars were less interested in theory than in the delineation of developmental laws; economics to them was an inductive discipline based on an assessment of all aspects of man's life in society. The empirical thrust of their interest led them in 1872 to found the Verein für Sozialpolitik (Social Policy Association), which was intended not only to encourage economic research and discussion but to promote social reform and to influence government policy. This Association, which continued to exert influence until the First World War, was never marked by a monolithic unity of views, although in general it was critical of *laissez-faire* economics. Of its leaders, Wagner and Schmoller favoured state paternalism and nationalization of major service industries, although Wagner was more autarchistic and more convinced of the primary importance of agriculture than Schmoller. Brentano, who fascinated the young Munich student Theodor Heuß by the eloquence of his lectures and the violence of his feuding with colleagues and public authorities, was, unlike Wagner, a free trader and an opponent of the landed interest, and his belief in social reform was rooted more in ethical duty than in considerations of state power. The vigour of his campaigns to improve the working conditions of coal-miners and women mill operatives and other groups often alarmed his fellow members in the Social Policy Association.[32]

---

[31] John Higham, with Leonard Krieger and Felix Gilbert, *History* (Englewood, N.J., 1965), p. 344.

[32] On Brentano, besides his own lively memoirs, *Mein Leben in Kampf um die soziale Entwicklung Deutschlands* (Jena, 1931), see Theodor Heuß, *Vorspiele des Lebens: Jugend-*

Of the other social sciences only brief notice need be taken here. At the beginning of this period, no departments of psychology existed in German universities, but the first signs of change were discernible when Wilhelm Wundt, who had begun his career as Helmholtz's assistant in Heidelberg, was called to a chair in philosophy at Leipzig in 1875 and, four years later, established the first psychological laboratory in the world. Modern German sociology had its beginnings when the Kiel Dozent Friedrich Tönnies published his *Community and Society* in 1887. This work, which posed the whole range of problems involved in the transformation from a society based on natural law and traditional values to political forms based on rational will, outlined all of the themes that were to occupy the attention of his successors in the decades before the war. The most important and influential of these were Georg Simmel, lecturer at Berlin, a pioneer in the study of social interaction, and Max Weber, whose *Protestant Ethic and the Spirit of Capitalism* (1904–5), published while he was a teacher at Heidelberg, awakened a lively interest in the sociology of religion, and whose studies of status, legitimacy, and bureaucracy had great seminal value.

IV

In Gustav Freytag's *Die verlorene Handschrift*, a novel that appeared in 1865, the protagonist, a professor named Werner, says proudly at one point:

No purple is nobler, no sovereignty more powerful than ours. We lead the souls of our people from one century to another; ours is the duty of watching over its learning and its thoughts. We are its champions against falsehood and against the ghosts of the dead past, which still wander among us, clad in the appearance of life. What we consecrate for life, lives, what we condemn, passes away. From us are required the old virtues of the apostles, to pay little attention to what is transitory, but to proclaim the truth.[33]

This is a typically liberal tribute to German scholarship and an expression of confidence in its practitioners. In fact, the confidence was misplaced. The majority of German professors were not the doughty fighters for truth that Freytag's words suggest, nor were they unprejudiced in their attitude towards the forces that influenced their people's thinking. In matters that touched in any way upon politics, they tended increasingly to conform to official opinion, as expressed by government agencies, and to lend their authority to the

---

erinnerungen (Tübingen, 1953), p. 217, and James J. Sheehan, *The Career of Lujo Brentano: A Study of Liberalism and Social Reform in Imperial Germany* (Chicago, 1966).

[33] Gustav Freytag, *Die verlorene Handschrift*, bk. V, Ch. 1.

support of government policies that appeared to more objective minds to be dangerous and irrational.

That this was perhaps inevitable can be illustrated by a brief description of what happened to academic freedom in Germany after 1871.[34]

No aspect of the German university system impressed foreign observers more or had more influence upon their own principles of university governance, particularly in the United States, than the concept of academic freedom. Three things were involved in this. The first was academic self-government, the principle that the internal affairs of the university should be governed by the professors themselves and their elected deans. The second was the idea of *Lehrfreiheit* or freedom of teaching, in accordance with which a professor or lecturer was free to teach what he wished to teach, guided by his own convictions and unhampered by political or other restrictions. This implied that no subject or issue was closed to investigation and exposition. In his inaugural lecture as Rektor at the University of Strasburg in May 1872, Anton Springer explained the meaning of this by saying: 'As its first and sacred right, German scholarship asserts the independence and freedom of investigation. No one shall prescribe its goal. No one shall determine in advance which way its involved road will go. . . . For how can it reach the truth if it does not have the right to test everything, to spare nothing, to dare all, to leave nothing aside out of fearful aversion?'[35] The third aspect of academic freedom was *Lernfreiheit* or freedom of study, in accordance with which the German student was free to attend the lectures of his choice or even to migrate from one university to another, restricted by no formal curriculum and responsible only, in the end, to his examiners.

In practice, these freedoms were always subject to certain limitations, and these increased in weight after 1871. Universities were, after all, state institutions and, since their fees were low and they had no property of their own, or very little of the revenue-producing kind, they were dependent upon governments for financial support. Their needs grew rapidly in an age in which the advance of natural sciences and technology required more elaborate facilities, and their

---

[34] On this subject there is a large literature. Apart from Samuel and Thomas, *German Education*, the most useful volumes are Friedrich Paulsen, *An Autobiography* (New York, 1938), Brentano's memoirs, and Fritz K. Ringer, *The Decline of the German Mandarins: The German Academic Community, 1890–1933* (Cambridge, Mass., 1969). See also Richard Hofstatter and Walter P. Metzger, *The Development of Academic Freedom in the United States* (New York, 1955), pp. 383–407.

[35] Brentano, *Mein Leben*, p. 217.

dependence increased to a degree that is indicated by a single statistic: in 1871 the Prussian Government was contributing 4,150,254 R.M. to its universities; in 1907–8 that had increased to 16,647,269 R.M. Inevitably, this led to a diminution of freedom, since there was a natural tendency to avoid jeopardizing grants of support by refusing to make concessions to government views about how the grants should be used and, by extension, how the universities should be governed. The government had to confirm the choice of the University's Rektor, and it also appointed professors—usually, although not necessarily, from faculty nominees; so there was in any case plenty of opportunity for government pressure, and, when there was a strong Minister of Education, it was apt to be exerted.

This was particularly true in the time of Friedrich Althoff, Prussian Minister of Education from 1897 to 1907, and head of its universities section for fifteen years before that. Althoff—a distorted but interesting portrait of whom appears in Hermann Sudermann's novel *Der tolle Professor* (1926)—cannot be considered an enemy of the universities; indeed, financially, he performed great services for those within his jurisdiction. But, like many former professors (he had been Professor of Law at Strasburg until 1882), he had scant respect for the collective wisdom or courage of academicians or for their sense of reality in matters of university government. He appears to have shared the view of his great predecessor Wilhelm von Humboldt, who on one occasion remarked that dealing with professors was like being the director of a company of travelling players.[36] His attitude toward academic freedom is illustrated by a comment of his to Friedrich Paulsen, to the effect that he had no intention of allowing the university to become a state within the state.[37] He showed that he meant this by violating the principle of academic self-government whenever he considered it to be necessary and, on occasion, by making appointments without consulting faculties. In 1900 he became interested in establishing a Roman Catholic Theological Faculty at the University of Strasburg as a means of increasing German influence upon public opinion in the Reichsland; and, in order to increase the chance of persuading the papal Curia to give its support to this plan, he decreed that there should be new professors of philosophy and history at Strasburg of Catholic faith and, on his own initiative, appointed a medievalist named Martin Spahn to the latter chair. This caused an uproar not

[36] *Wilhelm und Caroline von Humboldt in ihren Briefen*, ed. Anna von Sydow (7 vols., Berlin, 1906–16), ii. 19.
[37] Paulsen, *Autobiography*, p. 364.

only in Strasburg but in Munich, where the growth of ultramontanism was a matter of concern to university professors, and it elicited a petition of protest from the Bavarian university, and, from Berlin, a much-quoted statement from Theodor Mommsen in which the historian pointed out that, once appointments were made for political reasons, the whole future of German scholarship was jeopardized. None of this moved Althoff, whose appointment of Spahn had in any case been approved by the Emperor.[38]

Althoff had no hesitation about letting professors and lecturers know that he was opposed to their speaking or writing on current politics if their views did not coincide with those of the Imperial Government, and flagrant disregard of this invited punitive action on his part. In 1899, when Hans Delbrück, Professor of History at the University of Berlin, criticized the government's policy of Germanization in Schleswig-Holstein in the columns of his monthly journal the *Preußische Jahrbücher*, he was haled before a disciplinary court with a view to his dismissal, a punishment that was in the end averted partly by manifestations of support by his colleagues and partly by a speech that he delivered to a mass audience in support of the government's naval policy.[39] Less fortunate was Friedrich Tönnies, who, because he disregarded Althoff's demand that he sever his relations with the liberal Ethical Culture Society in 1893, was passed over for promotion in Kiel and had to wait for his associate professorship until 1908, after Althoff was dead.[40]

It is almost unnecessary to add that proclaimed Social Democrats had little hope of a successful academic career. In 1896–7 the Prussian Ministry of Education demanded that the *venia legendi* (the privilege of teaching) be withdrawn from a young physics lecturer at the University of Berlin named Leo Arons, because he was active in

[38] A full-scale account of the background and ramifications of the Spahn case and of the elaborate negotiations with the Vatican is to be found in John Eldon Craig, 'A Mission for German Learning: the University of Straßburg and Alsatian Society, 1870–1918' (Dissertation, Stanford Univ. 1973).

[39] Paulsen, *Autobiography*, p. 385.

[40] Tönnies was difficult in any case. Although he hoped that the publication of his *Community and Society* would assure his promotion, he confessed to Friedrich Paulsen in March 1889 that he foresaw difficulties since he could not take the oath of personal service to the King of Prussia which was expected of public officials, because it would deprive him of a sense of 'philosophical freedom'. See *Tönnies—Paulsen Briefwechsel* (Kiel, 1961), pp. 303–4. Max Weber believed that Althoff tried to block his appointment to Freiburg in 1893. See Wolfgang Mommsen, *Max Weber und die deutsche Politik* (Tübingen, 1959), p. 3; and Arthur Mitzman, *The Iron Cage: An Historical Interpretation of Max Weber* (New York, 1970), pp. 110 ff. The standard biography is Arnold Sachse, *Althoff und sein Werk* (Berlin, 1928).

socialist politics, although there was no evidence that this affected his teaching. The faculty baulked, refusing to do more than warn Arons to restrict his political activities. This was not enough for Althoff. He brought pressure to bear upon some of Arons's leading supporters—he told Friedrich Paulsen that he should not think that *he* was above reproach, since he had written an article on 'The German Universities and Subversion' for Maximilian Harden's journal *Die Zukunft*, a paper, Althoff said, that was guilty of lese-majesty in every issue[41]—and when these tactics did not work, simply went over the faculty's head. In 1898 the Prussian Government deprived Arons of his post by passing a law that declared that 'the deliberate promotion of Social Democratic purposes [was] incompatible with a teaching post in a royal university'. Nor was the Prussian Government alone in discriminating against scholars with unorthodox politics. In 1908 the young sociologist Robert Michels, one of Max Weber's most brilliant students, was denied the right to become a lecturer at Marburg because of his socialism and was forced subsequently to seek a position in Italy.

The pressures upon faculties did not come from the governments alone. Increasingly in the 1880s and 1890s the cry was heard in business and conservative-political circles that the universities were centres of subversion and that academic freedom was a screen behind which enemies of the state plied their trade. There were continual demands that something be done to get rid of the red professors, and these were generally supported by ill-informed patrioteers or enemies of all modern tendencies, like Julius Langbehn who wrote that 'the professor is the German national disease; the present German education of youth is a kind of massacre of the innocents'.[42] It is to the credit of a few great men that they fought back. Rudolf Virchow, Professor of Pathology at Berlin since 1856, member of the Berlin City Council and the Reichstag, where he was a prominent member of the Progressive delegation, did not allow official disapproval and right-wing criticism to blunt his attacks on Bismarck's policies or his doughty defence of the freedom of the University. In 1894, when the industrialist Stumm-Halberg, a notorious hunter for reds and one of the most passionate advocates of the Subversion Bill (Umsturzvorlage) which absorbed so much parliamentary energy before its defeat in 1895, attacked the economists Adolf Wagner, Gerhart von Schulze-Gävernitz, and Lujo Brentano by name, accusing them of disseminating socialism, his intended victims stood

[41] Paulsen, *Autobiography*, p. 365.
[42] Stern, *The Politics of Cultural Despair*, p. 166.

firm; and when Brentano was subsequently attacked by the conservative Press for showing sympathy for strikers in Hamburg, he responded by writing that his critics seemed to think that the possession of a university chair deprived him of his rights as a citizen, adding that he was of a different persuasion.[43]

Perhaps the most eloquent protest against the official enemies of academic freedom and their allies in the private sector was that of Theodor Mommsen. In 1901, in a public statement that echoed that of the Göttingen Seven of 1837, he wrote,

There goes through German university circles a feeling of degradation. Our life impulse is uninhibited inquiry, the kind of inquiry that does not discover what, after weighing objectives and considerations, it *should* discover or *wants* to discover or what would serve useful purposes outside the sphere of scholarship, but rather that which logically and historically seems right to the conscientious researcher—in a word, the truth. Upon loyalty to the truth depends our self-respect, our professional honour, and our influence upon youth. Upon it depends German scholarship, which has played its part in creating the greatness and strength of the German people. Who lays his hand on that puts an axe to the mighty tree in whose shade and protection we live and whose fruits benefit the world.[44]

There were, however, relatively few men like Virchow and Brentano and Mommsen. It was always easier to abandon unorthodoxy and uncomfortable colleagues and to join the establishment, and this is what most professors did. In some cases, they did so out of self-interest, motivated by the hope that political conformity and demonstrated loyalty would win them the title of Privy Councillor (Geheimrat) or some other preferment. In many more, they were doubtless moved by a genuine concern over the social, political, and moral results of the progress of industrialism in their country and a desire to reinvigorate older national and cultural values. Those who were driven by this concern were repelled by the materialism of the age and by the political influence of those who profited from it, the industrialists and the great capitalist landowners, but nevertheless their politics in important respects came to resemble that of these powerful interest groups. Thus a social and economic reformer like Adolf Wagner, who was attacked by Stumm for his 'socialism', held other views of which Stumm could only approve, including a strong bias against Jewish influence in German life and a fervent belief in the national cause.[45]

[43] Brentano, *Mein Leben*, pp. 200–5.   [44] Ibid., p. 220.
[45] Kenneth Barkin, 'Adolf Wagner and German Industrial Development', *Journal of Modern History*, xli (1969), 144.

It is no exaggeration to say that anti-Semitism, which had existed in Germany in many forms for a long time and had received an impetus from the financial crash of 1873, was given a spurious respectability when Heinrich von Treitschke declared in an article in the *Preußische Jahrbücher* in November 1879 that 'the Jews are our national misfortune'.[46] It is true that Treitschke regarded his essay, not as a racial attack, but as an appeal to German Jews to become better citizens; and it should be noted that he was refuted publicly by Mommsen and others of the academic fraternity and that Mommsen subsequently opposed (although without success) both his succession to the editorship of the *Historische Zeitschrift* and his admission to the Prussian Academy. Yet Treitschke probably spoke for a majority of his colleagues, if the statistics of professorial appointments in German universities mean anything. Although there were many Jewish instructors in university faculties in the pre-war years—in 1909–10 almost 12 per cent of all instructors, or 19 per cent if one counted converted Jews—there were many fewer professors, and in Berlin in those same years not a single faculty included a Jewish full professor. On no class in Germany did the identification of Jews with materialism and its political and cultural manifestations have greater influence than upon the self-proclaimed protectors of the national heritage, the university professors.[47]

At the same time, no more uncritical acceptance of the claims of German nationalism was to be found than in university faculties. The most extreme example of this failing was, once again, Heinrich von Treitschke.[48] For a quarter of a century students heard this deaf, hoarse-voiced, but compelling *preceptor Germaniae* fulminate against Germany's neighbours, calling for the destruction of British sea power, and glorifying war as a German destiny, provided by a beneficent Deity as a means of purging the nation of the sins of materialism and of allowing it to manifest and fulfil its cultural superiority. That his teachings left their mark upon the pre-war generation of German leaders is undeniable; and his influence is most painfully evident in the thought and actions of such of his auditors as Alfred von Tirpitz, Friedrich von Bernhardi, Carl Peters, the explorer, and Heinrich Class, the founder of the Pan-German League.

[46] On this and the dispute that followed, see *Der Berliner Antisemitismusstreit*, ed. W. Boehlich (Sammlung Insel, 1965) which gives Treitschke's article and the responses it elicited; Heuß, *Mommsen und das 19. Jahrhundert*, pp. 200–4; L. Wichert, 'Theodor Mommsen und Jacob Bernays', *Historische Zeitschrift*, 205 (1969), 265.

[47] See Ringer, *Decline of the Mandarins*, pp. 135–7.

[48] On Treitschke as teacher, see the biographies by Bußmann and Dorpalen and the editorial introduction to Craig's edition of the *History*.

His lectures were the embodiment of injustice and lack of objectivity, filled with emotional judgements and wildness of language. As a young man, Hellmuth von Gerlach sat at his feet in Berlin, for one lecture. In it he heard Treitschke compare Augustus the Strong of Saxony with Frederick William I of Prussia, to the great disadvantage of the former. Reflecting that Frederick William I had built an army, whereas Augustus had built Dresden, the most beautiful city in Germany, Gerlach decided not to attend any further lectures.[49] But Treitschke had no want of auditors, and what he taught them fed the stream of rabid nationalism that engulfed his country in 1914.

Nor was he a lonely example, except perhaps in the violence of his attitudes. On all of the critical issues of foreign affairs—fleet policy in 1900, for instance, and colonial policy in 1907—organized groups of academicians were to be found agitating for the government cause. Moved by the feeling that nationalism was, as Friedrich Naumann believed, the best way to woo the masses from Social Democracy or that patriotism might surmount the fragmentation caused by party politics, the professors were as aggressive in their nationalism as the Pan-Germans; indeed, after the Pan-German League was established in the 1890s, they bulked large in its membership. It is not an exaggeration to call them, as they were called before 1914, the intellectual bodyguard of the Hohenzollerns.

The same tendency toward conservatism was to be detected in organized university student life in the last years of the nineteenth century. By that time, what distinction had once existed between the older élitist corporations (Landmannschaften) and the more liberal Burschenschaften had disappeared, and student organizations in

---

[49] Gerlach, *Von rechts nach links*, p. 68. Compare the passage in Paulsen's autobiography. 'Treitschke carried his hearers away by the pompous force of his words. Hearing his monotonous and hollow voice for the first time, one could not help wondering why or how. I heard him lecture . . . at Berlin. Unfortunately, he was just speaking about England, and the invective he poured out in his blind hatred of English philosophy and the whole English mode of thinking became so intolerable to me that I walked out of the lecture room. His ungovernable temperament rendered him peculiarly insensitive to historical justice. He knew only two categories: for or against the good cause; and, in order to put down anything that warred against the latter, he regarded any means as justified—the good cause being the cause of Prussia. I wonder how England had really managed to incur his undying hatred, a hatred that knew no bounds. I can still hear his voice in the professor's room at Berlin when, on hearing of the fall of Khartoum and Gordon's death, he gave vent to his feelings in loud jubilation. "Just what ought to have happened!" he exclaimed. "Every one of them ought to meet with the same fate!" His deafness made it impossible to reply; his own voice was the only voice he ever heard, and this increased the intemperance of his emotions.'

general had become beer-swilling, duel-fighting, song-bawling fraternities. Many serious students doubtless felt repelled by this, like the one in Ernst von Wolzogen's play *Das Lumpengesindel* (1892), who says bitterly:

You corps students imagine that you have enjoyed the only real character-training because you have made a fetish of your childish ceremonial. . . . You have given up any thought of your own and especially any individuality and become congealed in rigid forms and empty prejudices; yet because you have done this you imagine that you are somehow better than the rest of mankind, who still think that their personal freedom has some value.[50]

In the 1880s a movement began which, in its first form, seemed designed to revive the moral and cultural values that had inspired the Burschenschaft movement in 1817. This was the Verein deutscher Studenten, which was founded in Berlin and spread rapidly to other universities, the various branches forming a federation and having a central organ called *Akademische Blätter*. The general invitation to the branch organizations issued at the time of the Kyffhäuser meeting of August 1881 recalled, in its language, the declaration of the first general convocation of the Burschenschaften in 1817; it spoke of 'the sinister powers of naked self-interest and cosmopolitan lack of patriotism' and of 'the sapping of morals and the de-Christianizing' that worked 'beneath the ancient sound foundation of our national character (*Volksthum*)'. Reminiscent of the history of the Burschenschaften also was the way in which the movement subsequently fell prey to rabid nationalism, anti-Semitism, and, in its south German branches, anti-Catholicism. At the same time, *Akademische Blätter* became a house organ for patrioteers who were active in Conservative and Pan-German circles, and those members of the movement who had hoped to make it a force for social reform, as Friedrich Naumann, a co-founder of the Leipzig branch, had done, were gradually eased out.[51]

All in all, the student organizations, of all varieties, like the universities of which they were a part, were the victims of the corrosive influence of materialism, feudalism, and nationalism.

---

[50] On the ceremonial aspects of beer-drinking and its effects, see the views of Gymnasialdirektor Max Nath in the 1880s, cited in Pross, *Jugend, Eros, Politik*, pp. 48–50. See also Hermann Sudermann's novel about the Bismarck period, *Der tolle Professor* (1926); Karl Kraus, *Die letzten Tage der Menschheit*, act IV, sc. 6; Gerlach, *Von rechts nach links*, p. 56; and, for the reaction of Max Weber's mother to his appearance after three semesters at Heidelberg, Mitzmann, *Iron Cage*, (New York, 1970), p. 24.

[51] See esp. Heuß, *Naumann*, pp. 40, 310.

V

'The woman's predicament', Ernest Rhys has written, 'is the test of the moral and human worth of any given state of society.'[52] Judged by this standard, Germany's condition in the nineteenth century was truly deplorable. Its ruling class was as intent upon keeping the female population in a state of dependence as it was upon combating socialism. All the expedients of the law, every form of financial and moral pressure, were employed to maintain male dominance in state, society, and the home. Women were denied basic civil rights (they could not vote and were in most states barred from membership in political organizations and trade unions) and were excluded from both any share in the governance of the country and employment in any of its administrative agencies. Moreover, unless they defied convention and won an independent position in the arts, their share in their country's cultural life was minimal, in comparison with that of their contemporaries in France.[53] The age of materialism did not produce figures like Rahel Varnhagen and Bettina von Arnim, nor did it provide its women with the educational opportunities that would have permitted them to aspire to such positions of influence.

In a man's world the very idea of higher education for women seemed ludicrous, and there was strong resistance to any suggestion that women deserved the same right to professional training as men. In most of Germany no secondary schools comparable to the Gymnasien existed for women until the very eve of the First World War, and in Prussia it was not until 1896 that women were even permitted to take examinations for the Reifezeugnis, the certificate proving that they had the equivalent of a Gymnasium education.[54] Not that this privilege helped them much, for until the turn of the century universities admitted no women students except those who came from abroad, and even after that barrier had fallen women in Prussian universities did not have the right to take the Staatsexamen or to qualify for higher degrees.[55] The first German woman to win a Ph.D. degree was Ricarda Huch, the distinguished historian and

[52] The introduction of the Everyman edition of *Anna Karenina*, quoted in J. P. Stern *Re-Interpretations: Seven Studies in Nineteenth Century German Literature* (London, 1964), p. 316.
[53] See Robert Minder, *Dichter in der Gesellschaft. Erfahrungen mit deutscher und französicher Literatur* (Frankfurt-on-Main, 1966), p. 20.
[54] Lange, *Berlin zur Zeit Bebels und Bismarcks*, pp. 570 f.
[55] *Deutsche Sozialgeschichte: Dokumente und Skizzen*, vol. ii: *1870–1914*, ed. Gerhard A. Ritter and Jürgen Kocka (Munich, 1974), p. 422.

novelist of the Weimar period, and she was forced to go to a Swiss university in order to earn it.[56]

Secondary education for women was available for those who wished to pay for it in *höheren Töchterschulen* and in private academies, but its quality was uneven, and it consisted for the most part of instruction in edifying subjects that would make middle-class girls good wives and charming hostesses—music and the useful arts, a superficial acquaintance with the German classics, conventional ethics, and the art of making polite and innocuous conversation. Lily Braun, who fled from this insipid pabulum into socialism, wrote in her memoirs that she was taught to believe that one judged a young woman less by her knowledge than by her comportment, and that all of her education had been directed to one goal, 'that I might one day be able to provide my husband with a proper domestic atmosphere (*eine hübsche Häuslichkeit*)'.[57]

Women who achieved that end were supposed to have fulfilled themselves, and, if they had second thoughts on the subject, soon discovered that the weight of public disapproval could be severe and, indeed, crushing. There exists no more moving description of the consequences of transgressing the moral code of middle-class society in the Germany of Bismarck and William II than Theodor Fontane's novel *Effi Briest*, which, in the incisiveness of its social analysis and its psychological insight into the predicament of women in the nineteenth century, bears comparison with *Madame Bovary* and *Anna Karenina*.[58] The heroine, whose outlook has been entirely shaped by the aspirations and taboos of the civil service aristocracy to which her parents belong, marries an honourable but dull man, many years her senior, and soon finds herself longing for something more than 'being rich and having a fine house'. She has a brief love affair with an army major, which her husband discovers six and a half years after its termination. Although he is aware of the irrationality of his behaviour, Effi's husband feels compelled to challenge the major to a duel, in which he kills him, to drive his wife from his home, although they have been happy together, and to take her daughter from her.

In the midst of these troubles Effi receives a letter from her mother, who, despite her love for her daughter, is as much a prisoner of social convention as the husband. For what it tells us of the *mores* of

[56] Albert Soergel and Curt Hohoff, *Dichtung und Dichter der Zeit: Von Naturalismus bis zur Gegenwart* (rev. edn., 2 vols., Düsseldorf, 1961), i. 296.

[57] Lily Braun, *Memoiren einer Sozialistin* (2 vols., Berlin, n.d.), ii. 149 f.

[58] See J. P. Stern's comparison of the three novels in *Re-Interpretations*, pp. 315 ff.

nineteenth-century middle-class society, it deserves to be quoted at length.

> . . . And now about your future, my dear Effi. You'll have to fend for yourself, and you may be sure of our support as far as material circumstances are concerned. You will do best to live in Berlin (these things are best got over in a big city) and so you'll be one of the many who are deprived of fresh air and clear sunlight. Your life will be lonely, and if you can't put up with that, you'll probably have to move out of your social class. The world in which you've been living will be closed to you. And the saddest thing for us and for you (for you, at least, if we are correct in thinking that we know you) is that your parents' house will be closed to you too. We can't offer you a quiet place in Hohen-Cremmen, a refuge in our home, for that would mean closing this house to all the world, and we are certainly not prepared to do that. Not because we are all that dependent on the world or that we would find it absolutely intolerable to bid farewell to what is called society. No, *not* for that reason, but simply because we have to show our colours and to make clear to everybody our—I cannot spare you the word—our condemnation of your behaviour, the behaviour of our only child, whom we loved so.[59]

For the married woman, infidelity was the unforgivable crime, to be punished by dispossession and *déclassement*. Against breach of the marriage contract by their husbands, however, German wives had no effective recourse, a kind of double standard being generally recognized in sexual behaviour; nor could they easily secure legal protection from, or redress for, marital abuse of their persons or their property. In this respect, conditions had not sensibly improved since the days when Ferdinand Lassalle was able to obtain justice for the wronged Countess Sophie von Hatzfeldt only by defying the statutes and making life so miserable for his client's husband that he voluntarily relinquished what he had, with the law's protection, stolen from his wife.

Isolated voices had been raised against these injustices for generations. Equality of the sexes had been one of the themes most persistently sounded by the Young German movement of the thirties and forties, and the first woman writers to champion the cause of emancipation—the novelist Countess Ida von Hahn-Hahn, Luise Aston, whose *My Emancipation, Censure, and Vindication* appeared in 1846, and the actress Wilhelmine von Hillern, whose novel *Die Geyer-Walley* (1875) shocked the prudish in much the same way as Gutzkow's *Wally, die Zweiflerin* had done forty years earlier—were influenced by that dedicated, but muddled, group of reformers. But it was only in the last years of the Bismarckian period that systematic efforts to promote women's rights got under way, when a middle-

---

[59] Fontane, *Sämtliche Werke*, vii. 391.

class emancipation movement that had its origins in pioneer work by Louise Otto-Peters in the sixties began to gather strength under the leadership of her disciple Helene Lange, and Socialist women's associations began to multiply under the guidance and inspiration of August Bebel, whose book *Die Frau und der Sozialismus* (1883) was so popular that it ran through fifty reprints before the outbreak of the war.

The Socialist associations focused their attention primarily upon inequality of treatment and pay of woman workers, and much of their activity—always hampered by legal prohibition against female membership in political organizations—was devoted to educating women concerning such things as the advantages of a shorter working day.[60] The bourgeois movement was, at the beginning, less single-minded about its goals and, on the whole, averse to preoccupation with social and political problems. In her memoirs Helene Lange wrote that the themes most debated in the 1880s were subjects like 'Female Character-Building', 'The Duty and Necessity of Self-Help', 'May Women Think?', 'The Woman Question as a Problem of Humanity', and 'The Woman Question and Male Misgivings'. In the 1890s, however, as social problems became acute, these concerns gave way to interest in more concrete things, like labour conditions, night work for women, social welfare for working mothers, female guardianship, prostitution, abortion, and, eventually, voting rights for women in community, Church, and state.[61] This shift brought some degree of convergence with the Socialist movement, whose leaders—Clara Zetkin and Lily Braun among others—had been critical of the lack of political consciousness among their middle-class counterparts.

As in the period before 1848, the fight for women's rights was reflected in the literature of the day, sometimes in unfortunate and self-defeating forms. Representatives of the Naturalist school like Richard Dehmel, Max Dauthendey, Otto Erich Hartleben, Otto Julius Bierbaum, and Karl Bleibtreu evinced a preoccupation with emancipation from conventional morality, free love, and the celebration of the prostitute as *Venus vulgivaga* that was more prurient than political; while, at the same time, the more militant spirits among the woman poets and novelists had a tendency to allow their earnestness to assume ludicrous forms. In a poem called 'Das moderne Weib' by Maria Janitschek, an affronted woman challenges the man who has insulted her to a duel and, when he hesitates to take up

[60] See Ottilie Bader, *Ein steiniger Weg. Lebenserinnerungen* (Berlin, 1931), pp. 32 f.
[61] Helene Lange, *Lebenserinnerungen* (Berlin, 1922), pp. 196 f.

weapons against her, on the grounds that 'woman exists for patience and forgiveness', reacts violently.

> 'So wisse, daß das Weib
> gewachsen ist im neunzehnten Jahrhundert!'
> sprach sie mit großen Aug, und schoß ihn nieder.[62]

On the other hand, it is probably true that the enormous popularity of the romantic novels of Amalie Schoppe, Luise Mühlbach, Eugenie Marlitt, and especially that phenomenon among German woman writers, Hedwig Courths-Mahler, who wrote more than 200 novels which had sold 27 million copies by 1950, helped to create sympathy for the vulnerability of women in contemporary society, although their works showed little appreciation of social reality, sentimentalizing the dilemmas of their shop-girl heroines and intimating that love will always find a way and that there is a natural affinity between kind hearts and coronets.[63]

On a more sophisticated level, the novels of Anna Croissant-Rust, Gabriele Reuter, Helene Böhlau, and Clara Viebig provided realistic descriptions of the problems of working-class and rural women, as well as poignant and persuasive insights into the humiliation that women felt in the face of society's denial to them of the spiritual opportunities available to men. It is worth remarking also that these champions of emancipation were not entirely unaware that the cost of freedom would not, for most women, be negligible. In one of the novels of Gabriele Reuter, an implacable opponent both of bourgeois convention and of the many Frau Briests who were its staunchest supporters, the author allows her heroine to say:

The woman of today, as art seeks to comprehend her in her essential character, has become a figure of longing. She neither grieves nor enjoys—her delicate slender limbs reach out toward something infinite, the lines of her profile betray a thirst for the inexpressible, her eyes yearn for the more than palpable behind the things of this common clay . . . her hands, weary but open with desire, grope uncertainly for the delights and fruits of knowledge which, visible only in her dreams, seem to float beyond them on blue zephyrs . . . Is mastery over the feelings of the man she loves still enough for the proud, unsatisfied woman of our time? Driven by a mysterious compulsion, she strives after a mystical union of souls and spirits. And yet—a new Eve—she already senses that the taste of that seductive fruit of knowledge will exclude her for ever from the paradise of her innocence and all the blessed happiness of blindness.[64]

[62] Soergel and Hohoff, Dichtung and Dichter i. 299. See Richard Hamann and Jost Hermand, Naturalismus (2nd edn., Berlin, 1966), pp. 73 ff.

[63] On Courths–Mahler, see esp. Gustav Sichelschmidt, Hedwig Courths-Mahler, Deutschlands erfolgreichste Autorin: Eine literatur-soziologische Studie (Bonn, 1967).

[64] Soergel and Hohoff, Dichtung und Dichter i. 303.

By the turn of the century there were more than 850 associations working for women's rights in Germany, with a combined membership that was approaching a million. The most important of these, and the one with the most comprehensive programme, was the Allgemeiner deutscher Frauenverein (ADF), led by Helene Lange and Gertrud Bäumer, who also published the nation's leading periodical for women, *Die Frau*, and edited the annual *Handbuch der Frauenbewegung*. The stated objective of the ADF was 'to bring the cultural influence of women to its fullest inner development and to unhampered social effectiveness'. Its more specific goals included improved secondary education for all woman graduates of the Volksschulen, reorganization of the superior Mädchenschulen so as to make them equal with comparable male institutions in the quality of the education provided, and unrestricted admission of qualified women to all scientific, technical, and humanistic institutions of higher learning; government recognition of marriage and motherhood as an occupation that must be protected legally and economically; increased opportunity for professional employment of women and, in the case of all woman workers, equality of pay with male workers performing the same work; an end to the double standard in sexual matters and to government protection of prostitution; reform of marriage laws so as to give equality of parental authority and property rights to the partners; reform of laws concerning children born out of wedlock so as to increase the responsibility of the father for the upkeep of mother and child; greater opportunity for employment of women in community and state administrations; admission of women to jury duty; abolition of limitations on women's rights of association; and participation of women in elections at every level.[65]

It cannot be said that many of these aspirations were fulfilled during the imperial period. Apart from the Social Democratic party and the Progressive party, which, under Friedrich Naumann's influence, admitted Else Lüders, a leader of the women's suffrage movement, to its national executive committee, none of the parties showed any sympathy for the women's objectives, and even the Progressives, who gave a lukewarm endorsement of the principle of votes for women in 1912, proposed no plan for making it effective. Regardless of party, most German males seemed to find the thought of their wives and daughters becoming emancipated and politically informed both alarming and repellent. Without always being willing

---

[65] Ritter and Kocka, *Sozialgeschichte* ii. 422–4.

to say so openly, they shared the sentiments, if not the treacly style characteristic of stories in the popular middle-class magazine *Die Gartenlaube*, of a Catholic notable who wrote in 1912:

In the realm of the heart, woman wields her gentle sceptre and 'with its magic makes the lowly hut a temple of bliss, a temple of peace'. Her mild and gracious being, whose silent influence no honest and sympathetic male heart can resist, creates for us that dear, intimate domesticity against whose firmly girt walls the raging storms of the outside world break in vain. And these quiet rooms, in which the active creative man sought and found peace and new strength after the day's hard work, are in the future to echo to the battle-cries of parties disputing over the programmes and interests of state and community![66]

The very thought was anathema, which explains why, with the exception of some improvement in educational opportunity and in the length of the working day in factories, little progress was made towards the emancipation of German women before the war. Their condition was hardly changed from what it had been thirty years earlier; and, when the fateful decisions of 1914 were made, it seemed entirely natural to those who ruled Germany that they should have no share in the determination of its fate.

VI

In 1885 Heinrich Hart wrote an article called 'Prince Bismarck and his Relationship to German Literature' in which he sternly criticized the Chancellor for his lack of interest in the arts and his failure to do anything to promote cultural activity in Germany. One would think, he said, that Bismarck included artists and writers among those unproductive members of society, the *Honoratioren*, whom he was always belabouring in the Reichstag. His attitude could only encourage the contempt for the arts that was already too prevalent.[67]

Although not entirely fair to Bismarck, this was a shrewd assessment of a real problem. In the national state that was founded in 1871 there was no productive relationship between politics and the arts, and part of the reason was to be found in the materialism of the age, which, with varied emphasis, dominated the thinking of scientists, politicians, and the great bulk of the comfortable middle class. This was not, of course, a uniquely German phenomenon,[68] but, because

[66] Ibid. 426.

[67] Heinrich Hart, 'Fürst Bismarck und sein Verhältnis zur deutschen Literatur', *Gesammelte Werke*, iii (Berlin, 1907), p. 257.

[68] Carleton J. H. Hayes, *A Generation of Materialism, 1871–1900* (New York, 1941), Chs. 3, 4, 9.

of the completeness of the victory over France and the remarkable economic development that followed, it assumed more exaggerated forms in Germany. In the 1870s it often seemed that creativity was not respected unless manifested in the production of material goods. Many a German artist came to feel that wealth and office were accorded more respect than the works of the spirit and that most of his fellow citizens were philistines in the spirit of the current song:

> Ich hab eine Loge im Theater,
> Ich hab auch ein Opernglas;
> Ich hab Equipagen und Pferde:
> Meine Mittel erlauben mir das!

> Ich rauche die feinste Havanna
> Zur Verdauung nach dem Frass.
> Ich liebe das ganze Ballettkorps:
> Meine Mittel erlauben mir das!

> Über Lumpen wie Kepler und Schiller,
> Rümpf ich nur verächtlich die Nas:
> Ich bin ein vollendetes Rindvieh:
> Meine Mittel erlauben mir das!

Feeling that way, he was apt to be resentful, to subscribe to Nietzsche's theory that 'power makes stupid',[69] and to explode like the young man in Conrad Alberti s novel *Die Alten und Jungen* (1889) who cries: 'I'll tell you what we need. We need a Sedan in which we play the part of the French. We need a Jena that will tear us out of this stinking, fouled, slovenly bed upon which the bourgeois has thrown us—so that the rabble that has ruled the fatherland since 1870, jobbers and N.C.O.s, will learn that there is something higher than stock market swindling and close-order drill.'[70]

But this is only half the story. The alienation of the artist in Imperial Germany was not solely attributable to the values of the middle class; it was in large part self-willed. Towards the real world, the world of power and politics, the German artist, in contrast to the French, always had an ambivalent attitude. He was drawn toward engagement in its affairs by his desire for recognition and community approval and by intellectual arrogance; he was repelled by a belief that to participate in politics or even to write about it was a derogation of his calling and that, for the artist, the inner rather than

---

[69] Nietzsche, *Götzendämmerung*, p. 122.
[70] Conrad Alberti, *Die Alten und Jungen* (1889), bk. i, Ch. 2.

the external world was the real one.[71] In general (one must make exceptions of Georg Forster, Heinrich von Kleist, Wilhelm von Humboldt, Ludwig Uhland, and Heine and Börne), the latter argument prevailed. Before 1914 it was only on rare occasions that German artists were interested, let alone stirred, by political and social events and issues, and, even when their attention was commanded, their response was rarely positive.

Not even the events of 1870–1 succeeded in shaking their political indifference. The victory over France and the unification of the German states inspired no great work of literature or music or painting. The emphasis upon heroism and aggressiveness and unconditionality that one finds in the work of the best painters of the 1870s—Anselm Feuerbach, Marées, Leibl, and Böcklin—and in the stories of Paul Heyse and Conrad Ferdinand Meyer doubtless owed something to recent events, but their authors had no further interest in the political developments of their time, which did not strike them as being poetic enough to challenge their talents.[72] What they really wanted was 'not reality but that *Jenseits von Gut und Böse* . . . that was accessible only to genius and demigods'.[73] As the infrastructure of the new Reich was being laid, German artists were writing about times infinitely remote or filling their canvasses with tritons and nereids and centaurs and Greek columns, while the greatest musician of the day, Richard Wagner, was composing musical dramas that, overtly at least, had only the remotest connection with the society in which he lived.[74]

[71] Robert Minder, *Kultur und Literatur in Deutschland und Frankreich* (Frankfurt-on-Main, 1962), pp. 5–43.

[72] In Wilhelm Raabe's *Horacker* (1876), Oberlehrer Dr. Neubauer is engaged in composing an epic poem about the Battle of Königgrätz, but it is clear that his colleagues (and the author) regard this as a comic enterprise and do not expect him to get much beyond his deathless line 'Schrecklich metzelt jetzt Steinmetz Schweinschädel erstürmend'. One of them says. 'Whether the hexameter and the historical facts are correct, I don't at the moment know, nor do I want to know' (Ch. 5). Among painters there were exceptions to what has been said above. Anton von Werner, godfather of the so-called 'Trompeter-von-Säckingen-Stil', painted, among other things, panoramas of Gravelotte and St. Privat and the often reproduced portrait of the Congress of Berlin. See Walther Kiaulehn, *Berlin: Schicksal einer Weltstadt* (Munich and Berlin, 1958), p. 298. Adolf Menzel, a greater painter, won Franz Mehring's praise for being one of the first artists to give a realistic representation of industrialism, as he did in his painting *The Iron Rolling Mill* (1875). Mehring, *Aufsätze zur Literaturgeschichte*, p. 333.

[73] Hamann and Hermand, *Gründerzeit*, p. 255.

[74] Schieder, *Kaiserreich*, p. 59. In Spielhagen's *Sturmflut* (bk. iii, Ch. 8), Schonau, using an ingenious blend of the philosophies of Hartmann and Schopenhauer, tricked out with references to the *Venusberg* and the *Zaubertrank*, makes an ironical defence of Wagner as one who expresses the salient characteristic of the age, namely, 'the

The 1880s brought a change in artistic style with the beginning of the so-called Naturalist rebellion, launched simultaneously by two groups of artists, one in Munich, a natural home of the Muses, where for two generations every seventieth person had been a writer, a painter, or a sculptor,[75] the other in Berlin, which, as a new *Weltstadt*, was the most exciting city in Germany.[76] The southern group was led by Michael Georg Conrad, who was inspired by Émile Zola's writings about the experimental novel and his focus, in works like *L'Assommoir* (1877), *Nana* (1879), and especially *Germinal* (1885), upon subjects and classes that had hitherto been considered unworthy of portrayal. In 1885 Conrad, in collaboration with Conrad Alberti and Karl Bleibtreu, founded the journal *Die Gesellschaft* in order to spread Zola's ideas and portray the social ills caused by industrialism. The Berlin movement was more a throw-back to the Young German movement of the 1830s, scorning everything that was classical and imitative of classicality, repudiating Goethe and Schiller and elevating Heine and Börne to their places in the pantheon, and focusing its attention upon contemporary social problems, such as the subordination of women in society and the plight of the urban poor. Its leaders were Heinrich and Julius Hart, who founded the journal *Kritische Waffengänge* in 1882, and Maximilian Harden, Paul Schlenther, and Otto Brahm, who with the Hart brothers founded the Verein Freie Bühne in 1889, an event of great importance in the history of the drama.[77]

The Naturalist movement had several positive results, which were not confined to literature. It liberated German painting from the decorative, pseudo-classical style of the 1870s and brought to the canvas scenes of everyday life and social situations. Max Liebermann's *Jam Makers* and Fritz von Uhde's *Drummers* represented a contemporaneity that was both refreshing and honest, a stylistic approach which, a decade later, in the Sezession movement of Liebermann, Corinth, and Slevogt, defied governmental pressure and saved German art from a return to artificial monumentality, and

---

conviction that life is meaningless and the correlative longing for nirvana, which is denied of expression only by the Will, which insists on draining life to the dregs'.

[75] See Max Halbe's memoirs of his youth in Munich in Hoefele, *Geist und Gesellschaft*, p. 229.

[76] Between 1871 and 1885 Berlin's population grew from 862,341 to 1,315,287. The exhilaration which people felt in this bustling metropolis is captured by Alberti in his novel *Die Alten und Jungen* (Ch.1), in which he speaks of the 'nervous, endlessly quivering Berlin air . . . which works upon people like alcohol, morphine, cocaine, exciting, inspiring, relaxing, deadly: the air of the world city'.

[77] Hamann and Hermand, *Naturalismus*, pp. 12–20, 278–82.

which, in the hands of Heinrich Zille, Käthe Kollwitz, and Balus-
chek, became a potent weapon of social criticism.[78] It put an end to
the parochialism of the German theatre by bringing the works of
Ibsen and Strindberg to the stages of Berlin and Munich, and this
encouraged German dramatists to turn to unconventional themes
which at first shocked audiences, as was true of Gerhart
Hauptmann's *Vor Sonnenaufgang* (1889) and the early plays of Arno
Holz and Hermann Sudermann. And in the field of the novel,
although Naturalism produced no one who could compete on equal
terms with Theodor Fontane, the first German novelist since Goethe
to enjoy a European reputation, it at least inspired dozens of novels
that were marked by a new attention to social injustice and new
insights into the progress of urbanization on the one hand and
industrialism on the other. Paul Lindau's portrayal of the life of the
upper bourgeoisie in Berlin (*Der Zug nach dem Westen*, 1886), Max
Kretzer's description of the fruitless attempts of independent craftsmen to compete with the factory system (*Meister Timpe*, 1883), and
Wilhelm von Polenz's *Büttnerbauer* (1895), which dealt with the
encroachment of capitalist agriculture upon the economic liberty of
the peasantry of West Prussia, represented healthy innovations in
German literature.

It would be a mistake, however, to regard the Naturalist movement as an awakening of conscience on the part of German artists,
for the attention that they accorded the deprived and ill-treated was
not entirely genuine, nor was it sustained. One cannot help feeling
that the interest in the proletariat that marks so many of these novels
was an expression of trendiness and would not have been so strong if
the controversy over Bismarck's Socialist Law had not sustained it;
certainly there was a perceptible diminution of this interest once that
law was repealed, Hauptmann, for instance, turning away from the
pseudo-radicalism of *Die Weber* (1892) and, with *Die versunkene
Glocke* (1896), reconciling himself to the aesthetic taste of the
bourgeoisie.[79] Nor can it be denied that, in focusing upon the drunkenness, disease, madness, and sexuality that were concomitants of
slum-living, the Naturalist writers were often either seeking to *épater
les bourgeois* or indulging in eroticism for eroticism's sake.[80] Finally,
among middle-class writers of the Naturalist persuasion, the socialism that was expressed in their pages was generally bogus, a mere

[78] Ibid., pp. 21–3, 60, 323, and Kiaulehn, *Berlin*, p. 308. Less useful is Donald Drew
Egbert, *Social Radicalism and the Arts: Western Europe* (New York, 1970), pp. 594, 621.
[79] Hamann and Hermand, *Naturalismus*, p. 265.
[80] Ibid., p. 284.

parlour socialism, if not a mask for the kind of élitism that Walter Hasenclever unconsciously expressed in 1915:

> Der Dichter träumt nicht mehr in blauen Buchten.
> Er sieht aus Höfen helle Schwärme reiten.
> Sein Fuß bedeckt die Leichen der Verruchten.
> Sein Haupt erhebt sich, Völker zu begleiten.
>
> Er wird ihr Führer sein.[81]

Ronald Gray has suggested that most German writers and thinkers, since the appearance of Goethe's *Farbenlehre* and Hegel's dialectic, have been fascinated by ideas of polarization and synthesis (*Steigerung*), and that this has led to a willingness to suspend criticism and accept evil as a part of life.[82] The behaviour of the Naturalist writers would seem to corroborate this. For a time, they were willing to use their skills to lay bare some of the ills of their society, but, even when they did so, their mood, more often that not, was one of scepticism rather than anger; they were often wholly fatalistic about the possibility of change (an attitude encouraged perhaps by a too slavish attention to fashionable sociological determinism); and their attention-span was very short.

It will be noted that the Naturalists never turned their attention to the political dangers that were inherent in the imperial system. Indeed, as those dangers became more palpable with the beginnings under William II of a frenetic imperialism, accompanied by an aggressive armament programme, the great majority of the country's novelists and poets averted their eyes and retreated into that *Innerlichkeit* which was always their haven when the real world became too perplexing for them. The 1890s saw the beginnings of Impressionism in Germany. Arnold Hauser has written that this movement was an artistic reflection of the new dynamism and the new feeling for speed and change that were introduced into European life by modern technology. If this was true, it was also true that, psychologically, German Impressionism was an attempt on the part of the artists and their upper-middle-class patrons to escape from the pessimism caused by the frightening outward thrust of political and economic forces by the cultivation of aestheticism. The striking characteristic of the novels and feuilleton articles of the late 1890s was the absence of political content, and the poets of the time—Richard Dehmel, Detlev von Liliencron, Stefan George,

---

[81] Walter Hasenclever, *Der politische Dichter* (1915).
[82] Ronald Gray, *The German Tradition in Literature, 1871–1945* (Cambridge, 1965), p. 1.

Richard von Schaukal, Rainer Maria Rilke, Hugo von Hofmannsthal—were equally unpolitical, subordinating reality to feeling and seeking to imprison on paper fleeting impressions, momentary moods, vague perceptions.[83]

> Kaum etwas auf der weiten Erde
> Birgt solche Poesie,
> Wie ein verlassener,
> Halb verwilderter,
> Lindenverwachsener
> Vogeldurchsungener Sommergarten.[84]

There were a few exceptions to this withdrawal, artists who
sensed that they lived in dangerous times and that it was their duty to
do what they could to expose and defeat the forces threatening
society. Out of the night-clubs of Munich came a remarkable moral-
ist, Frank Wedekind, remarkable because he seemed to many to be an
arch-immoralist, 'a genius of smut', as the critic Alfred Kerr wrote.[85]
In a series of powerful dramas—*Frühlings Erwachen* (1891); *Erdgeist*
(1895) and *Die Büchse der Pandora* (1904) (the famous Lulu plays
which were to be the basis of Alban Berg's opera); *Der Marquis von
Keith* (1900); *Hidalla* 1903)—which broke through the conventions
of the Naturalist theatre and opened the way to the Expressionist
drama of the 1920s and the theatre of the absurd of our own time,
Wedekind mounted a massive attack against Wilhelmine society and
the forces that ruled it. The governing philosophy of the day he
defined in one of his poems.

> Greife wacker nach der Sünde;
> Aus der Sünde wächst Genuß.
> Ach, du gleichest einem Kinde,
> Dem man alles zeigen muß.
>
> Meide nicht die ird'schen Schätz:
> Wo sie liegen, nimm sie mit.
> Hat die Welt doch nur Gesetze,
> Daß man sie mit Füßen tritt.

---

[83] See Arnold Hauser, *The Social History of Art* (4 vols., New York, 1958), iv. 166–70;
Impressionismus, ed. Richard Hamann and Jost Hermand (2nd edn., Berlin, 1966), p. 7,
and, at greater length, Georg Lukács, *Deutsche Literatur im Zeitalter des Imperialismus*
(Berlin, 1946), Ch. 3.

[84] Detlev von Liliencron, *Der Haidegänger* (1891), 'Ich war so glücklich.'

[85] Alfred Kerr, *Die Welt im Drama*, ed. Gerhard F. Hering (2nd edn., Cologne and
Berlin, 1964), p. 231. But see Wilhelm Emrich, 'Immanuel Kant und Frank
Wedekind', *Die Welt der Literatur* (Hamburg), 6 Aug. 1964, and Willy Haas, 'Den
Blicken der Philister preisgegeben', *Die Welt* (Hamburg), 24 July 1964.

Glücklich, wer geschickt und heiter
Über frische Gräber hopst.
Tanzend auf der Galgenleiter
Hat sich keiner noch gemopst.[86]

In his plays he made heroes out of pimps, whores, confidence men, and thieves, doing his best to demonstrate that, compared with the values of the supposedly respectable classes of society, their own were more honourable and more consistently observed. In *Frühlings Erwachen* and in the Lulu plays he contrasted the innocence of natural instincts with the motives of a society ruled by money, sex, and crime, not failing to make clear his belief that innocence would never be understood and would, in all likelihood, end by perishing, as Lulu perished, under the knife of the Ripper.

Wedekind's argument that dark forces of destruction were at large and had been given the keys of the kingdom by the bourgeoisie out of greed or cowardice or lack of wit was repeated with variations by Carl Sternheim and Heinrich Mann. Sternheim, with some justice, called himself the modern Molière, and his most important work was a cycle of five plays written with the spirit and wit of the French master, under the collective title *Aus dem bürgerlichen Heldenleben*. In these he laid bare with cold precision the frailties, petty triumphs, lies, and crimes of the German *Bürgertum* and showed how they were mirrored and magnified in the lives and activities of the ruling caste. In Sternheim's frigid aristocratic view, the emergence of bourgeois society had been a historical mistake that would be corrected, and he knew enough about the world of power to realize that the process of correction would have to be violent. In the third play of the cycle, *1913*, which was written before the outbreak of the war, Christian Maske, who has cast off his humble origins and, by wit and lack of scruple, fought his way successfully to great wealth and a patent of nobility, is forced to recognize that the industrial empire that he has created is being driven by its own insatiable appetites toward a holocaust. 'After us,' he warns his daughter, 'total collapse! We are ripe!'[87]

Heinrich Mann shared Sternheim's presentiment about the future. When he had decided as a young man to become a writer, he had told himself that Germany needed social novels about the contemporary scene, because German society was divided into strata with no understanding of each other and because this divisiveness and lack of

[86] Frank Wedekind, *Prosa, Dramen, Verse* (2nd edn., Munich, 1960), p. 43, 'Erdgeist.'
[87] Carl Sternheim, *Gesamtwerk*, ed. Wilhelm Emrich (Neuwied, 1964 and continuing), i. 285 (act III, sc. 2).

comprehension allowed the government to pursue its own dangerous courses without restraint. To reveal to his fellow citizens the
potentially tragic consequences of a continuation of their ignorance
and fecklessness in political matters was Mann's guiding motive as
he wrote his caustic analyses of Wilhelmine society, *Im Schlaraffenland* (1900)—the title itself revealing, since it means "In Cloud-
Cuckoo Land", the land of thoughtless, perilous innocence—*Professor Unrat* (1905), which Josef von Sternberg turned into
a powerful film starring Emil Jannings and Marlene Dietrich in 1931,
and *Der Untertan* (begun in 1907, although not published until 1918).
The last of these was a searing portrayal of the kind of byzantinism
that tolerated and supported the follies of William II and his paladins,
the tone of which is set in an early passage in which the protagonist
gazes reverently at the Emperor as he rides through the Bran-
denburger Tor.

On the horse, there under the gate of triumphal entries, rode Power! The
Power that rides over us and whose hooves we kiss! Which tramples over
hunger, defiance, and scorn! Against which we can do nothing because we
all love It. Which we have in our blood because we have submission in our
blood. An atom we are of It, a dwindling molecule of something It has spat
out! Each one of us a nothing, we nevertheless rise in ordered ranks, as
neo-Teutons, as military, Civil Service, Church and scholarship, as
economic organization and pressure group, moving upward in a cone-
shaped mass, up to that height where It stands, stony and glittering! To live
in It, to share in It, pitiless towards those who are further from It, and
triumphing even as It smashes us, for in this way It vindicates our love![88]

Power uncontrolled is always dangerous, and their recognition of
this explains the apocalyptic strain that runs through the works of
Wedekind, Sternheim, and Heinrich Mann. This note was even
stronger in the work of those young painters and poets of the years
immediately before the war who were in the vanguard of the Expressionist movement. In paintings like Emil Nolde's *Candle Dancers*
and Ludwig Meidner's *Burning City*, the sense of impending doom
was unmistakable, as it was in Georg Heym's disturbing poem 'Der
Krieg', written in 1911:

> Aufgestanden ist er, welcher lange schlief

and in Jakob van Hoddis's *Weltende*, written a year later:

> Dem Bürger fliegt vom spitzen Kopf der Hut,
> In allen Lüften hallt es wie Geschrei.
> Dachdecker stürzen ab und gehn entzwei
> Und an den Küsten—liest man—steigt die Flut.

[88] *Der Untertan*, conclusion of Ch. 1.

Der Sturm ist da, die wilden Meere hüpfen
An Land, um dicke Dämme zu zerdrücken.
Die meisten Menschen haben einen Schnupfen.
Die Eisenbahnen fallen von den Brücken.

Meidner wrote later about his work in these years: 'Day and night I painted my oppressive feelings on love, Last Judgments, the destruction of the world, etc., for in those days the toothy grin of the world storm already cast its frightening shadow over my plaintive brush.'[89]

The vision that this handful of writers and painters had was not shared by their fellow citizens or even by their fellow artists. The number of people who read Mann's kind of novel or looked at Meidner's kind of painting was very small, as Mann ruefully admitted when he allowed the jingoistic anti-hero of *Der Untertan* to explain to his wife that there was an order of rank among the arts.

'The highest is music,[90] therefore it is the German
     art form. Then comes drama.'
'Why?', asked Guste.
'Because it can often be set to music, and because
     you don't have to read it, and particularly—'
'What comes next?'
'Portrait painting, of course, because of the pictures
     of the Emperor. The rest are not so important.'
'What about the novel (*der Roman*)?'
'That's not an art form at all! At least, thank God!,
     not a German one. You can tell by the name.'[91]

More significant, however, is the fact that so few of Wedekind's fellow artists, or Sternheim's, or Heym's, felt as they did. They discovered that, even in their own guild, they were lonely Cassandras. Like the great majority of Germany's church leaders and the mass of the professoriate, those who followed the arts preferred to do just that and to leave the great issues of society and politics to those in authority. This elicited an outburst of contempt from Hein-

---

[89] Bernard S. Meyers, *The German Expressionists: A Generation in Revolt* (concise edn., New York, 1966), p. 61.

[90] Thomas Mann chose to view the First World War as one more phase in the struggle between 'music and politics, Germanness and civilization' (the latter, in his dictionary, a derogatory term). See Thomas Mann, *Betrachtungen eines Unpolitischen* (Frankfurt-on-Main, 1956), p. 24. It was not accidental that revolutionary literary movements in Germany always either scorned or distrusted music. This was true of the Young Germans; Gutzkow spoke contemptuously of music as 'the unnatural use of a chance dexterity'. The Naturalists suspected it because it was too romantic to serve the cause of truth. Heinrich Hart claimed that it was unreliable and aroused base instincts.

[91] *Der Untertan*, concluding pages of Ch. 5.

rich Mann. For a whole generation now, he wrote in 1910, the German artist had betrayed his proper function either by silence or by explicit approbation of the forces that were debauching Germany and which were now threatening to destroy her. 'For decades he has worked . . . for the justification of the unspiritual, for the sophistical exculpation of the unjust, for his enemy to the death: Power.'[92]

The anger was wated and the implied appeal in vain. Germany's artists and writers were not to arouse themselves for a new intervention in politics until after the war and the national collapse which their lack of political responsibility had helped to cause.

---

[92] Heinrich Mann, 'Geist und Tat' (1910), in *Essays* (Berlin, 1960), p. 13.

VII
The New Course and the Deterioration of Germany's Foreign Position
1890–1897

Überraschend, gegensätzlich
  Hirnerweichlich, zickzackplötzlich,
Phrasenfruchtbar, überreichlich,
  Zickzackplötzlich, hirnerweichlich.

ALFRED KERR[1]

Initiative without tact is like a flood without dikes.

FRIEDRICH VON HOLSTEIN (1895)[2]

O N 28 February 1859 the Prussian Crown Princess wrote a letter to her mother, Queen Victoria of Great Britain, on the subject that was uppermost in her mind, the birth of her first child, which had taken place a month earlier. 'Your grandson', she wrote, 'is exceedingly lively and when awake will not be satisfied unless kept dancing about continually. He scratches his face and tears his caps and makes every sort of extraordinary little noise. I am so thankful, so happy, he is a boy. I longed for one more than I can describe. . . .'[3]

The infant prince was christened Frederick William Victor Albert; he is remembered in history as William II. His character seems to have been formed at birth, for his conduct in later life was much like that described by his mother. He was never satisfied unless he was in motion and, if there are no records of his continuing to vent his feelings on his clothes, there is no doubt that he made many extraordinary noises. Even before 1888 this energetic behaviour exasperated and exhausted many of those close to him, including his mother, who may in the end have regretted praying so hard for a

---

[1] 'Es war einmal', in Alfred Kerr, *Caprichos: Strophen des Nebenstroms* (Berlin, 1926), p. 185.
[2] *Holstein Papers* iii. 577.
[3] *Letters of the Empress Frederick*, ed. Sir Frederick Ponsonby (London, 1929), p. 20.

boy, and after he became Emperor it had more fateful repercussions, since it contributed both to the government's failure to come to grips with critical domestic problems and to the increasingly irresponsible course of Germany's foreign policy.

I

This was not immediately perceived when William came to the throne in 1888. Most people were impressed by the new ruler's vitality, his openness to new ideas, the diversity of his interests, and his personal charm. As his Court Marshal wrote later, William was 'a dazzling personality who fascinated everyone who appeared before him. He was well aware of his ability to do this and developed this talent with much effort and refinement to an extraordinary perfection.'[4] He could talk to business men, archaeologists, leaders of *Männergesangvereine*, directors of steamship lines, theatre producers, and ministers of education about their own subjects with enthusiasm and an impressive amount of factual knowledge.[5] After the first impression faded, however, they were apt to suspect that the facts had been memorized for their effect, which was often true, and that the enthusiasm was a symptom of dilettantism.

In a bitter moment, the theatre critic Alfred Kerr once wrote of his sovereign:

> Was man klar an ihm erkannt
> War der Mangel an Verstand.
> Sonst besass er alle Kräfte
> Für die Leitung der Geschäfte.[6]

This was a little unfair, but only a little. William had as much intelligence as any European sovereign and more than most, but his lack of discipline, his self-indulgence, his overdeveloped sense of theatre, and his fundamental misreading of history prevented him from putting it to effective use. As his tutors themselves admitted, his formal education had been neither thorough nor balanced, partly because he was preoccupied in his youth by his determination to overcome the physical handicap of having been born with an almost useless left arm and partly because of differences with his parents. But he never admitted any deficiency in this respect or tried seriously to repair it. He never acquired the *Gründlichkeit* that is associated

---

[4] Graf Zedlitz-Trützschler, *Zwölf Jahre am deutschen Kaiserhof* (Berlin, 1924), p. 8.

[5] See the examples given in *Das Wilhelminische Deutschland: Stimmen der Zeitgenossen*, ed. Georg Kotowski, Werner Pöls, and Gerhard A. Ritter (Frankfurt-on-Main and Hamburg, 1965), pp. 11–15.

[6] 'ER', in Kerr, *Caprichos*, p. 97.

with the Germans and, in consequence, never learned anything thoroughly, least of all the basic facts of political life at home and abroad that might have moderated his enthusiasms and tempered his impetuosity.

Unlike his brother monarch in Vienna, who was capable of working sixteen hours a day for days on end in his office in the Hofburg, William preferred the open spaces to the dank air of the study. He was constantly on the move, travelling around the country to open exhibitions and speak at town halls, going on elaborate hunting expeditions, voyaging to England or Constantinople. A regular feature of his year was a cruise in northern waters in his yacht, a trip that was so lengthy that the Foreign Ministry found it prudent to assign one of its officials to accompany the Emperor in case a sudden crisis should arise. On William's side, there was no pretence at working. The cruises were occasions on which he surrounded himself with cronies who spent their time playing practical jokes on each other (William was as fond of these as his ancestor King Frederick William I)[7] or carrying on long discussions of fantastic and useless subjects. The intellectual level was usually low. During the 1891 cruise Alfred Kiderlen-Wächter wrote from Bergen to his friend Holstein in the Foreign Ministry:

I would like to make one more brief *résumé, for your ear alone*, of my impressions of our trip. They are not exactly favourable in one respect: since last year, H.M.'s autocratic tendencies have markedly increased. This *sic volo sic jubeo* obtains in matters great and small. And—quite between ourselves—it is not accompanied by any serious scrutiny or weighing of the facts; he just talks himself into an opinion. Anyone in favour of it is then quoted as an authority; anyone who differs from it 'is being fooled'. . . . I would like to add *for your benefit* an anecdote that throws a sidelight on H.M.'s thought processes. H.M. is growing a beard, a fact that provides one of the more interesting topics of conversation on board. 'This will fix the portrait-painters.' 'They'll have to alter the imprint on the ten-mark and twenty-mark pieces!' 'People will collect coins showing me without a beard.' 'Yes,' and he banged hard on the table, 'with a beard like this one could thump on the table so hard that your Ministers would fall down with fright and lie flat on their faces!!!!!!!!' Comment unnecessary.[8]

William's ministers came to dread these voyages, for their master was apt to coming bounding back from them, tanned and fit and

---

[7] These sometimes had unpleasant results. See the case of Lieutenant von Hahnke whose resentment over the Emperor's behaviour to him led to an incident and ultimately to his suicide. J. C. G. Röhl, *Germany without Bismarck: The Crisis of Government in the Second Reich, 1890–1900* (Berkeley, 1967), p. 29.

[8] *Holstein Papers* iii. 383.

with a new set of ideas and policies which, in his characteristic style, he required to be put into effect immediately. It was of no consequence to him that this might vitiate months of careful ministerial work, contradict prior understandings with the parties, or contravene state or Reich law. The Emperor had small regard for these things, least of all for the niceties of constitutional practice.

In this respect, he strongly resembled his great uncle, Frederick William IV, refusing to allow the constitution, which he boasted he had never read, to come between him and his people. Like that ruler, and with even less excuse, he believed in the divine right of kings and constantly reminded his subjects that they should do so too. 'You realize', he admonished the Provincial Diet of Brandenburg in February 1891, 'that I regard my whole position and my task as having been imposed on me from heaven, and that I am called to the service of a Higher Being, to Whom I shall have to give reckoning later.'[9] Opposition to the orders of such a ruler might be understandable on the part of those who, like the Socialists, had no belief in the law of God and no sense of the accomplishments of the Hohenzollern dynasty. But it was never justifiable and was not to be tolerated among that class that owed feudal loyalty to the Crown—'Eine Opposition preußischen Adliger gegen ihren König ist ein Unding!'[10]—or among those charged with the execution of his policies. As for those elements in Parliament or the public who appealed to the constitution against their sovereign's will, they must be defied, even at the cost of an adverse reaction among the people. William wrote with pathos to his Chancellor in July 1892:

We Hohenzollerns are accustomed only to advance slowly and painfully amidst troubles, conflict, party division, and lack of appreciation. How often have my ancestors, most recently my grandfather, who rests with God, had to battle for measures in direct opposition to the will of the uncomprehending populace, which first opposed, then criticized, and finally blessed them. What do I care about popularity! For, as the guiding principles of my actions, I have only the dictates of my duty and the responsibility of my clear conscience towards God.[11]

William's ministers had to contend not only with the absolutist but also with the warrior prince. The Hohenzollerns, at least the ones who were remembered in the history books—the Great Elector, King Frederick William I, Frederick II—had been soldiers; so had the

[9] Wilhelm II, *Die Reden in den Jahren von 1888 bis 1905*, ed. Johannes Penzler (Leipzig, n. d.), iii. 171.
[10] Ibid. 275.
[11] *Holstein Papers* iii. 420.

new Emperor's grandfather, who had fought against Napoleon, his uncle, a noted cavalryman, who had led the First Army at König-grätz, and his father, whose capture of the height of Chlum had decided that battle. When he was twelve, he had watched from a balcony as William I and his sons rode down Unter den Linden after the victory over France, and he never forgot that experience. He was determined to become a soldier himself and, with dogged per-sistance, acquired the ability, despite his physical infirmity, to con-trol heavy cavalry horses and to lead troops in tactical exercises. Even after becoming Emperor, he insisted, in the first years, on participating actively in army manœuvres, which filled his ministers with apprehension, since they were afraid he would kill himself, and exasperated the professional soldiers. After the manœuvres of 1890, Waldersee, who had succeeded Moltke as Chief of Staff, wrote: 'I am convinced that the monarch has a certain understanding of parade-ground movements, not, however, of real troop-leading. What is missing is an experience of war . . . [He] is extraordinarily restless, dashes back and forth, is much too far forward in the fighting line, intervenes in the leadership of the generals, gives countless and often contradictory orders, and scarcely listens to his advisers. He always wants to win and, when the decision of the judge is against him, takes it ill.'[12] In a later manœuvre, during the time of Schlieffen, William is supposed, after having led a cavalry attack and been repulsed, to have ordered the blowing of 'Das Ganze halt!', after which he detached a brigade from the enemy and resumed the attack, this time suc-cessfully. When this was reported to the Chief of Staff on the *Feldherrnhügel*, he sat silent for a moment, then adjusted his monocle and drawled, 'Originelle Idee!'[13]

Despite his dedication, the Emperor never became anything more than a not very gifted amateur. Nevertheless, during the twenty-six years that followed his accession, he played at soldiers. His happiest hours were those in which, beautifully uniformed, he galloped at the head of his regiment and impressed the crowds with his martial bearing and the gleam of his swung sabre. Military dress became an obsession with him, and he came to typify that cult of the uniform which Hermann Broch, in a passage in the novel *The Sleep-Walkers*, described as transforming the man in uniform into a property of what he was wearing.[14] He wore military dress whenever possible, if

---

[12] Waldersee, *Denkwürdigkeiten* ii. 145.

[13] *Die Weltbühne*, xxii (1926), pt. 2, 751.

[14] This was, perhaps, a sign of William's basic insecurity. Broch goes on to say: '. . . a generic uniform provides its wearer with a definite line of demarcation between his

not that of his own regiments, then of foreign ones with which he had an honorary attachment. He saw to it that wherever he went he was surrounded by a cloud of uniforms; he dined to *Ulanenmusik;* and he preferred military companions, manners, and advice to any other.

This last ominous circumstance is illustrated by the ordering of the Emperor's working week. To be sure, he never worked for very long even when at home, but there is no doubt that a disproportionate amount of the time he spent on official business was devoted to military matters. He rarely met any of his Prussian ministers in person, except the War Minister, who had a weekly audience. The Reich Chancellor, except on extraordinary occasions, saw the Emperor on Saturday afternoon, although this was not invariable. In contrast, the Chief of the General Staff and the Chief of the Admiralty (later replaced by the Chief of the Marine Cabinet) each had one regular audience a week, while the Chief of the Military Cabinet met the sovereign every Tuesday, Thursday, and Saturday morning.

This official schedule does not adequately describe the predominance of the military in William's councils. One of his first actions after becoming Emperor was to reorganize and enlarge the *maison militaire*, the group of adjutants and aides-de-camp who were customarily assigned to the court, and to transform it into a Royal Headquarters which included a significantly larger number of generals *à la suite* and Flügeladjutanten drawn from the Guards regiments, as well as the Chiefs of the Military and Marine Cabinets. This body was unified after 1889 under a Commandant of Headquarters who accompanied the Emperor when he was travelling, recorded and transmitted his orders on military and other matters, and was often privileged to be present at the audiences of other officials.[15]

This development marked a further step in the disintegration of

---

person and the world; it is like a hard casing against which one's personality and the world beat sharply and distinctly and are differentiated from each other; for it is the uniform's true function to manifest and ordain order in the world, to arrest the confusion and flux of life, just as it conceals whatever in the human body is soft and flowing, covering up the soldier's underclothes and skin, and decreeing that sentries on guard should wear white gloves. So when in the morning a man has fastened up his uniform to the last button, he acquires a second and thicker hide, and feels that he has returned to his more essential and steadfast being. Closed up in his hard casing, braced in with straps and belts, he begins to forget his own undergarments, and the uncertainty of life, yes, life itself, recedes to a distance.' Herman Broch, *The Sleep-Walkers*, trans. from the German by Willa and Edwin Muir (New York, 1947), pp. 20–1.

[15] On all this, see Craig, *Prussian Army*, pp. 238–40.

the unity of army organization that had begun in 1883;[16] but, more important, it represented the establishment of one more powerful and irresponsible agency in an already chaotic governmental structure. The influence of the adjutants, with whom the Emperor was always more intimate than with his civilian ministers, worried even his warmest admirers. Philipp Eulenburg noted with distress that his royal master appeared, under the combined influence of 'military Hohenzollernism and self-hypnotism', to have convinced himself that anyone in a Guards uniform was the quintessence of political wisdom.[17] This concern was justified, for the Emperor was soon employing spur-jingling aides-de-camp on diplomatic missions that would have been better left in the hands of professionals, and soliciting their advice on any problem that happened to be on his mind at the moment.

This greatly complicated the work of his ministers, not only in domestic affairs, as we shall see in the next chapter, but in the field for which William soon convinced himself that he had a special aptitude, namely foreign relations. His conviction in this regard was encouraged, certainly, by the maladroitness of those charged officially with the conduct of foreign affairs after 1890, but this did not change the fact that his ventures in diplomacy had deplorable results.

II

One can argue plausibly that the first foreign political action taken in what was sometimes grandiloquently called the Wilhelmine New Course was the most crucial of all those made between 1890 and the outbreak of the First World War and that it set in train the whole chain of calamity that led toward that catastrophe. If this is true, however, it has to be noted that, on this occasion, William II played an essentially passive role, the decisive force being exerted by the Foreign Ministry.

During the crowded week that saw Bismarck's dismissal and the resignation of his son Herbert from the post of Secretary of State for Foreign Affairs, the Emperor had a conversation with the Russian ambassador Count Shuvalov about pending negotiations for the renewal of the Reinsurance Treaty. William made it clear that he was willing to come to an agreement as soon as possible, and on 21 March 1890 he instructed his new Chancellor to take the matter in hand.

This was Leo von Caprivi, a soldier by profession who had served

[16] See above, Ch. V, p. 163.
[17] Johannes Haller, *Aus dem Leben des Fürsten Philipp zu Eulenburg-Hertefeld* (Berlin, 1924), p. 245.

with distinction in the wars against Austria and France and in the subsequent years of peace. He had a reputation for administrative skill, energy, and independence of mind, qualities that had been particularly marked during his term as Chief of the Admiralty in the years 1882–6, when, after introducing a series of reforms that did much to give the fledgling service a strategical doctrine and a sense of identification, he had resigned because the Emperor was consulting his bureau chiefs without his knowledge.[18] He was also possessed of a commendable sense of realism. He had not wanted to succeed Bismarck, because he had no illusions concerning the difficulties this would entail, not the least of which would be those arising from the inevitable unfavourable comparisons between his performance and that of his predecessor. He suspected that Bismarck's immediate successor was doomed to failure, and he accepted the assignment only because he felt it was his duty to do so.[19]

Caprivi's undeniable talents were balanced by grave deficiencies. In both domestic and foreign affairs he suffered from a lack of basic knowledge and of that intuitive sense upon which successful politicians rely. In the former, this led him in most things to follow a line that was characterized not by boldness but by diffidence and which not only underlined the difference in style between Bismarck and himself but involved him in difficulties that a more confident politician might have avoided. In foreign affairs, his awareness of his own limitations led him to defer to the experts.

When the Emperor approached him on the Russian matter, Caprivi had no Secretary of State to guide him, for Marschall von Bieberstein, who was to fill that post, had not yet been appointed. Caprivi therefore went to the Foreign Ministry himself to look for a copy of the treaty. The only senior official on duty was Friedrich von Holstein, the enormously knowledgeable but crotchety councillor who had been brought into the Ministry by Bismarck in 1876 and who had developed decided views of his own concerning what Germany's foreign policy should be. Holstein gave the Chancellor the necessary papers but was startled to learn that the Emperor was apparently ready to renew the treaty. In some agitation, he urged Caprivi to make no decision until he had discussed the matter with

---

[18] It was not unusual for a general to be chief of the naval service. Caprivi's predecessor, Ulrich von Stosch, had also been a soldier. On Caprivi's resignation, see H. O. Meisner, 'Der Reichskanzler Caprivi', *Zeitschrift für die gesamte Staatswissenschaft*, iii (1955).

[19] See J. Alden Nichols, *Germany after Bismarck: The Caprivi Era, 1890–1894* (Cambridge, 1958), pp. 29 ff.

the other senior councillors of the Ministry, and he arranged a meeting for 23 March.

To Holstein it was essential that the Emperor be persuaded to change his mind. The complexity and ambiguities of Bismarck's foreign policy had always distressed him, and he had convinced himself that the Reinsurance Treaty merely made his country vulnerable to Russian blackmail. In addition, another fear was now troubling him, namely that the renewed treaty might subsequently be used as a lever to bring Bismarck back to power, an event that would certainly eventuate in his own dismissal.[20] This last point Holstein did not see fit to mention when, together with Berchem, the Under-Secretary of State, and Ludwig von Raschdau, he sat down with the Chancellor on the arranged date. But his colleagues and he did emphasize heavily and unanimously the other objections that Holstein had often expressed in the past: namely, that the Reinsurance Treaty gave great advantages to Russia without any significant reciprocal advantage for Germany, since it neither protected Germany from a French attack nor excluded the possibility of Russia's concluding a treaty with France; that in recent years the Russian Government had shown little gratitude for these favours and had not hesitated to flirt with Germany's enemies in time of crisis; that the text of the treaty was incompatible with Germany's engagements to Austria-Hungary and Italy and clearly contradicted the obligations of its alliance with Romania; and that this fact gave the Russian Government the power either to weaken Germany's other alliances by revealing the precise nature of the tie between St. Petersburg and Berlin or to exact new concessions from Germany by threatening to do so. Renewal, in short, would perpetuate a policy that was disingenuous, needlessly complicated, and potentially dangerous. Far better to set a simpler, less hectic, and more honourable course.[21]

These arguments, which were soon supported by Schweinitz and Radowitz, convinced Caprivi, the more so because he was aware that these two Bismarckian ambassadors could not be described as instruments of Holstein; and in the days that followed they convinced the Emperor as well. Despite desperate attempts by the Russians to salvage at least a shadow of the old alliance,[22] the Russian tie was irretrievably snapped, and the old Bismarckian diplomatic system became a thing of the past.

The strongest intellectual force in the new order of foreign policy

[20] On this, see Rich, *Holstein* i. 316.
[21] See, *inter alia*, Raschdau, *Unter Bismarck und Caprivi*, pp. 142 f.
[22] See Schweinitz, *Denkwürdigkeiten*, ii. 435 ff.

that this action ushered in was Holstein, who was at the height of his influence between 1890 and 1897. Caprivi quickly acquired confidence in him;[23] and Marschall, a former Badenese envoy whose speciality was international law, was too insecure to question his judgement. According to Raschdau, Holstein had a good-natured contempt for these nominal superiors and when his fellow counsellor expressed concern about their lack of experience in foreign affairs, said: 'These matters we shall take care of if necessary *without* them and, if it comes to that, *in opposition* to them!'[24] Within the Foreign Ministry, Holstein's authority was virtually uncontested, particularly after Berchem, feeling that Marschall was slighting him, resigned and was replaced by Freiherr von Rotenhan, former minister to Argentina, who soon proved himself a complete misfit.

In these circumstances, Holstein's judgement became predominant also in the choice of the chiefs of mission abroad and, between 1890 and 1893, he was principally responsible for farreaching changes. Ambassadors who had made their careers under Bismarck were either encouraged to retire or transferred to capitals of lesser importance. Thus Kurd von Schlözer, with whom Holstein had served in Bismarck's St. Petersburg mission and whom he had disliked ever since, lost his post at the Vatican, and Ferdinand von Stumm, a self-declared Bismarckian, was forced out of Madrid. On the grounds that he was too pro-Russian, Radowitz was removed from Constantinople and given Stumm's post, the Embassy at the Sublime Porte falling to H. L. von Radolin-Radolinski, a close friend of Holstein. After complaining fruitlessly to Caprivi about this kind of favouritism in the Foreign Office,[26] Schweinitz gave up his assignment in St. Petersburg and was replaced by the former military plenipotentiary in the Tsar's suite, General von Werder.[27] Simi-

---

[23] See Caprivi's remarks about Holstein as reported in Radowitz, *Aufzeichnungen und Erinnerungen* ii. 326 f.

[24] Raschdau, *Unter Bismarck und Caprivi*, p. 142.

[25] See Kurd von Schlözer, *Petersburger Briefe*, ed. Leopold von Schlözer (Stuttgart, 1921) and *Letzte römische Briefe*, pp. 183 ff.

[26] Schweinitz says he told Caprivi: 'A personality who is not quite right in the head exercises too much authority in the Foreign Ministry' (*Denkwürdigkeiten*, ii. 443). He told his wife that he had also warned the Chancellor that 'the Holstein–Kiderlen administration [was] damaging the imperial service; everything is done in accordance with personal predilection or dislike; only insignificant people are given advancement; etc.' Caprivi said there was nothing he could do about it. Rogge, *Holstein und Hohenlohe*, p. 395. On Holstein's fears of Radowitz and Schweinitz, see Hatzfeldt, *Nachgelassene Papiere* ii. 766 f.

[27] Late in 1876 Werder infuriated Bismarck by misusing his office in St. Petersburg. For details, see Craig, *Prussian Army*, pp. 263–5.

larly, Graf Solms vacated the Embassy in Rome, apparently as a result of pressure brought to bear upon him by the Emperor at the behest of Philipp Eulenburg,[28] and Bernhard von Bülow, a confidant of both Eulenburg and Holstein, assumed his duties. Finally, Prince Reuß was encouraged to resign from his Vienna post, and his putative successor, Karl Graf von Wedel, later Staathalter in the Reichsland,[29] was moved to Stockholm instead so that the pleasant assignment on the Danube could be given to Philipp Eulenburg.[30] Only two of Bismarck's 'great prophets' retained their positions, Hatzfeldt in London, for whom Holstein had long felt respect and affection, and Münster in Paris, who was too lethargic to represent a political threat and too competent to replace easily.

This purge of the old guard was too thorough to escape public notice. Maximilian Harden, a shrewd and energetic political observer, launched a series of articles in his paper *Die Zukunft* describing the devastation in what he called 'The Marschall Islands';[31] and, on 24 October 1893, the satirical journal *Kladderadatsch* published an article called 'A Fourth at Skat' attacking Holstein, Kiderlen-Wächter, now his chief aide in the Foreign Ministry, and Eulenburg as influence-mongers. The latter article and those that followed it, revealing much embarrassing material about the methods of operation employed by the three associates, drove Holstein into fits of near hysteria in which he urged Eulenburg to secure the dismissal of the Berlin chief of police because he was unable to detect the author of the *Kladderadatsch* articles and expressed indignation that the Emperor had not made a public statement on his behalf.[32]

Holstein always responded with pathological fury to personal attacks, and this probably accounted for his exaggerated reaction on this occasion, which led Eulenburg to fear that it might result in a nervous breakdown. But at the same time Holstein was convinced that the Press attacks were part of a plot to bring the Bismarcks back to power, and he was aware that he was vulnerable to the attacks of those who advocated that course, not only because of the changes in

[28] See Rich, *Holstein* i. 404 n.

[29] See below, Ch. VIII, p. 297.

[30] See Wedel, *Zwischen Kaiser und Kanzler*, pp. 190 f.; Waldersee, *Denkwürdigkeiten* ii. 303 f., 310, 316.

[31] Raschdau, *Unter Bismarck und Caprivi*, pp. 227 f.

[32] The details are in Rich, *Holstein* i. 403 ff. The man who inspired the articles was apparently Geheimer Legationsrat von Bothmer of the Foreign Ministry, a Bismarckian and a friend of Raschdau. See Ernst Jäckh, *Kiderlen-Wächter der Staatsmann und Mensch* (2 vols., Berlin, 1925), i. 98.

the Foreign Service but because German foreign policy since Bismarck's fall had not been conspicuously successful.

Part of the rationale for jettisoning the Reinsurance Treaty had been that, once rid of that embarrassing arrangement, the German Government could create a healthier and more coherent system in which the junior members of the Triple Alliance and the Danubian federates of that combination would feel a stronger obligation to accept German leadership and in which Great Britain, already associated, since the Mediterranean Agreements of 1887, with Austria-Hungary and Italy, would be persuaded to give formal guarantees to protect the interests of those Powers and eventually to become a fully fledged member of the Triple Alliance. These hopes were almost immediately confounded. The effects of the lapsing of the Reinsurance Treaty were the exact opposite of what had been expected in the Foreign Ministry. The British saw no reason to increase their obligations. In 1887 it had seemed necessary to make commitments to the Austrians and the Italians in order to balance Russian power in the Near East and French power in the Mediterranean. Now this was no longer true, for, as the Russians did the obvious thing and began to move closer to France, it was clear that the Germans must protect the interests of their junior allies or see the dissolution of the Triple Alliance. As for the Austrians and Italians, the shift in European alignments had given them new leverage. They were now in a position to resist German demands or to raise the price of their continued collaboration by hinting that they might be forced to consider moving into the Franco-Russian orbit.

These unpleasant truths began to emerge almost immediately after the breaking of the Russian connection. In July 1890, presumably to remove a source of friction and to prepare the way for more comprehensive understandings, the Caprivi government concluded a colonial agreement with the British. It showed an unparalleled generosity on the part of the Germans and was much criticized for that very reason. In return for a narrow strip of territory that gave German South West Africa access to the Zambezi River, a common boundary between German East Africa and the Belgian Congo, and the island of Helgoland in the North Sea, the German Government accepted British claims to vast tracts of territory that gave them possession of the sources of the Nile and access to that river from the African east coast.[33] Caprivi and Holstein had no enthusiasm for

---

[33] On the negotiations of this agreement and its terms, see William Langer, *The Diplomacy of Imperialism* (rev. edn., New York, 1951), pp. 6 f. On its unpopularity in Germany, see Hatzfeldt, *Nachgelassene Papiere* ii. 782 ff. and notes.

colonial acquisition. To them, the lopsidedness of the bargain was inconsequential as long as it laid the basis for agreements with the British in Europe.

The British Government was not, however, prepared for anything like that. Lord Salisbury was pleased with the African agreement and with the state of Anglo-German relations; but, when Hatzfeldt raised the question of new agreements or argued that British support of Italy's ambitions in North Africa might discourage that Power from trafficking with the French, he was not interested. He seemed to be unsure of the judgement of the new government in Berlin and wrote to Lord Dufferin in Rome: 'I do not like to disregard the plain anxiety of my German friends. But it is not wise to be guided too much by their advice now. Their Achitophel is gone. They are much pleasanter and easier to deal with; but one misses the extraordinary penetration of the old man.'[34]

Salisbury was no more forthcoming a year later when Hatzfeldt returned to the charge. During the negotiations for the renewal of the Triple Alliance, the Italian Government had shown an alarming awareness of its new power of manœuvre. It had demanded that the German Government assume the obligation of maintaining the *status quo* in the whole Mediterranean area and had accepted a compromise reluctantly and only at the cost of an extension of Germany's pledge of 1887 to protect Italy's interests in North Africa and, in addition, some economic assistance to improve Italy's position in its current tariff war with France.[35] The negotiations had been accompanied by continued Italian hints that there were other ways to solve Italy's difficulties; and, when they were over, both Holstein and Hatzfeldt were convinced that there was a strong possibility of the Italians defecting to the French unless the British could be persuaded to give Italy a firm guarantee of support in case the French should attack them.[36] Hatzfeldt's attempts to convince Salisbury of the advisability of such a British pledge fell on deaf ears. The British Prime Minister pointed out that the prevailing sentiment in Parliament was opposed to new European involvements, and the discussions were broken off.

[34] Lady Gwendolen Cecil, *Life of Robert Marquis of Salisbury* (4 vols., London, 1921–32), iv. 374–5. On Hatzfeldt's attempts to interest him in supporting Italy, see Hatzfeldt, *Nachgelassene Papiere* ii. 793, 794, 798 f., 807.

[35] The reciprocal trade agreement of 1892 was Caprivi's means of satisfying this demand. See below, Ch. VIII, p. 253.

[36] Franco-Italian relations had reached a nadir as a result of the renewal of the Triple Alliance, and Crispi's fears of a French attack on the port of Spezia did not seem entirely incredible.

A month later, in July 1891, a French naval squadron visited the Russian port of Kronstadt and received an ecstatic reception. This was the first step in the Franco-Russian *rapprochement*, and its importance was not lost upon Holstein and his envoy in London. The chauvinists in both countries would be heartened and the chances of war greatly enhanced, Holstein felt.[37] Surely, the British would now see the light and make the kind of arrangements—a new treaty with Italy, a renewed guarantee of Turkey—that would commit them clearly to opposition to Franco-Russian ambitions. But the British did nothing of the kind. The Salisbury cabinet's position in the country was weakening rapidly, and the Prime Minister, faced with elections in 1892, had no intention of offending public opinion by making new commitments abroad. Hatzfeldt's attempts to encourage Anglo-Turkish security talks were as unsuccessful as his previous attempts to galvanize the British into activity. Moreover, there was little hope that he would be any more successful later, for when the elections came in July 1892, the Liberals came back into office, under the leadership of the pronounced isolationist Gladstone. When the anxious Hatzfeldt visited the new Foreign Secretary, Lord Rosebery, in order to discover whether the new government envisaged any major changes in foreign policy, he was unsuccessful in persuading Rosebery to admit the continued validity of the Mediterranean Agreements and had to be satisfied with a personal declaration that, if France should attack Italy without provocation, Britain would come to Italy's aid in its own interest.[38]

That Holstein's calculations had proved to be false was underlined by the fact that the Caprivi government, in November 1892, felt compelled to lay before the Reichstag a bill calling for sizeable increases in the army and to justify it by holding before the German people the threat of a two-front war.[39] All of this was grist to the mill of the Bismarckian Press which now pulled out all the stops and belaboured the Caprivi government for having brought the French and Russians together while following the will-o'-the-wisp of an alliance with Britain, a notoriously unreliable Power that was now clearly intent upon using the Triple Alliance for its own purposes while giving nothing in return. It was a plausible argument that was hard to refute, and it had a perceptible effect upon both public opinion, which was not used to the unsureness that now seemed to characterize German policy,[40] and the Emperor, who gradually

[37] Rich, *Holstein* i. 338.   [38] *G.P.* viii. 89.   [39] See below, Ch. VIII, p. 258.
[40] On the growing dissatisfaction of public opinion with imperial policy, see Sontag, *Germany and England*, Ch. 9.

began to feel that he should give the direction that was lacking.

Holstein and Hatzfeldt still believed that the logic of events would persuade the British that they must break out of their isolationist stance. Surely, it must occur to them that the increasing intimacy of France and Russia menaced them in the Far East, in Egypt, and in the Mediterranean, and surely, when the danger became evident, they would revise their position. But when, in the course of 1893, two events occurred that could be regarded as threats to British power, the British Government, to the exasperation of the Wilhelmstraße, did not react as it might have been expected to. In July 1893, when a confrontation between French and British forces on the Mekong River threatened war between them over Siam, the British abandoned the contested territory to the French. In October the visit of a Russian naval squadron to Toulon, a blatant advertisement of Franco-Russian naval strength in the Mediterranean, was no more successful in generating an effective British response, or, for that matter, in propelling Britain any closer to the Triple Alliance.[41]

These events completed the Emperor's disillusionment with Great Britain, which, he now concluded, would be worthless as an ally even if it deigned to become one. In his usual mercurial way, William II proceeded to talk himself into the notion that the breach with Russia was not a real one and that economic concessions and some assurances to the Russian Government concerning German disinterestedness in the Near East and the question of the Straits would nullify the new Franco-Russian association, which was not really directed against Germany in any case, and about which he was sure the Russians were not enthusiastic. He became particularly insistent on an economic accommodation with the Russians and, when Caprivi's negotiations for a trade treaty succeeded at the end of 1893, on terms that were very favourable to the Russians, he defied agrarian-conservative opinion and threw himself into the fight to secure acceptance by the Reichstag, reportedly saying that he had no desire for a war with Russia 'just for the sake of a couple of hundred stupid *Junker*'.[42]

Given the Emperor's impulsiveness, there was nothing extra-

[41] See Hatzfeldt, *Nachgelassene Papiere* ii. 919 ff., 930 f., 940 ff., 947 ff. The response came in the form of naval increases, but not until after Gladstone's retirement in March 1894. He had blocked earlier action by insisting that the fleet was adequate 'to perform all the purposes for which it exists'. See Langer, *Diplomacy of Imperialism*, p. 49.

[42] Hans-Jürgen Puhle, *Agrarische Interessenpolitik und der preußische Konservatismus im Wilhelminischen Reich 1893–1914* (Hanover, 1966), p. 299 n. 19. Caprivi had been negotiating with the Russians since 1891, the year in which he had concluded his other

ordinary about this volte-face. More surprising was the fact that the author of the foreign policy of the New Course followed his master's example. Holstein was never at his best in dealing with the British—his rigid mind was constantly exasperated by their insistent distrust of logic—and he became definitely disenchanted with them when the British electorate, at a time when the nation should have been finding new allies, returned Gladstone to office. In the course of the following year he actually began to speculate upon the advantages of leaving the English to their own devices, of allowing the Triple Alliance to expire without renewal, and of restricting Germany's commitments to alliances with Austria-Hungary and Russia, forswearing any interest in Romania, Bulgaria, Turkey, or the Straits.[43]

This was a return to the Bismarckian system with a vengeance, indeed, a return to the pre-1879 Bismarckian system, and it was of course utterly impractical. By the end of 1893 the Russians had concluded a military convention with France, and this was soon to be transformed into a formal defensive alliance. They were not going to abandon this for an outworn system that had never operated to their advantage in any case. Nor did they regard the prospect of tariff reductions as something that should divert them. There were people in Russian governmental departments who read German newspapers. They were perfectly aware of the rage that the tariff negotiations were causing among the East Elbian landowners; they knew about the agitations of the Bund der Landwirte; and they were conscious of the fact that a favourable trade agreement might be of short duration.[44] The belief of William II and Holstein that a revivification of the Russo-German alliance was a practical option was illusory, but, unfortunately for them, it was a long time before they realized this. Meanwhile it gave them a sense of false confidence, which lead them into some new and disastrous experiments.

III

In 1894 Paul Hatzfeldt sighed sadly that, if only his countrymen would learn to sit quietly and wait, broiled turtle-doves would fly

---

reciprocal trade agreements (see below, Ch. VIII). By 1893 the motivation had become political rather than economical.

[43] Rich, *Holstein* i. 358. As far as the Straits were concerned, the Emperor, in response to a question about what the Germans would do if Russia attacked them, told the Austrian Foreign Minister Kálnoky, in September 1893, that Germany would not consider this as a *casus belli*. See *G.P.* ix, nos. 2138, 2145.

[44] See below, Ch. VIII, p. 259.

into their mouths; as it was, however, they defeated their own interests, by 'incessant hysterical vacillations'.[45] Having swung from alliance with Russia to intensive wooing of Great Britain, they now fell back to a middle position, a policy of keeping all the options open—that is, of seeking to improve relations with Russia while not entirely abandoning their efforts in London. They soon, however, became impatient with this unheroic waiting game. Conscious of the fact that, in the eyes of public opinion, German policy seemed directionless and unproductive, they elected to add an element of vitality to it by becoming more active overseas.

This last idea seems to have been inspired by Paul Kayser, head of the Colonial Section of the Foreign Ministry, an ambitious man who had been brought into the service by Bismarck and given unusual preferment by him and had then been one of the first to abandon his benefactor in 1890.[46] Kayser's theory was that, in view of the interest of the German people in colonial affairs and the widespread disapproval of the Anglo–German Agreement of 1890, the government would gain prestige and perhaps profit by making its presence felt in overseas areas and by intervening in disputes between other colonial Powers, taking sides or acting as mediator as its interest dictated.

The trouble with this conception was that it was guided by no logical plan; it simply involved waiting for something to turn up and then deciding what to do about it. Moreover, it promised to involve Germany in continual embroilments with Great Britain, because Britain was the most active of the colonial Powers and consequently the one most likely to create opportunities for German meddling. To Kayser, however, and to William II, who adopted the idea with enthusiasm, this was an advantage, for it was an effective way of refuting charges that the government was too deferential to the British. Holstein had less faith than his sovereign in colonial involvements, but he nevertheless regarded the new departure as a possible means of demonstrating to the British that it was better to have Germany as a friend than as an enemy and of persuading them to be more amenable to the idea of strengthening their ties to the Triple Alliance.

From London Hatzfeldt protested that the whole business was inherently inconsistent. If the British were harassed by colonial disputes, they would hardly be inclined to draw nearer the Power

---

[45] Hermann von Eckardstein, *Lebenserinnerungen und politische Denkwürdigkeiten* (2 vols., Leipzig, 1919–20), ii. 161.

[46] Walter Frank, 'Der Geheime Rat Paul Kayser', *Historische Zeitschrift*, clxviii (1943), 320; Erich Eyck, *Das persönliche Regiment Wilhelms II* (Zurich, 1948), pp. 112 ff.

that generated them. Moreover, since they were aware that Germany wanted them to give concrete guarantees to the Triple Alliance, they would find it difficult to see why they should be expected to pay for the privilege of doing so by making colonial concessions as well.[47] The point was well taken, but it did not deter the implementation of the new policy. Nor did what appeared momentarily to be a major breakthrough in the negotiations with Whitehall.

In January 1894 Lord Rosebery instructed his new ambassador to Constantinople, Sir Philip Currie, to stop off in Vienna on his way to his post and to discuss Near Eastern affairs with the Austrian Foreign Minister, Kálnoky. Currie found that Kálnoky was fearful of imminent Russian action at the Straits and wanted to know whether Britain was prepared to maintain its traditional policy of defending Constantinople. If it were not, Austria would be forced, because of Italy's current weakness and Germany's disinterestedness, to retreat from the position it had adopted during the Bulgarian crisis and restrict itself in the future to defending its interests in the Balkans. Currie's reports to London galvanized Rosebery into action. At the end of January he told the Austrian ambassador in London: 'I assure you that I am absolutely determined to maintain the *status quo* in the Straits question, and that I would not recoil from the danger of involving England in a war with Russia.' On the other hand, he went on, if France should intervene, the British fleet could not defend Constantinople against the combined forces of the two Powers. 'In such a case, we should require the assistance of the Triple Alliance to hold France in check.'[48]

The Austrians were more than satisfied with this response, and it might have been expected that the Germans would have felt the same way, since Rosebery's proposal was marked by a greater degree of forthcomingness than the British Government had shown since 1890. Instead the Germans regarded it as a clumsy British trick, designed to get something for nothing. What the British were asking for, Caprivi answered,[49] was the right to go to war with Russia at a moment of their own choosing, while Germany would have to take on the onus of keeping France out or attacking if it came in, since it was obvious that France would not be deterred by the threat of

[47] Sontag, *Germany and England*, p. 286. See e.g. Hatzfeldt, *Nachgelassene Papiere* ii. 982 ff.

[48] *G.P.* ix, nos. 216 ff.; William L. Langer, *The Franco-Russian Alliance, 1890–1894* (Cambridge, Mass., 1929), pp. 376–9.

[49] Holstein seems to have had relatively little to do with the matter, for he was distracted by the *Kladderadatsch* affair and the Russian trade negotiations. See Rich, *Holstein* i. 364 n.

Austrian and Italian action alone. Moreover, the Triple Alliance was expected to give this pledge in advance, which was clearly impossible at a time when Germany was pursuing its goal of weakening the Franco-Russian connection by negotiating the new trade agreement with St. Petersburg.[50] 'We might jeopardize this success,' Caprivi wrote, 'if we gave England the opportunity to report to Russia any words of ours that were unfavourable to her in the question of the Dardanelles.'[51] The Austrians pleaded that the Rosebery offer might at least be taken as a basis for negotiations, and, although they could not budge Caprivi, continued their talks with the British until July 1894. But the Germans had already begun their overseas activities, and as a result the gulf between Great Britain and the Triple Alliance widened significantly.

No one could accuse the Germans of a lack of energy. In April 1894 they filed a claim for sole possession of the Samoan Islands;[52] in June they violently protested the legality of an Anglo-Congolese treaty concluded the previous month; and in the autumn of the year they quarrelled with the British over the recognition of the Sultan of Morocco, the boundaries of the Sudan, the future of Portugal's colonies, and the policy to be adopted toward Turkey as a result of the Armenian massacres.[53] Nor did Caprivi's supercession by Hohenlohe in October 1894 cause any slackening in this frenetic activity. The year 1895 saw an ill-considered German intervention in Far Eastern affairs that was inspired in the first instance by an unwarranted suspicion that Great Britain was about to seize Shanghai,[54] an announcement by the Emperor that the British Gov-

---

[50] The trade agreement was ratified in March 1894.

[51] For the German position, *G.P.* ix. 134–44. See also Langer, *Diplomacy of Imperialism*, pp. 52–6.

[52] The government of the Samoan Islands was, in accordance with a treaty of 1889, exercised jointly by Great Britain, Germany, and the United States. In March 1894 there was an insurrection, and the Germans thought that the U.S. Government wished to withdraw from the supervisory board. This led them to approach the British and ask, in effect, that the British withdraw too, leaving Germany in possession. This, Marschall explained to Hatzfeldt, would make an excellent impression on German public opinion. See Paul M. Kennedy, *The Samoan Tangle* (New York, 1974), pp. 108 ff.

[53] Rich, *Holstein* i. 374.

[54] In August 1894 war broke out between Japan and China over Korea. The Japanese quickly demonstrated their superiority, and the Chinese sued for peace in January 1895. The peace terms imposed by Japan were so onerous that the European Powers with Far Eastern interests were disturbed and France and Russia intervened. William II was convinced from an early date that the situation would lead to a general land-grab led by the English and was insistent that Germany should also intervene, despite the fact that it had virtually no interests, commercial or otherwise, in the Far East. For a scathing critique of German intervention, see Erich Brandenburg, *From*

ernment was intending to give the Straits to Russia and that he wouldn't allow it,[55] and the beginnings of friction over the Transvaal question. And 1896 was the year of the famous telegram from William II to President Paul Kruger of the Transvaal, which was occasioned by Dr. Leander Starr Jameson's attempt to overthrow Kruger's government and which brought Anglo–German relations to an all-time low.

It is not intended here to suggest that the German Government was always unjustified in taking the action that it did. The British could be extremely high-handed, and their actions on occasion deserved to be challenged. For example, certain articles of the Anglo–Congolese Treaty of May 1894 were questionable from the standpoint of both legality and elementary honesty and were patently designed to evade the provisions of the Anglo–German Agreement of 1890 (which provided for a common border between German East Africa and the Congo State) by giving the British a corridor that would at some future time assure the completion of the all-British route from Cairo to the Cape. The German Government had every right to object. Similarly, Jameson's raid into the Transvaal was an action sufficiently reprehensible to warrant some expression of German indignation.

But, even when they had sound grounds for their actions, the German interventions were apt to be abrupt and menacing, and the language used insulting or violent. In the Congo dispute,[56] the British agreed immediately to amend the offensive parts of the treaty, only to find that the Germans were not satisfied with this and had joined the French in an attempt to set the whole treaty aside. Later Lord Rosebery complained that, in the communications addressed to him, the German Government had adopted a tone 'which she might properly use in addressing Monaco'. The bullying style was in this case counter-productive. Rosebery responded to it by warning the other members of the Triple Alliance that German conduct might force the British Government to reconsider its whole position with respect to the Near East and the Mediterranean, a statement that caused much recrimination between Rome and

---

Bismarck to the World War (Oxford, 1933), pp. 53 ff. See also Langer, *Diplomacy of Imperialism*, pp. 167 ff. and esp. pp. 177 ff.

[55] In a conversation with Colonel Swaine, the British military attaché, on 24 October 1895, the Emperor made this accusation apparently on the basis of a speech of 15 August by Lord Salisbury in which he expressed doubts about whether the European Powers could preserve the integrity of the Ottoman Empire indefinitely.

[56] The best account of this dispute is in Langer, *Diplomacy of Imperialism*, pp. 101–44.

Vienna on the one hand and Berlin on the other.[57] Nor was this the only occasion on which the tone and language of German diplomatic communications left a legacy of bitterness behind. At Shimoneseki in April 1895, when the French, Russian, and German governments intervened to urge Japan to renounce the clause in the Sino-Japanese peace treaty that called for the cession of the Liaotung peninsula to Japan, the remarks of the German minister were both threatening and peremptory and were long resented in Tokyo.[58] Finally, it should be noted that the Emperor's personal interventions in foreign policy—and it was in these years that they increased rapidly in number and frequency—were marked by a higher degree of insult and injury than those of his diplomats.

Less offensive than the language but more puzzling to the other Powers affected was the murkiness of German motives, which was underlined by the lack of co-ordination and system between their separate actions. Marschall and Caprivi told Hatzfeldt in April and May 1894 that the acquisition of the Samoan Islands was absolutely essential in order to strengthen the government's prestige in the eyes of public opinion; to the ambassador's bewilderment, the importance of the islands had been completely forgotten in Berlin two months later. The tactics employed during the Congo dispute were even more baffling. Were they intended to call attention to the breach of law, or to serve as a diversion to allow the Germans to have their way in Samoa, or, in Hatzfeldt's words, to 'demonstrate the disadvantages of our hostility'?[59] No one in Berlin seemed to be quite sure. And what was the Emperor's primary motive in intervening in the situation created by Japan's defeat of China? The Emperor himself, who was the driving force behind this operation, seems initially to have thought of himself as protecting Japan from British intervention (and to have expected the Japanese to repay him by the cession of Formosa);[60] before long he was arguing that it was necessary for Germany to collaborate with France and Russia to offset Anglo-Japanese collusion.[61] The rapid shifts and turnings confused and irritated the governments that had to deal with the Germans: the Japanese, overwhelmed with friendship one day and heaped with

[57] Sontag, *Germany and England*, p. 294. See also *G.P.* viii. 129–33, 452, 455–7, 463 ff.

[58] See Brandenburg, *From Bismarck to the World War*, pp. 64 f.; Langer, *Diplomacy of Imperialism*, p. 186.

[59] Rich, *Holstein* i. 370. See Hatzfeldt, *Nachgelassene Papiere* ii. 984 f.

[60] Chlodwig, Fürst zu Hohenlohe-Schillingsfürst, *Denkwürdigkeiten der Reichskanzlerzeit*, ed. K. A. von Müller (Stuttgart, 1931), pp. 8, 16, 52.

[61] Ibid., p. 58.

contumely the next;[62] the French, who were first urged insistently to join in the attack on the Anglo-Congolese Treaty and were then, when they did so, abandoned; and most of all, the British, who failed to understand a diplomacy that combined professions of friendship and open threats in roughly equal proportions. Rosebery's Foreign Secretary, Lord Kimberley, wrote to Sir Edward Malet in June 1894: '. . . if this is to continue, it may have far-reaching consequences and it is difficult to understand what advantage they expect to gain by such a policy . . . I can't pretend to read the riddle, but your experience of German ways will enable you to enlighten me.'[63]

All of the faults of German diplomacy were revealed in the most glaring light during the Transvaal crisis of 1896. As has already been suggested, the Jameson raid merited some response from the German Government. The Transvaal, by an agreement made with the Gladstone government in 1884, was an independent state, although not permitted to conclude treaties with foreign Powers without British permission. There were thousands of Germans in Johannesburg and Pretoria, and they were prominent in the commercial and financial life of the area. Germans held the whisky and dynamite monopolies, controlled the National Bank, supplied the water, and imported iron and steel, chemicals, machines, and utensils. Krupp, Siemens and Halske, Goerz, Lippert, and the Deutsche Bank all had branches in the country, and Germans owned 20 per cent of all foreign capital invested in the country.[64] What happened to the Transvaal could not, therefore, be a matter of indifference to the German Government; and Marschall made this clear to the British ambassador immediately after receiving news of the raid. He then instructed Hatzfeldt in London to inquire whether the British Government had approved the raid and, if the answer were in the affirmative, to break off diplomatic relations.

On 1 January 1896 Berlin learned from London and South Africa that the raid had had no official encouragement. Marschall, however, whose conduct had been entirely correct up to this point, now became devious. On the one hand, he suggested to the French ambassador that co-operation would be desirable as a means of checking 'the insatiable appetite of the British'; on the other, in reporting this *démarche* to the German ambassador in Paris, he confided that, if this kind of pressure could be brought to bear, the British would cave in and join the Triple Alliance.[65] After their

---

[62] Waldersee, *Denkwürdigkeiten* ii. 347.
[63] Rich, *Holstein* i. 373 f.   [64] Langer, *Diplomacy of Imperialism*, p. 219.

Congolese experience, the French were not to be caught with this fly. All Marschall had succeeded in doing was to cast the usual doubt on German motives.

After this bad start, the Emperor took over the direction of German policy with respect to the Transvaal. William II was at this time not at his best, for the dispute over the Military Justice Bill was at its height and on New Year's Day he had had a discussion with the War Minister that reached such a degree of hysterical acrimony that Bronsart told Hohenlohe that he believed the sovereign was mentally unbalanced.[66] It was while he was in this emotional state that the Emperor heard of Jameson's raid, and it is perhaps understandable that his reaction should have been violent. But even his ministers and military and naval aides were astonished and aghast as they listened to the fantasies that poured from their master's lips—schemes for extending a German protectorate over the Transvaal, of sending troops to South Africa, and, in a mysterious way, of fighting a localized war against the British that would not extend to the seas or affect the European situation—and it was only to prevent the possibility of more drastic action that Marschall agreed to the dispatching of the telegram from the Emperor to the President of the Transvaal.[67]

That message congratulated Kruger and his people for having repelled an invasion by armed bands, and for succeeding 'in restoring peace and in maintaining the independence of the country against attacks from without'.[68] It was the last phrase that annoyed the British Government and infuriated the British Press, for the British regarded the Transvaal as lying within their sphere of influence and as being subordinate in matters of foreign policy. Apart from being a gratuitous intervention into the private affairs of the British Empire, the dispatch to Kruger seemed to corroborate all of the suspicions that had been engendered by the growth of German commercial

[65] See esp. Friedrich Thimme, 'Die Krüger-Depesche', *Europäische Gespräche* (May–June 1924), 201–44; K. Lehmann, 'Die Vorgeschichte der Krügerdepesche', *Archiv für Politik und Geschichte*, v (1925).

[66] Hohenlohe, *Reichskanzlerzeit*, p. 151, and below, p. 270.

[67] The troops that were to be used were apparently naval marines. At the meeting of 3 January 1896 to discuss the appropriate response to the raid, the three naval chiefs were present but no representative of the army. See Lehmann, 'Vorgeschichte' 171. The idea of a congratulatory telegram was accepted by the Emperor at the end of the meeting on 3 January. It was drafted by Paul Kayser, with emendations, including the final phrase, by the Emperor. When Holstein, waiting in the anteroom, objected, Marschall said, 'Oh, don't you interfere; you've no idea of the suggestions made in there. Everything else is even worse.' *Holstein Papers* i. 162.

[68] *G.P.* xi, no. 2610.

interest in the Transvaal and to prove that there was a conspiracy between Kruger and the German Government. *The Times* said solemnly: 'There is grave reason to suspect that hostile designs against this country have been in contemplation for a long time; and that the Transvaal was deliberately selected as the spot at which a blow might advantageously be struck';[69] and the majority of the Press rang changes on this theme. The public reaction was extraordinarily hostile, with the windows of German shops being smashed and the like, and for the first time anti-German feeling on the popular level became intense.

The complicated reasons for the extremity of the British reaction need not concern us here.[70] But it should be noted that it made a mockery of Marschall's hope that the Transvaal dispute might be used to bring Britain to terms with the Triple Alliance. When Valentine Chirol reported from Berlin that the telegram had been designed in part as 'a warning to England that she could only find salvation in closer contact with Germany and her allies', *The Times* answered stiffly, 'The paramount necessity of the moment is to bring home to the German mind the fact that England will concede nothing to menaces and will not lie down under insult.'[71] The German attempts to apply to foreign policy Frederick William I's prescription of using chastisement to compel love had been a miserable failure. In 1896 Anglo-German relations were at their lowest ebb, and Britain's relations with the junior members of the Triple Alliance all but severed. Considering the fact that the trade agreement with Russia had had no effect in checking the increasing economic collaboration between that country and France and that, in consequence, the Franco-Russian alliance was stronger than ever, German foreign policy, considered objectively, could only be considered as a failure.

IV

This was not, however, the opinion of that part of the German people that interested itself in foreign policy. Perhaps nothing that the Emperor ever did in his career was as popular as his telegram to Kruger. The Press was in an uproar of enthusiasm; the Colonial Union and the Pan-German League passed resolutions praising the government for its stand; and other groups, carried away by the heady

[69] Langer, *Diplomacy of Imperialism*, p. 242.
[70] It is thoroughly analysed in ibid., pp. 243 ff. with much illustrative detail.
[71] Ibid., p. 243. In December 1896 Hatzfeldt wrote to Marschall about the deterioration of relations caused by the Transvaal crisis. *Nachgelassene Papiere* ii. 1007 ff.

excitement of seeing Britain humiliated, followed suit. That the opportunism and arrogance of German policy over the past three years had already shifted the equilibrium of forces in Europe to Germany's disadvantage was lost upon most Germans. Ill-informed about the true nature of Germany's relations with other Powers, and told daily by the patriotic Press that the Triple Alliance was impregnable and the Franco-Russian alliance oriented exclusively against Britain, they were proud of the new course, which not only appeared to be a return to the assurance of Bismarckian policy after the lack of direction of Caprivi's first years, but also promised to be a worthy expression of Germany's new industrial and commercial strength.

The acceleration of Germany's economic development had been encouraged by the unification of the country, and, after the interruption of the crash of 1873 and the intermittent slumps in the years that followed, had been renewed in the 1890s in full force. In the ten years that followed Bismarck's dismissal, Germany had changed from a predominantly rural to a predominantly urban society, and, as urban industry brought the raw materials of the world to its mills and factories and transformed them into manufactured goods that could not be absorbed by the home market, from an inward-looking to an outward-looking country. German imperialism—if by that we mean the acquisition of overseas territory—had stopped after Bismarck's initial gains in the mid-eighties, but the extension of German interests around the globe had not. The chief agents in this outward march were the great banking combinations, particularly the so-called D-Banks, the Deutsche Bank, the Dresdener Bank, the Darmstädter Bank, and the Diskonto-Gesellschaft. These great organizations, which controlled about 40 per cent of Germany's commercial deposits, had been founded in part to promote industrial growth, but it was their purpose also, as stated by one of their publications, 'to foster commercial relations between Germany and other countries'.[72] They did this by investing in foreign banks and sharing in their operations or by establishing branches of their own and using their capital to support commercial opportunities. Their success in the 1890s was remarkable, as is illustrated by their creation of the Deutsch-Asiatische Bank in China,[73] and of subsidiaries of the Dresdener and Deutsche banks throughout Latin America, their activities, already noted, in South Africa, and their capital investment and acquisition of railway concessions in the Ottoman Empire.

[72] J. E. Clapham, *The Economic Development of France and Germany, 1815–1914* (4th edn., London, 1936), p. 393.
[73] Gustav Stolper, *German Economy, 1870–1940* (New York, 1940), pp. 55 ff.

In a sense, it can be said that Germany was a world Power before it began to act like one. When, in the last years of Caprivi and the chancellorship of Hohenlohe, it began to do so, clumsily, rudely, excessively—indeed, with all the deplorable characteristics of the parvenu—the change was greeted with enthusiasm, not only by those with material interests in overseas trade and investment, and not only by patriotic societies like the Colonial Union and the Pan-German League, but by ordinary citizens who were thrilled by the vision of the country's greatness. Nor were the writers who supported their enthusiasm mere time-servers and bought pens. Friedrich Naumann and Max Weber, who became interested in Germany's outward thrust in the 1890s,[74] Paul Rohrbach, the author of *The German Thought in the World* and *Onward to the Position of a World Power*, and his associate Ernst Jäckh were all true believers in a German mission that was hard to define but was predicted on the idea that, in the great changes that were taking place in the world as the old century died and a new one was born, German energy and German culture must play a worthy role. Almost fifty years later Rohrbach's wife was to write: '... my thoughts always wander back to that time when [we] cooperated in that fine effort: work for the Greater Germany, peaceful expansion and cultural activities in the Near East. . . . Vienna the gateway for these policies. Hamburg the portal to the seas and other continents... A peaceful Germany, great, honored and respected. . . Our methodical thought should be translated into technology and enterprise . . . Acknowledgement of our nation . . .'[75]

This desire for recognition, which was to be found in all sections of society, was the biggest political fact of the last years of the century. The aspirations of the German people coincided with the interests of expanding capitalism: both desired the transformation of Germany from a continental to a world Power. A cautious statesman, conscious of the weakening of Germany's position that had resulted from the first experiments in that direction, might have sought to divert the nation's attention to the essential tasks of achieving social peace and constitutional progress. But when the Hohenlohe ministry was reorganized in June 1897, the two men who stepped to the centre of the stage were not cautious men and they shared—indeed, they came to embody—the national temper. Bernhard von Bülow and Alfred von Tirpitz made world policy their

[74] See below, Ch. VIII, p. 275.
[75] Henry Cord Meyer, *Mitteleuropa in German Thought and Action, 1815–1945* (The Hague, 1955), pp. 101–2.

own and pursued it more aggressively and with greater assurance than their predecessors, confident that, under their direction, it would bring prestige, power, material advantage, public acclaim, and social peace.

VIII
Political Parties, Interest Groups, and the Failure of the Reichstag
1890–1914

For the creation of the German Reich, illusions of an enormous nature were necessary, which have now flown away with the honeymoon period of imperial unity, and which we are unable to reproduce by means of reflection.

MAX WEBER (1893)[1]

Scarron: Schauerlich. Für Politik kein Interesse?

Theobald: Ich war, was Bismarck tat, gespannt.

Scarron: Der ist lange tot!

Theobald: Nachher passierte nicht mehr viel.

CARL STERNHEIM, *Die Hose* (1908)[2]

THE dismissal of Bismarck did not remove the constitutional crisis that had led to it, and it was to remain unsolved. Caprivi and Hohenlohe strove valiantly with the problem, but neither of them possessed a scintilla of Bismarck's demonic will or of his virtuosic ability to reduce complexity to order, and they were unable to inspire the public and the political parties with either enthusiasm or confidence. As a result they were unsuccessful in overcoming the gulf between the Reichstag and the government and, for that matter, of controlling new splits and rivalries that soon threatened to reduce political life to chaos. Increasingly, politics came to resemble a *bellum omnium contra omnes*, in which the Chancellor, the Reichstag, the Prussian ministries, the state governments, the imperial court, organized economic interests, and various cabals contended against each other.

From this situation Bernhard von Bülow sought to escape by pandering to the desires of the most powerful economic groups in

[1] Quoted in Mitzman, *The Iron Cage*, p. 107.
[2] Sternheim, *Gesamtwerk*, i. 89.

the country in the hope that their union would give him the necessary support to pursue a dynamic foreign policy that would disarm
and eventually appease the left. This dual policy had some initial
success but gradually broke down because of the greed of Bülow's
social partners and the tendency of his diplomacy to alienate governments that had formerly been friendly. When he departed, having
worn out the patience of the country and of his royal master, Bülow
left to his successor, Theobald von Bethmann Hollweg, an intractable financial problem, to which the worsening foreign situation
contributed heavily, and a constitutional crisis as serious as the one
that had faced Caprivi.

Throughout these unhappy events, the country was afforded frequent new demonstrations of irresponsibility on the part of the
Emperor and the military establishment. It was a melancholy circumstance that the Reichstag, although given opportunities to bring
this dangerous and growing tendency under control, signally failed
to do anything of the kind.

I

In 1890 Caprivi's hope was that he might lower the tone of German
politics, so that there was less heroic posturing and fewer inflated
speeches and a greater willingness to co-operate in the interest of
efficiency and the general welfare. In the hope of reducing party
friction, he made it clear in his early speeches to the Prussian Landtag
and the Reichstag that he wished to follow a policy of non-
alignment, relying upon the co-operation of those individuals and
parties who placed the national interest above private and parochial
concerns. At the same time, in order to stimulate a new spirit and to
indicate that ideas that had been suppressed during Bismarck's personal dictatorship were welcome now, he announced that he
expected his ministers and secretaries of state to show initiative and
responsibility and would permit them to develop and promote their
own policies.[3]

Given the prevailing state of politics, these decisions were unwise.
The policy of non-alignment was greeted by most people with
scepticism or suspicion. Arthur von Brauer, the Badenese envoy in
Berlin, felt that Caprivi, like other soldiers who had held political
office, had a naïve belief that other people's sense of honour was as
highly developed as his own. 'He is succumbing to the delusion', he
wrote, 'that he can pursue a completely non-party "Policy of honest

---

[3] Nichols, *Germany after Bismarck*, pp. 43–4.

people" by "taking the good wherever one finds it"; he hopes to rally all "men of good will" to his banner.'[4] Such persons, Brauer intimated, were in short supply, most people being influenced more by self-interest than by loftier motives.

This was a shrewd and realistic view. Certainly, the mild enthusiasm with which the moderate and left parties greeted Caprivi's declaration of intentions was short lived, for the labour movement was not to be fobbed off with limitations on Sunday work and child labour (which represented the real as opposed to the rhetorical content of the Emperor's programme of social reform) and, by the middle of 1891, the Centre party was tired of waiting for educational concessions that were promised but never seemed to materialize. At the same time, even the limited support given to Caprivi by those parties alarmed the former partners of the Kartell. The National Liberals and the Free Conservatives feared that it forecast the kind of concessions to the Centre and Progressive parties that would encourage particularism at the expense of national unity, and they suspected that it was out of deference to those parties that Caprivi had begun to retrench in the matter of overseas expansion. The Conservatives feared that Caprivi was bent upon constitutional experiments that would subvert the political and social foundations of the Prussian state, a suspicion that was strengthened by the Chancellor's personal friendship with members of the Progressive party and particularly by his commercial policy. As part of his programme to reconcile the classes and in response to a worldwide economic *malaise* that was marked in Germany by a sharp increase in food prices, Caprivi in 1891 carried through the Reichstag a series of trade treaties with Austria, Italy, Belgium, and Switzerland, the conspicuous feature of which was a reduction of duties on imported wheat and rye from 5 to $3\frac{1}{2}$ R.M. per 1,000 kg in exchange for favourable rates for German exports of manufactured goods. The passage of these agreements was the greatest parliamentary triumph of Caprivi's term, but it was bought at the price of the bitter enmity of the East Elbian grain producers, who responded by establishing a highly effective pressure group to protect their interests, the Bund der Landwirte, which rapidly became the dominant influence in the Conservative party.[5] In general, Caprivi's receptivity to progressive ideas played a significant role in promoting the revolution in the

---

[4] Röhl, *Germany without Bismarck*, p. 75.

[5] Agitation for the establishment of such an organization began early in 1892, and the Bund der Landwirte was founded in February 1893. See Puhle, *Agrarische Interessenpolitik*, pp. 32–4.

Conservative party that took place in the early 1890s, the chief result of which was to overthrow the moderate leadership of Helldorf-Bedra and to deliver the party into the hands of Wilhelm von Hammerstein, the reactionary editor of the *Kreuzzeitung*, the Christian Social movement led by Stoecker, and the embittered agrarians. It was this alliance that saddled the party with the notorious Tivoli Programme of 1892 with its pronounced nationalistic and anti-Semitic flavour.[6]

Within six months of the passage of the commercial laws, most of the party support that Caprivi had attracted by their means was dissipated, and anti-government agitation was becoming general. In the first months of 1892, apparently in an attempt to win Centre support for other pending legislation, the Chancellor encouraged his Minister of Education in Prussia, Count Robert von Zedlitz-Trützschler, to propose a new Prussian School Bill, which restored to the Catholic Church moneys confiscated during the Kulturkampf, permitted one of the monastic orders to resume work in Germany, authorized the use of the Polish language in schools in Posen and West Prussia, and appointed a Pole as Archbishop of Posen and Gnesen. The details of the bill outraged the National Liberals, the moderate Conservatives, the Progressives, and even the Social Democrats, and there was strong public reaction against it which was encouraged when Bismarck spoke out from retirement against its provisions. Disagreeably affected by this uproar, the government made several attempts to compromise, efforts that were not helped by the Emperor's intervention in the affair, since the sovereign's advice was emphatic but changed radically from day to day. In the end, after attempts to water down the bill failed, it was withdrawn, so that, having alienated the moderate and left parties by introducing it, Caprivi ended by losing the support of the Centre by giving it up. The result was a decided slump in the government's fortunes.[7]

Caprivi's policy of deliberately narrowing the scope of his own office was also productive of trouble. From Bismarck he had inherited the position of Reich Chancellor and also those of Minister President and Foreign Minister of Prussia, as well as a tradition of centralization according to which all Reich and Prussian officials

---

[6] On the history of the Conservative party in these years, see Walter Tormin, *Geschichte der deutschen Parteien seit 1848* (Stuttgart, 1966), pp. 99 f., and, at greater length, Ludwig Bergsträsser, *Geschichte der politischen Parteien in Deutschland* (11th edn., Munich, 1965).

[7] On the School Bill, see Nichols, *Germany after Bismarck*, Ch. 5. On Holstein's important role in seeking a moderate solution, see Rich, *Holstein* i. 379–85.

were responsible directly to him and had no access to higher authority. He sought to reduce this accumulation of power first by appealing to the principle of collegiality and by giving his ministers and
secretaries of state freedom to develop and promote their own
policies. He carried this further in 1892 by relinquishing the post of
Prussian Minister President and, two years later, by abolishing the
special position of the Prussian Foreign Minister. The results of this
development might have been foreseen. Unless the affairs of Prussia
and the Reich were in the firm hands of one man, differences over
competence, and particularly over the question of where the initiative in legislation lay, were bound to arise. As soon as Caprivi
announced that he was giving the Prussian ministers the freedom
that Bismarck had denied them, he lost control over them, and some
of them began to intrigue against him. This was true, for example, of
his Finance Minister, Johannes von Miquel, an official of great ability
who reformed the Prussian tax system and introduced the graduated
income tax in 1891, but also a man who delighted in political
manœuvre and manipulation, which led him to maintain private
contact with Caprivi's agrarian enemies, the members of the Bismarck Fronde, and the Emperor's camarilla of confidential advisers.[8]
The situation became infinitely worse when the Chancellor yielded
the minister presidency to Count Botho Eulenburg in March 1892,
for Eulenburg, a self-willed Conservative from East Prussia, soon
demonstrated that he was not willing to support Caprivi in Reich
affairs unless his drastic ideas about solving the deadlock between the
government and the Reichstag were put into effect. Simultaneously,
as Caprivi lost control over the Prussian Ministry of State, he lost the
backing of the south German governments, who were as anti-
Prussian as ever and saw no reason why they should stand behind a
Chancellor who could not keep Prussian particularism in check.

By the middle of 1892, therefore, the government's authority was
in bad repair, and it is likely that Caprivi would not have survived in
office had it not been for the fear of those who had hitched their

[8] Miquel had played a prominent part in the formation of the National Liberal party
and had set its tone by his famous statement after Königgrätz: 'The time of ideals is
past. Today politicians must ask not so much as formerly what is desirable but rather
what is possible.' On his career, see Herzfeld's biography and that of W. Mommsen
(Stuttgart, 1928); and, for his financial achievements, W. Geiger, *Miquel und die
preußische Steuerreform 1890–93* (Groppingen, 1934). He was the author of the so-called
Sammlungspolitik, defined in a letter to Waldersee in 1897, in which he said, 'The
great task of the present is, without prejudice . . . to gather together all the elements
that support the state and thereby to prepare for the unavoidable battle against the
Social Democratic movement.' Herzfeld, *Miquel* ii. 183 f.

wagons to the Emperor's star that his fall might bring the Bismarcks back. During the manœuvres that accompanied the defeat of the Prussian School Bill, Friedrich von Holstein, the head of the Political Division of the Foreign Ministry and a man who realized that his career was at stake,[9] constantly warned of the possibility of Bismarck's returning in triumph and subjecting the Emperor to 'constitutional thumb-screws of the Belgian kind' and, through an intermediary, cautioned the sovereign to be discreet in his objections to the proposed legislation 'if we are not to cause Caprivi's fall'.[10] Such fears became more active in 1892 when influential supporters of Bismarck, including the Saarbrücken coal magnate Baron Carl von Stumm-Halberg, the industrialist Count Guido von Henckel-Donnersmark, and General von Waldersee, who was now Commanding General of the Ninth Army Corps at Altona, urged the desirability of an imperial reconciliation with the Bismarcks so persuasively that the Emperor, in his impulsive way, dispatched a telegram to Herbert von Bismarck, congratulating him on his engagement to the Austrian Countess Marguerite Hoyos. This alarmed Holstein, but not nearly as much as the news in June that Herbert von Bismarck's marriage was going to take place in Vienna and that his father not only intended to be present but planned to visit the capitals of Saxony and Bavaria.

To Holstein, and to Caprivi himself, who had been annoyed by a conversation between Waldersee and the Emperor in which the General offered to act as mediator between William and Bismarck, the trip to the southern capitals seemed part of an elaborate campaign to unseat the government and restore the old Chancellor to power.[11] Caprivi reacted energetically. He made it clear to his royal master that Bismarck's journey might well turn into a demonstration against the Emperor and his policies, a warning that so frightened William that he changed course abruptly, snubbed Waldersee, and wrote a letter to Emperor Francis Joseph, asking him not give any formal recognition to his 'rebellious subject' while he was in Austria.

[9] Holstein's fears were probably not exaggerated. The Bismarck family remembered his role in the Chancellor's dismissal, and Herbert von Bismarck described him as 'eine erbärmliche Personifizierung eitelster und kleinlichster Selbstsucht'. *Privatkorrespondenz*, p. 573.

[10] Röhl, *Germany without Bismarck*, pp. 83–4.

[11] The Bismarck Fronde had different ideas about what form a return to power would take. In Holstein's opinion, the majority view was that Bismarck himself would not take office but would be the guiding spirit of a government in which Herbert von Bismarck would be Foreign Minister and Waldersee Reich Chancellor. Rogge, *Holstein und Hohenlohe*, p. 391.

Simultaneously, with royal approval, Caprivi instructed the staff of the German Embassy in Vienna to decline invitations to any of the festivities attendant on the wedding.

When he became aware of these actions, Bismarck declared war upon the regime, and his public attacks upon its foreign and domestic policies during his visit to Vienna and his journey home were so violent that they put an end to any possibility of a reconciliation. This, unfortunately for Caprivi, did nothing to help him, for the publication of his letter to the Vienna Embassy had a highly injurious effect upon his public reputation and seriously weakened his national support at a time when he was forced to fight new and difficult parliamentary battles.[12]

Since the lapsing of the Reinsurance Treaty and the *rapprochement* between France and Russia,[13] German soldiers had been urging the necessity of a sizeable increase in army strength. In 1892 Waldersee's successor as Chief of Staff, Alfred Count von Schlieffen, calculated that Germany's principal antagonists had almost twice as many troops under arms or in reserve as Germany had, and he urged that all men capable of service must be trained. Caprivi was inclined to agree, but he was aware that the present Reichstag would be even less tractable when approached for heightened military appropriations than the Reichstag of 1887, and that conflict could be avoided only if the government could offer something in return. He wrote in a memorandum of April 1892:

There is no doubt that, unless a partial concession is made to the desire for annual establishment of the peacetime strength and the legal introduction of two-year service, a strengthening of the army is not to be attained. To conflict, dissolution, or even *coup d'état* we dare not allow it to come. The question is not whether the three-year service in itself is preferable to two-year service, but whether we will give up the three-year service for infantry troops in order to increase our peacetime strength by 77,500 men. . . . Any attempt to carry the increase through without introducing two-year service can lead only to defeat which must weaken the Emperor's government within the Reich and abroad.[14]

---

[12] On the trip and its political repercussions, see Rich, *Holstein* i. 385–90; Nichols, *Germany after Bismarck*, pp. 195–204; Waldersee, *Denkwürdigkeiten* ii. 240. The behaviour of Germany's ambassador in Vienna, Prince Henry VII of Reuß, who obliquely asked Herbert von Bismarck to be married somewhere else so that his position might not be endangered, struck the bridegroom as a grandiose example of 'byzantine cowardice', and he told his father that he was going to save the letters he had received from Reuß and his wife as 'kulturgeschichtliche Streiflichter auf unsere Zeit'. *Privatkorrespondenz*, p. 575.

[13] See above, Ch. VII, pp. 235–8.

[14] L. K. G. W. Rüdt von Collenberg, *Die deutsche Armee von 1871 bis 1914*, Forschungen und Darstellungen aus dem Reichsarchiv, Heft 4 (Berlin, 1922), p. 45.

After consulting Schlieffen and the War Minister, General Hans von Kaltenborn-Stachau, Caprivi decided that, in return for the necessary increases, the term of service must be shortened and that the Reichstag must be given the right to debate army strength every five, instead of every seven, years.[15]

Caprivi had had difficulties with the Emperor before, particularly during the dispute over the School Bill, but they were nothing to what he experienced now. Inflamed by exaggerated reports from the German military attaché in Paris about French strength and French intentions, William's demand for an acceleration of German armament verged at times upon the hysterical. On the other hand, the thought of giving up the three-year term of service, for which his grandfather had fought successfully in the constitutional conflict of the 1860s, was wholly repugnant to him, and opponents of the government like Waldersee were quick to exploit his sentimental view and to urge that there was no better issue upon which to fight the inevitable battle against the Reichstag.[16] Caprivi's negotiations with the parties were seriously handicapped by William's susceptibility to this kind of argument and his propensity for public outbursts of defiance against the Reichstag when under the spell of those who used it; and it says much for the Chancellor's patience and determination that he was able, not only to persuade William in the end to accept his bill, but to carry it through Parliament in 1893, roughly in the form in which he had devised it, although, to be sure, he managed this last only after a dissolution of the Reichstag, new elections, and further concessions to the opposition.[17]

For this, the Chancellor gained no gratitude from his royal master, who, as usual, had second thoughts almost immediately and, in this case, was encouraged to do so by the soldiers. They adopted Waldersee's argument that Caprivi regarded the army only 'as an object to be used in concluding deals with political parties',[18] and the Chief of the Military Cabinet, Hahnke, and other members of the Emperor's military suite insisted that Caprivi's excessive willingness to yield to the wishes of the Reichstag had forced upon the army a shortened term of service that was generally unpopular and a lot of

[15] Huber, *Heer und Staat*, p. 270.

[16] Waldersee, *Denkwürdigkeiten* ii. 214–15.

[17] Caprivi sought to popularize the bill by appointing an extreme nationalist, Major August Keim, to write propaganda tracts in favour of it, which he did with great success. See Röhl, *Germany without Bismarck*, p. 11. Even so, he had to reduce the demanded increase by 12,770 men. As a result, there were still eligible recruits who could not be called to the colours. Rüdt von Collenberg, *Die deutsche Armee*, pp. 45–9.

[18] Waldersee, *Denkwürdigkeiten* ii. 209–10.

half-strength battalions were militarily unsound.[19] To these arguments the Emperor was alarmingly vulnerable, and he was soon
believing that, in giving way to Caprivi on the term of service, he
had 'nearly done for himself with the army'.[20]

The Emperor seems to have convinced himself also that Caprivi
had lost a golden opportunity to 'chase the half-mad Reichstag to the
devil',[21] something which he was becoming more and more convinced was necessary. The elections of 1893 had not improved the
government's position in the slightest. Although the Progressives
had lost strength, the Socialists had gained 300,000 votes and could
be expected to be even more troublesome than in the past. It was
clear that the Emperor's plan to kill socialism with kindness had not
worked. Inevitably, his thoughts turned back to the solution that he
had rejected in 1890, Bismarck's plan for a *coup d'état*, and although
he knew that Caprivi was firmly opposed to the idea, he found
plenty of people who were ready to encourage him to take it up, not
only in his own Hauptquartier and Waldersee's headquarters at
Altona, but also in the Prussian Ministry of State.

In May 1894 Botho von Eulenburg announced his intention of
laying a bill to combat 'revolutionary tendencies' before the Reichstag. The wave of anarchist outrages that swept over Europe at this
time and culminated in the assassination of the French President,
Sadi Carnot, was the ostensible reason for this, although Eulenburg's proposed bill appeared to be aimed as much at Socialists and
trade-unionists as at anarchists and was clearly an attempt to revive
Bismarck's anti-socialist measures in a more extreme form. Like
Bismarck, Eulenburg expected that the Reichstag would baulk and
that the government would then take the necessary measures to set
aside the existing constitution and eliminate the forces of subversion.
In the course of this operation Caprivi would be removed also.
Eulenburg was in full sympathy with the agrarians, whose outrage
over the direction of the Chancellor's commercial policy had just
been increased by the conclusion of a trade treaty with Russia which
decreased the tariff on grain imports from 50 to 30 per cent.[22] Since
March, when the Reichstag approved the treaty, the Bund der
Landwirte and the extremists of the Hammerstein wing of the
Conservative party had been waging a demagogic campaign against
the Chancellor, which was secretly encouraged by the Minister

[19] Craig, *Prussian Army*, p. 245.
[20] Haller, *Eulenburg*, p. 201.
[21] Waldersee, *Denkwürdigkeiten* ii. 276.
[22] Eyck, *Das persönliche Regiment*, p. 76.

President and by Johannes Miquel for their own purposes.[23] This offensive, moreover, had supporters at court, the most powerful of whom was Botho von Eulenburg's cousin Philipp. It is a sad commentary upon the political style of the post-Bismarckian period that this bogus intellectual and composer of sentimental songs, whose self-esteem was as inflated as his political gifts were exiguous, should have possessed as much influence as he did, but his *Skaldenlieder* impressed the Emperor and his gifts of byzantine ingratiation persuaded William that he was a wise counsellor.[24] Even before his cousin's campaign began, Philipp Eulenburg was preparing the way for it by intimating to the Emperor that the Press agitation against Caprivi was greater than anything that Bismarck had ever had to withstand, that the demands of the agrarians could not be ignored forever, and that Botho von Eulenburg, if made Chancellor, could win their support;[25] and by the summer of 1894 he was one of the many voices close to the Emperor's ear that were insisting that the time was ripe for action against the forces of revolution but that Caprivi was not the man to lead the assault.[26]

It is likely that, despite the Emperor's enthusiastic reception of these ideas and his grandiloquent parole 'Onward to battle for religion, for morality and order against the forces of revolution!', Caprivi could have defeated these squalid intrigues and shored up his position as Chancellor if he had wished to do so. Despite his propensity for bellicose utterance, the Emperor was never a man of action, and his fundamental indecisiveness was made more anxious by a scathing attack by Caprivi in the Prussian Ministry of State upon Eulenburg's bill and the theory of the *coup d'état*, as well as by the fact that almost all of those who were advocating evasion or subversion of the constitution in the summer had changed their minds at least once by the autumn.[27] By that time the Foreign Secretary, Marschall

[23] It was characteristic of Miquel that, while recommending acceptance of the Russian treaty by the Reichstag, most of his speech dealt with the need of assistance for German agriculture, and privately he advised the Conservatives to vote against the bill. See Herzfeld, *Miquel* ii. 329.

[24] See Herzfeld, *Ausgewählte Aufsätze*, pp. 80 f.

[25] Röhl, *Germany without Bismarck*, p. 109.

[26] Ibid., p. 113.

[27] An interesting illustration of this is to be found in Gerlach, *Von rechts nach links*, pp. 134 f., where he describes a meeting of Conservative notables in Berlin at which a vote in favour of a *coup d'état* called for by Hammerstein failed because of the opposition of the young moderates of the party, a result that dimmed the ardour of the fire-eaters, although Hammerstein continued to believe that the only way out of Germany's difficulties was 'to provoke the workers and to shoot them'. See also Zechlin, *Staatsstreichpläne*, p. 125.

von Bieberstein, and Holstein, who remained faithful to Caprivi until the end, were sure that he had broken the back of the cabal opposing him, and the south German members of the Bundesrat were urging him to end the crisis by reassuming the post of Prussian Minister President. But Caprivi was tired of being sniped at by former comrades in arms, undercut by his Prussian Ministers of State, and belaboured by the Press lackeys of the Bund der Land-wirte;[28] he was disgusted by the anti-Semitic nature of some of the attacks made by the Conservatives against his policies;[29] and he had no desire to continue serving a sovereign as mercurial and as inconsistent as William II.[30] In October he submitted his resignation in such a way as to force Botho von Eulenburg to do the same, and the Emperor, after some vacillating, decided to let both men go.[31]

II

When he had done so, he is reported to have said to his friend Philipp von Eulenburg, 'I have no idea whom I can appoint. Do you know anybody?', to which Eulenburg answered ironically, 'A man who is neither conservative nor liberal, neither ultramontane nor a free-thinker, neither religious nor an atheist, is going to be hard to find.'[32] Whether this exchange ever took place or not is less important than the fact that it might have done so, given the dearth of obvious political talent on the one hand and the Emperor's preference for men without strong opinions on the other. His choice as Caprivi's successor was proof of this, for he fastened upon Prince Chlodwig zu Hohenlohe-Schillingsfürst.

Hohenlohe, it is true, had had a long and honourable career in German politics. As a Bavarian politician in the 1860s, he had been

[28] The Bund later took credit for bringing Caprivi down. See Puhle, *Agrarische Interessenpolitik*, p. 237.

[29] In December 1892 the Conservative party, in its Tivoli Programme, accepted an uncompromising anti-Semitic plank. During the debate on the army bill, its opponents accused the government of buying inferior weapons from Jewish firms, an argument that had been raised by the notorious anti-Semite Ahlwardt in a pamphlet called 'Jewish Rifles', which led to his imprisonment for libel. See, *inter alia*, Peter G. J. Pulzer, *The Rise of Political Anti-Semitism in Germany and Austria* (New York, 1964), p. 112, and Massing, *Rehearsal*, p. 91.

[30] In December 1891, after the Reichstag accepted the commercial treaties, the Emperor had lavished praise on Caprivi and made him a Count. See Nichols, *Germany after Bismarck*, p. 152. By mid-1893 he was saying that 'he was beginning to realize that the commercial treaties inspired by Caprivi had been a stupidity'. Herbert von Bismarck, *Privatkorrespondenz*, p. 577.

[31] For the details of the final crisis, see Röhl, *Germany without Bismarck*, pp. 112–17, and Zechlin, *Staatsstreichpläne*, pp. 119 and 129.

[32] Eyck, *Das persönliche Regiment*, pp. 199 f.

instrumental in breaking down the opposition in southern Germany towards the creation of the Empire, and he had subsequently served it as ambassador in Paris and as governor of the conquered territory of Alsace-Lorraine. But he had never been noted for forthrightness or self-reliance (one of his diplomatic colleagues had said caustically that his motto might be 'I may be weak but at least I am not a scoundrel'[33]) and he was older when he assumed the duties of Chancellor than Bismarck had been when he laid them down. There is little doubt that the Emperor appointed him as a respectable figurehead who would be easier to manage than his predecessor. William's judgement, in this as in other matters, was not perfect, for he overlooked Hohenlohe's reputation for stubbornness and evasiveness, which had led a member of his staff in Paris to say, 'It is quite impossible to make him do anything of which he disapproves. He flutters away like a little bird when you try to catch him.'[34] These qualities served to baulk some of the Emperor's more dangerous designs, and they justified Friedrich Naumann's description of Hohenlohe as 'an artist in the avoidance of catastrophe',[35] but they were no substitute for the kind of firm leadership that Germany needed at this juncture of its affairs. Under Hohenlohe the palace intrigues and the internecine warfare between agencies that had characterized Caprivi's last years continued and, indeed, became so intense as to defeat sound policy initiatives.

Nothing illustrates the new government's lack of energy and imagination more strikingly than its approach to the problem of the working class. In the Prussian Ministry of Commerce there was a dedicated group of civil servants, led by the minister Freiherr von Berlepsch and his chief assistant Theodor Lohman, who were convinced that the time had come to advance beyond the limitations of Bismarck's social welfare system, to provide the working class with a comprehensive code for the protection of the rights of labour, to encourage working-class participation in communal activities, and, by doing so, to satisfy its justifiable desire for equality and recognition.[36] These ideas, which were shared, with some modifications, by social reform groups within the Centre party, by Friedrich Naumann's National Social movement, by the Evangelical

[33] The remark was Werthern's—see Holborn, 'Bismarck und Werthern', 474—and the source Der Freischütz, act 3, finale.

[34] Bernhard Fürst von Bülow, Denkwürdigkeiten (4 vols., Berlin, 1930 ff.), iv. 464.

[35] Heuß, Naumann, pp. 199 f.

[36] See Hans Rothfels, Theodor Lohmann und die Kämpfejahre der staatlichen Sozialpolitik (Berlin, 1927) and Freiherr von Berlepsch, Sozialpolitische Erfahrungen und Erinnerungen (Mönchengladbach, 1925).

Workers' Union at Mönchengladbach, and by the so-called 'socialists of the chair' who belonged to the Social Policy Association, found little sympathy at the centre of the government; and, after the Emperor's brief flirtation with them in the first years of his reign, their proponents were gradually eased out of office, Berlepsch himself resigning in disgust in 1896.[37] The prevailing philosophy was that preached most stridently by the industrialist Stumm-Halberg, who believed that any kind of working-class organization was a threat to the existing social and political system,[38] and most apocalyptically by soldiers like Waldersee, who regarded military action as the best answer to the rise of socialism.

Hohenlohe's chancellorship was marked by an unending series of attempts to disable the Social Democratic party, either by legislative means or by threat of *Staatsstreich*, and, to the dismay of the Chancellor, and such perceptive public servants as Friedrich von Holstein, the Emperor was involved in all of them. The tone was set at the very outset of Hohenlohe's term by two speeches by Stumm-Halberg in January and February 1895, in which, along with much indiscriminate abuse of university professors, liberal pastors, and the Social Policy Association, he suggested that Social Democrats should be deprived of all rights of suffrage and that their leaders should be arrested and exiled.[39] These draconian recommendations were greeted with enthusiasm in Conservative and court circles, where Waldersee noted that 'people are thinking of a kind of *Staatsstreich* and of me as the right man to carry it out',[40] and where there was an insistent demand for the passage of the Eulenburg Subversion Bill of 1894.

Hohenlohe dug his heels in against the idea of subverting the constitution by means of a *coup*, in 1895 and whenever the idea resurfaced later on, making it clear to his sovereign that, if he wanted that sort of thing, he had better appoint a general as Chancellor;[41] but, presumably to head off William's more extravagant projects, he found it expedient to seek passage of the Eulenburg Subversion Bill, or as it was misleadingly called, the Bill for the Amendment and Amplification of the Criminal Code, the Military Penal Code, and

[37] On the circumstances of Berlepsch's resignation, see Gerhard A. Ritter, *Die Arbeiterbewegung im Wilhelminischen Reich: Die Sozialdemokratische Partei und die Freien Gewerkschaften 1890–1900* (Berlin, 1959), pp. 32–5.

[38] On Stumm-Halberg, see the biography of Fritz Hellwig, *Carl Freiherr von Stumm-Halberg* (Heidelberg, 1936).

[39] Heuß, *Naumann*, pp. 127 f.

[40] Waldersee, *Denkwürdigkeiten* ii. 338.

[41] See Hohenlohe, *Denkwürdigkeiten der Reichskanzlerzeit*, pp. 20 f.

the Press Law. This proved to be a mistake that bordered on the ludicrous, for, when the bill was sent to the Reichstag and referred to committee, it was subjected to so many amendments by parties wishing to direct its thrust against their own special enemies or against ideas that they reprobated that it threatened to become a new Syllabus of Errors, and, when it reached the floor of the House, it was promptly voted down.[42]

Infuriated by this set-back, the Emperor sent an open telegram to his Chancellor, saying, 'There remains for us, therefore, only fire-hoses for normal circumstances and cartridges for the ultimate'.[43] He refused, however, to accept this decision as final, and in the months and years that followed bombarded his ministers with demands for action against the threat from the left. In August 1895, nettled by the attitude of the Socialist Press towards the erection of a new statue of William I in Berlin (and by unkind references to what was described as his growing obsession with ancestor-worship), he asked his Prus-sian ministers for a new law of association, which would forbid organizations or meetings by Social Democrats, and although this failed, largely because of Hohenlohe's dilatory tactics, he came back to it frequently in the subsequent period. During the winter of 1896–7, impressed by a memorandum from Waldersee, who argued that a strike of the dock-workers in Hamburg marked the beginning of a comprehensive revolution and that preventive action by the state was urgently required, William made a speech before the Bran-denburg Landtag in which he announced that he intended to take up the struggle against subversion with all the means at his command, since 'the party that dares to attack the foundations of the state, that rises against religion and that does not even call a halt before the person of the All-Highest Sovereign . . . must be destroyed'.[44] Subsequently, he threw his support behind a plan formulated by Johannes Miquel which called for a redefinition of the suffrage law for Reichstag elections so as to weaken Socialist strength. When this proved to be impractical, because of reservations raised by the Centre and the liberal parties, he shifted his focus and encouraged the Reich Minister of the Interior, Count Posadowsky, to approach the governments of the other federal states for the purpose of concerting measures for restricting trade union activities. Finally, when this tactic was leaked to the Press and caused widespread public criticism,

---

[42] Ritter (*Arbeiterbewegung*, p. 29) says that in the end the bill was 'completely clericalized and [given] a strong emphasis against academic freedom'.

[43] Hohenlohe, *Reichskanzlerzeit*, p. 63.

[44] Rich, *Holstein* ii. 528.

he insisted that the Prussian Ministry of State begin work on a new law for the protection of labour and made an unheralded speech at Oeynhausen in which, to the stupefaction of his ministers, he announced that it would include provisions for prison terms for anyone who 'tries to prevent a working man who is willing to work from doing so or who encourages him to strike'.[45]

This irresponsible outburst, which led Hohenlohe to write to his son that he was 'more and more losing the desire to serve under this master',[46] led to a complete fiasco. The bill, which in its final form provided gaol sentences only in the case of strikes that imperilled the security of the Reich or of a federal state or were a threat to human life or property, was laid before the Reichstag after long delay in August 1899. It was defeated on its first reading and, when the Emperor insisted on its resubmission, was defeated again, paragraph by paragraph, without even being sent to committee and without a single representative voting in favour of the imprisonment clauses.[47]

The Emperor's attempts to solve the social question by variants of the Bismarckian formula and the violence of his public utterances alarmed many of his servants, who felt that they were undermining the authority of the government. 'The phrase current among all parties in the Reichstag,' Holstein wrote in November 1896, "That the behaviour of the Emperor can only be explained pathologically," is taking effect quietly but devastatingly, like a miasma.'[48] Walter Bronsart von Schellendorff, a soldier with a more sophisticated cast of mind than Waldersee, wrote sadly on the same theme: 'Much of what we did to cultivate the monarchical sense in the people, by means of a generation of wise domestic policy and the glorious accomplishments of the army, has, confound it!, crumbled away.'[49]

Moreover, apart from the fact that the Emperor's interventions were self-defeating—it was clear after the defeat of the Zuchthausvorlage in 1899 that the Reichstag was not going to be frightened into passing extraordinary legislation against socialism—their net effect was to embitter the working class and to deepen the gulf that had existed between it and the rest of German society since 1878. This was unfortunate, since there were forces at work within the working class that might, if properly appreciated, have led to the kind of reconciliation that men like Naumann and Lohmann and Berlepsch were working for.

[45] Ritter, *Arbeiterbewegung*, p. 39. [46] Hohenlohe, *Reichskanzlerzeit*, p. 458.
[47] Ritter, *Arbeiterbewegung*, p. 39. [48] Rich, *Holstein* ii. 521.
[49] Bogdan Graf Hutten-Czapski, *Sechzig Jahre Politik und Gesellschaft* (2 vols., Berlin, 1935–6), i. 309.

III

Despite the frightening picture painted by Stumm, and Waldersee, and their kind, the Social Democratic party's victory over Bismarck in 1890 had not inspired its leaders with new revolutionary fervour or encouraged them to begin planning the overthrow of bourgeois society. On the contrary, their electoral success, which had brought them a national vote of 1,472,000 and 35 seats in the Reichstag, strengthened the moderate or Lassallean tendencies in the party and awakened new respect for the possibilities inherent in parliamentary activity. Bebel himself, a devout and optimistic Marxist who once admitted that he never went to bed without the conviction that the revolution was only days away, was not unaffected by this; and he reacted savagely against the group of party intellectuals known as Die Jungen when, in the first days after the expiration of the Socialist Law, they criticized the party executive for its inactivity and accused it of timidity and surrender to petty-bourgeois values. Indeed, after holding a series of mass meetings in which he poured abuse and ridicule upon their pretensions, he hounded them out of their positions in the party Press.[50] Bebel wanted no new conflict with the state until the party had adjusted itself to post-Bismarckian conditions and had had time to make deliberate decisions about objectives and tactics. It was enough, he felt, for the party to reaffirm its faith in the doctrines of Karl Marx, as it did in its party conference at Erfurt in 1891, without making any ill-considered attempts to implement them.

Bebel's position was that of the cautious party bureaucrat. More forthright in their views and more persuasive in their arguments than Die Jungen were those party leaders who now called openly for a fundamental reorientation of the party along evolutionary rather than revolutionary lines. This note was first sounded by the highly respected Bavarian leader Georg Vollmar, who had generally been considered to be a member of the extreme left wing of the party. In a speech at the Eldorado-Palast in Munich on 1 June 1891, in which he emphasized the improvement of conditions for the working class and the party since Bismarck's fall, Vollmar declared that the best interests of the party would be served 'by an effort to bring about improvements of an economic and political nature on the basis of the present political and social order'. This, he argued, was both good sense and good socialism. 'Beside the general and ultimate good, we

---

[50] Lidtke, *The Outlawed Party*, pp. 300–14; Ritter, *Arbeiterbewegung*, pp. 82–6.

[must] see a nearer aim: the advancement of the *most immediate* needs of the people. For me, the achievement of the most immediate demands is the main thing, not only because they are of great propaganda value and serve to enlist the masses, but also because, in my opinion, this *gradual* process, this *gradual* socialization, is the method most strongly indicated for a progressive transformation [of the country].' Vollmar left no doubt in his auditors' minds that they should think of themselves as part of that country, not as outsiders; they should be proud of being Germans, and, indeed, of what their country stood for in the world. To the embarrassment of the party Press, Vollmar praised the Triple Alliance as a force for peace and said that any Power that broke the peace by an attack upon German soil would find the German working class arrayed against it.[51]

Vollmar's Eldorado speech was the basic manifesto of the movement that came to be known as revisionism.[52] It challenged the party to discard the outworn shibboleths of the past and become a practical movement for democratic reform, a prospect that frightened perceptive minds on the political right, like Johannes Miquel, who later described Vollmar as 'the most clever, ostensibly the most moderate, and hence the most dangerous' opponent of the existing order.[53] Vollmar's argument was elaborated later in the decade by the theoretical writings of Eduard Bernstein, who brought to it some of the refinements of British Fabianism;[54] but it would have made its way without Bernstein's help. The real force behind socialist reformism was the rank and file member of the party, who was basically patriotic and did not want to fight against the state if there were ways of co-operating with it, the Socialist members of south German and central German parliaments and communal assemblies who had discovered that co-operation was possible, and the leaders of the independent trade unions.

The unions had originally been the step-children of the Social Democratic movement, regarded as potentially useful centres for the political indoctrination of the workers but eliciting from the party

[51] Georg Vollmar, *Über die nächsten Aufgaben der Sozialdemokratie* (Munich, 1891).

[52] On revisionism there is an extensive literature. Useful general treatments can be found in G. D. H. Cole, *A History of Socialist Thought* (3 vols., London, 1953), George Lichtheim, *Marxism: An Historical and Critical Study* (New York, 1961), and Bertram D. Wolfe, *Marxism: 100 Years in the Life of a Doctrine* (New York, 1965). For more detailed accounts, see Carl W. Schorske, *German Social Democracy, 1905–1917* (Cambridge, 1955), J. P. Nettl, *Rosa Luxemburg* (2 vols., London, 1966), and Ritter, *Arbeiterbewegung*, esp. pp. 176 ff.

[53] Puhle, *Agrarische Interessenpolitik*, p. 327 (Miquel to Emperor William II, 10 Nov. 1894).

[54] Gay, *Bernstein*, Ch. 1.

leadership no real understanding of or support for their private economic interests.[55] This relationship changed after 1890, and particularly after 1895, when union membership began to expand rapidly, especially in the ranks of unskilled labour. In 1890 the unions had established a new central organization, the General Commission of Trade Unions, under the leadership of Carl Legien, a cool Realpolitiker who devoted his life to practical service for the German working man.[56] This body soon made it clear that it would no longer tolerate the indifference of Bebel and Liebknecht toward the concerns of union members,[57] the patronizing attitude of the party Press, Vorwärts in particular, and the arrogant assumption by party theorists that they had the right to control union policy. Nothing angered union leaders more than party attempts to make them abandon activities like the accumulation of funds for unemployment relief for their membership and the pursuit of collective bargaining agreements, on the ground that they would weaken working-class militancy. They were usually hard-headed and practical men, with little of the political fervour of their counterparts in France and with a profound distrust of intellectuals. They were willing to accord a contemptuous tolerance to the writers of articles in Die neue Zeit and the Sozialistische Monatshefte—'Laßt sie schwatzen!'—provided they did not impede union business, which was to gain benefits for their membership. To them preparations for a future revolution had no meaning; they were aware that it was to their interest to seek an accommodation with the society in which they lived rather than to indulge themselves with doctrinaire opposition to it. This view, they gradually imposed upon the Social Democratic party, forcing the executive, in return for their support, to modify its own conception of the class struggle. Indeed, in 1905 and 1906 the unions compelled the party to abandon its periodic agitation for the political mass strike, which in the view of the union leadership was a bootless doctrine 'advocated by anarchists and by individuals without any understanding of the class struggle'.[58]

[55] Ritter, Arbeiterbewegung, pp. 123 ff., 171 ff. As late as 1892 Carl Legien failed to persuade the party to pass a resolution pledging members to join unions in their trades.

[56] There is no adequate biography of Legien. See Theodor Leipart, Carl Legien, Ein Gedenkbuch (Berlin, 1929) and the sketches in the memoirs of Paul Löbe, Friedrich Stämpfer, and Carl Severing.

[57] Bebel apologized to the unions in 1900 for his previous attitude. August Bebel, Gewerkschaftsbewegung und politische Parteien (Stuttgart, 1900).

[58] Resolution passed by the Trade Union Congress at Cologne in May 1905. The account above is a much abbreviated version of a long and complicated struggle that began with Vorwärts's startled reaction to the establishment of the General Com-

In the last decade of the nineteenth century trade-unionism was the strongest of those forces that were changing the Social Democratic party, for all practical purposes, into a reformist democratic movement. The ability of union leaders to make agreements with representatives of industry and commerce, like the participation by representatives of labour in communal health, housing, and unemployment boards, and the collaboration between Socialist deputies and representatives of middle-class parties in town councils and provincial assemblies, was palpable evidence that neither the working class nor the political class that represented it was a force bent on the destruction of the existing political system. There were any number of examples to prove the opposite, like the effective coalition between the socialist and liberal parties in the Badenese Landtag. It was a tragedy for Germany—and the word, all things considered, is not too strong—that the ruling forces in Germany in the 1890s failed, or refused, to recognize this fact, preferring to portray the threat of socialism as Bismarck had done. There is no doubt that there were many who sincerely believed that no compromise with Social Democracy was possible, but there were more, in the councils of the Conservative, Centre, and National Liberal parties, and in the Bund der Landwirte and the Centralverband deutscher Industrieller, who saw that the price of collaboration with the working class was social and political change of a kind that they thought they could not afford.

Theodor Fontane wrote in 1896:

Everything that is interesting is to be found in the fourth estate. The bourgeoisie is frightful, and the aristocracy and clerics are old-fashioned, always the same old stuff. The new, the better world begins with the fourth estate. One would be able to say that even if he were talking only about aspirations and experiments. But that is not the way it is. What the workers think, speak, and write has in fact overtaken the thinking, speaking, and writing of the old ruling classes; it is all more genuine, more truthful, more

---

mission (an editorial entitled 'What is Going On?') and continued until the Congress of 1906 at Mannheim where the party virtually caved in in the face of union demands and where the General Commission announced that there was a good chance that in the future the unions would 'never again be endangered by theorists and writers who attach a greater value to mere revolutionary slogans than to the practical work in the labour movement'. In addition to the excellent account in Ritter, *Arbeiterbewegung*, pp. 125, 150 ff., 160, 164, 174 ff., see the older work of Theodor Cassau, 'Die Gewerkschaftsbewegung, Ihre Soziologie und ihr Kampf', in *Soziale Organisation der Gegenwart, Forschungen und Beiträge*, ed. Ernst Grünfeld, viii (Halberstadt, 1925); Selig Perlman, *A Theory of the Labor Movement* (New York, 1928), pp. 96 ff., 100 ff.; Franz Josef Furtwängler, *Die Gewerkschaften, Ihre Geschichte und internationale Auswirkung* (Hamburg, 1956), pp. 31 ff.; and Nettl, *Rosa Luxemburg*, i. 301 ff.

full of life. The workers have attacked everything in a new way; they not only have new goals but new methods of attaining them.[59]

What the novelist admired, however, the members of the ruling class in Wilhelmine society feared, and, because they did so, they preferred to ignore the possibilities of accommodation with the working class and to exaggerate the possibilities of conflict. The greatest failure of the Hohenlohe ministry was its inability either to check this tendency or to persuade the Emperor to stop associating himself with it. The fact that the monarch, publicly and repeatedly, described millions of his subjects as being untrustworthy, disloyal, and capable of helping Germany's enemies was a potent factor in alienating a large section of the working class. This did not necessarily persuade them to adopt the revolutionary stance attributed to them by their antagonists. Their ties to existing society, through their unions or communal organizations, were too strong for that. What it did mean, however, was that their integration in Wilhelmine society had to be what Guenther Roth has called a negative integration;[60] and the energy and spirit of democratic innovation that Fontane sensed in the working-class movement was left unused.

It is doubtful whether Hohenlohe had any appreciation of this. As a *grand seigneur*, he found it incomprehensible that the lower classes should be demanding a share in the governance of the state, and in any case he had no time to develop a more reflective attitude toward the problem. The romantic energies of his sovereign were not exhausted by his periodic campaigns against subversion. Hohenlohe was continually distracted by William II's abrupt *démarches* in foreign policy, which often had embarrassing consequences;[61] and, almost from the beginning of his term, the Chancellor had to wrestle with another of those intermittent conflicts of civil–military relations that plagued the history of the Second Empire.

This issue in this case was that of military justice, and it was posed because Hohenlohe's War Minister, Walter Bronsart von Schellendorf, undertook to revise the Prussian code of 1845, by modernizing trial procedures and providing for public hearings in most trials. Bronsart's initiative was hardly revolutionary, for the changes proposed had long been part of the judicial codes of other European

[59] Fontane, *Briefe* ii. 395 f.

[60] Roth, *Social Democrats*, pp. 159 ff., 315. According to Dieter Groh, the integration was positive enough to make the SPD an ineffective opponent of policies leading to war. *Negative Integration und revolutionärer Attentismus: Die deutsche Sozialdemokratie am Vorabend des Ersten Weltkrieges* (Frankfurt-on-Main, 1973), *passim*.

[61] See above, Ch. VII, 246.

military establishments, and the Kingdom of Bavaria had had public trials since 1869. There were, moreover, sound political reasons for the reform, since the Reichstag had passed resolutions in favour of publicity in 1870, 1889, and 1892, and since there were numerous interpellations on the subject in 1894. The Emperor, however, adamantly refused to accept the idea of reform, taking the line that it would constitute an attack upon the royal prerogative and saying pathetically that he would never be able to face his grandfather in heaven if he gave way to such a notion; and the Chief of the Military Cabinet, von Hahnke, brushed aside Hohenlohe's arguments about the intensity of public and parliamentary interest in the issue by saying curtly, 'The army must remain an insulated body into which no one dare peer with critical eyes'.[62] Three whole years passed before the issue was resolved, and in that period there were intermittent cabinet crises in the Prussian Ministry of State and in the federal government that led to the dismissal of one War Minister (Bronsart), one Foreign Minister (Marschall von Bieberstein, who had already offended the Emperor by attempting to restrain his wilfulness in foreign policy[63] and who now exhausted his tolerance by complicating the military justice dispute by making embarrassing disclosures about the operations of the Prussian Secret Police[64]), and two Prussian Ministers of the Interior (E. M. von Köller, because he revealed details of cabinet discussions to the Emperor's military entourage, and H. von Boetticher, presumably because he did not). In December 1898 the reform was finally accepted, largely because of persistent pressure by the Social Democratic, Progressive, and Centre parties, which in 1897 demonstrated their determination to have a modernization of the administration of military justice by forcing a cut of 12 million R.M. in the government's naval estimates and by launching a full-scale attack upon William II's personal regime and the influence of irresponsible agencies.[65]

[62] Hutten-Czapski, *Sechzig Jahre* i. 280–3; Hohenlohe, *Reichskanzlerzeit*, p. 116.

[63] See Eyck, *Das persönliche Regiment*, pp. 163 ff.

[64] In bringing suit against the newspaper *Berlin am Montag*, for accusations that he had leaked misleading information to the Press about foreign policy, Marschall disclosed that the leakage had come from the Secret Police through an agent called Tausch. The resultant trial of Tausch threatened revelations about the wider activities of the police network. This frightened a good number of people and infuriated the Emperor, who resented Marschall's stubborn loyalty to the constitution in pressing the case. See Dieter Fricke, 'Die Affäre Leckert-Lützow-Tausch und die Regierungskrise von 1897 in Deutschland', *Zeitschrift für Geschichtswissenschaft*, no. 7 (1960).

[65] For a fuller account of the dispute over military justice, see Craig, *Prussian Army*, pp. 246 ff.

By that time, Hohenlohe's credit with William II and with the nation had been pretty well exhausted. If he had served as a brake on the Emperor's more dangerous impetuosities, he had rarely taken a stand on principle, and he had not fought against the dismissal of Marschall and Boetticher, although they well deserved his support. Perhaps it can be said in his favour that his persistence in holding on to his office did Germany a minor service. If he had retired in 1895 or even in 1897, his successor might have been General von Waldersee. By staying until 1900, he made that impossible and assured the succession of Bernhard von Bülow. But one hesitates to assert too firmly that the country benefited from this substitution.

IV

No Chancellor, except Bismarck, had as varied and thorough a training in foreign affairs as Bernhard von Bülow. The son of a former Secretary of State for Foreign Affairs in Bismarck's service, he entered the Diplomatic Service in 1873 and, in the next fifteen years, served in a number of pleasant and important posts, including Rome, St. Petersburg, Athens, Vienna, and Paris. In 1878 he was secretary of the Congress of Berlin, the most impressive diplomatic omnium gatherum since Vienna. From 1888 to 1893 he was minister to Bucharest and, from 1893 to 1897, ambassador in Rome. In the latter year he returned to Berlin and, in the general shake-up of Hohenlohe's cabinet that was precipitated by the Emperor's displeasure by the failure of the naval estimates, the secret police trial, and the military justice dispute, he replaced Marschall von Bieberstein as Secretary of State for Foreign Affairs.[66]

From the beginning it was clear to insiders that this post was designed as a stepping-stone to higher things. Philipp Eulenburg, who considered Bülow to be one of his closest friends—they had been on a *Du und Du* basis for some time, and their letters were filled with expressions of affection that are embarrassing to modern ears[67]—had for years been describing him to the Emperor as the man who would solve all his difficulties. Indeed, as early as December 1895, infuriated by the Prussian Ministry of State's insistence upon the dismissal of his confidant E. M. von Köller, the Minister of the

---

[66] The cabinet changes included the substitution of Counter-Admiral Alfred von Tirpitz for Admiral Hollmann at the Imperial Naval Office, Graf Posadowsky-Wehner for Boetticher as Secretary of State for the Interior, and the appointment of Johannes Miquel, Prussian Minister of Finance, as Vice-President of the Prussian Ministry of State. See Hohenlohe, *Reichskanzlerzeit*, p. 364.

[67] Rich, *Holstein* ii. 550.

Interior,[68] William II had written: 'The Prince [Hohenlohe] is too old, he can no longer handle both foreign affairs and the Ministry of State, and the present Vice-Chancellor [Boetticher] is a cowardly milksop. Bülow shall become my Bismarck, and as he and my grandfather pounded Germany together externally, so we two will clean up the filth of parliamentary and party machinery internally. ... You may use this letter indiscreetly with Bülow.'[69] Not anxious at that time to become involved in a struggle with both the Ministry of State and the Foreign Ministry (William II's secondary target), Bülow did not respond to what others might have considered an invitation. He bided his time until it was clear that changes in the Hohenlohe ministry were inevitable and could not be described as the result of intrigue on his part. These tactics did not hurt him in the eyes of his imperial master, who was delighted when Bülow moved into the Foreign Ministry in June 1897 and who was soon writing to Eulenburg: 'Bernhard—superb fellow! . . . He has proved himself magnificently and I adore him! . . . What a joy to deal with someone who is devoted to one body and soul and who will and can understand one!'[70]

Bülow managed to retain his sovereign's confidence and affection not only for the three years during which Hohenlohe clung stubbornly to office,[71] but for most of the decade that followed his assumption of the old man's place. It is no exaggeration to say that he worked harder at keeping himself in the Emperor's good graces, upon which he knew that his position was absolutely dependent, than he did at any other aspect of his office, and he did not hesitate to employ the most byzantine forms of flattery to achieve his purpose. Shortly after becoming Chancellor, he sent a letter to Philipp Eulenburg which he was reasonably sure would reach the Emperor in one form or another.

I place my faith increasingly in the Emperor. He is so impressive! He is, along with the great King [Frederick II] and the Great Elector, the most impressive Hohenzollern who has ever lived. In a manner which I have never seen before, he combines genius—the most genuine and original genius—with the clearest good sense. He possesses the kind of fantasy that lifts me on eagle's pinions above all triviality and, at the same time, the

[68] On the Köller crisis, see Hohenlohe, *Reichskanzlerzeit*, pp. 123–40; Hutten-Czapski, *Sechzig Jahre* i. 284 ff.; and Eyck, *Das persönliche Regiment*, pp. 147 ff.
[69] Rich, *Holstein* ii. 501.
[70] Haller, *Eulenburg*, p. 240.
[71] Hohenlohe did not retire until October 1900 and even then only under great pressure. See Rich, *Holstein* ii. 624 f.

shrewdest appreciation of the possible and the attainable. And with it, what energy! What reflectiveness! What swiftness and sureness of conception.[72]

This unabashed pandering to the Emperor's worst qualities worried many in the top echelon of the government. Holstein's anxiety cost him the friendship of Eulenburg and the intimacy of Bülow. Waldersee, relegated to the army command at Altona by Bülow's arrival on the scene and forced to give up hopes of ever attaining the chancellorship, warned the Emperor's friend Albert Ballin, the managing director of the Hamburg-American Lines, that Bülow, by supporting all of the Emperor's enthusiasms and by never criticizing or opposing his wishes, was encouraging William II to overestimate his own abilities. Ballin refused to believe this, arguing that the Emperor was too clever to be taken in by crude adulation. Later, Waldersee records, Ballin returned and admitted that he had been wrong. 'Bülow', he said, 'is a misfortune for us and is destroying the Emperor completely.'[73]

To his credit, it must be said that Bülow had too realistic a view of developments in the world to cling to the reactionary social politics of his predecessors. With his accession to power, the likelihood of any attempt to stop the advance of Social Democracy by force disappeared. Bülow's programme for defeating the threat from the left had two components. First, he hoped to promote a union of the agrarian and industrial interests, based on the recognition and satisfaction of their economic desiderata, that would be strong enough to dominate the parliamentary situation in the Reichstag. This social-political formula had been conceived by Johannes Miquel in 1897 and given the name Sammlungspolitik,[74] and it had received the blessing of none other than Prince Bismarck, who recognized in it the spirit that had animated his Kartell of 1887 and who expressed his approval in an article in the Hamburger Nachrichten in March 1897. In this the former Chancellor declared: 'It is entirely in the interest of all producers, whether they produce grain or textiles or metals, to obtain the influence upon legislation that is due to them and which at

[72] Eyck, Das persönliche Regiment, pp. 190 f.

[73] Waldersee, Denkwürdigkeiten iii. 176, 220. On Ballin's shifting attitude towards Bülow, see Lamar Cecil, Albert Ballin: Business and Politics in Imperial Germany, 1888–1918 (Princeton, 1967), pp. 114 ff.

[74] On the Sammlungspolitik, see Herzfeld, Miquel ii. 183–4 and above, p. 255 n. 8. Also Dirk Stegmann, Die Erben Bismarcks: Parteien und Verbände in der Spätphase des Wilheminischen Deutschlands: Sammlungspolitik 1897–1918 (Cologne, 1970) and the criticism of Stegmann's interpretation in Wolfgang J. Mommsen, 'Domestic Factors in German Foreign Policy before 1914', Central European History, vi, no. 1 (Mar. 1973), 16–18.

the present time they do not exercise because of their disunity and because there are so many people making speeches in Parliament who make no contribution to the work of the nation'; and he went on to argue, as he had done earlier in a speech in 1895, that 'the bees' deserved more consideration than 'the drones', 'those drawing down salaries in state and communal offices, the professors, the pastors, and many other people' who played no part in the greatest task confronting the nation, that of 'combating Social Democracy and rendering it ineffective'.[75]

Bülow, with some private reservations, made this policy his own. To complement it and to provide an element of excitement and accomplishment that would impress the masses and fill them with a new love for and joy in the state, he embarked upon a spirited foreign policy on a global scale, a grandiose Welt- und Flottenpolitik. 'I am putting the main emphasis on foreign policy', he wrote in December 1897. 'Only a successful foreign policy can help to reconcile, pacify, rally, unite.'[76]

Inherent in this dual policy were, as we shall see,[77] the gravest kinds of risks, particularly in the field of foreign relations, for its inevitable consequence was the alienation of both Russia and Great Britain. But the economic gains that accrued to the partners in the agrarian–industrial condominium made them insensible to, or defiant of, these risks; and the supposed social-political advantages were irresistible to people who were frustrated by the failure of other attempts to check the rise of socialism. A man like Admiral Tirpitz, who had a professional stake in a policy based upon imperialism and navalism, had long been keenly aware of the political benefits it might bring. In addition to other reasons for Germany's adoption of such a policy, he wrote to Ulrich von Stosch in 1895, was the not-unimportant consideration that 'in the national purpose and economic gains consequent upon it lies a strong palliative against trained and potential Social Democrats'.[78]

Although somewhat removed politically from the Admiral, the sociologist Max Weber and the influential evangelical publicist and Progressive politician Friedrich Naumann shared his views. Weber's inaugural lecture at the University of Freiburg in 1895 demanded that the bourgeoisie shake themselves out of their 'soft eudaemonism' and take up the struggle for world power, since 'the goal of our

[75] Stegmann, *Die Erben Bismarcks*, pp. 67–8, 115.
[76] Röhl, *Germany without Bismarck*, p. 252.
[77] See below, Ch. IX.
[78] Alfred von Tirpitz, *Erinnerungen* (Leipzig, 1919), p. 52.

social-political labour is not world happiness but the social unification of the nation, which has been rent apart by modern economic
development, for the harsh struggles of the future'.[79] Naumann,
who had inherited from his mentor Stoecker a deep concern about
the gulf that existed between the working class and the rest of
Wilhelmine society, without accepting his prescriptions for their
solution, eagerly grasped at Weltpolitik as a means of social integration. In his influential book *Demokratie und Kaisertum*, written in
1900, he proclaimed, 'The new era will be imperialist and proletarian. . . . It is impossible at present to separate these two elements'.[80] Both he and Weber recognized the risks involved in competition with more firmly established world Powers, but seemed
exhilarated rather than deterred by them.[81] There is less evidence that
they were as conscious of the fact that the gains envisaged would be
enjoyed not by the nation but by the possessing classes.

The first tangible fruits of the Sammlungspolitik were the passage
of the Supplementary Naval Act of 1900[82] and the new tariff laws of
1902. That the agrarian party should have given its support to what
one of its leaders publicly called 'die gräßliche Flotte'[83] was due
partly to the hatred for England that affected it as a result of the Boer
War, an emotion caused less by sympathy for the underdog than by a
fear that a British victory in South Africa would herald a worldwide
victory of industrialism over the agrarian way of life and one that
must be resisted even at the cost of a fleet-building programme that
would bring undeniable profit to German heavy industry.[84] Equally

---

[79] Max Weber, *Gesammelte politische Schriften* (3rd edn., Tübingen, 1971), pp. 23–4
See also Mommsen, *Max Weber und die deutsche Politik*, pp. 32–4. Weber wrote later:
'Every successful imperialistic forcing play abroad normally strengthens, at least for
a time, the domestic prestige and with it the power and influence of those classes,
parties, estates under whose leadership the success is won.' *Grundriß der Sozialpolitik*,
iii. 2 (Tübingen, 1922), p. 626.

[80] Friedrich Naumann, *Demokratie und Kaisertum* (Berlin, 1900), p. 178.

[81] See Kenneth D. Barkin, 'Conflict and Concord in Wilhelmian Social Thought',
Central European History, v, no. 1 (Mar. 1972), 70. See also Werner Conze, 'Friedrich
Naumann. Grundlage und Ansatz seiner Politik in der nationalsozialen Zeit (1895 bis
1903)', in *Schicksalswege deutscher Vergangenheit*, ed. W. Hubatsch (Düsseldorf, 1950);
R. Nürnberger, 'Imperialismus, Sozialismus und Christentum bei Friedrich
Naumann', *Historische Zeitschrift*, clxx, no. 3 (1950), 525–48; and W. O. Shanahan,
'Friedrich Naumann: A German View of Power and Nationalism', in *Nationalism and
Internationalism*, pp. 352 ff.

[82] On the origins and development of navalism and its effects upon Germany's
foreign relations, see below, Ch. IX, pp. 303 ff.

[83] Eckhart Kehr, *Schlachtflottenbau und Parteipolitik 1894–1901* (Berlin, 1930), pp.
180 f.

[84] Kehr, *Economic Interest*, pp. 22–49 ('Anglophobia and *Weltpolitik*').

influential, however, were Miquel's negotiations, beginning in 1897, with the leaders of the Centralverband deutscher Industrieller and the Bund der Landwirte, which led to a private agreement that the government would bring in proposals to reform Caprivi's tariff laws and would be amenable to proposals from the grain producers for specific amendments.[85] The end-result of this was the passage of the new Tariff Law of December 1902, the principal feature of which was so great an increase of duties on imported grain that Russian grains were virtually excluded from the German market, a circumstance that redounded to the benefit of the East Elbian producers but significantly raised the price of staple foods in Germany.[86]

Although Bülow had been able, by appeals to the Centre, National Liberal, and Free Conservative parties, to force the modification of the most extreme agrarian demands, there was little doubt as to the real beneficiaries of the 1902 tariff. The Conservatives had in effect served notice on the Chancellor that their support of his policies was dependent upon his continued gratification of their economic interests. Bülow's recognition of this proved to be a serious limitation on his freedom of action in the subsequent period, when he was forced to face up to the financial difficulties caused by his aggressive foreign policy, his fleet-construction programme, and the slump of German trade during the economic recession that arose in 1903.

There was little doubt that the federal tax structure, as defined in the constitution and amended in 1879,[87] was badly in need of reform. Restricted on the one hand to dependence upon indirect taxes and to matricular contributions from the separate states and faced on the other by ballooning military and naval estimates and costly adventures like the seizure of Kiaochow and the war in South West Africa,[88] the Reich was faced with mounting deficits after 1903 which were in no way relieved by the new Tariff Law.[89] The financial question proved to be Bülow's most intractable problem, although he tried his best to avoid admitting this and to trivialize it with little

---

[85] Adolf Wermuth, *Ein Beamtenleben* (Berlin, 1922), pp. 218 ff.; Peter-Christian Witt, *Die Finanzpolitik des deutschen Reiches von 1903 bis 1913* (Lübeck and Hamburg, 1970), pp. 64–5.

[86] Witt, *Finanzpolitik*, pp. 71 ff. The National Liberals, Free Conservatives, and Centrists voted unanimously for the new Tariff Law. The Conservatives cast 30 votes for and 13 against, the dissenters for the most part being those who resisted the demands of the agrarians out of concern over their potentially ruinous political effects. See Wermuth, *Beamtenleben*, pp. 225–32.

[87] See above, Ch. II, p. 41 and Ch. III, p. 97.

[88] See below, Ch. IX, p. 310.

[89] See Witt, *Finanzpolitik*, pp. 74 ff.

jokes in the Reichstag, and in the end it brought him down, not least of all because of the intransigence of the agrarian interest.

Bülow's troubles began with the national elections of 1903. The unpopularity of the new Tariff Law was so great that the Social Democratic party, which had led the fight against it, gained 25 seats more than it had gained in 1898, while the left liberal parties, which had annoyed the voters by refusing either to vote for the tariffs or to join the Socialists in opposing them, lost 13 mandates. Although the National Liberals gained 3 seats, both Conservative parties lost, and the net result was a significant shift in the balance of forces in the Reichstag, which gave the Centre party a dominant position within the government coalition, since without its votes a majority was impossible. This was all the more infuriating to the other partners since the Centre had refused to join them in an electoral alliance for fear of losing votes by admitting solidarity with the agrarians;[90] and the Conservatives, in particular, showed they did not intend to forget this.

The resultant friction in the coalition was of critical importance in the wake of the elections, when the government tried to cope with the worsening budgetary deficit. It was characteristic of Bülow that at first he made no personal investment in this effort, pleading that foreign complications were engrossing all his time. The Chancellor knew that none of his predecessors had had much luck with tax increases, and tax increases were what was wanted now. But his failure to commit himself was in effect a new surrender to the agrarian forces (backed in this instance by the Prussian and Saxon governments) which were able to defeat both the Federal Treasury's attempts to win approval for new Reich taxes on tobacco and spirits and its efforts to introduce either a federal income tax or a comprehensive federal inheritance tax. In consequence, no rationalization of the tax structure took place.

By 1905 the budgetary situation had deteriorated so seriously that Bülow could no longer maintain his air of detachment. He told the Reichstag:

The finances of the Reich have gradually fallen into a state that requires speedy and thoroughgoing correction. The Reich's burden of debt has, because of lack of systematic amortization, steadily increased. The finances

---

[90] The Centre had voted for the tariff, but only after insisting that provision be made for the use of the increased income from duties to establish an insurance fund for widows and orphans. This paragraph, the so-called lex Trimborn, had no tangible result since the expected surpluses never materialized. John K. Zeender, 'The German Center Party, 1890–1906', *Transactions of the American Philosophical Society*, lxvi, pt. 1 (Philadelphia, 1976), 92.

of the federal states are suffering heavily because of the increased claims that the Reich makes on them. The nation's new political and cultural responsibilities (*Macht- und Kulturaufgaben*) are waiting upon the solution of this problem. It is incontrovertible that the Reich is in need of new income.[91]

This was a confession of his own weakness (the government had preferred in recent years to resort to loans rather than increase taxes) and the Reichstag was not impressed. The proposals that the government laid before it this time failed, on the one hand, because the Centre and the left parties refused to agree to the kind of taxes that would increase the burden on the ordinary taxpayer[92] and on the other because the Conservatives, without being able to prevent the institution of a Reich inheritance tax, found enough allies to help them weaken it by exclusion and deferment clauses, so that it had little financial significance.[93]

Meanwhile the cohesion of the governmental coalition had been further weakened. The independent line taken by the Centre during the debate on the abortive tax reform irritated both the Conservatives and the National Liberals, and the latter were further annoyed by the Centre's success, during the consideration of amendments to the Prussian School Law, in winning new concessions for Catholic institutions.[94] In the eyes of both these parties, moreover, the Centre appeared oblivious to the interests of either the government or the nation. In 1905, during the debate on the military appropriations, it had turned a deaf ear to all of Bülow's arguments about national security and had joined with the Social Democrats in striking requests for increases in the cavalry from the budget and imposing other restrictions.[95] In the same year, the rising star of the party, Matthias Erzberger, had begun to publish a series of startling reports about conditions in the German colonies, which accused the government of administrative incompetence, brutality in the treatment of natives, and subservience to the financial interests of large commercial enterprises, particularly the Tippelskirch and Woermann firms, which held a monopoly of shipping and supply to South West Africa and had used their position to charge the government exorbitant rates.[96] At a time when the government's prestige was

---

[91] Reichstag, *Verhandlungen* (1905), ccxiv. i ff.

[92] These included a proposal for a new tax on spirits and tobacco.

[93] On this complicated question, see Witt, *Finanzpolitik*, pp. 124–6.

[94] Ibid., p. 153.

[95] Ibid., p. 138.

[96] Zeender, 'Center Party' 99 ff.; Klaus Epstein, *Matthias Erzberger and the Dilemma of German Democracy* (Princeton, 1959), pp. 52 ff. For an account of the abuses and the administrative reforms passed in order to cope with them, see Jake Wilton Spidle,

being shaken by set-backs abroad, particularly the failure of its clumsy intervention in Moroccan affairs,[97] this behaviour seemed intolerable to the other Coalition partners, and they pressed Bülow to do something about it. He would doubtless have preferred to do so by means of negotiation,[98] but the discovery that influential Evangelical members of the Emperor's entourage were accusing him of excessive deference to Catholic views made him conclude that stronger action would be needed to shore up his sagging position.[99] He decided, therefore, to break with the Centre party and to create a new coalition by means of an electoral campaign based on nationalism, anti-socialism, and appeals to the latent anti-Catholicism that existed in certain parts of the country.

Bülow never displayed greater tactical virtuosity than during the election campaign of 1907, and, on the surface, he was brilliantly successful.[100] At the outset he succeeded by patient and adroit negotiation with the left liberal groups in persuading their leaders that they must throw their weight behind him in order to prevent the domination of the Reichstag by either a Red–Black alliance or a coalition in which the reactionaries had excessive influence. Subsequently, with the aid of a gigantic electoral fund contributed by financial and industrial interests and some of the larger trade associations, and with the aid of the Pan-German and Naval Leagues, he conducted a skilful propaganda campaign which, while rigorously avoiding any reference to domestic problems, appealed to the patriotism of the average voter, warning him that it was his duty to see that the enemies within the gates were made to suffer for their wilful neglect of the national interest.[101] The appeal did not fall on deaf ears. When the ballotting was complete, the parties of the so-called Bülow Bloc had won 216 seats (the Conservatives 60; the Free Conservatives 24; the Agrarian League and Economic Union 13; the Anti-Semites 16; the National Liberals 54; the Progressives 49).

jun., 'The German Colonial Civil Service: Organization, Selection and Training' (Dissertation, Stanford Univ. 1972), esp. Chs. 5, 6.

[97] See below, Ch. IX, p. 318.

[98] Indeed, he had tried to alleviate friction between the Centre and the new director of the Colonial Office, Bernhard Dernburg, by personal intervention in December 1906, but without success. Bülow, Denkwürdigkeiten, ii. 268 f.

[99] Rich, Holstein ii. 767; Bülow, Denkwürdigkeiten, ii. 261 f.; Theodor Eschenburg, Das Kaiserreich am Scheidewege: Bassermann, Bülow und der Block (Berlin, 1929), p. 37. Bülow was vulnerable because, among other things, his wife was a Roman Catholic.

[100] The election has been analysed by George D. Crothers, The German Elections of 1907 (New York, 1941).

[101] Ibid., pp. 105 ff., 118 f.; Dieter Fricke, 'Der deutsche Imperialismus und die Reichstagswahlen von 1907', Zeitschrift für Geschichtswissenschaft, ix (1961), 556 f.

Although the Centre actually gained 5 seats, increasing the size of its Reichstag delegation to 105, and the Poles had picked up 4, giving them a Fraktion of 20, the Socialists had lost 36 seats, falling from 79 to 43. Bülow had apparently won his gamble, escaping from the domination of the Centre without losing a working majority in the Reichstag.[102]

This had been achieved, however, at the cost of the lasting enmity of the Centre party. Its leaders, Spahn, Gröber, Hertling, and Erzberger, could not be expected to forget that they had been subjected to the kind of attack that the government Press had formerly reserved for the Socialists and that the German people had been told that 'the English, the French, and the Russians—all of our enemies in the world—desire the triumph of the allied Blacks and Reds because that would signify the end of German unity, power, and grandeur. Then our enemies would find it easy to overwhelm us and to make Germany once again the handmaid of others.'[103] It was only natural that they should wish to revenge themselves on the man who had authorized this sort of denigration of their integrity and in the sequel they found lots of opportunities to do so.

Bülow was, in fact, decidedly vulnerable. In the first place, having brought the left liberals into the Bloc, he had to persuade them that it was to their interest to stay. It was not long before they made it clear that the way to do this was to make concessions to their desire for change in Prussia, by liberalizing the school and association laws and reforming the three-class system of suffrage. Bülow's attempts to evade these demands by half-promises did not satisfy his new allies, although it alarmed his old ones; and, in 1907, when his new Reich Minister of the Interior and Vice-Chancellor, Theobald von Bethmann Hollweg, persuaded the Emperor to make a vague allusion to the possibility of change ('It is my will that . . . the suffrage of the lower house be developed in a manner corresponding to the economic development, the spread of education, as well as the political maturity and the strengthening of state consciousness. I consider this one of the most important tasks of the present'), the Conservatives were actively alarmed.[104]

---

[102] Crothers, *German Elections of 1907*, pp. 166 f.

[103] Witt, *Finanzpolitik*, pp. 158 f. To the National Liberals and Progressives, anti-Catholicism seemed to become the real point of the election, and Catholics began to talk about a new Kulturkampf. See Crothers, *German Elections of 1907*, pp. 119 ff.

[104] Konrad Jarausch, *The Enigmatic Chancellor: Bethman Hollweg and the Hubris of Imperial Germany* (New Haven and London), p. 58; Eschenburg, *Scheidewege*, pp. 72 ff. The Prussian suffrage issue had been revived by Friedrich Naumann in an article in the *Berliner Tageblatt* on 31 July 1907. Heuß, *Naumann*, pp. 331 ff.

In the second place, the problem of public finance had not been relieved by the tax bills of 1906, for the increase in yield was quickly absorbed by mounting naval costs.[105] With the national debt getting close to double what it had been in 1900, it was clear that a massive increase of federal income was needed, but it was equally evident that it would be difficult to make either the federal states or the parties of the Bloc agree on the form that new taxes should take. The Treasury officials convinced Bülow that he must call for 380,000,000 R.M. in new taxes on articles of consumption, 25,000,000 in increased matricular contributions, and 92,000,000 from an expansion of the existing inheritance tax. Knowing that this would cause a basic clash of interests, the Chancellor kept the details of the plan secret as long as possible, meanwhile mounting a propaganda campaign designed to bring so much public pressure to bear upon the parties and the state governments that they would not dare reject the tax package. In his instructions to his Press chief, Hammann, Bülow emphasized the fact that tax reforms must be presented as a question of 'To be or not to be' for the nation. He may have sensed that it might be the same for his personal position, although he pretended to be unaffected by this consideration. 'About my position', he wrote to Hammann, 'I am [not] concerned. A failure of the reform would give me *une très belle sortie*. But for our country, its internal welfare, it would be a blow that would not soon be overcome.'[106]

This tactic failed utterly. As usual, the agrarian interest proved impervious to public pressure, and the Bund der Landwirte and the Conservative leadership agreed in September 1908 to oppose any attempt to base reform on a Reich income or property tax, on an extension of the existing inheritance tax, or, indeed, on any scheme for increasing matricular contributions that would impose new burdens on the landholders. It was clear that, unless the Chancellor could persuade them to modify this stance, he would be unable to count on the support of the left liberals, who wanted new taxes on the land.

The Centre party, recognizing the Chancellor's dilemma, now moved quickly to exploit it. In a speech before the Bavarian Reichsrat, Graf Hertling, the leader of the southern and conservative wing of the party, announced that an extension of the inheritance tax would penalize the propertied class inequitably; and Matthias

---

[105] In addition to the Naval Bill of 1898 and the supplement of 1900, there had been another supplement in 1906. By 1908 the yearly budget of the Imperial Naval Office was 400 million R.M., about half that of the army. Ritter, *Kriegshandwerk* ii. 261.

[106] Witt, *Finanzpolitik*, p. 226.

Erzberger elaborated on these views in a newspaper article in which he also advanced a proposition already popular among Conservatives, namely that property should be subject to no new levies until a systematic effort had been made to tax mobile capital (stock market transactions, bank accounts, and the like).[107] Thus, before Bülow's tax reform was laid before the Reichstag, the Centre and the Conservatives were united in opposition to one of its principal features. Moreover, the Centre had made it abundantly clear to the *Junker* that it was not necessary for them to continue their uncomfortable coexistence with the liberals; another powerful ally was available to them. This was an invitation that the Conservatives were not prepared to disregard. They had become increasingly doubtful about Bülow's reliability and were becoming convinced that he would not hesitate, if his parliamentary position were threatened, to curry favour with the liberals by going beyond the inheritance tax and experimenting with more dangerous notions. By the end of 1908 a significant number of party leaders were ready to break with the Bloc in the hope of forcing Bülow's fall.

Constitutionally, it was true, the dissolution of the coalition need have no effect upon Bülow's position, for his retention of office was dependent on the Emperor's favour. But in November 1908 the Chancellor undermined his hitherto unassailable position with the Emperor by his handling of the crisis caused by the publication in the *Daily Telegraph* of London of an interview with William II in which the Emperor made a number of comments about foreign affairs that were calculated to harm relations with both Great Britain and Russia.[108] This new example of irresponsibility on the part of the sovereign aroused widespread criticism at a time when public respect for him had already been shaken by revelations of sexual deviance among some of his closest confidants;[109] and in the Reichstag there was a storm of resentment and a demand, shared momentarily by all parties, for the imposition of rigid restrictions upon the Emperor's political activities. Ironically, for once in his life, the Emperor had not acted unconstitutionally. Before authorizing publication of the interview, he had sent a transcript to Bülow for his

[107] Ibid., pp. 232, 234.

[108] Among other things, the Emperor took credit for having prevented Russia from attacking Britain during the Boer War and also for having devised the military plans that eventually enabled the British to end the war.

[109] These revelations were the result of Maximilian Harden's campaign, in the columns of *Die Zukunft*, against what he considered to be the dangerous influence of a court camarilla upon the Emperor. They effectively ended the career of Philipp von Eulenburg.

approval. In his airy way, the Chancellor had neglected to read it, passing it on to a junior official without indicating in any way that it should be treated cautiously. The Emperor's indiscretions, through no fault of his own, were allowed to stand and to make their way into print.[110]

Bülow did not see fit to admit this in the Reichstag, for to do so would have been to admit what the Austrian ambassador called the 'cascade de négligences' that had gone before.[111] Taking advantage of the public uproar and the demand of the parties and the federated governments for remedial action, he managed to obscure the events that preceded publication of the interview while intimating that he disapproved of it, adding that he was sure that the Emperor had meant well and would be more reticent in the future. If this were not so, he said blandly, neither he nor his successors could accept the responsibility of office.[112] Subsequently, with the encouragement of the Prussian Ministry of State and the Bundesrat's Committee on Foreign Affairs, the Chancellor extracted from his monarch a promise that, in the interest of the orderly conduct of state policy, he would henceforth be careful to observe the proper constitutional forms.[113]

Shaken by the storm that had blown up around him, William II acceded to these requests, but he did so resentfully, and relations between him and the Chancellor were never the same again. This need not have mattered had the *Daily Telegraph* crisis led, as it seemed for a time capable of leading, to a permanent constitutional change that would have increased the powers of Parliament at the expense of the monarchical principle. But the affair turned out to be just one more of those lost opportunities that marked the course of Germany's constitutional history; and the political parties, momentarily united in a demand for a diminution of the royal prerogative, a greater degree of responsibility of the Chancellor to the Reichstag, and the granting to that body of the right of interpellation, did not remain so. Having said A in brave determination, they said B doubtfully and without conviction. Theodor Eschenburg has written: 'The lack of discipline and solidarity, the formless excitement and

[110] Wilhelm Schüssler, *Die Daily-Telegraph-Affaire: Fürst Bülow, Kaiser Wilhelm und die Krise des zweiten Reiches 1908* (Göttingen, 1952); F. Freiherr Hiller von Gärtringen, *Fürst Bülows Denkwürdigkeiten: Untersuchungen zu ihrer Entstehungsgeschichte und ihrer Kritik* (Tübingen, 1956), pt. ii.

[111] Schüssler, *Die Daily-Telegraph-Affaire*, p. 27.

[112] Eschenburg, *Scheidewege*, pp. 149 f.; Hiller von Gärtringen, *Bülows Denkwürdigkeiten*, pp. 165–72.

[113] Witt, *Finanzpolitik*, p. 241; Eschenburg, *Scheidewege*, pp. 152 ff.

tendency to rhetorical excess that was common to the whole Wilhelmine era and the lack of a clear political objective let the whole Reichstag debate, upon which German public opinion had placed such hope, blow itself out without result.'[114]

The thought of exploiting both the public indignation over the Emperor's indiscretions and the financial crisis of the Reich in order to reform the Bismarckian constitution seems to have appealed to few of the parliamentarians. This was partly due to the fact that, unlike their colleagues in Britain and France, they were unschooled in the art of using their budgetary powers for political purposes. It was also an indication of the fact that the process by which the parties were being transformed from national political organizations into economic interest groups had already gone so far that it was virtually impossible for them to unite, as a parliamentary body, on any issue of great import. Two years later, Otto Hintze, the economic and social historian, was to point out that this tendency, which Bismarck had always encouraged, necessarily strengthened monarchical absolutism and weakened the influence of parliamentary bodies.[115] In 1909, among the bourgeois parties, only the followers of Friedrich Naumann sought to couple constitutional with fiscal reform, Friedrich Payer declaring that his vote for the government's tax proposals would be dependent upon the assurance of constitutional change.[116] Statements like this got little support from other Bloc members and merely strengthened the Conservatives' determination to force Bülow out of office before it was too late. They had been quick to note the Emperor's new coldness toward the Chancellor and were confident that, if the latter lost his majority, William would let him go. When formal discussions of Bülow's tax reform bill began, they therefore adopted an intransigent opposition to any concessions to their coalition partners, became increasingly intimate with the Centre leadership, and finally, on 24 March 1909, announced that they no longer regarded the financial question as a matter of Bloc politics. This declaration, which marked the end of Bülow's parliamentary alliance, was in effect his death-warrant.[117]

[114] Eschenburg, *Scheidewege*, p. 151. Friedrich Naumann claimed that this crumbling of the party front was due primarily to the refusal of Albert Bassermann, the leader of the National Liberal party, to allow his party to vote for any declaration against the Emperor or any list of demands for which the Social Democrats would vote. This proved, he said, the inability of the Reichstag to form any kind of majority that was not constructed by the Chancellor. Heuß, *Naumann*, pp. 342 ff.

[115] Otto Hintze, 'Das monarchische Prinzip', *Preußische Jahrbücher* (1911), 383 ff. The *Verwirtschaftlichung* of the parties is one of the major themes in Stegmann, *Die Erben Bismarcks*; see pp. 140–66, 219–43.

[116] Eschenburg, *Scheidewege*, pp. 158 ff.   [117] Ibid., p. 218.

This was not immediately clear, for the Chancellor held on for another three months until the financial issue was resolved. But in that time the direction of the negotiations concerning the tax structure slipped out of the hands of the government and into those of the Conservative and Centre leaders, who so dominated the work of the Reichstag Commission that the other parties, in May, refused to attend any further meetings. The final debate began on 16 June with a last appeal by the Chancellor for the inheritance tax; it was decided eight days later when that tax was voted down. Refusing to have his name associated with the successful Blue–Black substitute—taxes on mobile capital and on capital gains realized from the sale of land (a tax that affected urban landowners but not rural ones, since they rarely sold their proporty)[118]—Bülow asked the Emperor to dismiss him and went into retirement, after a farewell audience in which his sovereign, petulant because the crisis was interfering with his summer plans, acted, according to his former admirer, 'like a badly educated boy'.[119]

V

Before he passed from the scene, Bülow had one not insignificant triumph: he dictated the choice of his successor. The Emperor at first intended to appoint Graf Monts, the ambassador in Rome, a haughty and sardonic figure, sometime friend of Eulenburg and Holstein, with a critical bent and a talent for making enemies. With the collaboration of Valentini, the Chief of the Emperor's Civil Cabinet, Bülow was able to torpedo this.[120] William II then considered the Court Marshal August von Eulenburg and his cousin Botho, the putschist of 1894, but both of them were more conscious of their age and infirmities than the Emperor seemed to be, and they declined. William's agile mind then leaped to the possibility of bringing General Colmar von der Goltz back from Turkey, where he was serving as adviser to the Sultan's army. When it was pointed out that Goltz

[118] The Reichstag voted in favour of most of the excise taxes included in Bülow's plan and approved the 25,000,000 R.M. increase in matricular contributions. It made up for what the inheritance tax would have yielded by voting 40,000,000 R.M. new taxes on transfer of land and 70,000,000 R.M. of taxes on stock issues, stamps on dividend coupons, cheques, and bills of exchange. See Epstein, *Erzberger*, pp. 81 f.; Witt, *Finanzpolitik*, pp. 298 f.

[119] Bülow, *Denkwürdigkeiten*, ii. 525.

[120] Monts claimed that the Emperor had asked him in April whether he was prepared to accept the position and had told Albert Ballin that he was going to appoint him. In June, however, he wrote that democratic difficulties made the appointment inadvisable. A. Graf von Monts, *Erinnerungen und Gedanken*, ed. K. Nowak and F. Thimme (Berlin, 1932), pp. 145–7.

was indispensable in his present position, the Emperor gave way sulkily and accepted the man whom Bülow had pushed from the beginning, Theobald von Bethmann Hollweg.[121]

Once the decision was made, the Emperor, as mercurial as ever, was filled with enthusiasm for his choice. 'He is true as gold,' he told Bülow on 27 June, 'a man of integrity, also very energetic; he will straighten out the Reichstag for me. Besides, it was with him in Hohenfinow that I shot my first roebuck.'[122] Bülow was more cautious. 'For domestic policy Bethmann is certainly, all things considered, the best. He will keep the left on the string and bring back the Centre, and the Conservatives, as far as I know, are well disposed to him. Only he does not understand anything about foreign policy.' The Emperor brushed this aside. 'Foreign policy', he said gaily, 'you can leave to me!'[123]

There were those who regarded Bethmann as 'Bülow's revenge';[124] and Monts wrote spitefully to a friend: 'Bülow thinks that Bethmann will play the old tune, only with less virtuosity and grace . . . and then the world will finally recognize what a fine fellow *he* was'![125] Certainly the new Chancellor had little of Bülow's flair for the dramatic[126] and none of his delight in sensation, but this should have worried only those who had been taken in by Bülow's essential superficiality. Bethmann was the quintessential Geheimrat, who had made his way from the provincial administration of Brandenburg to the Prussian Ministry of the Interior and finally, in 1907, to the post of Secretary of State in the Imperial Office of Internal Affairs. He possessed all the best and worst qualities of the Prussian bureaucracy. He was a careful and energetic administrator, an effective negotiator, and a man of courage and honour in time of crisis; but, like Caprivi, he lacked creative talent, and his intellectual and political horizons were narrow. His ignorance of foreign affairs was, as Bülow had said, profound, and his knowledge of military problems minimal; and this robbed him of any confidence in two fields that were crucial for Germany's future. In other areas, too, he lacked

---

[121] R. von Valentini, *Kaiser und Kabinettschef* (Oldenburg, 1931), pp. 120 ff.

[122] This happened in 1877 when William was eighteen. Bethmann's father had provided half-tame bucks for the occasion, but the Prince missed three or four times before hitting one. See Jarausch, *Enigmatic Chancellor*, p. 35.

[123] Bülow, *Denkwürdigkeiten*, ii. 512.

[124] This was of Ballin's coinage. See Cecil, *Ballin*, p. 121.

[125] Hutten-Czapski, *Sechzig Jahre* i. 566.

[126] He would certainly never have gone to the length of rehearsing his speeches before a mirror, as Bülow did. See A. Zimmermann in *Front wider Bülow*, ed. F. Thimme (Munich, 1931), pp. 223 f.

verve and assurance. He was intelligent enough to see that the German political system was in need of reform (as Secretary of State of the Interior he had made a modest contribution to such reform by piloting a liberalization of the law governing political assembly through the Reichstag and proposing a reform of workers' insurance that was finally enacted in 1911), but he was too conservative in his views, and too opposed in principle to the idea of parliamentary government, to favour any fundamental change in the existing system. Given the pronounced leftward shift in national politics that began with the collapse of the Bülow Bloc, this meant that, after some ineffectual attempts to broaden his parliamentary backing, Bethmann became increasingly dependent upon non-parliamentary forces, the court, the bureaucracy, and the army. One of the consequences of this was that the militarization of Wilhelmine society reached its height during the peacetime years of Bethmann's chancellorship.

This was ironical, for Bethmann began his term with a keen awareness of how far that process had already been advanced as a result of Bülow's Weltpolitik and the activities of organizations like the Pan-German League, the Colonial Union, and the Naval League, which had not only conquered the *Bildungs- und Besitzbürgertum*, making it excitable, intermittently bellicose, and dangerously lavish in its support of military expansion, but had infected the lower middle class and portions of the working class with a high degree of *Hurrapatriotismus* as well.[127] Military values and military style influenced virtually all sections of society: a reserve officer's commission in a good regiment was something that every bourgeois entrepreneur desired for his son; the new brand of industrialists, whom Friedrich Naumann called 'Geheimratsübermenschen', ruled their firms as if they were fortress commanders;[128] and even right-wing Socialists were capable of striking military postures, as satirical magazines pointed out after the party congress of 1907.[129] Bethmann

---

[127] See Kehr, *Economic Interest*, p. 75. In 1911 Ludwig Frank wrote: 'Practically the whole bourgeoisie has become imperialistic as a result of the development of German industry and world trade; naval and colonial policy are no longer subjects of dispute within the bourgeois parties.' Cited in Stegmann, *Die Erben Bismarcks*, p. 113. The Pan-German League, founded in 1890 by Heinrich Clan, advocated colonial acquisition, vigorous support of German interests, by force if necessary, protection and support of *Volksdeutschen* everywhere in the world, and Germanization of minorities in Germany and Austria-Hungary. See Alfred Kruck, *Geschichte des Alldeutschen Verbandes 1890–1939* (Wiesbaden, 1954).

[128] Stegmann, *Die Erben Bismarcks*, p. 139.

[129] See the verse 'Noske schnallt den Säbel um' from *Lustige Blätter*, cited in Gustav Noske, *Aufstieg und Niedergang der deutschen Sozialdemokratie* (Zurich, 1947), pp. 29–30.

was not entirely immune to this himself (he made his first appearance before the Reichstag in the uniform of a major of the reserve), but he distrusted it when it appeared in strident and jingoistic forms, and he was resolved therefore to attempt to divert the nation's attention from problems of military power and foreign policy to essential tasks of domestic policy. In approaching these, he hoped—indeed, he felt that it was essential—to heal the political divisions caused by Bülow's fall and to bring the Conservatives, National Liberals, and Centre together in a programme of practical work that would alleviate some of the tensions of Wilhelmine society.

Bethmann soon discovered that this was not going to be easy. In the first place, the problems that contributed most to the political *malaise* were also the most intractable and divisive; in the second place, his legislative programme was handicapped by the chronic crisis in imperial finances. In the circumstances, the reforms that he proposed during his first years were modest to the point of timidity and met with little success. His attempt in 1910 to take the steam out of the perennial leftist agitation against the Prussian suffrage by modifying the existing law in such a way as to eliminate indirect voting and to diminish the plutocratic advantage found few supporters. Too radical for the Conservatives and not progressive enough for the National Liberals, Bethmann's bill aroused so much opposition in the Prussian Landtag that the Chancellor found it best to abandon it in May 1910, not without some bitter reflections about the way in which the stubborn opposition of the *Junker* to any change had further inflamed an issue that he had hoped to alleviate.[130] He was even less successful in his effort to ease relations between the Prussian Government and its Polish minority. Here again, the course he adopted—a deliberate slowing-down of the policy of Germanization that had been followed since Bismarck's time[131] and the establishment of a royal residence in West Prussia to bring William II into closer touch with the Polish nobility—aroused the suspicion of the Prussian Conservatives and the rage of the Hakatisten, the members of the extremely nationalistic Society of the Eastern Marches,[132]

Also Milorad M. Drachkovitch, *Les Socialismes français et allemand et le problème de la guerre, 1870–1914* (Geneva, 1953), pp. 216–75, 325–30.

[130] Jarausch, *Enigmatic Chancellor*, pp. 75–9.

[131] See Hans-Ulrich Wehler, 'Von den "Reichsfeinden" zur "Reichskristallnacht": Polenpolitik im Deutschen Kaiserreich 1870–1918', in his *Krisenherde des Kaiserreiches 1871–1918* (Göttingen, 1970), pp. 181 ff.

[132] This was usually called the HKT Society, after its leaders Hansemann, Kennemann, and Tiedemann. See R. W. Tims, *Germanizing the Poles: The H-K-T Society of the Eastern Marches, 1894–1914* (New York, 1941). On their influence, see Friedrich

without winning the appreciation of the Poles or the progressive elements in Germany. In the end, to preserve his credit with the Conservatives, the Chancellor found it expedient to implement Bülow's Expropriation Law and to begin sequestering Polish estates in the interests of the German peasantry, a decision that brought the wrath of the liberals, Progressives, Centre, and Socialists down upon his head and led to a vote of censure by the Reichstag early in 1913.[133] Finally, Bethmann's success in 1911 in securing legislative approval of a new constitution for Alsace and Lorraine, designed to integrate the Reichsland more fully with the Empire, was described by the reactionary but highly influential *Junker* politician Oldenburg-Januschau as 'a blow against Prussia's honour and prestige', and any benefit that the Chancellor derived from it was destroyed three years later by the incident at Zabern.[134]

If the parties of the *status quo* or, as he was wont to call them, the *staatserhaltende* parties found it impossible to co-operate on issues like this, Bethmann felt that he could not expect them to agree on the question of imperial finance. Yet, sooner or later, he knew, they would have to face it. The Blue–Black reform of 1909 had proved to be inadequate for anything but running expenses and interest on debts;[135] under the existing legislation any extension of social benefits or new experiments in Sozialpolitik were totally out of the question unless the Reich was willing to increase its already heavy burden of debt, and the same held true for naval or military expansion. This worried Bethmann, who, as early as 1910, was reflecting that unless new taxes were levied the security of the nation would be jeopardized,[136] but he saw no way of reconciling the differences between the parties, which had not been modified since Bülow had struggled with them. It would probably, he reflected, take the chastening experience of new Reichstag elections to bring the quarrelling groups to their senses. Meanwhile he decided to follow the course plotted by his capable Secretary of State of the Treasury, Adolf

---

Meinecke, *Die deutsche Katastrophe* (3rd edn., Wiesbaden, 1947), p. 39: 'The *Hakatisten* in Posen and West Prussia, the agitators of heavy industry, the *Junker* bureaucrats in the ministries and provincial governments, these were the specific supports of the internal power system whose complement externally was the Pan-German movement.'

[133] Jarausch, *Enigmatic Chancellor*, pp. 82–3.

[134] See Hans-Günter Zmarzlik, *Bethmann Hollweg als Reichskanzler 1909–1914: Studien zu Möglichkeiten und Grenzen seiner innenpolitischer Machtstellung* (Düsseldorf, 1957), pp. 93 ff.

[135] On the failure of the reform to raise the expected moneys, see Witt, *Finanzpolitik*, pp. 311 ff.

[136] Zmarzlik, *Bethmann Hollweg*, p. 49.

Wermuth, a policy of rigorous retrenchment, in which no government agency would be allowed to increase its expenditures unless savings were made to cover the additional outlay. This principle of 'keine Ausgabe ohne Deckung' Bethmann and Wermuth followed doggedly until 1912. Even after the Moroccan crisis of 1911 had produced a public clamour for a demonstration of Germany's armed might[137] and a series of excited demands from the Emperor, who wanted Bethmann to take advantage of the anti-English sentiment that the crisis had aroused to lay a bill for massive naval increases before the country and to go to the polls on that issue,[138] they held firm. The Chancellor had no desire to embark on a course that might very well lead to war,[139] and he was supported by his stubborn Secretary of State of the Treasury who, when imperial pressure threatened to become too much for Bethmann, made it clear that he would resign if any military increases were brought in until after the elections and who insisted that, even then, they must be part of a comprehensive financial plan. Anything less, Wermuth argued, would lead to a return of the bad old days when the military departments exceeded their budgets at will and made a shambles of orderly financial administration.[140]

The elections of 1912 were preceded by a campaign in which the Social Democratic party took advantage of the rising prices of food consequent upon crop failures to attack the government for its tariff and tax policies. The parties that supported the existing order did nothing to counter this, finding it impossible even to make inter-party agreements on how to co-operate during the run-off elections. The Conservatives spent most of their time attacking Bethmann, their leader Heydebrand accusing him of failing to defend German honour and German interests during the Moroccan negotiations. This forced the Chancellor to dissociate himself completely from the Conservatives during the campaign lest the British and French governments draw the wrong conclusions. Apart from calling upon civil servants to support the *staatserhaltende* parties, he played a curiously

---

[137] Ritter, *Kriegshandwerk* ii. 275.

[138] See, *inter alia*, Georg Alexander von Müller, *Der Kaiser . . . Aufzeichnungen des Chefs des Marinekabinetts Admiral Georg Alexander von Müller über die Ära Wilhelms II*, ed. W. Hubatsch (Göttingen, 1965), p. 102.

[139] The option of jingoism as a means of bringing the parties together was always available, but Bethmann opposed it at this time. 'Who today', he wrote in August 1910, 'will take upon himself the responsibility for rattling the sabre and painting the dangers of war on the wall, if the actual circumstances do not force him imperatively to do so?' Zmarzlik, *Bethmann Hollweg*, p. 48.

[140] On Wermuth's policy, see Wermuth, *Beamtenleben*, pp. 276 ff.; Witt, *Finanzpolitik*, pp. 337 ff.

detached role during the elections, confidently expecting the worst. The swing to the left was even greater than he had feared it might be. The Conservative Reichstag delegation was reduced to 43 (from 60), the Reichspartei to 14 (24), the Centre to 91 (105), the National Liberals to 45 (54), and the Progressives to 42 (49). In contrast, the Socialists won 67 new seats, which gave them 110 Reichstag deputies.

The elections had two unfortunate results. In the first place, they led to what Wolfgang J. Mommsen has called 'the stalemate of the party system'.[141] Theoretically, the Social Democrats were in a position to dominate the Reichstag, provided they could bring the liberals and the parties representing the national minorities to their side. But a Bassermann–Bebel bloc was hardly a practical matter. Despite the progress of revisionism in Socialist ranks, the traditions of the party militated against such a combination, and the left wing was big enough and loud enough to make it a virtual impossibility. In the same way, it was hard to imagine the right wing of the National Liberals being comfortable in an alliance with the Social Democrats. Nor did any other political grouping have the potential to make the Reichstag an effective body; a reconstitution of the Bülow Bloc, for example, seemed quite out of the question. In these circumstances, Bethmann was encouraged to have as little to do with parties as possible from now on, bypassing the Reichstag when he could and, when this was impractical, 'creating majorities from issue to issue',[142] and, on occasion, appealing to those sections of society that distrusted politics and politicians to support him against the quarrelling parliamentarians.[143] The Chancellor never shared, or at least never admitted to sharing, William II's opinion that the Reichstag was 'a troop of monkeys and a collection of blockheads and sleep-walkers',[144] but there can be no doubt that his policy of standing above the parties led to an increase in the kind of authoritarianism that the Emperor believed in, while at the same time making his own position more vulnerable to the influence that the military and the bureaucracy and the various private camarillas exercised upon the monarch.[145]

[141] Mommsen, 'Domestic Factors in German Foreign Policy', 27.

[142] Bethmann's own words, cited in Jarausch, *Enigmatic Chancellor*, p. 91.

[143] Fritz Fleiner once argued that the average German distrusts politicians and has a three-point credo that confirms him in his suspicion: (1) 'Der Staat sind die Beamten'; (2) 'Die Politik verdirbt den Charakter'; (3) 'Die beste Verfassung ist eine gute Verwaltung'. *Reden und Schriften* (Zurich, 1941), pp. 401 f.

[144] H. Lohmeyer, *Die Politik des zweiten Reiches* (Berlin, 1939), p. 240.

[145] Mommsen, 'Domestic Factors in German Foreign Policy', 28. See also Fritz

In the second place, the election results caused a virtual panic in precisely these groups. The sudden access of Social Democratic strength seemed to portend an imminent democratization of the country, if not something worse; and the bureaucrats and soldiers, fearful of the vulnerability of the monarchical system to internal as well as to external attack, became insistent upon building up the defences of the state as quickly as possible, increasingly sensitive to any attempt by the Reichstag or public opinion to impose restrictions upon them, and bitterly critical of the Chancellor when he did not defend their rights and privileges energetically enough to satisfy them. To protect his own position, Bethmann was often driven to actions which, with greater freedom, he might have tried to avoid.

This was particularly true in the field of imperial finance where he abandoned the principles that he and Wermuth had maintained in the period before the elections. To be sure, his position was a difficult one. With skill and pertinacity, and with much wear and tear upon the Emperor's patience, he had contained Admiral Tirpitz's campaign for a massive fleet increase by postponing any action upon it until after the excitement caused by the Moroccan crisis had quietened down and the elections were over and then by announcing a new increase in the army, which forced the Imperial Naval Office to curtail its expectations markedly. Even so, the Chancellor had to find over 100 million R.M. in new income, and Wermuth said that this sum could be raised only by the introduction of a Reich inheritance tax. Bethmann began negotiations to lay the basis for such an innovation but immediately ran into strong opposition in the Prussian Ministry of State, where Schorlemer, the Minister of Economics, declared that the Wermuth plan would put 'the tax screw (*Steuerschraube*)' in the hands of democratic elements in the Reichstag and that this 'would embitter the loyal and monarchically inclined population'. When this view was echoed by other Conservative ministers, Bethmann began to reconsider his position and, as Tirpitz and the Emperor began to complain of delays, he gave way completely. The idea of an inheritance tax was abandoned, and the money it was expected to provide was raised in part by the elimination of the tax exemption on spirits and in part from reserves that Wermuth had hoped to use to amortize debts. This surrender was

---

Hartung, 'Verantwortliche Regierung, Kabinette und Nebenregierungen im konstitutionellen Preußen 1848–1918', *Forschungen zur brandenburgischen und preußischen Geschichte*, xliv (1932).

too much for the Secretary of State of the Treasury, who resigned in disgust.[146]

From retirement Wermuth wrote an article in which he pointed out that the last years had witnessed a complete militarization of imperial financial policy, that all attempts to make the services observe the principles of sound financial planning had been defeated, and that they had been responsible for virtually every penny of the increase of state expenditure since 1911.[147] This was all perfectly true, and worse was to come, for the army now made it clear that the increases provided by the 1912 bill were inadequate to provide for national security.

In sharp contrast to the Imperial Naval Office, the army high command had, for almost twenty years, been remarkably modest in its demands upon the government. At the War Ministry, both von Gossler (1896–1903) and von Einem (1903–9) had resisted an expansion of the army's peacetime strength, partly because they believed that quality was more important than numbers and were satisfied that the German army was capable of withstanding any challenge, partly because they feared expansion would threaten the social homogeneity and political reliability of the officer and non-commissioned officer corps. They paid little attention to the complaints of Schlieffen (Chief of the General Staff, 1891–1906) and his successor Moltke the Younger, who argued that Germany's armed force was not adequate to implement their war plans; and, since neither of the staff chiefs desired to take issue to the Emperor, particularly in view of his strong predilection for the navy, the War Ministry had its way.[148]

The increase of international tension after 1911, however, made the new War Minister, von Heeringen (1909–13), more receptive to General Staff arguments, which were stated with a new cogency and emotion by Colonel Erich Ludendorff, head of the Mobilization

---

[146] The accounts of both Zmarzlik, *Bethmann Hollweg*, pp. 51 ff. and esp. 59, and Jarausch, *Enigmatic Chancellor*, pp. 91–5 are favourable to Bethmann, the former accusing Wermuth of one-sidedness and *Ressortpatriotismus*. Witt, *Finanzpolitik*, pp. 346–56 is more critical. See also Wermuth, *Beamtenleben*, pp. 304–16.

[147] Adolf Wermuth, 'Das Reichsfinanzprogramm', *Deutsche Revue*, xxxvii (July 1912), 8 ff.

[148] The best general discussion is Reichsarchiv, *Kreigsrüstung und Kriegswirtschaft* (Berlin, 1930). For the army bills of 1912 and 1913, see Hans Herzfeld, *Die deutsche Rüstungspolitik vor dem Weltkriege* (Bonn and Leipzig, 1923); Erich Ludendorff, *Mein militärischer Werdegang* (Munich, 1933); and Generaloberst von Einem, *Erinnerungen eines Soldaten 1853–1933* (Leipzig, 1933). An excellent brief account is to be found in Ritter, *Kriegshandwerk* ii. 256–81. See also Kehr, *Economic Interest*, pp. 50–75 ('Class Struggle and Armament Policy in Imperial Germany').

Section and, after October 1912, Moltke's closest adviser. Ever since 1910 Ludendorff had been arguing that Germany was dangerously exposed to foreign attack. 'The number of our enemies', he wrote in July of that year, 'is so great that it can become an unavoidable duty for us in certain cases to raise against them the totality of manpower capable of bearing arms. Everything depends upon our winning the first battles.'[149] What the army needed, he argued passionately, was not only an increase in over-all size but an energetic attempt to improve the organization and readiness of the reserve. 'We must once more become the people in arms', he wrote in 1912, 'to which we were once raised in a great time by great men. There must be no retreat for Germany, but only an advance!'[150]

In the general public there was, in the wake of the Moroccan crisis, strong support for these ideas, not least of all because of the activities of August Keim, a retired officer. At the beginning of 1912, without any official encouragement and apparently motivated purely by a private conviction that a major war was impending, Keim founded a propaganda organization called the Wehrverein for the purpose of 'awakening the whole nation to the understanding of a need for a larger army and of realizing this demand by the pressure of public opinion on the parties of the government'. The new union quickly surpassed the Navy League in effectiveness, and in 1912 and 1913 its chosen tactic of supporting all military bills until they were passed and then condemning them, in Keim's words, as 'completely inconceivable in their shortcomings' provided strong support for Ludendorff and his supporters in the General Staff and the War Ministry.[151]

The Army Bill of 1912 had added about 29,000 men to the peacetime strength of the army and introduced some technical improvements in weaponry, logistics, and organization. Before the end of the year, however, Ludendorff was demanding an increase of 300,000 recruits in two years and the raising of three completely new army corps. These figures alarmed Moltke, particularly when he discovered that Ludendorff expected his plan to be implemented, not over a period of years, but at once; and, when his impulsive subordinate refused to modify his views, the Chief of Staff transferred him to a regimental command. This did not mean that Moltke was any more satisfied with existing levels than Ludendorff. Indeed, after

[149] Ritter, *Kriegshandwerk* ii. 274.
[150] Ibid. 277.
[151] On the Wehrverein, see ibid. 276; Alfred Vagts, *A History of Militarism* (New York, 1939), p. 389; and, for its influence on thinking in the War Ministry, the memoirs of its Press chief H. Müller-Brandenburg, *Von Schlieffen bis Ludendorff* (Leipzig, 1925).

consultations with Heeringen, he now asked the Chancellor for what became the biggest army bill in German history, an increase of peacetime strength by 117,000 men and 19,000 officers and non-commissioned officers.

Bethmann reacted with some bitterness to these demands and was particularly shocked, he wrote, 'by our military's assessment of our relative strength in case of war. One must have a good deal of trust in God and count on the Russian revolution in order to be able to sleep at all. Because of the navy we have neglected the army, and our "naval policy" has created enemies all around us.'[152] Still, he did not waste time repining but threw himself into the effort to raise the necessary moneys to meet the army's needs.

The obvious dangers of the foreign situation made the task somewhat easier this time. The new Army Bill was greeted with enthusiasm and accepted by the Reichstag with no significant changes. Moreover, Bethmann was successful in raising funds to cover the increased costs. Despite difficulties with the Bundesrat, which was always reluctant to grant the Reich tax powers that might diminish the competence of the federal states in the field of direct taxation, that body concurred in the end in the Reichstag's demand for a tax on unearned increment, that is on the increase on the value of inherited land. For the first time in the history of the Reich, the federal government was given the right to tax property directly and, for the first time, an important financial law was accepted despite the opposition of the Conservatives.[153]

Perhaps more significant were two additional facts: namely, that this particular financial reform was designed solely to serve the military machine and that the Social Democratic party voted for it, despite its long tradition of opposing militarism in all its forms. The excuse given by Socialist spokesmen was that it was more important to assure the acceptance of the principle of Reich property taxes than it was to defeat the Military Bill. This was not disingenuous. Yet it was also true that the Socialist leaders were aware that a negative vote would not be understood by large sections of the working class, who, thanks to the integration process that had been taking place since 1890,[154] were just as patriotic and just as vulnerable to military influence as anyone else, particularly when—as Bethmann said in his speech introducing the bill—there seemed to be a real possibility of a war to defend Germany against the menace of Slavdom. A year later

---

[152] Jarausch, *Enigmatic Chancellor*, p. 96.
[153] Witt, *Finanzpolitik*, p. 372.
[154] See Ritter, *Arbeiterbewegung*, pp. 150, 170 ff.

the same feeling would dictate the voting of the war credits by the Socialist delegation.[155]

The most dramatic illustration of the growth of military preponderance in Germany and of the Chancellor's capitulation to it came in November 1913 in the Alsatian town of Zabern.[156] Here a young Prussian lieutenant named Forstner, by making insulting references to the people of Alsace in a speech to recruits that was reported in the Press, touched off a series of public disorders. Instead of reprimanding Forstner, the garrison commander, Colonel von Reuter, chose to regard the local protests as an insult to the army and, when they became more serious, abruptly superseded the civilian authorities, declared a state of siege, and instituted the wholesale arrest of people who assembled in the streets and jeered at his troops. The head of the Imperial Government in Alsace and Lorraine, Staathalter Karl von Wedel, was appalled by this behaviour, not because of any personal animus against the military (he was a soldier himself), but because he was aware that, unless the affair was settled quickly by the official disciplining of the officers responsible, it would irretreivably ruin everything that he and his predecessors had done to win the allegiance of the conquered population and would nullify the constitutional reform of 1911.[157]

The kind of solution Wedel hoped for was, however, made impossible by the fact that William II engaged himself in the affair immediately. Without taking any time for reflection, the Emperor accepted and approved a report sent to him by General von Deimling, the senior military commander in the Reichsland, that blamed the disorders on the sensational Press and local *provocateurs*.[158] When Wedel, who as Staathalter was immediately responsible to the Emperor, used this relationship to appeal for an audience with his monarch so that he might explain the political aspects of the matter, his request was indirectly but decisively refused. He was informed

[155] Witt, *Finanzpolitik*, p. 375.

[156] The most important items in the extensive literature on this incident are listed in Hans-Ulrich Wehler, 'Der Fall Zabern', *Die Welt als Geschichte*, xxiii (1963). See also Martin Kitchen, *The German Officer Corps, 1890–1914* (Oxford, 1968), Ch. XI.

[157] On the history of the Reichsland since 1871, see Hans-Ulrich Wehler, 'Unfähig zur Verfassungsreform: Elsaß-Lothringen von 1870 bis 1918', *Krisenherde*, pp. 17 ff. On the role and incomplete success of the University of Strasburg in promoting integration, which is what it was founded to do, see John Craig, 'A Mission for German Learning'.

[158] The Emperor at least refrained from indiscreet revelations of his personal views. Not so his eldest son, who sent a telegram to Reuter, congratulating him on punishing the 'Unverschämtheit des Zaberner Plebs' and urging more of the same, 'Immer feste druff!' See Wehler, 'Der Fall Zabern', 34.

that the Emperor would be briefed by the Chief of the Military Cabinet on the basis of reports sent to him by the responsible army command.

The Emperor had, in short, decided that the disposition of the incident at Zabern was a matter lying within the sphere of his royal power of command (*Kommandogewalt*), to be settled between his commanders and himself, without any civilian interference. He underlined this by remaining throughout the subsequent uproar at the Fürst von Fürstenberg's estate at Donaueschingen, where he was completely surrounded by his *maison militaire*. The lone exception in this uniformed galaxy was Councillor von Treutler from the Foreign Ministry, and the Emperor flatly refused to discuss Zabern with him.[159] At the beginning of December, when Wedel sent a comprehensive report of the incident and its consequences to Donaueschingen, William II covered it with critical marginalia. '[Wedel] forgets', the Emperor wrote, 'that the root of the whole business is purely military',[160] a remark that indicates how completely he had absorbed the philosophy of the soldiers, who had long since concluded that Alsace and Lorraine should be considered as a glacis for the war that they considered to be inevitable and that the local population should be regarded as potentially hostile and treated firmly. Of the inevitable domestic and international political repercussions of this attitude the Emperor seemed completely unaware.

Yet as early as 28 November Falkenhayn, the War Minister, had had to answer questions in the Reichstag about Lieutenant Forstner's behaviour in Zabern,[161] and, when the news of the arrests appeared in the Press, there was an outcry of protest that soon exceeded in violence that aroused by the *Daily Telegraph* interview. With the exception of the Conservatives and their friends in the self-styled Anti-Semite party, all of the parties in the Reichstag were disturbed, the Socialists and democratic left violently so; and it soon became clear that the Chancellor would be called to give some account to the angry parliamentarians.

It is characteristic of Bethmann that he never considered availing himself of the tactics of appeasement employed by Bülow in 1908. 'Bülow', he wrote scornfully later on, 'would have set off brilliant fireworks that would have pleased the crowds and singed the wings of the Kaiser and the army.' He could not do that, even though he

[159] Zmarzlik, *Bethmann Hollweg*, p. 115.
[160] Ibid., p. 118.
[161] Erwin Schenk, *Der Fall Zabern* (Stuttgart, 1927), p. 39.

agreed with Wedel that the army was entirely at fault. His fundamental opposition to parliamentarianism made it impossible for him
to join 'the vainglorious Bassermann arm-in-arm with Scheidemann
and Erzberger'.[162] As usual, he sought to follow the diagonal way.
He discussed with Falkenhayn the possibility of sending a high-
ranking officer to Zabern to liquidate the affair in a way that would
quieten the local agitation, among other things by relieving the
garrison commander; and, when the War Minister agreed to propose
this to William II at Donaueschingen, he wrote to the Emperor
urging him to agree to the plan, adding that this plea was motivated
by his 'consciousness of his bound duty to intervene with all [his]
energy on behalf of the authority of the army'. These words, as
Zmarzlik has commented, illuminate both the ambivalence of his
feelings and the awkwardness of the dilemma in which he had been
placed.[163]

The Emperor agreed to send Major-General Kühne to Zabern to
make an investigation and institute charges if necessary, but he
refused to permit the Chancellor to announce this to the Reichstag,
since in his view his action was a command matter and hence none of
its business. On 3 December, therefore, when Bethmann went
before Parliament, he had no means of moderating the passions of his
auditors. His speech, in which he admitted that excesses had been
committed but defended the local commander on the grounds that
he had been acting to liquidate a potentially dangerous situation, and
his stout declaration that 'the King's coat must be respected in all
circumstances', merely angered the deputies, and their anger turned
to fury when the War Minister barricaded himself behind the royal
power of command and refused to answer their questions. To the
accompaniment of violent speeches about this *dies ater* in German
history and philippics against Bethmann's weakness and the obliquities of the 'praetorian officers', a resolution was introduced declaring that the Chancellor's response to the Reichstag interpellation
on the Zabern incident was inadequate, and on 4 December this vote
of no-confidence was passed by a majority of 293 to 54.[164]

This was an impressive success for parliamentary government, or
would have been had the parties in the Reichstag demanded that the
government recognize the vote and yield to it. But a whole week

---

[162] Jarausch, *Enigmatic Chancellor*, p. 102.
[163] Zmarzlik, *Bethmann Hollweg*, p. 117.
[164] Wehler, 'Der Fall Zabern', 31. This was the second vote of no-confidence in
Bethmann's handling of affairs, the first, protesting expropriation of Polish estates,
having been passed on 30 January 1913 by a vote of 213 to 97.

passed before Philipp Scheidemann, speaking for the Socialists, called upon the Chancellor to resign on the grounds that he had lost all real authority and was being maintained in office only by 'the fetish of personal rule'; and Scheidemann's speech seemed only to embarrass the members of the other delegations who had voted together on 4 December.[165] Not used to authority, they were no more inclined than they had been at the time of the *Daily Telegraph* affair to make experiments in exercising it; the idea of using the boycott to force changes in the government frightened them. The militant mood of early December did not survive the Christmas season, and neither the dismissal in January of all charges against the officers who had caused the disturbances in Zabern, nor the resignation of Wedel, nor the appointment to the position of Staathalter of a reactionary conservative, who had opposed the constitutional reform of 1911 and Wedel's integration policy in Alsace-Lorraine,[166] had any power to revive it. The middle-class parties, which were composed of people who admired the military and imitated its values, could not be moved to more than momentary irritation over its faults, and a Reichstag that had voted the biggest peacetime military budget in history in October 1913 was not a body that was capable of disciplining the army three months later. The Reichstag did establish a commission in January 1914 to investigate means of delineating the legal boundary between civil and military authority, but this body disbanded, surreptitiously and without result, a month later.[167]

The firmness with which Bethmann had withstood the storm had won him some grudging respect in the nation at large and had strengthened his relationship with the Emperor. Despite his frequent irritation over the Chancellor's deliberate manner and his habit of weighing alternatives at inordinate length, William II appreciated Bethmann's unfailing loyalty and his refusal in the Reichstag to tolerate any attacks upon the Crown,[168] and he had come to recognize the merits of his moderate brand of conservatism. The Emperor was still capable of having temper tantrums about the Reichstag and of telegraphing the Chancellor, as he did in 1913, 'The sooner such *Halunken* are blown to smithereens the better! The

---

[165] See Schenk, *Der Fall Zabern*, pp. 51 ff.

[166] This was Johann von Dallwitz, Prussian Minister of the Interior from 1910 to 1914 and a leader of the Conservative opponents of reform. See Zmarzlik, *Bethmann Hollweg*, p. 127.

[167] Wehler, 'Der Fall Zabern', 41.

[168] The best treatment of relations between William II and Bethmann is Zmarzlik, *Bethmann Hollweg*, pp. 23 ff.

German parliamentarian and politician becomes daily more of a swine!', but he no longer thought of putsching against it. Indeed, in December 1913, he wrote to the Crown Prince: 'In Latin and Central America *Staatsstreiche* may belong to the instruments of the art of government. In Germany, thank God, they are not customary and must not become so, whether they come from above or below. People who dare to recommend such action are dangerous people, more dangerous for the maintenance of the monarchy than the wildest Social Democrat.'[169] With respect to domestic affairs, William II now generally followed Bethmann's advice.

Even so, the real victors in the Zabern affair were the military and their allies in the ranks of the Conservative party in Prussia, the agricultural and industrial associations and pressure groups, the service organizations and the Pan-German League. Despite the fact that they profited from Bethmann's loyalty to the monarchical principle and his energetic defence of the *status quo*, it was among these groups that the Chancellor was most bitterly hated and most vehemently denounced for flabbiness and proneness to dangerous constitutional experiments.[170] At the very moment when he was working patiently and skilfully to win the approval of the Reichstag and the Bundesrat for the staggering military budget of 1913, conspiracies were being hatched in the hope of unseating him. They were to continue without respite until his enemies brought him down in 1917.

[169] Ibid., p. 40.
[170] Stegmann, *Die Erben Bismarcks*, pp. 325 ff., 430.

IX
Weltpolitik, Navalism, and the Coming of the War
1897–1914

Ich seh durch blaue Nacht den Erdball rollen
und seh die lichten Flecken des Planeten:
es sind die Länder, draus wir blühen sollen.

Und näher! Auf den Meeren seh ich Scharen
grau-kleiner Punkte, die wie Möwen fliegen:
es sind die Schiffe, die durchs Weltmeer fahren.

Und näher noch: ein vielbevölkert Land
und viel Getümmel seh ich in den Städten,
doch allzu stumm den langen, langen Strand!

Daß Kraft und Luft und Licht in Deutschland wäre!
Oh, möchten sich wie hundert Schwäne wiegen,
wie Strahlen unsrer Kraft, wie Adler fliegen
einhundert Panzer auf beherrschtem Meere!

FRIEDRICH LIENHARD (1900)[1]

Alle Straßen münden in schwarze Verwesung.

GEORG TRAKL (1914)[2]

THE previous chapter has indicated the extent to which ideological, socio-economic, and institutional structures determined the general course of policy during the reign of William II. Foreign policy also reflected their influence, particularly after the introduction of the Sammlungspolitik of 1897. While recognizing this, the historian who undertakes to study its evolution after that date should nevertheless be wary about succumbing to a deterministic view and should remember Federico Chabod's comment that 'in a given situation, the work of the individual statesman

---

[1] 'Deutsche Weltmacht', in *Deutschland, Deutschland. Politische Gedichte*, ed. Lamprecht, p. 227. This poem appeared first in a collection called *Burenlieder*, and the author donated half of his profits to the Boer cause.

[2] 'Grodek', in Georg Trakl, *Selected Poems* (London, 1968), p. 120.

always intervenes incisively in the course of events, whether he allows himself weakly to be submerged by their flow or boldly succeeds in channelling them somehow, making them follow one rhythm or another, directing them to this goal or that, slackening their pace or quickening it'.[3] The behaviour of William II and his ministers is not a perfect illustration of this dictum, but it is close enough. Certainly, incisive intervention was a conspicuous feature of Wilhelmine diplomacy. Unfortunately, because its practitioners generally channelled events in illogical ways, set them to arrogant rhythms, directed them to dangerous goals, and quickened their pace instead of seeking to do the opposite, their boldness was self-defeating, and they allowed themselves fatalistically to be borne away by the flood in 1914.

I

With the exception of the Emperor himself, the persons who did most to give German foreign policy a European reputation for dangerous irrationality were Bernhard von Bülow and Alfred von Tirpitz. Bülow's character and objectives have already been touched upon. It is important now to consider the personality and ambitions of his dynamic colleague, for in the last analysis it was the naval policy that he inspired that gave a new dimension to the old colonial policy of the 1880s and early 1890s and transformed it into the Weltpolitik that entranced so many Germans as the new century dawned. And it was his policy, also, that contributed more than anything else to the total deterioration of Anglo-German relations.

The son of a lawyer and a doctor's daughter, Alfred Tirpitz joined the naval service in 1865 at the age of sixteen, as many other sons of wealthy middle-class families had done before him and were to do in the future, for the navy was the liberal service, having been born during the debates of the Frankfurt Parliament, and, unlike the army, it did not insist that its officers be aristocrats by birth. He served in the wars of 1866 and 1870, although the Prussian navy was too small and too badly armed to perform anything but scouting duty at that time, a circumstance that had led Bismarck to investigate the possibility of buying ships complete with crews from the United States Government. After the victory over France, the new German navy began to grow, and Tirpitz's career grew with it. He was, as one of his associates wrote years later, 'a very energetic character. He has too big a head of steam not to be a leader. He is ambitious, not choosy

<hr />

[3] Chabod, *Storia della politica estera italiana*, i, p. xiv.

about his means, of a sanguine disposition. High as the heavens in his joys but never relaxing in his creative activity, no matter how crushed he may appear . . . [He is] convinced of his own excellence.'[4] These qualities impressed the new Chief of the Admiralty, Albrecht von Stosch, who became particularly interested in Tirpitz's work on torpedoes and in 1877 made him leader of the Torpedo Section, an order confirmed by Caprivi when he took over the Admiralty in 1883.[5] Indeed, Caprivi, who was convinced that the navy should concentrate on defensive weapons rather than high sea vessels, gave him authority over fleet-training, dockyards, and workshops, and instructed him to expand, and prepare manuals of tactics for, the torpedo arm. In 1887 when Prince William went to England to attend the jubilee of Queen Victoria, Tirpitz commanded the torpedo flotilla that accompanied him and had long talks with his future sovereign, who was at that time just beginning his passionate love affair with the navy.

He must have impressed the Prince, for although German naval opinion turned against concentration on torpedoes once William had ascended the throne, the Emperor did not forget Tirpitz, who, after a year of sea duty in the Mediterranean and another as Chief of Staff of the Baltic Station, was appointed in January 1892 as Chief of Staff to the Executive Command and was personally commissioned by the Emperor to develop the tactical work of the High Sea Fleet. In this position, he completely recast the form of naval manœuvres, abandoned training formations that no longer corresponded to the state of naval technology, and introduced and developed line tactics. He accomplished this, however, at the cost of so much administrative friction that in 1895 he asked for a new assignment.

This was prompted by the awkward division of authority within the command structure. One of the first expressions of William II's interest in naval affairs had been the reorganization of the old Admiralty into three agencies: a new Naval Cabinet, under Kapitän zur See Freiherr von Senden-Bibran, which was similar in its functions to the Military Cabinet and was designed to facilitate communication

---

[4] Cited in Jonathan Steinberg, *Yesterday's Deterrent: Tirpitz and the Birth of the German Battle Fleet* (New York, 1965), p. 69.

[5] Stosch, like his successor Caprivi, was a soldier, with a distinguished career in the wars of 1866 and 1870. His political views were liberal and attracted the unfavourable attention of Bismarck, who forced him out of office in 1883. See Hollyday, *Bismarck's Rival*, and Roggenbach, *Im Ring der Gegner*. Tirpitz had great admiration for his work in the navy. 'Stosch took up again the broken thread of the Hansa; he was the first to feel his way towards a future for Germany overseas. He did a great deal also to breathe a fighting spirit into the navy.' *Erinnerungen*, Ch. 2.

between the Emperor and his commanders;[6] an Imperial Naval Office (Reichsmarineamt) as the supreme administrative agency of the navy, charged with all matters relating to its maintenance and development; and an Executive Command (Oberkommando) with responsibility for command, training, and planning, including all aspects of staff work. It soon became apparent that it was difficult to draw a clean line between the competence of the Naval Office, which was commanded after the autumn of 1889 by Rear-Admiral Friedrich von Hollmann, and the Executive Command, of which Tirpitz was the Chief of Staff, the more so because the former organization had the right to prepare and issue all fleet orders, including tactical ones.[7] When differences about tactics developed between Hollmann and Tirpitz, the former usually got his way,[8] and this prompted the younger man's request for reasssignment at the end of 1895.

In his memoirs, Tirpitz wrote that this step gave him 'the good fortune to obtain one more glimpse of Germany's interests before [he] took over the Admiralty and began building the fleet'.[9] In April 1896 he received his appointment as Chief of the Eastern Asiatic Cruiser Division and the specific commission to seek out a place on the Chinese coast where Germany could construct a military and economic base. The places that seemed most suitable to those who had studied the question earlier were Amoy, Samsah Bay, and the Chusan Islands, near Shanghai. Tirpitz inspected and rejected all three, on the grounds that their military advantages were unimpressive and their prospects of economic development, which he felt was essential, non-existent. He decided instead on Tsingtao, which had an enclosed bay (Kiaochow) and a well-populated hinterland. Once again his reports impressed the Emperor, and the acquisition of Kiaochow, which took place at the end of 1897, can be attributed directly to his influence.

[6] Senden, a lifelong bachelor, was devoted to the navy. His function at the beginning was to put the Emperor's impulsive ideas into comprehensible naval terms, for William II's knowledge of technical matters was exiguous. Because he saw the Emperor so frequently, Senden had great influence, which he used for the service he loved, since he was devoid of personal or political ambition. See Schmidt-Bückeburg, *Militärkabinett*, p. 213.

[7] On the administrative changes, see Walther Hubatsch, *Der Admiralstab und die obersten Marinebehörden in Deutschland 1848–1945* (Frankfurt-on-Main, 1958), pp. 49–57.

[8] Caprivi, who was opposed to the division of the old Admiralty, backed Hollmann, the more so because the office was subordinate to the Chancellor. On the skirmishing between Hollmann and Tirpitz and the alliance of the latter with Senden, see Steinberg, *Yesterday's Deterrent*, pp. 69–71.

[9] *Erinnerungen*, end of Ch. 7.

Before that happened, however, Tirpitz was back in Berlin as Secretary of State of the Imperial Naval Office, for Admiral Hollmann had proved himself incapable of satisfying the Emperor's demand for immediate and massive increases in naval strength. It was not entirely the Admiral's fault. The feuding between his office and the Executive Command, which had begun when Tirpitz was Chief of Staff, had become much more bitter, and Hollmann's attempts to keep a suspicious Reichstag in line were defeated by public speeches by Senden and Knorr, Chief of the Executive Command, which called for the approval of an extensive long-term building programme. These speeches were veiled attacks upon Hollmann's piecemeal approach to naval construction; and they succeeded in bringing him down, for, in response to them, the Reichstag in March cut 12 million R.M. from the naval estimates. Hollmann immediately resigned, and, although for constitutional reasons his resignation was not immediately accepted, he was replaced by Tirpitz two months later, when the Hohenlohe cabinet was reshuffled.[10]

During his year in the Far East, Tirpitz had had lots of opportunity to think about naval affairs in the total context of German policy, and the experience seems to have confirmed him in the belief, first, that Great Britain was Germany's chief enemy and, second, that the necessary instrument for countering British influence in the world was the battleship. He once wrote that his attitude towards the British was determined by family and profession, and this was doubtless true. His father had had the curious ambivalence towards England that often went with liberal views, and Tirpitz himself, as a German sailor, had probably not been uninfluenced by the condescension with which the English had treated him and his fellow officers in the 1860s when Plymouth was the main supply base for Prussia's minuscule navy.[11] But there can be little doubt that his feelings were also determined by his conviction that Britain was resolved to prevent Germany from becoming a world Power, and Tirpitz had believed that this was Germany's destiny ever since his service with Stosch.[12] It would be an unfulfilled destiny, however, until Germany had developed the kind of naval power that Britain

[10] On all of this, see Steinberg, *Yesterday's Deterrent*, pp. 97 ff.

[11] *Erinnerungen*, pp. 8 ff.

[12] 'As far back as the seventies Stosch was convinced that we must acquire colonies and that we could not continue to exist without some means of expansion. He considered that the prosperity of the young empire would only be ephemeral if we did not counterbalance the decided disadvantage of our position and history overseas before it was too late.' Tirpitz, *Erinnerungen*, Ch. 2.

would respect (it is significant that Tirpitz deplored the Emperor's telegram to Kruger because Germany had no significant sea power with which to back it up[13]), and the basic ingredient of that power must be the battleship. In the debate that was going on in naval circles in these years between those who believed the future lay in the construction of fast cruisers and torpedo boats and those who held to the old Nelsonian ideal of naval combat, Tirpitz, despite his long and warm association with what he called 'the torpedo gang', belonged to the latter school. Independently, he had arrived at the basic conclusions of the American theorist Alfred Thayer Mahan, namely that great issues between world Powers were determined not by commerce-raiding or conventional defensive measures, but by command of the sea, which was possible only by means of heavy battle fleets.[14] His ideas had been pushed by Senden and Knorr in their fight against Hollmann, and the Reichstag vote of March represented a defeat for them as well as for his hapless successor. Tirpitz was not dismayed by this and, within a remarkably short space of time, he had corrected it.

As soon as he became Secretary of State of the Imperial Naval Office, he began to transform it into the kind of organization that would prevent another humiliation like that of March 1897. The Naval Office became a propaganda centre whose objective was to make all Germans proud of their fleet—a task made easier by historical memories of the Hanseatic League and the role of the navy as a symbol of national unity in 1848—and anxious to strengthen it. Using the techniques of modern advertising, Tirpitz carried this message to all classes and to all ages—through the printed word, through lectures, through visits by junior officers to schools and by officers of higher rank to politicians, and through invitations to the public to board and inspect naval vessels.[15] He solicited and won the co-operation of the Pan-German League and the Colonial Union. More important, by identifying the fleet with the economic development of Germany, he won the support of those interests that had a stake in commercial and industrial expansion, starting with the chambers of commerce of the coastal cities, then enlisting some of the larger banking houses, and finally attracting the eager interest of heavy industry. His success in this last respect is shown by the fact

[13] See his letter of 13 February 1896 to Stosch, cited ibid., Ch. 7.

[14] On the state of world naval opinion at this time, see Langer, *Diplomacy of Imperialism*, pp. 421–37. On Mahan's influence in Germany, see Kehr, *Schlachtflottenbau*, pp. 38, 45, 101–10; and the work of an early popularizer of his views, Ernst von Halle, *Die Seemacht in der deutschen Geschichte* (Leipzig, 1907), p. 6.

[15] Kehr, *Schlachtflottenbau*, pp. 93 ff.; Ritter, *Kriegshandwerk* ii. 136, 176 f.

that in March 1898, when the cod-liver oil manufacturer Stroschein wanted to found a Naval League to mobilize the support of the lower middle class and was refused financial support by the Berlin banks, the industrialist Krupp supplied the necessary funds, through an intermediary. In its first year, the Deutscher Flottenverein was wracked with scandal and changes in directorate, but Krupp continued to support it, and it grew rapidly in strength, soon attaining a membership of a million people.[16] Finally, Tirpitz's propaganda for a larger fleet became an important element in the Sammlungspolitik of Miquel and Bülow,[17] attracting the support of all those who feared the threat of socialism and believed, as Tirpitz did himself, that Flottenpolitik would help defeat it.

With this backing and with a skill in negotiating with parties and in dealing with parliamentary committees that none of his predecessors had possessed, Tirpitz, in March 1898, persuaded the same Reichstag that had been so refractory in the previous year to vote 400 million R.M. for new naval construction, which was intended to bring the Imperial Navy up to a fixed strength of 19 battleships, 8 coastal armoured ships, 12 large and 30 small cruisers, and a supporting force of torpedo boats, special ships, and training vessels.[18] And two years later, using as an excuse the unsettling effects of the Spanish-American war in the Far East and the worsening situation in South Africa, he succeeded in carrying through a Supplementary Bill that called for a doubling of the number of battleships as quickly as possible.[19] These were undeniable triumphs for the new Secretary of State; undeniable also was the harm they did to Anglo-German relations.

When Hohenlohe laid the Naval Bill before the Reichstag on 6 December 1897, he disclaimed any intention of challenging other Powers. 'This measure shows you,' he said,

that we are not thinking of competing with the great sea powers, and for those with eyes to see it demonstrates that a policy of adventure is far from

---

[16] See esp. Kehr, *Economic Interest*, pp. 76–96 ('Social and Financial Foundations of Tirpitz's Naval Propaganda').

[17] See above, Ch. VIII, and for an extended discussion of the socio-political aspects of the naval policy, Volker R. Berghahn, *Der Tirpitz-Plan: Genesis und Verfall der innenpolitischen Krisenstrategie unter Wilhelm II* (Düsseldorf, 1971).

[18] On the story of the bill's passage through the Reichstag, see Steinberg, *Yesterday's Deterrent*, Ch. 5.

[19] This was to be effected in part by the transformation of the armoured coastal ships into battleships. See Ritter, *Kriegshandwerk* ii. 173 n. and Walther Hubatsch, *Die Ära Tirpitz: Studien zur deutschen Marinepolitik 1890–1918* (Göttingen, 1955), pp. 17 f. On the background and enactment of the supplement of 1900, see Berghahn, *Der Tirpitz-Plan*, pp. 157 ff., 205–48; and Kehr, *Schlachtflottenbau*, pp. 168 ff.

our minds. Precisely because we want to carry out a peaceful policy, we must make an effort to build our fleet into a power factor which carries the necessary weight in the eyes of friend and foe alike. . . . In maritime questions, Germany must be able to speak a modest but, above all, a wholly German word.[20]

These words, and those of Tirpitz, which echoed them, were intended to allay the suspicions of those parliamentarians who were opposed to a programme of unlimited expansion; but they were disingenuous. The basis of the 1898 bill was a memorandum which Tirpitz had sent to the Emperor on 15 June 1897, in which the Secretary of State expressed the view that German ships must be built to meet 'the most difficult situation in war into which our fleet can come', and went on to say, 'For Germany, the most dangerous enemy at the present time is England. It is also the enemy against which we most urgently require a certain measure of naval force as a political power factor.' Against an antagonist like England, commerce-raiding would be useless. 'Our fleet must be constructed so that it can unfold its greatest military potential between Helgoland and the Thames. . . . The military situation against England demands battleships in as great a number as possible.'

The new naval programme was, in short, from its very inception directed against Great Britain,[21] although this was not apparent to anyone who was not privy to the secrets of the Imperial Naval Office and the Naval Cabinet. Moreover, although it was not spelled out in detail until 1900,[22] the strategy that Tirpitz envisaged using against Britain was also implicit in his memorandum of June 1897. This was the Risk Theory (or Risikogedanke) which envisaged a German fleet stationed in home waters that was so strong that in the event of war with Great Britain it could take offensive action against the British home fleet. It would, indeed, pose so great a threat that, to deal with it, the British Government would have to recall its squadrons from the Mediterranean and the Far East at the cost of leaving its interests in these areas vulnerable to attacks by other Powers. As the German fleet grew in size, the British would perceive this and would, in consequence, be inclined to avoid conflict with Germany or to seek an accommodation with it on terms that would strengthen Germany's continental position and bring it other advantages, which

[20] Quoted in Steinberg, *Yesterday's Deterrent*, p. 164.
[21] Ibid., Ch. 4, from which these quotations are taken.
[22] In the memorandum 'Die Sicherung Deutschlands gegen einen englischen Angriff'. See Hubatsch, *Die Ära Tirpitz*, p. 16 n.

would include the kind of economic rewards that would gratify the German people and reduce their opposition to the Crown.[23]

From the strategic point of view, as opposed to the economic or socio-political, the fleet construction programme was supposed to give Germany secure coasts and great political leverage. But from the very beginning, this argument suffered from two grave logical flaws. It overestimated Germany's financial strength while at the same time assuming that the British people would be unwilling to pay the costs of maintaining their decided superiority in naval strength.[24] More important, it was singularly unreceptive to the possibility that Great Britain might seek an alliance with a Power other than Germany and to the fact that, if it did so, and if that Power were a naval Power, all of Tirpitz's calculations would prove to be false.[25]

For all of his great abilities, one is tempted to describe Tirpitz as the evil genius of German foreign relations from 1898 onwards. He had already made a powerful contribution to the worsening of Russo-German relations, for the seizure of Kiaochow in November 1897, which was inspired by his reports from the Far East, had infuriated the Russians, who regarded this as an intrusion into their sphere of influence and a threat to their projected domination of northern China.[26] Now his naval plans succeeded in putting an end to any remaining hopes the German Government might have about winning an alliance with Great Britain.

This was unfortunate, because there were still powerful forces in

---

[23] Berghahn argues that Tirpitz's thoughts ranged beyond a mere policy of black-mailing Britain into concessions and that, once the fleet had assumed its full strength, by accelerated building that would culminate some time after 1912, there would probably be a decisive battle with the British in the North Sea. Thus, in its one-sidedness, Tirpitz's strategy was comparable to the Schlieffen Plan. *Der Tirpitz-Plan*, pp. 184–5.

[24] Tirpitz was afraid that Britain might try to 'Copenhagen' the German fleet before it was fully developed. That this was not an idle fear is shown by the fact that Admiral Fisher suggested it to King Edward VII, who replied, however, 'My God, Fisher, you must be mad!' See esp. Jonathan Steinberg, 'The Copenhagen Complex', *Journal of Contemporary History*, i, no. 3 (1966), 23–46. The real threat was Britain's financial strength, which Tirpitz grossly underestimated. See Berghahn, *Der Tirpitz-Plan*, p. 595.

[25] Ritter, *Kriegshandwerk* ii. 185 ff. Technically, the strategy was also unsound in providing no effective response to a wide blockade. Ibid. 188 ff.

[26] The murder of two German Catholic missionaries in southern Shantung on 1 November 1897 gave William II an excuse for ordering the Far Eastern Naval Squadron, commanded by Admiral Diederichs, to seize Kiaochow. On the ensuing crisis, see Langer, *Diplomacy of Imperialism*, pp. 451 ff.; Hohenlohe, *Reichskanzlerzeit*, pp. 408 ff.; *G.P.* xiv, 67–151.

England that were working for a comprehensive Anglo-German agreement. In March 1898, for instance, Lord Balfour, Deputy Foreign Secretary, First Lord of the Treasury, and leader of the Conservative party in the House of Commons, had sought out Hatzfeldt and expressed a strong desire for better relations between the two countries.[27] As Great Britain's difficulties mounted in South Africa, Balfour's initiative was taken up by Joseph Chamberlain, the Colonial Secretary. In October 1899 Chamberlain sought to settle differences over Samoa, where the outbreak of civil war had divided the Powers, by offering the Germans a choice between their minimal demands in Samoa (the islands of Upolu and Savaii) and a more comprehensive scheme for large-scale concessions to Germany in the South Seas and Africa which, in Chamberlain's view, would 'settle at one blow all outstanding colonial difficulties between us'. To Hatzfeldt's disgust, the German Government ignored the possibilities implicit in the broader offer, as they had ignored Balfour's *démarche*, and yielded to the navy's insistence upon acquiring the two Samoan islands. The London ambassador telegraphed to Holstein, 'If our foreign policy depends on the views of Herr Tirpitz we will not go far in the world.'[28] But the fact was that German foreign policy was indeed coming to depend more and more on the views of Herr Tirpitz. Further overtures from Chamberlain and Balfour in November were given the same cool treatment as the earlier ones. 'The future task of the German government in my opinion', wrote Bülow at this time, 'is to preserve good relations with both Britain and Russia and, in the possession of a strong fleet, to await calmly and collectedly the future development of elemental events.'[29] The Emperor agreed with him whole-heartedly.

There seemed to be no intimation in the minds of the Emperor and his Foreign Secretary that the British might seek other alliances. At the very time that Chamberlain was committing himself publicly to the idea of a union between the Anglo-Saxon and the Teutonic Powers, William II was insisting upon the introduction of the naval supplement, brushing aside the doubts of his Chancellor with the imperious statement, 'In this question, which is a matter of to be or not to be, there is no more question of my retreating than there was for my grandfather in the question of the reorganization of the

[27] Rich, *Holstein* ii. 568; *Holstein Papers* iv. 64 ff.; *G.P.* xiv (1), 193 ff.; Hatzfeldt, *Nachgelassene Papiere* ii. 1153.

[28] Rich, *Holstein* ii. 598. See also Kennedy, *Samoan Tangle*, pp. 215–20.

[29] *G.P.* xv. 420. Quoted in Rich, *Holstein* ii. 612. See also Hatzfeldt, *Nachgelassene Papiere* ii. 1261 ff., 1278 f.

army.'[30] In the subsequent campaign for the bill, the government made no attempt to avoid either grandiose projections of German strength that were bound to alarm British opinion or anti-British rhetoric that was bound to offend it. The most effective way of persuading the general public that a big fleet was necessary was to depict Great Britain as a greedy and jealous Power intent upon stifling German commercial enterprise. Some of those who availed themselves of this argument seem to have believed it, Hohenlohe, the Chancellor, for one. 'We must not', he wrote at this time, 'expose ourselves to the danger of suffering the fate from England that Spain suffered from the United States. That the English are merely waiting for a chance to fall upon us is clear.'[31] But even government spokesmen who doubted that the English had such intentions did not hesitate to use the alarmist tactics. After all, they worked and, even if they annoyed the British, there was not much they could do about it, was there? Bülow, for one, who was discovering in these years that an occasional attack upon the British had excellent effects upon his popularity,[32] never concerned himself about how the British might respond. As late as 1903, when his ambassador in London warned him that the British might, if tried too far, make an accommodation with the French and the Russians, he brushed this aside in his usual airy manner. 'In my opinion', he wrote, 'we need not worry about such remote possibilities' ('Wir können die Dinge *meo voto* gar nicht pomadig genug nehmen').[33]

They were, of course, not remote. If the British Government and the British Press had received news of the passage of the Naval Bill of 1898 with equanimity,[34] they showed active alarm when the Supplementary Naval Bill was passed. The thought that the supplement promised to change the ratio between the strength of their own fleet and that of Germany from two to one to three to two was not comforting, and the suspicion was quick to grow that the Germans, who had the strongest army in Europe, were now seeking to build the strongest fleet as well. And given the unstable temperament of their ruler, where would that lead them? The abuse heaped upon the British army by German newspapers after the onset of the Boer War, and the failure of the German Government to do anything to control it, seemed to the British to belie all the professions of friendship that

---

[30] Hubatsch, *Die Ära Tirpitz*, p. 69.
[31] Langer, *Diplomacy of Imperialism*, p. 656.
[32] For an example of this, see Rich, *Holstein* ii. 668.
[33] *G.P.* xviii (2), 840.
[34] See Steinberg, *Yesterday's Deterrent*, pp. 196 f.

had come from Berlin over the years, and to make advisable some measure of self-defence.[35]

It is possible that the drift toward this solution might have been stayed as late as 1901 if Germany had been better served by its diplomatic representation in London. But Hatzfeldt had fallen seriously ill, and through most of this period his functions were being performed by the First Secretary, Baron Hermann von Eckardstein, a German aristocrat who had married into English society (Balfour called him 'that fat fellow who married Maples' daughter'[36]). Eckardstein burned with the desire to bring his native country and his adopted one into alliance, but his efforts were defeated by excessive zeal and a fatal propensity to exaggeration. He managed, not once but repeatedly, to mislead both Whitehall and the Wilhelmstraße by misrepresenting conversations and overstating the desire for alliance on both sides. What slim chance there was for an accommodation in 1901 evaporated because his inflation of conversations with Chamberlain and the new Foreign Secretary, Lord Lansdowne, led the German Government to believe that the British had expressed a desire for alliance and had then, for mysterious reasons, withdrawn it, while the British, receiving unsolicited messages from Berlin, were left feeling that the Germans wanted an alliance but wanted to impose impossible terms before the talks began. The result was an increase of distrust on both sides and a deepening of the estrangement.[37]

Those members of the British Government who had continued to regard a German alliance as desirable in a world in which Great Britain seemed to be ringed around with enemies were disappointed, but they did not, on that account, return to Salisbury's policy of avoiding foreign entanglements. The time had come, Lansdowne said in 1902, for the country to stop 'being swayed by musty formulae and old-fashioned superstitions as to the desirability of pursuing a policy of isolation. . . . *Prima facie*, if there be no countervailing objections, the country that has the good fortune to have allies is more to be envied than the country that is without them.'[38] The country seemed to agree, and the government was encouraged to begin the negotiations that led first to the Anglo-Japanese Alliance

---

[35] See E. L. Woodward, *Great Britain and the German Navy* (Oxford, 1935), pp. 55 ff.

[36] Rich, *Holstein* ii. 577.

[37] On Eckardstein's role, see Langer, *Diplomacy of Imperialism*, pp. 727 ff. and Rich, *Holstein* ii. 628 ff., 643–62.

[38] Nicholas Mansergh, *The Coming of the First World War: A Study in the European Balance* (London, 1949), p. 87.

and then, partly as a result of that, to the conclusion of the Entente of 1904 with France.

Bülow's policy of preserving good relations with both Great Britain and Russia had failed utterly. Thanks largely to his naval and imperialist policy, the British had been driven into the arms of France. Meanwhile Germany's relations with Russia, already strained by the seizure of Kiaochow, had deteriorated even further as a result of two other developments. In the first place, the East Elbian landholders demanded their compensation for having supported the naval appropriations and, in 1902, were granted the new tariff that virtually excluded Russian grains from the German market.[39] Secondly, the penetration of the underdeveloped lands of the Ottoman Empire by German banks, industrial firms, and railway interests, which had begun in the 1880s, was accelerated and given government support after the Emperor made an extraordinary trip to Damascus and Jerusalem in 1898. The Emperor's subsequent description of the projected Baghdad Railway, which was originally financed by an international consortium, as 'My railway', and Bülow's boastful talk about 'worming our way inch by inch down to the Persian Gulf', seemed to threaten Russian, as well as British, interests in that area; and, although compromises were reached on the railway issue with Russia in 1911 and with Britain on the eve of the war, much friction had been caused before those agreements, and this contributed to the alienation of Russia from Germany.[40]

II

The worsening of Germany's continental position that was caused by this revolutionary change in diplomatic alignments brought in its train a sharp increase in army interference in foreign policy.

In Germany's history this was not exactly new. In 1814 and 1815 the open dissatisfaction of Prussian soldiers with the peace terms signed by their government and their attempts to sabotage them aroused Castlereagh's alarm and prompted the Tsar of Russia to say, 'It is possible that some time we shall have to come to the aid of the

[39] See above, Ch. VIII, p. 277.

[40] See Friedrich Meinecke, *Straßburg, Freiburg, Berlin 1901–1919: Erinnerungen* (Stuttgart, 1949), p. 208; George W. F. Hallgarten, *Imperialismus vor 1914* (rev. edn., 2 vols., Munich, 1963), i. 223–49, 266–70, 306–8, 595–610; A. S. Jerussalinski, *Die Außenpolitik und die Diplomatie des deutschen Imperialismus* (2nd edn., Berlin, 1954), pp. 265 ff.; Christopher Andrew, 'German World Policy and the Re-shaping of the Dual Alliance', *Journal of Contemporary History*, i. no. 3 (1966), 137–51; Edward Mead Earle, *Turkey, the Great Powers and the Baghdad Railway* (New York, 1923); John B. Wolf, *The Diplomatic History of the Baghdad Railway* (Columbus, Mo., 1936); Lothar Rathmann, *Berlin–Baghdad* (Berlin, 1962).

King of Prussia against his army.'[41] The difficulties experienced by
Bismarck in enforcing military subordination to civil authority during the wars of 1864, 1866, and 1870 are well known;[42] and we have
already had occasion to refer to his vigorous reaction in 1887 to secret
military attempts to urge the Austrians to go to war with Russia.[43]
Since that time there had been relatively little overt military intervention in matters of foreign policy. Waldersee's attempt, during his
terms as Quartermaster General and Chief of the General Staff, to
convert the military attachés into a separate foreign service, reporting on political as well as military matters and sending their dispatches directly to the Emperor, had been baulked by Bismarck and
utterly defeated by Caprivi. Bismarck's successor made it clear that
the attachés must have their reports cleared by their chiefs of mission
and that they were to leave politics severely alone; and, to emphasize
the point, he rooted Waldersee's informants out of their posts in
Paris, Vienna, St. Petersburg, and Rome.[44] In the subsequent period,
the government had little occasion to complain about the military
attachés (with one conspicuous exception, in the case of Colonel
Schwarzkoppen in Paris who, by disobeying Count Münster's
specific prohibition against espionage, involved the embassy in the
complications of the Dreyfus affair[45]). The activities of the naval
attachés were, as we shall see, much more troublesome.

Even so, although Waldersee's successors had no interest in his
schemes and confined themselves for the most part to the technical
tasks of operational planning, their influence on Germany's foreign
policy was greater and more fateful than his. Count Alfred von
Schlieffen, Chief of the General Staff from 1891 to 1906, devised a
strategical plan for a two-front war whose technical virtuosity could
not disguise the fact that it would burden Germany with political
disadvantages in any conflict in which it was used. Helmuth von
Moltke, the nephew of William I's Feldherr, who served from 1906
until 1914, remained true to Schlieffen's legacy and interpreted the
plan in such a way as to impose grave limitations upon his country's
freedom of diplomatic action.

[41] See Gordon A. Craig, 'Problems of Coalition Warfare: The Military Alliance
against Napoleon, 1813–1814', in *War, Politics and Diplomacy* (New York, 1966), pp.
42–4.

[42] Craig, *Prussian Army*, Ch. V.

[43] See above, Ch. IV, p. 134.

[44] Craig, *Prussian Army*, p. 272; Alfred Vagts, *The Military Attaché* (Princeton,
1967), pp. 215 ff.

[45] See Friedrich Thimme, 'Botschafter und Militärattaché', *Europäische Gespräche*,
viii (1930).

Ever since 1871 German soldiers had brooded over the possibility that one day they would find themselves engaged in war with both France and Russia; and, long before the break in formal relations with St. Petersburg, the General Staff had been making plans for that contingency. Leaving aside problems of armament and logistics, the salient strategical problem was whether the bulk of Germany's forces should be directed against the eastern or the western antagonist. The older Moltke, who busied himself with this question in his last years, had flexible views which varied with changes in the European political situation, but, increasingly after 1879, he inclined to the view that, if a combination of political and military means were employed, Russia would be the easier enemy to defeat and that, therefore, Germany should conduct a holding operation in the west until a decision had been reached on the eastern front.[46] This was also the opinion of his successor Waldersee.

Schlieffen reversed this strategy. A pure technician who lacked Moltke's appreciation of the importance of non-military factors in modern war, he was less impressed by arguments about Russia's vulnerability to political attack (encouragement of insurrection among subject peoples like the Poles) than he was by the new fortifications that the Russians built at the end of the century in the area of Ivangorod, Brest-Litovsk, Kovno, and Warsaw (the so-called Narew line) and by the marked improvement of the Russian railway network in the same period. These changes argued against a quick victory in the east and led Schlieffen to study the possibilities inherent in an initial offensive in the west. From the start he ruled out any thought of a frontal attack against France's defensive line. The model he adopted was that of the Battle of Cannae in which Hannibal had crushed a numerically superior Roman army by attacking it in the flank and the rear. Schlieffen's studies led him to the conclusion that a quick and decisive victory over France could be achieved if the German army mounted a massive manœuvre of envelopment in which the bulk of its forces, pivoting upon Metz and Strasburg, drove through Belgium and the Grand Duchy of Luxemburg into the French rear, where they would cross the Lower Seine, wheel to the east, and pin the shattered French forces against their own fortresses and the Swiss frontier. Provided the right wing were made strong enough, even at the risk of allowing initial French penetration south of the hinge, Schlieffen was confident that the fighting power

[46] On the development of Moltke's ideas, see esp. Graf Moltke, *Die deutschen Aufmarschpläne*, ed. Ferdinand von Schmerfeld (Forschungen und Darstellungen aus dem Reichsarchiv, Heft 7) (Berlin, 1929).

of France would be destroyed in six weeks, and the Germans could shift their forces eastwards to deal with Russia.[47]

From a technical point of view, the plan was brilliant; from others it was disastrous. Not only did it completely overlook those psychological forces that have often in history made people defy their defeats and continue resistance by unconventional methods, but it made it inevitable that Germany would start the war it feared with the grave disadvantage of being labelled as an aggressor and a violator of international law, which would almost certainly deprive it of the sympathy and support of neutral Powers. This was of no great importance to Schlieffen, for he did not regard Belgium as a truly neutral state,[48] and, in any case, he was sure that the war would be over so quickly that neutral opinion would be of no consequence. But it should have been a matter of concern to the civil leadership of the state, who were apprised of the main features of the plan at an early date. Yet when Graf Hutten-Czapski, at Schlieffen's request, informed Holstein in May 1900 that, in the case of a two-front war, the General Staff did not intend to be restricted by international agreements and asked for his views on this, Holstein, after a long brooding silence, said, 'If the Chief of the General Staff, particularly such a pre-eminent strategical authority as Schlieffen, considers such a measure imperative, then it is the duty of diplomacy to concur in it and to facilitate it in every possible manner.'[49] Neither Hohenlohe nor Bülow raised objections to the plan;[50] and by the time Bethman Hollweg became Chancellor it was regarded as something that was no longer subject to political interference. By his own admission, Bethmann and F. L. von Jagow, his Foreign Secretary, knew about the projected violation of Belgian neutrality long before the war, but the Chancellor admitted in his memoirs that, during the years before 1914, no war council had ever been held in which the politicians had a chance to participate in discussions of military plans and preparations.[51]

[47] The most thorough treatment is Gerhard Ritter, *Der Schlieffenplan: Kritik eines Mythos* (Munich, 1956) which includes texts of the different drafts.

[48] In the memorandum of 1912 Schlieffen wrote that Belgium had fortified its German frontier but left its French frontier undefended. Ibid., p. 82.

[49] Hutten-Czapski, *Sechzig Jahre* ii. 37 ff.

[50] Bülow talked about the plan with both Schlieffen and Moltke. His account in his *Denkwürdigkeiten* (ii. 72 ff., 76 ff.) is self-serving and his description of how the Emperor, who also knew about the plan, threatened the King of Belgium in 1904 with invasion in the next war if he did not join Germany is unreliable. See Ritter, *Schlieffenplan*, p. 99.

[51] Theobald von Bethmann Hollweg, *Betrachtungen zum Weltkrieg* (2 vols., Berlin, 1919–21), ii. 7.

This was a kind of civilian capitulation to military expediency that Bismarck had never allowed, and it boded ill for the future. Yet, in the days that followed the British decision to abandon isolation and conclude a political agreement with France, there was little disposition in political circles to criticize the soldiers. After all, might not the solution to the problems now confronting Germany lie with them? During the sharp crisis that arose over Morocco in 1905, several of the chief actors on the German side seemed, for a time at least, to think so.

In accordance with the terms of their agreement with the British, the French Government in 1905 began to extend their control over Morocco. This undertaking the German Government decided to challenge; and in March 1905 the Emperor interrupted a Mediterranean cruise to make a theatrical landing at Tangier, where he visited the Sultan and promised to support his independence, and pointedly told the French consul that he knew how to defend German interests in Morocco and would expect the French to recognize that fact. The menace in these words was unmistakable; the Rouvier government in France recoiled in something close to panic; and on a sudden there was a widespread feeling that war was very near.

It is difficult to describe with any certainty the motives of the German Government in 1905. The visit to Tangier had been planned by Holstein and Bülow, who apparently intended not only to block France's Moroccan plans but to do so in such a humiliating way that the new Entente would be weakened or destroyed. But, if they were agreed on this (and that is by no means certain), they were agreed on little else. From the beginning, Bülow appears to have regarded the operation as one in which bluff would carry the day. Holstein was never one to rely on empty gestures. There is evidence, although admittedly circumstantial, that he wanted to provoke war with France.

Unlike Bismarck, Holstein was not in principle opposed to preventive war. Indeed, in 1887 he had been as eager as Waldersee to force war with Russia,[52] and since then he had been known to talk of war as a solution for Germany's difficulties.[53] He was aware that his

[52] H. Krausnick, *Holsteins Geheimpolitik in der Aera Bismarck* (2nd edn., Hamburg, 1942), pp. 117, 155 ff., 161.

[53] In December 1894, when Eulenburg talked of war as a means of bringing needed prestige to the government, Holstein answered, 'In one point I share your opinion, namely, that a *successful* war would have a very salutary effect'. He added, 'But as a precondition for this, a righteous cause as in 1870, would be necessary'. Students of the 1870 war will recognize that this would permit considerable latitude. Rich, *Holstein* ii. 488 ff. Again in 1897 Holstein wrote of the possibility of solving the internal problems of the Reich by means of a European war. Wehler, *Bismarck und der Imperialismus*, p. 499.

country could hardly hope for a better opportunity to deal with France than it had in 1905. The Russians were engaged in a disastrous war with Japan and were paralysed by revolution at home. The British army had not yet recovered from the long war in South Africa, and the British Government would hardly be eager to become involved in a continental war.[54]

That the German army, on the other hand, was ready for conflict, Holstein knew, for since Caprivi's chancellorship he had been on terms of personal friendship with Schlieffen, who often came to his office to read papers and to discuss the European situation. According to the testimony of Schlieffen's military associates, the Chief of Staff, who was working on the December memorandum which was to be the most complete formulation of his plan, was in a warlike mood. He had long been critical of the Bülow–Tirpitz policy, believing that it was a grave mistake to commit oneself to world policy before Germany's continental position was secure.[55] Now the time had come to correct that. In the summer of 1905 Schlieffen caused a sensation among General Staff officers by warning them that Germany might celebrate the hundredth anniversary of the Battle of Jena in sackcloth unless the soldiers had the courage to rise against the author of their troubles.[56] In September the Saxon military plenipotentiary reported that war against France was considered in the General Staff as a real possibility and that Schlieffen was confident about its outcome.[57] The testimony of his friends and the sequence of events would indicate that Holstein was thinking in the same terms.

Years later Graf Oskar von der Lancken, a diplomatist and friend of Holstein, wrote that the councillor told him in 1909 that Great

[54] For German discussion of this, see *G.P.* xix (1), 174–7. On the incoherence of German policy in the early stages of the Russo-Japanese war, the ill effects of which may have strengthened the desire for some kind of a success, see Jonathan Steinberg, 'Germany and the Russo-Japanese War', *American Historical Review*, 74 (1970), 1965–86.

[55] It was in Schlieffen's spirit that Wilhelm Groener, in a lecture to officers in General Headquarters on 19 May 1919, attributed the loss of the war to the fact that Germany engaged in 'a struggle with England for world mastery . . . before we had made our continental position secure'. Cited in Fritz Fischer, *Krieg der Illusionen: Die deutsche Politik von 1911 bis 1914* (Düsseldorf, 1969), p. 1.

[56] Wilhelm Groener, *Lebenserinnerungen,* ed. F. Freiherr Hiller von Gärtringen (Göttingen, 1957), pp. 83 ff. See also Peter Rassow, 'Schlieffen und Holstein', *Historische Zeitschrift*, clxxiii (1952), and Hugo Rochs, *Schlieffen. Ein Lebens- und Charakterbild für das deutsche Volk* (5th edn., Berlin, 1940), p. 40. For evidence of preventive-war psychology in the upper reaches of the army, see Einem, *Erinnerungen,* pp. 111–14, and *DDF* 2nd Ser. vi, no. 369.

[57] Fischer, *Krieg der Illusionen,* p. 99.

Britain's entente with France had convinced him that 'before the ring of the other Great Powers tightens around us, we must attempt with all our energies and with a determination that will not shrink from the utmost to break that ring. Hence the Tangier trip of the Emperor!'[58] Holstein had insisted on that venture, despite the hesitations of the Emperor; and in the subsequent period he was the driving force behind the bullying tactics that forced the dismissal of Delcassé, the French Foreign Minister, in June, the refusal to engage in direct negotiations with France over Moroccan affairs, and the insistence upon an international conference that was intended to create new opportunities for provocation.[59] He also stood behind the directive of December 1905 to the Press chief of the Foreign Ministry, which, apparently with the intention of sharpening the conflict, read: 'I am afraid that at the conference at Algeciras there will be a tendency on the part of the French, perhaps encouraged, but in any case not prevented, by England, to put Germany in a position in which it has only the choice between a heavy loss of prestige in the world or an armed conflict. Such a conflict in the spring is expected by many [in France] and desired by many.'[60]

But neither William II nor his Chancellor had the courage for this policy of *va banque*. The Emperor's heart had never been in the Moroccan enterprise, and his inconstant mind had, in any case, now turned to other projects. In July 1905 he startled the Foreign Ministry

[58] Oskar von der Lancken-Wakenitz, *Meine dreißig Dienstjahre 1888–1918* (Berlin, 1931), p. 56; Monts, *Erinnerungen*, pp. 191–2. Rich (*Holstein* ii. 699) points out that Lancken's memoirs are filled with error. While admitting the strength of the circumstantial evidence, he prefers to believe that Holstein's policy was not a war policy, but merely one of stupidity, although he has some trouble making out this case and seems to overlook the psychological evidence. There is admittedly no evidence in Holstein's dispatches and memorandums that he desired war in 1905. This is not surprising, especially when one remembers that Holstein's desire for war in 1887 is not documented by papers from his own hand either. The thesis that Schlieffen wanted war in 1905 has been vigorously attacked by Ritter (*Schlieffenplan*, pp. 102–33), who demonstrates the weakness of some of the evidence but does not explain away the testimony of Wilhelm Groener, a staff officer and disciple of Schlieffen, who during the crisis and for the rest of his life believed that the Chief of Staff desired to seize the opportunity to destroy France. It is interesting to note that, in two rather ambiguous passages in the introduction to his edition of Schlieffen's letters, Eberhard Kessel, while denying that Schlieffen's war plan of 1905 had 'a preventive war character', suggests that the Chief of Staff was thinking personally in terms of preventive war during the Moroccan crisis and says plainly that Schlieffen was as anxious to come to grips with France in 1905 as he had been in 1867. Generalfeldmarschall Graf Alfred Schlieffen, *Briefe* (Göttingen, 1958), pp. 13 f., 53 f., 205, 207, 208.

[59] See Richard von Kühlmann, *Erinnerungen* (Heidelberg, 1948), pp. 246 ff.

[60] Otto Hammann, *Bilder aus der letzten Kaiserzeit* (Berlin, 1922), p. 45.

by informing it by telegraph that he had invited the Tsar of Russia to meet him on his yacht in the Bay of Björko to sign a treaty of alliance. When this curious document was actually signed (one must suppose because the Tsar's powers of resistance were overborne by William II's enthusiastic garrulity), Bülow immediately conceived the idea that it might be used to solve the question of Morocco: that hapless land could be handed over to the French Government in return for an agreement to abandon the Entente and adhere to the new Russo-German treaty, which would thus become the nucleus of a continental league.

This was all moonshine. As soon as officials in the Russian Foreign Office had an opportunity to study the Björko treaty they concluded that, since it was restricted in its applicability to Europe, it had no attractions for them, and by the end of the year they had effectively killed it. By that time Germany's Moroccan policy was in hopeless disarray, compromised equally by its original bullying tactics and its recent attempts to win French adherence to the imaginary alliance by promises of concessions. The deplorable result of all of this was shown at the Algeciras Conference of 1906 where the French got exactly what they wanted, and the Germans found themselves isolated except for the support of Austria-Hungary.

It was after the set-back in Morocco that the fear of encirclement began to be a potent factor in German politics. It was understandable that this should be so. The crisis had not only strengthened the Entente but encouraged the beginning of talks between the French and British military staffs. Moreover, in the period that followed Algeciras, the Russians began their move towards London, prompted by the desire to protect their tie with France and also to secure British assistance in winning favourable peace terms in the Far East from Britain's ally Japan. Since the Italians had quite clearly lost their enthusiasm for the Triple Alliance by this time and were proving it by a serious political flirtation with France, it was clear even to the most short-sighted that Germany's diplomatic position was gravely weakened and that the principal result of Bülow's Welt- und Flottenpolitik had been to deprive the nation of all its allies save Austria-Hungary. The immediate result of the discovery was a nervous desire to make certain of Austria's continued loyalty. This took dangerous forms.

On 6 October 1908 the government of Austria-Hungary informed the Turkish Government that it had annexed the territory of Bosnia and Hercegovina, which it had administered since 1878. The annexation had in a sense been approved in advance by Izvolsky, the Russian Foreign Minister, in return for a promise that Austria would not object to Russia's winning the freedom of the Straits; but, under the pressure of his ministerial colleagues and the Pan-Slav Press, Izvolsky now repudiated that bargain and demanded that the Austrians be haled before an international conference to answer for what he described as a violation of the Treaty of Berlin. The Austrians flatly refused to consider this or to admit that Serbia, which had long coveted the seized area, was entitled to compensation. As the deadlock continued, the Serbs began to form armed bands along the Austrian frontier, and the Austrian army, whose chief, Conrad von Hötzendorf, had long desired a chance to smash the ambitions of the Great Serbian party, began to agitate for mobilization. It looked as if a shooting war was not far away.

The German Government had been disagreeably surprised by the Austrian action, which was, in the first instance, a blow at Turkey, a country where German economic interest had grown rapidly since the 1880s and promised, with the extension of the German-financed Baghdad Railway, to grow further and to bring political advantages in its wake. There was fear in Berlin that the Turks would react to the seizure by turning to Great Britain unless Germany dissociated itself from the action of its ally.[61] But Bülow was quick to discourage any such suggestion. In a revealing note, the Chancellor wrote:

> Our position would indeed be dangerous if Austria lost confidence and turned away. So long as we stand together, we form a bloc that no one will lightly attack. In eastern questions above all, we cannot place ourselves in opposition to Austria who has nearer and greater interests in the Balkan peninsula than ourselves. A refusal or a grudging attitude in the question of annexation of Bosnia and Hercegovina would not be forgiven.[62]

The German Government therefore not only supported Austria-Hungary in the Bosnian crisis but did so with a brutality that the situation did not require. In March 1909, as Izvolsky was painfully making up his mind to accept a face-saving formula, the Germans dispatched what can only be described as an ultimatum, instructing their ambassador in St. Petersburg to 'say to M. Isvolski . . . that we expect an answer—yes or no; we must regard any evasive, conditional, or unclear answer as a refusal. We should then draw back and let things take their course. The responsibility for further events would then fall exclusively on M. Izvolsky.'[63] The

---

[61] Marschall complained that the Austrian action had undone years of work in Turkey and William II was also indignant. See G. P. Gooch, *Before the War: Studies in Diplomacy*, i (London, 1936), p. 277.

[62] G.P. xxvi (1), 195.   [63] Ibid. (2), 693 ff.

Russians caved in, but the violence of the German note, which was probably designed to impress Vienna as much as St. Petersburg, was remembered with resentment and helped inspire Russian encouragement of Serbian activities against Austria in the subsequent period.

At the height of the crisis, in January 1909, Conrad, the Austrian Chief of Staff, wrote to Moltke, who had succeeded Schlieffen in January 1906, to ask what the German army intended to do in the event of an Austrian invasion of Serbia that provoked Russian intervention. Moltke's answer was completely in tune with Bülow's confession of dependence upon the Austrian alliance. Disregarding Bismarck's repeated insistence that the alliance of 1879 would involve German action only if Austria were attacked, Moltke assured Conrad that if Austria found it necessary to attack Serbia and was then confronted with Russian support of its foe, 'that would constitute the *casus foederis* for Germany'. As soon as Russia began to mobilize, Germany would call up its whole fighting force.[64]

In effect, Moltke had changed the treaty of 1879 from a defensive to an offensive treaty and placed his country at the mercy of the adventurers in Vienna. At the same time, he pointed out to Conrad that any war that resulted from Austro-Russian rivalry in the Balkans would have to be fought in accordance with Schlieffen's prescription. If Russia mobilized, France would mobilize too, and since 'two mobilized armies like the German and French will not be able to stand side by side without resorting to war . . . Germany, when it mobilizes against Russia, must also reckon on a war with France'.[65] That being so, the bulk of German forces would have to be used against France, although victory on the western front would come quickly, and full German aid to Austria would not be long delayed.

These were ominous words, for implicit in them was the belief that no matter where war might break out and no matter how Germany was involved, its participation must begin with an attack upon France. Limited war was now, in the thinking of the German

---

[64] See Craig, *Prussian Army*, pp. 288 ff. and the authorities cited. Ritter, *Kriegshandwerk* ii. 302 points out that Moltke expressed the opinion that it would be wise not to provoke war with Serbia, but to await its attack. But his point here was that this would deprive Russia of an excuse for intervening, and he did not suggest that this was a condition of German support. Certainly Conrad regarded Moltke's promises as 'binding written agreements'. See Feldmarschall Conrad von Hötzendorf, *Aus meiner Dienstzeit* (4 vols., Vienna and Berlin, 1921 ff.), ii. 85.

[65] Conrad, *Aus meiner Dienstzeit*, i. 381–2. See also Norman Stone, 'Moltke-Conrad: Relations between the Austro-Hungarian and German General Staffs, 1909–1914', *Historical Journal*, ix (1966), 204–11.

military, an impossibility: all conflict must be European in scope. Moltke told Conrad that he had informed the Emperor and Bülow of the nature of his communications to the Austrian Chief of Staff. They apparently did not object. This was more ominous still, for it indicated that, like the military, the civilian leadership of the state was giving way to a growing sense of fatalism.

III

In 1908 the Impressionist poet Detlev von Liliencron wrote a poem called 'Der Blitzzug' which began

> Quer durch Europa von Westen nach Osten
> Rüttert und rattert die Bahnmelodie.
> Gilt es die Seligkeit schneller zu kosten?
> Kommt er zu spät an im Himmelslogis?
> Fortfortfort Fortfortfort drehn sich die Räder
> Rasend dahin auf dem Schienengeäder,
> Rauch ist der Bestie verschwindender Schweif,
> Schaffnerpfiff, Lokomotivengepfeif.

This impetuous course ends disastrously, and the next day, in the smoking ruins of the train, are found what is left of its cargo: two spurs, a curling iron, some watches and money, a stock certificate, a book of poems entitled *Seraphic Tones*, and a little girl's doll.

A more timely poem could hardly have been written, or one more prophetic of what lay ahead. In 1908 the course was set for disaster; after that date, international crisis became commonplace and all Europe became involved in a runaway arms race.[66] One might suppose that poets would not have been the only ones to sense this, and that some form of public pressure might have been brought to bear upon governments in the interest of peace. Why was there no mobilization of conscience or of ethical disapprobation before 1914?

The answer is to be found perhaps in the fact that, during the nineteenth century, most Europeans who thought about the question at all had an ambivalent attitude toward war, and that even the most peace-loving among them had somewhere in the back of their

---

[66] The Peace Conferences at The Hague in 1899 and 1907 did nothing to relieve this. At the first of them, the German delegate, Colonel Schwarzhoff, with general approval, rejected the whole idea of limiting arms. He denied that the German people were suffering from excessive armaments or that excessive armaments would bring war or that arms reduction was practical. National military establishments, he held, were unique and complicated things, the end-result of the operation of history, tradition, administrative capacity, economic strength, and geographical position. They could not be submitted to any form of international regulation. On the 1907 conference, see below, p. 326.

mind wars that they considered justifiable and worth fighting. Apart from this, there were no independent groups or organizations capable of bringing real pressure to bear upon governments in the interest of peace. Political parties in all countries were split on questions of peace, war, and armaments, a fact that was true even of the Socialists, despite their doctrinaire anti-militarism. The established Churches were equally ineffective; weakened by a century of materialism and doctrinal strife, they generally took the safe line of supporting the government in political matters. The organized pacifist movement had more determination than the Churches, but it failed too, despite its by no means negligible following (160 separate European associations in 1914) and the wide circulation of its publications. The pacifist movement always had a bad Press and, in an age of hypernationalism, people were easily persuaded that it was filled with fanatics and cowards and illusionists who did not understand the facts of international life. No government paid more than passing attention to the movement's activities.[67]

It is possible that if the true horrors of modern war had been even dimly appreciated by the general public, things might have been different. But not even the professional soldiers had any inkling of what lay in store for them and, if they could not recognize the signs, the ordinary citizen could not be expected to do so, and it was only natural that he should leave all questions of foreign policy, war, and armaments to the government, which proceeded to stumble on its blind way to Armageddon.

When Bethmann Hollweg became Chancellor, he did, to be sure, try to halt that progress, by conducting foreign policy in a lower key, by discouraging the grandiose visions of the Pan-German League and the Colonial Union, and by limiting German expansion to moderate and attainable goals. 'We must', he said, 'drive forward quietly and patiently in order to regain that trust and confidence without which we cannot consolidate politically and economically.'[68] He wished to improve relations with all members of the Triple Entente and, in the case of Great Britain, he hoped, by reaching a settlement on naval affairs, to lay the basis for a political agreement.

In the Chancellor's view, the naval competition was both costly and self-defeating. The original calculations of the Tirpitz Plan had

---

[67] On the pacifist movement, see Roger Chickering, *Imperial Germany and a World without War: the Peace Movement and German Society, 1892–1914* (Princeton, 1975), esp. pp. 320–6, 384–419.

[68] Jarausch, *Enigmatic Chancellor*, p. 110.

been disrupted by the Anglo-French Entente, but neither this nor the subsequent failure to break the new combination by the strong line taken in Morocco had discouraged Tirpitz. In November 1905 the German Government announced a new naval supplement that not only provided for an increase in the tonnage of the ships authorized in 1900 but called for the construction of six large cruisers and forty-eight destroyers. This challenge the British met in 1906 by deciding to concentrate henceforth upon the construction of a new type of battleship, the Dreadnought, an 'all big-gun ship' that was intended to outrange all existing battleships in the heaviest armaments and to be superior to them in speed and ability to manœuvre.[69] The Liberal Government took this step reluctantly and, during the Peace Conference of 1907 at The Hague, sought to ameliorate its effect by proposing that Great Powers communicate to each other their projected plans for naval construction before they were entirely committed to them, so that there would be a possibility of negotiated agreements to moderate planned increases. This proposal was defeated, largely because of German opposition.[70] Tirpitz then began to press for another supplement, which Bülow, although he was aware that it would greatly complicate his plans for financial reform, had to accept because Tirpitz had secured the Emperor's support.[71] The new bill, which the Reichstag approved in 1908, shortened the life of battleships from twenty-five to twenty years, provided that each retired ship would be replaced by a Dreadnought, and, in general, marked a decided acceleration in construction. The fact that Tirpitz forbade the disclosure of full details concerning the projected programme, hiding them even from the Reichstag,[72] added to the disquiet with which the British reacted to the German action.[73] In 1909 an aroused public opinion forced the Liberal cabinet to make new increases in the naval estimates,[74] and it began to appear that this would be an endless competitive process.

Bethmann, nevertheless, hoped to stop it and, by persuading the British that Germany admitted British naval supremacy and was willing to limit its own construction, to win a promise of neutrality in case Germany were attacked by France or Russia or had to go

[69] Woodward, *Great Britain and the German Navy*, pp. 105 ff.

[70] Marschall boasted that Germany and Austria-Hungary had buried the British plan. Ibid., pp. 135-7.

[71] See Berghahn, *Der Tirpitz-Plan*, pp. 565 f.

[72] Ibid., pp. 566 ff.

[73] See Zara S. Steiner, *The Foreign Office and Foreign Policy, 1898-1914* (Cambridge, 1969), pp. 88 f., 112 ff.

[74] Woodward, *Great Britain and the German Navy*, pp. 219 ff.

to the defence of Austria. This was excessively ambitious in any case, and the Chancellor was handicapped in pursuing it by his own inexperience in foreign affairs, by the wilfulness of his colleagues, and by William II's pronounced views on foreign policy.

Bethmann's search for a political agreement was compromised almost immediately because he made the mistake of asking for too much too quickly. In a conversation with Goschen, the British ambassador, he expressed the view that 'the discussion of a naval agreement could lead to no practical result unless it formed part of a scheme for a general understanding and was based upon a conviction on the part, not only of the two governments but of public opinion in both countries, that neither country had any hostile or aggressive designs against the other'.[75] This cloudy formula alarmed the British, since it appeared to ask for a limitation on British freedom of diplomatic action in return for nothing that was tangible, for certainly Bethmann was extraordinarily vague when he was asked what naval concessions he was prepared to offer. This was understandable, since Tirpitz, who had the Emperor's ear, did not want to make any concessions at all.

The irritation that this caused in Whitehall changed to anger when Bethmann's Secretary of State for Foreign Affairs set out to reverse the verdict of Algeciras. Alfred von Kiderlen-Wächter was the last German diplomat of first rank to have had an intimate relationship with Bismarck. He had entered the Foreign Service in 1879, served under Münster in Paris and Radowitz in Constantinople, been a close friend of Holstein, who furthered his career, and was for ten years attached to the Emperor's suite as a representative of the Foreign Ministry during the monarch's cruises. At the height of the Bosnian crisis he had been called back to Berlin from his latest post, Bucharest, and made Acting Secretary of State, and in that capacity he had drafted the ultimatum that had forced Izvolsky to knuckle under. The incident was indicative of his style. He prided himself on being *ein Kerl* ('a tough guy') and was prone to displays of self-defeating violence.[76] Moreover, after he became Secretary of State in 1910, his self-confidence and arrogance blinded him to the necessity of keeping Bethmann fully informed of his intentions so that the unfortunate Chancellor was reduced on one occasion to the extremity of

[75] Jarausch, *Enigmatic Chancellor*, p. 114.
[76] The standard biography is Jäckh, *Kiderlen-Wächter*. More critical is W. Andreas, 'Kiderlen-Wächter: Randglossen zu seinem Nachlass', *Historische Zeitschrift*, cxxxii (1925).

getting his Foreign Secretary intoxicated in order to find out what was on his mind.[77]

In April 1911 the Moroccan question was abruptly reopened when the French Government, on the pretext of protecting foreigners from native disorders, dispatched troops to Fez. Technically, the action was a violation of the terms of the Algeciras Treaty. Kiderlen pointed this out and intimated that if, as he suspected, the French intended to remain in Fez, Germany would expect some kind of territorial compensation. The French ignored these suggestions for some weeks. This was a mistake, for on 1 July the German gunboat *Panther* hove to off the Atlantic Moroccan port of Agadir, and it was clear that it did not intend to leave until Germany had been paid to recall it.

This action aroused considerable enthusiasm in the patriotic Press—the *Kreuzzeitung* spoke of 'the nightmares of resigned discontent being dispersed by the rays of morning sun'[78]—and among those industrial groups that were interested in the mineral deposits of West Morocco. But this satisfaction was of short duration. In contrast to their behaviour in 1905, the French Government showed no disposition to be impressed by Kiderlen's menaces or receptive to his subsequent demand that Germany receive all of the French Congo as compensation for France's seizure of Morocco. Moreover, the British, nettled by Kiderlen's failure to consult them, took a decidedly hard line, when the Chancellor of the Exchequer, David Lloyd George, in a speech at the Mansion House on 21 July, said plainly that an attempt to treat Britain, 'where her interests were vitally affected, as if she were of no account in the Cabinet of Nations' would be a humiliation which Britain would not endure. In the wake of that speech Kiderlen's enterprise collapsed. He might argue lamely, as he apparently did to Bethmann and the Emperor at the end of the month, that German prestige required that Germany fight, regardless of the odds, unless the French gave way,[79] but no one was listening. The Emperor had no stomach for war; the navy chiefs were opposed to risking their fleet at this point in its development; Kiderlen's policy was criticized in the Bundesrat and in the Vienna Press; and talk of war led to a sharp decline in the stock market.[80] To add insult to injury, the French turned the screw by withdrawing

---

[77] Kurt Riezler, *Tagebücher, Aufsätze, Dokumente*, ed. Karl Dietrich Erdmann (Göttingen, 1972), pp. 178, 179.

[78] Fischer, *Krieg der Illusionen*, p. 121.

[79] Ibid., p. 129. Cf. Müller, *Der Kaiser*, p. 87.

[80] Fischer, *Krieg der Illusionen*, pp. 132 ff.

short-term loans from Germany. The Bethmann government decided to settle for what it could get: a large, but worthless, tract in Central Africa.

The fiasco had three fateful results. In the first place, it increased tension between Germany and the Entente Powers, accelerated the armaments race, and encouraged in the governing class a feeling that war was inevitable. Secondly, the completeness of the French victory in Morocco galvanized the Italians into moving into Tripolitania, lest the French Government consider doing so itself. The Italian action touched off a war with Turkey which, in its turn, encouraged the Balkan states to join together to despoil Turkey of what was left of its European possessions before they were anticipated by the Triple Alliance. A major role in forming this Balkan League, which soon had all of South-Eastern Europe in a state of perpetual crisis, was played by the Russian Government, now getting its own back for the humiliation suffered in 1909.

Finally, as a result of the set-back in Morocco, Bethmann's ability to cope with these new European complications with wisdom and moderation was seriously reduced. From this point on he was regarded by the conservative parties, the patriotic societies, and the soldiers as a weakling who had allowed a new Olmütz to be imposed upon the country. In view of what was to happen in the crisis of 1914, it is interesting to read the comment which Moltke, the Chief of Staff, made to his wife in August 1911: 'If we creep out of this affair with our tails between our legs, if we cannot be aroused to an energetic set of demands which we are prepared to enforce by the sword, then I am doubtful about the future of the German Empire. And I will resign. But first I will propose that we abolish the army and place ourselves under the protection of Japan. Then we will be able to make money without interference and to become imbeciles.'[81] Moltke did not, of course, resign; but he and many other officers were both embittered and determined that there must not be another climb-down like the one of 1911.

The outcome of the Moroccan crisis led Bethmann to redouble his efforts to win an agreement with Great Britain that would give Germany some hope that British aid to France would not be automatic in all contingencies. The key to improved relations was still, in his opinion, the naval question, and the reports he was receiving from the ambassador in London, Graf von Wolff-Metternich, gave him some reason to believe that the British might be amenable to the

[81] H. von Moltke, *Erinnerungen, Briefe, Dokumente* (Stuttgart, 1922), p. 362.

suggestion of a mutual reduction in the rate of construction. Unfortunately, the weight of Metternich's reports was reduced by those of his naval attaché, Captain Wilhelm Widenmann, who was encouraged by Tirpitz to represent all British overtures as attempts to dupe Germany. Although both Metternich and Bethmann remonstrated to the Emperor about the tendentiousness of Widenmann's reports,[82] their protests were unavailing, the Emperor expressing complete faith in the attaché's assessment of the situation and insisting that Metternich was naïve.[83] In consequence, the ambassador was prevented from making any progress towards laying the basis for productive talks, with the result that, when the British Secretary of State for War, Lord Haldane, a man long known for his sympathy for Germany, visited Berlin in 1912, to discuss an agreement, there could be no meeting of minds. Tirpitz, who made public another bill calling for additions to the navy on the day of Haldane's arrival, was opposed to any concessions unless the British were prepared to give an unqualified pledge of neutrality in the case of a Franco–German war. As long as this was the German position, there was no hope of accommodation.[84] Thus, when Winston Churchill, First Lord of the British Admiralty, proposed a naval building holiday in April 1912, the Emperor answered that this arrangement would be possible only between allies. Churchill's subsequent attempts to use the good offices of Sir Ernest Cassel and Albert Ballin to make the Emperor 'appreciate the sentiments with which an island state like Britain views the steady and remorseless development of a rival naval power of the very highest efficiency' also failed.[85]

William II still suffered from the illusion that he could frighten the British into coming to terms. After the failure of the Haldane mission, he had boasted '. . . I have shown the English that, when they touch our armaments, they bite on granite. Perhaps by this I have

[82] They were later supported by Kiderlen-Wächter who complained that Widenmann's reports 'breathed a hatred and distrust of England which, in my respectful opinion, are not justified and which . . . can only produce an unnecessary aggravation of the difficulties of our relations with England'. See Craig, *Prussian Army*, pp. 296 ff. and, for Widenmann's side of the story, Wilhelm Widenmann, *Marine-Attaché in London 1907–1912* (Göttingen, 1952).

[83] Metternich was recalled before the end of the year.

[84] The failure of the mission did not become apparent until after Haldane's return to England, and Albert Ballin, who was involved in the mission, was certain as late as mid-March that an alliance would be signed. But Lord Grey made it clear on 17 March that both technical and political obstacles stood in the way. See Cecil, *Ballin*, pp. 182–98.

[85] Randolph S. Churchill, *Winston S. Churchill*, ii (Boston, 1967), pp. 551 f. On all this, see Woodward, *Great Britain and the German Navy*, Chs. 18, 19, 20, 23.

increased their hatred but won their respect, which will induce them in due course to resume negotiations, it is to be hoped in a more modest tone and with a more fortunate result.'[86] This was the same illusion that had befogged German thinking about Britain since 1890, and it was now once more to be proved for what it was. In November, with some reluctance, the British took the step that invalidated the Tirpitz strategy. In an exchange of notes with the French ambassador, Lord Grey agreed that 'if either government had grave reason to expect an unprovoked attack by a third Power, or something that threatened the general peace, it should immediately discuss with the other whether both governments should act together'. The French Government immediately moved its fleet to the Mediterranean, as the British Admiralty, which had been forced to bring its Atlantic fleet home from Gibraltar and to move its Mediterranean fleet from Malta to Gibraltar, had been hoping it would do. No objective observer could deny that Britain's obligation to defend France from attack was now stronger than it had been and that Germany was responsible for this.[87]

In December Britain's position was made unmistakably clear. Europe was by now confronted with an extremely volatile situation in the Balkans, where a victorious war, waged against Turkey by the combined forces of Montenegro, Serbia, Bulgaria, and Greece, had put all existing frontiers in jeopardy and awakened the liveliest apprehension in Vienna. Once more Conrad and his followers were calling for war to put an end to the ambitions of the Great Serb movement, which seemed determined now to win access to the Adriatic; and it was obvious that this raised the danger of Russian intervention. At this juncture, doubtless with the intention of inducing caution in both Vienna and Berlin, Lord Haldane, clearly speaking with the authority of the government, told Lichnowsky, the German ambassador, that in the event of an Austrian invasion of Serbia, Great Britain could hardly remain a silent spectator. Then, with reference to a recent speech in which Bethmann had promised support for Austria if it were attacked by a third Power while pursuing its own interests, Haldane added that British opinion believed that the existing balance of forces in Europe should be maintained. It would not tolerate a defeat of France or the consolidation of all European power in the hands of a single state.[88]

This warning infuriated William II. In a meeting on 8 December

[86] Ritter, *Kriegshandwerk* ii. 235.
[87] Woodward, *Great Britain and the German Navy*, pp. 380 ff.
[88] *G.P.* xxxix. 111 ff.

with Tirpitz, Moltke, Heeringen of the Naval Staff, and Müller, the Chief of the Naval Cabinet, he upbraided the British Government and declared that, in view of its attitude, Germany must declare war against France and Russia at once. The discussion that followed was confused and without any positive result, and Bethmann Hollweg was not even informed that the meeting had taken place until more than a week had passed.[89] It is nevertheless significant that, in contrast to Tirpitz, who apparently argued that the navy was not ready for a major war and would not be for at least eighteen months, Moltke accepted the idea of a preventive war without hesitation, with the words 'the sooner, the better'. This was to remain the view of the Chief of Staff from now on. He was worried by the growth of Russian power, which he feared would invalidate all of the assumptions of the Schlieffen Plan if it continued unchecked. He made this clear in communications to his opposite number in Vienna[90] and in conversations with members of the government;[91] and his influence was probably behind the article in the *Kölnische Zeitung* of 2 March 1914, presumably written by one Oberleutnant Ulrich, which described Russia's military buildup, its growing economic strength, and the hostile nature of its policy and argued for a policy of firmness and a readiness to resort to arms if a crisis arose.[92]

Bethmann Hollweg was not prepared to surrender to the mood of the soldiers. He agreed with them about the dangers of the European situation, and he made this clear not only by the energy with which he threw himself into the effort to win support for the Army Bill of 1913 but also by the rhetoric he used to support it.[93] But, although he was willing to admit that circumstances might arise that would make it necessary for Germany to resort to preventive war, he refused to invite them. Instead of satisfying the Emperor's desire that the

[89] The main source for information on this meeting is Müller, *Der Kaiser*, pp. 124 ff. Fischer, *Krieg der Illusionen*, pp. 231 ff. and John C. G. Rohl, 'Admiral von Mueller and the Approach to War', *Historical Journal*, xii (1966) argue that this 'war council' determined the course of German policy from this time forward. This is clearly an exaggerated view, as Wolfgang J. Mommsen has pointed out in *Central European History*, vi, no. 1 (Mar. 1973), 12–14. See also his article 'The Debate on German War Aims', *Journal of Contemporary History*, i (1966), 47 ff. and 'Die deutsche "Weltpolitik" und der erste Weltkrieg', *Neue politische Literatur,* xvi (1971), 482 ff.

[90] See Conrad, *Aus meiner Dienstzeit*, iii. 670.

[91] The increase of the Russian danger did not induce him to abandon the Schlieffen Plan, even though he was aware of its political disadvantages, as he admitted to Jagow at the beginning of 1913. See Ritter, *Kriegshandwerk* ii. 271.

[92] Fischer describes this as a 'War in sight' article. See *Krieg der Illusionen*, pp. 546 ff., 552.

[93] See above, Ch. VIII, p. 296.

German people be prepared for the irrepressible conflict, he set himself the difficult task of solving the tangled Balkan situation 'through compromise in accord with England without undermining the firmness of our alliance with Austria'.[94] In pursuit of this goal, he refused to countenance any new increase in naval estimates, and he warned Berchtold, the Austrian Foreign Minister, against resorting to force 'as long as there is a slight chance to see the conflict through under considerably better circumstances'.[95] These cautionary steps facilitated the collaboration with the British Government that was largely responsible for the success of the ambassadorial conference that met in London to deal with the tangled territorial questions raised by Turkey's defeat. Later, when the victors fell out, and a second Balkan war began in June 1913, Bethmann's tactics were the same. Although Serbia was the chief beneficiary of the new conflict and Austria's Bulgarian ally the victim, the German Chancellor warned Berchtold to do nothing that might widen the conflict,[96] and he once more worked with Britain to reach a settlement.

Bethmann's hope was that the fragile international balance could be maintained as long as he had a practical working relationship with the British. He was heartened in the first months of 1914 by evidence that Anglo-German co-operation could extend beyond the Balkans. Thanks largely to the patient diplomacy of Richard von Kühlmann, First Secretary in the London Embassy, an agreement was worked out to provide for the peaceful division of the Portuguese colonies in the event that the government of Portugal decided to abandon them,[97] while at the same time the thorny question of extending the Baghdad Railway to the Persian Gulf was settled to the satisfaction of both parties by another agreement. 'If we both act together as guarantors of European peace, which as long as we follow this goal according to a common plan neither Entente nor Triple Alliance obligations shall prevent, war will be avoided', Bethmann wrote to Lichnowsky in London in June 1914. 'Sometimes you see things too pessimistically if you believe that in the case of war England will *undoubtedly* be found on France's side against us.'[98]

This can fairly be described as whistling to keep one's courage up. At other moments, and with increasing frequency, Bethmann was

[94] Jarausch, *Enigmatic Chancellor*, p. 137.

[95] Hugo Hantsch, *Leopold Graf Berchtold: Grandseigneur und Staatsmann* (2 vols., Graz and Vienna, 1963), i. 387–8.

[96] Ibid. ii. 441 ff.

[97] This was, in a sense, neutralized by an Anglo-Portuguese treaty providing for British financial aid to Portugal.

[98] *G.P.* xxxix. 628 ff.; Jarausch, *Enigmatic Chancellor*, pp. 141–3.

prey to the gloomiest of doubts about Germany's future. He knew that the Balkan wars, for all of his success in containing them, had left all of South-Eastern Europe in a state of unrelieved tension, which was exacerbated by the desire of the Serbs, with the hardly disguised backing of the Russians, to increase the territorial gains that they had made and by the determination of the Austrian Government to resist further Serbian expansion by resort to war if necessary, since the very fabric of the Habsburg monarchy was threatened by the Pan-Slav and Great Serb movements. In July 1913 Berchtold had made it clear to the German ambassador that Vienna could no longer tolerate having its interests neglected by its ally, adding 'we might just as well belong to the other *groupement*'.[99] Bethmann was not prepared to risk the realization of that threat. Moreover, he knew that the Austrian fears were not imaginary. The Russians, made self-confident by the success of their clients, were no longer amenable to the control of their allies. Russian dissatisfaction with the lack of support received from the west during the Albanian crisis of 1913 had had a sensible effect in Whitehall and the Quai d'Orsay;[100] and both the British decision to open naval conversations with Russia and Poincaré's decision to pay a visit to St. Petersburg were signs of an eagerness on the part of the Entente Powers to assure Russia that it could count on their future assistance. The importance of these steps was not lost on Bethmann,[101] and he became increasingly preoccupied with the Russian threat. 'The future belongs to Russia,' he said at the beginning of July 1914. 'It grows and grows and hangs upon us ever more heavily like a nightmare.'[102]

These gloomy reflections explain Bethmann's behaviour in the hectic days that followed the murder of the Austrian Archduke Franz Ferdinand and his wife in Sarajevo on 28 June 1914.[103]

---

[99] Hantsch, *Berchtold* ii. 449 ff., 460.

[100] On British concern over the possibility of losing Russia as an ally, see Harold Nicolson, *Portrait of a Diplomatist* (New York, 1930), pp. 216, 222 ff., 255, 300 ff., which describes the efforts made by his father, Sir Arthur Nicolson, then Permanent Under-Secretary for Foreign Affairs, to avoid anything that might give offence to the Russians. See also Zara Steiner, *The Foreign Office*, pp. 133–4, 150, 156–7.

[101] Riezler, *Tagebücher*, p. 182.

[102] Ibid., p. 183.

[103] On this, there is a mountain of literature. In addition to the older works, like Bernadotte Schmitt, *The Coming of the War, 1914* (2 vols., New York, 1930) and Luigi Albertini, *Le origini della guerra del 1914* (3 vols., Milan, 1942 ff.), one must consult the first chapters of Fritz Fischer, *Griff nach der Weltmacht: Die Kriegszielpolitik des kaiserlichen Deutschland 1914/1918* (3rd edn., Düsseldorf, 1964) and his *Krieg der Illusionen*, as well as Immanuel Geiss (ed.), *Julikrise und Kriegsausbruch 1914* (2 vols., Hanover, 1964). Fischer has a decided anti-Bethmann bias, which is contested effectively in

The Chancellor was a member of that now famous council of war summoned by William II on 5 July 1914, which was attended also by Zimmermann, the Under-Secretary of State for Foreign Affairs, Falkenhayn, the War Minister, Lyncker, the Chief of the Military Cabinet, and Generaladjutant von Plessen. The Emperor read a letter from the Emperor of Austria and a memorandum from the Ballplatz, both of which made it clear that the Austrians intended to demand satisfaction from the Serbian Government and to take military action if there was any hesitation in Belgrade about granting it; the Austrian Government wished, before it acted, to be assured of German support. All participants in the meeting were in agreement that their ally should be encouraged to go ahead, with the assurance that Germany would come to its aid in the event of Russian intervention. On the following morning Bethmann gave the 'blank cheque' to Szögyeny, the Austrian ambassador, telling him that the Austrian Government would have to decide how its relations with Serbia should be clarified, but that, in doing so, it could count firmly on Germany's support as ally and friend, whatever its decision might be.

For Bethmann, this was a decided change from the policy he had followed during the Balkan wars, and it cannot be attributed to the unanimous enthusiasm with which the previous day's decision was greeted in the General Staff. To his secretary Riezler, he described the policy on 7 July as a necessity arising out of the old dilemma that was posed whenever Austria considered action in the Balkans. 'If we urge them ahead, then they will say we pushed them in; if we dissuade them, then it will become a matter of our leaving them in the lurch. Then they will turn to the Western Powers, whose arms are wide open, and we will lose our last ally, such as it is.' 'This time,' he added, 'it is worse than 1912, for this time Austria is defending itself

Egmont Zechlin, 'Bethmann Hollweg, Kriegsrisiko und SPD 1914', Der Monat, xviii (Jan. 1966); Karl Dietrich Erdmann, 'Zur Beurteilung Bethmann Hollwegs', Geschichte in Wissenschaft und Unterricht, xv (1964), 525–40; and the third volume of Ritter's Kriegshandwerk. Decidedly critical of Bethmann is Dieter Groth, Negative Integration, pp. 331–9, 367–413, 663, 669–70, where the Chancellor is seen as resisting war only until he was certain of SPD support. See also James Joll, 'The 1914 Controversy Continued', Past and Present, no. 34 (July 1966), 100–13; the articles by Geiss, Klaus Epstein, and Wolfgang J. Mommsen in Journal of Contemporary History, i, no. 3 (July 1966); and those by Joachim Remak and Paul W. Schroeder in Journal of Modern History, xliii, no. 3 (Sept. 1971), 353–66, and xliv, no. 3 (Sept. 1972), 319–45. Balanced and unpolemical judgements are to be found in Jarausch, Enigmatic Chancellor and in Fritz Stern, 'Bethmann Hollweg and the War: The Limits of Responsibility', in The Responsibility of Power: Historical Essays in Honor of Hajo Holborn, ed. Leonard Krieger and Fritz Stern (New York, 1967), pp. 252–85.

against the intrigues of Serbia and Russia.'[104] The added words probably represented his deeper feelings. If those intrigues were allowed to succeed, Germany would lose more than an ally. Its whole position in the Balkans would be destroyed and any hope of maintaining itself as leading world Power would be illusory.

The blank cheque to Austria was therefore a necessary defensive measure. But it might also, if properly used, break the ring that was tightening around Germany. If Germany acted with sufficient determination in support of Austria's action against Serbia, the Russians might hesitate to support the Serbian Government, which was in any case implicated in the assassination at Sarajevo, and, if the Russians did not hesitate, the French or the British, or both, might shrink back from the threat of a general war and restrain the St. Petersburg government. To assure this result would require steady nerves and a studied avoidance of aggressive behaviour (Bethmann was disgusted, as the crisis mounted, by the jingoism of the Pan-German Press and the public support given it by the Crown Prince); but, provided the German Government acted with deliberate firmness, it might, if things worked out right, break the Entente.

But, of course, things did not work out right. The Austrians weakened their initially strong case by procrastination and by an ultimatum to the Serbian Government that seemed clumsy and impolitic even to those who were appalled by what had happened at Sarajevo. As for German behaviour, it was marked neither by steadiness of nerve nor by avoidance of menaces. The military became increasingly nervous about the element of time and its effect upon their mobilization schedules and, once Austria had declared war on Serbia, kept urging Bethmann to clarify French and Russian intentions; and Moltke, on his own, contributed to that clarification, and to the defeat of Bethmann's strategy, by secretly urging Conrad on 30 July to order full Austrian mobilization against Russia.[105] Moreover, not even this crude threat succeeded in intimidating the Russian Government, which was confident that it would be supported by France; and the news of Russia's general mobilization, on 31 July, put an end to Bethmann's hope that war, if it came, might be limited. Germany's mobilization, which followed immediately, was in accordance with Moltke's exchanges with Conrad in 1909, that is to say it activated the Schlieffen Plan. To defend Austria, Germany now attacked France by way of Belgium, the violation of whose territory brought Great Britain in on France's side. Thanks to the

---

[104] Riezler, *Tagebücher*, p. 183.
[105] Conrad, *Aus meiner Dienstzeit*, iv. 152.

soldiers' preoccupation with timing and the rigidity of their operational plans, Bethmann's gamble failed and led to a general war.

One wonders if he ever expected it to succeed. Germany's past record was not one to arouse much confidence in its ability to pursue foreign policy calmly and rationally. In July Bethmann spoke bitterly to Riezler about 'the earlier errors: a Turkish policy against Russia,[106] Morocco against France, fleet against England, all at the same time—challenge everybody, get in everyone's way, and actually, in the course of all this, weaken nobody. Basic cause: lack of planning, craving for petty prestige victories, and solicitude for every current of public opinion. The "national" parties who want to maintain and strengthen their political position by making a hullabaloo about foreign policy.'[107] And, apart from this, was not the nation showing the most alarming signs of spiritual degeneration? The political niveau had sunk to a miserable level; 'individuals as such [were] becoming smaller and smaller'; and in public life there was no sign of nobility or honour. As for intellectual life, its salient characteristic was the capitulation of the professors to the ugliest forces of the age.[108]

Bethmann was, in fact, a curious mixture of cultural pessimist and statesman, and it was perhaps his concern over the decline of values and intellectual vigour in his country and his hope that a daring action might have a remedial effect that directed his strategy in the summer of 1914. This would explain his cryptic remark to Riezler that his policy was 'a leap into the dark and the heaviest duty'.[109]

IV

That the Wilhelmine era ended in war and defeat was not, of course, Bethmann's fault, or Tirpitz's, or Schlieffen's, or even that of the ebullient ruler who gave the age its name and who certainly never wanted a war at all. Many things contributed to that tragic issue, not least of all the distortion of values that not only determined the garish style of the period but encouraged the tendency to over-value wealth

[106] Bethmann was thinking here not only of the Baghdad Railway policy but also of the appointment in the autumn of 1913, without the knowledge of the Chancellor or the Foreign Ministry, of General Liman von Sanders as chief of a military mission to Turkey and, simultaneously, as commanding general of the First Turkish Army Corps. The Russians reacted angrily, and Bethmann had to admit that the appointment had been ordered by the Emperor and carried out by the Military Cabinet. See Schmidt-Bückeburg, *Militärkabinett*, p. 226, and Eyck, *Das persönliche Regiment*, pp. 682 ff.

[107] Riezler, *Tagebücher*, p. 188.
[108] Ibid., p. 183.   [109] Ibid., p. 185.

and power. After the collapse and the revolution, Alfred Döblin was to write:[110]

Remember the time of the Wilhelmine regime. Not the fabulous boom, with which the dynasty had nothing to do. Think of the Siegesallee.[111] Of the ostentation of the parvenus. Of the byzantine emptiness and falsity of the spectacle and of the theatricality of the parades. Of the anti-popular exclusiveness. Of the 'comrades without a country'.[112] Of the conservative terrorism in the Prussian Chamber. Of the sovereign power of the *Junker* provincial councillors. Of the farce of the Reichstag. Of the special farce of the one-time Black–Blue bloc. Of the idolatry shown the officer. Of the wretchedness of the Agadir policy. The disinclination to consider curbing expansion and to busy one's self with spiritual matters. The growing atrophy of the bourgeoisie, which became divided into profiteers, lickspittles, the apathetic, and the discontented. The brooding atmosphere of this empire of money-grubbers, in which, from time to time, there sounded the rattling of sabres or the music of waltzes. This monstrousness, which sucked in even the working masses.

The time came when many Germans dwelt upon such things. In 1914, however, the gift of self-analysis was not yet highly developed.

[110] A. Döblin, 'Republik', *Die neue Rundschau*, i (1920), 78.

[111] This was a promenade in the Tiergarten lined with tasteless statues of the rulers of Brandenburg-Prussia. Inspired by William II, it was popular with Berliners, who are witty enough to appreciate *Kitsch* in the grand manner. It was largely destroyed in the Second World War, and the fragments dispersed.

[112] *'Die vaterlandslosen Gesellen'*, a term used publicly by William II to refer to those members of the working class who continued, despite all his efforts, to vote for the Social Democratic party.

X
The Great War
1914–1918

Frohlockt, ihr Freunde, daß wir leben,
Und daß wir jung sind und gelenk,
Nie hat es solch ein Jahr gegeben,
Und nie war Jugend solch Geschenk!

Wir durften stehn und durften schreiten,
So morgenwärts wie abendwärts,
Die größte aller Erdenzeiten,—
Uns brandet' sie ans junge Herz.

BRUNO FRANK (1914)[1]

IT is not easy for the historian to recapture the mood that affected the European peoples at the outbreak of the war in 1914. It was a curious compound of uncomplicated patriotism, romantic joy in the chance of participating in a great adventure, and naïve expectation that, somehow or other, the conflict would solve all of the problems that had piled up during the years of peace. Most Germans believed as fervently as most Englishmen and most Frenchmen that their country was the victim of a brutal assault; 'We did not ask for it, but now we must defend the homeland' was the common response, and it led to an impressive closing of the ranks. The Russian mobilization resolved the doubts of those who had been critical of the pre-war course of German policy; and, in the voting of the war credits by the Reichstag, the parties of the left stood shoulder to shoulder with their peacetime antagonists. The declaration of war released a heady excitement that swept the whole country. To the young it offered an exhilarating holiday from the dull routines of normal life—'War is like Christmas!', one newly commissioned lieutenant said happily[2]—and a promise of self-fulfilment.

Nor did one have to be called to the colours to sense that the

---

[1] Bruno Frank, 'Stolze Zeit, 1914', in *Der ewige Brunnen: Ein Volksbuch deutscher Dichtung*, ed. Ludwig Reiners (Munich, 1955), p. 440.

[2] Friedrich Meinecke, *Ausgewählter Briefwechsel*, ed. Ludwig Dehio and Peter Classen (Stuttgart, 1962), p. 326. The officer in question died of an accidental gunshot wound on the way to the front at Liège.

coming of war had changed everything or to believe that the change would be for the better. In one of the best novels to come out of the war, Ernst Gläser expressed what must have been the feeling of many older Germans who had long worried about the decline of values and the virulence of party strife in their country: 'At last life had regained an ideal significance. The great virtues of humanity . . . fidelity, patriotism, readiness to die for an ideal . . . were triumphing over the trading and shopkeeping spirit. . . . This was the providential lightning flash that would clear the air. . . . [There would be] a new world directed by a race of noble souls who would root out all signs of degeneracy and lead humanity back to the deserted peaks of the eternal ideals. . . . The war would cleanse mankind from all its impurities.'[3]

These illusions did not last long. The young recruits who went off to the front cheerfully bellowing

> Und unser allerschönstes junges Leben, Hurra!
> Liegt in dem Krieg wohl auf das Schlachtfeld hingestreckt

with no idea that anything of the sort could possibly happen to them, discovered at Langemarck that it could indeed,[4] and the innocent view of war as a glorious enterprise never recovered from that blow. At the same time, the idealism of the first days weakened as it became clear that important groups on the home front were more intent upon using the war for material gain than upon demonstrating the nobility of the German spirit. It was this latter development that caused the swift dissolution of that *Burgfrieden* which William II had so proudly announced on 4 August, with the words, 'I no longer recognize parties; I recognize only Germans.' It was soon evident that party strife was not dead, for the Socialist party and the trade unions were determined that their support of the war effort must be rewarded by significant progress toward democratic government

---

[3] Ernst Gläser, *Jahrgang 1902* (Berlin, 1929), pp. 188–9 (pt. 1: 'Das Schützenfest'). This belief was common to all belligerent countries. See the mocking account in Richard Aldington, *Death of a Hero* (London, 1929), pp. 225 f., 252 ff.

[4] To a greater degree than is true of the war songs of most other countries, German *Soldatenlieder* dwell heavily on death. See such well-known songs as 'Morgenrot', 'Kein schön'rer Tod ist in der Welt als wer vorm Feind erschlagen', 'Ich hatt' einen Kameraden', and the one quoted here, 'Nun ade, jetzt muß ich Abschied nehmen', the tune of which, somewhat modified, became the *Horst-Wessel-Lied*. On the mood of those who sang them in 1914, see Carl Zuckmayer, *Als wär's ein Stück von mir* (Vienna, 1966), pp. 207 f. At Langemarck raw recruits stormed French machine-guns and died by the hundreds with the *Deutschlandlied* on their lips. But no one sang, Zuckmayer writes, at Verdun or during the battle on the Somme or in the wasting war of attrition in Flanders.

and social reform,[5] while the parties of the right were equally determined to prevent this result and hoped to do so by debauching the working classes with a grandiose programme of territorial acquisition.

As early as the end of September 1914, the historian Friedrich Meinecke gave almost unconscious witness to the forces that were eroding the 'spirit of 1914'. 'I believe', he wrote to his friend Alfred Dove in Freiburg,

that this war, *even if it should end victoriously along the whole line*, will free us from a lot that troubled us until now. Of course, we must work hard afterwards, to see that our little bit of culture (*unser bißchen Kultur*) doesn't suffer harm. Our opponents ascribe to us military plans for the conquest of a new Roman empire—but trees don't grow up to heaven all at once. It is true that one hears of all kinds of continental appetites these days—Tirpitz is said to consider Antwerp indispensable and they say that Belgium is to be divided into four parts (one for us, one for Holland, one for France, which they want to spare, and one for Luxemburg)—which doesn't please me. The compactness and unity of our national state, upon which our present strength depends, ought not to be hurt by resistant appendages. Of course, we must at last beat England down to the point where it recognizes us as a world Power of equal rights, and I believe that our strength will be sufficient—despite the momentary squeeze in northern France—to achieve that purpose. The German–Turkish alliance is said to be concluded and the attack of the Turks on Egypt definitely set. Your doubts about all of these Napoleonic offensive manœuvres I, of course, surmise, but what are we to do? *Fert unda nec regitur*—that is what we must say about the task that destiny has given us and, with happy confidence, we must seek to accomplish it.[6]

Meinecke was a moderate, who was never taken in by those he called the *Schlagododros*, who believed that force would bring Germany mastery over Europe.[7] He hoped, from the very beginning, that negotiation might lead to a kind of Hubertusburg Peace, which would leave things much as they had been before 1914.[8] It was ominous therefore that, within two months of the onset of hos-

---

[5] At the end of August 1914 the Socialist Reichstag deputy Eduard David warned Delbrück, the Secretary of State, that his comrades who were making sacrifices for their country expected that their ideals and objectives would be recognized and that, if this were not the case, 'a void will open among the people that will not be bridged for decades'. Jürgen Kuczynski, *Der Ausbruch des Ersten Weltkrieges und die deutsche Sozialdemokratie* (Berlin, 1957), pp. 208 f.

[6] Meinecke, *Briefwechsel*, p. 47 (to A. Dove, 25 Sept. 1914). My italics.

[7] Ibid., p. 51 (to A. Dove, 11 Nov. 1916).

[8] The Hubertusburg Peace ended the Seven Years War in 1763. See Meinecke, *Straßburg, Freiburg, Berlin*, p. 198: 'I remember a characteristic conversation that I had in Hintze's house with the national economist Schumacher who was then at Bonn. I stated that already even a Hubertusburg peace would be a great victory for us. "Oh," he burst out, beaming with certainty, "we can hope for much more!" The first indication of the beginning of the division of minds.'

tilities, he should have discerned so clearly that military success would unleash—indeed, was already unleashing—greedy forces that would destroy what was best in Germany, *unser bißchen Kultur*, and it was even more ominous that he should have concluded that there was nothing much that he or other men who shared his views could do to change that, since Germany's course was determined by fate.[9]

I

The successes registered by the armed forces during the opening phase of the war were hardly impressive enough to justify the clamour for annexations that concerned Meinecke. One can argue, indeed, that the most striking aspect of the German war effort was the utter failure of the schemes upon which the two services had, in the pre-war period, lavished most of their intellectual and financial resources. The High Sea Fleet that Tirpitz had built as a weapon against England proved almost completely ineffective. In late August 1914 the Royal Navy penetrated the Helgoland Bight and sank the light cruisers *Ariadne, Mainz*, and *Köln* and the destroyer *V-187*, and damaged two other light cruisers. In January 1915 a brush between armoured cruisers off the Dogger Bank resulted in the loss of the *Blücher*. After that, the fleet remained in its home ports until May 1916 when it emerged to fight a full-scale battle against the British off Jutland, in which its losses were greatly exceeded by those of the enemy,[10] but were serious enough to persuade Admiral Scheer, who commanded the fleet in the battle, to advise the Emperor a month later that England could not be defeated by battles on the high seas but only by submarine pressure on its economic life.[11] The German fleet made some not very successful sallies from port after Jutland, but with its best officers and petty officers transferred to U-boats, its efficiency and spirit declined.[12] The reputation

[9] Meinecke had a tendency to give way to what E. R. Curtius once called the besetting German sin of taking refuge in destiny. This is the prevailing note in his book *Die deutsche Katastrophe*.

[10] The German fleet sank three British battle-cruisers, three light cruisers, and eight destroyers at the cost of one battleship, one battle-cruiser, four light cruisers, and five destroyers.

[11] In November 1914 the German China squadron, commanded by Admiral Spee, sank two British armoured cruisers off Coronel, but Spee's force was destroyed a month later in the battle of the Falkland Islands, and by the spring of 1915 there were no German fleet units or merchant vessels at large.

[12] An interesting, if highly polemical, account of the state of morale in the German navy is to be found in Theodor Plievier's novel *Des Kaisers Kulis* (1930). See also Daniel Horn (ed.), *War, Mutiny and Revolution in the German Navy: The World War I Diary of Seaman Richard Stumpf* (New Brunswick, 1967).

of its founder had by that time gone into eclipse. William II was bitterly disappointed in the fleet's record, blaming all of its losses upon Tirpitz and accusing him of building the wrong kind of ships and encouraging faulty design and inadequate armament; and he became so irritated by the Admiral's attempts to shore up his position by attacks on the Chancellor and upon fellow naval officers, that he dismissed him from office, at Bethmann's request, in March 1916.[13]

The collapse of the Schlieffen Plan was even more resounding. The story has been told too often to make a detailed description rewarding, and there would be even less point in becoming involved in the old debate about whether the plan might have succeeded if it had not been for alterations made by Moltke in the original distribution of forces.[14] The simplest explanation for what happened in August 1914 was that the Germans underestimated their opponents and paid the penalty for doing so. They had not expected the Belgian army, which was in the middle of a thoroughgoing reorganization, to oppose their projected sweep through their country. But the Belgians did oppose them, defending the ring of fortresses around Liège so stubbornly that, by the time the Germans had forced them back on Antwerp and begun the wheeling motion that was supposed to envelop the left flank of the French Fifth Army on the Sambre, they were four days behind schedule. That delay was costly. The German had supposed that whatever help the British might supply to the French would be late and would arrive at points remote from the decisive area of operations. But while they were still being held Liège, four infantry divisions and a cavalry division under the command of Sir John French had landed at Le Havre, Rouen, and Boulogne. They were able to reach Mons in time to prevent the French flank from being turned.

The stubborn Allied retreat from the Sambre to Le Cateau slowed the German drive, and the casualties caused by battle and fatigue were so great that the German command departed from the letter of the Schlieffen Plan and turned their forces to the east rather than the west of Paris. This was a fatal manœuvre, which enabled the French Commander-in-Chief, Joffre, to throw the reserves that he had been holding at Paris against the German flank and rear. Forced on to the defensive along the line of the River Marne, the Germans might yet

---

[13] Tirpitz's decline is charted in *Regierte der Kaiser? Kriegstagebücher, Aufzeichnungen und Briefe des Chefs des Marine-Kabinetts Admiral Georg Alexander von Müller 1914–1918*, ed. Walter Görlitz (Göttingen, 1959), pp. 43, 49, 52, 69, 75, 76, 89, 107, 122, 145, 163. See also Ritter, *Kriegshandwerk* iii. 26–9.

[14] On this question, see Ritter, *Kriegshandwerk* ii. 268 ff.

have regained their momentum, if Moltke, the Chief of Staff, had not made another radical departure from the plan by committing his left wing, to which Schlieffen had assigned a purely defensive function, to an offensive against Nancy. This exhausted resources that might have been used effectively on the Marne and locked the German forces into two violent and uncoordinated battles that soon proved to be beyond their strength. As the strategical situation threatened to become a shambles, Moltke's never very robust nerves gave way, and he resigned his post, after having allowed a subordinate, Lieutenant-Colonel Hentsch, to make the fateful decision that broke off the battle at the Marne and ordered a general retreat to the River Aisne.

One might think that the breakdown of the supposedly infallible plan would be received at home as a declaration of bankruptcy on the part of the General Staff. But the extent of the defeat was obscured by the language of the official communiqués,[15] and public opinion was confident that the German offensive would be resumed in the near future. In the last months of 1914 no one even dimly discerned the true shape that war was to assume in the west—the long bloody halt in the mud that was to destroy a whole generation of young men. This impercipience was due in part to what had been happening on the eastern front, where operations were characterized by great mobility and gratifying results.

In response to an urgent plea from the French Government, the Russians had invaded East Prussia with two armies at the very outset of hostilities, causing near panic in the headquarters of the commander of the Eighth Army, von Prittwitz, who sent an urgent plea to Moltke for reinforcements.[16] The Russian drive had, however, been ill prepared; logistical support of the forces employed was inadequate; and co-ordination between the two armies was faulty in the extreme.[17] Even before help arrived from the west in the persons of a retired general named Paul von Hindenburg, who replaced von Prittwitz, and Erich Ludendorff, now a major-general, who had distinguished himself in the taking of Liège, the staff at headquarters had become aware of the inviting gap that was opening up between the forces of the Russian general Rennenkampf and those of his

[15] See Meinecke, *Straßburg, Freiburg, Berlin*, p. 197.

[16] Moltke responded by dispatching two corps from the west, which may have weakened the right wing of his advance toward Paris.

[17] A graphic description of this and its consequences is to be found in Alexander Solzhenitsyn's novel *August 1914* (New York, 1971). See also Norman Stone, *The Eastern Front, 1914–1917* (New York, 1975), which emphasizes the role of accident in the result.

colleague Samsonov and had drawn up plans to take advantage of it. By a skilful use of railways, General François isolated and pinned Samsonov's force at Tannenberg until two other corps enveloped it from the rear, forcing it to surrender after heavy losses on 30 August. A week later Hindenburg fell upon the bewildered Rennenkampf and destroyed his army in the Battle of the Masurian Lakes. By mid-September East Prussia was free of Russian troops, and the German public had found the military heroes they had been longing for, in the team of Hindenburg and Ludendorff.

The enthusiasm aroused by the victory in the east was under-standable but excessive. It overlooked the fact that, while the oper-ations in East Prussia were moving towards their dramatic dénoue-ment, four Russian armies under General Ivanov had moved into Galicia to counter the offensive launched by Conrad von Hötzendorf at the beginning of August. By the first of September the Austrians had been badly mauled and were threatened by encirclement, and the Austrian Chief of Staff was forced to order a retreat that left all of Galicia in enemy hands. The defeat was doubly galling to Conrad, for his campaign against Serbia, begun on 12 August, was in deep trouble and, after his forces had suffered 227,000 casualties, it was broken off in December without result. In the battles of Galicia and Serbia, the Austrians lost the flower of their junior officers and their non-commissioned officers corps, and their morale was badly shaken. All of this Conrad blamed upon the Germans, because they had encouraged him in his over-ambitious plans and because they had betrayed what he considered to have been a promise to support his advance into Galicia by mounting a threat against Warsaw.

There was much justice in Conrad's charges, and one can carry them further. Well before the beginning of hostilities in 1914, the German General Staff must have known that, if war came, the Central Powers would be opposed by a military coalition with a decided numerical superiority. Awareness of this fact should have persuaded them that victory would be possible only on the basis of a truly joint military plan established on effective exploitation of interior lines, an offensive concentration against one major antagon-ist coupled with an essentially defensive posture on other fronts, and careful attention during that offensive lest the theatre of war be compressed so as to threaten the vital interests of either ally.[18] The fact was, however, that the Central Powers had begun the war without anything resembling a joint plan of war and, what was

[18] See 'West- oder Ost-Offensive 1914?', in Ludwig Beck, *Studien*, ed. Hans Speidel (Stuttgart, 1955), p. 158.

worse, without even adequate knowledge of the strength, organization, technical equipment, and capacity of each other's forces.
Instead of limiting the operations of the alliance to one major offensive, the German General Staff had authorized—indeed, insisted
upon—three: one through Belgium into France, one across the Drina
and Save into Serbia, and one into Galicia. All had failed, the latter
two so disastrously that the Habsburg armies never recovered from
the losses suffered in August and September 1914. Nor did the
mutual disenchantment caused by these initial defeats fade as the war
went on. When mixed units were employed in certain sectors of the
front, a practice that became increasingly frequent in 1915 and 1916,
the Germans had a tendency to claim credit for all the victories and to
blame the defeats on the 'schlappe Österreicher'. The Austrians were
quick to resent this, as well as the persistent German attempts to
subordinate their armies to a German Supreme Command, which
Conrad came to believe masked a desire 'to deprive us of all our
rights'. Their resistance made true military cohesion impossible and
contributed to the strategical disarticulation of the alliance in the last
stages of the war.[19]

Moltke's successor as Chief of the General Staff[20] was the Minister
of War, Erich von Falkenhayn, a West Prussian aristocrat whose firm
and at times arrogant defence of the army during the Reichstag
debate on the Zabern incident had angered many of the deputies.[21]
Falkenhayn had intelligence and energy, a sound analytical sense,
and good nerves in time of crisis, as he had demonstrated in bringing
the dangerously fluid situation on the Marne under control in mid-
September. His self-assurance and his preference for keeping his
own counsel, and his tendency to sarcasm in commenting on the
frailties of others, made him many enemies, including the Dioscuri
in the east, who were soon intriguing mightily against him; but no
one doubted his integrity, his strong sense of responsibility, and his
complete freedom from self-seeking. Unlike Ludendorff, he overestimated neither his own talents[22] nor his country's prospects in the
war.[23]

[19] On all this, see 'The Military Cohesion of the Austro-German Alliance,
1914–1918', in Craig, War, Politics and Diplomacy, pp. 46–57. On Austrian operations
in general, see Gunther E. Rothenburg, The Army of Francis Joseph (West Lafayette,
Ind., 1976), pp. 172–218.

[20] Falkenhayn's position was not clarified until November, when Moltke was
formally retired.

[21] See above, Ch. VIII, p. 298.

[22] After his dismissal, he assumed an army command without any apparent resentment. One cannot imagine Ludendorff doing anything of the sort.

[23] See H. von Zwehl, Erich von Falkenhayn, General der Infanterie: Eine biographische

It was Falkenhayn's cool assessment of Germany's situation that led him, in October and November 1914, to try to end the war with a decisive battle in Flanders. Starting on 10 October, he threw the Sixth Army, commanded by the Crown Prince of Bavaria, and the newly constituted Fourth Army of Duke Albrecht of Württemberg against the northern salient of the Allied line, hoping to break through to Calais and open the coast to the Somme. When this thrust failed, he reformed his forces and directed it at Ypres, the hinge of the Allied communications network. By the first of November he had made no impression here, although his forces had suffered 80,000 casualties in two weeks. Despite complaints from subordinate commanders, Falkenhayn refused to admit defeat. He resumed the assault on 10 November, this time committing four newly raised and imperfectly trained corps of young volunteers, who were cut to pieces by battle-tested British infantry in the hedgerows west of Langemarck. On 18 November, after the Chief of the Military Cabinet had warned of the imminent exhaustion of reserves and the Chancellor, for the first time in the war, had intervened in an operational matter by urging Generaladjutant von Plessen to persuade the Emperor to end the campaign, Falkenhayn called off the attack. By that time the army's losses were in excess of 100,000 and exceeded the total casualties of its British, French, and Belgian adversaries.[24]

This defeat filled Falkenhayn with a deep pessimism. In a conversation with Bethmann Hollweg, immediately after the securing of the Ypres operation, he startled the Chancellor by telling him that a German victory that would lead to an honourable peace was now impossible unless either France or Russia were detached from the enemy coalition. On the whole, he thought the most promising strategy was to stop thinking of any but the most modest of war damages (this must have made the Chancellor blink, for he had recently been informed of the extensive territorial ambitions of

Studie (Berlin, 1926); Karl-Heinz Janßen, *Der Kanzler und der General: Die Führungskrise um Bethmann Hollweg und Falkenhayn 1914–1916* (Göttingen, 1967), Ch. 1; Wilhelm Groener, *Lebenserinnerungen*, p. 187 and *passim* (Groener was one of his closest associates); and Ritter, *Kriegshandwerk* iii. 55 ff.

[24] On the battle, see *Der Weltkrieg 1914–1918*, bearbeitet im Reichsarchiv (12 vols., Berlin, 1925–39), v. 286–347, 393 ff., 577 ff.; C. R. F. M. Cruttwell, *A History of the Great War, 1914–1918* (2nd edn., Oxford, 1936), pp. 93 ff.; Cyril Falls, *The Great War, 1914–1918* (London, 1959), pp. 77–83; P. Guinn, *British Strategy and Politics, 1914–1918* (London, 1965), pp. 36 ff.; Erich von Falkenhayn, *Die Oberste Heeresleitung 1914–1916* (Berlin, 1920), pp. 23 ff.; Kronprinz Rupprecht von Bayern, *Mein Kriegstagebuch*, ed. W. Frauendienst (2 vols., Berlin, 1929), i. 194–261; Janßen, *Kanzler und General*, Ch. 2.

people like Stinnes, Kirdorff, Thyssen, Hugenberg, and other representatives of heavy industry) and to see whether the Russians would consider negotiations for a separate peace.[25]

Bethmann was shaken by this communication but doubted the possibility of persuading the Tsar to negotiate. His Under-Secretary of State for Foreign Affairs, Arthur Zimmermann, was even more critical of Falkenhayn's ideas. A peace with Russia should not, he argued, be considered until the power of Pan-Slavism had been definitively smashed and the Russians driven not only out of Galicia but also out of Poland.[26] This view found strong support in Hindenburg's headquarters, which Bethmann visited at the beginning of December. Hindenburg and Ludendorff bitterly reproached Falkenhayn for having used up troops in fruitless assaults at Ypres when they would, if shipped east, have enabled the Eastern Command to develop a massive flank attack against Russian armies advancing into Poland. There was no question, Ludendorff argued, that a total victory could be achieved in the east, provided they were given the troops to do the job.

When Bethmann reported these views to the Chief of Staff a few days later, Falkenhayn shrugged them aside as parochial illusions. The German army, he said, was 'a broken instrument', from which at the moment no decisive operation could be expected; it would be fortunate if it were able to maintain itself on all fronts.[27] Fresh from the heady optimism of the headquarters in Posen, Bethmann found these drastic statements distasteful; and it was from this point on that he began to work for Falkenhayn's replacement by Hindenburg and Ludendorff.[28] He would have been well advised to weigh Falkenhayn's arguments more carefully. Thanks to the hard experience at Ypres, the Chief of Staff had a more accurate appreciation of the strength of the Allied forces in the west than his critics on the eastern front. He was later to write:

[They] paid no heed either to the true character of the struggle for existence, in the most exact sense of the word, in which our enemies were engaged no less than we, or to their strength of will. It was a grave mistake to believe that our western enemies would give way, if and because Russia was beaten. No

[25] Ritter, *Kriegshandwerk* iii. 59 f.; Riezler, *Tagebücher*, p. 228.

[26] Egmont Zechlin, 'Friedensbestrebungen und Revolutionierungsversuche', in *Aus Politik und Geschichte* (Beilage, *Das Parlament*), Beilage 20/61, pp. 275–9; Beilage 22/63, pp. 3 ff. Riezler also argued against this idea. *Tagebücher*, p. 230.

[27] Ritter, *Kriegshandwerk* iii. 63.

[28] See Janßen, *Kanzler und General*, pp. 56 ff. Among those who helped strengthen his doubts about Falkenhayn were Riezler, Hertling, Lerchenfeld, and Ballin. See Cecil, *Ballin*, pp. 301, 306.

decision in the east, even though it were as thorough as it was possible to imagine, could spare us from fighting to a conclusion in the west.[29]

In November 1914 he tried to persuade the eastern commanders that their ideas were dangerously narrow and that to supply them with the troops they kept demanding would exhaust resources needed in the critical area of the war. 'Victories in the east', he wrote to Hindenburg on 26 November, 'that are achieved only at the cost of weakening our position in the west are worthless.'[30] It was sounder to forswear ideas of total victory in Russia and to limit operations there to the objective of persuading the Russian Government to treat for peace.

Falkenhayn remained true to these ideas in May 1915 when he scored one of the greatest German victories of the war on the eastern front. On the basis of a plan drafted by Conrad von Hötzendorf, he directed a combined thrust of Austrian and German forces against Gorlice and Tarnow in Galicia. Launched on 2 May 1915, this attack hit the Russians at a time when they were short of weapons, munitions, and food, and the result was a near rout. Their demoralized forces reeled back beyond Przemysl, Lemberg, Warsaw, and Brest-Litovsk until, after six weeks of desperate rear-guard fighting, they had been driven behind a line that ran from Riga on the Baltic to the Carpathians, 300 miles east of the positions they had held in August 1914. Falkenhayn refused, however, to push this stunning victory, which had cost the enemy 300,000 men and 3,000 guns, to the point that his eastern colleagues desired. He remained conscious of the threat in the west and the new strain placed on the Austrians by Italy's entrance into war on the Allied side. The Gorlice campaign remained limited in scope, designed not to crush the Russians but to persuade them to sue for peace.[31]

In retrospect, one can see that Falkenhayn's view of the situation was entirely sensible, given Germany's political and economic position in the middle of 1915. The failures of Germany's military strategy were real, and they had not been balanced by any conspicuous diplomatic victories, except the adherence of Turkey to the cause of the Central Powers, and that was almost inadvertent. On the eve of the war neither German diplomats nor German soldiers saw

[29] Falkenhayn, *Die Oberste Heeresleitung*, p. 61.

[30] Ritter, *Kriegshandwerk* iii. 60.

[31] On Gorlice, see Cruttwell, *Great War*, pp. 175 ff.; Falls, *Great War*, pp. 121–5; Janßen, *Kanzler und General*, Ch. 8; J. N. Danilov, *Rußland im Weltkriege* (Jena, 1925), pp. 467 f., 487 ff.; Oskar Regele, *Feldmarschall Conrad, Auftrag und Erfüllung 1906–1918* (Vienna and Munich, 1955), pp. 345 ff.; Stone, *Eastern Front*, pp. 128–43.

any advantage to be gained from a Turkish alliance, Moltke expressing the opinion that it would be unwise to reckon with Turkey 'in the foreseeable future as an asset for the Triple Alliance or Germany'. It was the Turks who took the initiative in seeking a closer tie, apparently in the belief that, if war came, a policy of neutrality might have calamitous consequences for them. Their first overtures, presented by Enver Pasha, the War Minister, on 22 July, were received without enthusiasm by Wangenheim, the German ambassador, and it was only after the Emperor had intervened personally on the day after the delivery of Austria's ultimatum to Serbia, that the Foreign Ministry became more receptive and, on the basis of formal Turkish proposals, began the negotiations that eventuated on 2 August in an alliance.[32]

The advantages that the Central Powers derived from this in the next two years were of considerable importance. Actual Turkish intervention in the war was postponed until November by the slowness of Turkish mobilization and the reluctance of the Grand Vizier and the majority of the ministerial council to take the initiative in precipitating hostilities with Russia. But the situation was clarified when the German admiral Wilhelm Souchon, who had diverted the Mediterranean squadron from Algerian waters to the Straits in August[33] and had subsequently been placed in command of the Ottoman fleet, took his ships into the Black Sea on 27 October and, deliberately exceeding his instructions, laid mines in shipping lanes, shelled Russian harbours, and sank several Russian vessels in port and on the seas. The Russians answered with a declaration of war on 2 November, in which they were joined a few days later by Britain, France, and Serbia. Once in the war, Turkish armies, sometimes with German and Austrian support, fought against the Russians in Anatolia, Transcaucasia, and Persia, and against British units in Mesopotamia, the Arabian peninsula, and the Palestinian area, from which they launched two major advances and several raids against the Suez Canal between January 1915 and the end of 1916. These operations benefited the Central Powers by diverting not inconsiderable numbers of Allied troops from the European theatre. Of even more importance was the successful Turkish defence of the Straits against Allied attack in 1915, which frustrated Winston Chur-

[32] On the treaty and its background, see Ulrich Trumpener, *Germany and the Ottoman Empire, 1914–1918* (Princeton, 1968), pp. 14–16.

[33] The squadron was composed of two cruisers, the *Goeben* and the *Breslau*. The story of their voyage to the Straits, which the British and French fleets tried fruitlessly to prevent, has often been told. See esp. Hermann Lorey, *Der Krieg zur See 1914–1918: Der Krieg in den türkischen Gewässern* (2 vols., Berlin, 1928–38), i. 1–28.

chill's grand design for establishing a sound connection with Russia[34] and also thwarted Allied hopes of persuading the Greek and Romanian governments to join their coalition. Finally, although it is not always remembered, the Ottoman Empire in the last two years of the war sent army divisions to fight in Romania, Galicia, and Macedonia. Although this war effort had to be sustained, because of Turkey's economic backwardness, by massive financial assistance and material support, the Ottoman contribution to the German war effort was, on balance, a positive one.[35]

On the other hand, in the competition for allies that went on during the first part of the war, the German Government suffered two major defeats. The first of these, the decision of the Japanese Government to join the Allied cause, was probably unavoidable, less because of Japan's existing ties with the British than because its military leaders saw in the war an opportunity to seize Germany's base on the Shantung peninsula and its holdings in the central Pacific, which had strategic importance for the defence of the home islands. There was nothing Germany could do to deflect this purpose or to defend its remote possessions; and the Japanese entry into the war marked the beginning of the dissolution of its colonial empire, which was to be completed at the Peace Conference in 1919.

More important for the conduct of the European war was the position of Italy. Although it was still formally a member of the Triple Alliance, its reliability had been doubted in Berlin and Vienna ever since the turn of the century, when French economic pressure had forced the Italian Government to abandon the former pro-German policy of Francesco Crispi; and those doubts were confirmed in August 1914 when the Salandra government announced that, since Austria's action against Serbia was not defensive in nature, Italy could not consider itself bound by the provisions of the alliance to intervene on the side of the Central Powers. This was a disappointment, but not a shattering one, since most Germans had little faith in the military capacity of their former ally, inclining to Bismarck's view that Italy had a large appetite but poor teeth. On the other hand, the German Government was well aware of the existence of pro-Allied sentiment in Italy and the desire on the part of Italian liberals, of deviant socialists like Benito Mussolini, and of

---

[34] The literature on this is enormous. See, *inter alia*, Reichsarchiv, *Der Weltkrieg* ix. 173–93; Alan Moorehead, *Gallipoli* (New York, 1956); Trumbull Higgins, *Winston Churchill and the Dardanelles* (New York, 1963); Martin Gilbert, *Winston S. Churchill,* iii: *1914–1916* (London, 1971), pp. 351 ff., 381 ff.; Cruttwell, *Great War,* pp. 204 ff.

[35] Trumpener, *Germany and the Ottoman Empire,* pp. 62–7.

nationalist demagogues like Gabriele d'Annunzio for intervention on the Allied side. If this were realized, it would at the very least increase the strain upon the Austrians, whose resources were already gravely depleted, while providing the British and French with new strategical opportunities. It was necessary therefore to do what was possible to strengthen the neutralist party, and for this purpose the German Government sent two agents to Italy, the former Chancellor, Prince Bülow, and the Centre party deputy, Matthias Erzberger. Bülow was chosen because of his many Italian connections (he had been ambassador to Rome in the nineties, had an Italian wife, and had maintained a residence in Rome since 1909); Erzberger, because he had contacts with the Vatican that might be useful.

This oddly assorted couple had no success, despite Bülow's suavity of manner and Erzberger's incorrigible optimism. There was no way that they could affect the tides of popular opinion that were swiftly eroding the foundations of Italian neutrality, and it had been clear from the very beginning of the war that the Salandra government would remain neutral only if paid to do so by concessions from Austria. Erzberger, partly because he never listened to other people very carefully, persisted at first in believing that 'the benevolent neutrality of Italy [could] be achieved for the entire duration of the war at the price of relatively small Austrian offers'. He was wrong. The Italian Government, at the least, wanted the cession of the Trentino, the Isonzo valley, Trieste, and parts of the Dalmatian coast. The Austrians were not prepared to buy Italian neutrality at that price (historically, the Habsburgs had always fought rather than surrender territory), and, although Erzberger seems to have felt that the German Government should pressure them into doing so, any action of that nature would have heightened the already existing tension within the Austro-German alliance to an intolerable degree.[36] For the Salandra government, the only real point of

[36] Emperor Francis Joseph was even more adamantly opposed to concessions of territory than his ministers, being stubbornly impervious even to appeals from the Pope and from his long-time friend Frau Schratt. For a time it appeared that the Austrian Government might be prepared to cede the Trentino, provided it were indemnified by the grant of part of Silesia by Germany. On this, see Egmont Zechlin, 'Das "schlesische Angebot" und die italienische Kriegsgefahr 1915', in *Erster Weltkrieg. Ursache, Entstehung und Kriegsziele*, ed. Theodor Schieder (Cologne and Berlin, 1969). But, of course, the Italians were after more than the Trentino. On 8 April Riezler wrote in exasperation, 'Italians never quite say how much they want, shove it off on the Austrians to make offers.' Five days later, when they gave an inkling of how extensive their claims might be, he wrote, 'Unverschämt. . . . Bestürzung, Wut.' *Tagebücher*, pp. 266–7.

negotiating with the Austrians at all was to drive up the price that the Entente Powers would be willing to pay for Italian intervention. By the time that Bülow and Erzberger had realized this and had begun to spend large sums of money in an attempt to bribe enough deputies to force Salandra from power, it was too late. In the Treaty of London of 26 April 1915 Italy obtained from the Entente the territorial pledges that it desired, and a month later Italian forces were advancing toward the Isonzo, just in time to complicate Falkenhayn's calculations during the Battle of Gorlice.[37]

The defection of Italy aroused fears that Romania might go the same way and, in June 1915, Bethmann sent Erzberger to Vienna and Budapest to discuss ways of preventing this. It is not quite clear why the Chancellor did not rely on his Foreign Service for this purpose, although it is likely that he wished to avoid giving a formal cast to the talks, which were designed to see how far the Austrians and Hungarians would be willing to go to buy off the Romanians. Erzberger discussed with Count Stefan Tisza the possibility of territorial concessions to Romania and various means of improving the lot of Hungary's Romanian minority and got a very dusty answer for his pains. The Magyar leader made it clear that he would tolerate no attempt to appease the Romanians, who, he said, were too cowardly to fight anyway.[38] The Romanians did, in fact, elect to stay on the sidelines, although it was the impressive German victory at Gorlice and the Allied fiasco at the Dardanelles, rather than timorousness, that determined their decision. This, in turn, had the effect of relieving the Bulgarian Government of some of the doubts that had prevented it from coming into the war on the side of the Central Powers, which it did in October, collaborating with the Austrians in an invasion of Serbia that overran that country and knocked it out of the war by the end of the year.

Optimists in Berlin might claim that these successes more than offset the loss of Japan and Italy and that, although Germany had been unable to prevent the opening-up of a new front in Southern Europe, the alliance with Bulgaria had eliminated one in the Balkans, while at the same time giving the Central Powers a firm land connection with their Turkish ally. But no amount of optimism could disguise the fact that the original war plan had failed, and that

---

[37] The principal actors in this diplomatic game have written their accounts, which should be read for what they are. See Bülow, *Denkwürdigkeiten*, iii, Chs. 15–18; Matthias Erzberger, *Erlebnisse im Weltkrieg* (Stuttgart, 1920), pp. 21 ff.; A. Salandra, *Italy and the Great War: From Neutrality to Intervention* (London, 1932). Epstein, *Erzberger*, pp. 118–40 is curiously uncritical of his hero.

[38] Epstein, *Erzberger*, p. 140.

the government had not devised a new one that promised to relieve the difficulties that flowed from that failure.

Not the least troublesome of those difficulties were the economic ones. Because the prevalent view before 1914 was that war, when it came, would be short—Schlieffen had, in fact, believed that in the modern age great nations cannot tolerate long wars—no preparations had been made to support a long war. Although the consumption of ammunition during the Russo-Japanese war had startled officials in the General Staff and the War Ministry and led them, in 1912, to start planning a new production programme, it had not yet been put into effect when war broke out. The result was that by October 1914 all existing stocks of ammunition had been used up and the army was dependent upon new production. This was so inadequate that on 14 November German artillery on the western front had only four days' supply of shells.[39] The question of repairing this situation and of producing other war materials in the amounts needed was complicated by the fact that the country began the war without any provision for a planned distribution of manpower between factory and front and because the desire to make the field army as strong as possible had left factories that were essential to war production without enough labour to keep them functioning. Again, production was dependent on available stocks of raw materials; and a survey by the Ministry of the Interior in August 1914 revealed the disturbing fact that the average large firm had a stockpile of raw materials that would last for only six months. On 8 August 1914 the head of the Allgemeine Elektrizitäts-Gesellschaft (AEG), Walther Rathenau, was shaken to hear from Falkenhayn that he had issued no orders that made provision for guarding against exhaustion of strategic materials and that he did not believe that an effective policy for this end could be devised.[40]

Rathenau was of a different persuasion, and he convinced the War Minister of the necessity of making a statistical survey of the supply situation and establishing a central authority to control distribution of materials. As a result, a War Raw Materials Section (Kriegs-rohstoffabteilung: KRA) was set up within the War Ministry, under Rathenau's leadership and with a staff composed of some of his closest associates in the AEG and of representatives of other industries using the materials that were to be controlled. Thanks to the enthusiasm of the first months of war, they were able to persuade the

[39] Gerald D. Feldman, *Army, Industry and Labor in Germany, 1914–1918* (Princeton, 1966), p. 52; Ritter, *Kriegshandwerk* iii. 59.

[40] Hutten-Czapski, *Sechzig Jahre* ii. 151 f.

governments of the separate states to accept their authority within their territories and, on that basis, working through a system of War Raw Materials Corporations (private stock companies established under the auspices of the government and authorized to buy, store, and distribute raw materials), they undertook to see that scarce materials were distributed only to firms that were engaged directly in the war effort and, also, that a system of priorities was established. By April 1915, when Rathenau handed his functions over to Major Josef Koeth, the KRA was operating effectively and had staved off a critical shortage of raw materials that might well have caused Germany's defeat.[41]

At the same time, the munitions crisis had been solved by a major scientific breakthrough, and the manpower problem alleviated by a series of intelligent decisions by the War Ministry. Munitions production depended upon nitrates, which were in short supply because the war had cut off the normal importation of Chilean saltpeter. This would have crippled the war effort had it not been for the pre-war discovery by Fritz Haber and Robert Bosch of a process for the mass utilization of nitrogen fixation, and the government's energy in launching a crash programme to build the necessary plants and in establishing a Chemicals Section in the KRA and a War Chemicals Corporation to co-ordinate the activities of the various chemical firms. Other aspects of munitions production were improved by the work of Major Max Bauer, the artillery expert of the General Staff, whose negotiations with leading industrialists succeeded in giving them a sense of the urgent necessity of accelerated production.[42]

The manpower situation was more difficult to correct, because the needs of the army and those of industry were in conflict. The right to decide which workers should be sent to the front and which should be exempted lay in the hands of the Deputy Commanding Generals of the various army corps districts, who had, by virtue of the Prussian Law of Siege, been given authority to maintain public safety in their areas of command.[43] The lack of uniformity between districts and the tendency of most generals to view the needs of the front with more sympathy than those of industry, caused loud complaints from producers, who sometimes refused to accept contracts for military supplies unless they were assured of a steady

[41] On this, see Feldman, *Army, Industry and Labor*, pp. 45–52.

[42] Ibid., pp. 52 ff.

[43] Ernst von Wrisberg, *Wehr und Waffen 1914–1918* (Leipzig, 1922), pp. 132 ff. For a critical view of the operation of the Law of Siege, see Albrecht Mendelssohn-Bartholdy, *The War and German Society. The Testament of a Liberal* (New Haven, 1937), pp. 108–12.

supply of skilled labour. At the end of 1914 the German Industry War Committee, which had been formed by the Central Association of German Industrialists and the League of German Industrialists, proposed to the War Ministry that exemption policy should be framed by a committee of factory owners. Aware that this would subordinate the control of military reserves to the private interest of industry, the Ministry rejected the suggestion. Instead it established an Exports and Exemptions Office (Abteilung für Ausfuhr, Einfuhr, und Zurückstellung: AZS) with authority to establish guide-lines for policy on exemptions and such related problems as the freedom of exempted labour to change jobs and their rights in wage disputes. Under the able leadership of Richard Sichler, a business man who had no connection with war industries, the AZS sought to persuade industry to supply its labour needs by training unskilled workers and using women and prisoners of war rather than by relying upon men who would normally be liable for military service. For the settlement of disputes about mobility of labour and wages, the AZS instructed the Deputy Commanding Generals to encourage the establishment of War Boards, composed of representatives of management and labour on terms of parity. This development was resisted bitterly, but without success, by industrialists who still held the pre-war view that a business man should be the master of his own concern and quite rightly perceived that a precedent was being established that would make it hard to maintain that philosophy in the future.[44]

The discontent of the industrialists on this score was alleviated by the fact that the high profits that they made from their military contracts were in no way threatened by a stringent taxation policy. From this they were protected both by the nature of the imperial constitution and by the fiscal philosophy of the man who became head of the Treasury at the end of 1914, Karl Helfferich. There was no national income tax, and the constitution excluded the Reich Government from the sphere of direct taxation. The coming of the war did not diminish the resistance of the separate states either to changes in this system or to the kind of extraordinary capital levy that had been imposed in 1913 to support the Army Bill of that year. Nor did Helfferich try to persuade them to mend their ways. Inflexibly liberal in his economic philosophy, he had an instinctive resistance to taxing profits, for he felt that this merely discouraged enterprise and initiative. The war did not persuade him to change his

[44] See Feldman, *Army, Industry and Labor*, pp. 64 ff., 73 ff.; Ernst von Wrisberg, *Heer und Heimat 1914–1918* (Leipzig, 1921), pp. 108 ff.

views. 'The compelling necessity for raising new taxes', he said in March 1915, 'does not exist for us, in contrast to England.' Germany, after all, was going to win the war. 'We hold fast to the hope of presenting our opponents at the conclusion of peace with the bill for this war that has been forced upon us.' Meanwhile all of the extraordinary expenses incurred by the conflict could be taken care of by loans.[45]

The inventiveness and the energy of men like Rathenau, Sichler, Bosch, and Haber, the support given to them by the acting head of the War Ministry, General von Wandel, and a fiscal policy which, by mortgaging the future, offered unlimited profits to the industrial class, brought the crisis of production that confronted Germany in 1914 under control. But this in no way alleviated the essential economic problem, which was one of surviving in a protracted conflict with a coalition of Powers that possessed superior resources and had command of the seas, enabling them to deny supplies to the beleaguered homeland. As early as 1915, the food problem in Germany was so serious as to cast doubt upon Germany's ability to hold out in a long war.

In the pre-war period Germany had been dependent upon the outside world for one-third of its food supply. The Allied blockade seriously reduced imports, and the resultant shortages, combined with an army purchasing policy that showed no regard for normal civilian needs, caused a sharp rise in the price of basic foodstuffs. In November 1914 the Social Democratic party demanded price ceilings and controls over producers and, by January, party and union leaders were warning the Secretary of State of the Interior that he could expect a collapse of the *Burgfrieden* if he did not do something to bring the situation under control.

The government responded by nationalizing wheat production, forcing farmers to declare their stores, forbidding the use of wheat and rye for fodder, and setting up a Wheat Corporation to buy up stocks and an Imperial Allocation Office to distribute them. By June 1915 bread rationing was in force throughout the country. These measures were approved by urban consumers but resented by the farmers, who, as price ceilings were extended to other agricultural products, began to evade them by selling on the black market. Their resistance increased after October 1915, when the government established an Imperial Potato Office and forbade the use of potatoes as

---

[45] See John G. Williamson, *Karl Helfferich, 1872–1924: Economist, Financier, Politician* (Princeton, 1971), pp. 121 ff., 141 ff. Matthias Erzberger later called Helfferich 'the most frivolous of Finance Ministers'. Epstein, *Erzberger*, p. 331.

fodder. Farmers were confronted with the choice of slaughtering their pigs and other animals or defying the law, and a not inconsiderable number chose the latter course. The situation was further complicated by the heavy-handedness of the Deputy Commanding Generals, who recognized that food shortages were potential sources of public disorder and sought to avoid trouble by imposing price ceilings and production quotas of their own and by penalizing farmers who did not conform to them. The result of this was more resistance, an increase of tension between the farming community and the consumers, and the beginning of food riots, demonstrations in front of food shops, and strikes.[46]

All in all, therefore, the economic balance-sheet was no more encouraging than the diplomatic one, and one might have supposed that this would have been appreciated by the more intelligent sections of society and might have induced them to take a very cautious view of Germany's prospects in the war. Yet in June 1915, when the military, diplomatic, and economic facts of Germany's position should have been reasonably well known to any perceptive person, the Pan-German League and a group of professors at the University of Berlin sponsored a congress on war aims which at the end of its deliberations sent an address to the Chancellor, defining in the most grandiose terms the extent of the empire in Eastern and Western Europe and overseas that the government must insist upon after the inevitable victory of German arms. Fifty years later a German historian who had been a front-line officer in 1915 wrote: 'Today we cannot, without a shudder of horror, look back to the dreadful contradiction that became apparent in the summer of 1915 between the deep concern with which the country's responsible statesman and its leading soldier regarded Germany's future and the tidal wave of expectations of victory and victorious demands which at that time submerged our nation ever more irresistibly.'[47]

II

In the lack of restraint with which they defined Germany's legitimate war aims, there was little difference between the political parties, the country's economic organizations, the intelligentsia, the armed services, and the federal princes. With respect to the last of these, the war had aroused dynastic passions almost as intense as those that complicated the diplomacy of the eighteenth century. On 14 August 1914, two weeks after the outbreak of war, King Ludwig III of

[46] On all this, see Feldman, *Army, Industry and Labor*, pp. 97 ff.
[47] Ritter, *Kriegshandwerk* iii. 91.

Bavaria informed the Prussian chargé d'affaires in Munich that he would expect his interests to be protected in the territorial adjustments that would follow the war and, when pressed to be more explicit, said that he was interested in a partition of the Reichsland Alsace-Lorraine and intimated that it would be appropriate also for Bavaria to acquire part of Belgium. This informal demand was soon elaborated into a scheme for a new Bavarian Burgundy that would include Dutch as well as Belgian territory and control the mouth of the Rhine. Nor did this exhaust Bavarian ambitions, for at a later date the Wittelsbachs became interested in acquiring the throne of a restored Poland, which was also the objective of Duke Wilhelm von Urach, Duke of Württemberg and member of the Catholic branch of the Württemberg royal family. The King of Saxony was as greedy for new possessions as his royal brother in Munich. In March 1915, under his direction, the Saxon Council of Ministers decided to demand an increase of Saxon territory at the end of the war, and in the subsequent period the Saxon Government expressed interest, not only in sharing in the partition of the Reichsland, but in acquiring title to land in the east, in Poland, in Lithuania, and particularly in Courland. The striking thing about the pretensions of these and other federal princes was their common assumption that Germany would, as a matter of course, acquire all of the areas for which they were competing.[48]

Among the political parties, only the Social Democrats continued to insist that the spirit with which the German people had accepted the unavoidable burden of war would be dishonoured if the conflict were turned into a war of conquest, and even they had a right wing that felt that, in view of the sacrifices made by the people, some material compensation should be expected.[49] All the other parties advocated some form of annexation, and the parliamentary bloc that controlled the Reichstag in the first two years of the war—the National Liberals, the Centre, and the Conservatives—were impassioned supporters of a programme of extensive claims in both Eastern and Western Europe. There was no essential difference in this respect between the rabid chauvinists in the Conservative party and Matthias Erzberger, who in September 1914 was so intoxicated by the dream of victory that he drafted a memorandum in which he

---

[48] The best study of this subject is Karl-Heinz Janßen, *Macht und Verblendung: Kriegszielpolitik der deutschen Bundesstaaten 1914–1918* (Göttingen, 1963).

[49] Thus the *Frankfurter Volksstimme* asserted in March 1915 that 'the renunciation of all demands of annexation is not in itself a serviceable programme'. See Hans W. Gatzke, *Germany's Drive to the West* (Baltimore, 1950), pp. 18–19.

called for the annexation of all of Belgium, plus the Channel coast as far as Boulogne, Belfort, the industrial area and rich ores of Longwy-Briey, and the French and Belgian Congo, as well as the transformation of Poland, the Baltic countries, and the Ukraine into German and Austrian satellites, and a staggering reparations bill that would, among other things, pay off the whole national debt.[50]

Even more important than the parties in exerting pressure in favour of annexations were organizations like the Pan-German League and the various economic associations. The collaboration of the League's president, Heinrich Class, and the chief Director of Krupp, Alfred Hugenberg, produced a memorandum on war aims at the beginning of 1915 that was more extensive than Erzberger's. This bill of particulars, which envisaged the acquisition of virtually all of France's mineral resources and, in order to balance this addition to Germany's manufacturing resources, 'an equivalent annexation of agricultural territory in the east', was signed by representatives of the Zentralverband deutscher Industrieller, the Bund der Industrieller, the Bund der Landwirte, the Deutscher Bauernbund, the Reichs-deutscher Mittelstandsverband, and the Christliche deutsche Bauernvereine and was sent to the Chancellor in May 1915.[51]

In order to invest these claims with respectability, the leadership of the Pan-German League undertook to mobilize the German intel-ligentsia, and particularly the university professoriate.[52] This was not difficult. The coming of the war had persuaded many professors that it was 'the duty of the intellectuals to encourage, to strengthen, and to vitalize the . . . people', and, since most of them believed that the Entente Powers bore the responsibility for the coming of the war, they were not all content, like the historian Otto Hintze, the economist Werner Sombart, and the psychologist and philosopher Wilhelm Wundt,[53] to limit the exercise of that duty to attacking the values of the enemy and exaggerating the cultural superiority of their own country and the nobility of its motives. From the very begin-ning of the war, there were professors who believed that the enemy must pay for his assault on Germany by being forced to cede ter-ritory. This was true of a group of scholars of Baltic origin, led by the

[50] Epstein, *Erzberger*, p. 106.

[51] Gatzke, *Drive to the West*, pp. 38–47.

[52] The plan for this originated in the pre-war period. See Heinrich Class, *Wider den Strom* (Leipzig, 1922), pp. 321 f. and, on the League's activity in general, Kruck, *Alldeutscher Verband*, pp. 66–80.

[53] Ringer, *Decline of the Mandarins*, pp. 183 ff.; W. M. Simon, 'Power and Respon-sibility: Otto Hintze's Place in German Historiography', in *The Responsibility of Power*, ed. Krieger and Stern, pp. 207 ff.

Berlin theologian Reinhold Seeberg and the historian Johannes
Haller, who demanded that the Russian Baltic provinces be freed
from 'the control of the barbarians', and of others who were cap-
tivated by Pan-German views of the necessity of acquiring lands in
Western Europe and expropriating their population, like the Bonn
economist Hermann Schumacher.[54]

In March 1915 the deputy chairman of the Pan-German League
held meetings in Berlin with Seeberg, the prominent agrarian von
Wangenheim, and Alfred Hugenberg, at the conclusion of which
Seeberg agreed to form a committee to draft and circulate a
memorandum on war aims that would then be sent to the Chancellor. This was the origin of the Petition of the Intellectuals (Intel-
lektuelleneingabe) of July 1915, which called for a programme of
annexations that was virtually identical with the Demands of the Six
Economic Organisations in May, although the emphasis was placed
less upon the material advantages that would accrue from these
acquisitions than upon the legitimacy of securing Germany from
future attacks and the civilizing mission that Germany could perform in the Slav lands. The petition was signed by 1,347 professional
men, theologians, school teachers, artists, writers, and academics,
the largest single group of signatories being university professors,
who numbered 352. These included such respected names as Ulrich
von Wilamowitz-Moellendorf, Eduard Meyer, Otto von Gierke,
and Adolf Wagner and, among the large number of historians, Erich
Marcks, A. O. Meyer, Erich Brandenburg, Dietrich Schäfer, and R.
Fester.[55]

The historian of the art of war and editor of the *Preußische
Jahrbücher*, Hans Delbrück, undertook the task of organizing a
counter-movement, an effort in which he was encouraged by the
economist Lujo Brentano, the editor of the *Berliner Tageblatt*,
Theodor Wolff, and the former Colonial Secretary, von Dernburg.
The Delbrück petition rejected the demands of the Seeberg group,

[54] See Klaus Schwabe, 'Die deutschen Professoren und die politischen Grundfragen
des Ersten Weltkrieges' (Dissertation, Philosophische Fakultät, Abert-Ludwigs-
Universität, Freiburg im Breisgau, 1958), pp. 143 ff., 152 f.

[55] The best source is Schwabe, 'Deutsche Professoren', pp. 160 ff. and 'Zur politischen Haltung der deutschen Professoren im Ersten Weltkrieg', *Historische Zeitschrift*,
193 (1961). See also Ringer, *Decline of the Mandarins*, p. 190 and Fischer, *Griff nach der
Weltmacht*, pp. 199 f. The names of Meinecke and Hermann Oncken appeared among
the supporters, apparently because of a failure of communication between them and
the organizers. See Meinecke, *Straßburg, Freiburg, Berlin*, pp. 202 ff. Hintze's signature
may also have been a mistake. The inclusion of all three shocked Hans Delbrück. See
his letter of 15 June 1915 to Hermann Oncken, in Schwabe, 'Deutsche Professoren', p.
189.

stressing the defensive character of the war and the danger that absorption of 'politically independent peoples and peoples accustomed to independence' would represent to the national integrity of the Reich. It did not flatly exclude territorial changes, but it insisted that 'the greatest prize that victory can bring will be the proudly achieved assurance that Germany need not fear even a whole world of enemies and the unprecedented testimony to our strength that our people will have given to the other peoples of the earth'. These views received the support of scientists of world reputation like Max Planck and Albert Einstein, of all of the leading 'Socialists of the Chair' (with the exception of Adolf Wagner), of the pacifists Ludwig Quidde and Walther and Levin Schücking, of the sociologists Max and Alfred Weber and Friedrich Tönnies, of the theologians Adolf von Harnack and Ernst Troeltsch, and of the historians Alfred Dove and Max Lehmann; but in all the petition attracted only 141 signatures and received relatively little publicity, compared with what Class and Hugenberg provided for the Petition of the Intellectuals.[56]

The Pan-German experiment in mobilizing the *clercs* was therefore a success. It is doubtless true that many of the professors who signed and circulated the Seeberg petition were politically naïve, like Hermann Schumacher who sought Friedrich Meinecke's support for the German acquisition of Calais by arguing 'Calais is really a very small port. The French will never miss it.'[57] Even so, the numbers who gave their names and who subsequently supported the Independent Committee for a German Peace, which was organized by the Berlin historian Dietrich Schäfer in November 1915 to work for extensive acquisitions in France, Belgium, and the Baltic lands,[58] were large and, in a country in which professors were accorded inordinate respect, impressive. There is little doubt that this kind of *Professorenpolitik* helped to confirm the German people in their irrational expectations.

In the support given by the military to the ultra-annexationist programme, economic considerations doubtless played some part, given the fact that the backbone of the officer corps had always been

---

[56] Schwabe, 'Deutsche Professoren', pp. 177 ff.; Gatzke, *Drive to the West*, p. 131; Fischer, *Weltmacht*, p. 201. In his anti-annexationist activities, Delbrück later received the support of Friedrich Meinecke, the Weber brothers, the politicians Solf and Schiffer, and the publicists Paul Rohrbach and Ernst Jäckh (Schwabe, 'Deutsche Professoren', p. 181). The fact that he had taken a leading role in organizing this movement led the Crown Prince to write to his father, urging that this 'unpatriotic scamp' (*vaterlandsloser Kerl*) be dismissed from his chair at the University of Berlin.

[57] Meinecke, *Straßburg, Freiburg, Berlin*, p. 203.

[58] Schwabe, 'Deutsche Professoren', p. 174.

supplied by the old landholding families of the east and, in recent years, an increasing number of army and navy officers had been drawn from the wealthiest middle-class families.[59] But these were certainly less important than what they considered to be Germany's security requirements. With these the continued independence of Belgium seemed to be wholly inconsistent, and the cession of Liège and the Flanders coast to Germany at the end of the war was regarded by most staff officers as the very least that Germany should demand. Even Falkenhayn, who in November 1914 was insisting that Germany's territorial ambitions should be held to the bare minimum and that in the west only the winning of Belfort was essential, changed his mind in the subsequent period. In 1916 he was telling the Chancellor that 'Belgium . . . must remain at our disposal as an area for the initial assembly of our troops, for the protection of the most important German industrial region, and as a hinterland for our position on the Flanders coast, which is indispensable for our maritime importance.'[60] The Chief of Staff remained opposed to extensive demands in other directions, but his colleagues were far less modest. General Hans von Seeckt, one of the coming men in the army, as a result of his brilliant work as Mackensen's Chief of Staff during the Gorlice campaign, believed that Germany must create a system of satellite states that would extend from the Channel coast to Persia.[61] Hindenburg, who seemed to think that periodic wars with Russia were part of the divine plan, believed that, in the interest of strategical manœuvrability, the Reich must acquire Poland and the Baltic states. Ludendorff, whose strategical views were reinforced by an awareness of the economic requirements of modern war, came in time, as we shall see, to have even more grandiose plans for annexation.

The views of the industrialists, the Pan-Germans, the members of the Wehrverein, the right-wing political parties, the professors who supported Schäfer's Committee for a German Peace, and the military establishment were influenced also by political and social considerations. They all wished to preserve the Bismarckian order and their place in it; they all feared that these were jeopardized by the forces of change that war always releases. They resented the intimation in the speech from the throne of 4 August 1914 that the end of the war would bring political and social reform—Heinrich Class had

[59] See Karl Demeter, *Das deutsche Offizierkorps in Gesellschaft und Staat 1650–1945* (Frankfurt-on-Main, 1962), pp. 26–9; Kitchen, *Officer Corps*, pp. 22 ff.
[60] Gatzke, *Drive to the West*, p. 81.
[61] Craig, *Prussian Army*, p. 311.

reacted to this with the bitter words, *'Um Gotteswillen! Damit ist der Krieg innenpolitisch verloren!'*[62]—and they were resolved, if possible, to prevent that. In November 1914 Alfred Hugenberg expressed both the fears of the ruling class and the tactics that they hoped would alleviate them.

The consequences of the war will in themselves be unfavorable for the employers and industry in many ways. There can be no doubt that the capacity and willingness of the workers returning from the front to produce will suffer considerably when they are subordinated to factory discipline. One will probably have to count on a very increased sense of power on the part of the workers and labor unions, which will also find expression in increased demands on the employers and for legislation. It would therefore be well advised, in order to avoid internal difficulties, to distract the attention of the people and to give phantasies concerning the extension of German territory room to play.[63]

This was, in short, a scarcely altered version of Tirpitz's pre-war prescription of imperialism as a cure for Social Democracy. The German people must be titillated by promises of a lucrative peace lest they insist on democratic reform. The argument was made with increasing insistence as the war went on and the possibilities of achieving grandiose war aims became more insubstantial. The Petition of the Intellectuals warned Bethmann Hollweg that a failure to achieve their desired objectives would not only cause 'the worst kind of dissatisfaction among the lower and middle classes because of the burden of taxes' after peace was restored, but would arouse 'bitterness that would extend into the ruling groups of society, would endanger domestic peace, and would even shake the foundations of the monarchy. The disillusioned nation would believe that it had sacrificed the bloom of its youth and the strength of its manhood in vain.'[64] Pan-German speakers constantly repeated the argument, warning of revolution if the people's hopes were disappointed by a renunciation of annexations;[65] and in May 1916 Generallandschaftsdirektor Kapp (the putschist of 1920) wrote to the Chancellor and warned him that a lukewarm peace would suck Germany down into 'the democratic swamp'.[66]

Subjected to these pressures, Bethmann Hollweg found it expedient to assume a highly equivocal position with respect to Ger-

[62] Class, *Wider den Strom*, p. 307; Kruck, *Alldeutscher Verband*, p. 90.

[63] Feldman, *Army, Industry and Labor*, p. 136.

[64] Schwabe, 'Deutsche Professoren', p. 169; Class, *Wider den Strom*, pp. 395–8.

[65] Craig, *Prussian Army*, p. 312.

[66] *The Fall of the German Empire*, ed. R. H. Lutz (2 vols., Stanford, 1932), i. 103.

many's war aims. 'I want to emphasize from the beginning,' he wrote in August 1914, 'that probably nobody is more imbued than I with the necessity of concluding this war, fought with such sacrifices of life and property, with a settlement that is advantageous in every respect for Kaiser and Empire.' On the other hand, he added quickly, domestic conditions would preclude 'turning the defensive struggle into a war of conquest'.[67] He had no doubt that government acceptance of anything as extreme as the Pan-German programme would destroy the *Burgfrieden* by alienating all of those who justified their support of the war by believing that Germany had no aggressive aims.[68] He hoped to resolve this dilemma by securing the kind of settlement that would satisfy Germany's will to power without forcible annexation of territory. Despite his willingness on occasion to study the feasibility of specific acquisitions, as in the case of the draft programme of war aims produced by his secretary Riezler in September 1915,[69] and to make tactical concessions to the military point of view, as in the case of the Kreuznach Conference of April 1917, his chief goal throughout the war was a German Mitteleuropa surrounded by willing vassal states which would include Belgium and Poland. As early as 18 August, in General Headquarters at Coblenz, he and his staff were discussing 'Poland and the possibility of a loose incorporation of other states with the Reich—a Central European system of preferential tariffs. Greater Germany with Bel-

[67] Jarausch, *Enigmatic Chancellor*, pp. 186 f.

[68] This seems to be the compelling argument against the view of Bethmann as an imperialist that one finds in Fritz Fischer's *Weltmacht*. The gulf that existed between Bethmann's thinking and that of the Pan-Germans is made clear in K. D. Erdmann, 'Zur Beurteilung Bethmann Hollwegs', *Geschichte in Wissenschaft und Unterricht*, xv (1964). See also Wolfgang J. Mommsen, 'The Debate on German War Aims', *Journal of Contemporary History*, i, no. 3 (1966), 63 ff.; Janßen, *Macht und Verblendung*, pp. 125 ff.; and Willibald Gutsche, 'Zu einigen Fragen der staatsmonopolistichen Verflechtung in den ersten Kriegsjahren', in *Politik im Krieg 1914–1918* (Berlin, 1964).

[69] First discovered by Fritz Fischer, this memorandum, which called for the annexation of at least parts of France and Belgium, has been strongly emphasized by those who regard Bethmann as no better than the Pan-Germans. But see Mommsen 'Debate' 65 ('There was . . . a world of difference between Bethmann's September Programme and Class's first big memorandum on war aims'), Fritz Stern, 'Bethmann Hollweg and the War', in *The Responsibility of Power*, ed. Krieger and Stern, p. 270, where it is pointed out that Riezler never mentioned the September memorandum in his diary and presumably thought of it as 'a provisional statement without any binding force', and Ritter's argument (*Kriegshandwerk* iii. 41–52) that it was never more than a preliminary, highly secret, completely provisional draft—more 'consideration' than 'decision'. See also Jarausch, *Enigmatic Chancellor*, p. 198: 'Germany's war aims continued to fluctuate and evolve in response to diverse pressures, justifying [Bethmann's] claim that he had "no plans but only *ad hoc* ideas which could be influenced through changes in the fortune of arms".'

gium, Holland, Poland as close satellites, Austria as more detached.'[70] Two and a half years later his objective was unchanged, Riezler writing: 'The policy of the Chancellor: to lead the German Reich which cannot become a world Power by the methods of the Prussian territorial state . . . to an imperialism of European form, to organize the continent from the centre outward (Austria, Poland, Belgium) around our undemonstrative leadership. . . .'[71] The advantages of acquiring associates who would accept German hegemony rather than disaffected subject nationalities was obvious. Such a policy would give Germany the reality of power without incurring the kind of resentment that had been caused by the annexation of Alsace and Lorraine in 1871 and without destroying the internal unity that had been created by the spirit of 1914. Indeed, since its domestic complement would be political and social reform, it would facilitate 'the reconciliation of democracy with a prudent policy of power'.[72]

The Chancellor's secretary had private doubts about the feasibility of this conception because of his pessimistic view of the political capacities of his people. 'The tragedy of the development of modern Germany', he wrote in December 1914. 'If it wins, all its powers will be expended on tasks for which the German has no talent—the kind of world domination that is antithetical to his spirit and his true greatness.'[73] 'The best in the German, his idealism and his honest courage, resists politics. . . . That shows now: he has no real command over all of the modern instruments of power . . . he knows only one, force. But how, even if he defeated the whole world, could he rule it with that alone?'[74] Bethmann was inclined to agree that the people who made decisions in Germany had no facility with, and took no pleasure in, indirect methods, in accomplishing thier objectives by co-operation with other peoples, but took satisfaction only in external shows of force and the flaunting of authority.[75] Still, it was clear to him, as the war stretched into 1915, that the brutal objectives of the industrialists and the Pan-Germans were not only politically indefensible but, given the limitations of Germany's military power, unattainable. It was therefore a matter of urgent necessity to defeat unreasonable ambitions and to win the country's

[70] Riezler, *Tagebücher*, p. 198.

[71] Ibid., p. 416.

[72] Ibid., pp. 268, 386, 416. See also Stern, in *Responsibility of Power*, pp. 270–3. On the concept of Mitteleuropa in German thought and the formulation given to it in the popular book of Friedrich Naumann, which appeared at the end of 1915, see Meyer, *Mitteleuropa*, esp. pp. 194 ff.

[73] Riezler, *Tagebücher*, p. 234.

[74] Ibid., p. 274 (22 May 1915).   [75] Ibid., p. 386 (2 Dec. 1916).

support for a programme of moderate aims, like those implicit in his Mitteleuropa plan.

Bethmann was handicapped in his attempts to achieve this by serious limitations on his authority. Even before the war, his enemies had been numerous, and the war increased their number. The conservative business groups and the nationalist associations recognized his lack of sympathy for their interests and did what they could to undermine his position in the hope that they could find a more congenial successor. In the Reichstag, the parties of the centre and the right (the Kriegszielmehrheit) were angered by his attempts to discourage discussion of war aims and his failure to agree with their views concerning territorial expansion and were suspicious of his plans for domestic reform. For their part, the Progressives and the Socialists distrusted his professions of support of constitutional reform because they were always accompanied with the reservation that change would have to wait until the war was over. Bethmann's authority in the Bundesrat was no more substantial, since several of the state governments and some of the princes resented his opposition to their plans of aggrandizement.[76] In the country at large he could count on little in the way of popular support, for he possessed none of the charismatic qualities of Bismarck and pretended to none, having a natural disinclination to appeals to the electorate. In the last analysis, his only real source of strength was the support of the Emperor, and that was unreliable, not because of any waning of William II's respect for his Chancellor, but rather because the war had brought a serious erosion of the power of the Crown.

This may have been due to the Emperor's own faults of character. He had never really recovered from the *Daily Telegraph* affair, and the lack of self-confidence caused by that incident was increased when the war brought down upon him a host of problems with which he was incompetent to deal. In peacetime, the soldiers had tolerated his military posturing; after war had become a reality, they had little interest in his views and kept him imperfectly informed. In November 1914, at a dinner-party where stories were told about the war in the air, the Emperor said to his guest of honour, 'I hear of such things purely by chance. The General Staff tells me nothing and never asks my advice. If people in Germany think I am the Supreme Commander, they are grossly mistaken. I drink tea, saw wood, and go for walks, which pleases the gentlemen. The only one who is a bit kind to me is the chief of the Field Railway Department [Colonel,

[76] Janßen, *Macht und Verblendung*, pp. 16–17, 124–5.

later General, Wilhelm Groener] who tells me all he does and intends to do.'[77] As the war continued, the Emperor became even more remote from its realities, living a life of peripatetic idleness, travelling incessantly between his various estates, making occasional visits to safe sectors of the front and less frequent ones to his capital, giving interviews to visiting dignitaries from countries allied with Germany, in which his tendency toward uncontrolled utterance became increasingly unrestrained, and alternating between fits of prolonged depression and frantic interest in trivialities, which made his staff worry about his mental stability. On the eve of the battle on the Somme, the Chief of his Naval Cabinet wrote, 'Conversation in the dining-car. His Majesty intends to reform society in Berlin after the war. The members of the aristocracy are to build palaces for themselves once more. He will forbid parties being given in hotels. He then proceeded to read us an article on the need for encouraging motor-racing in Berlin. And all this in such gloomy and uncertain times!'[78]

To help him in turning German policy towards moderate war aims, the Emperor, Bethmann realized, would offer little assistance. He therefore—and this proved to be a decision that encompassed his own downfall—turned to the military, or more specifically, to the leaders of the Eastern Command, Hindenburg and Ludendorff.

III

He was led to this fateful step by the disintegration of his relationship with the Chief of the General Staff. This had never been an easy one, partly because of tension caused by the lack of a clear constitutional delineation of the responsibilities of Chancellor and Chief of Staff in wartime,[79] but more because the two men were temperamentally incompatible. Falkenhayn's sarcastic manner was as offensive to Bethmann as Bethmann's heavy dullness was depressing to Falkenhayn. The Chancellor, in addition, regarded Falkenhayn as a dangerous gambler, with a tendency in his operations to play for higher stakes than he could afford. On his side, the Chief of Staff felt that Bethmann was so given to hesitations and second thoughts as to be incapable of action at critical moments.

The two wartime leaders were nevertheless able to rub along with reasonable efficiency until the end of 1915. Bethmann suppressed the doubts that had led him, in the wake of the Ypres campaign, to seek

[77] Müller, *Regierte der Kaiser?*, p. 68.
[78] Ibid., p. 208. See also pp. 97, 178, 197, 209–10, 221–2.
[79] See Craig, *Prussian Army*, Ch. V.

Falkenhayn's dismissal,[80] and, in the autumn of 1915, when Falkenhayn protested sharply against aspects of his diplomatic activity in the Balkans, he compromised in order to avoid a head-on clash of principle, like that in which Bismarck and Moltke became involved during the siege of Paris. He was willing to put up with minor annoyances of this nature because Falkenhayn had proved to be his strongest ally in his conflict with the navy, which in the course of 1915 threatened to widen the scope of the war. It was only after the Chief of Staff switched sides and joined the admirals that Bethmann decided that he must go.

The dispute had its origins in the navy's attempt to repair its shaken reputation by putting the submarine forward as the key to total victory. Conveniently forgetting his pre-war scorn of commerce-raiding and his advocacy of the doctrines of Alfred Thayer Mahan, Alfred von Tirpitz placed himself in the van of the new movement. In late November he granted an interview to the American journalist Karl von Wiegand, which was published on 22 December 1914, in which he announced a German submarine blockade that would close British waters to shipping. Tirpitz was not deterred in the least by the fact that, at the time of his declaration, Germany possessed only 21 U-boats, of which 12 were old models run by petroleum and incapable of operating as far away from their home ports as the English coast. With his usual sensitivity to the public mood, Tirpitz divined that the thought of a wonder weapon would excite public opinion to the point where it would demand enough submarines to defeat Britain, and, by and large, he was right.[81] From the very beginning of the war, the great mass of the public accepted the idea of unrestricted submarine warfare (that is, the sinking of ships without warning) with an uncritical enthusiasm and had no sympathy with the argument that resort to this kind of war would be an affront to humanity and would alienate neutral opinion.[82] Even the sinking of the Cunard liner *Lusitania* by a Ger-

[80] In November 1914, perhaps influenced by Hindenburg, Bethmann talked with Lyncker, the Chief of the Military Cabinet, and Generaladjutant von Plessen about the necessity of replacing Falkenhayn, presumably hoping that they would urge this on the Emperor. They showed no desire to do so and made it clear that the Emperor had confidence in Falkenhayn and was totally opposed to any change that would bring Ludendorff to the highest staff. See Ritter, *Kriegshandwerk* iii. 63 f.

[81] Ibid. 29 f., 145 ff.; Müller, *Regierte der Kaiser?*, pp. 76 f.

[82] See Riezler, *Tagebücher*, p. 335 (22 Feb. 1916), where he describes the enthusiasm for submarines as 'an orgy of uncontrolled indulgence in power that makes men drunk. . . . As one listens to the tumult, it appears that the English are just about right when they say the Germans are mad. Intoxication with the tools of power. No one seems to want to face up to the fact that there are limits to power. . . .'

man U-boat in May 1915, which cost the lives of 1,198 of the 1,959 passengers and crew aboard, including 440 women and 129 children and 128 United States citizens, stirred neither moral doubts nor political misgivings. In his memoirs the novelist Leonhard Frank, who became a pacifist and went into Swiss exile in 1915, described the reception of the news.

Michael (Frank) sat in the Café des Westens . . . Next to his table stood four guests, among them [a] journalist . . . For half an hour they had been talking with enthusiasm about the war. . . .
   Suddenly he saw that at the front of the room next to the entrance door, where the stock market reports and the bulletins from the front hung, grey-haired stock brokers were embracing each other with shouts of joy. He thought, the war is over. It was 7 May 1915.
   The journalist, a well-meaning man who later became editor of a socialist paper—after the war—hurried forward to the bulletin board. When he came back, he said, beside himself with excitement, 'We have sunk the *Lusitania*, with 1,198 passengers.' He said, 'The sinking of the *Lusitania* is the greatest act of heroism in the history of mankind.'[83]

Earlier in the year, Bethmann had shown that he was not entirely immune to the popular enthusiasm for the new weapon and the confidence of the sailors in its capabilities, for he had, under Admiralty pressure, agreed to an official declaration that Germany regarded the waters surrounding the British Isles as a war zone in which enemy merchant vessels could be sunk without warning.[84] The stern reaction of the United States Government to the declaration—President Wilson's note of 12 February, warning that he would hold the German Government to strict accountability for losses of American lives and property—had led him to doubt the wisdom of his action, and the threatening attitude assumed by the Americans after the sinking of the *Lusitania* persuaded him that concessions would have to be made, even if this meant a serious restriction of U-boat operations. The Chancellor was so concerned that he appealed to Falkenhayn, telling him that American intervention in the war would be inevitable unless the admirals curtailed the activity of their underwater fleet. Falkenhayn attended a meeting of 31 May at which Tirpitz and the Chief of the Naval Staff, Bachmann, presented arguments in favour of unrestricted submarine warfare and came down on Bethmann's side, insisting that the naval war be conducted in such a way as to avoid new political conflict. The decision that was reached, which amounted to ordering

[83] Leonhard Frank, *Links wo das Herz ist* (new edn., Munich, 1963), p. 64.
[84] Ritter, *Kriegshandwerk* iii. 152 ff.

U-boat captains to refrain from attacking large enemy or neutral passenger ships, was bitterly resented by the admirals—Tirpitz and Bachmann submitted their resignations, which William II indignantly rejected with some heated remarks about military conspiracy[85]—but Bethmann had his way. Because of Falkenhayn's support, he was able in August, when a new crisis arose because of the sinking of the British ship *Arabic*, a combined freighter and passenger ship, to extend the previous order so as to forbid attacks on all passenger ships regardless of size and origin.

By the end of the year, however, Falkenhayn had begun to reconsider his views. He had opposed the admirals largely because he wanted no complications with the neutrals during the Gorlice campaign and the Balkan operations that followed it. But his hopes that those hammer-blows would persuade the Russian Government to negotiate for peace were disappointed, and as the year came to an end the Chief of Staff found himself in a dilemma. He had grave doubts about the ability of the home front to support the war for more than another year. But where was a decisive victory to be attained in twelve months? Certainly not in Italy or at Salonika or in attacks against the Suez Canal, for such campaigns would merely be sideshows. Nor could anything more be achieved on the eastern front, unless Romania came in on the German side, for Germany could not safely detach enough troops from the west to support an eastern drive. Even in the critical western theatre of the war, possibilities were limited, the operations of 1915 having demonstrated that little was to be achieved by a frontal penetration of enemy lines. With what must have been a kind of desperation, Falkenhayn decided that the most promising plan was an attack upon a strong point that the French could not allow to be taken without grave damage to their morale and where, therefore, he could hope to draw in and destroy the best of France's remaining armies. He fastened upon the great fortress complex of Verdun and, in order to support his attack there, he called—with some reluctance but none the less insistently—for the institution of unrestricted submarine warfare against Allied shipping.[86]

It says much for Bethmann Hollweg's courage that he did not capitulate before what was now a united military front on the submarine question. On the contrary, with the help of Karl Helfferich, who provided him with critical analyses of the navy's statistics, the Chancellor fought a stubborn battle against the service

[85] Ibid. 162; Müller, *Regierte der Kaiser?*, p. 107.
[86] Ritter, *Kriegshandwerk* iii. 191–5.

chiefs and, in a series of meetings in March 1916, won the Emperor's support of his position. When Tirpitz once more submitted his resignation in protest, Bethmann was strong enough to persuade William II to accept it, and when the National Liberals and Conservatives tried to mobilize Reichstag opinion behind the once all-powerful Admiral, Bethmann was able to defeat this also, thanks to the aid of Matthias Erzberger, whose scepticism about navy claims led him to organize a Centre resolution supporting Bethmann's policy that received majority support in the Reichstag.[87]

Meanwhile the Chancellor's confidence in Falkenhayn, badly shaken by his change of front on the submarine question, was completely exhausted by the blood-letting at Verdun, which was as destructive of German strength and morale as it was of that of the enemy. Falkenhayn's hope of controlling the battle was frustrated from the beginning, for war has its own momentum and in this case it sucked fifty German divisions into the maelstrom. The rate of casualties left the Chief of Staff aghast. It made it impossible for him to break off the battle and to attempt a breakthrough in another sector of the weakened French lines, for he no longer had enough reserves to permit that and his sacrifice at Verdun had been so great that it had become a matter of prestige now to capture the strong point. But this hope was frustrated too by the offensive launched by the Russian general Brusilov in June, which broke the front of the Austrian Fourth Army at Lutzk, rolled over the Seventh Army as well, and in ten days pushed the Austrians back thirty-seven miles and took 25,000 prisoners.[88] To contain this massive drive, Falkenhayn had to divert reserves which he sorely needed in the west, with the result that his attempt later in the month to step up the assault upon Verdun in the hope of disrupting Entente plans for an offensive on the Somme failed completely. By July Verdun was still

[87] See Müller, *Regierte der Kaiser?*, pp. 147, 159 ff., 164 ff.; Williamson, *Helfferich*, pp. 155 ff.; Epstein, *Erzberger*, pp. 154 ff. Erzberger had a series of discussions with Admiralty officials and convinced himself that the navy did not have enough submarines to accomplish what they said they could accomplish. On the hullabaloo that followed Tirpitz's fall, which Hugo Stinnes compared with the fall of Bismarck, see Riezler, *Tagebücher*, pp. 339 ff., 342. On the irrationality of Tirpitz's supporters, see Conrad Haussmann's account of his discussion with Graf Zeppelin, who argued that the number of submarines available was unimportant. Germany must use those it had in order to demonstrate its will to the neutrals. *Schlaglichter*, ed. Ulrich Zeller (Frankfurt-on-Main, 1924), p. 59.

[88] *Österreich-Ungarns letzter Krieg 1914–1918*, ed. Österreichisches Bundesministerium für Heereswesen und Kriegsarchiv (Vienna, 1931 ff.), iv. 359–74; August von Cramon, *Unser Österreich-Ungarischer Bundesgenosse im Weltkriege* (Berlin, 1920), pp. 57–64; Rothenburg, *Army of Francis Joseph*, pp. 195 ff.; Ritter, *Kriegshandwerk* iii. 224 ff.; Falkenhayn, *Oberste Heeresleitung*, p. 204; Stone, *Eastern Front*, pp. 237–63.

swallowing up German divisions, while the British and French were attacking on the Somme in unexpected numbers and with a wealth of guns and munitions that indicated that, with American aid, they had now achieved a significant technical superiority.[89]

These disasters convinced Bethmann of the necessity of seeking peace on the best possible terms as soon as possible. At the same time, he was convinced that such an effort would receive popular backing only if it had the approval and support of Hindenburg and Ludendorff, whose public reputation had grown as Falkenhayn's had declined. Since May the Chancellor's associates in the Foreign Ministry, particularly Zimmermann, had been urging a change in the Supreme Command, arguing that the eastern chiefs were in fundamental agreement with Bethmann's views, an impression that Ludendorff and Hoffmann, the brilliant eastern Chief of Staff, both bitter enemies of Falkenhayn and both anxious for his power, were at pains to encourage. The Chancellor was now convinced that they were right and, on 23 June, in a telegram to General von Lyncker, Chief of the Military Cabinet, made it clear that he was pinning his hopes on the eastern commanders. 'The name Hindenburg', he wrote, 'is a terror to our enemies; it electrifies our army and our people, who have boundless faith in it. Even if we should lose a battle, which God forbid, our people would accept that if Hindenburg were the leader, just as they would accept any peace covered by his name. If this [change] does not take place, the length and varying fortunes of the war will in the end be blamed upon the Emperor by public opinion.'[90]

Lyncker resisted this suggestion, knowing that Hindenburg was merely a symbol behind which stood the reality of Ludendorff and agreeing with his assistant Marschall who predicted that, far from working for peace, Ludendorff 'with his boundless vanity and pride will continue the war until the German people are completely exhausted'.[91] Even more adamant in his opposition was the Emperor, who resented references to the public desire for a change in the command, remarking fretfully that this would be tantamount to his own abdication and the elevation of Hindenburg, as popular tribune, to his place.[92] He refused to listen to Bethmann's plea that 'what was at stake was the Hohenzollern dynasty; with Hindenburg

[89] Falkenhayn, *Oberste Heeresleitung*, pp. 200, 220 ff.; Guinn, *British Strategy*, pp. 143 ff.; Cruttwell, *Great War*, pp. 254 ff.

[90] Janßen, *Kanzler und General*, pp. 215 f.

[91] Dorothea Groener-Geyer, *General Groener, Soldat und Staatsmann* (Frankfurt-on-Main, 1955), pp. 59 f.

[92] Müller, *Regierte der Kaiser?*, p. 200.

he could make an advantageous peace, but not without him';[93] and on 24 August he reaffirmed his faith in his Chief of Staff.

But this was the last gasp of Falkenhayn's authority. On 27 August came the shattering news that the Romanian Government had declared war upon Austria-Hungary. Under this blow the Emperor collapsed completely, brokenly declaring that the war was lost and that Germany must sue for terms. The hysteria passed, but William II no longer had the spirit to withstand Hindenburg's supporters, who were now joined by Lyncker and Plessen and Falkenhayn's one-time trusted associate, the War Minister, Wild von Hohenborn. On the afternoon of 28 August 1916 the decision was made, and on the following morning Hindenburg and Ludendorff arrived at Schloß Pless and, in Bethmann's presence, were formally installed in office.

The Chancellor came away from the ceremony in a state of exhilaration, whereas William II had a bad case of the sulks.[94] The Emperor's political instinct was soon shown to be sounder than Bethmann's. He had all along sensed that the change in command would constitute a kind of political revolution, and he was right. The new Chief of Staff and his associate possessed an authority that neither Emperor nor Chancellor could command, the support of the German people, and they had no hesitation about using it against their nominal superiors in order to get their way. Within a matter of days, Bethmann was discovering, not only that he could not count upon the support of the new Supreme Command for his ideas about peace, but that he was going to have to defend himself against a new kind of military attack upon his prerogatives and his constitutional position. That Hindenburg and Ludendorff recognized no limitations to their mandate was shown early in September, when they addressed themselves to the problem of shoring up the situation in the badly shaken Austro-Hungarian army. Instead of confining themselves to plans for a new kind of field command, the military chiefs conceived an elaborate scheme for reorganizing the whole of the Habsburg Empire's political structure in order to increase German influence in Austrian affairs. Bethmann rejected this as impractical and politically naïve, only to receive a sharp note from Hindenburg in which the Field-Marshal claimed that a continuation of the policy of 'non-intervention in the internal affairs of Austria-Hungary' would make it impossible to strengthen Germany's ally and in which he brusquely asked the Chancellor to define his own

[93] Ritter, *Kriegshandwerk* iii. 241.   [94] Müller, *Regierte der Kaiser?*, p. 217.

views about Austria-Hungary. 'I must demand this in the name of the military,' he wrote, 'so that complete clarity will prevail in this matter.' Bethmann indignantly refused this request, writing, 'I must repudiate the explicit criticism of my direction of policy, which has been vested in me by His Majesty and for which I am solely responsible.'[95] The army chiefs yielded, but not because they were convinced by Bethmann's constitutional argument. They soon returned to the charge, and this time their dabbling in politics cut across a promising initiative for peace negotiations.

Falkenhayn had always hoped that Russia might be detached from the enemy coalition; and in an ironical way the Brusilov offensive, which helped to bring him down, gave some substance to that possibility. That drive had brought Russia's human and material resources close to the point of exhaustion, and in its wake there were indications that influential groups in Russia were ready to consider peace. In July the Vice-President of the Duma, Protopopov, had conversations in Stockholm with Hugo Stinnes and emphasized the readiness to treat, and the dismissal of the Foreign Minister, Sazonov, whose loyalty to the Entente was unqualified, gave substance to this intelligence.

The key to peace, however, was Russian Poland which had been in German hands since August 1915. As we have seen, Bethmann himself had no desire to see that territory restored to the Tsar, for Poland had an important role to play in his projected Mitteleuropa plan. On 12 August, indeed, the Chancellor had reached an agreement with the Austrian Foreign Minister Burián concerning the establishment of a kingdom of Poland allied to the Central Powers after the war. As rumours of Russian desires for peace grew, however, it seemed politic to make no announcement of these plans; the Emperor was particularly insistent on this point, and the Chancellor agreed.[96] Unfortunately, the soldiers did not. In July General von Beseler, the Governor-General of Warsaw, had prepared a memorandum in which he argued that the creation of an independent Poland would enable him to raise at least three divisions of Polish volunteers to fight on the German side, and Ludendorff had reacted with enthusiasm. Now in October 1916, paying no attention to the fact that new talks about peace had taken place between Protopopov and the German banker Warburg, and that the Swedish Foreign Minister Wallenberg had informed the German Government that the Russians were serious in their desire for negoti-

---

[95] Ritter, *Kriegshandwerk* iii. 257 f.   [96] Riezler, *Tagebücher*, pp. 371 n., 374.

ations,[97] Hindenburg informed the Chancellor that military considerations demanded the raising of a Polish contingent as soon as possible. Bethmann, demonstrating for the first time that he was incapable of standing up to the massive self-assurance of the Field-Marshal, deferred to his judgement; and on 5 November the German Government proclaimed the establishment of an independent Poland.[98]

This ended any hope of a separate peace with Russia, for it caused an outburst of nationalist indignation in the Duma that forced the Tsar to dismiss those ministers who had been working for an arrangement with the Germans. But it also failed to produce the military advantages that Beseler and Ludendorff had expected. The attempt to raise a Polish army that would be big enough to hold the north-eastern front and thus enable the Supreme Command to transfer German units to the west was a miserable failure, and this was because it became clear to the Poles that the independence offered them by the Germans was not genuine. Chiefly at fault was Ludendorff himself, whose brain had begun to teem with visions of a gigantic German empire in the east and who plainly intended to include Poland in it. By successfully opposing a clear delineation of Polish frontiers, the election of a Polish diet, and the creation of an independent Polish command, and by promising Wilna and adjoining districts to pro-German elements in Lithuania, where he hoped to create another satellite, Ludendorff alienated all of the Polish leaders who had been well disposed to Germany; and by the spring of 1917 Poland was a centre of disaffection and a receptive target for Allied propaganda.[99]

That Ludendorff's emergence as an annexationist would defeat Bethmann's hopes for attaining peace was illustrated not only by the lost opportunity in Poland but by the fate of the Chancellor's peace note of 1916. In August 1916 Bethmann had conceived the idea of informing the United States Government that Germany was prepared to enter peace talks and was willing to give up Belgium, on condition that its relations with that country be regulated by bilateral negotiation after the war, and that it would welcome American

[97] Müller, *Regierte der Kaiser?*, p. 226.

[98] On all this, see Werner Conze, *Polnische Nation und deutsche Politik im Ersten Weltkriege* (Cologne and Graz, 1958), pp. 203 ff.; Graf Westarp, *Konservative Politik im letzten Jahrzehnt des Kaiserreiches* (2 vols., Berlin, 1935), ii. 64 ff.; Hutten-Czapski, *Sechzig Jahre* ii. 290 ff., 304 ff.; Bethmann Hollweg, *Betrachtungen* ii. 94 ff.; Erich Ludendorff, *Urkunden der Obersten Heeresleitung* (2nd edn., Berlin, 1921), p. 300.

[99] See esp. Hutten-Czapski, *Sechzig Jahre* ii. 275 ff., 339, 340–3, 355–6, 366, 379; Fischer, *Weltmacht*, pp. 340–3.

mediation to advance that objective. No positive response came from Washington, where the presidential campaign was already absorbing the full energies of the government, and the Chancellor decided, with the Emperor's permission, to issue a declaration on his own initiative, defining Germany's war aims and indicating a willingness to negotiate on their basis. As he proceeded with the formulation of the note, by way of consultation with all interested parties, including the Austrian Government, he encountered serious obstacles from the military side. In November 1916, for example, Hindenburg made it clear that he would insist upon guarantees of Germany security in Belgium in the post-war period, and it soon became clear that, when translated into specifics, these would include at the least the possession of Liège, German ownership or control of Belgian railways, and a close economic relationship between the two countries. Bethmann was not opposed to all of these ideas, but he was aware that the disclosure of any of them would have the worst possible effect. As a result, when he forwarded the peace note in its final form to the United States Government on 12 December 1916, it contained no specific definition of war aims at all, amounting to nothing more than a declaration of German willingness to talk about peace and of determination to fight on to victory if the note were disregarded. Any positive effect that this ambiguous declaration might have had in London and Paris was negated by what the Allied governments were hearing at this time about the policy being pursued by the German military authorities in Belgium, which was characterized by accelerated exploitation of the Belgian economy, transportation of Belgian workers to Germany, and encouragement of a separatist movement in the Flemish districts of the country. When President Wilson issued a peace note of his own on 18 December, the Allied attitude was uncompromisingly negative, and Bethmann was unable to exploit this because of the restrictions placed upon his freedom of action by the military.[100]

From this point onwards, the erosion of the Chancellor's authority was swift. The energetic young officers on Ludendorff's staff—like Colonel Bauer, who was charged with improving the system of military procurement—were convinced that the civilian bureaucrats were incapable of dealing with the problems of total war and urged that the incompetents be rooted out and that the war effort be

[100] Erich Ludendorff, *Meine Kriegserinnerungen* (Berlin, 1920), pp. 243 ff.; Karl Helfferich, *Der Weltkrieg* (3 vols., Berlin, 1919), ii. 264 ff., 351 ff.; Gatzke, *Drive to the West*, pp. 151–61; Fischer, *Weltmacht*, pp. 375 ff.; Riezler, *Tagebücher*, p. 386.

increasingly militarized.[101] Their chiefs were not hard to convince. In November Hindenburg demanded and secured the dismissal of von Jagow, the Foreign Secretary, on the grounds that he was not a man 'who could bang his fist on the table'.[102] At the same time, the long-serving Press chief in the Foreign Ministry, Otto Hammann, was forced out of his position, presumably because his style lacked the militancy that the army chiefs desired. And in December Hindenburg told one of Bethmann's aides that he had lost all confidence in Karl Helfferich, the Minister of the Interior and the Vice-Chancellor.

Helfferich had incurred the displeasure of the Supreme Command because he had tried to brake their impulsive schemes for dealing with the problems of war production. The battles of Verdun and the Somme had created another munitions shortage, and this gave the steel-makers an opportunity to launch an attack upon the War Ministry, claiming that its bureaucratic procedures and its unrealistic labour policies were responsible for preventing industry from meeting the army's needs. The real reason for this criticism was to be found in resentment at restrictions imposed by the War Ministry on the profits made by producers and their concern over the Ministry's collaboration with unions. But the steel firms had a voice at court in the person of Colonel Bauer, and he was able to convince Hindenburg and Ludendorff that justice was on their side. The result was that the Supreme Command proceeded to withdraw most of the functions that the War Ministry had been performing effectively since 1914, including exemptions and control of manpower, and to hand them over to a new War Office (Kriegsamt) which was an adjunct of the General Staff and was commanded by General Wilhelm Groener. Moreover, they demanded a new Auxiliary Service Bill, which in its original form called for an extension of the draft to include all healthy males from the ages of 16 to 51, national service for women and persons not subject to the draft, reduction in the number of skilled workers returned from the front, the closing of

[101] On Ludendorff's views of total war, see Hans Speier, 'Ludendorff: The German Concept of Total War', in *Makers of Modern Strategy: Military Thought from Machiavelli to Hitler*, ed. Edward Mead Earle (Princeton, 1943), pp. 315 ff. On Bauer's political thinking, see Martin Kitchen, 'Militarism and the Development of Fascist Ideology: The Political Ideas of Colonel Max Bauer, 1916–1918', *Central European History*, vii, no. 3 (Sept. 1975).

[102] Bethmann tried briefly to protect Jagow but was told by Valentini, the Chief of the Civil Cabinet, that everyone was against Jagow and that his replacement by Zimmermann would improve Bethmann's own relations with the Supreme Command. See Riezler, *Tagebücher*, p. 383.

most universities, the closing-down of non-essential industries, and the retraining of their employees for war-work.

Helfferich rightly saw that, while all of this might have been acceptable in the first flush of patriotic enthusiasm in 1914, it would be viewed with suspicion by many people in late 1916. With the Chancellor's aid, he tried to gain time to negotiate with the leaders of the Reichstag and the representatives of labour. The Supreme Command had no patience with this. With a supreme indifference to political realities, they demanded legislative action, and Groener submitted a draft law to be laid before the Bundesrat and the Reichstag. Even if one grants that Helfferich did not show much skill in his attempts to steer the bill through those bodies, it was the irrational thrusting of the army chiefs that led to the débâcle. The Hilfsdienstgesetz (Auxiliary Service Law), which was supposed to militarize German society and also to give a preferred position in the production process to heavy industry, was rewritten in Reichstag committee, and what resulted was a law that did, in fact, provide for some increase in the draft and some rationalization of the use of labour, but which gave labour protection against arbitrary regulation of their freedom to choose employers, set up conciliation boards to settle disputes, and created a Reichstag committee to oversee the law's implementation.[103]

After the law had passed, Helfferich said sourly that one might almost say that it had been made by 'the Social Democrats, Poles, Alsatians and union secretaries'.[104] The Supreme Command was even more disgruntled than he was, and they blamed him for the failure of their design. Nor did their criticism stop there. They had been annoyed by Bethmann Hollweg's failure to yield to their urgency and his flat repudiation of Hindenburg's warning in mid-November that he would 'have to refuse responsibility for the continuation of the war if the homeland does not provide the necessary support'.[105] By the end of 1916 Hindenburg was beginning to share Ludendorff's already active dislike of Bethmann and was discussing the problem of succession with the leader of the Conservative party.[106]

Tension between the Chancellor and the military leaders was sharply increased at the beginning of the new year, when the sub-

[103] On this, see esp. Feldman, *Army, Industry and Labor*, pp. 149–249; Williamson, *Helfferich*, pp. 171 ff.

[104] Williamson, *Helfferich*, p. 183.

[105] Feldman, *Army, Industry and Labor*, p. 215.

[106] Westarp, *Konservative Politik* ii. 335.

marine question was raised once more. Bethmann had hoped that, on this issue, Hindenburg and Ludendorff would be on his side, but within a month of their assumption of office their concern over American munitions shipments to the enemy had begun to overcome their initial caution.[107] Meanwhile the Chancellor's position was weakened by the disintegration of the support he had formerly had in the Reichstag. In October 1916, when the U-boat question was raised by the parties of the right, it became clear that the majority of the Centre party now favoured the unrestricted use of the submarine, and, in order to mask its own divisions, the party sponsored a resolution that stated that, while the ultimate responsibility for deciding the question must rest with the Chancellor, he should be guided in his decision by the views of the Supreme Command.[108] In what can only be described as an act of collective irresponsibility in a matter affecting the very heart of the constitution, the principle of civilian dominance over the military, the Reichstag accepted this, and, in a very real sense, left Bethmann powerless. The failure of his peace initiative further strengthened the hand of those who demanded *guerre à outrance*. On 8 January 1917 the Chancellor received a telegram from Hindenburg requesting his presence at a conference at Pless to discuss the submarine issue. The invitation was in itself a kind of constitutional revolution, and Bethmann's presence at the conference the merest of formalities. When he arrived at Pless, armed with a careful brief prepared by Helfferich exposing the logical fallacies in the case for unrestricted submarine warfare, he learned that the Emperor had already been won over by the arguments of the army and navy chiefs. He did his best to alter the prevailing view, but, as he wrote later, he was confronted by men 'who were no longer willing to allow themselves to be talked out of decisions they had already made'.[109] Insisting that a new submarine campaign would bring material and psychological advantages to the armies in the field and make it easier for them to withstand the new enemy offensives expected in the spring, Hindenburg brushed Bethmann's concern about the American reaction aside as inconsequential. Unless the submarines were unleashed by 1 February, he insisted, he could no longer assume responsibility for the future course of operations.

---

[107] Helfferich believed that they had been converted to unrestricted use of the submarine by 31 August 1916. *Der Weltkrieg*, ii. 382.

[108] The resolution stated further that, if the Chancellor decided in favour of unrestricted submarine warfare, he 'could be assured of the approval of the Reichstag'.

[109] Bethmann Hollweg, *Betrachtungen* ii. 137 f.

A Bismarck, with a William I to appeal to, might have charged the Field-Marshal with insubordination. Bethmann lacked the self-assurance of his predecessor, and he could not help feeling that a policy that was backed by all of the military leaders, the Emperor, the Reichstag majority, and most politically active Germans might, after all, be sounder than he had believed. It may be that his tendency to fatalism helped persuade him to give way. Riezler wrote on the day after the fateful decision that it was 'a leap in the dark. We all have the feeling that this question hangs over us like a doom. If history follows the laws of tragedy, then Germany should be destroyed by this fatal mistake, which embodies all its earlier tragic mistakes.'[110] The Chancellor may have had something of this feeling, and this may have been why, when the decision was made, he did not resign, as Valentini urged him to do, but remained in office to bear his share of the responsibility for what ensued.[111]

For this he received no gratitude from the soldiers. Even his unavailing opposition to their advice was enough to convince Hindenburg and Ludendorff that he must go, and, although they were dissuaded from insisting on this immediately, they were soon given additional reason for demanding his head. For the Chancellor, as if sensing that the new policy would increase rather than relieve the burdens that the German people must bear, now sought to give it new assurance that its sacrifices would be rewarded by political reform. In a speech of 27 February 1917 he electrified the Reichstag by his declared commitment to this ideal, leading it a month later to establish an inter-party committee 'for the examination of constitutional questions especially in regard to the structure of the representative body of the nation and its relationship to the government'. Simultaneously, interest in the question of the Prussian franchise was revived, which led Bethmann to persuade the Emperor to issue a statement on 7 April, on the day following the United States declaration of war.[112] This 'Osterjeschenk', as it was called by irreverent Berliners, promised the abolition of the three-class electoral system and the reform of the Bundesrat as soon as the war was over. All of a sudden, in the fourth year of the war, Germany was in a ferment of political speculation and expectation,

[110] Riezler, *Tagebücher*, p. 395.

[111] See Müller, *Regierte der Kaiser?*, pp. 247–50; Valentini, *Kaiser und Kabinettschef*, pp. 147 ff.; Jarausch, *Enigmatic Chancellor*, pp. 300 ff.

[112] The United States Government had broken off relations with Germany in February. The decision to enter the war was influenced by Zimmermann's attempt to encourage Japan and Mexico to attack the United States. See Barbara W. Tuchman, *The Zimmermann Telegram* (New York, 1958).

and this was by no means confined to the Reichstag. April saw the first major strikes of the war, which filled some members of the old ruling class with foreboding, coming as they did on the heels of the March Revolution in Russia.

The soldiers considered all this a dangerous distraction from the war effort and blamed it upon the Chancellor. The government, Ludendorff wrote in his memoirs, 'increasingly let the direction of state business be taken out of its hands . . . by specific groups which, historically, were destructive rather than constructive [in their aims]'.[113] A demand by the Socialist party, in a manifesto issued in April, for immediate negotiations to secure 'a general peace without annexations and indemnities on the basis of the free international development of all peoples' increased their concern, for such a peace, they were sure, would unleash the full force of democracy and sweep away the system that they represented. It was necessary, a memorandum of the army's Propaganda and Intelligence Section stated some time later, to prove to the army and the people that 'a peace of renunciation or of understanding will not fulfil the needs of the German people but that only a victory and its consequences at the peace conference will bring about happy conditions for the German people and for each individual class'.[114] To further that end, the Supreme Command insisted that the government make a specific formulation of its war aims in terms that would hearten the war-weary people and, presumably, divert their thoughts from dangerous political ideas.

Bethmann, well aware of the boundless territorial ambitions of the annexationist groups, resisted this demand on the grounds that any statement that satisfied them would make negotiation with the enemy impossible. He was unable, however, to prevent the military from having their way and, after a series of discussions at Kreuznach at the end of April, felt compelled to put his signature on a pro-gramme of war aims that was more extravagant than anything hitherto envisaged, calling for the outright annexation of Lithuania, Esthonia, eastern Poland, the ore and coal basin of Longwy-Briey, the Grand Duchy of Luxemburg, and the southern tip of Belgium, plus extensive economic rights in the rest of Belgium and in the Romanian oil-fields and territorial compensation for Austria-Hungary in Romania and Serbia and for Bulgaria in the Dobrudja.[115]

---

[113] Ludendorff, *Kriegserinnerungen,* p. 357.
[114] H. Thimme, *Weltkrieg ohne Waffen* (Stuttgart, 1932), pp. 250 f.
[115] On the Kreuznach Conference, see Fischer, *Weltmacht,* pp. 447 ff., where it is

Admiral Müller, who was a critical observer at the final meeting, wrote in his diary: 'Valentini was quite right when he dubbed the whole thing as puerile. The thoughts of the Chancellor and Zimmermann could be read in their eyes: "It will do no harm if we ask for the maximum. We shall not get it." '[116]

Something of the sort may have been in Bethmann's mind. He gave his assent to the Kreuznach claims because he knew that the soldiers would demand his dismissal if he did not and because he was aware that the Emperor, who now seemed bent on proving to the right that he had not really meant what he had said in the Easter message, would not withstand that pressure. Even so, he had signed with an important reservation: 'I consider the agreed peace conditions attainable only if we can *dictate* the peace. Solely under this precondition have I assented.' He told the Bundesrat that, if a real chance of peace materialized, the Kreuznach terms would not stand in the way of its realization; and on 15 May 1917, speaking of the possibility of peace with Russia, he said that his goal was an agreement that would exclude 'any idea of rape' and would leave 'no sting, no trace of resentment'.[117]

The Chancellor had nevertheless compromised himself irretrievably. The right, which had long considered him to be a defeatist, was not taken in by his claiming to be 'in full agreement with the Supreme Command' while he continued to refuse to commit himself publicly to the annexationist cause. The left wing of the Social Democrats felt that Kreuznach had shown the real Bethmann and that he was no longer to be trusted. As for the parties of the middle, they became increasingly irritated by Bethmann's vacillations and increasingly doubtful about the quality of his leadership. This weakening of the Chancellor's parliamentary position strengthened the hand of the military, who were by June actively working for his dismissal by telling the Emperor that he was prolonging the war by giving the enemy reason to believe that an internal collapse was coming in Germany.[118] The energetic Colonel Bauer, Ludendorff's chief political agent, was doing his best to win over influential members of the middle parties in the Reichstag with the same arguments. He had established cordial relations with Gustav

---

argued that Bethmann's views did not differ substantially from that of the soldiers, and the critique of this position in Ritter, *Kriegshandwerk* iii. 505 ff.

[116] Müller, *Regierte der Kaiser?*, p. 279.
[117] Jarausch, *Enigmatic Chancellor*, pp. 223 ff.
[118] See Ludendorff, *Kriegserinnerungen*, pp. 358–9.

Stresemann of the National Liberals;[119] now, in June, he made an even more important conquest, in the person of Matthias Erzberger.

Erzberger had been making an independent study of tonnage figures and had reached the conclusion, which the navy rejected while refusing to refute his calculations, that the submarine campaign was a total failure and that Germany must seek a negotiated peace. On 10 June he had a conference with Bauer, who told him that Ludendorff shared his scepticism of naval claims, and was already planning a winter campaign. He painted a dark picture of Germany's military condition and the growing strength of the enemy and spoke of the necessity of preparing the people psychologically for the sacrifices that were to come. Erzberger seems to have proposed a plan for a special organization—'a kind of spiritual Kriegsernährungsamt'—to perform this function, and at a subsequent meeting the Colonel, after more gloomy comments on the military situation, said that Ludendorff accepted this idea.

Shaken by Bauer's revelations, Erzberger was also worried by two other matters. He was aware that the new Austrian Emperor Charles and his Foreign Minister, Czernin, were convinced that the Habsburg Empire must have peace before the end of the year; and he was concerned over intimations from the leaders of the Majority Socialists that, when the issue of war credits was posed again in July, they might have to vote negatively in order to protect themselves against their schismatic left wing, which at Easter time had organized an Independent Socialist party dedicated to the speedy termination of the war. Goaded on by these cares, the Centrist leader decided to share them with his parliamentary colleagues and did so with devastating effect. At the beginning of July the Main Commission of the Reichstag began its deliberations on war credits. In two speeches before this body, Erzberger gave a detailed and frightening picture of Germany's military prospects and called upon the Reichstag to pass a resolution expressing readiness to negotiate for a peace without forced annexations. Despite warnings by Bethmann and Helfferich that this would be considered by Germany's enemies as a sign of weakness, an Inter-Party Committee, representing the Centre, the National Liberals, the Progressives, and the Majority Socialists, was set up to draft such a resolution.

In the ensuing political confusion it soon became apparent that the Chancellor's position was seriously threatened. Bethmann himself recognized this and fought back. When he learned on 7 July that

[119] On Stresemann's role in the July crisis of 1917, see Marvin L. Edwards, *Stresemann and the Greater Germany, 1914–1918* (New York, 1963), pp. 139 ff.

Ludendorff had arrived in Berlin, obviously intent on exploiting the situation, he insisted successfully that the Emperor order the General to return to his post; and when the Inter-Party Committee raised the question of the Prussian franchise and of other reforms designed to promote parliamentary influence in executive agencies of Prussia and the Reich, he responded positively and, on 9 July, secured the Emperor's permission to advance on this front. But, ironically, both of these actions weakened rather than strengthened his cause. Erzberger had been one of the deputies whom Ludendorff had intended to see during his trip to Berlin. The Centre leader bitterly resented being baulked of the opportunity; on 8 July he publicly complained of the Chancellor's interfering with legitimate contact between the Supreme Command and the Reichstag; and on 9 July, when Stresemann demanded the Chancellor's resignation, there were strong indications that Erzberger was prepared to support this, partly because of wounded vanity and partly because he wanted to be sure of National Liberal votes for his desired peace resolution. As for the Chancellor's renewed commitment to democratic reform, it merely confirmed the military in their determination that Bethmann must go. They brought up their big guns now. On 12 July the Crown Prince had interviews with party leaders and reported to his father that the Chancellor's support was disappearing fast, and, on the same day, Hindenburg and Ludendorff telephoned their resignations to Berlin, saying that they could no longer work with Bethmann. The Emperor lamely explained to his Chancellor that he was placed in an impossible position, and Bethmann, not wishing to prolong his sovereign's discomfort, resigned on 13 July.[120]

In turning against Bethmann, Erzberger had convinced himself that the appropriate successor would be Prince Bülow, who (presumably with Erzberger's aid) would be able to collaborate effectively with, and if necessary to control, the Supreme Command. As it turned out, Bethmann's successor was not Bülow but an obscure Prussian civil servant named Georg Michaelis. Even so, Erzberger's plan for the succession bears thinking about, for it illuminates the political naïvety that flawed his career. In the crisis of July 1917 the soldiers had made much of him because they recognized that his aid was indispensable in bringing Bethmann down, which was their chief objective, and because they were confident that they could

---

[120] On the July crisis, see esp. Jarausch, *Enigmatic Chancellor*, pp. 373 ff.; Epstein, *Erzberger*, Ch. 8; Ritter, *Kriegshandwerk* iii. 551–84; Bethmann Hollweg, *Betrachtungen* ii. 232–5; Valentini, *Kaiser und Kabinettschef*, pp. 157 ff.; Ludendorff, *Urkunden*, pp. 408 ff.; Haussmann, *Schlaglichter*, pp. 101 ff.

frustrate his other plans once that goal was achieved. Whatever may be said about the sincerity of his desire for peace and for an extension of parliamentary government, he must bear a major share of the responsibility for having created a military dictatorship that would make both peace and political progress impossible until the Empire was in ruins.

IV

One of the principal reasons for the Supreme Command's campaign against Bethmann had been their conviction that he had failed to mobilize the nation's material and psychological resources for the war effort and had not maintained internal order. In March 1917 Colonel Bauer had summed up their dissatisfaction by claiming that the Chancellor was responsible for the insufficiency of food and coal supplies, which threatened the health of the workers and weakened productivity, and that his mismanagement of the Hilfs-dienstgesetz had encouraged 'an unfortunate upward movement of wages and far-reaching demands for political rights', to say nothing of the demoralization of the middle and productive classes and the decline of 'German loyalty, morality and sense of duty'.[121] The criticism was not restricted to the Chancellor. The secondary target for Bauer, his industrialist friends, and his superiors was the General who had administered the War Office since October 1916, Wilhelm Groener.

This was understandable. A pragmatic Württemberger with more flexible social and political views than most of his fellow officers, Groener had early concluded that the only way to master the prob-lem of production was to co-operate with the trade unions against both the attempts of the Independent Socialists to politicize the labour force (which became apparent for the first time during the strikes that followed the cutting of the bread ration in April 1917) and industrialist resistance to recognition of workers' rights.[122] This and his plan to check the strong inflationary tendency of the economy by seeking controls on both wages and profits made him a host of enemies in business circles, including such leaders of industry

---

[121] Feldman, *Army, Industry and Labor*, p. 371.

[122] Feldman writes: 'Groener sought to combine South German social egalitarian-ism with the Prussian tradition of reform from above, and his desire to grant substantive concessions to labour in the social sphere was designed to prevent the complete destruction of those authoritarian political and military traditions with which he identified himself. He was thus paving the way for the alliances of industry and labor and of the army and Social Democracy which were to determine the course of the Revolution.' Ibid., p. 404.

as Hugo Stinnes and Carl Duisberg of the Bayer dye firm. Their charges that Groener's policy weakened the war effort and threatened the social order were passed on by Bauer to Ludendorff; and the result was that the functions of his office were once more subordinated to War Ministry control, and he himself was assigned to a field command in August 1917.[123]

These changes, which restored to the Deputy Commanding Generals the independence that they had lost to the Kriegsamt, ushered in a period of increased military repression, which was characterized by severe restrictions on the right of assembly, stricter surveillance of meetings to discuss grievances, the return to military service of exempted workers who participated in strike agitation, and the use of force and militarization of factories as a means of forcing workers to return to work when strikes occurred. These measures did not help to restore the unity of national will that Ludendorff desired. On the contrary, they increased disaffection among the labour force of the industries affected and weakened the ability of the unions to discourage strikes, as was demonstrated in the wave of strikes that took place in Berlin, Kiel, Hamburg, Magdeburg, Cologne, and Munich in January 1918. Nor did the tightening of controls over the labour force have any effect upon the problems with which the great mass of the population had to cope by the end of 1917—the shortages of food and fuel and clothing and, in parts of the country affected by the expansion of war industry, of adequate housing at tolerable rents. By the beginning of 1918 the necessities of life were in very short supply and the hardships borne by the average German increasingly onerous.

The Reichstag's response to these conditions had been the passage on 19 July 1917 of Erzberger's Peace Resolution, which stated: 'The Reichstag strives for a peace of understanding and permanent reconciliation of peoples. Forced territorial acquisitions and political, economic, and financial oppressions are irreconcilable with such a peace.'[124] The Supreme Command's response was diametrically opposed to this and was based, as it had been all along, on the assumption that the war effort could be sustained, and political and social revolution averted, only by a real victory. They therefore resisted any implementation of the Peace Resolution, and

---

[123] Groener-Geyer, *Groener*, pp. 60 ff.

[124] The term 'forced acquisitions' was an escape, and Erzberger was later to say of the Peace Resolution, 'this way I get Longwy Briey by negotiation!' Prince Max von Baden, *Erinnerungen und Dokumente* (Stuttgart, 1927), p. 114. For Erzberger's own account, see *Erlebnisse*, Ch. XIX. Also Fischer, *Weltmacht*, pp. 522 f.

Bethmann's successor was speaking for them when he accepted the resolution with the damaging qualifying phrase 'as I interpret it'. In August and September 1917, when a papal note to all belligerents aroused a flurry of diplomatic activity, and when Michaelis's Foreign Secretary, Richard von Kühlmann, conceived the idea of secret talks with the British Government, the Supreme Command adopted a position that negated the possibility of success from the very beginning. After a discussion at Schloß Bellevue on 12 September, in which, in the presence of the Emperor, the civilian and military leaders considered proposals that might be laid before the British, Ludendorff torpedoed the projected talks by informing the Chancellor two days later that Germany must insist on an extended occupation of Belgium, the annexation of the iron basin of Lorraine and the Meuse valley as far as St. Vith, a number of new naval stations, and large African holdings.[125]

Meanwhile the Supreme Command had called into being a new movement that was designed to spread confidence in victory and an annexationist peace. This was the Vaterlandspartei (Fatherland party), founded in early September under the leadership of Admiral von Tirpitz. Its real authors were Lieutenant-Colonel Nicolai, the Chief of Military Intelligence, and Ludendorff himself, who encouraged Tirpitz and other known annexationists to found a mass party that would fight against the Peace Resolution and political reform and in support of an expansive imperialism. In terms of numbers, the new party was a tremendous success, for by July 1918 its membership exceeded that of the Social Democratic party. This effective organization of the bourgeoisie was made possible by the assistance given to the party by the army's propaganda service and the immense sums placed at its disposal by the Association of German Iron and Steel Industrialists and other organizations of that kind.[126]

It was, however, baleful in its consequences. The Fatherland party was instrumental in dulling the critical faculties of the German middle class and mobilizing them in support of war aims that Germany was now incapable of attaining. At the beginning of 1918 this

[125] On the papal peace note, see esp. M. Spahn, *Die päpstliche Friedensvermittlung* (Berlin, 1919). On Kühlmann's plans and the attitude of the military, see Kühlmann, *Erinnerungen*, pp. 471–3, 481–5; Georg Michaelis, *Für Staat und Volk* (Berlin, 1922), pp. 347–50; Ludendorff, *Urkunden*, pp. 428–33; Ludendorff, *Kriegserinnerungen*, pp. 413–19; Gatzke, *Drive to the West*, pp. 219–25, 228, 233.

[126] Fischer, *Weltmacht*, pp. 559 ff.; Feldmann, *Army, Industry and Labor*, pp. 429 ff. On the role of intellectuals in the Fatherland party, see Schwabe, 'Deutsche Professoren', pp. 355 ff. For acerbic comments on the effects of the party's propaganda, see Karl Kraus, *Die letzten Tage der Menschheit*, act 5, scenes 7, 50.

contributed to the government's failure to avail itself of what was probably its last chance to attain a moderate peace. In 1917 the coalition facing Germany was shaken by a series of set-backs. The great offensive of the French general Nivelle was a miserable fiasco and left the French army racked with mutiny and defeatism. Haig's push at Paschendaele in September was equally disastrous, and in its wake the former Foreign Secretary Lord Lansdowne publicly urged negotiations for peace. In October the Italians suffered a demoralizing defeat at Caporetto, which came close to knocking them out of the war. And, a month later, a second revolution in Russia brought the Bolsheviks to power, who immediately let it be known that they wished to terminate the war. In the view of Richard von Kühlmann, all of this added up to an opportunity to make peace with Russia and then to move to general peace on terms that would be better than any that could be attained by a further prolongation of hostilities. The essential first step towards this objective would be a moderate peace with the Bolsheviks, based on the principle of self-determination. This would bring some modest accretions of territory to Germany, but not such as to outrage the Reichstag majority, which was still true to the Peace Resolution, or to put propaganda weapons in the hands of the enemy. Indeed, such a peace might induce Russia's former allies, in their present mood of discouragement, to call for general peace talks.

But the Fatherland party was beating the drum for an annexationist peace, and Ludendorff, with its backing, defied Kühlmann's peace strategy. At a meeting with the Emperor and the Foreign Secretary in mid-December Ludendorff took the position that the Bolsheviks must be forced to recognize German annexation of the western half of Poland and a satellite status for Courland and Lithuania and to withdraw their own forces from Livonia and Esthonia. When Kühlmann, after talks with Czernin, the Austrian Foreign Minister, and Hoffmann, the German military plenipotentiary, simply ignored these desires in peace talks that began at Brest-Litovsk in late December, the Supreme Command hit back with full force. On 7 January Hindenburg wrote to the Emperor that he and his colleague had been deeply wounded by the fact that the advice of a military subordinate had been preferred to their own. With respect to Kühlmann's policy, the Field-Marshal wrote, 'Your Majesty will not demand that honest men, who have served Your Majesty and the fatherland loyally, should lend their authority and their names to negotiations [that they regard] with inner conviction as shameful for the Crown and Reich . . . I respectfully urge Your

Majesty to make a fundamental decision.' Hindenburg made it clear that he was prepared to resign on the issue; and, in a talk with the Chancellor a few days later, Ludendorff gave a strong intimation that he could no longer remain in service if Kühlmann and people who believed as he did retained their office.[127]

For a moment it appeared as if the generals had overstepped themselves. The Chancellor now was Count Georg von Hertling, who had replaced the bumbling Michaelis in October. Unlike his predecessor, this Bavarian elder statesman was no tool of the military, nor for that matter was he the creature of the Emperor. He owed his position to the pressure exerted by the Reichstag majority at the time of Michaelis's fall and was, in this sense, the first parliamentary Chancellor in the history of the Empire. This did not mean that he was fully in accord with the terms of the Peace Resolution, but he was no blind annexationist; he believed Kühlmann's prescription for peace more reasonable than the fantastic plans of the Fatherland party; and he was in no mood to sacrifice his Foreign Secretary to Ludendorff's whims. In consequence, on the basis of a report that he requested from Kühlmann, he wrote a memorandum that not only defended his tactics but, for the first time in the war, presented a constitutional rationale for the strict delimitation of military authority in the field of foreign affairs.[128]

This had little effect. In an acerbic marginal comment, Ludendorff said it was entirely up to the Supreme Commanders to decide how far their personal sense of responsibility would carry them. 'Even a decision by His Majesty cannot relieve the generals from the dictates of their conscience.' In view of this crippling reservation, Hertling's success in persuading Hindenburg to sign the memorandum had no meaning. Even for this token submission, the generals demanded a humiliating quid pro quo in the form of the dismissal of the Chief of the Civil Cabinet, Rudolf von Valentini. There was no logical reason for this demand, for Valentini had no influence on the Brest-Litovsk negotiations. He was merely a symbolic substitute for Kühlmann, who, the Supreme Commanders concluded, was untouchable at this time. The Emperor, furious over this arrogant infringement of his right to choose the members of his own household, fought desperately to save Valentini but finally capitulated to another threat of resignation by the military chiefs. It was a humiliation greater than the *Daily Telegraph* affair of 1908, and the Emperor never recovered

---

[127] Kühlmann, *Erinnerungen*, pp. 536–7.

[128] Ibid., pp. 538–42; Schmidt-Bückeburg, *Militärkabinett*, pp. 266 ff.; Ritter, *Kriegshandwerk* iv (Munich, 1968), 126 f.

from it. His influence in events from this time on was negligible and his attitude one of resigned apathy.[129]

The Supreme Command had its way also at Brest-Litovsk, where the terms imposed upon the Bolsheviks—after the breakdown of the talks in February, the resumption of hostilities, and Lenin's decision to surrender in March—were such as to satisfy the wildest dreams of the Fatherland party. Russia lost Poland, Lithuania, Courland, and western Livonia with Riga and the islands, and was forced to evacuate parts of the Caucasus and the rest of Livonia, Estonia, and Finland and to recognize the anti-Bolshevik government that had been set up in the Ukraine. Although final disposition of the severed territories was to wait on the expression of the desires of the populations, it was clear that there was little likelihood of their enjoying real independence if Germany won the war.[130]

The effects of this were, as has been indicated, generally unfortunate. It is true that the Brest-Litovsk Peace—and the Peace of Bucharest, by which the German Government imposed equally onerous terms upon Romania, which had made the mistake of entering the war on the Allied side at the time of the Brusilov offensive and had been soundly beaten for its pains—aroused exhilaration and a new confidence in peace in Germany. But this euphoric reaction, to which all of the parties which had voted for the Peace Resolution succumbed, with the exception of the Socialists,[131] was to have dire results and to make the psychological effects of the ultimate defeat doubly hard when it came six months later. Moreover, the treaty helped to make that defeat inevitable, for the shock of its terms not only ended the defeatism that had begun to rise in the west and strengthened the will of the Entente governments to fight on, but also aroused the resistance of the subject peoples of the east who could now see that only German defeat would bring them freedom. There were strikes and disorders in Poland even before the treaty was signed, and the assignment of Polish territory to the new Ukrainian puppet state caused revolts in the volunteer army that General von Beseler had raised so painfully, the defection of several units to the Bolsheviks, and the forced transfer of the rest to the

---

[129] Ritter, *Kriegshandwerk* iv. 129–31; Müller, *Regierte der Kaiser?*, pp. 344–5.

[130] The whole story of Brest-Litovsk is told in John W. Wheeler-Bennett, *The Forgotten Peace: Brest Litovsk* (London, 1938). See also Fischer, *Weltmacht*, pp. 621 ff.

[131] The SPD abstained in the vote on the treaty; the Independent Socialists voted no. The other parties of the Reichstag majority supported the treaty, Erzberger explaining that its terms were compatible with the Peace Resolution. See Ritter, *Kriegshandwerk* iv. 147; Epstein, *Erzberger*, p. 234.

Isonzo front.[132] Even more serious was the beginning of the dissolution of the Habsburg army, whose loyalty and discipline had
been the strongest integrative force in the troubled multilingual
empire. Now, worn down by its defeats and by the deficiencies of a
supply system that could no longer feed and clothe its troops adequately, the Imperial and Royal Army became increasingly susceptible to Entente propaganda, which made the most of the contrast
between the promises inherent in Woodrow Wilson's address of 8
January 1918 and the Brest terms, and to Bolshevik propaganda
brought home by prisoners released in Russia. Before long, Italian,
Yugoslav, and Czech deserters were beginning to form partisan
units behind the front.[133]

Finally, the Brest-Litovsk Treaty failed utterly to create a true
condition of peace on the eastern front. Because of the fragility of the
political situation in the Ukraine and the Baltic area, Germany had to
leave large numbers of troops in the east. In April 1918, after the
launching of the western offensive, one and a half million German
troops were stationed in the east, some forty divisions, half of which
were in the area that stretched from the Ukraine to the Don basin.[134]
Military necessity was not the only reason for this. Ludendorff,
whose mind was always resistant to the restraints of reality, seems in
these months to have begun to give way to the kind of megalomania
that was to affect Adolf Hitler in the Second World War. In any
event, he succumbed to a fantastic dream of creating a great south-
eastern Russian state under German influence that would extend all
the way to the Caucasus, of making a German Riviera on the
Crimea, and of building a bridge to Central Asia in order to threaten
the British position in India. This chimera he was to pursue until his
world collapsed in October 1918.[135]

That such a collapse was impending was clear to many perceptive
observers long before that date. The January strikes convinced the
leaders of the Majority Socialist party that, unless there was some
tangible evidence of progress toward peace and political reform,
there would be new violence and they might lose all control over the
masses. The influential *Frankfurter Zeitung* warned that continued
annexationist propaganda might very well defeat its purpose by
stifling what was left of the fighting morale of a war-weary army and

[132] Hutten-Czapski, *Sechzig Jahre* ii. 458–62.
[133] See esp. Rothenburg, *Army of Francis Joseph*, pp. 201–18; Arthur J. May, *The
Passing of the Habsburg Monarchy* (2 vols., New York, 1966), ii. 798 ff.; Ritter, *Kriegshandwerk* iv. 276 f.; and for a moving fictional account, Alexander Lernet-Holenia,
Die Standarte (Vienna, 1934).
[134] Ritter, *Kriegshandwerk* iv. 149.   [135] Ibid. 331–64.

people. In February 1918 Friedrich Naumann, Alfred Weber, Carl Legien, Robert Bosch, and others sent a memorandum to the Supreme Command arguing that the German people must not be asked to support a new military offensive until they were assured that every effort had been made to secure peace and emphasizing the necessity of Germany's giving an unequivocal pledge to liberate Belgium at the end of hostilities.[136]

All of these arguments Ludendorff either rejected or ignored, and in these last critical months of the war there was no authority in Germany except Ludendorff. Beside his dominant figure the Emperor and Hindenburg were insubstantial shadows; against his brutal will the aged Hertling had no power of resistance and the Reichstag majority was reduced to a dejected group of impotent criticasters. The parliamentarians' proposals of reform he regarded as 'a policy of surrender to the *Zeitgeist*' which was 'bound to lead to perdition'. With a reformed Prussian franchise, he wrote to a friend, 'we cannot live'.[137] As for giving up Belgium, this would be tantamount to admitting that Germany could not win the war, and this was an admission that he refused to make. Oblivious equally to the growing political discontent of the working class, to the increasingly serious food situation, to the serious deficiencies in army supplies and the shortage of reserves, made more critical by his grandiose schemes in the east, and, finally, to the near exhaustion of his allies, Ludendorff, surely the most terrible of the simplifiers of the First World War, insisted that his new offensive in the west would bring the total victory that would check the forces of democratic revolution and re-establish the Prussian absolutist order as a *rocher de bronze*.

On 21 March 1918 the great 'Michael offensive' opened with a crash of guns and with the might of the whole German army thrown upon the British front between St. Quentin and Arras. The British Third Army was thrust aside and Gough's Fifth overrun; Bapaume, Peronne, the line of the upper Somme were taken; and the hinge between the British and French armies threatened to snap and open the way to Paris. But Ludendorff's momentum was slowed down by the lack of fuel for his motorized units and by other logistical faults, and he lacked the reserves to keep up the pressure. When the expected gap did not appear between the Allies, he allowed himself

[136] Ibid. 162; Gatske, *Drive to the West*, pp. 252 f.; Heuß, *Naumann*, pp. 547 f.; Haussmann, *Schlaglichter*, p. 185. On Hans Delbrück's similar arguments, see Craig, *Prussian Army*, pp. 337 f.

[137] Ritter, *Kriegshandwerk* iv. 154; G. von dem Knesebeck, *Die Wahrheit über den Propagandafeldzug und Deutschlands Zusammenbruch* (Munich, 1927), p. 164.

to be diverted from his key objective and shifted his attack to points where it seemed easier to break through. In April he rolled over the Portuguese in Flanders and retook all of the ground lost to Haig in 1917. But the British held at Ypres, and Ludendorff changed direction again, developing a series of attacks between Soissons and Reims in May and crossing the Marne in the first week of June. The German thrusts were becoming weaker now and increasingly disarticulated. Within sight of the positions held in September 1914, the great offensive began slowly to grind to a halt.[138]

Belatedly, this inspired members of Ludendorff's staff to political reflection, and Colonel von Haeften, an officer with a wide acquaintance in circles long critical of the annexationist philosophy, wrote a memorandum in which he discussed the possibility of using political weapons to support the military offensive. 'Undoubtedly,' he wrote, 'the successes of our arms . . . have already had a great effect upon our enemies. . . . But these successes alone will not bring us peace. For that we need a political victory behind the enemy front.' When the memorandum was forwarded to the Chancellor and the Foreign Secretary, this passage impressed Kühlmann to such an extent that he dilated upon it in a speech before the Reichstag on 24 June, in which he said, '. . . an absolute end can hardly be expected from military decisions alone, without recourse to diplomatic negotiations'.[139]

For this eminently sensible observation, Kühlmann paid with the loss of his position. In an outburst of excited denunciation, the Conservatives, the National Liberals, and the Fatherland party accused him of undermining army and civilian morale, and the Supreme Command demanded, and got, his head. They also ordered Haeften to discontinue his political studies and then, in order to make their position perfectly clear, made a new statement on Belgium, indicating that it was their will that that unfortunate country should remain bound to Germany by economic and political ties and would be occupied by German troops for an indefinite period.[140]

Irrationality could hardly be carried further, given what now lay in store for these heedless annexationists. On 8 August Rawlinson's Fourth British Army, supported by French units, struck with drama-

---

[138] For an informed critique of Ludendorff's strategy, see *Ursachen des deutschen Zusammenbruches im Jahre 1918* (Berlin, 1920–9). For striking descriptions of the fighting, see Ernst Jünger, *In Stahlgewittern* (1920) and *Der Kampf als inneres Erlebnis* (1922).

[139] Reichstag, *Stenographische Berichte*, cccxii (1918), 5612; Kühlmann, *Erinnerungen*, pp. 572 f.

[140] *Ursachen des Zusammenbruches*, 4. Reihe, ii. 346–7.

tic suddenness east of Amiens, and masses of Allied tanks tore the German lines to shreds. This was 'the black day of the German army', and it recoiled, never to seize the initiative again. By the beginning of September the Allied armies were sweeping forward in every sector: the British were through the Somme and hammering at the Hindenburg line; the French were pushing forward in the Champagne; and the Americans, whom the German navy had vowed to keep out of Europe, had won their first fight at St. Mihiel and were advancing in the Meuse-Argonne.

And now, at the other end of Europe, the process of dissolution began. In mid-September Allied troops at Salonika attacked and breached the Bulgarian lines and began a headlong advance into Serbia. The Bulgars immediately sued for armistice terms. Turkey was left at the mercy of converging Allied armies, and its government hastened to follow the Bulgarian example. Even before these events had taken place, the Austrians, whose attempts to pierce the Piave line in June had broken on Italian resistance at a cost of 150,000 men, had informed Germany that they could fight no longer and had begun diplomatic exchanges with the Allies.

Even the indomitable Ludendorff could not stem this rush of events. At the end of September his strong nerves snapped, and he informed his government that it must sue for peace. Having brought Germany to the end of its resources, he left to the civilian leadership whose authority he had systematically undermined the hard task of seeing what could be saved from the ruins.

V

Later in the month Friedrich Meinecke wrote to a friend:

A fearful and gloomy existence awaits us in the best of circumstances! And although my hatred of the enemy, who remind me of beasts of prey, is as hot as ever, so is my anger and resentment at those German power-politicians who, by their presumption and their stupidity, have dragged us down into this abyss. Repeatedly in the course of the war, we could have had a peace by agreement, if it had not been that the boundless demands of the Pan-German–militaristic–conservative combine made it impossible. It is fearful and tragic that this combine could be broken only by the overthrow of the whole state.[141]

A peace by agreement might not have been as easy to attain as the historian supposed, but it would be hard to quarrel with his assignment of responsibility for the misfortunes that lay ahead for his country.

[141] Meinecke, *Briefwechsel*, p. 97 (to L. Aschoff, 21 Oct. 1918).

XI
From Kiel to Kapp: The Aborted Revolution
1918–1920

On the street at Potsdamer Platz, I saw
again, for the first time since the revolution,
an officer wearing epaulettes.

HARRY GRAF KESSLER (15 November 1918)[1]

In 1848 when Bakunin wanted to crown the
uprising in Dresden by burning down all the
public buildings and encountered opposition,
he declared, 'The Germans are too stupid for
that!' and went on his way.

OSWALD SPENGLER (1919)[2]

IN NOVEMBER 1918 the state that Bismarck had founded collapsed. It was replaced by a republic, which had fourteen years of troubled life before expiring as miserably, if not as noisily, as its predecessor. There were many reasons for the failure of the Weimar Republic, and, as will become clear, some of the forces that worked against its chances of survival were external in origin and beyond the capacity of Germans to control. Nevertheless, the Republic's basic vulnerability was rooted in the circumstances of its creation, and it is no exaggeration to say that it failed in the end partly because German officers were allowed to put their epaulettes back on again so quickly and because the public buildings were not burned down, along with the bureaucrats who inhabited them.

I

It is ironical that in the last month of the war the aspiration of liberals and democrats since 1848, of establishing a parliamentary monarchy in Germany, was finally achieved, without having the slightest influence on the course of events. At the end of September, when Luden-

---

[1] Harry Graf Kessler, *Tagebücher 1918–1937* (Frankfurt-on-Main, 1961), p. 32.
[2] Oswald Spengler, *Preußenthum und Sozialismus* (new edn., Munich, 1934), p. 9.

dorff told Field-Marshal von Hindenburg and Chancellor Hertling, that an immediate armistice was necessary, he also urged the formation of a government that would be capable of impressing the Allies by its representative character and its liberal philosophy. As a result, the majority parties in the Reichstag—the Progressives, the Centre, and the Social Democrats—accustomed to every kind of frustration and official obstructionism, suddenly discovered that they were actually being urged to carry out their desired reforms, including that of the antiquated Prussian suffrage. Completely unprepared for this change in their fortunes, they nevertheless ranged themselves behind a new Chancellor, Prince Max von Baden,[3] and in the course of October voted a series of laws, simultaneously approved by the Bundesrat, which not only provided for ministerial responsibility to Parliament but virtually eliminated the royal power of command over the armed forces, which were henceforth to be under the control of the civil government.[4] This was a constitutional transformation that at any other time would have transfixed the imagination of the country.

It did not do so now because the nation's attention was elsewhere. The news that the government was seeking an armistice—that, after all the fanfares of victory, the war was in fact lost—had had a universally shattering effect. On the one hand, it paralysed the will and energies of those who had been the most fervent supporters of the war effort; on the other, it destroyed the restraint with which the working and peasant classes had borne the deprivations that the conflict had forced upon them, undermined the discipline of the reserve forces and garrison troops stationed within the country, and galvanized the hopes and ambitions of the leaders of the extreme left. Before October there had been little evidence of anything that could be described as a desire for a truly revolutionary change of system. In the strikes of January 1918 nothing more radical in the way of political reform had been demanded than what had now been won by Prince Max's government, namely democratization and suffrage reform; and the strikes in Upper Silesia in June and July were purely economic in motivation. But on 22 October, when 300 workers in the Maybach motor construction plant in Friedrichshafen, Württemberg, went on strike, they not only shouted for peace and bread but chanted such slogans as 'The Kaiser is a scoundrel!' and

[3] 'The parties were commanded to take over power'. Theodor Eschenburg, *Die improvisierte Demokratie: Gesammelte Aufsätze zur Weimarer Republik* (Munich, 1963), p. 39.

[4] Reichsamt des Innen, Reichs-Gesetzblatt (1918), pp. 1273–5.

'Up with the German Republic!',[5] and this was not unique to this customarily quiet corner of Germany.

It is possible that the situation might have been stabilized if Emperor William II had realized, once the appeal for armistice had been made, that his own position was untenable, if only because of the widespread feeling that his going would ease a settlement with the enemy, and had surrendered the throne to one of his grandsons. This was the view of Friedrich Naumann and Friedrich Meinecke who, a few weeks later, when Germany was in the throes of revolution, wrote privately that it could have been avoided by an act of statecraft on the part of the monarch.[6] But even when the Emperor was made aware of the growing popular desire for his departure, he resisted the idea, preferring to indulge in fantasies in which he marched into Germany at the head of his loyal armies and restored the fealty of his subjects. His stubborn retention of office not only destroyed the last chance of a survival of his dynasty but helped to obscure the importance of the constitutional changes effected by Prince Max's government and to encourage the belief that it was not doing everything it could to secure peace.

This impression was strengthened by the fact that the armistice negotations were taking longer than had been expected. This was because President Wilson had responded to the German appeal with caution and, rightly suspecting that the German military might be hoping to use an armistice as a preparation for a renewed effort, had been defining conditions and seeking assurances that would make this impossible. The effect of this was, on the one hand, to increase the clamour for the abdication of the Emperor and, on the other, to encourage local efforts to end the war before it caused new bloodshed. The November Revolution was essentially the outgrowth of actions of this kind in the naval base at Kiel and the capital of Bavaria.

The troubles in Kiel originated in what can fairly be called an admirals' rebellion against Prince Max's government. Fearing that an armistice would require an ignominious surrender of the navy to the British fleet, Admiral Reinhard Speer, Chief of the Admiralty Staff, and his executive officer, Captain Magnus von Levetzow,

---

[5] William M. Hatch, 'Württemberg and the November 1918 Revolution' (Dissertation, Stanford Univ. 1973), pp. 129 f. Labour unrest had increased sharply in the first months of 1918, and Emil Barth, Klara Zetkin, and Ernst Thalheimer had formed an organization of revolutionary shop-stewards in Stuttgart.

[6] Meinecke, *Straßburg, Freiburg, Berlin*, p. 272; Heuß, *Naumann*, p. 575. See also Max Weber's views in mid-October. Ibid. p. 572.

attempted to order the High Sea Fleet to steam out from Kiel on a suicidal attack against the British navy that would redeem the honour of a force that had accomplished nothing notable since 1917. Rumours of the projected operation aroused resistance among the enlisted men, whose relations with the officers had for two years been marked by bitter disputes over rations and working conditions, and this led to open sabotage. Attempts by the naval command to discipline the leaders of the resistance merely exacerbated the temper of the mutineers who now formed a sailors' council, which not only insisted that their imprisoned comrades be released but also demanded the abdication of the Emperor and the immediate conclusion of peace.

Alarmed by what now threatened to become a rebellion against the state, the naval authorities appealed to the government for support, and Prince Max asked Conrad Haussmann, the Secretary of State, and the Majority Socialist Gustav Noske to go to Kiel and restore order. A forthright and energetic man who was to have a prominent part in the embroilments of the next two years, Noske arrived in Kiel on 4 November and in a remarkably short time ended a situation that had degenerated to the point where shots were being exchanged in the streets of the dock areas, secured the release of the prisoners, and persuaded the enlisted men to return to duty.[7]

He accomplished this by legitimizing the sailors' council, of which he had himself made chairman, and convincing the naval command and the civil authorities that it would be expedient to co-operate with it. This was a personal triumph of the first order, the more so because, in accomplishing it, Noske had been able to outmanœuvre the most radical elements in the sailors' movement. It did not, however, redound to the advantage of the government in Berlin. The councils distrusted Prince Max's government because it had been slow in responding to Noske's request for an amnesty and, flushed with success, saw no further reason to recognize its authority. There were many people who agreed with them, for their victory in Kiel inspired imitation. On 5 November a sailors' council took effective control of Germany's largest naval base at Wilhelmshaven; on the sixth columns of sailors and workers marched on the Rathaus in Hamburg and demanded that regulation of communications and food distribution be turned over to them, while a

[7] The events in Kiel are well described in Daniel Horn, *The German Naval Mutinies of World War I* (New Brunswick, 1969). See also *War, Mutiny, and Revolution in the German Navy*, ed. Horn. For a highly coloured account of the mood of the enlisted men before 1918, see Plievier's novel, *Des Kaisers Kulis*.

contingent of sailors from Kiel seized the police headquarters in Braunschweig and another, which had been held prisoner in the barracks of the 73rd Fusilier Regiment in Hanover, fraternized with their captors and arrested the commanding general; and on 7 November that performance was repeated in Cologne, where emissaries from the port cities subverted a garrison of 45,000 men and formed a council to govern the city. By the end of the first week of November the government could no longer rely on the garrisons in any of its northern cities.[8]

As in Kiel, so in Munich did the fear of the consequences of a continuation of the war serve to undermine local authority. The surrender of Austria-Hungary and the dissolution of the Hapsburg Empire made the Kingdom of Bavaria vulnerable to invasion from the south, and this aroused the liveliest apprehension in the capital, which was in no way alleviated when the government instituted measures of local defence. It was the fear of the war coming home to Munich that catapulted the left-wing Socialist Kurt Eisner to power. A student of Kant and Nietzsche, a journalist who had been on the editorial board of *Vorwärts* from 1898 to 1905, an ardent opponent of revisionism, and, since its founding in 1917, the leader of the Independent Socialist party in Bavaria, this extraordinary demagogue had spent most of 1918 in prison at Neudeck and Stadelheim because of his anti-war agitation. Released on 14 October, he sensed the popular temper and addressed himself to it. On 3 November, before an immense crowd on the Theresienwiese, he attacked a planned constitutional reform that had been initiated by the Bavarian Crown as both insincere and inadequate and declared, 'Across the border we greet the new Austrian Republic, and we demand that a Bavarian regime instituted by the people proclaim peace together with the German republicans of Austria in the name of Germany, since neither the will nor the power exists in Berlin to reach an immediate peace.'[9]

Words like this, which spoke to the main concern of the people of Munich, gave Eisner a moral ascendancy that enabled him to defy the royal government's attempts to hamper his activities and to outwit his Socialist rivals. On 7 November, taking advantage of another huge gathering on the Theresienwiese, at which Erich Auer,

[8] *Die deutsche Revolution 1918–1919*, ed. Gerhard A. Ritter and Susanne Miller (Frankfurt-on-Main, 1968), pp. 52–4; Horn, *Naval Mutinies*, p. 235; Richard A. Comfort, *Revolutionary Hamburg: Labor Politics in the Early Weimar Republic* (Stanford, 1966), pp. 30 ff.

[9] Allan Mitchell, *Revolution in Bavaria, 1918–1919: The Eisner Regime and the Soviet Republic* (Princeton, 1965), p. 87.

the Majority Socialist leader, counselled his audience to restrict themselves to peaceful demonstration, Eisner led his followers, who included soldiers and representatives of the Bavarian Peasants' League, in a march to the Guldein School, a temporary barracks, where they seized arms and then proceeded to the other city garrisons. By nightfall all military headquarters in Munich were in their hands, and before midnight bright red posters were being plastered on walls throughout the city announcing the establishment of a Bavarian Republic. On the following day, Eisner set up a cabinet of Independent and Majority Socialists, retaining the posts of Prime Minister and Foreign Minister for himself, promised that in due course a National Assembly would draft a constitution, and assigned the task of maintaining public order to councils that would be elected in the barracks, workshops, and villages. He justified the *coup* by declaring:

The democratic and social republic of Bavaria has the moral force to effect a peace for Germany that will protect it from the worst. The present overturn was necessary in order at the last moment to regulate the course of events by means of popular self-government without too great disruption before enemy armies flooded across the frontiers or demobilized German troops brought chaos into the land after the armistice.[10]

The events in Bavaria, which seemed to forecast the imminent dissolution of the Bismarckian Reich, decided the fate of the Hohenzollern dynasty. They convinced Prince Max that the situation was beyond his control and led him, on the morning of 9 November, to announce the resignation of his government. In a last effort to shore up the crumbling foundations of the state, he made it known that the Emperor and the Crown Prince intended to relinquish their rights to the throne and that the head of the Social Democratic party, Friedrich Ebert, was to be named Reich Chancellor and charged with the task of calling a Constituent Assembly to determine the form which the new state should take.[11] There was nothing in this announcement or in the words uttered by Ebert when he received the seals of office about establishing a republic, and Ebert himself was temperamentally attached to the monarchy, for which two of his sons had died. But it was too late to save it now. After Eisner's action in Munich, the tide was running so heavily in the direction of republicanism that Ebert and his colleagues felt it necessary to go with it if they were not to be passed by the not unskilful navigators of the extreme left. At 2 p.m. on 9 November, therefore, Philipp Scheidemann, the second ranking member of the Majority Socialist

[10] Ritter, *Die deutsche Revolution*, p. 58.
[11] Max von Baden, *Erinnerungen*, pp. 630–43.

executive, ended a speech before a mass demonstration in the Reichstag square by shouting, 'The Hohenzollerns have abdicated. Long
live the great German Republic!'[12]

The first half of that declaration was not strictly accurate, for it was
not until late in the evening that William II resigned himself to the
inevitable and fled across the border into Holland.[13] As for the rest, it
was merely an expression of hope in the viability of something that
few people had thought enough about to know whether they wanted
it or not. Their judgement would in the end depend upon what
substance was given to the word and by whom.

II

In the latter part of 1919 Oswald Spengler was to write scornfully of
the Majority Socialists, 'It is without parallel. They suddenly had
what they had been working for for forty years, full power, and they
regarded it as a misfortune.'[14] This should be taken for what it was,
an early example of right-wing polemics; as far as the facts go,
Spengler was accurate neither with respect to the mood of the party
nor to its actual situation. To talk of anyone having full power in
November 1918 was to close one's eyes to the fact that the political
confusion caused by revolutionary *coups*, the abdication of the
princes, and, after the armistice was concluded on 11 November, the
disorders caused by wandering bands of leaderless and undisciplined
troops was so great that it was literally impossible for anyone in
Berlin to know what was going on in much of the country. There
was nothing that Ebert and his colleagues could do for the time being
to affect the course of events in Munich or Braunschweig; and even
in Berlin itself their power—which, in the last analysis, derived from
an act of dubious constitutional propriety, Prince Max's surrender of
the chancellorship to Ebert—was challenged by the soldiers' and
workers' councils, the Independent Socialists, and the Spartacus
Union.

The most formidable of these opponents were the Spartacists. The
councils had developed no coherent programme and no leaders of
any consequence, and the Independents were a divided and, at critical
moments, indecisive party. A Dutch observer told Carl Sternheim at
the end of November that they reminded him of the muddled band

---

[12] See Philipp Scheidemann, *Memoiren* (2 vols., Dresden, 1928), ii. 310–14.

[13] On the background of the Emperor's flight, see Maurice Baumont, *The Fall of the
Kaiser* (New York, 1931) and *Das Ende der Monarchie 9.11.18*, ed. Werner Conze
(Berlin, 1952).

[14] *Preußenthum und Sozialismus*, p. 9.

of juvenile brigands in Max Reinhardt's production of Schiller's *Die Räuber*.[15] But the Spartacus Union, which was to become the Communist party of Germany (KPD) in January 1919, was a more serious threat, for it possessed two outstanding leaders, Karl Liebknecht, the son of one of the founders of the Social Democratic party, and the remarkable Polish revolutionary, Rosa Luxemburg. A theoretician of importance—Franz Mehring described her study of imperialism as 'a truly magnificent, fascinating achievement without its equal since Marx's death'[16]—Rosa Luxemburg deserves to be remembered even more for her insight into the nature of political action.[17] Her views had been shaped by her experience of the revolution of 1905 and by her progressive disillusionment with German Social Democracy, which in her opinion had withdrawn from the tasks of real life to devote itself exclusively to the growth of the party organization. She believed that revolutions were made by the spontaneous will of the masses but often baulked of their goals by the short-sightedness of party bureaucrats. A revolution would be 'great and strong as long as the Social Democrats don't smash it up'.[18] In 1918, intent upon a social and moral transformation of Germany, she regarded the quintessential party man Ebert as the enemy.

This was shrewd enough. Ebert had been chosen as head of the SPD when Bebel died in 1913 because of his administrative talents and because he represented the prevailing revisionist temper of the party.[19] Rosa Luxemburg's faith in the natural impulses of the working class he regarded as romantic and potentially dangerous. His view, expressed by Friedrich Stampfer in *Vorwärts*, was that 'Socialism is organization. Disorganization is the worst enemy of socialism.' He was determined, above all, that the scenes of violence and civil war that had accompanied the Bolshevik Revolution in Russia should not be repeated in Germany, and in order to prevent that he wanted to end the tumultuous transitional state into which Germany had fallen on 9 November by an act that would legitimize authority and restore the public law, the summoning of a National Assembly that would write a new constitution and lay the basis for the real-

[15] Carl Sternheim, 'Die deutsche Revolution' (1918), in *Gesamtwerke*, ed. Wilhelm Emrich, vi (Berlin, 1966), p. 86. This early judgement is borne out by the comprehensive study of the party, David W. Morgan, *The Socialist Left and the German Revolution: A History of the German Independent Social Democratic Party, 1917–1922* (Ithaca, 1975).

[16] Franz Mehring, *Briefe an Freunde* (Zurich, 1950), p. 84.

[17] See Nettl, *Luxemburg* ii, esp. 544 ff.

[18] Hannah Arendt, *Men in Dark Times* (New York, 1968), p. 52.

[19] Schorske, *Social Democracy*, pp. 123 ff.

ization of political democracy and a programme of systematic social-ization.

His efforts to promote this end by establishing an effective pro-visional ministry were blocked, in the first instance, by the Inde-pendent Socialists; and when he finally succeeded in forming a joint cabinet with them, the Council of People's Representatives, he was forced to give his assent to the principle that sovereign power resided in the soldiers' and workers' councils. The Berlin councils proceeded to elect an Executive Committee that henceforth claimed a right of control over the People's Representatives, a claim that Ebert was soon resisting because he convinced himself that the new body was a front for the left-wing Independents and the Spartacists. The tug-ging and hauling that ensued seriously weakened the Council's ability to maintain order in the capital, in which demonstrations, strikes, and armed mobs were daily occurrences in December and January. The fact that the cafés and *Kneipen* remained open and that the trams continued to run[20] is doubtless a tribute to the stubbornness of normal routine and a reminder that most people do not bother to participate in the events that determine the political circumstances of their lives. It does not alter the fact that the continuous alarums and excursions caused damage to property and loss of life,[21] and that the government's inability to control them was an ominous indication that this violence might become prevalent enough to dissolve the fabric of society completely.

Confronted with this possibility, Ebert made the decision that has, in judgements of his career, overshadowed anything else that he ever did. He decided to ally himself with the Supreme Army Command against the threat of the extreme left. There is no doubt that he was disposed to do so even before the threat became manifest. On the night of 9 November he had received a telephone call from General Wilhelm Groener, who had replaced Ludendorff in the Supreme Command when that volatile commander had counselled a breaking-off of the armistice discussions and a resumption of the war. Groener was a Württemberger with political ideas that were less anachronistic than those of most of his colleagues; as head of the Kriegsamt during the war, he had shown the ability to work effec-tively with the trade unions; and he was realist enough to see the advantages, for the country and for the army, of a continuation of

---

[20] Kessler, *Tagebücher*, p. 28. See also Ernst Troeltsch, *Spektator-Briefe. Aufsätze über die deutsche Revolution und die Weltpolitik 1918–22* (Tübingen, 1924), p. 30 (14 Jan. 1919).

[21] See e.g. the eyewitness account of the bloodshed at the Oranienburger Tor on 6 December, in *Die deutsche Revolution*, pp. 118–19.

this partnership in expanded form. When he telephoned Ebert, Groener placed the army at the disposal of the new Chancellor, asking in return that the government make every effort to prevent the disruption of the railway system during the withdrawal of the field army from France and that, above all, it promise to combat the forces of Bolshevism on the home front. It is understandable that, in the confusion that reigned in the first hours after his assumption of office, Ebert should have grasped at this implied recognition of the new government by the Supreme Command.[22] More questionable was the stubbornness with which he remained true to this telephonic pact in the subsequent period, when it was more difficult to justify it.

It has been argued persuasively that the Chancellor took an exaggerated view of the Red menace and missed an opportunity to exploit the energy and will represented by the soldiers' and workers' councils in order to mobilize working-class enthusiasm for the new regime. Whatever influence the Bolshevik model may have had in stimulating the council movement in the first place, the majority of its members, as Noske had discovered in Kiel, were moderate in their views and objectives and far more interested in the restoration of civil order and economic security than in ideological issues.[23] Ebert was given an indication of this at an early date, when a Congress of Councils from all over the country assembled in the Zirkus Busch in Berlin on 16 December. The widespread expectation that this would offer an opportunity for a leftish putsch proved to be without foundation. Indeed, the assembled delegates refused to give the Spartacus Union any voice in their deliberations, elected a new executive that was composed entirely of Majority Socialists, and placed themselves squarely behind Ebert's plan for the election of a National Constituent Assembly at the earliest possible date.

On only one subject did the Congress show a will of its own, and that was the future constitution of the military establishment. The delegates voted for the immediate dismissal of Field-Marshal von Hindenburg and the dissolution of the schools (Kadettenhäuser) which had in the past been the first stage in the education that produced the officer corps. Not content with that, they showed

---

[22] On the famous telephone call, see Sir John W. Wheeler-Bennett, *The Nemesis of Power: The German Army in Politics, 1918–1945* (London, 1953), p. 21. On Ebert's motives, see Arthur Rosenberg, *Geschichte der Weimarer Republik*, ed. Kurt Kersten (Frankfurt-on-Main, 1961), pp. 37 f.

[23] See esp. F. L. Carsten, *Revolution in Central Europe, 1918–1919* (London, 1972), pp. 68 ff., 127 ff., 325 ff.

overwhelming approval for a seven-point programme proposed by Walter Lampl of Hamburg which called for the replacement of the old military system by a popular militia (Volkswehr) that elected its own officers and was under the over-all command of the cabinet and the Executive Committee.[24] These were not new demands. They had been made in the Prussian Constituent Assembly in May 1848 only to be dropped when a sudden flaring-up of mob violence in the capital and the incapacity of the civil guard to deal with it destroyed confidence in the idea of a militia.[25] In December 1918 the proposals for a radical reorganization of the military establishment suffered a similar fate.

As soon as the Congress had finished its deliberations, Ebert received a visit from General Groener and his chief aide, Major Kurt von Schleicher, who informed him that unless the Lampl resolutions were rejected out of hand the assurances made by Groener in the army's name on 9–10 November would be revoked and the government left to its own resources. It is impossible to say how Ebert would have responded to this threat if he had been given time for reflection. His immediate answer was temporizing, a rather ambivalent promise that Lampl's resolutions would not apply to the field army.[26] This, unfortunately, was immediately interpreted by the Independent Socialists as a betrayal and led ultimately to their withdrawal from the cabinet. Even before they had taken this step, one of their ministers, Emil Barth, an impetuous man of small judgement, had begun to stir up the sailors' and workers' councils of Berlin. The result was a rash of new disorders, beginning on 23 December, when the most radical and undisciplined of the councils, the People's Naval Division, surrounded the Reich Chancellery and for a time held the government captive, and escalating day by day until 5 January, when 200,000 workers, carrying flags and weapons, marched in the streets to protest against a government attempt to restore discipline in the security police by dismissing its commander. Under the pressure of these events and of clear signs that the Spartacists were not only fomenting the agitations but were planning a *coup*, Ebert abandoned

[24] See *Allgemeiner Kongress der Arbeiter- und Soldatenräte Deutschlands: Stenographische Berichte* (Berlin, 1918), pp. 61–5.

[25] Craig, *Prussian Army*, pp. 111–12; Erich Kaeber, *Berlin 1848* (Berlin, 1948), pp. 115 ff., 168 ff.

[26] Ebert's modifications of the points, made at a meeting of the Provisional Government and the new Executive Council with Groener on 20 December, also exempted the frontier defence forces and the navy. See Holger H. Herwig, 'The First German Congress of Workers and Soldiers Councils and the Problem of Military Reforms', *Central European History*, i, no. 2 (June 1968), 160–3.

any thought he may have had about implementing the military demands of the Congress.

He was certainly influenced in this decision by the patent unreliability of existing militia forces. Ever since November attempts had been made to form watch regiments and security guards and republican defence corps in the major cities, and these efforts were redoubled at the end of December when Ebert appointed Gustav Noske to one of the seats in the cabinet vacated by the Independents and empowered him, as Minister of Defence, to raise a force capable of defending the government. Noske quickly discovered that there was no disposition on the part of the working class to assume military duties of any kind and that the existing republican units and the few new ones that he succeeded in forming could not be counted on to control and disperse anti-government demonstrations.[27] When the Spartacists (now the Communist party) decided, after much vacillating, to make a serious attempt to capture the centre of Berlin and, on the night of 5–6 January, assaulted and captured such positions as the *Vorwärts* building and the Wolff Telegraph Bureau, the Berlin Sicherheitswehr proved to be as ineffectual as the Bürgerwehr had proved to be during the attack upon the Berlin armoury in June 1848. Apart from a few isolated exceptions, they surrendered without firing a shot.

Faced with what appeared to be an imminent Communist takeover of the capital and alarmed by reports of Polish incursions in Posen and Silesia and Bolshevik activity in the Baltic lands, uncomfortably close to East Prussia, Ebert and Noske fell back upon the support of the Supreme Command. By this time Hindenburg and Groener had few reliable units of the regular army left at their disposal, but in December, prompted by a memorandum from General Ludwig von Maercker, the former Commander of the 214th Infantry Division, they had begun to encourage former officers to recruit volunteer forces on their own. The ease with which these free corps were raised was in sharp contrast to the abortive efforts to form an effective Volkswehr.[28] Demobilized lieutenants and N.C.O.s who found it difficult to adjust to civilian life, university students and adventurers, patriots and drifters responded to appeals like the one posted by Maercker:

The place of the Imperial Government has been taken by that of Reichs-

---

[27] Harold J. Gordon, jun., *The Reichswehr and the German Republic, 1919–1926* (Princeton, 1957), pp. 18–21; Troeltsch, *Spektator-Briefe*, p. 36 (28 Jan. 1919).

[28] On the origins and development of this idea, see Robert G. L. Waite, *Vanguard of Nazism: The Free Corps Movement in Germany, 1918–1923* (Cambridge, Mass., 1952).

kanzler Ebert. . . . It needs strength for the struggle on our borders and the struggle within. In the east the Russian Bolsheviks, the Poles, and the Czechs are standing on Germany's frontiers and threatening them. Inside the Reich chaos is mounting. Plunder and disorder are everywhere. Nowhere can one find respect for law and justice, respect for personal and government property. . . . Therefore, we must intervene![29]

Their devotion to the fatherland was undeniable, but—as Friedrich Meinecke asked himself as he listened to a column of troopers near the Luisenstift on the Podbielski Allee in Dahlem Dorf, whistling 'Heil dir im Siegerkranz'—how loyal would they be to the Republic?[30] When Colonel Wilhelm Reinhard, one of the first free corps commanders, was asked by a journalist whether he had not called the government a rabble and the new flag a Jewish rag, he cheerfully admitted having said something of the sort and then added, under further questioning, 'I make no bones of the fact that I am a monarchist. My God! when one has served his king and his country faithfully for thirty years, he can't suddenly say, "Starting tomorrow I'm a republican!" But you don't have to be afraid. I don't believe it's possible to set up a monarchy again in a minute. The Allies wouldn't let us do that in any case. But what will happen in ten years time—.'[31]

It was upon units led by men like Reinhard, armed and supplied from regular army depots, and placed under the over-all command of General Walther Lüttwitz, that Ebert and Noske believed they had to rely if their government was to survive in January 1919. The free corps gave them the order that they wanted, but at fateful cost. On 10 January the Reinhard Brigade opened the bloody and protracted campaign against Communism by a successful assault upon Spartacist headquarters at Spandau, while the Potsdam Free Corps of Major Stephani, using flame-throwers, machine-guns, mortars, and artillery, retook the *Vorwärts* building. On the eleventh Noske himself, at the head of 3,000 men, marched from his headquarters in Dahlem by way of Potsdamerstraße and Leipzigerstraße to the Tiergarten, Wilhelmstraße, and the Berlin Rathaus, receiving cheers in middle-class Charlottenburg and being unopposed elsewhere. Further columns entered Berlin from Lichterfelde and Zehlendorf and proceeded methodically to bring the city under control. There was little organized fighting—the Spartacist action had been ill pre-

[29] *Das Heer und die Republik: Quellen zur Politik der Reichswehrführung 1918 bis 1933*, ed. Otto-Ernst Schüddekopf (Hannover and Frankfurt-on-Main, 1955), p. 48.
[30] Meinecke, *Straßburg, Freiburg, Berlin*, p. 277.
[31] Schüddekopf, *Heer und Republik*, pp. 50 f.

pared and badly supported—and the rebel dead numbered not much above 100, at the cost of 13 free corps men killed and 20 wounded.[32]

Among the Communist casualties were Karl Liebknecht and Rosa Luxemburg, who were captured on 15 January, along with Wilhelm Pieck, a member of the Revolutionary Committee, by units of the Garde-Kavallerie-Schützen-Division. Pieck managed to survive and lived to become the first President of the German Democratic Republic after 1945. Luxemburg and Liebknecht were not so lucky. Interrogated in the Eden Hotel, they were escorted from that place on the pretext of being taken to the Moabit prison. As they left the hotel, they were hit over the head by a rifle-butt wielded by a soldier named Runge and then dragged into separate cars. Liebknecht was forced out of his motor car as they passed through the Tiergarten and was shot by a Captain Pflug-Hartung for 'trying to escape', his body then being delivered to a mortuary without any identifying information. Luxemburg was shot by a Lieutenant Vogel and her body thrown into the Landwehrkanal, where it remained undiscovered until the end of May.[33] These brutal murders inflicted a wound upon the German working-class movement from which it did not recover. Even those who had joined the Spartacus Union in 1918 and had subsequently become disillusioned with the course of German Communism found it difficult, if not impossible, to return to the party that had condoned, or seemed to condone, these vindictive executions.[34] The memory of Liebknecht and Luxemburg was to be one of the most potent factors in preventing a true reunion of the left even when Adolf Hitler was standing at the gates.

There was no time in Noske's busy headquarters to dwell upon what might be the future consequences of present action. Berlin was not the whole of Germany, and what happened in January in the capital had an inflammatory effect upon radical groups in other cities. But at the end of January Lüttwitz told the Minister of Defence that he had enough troops under arms to deal with the other centres of disaffection without endangering the security of the government, and he was as good as his word. In February and March the free corps of Maercker and Lichterschlag liquidated Spartacist insurrections in Bremen, Cuxhaven, and Wilhelmshaven, in Mülheim and Düsseldorf, and in Halle. In the second week of March a general strike in Berlin, called by the Independents and the Communists, led to heavy fighting in the streets and assaults upon police stations by Communist-led factory workers from Spandau, Hennigsdorf, and

[32] Gordon, *Reichswehr*, pp. 26–30.   [33] Nettl, *Luxemburg* ii. 774 f.
[34] Arendt, *Men in Dark Times*, p. 36.

Marienfelde, supported by the People's Naval Division and elements of the volatile Republican Defence Corps. Noske immediately concentrated 42,000 troops on the city and issued a notorious order that authorized the immediate execution of anyone taken with arms in hand. Spearheaded by Reinhard's troopers and the Guard Cavalry Rifle Division of the equally ruthless Captain Pabst, the free corps took liberal advantage of this *carte blanche*, and before resistance came to an end, killed 1,200–1,500 of their antagonists at a cost of 75 dead, 150 wounded, and 38 missing.[35]

Nor did the killing stop there. In April Maercker's Rifles restored order in Braunschweig and Magdeburg, while the free corps Goerlitz and Faupel took Dresden. In early May Maercker and Hülsen pacified Leipzig; and, finally, in the same month, the great *Säuberungsaktion* reached its climax with the conquest of Munich.

Kurt Eisner's fortunes, having mounted like a rocket, came down like a stick. While he gave himself over to a vain attempt to secure peace by establishing personal contact with Woodrow Wilson,[36] Bavaria experienced a marked economic deterioration, characterized by food and fuel shortages, rising prices, heavy unemployment, and the threat of insolvency because of unrealistic social welfare policies adopted in November. When parliamentary elections were held in January, Eisner's party suffered a humiliating defeat, and the Majority Socialists who were the chief beneficiaries of this insisted that he recognize these results and surrender his office to make way for a return to normal parliamentary practice. After trying to avoid this by appeals to Socialist unity and the objectives of the revolution, Eisner gave in. On 21 February, however, as he walked with his secretaries and armed guards towards the Landtag building to make his speech of resignation, he was shot and killed by a young nobleman named Arco-Valley. An hour later, in retaliation, a member of the Revolutionary Workers' Council entered the Landtag and gravely wounded the Majority Socialist leader, Erich Auer.[37]

The shots fired on 21 February marked the opening of a second wave of revolution in the Bavarian capital. Although the Landtag on 18 March authorized a cabinet under the Majority Socialist Johannes

[35] Craig, *Prussian Army*, pp. 360 f.; Gordon, *Reichswehr*, pp. 30–3.

[36] On 10 November F. W. Foerster, the well-known German pacifist, had carried an appeal for peace that had been drafted by Eisner to Professor George D. Herron in Switzerland and asked him to transmit it to the President, whose confidential agent he was widely supposed to be. See Herron Papers, Hoover Institution, Stanford University, II, Documents lxiii–lxv; Mitchell, *Revolution in Bavaria*, pp. 131 ff.; Mitchell Pirie Briggs, *George D. Herron and the European Settlement* (Stranford, 1932), pp. 64 ff.

[37] Mitchell, *Revolution in Bavaria*, esp. Ch. VIII.

Hoffman to issue the laws and proclamations necessary to restore order in the *Land*, the new Prime Minister was unable to alleviate the growing polarization between the parliamentary parties and the local soldiers' and workers' councils which, since the beginning of the year, had been infiltrated by the Communists. By the beginning of April large meetings of unemployed in the beer cellars of Munich were calling for revolutionary action, and the temper of the town had become so ugly that Hoffman felt it expedient to move his government to Bamberg. Into the vacuum created by his flight moved as strange a band of tribunes as had been seen since the days of the Paris Commune—the anarchist philosopher Gustav Landauer, the young dramatist Ernst Toller, the poet of the Bohemian life, Erich Mühsam, whose chief political act was the writing of some verses called 'Der Lampenputzer' which slanged the Majority Social-ists, and a demented academic named Dr. Franz Lipp, who assumed the post of Foreign Minister and immediately dispatched a telegram to 'Comrade Pope, Peter's Cathedral, Rome', in which he accused Hoffman of having absconded with the key to his toilet and quoted Kant's *On Perpetual Peace*.[38]

The antics of this self-styled Soviet Republic were a reversion to the revolutionary play-acting that Alexander Herzen commented on after passing through Germany in 1848. They lasted only six days before their enterprise was hijacked by a more serious junta led by Eugen Leviné, a Russian-born follower of Rosa Luxemburg who was under orders of the Communist Executive in Berlin to take over the party in Bavaria. On 13 April, backed by a newly constituted executive of factory and soldiers' councils of Munich, Leviné pro-claimed the dictatorship of the proletariat and began rapidly to recruit a Red Army to defend Bavaria against external attack. It was a vain endeavour. A month earlier, when Béla Kun's Soviet was still functioning in Budapest and when there was a possibility of the Communists taking over in Vienna, Leviné might have expected support if he needed it, but in both those capitals communism was in retreat by mid-April, and there was nothing to dissuade the Ebert government from trying to do to Bavaria what it had already done in the rest of Germany.

The day after Leviné's Soviet was proclaimed, Johannes Hoffman, recognizing with some bitterness that his own forces lacked the numbers and the spirit to recapture his capital, appealed to Berlin for

---

[38] The telegram is reproduced in Tankred Dorst, Peter Zadek, and Hartmut Gehrke, *Rotmord oder I was a German* (Munich, 1969). This is a television play based on Dorst's play *Toller*.

assistance. Noske responded enthusiastically, ordering 20,000 troops to move south. Only half of these arrived in time for the *dénouement*, but these joined with free corps raised in northern Bavaria, like Epp's Bayrisches Schützenkorps and Freikorps Oberland, and with troops sent from Württemberg to form a well-equipped force of 22,000 men which advanced on Munich under the command of the Prussian Major-General von Oven. Its advance units, enraged by news that the Red Army had murdered ten hostages, broke into the city on 1 May and retaliated indiscriminately, shooting dozens of people on mere suspicion of revolutionary activity. The Bavarian Soviet collapsed quickly, and its leaders were rounded up. Landauer was beaten to death by soldiers; Leviné was tried and executed for treason; Toller and Mühsam received prison terms of ten and fifteen years respectively. In the streets a veritable White Terror reigned for weeks, during which almost a thousand people lost their lives.[39]

These liquidations in Munich removed the last threat to the Ebert government from the left. The consolidation of the government's authority had been achieved by violence and the employment of agents whose devotion to republican principles was exiguous. It is worth noting in passing that many of the praetorians who combated the Spartacus Union in 1919—and this number included Pflug-Hartung and Vogel, and Pabst, Faupel, and Reinhard—ended their careers as enthusiastic servants of Adolf Hitler. Yet even if Ebert had been fully aware of the risks that he was running when he placed his faith in the Supreme Command, it is unlikely that he would have followed a different policy than the one he chose. From the beginning his objective had been to preserve the unity of the Reich, to prevent a recurrence of the Russian tragedy on German soil, and to broaden the basis of the government of 9 November by means of an act of national legitimation,[40] and in his view the support of the Supreme Command and the free corps had been indispensable in assuring the election and assembling of the National Assembly that symbolized the attainment of that goal.

When the German people went to the polls in mid-January 1919, Ebert's Majority Socialist party received a total of $11\frac{1}{2}$ million votes and secured 163 of the Assembly's 421 seats. In contrast, the Independents, who had supported the council movement, polled only $2\frac{1}{4}$ million votes for 22 seats, and the Communists, who abstained, were unrepresented. The parties that came closest to matching the Major-

[39] Mitchell, *Revolution in Bavaria*, pp. 307 f., 319 ff.

[40] See e.g. D. K. Buse, 'Ebert and the German Crisis, 1917–1920', *Central European History*, v, no. 3 (Sept. 1972), esp. 245 ff.

ity Socialists were the ones that had been associated with them during the war and would be their closest associates in the days ahead—the Centre, with 6 million votes and 91 seats, and the German Democratic party (DDP), the heir of the old Progressive tradition, with 5½ million votes and 75 seats. The Conservatives, now renamed the German National People's party (DNVP), won 3 million votes and 44 seats, and the new German People's party (DVP) of Gustav Stresemann, the successor of the National Liberal party, won 19 seats with a vote slightly in excess of 1 million.

These results, whatever else they proved, hardly constituted a strong vote of confidence for Ebert's party, which won only 38 per cent of the vote. Indeed, the returns seemed to show that something like the pre-war balance of parliamentary power had been restored.[41] What that meant was that, if socialist unity was the first casualty of Ebert's policy, socialization was the second, for the Majority Socialists were no longer strong enough to implement it alone.

It is, however, doubtful that Ebert and his closest associates regarded this as a loss. In November the Council of People's Representatives had recognized the appreciable party pressure for a thoroughgoing social and economic transformation of the country and had set up a special Socialization Commission to advise the government on means of achieving such a change. This nine-man board of experts, which included Karl Kautsky and Rudolf Hilferding and, at a later date, the economist Joseph Schumpeter, began to draft plans for the speedy nationalization of heavily concentrated industries like coal and iron. But from the start its work was regarded with suspicion by party dignitaries who feared the disruptive effects of precipitate experimentation and who believed that the important thing was to achieve labour peace and full production as soon as possible. Ebert's speech on 10 December, in which he asserted, 'Work is the religion of socialism', expressed this feeling.[42]

The Commission encountered strong opposition also from Rudolf Wissell, who joined the Council of People's Representatives with Noske in December 1918 and became head of the Ministry of Economics in February, and his closest collaborator in that ministry, Wichard von Moellendorff. An engineer with a consuming interest in industrial organization, Moellendorff had been an associate of Walther Rathenau during the war and had been the author of the proposal for a raw materials board that was the basis for Rathenau's

[41] Helmut Heiber, *Die Republik von Weimar* (Munich, 1966), p. 31.

[42] Friedrich Ebert, *Schriften, Aufzeichnungen, Reden* (2 vols., Dresden, 1926), ii. 129.

Kriegsrohstoffabteilung.[43] He was an opponent equally of the kind of highly competitive free economy that, in his view, had helped cause the war and of the simplistic ideological faith that expropriating the expropriators would solve all economic problems. Instead he favoured a controlled economy with marked autarchic overtones, based on the collaboration of management and labour and managed by technocrats. Moellendorff's socialism was close to that preached by Spengler in *Preußenthum und Sozialismus* (1919), a book that had a profound effect on him; it emphasized nationalism rather than internationalism and discipline rather than voluntarism. Wissell, whose career had been in the trade union movement and who had the typical union functionary's distrust of party intellectuals and respect for discipline, as well as a personal dedication to the cause of social reform, strongly supported his aide's ideas.[44]

So strongly, indeed, that the Socialization Commission could make no headway with its plans and faded out of existence in March 1919. But nothing much came of the Wissell–Moellendorff schemes for a totally controlled economy either, apart from a Socialization Law, which stated in general terms that collectivity should be the goal of the government and the duty of all citizens, and a law for the national cartellization of the coal industry, which established a council of experts composed of equal numbers of members from government, management, and labour to supervise its implementation. Both these laws were voted by the National Assembly, without much enthusiasm, in March 1919. They had negligible results, and attempts by Wissell and Moellendorff to proceed to more elaborate and comprehensive forms of economic management, in which economic 'self-governing bodies' which bore a faint similarity to the workers' councils of 1919 and borrowed some features from British guild socialism played a prominent role, failed to win the support of either management or labour and were strongly opposed by the SPD's parliamentary allies, the Democrats and the Centrists. In July 1919 both men resigned from the Ministry, and socialization became a dead letter.

This was probably inevitable. The government was confronted with too many other problems and crises in 1919 and 1920 to be able to devote much time to serious economic and social planning.

[43] See above, Ch. X, p. 354.

[44] On Wissell, see David Edward Barclay, 'Social Politics and Social Reform in Germany, 1890–1933: Rudolf Wissell and the Free Trade Union Movement' (Dissertation, Stanford Univ. 1974), esp. Ch. III.

III

The delegates who had been elected to the National Assembly in mid-January assembled a month later in Weimar, the home of Goethe and his patron Carl August and of the mighty poet who had sought to teach his countrymen that greatness should be defined not in terms of material power but of moral stature and devotion to liberty. Cynics might suggest that in an age in which the words of Schiller's hero Wallenstein seemed to be all too true—'Dem bösen Geist gehört die Erde, nicht dem guten'—this home of the Muses was perhaps rather remote from the real world, but few could deny that it was a more appropriate locale for the laying of the foundations of a free Germany than Potsdam or Berlin. And that was the task that engaged it—after it had elevated Friedrich Ebert to the office of Reichspräsident and authorized his party to undertake negotiations with the others for the formation of a government—from February until August, when the Weimar constitution was promulgated.

In its time this document was celebrated for the consistency and thoroughness of its embodiment of the idea of popular sovereignty; with the benefit of hindsight, we are more apt to be impressed by the hidden flaws, some of them inherent in its virtues, that contributed to the downfall of the Republic that it was designed to preserve. Its clauses assumed a desire for democracy and an understanding of the responsibilities that go with it that were not nearly as widespread in the Germany of 1919 as its drafters seemed to believe. Many of those who were loudest in their professions of democracy were in their hearts as monarchist as the outspoken Colonel Reinhard. They adopted democracy as a means of persuading the Allies to grant Germany lighter peace terms, and when the victorious Powers in Paris refused to oblige, they reverted to their true sentiments with a vengeance. As for the great majority of the German people, they had not been prepared by the course of their country's history or the example of their great men to understand or desire democratic government. What, after all, was to be expected of the ordinary German when a Thomas Mann could say in 1918: 'I don't want the trafficking of Parliament and parties that leads to the infection of the whole body of the nation with the virus of politics. . . . I don't want politics. I want impartiality, order, and propriety. If that is philistine, then I want to be a philistine.'[45] It was indeed philistine—a variant of the *spießbürgerliche* belief that 'the best government is a good

[45] Thomas Mann, *Betrachtungen*, p. 253.

administration'. It was not a very good foundation for a democratic republic.

This was nevertheless what the constitution, in its first article, proclaimed the German Reich to be, adding bravely, 'Political authority derives from the people'; and the later articles underlined the people's powers and rights and guaranteed them as far as words were capable of doing so. They were to elect the Reichspräsident by secret, direct, and universal suffrage; their will was to be given legislative expression in the Reichstag, whose powers were more considerable than those of its imperial counterpart, whereas those of the Reichsrat, which represented the member states, were purely nominal. All legislation was to originate in the Reichstag, and before its members the Chancellor and other cabinet ministers had to defend their policies.

In their zeal to achieve the fullest possible expression of democratic government, the framers of the constitution provided for the use of proportional representation in elections to the Reichstag and introduced the wholly untried practice of popular initiative and referendum. Much disruption was to result from these innovations. Proportional representation is doubtless the most effective method of assuring that all shades of opinion find expression, but it works best in time of political and social peace and in situations where there is general acceptance of rules of political intercourse and competition. Neither of these conditions obtained in post-war Germany, and the new electoral method had the effect of complicating the legislative process by increasing the number of parties and making it unlikely that any single party would command a majority. This made coalition government inevitable, while also jeopardizing the security of the Republic by giving representation and an opportunity for publicity and growth to anti-republican splinter groups that might otherwise have died of lack of attention. All of this made for an inherent instability that manifested itself in what appeared to the bemused spectator to be a continuous game of musical chairs as coalitions were made and unmade and ministries formed and reformed. This and the too frequent dissolution of the Reichstag, and the new elections that this necessitated, tended to reduce general respect for parliamentary government.

In the same way, the institution of initiative and referendum, partly because it was unaccompanied by safeguards against misuse, had unfortunate results. The conditions for making a referendum necessary on any issue were so easy to fulfil that enemies of the Republic could use it for purposes of obstruction, as they did, for example, during the debate over the Young Plan in 1929, which was one of the major stepping-stones in Adolf Hitler's ascent to power. It is not too much to say that their faith in democracy led the framers of the constitution to overlook the cautionary advice of the great nineteenth-century liberal advocates of representative government, like John Stuart Mill, and to give a dangerously exaggerated role to the plebiscitary power, which could be used to set aside considered votes in either Reichstag or Reichsrat.

The plebiscitary counterpoise to parliamentary power found expression also in the position of the President, who was elected by direct vote of the people for a period of seven years and given extensive powers. In addition to the command of the armed forces, these included the right to appoint and dismiss the Chancellor, to dissolve Parliament and order new elections, and, in certain contingencies, to call for national referenda. It has sometimes been said that, in defining the President's powers, the members of the National Assembly were overcome by historical sentimentality and subconsciously created an Ersatz-Kaiser. But even the old Emperor had never been specifically authorized to set aside the basic law of the land, as was true in the case of the Reichspräsident. Article 48 of the Weimar constitution stated explicitly: 'Should public order and safety be seriously disturbed or threatened, the President may take the necessary measures to restore public order and safety; in case of need, he may use armed force . . . and he may, for the time being, declare the fundamental rights of the citizen to be wholly or partly in abeyance.' The majority that approved this sweeping grant of power were doubtless thinking of the troubles that had filled the first six months of the Republic's existence and were making sure that the executive had enough power to deal with renewed Communist disorders. They thought that they were making a sensible provision for exceptional conditions and can perhaps be forgiven for their failure to conceive of the exceptional becoming the normal. That failure of imagination, nevertheless, made representative government vulnerable to attack by any extra-parliamentary force that was supported by the President's emergency powers. This was a constitutional anomaly that became critical in the years after 1930.

Not all of the weaknesses of the constitution were rooted in excessive democratic zeal. One at least arose from a change that could be considered undemocratic—a reform of the electoral law to abolish the single-member constituency and to base representation in the Reichstag on party lists. This tended to elevate the party caucus to a dominant position and to reduce the independence of the party's

Reichstag delegation in general and of those who served as ministers in coalition governments in particular. Ministries came to exist at the sufferance of party organizations which had the power to order their representatives to withdraw if their wishes were not met, a fact that greatly increased the normal instability of coalition government, while vastly complicating the task of forming viable combinations of parties.[46]

Other problems were posed by the National Assembly's failure to deal with the old issue of centralization versus states' rights. Throughout the history of the Republic there was intermittent discussion of *Reichsreform*—the idea of re-ordering the federal structure of Germany in such a way as to centralize power in the national government and to reduce the rest of the country to homogeneous and identical units with uniformly subordinate institutions—but it remained an aspiration. The enduring strength of particularism was demonstrated even during the tumultuous period that began in November 1918, for the various states had their own revolutions that were often little influenced by the course of events in the national capital. One of the factors that contributed to the decline of Johannes Hoffman's prestige in Bavaria and made him vulnerable to the attack of the extreme left was his failure to take an intransigent stand against any diminution of Bavaria's pre-war privileges during the National Assembly's discussions of the question of states' rights. Other provincial leaders were more determined opponents of centralization than Hoffman was; and as the debate went forward many who might have been expected to be centralizers wavered or swung to the other side. It was clear, for example, that *Reichsreform* would make little sense unless Prussia's position in the Reich were reduced. But could the SPD, which favoured centralization in principle, really be expected to support the old cry of 1848 'Preußen muß aufgehen!' at the cost of their own political dominance in Prussia and the influence it gave them over most of Germany? Many Socialists did not believe so and were at one with the soldiers and the bureaucrats in wanting no change.[47]

[46] Godfrey Scheele, *The Weimar Republic* (London, 1946), p. 49.

[47] See Heiber, *Republik*, pp. 40–1. A diminution of Prussia's role, moreover, might be expected to mean the partition of that state. Opponents of this feared that it would lead to French domination of a new Rhine province. See Karl Dietrich Erdmann, *Adenauer in der Rheinlandpolitik nach dem Ersten Weltkrieg* (Stuttgart, 1966), pp. 212 ff.; Henning Köhler, *Autonomiebewegung oder Separatismus: Die Politik der 'Kölnischen Zeitung' 1918–1919* (Berlin, 1974), pp. 61 ff. On the frustrations of those who believed in *Reichsreform*, see Arnold Brecht, *Aus nächster Nähe: Lebenserinnerungen 1884–1927* (Stuttgart, 1966), pp. 413 ff. and *Mit der Kraft des Geistes: Lebenserinnerungen 1927–1967 Reiches vom 11. August 1919* (11th edn., Berlin, 1929), pp. 89 ff.

And that is pretty much what they got. There was some diminution in the powers of the separate states. Those that had been left by Bismarck with control over their own armed forces and the right of independent representation in foreign affairs now forfeited those privileges, and all federal states lost what had in the past been their principal means of exerting financial control over the Reich government when the old system of *Matrikularbeiträge* came to an end and the federal government received the right to assess direct taxes. But while they gave way on this, and while they acknowledged the national government's exclusive jurisdiction over foreign and colonial affairs, national defence, currency, customs duties, posts, telegraph, and telephone, and railways, and paid lip-service to the priority of its laws over local law and its right to lay down normative regulations, the separate states retained much power. They had concurrent rights in the matters that affected the lives of citizens most directly, notably in the area of civil and criminal law, religion, education, and social welfare. This overlapping of jurisdiction, and the additional fact that Reich laws on certain subjects could be effective only if implemented by state regulations, made quarrels over competence and open conflict inevitable.[48] The knowledge that the legitimacy of the Republic was widely challenged encouraged its enemies to exploit the ambiguities in the relationship between the separate states and the national government in order to defy the policies of the Reich, and, when this happened, it was not always easy for the national government to make a legal case for intervention. The year 1923 was to demonstrate how dangerous this clumsiness, which was perhaps unavoidable, could be.

Finally, the health and stability of the Republic were to suffer from faults of commission and omission with respect to the Civil Service, the administration of justice, and the educational system.

During the November days, both Reich and state governments were agreed that a radical reform of the Civil Service that included the dismissal of all officials who had served the Empire or local dynasties would be impractical and would merely increase the prevailing disorganization and confusion. This decision was confirmed by the Weimar constitution, which gave all members of the state service a guarantee of their 'well-earned rights' (Article 129, Paragraph 1) and recognized their freedom of political opinion and expression and association as long as this did not conflict with their loyalty to the state (Article 130, Paragraph 2). The result of this was

[48] On this complicated question, see Gerhard Anschütz, *Die Verfassung des Deutschen Reiches vom 11. August 1919* (11th edn., Berlin, 1929), pp. 89 ff.

that the administration of the Republic's business was left in the hands of professional civil servants who were perhaps not overtly anti-republican but shared a basically anti-democratic approach to government. This was particularly true in Prussia, where the effect of the Puttkamer reforms of the 1880s had impregnated the bureaucracy with an absolutist caste spirit that proved to be impossible to eradicate. Below the ministerial level, the great majority of the bureaucrats were more intent upon preserving the administrative methods of the Wilhelmine period than they were on adjusting to the requirements of a pluralistic society with a parliamentary government. Their scarcely concealed disdain of the ministerial instability caused by the constantly shifting coalitions was a silent manifestation of their true feelings about the Republic.[49]

More flagrant in the way in which they abused their positions were the judges. Article 54 of the constitution guaranteed their positions, and this was interpreted by many of them as giving them licence to express their prevalently monarchist sentiments from the bench, both in word and in deed. The Socialist jurist Gustav Radbruch, during his term as Reich Minister of Justice, complained that there existed 'a state of war between the people and the judiciary',[50] and his party colleague Julius Leber, who had like Radbruch felt it necessary in 1918 to insist upon the irremovability of judges, admitted later that it had been a mistake not to start with a clean slate.[51] In many German court-rooms after 1918, libellous attacks upon republican ministers and defamation of the Republic and its symbols were more likely to be commended than punished, and in the case of attempts to overthrow the Republic putschists of the right could generally expect more lenient treatment than left revolutionaries. Bavarian justice was notorious in this regard, and the excoriating pages that Lion Feuchtwanger devoted to it in his novel about Bavarian politics, *Erfolg*, are not exaggerated. This is illustrated by the difference between the harshness of the sentences

---

[49] Karl Dietrich Bracher, *Die Auflösung der Weimarer Republik: Eine Studie zum Problem des Machtverfalls in der Demokratie* (2nd edn., Stuttgart, 1957), pp. 177, 180 ff., 189, 190 f. See also Troeltsch, *Spektator-Briefe*, p. 89 (19 Dec. 1919).

[50] See Eugen Schiffer, *Die deutsche Justiz* (Berlin, 1928), p. 15, and Radbruch's memoirs, *Der innere Weg* (Stuttgart, 1951), p. 141 ff. Important also are Ernst Fraenkel, 'Die Krise des Rechsstaates und die Justiz', *Die Gesellschaft*, viii (1931), and Eckart Kehr, 'Zur Genesis der preußischen Bürokratie und des Rechtsstaates', ibid. ix (1932), reprinted in Kehr, *Economic Interest*, pp. 141–63 ('The Genesis of the Prussian Bureaucracy').

[51] Julius Leber, *Ein Mann geht seinen Weg: Schriften, Reden und Briefe, herausgegeben von seinen Freunden* (Berlin, 1952), pp. 127 ff.

imposed upon the members of the Bavarian Soviet after its liquidation in May 1919 and the ludicrous leniency given to the murderers of Kurt Eisner and Gustav Landauer. Count Arco's initial sentence of death was commuted to a brief term of fortress imprisonment; the soldier who kicked Landauer to death after shooting him received five weeks of fortress detention, while Major von Gagern, who watched the murder, got off with a fine of 300 R.M.

It would be a mistake to draw too sharp a distinction between Bavaria and other states in the way in which the law was applied in political cases. The federal penal code stipulated that anyone seeking by force to overthrow the constitution of the Reich or that of any of the single states should be punished by life imprisonment. The Prussian judges who tried the participants in the Kapp Putsch in 1920 and the Bavarian magistrates who sat in the case of Adolf Hitler, General Ludendorff, and their associates after the abortive revolution in November 1923 were alike in turning a blind eye to this statute and in meting out sentences that were nominal. Against this kind of encouragement of the Republic's enemies, the constitution gave no protection.[52]

Nor did it do anything to defend Germany's new democracy against the more subtle erosion of its foundations that was caused by the delinquencies of the educational system, which continued to be what it had been before the war, a buttress of the existing social system and a stronghold of uncritical nationalism, and which now took on a pronounced anti-republican colouration.

There were many people in 1918 and 1919 who believed that the political attitudes of German professors during the war had shown the need for a thoroughgoing shake-up of the system of faculty recruitment and promotion in the universities; and there was no lack of social reformers who wanted to equalize opportunity in secondary education and to remodel school curricula so as to inculcate democratic ideas. Their designs were defeated by the forces of particularism and religious differentiation, and also by a sedulously cultivated notion that, at a time when Germany was being treated as a pariah by the victorious democracies, its self-respect demanded that it should refuse to accept their values but reassert its own traditional ones.[53] The framers of the Weimar constitution yielded to

[52] See the uncompromising statement of Troeltsch in July 1922. *Spektator-Briefe*, p. 284.
[53] This was the argument, for example, of Carl Heinrich Becker, Prussian Minister of Education from 1925 to 1930, in his *Kulturpolitische Aufgaben des Reiches* (Berlin,

the stronger pressures and decided not to be innovative. While asserting the federal government's right and intention to issue normative regulations in educational matters (later fulfilled in the form of periodic Reich School Conferences), they left education as before in the hands of the separate states.

There was, in consequence, a paucity of reform on every level. In the universities the most notable changes were the increase in the number of women students (the introduction of women's suffrage had finally broken the stubborn resistance of the universities to admission of women, which had, in Prussia, continued until the eve of the war) and the establishment of democratically elected committees (Allgemeiner Studentenausschuß or ASTA) to represent student opinion. But the mandarins of the academic establishment fought implacably against any change in the governance or the curriculum of the universities. The monopoly of power remained in the hands of the full professors, a group that was almost monolithically conservative. They showed this by excluding from their ranks and privileges colleagues with unconventional views or research interests of which they disapproved for political reasons. In the field of modern history, as the young Berlin scholar Eckart Kehr pointed out in an angry attack upon the establishment, anyone who sought to investigate the economic and social history of the recent past was frozen out,[54] whereas praise and preferment were heaped on chroniclers like Adalbert Wahl, whose German History exceeded that of Treitschke in its scorn of liberal values and its latent anti-Semitism, and Konrad Bornhak, who wrote a laudation of the reign of William II that ran through several editions.[55]

The professors' opposition to democracy within the universities was reflected in their repudiation of the Republic. In using their lecture rooms for attacks upon 'the system', the natural scientists and professors of medicine were almost as unabashed as the historians, jurists, and Germanisten. Few of these pundits had any practical alternative to the regime they opposed; they were inveterate supporters of a dead past. There is no doubt that they helped infect their auditors with contempt for the Republic, although the students had no patience with the reactionary nonsense that they preached, much preferring, as time went on and the government's troubles mounted,

---

1919). On Becker's policies, see Kurt Düwel, 'Staat und Wissenschaft in der Weimarer Epoche', Historische Zeitschrift, Beiheft 1 (1971), 31 ff. On reform proposals and their fate, see Ringer, Mandarins, pp. 67–80.

[54] See Kehr, Economic Interest, pp. 174–88 ('Modern German Historiography').

[55] See Eschenburg, Improvisierte Demokratie, p. 291 n. 88.

to imbibe headier nostrums, like National Socialism, which by 1929 was the strongest movement in student politics in nineteen of Germany's universities.[56] The tendency might not have been so pronounced if anything had been done to broaden the social base of the student body, but this did not happen. In 1928 only 4·03 per cent of male students and 1·17 per cent of female students in German universities had working-class or lower-middle-class backgrounds, and the comparable figures for technical universities were 2·68 and 1·96 per cent.[57]

With respect to the lower schools, the constitution met the reformers' demand for equality of opportunity by specifying a uniform type of elementary school for all children (Articles 146, 147). The effect of this was somewhat reduced by the continued existence of preparatory schools for those who could afford the fees and the preference given to students of these schools by some secondary institutions. With respect to the latter, the constitution stipulated that admission was to be governed by talent rather than by the economic resources of the parents and urged regional and local authorities to provide financial assistance for poor children. During the period of the left-wing coalition government in Thuringia in 1922–3 something was done to implement these principles, but this did not last, and elsewhere financial stringency was widely used to evade the constitution's intention.

The most notable feature of secondary education during the Weimar period—apart from a healthy tendency, promoted by the Reich School Conferences of 1920–3, to raise the status of women's secondary education—was its retention of the social characteristics and intellectual values of the pre-war period. Even innovations pointed backwards. Thus, when the Prussian Ministry of Education established a new kind of rural secondary school, it was with the declared intention of nurturing 'the forces, found in village and small town, of healthiness, sureness of instinct, and indigenous characteristics' and of preventing the dominance of 'the spirit of the large city'. This was a veiled attack upon the Republic, the implication being that its leadership was un-German. The anti-republican tone

[56] See Walter Laqueur, *Weimar: A Cultural History* (New York, 1975), pp. 193 ff. See also Edward Yarnell Hartshorne, jun., *The German Universities and National Socialism* (Cambridge, Mass., 1937). A more differentiated study of susceptibility to National Socialism is Wolfgang Kreutzberger, *Studenten und Politik 1918–33: Der Fall Freiburg-im-Breisgau* (Göttingen, 1972).

[57] R. H. Samuel and R. Hinton Thomas, *Education and Society in Modern Germany* (London, 1949), p. 126. See also Hans Speier, 'Workers turning Bourgeois', in *Social Order and the Risks of War: Papers in Political Sociology* (New York, 1952), p. 61.

of the books placed in the hands of students of these and other schools was more intrusive and, indeed, often strident. History, government, and geography texts and anthologies of poetry not only abounded in aggressive nationalism and praise of the monarchical past but placed the responsibility for all of Germany's present misfortunes at the door of foreign Powers and the republican government. The handbooks in history in general use not only denied that Germany had any share in causing the war but insisted that its armies had not been defeated. As one Prussian text maintained:

In hand to hand fighting the German showed his superiority up to the last moment. But . . . the resistance of the Austrians, Bulgars and Turks had collapsed. . . . Worse news came: 'Sailors revolt in Kiel!'—'Revolution in Berlin!'—'The Emperor in Holland!' Thus, all possibility of a final resistance on the shortened line between Antwerp and Strasburg was gone!

Germany had, in short, been defeated by the very people who were now ruling it.[58]

The failure of those who wrote the Weimar constitution to draft regulations that would have prevented or corrected this sort of literary sabotage was, like their other failures, understandable, given the circumstances and the balance of political forces in 1919. But, of all their shortcomings, this was perhaps the most critical, for it allowed the post-war generation to be systematically indoctrinated with anti-democratic ideas.

IV

No subject agitated the textbook writers more or gave them a better excuse for oblique attacks upon the Republic than the Versailles Treaty. This was inevitable, for there were few Germans who were not left aghast when its terms were revealed. Having placed their faith in the American President and convinced themselves, by an extraordinary feat of wishful thinking, that the decisions made at Paris would be guided by the spirit of reconciliation that he had expressed in the speech announcing the Fourteen Points, they were outraged to discover that the victors intended to apply that older principle of settlement, *vae victis*. Most indignant, naturally, were those who had least cause to complain, the people who had luxuriated in the most grandiose dreams of conquest and material acquisition during the war. But even more reasonable persons, who had expected the terms to be severe and had even believed that their country deserved to be punished, were shocked by what appeared to

[58] On this, see above all Samuel and Thomas, *Education and Society*, esp. pp. 73 ff.

them to be the Entente's flagrant violation of their own declarations (for example, in their plundering of Germany's colonial empire), of the facts of history (in their attribution of exclusive responsibility for the war to Germany and its allies), and of the rules of economic reason (in the horrendous load of reparations that the war–guilt clause was intended to justify), and were left incredulous by their apparent lack of interest in the question whether Germany was to become a viable democracy or not (else why would they heap these indignities upon the new Republic?).

There is something to be said for this reaction. Apparently, the victorious Powers thought seriously about the relationship between Germany's domestic politics and the treatment to be accorded it only during the period when Béla Kun's Soviet seemed to be taking hold in Budapest. At that time, General Smuts and others urged the advisability of appeasing Germany in order to make it a reliable bulwark against Bolshevism, and Lloyd George was not unimpressed. But Béla Kun did not last, and the advocates of a Carthaginian peace had their way.[59] It would be too simple to say that their victory made the downfall of the Weimar Republic inevitable, for that was the result of many interconnected factors. But certainly the Versailles Treaty was directly responsible for two crises in 1919 and 1920 that seriously shook the authority of the new republican government and, incidentally, cast serious doubt on the reliability of its military allies.

The first of these came when the German Government received the terms of the Treaty on 7 May. The initial reaction of the Scheidemann cabinet was unanimously negative, and, in a speech in the Aula of the University of Berlin on 12 May, the Chancellor accused the Entente Powers of seeking to make the Germans 'slaves and helots . . . doing forced labour behind barbed wire and prison bars' and declared that acceptance of the Treaty would be incompatible with German honour. When the Allies, however, rejected German proposals for extensive amendment and, on 16 June, sent an ultimatum demanding acceptance within five days, the unity of the cabinet dissolved. Scheidemann, Brockdorff-Rantzau, the Foreign Minister, the Socialist Otto Landsberg, and the three Democratic party ministers held firm, but they were opposed by the rest of the cabinet, who were responsive to the arguments of Matthias Erzberger, who had led the delegation that signed the terms of the Allied armistice in November and now argued for acceptance of the

[59] See esp. Arno J. Mayer, *Politics and Diplomacy of Peacemaking: Containment and Counterrevolution at Versailles, 1918–1919* (New York, 1967), Chs. 15, 16, 17, 21, 22.

Treaty with a persuasive fatalism—which was to be remembered and made the excuse for his murder by rightist thugs in August 1921.[60] What was most galling to the Chancellor was that his Socialist colleagues in the cabinet and the Reichstag delegation failed to support him, the Fraktion voting 75 to 39 for acceptance of the Treaty. On 20 June, therefore, Scheidemann submitted the resignation of his cabinet to Ebert.

This first cabinet crisis in the Republic's history was complicated by what promised to become a soldiers' revolt. The military had special reasons for repudiating the Treaty. It stipulated that the army was to be reduced to 100,000 officers and men, without aircraft, armour, or offensive weapons, and that its General Staff, war academy, and cadet schools were to be dissolved. Until this reduction was accomplished, the Rhineland, which was to be permanently demilitarized, would be occupied by Entente troops. Simultaneously, the fleet, upon which William II and Tirpitz had lavished so much devotion, was to become a token force with no vessels exceeding 10,000 tons and no submarines. Finally, the Emperor and other war leaders were to be surrendered for trial on charges of violating the laws of war. The German officer corps felt insulted and demeaned by these terms, which also promised to destroy the calling to which they had devoted their lives.

As early as 15 May, a group of high-ranking officers, including General Walther Reinhardt, the commander of the provisional Reichswehr that was now being organized to take place of the old army, General von Below of the XVII Corps, and General von Loßberg of the army of the south, were discussing the possibility of rejecting the Treaty even at the cost of renewed military action, and they proved unresponsive to warnings from General Wilhelm Groener at the headquarters of the still existing Supreme Command that their ideas were impractical and potentially disastrous. The split in the cabinet and the highly ambiguous position adopted by Field-Marshal von Hindenburg encouraged Reinhardt and his friends to call a conference of commanding officers at Weimar on 19 June that was clearly designed to force the government to defy the Allies. On the eve of the meeting, indeed, Reinhardt asked Groener whether the Supreme Command would be willing to break with the government if it acceded to the terms and to lead an insurrectionary movement in the east. Groener indignantly rejected this proposal and, in order to bring the hotheads to their senses, mobilized an

---

[60] See Epstein, *Erzberger*, pp. 314–27, where the ratification of the treaty is called 'Erzberger's greatest single achievement'.

impressive group of municipal and provincial officials and parliamentarians. These persons made no bones of the fact that a military rising would receive minimal public support and might, indeed,
be greeted with resentment and sabotage. This shook the junta's
confidence, but they were stubborn and continued to insist that,
rather than accept the war-guilt clause, they would go ahead with
their military plans.

How serious they were about this was shown a few days later,
when the Allies, approached by the reconstructed cabinet led by the
Socialist Gustav Bauer with a request for the elimination of the
offensive clauses, curtly refused and demanded acceptance of the
Treaty by 23 June. The soldiers immediately prepared for action.
Below and Loßberg began to plan a defensive line along the Elbe; in
Berlin, General von Lüttwitz discussed contingency plans with his
staff; and the inspirer of the free corps, General Maercker, actually
went to Gustav von Noske with a proposal that he become the leader
of a military dictatorship.

What Noske would have done if left to his own devices it is
impossible to say. He had vacillated badly on the question of accepting the terms, but on the whole favoured rejection, and he was
always susceptible to the opinions of the soldiers and flattered when
they deferred to him. There is little doubt that he flirted with the
notion of following the course proposed by Maercker. He was,
however, prevented from doing anything of the sort by Ebert, who,
unlike his Minister of Defence, was not given to wavering in
moments of crisis. On 23 June, as the time-limit set by the Entente
ran out, the President telephoned Wilhelm Groener and told him that
he would throw his considerable weight on the side of rejection, if
the Supreme Command thought there was the slightest chance of
resistance being successful. He asked for an unequivocal answer by
mid-afternoon.

Groener answered for the Field-Marshal, who was adroit in avoiding responsibility for hard decisions. If the terms were rejected and
fighting were resumed, he told Ebert, Germany's position would be
hopeless, as all but the most romantic of the soldiers realized. There
was no alternative to acceptance. If the government took a firm line,
and if Noske as Minister of Defence made a public appeal to the
armed forces, explaining the necessity of the decision and calling for
the loyal support of every officer and man, the military resistance
would evaporate. Once again, as in the previous November, Ebert
was reassured by Groener's words. He followed his advice to the
letter, advised the cabinet to do their unhappy duty, and drove the

doubtful Noske into the breach. Within minutes of the expiration of
the ultimatum, the Versailles Treaty was accepted.[61]

Nevertheless, Groener rather underestimated the depth of the
military resentment, largely, one must suppose, because he regarded
all the generals involved, with the exception of Reinhardt, as intellectual light-weights. But even light-weights can be stubborn, and
men like Lüttwitz proved to be very much so. Their resistance to the
terms of the Treaty and their dissatisfaction with the government did
not end in June 1919. There was an unhappy sequel nine months
later.

This was prompted by the insistence of the Entente Powers that
the force limits set by the Treaty be met as quickly as possible and
that, to facilitate this, the disbanding of auxiliary forces begin forthwith, since the state of public order in Germany no longer warranted
their existence. In June 1919, and again with a more peremptory
urgency in August, the Council of Principal Allied Powers in Versailles ordered that all German forces be withdrawn from territory
that had belonged to Russia before 1914. This referred to the mixed
force of free corps and Baltic militia units which, in conjunction with
the forces raised by the Baltic governments and under the command
of General Rüdiger Count von der Goltz, had been engaged since
February 1919 in operations against the Bolsheviks in Lithuania and
Latvia. This campaign had succeeded in stemming the western surge
of Bolshevism, but, by June, friction had developed between Goltz's
insubordinate commandos and their Baltic hosts, and the Entente
governments thought it high time they be recalled and disbanded.[62]
At the same time, they became increasingly concerned about the
proliferation of private troops and local defence units that had taken
place in Germany during the first half of 1919. It was difficult to say
how significant a force these represented—somewhat later Lloyd
George was to complain about $3\frac{1}{2}$ million weapons in German
hands—but presumably there were more people under arms than the
Treaty authorized, and the Entente wanted to correct that situation.

There is no doubt that their policy was inconsistent and even
disingenuous. Just as they had tolerated the existence of Goltz's force
until it had, to their advantage, removed the Red threat to the Baltic,

---

[61] On this whole affair, see Craig, *Prussian Army*, pp. 367–73, and the authorities
cited there; also Schüddekopf, *Heer und Republik*, pp. 72–4, 92–6.

[62] On the Baltic adventure, see Waite, *Vanguard*, Ch. 5; E. O. Volkmann, *Revolution
über Deutschland* (Oldenburg, 1930), pp. 237–45, 306–11; Rüdiger Graf von der Goltz,
Meine Sendung in Finnland und im Baltikum (Leipzig, 1920) and *Als politischer General im
Osten 1918–1919* (Leipzig, 1936).

so did they, for a long time, avert their gaze from the Bavarian local defence force, the Einwohnerwehr, which under the energetic leadership of Georg Escherich reached a total membership of 250,000 by February 1920 and included mobile brigades of considerable size, one of them, Bund Oberland, numbering 9,600 men. This appears to have been due to speculation in certain agencies of the French Government about the possibility of using the Einwohnerwehr as a ploy in a scheme to loosen Bavaria's ties to the Reich and even to encourage separatism.[63] But apart from Bavaria Entente policy was reasonably unambiguous by the middle of 1919. The Baltic units were forced to come home, and the Allies pressed for their dissolution, together with that of all other units that could not be absorbed in the new Reichswehr without exceeding the figure of 100,000 laid down in the Treaty.

The government's attempts to comply led to a series of mutinous acts on the part of the soldiers. As early as July 1919, Captain Waldemar Pabst ordered units of the Guards Cavalry Rifle Corps to march on Berlin on the pretext that the Communists were about to seize the capital. This order was intercepted by Pabst's astonished superiors, and Pabst was dismissed and the Rifle Corps dispersed throughout the country.[64] But this was merely an earnest of more serious things to come. Pabst soon resurfaced as a leading spirit in a political organization called the National Association (Nationale Vereinigung) to which the most determined anti-republican leaders gravitated and which also attracted notables like General Ludendorff and his wartime associate, the sinister Colonel Bauer. Under the leadership of General von Lüttwitz and a not very distinguished East Prussian politician named Wolfgang Kapp, this body began to lay serious plans for the overthrow of the republican government.

Kapp had enough political intelligence to realize that this would involve careful groundwork and negotiation with potentially friendly elements in the party and industrial structure.[65] These refinements were lost on Lüttwitz, a stupid and arrogant man who believed that if one pounded the table hard enough civilians were bound to yield in terror. It was his discovery that this was not true that led him to launch the action that is remembered as the Kapp

[63] On the Einwohnerwehr, see the forthcoming study by David C. Large.
[64] See Gordon, *Reichswehr*, pp. 97–8.
[65] Most business men were surprised and angered by the putsch and did not support it, although this was not because of their devotion to the Republic. See Gerald D. Feldman, 'Big Business and the Kapp Putsch', *Central European History*, iv, no. 2 (June, 1971), esp. 101, 128 f.

Putsch. In February the government ordered the disbandment of two first-rate free corps, the Baltikum Brigade of Bisschoff's Iron Division, which had distinguished itself in the capture of Riga from the Bolsheviks in May 1919, and the 2nd Marine Brigade of Captain Hermann Ehrhardt. Their commanders appealed to Lüttwitz, and the choleric General stamped into Ebert's office and demanded the revocation of the orders, the cessation of the whole policy of troop reduction, the dismissal of the present head of the Reichswehr, General Reinhardt, who, despite his role in the crisis over the reception of the peace terms, was known for his republican sympathies,[66] new elections, and the appointment of a non-party government of experts. Somewhat overwhelmed by this bill of particulars, Ebert rejected them out of hand, and Noske, who was present, told the General that, if he were not prepared to obey the government's policy, he should hand in his resignation. Instead of doing so, Lüttwitz sent orders to Ehrhardt at Döberitz to begin the action against the Republic by marching on Berlin.

Warned by a journalist of what impended, Noske hastily called a meeting of headquarters staff in the Ministry of Defence in the course of which he discovered to his stupefaction that he could not count on the army to resist the mutineers. Although Reinhardt called for action, the local commanders took their line not from him but from General Hans von Seeckt, Chief of the Troop Bureau of the Reichswehr and, in effect, the army's Chief of Staff. A man who was universally respected by his fellows for his outstanding record on the eastern front during the war, Seeckt set his face inflexibly against an armed defence of the capital. The army could not fire upon its wartime comrades without destroying itself. The government would have to find its own protectors.

And that is what the cabinet did. While Seeckt elaborately took leave and withdrew to his quarters and Ehrhardt's jubilant troopers surged into Berlin, Ebert and his colleagues prudently retreated by car to Dresden and then, by train, to Stuttgart, from where they appealed to the working class to defend the Republic. The general strike that followed made a quick end of the hapless government of the Nationale Vereinigung that was set up in Berlin on 13 March. Kapp and Lüttwitz, who headed it, had no idea of what to do with the power that Ehrhardt put in their hands, and the breakdown of public services and the signs of disaffection in some of the Berlin

---

[66] On Reinhardt, see esp. Fritz Ernst, 'Walther Reinhardt (1872 bis 1930)', *Zeitschrift für Württembergische Landesgeschichte*, xvi (1957), 331–64, and *Aus dem Nachlass des Generals Walther Reinhardt* (Stuttgart, 1958).

garrisons bewildered and defeated them. By 17 March their adventure was over.[67]

It had, however, made one thing clear: that the leaders of the army had not been as faithful to the bargain struck on 9 November 1918 as Ebert had. Seeckt's neutrality during the putsch seemed to show that the army would defend the Republic against attacks from the left but did not feel obliged to adopt a similar attitude towards the 'national' opposition. If that were so, asked some of Ebert's colleagues, why should the government show any further regard for the views of the generals? Was not this the time to do what should have been done at the beginning, to destroy the old officer corps and build a genuinely republican force?

If the logical answer was affirmative, it was belied by circumstances. The general strike that had been used against the Kappists was so successful that it reawakened hopes of revolution among the Communists and touched off extended disorders in the Ruhr, during which a 'Red army', estimated as being 50–80,000 strong, captured the main industrial centres and, by 20 March, dominated the entire area east of Düsseldorf and Mülheim. To put down what seemed to be a renewal of the Spartacus troubles on a wider scale, Ebert felt compelled to call upon the very men who had failed him earlier in the month. General von Seeckt was appointed as commander of all of the nation's armed forces and was authorized to restore order in the Ruhr. This he did with dispatch, using the free corps of Rossbach, Faupel, Pfeffer, and Epp and, as back-up troops in central Germany, those of Ehrhardt and Bisschoff. This was not meant as a provocation; Seeckt was soon going to demonstrate an insistence upon discipline that was to disappoint the self-willed commando leaders. But the salient point is that any idea of disciplining those who had failed to defend the Republic in March 1920—including the Security Police in Berlin, which had been singularly remiss in its duty[68]—was abandoned. The only one who was punished for what had happened was Gustav Noske, who lost his post because his party held him responsible for failing to control Lüttwitz. As things turned out, his successor was to have even more difficulty in restraining Seeckt, who, while carefully refraining from

---

[67] On the Kapp Putsch, see esp. Johannes Erger, *Der Kapp–Lüttwitz Putsch. Ein Beitrag zur deutschen Innenpolitik 1919–20* (Düsseldorf, 1967); Waite, *Vanguard*, Ch. 6; Gordon, *Reichswehr*, pp. 101–43; Schüddekopf, *Herr und Republik*, pp. 100–14; Wheeler-Bennett, *Nemesis of Power*, pp. 60–82. On the attitude of the police, see Hsi-Huey Liang, *The Berlin Police Force in the Weimar Republic* (Berkeley, 1970), p. 47.

[68] Liang, *Berlin Police*, p. 49.

putsches, made the army an autonomous body within the state, with policies that did not always accord with those of the government.

If this spelled future trouble, so did one further consequence of the Kapp Putsch. The preparations for that action had been known to the commander of the Bavarian Einwohnerwehr, Georg Escherich, and had led him to discuss a parallel action with the President of the Upper Bavarian district, Gustav von Kahr, and the chief of the sizeable Provincial Police, Ernst Pöhner. When the news of Ehrhardt's capture of Berlin reached Munich, this trio urged the local Reichswehr commander, General von Möhl, to declare martial law and assume dictatorial powers. Möhl, who had been in touch with Lüttwitz, did not need much persuasion. He went to Hoffman, the Socialist Prime Minister, and told him that he could not be responsible for public order unless Hoffmann resigned. Worn out by a term of office that had known nothing but trouble, Hoffman complied, and his Socialist colleagues followed his example. On 17 March Kahr became Prime Minister and appointed a cabinet without any representation of the left. The general strike that had stopped Kapp was powerless to undo this radical shift to the right in a state whose politics had always been opposed to the authority of the Reich and which were now, in addition, to become pronouncedly anti-republican.

V

The Socialist set-back in Bavaria was followed by a more general political defeat that led to a significant change in national politics. In the Reichstag elections of 6 June 1920, the first national poll since the ballot for the National Assembly eighteen months earlier, all three members of the Weimar coalition suffered severe losses. The Democratic party was hardest hit, beginning its rapid slide to political irrelevance by dropping from its 1919 total of 5,641,800 votes to 2,333,700 and losing 36 of its 75 Reichstag seats. The popular vote of the Centre party fell from 6 million to 3,845,000 although this was offset by the fact that 1,200,000 of the deficit was caused by a shift of voters to the Bavarian People's party (BVP), which could be expected to vote with the Centre on many issues. Henceforth the Centre would have 64 instead of 91 seats, and the BVP 21. The effect of the Kapp Putsch on the SPD was even more notable: from a total of 11,500,000, the party dropped to a mere 6,100,000, retaining only 102 of its 163 seats. The beneficiary of this débâcle was the Independent Socialist party which, in a misleading and temporary success (it was to fall victim to its innate fissiparous tendencies before the year was out), increased the size of its Reichstag delegation from 22 to 84 members. The Communists added to the SPD's discomfiture by winning 4 seats.

The swing was to the right, as was shown by the emergence of the BVP and the marked recovery of the other middle-class parties. Stresemann's DVP, now beginning to benefit from the support of business interests, increased its representation from 19 to 65 seats. This was exceeded by the Nationalists, who now became the strongest of the bourgeois parties with a gain of 27 seats, for a total of 71. All things considered, it was painfully apparent that control of the Republic's policies had slipped, for the moment at least, from the hands of the republicans, for the Weimar Coalition controlled only 205 of the Reichstag's 452 seats.

Ebert's party now made a critical decision. Unwilling to serve in a coalition with a widened bourgeois representation and failing to persuade the USPD to become its associate in government, the SPD withdrew and made way for the formation of the first all-bourgeois government. Nor was its departure a temporary one, for, although it was to participate in the Stresemann cabinet in 1923 and the Müller cabinet of 1928–30, it seemed even on those occasions to be hankering after the relative irresponsibility of opposition. This created an anomalous situation in which the party with the strongest democratic instincts, which had preserved the unity of the Reich in 1918 and 1919 and stood fast against the forces of political extremism, seemed to prefer a situation in which the Republic was governed by parties less devoted to its preservation than it was itself. One understands why a distinguished historian of the left described the elections of June 1920 as 'a catastrophe for the Weimar Republic'.[69]

[69] Rosenberg, *Republik*, p. 99. See too the contemporary judgement of Ernst Troeltsch, who also used the word 'catastrophe'. *Spektator-Briefe*, pp. 18, 141–9.

XII
Reparations, Inflation, and the Crisis of 1923

Wir versaufen unser Oma ihr klein Häuschen,
  ihr klein Häuschen,
Wir versaufen unser Oma ihr klein Häuschen,
  und die erste und die zweite Hypothek.
                                        Popular song (1922)[1]

If we don't get done with these everlasting government crises, if
we don't find a strong man who doesn't care a fig whether the
parties have confidence in him or not and simply makes a clean
sweep of them, then we might as well close up shop in Germany.
                        Nordwestdeutsche Handwerkszeitung (1923)[2]

THERE were many Germans after 1918 who found it impossible
to reconcile themselves to the political results of the war, and
Kurt Tucholsky was not exaggerating greatly when he wrote
that the first article in the credo of the bourgeoisie was 'Under the
Kaiser everything was better.'[3] An important ingredient of this
feeling, of course, was sentimentality, and this might have been
expected, in the normal course of events, to diminish in intensity and
to give way to a resigned acceptance of the new conditions. At least,
this could have been expected if Germans had been able to return to
the kind of 'normalcy' to which Warren G. Harding led his American countrymen.

For the Weimar Republic no such possibility existed. Its normal
state was crisis. Upon the political shock of the military defeat and

---

[1] Hans Ostwald, *Sittengeschichte der Inflation: Ein Kulturdokument aus den Jahren des
Marksturzes* (Berlin, 1931), pp. 218 f. For a description of the song being sung in
macabre circumstances, see Ernst von Salomon, *Die Geächteten* (new edn., Hamburg,
1962), p. 205.

[2] Heinrich August Winkler, *Mittelstand, Demokratie und Nationalsozialismus: Die
politische Entwicklung von Handwerk und Kleinhandel in der Weimarer Republik* (Cologne,
1972), p. 78.

[3] Kurt Tucholsky, 'Die Glaubenssätze der Bourgeoisie', in *Ausgewählte Werke* (2
vols., Hamburg, 1965), ii. 148.

the humiliation of the peace terms followed the harrowing experience of the inflation. Before it had run its course, millions of Germans who had passively accepted the transition from Empire to Republic had suffered deprivations that shattered their faith in the democratic process and left them cynical and alienated. Their feelings were reflected in a series of new political threats to the Republic in 1923. It overcame these. Unfortunately, it was less successful in mastering the crisis of confidence caused by the financial collapse that preceded them.

I

Despite everything anti-republican propagandists were to say later on, the inflation originated neither in the iniquities of the peace treaty nor in the flabbiness of leaders brought to power in November 1918. It was rooted rather in the fiscal policy of the Imperial Government during the war years and, specifically, in its decision to finance the war by loans rather than taxes. In August 1914, when the Reichstag authorized the government to borrow up to 5 billion R.M. for war expenditures, it also approved provisions for the suspension of the customary restrictions placed by law upon the circulation of notes not covered by gold reserves and for the organization of auxiliary agencies (Loan Banks) with the right to extend credit on collateral that did not qualify for Reichsbank loans under pre-war regulations. As a result, the printing-press became the principal means of meeting the needs of government and business, and, as wartime expenditures increased, the amount of money in circulation increased also, so that by the end of the war it had quintupled. There was in consequence a decided slippage of the currency's value on the international market, so that the mark had declined to about half of its gold parity by 1918.[4]

Until the end of the war, the absence of normal market activity and the pervasiveness of government economic regulation hid this from the German people, but once the conflict was over the truth was out, and the resultant slump of national confidence in the currency accelerated the wartime depreciation. The inexperience of the first post-war governments and the distraction of their energies to the tasks of maintaining civil order doubtless prevented them from taking measures that might have brought the growing inflation under control. But, as a British Treasury official was to write with surprising candour in November 1921, the main reason for their failure was 'that the task had been rendered impossible by the mag-

---

[4] Stolper, *German Economy*, p. 60. On the Treasury's policy during the war, see above, Ch. X, pp. 356 f.

nitude of the financial and economic burdens imposed upon Germany in the early years after the Armistice'.[5] An already serious problem had been made much more so—had, according to this British view, been made insoluble—by the economic terms of the Versailles Treaty and the reparations policies of the victorious Powers.

The use of the plural form of the last noun is deliberate and denotes an important aspect of this complicated matter. From the beginning, the Powers at Paris were divided in their views of the purpose and desirable scope of reparations. In a moment of exasperation in the summer of 1919 the American expert Norman H. Davis wrote, 'Some of the delegates wanted to destroy Germany, some wanted to collect reparations, and others wanted to do both. Some wanted to collect more than Germany had agreed to pay or could pay; and others wanted to take all her capital, destroy her, and then collect a large reparations bill.'[6] Two circumstances underline the essential fairness of this judgement. The first was the victors' decision to expand the definition of reparations from 'compensation . . . for all damage done to the civilian population of the Allies and to their property by the aggression of Germany by land, sea, or from the air'[7] so as to make it include the cost of all pension payments to Allied combatants as well, an addition that increased the burden imposed on Germany to inordinate dimensions. The second was the Allied refusal to face up to the problem of how reparations payments were to be made.

It was common knowledge, at least among the financial advisers of the Allied governments, that they could not be made by transfers of gold, since the gold reserves of the Reichsbank, which amounted to only about 2·4 billion gold marks, were clearly inadequate to satisfy Allied expectations. The alternatives were labour services (the restoration of devastated areas by German working forces) and exports of manufactured and other goods. The French and Belgian governments, while willing to discuss the first of these possible solutions, were too conscious of the lively opposition of their trade unions and construction companies to go very far towards implementing it. The British, who were cordially disposed toward German labour payments to their Allies, were, as Lloyd George made

[5] Hermann-Josef Rupieper, 'Politics and Economics: The Cuno Government and Reparations, 1922–1923' (Dissertation, Stanford Univ. 1974), p. 47.

[6] Ibid., p. 14.

[7] This was the original view of the American delegation, based upon the spirit of the Fourteen Points.

very clear in the spring of 1919, definitely opposed to payments in the shape of manufactured goods. In any case, the Allied governments crippled Germany's ability to mount a significant export programme by confiscating its merchant fleet and a considerable amount of its rolling stock and, subsequently, by erecting tariffs against German goods. This prompted another American adviser, Bernard Baruch, to warn his government not to agree 'with our associates in the war, that Germany is to pay a certain indemnity and yet making it [sic] impossible for her to pay'.[8]

The Americans could, of course, afford to be more detached than the European governments, who had promised their constituents that the Germans would pay the full cost of the war. Yet the gap between their promises and what their experts told them might be possible was sufficiently great to persuade Lloyd George and Clemenceau that some reduction of expectation might be necessary and that they had better prepare the voters for this. Since this would take time, they decided not to set a definite figure until a Reparations Commission had made a thorough study of the matter. As Lloyd George said ingenuously, 'If figures were given now, they would frighten rather than reassure the Germans. Any figure that would not frighten them would be below the figure with which he and M. Clemenceau could face their peoples in the present state of public opinion.'

The Allied governments nevertheless demanded that payments begin in August 1919 and that they reach 20 billion gold marks by 1 May 1921, when the Reparations Commission would make its report. Part of these transfers, and of the payments made after May 1921, would be in the form of deliveries in kind, specifically at least 38 million tons of coal a year for a period of ten years, plus large amounts of timber, chemicals, and other goods. In addition, the Germans were obliged to pay all the costs of the Allied occupation of the Rhineland, although their expenditures for this were not to be credited against their reparations obligation.

These preliminary terms were sufficiently drastic to cause the German Government serious difficulties, which were, unfortunately, compounded by self-defeating exhibitions of defiance. When they fell behind in their shipments of coal in the spring of 1920—a circumstance for which the disruption caused by the Kapp

---

[8] Rupieper, 'Politics and Economics', p. 15. On German views of the problem of payment, see Peter Krüger, *Deutschland und die Reparationen 1918/1919. Die Genesis des Reparationenproblems zwischen Waffenstillstand und Versailler Friedensschluß* (Stuttgart, 1973).

Putsch and the general strike were in large part responsible—the Allies showed some willingness to consider alternate plans for payment. The Germans were invited to present their views at a conference at Spa in July 1920, and a delegation headed by the Chancellor, the venerable Centrist politician Konstantin Fehrenbach, and Walter Simons, the Foreign Minister, duly appeared. The meeting proved to be a fiasco. Because the question of arms reduction was also on the agenda, the German delegation included General von Seeckt and several of his staff, all wearing uniform and medals. This had an effect upon the emotions of their late antagonists that was hardly conducive to objective discussion, and a series of unfortunate remarks to the Press by the new German Minister of Defence, Otto Gessler, about his country's inability to reduce its forces to the limits defined by the treaty did not improve things.[9] In this highly charged atmosphere an explosion on the part of Hugo Stinnes, the Rhenish mining magnate, who had also been invited to come to Spa as an expert, ruined any possibility of achieving an alleviation of the delivery problem. Josef Wirth was later to describe Stinnes as 'the typical *Katastrophen-Politiker*',[10] and there is no doubt that, although he was a virtuoso in the field of business and finance, he had no inkling of the arts of political negotiation. Impatient with the technical discussions of the deficit in coal shipments, he undertook to resolve the problem by lecturing the Allies on the arrogance of victory and by threatening them with a complete stoppage of deliveries. As his anguished colleagues feared, the Allies retorted with an ultimatum, stating that, unless the Germans, within seventy-two hours, signified their willingness to make up the default at once, they would occupy the Ruhr. Thanks to some fast footwork by M. J. Bonn, a financial expert who had friends in the British delegation, these terms were modified to some degree, but there was no disguising the fact that, in general, Spa was a lost opportunity and that German maladroitness had strengthened the impression that the Germans were unregenerate.[11]

Even Lloyd George, who had had doubts about the justice and viability of the economic settlement and was anxious to temper the harder line of the French, found it difficult to resist this feeling, for

[9] See Craig, *Prussian Army*, pp. 390 f.

[10] Kessler, *Tagebücher*, p. 559.

[11] On the Spa Conference, see W. M. Jordan, *Great Britain, France, and the German Problem, 1918–1939* (London, 1943), pp. 71, 85–8, 115, 136; Viscount d'Abernon, *An Ambassador of Peace* (3 vols., London, 1929), i. 56–75; Harold Nicolson, *Curzon: The Last Phase, 1919–1925* (new edn., New York, 1939), pp. 203, 226–30; M. J. Bonn, *Wandering Scholar* (New York, 1948), pp. 251–8.

German behaviour continued to reinforce it. The fact that Stinnes became a kind of national hero because of his theatrics and the news that the German People's party was openly disaffected with its government partners because of their support of the German delegation's surrender at Spa discouraged any desire to make concessions to Berlin. In January 1921, therefore, the British Prime Minister agreed, after some initial reluctance, to support a French plan for the payment of the reparations bill that required the Germans to make annual payments that would increase from two to six billion gold marks over a period of forty-two years and, in addition, to pay 26 per cent of the proceeds of German exports during that period.

The best that can be said for this 'preposterous plan', as Gustav Stolper has labelled it,[12] is that it allowed the German Government to make a counter-proposal. When they did so, their position struck the Allies as being disingenuous, for they offered a total of only 30 billion marks, to be made in easy payments. The German experts had settled on this figure by deducting 8 per cent interest from the total of the projected payments and reaching a present value of 50 billion marks, from which they subtracted the 20 billions that they were obliged to pay by May 1921, on the grounds that it had in fact already been paid. Upon examination, these calculations proved to be highly dubious, in part because they were based upon an over-valuation of assets, like the Saar mines, that had passed into Allied control, and upon a claim for credit for the fleet that had been scuttled at Scapa Flow.[13] Infuriated by this scheming, and doubtless also by evidence of Germany's continued failure to meet the military terms of the treaty and reports of the rapid growth of the Bavarian Einwohnerwehr and of illegal shipments of arms from its offshoot Orgesch into Austria, the Allied governments resorted to sanctions and, in March, occupied the towns of Düsseldorf, Duisburg, and Ruhrort and impounded the customs receipts of the occupied territories.

Before the German Government had recovered from this shock, it was confronted with the long-expected report of the Reparations Commission with respect to the exact extent of the reparations debt. At the end of April, by unanimous vote, this body set the sum at 132 billion gold marks. This figure was, to be sure, modified by the arrangements that the Commission recommended for its payment.

[12] *German Economy*, p. 77.
[13] See Erich Eyck, *A History of the Weimar Republic* (2 vols., Cambridge, Mass., 1962), i. 174–5.

The debt was to be divided into three sets of bonds which the German Government had to deliver to the Allies. The first set, the A Bonds, due on 1 July 1921, would be valued at 12 billion gold marks and would represent the unpaid balance of the 20 billions that the Germans were supposed to have paid by 1 May; the second series, or B Bonds, to the value of 38 billion gold marks, were to be delivered to the Commission by 1 November 1921. Both of these series could be issued by the Commission as it saw fit and would bear 5 per cent interest. A third series of bonds to the value of 82 billion gold marks was also to be delivered by 1 November, but the Commission could not issue them until German payments were sufficient to cover the charges of interest and sinking funds connected with Series A and B. Since such payments would have to be made by a tax on exports and since the British were uncomfortably aware that they would suffer from any expansion of German trade great enough to meet the charges on the first two bond series, it is doubtful whether anyone with any sophistication in matters of international finance believed that the C Bonds represented anything but a fairly empty threat to turn the screw harder if the Germans were not co-operative. To all intents and purposes, the German debt had been set at 50 billion gold marks.[14]

This was a diminution, however, without much actual meaning, for the gold mark was an abstraction based upon the pre-war relationship of the mark to the United States dollar, which was 4:1. A debt of 50 billion gold marks, then, was a debt of 12·5 billion dollars. But in May 1921 it would have taken 750 billion paper marks to pay off such a debt, for the mark had already fallen to sixty to the dollar. It was to fall further. When the Allies made the Commission's figure known to the German Government on 5 May 1921, their note included an ultimatum demanding unconditional acceptance of the total obligation and the remission of a billion gold marks (250 million dollars) within twenty-five days. That sum was paid by the German Government, but only by selling newly printed paper marks on the foreign-currency exchanges. As a result, depreciation was accelerated, and by November the paper mark had slid from 60 to 310 to the dollar.[15] The inflation begun during the war was now

[14] Sally Marks, 'Reparations Re-Considered: A Reminder', *Central European History*, ii, no. 4 (Dec. 1969), 358–60. Charles S. Maier, *Recasting Bourgeois Europe: Stabilization in France, Germany and Italy in the Decade after World War I* (Princeton, 1975), pp. 241–2.

[15] David Felix, 'Reparations Re-Considered with a Vengeance', *Central European History*, iv, no. 2 (June 1971), 172–4.

tremendously stimulated, and it was to increase remorselessly until the government was bankrupt.

Even before the Allied note of 5 May, the Fehrenbach government, discouraged by the failure of a plea that it had made to the United States Government for mediation and weakened by the defection of the People's party, had handed in its resignation. The burden of meeting the ultimatum—which, in addition to its financial requirements, demanded the disbanding of the Bavarian Einwohnerwehr and strict adherence to the military terms of the treaty—fell upon a new government headed by two of the most gifted, although not the most fortunate, men in public life, Josef Wirth and Walther Rathenau.

In the Centre party, Wirth had been overshadowed by Matthias Erzberger until that ebullient figure's career was ended by the revelations of bad judgement that emerged from his libel suit against Karl Helfferich in 1920.[16] Wirth succeeded Erzberger as Minister of Finance and soon demonstrated that, although he did not possess the technical knowledge of his predecessor, he was just as energetic and possessed rather more candour and perspective. Optimistic by temperament, he was not easily daunted by adversity, and among German politicians he was singular in his willingness—indeed, his joy—in making decisions.[17]

Wirth's bluff temperament contrasted sharply with that of his introverted colleague Rathenau, who now crowned his public career by serving as Minister of Reconstruction and, after February 1922, as Foreign Minister. There was no doubt about Rathenau's qualifications for dealing with Germany's economic problems, although his technical abilities were to some extent offset by personal shortcomings, notably a fertility of imagination that made it easier for him to devise new schemes than to hold firm to established ones. The art of digging in his heels was not highly developed in him, and he was prone to fits of discouragement and melancholia. The fact that he was a Jew who was secretly ashamed of that fact doubtless contributed to his periodic depression; certainly his Jewishness was a handicap after he became Foreign Minister, for his appointment was regarded as an outrage by the apoplectic patrioteers of the right.[18]

[16] On this case, which originated with Erzberger's attack on Helfferich's wartime policy, see Epstein, *Erzberger*, Ch. 14 and Williamson, *Helfferich*, pp. 292–3, 295–302, 313–28.

[17] The best book is Ernst Laubach, *Die Politik der Kabinette Wirth 1921/22* (Lübeck and Hamburg, 1968). For the reasons why his energy and optimism were unavailing, see Maier, *Bourgeois Europe*, pp. 271–2.

[18] Perceptive assessements of Rathenau's character and career can be found in

Whatever the lunatic fringe might think of him, Rathenau had the courage to recognize and advocate the necessary. There was no doubt in his mind about the determination of the Allies and the lack of an alternative to yielding to the ultimatum. In his first speech to the Reichstag, therefore, he boldly argued for acceptance and for scrupulous fulfilment of the Allied terms, reminding his auditors—in one of the elaborate analogies to which he was addicted and which led coarser-fibred politicians to regard him as an over-educated windbag—of the Beethoven quartet movement (Opus 135, final movement) that 'begins with slow tones "Must it be?" and closes with a decided and powerful "It must be!" . . . whoever comes to his task without that "It must be!",' he added, 'comes with only half a will to the solution [of Germany's problems].'[19]

The Wirth–Rathenau policy of fulfilment was neither negative in nature nor animated purely by a spirit of resignation. Rathenau was a firm believer in negotiations—Lord d'Abernon wrote that he had 'taken to international conferences with a passion. He wants them to go on all the time'[20]—and it was his view that, if one avoided the intractable questions of principle and focused on concrete issues, one might discover unexpected areas of agreement that would gradually widen until at last what people were calling the 'iron curtain' between Germany and the West was torn away.[21] This was an approach that found little support among irreconcilables like Stinnes, who delighted in sabotaging it as far as he could; but for a time it seemed that it might strike a responsive chord in French government circles. In October 1921 talks between Rathenau and Louis Loucheur led to the so-called Wiesbaden Agreement, which was designed to modify the schedule of payments by increasing the delivery of reparations in kind to France.

This sign of progress was illusory. Although the agreement was at first approved by the French Press, it soon became the object of a concentrated attack by heavy industry and chemical and electrical interests, which feared German competition, and these opponents

---

Count Harry Kessler, *Walther Rathenau: His Life and Work* (New York, 1930); James Joll, *Three Intellectuals in Politics* (new edn., New York, 1965), pp. 106 ff.; Walter Struve, *Elites against Democracy: Leadership Ideals in Bourgeois Political Thought in Germany, 1890–1933* (Princeton, 1973), pp. 149–85; Eric Kollmann, 'Walther Rathenau and German Foreign Policy: Thoughts and Actions', *Journal of Modern History*, xxiv (1952), 128 ff.; Troeltsch, *Spektator-Briefe*, pp. 285 ff.

[19] Walther Rathenau, *Gesammelte Reden* (Berlin, 1924), p. 203.
[20] D'Abernon, *Ambassador of Peace* i. 255.
[21] For uses of the term 'iron curtain' in the twenties, see ibid. iii. 101, 211, and Gustav Stresemann, *Vermächtnis*, ed. H. Bernhard (3 vols., Berlin, 1932–3), iii. 327.

were soon joined by chambers of commerce and trade associations representing construction companies and producers of agricultural machinery. The French right, led by Raymond Poincaré, used the Wiesbaden understanding as a stick with which to belabour the policies of the Prime Minister, Aristide Briand, who had shown some signs of becoming responsive to Lloyd George's pleas for concessions to German weakness; and they did this so successfully that, in the wake of a conference with the British Premier at Cannes which aroused unfavourable public reaction,[22] Briand abruptly resigned at the beginning of 1922. He was replaced by Poincaré, whose policy of rigorous enforcement of the treaty frustrated any hope of alleviating the reparations problem for another two years.

Leaving the question of personality aside, this was probably inevitable in any case. The problem was complicated by the question of Allied debts to the United States, and Washington made it clear that it expected them to be paid. This forced the British Government, in the course of the new year, to notify its allies that it must ask them to liquidate their debts to Britain, and this admonition, expressed unequivocally in the Balfour note of 1 August 1922, undercut Lloyd George's attempt to lighten Germany's load, for it led the French, Belgian, and Italian governments to remain uncompromising with respect to the German obligation.[23]

The policy of fulfilment was not, in these circumstances, capable of meeting Rathenau's expectations. Far from being sympathetic to Germany's financial plight, Poincaré took the line that Berlin was deliberately destroying the mark in an elaborate attempt at blackmail and that the Allies should impose financial controls upon their former antagonist and insist upon productive pledges—the seizure of territories capable of producing revenue—as the price for a reparations moratorium or any other form of relief.

Any chance that Rathenau might have had of overcoming this obduracy was lost in April 1922 during the economic conference at Genoa, where the Foreign Minister demonstrated that he could be as maladroit as Stinnes had been at Spa. Feeling that he was being snubbed by Lloyd George, who was having his usual clubby talks with everyone but the Germans, and fearing that this portended some new anti-German stroke, Rathenau allowed himself to be

[22] Newspaper photographs of Lloyd George giving Briand instruction in golf encouraged the impression that the Prime Minister was too deeply under British influence. See, *inter alia*, A. J. Sylvester, *The Real Lloyd George* (London, 1947), pp. 71–4.

[23] On the Balfour note, see Keith Middlemas and John Barnes, *Baldwin. A Biography* (London, 1969), pp. 132 f.

talked into a separate treaty of friendship with the Soviet Union. There is no real evidence that this Rapallo Treaty, to which historians have devoted so much time, was much more than an expression of Rathenau's moodiness,[24] and it is highly unlikely that its conclusion destroyed the possibility of a comprehensive reparations settlement at Genoa, although this was later asserted.[25] But it is clear that Rathenau's action seemed provocative to Poincaré, whose distrust of the Soviet Union was exceeded only by his suspicion of Germany.[26] Within two months of his signature of the treaty the German Foreign Minister was dead, murdered by nationalist zealots who were convinced that they were doing their country a service by removing him.[27] It is possible that, before this happened, he had realized that his diplomacy had been self-defeating and that the policy of fulfilment was bankrupt. Otto Gessler claimed in his memoirs that Rathenau told him, shortly after Genoa, that a French occupation of the Ruhr was inevitable.[28]

Rathenau's death took the spirit out of the Wirth cabinet; and, although the Chancellor tried to shore it up by persuading the SPD to join the coalition, his plan foundered on the incompatibility of the

[24] See, inter alia, Kessler, Rathenau, pp. 304–40; Kessler, Politische Tagebücher, p. 301; d'Abernon, Ambassador of Peace i. 308 ff.; Bonn, Wandering Scholar, pp. 267–9; Kollmann, 'Rathenau', 136; H. Graml, 'Die Rapallo-Politik im Urteil der Westdeutschen Forschung', Vierteljahrshefte für Zeitgeschichte, xviii (1970); Laubach, Kabinette Wirth, pp. 180 ff.; Theodor Schieder, 'Die Entstehungsgeschichte des Rapallo Vertrags', Historische Zeitschrift, 204 (1967); and H. Pogge von Strandmann, 'Großindustrie und Rapallopolitik', Historische Zeitschrift, 222 (1976), 265 ff. and esp. 294–9, which describes the interest of powerful industrial concerns in a Russian treaty and throws doubt on the theory that Rathenau's decision to interrupt his fulfilment policy by concluding a treaty was entirely impulsive.

[25] The Swedish financier Marcus Wallenberg later claimed that English, Dutch, and Swedish experts had worked out such a plan. Wipert von Blücher, Deutschlands Weg nach Rapallo (Wiesbaden, 1951), p. 164 n. For some perceptive contemporary remarks on the treaty's effects, see Troeltsch, Spektator-Briefe, pp. 274 ff.

[26] This feeling was reciprocated by Wirth, who told a meeting of minister presidents of the separate states in March that French influence in Europe was excessive and that in view of the aggressiveness of Poincaré's policy German foreign policy must become more active. Akten der Reichskanzlei. Die Kabinette Wirth, ed. Ingrid Schulze Bidlingsmaier (2 vols., Boppard, 1973), i. 646.

[27] On Rathenau's death and the reasons for it, see the accounts of Ernst von Salomon, who was implicated, in Die Geächteten, pp. 189–229 and Der Fragebogen (Hamburg, 1951), pp. 103–12, and E. I. Gumbel, Verschwörer: Beiträge zur Geschichte und Soziologie der deutschen nationalistischen Geheimbünde seit 1918 (Vienna, 1924), pp. 48 ff. David Felix, Walther Rathenau and the Weimar Republic: The Politics of Reparations (Baltimore, 1971), esp. p. 168, over-emphasizes anti-Semitism as the motive.

[28] Otto Gessler, Reichswehrpolitik in der Weimarerzeit, ed. Kurt Sendtner (Stuttgart, 1958), p. 239. The failure of the policy of fulfilment is analysed in Maier, Bourgeois Europe, pp. 281–8.

Socialists and the DVP. Amid mutual recriminations Wirth resigned in November 1922, creating a major political crisis. The situation called for new leadership and vision, but there was no obvious successor to Wirth, and none of those mentioned as candidates—Stresemann of the DVP, the Oberbürgermeister of Cologne, Konrad Adenauer, the leader of the Catholic trade union movement, Adam Stegerwald—could hope to command a majority in the Reichstag. In the end, as on earlier occasions, it was Friedrich Ebert who took the initiative in proposing a solution. In November he authorized Wilhelm Cuno, head of the Hamburg-American Shipping Line, to form a cabinet.

This choice was not as surprising as it seemed to some contemporaries. Cuno had been on his way to a distinguished career in the Imperial Civil Service before he was persuaded to join Hapag in 1917 by Albert Ballin, whose successor he became. His brilliant direction of its affairs, and particularly his negotiation of an agreement in June 1920 with Averell Harriman's American Ship and Commerce Company, which restored Hapag's pre-war position, had made an impression on the world of politics. He had subsequently been invited to participate in reparations talks with the Allies; he was mentioned as a successor to Erzberger as Minister of Finance in 1921; and Wirth had offered him the Foreign Ministry after Rathenau's death. He was a man with acknowledged administrative talents and energy.

It is difficult, nevertheless, to find anything to commend in this turn in Germany's political fortunes. Ebert's decision to avoid new elections and to permit Cuno to form a government without responsible party ties could easily be interpreted as an admission of doubt in the continued viability of the parliamentary system, and it was startling that the republican parties, including the SPD, should acquiesce so tamely in the setting of this ominous precedent. This was all the more surprising in view of the fact that Cuno had made no secret of his scorn for politicians and their art, of which, as M. J. Bonn was later to remark, he knew less 'than an average trade union leader who had tumbled into a minister's chair'.[29] Both Cuno and Ebert seem to have believed that a solution of Germany's problems would be facilitated by the greater degree of collaboration between government and business that Cuno would provide. This was surely naïve. With respect to the country's principal problem, the deterioration of the currency, the industrialists and the bankers had from the beginning taken the view that this was the government's problem

[29] Bonn, *Wandering Scholar*, p. 279.

rather than their own and had resisted any suggestion that they contribute to its solution by acquiescing in sequestration of their property or special levies in gold that might be used to brake the depreciation. They had also opposed proposals by the Wirth government for reform of currency-control regulations and increases in the discount rate as prejudicial to the foreign interests of German industry.[30] If there was a common denominator in the various proposals put forward by representatives of business in the last months of 1922 it was the assumption that the sacrifices would be made by others and that a return to normal economic conditions would require the elimination of the gains made by labour in 1918–19 (the eight-hour day, collective bargaining, and the recognition of the trade unions as bargaining agents) and of unemployment benefits, as well as a reduction of property taxes and a stabilization of the currency by safe means—that is, by taking the advice of people with a decent respect for free private enterprise rather than by listening to government experts who would prefer to check devaluation by using the tax weapon or the Reichsbank gold reserve.[31] These were ideas that implied so fundamental a change in the Weimar system that they could be implemented only at the cost of renewed civil disorder.

When he took office, Cuno believed that he could count on the support of industry and banking in his efforts to reach an agreement with the Allies for a final settlement of reparations. He soon discovered that he was in no better a position in this regard than his predecessor, and that leaders of the business community showed profound distrust of any initiative on his part that did not leave the power of decision in their hands. Thus on 11 December 1922, when the Chancellor was trying to win back some of the initiative lost by the Wirth–Rathenau government in its last days, by making a new offer for a temporary *modus vivendi*, his *démarche* was attacked furiously by the Stinnes Press.[32]

Instead of asserting the authority of the government against his refractory associates, Cuno showed a dangerous tendency to defer to their wishes; and this contributed to the weakness of his position

---

[30] Constantino Bresciani-Turroni, *The Economics of Inflation. A Study of Currency Depreciation in Post-War Germany* (London, 1937), p. 105.

[31] See the discussion of the proposals of Hermann Buecher and others in Rupieper, 'Politics and Economics', pp. 130 ff. For illustrations of irreconcilable differences between the Wirth government and leading business circles, see Maier, *Bourgeois Europe*, pp. 287 f. and Gerald D. Feldman, *Iron and Steel in the German Inflation, 1916–1923* (Princeton, 1977), pp. 285–6.

[32] Rupieper, 'Politics and Economics', pp. 143 f.

when it became apparent that the French Government intended to use a German default in shipments of coal and timber as an excuse for occupying the Ruhr. The British Government could not be counted upon to restrain Poincaré, because they were dependent upon French co-operation to protect their Middle Eastern interests in the difficult negotiations that were currently taking place at Lausanne, and the Begians, while secretly disapproving of French policy, felt compelled to support it for economic reasons.[33] Only an impressive and plausible German proposal could be expected at this late date to stay Poincaré's hand. Cuno failed to produce it because he relied upon the bankers and industrialists to tell him what it should include, and they proved incapable of rising above their special interests. The German note of 2 January 1923 offered a payment of 20 billion gold marks, which was to be raised by an international loan, and made even this unimpressive figure conditional upon the restoration of German equality on the world market, the evacuation of Düsseldorf, Duisburg, and Ruhrort, and assurances concerning the eventual evacuation of the Rhineland.

That Cuno himself had little faith in this bill of particulars is shown by the fact that he attempted to impress Poincaré by an extraordinary *démarche* in mid-December. He informed the United States Government that Germany would be prepared to sign a peace treaty with all countries bordering on the Rhine for a period of thirty years, this engagement to be guaranteed by the United States.[34] This proposal was an interesting precursor of the Stresemann guarantee plan that eventuated in the Locarno treaties of 1925,[35] but the ground had not been properly prepared for it, and it struck diplomatic observers as being nothing more than a gesture of desperation. This was Poincaré's expressed view when he rejected it out of hand. As for the German reparations offer, it was never considered by the

[33] Stephen A. Schuker, *The End of French Predominance in Europe: The Financial Crisis of 1924 and the Adoption of the Dawes Plan* (Chapel Hill, 1976), pp. 22 f., 178–9 argues that Poincaré was convinced that 'the Germans were deliberately ruining their own currency to give a fraudulent impression of national bankruptcy' and that he decided to occupy the Ruhr reluctantly and because he could think of no other way of defeating the German campaign to sabotage and destroy the reparations system. On Belgian policy, see J. E. Helmreich, 'Belgium and the Decision to Occupy the Ruhr: Diplomacy from a Middle Position', *Revue belge de philologie et d'histoire*, li (1973), 822–39. On Anglo-French difficulties in the Middle East and the Lausanne Conference, see Nicolson, *Curzon*, pp. 258 ff., 273 ff., 279 ff., 281 ff., and Roderic H. Davison, 'Turkish Diplomacy from Mudros to Lausanne', in *The Diplomats*, esp. pp. 202–3.

[34] Rupieper, 'Politics and Economics', p. 171.

[35] See below, Ch. XIV, p. 517.

Allies at all, largely because Poincaré did not wait for it. The Reparations Commission had declared Germany in default on 26 December. The decision was confirmed by the French, Belgian, and Italian governments on 9 January, and two days later French and Belgian troops began to move into the Ruhr.

II

No plans had been made for this contingency, for Cuno had persisted in believing until the last moment that something would intervene to stop Poincaré. His response to the French action, therefore, was not based upon any reasoned calculation of German capabilities, although it is important to note that he was not the sole culprit in this respect. The cabinet council that met to consider retaliatory measures was presided over by Ebert and included General von Seeckt and the Social Democratic Minister President of Prussia, Otto Braun. Ebert insisted that Germany must show the world that it would not yield to military force, and those present were unanimous in their decision to organize passive resistance against the occupation.[36] In the days that followed, this resolution received strong support from the parties and the trade unions and was acclaimed in the Press. Thus, in a passion of unreflective patriotism, the government committed itself to a policy which, as experience would prove, was as difficult to abandon as it was impossible to support.

From the very beginning its costs were staggering. When the government ordered German officials and railway and factory workers in the Ruhr to refuse to co-operate with the occupying Powers, the French responded by putting officials of their own in charge of civil affairs and the administration of transport facilities, by sequestering bank reserves and factory inventories, and by responding to strikes with intimidation, eviction, and imprisonment. This imposed upon the German Government the obligation of supporting the victims of this treatment and their families. At the same time, the systematic conversion of the Ruhr into an economic system under foreign control deprived Germany of vital raw materials (85 per cent of German coal came from the Ruhr), disrupted production, and eventually increased unemployment in the rest of Germany. This greatly increased the number of those who felt they had a legitimate claim for government compensation.

It was impossible for the Reich Treasury to meet these extra-

---

[36] *Akten der Reichskanzlei. Das Kabinett Cuno*, ed. Karl-Heinz Harbeck (Boppard, 1968), no. 37, 9 Jan. 1923.

ordinary obligations with its existing resources. It was already heavily burdened with the costs of servicing its war debts, paying pensions to the victims of the war, and supporting a greatly expanded social welfare programme. Although reparations to France and Belgium had stopped as a result of the invasion, the government considered it necessary to continue payments to Great Britain and Italy, because it hoped to solicit their aid in defeating the occupation. Yet because they feared anything that suggested nationalization or disguised socialism, the bourgeois parties opposed resorting to emergency capital levies as a means of raising new revenues, and industry's attitude toward forced loans and new taxes remained unchanged. In February 1923, when Havenstein, President of the Reichsbank, and Hermes, the Minister of the Treasury, were seeking to shore up an already desperate financial situation by floating a dollar loan among industrialists, Hugo Stinnes (who had already made it clear to the government that he would not allow the policy of passive resistance to interfere with his private contracts with French firms and who was suspected by some shrewd observers of using government credits to buy foreign exchange) flatly refused to subscribe.[37] It was not until August, when the country was experiencing food riots, that self-interest and fear persuaded the representatives of industry to agree to a sizeable loan.[38]

The failure to devise a schedule of taxation that would correspond to government needs was partly due to Cuno's lack of leadership and his inability to resolve differences between Havenstein, Hermes, and the Minister of Economics, Johann Becker; but the parties were also at fault. In March and July they completely redrafted government tax bills so as to protect special interests that supported them. Later on, when the experts of the Dawes Commission studied the tax record of the inflation years, they wrote:

It can be said with confidence that the wealthier classes have escaped with far less than their proper share of the national burden, and we have put it as a matter for serious consideration by the German Government whether they should not, facing even the admitted administrative difficulties, review the assessments of recent years in the case of those particular classes of taxpayers and reassess their liability upon a gold basis.[39]

[37] Ibid., no. 138, 23 Apr. 1923; *Der Nachlass des Reichskanzlers Wilhelm Marx*, ed. Hugo Steilkaemper (4 vols., Cologne, 1969), iii, no. 213, 21 Sept. 1923.

[38] *Akten der Reichskanzlei: Cuno*, nos. 234, 235, 1, 2 Aug. 1923.

[39] Harold G. Moulton, *The Reparation Plan. An Interpretation of the Reports of the Expert Committees Appointed by the Reparations Commission* (new edn., Westport, 1970), p. 198, cited in Rupieper, 'Politics and Economics', p. 342.

Apart from its inequity—the fact that wage and salary workers paid more than their fair share—the great deficiency of the Cuno government's tax policy was that it did not produce enough revenue to meet its obligations. For the years from 1920 to 1923, the excess of government expenditure over income was, respectively, 7,175 million R.M., 6,728 million, 6,136 million, and 11,732 million. These deficits were covered by 'floating debts', a euphemism for resort to the printing-press.[40] By the end of 1923, 133 printing-presses had 1,783 presses running day and night to print Reichsbank notes, which had to be transported to banks of issue in large straw crates carried by armies of porters.[41] The effect of this upon the value of the mark, measured in relation to the dollar, was catastrophic.[42]

Dollar Quotations for the Mark;
Selected Dates, 1914 and 1919–23
(monthly averages)

July, 1914	4.2
January, 1919	8.9
July, 1919	14.0
January, 1920	64.8
July, 1920	39.5
January, 1921	64.9
July, 1921	76.7
January, 1922	191.8
July, 1922	493.2
January, 1923	17,972.0
July, 1923	353,412.0
August, 1923	4,620,455.0
September, 1923	98,860,000.0
October, 1923	25,260,208,000.0
November 15, 1923	4,200,000,000,000.0

Even now, in an age in which inflation has become a household word, it is difficult to convey a sense of the meaning of this plunging decline in the worth of the one commodity that more than any other serves man as a means of rational measurement of his situation. For millions of Germans these figures created a lunatic world in which all the familiar landmarks assumed crazy new forms and all the old

[40] Stolper, *German Economy*, pp. 81 f. The mark used here is the paper mark divided by a cost-of-living index.
[41] See the photographs in Ostwald, *Sittengeschichte*, pp. 116 ff.
[42] Stolper, *German Economy*, p. 83.

signposts became meaningless, in which the simplest of objects were invested by alchemy with monstrous value—the humble kohlrabi shamefacedly wearing a price-tag of 50 millions, the penny postage stamp costing as much as a Dahlem villa in 1890—but in which all value was illusion and monetary fortune fleeting. 'In 1923,' says the protagonist of Remarque's *Drei Kameraden*, 'I was advertising chief of a rubber factory. That was during the inflation. I had a monthly salary of 200 billion marks. We were paid twice a day, and then everybody had a half-hour's leave so that he could rush to the stores and buy something before the next quotation on the dollar came out, at which time the money would lose half its value.'[43] It was possible, Malcolm Cowley was to write in his memoir of the 1920s, to 'gamble in Munich for high stakes, win half the fortune of a Czechoslovakian profiteer, then, if you could not be spend your winnings for champagne and Picasso, you might give them day after tomorrow to a beggar and not be thanked. Once in Berlin a man was about to pay ten marks for a box of matches when he stopped to look at the banknote in his hand. On it was written, "For these ten marks I sold my virtue." He wrote a long virtuous story about it, was paid ten million marks, and bought his mistress a pair of artificial silk stockings.'[44]

For those who had the wit to master the rules for surviving in this world of wildly fluctuating values and who—and this was more important—possessed enough tangible property to give them manœuvrability, these were congenial and lucrative times. With property, one could secure credit from banks for plant expansion or investment in other properties. The investment brought profit without risk, and the loan was paid off in depreciated currency. Huge fortunes were accumulated in this way, and the example of Hugo Stinnes is, if the most extraordinary, only one of many examples that could be cited. Stinnes was a man of substance before 1918, for he controlled the German–Luxemburg Mining Company and the Rhine Westphalian Electric Company, the leading power supplier in the Ruhr, and had begun to acquire interests in transportation. But it was the manipulation of credit made possible by the inflation that enabled him to buy up whole forests to supply pit-props for his mines, to acquire the Styrian Erzberg, the largest coal-mine in Europe, to invest in iron and steel plants in Hungary and chemical, aluminium, and timber interests in Romania, and to build an empire

[43] Erich Maria Remarque, *Drei Kameraden* (1938), Ch. 1.
[44] Malcolm Cowley, *Exile's Return: A Literary Odyssey of the 1920's* (new edn., New York, 1951), p. 81.

of 150 periodicals and newspapers. At the end of his career he had a large share in 69 construction companies, 66 chemical, paper, and sugar works, 59 mines, 57 bank and insurance companies, 56 steel and iron works, 49 brown coal works, 37 oil fields and petroleum factories, 100 metallurgical works, 389 commercial and transport concerns, 83 railway and shipping companies, and over a hundred other miscellaneous businesses. When he died in April 1924, the satirical journal *Simplicissimus* showed Saint Peter ringing the bell of heaven to summon the angels and saying, 'Stinnes is coming! Wake up, children, or in a fortnight he'll own the whole works!'[45]

There was money being made during the inflation days, by the manipulators of high finance and by the thousands of small speculators, the *Raffke* and *Schieber*, who knew how to profit from the distress of others, who bought the treasured possessions of the desperate for a pittance and sold them across the border in Holland or Belgium, who operated skilfully on the black market, who cornered foodstuffs in short supply and sold them in adulterated form. And much of what was made was squandered, lavishly, ostentatiously, frenetically, on garish entertainments and empty luxuries—all of which contributed to the erosion of moral standards, the growth of crime, and the defiant cynicism that rang through the songs, the plays, and the satirical writing and pictorial art of the period. The precipitous fall of the mark was accompanied, paradoxically, by a hectic gaiety, one of the more innocent manifestations of which was a rage for dancing that seemed to overcome Germans of all classes, leading them to dance at luncheon and at tea, in hotel ballrooms and garden restaurants and night-clubs, on the beach and in the streets, to the strident sound of American jazz and *Schlager* like 'Yes, We Have No Bananas', 'My Parrot Eats No Hard-Boiled Eggs', and 'Was tut der Meyer in der Himalaya.' This poignant grasping after pleasure and the all too insistent elaboration on the theme 'Man lebt ja nur so kurze Zeit und ist so lange tot' struck many contemporaries as an ominous sign of social disintegration.[46]

But there was more tangible evidence of that than was represented by the not unnatural amount of whistling to keep one's courage up. It was to be found among the large numbers of middle-class people who were impoverished by the depreciation and who were left with a bewildered sense of having been victimized for their loyalty to the values of frugality, thrift, and provision for the future that had been

---

[45] Gert von Klass, *Stinnes* (Tübingen, 1958), pp. 274, 350.

[46] See Ostwald, *Sittengeschichte*, pp. 111 ff., 204 ff.; Stefan Zweig, *Die Welt von Gestern: Erinnerungen* (Frankfurt-on-Main, 1970), p. 227.

drilled into them in their youth. Persons with fixed incomes, possessors of savings accounts, war bonds, debentures, insurance annuities, and mortgages found that years of hard work and delayed gratification had gone for nothing and that their plans and dreams for themselves and their families had to be abandoned. In Remarque's *Der schwarze Obelisk*, perhaps the most successful of the novels that have sought to capture the atmosphere of the inflation, a widow explains the suicide of her husband by saying: 'It was because of the money. It was in a guaranteed five-year deposit in the bank, and he couldn't touch it. It was the dowry for my daughter from my first marriage. He was the trustee. When he was allowed to withdraw it two weeks ago, it wasn't worth anything any more, and the bridegroom broke off the engagement. . . . My daughter just cried. He couldn't stand that. He thought it was his fault.'[47] Many similar tragedies were acted out in Germany in 1923. At the end of the year there were three times as many public relief recipients as there had been in 1913, and most of these were old people and widows who normally would have lived comfortably on their pensions and savings.[48]

Many persons who were self-employed also ended on relief rolls. Small traders and business men did not find it as easy to get credit as Stinnes, nor did they possess the foreign properties that would have enabled them to liquidate their debts and otherwise free themselves from the problems created by depreciation. Dependent entirely on the local market, and confronted with mounting costs for their materials, they were prevented by government price regulations in July 1923 from offsetting these in the usual manner; and, as has already been indicated, they were also forced to bear a disproportionate share of the burden of taxes. All things considered, the inflation hit the self-employed middle class harder than the war, and it is not surprising that many of its members were unable to maintain their independence.[49]

Manual workers tended to weather the inflation rather better than artisans and small tradespeople, because in the early stages of the inflationary spiral unemployment was low and, thanks to their union protection, their wages were revised upwards. But after the rapid slump of the mark set in at the end of April, their position

---

[47] Erich Maria Remarque, *Der schwarze Obelisk: Geschichte einer verspäteten Jugend* (3rd edn., Cologne, 1971), p. 67.

[48] Jürgen Kocka, 'The First World War and the *Mittelstand*: German Artisans and White Collar Workers', *Journal of Contemporary History*, viii, no. 1 (Jan. 1973), 122.

[49] Ibid.; Winkler, *Mittelstand*, p. 76.

deteriorated. Even those who had jobs saw their savings disappear, while the gap between real wages and the cost of living widened perceptibly; and they were soon in the minority. By the end of 1923 only 29·3 per cent of the total German labour force was fully employed. Of those workers who belonged to trade unions, 23·4 per cent were unemployed, and 47·3 per cent worked only part time.

Unable to protect their members' jobs, the unions proved equally ineffective in maintaining the rights won by the labour movement in 1918–19. Weakened by the depreciation of their pension funds and other savings, they did not have the resources to withstand attacks upon labour participation in plant management, collective bargaining, and the eight-hour day. The agreement made by Hugo Stinnes and Carl Legien in 1918 for common governance of industry by a Zentralgemeinschaft broke down completely. At the same time, employers succeeded in establishing the principle that a working day longer than eight hours could be established in individual plants and industries with government permission or negotiated contract. As a result of this and the reappearance of yellow-dog unions, the ten-hour day tended to become normal in much of German industry. It was significant also that during 1923 large numbers of workers tore up their union cards and that the Allgemeiner deutscher Gewerkschaftsbund, which had seven million members at the beginning of the year, had dropped to four million by 1924. This was not permanent, but something had been lost beside numbers. After the inflation the trade union movement as a whole had less of the cohesive spirit and militancy that had been so effective in defeating the Kapp Putsch in March 1920.[50]

The persons, however, who proved to be most vulnerable to the effects of the inflation were the sick and the young. The mounting cost of hospital care and the increase in doctors' fees placed adequate medical treatment beyond the capacity of millions at a time when the ballooning price and frequent shortage of essential foodstuffs were causing widespread malnutrition and the reappearance of diseases

---

[50] See, inter alia, Theodor Leipart, Zehn Jahre deutscher Geschichte 1918–1928 (Berlin, 1928), pp. 340–3; Furtwängler, Gewerkschaften, pp. 59–61; Helga Timm, Die deutsche Sozialpolitik und der Bruch der Großen Koalition im März 1930 (Düsseldorf, 1952), pp. 26 f., 44 f.; Bracher, Auflösung, pp. 201–2. On the changing attitude of the unions toward the Ruhr struggle, see Lothar Erdmann, Die Gewerkschaften im Ruhrkampf (Berlin, 1924). The dispute over the eight-hour day caused a crisis in October that threatened to break up the Stresemann government but was ended by a compromise that allowed the 'temporary' suspension of the eight-hour day, while confirming it as the normal standard. Henry Ashby Turner, jun., Stresemann and the Politics of the Weimar Republic (Princeton, 1963), pp. 120–3.

that had been common during the worst days of the Allied blockade. The death rate in cities of more than 100,000 inhabitants rose from 12·6 to 13·4 per thousand for the year 1921–2, and the figures for 1922–3 were worse. The suicide rate also went up, and deaths from hunger, and from ailments aggravated by malnutrition, were common.

Children up to the age of fourteen suffered as heavily as the aged and sick. Lack of proper nutrition left schoolchildren all over the Reich listless and prone to illness. The Oberbürgermeister of Berlin reported in 1923 that 22 per cent of the boys and 25 per cent of the girls in the elementary schools were below normal in height and weight. Thirty-one per cent of all children were unfit for work for reasons of health. In all districts the incidence of tuberculosis rose rapidly: in Neukölln, for example, form the 1914 figure of 0·5 per cent to 3·2 per cent in 1922. The incidence of rickets in schools in Berlin-Schöneberg increased from 0·8 per cent in 1913 to 8·2 per cent for 1922.[51]

To detached observers, it was clear that the unhappy social effects of the inflation could not reasonably be blamed upon the republican regime. The troubles in which the country was involved were the result of the lost war and the treaty that was its price, and, if they were complicated by mistakes made by republican governments, that contribution was insignificant in comparison with that made by the self-interest and irresponsibility of German business, which was known for its anti-republican posture. But people who are treated outrageously are not prone to the balanced view; and many of those whose security and hopes had disappeared struck back at the most convenient target. Organizations representing the artisans and the small trades accused the government of flagrant violation of the constitution, Article 164 of which, the so-called Mittelstandsartikel, stated unequivocally that it was the responsibility of the government to protect and promote economic freedom by maintaining an independent middle class in agriculture, trade, and commerce. According to a complaint by Saxon artisans in October 1923, the government had sacrificed the interests of the handicrafts to the powerful and entrenched economic interests on the one hand and organized labour on the other, and consequently no longer deserved middle-class support. Without any objection from his *Mittelstand*

---

[51] Ostwald, *Sittengeschichte*, p. 194. See the speech of the President of the Reich Department of Health, 20 February 1923, in *Verhandlungen des Reichstags: Stenographische Berichte*, ccclvii. 9779–84, the bulk of which is in *The German Inflation of 1923*, ed. Fritz K. Ringer (New York, 1969), pp. 112–18.

audience, a speaker in Hamburg declared '. . . we have lost confidence in the state'.[52]

This was a loss that was not made good after the currency was stabilized. Among those groups who had been actually or psychologically expropriated, the resentment was lasting and was reflected in political attitudes hostile to democracy. When National Socialism became a mass movement in the thirties, the *Mittelstand* was, in relation to its size, over-represented in it. The same tendency was manifest among white-collar workers. In 1920 the right-wing Gesamtverband deutscher Angestelltengewerkschaften (Gedag) was decidedly weaker in numbers than the Social Democratic Allgemeiner freier Angestelltenbund. Ten years later the latter organization had lost 30 per cent of its members, and Gedag had a commanding lead, while, at the same time, white-collar workers comprised the largest occupational group in the National Socialist Reichstag delegation.[53] The tendencies that led to these results originated in the inflation of 1923.

But it would be a mistake to dwell upon the remote political repercussions of the economic disaster before discussing the immediate ones. These were serious enough. Before the year was over the government had to face threats of revolution from both left and right, and these were so formidable that they might have ended the republican experiment if it had not been for the play of chance and personality.

III

After June 1923 the Cuno government had no effective control over the country, and by the first week of August it was ready to admit it. The policy of passive resistance had proved to be insupportable, and its continuation promised to bankrupt the state. At the same time, nothing seemed capable of stopping the relentless fall of the mark, which now began to have menacing social and political results. Between June and August a wave of strikes swept across the country. Protesting the failure of their wages to keep pace with the cost of necessities, thousands of industrial workers and miners walked out of their plants in Upper Silesia in June. Strikes followed among merchant seamen in Hamburg, Bremen, and Emden, and among metal workers in Saxony, Brandenburg, and Mecklenburg. In July the great metal industry of Berlin was affected, and 100,000 workers

---

[52] Winkler, *Mittelstand*, pp. 73, 76 ff.

[53] Herman Lebovics, *Social Conservatism and the Middle Classes, 1914–33* (Princeton, 1969), pp. 31–2; Kocka, 'First World War and the *Mittelstand*' 122 f.

were idle. In July and August unrest among agricultural labourers, which had been intermittent since May, spread from Silesia to other areas and began to assume a violent aspect. Simultaneously, in places affected by heavy unemployment, like the Wiesenthal in Upper Baden, there were agitations and riots throughout the summer months. Something dangerously like a mass movement of hunger and desperation seemed to be gathering, and the possibility of a return to the situation of 1918 suddenly became very real to the parties that had been supporting Cuno.

Their tolerance evaporated completely when a lame attempt by the Chancellor to justify his policy, in a speech in the Reichstag on 8 August, was given the lie on the same day by a strike vote by the typographical union. When the printers walked out, they stopped the government presses and left the capital with a frightening short-age of paper money. Municipal railway workers, operators of the city power plants, construction hands, and hospital personnel joined the printers, and a general strike seemed possible. Aware that the reinvigorated Communist party was profiting from all this, the Socialist Reichstag delegation informed Cuno on 11 August that he no longer had their confidence. This seems to have come as a surprise to Friedrich Ebert, but he did not try to save the man he had made Chancellor nine months earlier. Nor did Cuno try to fight for his job. He was happy to return to the simpler world of Hapag.[54]

The man who stepped into his place was to be the dominant figure in German politics for the next six years, during which he came to represent for many people the last remaining hope for the survival of the Republic. Gustav Stresemann was a rather improbable candidate for such a role. As a young man in the pre-1914 National Liberal party, he had been an admirer of Bülow's Weltpolitik and, during the war, he was an outspoken annexationist, one of the chief figures in the intrigue that brought Bethmann down, and so uncritical a sup-porter of the military that he was known as 'Ludendorff's young man'.[55] Nor had the defeat of 1918 brought an immediate change of heart. A convinced monarchist, he abandoned his hope of a restor-ation slowly and reluctantly. In 1920 his sympathies were with the Kappists, although the failure of the putsch opened his eyes to the short-sighted incompetence of the die-hards. It took the murders of Erzberger and Rathenau, which shocked him deeply, to complete his

[54] Werner T. Angress, *Stillborn Revolution: The Communist Bid for Power in Germany, 1921–1923* (Princeton, 1964), pp. 350 ff., 370–2; *Akten der Reichskanzlei: Cuno*, nos. 243–8, 10–12 Aug. 1923.

[55] On Stresemann's early career, see Edwards, *Stresemann, passim*.

disillusionment with the so-called national opposition. He became a supporter of the Republic because he gradually convinced himself that the alternative was dictatorship of the right or, more likely, the left. In either case, the circumstances would be unfavourable for the realization of the things he considered important: the adaptation of the best features of the old order to the conditions of twentieth-century Europe, the economic recovery of the country, and its rehabilitation as a strong and respected member of the European comity of nations. In 1920, when Stresemann first led the DVP into the government, he had done so with reservations. In the crisis following Cuno's fall, at a time when Communism seemed to be establishing itself in Saxony and Thuringia and alarmed conservatives were calling for military rule, he threw himself whole-heartedly into the struggle to save constitutional government.[56]

Stresemann had been chairman of the Reichstag's Foreign Affairs Committee since 1920, and during the struggle in the Ruhr he had won the respect of all parties by his informed and articulate attacks on French policy, which were often quoted in the foreign Press. At the same time, he had been a sharp critic of the selfishness of the business community during the inflation, and his call for a tax upon capital goods had won the support of the SPD. In consequence, he was the unanimous choice of the moderate parties and the Socialists to succeed Cuno and was able to form a more broadly based government than any in the Republic's history. Whether that was to mean anything depended on this Great Coalition's ability to move swiftly to halt the runaway inflation and meet the threats to the Republic that social disintegration was encouraging.

In the new Chancellor's mind, the key to the situation was passive resistance, which had been an unmitigated disaster but had become so invested with symbolic importance that to abandon it would strike many as a betrayal. But what was the alternative? Poincaré was now standing pat, deaf to any proposals for new talks until the Germans should satisfy his *amour propre* by giving up their opposition. The British were not inclined to intervene; indeed, on 19 September the Baldwin government endorsed the French position. Stresemann concluded that the bitter medicine would have to be swallowed in the hope that a cure would follow. On 26 September, with the full support of the President and the cabinet, he announced the termination of passive resistance in the Ruhr.

Despite Stresemann's careful preparations for this step and his

---

[56] He had been concerned about dictatorship since Cuno's appointment. See Turner, *Stresemann*, pp. 103 f.

patient efforts to convince all political factions of its unavoidability, he was bitterly attacked, and not only by the extreme patriotic Press. He brushed these criticisms aside. 'Giving up passive resistance', he said, 'is perhaps more patriotic than the phrases used to combat it. I knew when I did it . . . that I was putting my own political position in my party—yes, and even my life—in jeopardy. But what is it we Germans lack? We lack the courage to take responsibility.'[57] The hard decision made possible the opening of talks between the occupying authorities in the Ruhr and the local industrialists that eventuated in the so-called MICUM (Mission interallié de contrôle des usines et mines) agreements of 23 November, which established a working arrangement for reparations for the period ending on 15 April 1924.[58]

This was an important first step, but other problems were now crowding in, and it seemed advisable to meet them not by normal legislative procedures but by means of an enabling act by the Reichstag that would give the government freedom to operate by decree. After some objections from the Socialists, which threatened to break up the Great Coalition in October,[59] the Reichstag passed the necessary legislation on 13 October. It was none too soon. The country was alive with rumours of impending *coups*, and, in three instances, these possessed a menacing substance.

In the first place, the government narrowly escaped another Kapp Putsch. In February 1923, shortly after the Lithuanians had seized Memel and amid fears that the French might try to use their occupation of the Ruhr to promote separatism in the Rhineland, the Cuno government had decided to build up a secret reserve army. With the approval of the Prussian Ministry of the Interior and the army high command, an arrangement was made for the recruitment and training of 'labour battalions' (*Arbeitskommandos*), and by September 50,000 to 80,000 men had been enrolled in what came to be called the Black Reichswehr, and were being trained in various Reichswehr centres. Four battalions were stationed at Küstrin, not far from Berlin, under the command of Major Bruno Buchrucker, an officer of more energy than judgement, who, having played a major role in raising the illegal force, was anxious to lead it into action. He convinced himself that, if he marched on Berlin and deposed the government, the chief of the army command, General Hans von

---

[57] Quoted in Martin Göhring, *Stresemann, Mensch, Staatsmann, Europäer: Gedenkrede gehalten am 8. Juli 1956* (Mainz, 1956), pp. 19 f.

[58] Turner, *Stresemann*, p. 120.

[59] See n. 50 above.

Seeckt, would support him with the full resources of the army; and he drew up an elaborate operational plan that was meant to go into effect in October.

The signals that Buchrucker received from the enigmatic army chief and those near him, however, were so sybilline as to defy interpretation, and this substitute Wallenstein was beset with as many doubts as the original. He tried to call the operation off, found that his subordinates were determined to act without him, decided to inform on them, and in general created such an embarrassing muddle that the Reichswehr had to step in and arrest everyone in sight and seize all the incriminating evidence lest it get into the newspapers.[60]

Apart from casting a curious light upon the army's reliability, a subject to which we will return, the main importance of the abortive putsch was its indication of the general instability of political conditions. A more dangerous manifestation of this followed almost immediately, when the Communists tried to launch a revolution.

The history of German Communism since 1919 had been an unedifying one. The idealism, the open exchange of ideas, the vision of a united working class marching to a common goal that had characterized the movement in its early days did not survive the death of Rosa Luxemburg. Factionalism became prevalent within party councils, which had the result of driving out talented members, like Paul Levi in 1921 and Ernst Reuter a year later, and of subordinating the party increasingly to control from Moscow. Competition rather than co-operation came to characterize its relations with the trade unions and other working-class organizations, so that even when it proclaimed its support of the principle of the united front its behaviour was so patently disingenuous that it repelled potential allies. When the Independent Socialist party split in December 1920, its left wing joined the KPD, but many Independents regretted this step and found their way back to the SPD. As the grip of Moscow tightened, the KPD's ability to make concessions to non-Communist groups, which was never very great, diminished; and the bulk of the working class instinctively reacted to its overtures with suspicion.

Finally, for a party that talked so much about scientific socialism and venerated Lenin, who had scorned ill-considered and untimely revolutionary action, the KPD developed a fatal penchant for adventurism. In March 1921 the party leadership eagerly embraced a plan

---

[60] The fullest account in English of the Küstrin affair is in Waite, *Vanguard*, pp. 242–54. See also Gumbel, *Verschwörer*, p. 109; Gordon, *Reichswehr*, pp. 233–5; Schüddekopf, *Heer und Republik*, pp. 167–9.

for an armed insurrection in Saxony which was urged upon them by the Hungarian revolutionary Béla Kun, with the backing of the Comintern. This was a tragic failure, costing at least 150 lives, and it caused a drop in KPD membership from 350,000 to 180,000.[61]

The inflation and its attendant miseries helped repair these losses. By September 1922 the party had 224,389 card-carrying members, and its voting strength was considerably in excess of that. In Thuringia and Saxony, a centre of lignite, copper slate, and potash deposits, with numerous steel and processing plants and the important Leuna petrol and chemical works, the KPD made considerable inroads into districts which normally voted Socialist and in the autumn elections for the two diets increased its vote, respectively, from 8,131 (the 1921 figure) to 73,686 votes, and from 117,359 to 226,864.[62] These handsome gains, and some impressive evidence of success in infiltrating unions and factories both in central Germany and in the cities of the north, served both as anodyne and stimulant upon some of the members of the party Zentrale. All memory of the March fiasco dropped from the minds of activists like Ruth Fischer and Arkadi Maslow, and they began to complain about the passivity of the more cautious leader Heinrich Brandler. They were encouraged by the Comintern leadership, which once more decided that Germany was ripe for revolution.

Events in Thuringia and Saxony lent credibility to this view. In the former state, the Socialist government had been defeated in the Chamber in May, and the Reich Government had felt compelled to put responsibility for the maintenance of public order in the hands of the Commander of the Fifth Military District, General Walther Reinhardt. His clumsy attempts to regulate political activity threatened to drive the Socialists into the KPD's arms. In Saxony the situation was even more critical. After a similar parliamentary setback, the Socialists had made a pact with the KPD whereby, in return for Communist support, a new Socialist government would establish agencies that would give the working class regulatory powers over industry and would sponsor the formation of proletarian defence units (hundreds) to secure the state against Fascist attack. On 21 March, by a narrow vote, the Saxon Diet had elected the left-wing Socialist Dr. Erich Zeigner as Minister President; and, in the months that followed, he not only alarmed middle-class opinion in Saxony by keeping his promises to the KPD and by instituting a communal reorganization that seemed to foreshadow a decided shift of com-

[61] On the March action, see esp. Angress, *Stillborn Revolution,* Ch. 5.
[62] Ibid., p. 250.

munity power to the lower classes, but kept up a steady drumfire of criticism of the federal government, accusing it of pursuing a policy in the Ruhr that benefited big business and of protecting anti-republican paramilitary bands. The fall of the Cuno government seemed to accelerate this drift to the left. On 9 September there was a muster of the proletarian hundreds in Dresden, at which a Socialist speaker predicted an imminent struggle between left and right and exhorted his 8,000 auditors to fight, when that moment came, for the dictatorship of the proletariat.[63]

Finally, as if this were not enough, Stresemann had to worry about the situation in Bavaria. Since 1919, when the free corps had liquidated the Munich Soviet, Bavarian politics had been complicated, and in 1923 it became dangerously so as a result, on the one hand, of the revival of left extremism, and on the other, of the proliferation of nationalistic racist associations (Wikingbund, Reichsflagge, Bund Oberland, and others) led by former officers and soldiers of fortune like Hermann Ehrhardt and Ernst Röhm. In the summer of 1923 these groups formed what they called a Kampfbund with another militant organization, the National Socialist Workers' party (NSDAP), which was led by a young man of outstanding oratorical ability and unlimited political ambition named Adolf Hitler.

The government of Eugen von Knilling, conservative in tone and based on the moderate parties, became concerned lest prevailing economic distress and the tension caused by events in the Ruhr and neighbouring Thuringia and Saxony create a situation like that of 1918–19 and decided, in the late summer of 1923, to appoint a General State Commissioner with special powers in matters of public security. For this post they chose the former Prime Minister, Gustav von Kahr, a monarchist with ties to the old Pan-German movement and strong personal ambitions. Kahr immediately entered into close relations with the local Reichswehr commander, General von Lossow, and the head of the provincial police force, Hans Ritter von Seisser. Triumvirates seem prone to adventurism, and this one was no exception. The partners seem to have hoped, with the support of the fighting groups, to free themselves from Knilling's leading strings and to implement their own anti-republican policy. Kahr was in touch with Friedrich Minoux, former right-hand man of Hugo Stinnes, who had convinced him that the Stresemann government would soon be replaced by a four-man directorate composed of Otto von Weidfeldt, the German ambassador in Washington, General Director Henrich of the Siemens Corporation, General von Seeckt, and himself. Kahr, Lossow, and Seisser thought they could hitch their wagon to that star.[64]

The presence of the names of two soldiers in this improbable cast of characters throws light upon another of Stresemann's difficulties as he worried over the Bavarian and central German problems. He could not be entirely sure of the support of the army, particularly if he ordered it to act against the nationalist opposition. In October Lossow proved to be wholly unresponsive to attempts by the Ministry of Defence to make him end his involvement in Bavarian politics, but it was difficult to do anything about it because Seeckt was disinclined to discipline his subordinate. The possibility of Seeckt collaborating in an anti-republican putsch was not a figment of the imagination of the Munich triumvirate. Throughout the crisis months of 1923 the General was seriously considering the possibility of taking power into his own hands, openly or by disguised means. He was in touch with Kahr and, in a letter to him in November, was to express his antagonism to Social Democracy, his antipathy to the constitution, and his confident expectation that it would soon be changed.[65] On the other hand, as one intellectual of the right commented bitterly, Seeckt was the kind of man who marched bravely up to the Rubicon and then decided to go fishing.[66] He tried, at one critical moment, to persuade President Ebert that Stresemann was incapable of mastering the situation and had lost the army's confidence—a suggestion that Ebert repudiated with indignation—but he always shrank back from seizing the initiative himself.

Stresemann had no way of knowing that this would be true, and his uncertainty about Seeckt's intentions affected his tactics as the Bavarian situation developed. Although the Munich Government encouraged Lossow in his insubordination, and although Kahr publicly attacked the federal government in terms that hinted at an imminent break, the Chancellor refused to rise to the challenge, preferring to play a waiting game while he dealt with the situation in

[64] Harold J. Gordon, jun., *Hitler and the Beer Hall Putsch* (Princeton, 1972), p. 246. For the political atmosphere in Bavaria in 1923, see also Lion Feuchtwanger's novel *Erfolg* (1930).

[65] Seeckt Papers: Seeckt to Kahr, 5 Nov. 1923. See Craig, *Prussian Army*, p. 417. Cf. Kitchen, *Military History*, pp. 253–4. Seeckt's thinking at this time is discussed in Eberhard Kessel, 'Seeckts politisches Programm von 1923', in Konrad Repgen and Stephan Skalweit (eds.), *Spiegel der Geschichte: Festgabe für Max Braubach* (Münster, 1964), pp. 899–914; and Hans Meier-Welcker, *Seeckt* (Frankfurt-on-Main, 1967), pp. 389–405, 411–16. See also George W. F. Hallgarten, *Hitler, Reichswehr und Industrie: Zur Geschichte der Jahre 1918–1933* (Frankfurt-on-Main, 1962), pp. 19–38.

[66] Salomon, *Fragebogen*, p. 343. The observation was Hans Zehrer's.

Saxony and Thuringia, which he regarded as the more immediate threat to the Republic's security. This was sound enough, for the Zentrale of the KPD had been summoned to Moscow in September and instructed by Trotsky, Radek, and Zinoviev to seize the opportunity afforded by the economic disintegration of Germany to launch a revolution. Stresemann did not know this, but he could not ignore clear warnings of action in a speech by Remmele, the Communist deputy, in the Reichstag on 8 October and in appeals to the working class that were appearing in the *Rote Fahne*. On 10 October, when the Communist journal printed a letter to the editor from Josef Stalin, which began with the words 'The approaching revolution in Germany is the most important world event in our time', Stresemann felt that he must move against Saxony, partly because he was afraid that the Bavarians might if he did not.[67]

The hapless victim of his decision was Zeigner, the Minister President. He was not a Communist, but he was so deeply concerned by the tendency of Bavarian politics and by what things like the Küstrin affair portended that he was determined to make Saxony a bastion of Social Democracy. To this end, he felt it necessary now to get a stronger commitment of support from the Communists and tried to accomplish this by giving them three ministerial posts and forming a united front government. This accorded well with the plans of the KPD, and the party Zentrale promptly moved from Berlin to Dresden. They might have saved themselves the trip. On 13 October General Müller, the Commandant of the Fourth Military District, ordered the immediate dissolution of the proletarian hundreds and, when the Zeigner government sought to defy this order, took over command of the local police and moved Reichswehr units into the capital in order, as he informed the Minister President, 'to restore and maintain constitutional and orderly conditions in the Free State of Saxony'.

This not only aborted the secret Communist plans but brought Zeigner down. At a conference of representatives of all labour factions at Chemnitz on 21 October, it became clear that there was no disposition to take any effective retaliatory action. A violent appeal by Heinrich Brandler for a general strike against the Reichswehr met with an embarrassed silence, and its only real effect was to give the Stresemann government an excuse to take another step forward and liquidate the Saxon problem once and for all. On 27 October the Chancellor ordered Zeigner to expel his Communist ministers, since

---

[67] Angress, *Stillborn Revolution*, p. 428.

their presence in his cabinet was 'incompatible with constitutional conditions', and, when the embattled Minister President refused, instituted proceedings under Article 48 for his deposition. Similar measures followed in Thuringia, without any effective resistance in either of the *Länder*.

This forthright action by the federal government left the Communist Zentrale in complete disarray, which probably explains why, as it was glumly facing up to reality in Dresden, it was unable to prevent its local organization in Hamburg from attempting a *coup* in the city on 23 October. The elaborate battle plan devised by the Hamburg leaders was beyond the capacity of a force that included no more than 400 shock troops and some poorly armed hangers-on; and local police, supported by navy troops and detachments of the Socialist militia, the Vereinigung Republik, had put down the futile adventure within twenty-four hours. Its reverberations, however, were far-reaching. Together with the Communist fiasco in central Germany, it contributed to the loss of influence of those people in Moscow who had been most insistent on a revolutionary policy in Germany. Within the German party this led, after the deposition of Brandler and the brief reign of Ruth Fischer as head of the Zentrale, to the complete subordination of the KPD to the direction of Josef Stalin.[68]

The collapse of the threat of revolution from the left and the simultaneous spluttering-out of what had for a time seemed to be a serious separatist movement in the Rhineland[69] did not sensibly relieve Stresemann's situation, for the Bavarian problem was still unresolved. Indeed, the very fact that this was so led to a new attack upon him by the SPD. The Socialists had been gravely troubled by Zeigner's dismissal, and they demanded that the Chancellor take a similarly hard line against the Bavarians, who in late October had

[68] On all this, see ibid., Ch. 13; Ossip K. Flechtheim, *Die Kommunistische Partei Deutschlands in der Weimarer Republik* (Offenbach, 1948), pp. 95 ff.; Ruth Fischer, *Stalin and German Communism. A Study in the Origins of the State Party* (Cambridge, Mass., 1948), Chs. 15, 16; Lothar Danner, *Ordnungspolizei Hamburg: Betrachtungen zu ihrer Geschichte 1918 bis 1933* (Hamburg, 1958), pp. 74–131; Jan Valtin, *Out of the Night* (New York, 1941), pp. 70 ff. On the 'Vereinigung Republik', which later became part of the national republican militia, the Reichsbanner, when it was founded in February 1924, see Karl Rohe, *Das Reichsbanner Schwarz-Rot-Gold* (Düsseldorf, 1966), p. 37.

[69] See Carl Severing, *Mein Lebensweg* (2 vols., Cologne, 1950), i. 435–6; Hans Spethmann, *Zwölf Jahre Ruhrbergbau 1914–1925* (4 vols., Berlin, 1930), iv. 212–38; Walter Ulbricht, *Zur Geschichte der deutschen Arbeiterbewegung,* i (Berlin, 1953), pp. 131–2; Erdmann, *Adenauer in der Rheinlandpolitik, passim*; Henning Köhler, *Anatomie-bewegung oder Separatismus, passim*.

required all Reichswehr troops in their *Land* to take an oath of allegiance to the Munich Government. This was more provocative than anything that Zeigner had done, and the Socialists refused to be persuaded by the Chancellor's argument that *Reichsexekution* in the south might lead to civil war. When he indicated that he intended to continue to play the role of Fabius Cunctator, the SPD ministers, on 2 November, resigned from the cabinet.[70]

This did not lead to an immediate termination of Stresemann's chancellorship, for President Ebert was willing to prolong the Reichstag recess so that the Chancellor's lack of a parliamentary majority could not be demonstrated, thus forcing his resignation. But this could not go on indefinitely, and meanwhile the departure of the Socialists distracted Stresemann's energies by necessitating laborious discussions with party leaders and made him vulnerable to attacks by the right wing of his own party—which, under Stinnes's influence, wanted an agreement with the Nationalists—and intrigues by those who were thinking in terms of authoritarian solutions. The number of influential people who were apparently willing, not only to jettison Stresemann, but to abandon constitutional government, was so large that a successful rightist revolution in Bavaria might very well have received enough support in the capital to end the democratic system.

That it did not come to that was due to the fact that Kahr and his associates had been sufficiently impressed by the liquidation of the Communist threat and by Stresemann's differences with the SPD to reassess the situation and become less headstrong in their tactics. This deceleration goaded Adolf Hitler and his hungry Nazi troopers into the much-celebrated Beer Hall Putsch of 8 November 1923 in which, with the moral encouragement of General Ludendorff, the young leader tried to take over the faltering enterprise and inaugurate the awakening of Germany. The triumvirate did not take kindly to this presumptuous behaviour, and they let Hitler go his own way, which, on the morning of 9 November, led up the narrow Residenzstraße past the Feldherrnhalle to the opening of the Odeonsplatz, where a ragged volley from the rifles of the Landespolizei ended the march on Berlin, led to the Führer's capture and imprisonment, and gave the National Socialist movement its first martyrs.[71]

It also ended the last of the political crises that had made the survival of democratic government so problematical in 1923. After

[70] On this crisis, see Turner, *Stresemann*, pp. 128 ff.
[71] The fullest account is Gordon, *Beer Hall Putsch*, Ch. 12.

9 November the anti-republican tone of Bavarian politics waned perceptibly. Although Kahr survived as a figure of consequence until Hitler took his revenge in the Night of the Long Knives in 1934, he gave up his grandiose schemes; and the government of Heinrich Held which took over from Knilling in 1924 and lasted until 1933 showed no desire to revive particularist passions. Stresemann's Fabian tactics had been successful after all. The SPD, however, was not ready to admit it. When the Reichstag reconvened on 20 November, they renewed their attacks on the Chancellor's Saxon policy and, on 23 November, joined with the Nationalists to defeat his government. Ebert was furious with his party. 'The reasons why you have felled the Chancellor will be forgotten in six weeks,' he said, 'but you will feel the effects of your stupidity for the next ten years.' It is possible that some of them did regret their vote later on, but, if so, it did not affect their subsequent behaviour. Stresemann's was not, sadly, the last Great Coalition that they were to destroy.

IV

Before he was forced to relinquish the chancellorship, Stresemann had put in train the measures that finally led to the stabilization of the currency and the end of the inflation. After Rudolf Hilferding, his Socialist Minister of Finance, had proved unsuccessful in coping with the intractable problem, the Chancellor took advantage of the reconstruction of the cabinet in October to replace him with Hans Luther, former mayor of Essen and Minister of Food under Cuno. Luther was a sanguine and, what was more important, a tough-minded man, who was incapable of being intimidated by the industrialists and financiers who had profited from the inflation; and he soon acquired a partner even more ruthless than he, when Havenstein, President of the Reichsbank, died and was replaced by Hjalmar Greeley Schacht, to the dismay of the banking community, who favoured Karl Helfferich, a man more sympathetic to their interests. To replace the old mark, which was by this time worth no more than the trillionth part of a dollar, Luther established a new bank of issue, whose notes (Rentenmark) were covered by mortgage bonds based on the assets of industry and agriculture. Schacht prevented the new currency from being debauched by those whose speculation had fed the depreciation of the old by imposing rigid limits on the amount issued, by cutting off new credits to industry, and by compelling the speculators to sell the $1\frac{1}{2}$ billion dollars of foreign currency that they had accumulated to the Reichsbank. The virtual doubling of the bank's gold and foreign exchange reserves that followed from this in

1924, and the simultaneous cut-back in government expenditures made possible by the ending of passive resistance, balanced the budget and restored national confidence, and the inflation came to an end.[72]

Its political cost had been great, and it left wounds in the collective psyche that did not heal in the years of relative stability that now, thanks to the achievements of Stresemann's chancellorship, began for the German Republic.

[72] On the stabilization of the currency, see Bresciani-Turroni, *Economics of Inflation*, Chs. 9, 10; Bonn, *Wandering Scholar,* pp. 281–6; Hans Luther, *Politiker ohne Partei* (Stuttgart, 1960), pp. 109–247; Williamson, *Helfferich*, pp. 383–94; Hjalmar Schacht, *Confessions of 'The Old Wizard'* (Boston, 1956), pp. 162–78.

XIII
Weimar Culture

. . . unsere merk würdige Zeit: die trübe, verzweifelte, und doch
so fruchtbare Zeit nach dem großen Krieg.
                    HERMANN HESSE, *Morgenlandfahrt* (1932)[1]

L'Allemagne n'est pas une entreprise sociale et humaine, c'est
une conjuration poétique et démoniaque.
                    JEAN GIRAUDOUX, *Siegfried* (1928)[2]

WHEN the Nationalist Socialists came to power, they instituted a policy of general denigration of the culture of the
Weimar period, dismissing it as *Kulturbolschewismus* and
pretending that nothing that was created between the end of the war
and 1933 was worth looking at, listening to, reading, or thinking
about. Adolf Hitler is supposed to have said scornfully, 'Fourteen
years, a junkyard! (*Ein Trümmerfeld!*).'

It would be difficult to find any scientific or humanistic achievement by the Nazis that gives a scintilla of support to this attitude. As
we shall have occasion to see, Nazi culture was a *contradictio in adjecto*
and, in most of its manifestations, eminently forgettable. But the
poetry of Rilke and George and Benn has not been forgotten, nor
have the novels of the brothers Mann and Hermann Hesse and
Alfred Döblin, or the drama of Expressionism, or the work of the
Bauhaus, or the music of Schönberg. And these are but a few of the
works of the spirit and the imagination that make it justifiable to say
that, in the richness and variety of its cultural accomplishments, the
Weimar period is second to none in German history.

This achievement was possible in large part because of the freedom and encouragement that the Republic, in contrast to most other
regimes at the time, gave to its artists and intellectuals so that they
could express themselves as they wished. It is interesting to note how
few of them seemed to feel any reciprocal obligation or any inclination to come to the Republic's defence when, in the years of the
great depression, its many foes gathered for their final assault upon
German democracy.

---

[1] Hermann Hesse, *Morgenlandfahrt* (1932), Ch. 1.
[2] Jean Giraudoux, *Siegfried. Pièce en 4 actes* (Paris, 1928), act I, sc. 2.

I

Weimar Germany has so often been described as a cradle of modernity that we do well to remind ourselves that most of the movements that we associate with it—Expressionism in art and literature, Bauhaus architecture, the physics of relativity, psycho-analysis, and depth psychology, the sociology of knowledge, and atonal music—had their origins before the war, and in some cases —Expressionist poetry, for example—had produced their finest fruits in the pre-war period.[3] The description is nevertheless justified. Although the epochal discoveries of de Broglie, Planck, and Einstein, and of Freud, Adler, and Jung, were made earlier, it was only in the twenties that they entered into the popular consciousness and began to affect people's attitudes about themselves and the world they lived in. It was only now that the word relativity was charged with cosmic meaning and that quite ordinary people talked about frustrations and about inferiority and Oedipus complexes.[4] Similarly, while painters like Kirchner, Schmidt-Rotluff, and Nolde had developed their characteristic styles before 1914, their work was not widely seen, partly because William II proclaimed that art that ventured 'beyond the laws and limits imposed by Myself' was not art at all and because the directors of state-supported galleries accepted this as a guide-line for acquisition. It was in the 1920s that these restrictions fell away, that special exhibitions were arranged for modern artists, and that visitors to museums became used to seeing paintings that broke with all of the formalistic canons of the past.[5]

Weimar culture was pre-eminently modern also because those who created it felt that it was and believed that they were living in a new age in which everything had to be created afresh. The great caesura of the war gaped between them and a past whose institutions, traditions, and values had been smashed beyond repair, and they felt this as a release and a challenge. In a book called *The Collapse of German Idealism*, published in 1919, the conservative writer Paul Ernst expressed this feeling by crying, 'Our age is over! Thank God, it is over! A new age dawns that will be different!'[6] This sense of beginning anew, this eagerness to be different and to do things in different ways, was characteristic of the style of the twenties. At its

[3] See above, Ch. VI, pp. 221–2.
[4] Bruno E. Werner, *Die Zwanziger Jahre von Morgens bis Mitternachts* (Munich, 1962), p. 37.
[5] Laqueur, *Weimar*, pp. 164–5.
[6] Werner, *Die Zwanziger Jahre*, p. 17.

worst, it led to the kind of trendiness that Franz Werfel made fun of in verse that portrayed modern man as prone to every fad that came along from Communism to African art and from eastern mysticism to ballroom-dancing.

> Eucharistisch und thomistisch,
> Doch daneben auch marxistisch,
> Theosophisch, kommunistisch,
> Gotisch kleinstadt–dombau–mystisch,
> Aktivistisch, erzbuddhistisch,
> Überöstlich taoistisch,
> Rettung aus der Zeit-Schlamastik,
> Suchend in der Negerplastik,
> Wort und Barrikaden wälzend,
> Gott und Foxtrott fesch verschmelzend.[7]

At its best, it manifested itself in a keenness to experiment with new ideas and new forms so that the quality of life and the values that guided it might be improved. This was true, for instance, of the drama of the early Weimar period, of the work of Walter Gropius and his associates at the Bauhaus, and, to a lesser extent, of musical composition and performance.

In his memoirs the actor Fritz Kortner has left a stirring description of the première of Leopold Jessner's new production of Schiller's *Wilhelm Tell* at the Staatliches (formerly Königliches) Schauspielhaus in Berlin in the spring of 1919. The performance aroused furious indignation among a large part of the audience, not only because the entrance of the tyrant Gessler, played by Kortner in a uniform festooned with decorations from all branches of the old army, was heralded by the sound of a horn similar to that used on the late Emperor's car, but because the stage was completely bare of the conventional trappings of the Naturalistic theatre. Thus, when Ernst Basserman began Tell's famous soliloquy

> Durch diese hohle Gasse muß er kommen
> (Through this empty pass he must come)

the action was interrupted by angry shouts of 'Where is it?' and chanted choruses of 'Jewish swindle! Jewish swindle!'[8]

Those who demanded opulence and overstuffed sets from the theatre continued to find what they wanted at Hans Poelzig's extraordinary Großes Schauspielhaus (one of the few examples of Expressionism in architecture), which presented grandiose revues like Benatzky's *Das weiße Rössl*, or at the Metropoltheater, where

[7] Franz Werfel, *Spiegelmensch* (Berlin, 1920), p. 130.
[8] Fritz Kortner, *Aller Tage Abend* (Munich, 1959), pp. 351–60.

Fritzi Massary and Richard Tauber sang the Lehar operettas *Land des Lächelns* and *Friedericke*, or in the extravaganzas of Max Reinhardt, who lived up to his pre-war reputation for elaborate effects with his production of Vollmoeller's *Mirakel* in 1923 and the famous production of Hofmannsthal's *Jedermann* at the Salzburg Festival. But the best writers and producers followed Jessner's lead, and, when we think of theatre in the Weimar period, our minds turn to their experimentation with unconventional techniques and their attempts, not always successful, to substitute imagination for furniture.

Germany's greatest dramatist once wrote an essay in which he argued that the theatre was a moral institution, 'the common channel through which the glow of wisdom flows from the intelligent, superior part of society and spreads itself in gentle streams through the whole state'.[9] In the first years after the war the German theatre generally shared this view of itself and its purpose, and moral earnestness played its part even in the comedy of manners as written by Feuchtwanger, Sternheim, and Rehfisch. It was most pronounced, however, in the productions of Erwin Piscator at the Theater am Nollendorfplatz in Berlin, where a variety of techniques, including the use of film-strips and newspaper montage, were employed to carry the gospel of social revolution to fashionable west-end audiences,[10] and in the Expressionist theatre.

Lothar Schreyer once described Expressionism as 'the spiritual movement of a time that places inner experience above external life', and the Expressionist dramatists seemed to agree, for they relied heavily upon abstraction and symbolism, often giving their characters no names and identifying them only by occupation, and having them communicate with each other in bursts of ecstatic incantation rather than in ordinary language.[11] 'Words are confused speech,' Gerhard Hauptmann wrote in his Expressionist play about Montezuma and Cortez. 'Screaming is clarity! Screaming is truth!'[12]—words that may have prompted Thomas Mann's portrayal in *Der Zauberberg* of Pieperkorn/Hauptmann delivering a

---

[9] 'Was kann eine gute stehende Schaubühne eigentlich wirken?', in Friedrich Schiller, *Sämtliche Werke*, ed. Gerhard Fricke and Herbert G. Göpfert (2nd edn., 5 vols., Munich, 1960), v. 828.

[10] On Piscator, see Jürgen Rühle, *Theater und Revolution* (Munich, 1963), pp. 132–58.

[11] On Lothar Schreyer and the literature of ecstasy, see Soergel and Hohoff, *Dichtung und Dichter* ii. 162–7.

[12] *Der weiße Heiland*, sc. 8, in Gerhard Hauptmann, *Gesammelte Werke in sechs Bänden* (Berlin, n.d.), suppl. vol. ii. 136 f.

harangue beside a waterfall that makes it inaudible and his later reference in his story about the inflation period, *Disorder and Early Sorrow*, to 'artists of the new school who stand on the stage in strange . . . and utterly affected dancing attitudes and shriek lamentably'.[13] But the rhapsodic style, and the use of stark sets that facilitated movement and choral effects were intended to enhance the didactic purpose, overwhelming the audience not by dramatic argument but by the emotion engendered by these technical innovations. In this way, the Expressionist drama sought to advance the liberation of mankind from ancient error, from war and nationalism (Reinhard Goering's *Seeschlacht* and Fritz von Unruh's *Heinrich aus Andernach*), from social and economic conditions that enslaved and corrupted the masses (Toller's *Massemensch* and Georg Kaiser's *Gas*), and from false systems of values and religious codes that stifled the soul (Bert Brecht's *Baal* and Ernst Barlach's *Sündflut* and *Der blaue Boll*).

The experimental theatre received some of its technical inspiration from a movement that did more to change the appearance of the modern world than any other force that was active in the twenties. This was the Bauhaus, which originated in a proclamation made in 1919 by a 36-year-old Berlin architect named Walter Gropius, announcing the establishment of a new school of art, architecture, and design at Weimar, the purpose of which would be to 'break down the arrogant barrier between craftsman and artist', to achieve a new unity of art and technology, and to 'conceive and create the new building of the future'. At Weimar (and later at Dessau) Bauhaus students first took a course on basic design planned by the Swiss artist Johannes Itten, in which they were encouraged to forget everything they had learned about art and to rely upon their spontaneous impulses in developing their sense of touch, colour, and space. They then moved to practical design and production, working with skilled craftsmen and a faculty of talented artists like Lyonel Feininger, Paul Klee, Wassily Kandinsky, and Josef Albers (painting), László Moholy-Nagy (photography and other arts), Herbert Bayer (graphics), Anni Albers (textile weaving), Oskar Schlemmer (stage design), Gerhard Marcks (sculpture), and Marcel Breuer and Mies van der Rohe (architecture and furniture design.)

Almost from the beginning the Bauhaus was a happy experiment, and its first exhibition, in the summer of 1923, was a landmark in the history of modern art. The high points in this week-long festival,

---

[13] Thomas Mann, *The Magic Mountain*, trans. H. T. Lowe-Porter (New York, 1945), pp. 620–1 (Ch. 7); *Stories of Three Decades*, trans. H. T. Lowe-Porter (New York, 1945), pp. 501–2.

which, partly because of Herbert Bayer's brilliant posters, attracted 15,000 visitors, were the stunning display of varied products that illustrated the exhibition's theme, 'Art and Technics: A New Unity', and the showing of a model house, designed by Georg Muche, with interior furnishings by Marcel Breuer. The programme also included a performance of Schlemmer's *Triadic Ballet*, which combined new concepts of stage design and costume with the use of puppets and automata in the dance, a programme of musical works by Stravinsky and Hindemith, who were frequent visitors at the Bauhaus, and a concert of Dadaistic music and improvised jazz by the student band.

Throughout its career the Bauhaus was under fire from right-wing groups who sensed nefarious political purpose behind its activities or were outraged by its flaunting of tradition. Financial pressures resulting from this prompted the move to Dessau in 1924 and, shortly before Hitler's accession to power, a second migration from Dessau to Berlin. It soon became apparent that it could not survive the intellectual climate of triumphant National Socialism, and Mies van der Rohe, who had become director in 1930, dissolved the movement and went, like Gropius, Moholy-Nagy, Breuer, Bayer, and Albers, to the United States, where they were greeted with open arms. This reception was understandable. In their fourteen years of collaboration they had demonstrated that objects of everyday living like furniture, cutlery, china, and lamps could be made to combine simplicity, strength, and beauty, and they had revolutionized industrial design and helped invent a new architecture. This was no mean achievement. The Bauhaus had come a long way towards fulfilling the challenge made by Walter Gropius in his inaugural address in 1919, when he said, 'Let us create together the building of the future . . . as a crystalline symbol of a new and rising faith'.[14]

Germany's contributions to modern music during the Weimar period were somewhat less impressive, but nevertheless notable. The great musical revolutionary of the pre-war period, Richard Strauß, continued to produce works that were well received—*Die Frau ohne Schatten* (1919), *Intermezzo* (1924), *Die ägyptische Helena* (1928), and *Arabella* (1933)—but none of them had the originality

---

[14] On all this, see esp. Wolf von Eckardt, 'Bauhaus', *Horizon* (Nov. 1961), 60–74. See also Hans M. Wingler, *The Bauhaus* (New York, 1969); Barbara Miller Lane, *Architecture and Politics in Germany, 1918–1945* (Cambridge, Mass., 1968); and *Paul Klee in Selbstzeugnissen und Bilddokumenten*, ed. Carola Giedion-Welcker (Reinbeck bei Hamburg, 1961), pp. 67 ff.

and excitement of his earlier creations. The new forces were Hindemith and Schönberg. A remarkably versatile composer with considerable influence both in Germany, where he was head of the composition class at the Berlin Hochschule für Musik after 1927, and abroad, Hindemith wrote string quartets, song-cycles based on the poetry of Rilke and the Expressionist Georg Trakl, jazz music, and operas, two of which—*Cardillac* (1926) and *Mathis der Maler* (1934)—established themselves in the European repertory. Less prolific, but more revolutionary in his technique, was the creator of the twelve-tone scale and of atonal music, Arnold Schönberg, who became a favourite target of the traditionalists without allowing this to affect his work, of which the *Gurrelieder* and *Verklärte Nacht* are the most frequently heard products. Schönberg's influence was carried further by his students Anton Webern and Alban Berg, the composer of the operas *Wozzek* and *Lulu*. Other gifted innovators, whose style was less inaccessible to the general public than the composers of the Schönberg school, were Ernst Krenek, whose jazz opera *Jonny spielt auf!* was hailed enthusiastically at the time of its première in 1927 but is now not often heard, and Kurt Weill, whose music for Brecht's *Dreigroschenoper* (1928) and *Mahagonny* (1930) was to win him a world reputation.[15]

It was a sign of the openness of Weimar cultural life to new ideas that performances of the new music were not restricted to the largest cities. The premières of Strauß's *Die ägyptische Helena* and *Arabella* were in Dresden; Darmstadt, a town of 100,000 with an opera repertory that had seldom in the past strayed far from Mozart, Wagner, Bizet, and Lortzing, experimented with Auber's revolutionary opera *The Dumb Woman of Portici* (1828) in 1928 and was the first place apart from Berlin to hear Berg's *Wozzek*;[16] and other provincial theatres were no less progressive. As the musical capital of the country, Berlin, with three opera-houses—the State Opera under Eric Kleiber's direction, the Kroll Opera (Otto Klemperer), and the Municipal Opera (Bruno Walter)—with other leading conductors like Wilhelm Furtwängler, Fritz Busch, and the young Herbert von Karajan, and with a wealth of symphony orchestras, string quartets, and choral groups, showed both the greatest variety and the greatest willingness to experiment. Milhaud, Schönberg, Shostakovich, and Hindemith received the same attention as more familiar composers; the first performance of *Wozzek* at the Kroll Opera was followed by an equally triumphant première of

---

[15] On the musical scene, see Laqueur, *Weimar*, pp. 155–62.
[16] Rudolf Bing, *Five Thousand Nights at the Opera* (New York, 1972), p. 36.

Leoš Janáček's *Jenufa*, directed by Eric Kleiber. In 1931, when Carl Ebert succeeded Walter as musical director of the Municipal Opera, he not only mounted a new production of Mozart's *Die Entführung aus dem Serail*, which broke with the orthodox treatment of that work, but also started a Verdi revival of some consequence. Interest in the Italian composer had been aroused by Franz Werfel's novel about him in 1924, a book that was both a farewell to Expressionism on the author's part and an attack upon the musical dominance of Wagner.[17] Now Ebert staged *Macbeth*, which had not been done since the nineteenth century, with sets by Caspar Neher and with Fritz Stiedry on the podium, and he followed this with an impressive production of *Un Ballo in Maschera*, with Neher and Fritz Busch.[18]

In literature and the theatre, in the visual arts and music, the forces of modernity were strongly at work throughout the republican period and were encouraged both by the prevailing post-war temper and by the moral, and sometimes tangible, support given by the federal and state governments. In this connection it may be noted that, on the state level, the arts received more generous treatment when Social Democrats were in power than otherwise. The clerical government of Bavaria was always suspicious of literary men with advanced ideas, and it was the victory of conservatism in Thuringia after 1923 that forced the Bauhaus to move from its original home.

II

The Weimar Republic also experienced a revolution in manners and morals that justified its claim to modernity. As in other countries, the war had wrought profound changes in such things as dress, social behaviour, attitudes toward work and leisure, family relationships and the privileges of young people, religious faith, and the relations between the sexes; and in the case of some of them the changes had been further influenced by the instability of the post-war years, the intermittent collapse of public order, and the chaotic conditions caused by inflation.

To speak in the most general terms, the net result of all this had been to weaken the pillars of orthodoxy. The Churches, largely because of their excessively patriotic stance during the war and their clinging to past loyalties, had lost much of their former influence. Revolt against parental authority was a commonplace of Expressionist literature, the tone having been set by Walter Hasenclever's *Der Sohn* (1914) and Franz Werfel's short novel *Nicht der Mörder, der*

---

[17] See Peter Gay, *Weimar Culture: The Outsider as Insider* (New York, 1968), p. 123.
[18] Bing, *Five Thousand Nights*, pp. 41 ff.

Ermordete ist schuldig (1920). The parallel repudiation of the surrogate father, the schoolmaster, was so constant a feature of the novel and the cinema—found equally in Leonhard Frank's *Die Ursache*, in which a young man murders his former teacher, in Wilhelm Suskind's *Jugend*, and in films like Sternberg's *The Blue Angel* (based on Heinrich Mann's novel *Professor Unrat*) and Carl Froelich and Leontine Sagan's *Mädchen in Uniform*—that there is no doubt about its pervasiveness.

It was no longer possible to make the kind of complaint voiced in 1912 by Gustav Wyneken, the leader, with Hans Blüher, of the pre-war Jugendbewegung. Wyneken had written:

> Should it not fill us with terror to think that these young people, who are subordinated for the greatest part of the day to the routine of a uniformed book-learning, who are dressed in ridiculous bits of clothes and carry the signs of the myopia of our century on their faces, and who arouse our pity and our anger as they trot from house to school and from school to house—to think that these impoverished existences . . . glow with life and could sparkle and shine . . . and yet have no inkling of it or longing for it? . . . We need a new culture of youth—at long last, of youth!—for such a thing has never existed among us. We need a new, a real, youth, for we still hardly know what youth looks like.[19]

The liberation that Wyneken desired had now been largely accomplished. Young people were no longer deferential to their parents and their teachers and their codes of behaviour and morality. They were more critical and more flexible than young people before the war, for they were all too aware of the transitory nature of things. As one of their number, Klaus Mann, wrote:

> We are in the peculiar position of regarding everything as possible, and that keeps us ready and protects us from torpidity. Will we have a monarchy and an emperor in the country next week? We would not be in the least astonished by that. Will we have a Communist Soviet state with terror and a red murder tribunal the day after tomorrow? We are prepared for anything.[20]

This did not mean, however, that German youth had won a new sense of assurance or a knowledge of what it wanted to accomplish in

[19] Soergel and Hohoff, *Dichtung und Dichter* ii. 325. On Wyneken and the pre-war movement, see Walter Laqueur, *Young Germany: A History of the Youth Movement* (New York, 1962), esp. Chs. 4, 6; and Pross, *Jugend, Eros, Politik*, pp. 130 ff., and *Vor und nach Hitler* (Olten and Freiburg im Breisgau, 1962), pp. 104 ff.; George L. Mosse, *The Crisis of German Ideology: Intellectual Origins of the Third Reich* (New York, 1964), esp. Chs. 9. 11; John Gillis, *Youth and History: Tradition and Change in European Age Relations, 1770–Present* (New York, 1974), pp. 149 ff.

[20] Klaus Mann, *Heute und Morgen* (Hamburg, 1927), p. 13.

life. Klaus Mann himself admitted, 'We are a generation that is united, so to speak, only by perplexity. As yet, we have not found the goal that might be able to dedicate us to common effort, although we all share the search for such a goal.'[21] The liberation of German youth tended, in short, to transform itself into a nagging 'Problem of German Youth', and it was, indeed, widely and incessantly discussed as such. This and the neo-romantic idealization of adolescence that was characteristic of much of what was left of the old youth movement played their part in the politics of the Republic's last years.

The liberation of German women from the fetters of the past also had its ambiguities.[22] Women now had the vote; their educational opportunities had greatly improved; the world of business had opened to them, and in the twenties eleven million of them were working full time, although still for the most part in relatively menial positions and at rates of pay inferior to those of their male compeers. In the cultural activities of the time their role was prominent; indeed, the memory of the Weimar period is inseparably associated with names like Elisabeth Bergner, Tilla Durieux, Fritzi Massary, and Trude Hesterberg in the theatre, Sigrid Onegin and Frida Leider in the opera, Mary Wigman in the dance, Else Lasker-Schüler, Gertrud le Fort, and Mechtilde Lichnowsky in literature, and Ricarda Huch in history. Armed with hard-earned degrees, many others were storming the barricades of the professions, and making their way in fields like psychology and sociology, which were less tradition-bound than some of the older disciplines.

German women had freed their bodies from the ugly and form-concealing garments of the pre-war period, abandoned the corset, and had their cascades of hair abbreviated to the styles known as the *Bubikopf* and the *Herrenschnitt*. They had also escaped from the time-worn prescriptions of what was or was not proper behaviour for women and had jettisoned ancient taboos against unaccompanied appearances in public places, the use of tobacco and liquor, and pre-marital sexual relationships. In Weimar Germany there were doubtless still many Effi Briests, whose lives were guided by older conventions and the fear of social disapproval, but one would not choose one of them as a representative of the new woman. A more likely fictional model would be the indomitable heroine of Vicki Baum's novel *Stud. chem. Helene Willfüer*, who makes her way to her goal despite financial want, personal tragedy, frustrated love, a child born out of wedlock, and the distraction of enormous quantities of

<hr>

[21] Ibid., p. 6.   [22] See above, Ch. VI, pp. 207–13.

time and energy to the dilemmas of her friends, never daunted by problems before which her male colleagues quail, asserting her moral superiority even over that adamantine figure of nineteenth-century fiction, the German professor, and establishing herself in the end as a research scientist with a reputation sufficient to allow her to dictate her own terms of employment. The tremendous success of the book, which went through seven editions, probably indicates that many women accepted Helene Willfüer as a figure to be admired and, if possible, emulated.

Yet even among the most liberated women there was some ambivalence. As Walter Laqueur has written, they welcomed the disappearance of the old moral conventions but regretted it at the same time; and, more often than not, they used their political power to vote for parties that had opposed giving it to them.[23] What their proper role should be was not at all clear to many of them, and, while they were thrilled by the sensation-packed pages of Vicki Baum, they also read the novels of a more respected writer, Ina Seidel, who constantly emphasized, as fundamental responsibilities of the German woman, motherhood, the family, the home, the soil.[24]

III

A notable feature of the cultural life of the Republic was the antipathy of its leading representatives towards the Weimar constitution and those who served it in government and Parliament. It goes without saying that support for the regime could not be expected from Communist intellectuals, who lived in the expectation of another and more successful Spartacist week or Hamburg rising and who, meanwhile, in journals like *Die Linkskurve*, preached the message that the Republic was nothing but a disguised form of Fascism that would disappear when the working class recognized its true character.[25] This view of the Republic as a transitional stage in German history was also the stock-in-trade of these ideologues of the New Right who will concern us in the next section, and their detestation of the constitutional system was as unalloyed as the publicists of the KPD. As for the university professors and those aspiring to academic chairs, they were, with few exceptions, solidly

[23] Laqueur, *Weimar*, p. 32.
[24] On Ina Seidel, see Soergel and Hohoff, *Dichtung und Dichter* ii. 677–82.
[25] See Werner T. Angress, 'Pegasus and Insurrection: *Die Linkskurve* and its Heritage', *Central European History*, i (1968), 35–55; Alfred Döblin, 'Katastrophe in einer Linkskurve', *Das Tagebuch*, 3 May 1930, reprinted in *Die Welt* (Hamburg), 6 June 1964; Jürgen Rühle, *Literatur und Revolution: Schriftsteller und Kommunismus* (Cologne and Berlin, 1960), pp. 184 f.

arrayed against a regime that periodically, if ineffectually, sought to limit their privileges and whose economic policies had, in their view, been responsible for the drastic reduction of their financial emoluments that resulted from the inflation.[26]

But the opposition of these groups, which was to be expected in any case, was probably less damaging psychologically than the mixture of indifference, disdain, and nagging criticism that came from many intellectuals who owed to the Republic their freedom to pursue their artistic objectives in their own way. It is true that this opposition included a good many journalists, writers, artists, professional men, and undomiciled academicians on the fringes of the literary world whose political views were naïve and muddled and whose opposition was important only because it was so general and because the Republic had so few vocal defenders. But among them there were also a not inconsiderable number of people whose achievements commanded wide respect and whose silence or ambiguity of attitude did the Republic a grave disservice.

It is not difficult to understand why the left-wing intelligentsia took the position they did. Many of them—and this included most of the Expressionist writers and artists who became interested in politics at the end of the war—had entertained the most unreasonable expectations of the Revolution of 1918 and of the role of leadership that they would have in the new dispensation, while remaining unwilling to acquire the political skills that would be needed if those ambitions were to be realized. Indeed, in their hearts, the Expressionist activists were contemptuous of politics and its practitioners. 'I cannot describe to you', Franz Werfel had written during the war, 'how contradictory to me are the concepts poetry and politics! The politician looks at life coldly; the evil of power has triumphed over him.' Under his leadership, it was believed, mankind had been induced to betray its best instincts and to accept the institutionalization of brute force, hatred, and greed. Only by casting off old political forms and outworn leadership and by a radical commitment to the belief that human beings are essentially good could society be transformed, a process that would be effected, the poet J. R. Becher wrote, by 'simple, brotherly, wholly natural love, the love of man for man, the unambiguous, irresistible faith in the evolution of

[26] See above, Ch. XI, pp. 452–4. Before the inflation, a professor's salary was seven times that of an unskilled worker; afterwards, the ratio was closer to 2 to 1. The economic troubles of the early 1920s also reduced state appropriations for higher education and sharply reduced funds for things like library purchases. All this deepened anti-republican feeling among the professoriate. See Ringer, *Mandarins*, pp. 63 ff.

humanity, in the way of God, endlessly proven in history, the final magnificent triumph of the good idea'.[27]

This—repeated in Leonhard Frank's widely read novel *Der Mensch ist gut* and in the often incoherent verse of dozens of contributors to Franz Pfemfert's journal *Aktion*—was heady but insubstantial stuff. The number of Expressionist activists who were active in any political sense, or who, like Ernst Toller and Erich Mühsam, went to the barricades to try to give a concrete form to their philosophy, was small. The great majority relied upon their eloquence to achieve their desires, and found that not very many people were listening. From the working class, whom they tended both to idealize and to patronize, and to whom they offered themselves as leaders, like the Billionaire's son in Kaiser's *Gas*, their mixture of anarchism and utopianism elicited no response. As Georg Lukács said aptly, they had no real way of communicating with the proletariat because 'their formulations of social problems were always on the level of a subjective idealism or a mystical objective idealism that showed no understanding of the actual social forces'.[28]

Unwilling to master those actualities, the Expressionist activists reacted with a sense of betrayal when other more practical persons strove with the intractable problems of the first post-war years and gradually created the conditions necessary for social order. The compromises that had been the price of that achievement they found repellent; and, in the stabilized republic made possible by Stresemann's chancellorship, they saw only a society that had given a new lease of life to the very things that they had hoped, by ecstatic utterance and appeals to humanity, to destroy: the authoritarian bureaucracy, the old military caste, the pre-war social system, and bourgeois ethical and moral standards. Ernst Toller expressed his personal feeling of outrage at this result in his late play *Hoppla wir leben!* (1928), the protagonist of which, a revolutionary who has been in an asylum for eight years because of a breakdown, returns to society and discovers that all of the things that he had fought to overcome have survived and that all of his former comrades have sold out to the established order in one way or another. An unregenerate rebel, he seeks to resume the struggle but is arrested and executed for a crime that he did not commit.

This kind of alienation was felt by all of the Expressionist activists,

---

[27] Victor Lange, 'Ausdruck und Erkenntnis: Zur politischen Problematik der deutschen Literatur seit dem Expressionismus', *Die neue Rundschau* (1963), 96 ff.; Rühle, *Literatur und Revolution*, pp. 275 ff.

[28] Georg Lukács, *Probleme des Realismus* (Berlin, 1955), pp. 155 ff.

and it is worth noting that none of them became a convinced supporter of the Republic. Those members of the movement who
retained an interest in politics after 1924 turned to extremer creeds,
Ludwig Rubiner, J. R. Becher, and Bertolt Brecht to Communism,
Arnolt Bronnen and Hanns Johst to National Socialism. Others, like
Werfel and Hasenclever, found substitutes for their old revolutionary enthusiasm in religion or occultism or existentialism or
retreated into that *Innerlichkeit* that regarded politics as something
with which the man of the spirit need have no concern.

It was one of the tragedies of the Weimar Republic that, at the very
moment when it was being given new hope of life by the political
and economic stabilization, this defection, which was not limited to
the Expressionists, should have taken place. Weimar democracy
needed all the friends and supporters it could find; it found few in the
world of literature. It is true, perhaps, that the country's two greatest
writers were temperamentally disposed in favour of the Republic,
but they did not seem to believe it capable of long life. Both Thomas
Mann and Hermann Hesse were fascinated by the general decline of
Western society, with the increasing materialism, and with what
seemed to them to be the pending conflict between anarchy and
authoritarianism. This, essentially, was the theme of Mann's novel
Der Zauberberg (1924), an impressive but ambiguous work, which
betrayed serious doubt about the ability of rationality to sustain
society in an age of crisis. Hesse not only shared this doubt—'For us
in old Europe', he wrote in *Klingsors letzter Sommer* (1920), 'everything has died that was good and unique to us. Our admirable
rationality has become madness, our gold is paper, our machines can
only shoot and explode, our art is suicide; we are going under,
friends'[29]—but at times expressed it in ways that appeared to be
veiled attacks upon the Republic. In his influential book *Steppenwolf*,
which appeared in 1927, there is a curious dream sequence in which
his protagonist finds himself occupied, together with a retired professor of theology, in ambushing motor cars and shooting their
occupants. They talk about the justifiability of this behaviour and
conclude that, because there are too many people anyway, they are
performing a useful service. The protagonist says:

Yes, what we are doing is probably mad, and probably it is good and
necessary all the same. It is not a good thing when a man overstrains his
reason and tries to reduce to rational order things that are not susceptible of
rational treatment. Then there arise ideals such as those of the Americans and

[29] Herman Hesse, *Klingsors letzter Sommer* (Insel-Bücherei, no. 502, n.d.), p. 51.

the Bolsheviks. Both are extraordinarily rational, and both lead to a frightful oppression and impoverishment of life, because they simplify it so crudely. The likeness of man, once a high ideal, is in process of becoming a machine-made article. It is for madmen like us, perhaps to ennoble it again.[30]

This sounds like a plea for irrationalism and for methods of government similar to those adopted later by Hitler. It was not, of course, anything of the sort, but rather, like its predecessor *Demian* (1919), a thoughtful book about the human dilemma and a plea for the full realization of human capabilities. But passages like this could be read with comfort and even with enthusiasm by the most inveterate opponents of the Republic.

More deliberate in their attacks upon the Republic and its values and institutions were the writers who were associated with the movement known as The New Objectivity or Matter-of-Factness (Die neue Sachlichkeit). Inaugurated in the mid-twenties by Joseph Roth, Hermann Kesten, and Erich Kästner, this group, 'in contrast to the simplifying pathos-mongers of the Expressionist movement, was made up of complete ironists, embittered critics of the ruling society, pure satirists, and Voltaireans', or so Kesten remembered their common bond thirty-five years later.[31] They regarded their function as one of exposing the weaknesses, injustices, and hypocrisies of their time, but they seemed to have little hope that anyone would do very much to correct the ills they exposed. If the Expressionists had had perhaps too naïve a faith in man's capacity for development, the New Objectivists were, in Alfred Döblin's description, 'disenchanted and disillusioned people'.[32] In Döblin's greatest novel, *Berlin Alexanderplatz* (1929), this pessimism was almost unrelieved. Not only is the hero, who comes out of prison determined to make himself a good citizen, corrupted, and broken, and in the end forced into submission by collective forces that are indifferent to individual hope and aspiration, but the drama of his life is played out in Berlin, the city that had been the pride of the old Empire, now portrayed as 'Sodom on the eve of its destruction'.[33]

Erich Kästner's novel of the depression years, *Fabian. Die Geschichte eines Moralisten* (1931), took an even gloomier view of

---

[30] Herman Hesse, *Steppenwolf*, trans. Basil Creighton (new edn., New York, 1957), pp. 266–7.

[31] Hermann Kesten, 'Brutstätte allen Unheils', *Die Zeit*, 22 Sept. 1961. An interesting account of the movement is Helmuth Lethen, *Die neue Sachlichkeit: Studien zur Literatur des 'Weißen Sozialismus'* (Stuttgart, 1970).

[32] Alfred Döblin, *Schicksalsreise* (Frankfurt-on-Main, 1949), p. 165.

[33] Walter Muschg, *Die Zerstörung der deutschen Literatur* (3rd edn., Berne and Munich, n.d.), Ch. 4.

contemporary German society and was not lightened by the crumbs of religio-philosophical comfort that Döblin offered his readers.[34] Through the lips of one of his characters, Kästner advances a theory of general guilt.

We are perishing because of the spiritual ease of all concerned. We want things to change, but we don't want a change in ourselves. . . . The bloodstream is poisoned . . . and we are content to paste a plaster on each place on the world's surface where sores appear. Can you cure blood-poisoning in that way? You cannot. The patient will one day collapse, covered from head to toes with plasters.[35]

About the capital of the Republic, Kästner was even more uncompromising than Döblin. 'In so far as this gigantic city consists of stone,' Fabian says, 'it has hardly changed. But with respect to its inhabitants, it has long resembled a madhouse. On the east side resides crime; in the centre, chicanery; on the north side, misery; on the west side, depravity; and on all sides dwells decadence.'[36]

The view that the moral fabric of society was eroded beyond repair was so common that it assumes significance. It was surely no coincidence that the figure of the *Hochstapler*, or confidence man, should play so large a part in the literature and drama of the time—in Rehfisch's *Das Duell am Lido*, for example, in which Marlene Dietrich had one of her first triumphs on the stage, in Thomas Mann's fragment of a novel, *Felix Krull* (1923), in Vicki Baum's *Menschen im Hotel*, in Brecht's *Dreigroschenoper* (1928), and in Wedekind's *Marquis von Keith*, which was revived with success in 1929.[37] When one glorifies the criminal, the hidden assumption is that the system he is preying on is not worth defending.

This assumption was certainly implicit in the politics of the New Objectivists. The title of Leonhard Frank's autobiographical novel, *Links wo das Herz ist*, fitted them as far as temperament was concerned. Their views on political and social questions ranged from the progressive to the radical, and they were instinctive opponents of capitalism, imperialism, militarism, the *Junker*, the conservatism of the Churches and the courts, and bourgeois conventions and values. But if they belonged to the left, they had no habitation there. Politically, they were homeless, because they would not tolerate party discipline. Contemptuous alike of the opportunism of the Social

[34] On this aspect of Döblin's novel, see Soergel and Hohoff, *Dichtung und Dichter* ii. 530–3; and Benno von Wiese, *Der deutsche Roman* (2 vols., Düsseldorf, 1963), ii. 291 ff.

[35] Erich Kästner, *Fabian. Die Geschichte eines Moralisten* (new edn., Cologne and Berlin, 1950), p. 37 (Ch. 3).

[36] Ibid., pp. 102–3 (Ch. 10).

[37] See Werner, *Die Zwanziger Jahre*, pp. 128–9.

Democratic party and the rigidity of the Communists, they added to the fragmentation of Weimar politics by forming short-lived splinter groups of their own, conscious of their isolation and compensating for it by an increasing degree of irresponsibility. This was also the hallmark of their journalistic activity, in which, with a fine disregard for political perspective, they were as critical of the Republic and the parties that defended it as they were of the enemy on the right.

This was true, for example, of Kurt Tucholsky, that nonpareil of comic invention, the greatest German satirist since Heine. On the staff of Carl von Ossietzky's independent left-wing journal *Die Weltbühne*,[38] he was easily the most prolific writer, so much so that he used four noms de plume, and he was an indefatigable fighter against anti-democratic forces and a merciless critic of what he considered to be the bourgeoisie's lack of civic virtue and its secret hankering after authoritarian government. Yet his political judgement was flawed by a lack of moderation and a violence of tone that served the cause of the people he detested. He never overcame his belief that Germany would have entered into an existence of milk and honey if it had not been for the failure of Social Democratic leadership in 1918, and his attacks upon 'the November criminals' were as intemperate as anything written by the ideologues of the extreme right. His detestation of Ebert exceeded even his hatred of Seeckt, and he did not hesitate to describe him as 'a functionary of mediocre talents' and 'a mediocre bourgeois, the worst mixture that one can imagine: personally incorruptible and professionally dirty' and to say that 'the complete victory of the German reaction . . . was Ebert's fault'.[39]

Nor did Tucholsky limit himself to criticizing the sins of omission of 1918. He showed the same skewed perspective in judging the politics of the stabilization period. He was capable of writing in 1927, in an essay on the veterans' organization called the Stahlhelm, which was a source of some concern to the French Government and to others who worried about the growth of paramilitary forces:

The great danger for European peace . . . does not lie in the Stahlhelm. . . . The real danger in Germany is the intra-party Stresemann type. . . . Since 1913 I have belonged to those people who believe that the German spirit is poisoned almost beyond recovery, who do not believe in an improvement, who regard German democracy as a façade and a lie, and who, despite all

[38] See Istvan Deak, *Weimar Germany's Left-Wing Intellectuals. A Political History of the Weltbühne and its Circle* (Berkeley, 1968), and Raimund Koplin, *Carl von Ossietzky als politischer Publizist* (Berlin, 1964).

[39] Kurt Tucholsky, *Gesammelte Werke*, ed. Mary Gerold-Tucholsky and Fritz J. Raddatz (8 vols., Hamburg, 1962), ii. 287, 322, 972, 1302.

assurances and optimistic touches, believe that an empty steel helmet is not as dangerous as a silk hat.[40]

Two years later, in his picture-book with text called *Deutschland, Deutschland über alles*, he included a number of cheap slurs on republican leaders that showed a staggering naïvety about the foreign and domestic problems with which they had to cope. All in all, it is difficult not to agree with Paul Sethe, who, in an otherwise generous appreciation of Tucholsky's talents, wrote that, while democratic politicians 'exhausted their energies in hard combat with Hugenberg and Hitler, [he] stood aside and jeered at them. They could have used help. All they got was scorn and laughter.'[41]

Tucholsky's attitude was all too common among the left-wing intellectuals, and their continual variations on the theme of the degeneracy of the society in which they were living could not help but hearten those bent upon the destruction of the Republic.

IV

Not all of the Weimar intellectuals were to be found on the left. The right had its ideologues too, and their influence, particularly upon German youth, was formidable enough to worry the supporters of democracy. This would not have been true had they been mere *laudatores temporis acti*, recommending a return to a past that was rapidly dimming in memory. Their distinguishing characteristics were their repudiation of both the Republic and the Empire it had replaced and their apocalyptic vision of a new revolution that would smash all systems and transform all values and lead to the emergence of a new Reich of incomparable strength and moral integrity. In their pursuit of this objective, they refused to be guided by traditional criteria, they rejected the view that political action must be rational in motivation and goal, and they idealized violence, not only for its efficacy in achieving the kinds of goals they sought, but for its inherent value. Most of them were patriots and idealists, a fact that lent a high moral tone to their literary exercises that contrasted with the cynicism of much of the writing of the New Objectivists; but they were also nihilists and irrationalists. In a real sense, they were the intellectual advance guard of the rightist revolution that was to be effected in 1933; and, although most of their outstanding figures

[40] Ibid., 789 ff.

[41] Paul Sethe, 'Tucholskys tragische Irrtümer', in *Die Zeit*, 10 Apr. 1964. These comments, and much else in this section, are based on, and reproduce in part, my article 'Engagement and Neutrality in Weimar Germany', *Journal of Contemporary History*, ii, no. 2 (1967), 49–63.

were contemptuous of National Socialism and its Führer, they did much to pave his road to power.[42]

The most influential of these intellectuals of the radical right, or neo-conservatives as they are sometimes called to distinguish them from run-of-the-mill reactionaries or supporters of the new Nationalist party, were Arthur Moeller van den Bruck and Oswald Spengler. The former was a descendant on his father's side of a long line of Prussian soldiers, bureaucrats, and Evangelical pastors and was a writer of established reputation before 1918; the latter, a retired schoolmaster who lived in obscurity until he startled the world in 1918 with a very large book called *The Decline of the West*. The difference in background did not impair the natural affinity of their political and philosophical views. Both were cultural pessimists in the tradition of Nietzsche, Paul de Lagarde, and Julius Langbehn; both were opposed to 'the frightful form of soulless, purely mechanical capitalism, which attempts to master all activities and stifles every free independent impulse and all individuality' and to modern science, which was its handmaiden;[43] both were convinced that a society dominated by these forces and by the debilitating philosophy of liberal democracy was degenerate and doom-laden; and both called for the creation of an élite of heroes to save Germany from this impending fate.

Even before the defeat of 1918 had given new urgency to his writing, Moeller van den Bruck had elaborated what were to be the main features of his political philosophy. In his view, the arch-enemy of German culture was liberalism, which he equated with everything that was flabby and corrupt,[44] and which he believed destroyed the heroic spirit of men by the emphasis it placed upon goodness and rationality and the encouragement it gave to indiscipline and moral laxity, in the name of freedom, and to money-grubbing and wasting luxury, in the name of progress. Liberalism falsified the true nature of life and stunted the instincts and drained the energies that men should have to cope with its harsh realities; it promoted the decline of nations by sapping their moral fibre and depriving them of passion and the will to power. Evidence of this was already to be found in the nations of Western and Southern Europe, which were showing all the signs of decrepitude, and Germany would succumb to the same

---

[42] Kurt Sontheimer, *Anti-Demokratisches Denken in der Weimarer Republik* (Munich, 1962), p. 178, and the essay with the same title, in *Der Weg in die Diktatur*, ed. Christian Gneuss (Munich, 1962), p. 67.

[43] Oswald Spengler, *Briefe 1913–1936*, ed. Anton M. Koktanek and Manfred Schröter (Munich, 1963), p. 203 (Eduard Meyer to Spengler, 25 June 1922).

[44] Stern, *Cultural Despair*, p. 197.

disease unless a will to resistance were inspired in the bosoms of its young men. To provide them with models was the purpose of Moeller's pre-war writing, his multi-volume series of historical portraits of German heroes from Hermann the Cherusker to the great Frederick (*Die Deutschen*, 1904–10) and his appeal for a return to the antique Prussian virtues of simplicity, honour, and courage, which were in danger of being eaten away by the prevalent cultural relativism (*Der preußische Stil*, 1914).[45]

The war convinced Moeller that the Germans had not lost the heroic virtues, and the defeat of 1918 did not persuade him that they must now lapse into desuetude. He was one of the first and most influential preachers of the 'stab-in-the-back' theory, arguing that Germany had been robbed of victory by the cleverness of the Allies, who had used the shop-worn ideals of liberalism and democracy to persuade the gullible Americans to come to their aid and had then used the false promise of a magnanimous Wilson peace to trick the war-weary German people into giving up the fight. But 'a people is never lost if it understands the meaning of its defeat'. The Germans must rid themselves of the system built on the betrayal of 1918 in a new revolution that would destroy the system of values that had led them to their present lowly situation and would usher in the Third Reich.

What the precise nature of the new order was to be Moeller never made very clear. He seemed to have in mind a society that would be freed of anything resembling the Weimar party system and would have a corporative form of government under the direction of leaders who would combine the talents of Frederick the Great, Bismarck, and Hugo Stinnes. Even in Moeller's last book, *Das Dritte Reich* (1925), the precise outlines of the Third Empire were obscured by the mist of rhetoric. What, after all, was one to make of the following statement?

German nationalism champions the Final Reich. This is always promised. And it is never fulfilled. It is perfection that can only be achieved in imperfection. . . .There is only one Reich, as there is only one Church. Others claim the name—the State, the community, the sects. But there is only *the* Reich. German nationalism fights for the possible Reich. The German nationalist of this age is, as a German, still and always a mystic, but as a political being he has become a sceptic. He knows that the realization of an idea is always increasingly postponed, that the spiritual in the actual usually—and this is very political—looks very human, and that nations

---

[45] Klemens von Klemperer, *Germany's New Conservatism: Its History and Dilemma in the Twentieth Century* (Princeton, 1957), pp. 155 ff.

always realize the idea that is laid upon them only to the extent that they succeed in asserting themselves historically.[46]

Yet perhaps precision and definition were less important than passion and the conviction that change was coming because it must come. Alienated and disoriented young people, who saw no remedy for their discontents in the prescriptions of the established parties, were drawn to Moeller's programme because it attacked all the things that they hated themselves and because it held out the hope of a new dispensation in which their willingness to believe and their special talents would be rewarded. The very abstractness of Moeller's thought made them think that it was profound, and clubs were founded to discuss his ideas and how they should be effected. One of these, the Juni-Club, founded in June 1919, became the centre of the whole neo-conservative movement, attracting people like Paul Fechter, one of Stinnes's editors, Rudolf Pechel of the *Deutsche Rundschau*, the novelist Hans Grimm, Walter Schotte of the *Preußische Jahrbücher*, and Otto Strasser, later a member of the National Socialist movement and still later a dissident from it. The house organ of this group was the journal *Gewissen*, edited by Eduard Stadtler, a conservative review that became increasingly insistent upon a radical change in the political system, attacking the basic premisses of parliamentary government and intimating, ever more unambiguously, that dictatorship was the only practical method of tackling the nation's problems.[47]

It was through the June Club that Oswald Spengler came into contact with Moeller, and the meeting, and the mutual admiration that resulted from it, seem to have modified the extreme pessimism that characterized the first volume of *The Decline of the West*. That work, a morphological view of history, based on a loose comparison between our own time and the later centuries of the ancient world and tricked out with elaborate biological analogies,[48] has been described succinctly as 'a sombre murky vision of the doom of our civilization'.[49] The considerable stir caused by its appearance was due partly to the inference drawn by many readers that Spengler's clotted

---

[46] Moeller van den Bruck, *Das Dritte Reich* (3rd edn., Hamburg, 1931), pp. 320–1.

[47] See Stern, *Cultural Despair*, p. 231. On the ideas of this group, see Armin Mohler, *Die konservative Revolution in Deutschland 1918–32: Grundriss ihrer Weltanschauungen* (Stuttgart, 1950) and Otto-Ernst Schüddekopf, *Linke Leute von Rechts: Die national-revolutionären Minderheiten und der Kommunismus in der Weimarer Republik* (Stuttgart, 1960).

[48] Oswald Spengler, *The Decline of the West*, trans. Charles Francis Atkinson (2 vols., New York, 1926, 1928), i. 3.

[49] H. Stuart Hughes, *Oswald Spengler: A Critical Estimate* (New York, 1952), p. 7.

and pedantic prose not only explained, and to some extent palliated, Germany's defeat but proved that the victors were really in the same boat, since all members of Western culture were going down at the same time. After meeting Moeller, however, Spengler detected gleams of hope. Impressed by Moeller's view that a defeated Power that faced up to its situation possessed important advantages over victors who were unaware that their success had been adventitious, he seems to have begun to wonder whether Germany might not emerge as the one vigorous Power in an age of general decline. He joined the campaign to persuade German youth to make this possibility come true, supporting Moeller's call for action: 'The beast in mankind is creeping upon us. The shadow of Africa darkens Europe. We must be the guardians at the threshold of our values.'[50]

Spengler was an ambitious man who longed to be a mover and shaker, a confidant of people in high places, a person of influence in the chancelleries of the Great Powers, but he was incapable of inspiring confidence in people in responsible positions, and his efforts to play a role in the political intrigues of 1923 led General von Seeckt to write that he wished Spengler 'had gone down with the West—a political fool!'[51] Nor did his later writings live up to the impression made by his first work; he had a tendency, when dealing with contemporary politics, to make the most trivial and irresponsible charges against people and institutions he disliked and then to be exposed as incapable of corroborating them.[52] Seeckt was not alone in thinking him a fool. Harry Kessler heard him lecture at the Nietzsche-Archiv and came away feeling that he was 'a half-educated charlatan . . . a fat pundit with a flabby chin and a brutal mouth who for an hour poured out the tritest and most trivial stuff. . . . Not *one* original idea, not even *false* diamonds. Everything uniformly insipid, colourless, flat, boring. Yes, Spengler managed to make even Nietzsche boring!'[53]

It is a mistake, however, to assess a writer's significance solely on the basis of the impression that he makes on cultivated minds. There were many young Germans, perhaps less sophisticated then Kessler, who did not find what Spengler had to say either trivial or platitudinous; and awareness of this fact worried more traditional conservatives like Thomas Mann and the distinguished scholar Ernst

[50] Moeller van den Bruck, *Das Dritte Reich*, p. 322.
[51] Struve, *Elites against Democracy*, pp. 236 ff., 244.
[52] Hughes, *Spengler*, pp. 110 ff.; Spengler, *Briefe*, pp. 334–6, 341–2, 343–6 (letters of 12 June, 25 June, 5 Aug., 12 Aug. 1924).
[53] Kessler, *Tagebücher*, pp. 545 f.

Robert Curtius. These men experienced a mixed feeling of outrage and fear when they read Spengler's speech 'On the Political Duties of German Youth' (1924), in which he counselled his auditors to cast aside cultural and ethical baggage that would weigh them down on the difficult journey they must undertake, and in which he said:

Whether one is right or wrong—that doesn't amount to much in history. Whether or not he is superior to his adversary in a practical way, that is what decides whether he will be successful. . . . To be honourable and nothing else—that's not enough for our future. . . . To train oneself as material for great leaders, in proud self-denial, prepared for personal sacrifice, that is also a German virtue. And, given the case that, in the hard times ahead, strong men will appear, leaders to whom we must entrust our fate, then they must have something upon which they can rely. They need a generation such as Bismarck did not find, which appreciates their kind of action and does not reject it for romantic reasons, a dedicated band of followers who have, by way of long and serious self-training, come to the point of understanding the necessary and do not—as would doubtless be true today—reject it as un-German.[54]

This contemptuous dismissal of the values that had animated their own lives was bitterly offensive to Mann and Curtius. No less so was the brutal determinism of Spengler's philosophy, his insistence that it was 'the unalterable necessity of destiny' that had defined this generation's task and made obedience to it a duty. 'We Germans seek recourse too easily in destiny and tragedy,' Curtius wrote sadly, recognizing perhaps that, for perplexed and disillusioned people, destiny serves both to excuse and to ennoble their failure to assume responsibility for facing up to reality,[55] and that it was precisely this that made Spengler and Moeller (for fate bulked large in his system of ideas also) such dangerous preceptors of German youth.

There can be little doubt that their teaching, and that of other neo-conservatives with whom they were associated, encouraged three tendencies that were already all too prevalent in Germany: anti-intellectualism, the acceptance of violence, and political indifferentism. When they set off to the magic castle of their misty Third Reich, the intellectuals of the New Right turned their backs upon reason and its uses and then, defiantly, made a virtue of what they had done. In *The Decline of the West*, Spengler had argued that the idea of destiny was the answer to the narrow and lifeless theory of

---

[54] *Die Zerstörung der deutschen Politik: Dokumente 1871–1933*, ed. Harry Pross (Frankfurt-on-Main, 1959), pp. 88–9.

[55] Von Klemperer, *New Conservatism*, p. 172. See also Thomas Mann, 'Von deutscher Republik' (1922), in *Reden und Aufsätze* (Stockholmer Gesamtausgabe, 2 vols., Oldenburg, 1965), ii. 41 f.

causality used by historians and that 'the destiny-logic of the world-becoming' was to be preferred to 'the causal logic of notion and law' and 'the realm of direct intuitive vision' to be valued over 'that of a mechanical system of objects'.[56] Ernst Jünger, upon whom Spengler's book had great influence, not only accepted this position but boasted that it was a privilege to take part in the intellectuals' high treason against intellect.[57] He and his associates professed the belief that considered action was a sign of unmanliness, that the viscera were sounder guides than the mind, and that passion and sweat and blood would solve all problems. Jünger was always fascinated by barbarism. By writing in this vein, he took a long step toward it.

Closely connected with this was an attitude towards violence that amounted to idealization. In sharp contrast to the intellectuals of the left, to whom hatred of war and anti-militarism were articles of faith, the neo-conservatives not only justified war as an instrument of national policy but glorified it as an ennobling experience. A *Frontkämpfer* who had been wounded three times during the war, Jünger wrote in his volume of essays *Der Kampf als inneres Erlebnis* (1922): 'Combat is one of the truly great experiences. And I have still to find someone to whom the moment of victory was not one of shattering exaltation (*Rausch*) . . . I should not like to do without this force among the complex of emotions that drive us through life.' War was a necessity and a release. In it 'the true human being makes up in a drunken orgy for everything that he has been neglecting. Then his passions, too long dammed up by society and its laws, become once more uniquely dominant and holy and the ultimate reason.' In battle, in combat and death in the trenches, men find their way back to the elements, to the sources of life, to true being. War is thus fulfilment, but also preparation. For, as Jünger wrote of the 1914–18 War:

This war is not the end, but the chord that heralds new power. It is the anvil on which the world will be hammered into new boundaries and new communities. New forms will be filled with blood, and might will be hammered into them with a hard fist. War is a great school, and the new man will be of our cut.[58]

---

[56] Spengler, *Decline* i. 141.

[57] Ernst Jünger, *Werke*, vi (Stuttgart, 1964), p. 48 (*Der Arbeiter*, originally published in the autumn of 1932). See also Hans-Peter Schwarz, *Der konservative Anarchist: Politik und Zeitchronik Ernst Jüngers* (Freiburg im Breisgau, 1962), pp. 40–5.

[58] Ernst Jünger, *Der Kampf als inneres Erlebnis* (new edn., Berlin, 1925), pp. 76 f.; Schwarz, *Der konservative Anarchist*, pp. 67–8.

Jünger's eloquent pen had a good deal to do with the revival of war literature in the Weimar period, and it was not long before glorifi- cations of the recent holocaust were pouring from the presses in numbers that soon swamped the editions of anti-war books like Ludwig Renn's *Krieg* (1928) and Remarque's *Im Westen nichts Neues* (1929). Rudolf Binding's memoirs, *Vom Kriege* (1924), Georg von der Vring's *Soldat Suhren* (1927), Werner Beumelburg's *Trommelfeuer um Deutschland* (1929) and *Gruppe Bösemüller* (1930), and E. E. Dwinger's trilogy *Deutsche Passion* (1932) stressed the heroic aspects of the conflict rather than the suffering it entailed and, like Jünger's works, helped to persuade the generation that had not fought in the trenches in Flanders that their lives were still incom- plete without the ultimate experience.

This acceptance of the legitimacy and, indeed, positive value of external violence was accompanied by a condoning of the use of violence on the home front. If, as Moeller and the others said, the old past was bad and must be destroyed so that the true Germany might emerge, then surely it was permissible to use force against those who were seeking to preserve it. Thus, one of Rathenau's murderers argued, with the kind of logic that Spengler admired, that, while he had a high opinion of the Foreign Minister's abilities, he had to kill him because of them, for if allowed to live Rathenau might see to it that 'greatness grew once more out of this crumbling and despised time'.[59] Apart from this, the radical right had a pragmatic approach to domestic violence. In the absence of real war, it could, after all, serve as a surrogate school of heroism and collective action. Thus the young Adolf Hitler encouraged his Brown Shirts to engage in street-battles and even gave medals to participants in these bloody affrays. He recognized that organized violence was a means simul- taneously of training his private army, of weakening his rivals, of demonstrating the weakness of the existing regime, and of both intimidating and impressing the ordinary citizen. The intellectuals of the right were the first people to realize the propaganda value of violence and terror and to regard this as legitimizing their use.

Finally, not the least baleful of the influences of the neo- conservatives was the political indifference that they encouraged among the younger generation by telling it, in many ways and with ceaseless iteration, that the Republic was contemptible and un- worthy of support and that the sooner it fell the better. Even after 1930, when the tiger was at the gates, and when it was not difficult to guess that what followed a collapse of the Republic would bear little resemblance to the vision of Moeller van den Bruck, the ideologues of the right were unmoved and continued to preach political abstention.

The successor of the June Club in the Republic's last days was the Tat Circle, named after the influential journal edited, since 1929, by Hans Zehrer, a man with a nimble but somewhat miscellaneous mind, whose approach to political problems was strongly influenced by the writings of Max and Alfred Weber, Karl Mannheim, and Vilfredo Pareto. Zehrer was interested in the role of the intellectual in society and in the problem of generational conflict, which was becoming acute in the 1930s as the universities turned out twice as many graduates as there were jobs appropriate to their talents. He shared the resentment of these young academicians and fed it, by encouraging them to turn it against the Republic, and by talking about the necessity of developing the new élite that would rule Germany from their ranks. He elaborated plans to activate this idea, drawing on the experience and the language of the various leagues for young people, so that political analyses in *Die Tat* often resembled a fusion of Pareto's theory of élitism with slogans from the Youth Movement.[60] At the same time, the journal's editorial policy became increasingly anti-republican, and its position on the question of taking political responsibility in the present crisis uncompromisingly negative. Zehrer's parole for young Germany was a ringing call to inactivity. 'Achtung, junge Front! Draußenbleiben! (Attention, young front! Remain uncommitted!)'[61]

In 1919 Carl Schmitt, a brilliant political scientist who admired and shared the views of Moeller van den Bruck and Ernst Jünger, wrote, 'Everything romantic stands in the service of other unromantic energies.' These were prophetic words. The neo-conservative intellectuals were all romantics, whose approach to life and its problems was irrational, who confused rhetoric and aestheticism with political wisdom, but were as impatient as the Expressionist activists had been with the labours involved in mastering the political realities of their day. The Third Reich that was coming was not the one of which they had dreamed, nor were they to be its élite. Indeed, almost all of those who have been mentioned here refused to serve its leader, and some became part of the underground resistance to his rule. Even so, in the days of their greatest influence, they had

---

[60] Struve, *Elites against Democracy*, pp. 367–8 and, for an interesting analysis of Zehrer's thought, pp. 353–76.

[61] Von Klemperer, *New Conservatism*, p. 131.

been in his service, and he was the beneficiary of their attacks upon the values of the past, their repudiation of morality and rationality as the criteria of private and public conduct, their idealization of violence, and their contribution to the political irresponsibility of German youth.

V

No account of cultural tendencies in the Weimar years would be complete without some reference to the emergence of new forms of popular entertainment, and particularly to the film. The period was a golden age for the German cinema, a time of great directors like Carl Mayer, F. W. Murnau, and G. W. Pabst, of artists whose fame spread far beyond the boundaries of Germany, like Asta Nielsen, Conrad Veidt, Emil Jannings, and Marlene Dietrich, and of masterpieces like the Expressionist film *The Cabinet of Dr. Caligari* and such early sound-films as Josef von Sternberg's *The Blue Angel* (1930) and Fritz Lang's *M* (1931).

The films of the republican era have been subjected to extensive sociological and psychological analysis by authors seeking to find explanations for the failure of democracy or premonitions of things to come. In one fascinating study, Siegfried Kracauer has undertaken to demonstrate that there was, in the serious film of the period, an obsessive fascination with fate and authority and with the dilemma of the individual caught between the unavoidable alternatives of tyranny and chaos.[62] One should be cautious about generalizing from these findings; this is the same Kracauer who had written earlier that the Tiller Girls, an American troupe that delighted Germans during the inflation years with the beauty of their legs and the precision of their dancing, were a symbol of the Taylorization of art, of the disenchantment of society by means of capitalist rationalization, of the destruction of the 'mythic forces' by *Technisierung*.[63] The films that supported such portentous conclusions were more than balanced by the large number of technically sophisticated but essentially trivial motion pictures that attained tremendous popularity, like Erik Charrell's *The Congress Dances* (1931), with Conrad Veidt as Metternich, Willi Foertsch as Alexander I, and Lilian Harvey as the little milliner whose bitter-sweet romance with the Tsar was played out to the accompaniment of a sentimental song that reminded the audience that 'Das kommt nur einmal/ Das kommt nicht wieder.'

[62] Siegfried Kracauer, *From Caligari to Hitler: A Psychological History of the German Film* (Princeton, 1947).
[63] Lethen, *Neue Sachlichkeit*, p. 43.

The film was a source of entertainment and also of instruction. As Hans Harbeck wrote in 1929, in a poem called 'Kino, Kino über alles', one got more than the main feature for the price of admission. There were short features, often with comedians like Chaplin, Keaton, and Lloyd; there were travelogues; and there was always the newsreel.

> Das Boxendenkmal, festlich eingeweiht,
> das Dichtergrab, verweht und eingeschneit,
> das Schiff, das eine Beute ward der Wellen,
> der Inbegriff all dessen, was hienie-
> den gilt als Sensation und *dernier cri*,
> man sieht's, husch, husch, an sich vorüberschnellen.[64]

The world of the film, the poet wrote, was 'work of art and relaxing bath for the nerves'. He might have added that it was widener of horizons and passport to the world as well.

Radio broadcasting came later. In 1925 there were only 600 broadcasting stations in the whole world, and it was not until the early thirties that all major cities in Germany had stations of their own (Poelzig built his Haus des Rundfunks in Berlin in 1930) and ordinary citizens began to dream of buying their own sets. But by that time, there was usually at least one receiving set even in villages too small to have a cinema-house, and in such cases the practice of collective listening brought entertainment and instruction to the community and helped to reduce cultural parochialism.

Before the First World War spectator sports enjoyed little popularity in Germany; in the 1920s they fascinated persons of both sexes and every class. It was a decade of champions: Tilden, Cochet, Lenglen, Wills on the tennis-courts; Paavo Nurmi, the world's fastest human, on the track; Dempsey, Carpentier, and Schmeling in the ring; Gertrude Ederle conquering the Channel; Elly Beinhorn flying around the world. When they could not be seen in person, their exploits could be seen on the newsreel or listened to on the wireless. There were races between champion eights on the Havel in Berlin, and association football, now drawing monstrous crowds, in all large cities. Automobile racing was popular enough to justify the building of the Avus in Berlin for such contests; and most popular of all, in Berlin at least, was six-day bicycle racing, which drew thousands of people, proletarians and society swells, comfortable *Bürger* and stars of screen and stage, to the Sportpalast, where they sat above the whirring wheels, eating sandwiches and listening to the

---

[64] *Hier schreibt Berlin: Ein Dokument der 20er Jahre*, ed Herbert Günther (Munich, 1963), p. 49 f.

music, and, periodically, when there was a sudden acceleration of tempo and the cyclists burst into a sprint, being caught up in the frenzied excitement that fascinated the absconding cashier in Kaiser's *From Morn to Midnight*.

Childish, this sport. One rider must win because the other loses. Look up, I say! It's there, among the crowd, that the magic works. Look at them—three tiers—one above the other—packed like sardines—excitement rages. . . . From boxes to gallery one seething flux, dissolving the individual, recreating passion! Differences melt away, veils are torn away; passion rules! The trumpets blare and the walls come tumbling down. No restraint, no modesty, no motherhood, no childhood—nothing but passion! There's the real thing. That's worth the search. That justifies the price![65]

None of the official activities of the republican government of Weimar was capable of arousing the kind of enthusiasm and emotional commitment that these forms of popular entertainment were able to generate. This was not lost on certain of the Republic's enemies, who speculated about the possibility of harnessing these media of mass communication to their own purposes and making use of their techniques in the elaboration of a new political style that would win mass support for an all-out assault on Weimar democracy.

[65] Georg Kaiser, *From Morn to Midnight*, trans. Ashley Dukes (the Theater Guild version) (New York, 1922), pp. 88, 91. On sport, see Werner, *Die Zwanziger Jahre*, pp. 80–1.

XIV
Party Politics and
Foreign Policy
1924–1930

> The formation of parties is the Nessus shirt of freedom. They stick
> to the people just as painfully as dynasties. . . . In the existing
> parliamentary system, we have a ruling authority no less unbear-
> able than the earlier one, which was based upon conquest, pre-
> scription, and divine right. This one, however, rests upon sys-
> tematically sanctioned deceptions.
>
> ALFRED DÖBLIN (1920)[1]

> If you have not understood that the maintenance of democracy and
> the Republic is the most important interest of the party, then you
> have not learned the ABC of political thinking.
>
> RUDOLF HILFERDING (1927)[2]

FOR the German Republic the six years that began in 1924 were
marked by foreign success and domestic failure. These were the
years in which Stresemann's diplomacy effected the removal of
nearly all of the restrictions placed by the peace treaty upon German
sovereignty and brought Germany back into the comity of nations
on terms of equality with the other Powers in every respect save that
of armament. This was an undoubted achievement, recognized by
contemporaries as being comparable with Bismarck's transformation of Prussia's status in the years after 1862, and it was all the
more remarkable in that it was jeopardized at every step by opposition and crisis at home. Indeed, the divisiveness of Weimar politics
increased proportionately to the strengthening of Germany's international position, and Stresemann's last success was followed,
within a matter of months, by so striking a failure of parliamentary
government that it began to occur to thoughtful observers that the
Republic might not survive long enough to profit from his work.

---

[1] *Die neue Rundschau* (1920), i. 75.
[2] At the Kiel Party Convention of the SPD in 1927. Quoted in Timm, *Sozialpolitik*,
p. 52.

I

The erosion of the strength of parliamentary democracy was due in considerable measure to the nature of party politics, surely one of the most melancholy aspects of the Republic's history. The ability of the parties to collaborate in giving effective government to the country was vitiated by weaknesses to which all of them were prone to a greater or lesser extent. These included a failure of leadership that was reflected either in growing bureaucratization or in debilitating factionalism, a lack of imagination that manifested itself either in clinging to outworn doctrines or in excessive readiness to consider anti-democratic solutions to the country's problems, and a tendency to subordinate the interests of the nation to those of special professional or economic groups. As a result, even before the world depression brought the country's brief period of material well-being to an end, parliamentary ineffectuality was so patent that increasing numbers of private citizens were referring contemptuously to 'the system', the 'Bonzen' who battened on it, the 'Parteiwirtschaft' that was its salient characteristic, and the muddle and instability that was its result. For these people the 'elderly and slightly intoxicated gentleman' in Tucholsky's sketch was a kind of spokesman, when he explained his predicament by saying engagingly: ' . . . ick bin sosusahrn ein Opfer von unse Parteisserrissenheit'.[3]

The parties which had been loyal to the Republic from the beginning suffered as seriously from the ills mentioned above as those whose devotion to democracy was doubtful. The ability of the Social Democratic party, for example, to support the regime that it had been largely responsible for creating was always handicapped by inability or unwillingness to free itself from the dead hand of the past. Both its history since 1890 and the concrete objectives set down in the Heidelberg Programme of 1925 made it clear that it had become a reformist party, seeking to promote democratic socialism by evolutionary means, and its social composition and economic condition underlined this fact. By the end of the twenties only 60 per cent of its membership were workers, the rest being white-collar employees (10 per cent), civil servants (3 per cent), housewives (17 per cent), and schoolteachers, members of the professions, independent business men, and intellectuals. At the same time, the party owned almost 200 newspapers and had a considerable financial stake in union funds, consumers' co-operatives, and the Bank der Arbei-

---

[3] 'Ein älterer, aber leicht besoffener Herr', in *Ausgewählte Werke*, ii. 153 f.

ter, Angestellten und Beamten. It had clearly become a party of people with more to lose than their chains.[4] Unfortunately, it had few leaders who were willing to admit this.

The Lübeck Socialist Julius Leber, whose role in the resistance to Hitler contributed to the revitalization of his party after 1945, believed that it had been held captive, in the Weimar period, by 'an absolute and intolerant ideology'.[5] Unwilling to admit that they no longer regarded revolution as a necessity because they feared KPD charges that they were betraying the working class, SPD spokesman clung to the rhetoric and the formulations of revolutionary Marxism while quietly abandoning its substance. Thus the Heidelberg Programme, based on a draft of Karl Kautsky, who had written the Erfurt Programme of 1890, repeated in large part the language of the earlier document, while also—doubtless in the hope of strengthening the loyalty of the USPD members who had returned to the fold in 1922—voicing approval of increased use of Councils (Räte) in the regulation of the country's economy.[6]

This obeisance to the past was more than verbal, for it was reflected in a doctrinaire rigidity on important issues. A salient weakness of the party in the days of the Empire had been its failure to develop a programme that might have appealed to agrarian workers and small farmers, the party theorists offering them no remedy for their distressed conditions but ideological explanations. This deficiency was not made good now.

The Weimar party was always ready with ringing declarations about the necessity of expropriating the princely families or breaking up the great estates east of the Elbe, but it never succeeded in focusing its attention on the problems that faced small farmers in areas like Schleswig and Holstein, where, in 1929, there were tax strikes, mass demonstrations, and the bombing of government offices in protest against the prices of fodder and the interest rates on loans.[7] Insen-

---

[4] Sigmund Neumann, *Die Parteien der Weimarer Republik* (new edn., Stuttgart, 1965), pp. 27 ff.; Friedrich Stampfer, *Die vierzehn Jahre der ersten deutschen Republik* (Karlsbad, 1936), pp. 475 f.; Richard N. Hunt, *German Social Democracy, 1919–1933* (New Haven, 1964), Ch. 4.

[5] Leber, *Ein Mann geht seinen Weg*, p. 213.

[6] Timm, *Sozialpolitik*, pp. 48 ff.

[7] Interesting accounts in the form of novels are Hans Fallada, *Bauern, Bonzen und Bomben* (1931) and Ernst von Salomon, *Die Stadt* (1932). See also the report of the Minister of the Interior, Karl Severing, 'Zur innenpolitischen Lage in Deutschland im Herbst 1929', *Vierteljahrshefte für Zeitgeschichte*, viii (1960); on national agrarian policy, John B. Holt, *German Agricultural Policy, 1918–1934* (Chapel Hill, N.C., 1936); and on the activity of rightist radicals in the riots, Schüddekopf, *Linke Leute von Rechts*, pp. 306 ff.

sitive both to the farmers' attachment to the soil and their innate suspicion of a government that had long ignored their needs, the SPD allowed rural Germany to fall under the political influence of National Socialism.[8]

It was equally short-sighted in military affairs. Perhaps because its collective conscience still smarted as a result of its failure to create a new-style republican force in 1919, the SPD was never able to come to terms with the military establishment or to respond to gestures of accommodation from the military side. That it was zealous in exposing illegitimate political activities on the part of soldiers was understandable; less so was its tendency to adopt an extreme pacifist position whenever armament bills were before the Reichstag. This gained for it, in the opinion of many independent voters, the reputation of being both un-patriotic and incapable of understanding the realities of international life. At the Magdeburg Party Conference of 1929, Leber warned his party comrades that a republic in which there was an unbridgeable gulf between the armed forces and the working class could not possibly survive. No one responded to his remarks, the discussion remaining on a comfortable theoretical level.[9]

The party leadership prided itself on being composed of hard-headed realists. To the country at large they seemed rather a group of functionaries who were so uniformly colourless as to be practically indistinguishable from each other and whose realism consisted of carefully avoiding risks and discouraging initiative and imagination. In retrospect, this judgement does not seem unjust. The number of trade union secretaries and party bureaucrats in the executive was so great that the word *Bonzentum* was widely used within the party itself to refer to their monopoly of power and their mandarin-like imperviousness to unorthodox ideas. Since most of their procedures and tactical ideas had been formulated for the use of a party that was generally in opposition, they had fallen into the habit of assuming that this was not only the normal, but the desirable, state and were unwilling—as they demonstrated in 1923, 1926, and 1930—to make the concessions and accommodations that might bring them, or allow them to retain, power and responsibility. There were no Lassalles or Vollmars in the Weimar party, and those who might have developed into spirited or flamboyant tribunes were soon

[8] The best study of this development is Rudolf Heberle, *From Democracy to Nazism: A Regional Case Study on Political Parties in Germany* (Baton Rouge, La., 1945).

[9] Leber, *Ein Mann geht seinen Weg*, pp. 146 ff., 223 ff.; Stampfer, *Vierzehn Jahre*, p. 483. On the military policy of the SPD, see Gordon Douglas Drummond, 'The Military Policy of the German Social Democratic Party, 1949–1960' (Dissertation, Stanford Univ. 1968), Ch. 1.

discouraged and went away. The note of passion was rarely heard, least of all in party propaganda, which was characterized by depressing rationality and dogmatism. It is no wonder that the SPD tended increasingly to become a party of old men, with less than 10 per cent of its membership in 1930 under twenty-five years of age.[10]

The fatal ills of the SPD—and this was recognized by post-1945 leaders like Kurt Schumacher, Carlo Schmitt, Fritz Erler, and Willy Brandt—were complacency and parochialism. Instead of making an effort to transform the party into one that could appeal to all classes and rally them to the defence of the Republic, its leaders acted as if they owed responsibility only to the working class. In practice, this meant taking their lead from the trade unions and doing nothing that might jeopardize their support. This was to do irreparable harm to the party and the Republic in 1930.

If the SPD suffered from doctrinaire rigidity, the principal weakness of the Democratic party was the opposite. From the beginning the DDP had difficulty in making voters understand what it stood for and why, and its efforts to correct this failing led to intramural bickering, frequent resignations from its directorate, and, finally, the adoption by a rump leadership of doctrines that belied the party's name, which was, indeed, changed in the same year that saw its expiration.

In 1919 the DDP was the third largest party in the country, with 75 seats in the National Assembly. Within a year this strength had been almost cut in half, and the party's Reichstag delegation in 1920 numbered only 39, a strength that it was never again able to achieve. This galloping anaemia was due to the dearth of political skill among the party's founders, who were largely drawn from the pre-war Progressive party and from academic and professional groups that had previously played no direct part in public affairs.[11] Many of them, influenced by the blend of idealism and nationalism that was

---

[10] Neumann, *Parteien*, pp. 27–32; Leber, *Ein Mann geht seinen Weg*, pp. 200 f.; Hunt, *Social Democracy*, Ch. 7; Adolf Sturmthal, *The Tragedy of European Labour, 1918–1939* (New York, 1943), pp. 35–41.

[11] On the origins of the party, see Otto Nuschke, 'Wie die Demokratische Partei wurde', in *Zehn Jahre Deutsche Republik*, ed. Anton Erkelenz (Berlin 1928), pp. 24 ff. For its history and the ideas of its leading members, see Robert A. Pois, 'The Bourgeois Democrats of Weimar Germany', *Transactions of the American Philosophical Society*, N.S. 66, pt. 4 (1976). Useful also are Bruce B. Frye, 'The German Democratic Party, 1918–1930', *Western Political Quarterly*, xvi (1968), 167–79, and three articles by Attila Chanady, 'Anton Erkelenz and Erich Koch-Weser: A Portrait of Two German Democrats', *Historical Studies: Australia and New Zealand*, xii (1967), 'The Dissolution of the German Democratic Party', *American Historical Review*, 73, no.5 (1968), and 'Erich Koch-Weser and the Weimar Republic', *Canadian Journal of History*, vii (1972).

the distilled essence of the writings of Friedrich Naumann and Max Weber, were not democrats by instinct and were ill at ease in the pluralistic Weimar system, which seemed to stand in the way of their achievement of social reconciliation in the interest of national strength. Their hope of making the DDP the instrument of that process and of transforming it into a mass party was rendered idle by their inability to speak to the electorate in terms that the ordinary voter could understand. They always gave the impression of being more interested in abstractions than in the issues that moved the people, and when they took strong stands (resigning from the government over the peace treaty, for example, and opposing the compromises reached by the other parties in 1919 with respect to education in elementary schools),[12] their reasons for doing so were neither clear nor persuasive.[13] At an early date they appeared to many to be a body of impractical intellectuals. As time went on, thanks to the composition of their executive and the support the party received from the Mosse-Ullstein Press, and particularly the *Berliner Tageblatt*, whose chief editor, Theodor Wolff, had been one of its founders, the DDP was widely regarded as the party of the Jews.[14]

Its failure with the voters, which became more evident in the 1924 elections, when its Reichstag representation fell to 25 seats, had the effect of destroying the internal homogeneity of the party and encouraging a drift to the right. The *étatiste* strain grew stronger and began to assume illiberal characteristics. To the dismay of the left wing, which was led by Wolff, Anton Erkelenz, Willy Hellpach, and Ludwig Quidde, the party majority dissociated itself from the SPD's criticism of army meddling in foreign policy in 1926, and its subsequent support of a bill (the Schund- und Schmutzgesetz) that placed restrictions upon freedom of publication in the interest of public morality led to Wolff's resignation. His friends soon followed him, for the party leader Erich Koch-Weser and Naumann's successor as editor of *Die Hilfe*, Gertrud Bäumer, became increasingly critical of parliamentary practice and began to lend themselves to flights of political romanticism, Bäumer in particular talking of breaking the ties with the Berlin Press and seeking '*völkisch* (racist) and soil-bound strengths'. As the Republic entered its last phase, the sadly depleted DDP, which had been a member of the original

---

[12] See Wilhelm Ziegler, *Die deutsche Nationalversammlung 1919–20 und ihr Verfassungswerk* (Berlin, 1932), pp. 209 ff.

[13] Neumann, *Parteien*, pp. 46 ff.

[14] Heuß, *Naumann*, pp. 591 ff.; Kiaulehn, *Berlin*, pp. 500–4; and Pois, 'Bourgeois Democrats' 81 f., who analyses the anti-Semitism of some leaders of the party.

Weimar Coalition, was flirting with the idea of fusion with the Young German Order (Jungdo), an anti-republican, anti-Semitic offshoot of the Youth Movement,[15] and representative of the kind of Teutomania that had aroused Heine's fascination and contempt.[16]

The third member of the original Weimar Coalition had more inner stability than the DDP but was also increasingly subject to anti-democratic tendencies. Unlike the DDP, the Centre party was strong in all parts of the country; it was predominantly Roman Catholic, but not overwhelmingly so (some of its Reichstag deputies were Protestants) and was balanced socially so that its Fraktion included union officials and workers' representatives (20 per cent), teachers and writers (11·5 per cent), clerics (5·7 per cent), and industrialists, business men, landlords, and small farmers. The party's variegated social composition made its leadership more pragmatic and flexible than the SPD and more atune to popular currents than the DDP. It believed in compromise—one of its leaders, Joos, described it as a party not of 'Either-or' but of 'Why not both?'—and thus was able to ally with parties to the left of it (as it did in Prussia) or to the right (as it generally did in national politics).[17]

Because of the fragmentation of party politics, it had become clear by 1925 that no government could command a parliamentary majority without the participation of the Centre.[18] This was healthy neither for the Reichstag nor the party, inflating the Centre's self-confidence to a dangerous degree and encouraging an always latent opportunism. As long as men like Wirth, Joos, and Marx were in control, there was little risk of dangerous anti-republican experiments, for they were democrats by conviction and skilled operators in the game of party politics. But in 1928, worn out by the strain of serving four times as Reich Chancellor, Marx resigned the party leadership and was replaced by Monsignor Kaas, who insisted that Heinrich Brüning be made head of the Reichstag delegation.[19] The new team, which took over on the eve of the depression years, were less patient with the shortcomings of parliamentary practice than their

[15] See Kurt Pastenaci, 'Der Jungdeutsche Orden und die deutsche Jugendbewegung', *Süddeutsche Monatshefte*, xxxv (1926), 177 ff. See also Pois, 'Bourgeois Democrats' 62–6, 74 ff. on Gertrud Bäumer and her role in turning the party toward the Order.

[16] Heinrich Heine, *Werke*, ed. Martin Greiner (2 vols., Cologne and Berlin, n. d.), ii. 752–3.

[17] Neumann, *Parteien*, p. 40. An excellent account of the party's role in the coalition politics of the early years is Rudolf Morsey, *Die deutsche Zentrumspartei 1917–1923* (Düsseldorf, 1966).

[18] Leber, *Ein Mann geht seinen Weg*, p. 44.

[19] Eyck, *Weimar Republic* ii. 220 f.

predecessors and more willing to consider other solutions. Encouraging them to do so, and fully prepared to show the way if they did not, were less scrupulous politicians, like the ineffable Franz von Papen, who had made opportunism a fine art.

Of the three original Weimar parties, therefore, two were showing anti-democratic tendencies by the end of the 1920s. This was even more notable in the case of the People's party (DVP) and the German National People's party (DNVP). The first of these, founded in 1919 by Gustav Stresemann to carry on the tradition of the pre-war National Liberals, had come to the support of the Republic in 1923, when it participated in the Great Coalition. The collaboration with the Socialists had not been easy, offending many of Stresemann's colleagues, who felt that the party should remain loyal to its slogan

> Von roten Ketten macht euch frei
> Allein die Deutsche Volkspartei.

From the beginning the DVP was the party of *Besitz und Bildung*, and increasingly it was the former that called the tune.[20] While it served as the political voice of a large part of the academic community, its salient characteristic was the appeal it made to business circles, which early found the party executive eager, in return for financial support, to proclaim the message that what was good for industry was good for the nation.[21] Before long, prominent industrialists were playing leading roles in party councils; in the twenties men like Stinnes, Vögler, and Kalle were members of the DVP Fraktion in the Reichstag, and in 1930 ten DVP deputies had between them 77 company directorships.[22]

This tendency worried Stresemann, who had hoped that his party would become the centre of a vital and realistic liberalism, but discovered that his views were considered to be too advanced by many of his colleagues. In July 1925, in a bitter note in his diary, he wrote that, after he had saved the party in the previous year's elections, the party's Reichstag delegation, instead of being grateful, seemed all too anxious to get rid of him;[23] and three years later, when the fact that he and his colleague Curtius joined the Müller cabinet elicited grumbling in the party, he exploded and accused the Fraktion of lacking the courage 'to take a position contrary to that of the big employers' groups and industrial associations', noting that 23

---

[20] S. Brant, 'Politische Chronik', *Die neue Rundschau* (1921), i. 554.
[21] Bracher, *Auflösung der Weimarer Republik*, p. 297.
[22] Neumann, *Parteien*, p. 53. [23] Stresemann, *Vermächtnis*, ii. 153.

members of the delegation were closely associated with large business firms.[24]

Because of his concern over the growing influence of vested interests in the DVP's councils, Stresemann began to think that national legislation might be necessary to limit private contributions to the parties, replacing them with state assistance. In 1929 he also speculated about the possibility of a fundamental reorganization of the party's structure that might form the basis for a fusion with the Democratic party.[25] The distractions of foreign policy and his own waning energies prevented him from giving substance to these ideas, and it is doubtful whether they were practical in any case. Before 1929 was over, the country was faced with too many serious economic problems for anyone to spend much time thinking about party finance, and it was unlikely that the failure to create a vital liberal party in 1919, which was the result of the mutual antipathy of Stresemann and the DDP leadership at that time,[26] could be made good at this late date, when the Democrats were in ideological disarray and when the DVP had a right wing oriented towards business that would probably have responded to a proposal of fusion by decamping to the Nationalists. It was too late to think of checking the party's willing subordination to the interest of the business community that financed it, and, when Stresemann's strong personality was removed by death, the party, under the leadership of Ernst Scholz, moved steadily to the right. Its fateful behaviour in 1930, which will engage our attention below, was a logical culmination of a trend that was apparent as early as 1924.

A similar progression took place within the German National People's party, which was plagued by internal incoherence and ideological ambivalence from the beginning and which succumbed in the end to the influence of its most violent elements. The party began its existence with a much less homogeneous membership than the pre-war Conservative party, embracing not only former members of that party and the Free Conservative party, but what was left of the old *völkisch* groups and the Christian Social party, and a large number of former National Liberals who did not heed Stresemann's call to the DVP. It was no longer as exclusively agrarian and East Elbian as the old party, for half of its voting strength now came from western Germany, and its Reichstag Fraktion represented the urban upper bourgeoisie, industrial associations, associations of salaried employees, like the Deutschnationaler Handlungsgehilfenverband,

---

[24] Timm, *Sozialpolitik*, pp. 87 ff.   [25] Turner, *Stresemann*, pp. 253–6.
[26] Ibid., pp. 18–25.

and various professional groups, in addition to the great proprietors and grain producers. This was reflected in a certain philosophical inconsistency, for, if most of its members felt that the party's chief mission was to fight for revision of the treaty and against the democratic system, they could not neglect the material interests of groups that supported the party but found it necessary to make an accommodation with the regime. Inveterate and unalloyed opposition to the Republic seemed to be impolitic, and a party declaration of 1918 had admitted the necessity of working 'on the basis of the parliamentary form of government, which is the only possible one after recent events'. The fiasco of the Kapp Putsch underlined the wisdom of this attitude, which was confirmed at the Görlitz Party Conference of 1922, during which it appeared that the party was on the point of breaking definitively with primitive *Junkertum* and radical anti-Semitism.[27]

This was misleading. The DNVP was so heterogeneous in membership that it always included some elements that were discontented with its stance on particular issues and, whether participating in government on the national level or abstaining, it always appeared to be in a state of high indignation. After Karl Helfferich's death, moreover, it seemed bereft of leaders who were capable of directing its interest to real rather than symbolic issues. Hergt and Westarp enjoyed none of the respect that Helfferich had commanded, being rejected equally by the Prussians of the old *Kreuzzeitung* school like Oldenburg-Januschau, who considered them flabby and unprincipled, and the younger and more progressive party members, who felt they lacked the imagination to increase the party's popular appeal.[28]

It was an initiative on the part of one of these young Turks, coming on the heels of a disappointing performance in the elections of 1928, that caused a fateful shift in the party's direction. This was an article by Walter Lambach of the Handlungsgehilfenverband, in which he argued that the time had come for the party to make an explicit declaration of its willingness to work henceforth within the framework of the present state. Lambach criticized those who continued to talk as if the restoration of the Hohenzollerns was in the

[27] On the early history of the party, see esp. Werner Liebe, *Die Deutschnationale Volkspartei 1918–1924* (Düsseldorf, 1956) and Lewis Hertzman, *DNVP. Right-Wing Opposition to the Weimar Republic, 1918–1924* (Lincoln, Nebr., 1963).
[28] Stampfer, *Vierzehn Jahre*, pp. 388 ff., 462 f., 485–6. The difficulties of drafting a programme that would bridge the differences is described in Attila Chanady, 'The Disintegration of the German National People's Party, 1924–1930', *Journal of Modern History*, xxxix, no. 1 (Mar. 1967), 65–91.

realm of practical politics and called for the opening of the party to all Germans in the interest of a truly national conservatism.[29]

This infuriated the party majority, whose first impulse was to expel Lambach from their ranks, and it played into the hands of the man who was fated to be the DNVP's nemesis. Alfred Hugenberg, former director of Krupp, owner of a newspaper empire that had evolved from his purchase of the Scherl Verlag after the war, and owner after 1927 of Ufa, Germany's largest film company, was not content with the triumphs that were to be won in the marts of trade. An established figure in rightist politics since he had helped found the Pan-German League and the Vaterlandspartei, he was inflexibly opposed to the Republic and contemptuous of those who believed in the possibility of anything more than a truce with it. In a letter to Count Westarp in September 1927, he spelled this out.

Anyone who accepts this parliamentary system belongs, from the historical perspective, to those [nameless] figures who keep passing (or staggering) [across the historical stage]. History will decide whether they are going to be stand-ins for those elements which will destroy Germany completely, or—if everything goes well—will just be carters attending to their menial job without any creative idea. Whoever believes theoretically in the necessity of a complete innovation and reconstruction of our public life, whoever is contemptuous of today's state and yet builds his personal fortune and future on his collaboration with the parliamentary system, is a moral cripple.[30]

The Lambach article, which seemed to prove that the number of party members who were willing to compromise was growing, exercised Hugenberg greatly and aroused his determination to end their influence. He did not discourage his friends, therefore, when they put his name forward as successor to Westarp, who resigned after the 1928 elections, and he was elected party chief in October.

Hugenberg's victory marked the end of moderate conservatism and ranged the DNVP with those forces that were irreconcilably opposed to the democratic system. This became abundantly clear in 1929, when Hugenberg brought it into alliance with Hitler's NSDAP and Franz Seldte's Stahlhelm in the fight against the Young Plan. This campaign fell short of its objective. It also gave the Hitler movement a respectability and legitimacy that it had not possessed before, while causing the resignation of 14 prominent members of the DNVP and leaving a larger number disaffected. These results

[29] Walter H. Kaufmann, *Monarchism in the Weimar Republic* (New York, 1953), pp. 182–5; Bracher, *Auflösung*, pp. 313–15.

[30] Andreas Dorpalen, *Hindenburg and the Weimar Republic* (Princeton, 1964), p. 129.

might have given a shrewder politician pause, but Hugenberg was heedless and self-confident and did not deviate from the course he had set until he had effected the destruction of both the Republic that he hated and the party that had accepted his leadership.[31]

Given the nature and tendencies of the five leading parties, one is not surprised to learn that, between February 1919, when Philipp Scheidemann became the Republic's first Chancellor, and June 1928, when Hermann Müller put together his government, fifteen separate cabinets passed across the political stage, none performing for longer than eighteen months and several disappearing into the wings in less than three. The high mortality rate was due, as has been noted, to the fact that representation in the Reichstag was shared by so many parties that majorities could be obtained only by coalitions, and to the additional circumstance that the number of working combinations was severely limited. Because of the DDP's rapid decline in strength, the original Weimar Coalition (SPD, Centre, DDP) could no longer dominate the Chamber. The number of combinations that might do so was restricted by the fact that the SPD and the DNVP would not serve together. In practice, the only groupings that had a decent chance of survival were governments of the Great Coalition, including the SPD and all of the strong parties to the left of the DNVP, and governments of the Bourgeois Coalition, including the DNVP and all of the major parties to the right of the SPD.

But even these potentially viable combinations were at the mercy of the whims of party executives, which kept their ministers on tight leading-strings, and were constantly jeopardized by the pressures exerted upon them by special interests and by sudden gusts of ideological zeal. Whenever the SPD was in the national government, its struggles with its own conscience and its nervous habit of looking over its shoulder to see how the trade unions were reacting placed a heavy strain upon the tolerance of its partners, and the growing antipathy between the SPD and the DVP made coalitions of the left increasingly hard to form and maintain. Thus in the spring of 1926, after the fall of the second Luther government, the opportunity to form a Great Coalition government under the leadership of the energetic Mayor of Cologne, Konrad Adenauer, failed because the leader of the DVP, Ernst Scholz, told Adenauer that the DVP was unwilling to join a Socialist-dominated government.[32] Similarly, the

---

[31] The wilfulness of Hugenberg's leadership is described in Chanady, 'Disintegration' 82–90.

[32] On this incident, and on the possibility that the Adenauer candidacy failed because of Stresemann's dislike of the Mayor, see Fritz Stern, *The Failure of Illiberalism:*

spasms of reaction from which the DNVP suffered had a de-
stabilizing effect on Bourgeois Coalitions, making it difficult for the
left wing of the Centre to remain in harness with the Nationalists and
prompting sudden walk-outs by the latter, as was the case after the
conclusion of the Locarno treaties in 1925. This meant as often as not
that the Republic was governed by minority cabinets, living from
issue to issue by means of scratch majorities and always at the mercy
of votes of no-confidence in which they could be sure that the
totalitarian parties, the KPD and the NSDAP, would cast their votes
with the opposition.

More and more, parliamentary politics came to resemble an endless cabinet crisis, with more time and energy expended on the task
of filling the ministerial chairs than in governing the country. This
bored the mass of the voters and led them to turn to more diverting
subjects. But it was a source of deep concern to people who realized
that, in certain circumstances, boredom might be transformed by the
totalitarian movements into a weapon against the Republic, and at
the SPD Party Convention at Kiel in 1927 Rudolf Hilferding warned
his colleagues that, in their jealous regard for party interest, they
should not forget that the future of socialism depended upon the
Republic's survival.[33]

No less concerned than Hilferding over the parochialism of the
parties was the Republic's second President, Field-Marshal von Hindenburg. After Ebert's sudden death in February 1925, Hindenburg
had responded to the appeal of friends and allowed his name to be put
forward as the national candidate for the presidency, subsequently
defeating Marx, the former Chancellor, by a narrow vote
(14,655,000 votes to 13,751,000, with an additional 1,931,000 cast for
the Communist candidate, Ernst Thälmann). Many regarded his
election as a grave blow to German democracy, but nothing that
Hindenburg did in his first years confirmed this impression. At the
ceremony in which the Marshal took his oath to the constitution,
Harry Kessler was struck by the emphasis that he placed in his
remarks upon popular sovereignty and the democratic and republican nature of the constitution, and Kessler recorded the view of a
friend from the Riga Embassy, who said to him, as they left the
Reichstag, 'We have just experienced the *birth* of the German

Essays on the Political Culture of Modern Germany (New York, 1972), pp. 162 ff. and esp.
182–90.

[33] See epigraph on p. 498. On the party's inhibitions and on the general problem
of finding viable combinations, see Michael Stürmer, *Koalition und Opposition in der
Weimarer Republik 1924–1928* (Düsseldorf, 1967), pp. 258–60, 265 ff.

Republic.'[34] In the five years that followed, Hindenburg's role in politics was a positive one, and in the cabinet crises of those years, he used his authority judiciously and worked with the parties to find ways out of the dilemmas created by their internecine strife.

This was not to last, partly because the President was not tough-minded enough to withstand complaints by his Nationalist friends that he was tolerating November criminals and unpatriotic ele-ments. But it is worth asking whether he would have become as susceptible to this anti-democratic propaganda if the parties had acted differently. In his speech to the Reichstag when he took the constitutional oath, he had appealed to them to aid him in restoring national unity, saying: 'This noble task I can fulfil more easily if the parties in this High House will not indulge in petty quarrels about advantages for a party or an economic group but will compete with each other in serving our hard-pressed people faithfully and effec-tively.'[35] It cannot be said that the parties showed any disposition to heed that appeal, and their behaviour in the subsequent period gradually exhausted both his energy and his patience. His military temperament became increasingly offended by what seemed to him to be a fundamental lack of discipline and loyalty that endangered national security, and it was not long before he was listening to people—some of them former army associates who shared his dis-comfort with the untidiness of the pluralistic system—who argued that strict adherence to the constitution and the rules of parliament-arianism merely encouraged party anarchy and that there were better ways of using presidential authority in the interest of people and state.

President von Hindenburg did not begin to yield seriously to those counsels until 1930. Until then the parties continued on their unruly way, complicating the professional life of another man whose assigned task was to maintain and promote the national interest. This was the Foreign Minister, Gustav Stresemann.

II

As a general rule, Stresemann's foreign policy received the support of the parties of the moderate left and the middle, while being consistently opposed by the Nationalists, the Nazis, the Com-munists, and the right wing of his own party. Especially after the Locarno treaties of 1925, many persons in the former camp believed that the Foreign Minister had repudiated his imperialist past and was

[34] Kessler, *Tagebücher*, pp. 441–2.   [35] Dorpalen, *Hindenburg*, p. 88.

working to create a new Europe that would contain and eliminate nationalism and militarism. The rightist parties were inclined to accept this view, as many liberal historians have done,[36] while reprobating it and accusing the Foreign Minister of working in the interest of Germany's enemies, while the Communists professed to believe that his policy was designed to prepare the way for a joint assault on the Soviet Union by the Locarno Powers. Now that Stresemann's private papers are open to historians, it is clear that both his supporters and his detractors were wrong in their evaluations of his motives and objectives.

Stresemann was no more a 'good European' than Austen Chamberlain or Aristide Briand or any other of the leading statesmen of his time. He was capable of using the sentimental rhetoric that was the characteristic style of the proponents of a future United States of Europe, but he was no believer in that grand design. As a German statesman, he felt that it was his obligation to concern himself with urgent national requirements, and the goal he set himself was to regain full sovereignty and independence for his country so that it was no longer at the mercy of others and could protect itself against attack or dictation or indirect pressure. This would be possible only after more specific goals had been attained: the diminution and eventual removal of the financial burdens imposed by the Versailles Treaty; the evacuation of German soil by foreign troops; the attainment of military parity with other Powers; and, finally, the rectification of its eastern frontier and, perhaps, the regulation of its relationship with Austria by anschluss or fusion.

These were objectives that most people in the rightist parties regarded as desirable. The trouble was that they wanted them to be proclaimed publicly and to be accomplished forthwith, and many of them, in addition, were not content with Stresemann's modest desire for the return of Germany's pre-war possessions in the east but lusted after Poland and the Ukraine. They would not understand that the realities of the European situation made patience, ambiguity, and opportunism requirements of German foreign policy. Unconditional men with a proneness to over-simplification, they had no sympathy with a minister who was always as acutely aware as Bismarck had been of the limitations of foreign policy and who said on one occasion, 'So ist das Leben, and it would be foolish if we sought

---

[36] See, inter alia, Antonina Vallentin, Stresemann. Vom Werden einer Staatsidee (Leipzig, 1930); Rudolf Olden, Stresemann (Berlin, 1929); Felix Hirsch, Gustav Stresemann, Patriot und Europäer (Göttingen, 1964); Henry L. Bretton, Stresemann and the Revision of Versailles: A Fight for Reason (Stanford, 1953).

to guide our foreign policy in accordance with rigid systems of ideas. We must take people and things as they are.'[37]

This was not heroic enough for the patrioteers in the DNVP and the Nazi party, and the drumfire of their criticism was unrelenting. This opposition would have been a crippling handicap if it had not been for the support that Stresemann received from the Socialists and the Centre. But even this was by no means automatic. The Foreign Minister's realism could be as offensive to the moderates as it was to the nationalists and, when it became too obtrusive, they became angry, with results that were sometimes embarrassing.

Stresemann was aware, for example, of secret agreements between the Reichswehr and the Red Army that provided the German soldiers with weapons and training in specialties denied them by the treaty.[38] He did not particularly approve of these arrangements, but he made no energetic attempt to discourage them. To do so would have embroiled him with General von Seeckt, the author of the arrangement, and increased the already considerable intensity of his opposition and that of Count Ulrich von Brockdorff-Rantzau, the ambassador in Moscow, to the accommodation with the Western Powers that was achieved at Locarno and became the fulcrum of Stresemann's foreign policy. Moreover, although he never shared Seeckt's dreams of a joint Soviet–German war to destroy Poland, the Foreign Minister could not exclude the possibility that a revision of the eastern frontiers might be possible only by means of military pressure; if that were so, the Russian military tie might prove useful. In view of this, Stresemann turned a blind eye to the connection, with the result that in 1926, when the *Manchester Guardian* exposed it, the SPD's anger was turned as much against him as against the army, and it was deaf to his warnings that further disclosures on their part would jeopardize pending negotiations.[39]

Despite the constant party sniping and the unwavering foreign suspicion that it fed, Stresemann was able, within five years, to accomplish a fair share of his objectives, partly, to be sure, because of basic differences between the French and British governments with respect to Germany, but more because of his superb gifts as a negotiator. No German statesman since Bismarck's time had demonstrated, as brilliantly as he was to do, the ability to sense

[37] Stresemann, *Vermächtnis*, ii. 231 ff.

[38] On this, and the rich literature dealing with it, see Craig, *Prussian Army*, pp. 408 ff.

[39] Eyck, *Weimar Republic* i. 291–3, 303 ff. On the Polish question and the kind of pressure Stresemann regarded as potentially effective, see the persuasive article by Robert Grathwohl, 'Gustav Stresemann: Reflections on his Foreign Policy', *Journal of Modern History*, xiv, no. 1 (Mar. 1973), esp. 64–70.

danger and to avoid it by seizing and retaining the initiative, the gift of maintaining perspective and a sense of relative values in the midst of a changing diplomatic situation, and the talent for being more stubborn than his partners in negotiation and for refusing to allow their importunities to force him to accept second-best solutions.

Stresemann's termination of Cuno's policy of passive resistance drove the first wedge between the British and French governments. Already uneasy about the long-term consequences of the French hard line, the British took advantage of Stresemann's action to take up a suggestion made originally by Charles Evans Hughes, the American Secretary of State, that the reparations problem be regulated by an international commission of financial experts. On 12 October 1923 the British Government asked Washington whether it would be prepared to participate in such an undertaking and, when it received an affirmative reply, proceeded, despite French objections to organize the meetings in London from which the Dawes Report (named after the American president of the board of experts) emerged in the spring of 1924. In brief, this report, which was accepted with some modification by a conference of the interested governments in London in August, ended the French exploitation of the Ruhr and determined that sanctions could be applied in the future only in case of a flagrant default that had been declared as such by a board of arbitration. The reparations obligation was reaffirmed and productive pledges were required of Germany in the form of mortgages on railway plant, industrial debentures, and guarantees based on the income from import and excise taxes; but the annuities required were scaled down, and the schedule of payments modified in the German interest. The plan as a whole was designed to alleviate a problem that was now recognized generally as disruptive of European harmony and to encourage the Western nations to advance new credit to Germany and to participate in the expected upswing of its economy.[40]

To many Germans the acceptance of any obligation to continue paying reparations seemed unpatriotic, and the Reichstag debate on ratification in late August was stormy, with the Nationalists, the Communists, and the *völkisch* groups vying with each other in the violence of their assaults upon the 'policy of enslavement' and an apoplectic Ludendorff shouting, 'This is a disgrace to Germany! Ten years ago I won the battle of Tannenberg. Today you have made a

---

[40] On the London Conference and the effects of the settlement on European relations, see Schuker, *French Predominance*, Chs. 7 and 8 and pp. 385–6, where the effects upon French security are emphasized.

Jewish Tannenberg!'[41] The Foreign Minister found this posturing irresponsible. Confronted with the Dawes arrangement, he said later, he had been in the position of a condemned man who is offered a year of life if he will teach the king's horse to fly. One does not turn down such an offer; after all, 'before the year is out, the king, or I, or the horse may die, and anyway, who knows? Perhaps the horse will really learn to fly.'[42] The plan offered tangible advantages—it freed the Ruhr, and it involved other countries in Germany's economic future through the investments of their citizens—and who could say whether it might not have unexpected dividends? Perhaps the contacts that Stresemann had made in London with Eduard Herriot and Ramsay MacDonald might facilitate agreement on other subjects, particularly the evacuation of the Rhineland and the withdrawal of the Inter-Allied Military Control Commission (IMCC), which was charged with the task of seeing that the military terms of the Versailles Treaty were enforced.

These hopes seemed to be dashed, however, when, shortly after the Reichstag had ratified the Dawes Plan, the IMCC made a general inspection of German factories and military installations and reported such widespread evasions and violations that the Conference of Ambassadors announced that the evacuation of the Cologne zone, scheduled for January 1925, would not take place.[43] This had a profoundly depressing effect in Berlin. 'The policy of the London Conference', Stresemann told the cabinet, 'carried with it not only the idea of an economic and financial settlement, but a settlement of the whole world-political situation. The non-evacuation of Cologne puts the continuation of this policy in the greatest danger.'[44]

This seemed all the more true when December brought the fall of the Labour Government in England and a spate of rumours concerning the pro-French sympathies of the new Conservative Foreign Secretary, Austen Chamberlain. The British ambassador, Lord d'Abernon, warned the Wilhelmstraße that the French were urging an alliance on Chamberlain and that they would probably be successful if the Germans did not try a diversionary manœuvre;[45] and

[41] Stresemann, *Vermächtnis*, i. 524.

[42] Anneliese Thimme, *Gustav Stresemann, eine politische Biographie zur Geschichte der Weimarer Republik* (Hannover and Frankfurt-on-Main, 1957), pp. 69 ff.

[43] Michael Salewski, *Entwaffnung und Militärkontrolle in Deutschland 1919–1927* (Munich, 1966), pp. 271–81, 285.

[44] Ibid., p. 283.

[45] F. G. Stambrook, ' "Das Kind"—Lord d'Abernon and the Origins of the Locarno Pact', *Central European History*, i (1968), 237, 247, 250.

Stresemann took the warning to heart.[46] He feared that a new Anglo-French agreement would prolong the occupation and have the additional effect of leaving Germany so isolated that it would be driven into a dangerous dependence on the Soviet Union.

It was to forestall this danger that the Foreign Minister took the first step on the road that was to lead, through many difficult bypaths, to Locarno. On 20 January 1925 the Under-Secretary, Carl Schubert, asked Lord d'Abernon to forward to his government, unofficially and confidentially, a proposal for an international guarantee of the *status quo* in Western Europe. This was not a plan of striking originality (something of the sort had been proposed without success by the Cuno government in 1922) but it made up for that deficiency by its timeliness. The question of supplementing the rather vague peace-keeping paragraphs of the League of Nations Covenant by means of security plans with effective sanctions was engaging the attention of all governments. In 1923 the Draft Treaty of Mutual Assistance had failed of general acceptance, largely because of British opposition; in 1924 the Geneva Protocol was before the League, another arrangement that the British found unacceptable, partly, as Chamberlain told a bemused Assembly, because it was too logical to appeal to his countrymen,[47] more because it would have implied a British obligation to oppose aggression in Eastern Europe. The British Government was concerned lest a flat rejection expose them to charges of standing in the way of a resolution of the security problem. The Stresemann proposal offered a way out of the dilemma, and Chamberlain, aware that his own preference for a simple Anglo-French alliance had no chance of cabinet support, accepted it, rather unhappily, and persuaded the French to do the same. This last was not as difficult as it might have been if Poincaré had still been in power, but his German policy had been repudiated at the polls in 1924, largely because of the unhappy repercussions of the occupation of the Ruhr, and the French acceptance of the Dawes Plan in August was an admission that security policy must be based henceforth on collective rather than unilateral action.[48]

[46] See his speech to the Foreign Affairs Committee of the Reichstag, quoted in Thimme, *Stresemann*, pp. 80–1. See also Ludwig Zimmerman, *Studien zur Geschichte der Weimarer Republik* (Erlangen, 1956), p. 54.

[47] Gordon A. Craig, 'The British Foreign Office from Grey to Austen Chamberlain', in *The Diplomats, 1919–1939*, ed. Gordon A. Craig and Felix Gilbert (Princeton, 1953), pp. 40, 43.

[48] Jon Jacobson, *Locarno Diplomacy: Germany and the West, 1925–1929* (Princeton, 1972), pp. 14 ff., 26 ff. On the reasons for the abandoning of Poincaré's policy, see Schuker, *French Predominance*, pp. 229–31.

Stresemann's initiative was therefore successful, but his difficulties were just beginning. In the negotiations that eventuated in October 1925 in the conclusion of the Treaty of Mutual Guarantee, by which the states bordering on the Rhine abjured the use of force in their mutual relations and, together with Britain and Italy, guaranteed the demilitarization of the Rhineland and the existing western frontiers, and in the parallel negotiations on the terms for Germany's admission to the League of Nations, Stresemann was forced to manœuvre, in Bismarck's phrase, like a dog moving through a thick wood with a long stick in his jaws. His view was that the Rhineland Pact and Germany's willingness to enter the League were positive contributions to European security and that their logical consequence should—as he told the American ambassador—be the evacuation of the whole of the Rhineland before 1930, the date set by the treaty.[49] The French, while welcoming the German renunciation of the use of force in the west, felt, not unnaturally, that a guarantee should be extended to their eastern allies as well and were insistent that, if Germany were admitted to the League, it must assume the same obligations as other members. To have accepted the first of these demands would not only have baulked Stresemann's desire to move by stages towards revision of the frontiers (an intention that he made unmistakably clear in a letter to the former Crown Prince in September 1925),[50] but would have weakened public support of his policy and alienated the army leadership. As for the League, the Foreign Minister felt it essential that Germany be granted an exemption from the military obligation implicit in Article 16 in order to underline its lack of equality in armaments and also to reassure the Soviet Government that entrance into the League was not a potential threat to Moscow. Stresemann had none of the romantic fascination that his predecessor Rathenau had for the Soviet Union, nor did he share Brockdorff-Rantzau's belief in a 'brotherhood of destiny' between Germany and the great eastern Power. He never forgot that Moscow was the home of the Comintern and the source of some of his internal problems. But he saw no point in alienating a government whose military assistance might one day be useful or of sacrificing the balance that Rapallo had brought to German foreign relations for the undoubted advantages that membership of the League would bring for advancing his objectives by propaganda and personal diplomacy. 'We would not', he said later to some members of the DNVP, 'permit ourselves to be used as a tool against Russia;

[49] Stresemann, *Vermächtnis*, ii. 261–2; Jacobson, *Locarno Diplomacy*, p. 55.
[50] Eyck, *Weimar Republic* ii. 20–3.

therefore, we insisted on our reservations with respect to the League.'[51]

In the end, Stresemann won his primary objectives, and a bit more, through patience and a superb sense of timing and by exploiting the unwillingness of the British and French to have the negotiations fail once they had become public. In the talks that preceded the gathering of the diplomats at Locarno, the Foreign Minister had failed to win the assurances that he required concerning the eastern frontiers and the League; once the conference began and the Press had begun to talk of 'the spirit of Locarno', it was hard for the Western Powers to refuse concessions without seeming unreasonable to European public opinion. Already protected from a general guarantee of the eastern *status quo* by British disinclination to make commitments in that area, Stresemann was able at the conference to block a plan for a French guarantee of the arbitration treaties that the German Government had agreed to conclude with Poland and Czechoslovakia. Similarly, he won exemption from the sanctions obligation stipulated in Article 16 of the Covenant.[52] In both cases, he had his way by being more stubborn than Chamberlain and the leader of the French delegation, Aristide Briand. Indeed, sensing their vulnerability to public opinion in their countries, he resorted successfully to tactics that Chamberlain bitterly described as 'blackmail', making his signature of the Locarno treaties contingent upon the evacuation of the Cologne zone and an agreement in principle that the Allies would drop some of the complaints they had made in December about German violations of the arms clauses, and that they would reduce the size of their occupation forces and would phase out the IMCC.[53]

Although the last two matters were to be haggled over for another two years, Stresemann had reason to be satisfied with the results of Locarno. No real restrictions had been placed upon German freedom of action in the east, despite the arbitration treaties, for it was the German view, made clear to the British before Locarno, that no such

[51] Hans W. Gatzke, 'Von Rapallo nach Berlin: Stresemann und die Deutsche Rußlandpolitik', *Vierteljahrshefte für Zeitgeschichte*, iv (1956), p. 9 n. 49; and the same author's 'Russo-German Military Collaboration during the Weimar Republic', *American Historical Review*, lxiii (1958), 565 ff.; and in general, his *Stresemann and the Rearmament of Germany* (Baltimore, 1954).

[52] Jürgen Spenz, *Die diplomatische Vorgeschichte des Beitritts Deutschlands zum Völkerbund 1924–1926: Ein Beitrag zur Außenpolitik der Weimarer Republik* (Göttingen, 1966), pp. 96–106; Piotr Wandycz, *France and her Eastern Allies, 1919–25* (Minneapolis, 1962), p. 360; F. Gregory Campbell, *Confrontation in Central Europe: Weimar Germany and Czechoslovakia* (Chicago, 1975), pp. 149–54.

[53] For details, see Jacobson, *Locarno Diplomacy*, pp. 60–6.

treaty could exclude the possibility of resort to force if arbitration failed.[54] On the other hand, he could claim that the Rhineland Pact had drawn the teeth of the Franco-Polish alliance, by freeing Germany of the fear of an automatic French attack in the event of a war with Poland in which Germany was not clearly the aggressor,[55] and that the treaties and the entrance into the League would create a psychological atmosphere that would promote German territorial interests in both east and west.

These arguments were lost upon nationalist opinion at home. The National Socialist Press spread the rumour that Stresemann's sister-in-law was married to Poincaré and suggested that assassination was the only appropriate reply to the treason of Locarno. DNVP papers were hardly less restrained, although they focused their attention upon the surrender of Alsace-Lorraine, which was implied by the Rhineland Pact. To the embarrassment of Martin Schiele and other members of the DNVP Reichstag delegation who favoured the treaties, the party executive voted on 23 October to withdraw their ministers from the cabinet and instructed the Fraktion to vote against ratification. This infuriated the Chancellor, Hans Luther, who had accompanied Stresemann to Locarno. 'We have achieved', he thundered at Count Westarp, 'one hundred per cent of what we undertook to achieve at Locarno! Never has a delegation had such a success! We were a people of helots, and today we are once more a state of world consequence! A storm of resentment will sweep the German Nationalist party away if it mutilates this achievement!' His anger was unavailing, and the domestic price of Locarno was a prolonged cabinet crisis.[56]

This did not pose a real threat to the treaties, for SPD votes were enough to assure Reichstag ratification. But the Nationalist defection worried the Reichspräsident, who was already the recipient of complaints from Brockdorff-Rantzau in Moscow and from people close to General von Seeckt that the Foreign Minister was delivering the country into the hands of the Western Powers. Hindenburg's knowledge of foreign affairs was rudimentary at best, and he had little confidence in Stresemann, on one occasion admitting that he preferred foreign ministers who knew how to pound their fists upon

[54] See Gaines Post, jun., *The Civil-Military Fabric of Weimar Foreign Policy* (Princeton, 1973), pp. 28–31.

[55] Anneliese Thimme, 'Gustav Stresemann, Legende und Wirklichkeit', *Historische Zeitschrift*, clxxxi (1956), 315 f.; Zigmunt J. Gasiorowski, 'Stresemann and Poland before Locarno', *Journal of Central European Affairs*, xviii (1958), 47.

[56] Luther, *Politiker*, p. 387; Turner, *Stresemann*, pp. 214–18; Stürmer, *Koalition*, pp. 124–7.

the table. He distrusted the League and was confused by the terms of the treaties, and it took skilful pleading on Luther's part to persuade him of the advantages of the settlement.[57]

The criticism did not die away, and for the rest of his career Stresemann had to expend much of his warning energies on defending himself against people like Brockdorff and Seeckt who wanted an exclusively pro-Soviet foreign policy and the irrationalists of the extreme right who had no clear policy of their own but were adamant in calling for the rejection of Stresemann's. His defence was handicapped, moreover, by the fact that Locarno was not followed by the gains he had envisaged when the treaties were ratified. Indeed, he quickly encountered set-backs that left him discouraged and embittered.

The first of these was the unexpected deadlock that developed within the Council of the League in March 1926, when the governments of Poland, Spain, and Brazil reacted to the prospect of Germany receiving a permanent Council seat by demanding equal treatment.[58] Stresemann and Luther had gone to Geneva to be present at Germany's induction; they had to return, irritated and embarrassed, to face a hostile Press that made much of the 'national humiliation'. It was partly to calm this storm and to put an end to the persistent and skilful campaign that the Soviet Government had been waging against Germany's adhesion to the League of Nations that Stresemann found it expedient to negotiate a new agreement with the Soviet Union, the Treaty of Berlin, in April 1926. This effected no significant change in the terms of the Rapallo Treaty of 1922, merely underlining the intent of the signatories to consult in time of crisis and the obligation of each to remain neutral in the case of an attack upon the other. If, as Lord d'Abernon said, Stresemann signed the new engagement because he had to, he did not give anything to the Russians that they had not had before. Moreover, one of Stresemann's diplomatic talents was his ability to derive advantage from the necessary, and it can be argued that he did so here, improving his bargaining position with his Locarno partners as a result of the Berlin Treaty.

The immediate reaction in London and Paris was one of shock and outrage, and before the end of the month both governments had informed the Wilhelmstraße that any troop reduction in the occu-

[57] Luther, *Politiker ohne Partei*, p. 398; Dorpalen, *Hindenburg*, pp. 95–6.

[58] On this crisis, see F. P. Walters, *A History of the League of Nations* (2 vols., London, 1952), i. 316–27; and Erik Lönnroth, 'Sweden: The Diplomacy of Östen Undén', in *The Diplomats*, pp. 88–99.

pation zones was out of the question for the time being. Austen
Chamberlain, who had domestic reasons for wishing to withdraw
British garrisons from the Rhineland and had become critical of
French resistance to reductions, wrote to Lord d'Abernon: 'My
earnest desire was to make progress with the changes which Locarno
had rendered possible. At the present moment, however, it would be
useless to talk of further concessions. . . . In the excitement and
perturbation caused by the Russo–German negotiations, we could
make no progress.'[59]

But the considered opinion of the Western governments was that,
in view of Germany's other options, it might be unwise to be too
resistant to its demands. In May 1927 Chamberlain reminded
Briand: 'We are battling with Soviet Russia for the soul of Germany.
We had won a success at Locarno. We had confirmed it when
Germany entered the League; but the more difficult our relations
with Russia became, the more important was it that we should attach
Germany solidly to the Western Powers.'[60] This helps to explain
why the coolness between Berlin and the West was of relatively
short duration, and why Stresemann was able in December 1926 to
persuade Chamberlain and Briand to make good the promises they
had made after Locarno by cutting their occupation forces to 60,000
men and by withdrawing the IMCC from German soil. These new
concessions were unaffected by the hullabaloo caused in Germany in
October by General von Seeckt's unauthorized invitation to a
grandson of the former Emperor to attend military manœuvres—an
action that led to the dismissal of the 'genius with the monocle'[61]—or
by the more considerable row touched off by the *Manchester Guardian's* article about the secret collaboration between the Reichswehr
and the Red Army and the SPD's attack upon the government in
December for its complicity in this.[62] The Western Powers were, of
course, aware of this connection and seem to have convinced themselves that it offered Germany no significant military advantages;[63]
but it seems clear that they felt that it would be inexpedient to
continue to use Germany's association with the Soviet Union as an
excuse for reneging on earlier pledges, particularly since the general
euphoria induced by Locarno had been reinforced by Germany's

[59] Jacobson, *Locarno Diplomacy*, p. 82.
[60] Ibid., p. 123.
[61] See Reginald H. Phelps, 'Aus den Seeckt-Dokumenten: Die Verabschiedung
Seeckts 1926', *Deutsche Rundschau*, Sept. 1952; and Gordon, *Reichswehr*, pp. 261–8.
[62] Craig, *Prussian Army*, pp. 423–4 and notes; Turner, *Stresemann*, pp. 227 f.
[63] Jacobson, *Locarno Diplomacy*, p. 110 and n.

belated admission to the League in September 1926 and by the exuberant rhetoric that had marked that occasion.[64]

On the other hand, nothing came of the elaborate plan for a comprehensive settlement of all outstanding differences between France and Germany that Stresemann and Briand had discussed in a private meeting at Thoiry in the French Jura immediately after the session in Geneva. On that occasion, the French Premier had talked of the possibility not only of a complete evacuation of the Rhineland but of a reunion of the Saar with Germany without the plebiscite stipulated in the treaty, in return for a sizeable reparations payment in advance of the Dawes schedule.[65] By 1927 Briand had become much more reserved and, while denying that his attitude had changed, generally took the line that French public opinion and the attitude of the General Staff made new concessions difficult. Poincaré's stabilization of the franc in December 1926 had something to do with this, for it reduced the necessity of bargaining on the basis of reparations, but there is little doubt that Briand was becoming disturbed by developments inside Germany—the continued attacks upon Locarno and German membership in the League, the growth of paramilitary forces like the Stahlhelm and the apprehension they were causing on the German left (Professor F. W. Foerster warning that for every French soldier who left the Rhineland ten Stahlhelm troopers would spring up), persistent rumours that, although the Germans had complied with demands that they dismantle fortifications around Königsberg, they were continuing to build strong points on the right bank of the Oder to facilitate future operations against the Polish corridor,[66] and a provocative speech by President von Hindenburg on 18 September 1927, on the occasion of the dedication of a memorial at Tannenberg, in which he denied categorically that Germany was responsible for the outbreak of the war.[67] To Briand these seemed signs of future trouble, and he now accepted the view of the French Superior Council of War that anything like a complete evacuation of the Rhineland would have to await the completion of a new system of fortifications along France's eastern

[64] Brigadier J. H. Morgan, a member of the IMCC, claimed later that the withdrawal of the Commission, despite known German violations, was 'the price of Locarno'. *Assize of Arms: The Disarmament of Germany and her Rearmament, 1919–1939* (New York, 1946), p. xiii.

[65] On Thoiry, see Stresemann, *Vermächtnis*, iii. 17–23; and Georges Suarez, *Briand, sa vie, son œuvre* (5 vols., Paris, 1938–52), iv. 203–28.

[66] On the paramilitary forces and the eastern fortifications, see Salewski, *Entwaffnung*, pp. 339, 369–72.

[67] Dorpalen, *Hindenburg*, p. 131.

frontiers. In September 1927, when the Locarno partners met in Geneva, he refused to discuss the subject at all.[68]

This could not but be frustrating to Stresemann. He had been a successful Foreign Minister, a fact attested to not only by the Dawes Plan, the Rhineland Pact, the admission to the League, and the withdrawal of the IMCC but also by the co-ordination he had brought to German foreign policy. The civil–military problem that had so often hampered the efficiency of the country's foreign relations in the past had been largely overcome even before Seeckt's dismissal; there was a high degree of unity and even collaboration in planning between the Foreign and Defence Ministries; and even with respect to policy towards the Soviet Union, the soldiers had come to admit the primacy of the Foreign Minister.[69] But he had not yet done for his country all he had set out to do and, until he had persuaded the West to complete the evacuation of Germany, it was not feasible to turn to the objectives upon which both his ministry and the Defence Ministry had their eyes fixed, the revision of the eastern frontiers and the beginning of negotiations to improve Germany's position with respect to armaments.[70] Stresemann's views were not identical with those of the soldiers—he had more confidence than they in the possibility of solving the former question by negotiation and, with respect to armaments, he was more interested in attaining parity than in winning complete freedom of action[71]—but there was no question in his mind that the restoration of Germany's sovereignty would not be complete until these problems had been settled.

The Foreign Minister resolved, therefore, to make a renewed effort to achieve the evacuation of the two remaining zones of occupation, and, in order to deprive the French as far as possible of excuses for delaying further, he was anxious to enter the negotiations with the backing of a government that had strong parliamentary support and was demonstrably republican in character. In the spring

[68] Jacobson, *Locarno Diplomacy*, pp. 137 f.

[69] On this relationship, see Post, *Civil-Military Fabric*, esp. pt. 2.

[70] On the general correspondence of their views, compare Stresemann's speech of 14 December 1925 to the Arbeitsgemeinschaft deutscher Landsmannschaften in Großberlin with the memorandum on policy objectives prepared by Joachim von Stülpnagel of the Defence Ministry in March 1926. *Akten zur deutschen auswärtigen Politik*, Ser. B, 1925833, I, i (Dec. 1925–July 1926), 341 ff., 27 ff.,738, 740. See also the letter to the Crown Prince in *Vermächtnis*, ii. 553–4.

[71] See Henry Ashby Turner, jun., 'Stresemann und das Problem der Kontinuität in der deutschen Außenpolitik', in *Grundfragen der deutschen Außenpolitik seit 1871*, ed. Gilbert Ziebura (Darmstadt, 1975), pp. 299–303; Andreas Hillgruber, *Kontinuität und Diskontinuität in der deutschen Außenpolitik von Bismarck bis Hitler* (Düsseldorf, 1969), pp. 18–20.

of 1928, therefore, when the fourth Marx government was defeated in a dispute over a new Elementary School Bill and when the May elections showed a shift to the left, Stresemann worked actively for the creation of a Great Coalition government and, despite difficulties with his own party, whose right wing was greatly strengthened by the elections, and health problems that confined him to a sanatorium in the early summer months, he appeared to be successful. By 28 June 1928 Hermann Müller of the SPD had put together a cabinet that included three Socialist ministers besides himself, two from the DDP, one each from the Centre and the Bavarian People's parties, and Stresemann and Julius Curtius from the DVP.[72]

The new combination, however, soon proved itself to be the *reductio ad absurdum* of Weimar party politics, and the spectacle it provided of Germany's internal divisions was hardly likely to inspire confidence abroad. The effort of holding it together was a serious drain upon the Foreign Minister's strength as he pursued his foreign goals, and after his death in October 1929 it collapsed ignominiously.

III

From the outset it was apparent that the members of the Müller cabinet had other, and to them more important, things on their minds than foreign affairs. Stresemann's own party was unresponsive to his argument that a united government was essential for the successful pursuit of foreign policy and refused to commit itself to the support of the government unless it were paid to do so by being given some representation in the Prussian Government and the patronage that went with it. The Centre proved equally incapable of rising above selfish interest, frustrating the DVP's Prussian ambitions because that party would not support the Prussian concordat with the papacy, and seeking to blackmail its partners into granting it an additional cabinet seat by withdrawing its one minister for a period of three months. As for the SPD, it tended to subordinate all issues to the economic one and to the trade union interest. Because of these attitudes, the Müller government never became a Great Coalition in any meaningful sense. Its members shared no common ground, and their willingness to support any policy announced by the cabinet was always adventitious.

Even before the new ministers had settled into their seats, this had become painfully clear. During the summer recess of 1928 the cabinet voted to proceed with the construction of the first of four

[72] On the process of forming the cabinet and Stresemann's difficulties with his party, see Turner, *Stresemann*, pp. 238–42.

armoured cruisers that were authorized by the Versailles Treaty. The *Panzerkreuzer* had already been approved by the previous Reichstag, and public opinion was generally favourable, knowledgeable people appreciating the fact that the new ship would improve German security in the Baltic area. Neither these considerations, however, nor the fact that a Socialist Chancellor had presided over, and voted for, the cabinet's decision deterred the SPD from treating the country to a demonstration of doctrinaire irresponsibility of the most self-defeating kind. During the May elections they had campaigned with the slogan 'Not armoured cruisers but food for children!', and they refused to disavow that now. On 15 August the party executive and the Reichstag delegation voted two mutually inconsistent resolutions, the first criticizing their ministers for having voted for the ship, the second declaring that continued SPD membership in the government was essential 'out of consideration for the general interests of labour'. This at least had the advantage of ambiguity, but the SPD proceeded to throw this away and to allow themselves to be goaded by a Communist demand for a referendum on the issue of the cruiser to introduce a motion in the Reichstag for the halting of construction and to require all members of the Reichstag delegation, including the ministers, to vote for it.[73]

This behaviour was not even justified by party history, as Julius Leber pointed out. 'Do we', he asked, 'stand with Bebel, Jaurès, the Erfurt Programme, and the French socialists, all of whom accepted far-reaching legislation for the defence of the fatherland, or are we adopting the position that socialists everywhere, without regard for the conditions of armaments in other countries, must be in favour of total disarmament for their own country?'[74] The latter seemed to be true and, although the *Panzerkreuzer* bill passed handily when the vote was taken, thanks to some energetic lobbying among the parties of the right by the new Defence Minister, General Wilhelm Groener, the Socialists, with monolithic obtuseness, struck a blow at the government's credibility from which it never recovered.

If Stresemann was appalled by the thought of the impression this must create abroad, he had more reason for concern over the behaviour of his own party. He had been so completely absorbed in foreign affairs since 1924 that he had been able to devote little attention to its inner development. In December 1928, when its right wing openly sided with iron producers who were defying a government arbitral award in an ugly industrial dispute, and in the first

[73] Eyck, *Weimar Republic* ii. 162–5.
[74] Leber, *Ein Mann geht seinen Weg*, pp. 143 ff.; Stampfer, *Vierzehn Jahre*, pp. 481 f.

months of 1929 when the DVP revenged itself for its disappointment in Prussia by announcing that it could not be counted upon to support the Müller government unless its fiscal policies were reformed in ways that would have been intolerable to the other government parties, he realized belatedly that this was no longer the party that he had founded. He had wanted it, he wrote to an associate in mid-March, to be 'the bridge between the old and the new Germany'; it had, in fact, lost any desire to take the responsibility that such a role would involve. It had ceased to be 'a party of *Weltanschauung*' and was becoming 'more and more a purely industrial party', and its members no longer wanted to govern but to join the national opposition, where they could 'let go with all the catchwords they have learned from the Stahlelm and from Hugenberg'.[75]

Stresemann did what he could to postpone what he feared would be the inevitable result of these tendencies, while he pursued the exhausting negotiations that led to his last diplomatic success. He had laid the basis for this in August 1928, when he finally persuaded the French to give serious consideration to an early evacuation of the Rhineland and to agree to a new review of the reparations obligation. In February an international board headed by the American banker Owen D. Young began this assessment, which was completed in June and submitted in August to a conference of the interested Powers at The Hague. When he led the German delegation to the Dutch capital, Stresemann was not unnaturally interested in the substantial reductions that the plan promised to bring in reparations annuities, but he was determined to make the other Powers see that no new financial arrangement would impress the German people, five years after the Dawes Plan, unless it were accompanied by an evacuation of the Rhineland on schedule, that is, in 1930. As it turned out, the gaining of this point required no great feat of persuasion on his part. The conference at The Hague was largely dominated by a running conflict between the financial experts of the other creditor nations and Philip Snowden, the Chancellor of the Exchequer in the new British Labour Government. An atrabilious man with a wounding tongue, who was convinced that British policy had been weak and ineffective under the Conservatives, Snowden cared nothing for the spirit of reconciliation associated with Locarno and the amenities that had accompanied it. His concern was exclusively for the British taxpayer, in whose interest he wanted the largest possible share of the receipts from the Young Plan and the speediest possible elimi-

---

[75] Turner, *Stresemann*, pp. 251 f.

nation of allocations for the support of troops in Europe. Once he was satisfied with respect to the first point, he made short shrift of Briand's hesitations on the evacuation issue, threatening to withdraw British troops independently if the French did not yield. The German Foreign Minister had a couple of unusually acrimonious sessions with Briand before agreement was reached on the final date of evacuation (30 June 1930), but it was the British attitude that settled the main issue.[76]

Stresemann's belief that this would impress German opinion and facilitate ratification of the Young Plan was probably justified, although it is also probably true that his domestic opponents weakened their case by the very excessiveness of their reaction. Hugenberg, the new leader of the DNVP, had begun to make plans for the campaign against the settlement as early as June 1929 and had formed a committee to direct it that included Heinrich Class of the Pan-German League (who set the moral tone of the movement by describing Stresemann as 'the essence of all the dangerous tendencies of our nation [whose] psychic degeneracy is clearly derived from his political decadence'), Franz Seldte of the Stahlhelm, Fritz Thyssen of the Reichsverband der deutschen Industrie, and—*salonfähig* for the first time thanks to Hugenberg's invitation—the man who was going to destroy all of his new associates, Adolf Hitler. In September this group sent to the Federal Minister of the Interior the draft of a law for submission to national referendum. This required the government to repudiate the war-guilt clause of the Versailles Treaty and to demand immediate evacuation of the occupied areas; it forbade the government to assume any new obligations that would imply a recognition of responsibility for the coming of the war; and it made any minister who signed treaties incurring such obligations liable to trial for treason. This fantastic document—which Friedrich Stampfer aptly described as 'a coolly calculated gamble on the stupidity and ignorance [of the German people'][77]—attracted 4,135,000 signatures, enough to satisfy the legal requirement for having it laid before the Reichstag and made subject to national plebiscite; but after that initial success it rapidly ran out of momen-

---

[76] On the conference at The Hague, see, *inter alia*, J. W. Wheeler-Bennett, *Information on the Reparation Settlement, Being the Background and History of the Young Plan and the Hague Agreements, 1929–1930* (London, 1930); Robert Skidelsky, *Politicians and the Slump: the Labour Government of 1929–1931* (London, 1967); Philip Snowden, *An Autobiography* (2 vols., London, 1934), ii. 783–817; Stresemann, *Vermächtnis*, iii. 548 ff.; Jacobson, *Locarno Diplomacy*, pp. 309–43.

[77] Stampfer, *Vierzehn Jahre*, p. 502.

tum. In the Reichstag debate less than 100 members voted for the first three paragraphs of the so-called Freedom Law, and on the fourth, which Julius Curtius described as 'an infamy that is not excused by even the most bitter political differences', even the DNVP broke, only 55 of its delegation supporting Hugenberg. This resounding defeat was not without effect when the popular referendum was taken in December, for the document fell far short of the vote required to make it law.[78]

Even so, the fact that the 5,825,000 Germans who voted for the Freedom Law were apparently willing to repudiate the work of the Republic's greatest statesman, to brand him and his associates as traitors, and to opt for a policy that defied the rest of the world and its notions of the public law was surely not insignificant. This and the techniques employed to effect that result were ominous signs of the radicalization of German politics and the beginning of attempts to mobilize the masses against the parliamentary system. In the Reichstag Curtius described the work of the Hugenberg committee as 'an attack against the authority of the state'. It would have been more accurate to call it a repudiation of the legitimacy of the democratic Republic, an attitude that increasing numbers of Germans were to share in the years ahead.

Until his death on 3 October 1929 Stresemann was able to prevent his party from joining them. His last service to his country was in a gruelling meeting of the DVP's Reichstag delegation on 2 October, where he used all of his diplomatic gifts to persuade his colleagues not to jeopardize what had been gained at The Hague by overthrowing the government on a question of financial policy, as the right wing apparently wanted to do. He retired to his bed without knowing what the issue would be, but, in fact, he had won a narrow victory. The DVP remained in the government until the Young Plan was ratified and the Rhineland evacuation well under way.

The fall of the Müller cabinet could, nevertheless, already be descried, and the operative cause was the question that had been agitating the DVP Fraktion on 2 October. During the previous winter the country had slipped into a worrisome economic recession that failed to respond to treatment. By the spring of 1929 the number of registered workers who were applying to the Reichsanstalt für Arbeitsversicherung (RAV) for relief was approaching 1,500,000 (this did not, of course, represent the total number of unemployed, which included people who had never had a job and was much higher). The unemployment insurance fund, which was made up of contributions from employed workers and their employers, was running a sizeable deficit, and its administrators were seeking a government subvention of almost 400 million R.M. to tide it over until June. The government was already having difficulty in meeting its normal obligations, and an attempt in May to alleviate its situation, by offering the public an issue of bonds to the value of 500 million R.M. with 7 per cent interest and generous tax benefits, failed dismally, less than two-fifths of the amount being subscribed. It was clear that some adjustment in the unemployment insurance system was advisable, even though it was simplistic to claim, as the Hugenberg Press and some of the trade associations sought to do, that the system was the *fons et origo* of all the nation's economic troubles and ought to be dismantled. This kind of propaganda could not help but arouse the strongest suspicion of the trade unions and create an atmosphere that made rational discussion of the financial problem extremely difficult.

This became apparent in September, when the Minister of Finance, Rudolf Hilferding, and the Minister of Labour, Rudolf Wissell, with the aid of the Prussian Government, formulated a plan for maintaining existing levels of relief by increasing the contributions of both workers and employers. This brought a storm of protest from the Federation of German Manufacturers and the German Employers' Union, which were now accepting the Hugenberg view that the road to economic salvation lay in lower relief payments, proof of need by recipients, and elimination of certain categories of workers from the rolls, combined with major fiscal reform that would make it possible to lower taxes. It was the DVP's reflection of these views that was the occasion of Stresemann's last stormy meeting with his party. The government plan was nevertheless approved by the Reichstag, but this brought no sensible lightening of the atmosphere. On the contrary, before the month of October was over, the stock market crash in New York suggested that the country's problems were just beginning.

It is not easy, as one studies the evolution of the deepening economic crisis,[79] to find anyone with political influence in Germany who cared so deeply about the possible consequences of failing to master the national emergency that he was willing to subordinate his own personal or professional interests to the common cause. It was a

[79] The best accounts are Timm, *Sozialpolitik*, pp. 97 ff., 139 ff., and Stampfer, *Vierzehn Jahre*, pp. 503 ff., but see also Eyck, *Weimar Republic* ii, Ch. 8, and Bracher, *Auflösung*, pp. 291 ff.

time in which organized selfishness was more evident than courage and imagination and in which fatalists and opportunists dominated the scene. Hermann Müller, a decent but unimaginative man, presided over the deteriorating situation with a lack of vigour that was partly due to the liver ailment that was to lead to his death in March 1931. Under his slack leadership, the coalition satraps and horse-holders—Scholz of the DVP, Brüning of the Centre, Wissell of the SPD—went their own ways without worrying over-much about cabinet solidarity, while directors of government agencies showed no scruples about adopting positions that were at variance with ministerial plans. In the last months of 1929, for instance, the President of the Reichsbank, Hjalmar Schacht, an able but arrogant and extremely ambitious man, began a series of harassing tactics against the government, seeking to deny it further credits for the support of the insurance funds unless it instituted fiscal reforms of his own prescription. When Johannes von Popitz, Secretary of State of the Ministry of Finance, sought to circumvent him by negotiating an agreement for short-term credit with the American banking firm of Dillon and Read, the Reichsbank President, on 6 December, issued an extraordinary manifesto, accusing the government of fiscal irresponsibility, which frightened the Americans off and led to the resignation of Popitz and his chief Hilferding.[80]

The new Minister of Finance, Paul Moldenhauer of the DVP, sought to accommodate his policy to Schacht's demands, while at the same time hoping that some relief would come from a new agricultural tariff, new taxes on tobacco, and the reductions in reparations that would follow implementation of the Young Plan, the final details of which were worked out in a second conference at The Hague in January. He was disappointed on both counts. At the end of January he was forced to announce that the prospective savings in reparations annuities would barely cover the current year's deficit, a prognosis that fiscal experts regarded as excessively optimistic. As for Schacht, he was unappeasable. After a faintly ridiculous visit to The Hague, where he tried briefly and vainly to dominate the proceedings, he satisfied his now obsessive desire to see his name in headlines by resigning abruptly from his position at the Reichsbank in what the *Frankfurter Zeitung* called an obvious demonstration against the government.[81]

---

[80] Lutz Graf Schwerin von Krosigk, *Es geschah in Deutschland: Menschenbilder unseres Jahrhunderts* (Tübingen, 1951). For Schacht's own account, see Hjalmar Schacht, *Das Ende der Reparationen* (Oldenburg, 1931), p. 154, and *Confessions*, pp. 237 ff.

[81] Timm, *Sozialpolitik*, p. 173.

His example inspired imitation. Scholz and the DVP were already invoking Schacht's name to support their argument that the government was shirking its duty by not cutting back on insurance payments, and now the new leader of the Centre party's Reichstag delegation began to sound Schachtian in his turn. In February, when the Young Plan was brought before the Reichstag for ratification, Heinrich Brüning announced that his party could not accept the proposals unless it received a clear picture of the financial condition of the country and the probable effects of the plan. Although he decided in the end not to block ratification, Brüning nevertheless carried his concerns to the President's Palace, in a visit ostensibly motivated by a desire to observe the proprieties by paying his respects to the Field-Marshal as new Fraktion leader. It was an odd meeting, in which Brüning clearly had other things on his mind besides fiscal reform. He spoke of the respect his delegation had for Hermann Müller and their intention of continuing to work with him as long as he was willing to promote necessary reforms, which he did not apparently specify. At the same time, he made it clear that the majority of his party colleagues were, like him, temperamentally inclined toward co-operation with the right and had been forced into collaboration with the Social Democrats by Hugenberg's excesses, at whose name, according to Brüning's account, 'a sad look came over the Reichspräsident's features, carved as if from oak, but also a certain firmness and determination'. Brüning pointed out that the President had many friends among the Nationalists, and even in the SPD, and that he hoped he would use 'his great authority' to build a bridge between the constructive elements of left and right. If so, he would do his best to support the President's efforts. Hindenburg, who had always been a great weeper, now became demonstrably lachrymose and seizing Brüning's hands, said brokenly: 'Throughout my life everybody has abandoned me. You must promise me that you and your party will not leave me in the lurch at the end of my life.'[82]

It is difficult to avoid the conclusion that Brüning was protecting his future against a collapse of the cabinet that he regarded as imminent and that he was already thinking about a radical departure from normal parliamentary government if he should himself be called to power. If this is true, his calculations about the continued viability of the Müller cabinet were accurate. It was no longer possible to avoid a confrontation on the question of the future of unemployment insur-

[82] Heinrich Brüning, *Memoiren 1918–1934* (Stuttgart, 1970), pp. 148–9.

ance. Either the contributions to the insurance fund would have to be increased, which business in general opposed and which the DVP would not accept, as Moldenhauer discovered on 24 March, when he brought in a financial package that included a proposal for such an increase, or the benefits would have to be reduced, an idea that was anathema to the trade union movement, which suspected that it would be the preface to a general reduction of wages. As the cabinet struggled with this intractable problem, a DDP deputy named Oscar Mayer devised a compromise which he persuaded Brüning to sponsor and which for a moment seemed capable of uniting the dissident elements. This would have given the unemployment fund an annual government subsidy the extent of which would be decided in the budget debate. If this proved to be inadequate, the RAV would have the authority to raise the rate of contributions from employers and workers by 0·025 per cent.

This won the assent of all members of the coalition except the Bavarian People's party (which was sulking because of the inclusion of a new beer tax in Moldenhauer's financial scheme) and the SPD. The decisive influence in Socialist councils at this time was not the Chancellor, or the Minister of Economics, Robert Schmidt, or the Minister of the Interior, Carl Severing, all of whom were ready to accept the Mayer–Brüning compromise, but Rudolf Wissell, who had spent his life in the trade union movement and who was the party's most ardent advocate of social policy, one manifestation of which was unemployment insurance. To Wissell, the compromise was a disguised attack upon the integrity of the system and would lead to its gradual emasculation. His refusal to accept it made it necessary to submit the issue to the party's Reichstag delegation, and that body, under Wissell's influence and mindful of its dependence upon trade union support, voted overwhelmingly to reject the Mayer–Brüning plan.[83] With the cabinet in complete disarray, and Moldenhauer flatly refusing to clean up after this disastrous smashing of the crockery, Müller submitted the resignation of his cabinet to Hindenburg, who accepted it.

Gustav Noske, who had had his own troubles with his party comrades, described in his memoirs how Rudolf Hilferding once talked to him about 'the truly intolerable situation of having a party behind one which is utterly without leadership or direction . . . [and whose] policies are determined by people who were ready to let

---

[83] For a fuller account of Wissell's position in this crisis see David Barclay, 'Social Politics and Social Reform: Rudolf Wissell and the Free Trade Union Movement', Ch. 5.

German democracy and the German Republic go to the devil . . .
over the question of thirty pfennigs for the unemployed'.[84] In view
of the Socialist delegation's blindness, in the crisis of March 1930, to
anything save the reaction of the unions to their decision, this can be
described as a true bill.[85] But it would be a mistake to regard the SPD
as the sole, or even the most important, author of the Müller
cabinet's fall. The behaviour of the DVP during the eighteen months
that preceded the final crisis had reflected a growing conviction that
the maintenance of the capitalist free enterprise system was incompatible with the continuation of parliamentary democracy;[86]
and the Centre, under Kaas and Brüning, was already succumbing to
the fateful opportunism that was to be its salient characteristic for the
next three years. None of the parties, inside the coalition or out, can
be exempted from responsibility for the failure of the Republic's last
democratic government, or for the fall of the Republic that was not
long delayed.

[84] Noske, *Aufstieg*, p. 309.
[85] See Leber, *Ein Mann geht seinen Weg*, pp. 220, 233 f.
[86] Timm, *Sozialpolitik*, p. 201.

XV
The End of Weimar

Durch die letzten Tagesblätter
Rauscht die welke Politik
Greise schauen nach dem Wetter
Gibt es Putsch?
Futsch ist futsch
     Du deutsche Republik!

WALTER MEHRING (1931)[1]

This man is not of our race. There is something totally alien about him, something like an otherwise extinct primordial race that was totally amoral.

OTTO HINTZE (1931)[2]

PARLIAMENT having demonstrated its incapacity to give effective government to Germany, the country now passed into a condition similar to that which prevailed in Rome in the fifth decade before Christ, when the civil power lost its authority and the soldiers and demagogues took over. The fall of the Müller cabinet marked the beginning of a degree of military intervention in German politics that had been exceeded only by the behaviour of the Third Army Command in the years 1916–18. On this occasion, however, the military politicians lacked the will to take responsibility boldly and openly into their hands. They preferred to operate through chosen agents whom they could control and of whom they could dispose when they had outlived their usefulness. This was a difficult game at best, and they weren't very good at it. In the end they lost heart, and their last agent became their master.

I

The increased political activity of the military was inspired by the active concern of its chiefs over the disintegration of public order that accompanied the rising unemployment of the last months of 1929 and the evidence of growing extremism that was afforded by gains made in local elections by the National Socialist and Communist

---

[1] 'Ein Leichenwagen fährt vorüber', in Walter Mehring, *Der Zeitpuls fliegt: Chansons, Gedichte, Prosa* (Hamburg, 1958), p. 27.
[2] Meinecke, *Deutsche Katastrophe*, p. 89.

parties. It seemed to them that, unless these developments were halted, the country would drift into a condition similar to that of 1918 and that national unity might dissolve in a civil war in which the army itself, the last bulwark of state authority, would be torn asunder.

So palpable did this danger appear to Müller's Defence Minister that in January 1930 he issued an extraordinary general order to the armed forces, warning them against becoming infected by party strife or the blandishments of demagogues and exhorting them to remember that the Wehrmacht was 'the necessity and most characteristic expression' of national unity and will.[3] The author of this document, Wilhelm Groener, had reason to remember the situation of 1918 with particular clarity, so much so that he was not content to rely upon rhetorical appeals but concluded that, as in that earlier crisis, the army must now again take the initiative in ending the divisions that threatened the Reich. Throughout the winter months of 1929–30 Groener and the man he called 'my Cardinal *in politicis*', General Kurt von Schleicher, head of the Defence Department's Ministeramt, or political bureau, were deeply involved in plans and negotiations for a new kind of government that would replace Müller's cabinet when it finally tottered to its fall. The model that seemed best calculated to cope with the national emergency was a cabinet of men who were not restricted in any way by party allegiance, who would work together as a team guided only by national interest, and who relied for their ultimate authority upon the powers of the President.[4] The man best qualified to lead such a government was Heinrich Brüning.

Brüning commended himself to the military chiefs for several reasons in addition to the obvious one that he would presumably be able to count on the support of his own party, which was one of the larger ones. He was known to have conservative fiscal views, which would reassure the business community; his voting record showed consistent support of military appropriations, and he was a firm believer in the necessity of revising the arms clauses of the Versailles Treaty on Germany's behalf; he shared Schleicher's hostility toward Social Democracy, which he believed had encouraged materialism, moral laxity, and unreasonable expectations in a large part of the population; and, as an ardent Roman Catholic, he was not disinclined to consider authoritarian solutions for serious problems. In his talks with the Field-Marshal, Schleicher, who played the key role in persuading the old man of the need for a radically new approach in

---

[3] Craig, *Prussian Army*, p. 433.
[4] Ibid., pp. 436–7 and notes; Dorpalen, *Hindenburg*, pp. 170 ff.

government, stressed all of these points when he talked about Brüning, and he also disarmed Hindenburg's uneasy suspicion of Catholicism by emphasizing Brüning's excellent war record and the fact that he had won an Iron Cross, First Class as a front officer.[5]

These tactics were successful. In a long conversation with Brüning on 27 December, as they walked in the Potsdam woods, Groener informed the Centre leader that the President was resolved to ask him to form a government when Müller fell and urged him to heed the call of duty. When Brüning asked whether it might not be better for a general to become Chancellor—Groener himself, or Schleicher—the Defence Minister brushed the question aside by saying—with less than perfect logic, in view of his own present activities—that this would contradict all of his efforts to keep the army out of politics. He insisted that Brüning was the man of the hour and assured him (rather too easily, as events would show) that he could guarantee the reliability of the President's support because he had done the Field-Marshal so many services in the last twelve years that it would be 'humanly impossible' for Hindenburg not to follow his advice, which would be steadfastly exerted on Brüning's behalf.[6]

When the call came to him from the President's Palace on 27 March 1930, Brüning was, therefore, prepared for it, and it did not take him long to make up his mind about it. In his interview with Hindenburg the next morning, he explained that he intended to form a cabinet capable of pursuing an independent course but that this would be possible only with the backing of the presidential emergency powers. This aid the Field-Marshal promised to give, addding, 'But naturally only in so far as it is consistent with the constitution, which I have sworn before God to maintain.'[7] This was enough for Brüning. He accepted the assignment and got down to the job of selecting his ministers, which, in defiance of all precedent, he completed within forty-eight hours.

At first blush, the new cabinet did not differ radically from its predecessor. The four Socialist ministers were gone, but seven members were relics from the Müller government. The new faces were Gottfried Treviranus of the Volkskonservativen, Brüning's most enthusiastic follower—his *treuer Knappe*, in the current

---

[5] Otto Meissner, *Staatssekretär unter Ebert–Hindenburg–Hitler: Der Schicksalsweg des deutschen Volkes von 1918–1945, wie ich ihn erlebte* (Hamburg, 1951), pp. 187–8; Schüddekopf, *Heer und Republik*, p. 248 and n.; Schwerin von Krosigk, *Es geschah in Deutschland*, p. 117.

[6] Brüning, *Memoiren*, pp. 158–61.

[7] Ibid., p. 161.

phrase—who became Minister for Occupied Territories,[8] Martin Schiele, like Treviranus a dissident from the DNVP, who went to the Ministry of Food, J. V. Bredt of the new and short-lived Wirtschaftspartei, who headed the Ministry of Justice, and Brüning himself. Nor, at least in the first stage, were all of its members as free from party influence as its patrons had hoped. Only Groener, Treviranus, and Schiele were truly independent, and party pressure was strong enough to force both Bredt and the Finance Minister, Moldenhauer of the DVP, to withdraw from the cabinet at an early date.[9] But the new combination had two distinctive characteristics. It was a younger cabinet than Germany was accustomed to, with six former *Frontkämpfer* among its members, a circumstance that promised vigour and new ideas; and it was solidly united in its respect for Brüning. Because of the loyalty and support that he received from his colleagues, Brüning was the first Chancellor, since Stresemann's hundred days in 1923, who really led his cabinet.[10]

Brüning had undeniable gifts, although it may be doubted whether they were quite the ones needed in the situation that confronted him. About his selfless devotion to his country there can be no question; and it is clear that his moral purpose was supported by intellectual resources and a mastery of the technical aspects of the questions with which he had to deal that were superior to those of most of his predecessors. Groener was not merely giving way to *Schwärmerei* when he told a friend that he had never known 'a statesman, chancellor, minister, or general who combined in his head as much positive knowledge and political clarity and adaptibility as Brüning'.[11] The Chancellor had the same effect upon the hard-headed British ambassador, Sir Horace Rumbold, and upon his American colleague, Frederic M. Sackett, who told the Secretary of State, Henry L. Stimson, that the German Chancellor was 'the discovery of Europe, a really great man'.[12]

These qualities of mind were not accompanied, however, by the psychological gifts that politicians need if they are to be successful. Brüning was a man who thought in terms of measures rather than

[8] For details of their association, see Gottfried Reinhold Treviranus, *Das Ende von Weimar: Heinrich Brüning und seine Zeit* (Düsseldorf and Vienna, 1968).

[9] Bracher, *Auflösung*, p. 325; Horst Hausen, *Das Präsidialkabinett. Eine staatsrechtliche Betrachtung der Kabinette von Brüning bis Hitler* (Erlangen, 1933).

[10] Eschenburg, *Improvisierte Demokratie*, p. 248.

[11] Craig, *Prussian Army*, p. 438.

[12] Brecht, *Kraft des Geistes*, p. 130; *The Politics of Integrity: The Diaries of Henry L. Stimson, 1931 to 1945*, ed. Francis Loewenheim and Harold Langley (New York, 1978), 4 May 1931.

people, and he over-valued the power of reason and logic. When he was convinced of the rightness of his course, he fully expected others to see and be persuaded by that rightness, and he neglected to ask himself what would happen if they did not do so, if they, indeed, defied reason and logic because they felt too strongly to want to be persuaded against their will. This not only betrayed him into serious miscalculations of the public mood but made him vulnerable to the designs of less honourable men. In an age of passion and intrigue and widespread popular despair he was the pure technician, possessing neither the passion that inspired Bismarck's use of political power nor the charisma and the buoyant optimism that characterized his great contemporary, Franklin Delano Roosevelt. To the German people, who like leaders who are not afraid to show their feelings, he seemed cold, over-intellectual, and unsympathetic, and this, as much as anything, was the cause of his undoing.

He was, moreover, prone to a stubborn wilfulness in action that compounded the already formidable problems with which he had to deal, and nothing illustrates this better than his tactics during his first months in office. Although his cabinet did not command a majority in the Reichstag, it started off with certain advantages that an adroit parliamentarian could have exploited. It was no secret that Brüning was counting on Hindenburg and that failure to co-operate with him would probably lead to a dissolution of the Reichstag. This was something that most members of Parliament wished to avoid, and Hugo Breitscheid, whose party was somewhat chastened by the consequences of its stubbornness during the Müller crisis, intimated to the Chancellor at an early date that the SPD was ready to co-operate in finding parliamentary solutions to the country's economic problems. Had Brüning been willing to compromise on individual items of his programme, he might have found it unnecessary to invoke presidential authority at all.

But Brüning showed no willingness to consider this offer. In his view, the key to Germany's troubles—the depression, unemployment, the growing political divisiveness of the country—was fiscal reform, the ruthless and unconditional restoration of financial responsibility by means of an integrated deflationary programme of savings, tax increases, and reduction of government expenditures. This would admit of no compromise or amendment. Parliament must either accept it as a whole, or see itself bypassed and the programme effected by other means.[13]

---

[13] Bracher, *Auflösung*, p. 337.

The challenging tone of Brüning's opening declaration in the Reichstag on 1 April indicated that the Chancellor was already committed to the second alternative. A friend who talked to him during these first months reported that he was 'determined to go to the limit and deeply inspired by the consciousness of the hour of destiny at which the German people finds itself'.[14] He made no attempt to hide his feelings from the attentive parliamentarians. His was a new kind of government, he informed them, not tied to the usual coalition of parties. It had a programme that it was determined to put into effect without delay. The co-operation of the Reichstag would be appreciated, but, if it were not forthcoming, this would be 'the last attempt to accomplish this with the aid of the present Chamber'.

When the first instalments of the programme were delivered in June, the parties found many things to complain of. To the DNVP and the DVP, the sharp increases in taxes, particularly upon the upper brackets and on unmarried persons, were intolerable, the more so because the Young Plan payments and unemployment relief were to be continued; to the SPD, the proposed savings were inadequate because they did not include any provision for a reduction in military expenditures. On 16 July these parties, joined by the inveterate spoilers, the Nazis and the Communists, voted down essential parts of the financial package; and, when Brüning responded immediately by promulgating his budget, with the controversial measures, by emergency decree, the Reichstag majority, two days later, demanded that these decrees be abrogated, the SPD arguing that they represented an attack upon popular sovereignty. In obedience to the constitution, the Chancellor complied, but he was not stayed. He now dissolved the Reichstag and postponed the new elections until 14 September, the latest date that was constitutionally valid. Meanwhile he put his financial programme into effect by presidential authority.

In his memoirs the distinguished German scholar and civil servant Arnold Brecht recalled a passage from Sallust, in which the Roman historian described a speech made by the young Julius Caesar in the year 63 B.C., when Cicero, as consul, had used measures of dubious constitutional validity against five followers of the conspirator Catiline. Caesar pointed out that all dangerous precedents had their origins in good causes and created arguments with which bad men could later justify their crimes.[15] That Brüning's purpose was hon-

[14] Max Miller, *Eugen Bolz, Staatsmann und Erkenner* (Stuttgart, 1951), p. 374.
[15] Brecht, *Kraft des Geistes*, pp. 124 f.

ourable goes without saying, but in pursuing it he had made the first significant—and, as it turned out, irreparable—breach in the Weimar constitution and shown the way to the more ruthless men who would soon shove him aside and complete the destruction of democratic government in Germany.

It has been said that he would hardly have followed the course he had chosen if he could have foreseen the results of the September elections,[16] and it is doubtless true that his insensitivity to the popular mood and the passions that inspired it misled him. But why did he not listen to others? There were dozens of politicians in Germany in 1930 who had the gravest misgivings about holding elections in the middle of a deepening depression, when people were bewildered and resentful and all too ready to listen to radical tub-thumpers. There had been enough straws in the wind to show the direction in which it was blowing; in the June elections in Saxony the Nazis had shown surprising strength, and Communist meetings were attracting outsize audiences. The election campaign itself was bound to be so violent that it would jeopardize civil order, and the Reichstag that resulted from it would almost certainly be less effective and manageable than the present one, which still had two years to run. Unless one were willing to abolish the Reichstag entirely—and not even the military politicians had reached that point yet—new elections might make the government's position intolerable.

Brüning must have heard all of this, but he closed his ears to it. He was convinced not only of the soundness of his fiscal programme but of the rightness of the course he had taken to effect it; and he went his way with heedless impetuosity because he was sure that the German people would respond to his vigorous leadership by repudiating the obstructionist Reichstag and electing the kind of Parliament that would support his reforms. 'The election', he wrote later, 'became a plebiscite on the emergency decrees, but at the same time a fight for decision between a senseless form of parliamentarianism and a sound and judicious democracy, in which the government, in order to save public finances from collapse, had to take up the struggle for this objective before the whole people in face of the intriguing and the foolishness of the existing Reichstag.'[17]

Had Brüning been a Bismarck, he might, despite the daunting economic circumstances, have been able to pull this off, by dramatizing the conflict of principle in his own person. But the Chancellor was incapable of this. Before large audiences he was awkward and

---

[16] Ibid., p. 125.   [17] Brüning, *Memoiren*, p. 182.

curiously bloodless, and his speeches lacked any ability to inspire, which was natural enough since they spoke largely of sacrifices that had to be endured. Before long he was being called the Hunger Chancellor, hardly a sobriquet that would attract votes. His image might have been enhanced if he had received the open and enthusiastic support of the President, who was still a force capable of generating a loyal response from the masses. But although the Brüning government was his government in a sense that no earlier one had been, and although his name was on the decree that had put the budget in force, Hindenburg remained almost completely passive during the campaign. 'As a matter of principle,' his office announced, 'the Reich President does not intervene in the election campaign.'[18] This attitude blunted all of Brüning's arguments about the justifiability of using presidential power against a recalcitrant Reichstag, and it confused an already troubled electorate who could not make out, from listening to the contradictory speeches of Brüning's colleagues, whether they were attacking or defending democracy and what the consequences of either course were likely to be.

Before the campaign was over, a very large proportion of the electorate had simply stopped listening and adopted a kind of 'plague on both your houses' attitude. As a result, the elections of 14 September confirmed the worst fears of those who had counselled against dissolution in July. The 35 million Germans who went to the polls—4 million more than in 1928 and the largest percentage of the registered voters (82 per cent) to vote since 1918—did indeed repudiate the Reichstag that Brüning had dissolved, although hardly in the manner he expected or desired. The liberal parties were seriously weakened and now went into a terminal decline: the DVP losing a million votes and a third of its seats (falling from 45 to 30); the DDP, under its new name, the Staatspartei, electing a riven delegation that sank from 20 to 14 seats when the representatives of the Young German Order resigned a few weeks after the election; the new Wirtschaftspartei barely keeping itself alive.

This did not surprise Brüning, for he had not expected a recovery of a German liberalism whose parliamentary strength had fallen from 23 per cent of the mandates in 1919 to 13 per cent in 1928 and which, since Stresemann's death, had shown every indication of being moribund. But he had set his hopes on heavy defections from Social Democracy and a repudiation of Hugenberg that would operate in the interest of the moderate conservatives and make possible

[18] Dorpalen, *Hindenburg*, p. 193.

the formation of a strong nationalist coalition of the moderate right; and he was disappointed on both counts. The Social Democratic party lost 10 seats and about 600,000 votes, but with 143 Reichstag seats it was still the strongest of the parties. Even more disturbing for Brüning was the fact that 4,600,000 Germans had cast their votes for the KPD which now, with 77 seats, possessed a greater potential for obstruction than at any time since its founding.

Brüning's own party and its southern German counterpart, the Bavarian People's party, held their own, the Centre increasing its mandates from 62 to 68. But the strong moderate right, which the Chancellor had hoped would help him dominate the new Reichstag, never materialized at all. Hugenberg's follies, to be sure, revenged themselves upon him, and the DNVP lost almost 2 million votes and had to be satisfied with only 41 of the 73 seats it had won in 1928. But this did not work to the advantage of the Volkskonservativen of Westarp and Treviranus, who polled less than 300,000 votes and obtained only 4 seats, nor did it help any of the other independent conservative groups. The voters who turned from Hugenberg, like most of those who abandoned the liberal parties and a presumably large percentage of the 4 million new voters, cast their ballots for the party that Brüning had overlooked, Adolf Hitler's NSDAP.[19] In 1928 the Nazis had polled 809,000 votes and won 12 Reichstag seats; in September 1930 their vote was 6,400,000, which meant that 107 brown-shirts were going to march into the new Reichstag.[20]

These results gravely compromised the Brüning experiment. His efforts to solve Germany's problems now took on an air of desperation, and he turned his energies increasingly to the field of foreign affairs in the hope that he might win a diplomatic success impressive enough to enable him to contain the forces of radicalism that the September elections had released. Meanwhile the tone of German politics became violent and brutal to an unprecedented degree. That perceptive observer Harry Kessler, who was in Berlin at the time of the opening of the new Reichstag in October, wrote:

The whole afternoon and evening great Nazi masses who demonstrated and, during the afternoon in the Leipzigerstraße, smashed the windows of the department stores of Wertheim, Grünfeld, etc. In the evening, in the Potsdamer Platz, crowds that shouted, 'Deutschland erwache!', 'Juda verrecke!',

---

[19] In 1944 Brüning wrote to Arnold Brecht that he had not overlooked the NSDAP and had, in fact, thought it possible that they might win as many as 140 seats. Brecht, Kraft des Geistes, pp. 125, 415 ff. If this were true, it would be even more difficult to understand his decision to dissolve the Reichstag.

[20] On the elections, see Bracher, Auflösung, pp. 364 ff.; Eyck, Weimar Republic ii. 278 ff.

'*Heil! Heil!*' and were continually dispersed by the *Schupo*, patrolling in vans and on horses. . . . The scene in the streets reminded me of the days shortly before the revolution, the same crowds, the same Catilinarian types loung-ing about and demonstrating.[21]

II

The astonishing success won by the National Socialists in the elec-tions of September 1930 can be explained only in part by the prevailing economic distress of the country and the deepening dis-enchantment with the Weimar party system. The fact that the Nazis were the chief beneficiaries of these things was due rather to the character and political gifts of their leader and the nature and appeal of the party that he had rebuilt and nurtured after the débâcle of 1923.

In the years after 1933 one often saw on the wall of a village *Krug* or urban *Kneipe* a framed lithograph showing three heads in profile: those of Frederich the Great, Bismarck, and Adolf Hitler. The artist, who was commissioned by Josef Goebbels's Propaganda Ministry, had obviously been set the task of demonstrating the legitimacy of the regime by means of a pictorial representation of historical con-tinuity; and his creation may indeed have had a reassuring effect upon those who eyed it over their beer, alleviating any doubts they might be having about the Führer's policies.

But if they believed what was implied in the picture, they were wrong, just as those German historians of the modern school who argue that Hitler is part of a continuum that includes Bismarck, William II, and Stresemann are wrong. The similarities of thought and action that have been adduced to prove Hitler's kinship with other German statesmen or to demonstrate the native roots of his political behaviour are too trivial to be persuasive. Adolf Hitler was *sui generis*, a force without a real historical past, whose very German-ness was spurious because never truly felt and in the end, in the moment of defeat, repudiated, self-contained, and self-motivated, dedicated to the acquisition of power for his own gratification and to the destruction of a people whose existence was an offence to him and whose annihilation would be his crowning triumph. Both the grandiose barbarism of his political vision and the moral emptiness of his character make it impossible to compare him in any mean-ingful way with any other German leader. He stands alone.

In the years of his ascent to power that loneliness, that uniqueness, played its part. It created that distance between him and his party

[21] Kessler, *Tagebücher*, p. 646.

comrades that he deliberately cultivated for the psychological advantages that it brought him, and this was not the least important factor in reinforcing the principle of leadership in the party and in making his personal ascendancy indisputable. It lent a nimbus of mystery to his figure that awed many who entered his presence, and left few unimpressed. It exuded its own magic force on the multitudes who came to hear him and captured and bound them to him even before he had begun to speak.

His uniqueness had another aspect. Among all of the prominent figures of the Weimar period, he is the only one of whom it can be said unequivocally that he possessed political genius. There were some who had particular gifts that he did not equal—Stresemann's talents as a negotiator spring to mind—and there were many who had qualities of mind and character that were entirely lacking in him and, indeed, entirely beyond his powers of appreciation. But as a political animal, he was a nonpareil in his own time. In his person were combined an indomitable will and self-confidence, a superb sense of timing that told him when to wait and when to act, the intuitive ability to sense the anxieties and resentments of the masses and to put them in words that transformed everyone with a grievance into a hero in the struggle to save the national soul, a mastery of the arts of propaganda, great skill in exploiting the weaknesses of rivals and antagonists, and a ruthlessness in the execution of his designs that was stayed neither by scruples of loyalty nor by moral considerations.[22]

It was Hitler's complete faith in himself and his belief that he was destined to become the leader of the nation with which he identified his fate after 1919 that had impressed the motley assortment of nihilists, disinherited intellectuals, and *condottieri* who had been the backbone of the original party; and during the long winter of discontent that followed the collapse of the November Putsch, it was his apparent imperviousness to doubt that bound them ever more firmly to him. Ambitious men who were greedy for recognition and power, they were, in their sober moments, prone to discouragement and thoughts of surrender. Repeatedly, the movement was saved from disintegration by Hitler's faith and will, until its subordinate leaders came to believe in his mission as fervently as he did himself.

[22] See the excellent appreciation of his political gifts in H. R. Trevor-Roper's introduction to *Hitler's Secret Conversations* (New York, 1953), and the incisive analysis in Ch. 7 of Alan Bullock, *Hitler: A Study in Tyranny* (rev. edn., New York, 1964). Enlightening also is Joachim C. Fest, *Hitler. Eine Biographie* (Frankfurt-on-Main, 1973), pp. 367–400, 448–63.

Josef Goebbels was capable of great cynicism, but he was not being cynical when he wrote in hymnic accents in *Der Angriff* in November 1928:

Many people are capable of perception, and still more of organization, but only one man in Germany is capable, by means of fate-given perception and the power of the word, of creating political works for the future. Many are called, but few are chosen. We are all convinced, so that our conviction can never be shaken, that he is the mouthpiece and the pathbreaker of the future. Therefore, we believe in him. Beyond his human form, we can see in this man the active grace of destiny, and we cling to his thought with all our hopes and bind ourselves to that creative power that drives him and all of us forward.[23]

Perhaps because his faith in himself was so unalloyed, Hitler had tremendous resources of patience. He knew by instinct that, in politics as in war, a sense of timing is an indispensable gift. The events of 1923 had taught him the perils of precipitate action; thereafter, he played a waiting game. In the period that followed the elections of September 1930, this proved to be of inestimable importance and may with justice be described as the key to his ultimate success. The closer the party got to power, the more eager were Hitler's subordinates to enjoy its privileges, and there was always a danger that their eagerness would make them vulnerable to attractive but insubstantial offers, so that they would in the end be gulled and fobbed off with trifles. It was Hitler's ability to wait that prevented this. He had his own inner clock, and he was capable of resisting any amount of argument and pressure until it told him that the time had come for action.

When that happened, he could move with blinding abruptness and with a total disregard of the risks involved. His later career was rich in occasions on which he dared actions that filled his party comrades, his diplomats, and his soldiers with trepidation and presentiments of disaster, and repeatedly his resolution was justified by the results. This was an essential ingredient of his diplomatic style after 1933, and it paid rich dividends, but even in the earlier years it was the necessary concomitant of his Fabian tactics, lending an element of incalculability to his politics that his antagonists came to appreciate and dread.

The talent that had, in the first instance, transformed him from a rootless vagrant to a politician of consequence was his ability to attract the masses and win their allegiance, and this was manifested in his success as an orator. Anyone who has seen Leni Riefenstahl's film

[23] Bracher, *Auflösung*, p. 119 n. 95.

of the 1934 Party Convention in Nuremberg, *Triumph des Willens*, can understand why this was so, even if he does not understand German, for the power and passion that animated Hitler's speeches are manifest and disturbing despite the more than forty years that have passed since they were recorded. No popular tribune in German history had ever been as successful as he proved to be in breaking down the emotional resistance of his audiences, in driving them to transports of rage and exaltation, in forcing them to merge their wills with his own.

But essential to this ability to dominate and mesmerize his hearers were his remarkable intuitive powers, which enabled him to sense their moods and divine their fears and longings and say the things that they wanted to hear, the things that would tell them that they were right in feeling deprived and victimized, that their resentments were justified, that the real Germans were surrounded by crafty and unrelenting foes, the worst of whom were in their midst, posing as Germans, but that their time would come, inevitable as a storm in the spring, and heads would roll. Otto Strasser, an early follower who later broke with the Führer, said once:

Hitler responds to the vibrations of the human heart with the delicacy of a seismograph. . . . [He possesses] an uncanny intuition, which infallibly diagnoses the ills from which his audience is suffering. . . . [He] enters a hall. He sniffs the air. For a moment he gropes, feels his way, senses the atmosphere. Suddenly he bursts forth. His words go like an arrow to their target; he touches each private wound on the raw, liberating the mass unconscious, expressing its innermost aspirations, telling it what it most wants to hear.[24]

Since the resentments of his auditors were diverse and unfocused, it was his purpose to direct them to specific targets, among which the Versailles Treaty, the Young Plan, the League of Nations, the parliamentary democracy that tolerated these things, and the Jews who were prominent in its political and economic life took pride of place. In undertaking to make the average German believe that these were the primary sources of all his problems and anxieties, Hitler showed a mastery of propaganda technique, which nevertheless revealed a basic contempt for the intellectual capacity of the common people. In *Mein Kampf*, the book he had written during his prison term in Landsberg in 1924, he stated the principle that 'all propaganda must be popular and its intellectual level must be adjusted to the most limited intelligence among those it is addressed to. Consequently, the greater the mass it is intended to reach, the lower its purely intellectual level will have to be.' And again:

[24] Bullock, *Hitler*, p. 341.

The receptivity of the great masses is very limited, their intelligence is small, but their power of forgetting is enormous. In consequence of these facts, all effective propaganda must be limited to a very few points and must harp on these in slogans until the last member of the public understands what you want him to understand by your slogan. As soon as you sacrifice this slogan and try to be many-sided, the effect will piddle away. . . .[25]

Hitler's didactic approach to his audiences was based upon these principles and an awareness of two other psychological principles: first, that arguments are weakened by qualifications or concessions to the other side, so that the uncompromising and categorical style tends to be the most convincing; second, that prevarication is best cast in the most exaggerated forms. The masses indulge in petty falsehoods every day, he once said cynically, but it would never come into their heads to fabricate colossal untruths and they are not 'able to believe in the possibility of such monstrous effrontery and infamous misrepresentation in others'. The bigger the lie, therefore, the more likely was it to be believed. Besides, 'even the most insolent lie' always leaves traces behind it, even after it has been nailed down.[26] This cynical wisdom guided the vicious campaigns of character assassination that Hitler and his paladins used against people who stood in their way or whose reputation they felt it necessary to tarnish. Both Stresemann and Brüning suffered from it, and so did many less prominent figures, like the unfortunate Dr. Weiss, the Deputy Police President of Berlin, whom Goebbels persecuted implacably, according to the prescriptions laid down by his master.[27]

In the field of visual propaganda, Hitler also showed a great talent—he designed the highly effective swastika party banner himself,[28] and had some success at self-dramatization by means of dress, the distinctiveness of his personal motor car, and his revolutionary use of the aeroplane for campaigning—and he also chose subordinates who were gifted in producing startling and impressive effects to enhance the activities of the party. Even the simplest Nazi meeting was a staged affair, with ceremonial and pageantry and flags and music; one at which the Führer spoke was a religious ceremony; and the annual party conference was a grandiose extravaganza designed to hearten the faithful, impress the foreign observer, and daunt the potential foe by its demonstration of united will and disciplined power. It would be difficult to prove the degree to which

[25] Adolf Hitler, *Mein Kampf*, trans. Ralph Manheim (Boston, 1962), pp. 180–1.
[26] Ibid., pp. 231 f.   [27] Liang, *Berlin Police*, p. 153.
[28] Hitler, *Mein Kampf*, p. 496.

this contributed to the party's victory at the polls in September 1930 or to the Nazi regime's foreign successes after 1933; but that there was an important contribution cannot be doubted.[29]

The effectiveness of Hitler's powers of persuasion was not confined to mass meetings. In the course of his career he showed an unusual capacity for ingratiating himself with people who were originally suspicious or antagonistic and winning them over to his point of view. His success in this was due partly to a kind of verbal sleight of hand that made them think that doing things his way would demonstrate the validity of *their* principles (a fine example of this from the late thirties was his masterful use of the word 'realism' in negotiations with the self-styled realist Neville Chamberlain),[30] and partly to his skill in detecting and playing upon their weaknesses. The latter talent he used with effect in foreign affairs after 1933, but it played an important part in his domestic policy also and, from the beginning, had been an effective means of strengthening his authority in his party. It was part of his technique to play upon the ambition and jealousy and greed of his subordinates, using favours and preferments to establish obligations or dependence, allowing rivalries to develop, pitting one individual or group against another. The National Socialist party was never the monolithic centralized structure that its official propaganda portrayed it as being, for its Führer kept it atomized into countless rival agencies that were balanced and controlled by his personal authority. His skill in managing this was not the least important of his political gifts.

Finally, Hitler's unconditionality, his utter ruthlessness in action, was also an important element in his political success. He was aware that violence and terror have their awful fascination and that the brutal employment of force attracts as many people as it repels. In the early days of the party he became convinced that a bloody affray in the streets was a better advertisement for the party than a dozen pamphlets; as time went on, he had grounds for believing that the deliberate liquidation of political opponents was no less effective as a means of impressing the world by the firmness of Nazi purpose. If the bigness of the lie lends credibility to it, so does the enormity of the crime increase the likelihood of its intimidating enemies and persuading neutrals to join the cause. The important thing is to be

[29] See Z. A. B. Zeman, *Nazi Propaganda* (2nd edn., London, 1973), Chs. 1, 2; George L. Mosse, *The Nationalization of the Masses: Political Symbolism and Mass Movements in Germany from the Napoleonic Wars through the Third Reich* (New York, 1975), Ch. 8; Albert Speer, *Inside the Third Reich: Memoirs* (New York, 1970), Chs. 5, 6.

[30] Craig, *War, Politics and Diplomacy*, p. 213 n. 18.

taken seriously, and the dangerous man is always taken so. Hitler's matter-of-fact acceptance of this truth and his unscrupulous application of it in his political behaviour should not be omitted when the nature of his political genius is being analysed.

Although Rudolf Hess was asserting a truism when he used to shout, at the height of the annual Nuremberg jamboree, 'The Party is Hitler! Hitler is the Party!', this does not obviate the necessity of our inquiring into the nature of the NSDAP in 1930 and the social groups on which it exercised the strongest appeal.

In contrast to almost all of the other parties in the Weimar period, the Nationalist Socialist Workers' party did not direct its propaganda towards a single social or economic class or grouping of interests. This had not always been so. In its early days the party regarded itself, and was thought of by a middle class that was still traumatized by the events of 1918, as a party of the left. As late as 1922–3, although it included a not inconsiderable number of soldiers of fortune, misfits, and nihilists (the group that in 1930 prided itself on being the old guard of the party), it also had a disproportionately high number of manual workers in its membership,[31] and its appeals were beamed with particular urgency towards the working class. During the election campaign of 1924, the *Nordwestdeutsche Handwerkszeitung* described the NSDAP as 'a pure workers' movement' and warned its readers against 'Bolshevik poison in black, white, red packing'.[32] But when Hitler came out of Landsberg in December 1924 and began the reorganization of the party and its shift from the tactics of revolution to those of legality, he also recognized that the effort to win the working class from its Marxist parties had failed. Nazi propaganda changed its tone, and the party began to seek the support of other social groups.[33] It stopped pretending to be a *Klassenpartei* and became a *Sammelpartei*, open to anyone who felt strongly about the state of the Germany and the obliquities of the republican government. Although it still called itself a workers' party, its occupational profile in 1930 indicated that the working class was decidedly under-represented. The percentage of total party membership claimed by salaried employees (25·6 per cent), persons who were self-employed or had independent means (20·7 per cent), civil servants (8·3 per cent), farmers (14 per cent) was greatly in

---

[31] See Michael H. Kater, 'Zur Soziographie der frühen NSDAP', *Vierteljahrshefte für Zeitgeschichte*, xix (1971), 124 ff.

[32] Winkler, *Mittelstand, Demokratie und Nationalsozialismus*, p. 159.

[33] Jeremy Noakes, 'Conflict and Development in the NSDAP, 1924–1927', *Journal of Contemporary History*, i, no. 4 (1966), 3 ff.; Dietrich Orlow, *History of the Nazi Party, 1919–1933* (Pittsburgh, 1969), pp. 76 ff.

excess of, and in the first two cases double, their percentage of the national population. The percentage of manual workers (28·1 per cent) was almost 18 per cent lower than its national percentage.[34]

With a membership so diverse, the NSDAP could not hope to be ideologically consistent, and this explains why it was easier to say what the Nazis were against than what they were for. Thus perhaps the best definition of the movement was that given by Gregor Strasser in a speech in the Berliner Sportpalast in 1932: 'National-sozialismus ist das Gegenteil von dem, was heute ist!,[35] It is true that there was a party programme, the so-called Twenty-Five Points, but this was a confused mixture of nationalistic, anti-Semitic, and pseudo-socialist demands, which were either exasperatingly vague or mutually contradictory.[36] The Führer paid little attention to the programme's economic points, which were, in his mind, conditional in any case, since he regarded the purpose of domestic policy as being, not to realize specific economic or social plans, but to pre-pare the German people for the great tasks of foreign policy that awaited them.[37] Josef Goebbels regarded the programme as a whole as an embarrassment, saying frankly, 'If I had founded the party, I wouldn't have laid down any programme at all!'[38] Nazi speakers discouraged attempts on the part of their audiences to seek enlightenment about the precise meaning of the Twenty-Five Points and fell back on Strasser's formula. Peter Drucker once heard one of them shouting at a gathering of farmers: 'We don't want higher bread prices! We don't want lower bread prices! We don't want unchanged bread prices! We want National Socialist bread prices!'[39]

The defects of logic that contemptuous outsiders could point to in no way diminished the party's appeal, particularly to those elements of the middle class who constituted the most marginal stratum in Germany, squeezed as they were between the wealthy bourgeoisie on the one hand and the organized working class on the other, and apprehensive over what appeared to be the deterioration of their economic social condition. This *Mittelstand*, the centre of German

---

[34] Wolfgang Schäfer, *NSDAP, Entwicklung und Struktur der Staatspartei des Dritten Reiches* (Marburg, 1957), p. 17.

[35] Bracher, *Auflösung*, p. 108.

[36] Wolfgang Mommsen, *Deutsche Parteiprogramme* (Munich, 1960), pp. 547 ff.

[37] *Hitler's Secret Book*, trans. Salvator Attanasio with an introduction by Telford Taylor (New York, 1961), pp. 32, 34. See also Eberhard Jäckel, *Hitler's Wel-tanschauung*, trans. Herbert Arnold (Middletown, Conn., 1972), pp. 68–75.

[38] Bracher, *Auflösung*, p. 108.

[39] Peter Drucker, *The End of Economic Man: A Study in the New Totalitarianism* (New York, 1939), pp. 13 f.

philistinism and *Kitsch* and the butt of Georg Grosz's savage cartoons, was potentially the most revolutionary class in the country, because of its structural fluidity, its lack of leadership, and its resentment; and its steady gravitation toward National Socialism after 1929 was portentous.

Inconsistency of programme did not bother this class as a whole, or its more organized elements in the handicrafts and small trades. One of their spokesmen said in 1930 that it would be foolish to conclude that all those who voted for the NSDAP accepted the party programme in its entirety. The point was that 'private rejection of individual points of the programme weighed less heavily with those voters than the hope that only National Socialism still had the strength to drag the mired cart out of the muck'.[40] Similarly, the small farmers who voted for National Socialism were probably attracted less by specific points of the agricultural programme that the party developed after 1930 than by the anti-Semitic and anti-capitalist slogans used by Nazi orators and the promise that in a National Socialist state agriculture would be restored to the position of honour and respect that it deserved. Finally, the hordes of middle-class youths who turned to National Socialism after 1929—a phenomenon that so impressed army leaders that, according to the British military attaché, they were saying, 'It's the youth movement. It can't be stopped!'[41]—probably did not bother to read the programme at all, being attracted rather by the movement's invocation of ideals that they admired—comradeship, loyalty, courage, sacrifice—and the fact that it offered them a psychic outlet for their repressed or unfulfilled emotions and ambitions.

The party sought to strengthen its influence among all these groups by infiltrating and, whenever possible, taking over existing middle-class organizations. They had conspicuous success in the case of the Deutscher Handlungsgehilfenverein (DHV), where they gradually turned the younger functionaries against their leader Max Habermann, who had connections with the Volkskonservativen and was a supporter of Brüning. By 1931 the DHV had become an adjunct of the NSDAP, highly useful in opening up new opportunities for it to win over other groups of white-collar workers and, incidentally, bringing it significant financial support as well. In Schleswig-Holstein, a centre of agitation by the small farmers, the Nazis moved

---

[40] Winkler, *Mittelstand, Demokratie und Nationalsozialismus*, p. 178.

[41] *Documents on British Foreign Policy, 1919–1939*, ed. E. L. Woodward and Rohan Butler (London, 1949 ff.), 2nd Ser. i. 512 n. (hereafter cited as *BD*). See also Meinecke, *Deutsche Katastrophe*, pp. 70–1.

into the regional branches of the Farmers' Association and the village associations, which were known as Schicksalsgemeinschaften, and in 1931 the NSDAP leadership ordered its local members to join the Land- und Bauernbund and brought that organization under its control. Even more important was the effectiveness of Nazi tactics in penetrating the bastion of the national Rural League, an offshoot of the pre-war Bund der Landwirte which, until 1930, had been controlled by the great landed proprietors of eastern Germany. After September 1930 the RLB felt the need of more substantial political support than could be provided by the DNVP and the short-lived Christian National Farmers' and Rural People's party and sought a *rapprochement* with the victorious NSDAP.

The technique of winning influence in local branches of economic organizations and then mobilizing the membership against the national committees was effective also in the case of the handicrafts' associations, like the Nordwestdeutscher Handwerkerbund and the Reichsverband des deutschen Handwerks; while the rabidly anti-Semitic campaign against department stores and consumers' unions, which the Nazis launched in 1929, gradually brought most of the *Mittelstand*'s trade associations under the control of the National Socialist Kampfgemeinschaft gegen Warenhaus und Konsumverein. Finally, Nazi success in the university student organizations, which first became evident in the ASTA elections of 1929, was promoted by the same tactics of infiltration and co-ordination, the National Socialist youth groups demonstrating skill in manipulating the nationalist and racist student corporations and fraternities for their own purposes.[42]

Thanks to the extraordinary talents of its leader, the wide appeal of its propaganda, and the success of its tactics in dealing with *Mittelstand* organizations, the National Socialist party exuded strength and confidence in the months that followed its great electoral victory. But it was not yet in power, and whether it ever would be would depend upon its ability to maintain its momentum and retain the support that it had won. Its weakness was that, unlike the SPD

---

[42] On all this, see, *inter alia*, Karl Dietrich Bracher, *The German Dictatorship: The Origins, Structure and Effects of National Socialism* (New York, 1970), pp. 152–6; Heberle, *Democracy to Nazism*, pp. 84–9; Horst Gies, 'NSDAP und landwirtschaftliche Organisationen in der Endphase der Weimarer Republik', *Vierteljahrshefte für Zeitgeschichte*, xv (1967), 341–76; Winkler, *Mittelstand, Demokratie und Nationalsozialismus*, pp. 172–82; Wolfgang Zorn, 'Student Politics in the Weimar Republic', *Journal of Contemporary History*, v (1970), 128 ff.; H. P. Bleuel and A. Klimert, *Deutsche Studenten auf dem Weg ins Dritte Reich* (Gütersloh, 1967). Michael H. Kater, 'Der NS-Studentbund von 1926 bis 1928', *Vierteljahrshefte für Zeitgeschichte*, xxii (1974), 148–90.

and the Centre, it did not possess an inherent stability and staying power. As Karl Dietrich Bracher has written,[43] it was a *Glückseligkeitsreligion*, which appealed to discontented people and would have to prove its ability to allay their discontents in reasonably short order if it were not to lose the converts to new demagogues.

For Hitler and his followers the electoral success of September 1930 raised difficult but urgent new problems of tactics and timing. Because he remembered the consequences of the fiasco of 1923, and also because he was sure that Hindenburg, Brüning, and Groener would not hesitate to use the full resources of state power against a putsch, the Führer had resolved to seek power by legal means, that is by establishing his right to the chancellorship through electoral strength and parliamentary manœuvre. 'In principle,' he explained to his followers in Munich shortly after the elections, 'we are not a parliamentary party because this would contradict our whole conception. We are merely forced to be a parliamentary party and what forces us is the constitution. . . . The victory that we have just won is nothing less than the acquisition of a new weapon for our struggle.'[44] This sounded somewhat lame and apologetic, a plea to the expectant faithful not to presume too much from recent events, to be patient, to realize that these things take time.

But what if time were not on Hitler's side after all? What if Brüning recovered from the blow that he had suffered on 14 September and, by means of a turn in the economic tide or a diplomatic victory that impressed public opinion, consolidated himself in power? These questions must have been much in Hitler's mind as the year 1930 came to an end.

III

Meanwhile, however, everything seemed to conspire against Brüning. No matter how anxiously he eyed the economic skies, there was no sign of a break in the clouds. When he came to office, the number of registered unemployed stood somewhere in the neighbourhood of 3,000,000; in December 1930 the figure was 4,380,000; twelve months later it was to jump to 5,615,000. There was no possibility of the Chancellor's entrenching himself in power when the number of unemployed was approximately a tenth of the total population, the more so because he held stubbornly to an economic policy which, like that of the Hoover administration in the United States, seemed to be based on the assumption that depressions, like storms at sea,

---

[43] Bracher, *Auflösung*, p. 108.   [44] Quoted in Fest, *Hitler*, p. 405.

were not amenable to human control but must simply be allowed to blow themselves out.

At the same time, Brüning's attempt to take a leaf out of Bismarck's book and solve his domestic problems by means of diplomatic triumphs failed, not least of all because of mistakes for which he must bear the responsibility. His specific goals were a scaling-down of the Young Plan payments, if not their complete elimination, an objective that he believed would be advanced by, and would complete, his reform of Germany's finances.[45] Beyond that he looked towards a greater triumph, the regaining of his country's parity in armaments with the consent of the other Powers. This was something that all parties, from the right wing of the SPD to the NSDAP, regarded as essential,[46] which meant that it could hardly fail to rally support behind the government; and it was also a matter very much on the minds of Brüning's patrons, Groener and Schleicher. His objectives, therefore, were logical enough; it was the tactics he used in pursuing them that were at fault.

Admittedly, his position was difficult. He was forced, by the harsh realities of German politics, to follow a foreign policy that would seem properly nationalist at home but conciliatory abroad. He had not only to seek concessions from the other Powers but, for the sake of public opinion, to demand them. Since this was bound to alarm the French Government, already concerned about what the September elections might portend, he had to persuade the British and the Americans that he was really working for a *rapprochement* with France and that the French were being unreasonable in not appreciating this and to solicit their assistance in gentling the French toward a comprehensive settlement. Thus in December 1930 he told Sackett, the United States ambassador, that he believed that 'a complete understanding with France was the truly decisive goal for a pacification of the politics of the whole world' but that this could not be accomplished by means of direct talks because of 'French internal political factors'.[47] Sackett was impressed by this and by Brüning's suggestion that the United States Government might consider calling an international conference to deal with all of the outstanding troublesome questions in a co-ordinated manner.

[45] See, above all, Wolfgang J. Helbich, *Die Reparationen in der Ära Brüning* (Berlin, 1962), esp. Ch. 3.

[46] For the SPD's diverse views, see Gustav Adolf Caspar, *Die Sozialdemokratische Partei und das deutsche Wehrproblem in den Jahren der Weimarer Republik* (Frankfurt-on-Main, 1959), pp. 20 f., 69.

[47] Edward W. Bennet, *Germany and the Diplomacy of the Financial Crisis, 1931* (Cambridge, Mass., 1962), p. 32.

The British, while sympathetic to Brüning, were more doubtful, noting that the German Chancellor was asking for a great deal and offering nothing in return but the hope that, if he got it, right extremism in Germany might be contained. The Foreign Office was, moreover, displeased by the hectoring tone adopted by Brüning and his associates in their public pronouncements on foreign policy. As early as July 1930, in a cabinet memorandum, the Permanent Under-Secretary for Foreign Affairs, Sir Robert Vansittart, pointed to recent speeches by Curtius and Treviranus in which the existing status of the Saarland had been described as unnatural and the statement had been made that Germany could not 'rest content with her present frontier in the east'. The German Government seemed bent, he warned, on opening a Pandora's box of troubles, and one should not be surprised if they began to talk about anschluss next.[48]

This was a sound guess. The set-back in the September elections lent a new urgency to Brüning's diplomatic campaign and an increased shrillness to his domestic statements on foreign affairs. 'We have recently been struck', an official in the British Foreign Office wrote to the Berlin Embassy in October, 'by the sudden . . . unexpected emergence of a demand in Germany for the abolition of the demilitarization restrictions in the Rhineland.'[49] Brüning's condoning of this was hardly an earnest of his desire for general appeasement; nor was his insistence upon proceeding with the construction of a second armoured cruiser consistent with his poverty-stricken air when demanding a revision of the Young Plan.[50] Far more disturbing, however, was the confirmation given to Vansittart's apprehensions in March 1931 by the sudden announcement in the Press that the German and Austrian governments intended to establish a customs union (Zollunion) between their two countries.[51]

It is doubtful whether this project could, even by the most ingenious legal casuistry, have been squared with the provision of the peace treaty and the Geneva Protocol of 1922, although it is theoretically possible that the legal obstacles might have been removed by negoti-

[48] *BD* 2nd Ser. i. 501 n.   [49] Ibid. i. 517.

[50] Ibid. ii. 104, 115, 116, 124, 148 f., 207; *Foreign Relations of the United States, 1931*, i. 97 f., 108, 130 f.

[51] See esp. Oswald Hauser, 'Der Plan einer Deutsch-Österreichischen Zollunion von 1931 und die europäische Föderation', *Historische Zeitschrift*, 179 (1955), 57 ff.; Wolfgang J. Helbich, 'Between Stresemann and Hitler: The Foreign Policy of the Brüning Government', *World Politics*, xii (1959), 24–44; F. G. Stambrook, 'The German–Austrian Customs Union Project of 1931: A Study of German Methods and Motives', *Journal of Central European Affairs*, xxi (1961), 24–40; Julius Curtius, *Sechs Jahre Minister der deutschen Republik* (Heidelberg, 1948); and Bennett, *Diplomacy of the Financial Crisis*, Ch. 3.

ation. But the striking feature of the joint announcement was that it had not been preceded by the kind of diplomatic sounding that Stresemann had always employed; nor had any attempt been made to consult the French or the League of Nations. It was an exercise in diplomatic improvization, a forcing manœuvre in the Wilhelmine manner; and its failure was so shattering that it is now virtually impossible to discover who originally inspired it. Meissner, the State Secretary, believed that the Foreign Minister, Curtius, talked a reluctant Chancellor into accepting the scheme;[52] Brüning himself claimed that it was initiated by the Foreign Ministry during the Müller period and generated its own momentum.[53] The question is academic; the reality, that Brüning had the responsibility and had to pay the price when the French and the Czechs correctly recognized the deliberate political thrust of the project[54] and blocked it by insisting that it be submitted to the World Court, where it was declared in violation of treaty law. The diplomatic set-back was humiliating enough. Worse was the fact that, by making the Powers suspicious of Germany's intentions, it blocked the concessions that Brüning was seeking and, since it was probably responsible for the French Government's delay in accepting President Hoover's suggestion for a moratorium on war debts, reduced the possibility that that plan might alleviate Germany's economic condition.

The result of this was a steady decline in Brüning's popularity and the authority of his government, which was reflected in an increase of domestic violence—crime, industrial unrest, political terrorism, and bloody street-fighting between Nazi storm-troops and Communists. Hitler may have pledged himself and the NSDAP leadership to legality, but he did not attempt to restrain the activities of his local organizations. On the contrary, in his much-publicized speech to the Industry Club of Düsseldorf in January 1932 he justified them in words charged with pathos:

I know perfectly well, gentlemen, that when the National Socialists march through the streets and there is sudden tumult and uproar, the *Bürger* draws his curtains back, looks out, and says, 'They're disturbing my rest again, and I can't sleep.' . . . But don't forget that it is also a sacrifice when hundreds of thousands of men of the SA and the SS [Sturmabteilung and Schutzstaffel] have to get into trucks every day, and protect meetings, and make marches, only to come back in the grey of the morning and have to go to their job or their factory or collect their few pennies dole as unemployed. . . . If the whole

---

[52] Meissner, *Staatssekretär*, p. 198.

[53] Brüning, *Memoiren*, pp. 264 ff.

[54] See Bennett's discussion of the question of political intent in *Diplomacy of the Financial Crisis*, pp. 78 ff.

nation had the same faith in its calling as these hundreds of thousands, if the whole nation possessed this idealism, a quite different Germany would be standing before the world today.[55]

Apart from exaggerating the numbers of his troopers in order to impress his audience, Hitler was drawing a veil of patriotic romance over crimes of assault and murder committed nightly by youthful thugs wearing the insignia of his party. During 1931 hardly a week passed that was not marked by shootings and bombings and deliberately planned 'actions' that left damage to property and casualties in their wake.[56]

The real target of these assaults upon the public order was Brüning, but the Chancellor did not fight back. He was too busy with what Groener called his 'Spiel mit fünf Kugeln à la Bismarck',[57] his search for the elusive foreign triumph that he had set his heart on, to have much time left for domestic affairs, and, as he travelled from capital to capital in the latter part of 1931, he left the problem of internal security to his Minister of the Interior—a position that Wilhelm Groener filled after October 1931, while continuing to serve as Minister of Defence—and to the state governments. This did not please all of the Länderregierungen, who were closer to the Nazi outrages than the Chancellor and more apprehensive about where they might lead. In November the Frankfurt police came into possession of a set of papers (the 'Boxheim documents') which turned out to be circumstantial plans for the seizure of power by the SA and other Nazi organizations in the event of an attempted Communist Putsch and the establishment of a dictatorship, which would abolish private property and taxes and make short shrift of enemies of the state and Jews.[58] Who was to say that the Nazis might not implement such a plan at an appropriate moment, perhaps during the spring of 1932, when there would be Landtag elections in Prussia and the other states? Several of the state governments felt that something should be done to forestall this before it was too late and, when their advice went unheeded, became increasingly dissatisfied with Brüning and critical of his lack of leadership.

They were not alone. The disenchantment of the *Mittelstand* was complete by the spring of 1932, for the relief and protection that they had expected from Brüning's emergency decrees had not material-

[55] Max Domarus, *Hitler, Reden und Proklamationen 1932–1945, kommentiert von einem deutschen Zeitgenossen* (2 vols., Neustadt a.d. Aisch, 1962–3), i. 68 ff.
[56] Arnold Brecht, *Prelude to Silence* (New York, 1944), p. 63.
[57] Craig, *Prussian Army*, p. 442.
[58] On the Boxheim papers, see Eyck, *Weimar Republic* ii. 337–8.

ized.[59] Some of the country's leading industrialists, noting that the Chancellor had been forced increasingly to depend upon SPD support in order to avoid a Reichstag vote of no-confidence or demands for the repeal of the decrees, feared that he was becoming a Socialist pawn and that this would be reflected in his taxation policy.[60] This fear did not lead them to rush into Hitler's arms—the amount of industrial contributions that were made to the NSDAP before 1933 has been greatly exaggerated[61]—but the invitation to Hitler to speak at the Industry Club in Düsseldorf was at least a sign that big business was keeping its options open, and to the extent that it brought any money to Hitler it hurt Brüning. The East Elbian landed proprietors, who lived in perpetual fear of a cessation of state subventions and proposals for the division of large estates, convinced themselves simultaneously that Hans Schlange-Schoningen, who became Commissioner for Eastern Aid (Osthilfe) in November 1931, was an advocate of what they called agrarian Bolshevism, and their enthusiasm for Brüning, never very warm in any case because of his religion, cooled rapidly.[62]

The President himself became discontented with his Chancellor after Brüning had failed to persuade the Nazis to join with other parties in an agreement to prolong the presidential term, so as to avoid a new election and the disturbance of public order that would surely attend it. It seemed demeaning to him to have to run against a Communist (Ernst Thälmann) and a former corporal (Hitler), and it was humiliating to learn, when the first poll was taken in March 1932, that almost half of the nation had voted against him, including the inhabitants of Tannenberg and the Masurian Lake district, where he had won his greatest military victory. In the run-off election in April he won easily enough—19·4 million votes, to Hitler's 13·4 million and Thälmann's 3·7 million—but only by means of Centre and Socialist votes, while many of his old friends and associates went into Hitler's camp. The elections affected the Field-Marshal with an irrational resentment against the Chancellor that was important in the sequel.[63]

Most fateful for Brüning was the fact that the military lost confidence in him. This was not true of Groener, who remained loyal to

[59] Winkler, *Mittelstand, Demokratie und Nationalsozialismus*, pp. 140–6.

[60] Bracher, *Auflösung*, p. 438 n.

[61] See esp. Henry Ashby Turner, jun., 'Big Business and the Rise of Hitler', *American Historical Review*, lxxv (1969), 56–70 and 'Großunternehmertum und Nationalsozialismus 1930–33', *Historische Zeitschrift*, 221 (1975), 18–68.

[62] Bracher, *Auflösung*, p. 439 n.

[63] On the presidential elections, see Dorpalen, *Hindenburg*, Ch. 8.

the Chancellor to the end. But by the spring of 1932 the cold gambler Schleicher had concluded that the Brüning experiment had been a failure. Not only was the Chancellor's dependence upon the SPD in the Reichstag alienating the political forces he had been meant to attract, but his foreign policy was stalled and, indeed, misdirected. Schleicher was convinced that an expansion of the army was absolutely essential for reasons of national security and domestic tranquillity; it would make impossible another defeat like the failure of the Zollunion and would enable the army to absorb Hitler's SA, thus ending a threat to the Reichswehr's legitimate monopoly of power. In his view, Brüning should take advantage of the forthcoming Disarmament Conference in Geneva to demand armed equality with Germany's neighbours and should sabotage the conference if his wishes were not met. When it became clear that Brüning would not accept these tactics, that he intended, indeed, to give priority to the reparations question and was more interested in parity and reduction than in freedom to arm *ad libitum*, Schleicher resolved that he must go.[64]

The lever that he used to prise the Chancellor from his position was handed to him by his chief. In mid-April, in response to insistent pressure from the state governments, especially the Socialist Government of Prussia, Groener, as Minister of the Interior, convinced Brüning and Hindenburg that Hitler's SA and SS must, in the interest of internal security, be banned by emergency decrees. Although he pretended at first to agree that this step was necessary, Schleicher orchestrated the chorus of protest from military and nationalist circles that immediately rattled the windows of the Defence Ministry and the President's Palace. In an attempt to divert the storm from Brüning's head, Groener resigned as Minister of Defence.[65] This was not enough. Bombarded by letters from senior army officers who complained that the dissolution of the SA was a serious blow to the country's military potential, by insinuations from his son, who was a confidant of Schleicher, that the exemption of the republican Reichsbanner organization from the decree was another sign of Brüning's subservience to the SPD, and by furious protests from his agrarian friends against the announcement in May

---

[64] On the military differences, see Post, *Civil-Military Fabric*, pp. 304 ff.; Hillgruber, *Kontinuität*, pp. 20–2. Cf. Michael Salewski, 'Zur deutschen Sicherheitspolitik in der Spätzeit der Weimarer Republik', *Vierteljahrshefte für Zeitgeschichte*, xxii (1974), 135, 140–3.

[65] On the origins of this crisis, see Craig, *Prussian Army*, pp. 439–53. On Groener's defence of the Reichsbanner's exemption from the decree's application, for which he was criticized by the right, see Rohe, *Reichsbanner*, p. 423.

that the government intended to push a plan for land resettlement, President von Hindenburg concluded that he was being gulled by the Chancellor and his colleagues. On 29 May he told Brüning that his government had been badly discredited and that he would sign no new emergency decrees proposed by it. This was a death sentence, and Brüning recognized it as such. He submitted the resignation of his cabinet on the following day.

IV

Of all of Hitler's antagonists in the last months before his accession to power, Kurt von Schleicher was the most able and the most dangerous. A cultivated man of charm and cynical wit, with the ability to ingratiate himself with people from widely different milieux (he was as close to the Jewish financier Jakob Goldschmidt as he was to Oskar von Hindenburg, the President's son), this quintessential *Bürogeneral* possessed a cold political intelligence, strategical gifts of the first order, and great resources of courage and patience. His salient weakness was his preference for operating in the *coulisse* and relying upon others to execute his designs. This made him vulnerable to the weaknesses of his agents and deprived him of perfect control over the delicate operations that he set in train. In addition, he forgot that there is such a thing as being too clever and fell victim to his own reputation for being so.

One of Schleicher's reasons for precipitating Brüning's fall was his belief that that statesman had made a mistake in trying to destroy Hitler by direct attack and that this had contributed to the Führer's success in the state elections of 24 April 1932; the NSDAP was now the strongest party in all the diets except that of Bavaria.[66] As long as Hitler was a putative Messiah to large numbers of people, actions of this kind would only win sympathy for him. The effective way of dealing with him was to induce him to accept membership in a broad national coalition in which he would have to share the praise or blame for the decisions that had to be taken and in which, as time went on, he could be systematically shorn of his present resources of power. The Papen government, which was Schleicher's invention, was intended to be the nucleus of such a coalition.

In urging Hindenburg to appoint Franz von Papen as Brüning's successor, Schleicher believed that his nominee would have no strong convictions of his own and would be amenable to his direction. He was aware that Papen's strength lay in his connections—he

[66] See Dorpalen, *Hindenburg*, p. 309, where Schleicher's papers are cited to support this.

THE END OF WEIMAR

was a Catholic nobleman and a former Guards officer and had married the daughter of a Saarland industrialist—rather than in his intelligence; and when a friend remarked that the new Chancellor was not known to have a strong head, he had answered, 'He doesn't have to have. He's a hat!' Papen's colleagues, in whose selection Schleicher had a good deal to say, were no more impressive than their leader; for the most part they were men without parliamentary connections or backing, aristocrats and bureaucrats of such pronouncedly conservative views that Harry Kessler said that their collective philosophy represented a combination of stupidity and reaction that had not been seen since the Polignac government of 1830.[67] The country's first reaction to the new combination was a mixture of disbelief and indignation, which was not greatly diminished when the Western Powers, at the Lausanne Conference in June, gave the new Chancellor what they had denied Brüning, the abrogation of the Young Plan and the end of reparations. Like other concessions made to the Weimar Republic, this came too late to do it any good.

The Brüning government had depended in the Reichstag upon the tolerance of the SPD; to give its successor time to settle into office, Schleicher secured a promise of similar forbearance from the leader of the NSDAP. The price was a promise of new elections and the revocation of the decree prohibiting the public appearance of the SA and SS. Ernst Thälmann said that the latter was an open invitation to murder, and it is hard to deny the truth of this in view of what happened when the prohibition was lifted. In the next five weeks, in Prussia alone, there were nearly 500 brawls between the triumphant storm-troopers and their chosen enemies, in which 99 persons were killed and more than a thousand hurt; on 10 July 17 persons died in street fights in various parts of the country; and on 17 July a Nazi parade through the working-class districts of Hamburg-Altona led to a battle in which 17 more people lost their lives.[68]

It is one of the ironies of which the history of the Weimar Republic is full that these crimes became the excuse for an attack, not upon their authors, but upon the last real bulwark of German democracy. On 20 July 1932 Papen deposed the Prussian Government by decree on the grounds that it was incapable of maintaining public order and became Reich Commissioner with full powers over the state. Neither from the deposed ministers, nor from the police, nor from the Reichsbanner was there any resistance; and the trade unions,

[67] Kessler, *Tagebücher*, p. 670.
[68] On the Altona affair, see Severing, *Mein Lebensweg*, ii. 345 f.

which had stopped the Kapp Putsch in 1920, did not attempt to repeat that triumph. Respect for formal law and fear of unemployment conspired in Papen's interest, and by his *coup de main* he ended the old dualism between Prussia and the Reich and took over the resources of the largest of the federal states, along with a well-equipped police force of 90,000 men.[69]

Papen's action was popular with the army which had always regarded the dualism—a logical arrangement from their point of view under the Empire—as potentially dangerous to them during the years of Socialist domination of Prussian politics. Schleicher had good reason to be pleased with his new Chancellor, who had not only given him, as Defence Minister in the Papen cabinet, a free hand to determine the tactics to be followed in the Disarmament Conference in Geneva,[70] but whose *coup* promised to deprive Hitler, if he should form a government in Prussia on the basis of his victory in the Landtag elections in April, of resources that could be used against the Reich.[71] The *Staatsstreich* was also the kind of evidence of strength that might persuade Hitler to consider joining forces with Papen and thus enable Schleicher to capture him.

But Hitler had no thought of coming into the government except on his own terms. The Reichstag elections that were part of the price for his toleration of Papen were held on 31 July and increased the number of Nazi seats from 107 to 230. Although their popular vote had not increased since the second presidential poll, and although some observers were saying that their high tide had been reached, their leader felt justified, when Schleicher invited him to a meeting at Fürstenberg on 5 August, to ask for full power: the chancellorship for himself, the Ministries of the Interior, Justice, and Agriculture for his party, as well as the premiership and the Ministry of the Interior in Prussia, and an enabling act to permit him to rule by decree. Schleicher was non-committal, and Hitler appears to have taken this for assent. He was bitterly disappointed. On 13 August Schleicher and Papen rejected all of his demands, offering him only the vice-chancellorship in the existing cabinet and a vague promise that Papen would yield his position to him after a reasonable time; and, on the same afternoon, President von Hindenburg, after asking him if he intended to support the government and receiving a negative

[69] Eric Matthias, 'Der Untergang der alten Sozialdemokratie', *Vierteljahrshefte für Zeitgeschichte*, iv (1956), 250 ff.; Brecht, *Kraft des Geistes*, p. 173; Eyck, *Weimar Republic* ii. 414, Liang, *Berlin Police*, pp. 152 ff.; Rohe, *Reichsbanner*, pp. 426–37.

[70] On Schleicher's bypassing the Foreign Ministry in this respect, see Post, *Civil-Military Fabric*, p. 314.

[71] See Schüddekopf, *Heer und Republik*, p. 347.

answer, gave him a lecture on duty and—what was worse—provided the Press with an account of the interview that made the Field-Marshal's displeasure painfully clear.

There is no doubt that the events of 13 August, which were doubtless carefully stage-managed by Schleicher, hurt Hitler, and they would have hurt him more if he had given way completely to the berserker rage that affected him in the days immediately following the interview. If ever he came close to yielding to the demands of those hot-headed party *Revoluzzer* who wanted to take power by forceful means, it was in this period, and if he had done so, he would almost certainly have destroyed his chances for all time. As it was, his desire for revenge betrayed him into a serious miscalculation. On 12 September he broke the truce with Papen and forced the Chancellor, in order to stave off a vote of no-confidence, to dissolve the Reichstag. In the new elections of 6 November 1932 he paid the price for this. The fiasco of 13 August and Hindenburg's well-publicized dressing-down of the corporal, the moral outrage that many people felt when Hitler publicly defended five SA men who had brutally murdered an unarmed Communist in Potempa in August, and the fact that a significant number of people were tired of waiting for Hitler to take power and were either lapsing into political indifference or defecting to the KDP combined to cause the first heavy set-back in the NSDAP's march towards power. The party lost 2 million votes, with serious defections even in districts like Schleswig-Holstein, which had been considered Nazi strongholds, and had to give up 34 Reichstag seats (while the KPD gained 11.) In Schleicher's view, these results could hardly fail either to make Hitler more receptive to offers of shared power or to tempt elements in his party to seek an accommodation with the government before it was too late.

There was, however, a serious obstacle to testing these hypotheses. 'What do you think,' Schleicher joked ruefully, 'little Franz has discovered himself!'[72] The gentleman jockey Papen was, indeed, seeking to become a real man on horseback. Weary of his attempts to persuade Hitler to abandon his isolation, he had, in collaboration with his Minister of the Interior, Freiherr von Gayl, a rather primitive *Junker* backwoodsman, devised a basic constitutional reform that was to be effected by presidential authority and would transform the democratic Republic into an authoritarian corporative state, in which popular sovereignty would be eliminated

[72] Fest, *Hitler*, pp. 484 f.

and a propertied élite would rule over the great mass of the unprivileged. It was a scheme of such stupefying naïvety that it hardly deserved attention, or would not have done so had it not been for the fact that there was some possibility that it might be tried. Papen had many friends in the business community and, through Gayl, in the East Elbian aristocracy. More important, he had gained such an ascendancy over Hindenburg in his few months of power that there was no telling what the old man might be prepared to do for him.

Schleicher has had such a bad press that it is often assumed, without hard evidence to support it, that he was always motivated by personal ambition and desire for power. It is difficult to find any trace of that kind of selfishness in his decision to stop Papen, and it is much easier to believe that he was thinking primarily of his country and of the army to which he had devoted his life when he commissioned Lieutenant-Colonel Eugen Ott of the Wehrmachtabteilung of his ministerial bureau to conduct a war game on the problem of managing a crisis that involved a general strike and the complications arising from it. Quite properly, Ott assumed the worst possible case. Bearing in mind the recent collaboration between Nazis and Communists in a transport strike that had tied up the whole city of Berlin, he took it for granted that this would be repeated in a major political crisis, perhaps on a greater scale, since together they had 18 million voters who might, in some part, be mobilized. The war-gaming group concluded that the government did not have at its disposal forces (army, police, emergency civilian organizations) sufficient to deal with such a contingency and at the same time to defend the eastern frontiers if the Poles should take it into their heads to take advantage of the situation.[73]

In a tense meeting in the Reichskanzlei on 1 December, Schleicher tried to convince Hindenburg that Papen's scheme was both dangerous and superfluous, since fissiparous tendencies were becoming perceptible in the NSDAP and could be encouraged. He had no success, and even his pointed remark that Hindenburg would be breaking his oath to defend the constitution if he should do what Papen desired had no effect upon the Field-Marshal, who obstinately stood by the Chancellor. It was not until the next day, when Schleicher produced the report of the Ott group, that Hindenburg gave way, in a tearful scene described, with perhaps too purple a

---

[73] See Post, *Civil-Military Fabric*, pp. 319–21; F. L. Carsten, *The Reichswehr and Politics, 1918–1933* (Oxford, 1966), pp. 378 ff.; Thilo Vogelsang, *Reichswehr, Staat und NSDAP* (Stuttgart, 1962), pp. 333–4, 484–5; Bracher, *Auflösung*, pp. 673 ff.

prose, in Papen's memoirs. The Field-Marshal was not too feeble to recognize military realities when they stared him in the face. 'But I am too old', he said, 'to assume responsibility for a civil war at the end of my life. So we must, in God's name, let Herr von Schleicher try his luck.'[74]

V

Adolf Hitler was two short months from the power he sought when Schleicher, against his will but in default of other candidates, became Chancellor. The Führer had, of course, no way of knowing that. For months he had been doing what is always the hardest thing for a politician to do in a situation that seems to be changing to his disadvantage: namely, resisting the pressure of his followers to settle for what he can get before it is too late. Later, he was justifiably proud of his stubbornness and boasted, 'Unless I have the inner, incorruptible conviction, this is the solution, I do nothing, not even if the whole party tries to drive me into action.'[75] But it could not have been quite as easy as that sounds, and there was always the possibility that the party would tire of his intransigence and leave him.

This was what Schleicher was counting on. He could sense the impatience of Hitler's followers. Since August he had been in contact with Gregor Strasser, the popular head of the Nazi party bureaucracy and a man who was well informed about the anxieties of the rank-and-file party members. Even before the Papen crisis had come to a head, Schleicher had received intimations that Strasser was ready to break away from his party and that, if he did so, he would not be alone. This possibility promised to give substance to an idea that had been germinating in Schleicher's head for some time—that of a coalition between labour groups (Catholic and independent trade unions and Nazi labour organizations) that would receive the strong backing of the army and would be able to effect not only a political but a healthy spiritual revolution. The similarities between Schleicher's scheme and the ideas expressed in works like Spengler's *Preußenthum und Sozialismus* and Jünger's *Der Arbeiter*, and in leading articles by his friend Hans Zehrer in *Die Tat* are striking, although it is admittedly impossible to say how directly these writings affected the thinking of this pragmatic practitioner of politics. Ideology aside, in a country that was becoming increasingly anti-capitalist, and in which respect for the army was deeply ingrained in all classes, a

---

[74] Franz von Papen, *Memoirs*, trans. Brian Connell (London, 1952), pp. 216–24; Dorpalen, *Hindenburg*, pp. 384–96.
[75] Rauschning, *Hitler Speaks*, p. 181.

military–labour alliance seemed infinitely more practical than Papen's reactionary fantasies.[76]

But the proof of this lay, of course, in the willingness of those whom Schleicher desired as allies to serve under his banner, and that proved to be insubstantial. In their initial stages, the General's approaches to the trade unions had been successful, and Theodor Leipart and Wilhelm Eggert of the SPD and Bernard Otto of the Catholic union movement showed almost an eagerness to cooperate. But before any agreement could be reached, Hugo Breitscheid of the SPD had dampened the enthusiasm of his party comrades by reminding them of Schleicher's support of Papen's extinction of the Socialist Government in Prussia and warning them that he could not be trusted, and after that there was little likelihood that the unions would give the Chancellor any appreciable backing.[77]

Even more crucial was the collapse of the Strasser plan. Here once again Schleicher was betrayed by one of his agents, for Strasser proved to be not only indecisive but so politically maladroit that, when he finally made up his mind to break with Hitler, he made the fatal mistake of going off for a holiday to Italy instead of bending his full efforts to promoting a mass exodus from the NSDAP. It was Hitler who rose to the occasion in this crisis of the party, and in an awe-inspiring release of all the passions and tensions that had been pent up within him during the long months of waiting, he terrified the doubtful brethren into submission, abolished the party's central administrative agency, the Political Organization that Strasser had dominated, and set up a new central party office under Rudolf Hess that assured him of the support of a united party.

That was the end of Schleicher's grand design. He did not immediately admit his defeat; he was a courageous man and a stubborn one, and he went on trying to mobilize labour support by introducing a new public works programme as a means of easing unemployment and by reviving the land resettlement programme first proposed in Brüning's time. These measures did not move the people they were meant to impress, being regarded as clever improvisations designed to attract votes rather than to improve conditions, and they completely alienated the business and landholding constituencies. Schleicher's political skills were clearly proving to be

---

[76] See Struve, *Elites against Democracy*, pp. 353–76; Hans Otto Meissner and Harry Wilde, *Die Machtergreifung: Ein Bericht über die Technik des nationalsozialistischen Staatsstreichs* (Stuttgart, 1958), pp. 93 f.; Vogelsang, *Reichswehr, Staat und NSDAP*, pp. 267–9.

[77] Noske, *Aufstieg und Niedergang*, p. 310; Bracher, *Auflösung*, pp. 669 f.

self-defeating, and on 23 January he was forced to go to Hindenburg, admit that his attempt to build a new majority had failed, and ask for the dissolution of the Reichstag and the banning of both NSDAP and KPD by decree. Pointing out that this would merely create the same kind of emergency that the General had described, only two months earlier, as being beyond the capacity of the armed forces to contain, Hindenburg refused and, five days later, when Schleicher repeated his request, refused again. In the interim the Chancellor had learned that the President had been conducting secret talks with Papen concerning the formation of a new government, and he angrily resigned his post, accusing Hindenburg of breach of faith.

In January 1933 it was widely believed in the outside world that what would follow now would be an open military dictatorship, since the army would not tolerate the elevation of the murderer of Potempa to the position that Bismarck had once held. This theory was mistaken on two counts. First, the officer corps as a whole was heartily tired of the Groener–Schleicher policy of military involvement in parliamentary politics. This activity appeared to them to be a violation of Seeckt's theory of the army above politics, to which they were anxious to return. In the second place, they had no strong animus against Hitler. On the contrary, ever since the Ulm trial of 1930, when three lieutenants were tried for disseminating Nazi literature among their fellows, National Socialism had made steady progress among the junior ranks, who were attracted by the nationalist appeals of the movement and by the promise of action and promotion when it came to power.[78] Even among the senior officers there were a significant number in key positions who were sympathetic towards the movement and its leader, General Werner von Blomberg and General Walter von Reichenau being well known for their views in this respect. If Hitler had reverted to the tactics of 1923, the army would doubtless have done its duty and stopped him. There was no likelihood that it would resist if he were invited by the President to take power, and it is significant that, for all of his disappointment over his failure to outmanœuvre Hitler, Schleicher never considered appealing to the army to baulk the Führer of his success at the last moment.[79]

The army therefore remained neutral in January 1933 and allowed the Republic, which had given it support and honour ever since the Ebert–Groener agreement of 1918 and which it was pledged to defend, to be handed over to a man who had made it perfectly clear

---

[78] On the Ulm trial, see Schüddekopf, *Heer und Republik*, pp. 265 ff.
[79] See Carsten, *Reichswehr and Politics*, pp. 390 ff.; Craig, *Prussian Army*, pp. 464 ff.

that he was determined to destroy it. The only soldier who made an effort to keep Hitler from the chancellorship was Hindenburg, who did not like the corporal and who wanted his favourite Papen back at his side. But Papen himself had seen that that was impossible and that the only way to get the support of the NSDAP, which a government would need if it were to be strong enough to restore stability and stop the growth of Communism, was to give Hitler the post he coveted. He must, however, be forced to share power with men who would be able, if necessary, to restrain him; and Papen had been presiding over talks with the Nazi leadership and the chiefs of the various nationalist groupings in order to find the right combination. By 30 January agreement had been reached and the presidential assent secured. Hitler became Chancellor in a coalition cabinet, with Papen as his Vice-Chancellor, Hugenberg of the DNVP and Seldte of the Stahlhelm as Ministers of Economics and Labour respectively, and Blomberg as Minister of Defence. The new cabinet included only two Nazis besides Hitler, Wilhelm Frick as Minister of the Interior and Hermann Goering as Minister without Portfolio.

Papen and his friends were well satisfied with the result. 'We have him framed in,' one of them said.[80] The remark should be included in any anthology of famous last words.

[80] Fest, *Hitler*, p. 502.

XVI
The Nazi Dictatorship: the Instruments of Power

Wir werdend Volk, wir sind der rohe Stein—
Du, unser Führer, sollst der Steinmetz sein;

der Steinmetz, der mit schöpf'rischer Gewalt
den Stein erlöst von seiner Ungestalt.

Schlag immer zu! Wir halten duldend still,
da deine strenge Hand uns formen will.

HEINRICH ANACKER (1931)[1]

T HE latest turn in German politics caused no great sensation in the international Press, which was less interested in what was happening in Berlin than it was in Franklin D. Roosevelt's arrival in Washington and in the preparations for the World Economic Conference in London. Those correspondents who wrote about the new German Chancellor did so without any apparent expectation of significant impending change and certainly without any sense of foreboding with respect to the future. Most of them emphasized the fact that the Nazis had acquired only three seats in the new cabinet and argued that this was too insecure a power basis to ensure long tenure in office. Those who ventured any kind of prediction seemed to feel that, despite his revolutionary posturing in the past, Hitler would be tamed by the experience of office and that, in any case, he would be kept under careful restraint by a conservative consortium led by Papen, Hugenberg, and the leaders of the army, the new Reichswehr Minister, Blomberg, and the Chief of the Army Command, Werner von Fritsch.

This appraisal of the situation accorded with that of the non-Nazi members of the new cabinet, who had convinced themselves that, in yielding the chancellorship to Hitler, they had fobbed him off with the shadow rather than the substance of power, while putting themselves in a position to capture his movement for their own purposes.

---

[1] From Heinrich Anacker, *Die Trommel. SA Gedichte* (1931), quoted in *Deutschland, Deutschland. Politische Gedichte*, ed. Lamprecht, p. 380.

'We have hired him!' Papen bragged to one of his friends,[2] and to another, who had expressed doubts on this score, 'What do you want? I have Hindenburg's confidence. Within two months we will have pushed Hitler so far into the corner that he'll squeak!'[3]

These forecasts were the first of many that were, in the course of Hitler's career, to be confounded by actuality. Papen's boast, in particular, was ludicrously wrong and shows how little that flocculent amateur had learned about the Nazi leader during his not infrequent contacts with him. Hitler had no intention of being manœuvred by his cabinet colleagues. He was resolved not only to escape their restraining influence but to subordinate the whole machinery of the state to his own will and direction and, while he was about it, to smash all independent agencies and institutions which might, because they possessed an inherent spontaneity, stand in the way of his vaulting ambitions for his Third Reich.[4] The two months that Papen thought would finish the new Chancellor were, in fact, all that he needed to lay the basis for that process of conquest and subordination. Upon it, in the years that followed, rose the structure of the totalitarian state.

Seen from either a stylistic or a logical point of view, it was never a uniform or a logical structure. In it traditional and revolutionary elements commingled uneasily and lent an air of incoherence to the whole. The functions performed in some of its parts seemed to serve no purpose except to offset what went on in others, and there were some sections that seem to have been stuck on in a fit of absent-mindedness and then to have been forgotten. It was always difficult for those in one part of the building to know what was going on in others, and lateral communication was often quite impossible. The only clear channels of communications were those that ran to and from the apartments of the architect, and this had been the guiding principle of his creation, consciously intended to make all parts of the whole dependent upon his commands. It was imposing enough in its external appearance to impress a distracted and credulous world—resembling, in this respect, as in its internal incoherence, that curious amusement centre called Haus Vaterland that stood on the Potsdamer Platz in Berlin[5]—but it was not, as the Germans say, *sturmfrei*, and in time the storms came.

    [2] Schwerin von Krosigk, *Es geschah in Deutschland*, p. 147.

    [3] Bracher, *German Dictatorship*, p. 195.

    [4] Franz Neumann, *Behemoth: The Structure and Practice of National Socialism* (2nd edn., New York, 1944), p. 367.

    [5] Built during the Wilhelmine period, Haus Vaterland remained, until its destruction in the war, a favourite attraction for visitors from the provinces. It comprised

I

The insubstantiality of the conservatives' hopes that they could control the new Chancellor was apparent from the very beginning. His first victory over his Nationalist colleagues came even before he had taken the oath of office, when he successfully insisted upon an immediate dissolution of the Reichstag, with new elections to follow in March. Hugenberg, who sensed that Hitler's mass party could hardly help but be the beneficiary of any success won by the government, opposed this stoutly but was unable to hold the others in line, so that the Nazi leader got what he wanted, the opportunity to make a new appeal to the German people, this time with the considerable advantages provided by the authority inherent in his position and by the support of the President. Almost immediately he began to distance himself subtly from the non-Nazi cabinet members. In his speeches, beginning with the programmatic declaration of 1 February,[6] he managed to leave the impression that they still languished in the kind of thinking that had done so much disservice to Germany during the last fourteen years and that they did not really understand the new politics which his party comrade Frick concisely defined as being characterized by 'the will and the strength to act'. The unspoken premiss in these utterances was that the sooner Hitler was permitted to make policy in his own way, the better for Germany. This was true also of Hitler's long speech to the commanders of the Reichswehr in the apartment of General von Hammerstein on 3 February, which was clearly designed to ingratiate himself and his movement with the armed forces and to persuade them that their own interests would be best served by the 'strictest kind of authoritarian state leadership', since only that could extirpate Marxism and pacifism and prepare the way for the elimination of the disabilities imposed by the Versailles Treaty.[7]

In this disquisition to the generals Hitler had been careful to assure his audience that he regarded the Wehrmacht as the only legitimate instrument of armed power within the state. He did not hesitate, however, in what Konrad Heiden called the decisive revolutionary

a bewildering conglomeration of restaurants, bars, dance-halls, and other amusements, including a Hamburg sailors' *Kneipe,* a Grinzing *Weinstube,* a terrace overlooking the Drachenfels, and a *Wild-West-Stube* which featured a band in cowboy costume and, periodically, a violent storm in what appeared to be the Rocky Mountains.

[6] Domarus, *Hitler: Reden* i. 191 ff.

[7] Thilo Vogelsang, 'Hitlers Rede an die Generäle, 3 Februar 1933', *Vierteljahrshefte für Zeitgeschichte,* ii (1954), 434 ff.

act of National Socialism,[8] to lay his hands upon those forces that lay outside the army's direct control, namely the police. His instrument in this regard was Hermann Goering who, in his capacity as Prussian Minister of the Interior, acted with a brutal heedlessness and contempt for law and tradition that simply overwhelmed his nominal superior, the Vice-Chancellor and Reich Commissioner for Prussia, Papen, who weakly let him have his way. Goering started by placing fourteen police presidents of Prussian towns on the retired list and unceremoniously firing dozens of subordinate officials, and then appointed the Berlin SS Oberführer Kurt Daluege as 'Commissioner on special assignment' and charged him with the task of purging the whole police force of unreliable elements. On 17 February he ordered all local police offices to establish good working relations with the SA, the SS, and the Stahlhelm and to co-operate with them in their efforts to combat the left, 'if necessary, by resort to the unconditional use of weapons'. With that mixture of levity and lack of moral scruple that constituted his characteristic style, Goering elaborated on this order by stating, 'Every bullet that now leaves the mouth of a police pistol is my bullet. If you call that murder, then I am the murderer, for I gave the order, and I stand by it.' Five days later he ordered the police to avail themselves of auxiliaries, in view of the growing threat from the radical left, and made it clear that only members of the *nationale Verbände* should be accepted as such. In practice, this legitimized Nazi terrorism in the streets, for, despite assurances that auxiliaries would always be under the command of regular police officers, this was rarely the case.[9]

In improving the electoral fortunes of the party, Goering's policy was of unquestioned importance, for SA units, wearing Hilfspolizei brassards, could now break up the meetings of other parties with impunity. Useful in this respect also was the presidential decree of 4 February which authorized the prohibition of newspapers or public meetings that 'abused, or treated with contempt, organs, institutions, bureaus or leading officials of the state' or broadcast false information that might 'endanger the vital interests of the state'. Under the authority of this sweeping decree, which had, ironically, been drafted by Hitler's predecessors in office with an eye to con-

[8] Konrad Heiden, *The Fuehrer* (Boston, 1944), p. 59.

[9] K. D. Bracher, Wolfgang Sauer, and Knut Schulz, *Die nationalsozialistische Machtergreifung. Studien zur Errichtung des totalitären Herrschaftssystems in Deutschland 1933/34* (Cologne and Opladen, 1960), pp. 72 ff. See also Erich Gritzbach, *Hermann Goering, Werk und Mensch* (2nd edn., Munich, 1938), pp. 31 ff.; Rudolf Diels, *Lucifer ante portas* (Stuttgart, 1950), pp. 182 ff.; Liang, *Berlin Police*, pp. 171 ff.

trolling the activities of his own party, Goering proceeded not only to suppress the Communist Press but to impose crippling restrictions upon the national and provincial papers of the SPD and the Centre as well. Attempts to protest against this flagrant attack on the liberty of the Press were fruitless. When a congress of intellectuals and artists was held for this purpose in February, in the Kroll Opera House, it was dissolved by the police, after the reading of a statement by Thomas Mann, on the grounds that it had included atheistic observations that threatened public morality.[10]

This kind of harassment reduced public expression of opposition to a minimum and gave a decided advantage to the government parties, who also had the benefit of access to the radio, which was under state control. In the election campaign it was the Nazis who made the most skilful use of this still relatively unknown instrument of mass persuasion. In Josef Goebbels they possessed a propagandist of genius who immediately sensed the potentialities of the new medium and saw to it that Hitler's principal speeches were broadcast by all stations and that they were accompanied by his own commentary, which was skilfully designed to communicate to the home listener a sense of the enthusiasm of the Führer's audience. In a back-handed tribute to Goebbels's artistry, wits were soon recommending an addition to the table of weights and measures: a Goeb, signifying the amount of power needed to turn off 100,000 radio sets at the same time.[11]

In February and March 1933 enough of them were not turned off to enhance the Nazi party's electoral chances, although it is a matter of pure speculation whether this was any more important than the tactics of persecution and intimidation used against the parties of the left. It is true, however, that the latter became more intense and more flagrant as a result of the burning-down of the Reichstag building on 27 February.

The debate over the authorship of the fire still continues and will probably never be resolved to everyone's satisfaction. Despite recent attempts, however, to support the case against Marinus van der Lubbe, the half-witted Dutch vagrant who was tried and executed for the crime, the evidence collected by an international committee headed by Walther Hofer of Berne strongly supports the conclusion that the blaze was set by an SA/SS Sondergruppe under the direction of Himmler's associate, Reinhard Heydrich, and the director of the division of police in the Prussian Ministry of the Interior, Kurt

[10] Martin Broszat, *Der Staat Hitlers* (Munich, 1969), pp. 93–4.
[11] Max Vandry, *Der politische Witz im Dritten Reich* (Munich, 1967), p. 33.

Daluege.[12] The cause of the fire was, in any case, less important than the result. Hitler and Goering wasted no time in laying the deed at the doorstep of the Communist party and in using this charge to justify a crippling blow at what was left of the democratic system. Before the morning of the twenty-eighth had dawned 4,000 Communist officials and party members had been arrested, along with intellectuals and professional men who had incurred the wrath of the Nazi party, some of whom—the anarchist Erich Mühsam, for example, and the editor of *Die Weltbühne*, Carl von Ossietzky—were not to survive the ordeal that awaited them. Before noon Hitler had induced a shaken President, who was persuaded that a Communist revolution was imminent, to sign the most fateful of all of the emergency decrees that bore his name.

This decree suspended all of the basic rights of the citizen for the duration of the emergency, authorized the Reich Government to assume full powers in any federal state whose government proved unable or unwilling to restore public order and security when the situation required it, and ordered death or imprisonment for a series of crimes, some of which were newly invented, including treason, assault upon members of the government, arson in public buildings, incitement to riot, and resistance to the provisions of the decree.[13] It was another indication of the incompetence and the fecklessness of the Nationalist members of the cabinet that they should have agreed to this extraordinary grant of power to the Nazi leader. The decree was accompanied by no normative regulations by the Reich Minister of the Interior, its interpretation being left to each Minister of the Interior in the separate states, a provision which gave Herman Goering a frightening latitude in Prussia. Even worse, unlike similar decrees issued by President Ebert in 1923, this one did not include any provision guaranteeing an interned person a prompt hearing and the right of counsel, appeal, and redress for false address. This, as Arnold Brecht wrote later, was 'a dreadful omission'.

The police could arrest . . . persons and extend the time of detention indefinitely. They could leave the relatives without any information regarding the prisoner's whereabouts and fate. They could prevent any lawyer or other person from visiting him or from looking into the records. They could treat

---

[12] See Walther Hofer and Christoph Graf, 'Neue Quellen zum Reichstagsbrand', *Geschichte in Wissenschaft und Unterricht*, 27, Heft 2 (1976), 65–88; *Das Gewissen steht auf*, ed. Annedore Leber (Berlin, 1954), pp. 106 f. Compare F. Tobias, *Der Reichstagsbrand. Legende und Wirklichkeit* (Rastatt, 1962); Hnas Mommsen, 'Der Reichstagsbrand und seine politischen Folgen', *Vierteljahrshefte für Zeitgeschichte*, xii, Heft 4 (1964).

[13] For this decree 'zum Schutze von Volk und Staat' and the supplementary decree 'gegen Verrat an deutschen Volk', see *Reichsgesetzblatt* (1933), pp. 83 f.

him as they saw fit, e.g. overload him with work unsuited to him, feed and house him badly, force him to say formulae or to sing songs he detested, maltreat him in order to get him to confess or to divulge the names and acts of others; and . . . whip him or shoot him. . . . They could do all this, provided only their superiors allowed them to do so.[14]

On 2 March 1933 a correspondent of the *Daily Express* asked Hitler whether the suspension of individual liberties was to be permanent. The Nazi leader answered with a decided negative, adding: 'When the Communist danger is eliminated, the normal order of things will return.'[15] In reality, the decree of 28 February created an important aspect of the normal order of National Socialism. Its provisions and the practices and institutions they created—arrest on suspicion, imprisonment without trial, and all the horrors connected with the concentration camps that now began to proliferate like a malignant disease in Germany—persisted until the end of the Third Reich; and the paper that Hindenburg signed was used to justify the execution of those of his comrades in arms who tried in July 1944 to undo his tragic error.

Immediately, in the days that followed its promulgation, the decree was turned against the real and fancied enemies of the Nazi party. In the last weeks of the election campaign the entire Marxist Press was silenced; the SPD found it impossible to campaign effectively; and even respected bourgeois party leaders like Brüning and Stegerwald of the Centre had their meetings broken up by ruffians and, on more than one occasion, were in peril of their lives.

Despite all this, Hitler's party fell far short of an absolute triumph in the elections of 5 March 1933. With its cabinet allies, it succeeded in winning a clear majority of the seats in the Reichstag, as the table indicates; but the SPD and the Centre had held firm and come close to winning their usual number of seats, and even the KPD had polled almost 5 million votes and won 81 seats. If the cabinet remained united, it could pass ordinary legislation; but it could not legally alter the constitution, because that would require a two-thirds vote which the other parties still had the power to block.

Whether they had the will to do so was, however, the real question, and the signs multiplied after 5 March that they had not. The Nazi Press hailed the results of the Reichstag elections and the significant increases in the party vote in the Landtag elections in the federal states as a revolution, and the local organizations of the party celebrated the results with an orgy of arrests, looting of Jewish depart-

---

[14] Brecht, *Prelude to Silence*, p. 91.
[15] Rohe, *Reichsbanner*, pp. 461–6; Broszat, *Der Staat Hitlers*, p. 104.

Election Results, 5 March 1933

	SEATS
NSDAP	288
Kampffront Schwarz–Weiss–Rot	52
Zentrum	73
Bayerische Volkspartei	19
Deutsche Volkspartei	2
Christlich-Sozialer Volksdienst	4
Deutsche Staatspartei	5
Deutsche Bauernpartei	2
Württembergischer Landbund	1
SPD	120
KPD	81

ment stores, attacks on the oppositional Press, and violence in the street that reflected a belief that anyone wearing a brown shirt was freed from the customary restraints of law. Hitler himself showed a new heedlessness, by turning the provisions of the decree of 28 February against those *Länder* in which oppositional elements were still significant. In the two weeks that followed the election, using the argument that local authorities were incapable of maintaining order, which was being disrupted in the main by drunken troopers of the SA and SS, the government dispatched troops or units of the SA and SS into Württemberg, Baden, Bremen, Hamburg, Lübeck, Saxony, Hessen, and Bavaria and, on the pretext of defending the Weimar constitution, replaced the legally constituted governments with Reich Commissioners. In Bavaria the Held government made energetic attempts to appeal to the President against his headstrong Chancellor, only to be informed by Meissner, the Secretary of State, that complaints should be addressed to the government, which, in Hindenburg's opinion, had acted 'on its own competence'. Held was forced to yield his seals of office to Franz Ritter von Epp, the former free corps leader who had helped crush the Munich Soviet in 1919.[16]

These successes induced a growing fatalism in the ranks of those who had opposed National Socialism. Members of the republican Reichsbanner organization began to apply for admission to the Stahlhelm; the leadership of the ADGB, the federation of trade unions, announced in March that it was ready to break its tie with the

[16] Erwein von Aretin, *Krone und Ketten* (Munich, 1955), pp. 155 ff.; and esp. Karl Schwend, *Bayern zwischen Monarchie und Diktatur* (Munich, 1954), pp. 506 ff. and *passim*.

SPD and co-operate with the new government; and thousands of individual members of the middle parties joined the NSDAP, acquiring, as they did so, the unflattering title *Märzgefallene*.[17] Even before Hitler formally asked for a grant of full powers, therefore, the potential opposition to this was fatally compromised, particularly in view of the fact that influential bishops of the Catholic Church were beginning to urge the necessity of an accommodation with the Nazi movement.

On 21 March, in an elaborate ceremony upon which Joseph Goebbels, since 11 March Reich Minister for Public Information, had lavished all of his resources of energy and art, Hitler stood with the aged President in the Garnisonkirche in Potsdam, whose chimes had admonished generations of soldiers to be loyal and God-fearing—

> Üb' immer Treu' und Redlichkeit
> Bis an das kühle Grab
> Und weiche keinen Fingertritt
> Von Gottes Gnade ab—

and symbolically pledged allegiance to the traditions and values of the past. This travesty was intended as psychological preparation for the vote on the Enabling Act which Hitler demanded two days later when the Reichstag assembled in the Kroll Opera House; but, lest it fail of effect, the SA and SS, which had stood in disciplined ranks at Potsdam, acted on the latter occasion like a band of bloodthirsty *Landsknechte*, sealing off all approaches to the Opera House and filling the air with murderous howls of 'Wir fordern das Ermächtigungsgesetz—sonst gibt's Zunder!' To this menacing accompaniment, Hitler asked for a law of four years' duration that would enable the government to dispense with constitutional forms and limitations as it formulated regulations for dealing with the country's problems, promising that the law would be used only to assure the German people of the comptence and stability of its government and that no action would be taken that would infringe the rights of the Reichstag, the Reichsrat, the Presidency, or the separate states.

Although none of the 81 elected KPD deputies was in his seat (the melancholy witticism of the day was that they were 'postalisch unauffindbar'[18]) and although 26 Socialist deputies had also been prevented from reaching the hall, the Nazis, even with their Nationalist allies, lacked the necessary two-thirds of the voting members to assure passage of the proposed bill. Since it was made clear, in a courageous speech by Otto Wels, that the SPD would

[17] Broszat, *Der Staat Hitlers*, pp. 113 f.
[18] Helmut Heiber, *Adolf Hitler* (Berlin, 1960), p. 83.

stand firm, the decision lay with the Centre party and its associate the Bavarian People's party. Heinrich Brüning was later to claim that the Centre had made its assent conditional upon modifications of the decree of 28 February and had voted for the bill only when Hitler had agreed, only to break his promise later.[19] That the Centre leadership did make some effort to impose conditions is doubtless true, although their efforts were largely directed toward getting some assurance that Hitler would not attack Catholic schools or abrogate the concordats between the Vatican and the separate states. There is reason to believe, however, that the attitude of the Catholic parties on 23 March was determined by Monsignor Kaas's argument in the party meeting that, if Hitler did not get what he wanted by means of the Enabling Act, he would secure it by more unpleasant means and that it would be wiser to concede and hope for favours in return.[20]

In the end only the 94 Socialists voted against the Enabling Act and, with 58 votes to spare, Hitler, on the afternoon of 23 March 1933, became dictator, 'created by democracy and appointed by parliament',[21] free from any real control by his cabinet colleagues or, for that matter, by the President, and empowered to mould Germany's governmental and social system as he wished.

II

The elaboration of the new dictatorial regime was preceded by the elimination of those institutions and structures of the Weimar system that no longer served a useful purpose in a National Socialist state and the disciplining and co-ordinating of those that were indispensable. The term used to describe this process was *Gleichschaltung*—literally, 'putting into the same gear'—a word so cryptic and impersonal that it conveys no sense of the injustice, the terror, and the bloodshed that it embraced. Specifically, *Gleichschaltung* meant in its first stage the purging of the Civil Service, the abolition of the Weimar party system, the dissolution of the state governments and parliaments and of the old Federal Council (Reichsrat), and the co-optation of the trade union movement. Before it had run its course, it had led to a disciplinary blood-letting within the National Socialist party itself, an event which, by compromising the army leadership, marked the beginning of the *Gleichschaltung* of the armed forces that was to be completed in February 1938.

[19] Heinrich Brüning, 'Ein Brief', *Deutsche Rundschau*, July 1947.
[20] See the protocol of the Centre party meeting in *Vierteljahrshefte für Zeitgeschichte*, iv, Heft 3 (1956), 306–7.
[21] Heiden, *The Fuehrer*, p. 579.

No one recognized more clearly than Hitler how effectively an independent and unreconstructed Civil Service could sabotage the intentions of a government. He had no intention of allowing a repetition of what had happened as a result of the Republic's failure to discipline the bureaucracy and the judiciary, and he moved swiftly to assure himself, if not of ideological conformity, at least of total obedience. On 7 April 1933 he promulgated a Law for the Restoration of the Professional Civil Service, subsequently amended and expanded by a series of interpretative decrees, which eliminated tenure and other legal safeguards in the case of officials who did not meet their superiors' standards of suitability or could not prove their political reliability or their pure Aryan descent. An indication of the effect of these regulations is the fact that, out of 1,663 members of higher Prussian Civil Service, 12·5 per cent were eliminated for political or racial reasons and 15·5 per cent for lack of qualification. In other states, where the numbers of SPD officials were smaller and where the law was applied less rigorously, the corresponding averages were 4·5 and 5 per cent.[22] Virtually all officials of Jewish descent fell victim to this law (war veterans were, for a time, exempted in most states, as well as most non-Jews who had not made themselves conspicuous by their independence of mind or the intensity of the democratic convictions). Those who survived this purge had no reason to feel secure. It was abundantly clear that the price of tenure was *Kadavergehorsam*, corpse-like obedience.

No immediate attempt was made to purge the judiciary or to interfere with the independence and acquired rights of judges, although the new masters of the state were careful to see that new judicial appointments were characterized by ideological orthodoxy. But it was difficult to believe in the independence and impartiality of German justice after Hitler, in the wake of the murders of 30 June 1934, had declared himself to be Germany's 'supreme judge' and after magistrates and civil servants had accepted that claim by taking an oath to serve him; and in April 1942 the Reichstag put an end to any illusions that may have persisted by approving Hitler's request for the power to remove any judge whose sentences he regarded as being too lenient or whose conduct of office seemed insufficiently inspired by loyalty to National Socialism. Even before that time, political interference with legal process had become notorious, and verdicts were often flagrantly ignored by party agencies. The demoralization of the judicial system was well advanced long before

---

[22] Hans Mommsen, *Beamtentum im Dritten Reich* (Stuttgart, 1966), p. 56.

the law of 1942 and long before the People's Courts, administered by the hyena-like Roland Freisler (corrosively depicted in Fallada's well-researched novel *Jeder stirbt für sich allein*), had made a travesty of German justice with their show trials with pre-arranged results.[23]

In dealing with the legal profession as a whole, the new regime showed less delicacy than they employed in the case of the judges. In National Socialist theory, lawyers were to be regarded as servants of the movement, guided by its objectives and its conception of the needs of the German people. To assure the existence of a legal corps of this nature, the government, on the same day that it issued its Law for the Restoration of the Professional Civil Service, handed down a Law on Admission to the Practice of Law that imposed stringent racial and political qualifications. At the same time, lawyers were dragooned into party-controlled 'fronts' and 'academies' established for their indoctrination and were forced to be responsive to the directives of the future Governor-General of Occupied Poland, Hans Frank, who, on the basis of his legal services to the movement during its *Kampfzeit*, was appointed Reich Commissioner for the Co-ordination of Justice in the States and for the Renewal of Juris-prudence.[24]

If there were still a place, however circumscribed, in the new dispensation for lawyers, it soon became clear that there was none for politicians of the old school. The days of the pluralistic political system came to an end with the passage of the Enabling Act, although it was some months before this was fully realized. The Communist party had, of course, been declared illegal in February, in the wake of the Reichstag fire; and, after Otto Wels's defiant speech during the debate on the Enabling Act, the Socialist leadership had good reason to believe that their days were numbered too. Although their subsidiary organizations, particularly the Reichs-banner, came increasingly under attack in the separate states, how-ever, the executive continued for months to be divided into those who believed it imperative to move party headquarters to Prague and to mount an offensive against National Socialism from that capital, and those who continued to hope that an arrangement might be reached with the new government that would make this unneces-sary.[25] This debate was rudely terminated on 22–3 June when the

[23] See, in general, Ilsa Staff, *Justiz im Dritten Reich* (Frankfurt-on-Main, 1964). The Freisler portrait is in Chs. 61 and 62 of Fallada's novel.

[24] Bracher, *German Dictatorship*, pp. 213–14.

[25] See Rohe, *Reichsbanner*, pp. 465 ff. On the party debate, see E. Matthias, 'Der Untergang der Sozialdemokratie 1933', *Vierteljahrshefte für Zeitgeschichte*, iv (1956), Heft 2, 181 ff.; Heft 3, 250 ff.

government forbade further SPD activities in the Reich, declared it to be an organization that was inimical to the state and the German people, and confiscated its property.

The ban on SPD activity issued by the Prussian Government applied also to the Deutsche Staatspartei (the last incarnation of the DDP) which had had electoral arrangements with the SPD during the March elections. This was enough to drive the Staatspartei into liquidation. It was rapidly followed by the pitiful remnant of the DVP which gave up the ghost on 29 March. It is possible that, if Gustav Stresemann had still been alive, he would have derived some satisfaction from the fact that his creation survived longer than the DNVP. The strength of the Nationalist party was undermined by a growing feeling among its supporters and its delegation in the Reichstag that their best course was to seek fusion with the NSDAP, a movement that gathered momentum after Franz Seldte joined the Nazis in April and offered the leadership of the Stahlhelm, which included many DNVP members, to Hitler. Hugenberg's stubborn attempts to maintain an independent position by transforming the party into a German National Front merely succeeded in provoking Hitler into encouraging a campaign of harassment against the new formation at the state level and an all-out attack on Hugenberg's policies as Minister of Economics and Agriculture by Nazi agencies that represented the interests of the *Mittelstand* and by the party's agricultural expert Darré. Hugenberg's position within the cabinet became completely untenable as a result of his arrogant and ineffectual behaviour at the World Economic Conference in June, and his resignation on 26 June led to the dissolution of the party a day later.[26]

By this time only the Catholic parties remained, and they now fell victim to the opportunism that had marked the Centre's politics ever since its foundation in the wake of Königgrätz. Since March leading members of the Catholic hierarchy in Germany, including Cardinals Faulhaber of Munich and Bertram of Breslau, had been moving to the conclusion that the continued existence of the party might jeopardize confessional interests, and this sentiment grew stronger when Hitler, in his first foray into the field of foreign policy, indicated his willingness to conclude a Reich concordat with the Vatican. In the ensuing negotiations, both Monsignor Kaas, who had resigned his leadership of the Centre to devote his full time to church affairs, and the Papal Secretary of State Eugenio Pacelli (later Pope Pius XII) strongly supported a policy of accommodation in order to

[26] Broszat, *Der Staat Hitlers*, pp. 121–3. For details, see *Das Ende der Parteien 1933*, ed. E. Matthias and R. Morsey (Düsseldorf, 1960), pp. 650 ff.

assure the continued existence of Catholic schools and other organ-izations in Germany. To this end the Vatican showed itself willing to yield to Hitler's insistence that the concordat include an article deny-ing Catholic clergy the right to engage in political activity.[27] The conclusion of the Reichskonkordat, which was warmly received by Catholic opinion in Germany, completely disarmed the party lead-ership, and after some frantic last-minute efforts to win some assur-ances from the Nazis concerning the personal safety and professional future of its leading members (assurances which were not suf-ficiently unequivocal to dissuade Brüning and others who had offended the Nazis in the past from leaving the country), the Centre executive dissolved the party on 5 July. The Bavarian People's party had taken similar action the day before.[28]

Hard upon this melancholy series of collapses came the law of 14 July 1933 which declared that the NSDAP was the only legal party in Germany and that any attempt to try to found a new party, or to continue to work within the shell of the old, would be pun-ishable by imprisonment of up to three years. The effect of this was to transform the once contentious but occasionally creative Reich-stag into a sounding-board for the Führer's voice or, in the descrip-tion of one anonymous wit, into the most expensive glee club in the country. It was not, however, completely innocuous. Hitler found that it afforded an impressive setting for his programmatic declar-ations and for declarations on foreign policy; and it was useful also as a means of giving sanction to laws that violated the wording or the spirit of the Emergency Decree of 28 February and of expediting *démarches* that would have been delayed if handled through normal diplomatic channels. But there was no resemblance between the new Reichstag and a genuine parliamentary chamber, and, after July 1933, an independent speech from the floor on any subject would have caused the very pictures to fall from the walls.

It would have been an anomaly to allow the parliaments of the separate states to retain powers more extensive than their national counterpart. In fact, the whole governmental structure of the federal states was systematically dismantled in the course of 1933. The process began in March with the series of depositions already men-tioned and the institution of Reich Commissioners or Reichs-statthalter in most states. At the end of March a Reich decree author-

[27] See K. D. Bracher, *Nationalsozialistische Machtergreifung und Reichskonkordat* (Wiesbaden, 1956).

[28] *Das Ende der Parteien*, pp. 368 ff.; Günther Löwy, *Die katholische Kirche und das Dritte Reich* (Munich, 1965), pp. 44 ff., 53 ff.

ized the new governments to issue laws and regulations without the assent of their Landtage, and on 7 April 1933 a new Gesetz zur Gleichschaltung der Länder mit dem Reich increased the powers of the Statthalter and declared that the Landtage were not permitted to pass votes of no-confidence in the actions of the Statthalter or his government. The fate of the state governments was finally regulated by a constitutional amendment passed by the new Reichstag on 30 January 1934 (Gesetz über den Neuausbau des Reiches) which stated that the parliaments of the separate states were dissolved, that their sovereign rights now devolved upon the Reich, that their governments would henceforth be subordinate to that of the Reich Government, and that their Statthalter would be supervised in their functions by the Reich Minister of the Interior.[29]

That this law was not as unambiguous as its lapidary style seemed to suggest soon became evident, and the reasons for this and the disputes to which it gave rise will engage our attention later. But the promulgation of the law of 30 January 1934 at least made it clear that the federal principle of government that had existed since 1867, and the forms in which it was expressed, were dead. The abolition of the Reichsrat in February, by means of a law that ignored the fact that it violated the assurances made at the time of the passage of the Enabling Act, underlined the transition from the system that Bismarck and his republican successors had found it expedient to maintain to one of centralization and national concentration.

While the dismantling of the constitutional framework was taking place, the National Socialist leadership was also effecting the *Gleichschaltung* of all of those economic organizations that had exercised political influence during the Empire and the Republic. After a period of some confusion and, on the part of the ADGB, some ignominious attempts to curry favour with the new regime, the trade unions were subjected to an invasion by the SA and the SS on 2 May 1933 and were subsequently swallowed up in a gigantic Labour Front (Deutsche Arbeitsfront: DAF), the chief of which was the Gauleiter of Cologne, Robert Ley, a man known more for his capacity for strong drink than for any interest in working-class problems. This was not a disability, for the DAF was not intended to perform the usual functions of labour organizations but rather to serve as a control mechanism, and to keep labour in an atomized and powerless condition with no leaders or representation of their own.[30]

---

[29] *Reichsgesetzblatt* (1934), p. 75.

[30] Hans-Gerd Schumann, *Nationalsozialismus und Gewerkschaftsbewegung* (Hanover, 1958), pp. 168 ff. See below, Ch. XVIII, p. 624.

The old *Mittelstand* organizations, which had played a prominent role in building opposition to the Brüning government in the years 1930–2, had much the same experience. Taken over in the spring of 1933 by the National Socialist Fighting League of the Industrial Middle Class (NSKB), they sought under its energetic leader Theodor von Renteln to achieve their old goal of liquidating the large department stores, like Wertheim and Tietz in Berlin, in the interest of small business. But the political advantage to be gained from encouraging this objective was no longer as important to the party as it had been before 1933, and when officials from the Economics Ministry pointed out the economic costs of closing the stores, in terms of jobs and investments lost, and the effects that this would probably have on recovery, the party leadership hastily called off the action, Hitler himself—not without some irritated resistance—agreeing that the stop should apply even to concerns under Jewish management like that of Hermann Tietz. Simultaneously, the Führer's Chancellery dissolved the NSKB and in September 1933 assigned its component parts to a newly created Nationalsozialistische Handwerks-, Handels- und Gewerbe- Organisation (NS-Hago) which, it soon became clear, was intended to have a purely representational function.[31]

The fate of the various agricultural associations was no less melancholy. Since the 1870s the producers' organizations had been influential in the politics of German conservatism, but their power had suffered from the same process of emaciation as the German Nationalist party, and when the DNVP gave up the ghost, they dissolved themselves. The political organizations of small farmers came, after January 1933, under the control of local Nazi peasant leaders, whose activities were co-ordinated by a new Reich Nutrition Estate directed by Walter Darré, who became Reich Peasant Leader in January 1934.

The representative bodies of heavy industry were successful in escaping the most stringent forms of *Gleichschaltung* in large part because of Hitler's respect for the industrial magnates. He had said to Otto Strasser in October 1930: 'Do you think I'd be so crazy as to destroy German heavy industry? Those producers worked their way to the top by their own merits, and, because of this process of selection, which proves that they are an élite, they have a right to

---

[31] Winkler, *Mittelstand, Demokratie und Nationalsozialismus*, pp. 185–7; Heinrich Uhlig, *Die Warenhäuser im Dritten Reich* (Cologne, 1956), pp. 111–12; Broszat, *Der Staat Hitlers*, pp. 212 ff.

lead!'[32] With this kind of protection and their intimate personal associations with people like Herman Goering and Hjalmar Schacht, the leaders of German industry did not find it difficult to defeat clumsy attempts to seize power like that of the SA in April 1933 to purge the leadership of the Reichsverband der deutschen Industrie and to infiltrate the organization with their own people. There was a good deal of talk in the early years about a reorganization of industry on the corporative principle, to be effected by the business leaders themselves, and Fritz Thyssen received Hitler's authorization to elaborate this idea, but nothing came of this. The fact of the matter was that there was a community of interest between industrial management and the Nazi leadership that made the kind of *Gleichschaltung* that other institutions had to suffer unnecessary in this case. Industry therefore received a large measure of freedom, for which it paid by having to assume the burden of complicity in Hitler's designs.

By the beginning of 1934 the foundations of the totalitarian state had been well and truly laid, and its creator had freed himself from the restrictions of the democratic constitution and from the possibility of serious opposition from autonomous political or economic organizations.[33] There were now only two sources of potential danger to his authority: the armed forces, which had, so far, been immune to the process of *Gleichschaltung*, and his own party, which, like other revolutionary movements in history, had fallen prey to internal discontents that encouraged the rise of a sizeable dissident element. The coincidence of these problems, while troubling, opened the way to their simultaneous solution in June 1934, by means that gave the world a startling demonstration of the ruthlessness and unconditionality of which Germany's new leader was capable.

On the whole, the armed forces had reason to be satisfied with Hitler's conduct during his first year of office. His speech to their commanders in February 1933 and his address in the Garnisonkirche in March seemed to indicate both a decent respect for historical tradition and an intention of respecting the rights and advancing the interests of the military establishment; his new army law of 20 July 1933 had eliminated features of the Republic's Heeresverfassung that had been unpopular with the officer corps (the jurisdiction of civil

[32] Heiber, *Adolf Hitler*, p. 68.
[33] For an account of how this atomization of society worked on the local level, see William Sheridan Allen, *The Nazi Seizure of Power: The Experience of a Single German Town, 1930–1935* (Chicago, 1965), Ch. 14.

courts in certain kinds of cases involving military personnel, and the system of giving elected representatives of the rank and file a role in command decisions).[34] He had, on the whole, not interfered with appointments to higher staff; and, on the one occasion in which he had sought to do so—his nomination of General Walter von Reichenau as Chief of the Army Command after Hammerstein's retirement in the spring of 1933—and was baulked by the opposition of the group commanders Rundstedt and Leeb and the flat refusal of Hindenburg to accept his suggestion, he had yielded with good grace and accepted the appointment of Colonel-General Werner von Fritsch to the post.[35] Those high officers who shared Seeckt's prejudices in foreign policy were disturbed by his termination of the military collaboration with the Red Army and the conclusion of the pact of friendship with Poland in January 1934,[36] but their concern on this score was balanced by their satisfaction with the Führer's decision to withdraw the German delegation from the Disarmament Conference in Geneva in October 1933 and his subsequent intimations to the army chiefs that the Truppenamt could begin to revise its peacetime mobilization schedules in an upward direction and that it could expect to receive real tanks in the next months.[37]

On the other hand, the leaders of the armed forces were becoming increasingly apprehensive about Hitler's ability to control the wilder spirits in his party, whose ambitions, if fulfilled, would seriously affect the army's position in the state; and in the first months of 1934 their concern on this score made their attitude towards Hitler dangerously critical.

The source of this alarm was the SA. Until very recently, the leaders of the army had regarded the brown-shirted legions with sympathy and, as late as April 1932, they had been unhappy about the attempt of the Brüning government to dissolve them, since, in the army's view, they might serve as a valuable reserve in case of war. But in recent months the SA had been expanding rapidly (its absorption of the Stahlhelm after Seldte's capitulation to Hitler brought it to a strength that some placed well above a million men); it was acquiring sophisticated weaponry and specialized units that

[34] Wheeler-Bennett, *Nemesis of Power*, p. 300.
[35] Walter Görlitz, *History of the German General Staff* (New York, 1953), p. 282 and *Hindenburg: Ein Lebensbild* (Bonn, 1953), p. 417.
[36] See below, Ch. XIX, p. 680.
[37] Görlitz, *General Staff*, p. 247; B. H. Liddell Hart, *The Other Side of the Hill* (rev. edn., London, 1951), p. 121; and, in general, Post, *Civil-Military Fabric*, pp. 311 ff., 354 f.

were not appropriate to its past role as a predominantly political force; and there was a persistent rumour that its commander, the tough soldier of fortune Ernst Roehm, aspired to make it the army of the new age, of which he would be the Scharnhorst, and in which the professional Reichswehr would be submerged in the brown flood.

This was not an idle rumour, and the army leadership was not alone in being alarmed by it. Since the middle of 1933 Hitler was aware of accumulating resentment in the ranks of the SA over the government's refusal to gratify their inflated expectations with respect to the Nazi *Machtübernahme*. Many of the troopers who had fought the battle of the streets for the Führer had naïvely believed that when he came to power they would be given the keys to all the bank vaults and the choice of all the jobs that would be vacant after they had chased the enemies of the people from office. They were bitterly disappointed when Hitler refused to make party loyalty the sole criterion for preferment, and Roehm did not hesitate to play upon this feeling. In June 1933, in an article in the *National-sozialistische Monatshefte*, he launched a sharp attack upon office-holders who called themselves National Socialists but had in fact betrayed the revolution, and warned: 'Whether it suits them or not, we will continue our fight; with them, if they finally realize what is at stake; without them, if they do not want to do so; and, if it has to be, against them!'

This was challenging enough to elicit a direct answer from Hitler, who, in a speech to his Reichsstatthalter on 6 July, said plainly: 'Revolution is not a permanent condition. . . . One must lead the stream that has been freed by the revolution into the safe channel of evolution. In this process, the most important thing is to educate people. . . . The ideas in our programme impose an obligation upon us, not to act like fools and to overthrown everything, but to actualize our thinking cleverly and carefully.' On the other hand, the Führer preferred not to force the issue, relying rather on a mixture of veiled threats (like the sharp reference, in his speech to the Gauleiter on 2 February 1934, to 'fools that say that the revolution is not ended') and efforts of appeasement (like the appointment of Roehm as Minister without Portfolio in the Reich Government in December 1933) in the hope that the SA leader would come round to his point of view.[38]

These tactics were unavailing, the more so because Hitler was completely unresponsive to Roehm's ideas about a reorganization of

[38] Domarus, *Hitler: Reden* i. 286 f., 363; Broszat, *Der Staat Hitlers*, pp. 259, 266.

the armed forces. In an interview with Hermann Rauschning in the first months of 1934, which was as remarkable for its lack of caution as for the rage and disappointment that characterized it, Roehm said:

Adolf is a swine. He will give us all away. He only associates with the reactionaries now. . . . Getting matey with the East Prussian generals. They're his cronies now. . . . Adolf knows exactly what I want. I've told him often enough. Not a second edition of the old imperial army. Are we revolutionaries or aren't we? *Allons, enfants de la patrie!* If we are, then something new must arise out of our *élan*, like the mass armies of the French Revolution. If we're not, then we'll go to the dogs. We've got to produce something new, don't you see? A new discipline. A new principle of organization. The generals are a lot of old fogeys. They never had a new idea. . . . I'm the nucleus of the new army, don't you see that? Don't you understand that what's coming must be new, fresh and unused? The basis must be revolutionary. You can't inflate it afterwards. You only get the opportunity once to make something new and big that'll help us lift the world off its hinges. But Hitler puts me off with fair words.[39]

It is impossible to say how long Hitler would have put up with this kind of indiscipline if he had been completely free to make his own decisions. But from the spring of 1934 onwards he was made aware of the growing dissatisfaction of the Reichswehr command over his failure to discipline Roehm, and this was something that he dared not disregard. Hitler knew that President Hindenburg, now eighty-four years old and visibly ailing, could not cling to life much longer. When the inevitable happened, he wanted to succeed to Hindenburg's office and to the military prerogatives that accrued to it. It was painfully clear to him that an army that felt that its existence was threatened by his storm-troops would try to block that succession and might very well succeed in doing so.

The extent to which the generals were able to exploit Hitler's feeling of vulnerability and the methods they employed in doing so are still a matter of conjecture.[40] What is clear is that from March onwards Hitler moved—erratically and with spells of doubt and indecision—towards a show-down with the SA and its rebellious chief, and that his accomplices, when the bloody test came, included not only such personal rivals and antagonists of Roehm as Hermann Goering and the chief of the SS, Heinrich Himmler, but the leaders of the armed forces as well. There is no longer any doubt about the army's collusion in the Night of the Long Knives, 30 January 1934, when Roehm and dozens of other SA leaders were snatched from their beds and shot without trial by SS troopers in the Stadelheim

[39] Rauschning, *Hitler Speaks,* pp. 154–5.
[40] See, *inter alia,* Craig, *Prussian Army,* pp. 476–7.

prison in Munich and the concentration camp at Dachau. Blomberg and Reichenau, Fritsch and the head of the Truppenamt, Lieutenant-General Ludwig Beck, were probably shocked and dismayed when they learned that the action had taken the lives of a number of people who had no connection with the SA at all: Gustav Kahr, who had double-crossed Hitler in 1923, Gregor Strasser, who had broken with him in November 1932, Edgar Jung and Erich Klausener, associates of Papen and suspected dissidents, and, worst of all, two distinguished military officers, Kurt von Schleicher and his former aide, General von Bredow. But they had all known of the projected operation; they had helped to assure its success by supplying transportation and weapons for the SS units that were dispatched to Munich with orders to liquidate Roehm's staff; and they had placed regular army units on the alert so that they might intervene in the event of strong SA resistance.[41]

Nor did they make any attempt to register their disapproval after they learned that it had gone further than they expected. On 1 July the Defence Minister, General von Blomberg, issued an order of the day to the armed forces in which he spoke of the Führer's 'soldierly decision and exemplary courage' in wiping out 'mutineers and traitors', whose number presumably included—at least, he said nothing to the contrary—Blomberg's dead comrades, Schleicher and Bredow. And a month later, when Hindenburg died, the army chiefs showed no hesitation about permitting the man who had relieved them of the challenge posed by Roehm's SA to step into the Field-Marshal's place. Not only did they tolerate Hitler's announcement of the amalgamation of the offices of Chancellor and President and his assumption of the dual post under the title Führer und Reichskanzler, but on 2 August 1934, along with every officer and man in the armed forces, they bound themselves to him with the declaration:

I swear by God this sacred oath, that I will yield unconditional obedience to the Führer of the German Reich and *Volk*, Adolf Hitler, the Supreme Commander of the Wehrmacht, and, as a brave soldier, will be ready at any time to lay down my life for this oath.[42]

In return for this sweeping commitment, the leaders of the army got what they thought they needed, a formal promise from Hitler, in a letter to Blomberg on 20 August, 'to intercede', whenever necessary, 'on behalf of the stability and inviolability of the

[41] Klaus-Jürgen Müller, 'Reichswehr und Röhm-Affäre', in *Militärgeschichtliche Mitteilungen,* i (1968), 117.

[42] *Militärwochenblatt*, xix, no. 8 (25 Aug. 1934), 283–4.

Wehrmacht, in fulfilment of the testament of the late General-feldmarschall, and, in accordance with my own desire, to fix the army as the sole bearer of arms in the nation'. It is possible that Hitler meant these words when he wrote them; the process which was to transform the SS into a much more formidable competitor of the Reichsheer than the SA had ever been did not begin until later in the year. In any case, the letter was a small price to pay for what can only be called a moral capitulation on the part of the army leadership. With the oath of 2 August 1934 the army had acquiesced in its own *Gleichschaltung*.

III

When he assumed the functions of the old Field-Marshal in August 1934, Hitler abolished the title Reichspräsident and designated himself Führer und Reichskanzler. The change was made not to honour Hindenburg by allowing his office to die with him, although Hitler said so at the time, but rather to lay the basis for a claim that Hitler's authority had greater legitimacy than that of any of his predecessors, that it rested not upon the mere fact that he had inherited the organized power of the state but upon his historical mission as the leader of a movement that embodied the yearnings and aspirations of the German people.

National Socialist political theorists were quick to elaborate upon this theme. Thus Ernst R. Huber, a writer who was skilful in devising impressive, if not always plausible, formulations to justify Nazi claims, wrote that the *Führergewalt* had replaced all previous forms of authority and that its justification was inherent in its very scope.

The Führer unites in himself the whole sovereign power of the Reich; all public power in the state as in the movement stems from the Führer's power. We must speak, not of state power, but of Führerpower (*Führergewalt*), if we want to describe political power in the *Völkisches Reich* correctly. For it is not the State as an impersonal unity that is the carrier of political power, but rather the Führer as the executor of the whole people's will (*des völkischen Gemeinwillens*). The *Führergewalt* is comprehensive and total; it unites in itself all the instruments of political organization; it extends to all the special areas of popular life; it comprehends all members of the community (*Volksgenossen*), who are obliged to give loyalty and obedience to the Führer. The *Führergewalt* is not hemmed in by conditions and controls, by autonomous preserves or shelters and jealously guarded individual rights, but is free and independent, exclusive and without restriction.[43]

---

[43] E. R. Huber, *Verfassungsrecht des Grossdeutschen Reiches* (2nd edn., Berlin, 1939), pp. 213, 230. On other theorists who wrote in the same spirit, see Bracher, *German Dictatorship*, Ch. 7.

This passage is categorical rather than persuasive, amounting to little more than a justification *post factum* of the process of *Gleichschaltung*. We need not linger over the question of whether Hitler had any real title to the great power that he had accumulated by August 1934; but we cannot avoid asking how effectively he used that power in the governing of Germany. During the 1930s a good many people in the West, discouraged by the failure of their own governments to find easy solutions to their problems, allowed themselves to be persuaded by Nazi propagandists that totalitarian dictatorship in Germany was proving its superiority to pluralistic democracy and were intimidated by the very thought of possible conflict with such a paragon of efficiency. It was not until that conflict finally came that they began to discover that their fears had been exaggerated; and post-war analyses of the structure of government during the Third Reich have demonstrated that the smoothly functioning Nazi state was never much more than a myth. Instead of party and state being bound together in a harmonious union directed by the will of the Führer—an image that Nazi ideologues were fond of evoking—relations between the two were characterized by mutual suspicion, competition, and duplication of function, which Hitler attempted neither to correct nor to discourage. Even the most cursory examination of government on the national and local levels yields startling evidence of this.

As before 1933, the bulk of Reich business was performed in the various Ministries of State by men of long years of professional experience. The leadership of the ministries was generally of high quality. Whatever might be said about the lack of *Zivilcourage* on the part of General von Blomberg and his aides, they were proficient in carrying out their military duties, and, although Hitler sometimes complained that they were too unimaginative to seize upon opportunities that he gave them for rapid expansion of the armed forces,[44] their careful and methodical work was largely responsible for the brilliant German victories of 1939 and 1940. Until the end of the decade the Foreign Office, particularly at the level of Under- and Assistant-Secretary, was as rich in talent as any department of external relations in Europe. The Ministries of Finance and Economics had strong and imaginative leaders in Count Schwerin von Krosigk and Hjalmar Schacht; and the Minister of Justice, Franz von Guertner, and his assistant Hans von Dohnanyi showed an admirable respect for the traditions of their department and great courage

[44] See Craig, *Prussian Army,* p. 485.

in attempting to defend them. Of the ministries headed by old Nazis, the Propaganda Ministry was the most outstanding, and its chief Joseph Goebbels was probably without equal in Europe for technical virtuosity.

Yet all of the resources of energy and invention that were to be found in these departments were offset by external circumstances. For one thing, they suffered from a lack of any systematic machinery for co-ordinating their policies or even keeping each of them informed about what the others were doing. The old cabinet system had been a victim of Hitler's rapid emergence as dictator. The cabinet had not, to be sure, been abolished, but it met rarely and in circum-stances that permitted no opportunity for any real discussion or inter-change of information, and Schwerin von Krosigk was to complain that he and his colleagues learned about such important events as the repudiation of the arms clauses of the Treaty of Versailles in March 1935 and the formation of the Axis in November 1936 only from the newspapers. [45] The Reich Chancellery, which existed ostensibly to provide a link between Hitler and the ministries, did not serve as an adequate means of communication and co-ordination, and its chief Heinrich Lammers spent more time in bringing ministerial business and state papers to Hitler's attention than he did in keeping the ministries properly informed or, for that matter, in trying to per-suade Hitler, in the interest of efficiency, to protect them from other threats to their efficiency and independence.

Such attempts would probably have been fruitless in any case, for Hitler was himself the author of the ministries' woes. He had at his disposal not only one Chancellery but three—that presided over by Lammers; a Presidial Chancellery, directed by Otto Meissner; and the Party Chancellery which was headed by Rudolf Hess, the Führer's Deputy, and his chief aide, and, in 1941, his successor, Martin Bormann—and he made no very precise delineation of their func-tions. Meissner, who had served both Ebert and Hindenburg as Secretary of State, was more interested in retention of office than in power, and Hess was a moody and introverted man, who was given to long periods of inactivity. But Bormann was both energetic and hungry for power, and he took advantage of the passivity of his chief and Hitler's lack of method to concern himself with everything and to meddle in everyone's business. As his influence grew, he became increasingly interested in the operations of the various ministries and, in particular, their personnel policies, making himself the

---

[45] Schwerin von Krosigk, *Es geschah in Deutschland*, p. 202.

champion of the principle of ideological purity in selection and promotion procedures.[46]

Regarded at first as a mere nuisance, Bormann developed into a major threat to departmental efficiency, and the late thirties and the early war years were marked by frequent ministerial complaints about his meddling. The official most affected by his activities was the Minister of the Interior, Wilhelm Frick, who, as the author of the German Civil Service Law of 26 January 1937, was dedicated to the protection of departmental staffs against party attempts to impose the wrong kind of criteria for advancement and Bormann's insistence that loyalty to the party should be considered more important by Beamten than obedience to the orders of their superiors. Frick won a series of hard-fought battles but was in the end worn down by the dogged pertinacity of his opponent who, by his skill in finding ever new causes for complaint (failure to dismiss Beamten with Jewish wives, for example, or having a minority of party members on promotion lists), gradually won Hitler over to his point of view. In November 1941 Frick complained in writing to Hitler about these constant attacks, which were defeating his own attempt to make the professional Civil Service a reliable pillar of the state, inspired both by the Prussian concept of duty and the National Socialist character and vision. 'In ever increasing intensity', he wrote, 'come reports of an officialdom that is embittered because of a lack of appreciation of their accomplishments.' The feeling, he added, was understandable, given the fact that

the Civil Service is exposed publicly, even in the party Press, to every possible kind of attack, based in part on faulty information, in part on a lack of expert knowledge, and sometimes even on malicious distortion; and occasional mistakes, such as occur in all large organizations, are made the occasion for irresponsible generalizations which remind one of the worst days of the class war. . . . The Civil Service suffers deeply, moreover, from the fact that new tasks are assigned not to it but to party organizations, although they are really administrative matters.

This appeal did not succeed in improving the situation, and indeed, before the year was out, Frick had given up the fight and agreed to accept one of Bormann's men to administer his personnel department. This completed the demoralization of the service and was inevitably reflected in a decline of standards of performance in the ministries.[47]

[46] On Bormann, ibid., p. 245.
[47] The basic work is Mommsen, Beamtentum, esp. pp. 81 ff., but see also Edward N. Peterson, The Limits of Hitler's Power (Princeton, 1969), pp. 86–102.

Frick's reference to the assignment of administrative tasks to other agencies is worth dwelling on. From the very beginning of the regime the ministries had had to contend with the inevitable wrangles over competence that this duplication caused. Hitler had a fondness for setting up special authorities and agencies to deal with problems that could, with greater administrative economy, have been handled within the existing ministerial structure, and these sometimes, by a process of bureaucratic imperialism, deprived the appropriate ministry of any useful function. The Reich Ministry of Labour, despite the fact that it had been assigned to a Nazi of some prominence, Franz Seldte, experienced this process of involuntary debilitation, being overshadowed from May 1933 onwards by Ley's Deutsche Arbeitsfront and, at a later date, losing other functions to the General Plenipotentiary for Work Mobilization, Fritz Sauckel.[48] After Hitler instituted the Four Year Plan in 1936, Herman Goering, who was charged with its direction, built up an organization that virtually submerged the Ministry of Economics. The ministerial staffs who were victimized by this kind of aggrandizement may have derived some grain of satisfaction from the fact that the special authorities often lost their gains in wasting power struggles with each other. Goering's authority was gradually eroded by the rapid rise of Fritz Todt, who became General Inspector for the German Road System in June 1936, with the mission of constructing a new highway system and who was so successful that in 1938 Hitler appointed him General Plenipotentiary for the Regulation of Construction within the framework of the Four Year Plan Organization. Responsible to Hitler rather than to Goering, Todt rapidly built an empire of his own, which comprised a network of agencies for the planning and administration of projects like the construction of Germany's western defences and for the regulation of contracts with private firms and mobilization of labour. Todt reached the height of his influence in 1940, when he added the post of Reich Minister for Armaments and Munitions to his other functions; but by that time his accumulation of power was attracting the jealous attention of other party notables and, although he was protected by the unstinted admiration and support that Hitler gave him, his successor Albert Speer soon found himself engaged in unremitting warfare with people like Sauckel, Bormann, and the rising star, Heinrich Himmler.[49]

[48] Schwerin von Krosigk, *Es geschah in Deutschland*, p. 181.
[49] Ibid., pp. 298–30; Broszat, *Der Staat Hitlers*, pp. 328–32; Albert Speer, *Inside the Third Reich* (New York, 1971), Chs. 18, 22.

The ministries that were most free from interference and competition were those whose subject-matter was technical enough to discourage amateurs. At the Finance Ministry, Schwerin von Krosigk was generally left to himself, and the chiefs of the army did not have to worry seriously about incursions into their sphere of special competence until the war years, when Hitler increasingly arrogated to himself powers of decision in the strategical and even operational sphere and when Himmler revived Roehm's scheme of submerging the professionals in a new Volksarmee.[50] The Foreign Ministry, however, which, in Stresemann's time as in Bismarck's, had had the same kind of monopoly in its field as the army, had from the beginning to suffer the competition of party agencies that carried on foreign policies of their own or claimed to possess an expertise in aspects of foreign relations that was not possessed by the professional diplomats. These included the Aussenpolitisches Amt der NSDAP (APA) established in April 1933, whose director, Alfred Rosenberg, fancied himself as the man who would refashion German foreign policy on strictly ideological lines, but who quickly undermined his own position by a quite extraordinary degree of looniness; Dienststelle Ribbentrop, whose chief, a former traveller in wines, so impressed Hitler by his knowledge of foreign languages and his supposed connections with the international *haute monde*, that he not only took his reports seriously but, to the fury of the professionals in the Wilhelmstraße, made him Special Envoy for Disarmament in 1934 and ambassador to Great Britain a year later; and the Auslandsorganisation der NSDAP (AO) and the Volksdeutsche Mittelstelle, which maintained contacts with Germans abroad with results that were often disruptive of regular diplomatic business. The muddle that resulted from this proliferation of offices was not relieved until Ribbentrop became Foreign Minister in 1938, and even then the improvement was not great, since he brought his own kind of incoherence into the office with him.[51]

This duplication of function cannot be ascribed solely to Hitler's administrative carelessness and the ambition of his party comrades, for there was an element of design at work as well. During the *Kampfzeit* Hitler had learned the old lesson of divide and rule and had become adroit in devising checks and balances that protected his

[50] See Gordon A. Craig, 'The German Army and the Home Front during the Second World War', in *Comité international des sciences historiques: XIème Congrès international: Rapports*, iv: *Méthodologie et histoire contemporaine* (1965).

[51] See, *inter alia*, Paul Seabury, *The Wilhelmstrasse* (Berkeley, 1954), pp. 58 ff.; Gordon A. Craig, 'The German Foreign Office from Neurath to Ribbentrop', in *The Diplomats*, pp. 427 ff., 433 ff.

own position by making the contenders dependent upon his arbit-
rament of their disputes. Offsetting every grant of authority with a
counter-grant to someone else became the hallmark of his administrative practice after he assumed office. Not even old comrades like
Goebbels were immune to its application. His mandate as Minister
of Propaganda included control over all German publications, but
his attempts to actualize this power met strong opposition from Max
Amann and Dr. Otto Dietrich, whom Hitler had appointed as Reich
Leader of the Press and Reich Press Chief respectively. Goebbels got
no satisfaction when he appealed to Hitler for a clarification of the
relationship between these posts or, for that matter, when he tried to
protect his control over cultural propaganda from incursions by
people like Rosenberg and Goering and over foreign propaganda
from the pretensions of Ribbentrop. It was not until the second half
of the war, when he had retired to the *Wolfsschanze* to devote his full
energies to the direction of operations, that Hitler gave Goebbels full
control over propaganda in all its ramifications and charged him
with the moral mobilization of the nation for total war.[52]

Dualism, struggles over competence, and duplication of function
also characterized local government during the Third Reich. At the
municipal level, the mayor was supposed to be the sole responsible
and governing leader of his community, as specified by the municipal ordinance of 30 January 1935, but unless he was also the local
party leader, which was generally true in small towns but in only 60
per cent of the cities, friction between party and state was almost
inevitable. On the state level, the situation was more complicated.
The law of 30 January 1934 had dissolved the old state parliaments in
what seemed to be the first step toward a comprehensive reform that
would eliminate the last vestiges of particularism. This never
materialized and, if the parliaments disappeared, the states remained
with all of their old prejudice against the central government in
Berlin. That government's authority was represented in the states by
the Reichsstatthalter and the State Minister of the Interior, both of
whom were responsible to the Reich Minister of the Interior, Wilhelm
Frick, a champion of *Reichsreform* in the direction of centralization,
and whatever other local ministers had been co-ordinated with the
appropriate Reich ministries, which was true of the State Ministries
of Justice after April 1935. The forces of particularism varied in

---

[52] Otto Dietrich, *Zwölf Jahre mit Hitler* (Munich, 1955), pp. 130 ff.; Helmut Heiber,
Josef Goebbels (Berlin, 1962), pp. 144 ff.; Oren J. Hale, *The Press in the Third Reich*
(Princeton, 1964), pp. 76 ff., 297 ff.; E. K. Bramsted, *Goebbels and National Socialist
Propaganda* (Lansing, Mich., 1965), pp. 278 ff.

nature, but generally included the mayors of larger cities, district party leaders, and especially the Gauleiter (or at least those Gauleiter who had not been co-opted by being made Reichsstatthalter or given other state positions). As party leaders with long records of loyalty to Hitler, the Gauleiter were confident that the Führer would not disregard their views, and they had no hesitation about sabotaging a policy of centralization which they believed was tantamount to handing the country over to bureaucrats. Gauleiter Fritz Sauckel's powerful attack in January 1936 upon the debilitating effect of centralization and his insistence that the strength of the National Socialist movement depended upon the vital forces that were to be found only in the Gaue and could be mobilized only by local leaders probably put an end to any possibility of a truly comprehensive *Reichsreform*. This was not, however, admitted by either Hitler or Frick. The latter continued to attempt to rationalize relations between Reich and *Land* and state and party, while the former continued to be enigmatic about his intentions. In the circumstances, government in Germany became an increasingly anarchic jungle of agencies whose conflicts the Reich Chancellery confessed that it was unable to resolve,[53] in the midst of which powerful satraps built their own centres of power, which they ruled like lords of the march in the name of a remote emperor.[54]

If efficency means making the most of one's material and intellectual resources for the achievement of rational goals which will redound to the common good, it is clear that this kind of system would not produce it. The energy and early success of Hitler's foreign policy prevented a great many people, at home and abroad, from seeing this and from realizing further that the force that prevented the regime from dissolving into revolution and chaos was terror, and its instrument was the SS.

The origins of the SS go back to the year 1925, when Hitler was rebuilding the NSDAP after his release from Landsberg prison. Finding it impossible to organize the original fighting organization of the party, the SA, as he wished (even in those days its commander Roehm wanted more independence than Hitler was willing to give him and resigned when he did not get it), the Führer asked one of his old bodyguard from the days of the Munich Putsch to raise a new unit that could be used to protect him and other party leaders, to give security at party meetings, and to perform other tasks assigned to it,

[53] See the Reichskanzlei note of 8 October 1941, cited by Broszat, *Der Staat Hitlers*, p. 172.
[54] Ibid., pp. 140 ff., 151 ff.; Peterson, *Limits of Power*, pp. 102–25.

including the recruiting of members and selling advertisements for the party newpspaper, the *Völkischer Beobachter*. By the late summer this Stabwache was in existence and had been renamed Schutzstaffel, but it did not seem to have much of a future. When the SA was reorganized in November 1926 under Captain von Pfeffer, the SS was subordinated to the new leadership and regarded as being of no particular significance.[55]

This changed with the appointment of Heinrich Himmler as the new Commander of the SS, for this rabbity-looking fanatic, who subscribed to the most extreme forms of racism and blood theory and veneration of the soil, was also a shrewd practitioner of power with an eye to the main chance. He noted coldly that, as the SA grew larger and more proletarian in character and rowdier in behaviour, its usefulness and reliability decreased, and he set out to make the SS the embodiment of everything the SA was not—a disciplined élitist force, selected in large part from former officers and from unemployed academicians, and characterized by its complete devotion to the Führer. From the beginning Himmler thought of the SS as more than a bodyguard, indeed as the training-ground for the leaders of the future National Socialist state, and it is probable that he already dreamed of the elaborate experiments in breeding for the future that led in later years to the establishment of the notorious Ordensburgen, which were supposed to produce a new race of Germanic Knights.

Hitler was impressed by the progress made by the SS under Himmler's leadership and by the qualities that inspired it, and he bestowed upon it the parole 'Deine Ehre heißt Treue.' Other more substantial preferments were to follow. In 1932, after the republican police had made damaging revelations about the activities of the SA's intelligence and espionage section, Hitler gave the SS a monopoly in this field, and Reinhard Heydrich, a former naval intelligence officer, who became Himmler's right-hand man, quickly built up a formidable Sicherheitsdienst (SD), the purpose of which was, in the first instance, to combat Communism and other ideological tendencies that threatened the German *Volk*-soul, and which was designed ultimately to bring the thinking of all Germans under close control.[56] This was a significant expansion of the SS's function and marked the beginning of its ideological activities, which also found

---

[55] Hans Buchheim, 'Die SS—Das Herrschaftsinstrument', in *Anatomie des SS-Staates*, ed. Hans Buchheim, Martin Broszat, Hans-Adolf Jacobsen, and Helmuth Krausnick, i (Olten and Freiburg im Breisgau, 1965), pp. 31 ff.

[56] Ibid., pp. 67 ff.

expression in the establishment of a Bureau on Race (Rasseamt) under the leadership of Walther Darré, a blood-and-soil enthusiast who later became Reich Peasant Leader. The SS's later claim to the right of directing the party race and land settlement policy stemmed from this creation of 1932.

The acquisition of political power of significant degree did not begin, however, until after the *Machtübernahme* of 1933. Heydrich is supposed to have boasted in March 1933 that the party had played its role by opening the way to power and could now be dispensed with. 'Now the SS will infiltrate the police and create with it a new organization.'[57] This proved to be not quite as easy as he seemed to believe, but his tactical direction was correct enough. In March 1933 Himmler took the post of police chief in Munich and used this relatively minor post as a means of gaining influence over the Gauleiter and Minister of the Interior, Adolf Wagner, who within two months had made him commander of all Bavarian police forces and given him control over Dachau and the other concentration camps in the state. The brutal efficiency with which he used these powers commended him to other local party chiefs who were aware that Frick, the Reich Minister of the Interior, had plans for bringing all state police forces under his own control. The Statthalter preferred to follow Wagner's example and entrust their forces to Himmler, particularly since he promised to continue to respect their over-all authority and was generous with his offers of positions in the SS for them and their staffs. By the beginning of 1934 Himmler and Heydrich had control of all political police forces in Germany except those in Prussia, and in April 1934 they were successful there too, for the show-down with Roehm was approaching, and Hermann Goering, who exercised personal control over the Prussian secret police (Gestapo), wanted to be sure of Himmler's support in the power struggle that was approaching. Accordingly, on 20 April he agreed to Himmler's appointment as Deputy Chief and Inspector of the Gestapo and, two days later, that of Heydrich as head of its central office. Goering's control over his new associate was purely nominal—in November he ordered that correspondence dealing with the Gestapo be sent not to the Minister President's office but directly to Heydrich—and Himmler's police power in Prussia was henceforth as untrammeled as it was in the other states. This rapid accumulation of power alarmed the Reich Minister of the Interior who after the the events of 30 June 1934 warned Hitler that, unless checked,

[57] Peterson, *Limits of Power*, p. 126.

Himmler would be a greater danger than Roehm had been. This fell on deaf ears, and Frick's subsequent attempts to keep Himmler's activities under some measure of state control were unavailing. An order from Hitler on 17 June 1936 authorized Himmler to co-ordinate all police activities (criminal as well as political) throughout the country and gave him the title Reichsführer-SS und Chef der Deutschen Polizei im Reichsministerium des Innerns. Frick could derive little satisfaction from the last phrase. His authority was as nominal as Goering's, although he continued to be a source of nuisance to Himmler until 1943 when the Reichsführer himself became Minister of the Interior and Frick was packed off to Bohemia as Reichsprotektor.[58]

The successful operation against Roehm, in which the élite SS Leibstandarte Adolf Hitler, commanded by Sepp Dietrich, played a leading part, brought Himmler new powers, for he now received responsibility for administering the detention camps that had been run by the SA, like the one at Oranienburg near Berlin, as well as those already under his control. In the more than fifteen concentration camps that were already in existence, there were wide variations in procedures, work routines, and punishments. Using as a model the structure and regulations that Theodor Eicke had devised for the concentration camp at Dachau, which the SS had administered since the spring of 1933, Himmler rationalized and unified the whole camp system, making Eicke, a pioneer in the bureaucratization of terror, his Inspector of Concentration Camps and SS Guard Units. These last, with a total strength of 2,000 men at the end of 1934, expanded rapidly after that date; they were the dreaded Order of the Death's Head (Totenkopfverbände) who carried out the mass murders at Auschwitz and Buchenwald and Treblinka once Hitler had instituted the Final Solution of the Jewish Question, and they committed innumerable other bestialities before that time came.[59]

The leaders of the army had welcomed the action of the SS armed units against the SA in June 1934. They were less pleased when, in the year that followed that blood-letting, Himmler added two new regiments to that commanded by Sepp Dietrich. This revived the very ghost that the military though they had laid, and they invoked Hitler's

[58] Ibid., pp. 130 f.; Buchheim, 'SS', pp. 35–67.
[59] See Heinz Höhne, The Order of the Death's Head (New York, 1970), pp. 353 ff.; Gerald Reitlinger, SS: Alibi of a Nation, 1922–1945 (New York, 1957), pp. 253 ff.; Eugen Kogon, The Theory and Practice of Hell: The German Concentration Camps and the System Behind Them (New York, 1950), passim.

promise to respect the army's monopoly of military force in order to prevent new expansion. They had only temporary success. On 17 August 1938 Hitler gave Himmler permission to exceed existing limits by the transfer of SS men on general duty to the armed units and by recruitment. By the end of 1938 the so-called *Verfügungstruppen* and the Death's Head units together numbered 20,000 men. This was the nucleus of the Waffen-SS with which the Reichsführer hoped one day to replace the regular army.[60]

In the muddle of competing agencies that constituted the governmental system of the Third Reich, the SS was the effective instrument of domination. Unfettered by the normal restraints of law and accountable only to its commander, and beyond him the Führer himself, it exercised sovereign control over the lives and liberties of German citizens, arresting and detaining them on any pretext, imprisoning them for long periods for unproved or invented crimes (even after the regime was presumably stable and consolidated, there were never fewer than 10,000 Germans in concentration camps), subjecting them to inhuman physical torments, and murdering them for daring to criticize the realities of National Socialism and the crimes of its leadership. The knowledge of the enormities that the SS perpetrated daily, the knowledge that the camps were always waiting for new inmates, the knowledge that many who entered them were never heard of again was never absent from the minds of German citizens, and the fear that it induced was a potent force in maintaining their obedience to the dictatorship. In the Third Reich, terror was the greatest of political realities, and it was in recognition of this fact that the Reichsführer-SS told his followers in 1937 that their task was not merely to safeguard, but rather to create, the new political order.[61]

---

[60] See George Stein, *The Waffen-SS* (Ithaca, 1966); Höhne, *Order of the Death's Head*, pp. 436 ff.

[61] Bracher, *German Dictatorship*, p. 354.

XVII

The Nazi Revolution: Economic and Social Developments

I am not, after all, the little man who makes ducats.
HJALMAR SCHACHT to WALTHER DARRÉ (24 March 1936)[1]

The people does not exist for the economy or for economic leaders or for economic and financial theories, but finance and economy, economic leaders and all theories have the exclusive duty of supporting the battle of our people for self-assertion.
ADOLF HITLER (August 1936)[2]

All things considered, it must be said here that we Germans must finally learn not to regard the Jew and members of any organization who have been taught by the Jew as people of our kind or representatives of our manner of thinking.
HEINRICH HIMMLER (5 March 1936)[3]

IN his masterful study of the structure and practice of National Socialism, written in 1941, Franz Neumann recognized that terror was the most effective of the instruments that held together a society in which all of the old structures and loyalties had been systematically destroyed by the process of *Gleichschaltung*. But he also emphasized the importance of material progress as an integrative force and did not hesitate to describe such achievements of the German economy as the ending of unemployment, the increase of production, and the development of new industries as 'astounding'.[4] Coming from a man who had been forced to leave his country and who was not given to encomiums of the regime that had made this

---

[1] Dieter Petzina, *Autarkiepolitik im Dritten Reich: Der nationalsozialistische Vierjahresplan* (Stuttgart, 1968), p. 34. The reference is to the *Dukatenmensch* who is carved on the east wall of the Hotel Kaiser Worth in Goslar in the Harz, a squatting figure with posterior bared to the public, making gold coins.

[2] Hans-Adolf Jacobsen and Werner Jochmann (eds.), *Zur Geschichte des Nationalsozialismus: Ausgewählte Dokumente* (Bielefeld, 1961), Dok. VIII 1936, p. 2.

[3] *Heinrich Himmler: Geheimreden 1933 bis 1945*, ed. Bradley F. Smith and Agnes F. Peterson (Frankfurt-on-Main, 1974), p. 57.

[4] *Behemoth*, pp. 221 f.

necessary, this judgement is arresting enough to prompt some investigation of Hitler's economic policy, the degree of success achieved by it, and its social effects and costs.

I

It seems clear that, when he was appointed Chancellor in January 1933, Hitler had no very clear idea of the kind of economic policy he would follow. His political instinct, however, must have warned him that the consolidation of his authority would depend upon his success in correcting the conditions that had been disastrous to his predecessors in office. Although there were signs that the world depression might be easing, unemployment still stood at about 4½ millions, and agriculture was still suffering from the impoverishment and indebtedness that had caused peasant riots to spread from Schleswig-Holstein across the whole of northern Germany in 1932.

Until the March elections were past and the policy of *Gleichschaltung* fairly launched, the Führer was unable to turn his attention to these problems, but it was notable that he closed his ears to those party members who advocated radical economic solutions and who argued that the time was ripe for the implementation of the economic clauses of the party programme and the fulfilment of the promises made to the *Mittelstand* organizations. As has been indicated above, Hitler was no socialist, and, as an admirer of power, he had not the slightest intention of indulging those who had romantic notions of breaking up the great aggregates of economic strength so that the country might return to the simpler past. To have done so would have made impossible the fulfilment of his already well-developed ambitions in the field of foreign policy, which would, he never seems to have doubted, depend upon the effective use of the capitalist structure and the managerial and technological skills of industry that had in the past been largely responsible for making Germany a Power of the first rank.

That his thinking ran in this direction was shown by his appointment of Hjalmar Schacht as President of the Reichsbank in March 1933. No one who remembered the part played by this stubborn defender of capitalist values during the cabinet crisis of 1930 could doubt that this was a gesture of reassurance to the big business community and a sign that, despite the continuing economic *malaise*, there was no danger of wild experiments. A month earlier the Chancellor had announced that the national government would 'achieve the great task of reorganizing the economy of our *Volk* by means of two great four-year plans: for the salvation of the German farmer, in order to maintain the food supply and, in consequence, the very basis of the nation's life; for the salvation of the German worker, by means of a powerful and comprehensive attack upon unemployment'.[5] Apart from continuing the work-creation policies of his predecessors, however, he did nothing to fulfil these pledges until he had solicited the advice of leading industrialists, and it was not until the summer that a programme was inaugurated that could be described as National Socialist.

The Reinhardt Plan, named after the Secretary of State of the Finance Ministry, poured over a billion R.M. into a variety of public works projects for the construction of roads, canals, official buildings, and the like, provided subventions to private construction firms for the renovation of dilapidated dwellings and for new housing complexes, and encouraged and stimulated plant expansion in the machine tool and agricultural machinery industries by granting tax advantages. The emphasis upon pump-priming in the private sector won the approval of German business circles, and this grew to enthusiasm as a result of the rapid development of one aspect of the programme, the projected creation of a national network of highways. The building of the autobahnen, which not only provided jobs for thousands of construction workers and engineers and architects but also stimulated the automotive industry and allied trades, struck the national fancy and had a similar role in German recovery to that played in Franklin Roosevelt's New Deal by the National Recovery Administration. Nazi propagandists pulled out all the stops in advertising this as dramatic proof of the energy and earnestness with which the regime was tackling the country's basic problems; and the newspapers and the radio supplied circumstantial accounts of the actual work of construction, in which they emphasized the number and variety of workers involved and described the project as symbolic of the emergence of a new *Volksgemeinschaft*. All this was not without effect, even upon labourers who had been deprived in May of the right to belong to trade unions of their own; it enhanced the Führer's personal position; and it had the psychological effect of persuading people that conditions were improving.

With respect to employment this was doubtless true, for the public works programmes, the revival of private production as a result of government support, the encouragement of work-sharing, the establishment by the party of formally voluntary labour and agricul-

[5] Speech of 1 Feb. 1933. Domarus, *Hitler: Reden* i. 191 ff.

tural services, and the Labour Front's vocational training pro-gramme sharply reduced the number of people without occupation.[6] How stable these gains were and whether they would in themselves have served as the basis for a healthy and developing economy it is impossible to say, for all these programmes were soon over-shadowed by the beginning of what has been called the command economy, based upon a massive rearmament effort.

In his conversation with the commanders of the armed forces on 2 February 1933, Hitler had revealed that he intended to begin rearmament on a large scale as soon as possible. 'The build-up of the Wehrmacht', he said, was 'the most important of the prerequisites for the attainment of our goal: the reconquest of political power'. Implicit in the process, however, were dangers; Germany's military recovery would 'show whether France still has statesmen'.[7] For most of the year that followed Hitler refrained from testing French resis-tance by a too provocative action, like the resumption of universal military service, which he had promised the generals but now post-poned, or a readily detectable increase of arms production. But after October 1933, when he terminated German membership in the Disarmament Conference and the League of Nations without hav-ing to suffer Western reprisals, he became less cautious, and re-armament on a serious scale began. The year 1934 showed a sharp increase of state expenditures for this purpose, and the amount more than doubled between 1934 and 1936 and went on increasing, $44\frac{1}{2}$ billion R.M. being spent in expanding the arms effort between 1933 and 1938 and 30 billion more in 1939.[8] Translated into jobs, this was enough to bring full employment in the country, the more so because the armament effort had the effect of creating new industries as it grew. This was the consequence of Hitler's early acceptance of self-containment, or autarchy, as the concomitant goal of the Ger-man economic effort.

The Führer was doubtless impelled towards this conclusion by his memory of the ruinous effects of the British blockade upon Ger-many's war effort in the First World War and by his awareness of the country's dependence upon the outside world for strategical mat-

[6] For a critical view of the work-creation programme, see Timothy W. Mason, *Arbeiterklasse und Volksgemeinschaft: Dokumente und Materialien zur deutschen Arbeiter-politik 1936–1939* (Opladen, 1975), pp. 46 ff. For a more positive view of local results, see Allen, *The Nazi Seizure of Power*, pp. 258–71.

[7] Jacobsen and Jochmann, *Zur Geschichte des Nationalsozialismus*, Dok. 3 ii 1933.

[8] See the estimates in René Erbe, *Die nationalsozialistische Wirtschaftspolitik 1933–1939 im Lichte der modernen Theorie* (Zurich, 1958), pp. 25, 34. See also Mason, *Arbeiterklasse*, p. 101.

erials like india-rubber, copper, base metals, and mineral and fuel oils. He had become interested at an early date in the production of ersatz materials. In 1934, in another example of that administrative dualism to which he was prone, he had authorized his special adviser on economic affairs, a party official named Wilhelm Keppler, to set up an agency that would investigate the problems of synthetic production, which the more orthodox Ministry of Economics considered too impractical and expensive to waste time on; and the resultant Dienststelle Keppler began basic research on the possibilities of producing artificial rubber (*Buna*), synthetic fats, and cheap metals that proved useful after 1936 in facilitating the synthetics programme of the Four Year Plan.

These experiments were strongly encouraged by heavy industry and the leading chemical concerns on the one hand, and by the military on the other. The production of synthetics, either by means of polymerization or by the hydrogenation of coal, required investments for new plant and machinery that were beyond the resources of even the most thriving firms. If these costs could be assumed by the state, on the other hand, they were more than willing to cooperate, the more so because the new techniques that were developed might very well have profitable by-products. As early as December 1933 the great dye concern I. G. Farben had received a state subvention for work on synthetic fuels at its Leuna plant; and in the following year it joined with the country's leading potash concern, Wintershall, and the principal producers of brown coal to form a state-supported corporation Braunkohle Benzin A.G. (Brauhag) for the production of petrol from lignite. Similar corporations were the basis for the development of a new cellulose wool industry and for new firms that exploited low-grade ores in metal production.[9]

I. G. Farben's experiments with synthetic fuels aroused active interest in the Reich Air Ministry, for obvious reasons. The most enthusiastic and consistent support for autarchy on the military side came, however, from the army, where an energetic major named Georg Thomas, in the Wehrmachtsamt, had been seeking with some success to indoctrinate his superiors, including the Minister of War, General Werner von Blomberg, in the basic concepts of war economy (*Wehrwirtschaft*). Thomas was not an enthusiastic supporter of Adolf Hitler—indeed, he was arrested after the *attentat* on Hitler on 20 July 1944 and remained in detention in concentration camps in Berlin, Flossenbürg, Dachau, and Toblach until the

---

[9] Neumann, *Behemoth*, pp. 277 ff.

end of the war because the SS found evidence of oppositional activity on his part in 1938 and 1939—but he had been in charge of the army's Economic Mobilization Section since 1928, and his zeal for his specialty proved stronger than his concern over the possible consequences of Hitler's policy. In his memoirs he wrote, 'When at the end of 1934 I was given the assignment of bringing Germany's economy to a state of war-readiness, I accepted this task with my whole heart, because it was my view that for Germany to be defenceless in the midst of highly armed states was impossible and a danger to the peace. In violation of the Versailles Treaty, the Western Powers had not disarmed; Russia was re-arming comprehensively; therefore, something must happen in Germany.'[10] Thomas not only supported rearmament but was an advocate of thoroughgoing economic mobilization. In a memorandum written to his superiors in the winter of 1933–4, he not only called for the systematic build-up of plants for the production of ersatz materials, but—with a kind of throw-back to the work of Walther Rathenau—urgently suggested the appointment of Raw Materials Commissioners, who would undertake the task of stock-piling strategical materials and pin-pointing significant deficiencies.[11]

The effect of all this activity on the employment situation was positive, but this progress was not achieved without causing other problems. Not all branches of German business benefited from the rearmament programme and the application of the new technology—consumer goods industries and those that depended on the export trade (light wares, electro-industry, shipping trades, and the like) could claim, with some justification, that they were disadvantaged by it—and some industries that might normally have shared in the boom in weaponry soon discovered that the government preferred to give its contracts to the largest and technologically most advanced firms. As the tempo of armament increased, so did the tendency towards increasing centralization and monopoly, and even business men who thought that they had a claim on the regime's gratitude because they had supported it before 1933 found that this was no protection against elimination or confiscation, as the Thyssen combine was to discover. Small producers and retailers were particularly vulnerable, especially after the introduction of the Four Year Plan in 1936, and many of them fell victim to regulations

[10] Wolfgang Birkenfeld (ed.), *Georg Thomas, Geschichte der deutschen Wehr- und Rüstungswirtschaft 1918–1943–1945* (Boppard, 1967); Wilhelm Treue, 'Ein General im Zwielicht', *Die Zeit* (24 Jan. 1967), p. 12.

[11] Petzina, *Autarkiepolitik*, pp. 26–7.

that were designed ostensibly to eliminate inefficient and unreliable businesses but were really intended to aid the war economy by promoting rationalization of production and of labour supply. Not unnaturally, firms in difficulty sought to shore up their positions by appealing to friends in high places in the government or the party, and the results were not only unedifying but disruptive of bureaucratic and economic efficiency.

A more serious problem was posed by the unfavourable balance of payments. The new synthetic industries could not be expected to meet Germany's needs for strategical materials quickly, which meant that large quantities of metals and fuels and rubber had to be imported. Normally, this would have been paid for by the proceeds of German exports, but these were now inadequate for that purpose, partly because of a decline in the prices of finished goods at a time when the cost of raw materials was rising, partly because of foreign tariffs and quotas that were the result of the economic nationalism promoted by the world depression, and partly and significantly because reports of Nazi brutality towards opponents of the regime made foreigners disinclined to buy German products and led, particularly in the United States, to local boycotts. As President of the Reichsbank and, after August 1934, Minister of Economics as well, Hjalmar Schacht tried to overcome this deficit by means of the New Plan of September 1934, which was an attempt to increase German trade by means of bilateral agreements with countries whose governments agreed to accept credit for German purchases and to use it to buy in German markets. This was a deliberate departure from the most-favoured-nation principle and from normal conceptions of multilateral trading, and it aroused considerable criticism in Western countries, but Schacht succeeded in concluding offset agreements with twenty-five countries, mainly in the Balkans and South America, and in increasing Germany's export trade by 19 per cent between 1934 and 1936. In normal circumstances this would have permitted Germany to satisfy its import requirements without difficulty.[12]

This was made impossible, however, by the insatiable demands of the war industries for raw materials, particularly after March 1935, when Hitler repudiated the arms clauses of the Versailles Treaty and reintroduced universal military service, and by the simultaneous increase in necessary imports of food.

The latter problem was only partly due to crop failures. National

---

[12] Schacht, *Confessions*, pp. 301–3.

Socialist agricultural policy was largely to blame, because it gave higher priority to politics and ideology than to economic considerations. The first half of 1933 was given over to the elimination of the leadership of the old agrarian organizations—Andreas Hermes, for example, the president of the Union of Christian Peasant Societies and of the Reich Association of Agricultural Communities (Reichsverband der deutschen landwirtschaftlichen Genossenschaften) had been an outspoken opponent of the NSDAP and had long been marked for retribution[13]—and the co-ordination of these associations under Walther Darré, who was designated Reich Peasant Leader in May and who succeeded Alfred Hugenberg as Minister for Food and Agriculture when the former Nationalist party leader relinquished his office in June. As Schacht has written, Darré was more a philosopher than a practical administrator;[14] he took seriously the rhetoric about the mystique of the soil that had been the stock-in-trade of party orators in rural parts before 1933, and dreamed of re-agriculturalizing Germany. His instrument for this purpose was the Hereditary Farm Law (Reichserbhofgesetz) of 29 October 1933, which designated about a third of Germany's farms, all of medium size (not over 125 hectares) and worked by pure-blooded Germans, as Hereditary Farms and gave their proprietors the sole right to call themselves *Bauern*. These farms were henceforth inalienable and inseparable, and a limit was placed on the amount of debt that their farmers could incur. The law was intended to stabilize the rural population by making it an honour to have such a holding, but to many farmers its salient feature seemed to be to tie small farmers to the soil where they continued to be subject to the competition of the great landowners who did not suffer the credit restrictions that bore upon them and prevented them from modernizing and mechanizing their farms. The net result of the law was resentment and stagnation, as well as a continued flight from the soil, which was encouraged by the lucrative opportunities to be found in industry.[15]

If this was bad for agricultural production, so was the operation of the law of 15 August 1933 for 'the expansion of agriculture' and that of 13 October, which set up a Reich Food Office with powers to regulate production and prices. Darré's attempts to raise the agricultural standard of living by reducing the acreage under cultivation were maladroit and had disastrous results. Between 1933 and 1935 the yield of wheat, barley, and fodder grains had declined by an

---

[13] He was arrested on 20 March 1933. See Broszat, *Der Staat Hitlers*, p. 230.

[14] Schacht, *Confessions*, p. 302. [15] See Broszat, *Der Staat Hitlers*, pp. 234 ff.

average of 15 per cent; the production of potatoes fell off by 10 per cent and there were corresponding declines in meat production and dairy products. It became clear that, unless these deficits were balanced by increased imports, there was going to have to be a considerable amount of belt-tightening, and the last thing that the party wanted to have to admit was that National Socialism had resulted in a lowering of nutritional standards. Since Germany was currently importing only 64 per cent as much food products as it had in 1928, some increase in volume was not unreasonable. On the other hand, with imports of raw materials increasing and with 83 per cent of Germany's foreign trade on a barter basis, so that the country received free foreign exchange for only 17 per cent of its exports, any increase of food imports must lead to balance of payments difficulties.

On this point, Darré and Schacht clashed seriously in 1935, when the Reich Peasant Leader was forced to ask for credits to cover additional imports of fats. Already appalled by both the immensity of the arms drive and the costs of experimentation with the production of synthetics, of which he strongly disapproved, and intent upon using the Reichsbank's control over foreign currency (*Devisen*) to brake these tendencies, Schacht seems to have decided to use Darré's request as a means of dramatizing the problem. When he refused to authorize the credits requested, however, Hitler instructed Hermann Goering to adjudicate the conflict and to reach a decision that would protect 'the nourishment of the German people', and Goering—whose drive to expand the Luftwaffe was a contributory factor to Schacht's difficulties—authorized the expenditure of 12,400,000 R.M. in foreign exchange for that purpose. The mediation marked the first step in Goering's ascent to the position of National Socialism's economic tsar, but it solved neither the food problem nor that of credits. In 1936 Darré was back with new requests, for food shortages were now so serious that prices of some commodities were 50 per cent higher than in the previous year. Moreover, the balance of payments problem sharpened critically when the Soviet and Romanian governments announced in the spring of 1936 that they were placing restrictions upon exports of oil and would require payment in cash (*Bardevisen*) for all future shipments. There was every indication that other suppliers of raw materials might follow suit, for Germany had an exchange deficit of more than 500 million R.M. and was beginning to look like a bad risk.[16]

[16] On all this, see Petzina, *Autarkiepolitik*, pp. 30–6.

Schacht's formula for dealing with the problem was an eminently orthodox one: if the country was buying more than it could pay for, then it must begin to economize. It could not have both guns and butter, because the income from taxation and exports was not great enough to meet the cost. Since the Führer had just indicated that he was not willing to impose restrictions upon the food supply, economies would have to be at the cost of the guns. Already in December 1935 Schacht had written to General von Blomberg, 'You expect me to furnish sufficient foreign exchange to meet your requirements. In reply, I beg to state that under prevailing circumstances I see no possibility of doing so.'[17] In the first months of 1936 he pushed this argument energetically in meetings with provincial presidents and Gauleiter, who were beginning to be seriously concerned about tax and price levels, and had private discussions with Hitler and other party leaders.

It is difficult to decide whether it was naïvety or arrogance that led Schacht to believe that he could persuade Hitler to reduce the pace of rearmament by arguing that fiscal orthodoxy and the conventions of international trade required it. His preachments about the necessity of balancing the budget and following approved practice in dealing with creditors must have struck the Chancellor, if he bothered to think of them at all, as being quaint and irrelevant. Armies, Hitler must have thought in his brutally simple way, are, to be sure, expensive things, but if they fulfil the purposes for which they are raised, they pay their own way in the end. Ministers of Economics should realize this and, instead of worrying about debts, should bend their minds to devising ways to tide the country over in the interval between the time when they are incurred and the conquests that will pay for them or make them meaningless. The Führer did not, of course, open his mind to the Reichsbank President. Instead, he seems to have concluded that there was a fundamental incompatibility between Schacht's philosophy and his own, and that the economic preparations for the effort that would fulfil his grandiose ambition in foreign policy (ambitions that had just been encouraged in March by the failure of the Western Powers to resist his military occupation of the Rhineland[18]) would benefit from a new psychological offensive under the direction of someone who was a true believer rather than a sceptic. The new offensive was the Four Year Plan and the new director was Hermann Goering.

[17] Schacht, *Confessions*, p. 331.
[18] See below, Ch. XIX, p. 690.

II

In August 1936, in his eyrie at Obersalzburg, Hitler composed a long memorandum on rearmament and economic policy that was so frank in revealing his intimate thoughts that he decided to keep its contents secret from everyone but Goering and Blomberg.[19] It began with a description of the threat that Bolshevism posed to Europe and a prediction that, unless Germany were prepared to meet and defeat it, it would suffer, not another Versailles, but complete annihilation. 'If we are not able in the shortest possible time', Hitler wrote, 'to make the German Wehrmacht, in training, in the disposition of its formations, and, above all, in its psychological readiness, the first army in the world, then Germany will be lost! . . . To the achievement of this goal, all other considerations must be unconditionally subordinated!'

Those charged with making economic decisions should remember that their sole duty was to enable the German people to assert itself in the world of politics. The time was past for fruitless debates over shortages in foodstuffs and raw materials or for irresponsible suggestions that either could be solved at the cost of the national armament programme. Such proposals betrayed 'a complete lack of appreciation—not to use a stronger term—of the tasks and military requirements that face us'. Definitive solutions for Germany's economic problems could in any case be found only by the acquisition of greater living space for its population.

The task confronting the economy, therefore, was a twofold one: first, to find provisional solutions for the problems of food and raw materials, and second, to create the basis for the 'struggle for self-realization'. Hitler called for an economic mobilization comparable to the military one, which would maintain food supplies without jeopardizing the armaments effort and would attain self-sufficiency in strategic materials. In particular, he demanded the solution of the fuel problem within eighteen months, the mass production of synthetic rubber, the immediate expansion of the iron and steel industry and a heightened effort to produce metal from low-grade ores, the freeing of the supply of industrial fats from dependence upon imports, and the development of light metals.

Through all this ran an unmistakable note of menace. Four costly years had been lost, and the reason, in part at least, had been bureau-

---

[19] A third copy was given to Albert Speer in 1944. Schacht, who had not been previously aware of its contents, learned of them during the Nuremberg trial. See Schacht, *Confessions*, pp. 341 f.; Petzina, *Autarkiepolitik*, p. 48

cratic interference by the Ministry of Economics in the productive process and 'lamentations and demonstrations of our lack of foreign exchange'. With respect to the latter, it was essential that there be an immediate investigation of German holdings of foreign exchange abroad, the very existence of which hinted at sabotage of the national effort and the country's security. It would be necessary, Hitler wrote, for the Reichstag to pass two laws, one providing the death sentence for economic sabotage, the other making the whole Jewish community responsible for all damage to the economy by single acts of sabotage. There must be no more time wasted. 'The German army must be operational in four years. The German economy must be capable of supporting war in four years.'[20]

Hermann Goering read excerpts from this document to Schacht and other ministers on 4 September, adding cheerfully, 'Everything we do now must be as if we were in a state of immediate danger of war.'[21] He knew by now that he was to be the director of the new Four Year Plan that Hitler formally announced at the Nuremberg Party Convention on 9 September. He was ready to accept the responsibility with that boundless self-confidence that was always characteristic of him but was so often belied by his tendency to underestimate the magnitude of problems, by his proneness to inattention to detail, and by that tendency to self-indulgence that Claire Waldoff mocked in her cabaret song:

> Rechts Lametta—links Lametta
> Und der Bauch wird imma fetta!
> In de Luft, da is er Meesta—
> Hermann heeßta! Hermann heeßta!

The powers granted him in Hitler's Decree for the Administration of the Four Year Plan on 18 October 1936 were, on the surface at least, impressive. Asserting the importance of a 'united direction of all of the powers of the German people and the disciplined co-ordination of all appropriate agencies of Party and State', the Führer empowered Goering to issue 'legal ordinances and general administrative instructions' and to 'survey and interrogate all administrative authorities, including the superior offices of the Reich, as well as their individual departments and their attached agencies, and to issue directives to them'.[22] It cannot, however, be claimed that Goering made very effective use of this extensive authority.

---

[20] The memorandum is printed in full in Jacobsen and Jochmann, *Zur Geschichte des Nationalsozialismus*, Dok. VIII 1936.

[21] Petzina, *Autarkiepolitik*, p. 53.

[22] *Reichsgesetzblatt* (1936), i. 887.

For one thing, he expended the major part of his energies in his first year in carrying on intermittent warfare with rival agencies. These internecine conflicts, which were to be found in every part of the National Socialist political structure, were particularly bitter in the field of rearmament. Even before the inception of the Four Year Plan there had been struggles over competence and goals inside the Wehrmacht—between the separate services, for example, but also between the services as a whole and the War Ministry's War Economy Department—as well as between the Wehrmacht and Schacht, who in addition to his other offices held that of Plenipotentiary for War Preparedness. Goering now plunged into conflict with both Schacht and Blomberg. There were, of course, fundamental differences of view between him and the Economics Minister; but even after Schacht's constant complaints had led Hitler to deprive him of his ministerial functions in November 1937, the interdepartmental infighting did not slacken, for Goering was soon involved in conflict with Schacht's successor, Walter Funk, while at the same time stubbornly doing everything he could to deprive the War Ministry's experts of any influence in the sphere of economic planning. This latter endeavour may have been rooted in latent animosity towards the army leadership and a desire to supplant it; at least, this is suggested by the part that Goering played in the revelations that forced Blomberg from office and led to a reorganization of the structure of command in February 1938.[23] All this diverted Goering's attention from the task of building an effective organization for the administration of the Four Year Plan and led him to set up a structure that kept expanding and adding new sections to duplicate the work of potential rivals. The resultant structure was too elaborate and clumsy to work and, in September 1938, it was forced to undergo basic reorganization.

Goering's policies as director of the economy were reflections of his temperament: egocentric, dashing to the point of rashness, and generally lacking in perspective. Sporadically, he sought to ease the balance of payments problem by confiscations and special levies. In the spring of 1937, responding perhaps to a suggestion made in Hitler's secret memorandum of the previous year, he seized all foreign securities in German possession at home and abroad, while at the same time speeding up the collection of export debts. Coming just at the moment when world trade was beginning to revive, this was ill timed and self-defeating; and in a barely civil letter to the

[23] See below, Ch. XIX, p. 700.

Reichsmarschall, Schacht said that he had 'plundered part of our capital and deprived our current foreign exchange income of regular payments in interest and dividends accruing therefrom'.[24] Even when his economic strategy showed imagination, its author's refusal to be content with modest gains had negative results in the long run. After the outbreak of the Spanish Civil War Goering organized a corporation by the name of Rovag in Germany to work with a corresponding Spanish–German body called Hisma in facilitating the exchange of Spanish metals for German manufactured goods, and his chief agent in Spain later claimed that in 1937 Hisma had shipped 1,620,000 tons of iron ores, 956,000 tons of pyrites, and 7,000 tons of miscellaneous ores to Germany.[25] Subsequently, however, his attempts to persuade the Spanish Government to grant Germany a majority of the shares in the most important mining companies in Spain and Morocco,[26] and the intrigues of his agents, not only against other foreign mining interests, but also against representatives of the German Economics Ministry and against the German ambassador and his staff[27] alienated General Franco to the point that he made economic concessions to the Germans reluctantly, only when the fortunes of war required it, and even then as slowly as possible. In May 1939, when the civil war dragged to its end, Franco refused to meet Goering to discuss future policy, although the Reichsmarschall was lingering off shore in a German ship waiting for an invitation.[28]

The statistical evidence is inadequate to provide the basis for a balanced assessment of the Four Year Plan's contribution to Germany's economic development between 1936 and the outbreak of war. It is clear, however, that it did not fulfil the goals laid down in Hitler's memorandum of August 1936. With production of fuels, industrial oils and fats, and light metals far below target, the synthetics programme had not made enough progress by the autumn of 1939 to justify any talk about autarchy. The result was that foreign exchange was still in critically short supply, although it was intermittently relieved by surprises like the unexpected upswing of world trade in 1937, which increased German exports, particularly of machinery and marine and electrical equipment, by 23 per cent and contributed to a saving of about 150 million R.M. of *Devisen*, and by

[24] Schacht, *Confessions*, p. 341.

[25] *Documents on German Foreign Policy, 1918–1945*, (Washington, D.C., 1949 ff.), Ser. D (1937–41), iii, nos. 80, 101, 507 (hereafter cited as *GD*).

[26] Ibid., nos. 464, 470, 596, 632, 682, 690, 691, 692, 698, 700.

[27] Ibid., nos. 474, 496, 791, 794.

[28] Ibid., nos. 793, 798, 799, 800, 811.

windfalls like the 295 million R.M. of gold and foreign exchange that were gained as a result of anschluss with Austria.[29]

Goering always treated the exchange problem with considerable levity, as if it were unimportant. In a sardonic comment on the Reichsmarschall's speech in Vienna immediately after the triumphant entrance of German troops in March 1938, the French ambassador, André François-Poncet, wrote:

M. Goering poured over the heads of his auditors the contents of an immense horn of plenty. One would have said, a Gulliver surfeiting the Lilliputians. It seemed that the Marshall had in his pockets inexhaustible riches. The question of money evidently had no importance in his eyes. The Reich's debt, which has already reached the figure of 57 billion mark, is going to go on rising.

All the procedures that have been applied in Germany will be repeated in Austria, doubtless for the same ends. It is characteristic that at the head of the remedies promised by M. Goering were rearmament, the expansion of factories for war materials, and the creation of new aircraft factories and air bases.[30]

There was perhaps something to be said for this carefree attitude. With reference to Germany's continued dependence upon world trade despite all its efforts to free itself, the most authoritative analyst of the Four Year Plan has written, 'If the foreign governments had answered Hitler's foreign policy with a comprehensive economic blockade, the weaknesses of the economic "mobilization" would have become apparent.'[31] But of course they did not. In 1938 and 1939 the Western Powers seemed to believe that economic appeasement would persuade Hitler to become a peaceful and satisfied member of the international community, and they not only did not insist that the German Government make good its deficits in trading accounts and pay its debts to their citizens, but redoubled their efforts to confer economic advantage upon Hitler whenever he committed an outrageous action. In March 1938 the British Government willingly authorized the Bank of England to hand the assets it held on behalf of the Austrian National Bank over to the Reichsbank; and, after German troops entered Prague in March 1939 and completed the destruction of Czechoslovakia, the British Treasury did not attempt to prevent the transfer of £6 million of Czech gold deposits held by the Bank of England in the name of the Bank for International Settlement, and there was some disposition

---

[29] Petzina, *Autarkiepolitik*, pp. 109 ff., 112.   [30] *DDF* 2nd Ser. ix. 117.
[31] Petzina, *Autarkiepolitik*, p. 195.

to hand over blocked Czech assets as well.[32] In view of this sort of action, Goering and his master must have been tempted more and more strongly to seek escape from the economic pinch by a *Flucht nach vorne*. New adventures might not only conceal internal economic strains but ease them.

The failure of the synthetics programmes to live up to expectations should not, however, be allowed to disguise the fact that they had none the less led to a considerable expansion of industry and to the creation of important new techniques of production, particularly in the field of leather articles, cellulose, plastics, artificial silk, and rubber goods. Nor was this the only change in the structure of the German economy that can be attributed to the Four Year Plan. It not unnaturally caused some shift in investment patterns, so that the percentage of investment in housing and consumer goods tended to decline, although this was not pronounced until the war years.[33] More important, it effected a significant change in the regional structure of industry, shifting the balance from western to south-central Germany. Partly for strategic reasons, partly because of the presence of deposits of lignite, the great synthetics plants set up by the Four Year Plan were located in the area between Braunschweig, Magdeburg, and Halle-Leipzig, with the Leuna works near Merseburg, Buna works at Shkopau, aluminium works at Bitterfeld, and synthetic fuel plants at Zeitz, Magdeburg, and Böhlen.

Finally, the Four Year Plan strengthened the already strong tendency towards concentration and monopoly of economic power by the largest firms. An example is seen in the rise of I. G. Farben, whose influence became ascendant when Goering appointed Carl Krauch of that company as his deputy for special problems of chemical production and then, in August 1938, gave him oversight of mineral oil, rubber, light metals, and explosives production. Goering used Krauch as his agent in reducing the functions of the Wehrmacht in economic planning and in restricting it to problems of weapons and munitions production. Krauch performed this mission successfully by providing his chief with plausible evidence concerning the inefficiency of the military planning staffs; and he then went on to establish I. G. Farben as the giant in the field of synthetics and the

[32] See Paul Einzig, *Appeasement before, during and after the War* (London, 1941), pp. 122 ff. and *In the Centre of Things* (London, 1960), pp. 186 ff. See also Martin Gilbert and Richard Gott, *The Appeasers* (London, 1963), pp. 208–11. The gold, while transferred to the Reichsbank's account, does not seem to have left London.

[33] Petzina, *Autarkiepolitik*, p. 187.

symbol of the partnership of big business and the state in the war economy.

The striking aspect of this collaboration was the latitude granted to business to make decisions about the use of resources and about methods and goals. This was perceived by François-Poncet, who wrote in July 1937:

The enterprise pursued by the Hitler government escapes, in its empiricism, categorical formulas. While augmenting their means of control and pressure upon key industries, the directors of the Third Reich have never seemed anxious, at least up till now, to assume direct control or to substitute *étatisme* for the system of capitalist exploitation. . . . The recent decisions taken by General Goering, 'the delegate of the Führer for the execution of the Four Year Plan', consist on the one hand of legislative arrangements of an extensive character which virtually confer on the state the possibility of controlling production . . . and, on the other hand, a measure of execution that is characterized by much more restraint.[34]

The liberties granted to the great concerns were, however, dependent upon a willing complicity in the state's designs, which they helped to promote. There was good reason for the directors of I. G. Farben and similar firms to stand in the dock at Nuremberg after the war.

III

In his secret memorandum of August 1936 Hitler had insisted that the Wehrmacht be ready for war within four years. To what extent can it be said that his goal was met?

There is no question that the armed forces had acquired a formidable strength by August 1939. They comprised 103 fully equipped army divisions, including five armoured and four semi-armoured divisions with a total strength of 3,200 tanks, more than 3,646 operational aircraft, and a navy with 57 submarines, 22 destroyers, 9 cruisers, and 6 'pocket battleship' (*Panzerkreuzer*). Although the naval component was weaker than the British, the total force was greater than that of any of Germany's neighbours, and its state of readiness was a potent factor in the crises of 1938 and 1939.[35]

At the same time, there is no doubt that this force was inadequate

---

[34] *DDF* 2nd Ser. vi. 517–18.

[35] See Russel Henry Stolfi, 'Equipment for Victory in France 1940', *History*, l, no. 183 (1970), 1–20 and, at greater length, 'Reality and Myth: French and German Preparations for War, 1933–40' (Dissertation, Stanford Univ. 1966). See also Andreas Hillgruber, *Hitlers Strategie 1940–1941* (Frankfurt-on-Main, 1965), pp. 33–40, and B. Mueller-Hillebrand, *Das Heer, 1935–45*, i (Darmstadt, 1954), pp. 68–71.

for the uses to which Hitler wished to put it and that a greater degree of unity and will on the part of his antagonists would have proved this immediately. The Polish campaign of 1939 was not particularly gruelling for the Germans, yet the gaps it left in munitions supply and availability of vehicles proved so hard to fill that the army as a whole was incapable for some months of mounting another offensive. In October 1939, according to the army's Quartermaster General, there was only enough munitions on hand to supply a third of the operational divisions for four weeks; spare parts for damaged tanks and trucks were hard to come by, and the motorized divisions were not fully ready for action until April 1940; and tyres and fuel were in very short supply. If Hitler had persisted in his desire to attack France before Christmas 1939, the result, according to his generals, would almost certainly have been disastrous.

These deficiencies came as no surprise to those in the military who were best qualified to give advice about economic-military mobilization. As early as November 1936, in a speech before the Reich Chamber of Labour, Colonel (later General) Georg Thomas had pointed out with considerable vigour that the achievement of the goal set by Hitler would depend upon a comprehensive programme that would include restrictions upon sectors of the economy that were not involved directly in armaments production, firm regulation of the labour market and controls on wages and prices, and a conscientious husbanding of raw materials and other resources.[36] Thomas continued to press these arguments for the next four years, and was supported in his views by the Reich Commissioner for Price Regulation, Josef Wagner, and the Reich Peasant Leader, Walther Darré.[37] The logic of his case was incontrovertible, but no attempt was made to satisfy his bill of particulars. Indeed, whenever there was any question that this might be done, either powerful party agencies intervened to prevent it or the leadership of the state refused to take responsibility for issuing the necessary orders. What has often been called the command economy in fact suffered from a failure to command. Far from being totalitarian, economic policy after 1936 suffered from a continuation of Darwinian practices, in which there was a high degree of wasteful competition for raw materials, skilled labour, and foreign exchange between the arms industry, consumer goods, and party projects like Hitler's urban beautification programme, while at the same time high wages in the production goods industries set up inflationary pressures and encouraged a flight from

[36] Birkenfeld, *Georg Thomas*, Chs. 17–19.
[37] Mason, *Arbeiterklasse*, pp. 138–9, 157, 179–88.

the land that endangered the food supply. And the basic reason for this situation was an uneasy feeling in the upper ranks of the NSDAP that the German people, and in particular the German working class, would not tolerate the sacrifices necessary to correct it.

It is not easy to draw an objective balance between what German workers as a class gained and lost as a result of National Socialism or to make any realistic generalizations about their political and psychological attitude towards the regime. The process of *Gleichschaltung* had deprived German workers of rights that they had won only after years of patient effort—their right of political choice, their right to organize and bargain collectively through their own agents—and in the years that followed they sometimes suffered restrictions (which were, to be sure, often laxly administered) upon their freedom of movement and vocational choice. To the older generation, these were infringements of liberty that could not be taken lightly; on younger workers, who had never belonged to a trade union or cast a vote for any party but the NSDAP, these losses had far less psychological impact.

They were, in any case, even for those who felt them most keenly, offset by certain undeniable gains, the chief of which was employment. The number of people without jobs fell from somewhat more than six million at the beginning of 1933 to one million in 1936, and the latter figure was unrealistic because it included structural and seasonal unemployment, as well as unemployment caused by temporary shortages of raw materials. In effect, for the period after 1936 it is accurate to talk about full employment in Germany. Official figures indicate that between August 1937 and August 1939 the number of employed persons rose from 19,660,000 to 21,650,000, while unemployment fell from half a million to 34,000. In the autumn of 1938 the number of employed was at an unprecedented high, despite the fact that almost a million young men were in the armed services; and the Reich Labour Minister calculated that the economy was suffering from a labour deficit of a million workers.[38]

The fact that everyone capable of working and desirous of doing so, with the exception of the Jews, could find employment (and that most of those who suffered disabilities, with the same exception, received support from party agencies like the Winter Relief) is more important than the controverted question about whether wages were higher or lower than in republican times, a question that is of more interest to economists than it would have been to German

[38] Ibid., pp. 56, 59, 104.

workers in 1936. In general, it can be noted that real wages were sustained throughout the pre-war period by norms set by the government that were effective in curbing runaway inflationary tendencies but were not administered so rigorously as to destroy incentives. Skilled labour was well rewarded, and the growing difference between the wages of the skilled and the unskilled encouraged increasing numbers of young workers to enrol in state-supported vocational programme. The wages of the average worker kept pace with the cost of living, despite the fact that 18 per cent of his pay packet was deducted for unemployment, health, and accident insurance, income and poll taxes, and contributions to party relief agencies. The price of cereals and other basic foods tended to rise in the early years of the regime because of bad harvests and administrative miscalculation (although the tightened price regulations of the Four Year Plan alleviated this to some extent), and the cost of clothing was 13 per cent higher in 1937 than it had been in 1928; but there was a decline in the cost of heating and light, and rents were controlled by the state. Since housing construction was by 1937 almost equal to the 1929 level, most people were adequately housed, and, since *per capita* calorie consumption had recovered from its 6 per cent decline in the years 1929–32, they were adequately fed. Indeed, David Schoenbaum has suggested that the trend from margarine to butter and the increased consumption of meat and coffee pointed to an over-all rise in the living standard. [39] The best-paid workers were those in the technologically advanced trades and to a lesser extent in the metal trades, construction, and mining, and their relative affluence contributed to the stimulation of the consumer goods industries and the rise in imports of woollen goods, tobacco, coffee and cocoa, and luxury goods, with resultant pressure upon foreign exchange resources. The number of radio sets, vacuum cleaners, and kitchen appliances being produced and purchased in 1939 was a source of worry to General Thomas but an indication of some improvement in the quality of daily life. [40]

In addition to these undeniable gains, German workers received significant supplementary benefits from the state. The party conducted a systematic and impressively successful campaign to improve working conditions in industrial and commercial plants, with

[39] David Schoenbaum, *Hitler's Social Revolution: Class and Status in Nazi Germany, 1933–39* (New York, 1967), p. 100. See also Gerhard Bry, *Wages in Germany* (Princeton, 1960), pp. 235–9, 245, 263; C. W. Guillebaud, *The Economic Recovery of Germany* (London, 1939), pp. 178, 187, 204; Mason, *Arbeiterklasse*, pp. 62–4, 76–7, 113–14.

[40] Mason, *Arbeiterklasse*, pp. 115–16.

periodic drives designed not only to see that health and safety regulations were enforced, but to encourage some alleviation of the monotony of daily labour at the same task by means of amenities like music and growing plants and special awards for achievement.[41] Where employers were reluctant to yield to these not inexpensive innovations, they were talked around by the trustees of labour and the labour councils that the Law on the Regulation of National Labour of 20 January 1934 had established as features of industrial management, while making sure that they were under close party control.

Perhaps more appreciated than these important but unexciting reforms were the varied recreational opportunities provided by the Strength through Joy (Kraft durch Freude: KdF) programme. The number of paid holidays for the average worker had doubled since the Weimar period, totalling now as much as 12 to 15 days. The party undertook to organize that free time as far as possible by making available any number of sports and cultural programmes and by going into the travel business on a large scale. On its own cruise ships, the KdF organization took thousands of people to the Norwegian fjords and the sunshine of Madeira and Majorca, and there were many less elaborate expeditions within Germany itself. This regulation of leisure time had its ideological purpose, but the trips were so inexpensive (they were subsidized in part by the confiscated assets of the trade unions) as to be within the reach of many German families who had never been able to afford a real holiday before. In 1938 alone, according to official statistics, 180,000 Germans went on cruises, and 10 million—three-fifths of them workers—went on holiday trips of all types.[42] The KdF promised to expand these travel opportunities even further by making it possible for the German worker to own a motor car of his own; and, although this pledge was baulked of fulfilment by the coming of the war, the knowledge, after 1937, that the Volkswagen was in production probably had a positive effect upon the attitude of many workers toward the regime.[43]

It seems likely, indeed, that the NSDAP's attempts to convince the working class that it had its interests at heart were not unavailing. In a country that had always been characterized by a rigid system of social stratification, such things as the abolition of the distinction

[41] On the party's elaborate Beauty of Labour programme, see the excellent article by Anson G. Rabinbach, 'The Aesthetics of Production in the Third Reich', *Journal of Contemporary History*, xi, no. 4 (Oct. 1976), 43–74.

[42] Richard Grunberger, *The 12-Year Reich: A Social History of Nazi Germany, 1933–1945* (New York, 1971), pp. 216–18.

[43] Schoenbaum, *Social Revolution*, p. 105.

between white-collar and blue-collar workers with respect to rights and privileges—a conspicuous feature of both the Law on the Regulation of National Labour and the Hours Law of 1938—were bound to have greater effect than they might have had elsewhere. Nazi propaganda sought to bridge the gap that had yawned between the working class and the rest of society during the Empire and even during the Republic,[44] by emphasizing the essential nobility of hard work and its vital importance to national recovery. In the period before 1936, when the Labour Service was an important factor in overcoming unemployment and was made mandatory for school-leavers and persons without skills vital in other parts of the economy, membership was pictured as a privilege and an honour, and the men who worked at reclaiming the marshes and building dykes against the Baltic Sea and helping to harvest the East Elbian grain were described as soldiers in the service of their country. That the psychological impact of this was not negligible can be seen in Leni Reifenstahl's film of the 1934 Party Convention, *Triumph des Willens*, in which the Labour Service is reviewed by the Führer.

Nor was that of the egalitarian aspects of Nazi economic administration. The Law on the Regulation of National Labour insisted that factories and workshops were to be considered as *Betriebs-gemeinschaften*, in which, to be sure, there was an observation of the principle of leadership (the entrepreneur was the *Betriebsführer* and the workers his *Gefolgschaft*) and a hierarchy of responsibilities, but in which no class distinctions were to be recognized, since to be effective the *Betrieb* must operate as a community of equals.[45] This equality of status was supplemented by equality of opportunity. Ideally, all workers were regarded as being upwardly mobile. They were rewarded for achievement and initiative and could improve their economic position as a result; and they were encouraged to do so by vocational programmes and opportunities to acquire new skills. 'The worker is ever more aware', a Labour Front official boasted in January 1939, 'that he has the opportunity to reach the highest levels in his plant commensurate with his merit.' That this ideal was often violated by favouritism and that the chance of advancement was never open to anyone whose political views were suspect was, of course, true,[46] but there must have been thousands of workers whose ambitions for the future of their families were strong

---

[44] See Roth, *Social Democrats;* and, for a dramatic illustration of the gap, the concluding three chapters of Hans Fallada's novel *Kleiner Mann—was nun?* (1930).

[45] Mason, *Arbeiterklasse*, p. 41.

[46] See Hans Fallada, *Jeder stirbt für sich allein* (1949), Ch. 6.

enough to make them willing to pay the price of the benefits offered them.[47]

In September 1933, speaking before the General Economic Council, Hitler said: 'You have to educate a people to the point where it will march through thick and thin with its government and will feel absolutely united with its government, a people to which you can in a moment give the necessary psychological impulse, which you can stir to action, which you can inspire, which you can sweep away with you. If that isn't possible, then everything you do is impossible, and you have to capitulate.'[48] To what extent had the socio-economic policies of the Nazi regime been able to give that kind of education to the working class?

Whatever the answer to that question—and it would be impossible to answer it with any assurance of being correct—it is clear that influential officials and agencies in the National Socialist movement were sure that the desired pedagogical goal had not been achieved and that one could not, despite all the benefits that had been made available to the working class, count on the kind of loyalty that Hitler had described as necessary.

Among these was the German Labour Front (DAF), which had been established in May 1933, immediately after the liquidation of the trade union movement, with the goal (defined belatedly in November) of 'educating all Germans engaged in the life of labour in National Socialist conviction (*Gesinnung*)'.[49] The chosen leader of the DAF, Robert Ley, had underlined the cost of failing to accomplish this task. Speaking of those who had belonged to the trade unions, Ley said:

. . . Nothing is more dangerous to a state than homeless men. In such circumstances, even a bowling club or a skat club assumes a state-maintaining function. A person goes there in the evening and knows that he belongs. . . . It was of tremendous value that the Labour Front put these twelve million people back in their place in the state. They were, to be sure, in some part, oppositional, and in addition filled with distrust and hatred. But if the state had said: No, you don't count; we want nothing to do with you; perhaps, one day, your children, but, as for you, you're excluded —believe me, that would have been disastrous.[50]

---

[47] See Schoenbaum, *Social Revolution*, pp. 75–80, 110–12.

[48] Mason, *Arbeiterklasse*, p. 100. See *Völkischer Beobachter*, no. 265 (22 Sept. 1933).

[49] Mason, *Arbeiterklasse*, p. 40. The functions of the DAF were elaborated in an order of Hiter's on 24 October 1934. See Jacobsen and Jochmann, *Zur Geschichte des Nationalsozialismus*, Dok. 24 x 1934.

[50] Mason, *Arbeiterklasse*, p. 36.

The defensive—indeed, worried—tone struck here became more pronounced in the years that followed. Like other Nazi hierarchs, Ley devoted much of his energy to attempts to broaden his own sphere of competence, to usurp for the DAF the tasks performed in the governance of plants by the trustees of labour, who were responsible to Franz Seldte, the Minister of Labour, and to win a controlling influence over the Economics Ministry's activity in the field of vocational training.[51] But his rationale for this empire-building was always that the DAF understood the working class better than the other agencies and had a greater appreciation of the limits of its support of the regime.

Indeed, the DAF very quickly abandoned education for advocacy. It never attempted to include in its indoctrination programme any strong intimation that the consolidation and expansion of National Socialism would require discipline and a not inconsiderable degree of sacrifice on the part of the working class. On the contrary, Ley's opposition to Seldte was largely motivated by the fact that the Labour Minister did believe that sacrifice would be required and, like Georg Thomas, was an advocate of a planned economy directed toward all-out armament. But in the period from 1936 onwards, whenever suggestions were made for increased controls over allocation of manpower or over wages and hours, for restraint on the consumer goods industries, or for firm anti-inflationary measures, Ley and the DAF could be counted on to oppose such restraints with the argument that the working class would not tolerate them.

Ley's position in the NSDAP—he and Rudolf Hess between them controlled the organization of the party—made it impossible to overlook his views; but even if he had been of less consequence, he could have counted, in this question, upon the aid of powerful allies. The great majority of the Gauleiter believed, as he did, that the party's support among the working class would become questionable if serious checks were placed upon their economic freedom, and this view was generally shared by Josef Goebbels and the party Press. In the minds of these people there was, of course, no fear of anything resembling a popular revolt. They knew that the formidable power of the SS made that impossible. But there might be sabotage and slow-downs and forms of passive resistance that would be troublesome, and these, it was felt, must be avoided.

Against these arguments the Wehrmacht and Seldte and Darré, who wanted more controls, were powerless. Hitler always put con-

---

[51] Ibid., p. 132.

siderable stock in what his Gauleiter said,[52] and in this case their advice, and Ley's, supported his own inclination to avoid action that might be politically disadvantageous. He was not much interested in economic questions in any case, and was inclined to believe here, as in other questions whose complexity exceeded his grasp, that difficulties can always be resolved by an effort of will. If, as the soldiers said, the armed forces were suffering from shortages of material, there were other ways of repairing that situation than by demanding sacrifices of the German people at the cost of one's popularity. The Führer followed the advice of the leaders of the party and closed his ears to those who insisted that he had to choose between more regulation and inadequate military preparedness. He refused to admit the dilemma and was encouraged to do so by the gains his foreign policy brought him. In March 1939, when German troops occupied what was left of Czechoslovakia, a staff officer wrote:

Considerable amounts of war material of every kind already on their way back to Germany, a colossal increase of strength. So far, a thousand aircraft that can be used in war. The Führer is beaming. . . . Very big stocks of raw materials. . . . Fuel stocks for six weeks. Lots of coal. . . . Lots of money and foreign exchange on hand. . . . The Führer can't wait to get an estimate of the war material we have gained and keeps pressing for it.[53]

The labour regulations of the command economy, therefore, remained half-measures. The measures that would have been necessary to create the kind of total economic mobilization that Thomas wanted—a lower standard of living, longer hours, greater work discipline, restrictions upon changing jobs and on competition for skilled labour, and the like—were never really tried. The Compulsory Labour Service Law of 14 March 1938, which was intended to mobilize unused labour reserves for national tasks, and the Dienstpflichtverordnung of 22 June 1938, which was issued because of the necessity of raising a labour force of 400,000 to build a western line of fortifications, were never applied with full vigour, and most terms of compulsory labour service were of short duration.[54] The Decree on Regulation of Wages of 25 June 1938, intended to restore work discipline and reduce changing of jobs, was watered down in the same way. Until the outbreak of the war, and even afterwards, the

[52] Peter Huttenberger, *Die Gauleiter* (Munich, 1969); Speer, *Inside the Third Reich*, pp. 404 ff.

[53] Elisabeth Wagner (ed.), *Der Generalquartiermeister. Briefe und Tagebuchaufzeichnungen des Generalquartiermeisters des Heeres, General der Artillerie Eduard Wagner* (Munich, 1963), pp. 82–3, 124–5.

[54] Mason, *Arbeiterklasse*, pp. 152–3, 154–7, 726 ff.

working class was permitted to enjoy the economic and social gains it had made without having to pay, or even to know about, their true cost.

IV

In 1933 and 1934 a campaign to enforce the withdrawal of married women from the labour force was one of the measures employed by the Nazis to overcome the economic troubles that they had inherited; in 1939 the government's refusal to order a general conscription of women for work in war industries was an important reason for the continuation of labour shortages and curtailed production. These incidents illustrate the important role of women in the economy of the National Socialist period, but they also throw light upon the ideological presuppositions of the Nazi movement and the way in which they contributed to the most original and daring of the regime's social experiments.

There is no doubt that in its attitudes toward women the National Socialist order was as repressive and reactionary as that of Italian Fascism, while also being more consistent and efficient in implementing its anti-feminism. In the eyes of its ideologues the progress made during the republican period in freeing women from the disabilities and oppression of the Wilhelmine period was anathema, and the emancipated *Berlinerin* of the 1920s, celebrated in the chansons of Walther Mehring and Kurt Tucholsky, represented a threat alike to male supremacy, bourgeois morality, and the future of the race. To them it was unnatural for women to aspire to careers in politics or the professions or to indulge in any activity that removed them from the sphere to which their sex had assigned them. 'Can woman', asked one of the popular purveyors of Nazi thought, 'conceive of anything more beautiful than to sit with her beloved husband in her cosy home and to listen inwardly to the loom of time weaving the weft and warp of motherhood through centuries and millenia?'[55]

The National Socialist party made its position clear as early as 1921 when it excluded women from membership in the party executive, and subsequently when it extended this principle of exclusion down through its political and bureaucratic structures. There were no women among the 107 brown-shirted deputies who stormed into the Reichstag in September 1930, although the other parties could

---

[55] Dr. Kurt Rosten, quoted in Grunberger, *The 12-Year Reich*, p. 278. On Rosten, see also Joachim C. Fest, *Das Gesicht des Dritten Reiches: Profile einer totalitären Herrschaft* (Munich, 1963).

boast of skilled parliamentarians like Clara Zetkin and Toni Sender and Gertrud Bäumer and Maria Luders. After they had conquered the state, the Nazis set about de-feminizing the whole of the public service, as well as the agencies that supplied it with talent. Many married women who were superior civil servants and doctors were dismissed immediately; a decree of the Prussian Ministry of the Interior in April 1934 dismissed all women public employees who could be supported at home; and a purge of the legal profession culminated in 1936 with the denial to women of the right to act as judges, prosecutors, or assessors. The number of women teachers in elementary and secondary schools was reduced; the curricula in girls schools were modified so as to emphasize domestic sciences; and there was a sharp curtailment of admissions of women to universities, only 1,500 of 10,000 eligible candidates being admitted in 1934.

In their approach to the employment of women in other occupations the Nazis were more selective. They did not, of course, try to do anything about the more than four million women who were classified in the census as 'family assistants' and who worked, often for long hours at no pay, on farms or agricultural allotments belonging to their husbands or in family shops or handicrafts. Indeed, they classified these occupations as 'womanly work', admitted their social importance, and even supported them by establishing a Labour Service for girls, at first voluntary but made compulsory in January 1939 for all women under twenty-five, to 'reinforce the farm and household economy, particularly the farm women and the mothers of large families'.[56] Nor did the party attempt to compel women to give up their positions in occupations in which they were wage-earners competing with men, although, in the early years when unemployment was still high, there was strong feeling among the party rank and file that this should be done. It worked instead by pressure and inducement, on the one hand authorizing local authorities to persuade families in which there was double employment (man and wife, or father and daughter) to surrender the woman's job in the interest of social sharing, and on the other, offering interest-free loans averaging 600 R.M. to young women who were willing to withdraw from the labour market and get married.[57]

While these last measures had the temporary effect of helping to

[56] Schoenbaum, *Social Revolution*, p. 183.
[57] Tim Mason, 'Women in Germany, 1925–1940: Family, Welfare and Work', *History Workshop*, Issue i, (spring 1976), 92–3.

alleviate unemployment, they did not in the long run reduce the number of married women working in trade and industry. The rationalization of industry increased the number of jobs they were capable of performing, they were often more adaptable than men, and the fact that they worked at cheaper hourly rates of pay commended them to employers. The number of working women increased from 4·52 million to 5·2 million between 1936 and 1938, the percentage of increase being greater in the production goods industries than in consumer goods. No industry remained closed to them except those in which a high degree of physical strength was required of workers, like mining and metallurgy and the building trades. In the chemical, electrical, and rubber industries, as well as in textile and food industries, women workers were in such demand by 1939 that their wage rates were beginning to increase.[58]

The early campaign to reduce the number of women in the labour force did, however, succeed in fulfilling another purpose. Like other totalitarian regimes, this one was concerned about the birth rate, and one of its objectives was to reverse the sharp decline from 2 million live births per annum at the beginning of the century to 1·3 million in 1925 and 971,000 in 1933. The marriage loans offered to young women who were willing to surrender their jobs was only one of a number of incentives offered to promote fertility. The doubling of income tax allowances for every dependent child in 1934 (and the raising of taxes on unmarried persons), generous maternity benefits, family allowances that increased geometrically with the number of children, allowances for the education and vocational training of older children, health services at reduced rates and cheap railway tickets for large families, and special welfare benefits from agencies like the Winter Relief were available to young couples who might otherwise hesitate, for financial reasons, to start a family. In addition, they received the psychic satisfaction provided on the one hand by party organizations like the Mothers' School, which taught pregnant women how to cope with the problems of maternity, hygiene, and family management, and on the other by never-ending propaganda that stressed the nobility and patriotism of motherhood and bestowed decorations upon particularly fecund examples of it, mothers of eight children, for instance, being awarded the Mother's Cross in gold.[59]

Although population experts may question the causal relationship, National Socialist Germany, alone among countries peo-

[58] Schoenbaum, *Social Revolution*, pp. 184–6.
[59] Mason, 'Women in Germany' 96–101.

pled by whites, succeeded in attaining some increase in fertility. There were 1,200,000 live births in 1934, an increase of 31,000 over the previous year, and the rate of increase was steady thereafter, 1,410,000 births being recorded in 1939. In the period from 1933 to 1939 the number of births per 1,000 women of child-bearing age rose from 58·9 to 84·8.[60]

For those women who hankered after public activity, the party offered what Tim Mason has called an element of surrogate emancipation by encouraging them to organize and indoctrinate other women in associations like the National Socialist Frauenschaften, which came to embrace some 7 million members and engaged in a range of activities from publishing magazines for women to administering educational and cultural programmes. The Nazi Press also sought to demonstrate the compatibility of loyalty to party ideals with prominence in the arts, social service, and other activities and celebrated as models women like the film producer Leni Riefenstahl,[61] the aviatrix Hannah Reitsch, Gertrud Scholz-Klink, mother of four and leader of the Nazi Women's League, Emma Goering, a former actress, and Magda Goebbels, whose interest in fashion encouraged German women to believe that it was not absolutely necessary for good National Socialist women to dress in the unadorned style of the Bund deutscher Mädchen. Any attempt to return to older feminist notions, however, or to be too obtrusive about working for more opportunities for women in the party, was frowned upon, and Sophie Rogge-Börner, who objected to male supervision even of the work of the Frauenschaften, was officially silenced in 1937.[62]

Yet there does not seem to have been much disposition, on the part of women, to object to the official attitude toward them. The evidence points rather in the opposite direction. The frequently made comparison between Nazi anti-feminism and anti-Semitism is not entirely inaccurate—both served to concentrate varied resentments against single targets—but in the former case the majority of the victims do not seem to have felt victimized. The contrast that Hitler made in a speech to the National Socialist Frauenschaften at the 1934 Party Convention between the world of man—the state and the struggle for the community—and 'the world of the woman . . . a smaller world . . . her husband, her family, her children, and her home' was acceptable to a generation of women who had been

[60] Ibid. 102.   [61] See below, Ch. XVIII, p. 656.
[62] Clifford Kirkpatrick, *Nazi Germany: Its Women and Family Life* (Indianapolis, 1938), p. 97.

denied the comforts of that smaller world, and it was strongly approved by influential feminist groups that were connected with the Nationalist party and the Evangelical Church. Goebbels's argument, moreover, that the 'displacement of women from public life occurs solely to restore their essential dignity to them', was persuasive to many middle-class women who were flattered by the cultism that the Nazis developed to celebrate the ideal German wife and mother. For those who were not or were denied these gratifications by material circumstances, the country's economic development under Hitler brought other advantages. With the coming of more affluent times after 1936, the pressures against the employment of women in trade and industry were relaxed, and the opportunities and rewards open to them steadily improved. Paradoxically, the regime that was ideologically reactionary in its approach to women's place in society helped in some ways to improve it.[63]

As for Adolf Hitler, he was, as is well known, not only popular with the great majority of German women but a figure of adulation and veneration, never, in their eyes, responsible or blemished by the crimes of his regime, which they blamed upon his underlings, the object of an uncritical loyalty that remained unshaken until the Third Reich tumbled down around their ears.

V

In his memoirs Albert Speer writes of passing through the Fasanenstraße in Berlin on 10 November 1938, on the morning after the dreadful pogroms of Krystallnacht, during which the Berlin synagogue was razed to the ground, synagogues and Jewish community houses in other towns gutted or badly damaged, over 7,000 Jewish businesses destroyed, nearly a hundred Jews killed, and thousands beaten and intimidated. Speer writes that, although he did not realize it at the time, more had been smashed than glass that night, that Hitler had crossed a Rubicon, that 'something was beginning that would end with the annihilation of one whole group of our nation'.[64]

Speer was a singularly obtuse observer. The origins of the annihi-

---

[63] Mason, 'Women in Germany' 75; Grunberger, *The 12-Year Reich*, p. 276. By 1941 Goebbels was arguing not only that compulsory labour service for women was necessary for the war effort but that it would be useful in 'overcoming an outdated class attitude' among the wealthier classes. See *The Secret Conferences of Dr. Goebbels: The Nazi Propaganda War, 1939–1943*, sel. and ed. Willi A. Boelcke, trans. from the German (East Lansing, Mich., 1965), pp. 119 ff.

[64] Speer, *Inside the Third Reich*, p. 161.

lation of the German Jews were much more remote in time than the events of Krystallnacht. They are to be found in popular reactions to the dislocations that accompanied Germany's belated but headlong rise as an industrial Power in the nineteenth century and in the growth of a virulent form of racist anti-Semitism in the Wilhelmine period, which remained latent until military defeat and economic collapse turned it into a potent rallying-cry for the rightist fanatics and demagogues who led the attack upon the Weimar constitution. The most gifted of these, Adolf Hitler, was also the one most obsessed with hatred and fear of the Jews. As Lucy Dawidowicz has written, 'the Jews inhabited Hitler's mind. He believed that they were the source of all evil, misfortune, and tragedy, the single factor that, like some inexorable law of nature, explained the workings of the universe . . . the demonic hosts whom he had been given a divine mission to destroy.'[65] There is little doubt that Krystallnacht and much worse was in Hitler's mind long before he came to power, and premonitions of the horrors to come were to be found in the anti-Jewish legislation that he authorized immediately after the passage of the Enabling Act in March 1933 had given him the freedom to do as he wished. If his anti-Semitism showed some restraint in the first years, it was not because he had developed doubts about his ultimate purpose, but merely because of concern over foreign reaction to attacks upon the Jews and the possibly crippling economic consequences of too-hasty action.

The wave of anti-Jewish violence that followed Hitler's appointment as Chancellor—window-smashing and plundering forays in Jewish department stores and assaults on Jewish professional men, often by mobs dressed in SA uniforms—outraged foreign opinion and, in the Western democracies, led to discussion of joint reprisals and a not inconsiderable amount of voluntary boycotting of German goods. It was symptomatic of Hitler's belief in a worldwide Jewish conspiracy that he thought that these foreign protests stemmed exclusively from Jews and could be stopped by a general boycott of Jewish business in Germany. 'Perhaps', he told Goebbels on 26 March, 'the foreign Jews will think better of the matter when their racial comrades in Germany begin to get it in the neck.'[66] The boycott was declared at the beginning of April and lasted three days but failed utterly to fulfil its purpose; and the economic experts, with Schacht, the Reichsbank President, in the van, strove to make Hitler

[65] Lucy S. Dawidowicz, *The War against the Jews, 1933–1945* (New York, 1975), p. 21.
[66] Josef Goebbels, *My Part in Germany's Fight* (London, 1935), pp. 269–70.

understand the fragility of Germany's trade and credit balance and what could happen to the country if foreign business men turned their backs upon it. If we can believe his own account, Schacht was particularly outspoken and, after he had become Minister of Economics, kept dinning into Hitler's ears the message that 'the agonizing persecution of Jewish individuals under the direction or with the connivance of party groups, and the failure of state machinery to take any effective countermeasures, causes an ever repeated tightening of the Jewish boycott of German exports; for each incident, even the smallest, is magnified and spread abroad'.[67] Other advisers pointed out that uncontrolled SA attacks upon Jewish shops were bad for all business in the district affected and that outrages in department stores like Wertheim and Tietz in Berlin were resented by people whose shopping habits revolved around these models of efficiency, variety, and economy, to say nothing of the thousands of sales staff whose pay-packets were diminished by constant disruptions.

The last argument was particularly persuasive in the days before full employment had set in, and what had started as a drive to close down Jewish businesses turned into an effort to insist that they continue to operate lest their closing contribute to the prevalent economic distress. In the clothing and retail trades, Jewish firms continued to operate profitably until 1938, and in Berlin and Hamburg, in particular, establishments of known reputation and taste continued to attract their old customers despite their ownership by Jews. In the world of finance, no restrictions were placed upon the activities of Jewish firms in the Berlin Bourse, and until 1937 the banking houses of Mendelssohn, Bleichröder, Arnhold, Dreyfuss, Straus, Warburg, Aufhäuser, and Behrens were still active.[68]

While this modicum of freedom was being granted them, however, German Jews were being systematically stripped of all their other rights. Through the operation of the Law for the Restoration of the Professional Civil Service and supplementary decrees, Hitler deprived them of their positions in the state bureaucracy, the judiciary, the professions, and the universities, [69] while the Law against the Overcrowding of German Schools and Institutions of Higher Learning (25 April) denied their children the right of higher education, and the establishment of the Reich Chamber of Culture

---

[67] Schacht, *Confessions*, pp. 315 f.; Dawidowicz, *War against the Jews*, p. 63.
[68] Schacht, *Confessions*, p. 323. For the experience of a banker in a small town, see Allen, *The Nazi Seizure of Power,* pp. 211–12.
[69] See above, Ch. XVI, pp. 579–80.

(29 September) and the enactment of the Press Law (4 October) laid the basis for their exclusion from the world of arts and letters. To clarify the implementation of these laws, and others like the Law on the Revocation of Naturalization (14 July), which revoked the citizenship of East European Jews and other 'undesirables' who had been naturalized during the Weimar period, a decree of 11 April defined a non-Aryan as anyone descended from non-Aryan, especially Jewish, parents or grandparents; and civil servants had henceforth to prove their Aryan descent by submission of convincing documentation.

Hitler's first significant victories in foreign affairs—his triumph in the Saar plebiscite in January 1935 and his successful repudiation of the arms clauses of the Versailles Treaty in March[70]—touched off a wave of exultation among the party faithful which was reflected in savage new attacks against Jewish property and personal rights. In the summer of 1935 the Tauentsienstraße in Berlin was festooned with placards reading 'Anyone who buys from Jews is a traitor to his people!', and lawns in Munich parks bore signs warning that 'Jews are not wanted here'. New interventions by Schacht and wariness about the possibility of overt anti-Semitism reducing the number of participants and visitors expected for the 1936 Olympic Games in Berlin induced the government to bring these disorders under control; but, as if to reassure his followers that he was making no concessions to international Jewry, Hitler used the occasion of the Party Convention of September 1935 to strip German Jews of their nationality and of any last hope that they might have entertained about the protection of the law. The Reichsbürgergesetz of 15 September made Aryan blood a requirement of citizenship and stipulated that 'only the citizen is the beneficiary of full political rights under the provisions of the laws'. The Law for the Protection of German Blood and German Honour, issued on the same day, began with a preamble in which the Reichstag expressed its collective conviction that 'the purity of German blood is the prerequisite for the continued existence of the German people' and its 'inflexible determination to secure the German nation for all time'. It then forbade marriage between German citizens and Jews and made it, and extra-marital relations between citizens and Jews, punishable by imprisonment.[71]

The Nuremberg Laws of 1935 resembled the action of a primitive

---

[70] See below, Ch. XIX, pp. 683–4.

[71] Jacobsen und Jochmann, *Zur Geschichte des Nationalsozialismus*, Dok. 15 IX 1935. See also Bracher, Sauer, and Schulz, *Machtergreifung*, pp. 286–7.

tribe that casts unpopular members into the outer darkness where they become anyone's prey. It was no coincidence that members of Hitler's government began now to speculate about the most effective ways of despoiling the alien. Once the Olympic Games were out of the way and it was no longer imprudent to launch new anti-Jewish policies, Hitler himself devised a novel method of exacting booty from his hated enemy. In the memorandum of August 1936 he laid down the principle that the Jewish community as a whole should be responsible for any damage done to the German economy by individual Jews and asked that this be enacted as law. Hermann Goering sought to implement this principle in his seizure of Jewish foreign exchange holdings in the spring of 1937 and again after Krystallnacht, but in both cases the yield was disappointing, and the director of the Four Year Plan began to think that a policy of direct expropriation would be more profitable.

He was perhaps persuaded of this by his experiences in Vienna during the anschluss, where he and other Germans were at first impressed by the enthusiasm and thoroughness with which the Austrians gave themselves to the task of looting their Jewish fellow citizens—going about the job, the SS paper *Schwarzer Korps* wrote admiringly, 'with honest joy' and managing 'to do in a fortnight what we have failed to achieve in this slow-moving ponderous north up to this day'.[72] A month later Goering instituted the first of a whole series of expropriation laws. A fundamental Decree regarding the Reporting of Jewish Property (26 April 1938) required all Jews to make a complete reporting of their domestic and foreign property in excess of 5,000 R.M. in value and stipulated that 'the plenipotentiary for the Four Year Plan may take measures to insure that the use of property made subject to reporting will be in keeping with the interests of the German economy'. Aryanization of Jewish businesses began in earnest in June; a month later Jewish physicians were notified that they must liquidate their practices within three months; in September Jewish lawyers were given until 30 November to do the same; and in October Goering announced that it was necessary for the Jews to be completely 'removed from the economy'.[73] The outrages of Krystallnacht, touched off by the murder of a German diplomatic secretary by a Polish Jewish student in Paris on 7 November, followed, as a result of which the Jews were ordered to pay a collective fine of one billion R.M., in addition to the cost of the damages to their own property (which the state collected by con-

[72] Grunberger, *The 12-Year Reich*, p. 507.
[73] Dawidowicz, *War against the Jews*, pp. 96–7.

fiscating their insurance payments). On the same day that Goering levied this exaction, he issued a Decree on Eliminating the Jews from German Economic Life, which excluded Jews from retail stores, mail-order firms, independent crafts, sales, service, and management.[74] In short, by the beginning of 1939 the Jews had been abused and plundered, deprived of their citizenship, and, finally, deprived of their livelihood.

One might ask, at this point, who gained from this forced transfer of property. Goering, as director of the war economy, always insisted that it was not intended to be 'a charitable scheme for incompetent party members', a reference perhaps to the further development of the Austrian situation, where, by the end of 1938, 3,500 party members had become 'commissioners' over seized Jewish properties. The director of the Four Year Plan insisted that Jewish property belonged to the Reich.[75] In reality, however, as the *Frankfurter Zeitung* pointed out in May 1935, the chief beneficiaries had, from the beginning, been the giant enterprises that rounded out and extended their holdings by buying out Jewish firms that were under pressure; and this process continued, in different forms, when Aryanization became official policy in 1938. The expropriations, in short, stimulated the already pronounced tendency towards capital concentration and monopoly. Between 1932 and 1939 the number of German banks decreased from 1,350 to 520, and most of those that were swallowed up were Jewish houses like S. Hirschland of Essen. The acquisition of Jewish property made possible the establishment of important new combines in the textile industry and, in general, benefited already mammoth firms like Otto Wolff, which acquired the Thale iron and steel works, Friedrich Flick, which took over Rawack and Grünfeld Montaninteressen, and Mannesmann, which assumed control of the Wolff–Netter–Jacobi firm and the Hahnsche Werke.[76] The resultant concentration in the iron and steel industry may have aided the armament effort; but it would be difficult to argue that the process of monopoly contributed anything to the retail trade except inflated profits for the monopolists.

VI

In the discussions that eventuated in the Decree on Eliminating the Jews from German Economic Life, Reinhard Heydrich, who was head of the Security Service (SD) in Himmler's SS and whose office had since 1934 had a separate section for Jewish affairs charged with

---

[74] Ibid., p. 103.   [75] Ibid., p. 97.
[76] Neumann, *Behemoth*, pp. 116–20, 275, and notes.

developing a long-range solution of the Jewish question, told Goering that to drive the Jews out of their businesses was at best a half-solution. 'The main problem, namely, to kick the Jew out of Germany, remains.' The formidable security chief suggested that Goering might consider the policy of emigration that his agent Adolf Eichmann had devised in Vienna after the anschluss, a policy that gave Jews a choice between forced labour and detention on the one hand, and leaving the country on the other.

Goering agreed, apparently with the proviso that a way would have to be found to make emigration more profitable for those compelling it; and, in January 1939, a Reich Central Office for Jewish Emigration was established under Heydrich's direction and was charged with working out procedures. But events moved too fast in 1939 to permit the elaboration of this plan, and the coming of war soon made emigration impossible. In any case, Hitler's thinking had already gone beyond Heydrich's solution. On 21 January he spoke in confidence to Chvalkovsky, the Czech Foreign Minister, and said: 'We are going to destroy the Jews. They are not going to get away with what they did on 9 November 1918. The day of reckoning has come.'[77] A week later, in a speech marking the seventh anniversary of his accession to power, he told the Reichstag that, if international Jewry once more plunged the world into war, 'then the consequence will not be the Bolshevization of the world and a resultant victory for the Jews, but, on the contrary, the destruction of the Jewish race in Europe'.[78]

[77] Helmuth Krausnick, 'The Persecution of the Jews', in Buchheim *et al.*, *Anatomy of the SS State* (New York, 1968), p. 44.
[78] Domarus, *Hitler: Reden* ii. 1058.

XVIII
Cultural Decline and Political Resistance

Thickly thronged were the thousands who welcomed Minister Dr. Goebbels with the German Greeting. Fanfares blared; the horns of the State Band struck the festival note. Then, under Peter Raabe's assured baton-wielding, the Philharmonic Orchestra supplied an accompaniment of Beethoven chords for the powerful and direction-setting words that the Fuehrer devoted, in his book *Mein Kampf*, to the relationship between Art and the People. Staatsschauspieler Lothar Müthel spoke them quite simply, with compelling clarity. Then again, music, this time from Pfitzner's 'The German Soul.'

Deutschland, erwache!, the electrifying call rang through the hall. Shouts of *Heil!* greeted Dr. Goebbels once more as he mounted to the podium. The minister began with a historical retrospective and recalled his earlier words about creative freedom, about art that remains free within its own laws of development but is bound to the moral, social, and national principles of the State.

'It is not an expression of the loyalty that the creative artist owes to the State,' the Minister continued, 'when National Socialist demands which find their justification in the militant Movement are scorned and discredited by certain circles. For National Socialism is not only the political and social, but also the cultural conscience of the nation.'

Berliner Lokal-Anzeiger (7 December 1934)

Ein Land ist nicht nur das, was es tut—es ist auch das, was es verträgt, was es duldet.

KURT TUCHOLSKY to ARNOLD ZWEIG (1934)

IN an appallingly frank interview with the foreign Press corps in November Adolf Hitler expressed his distaste for intellectuals. 'Unfortunately,' he added, 'one needs them. Otherwise, one might—I don't know—wipe them out or something. But, unfortunately, one needs them.'[1]

---

[1] Rede Hitlers vor der deutschen Presse 10. November 1938', *Vierteljahrshefte für Zeitgeschichte*, vi, Heft 2 (1958), 188. On the intellectuals and their role in the Third Reich, see Fest, *Gesicht des Dritten Reiches*, pp. 338–55; Bracher, Sauer, and Schulz, *Machtergreifung*, pp. 288–307.

It was the practical politician rather than the baulked artist who was speaking here. The Führer knew that the solid support of the intellectual community was one of the most effective means of reinforcing the ordinary citizen's confidence in his country's government, and that the lack of this resource had been one of the salient weaknesses of the Weimar Republic. From the beginning of his chancellorship he was intent upon winning the loyalty of German artists and writers and scientists, and he had remarkable success. It is true that many of Germany's most distinguished representatives of the mind and spirit went into exile as soon as they were able to do so, and that Germany was consequently deprived of the wisdom and skills of writers like Thomas and Heinrich Mann, and Arnold and Stefan Zweig, and Franz Werfel and Jakob Wassermann, of all of the important masters of the Bauhaus school, of painters like Beckmann, Kokoschka, and Schwitters, of architects like Mies van der Rohe and Marcel Breuer, of musicians like Kurt Weill, of masters of the film like Sternberg and Fritz Lang, and of scholars and teachers whose talents would profit other countries than their own. But in numbers the *émigrés* were not to be compared with the leading figures in every field of intellectual endeavour who hailed the advent of National Socialism and pledged support to its Führer with every evidence of enthusiasm.

I

It is not difficult to account for this positive response. It was the result in many cases of the political naïvety that was the price of the traditional aloofness of German *Dichter* and *Denker* from practical affairs, and of the contradictory longing for community that was often the hidden corollary of this *Innerlichkeit*. It was influenced by a surprisingly pervasive feeling that German culture had become too 'international' during the republican era—a feeling that had led to a noisy secession from the Prussian Academy of Arts in 1931—and a belief that the time had come for the renewal and strengthening of national values and that that was what Hitler meant when he talked about the necessity of a vital connection between *Volk* and culture. It was often the consequence of resentment over a fancied lack of appreciation and of the hope that under National Socialism neglected talent would be recognized and rewarded. It was not unaffected by the admiration of violence and terror and brutality to which many intellectuals are prone. And finally, in all too many cases, it was the result of fear of the consequences of not supporting the regime.

It was this last, most primitive emotion that prompted the deplorable examples of personal betrayal and cowardice that Thomas Mann recorded in his diary in 1933: the successful Berlin architect who, in order to protect his career, admitted that his wife was Jewish but insisted that he had had no intimate relations with her for eight years; and the artists of the Munich satirical journal *Simplicissimus*, who sought to explain away their past loyalty to the Republic and their many wounding anti-Nazi cartoons by maintaining that they had been led astray by one of their number, Theodor Heyne.[2] But no such compulsion explains why men of assured position and reputation like Gerhard Hauptmann and Carl Schmitt and Martin Heidegger and Gottfried Benn turned voluntarily to National Socialism and, in doing so, gave party propagandists an answer to those who claimed that the regime had been repudiated by the country's best minds and most distinguished artists.

One suspects that Hauptmann would have found reasons to support any regime that had come to power in 1933. The lean young radical of the 1890s, whose play *Die Weber* had shocked and agitated audiences, had, over the years, swollen to an imposing establishment figure, proud of his supposed resemblance to Germany's greatest poet, which he tried, in every possible way, to enhance (to the great amusement of Josef Goebbels, who called him a 'trade-union Goethe'), and very fond of the limelight. Hauptmann's political views were always ill defined and inconsistent, and throughout the war years and the Weimar period he had chopped and changed with a ludicrous regularity, always in the end giving a resounding vote of confidence to the policies and parties that were in the ascendancy. His attitude toward National Socialism was in doubt, therefore, only as long as its success was questionable. Once Hitler had consolidated his power, Hauptmann became his warmest admirer, capable of writing, after a speech in which the Führer called Winston Churchill an 'insane drunkard' and referred to the Jews as 'the arsonists of the world', that Hitler was really 'a complete Platonist, therefore a man of ideas, truly human, national, and both European and universal'.

Hitler's triumphs in foreign policy enraptured him—'I feel the event in my blood!', he wrote after the occupation of the Sudetenland—and he never seems to have wondered whether their price in the end might not be ruinous, or, indeed, about the consequences of any other aspect of National Socialist rule. 'I must', he wrote in 1938, 'finally put this sentimental Jewish question completely out of my head. There are more important, loftier German things at stake—and

---

[2] Thomas Mann, *Reden und Aufsätze*, ii. 456.

one feels the grandeur and strength of the organization.' Hans von
Brescius has argued that in all this there was more innocence than
opportunism and that Hauptmann should properly be regarded as
the quintessential example of the seductibility of the bourgeois
mentality.[3] However that may be, this *naïf* was a man of prominence,
and his 'Ich sage, Ja!' to National Socialism before the elections of
March 1933 doubtless influenced the attitude of the kind of people
who take the political opinions of film stars and other celebrities
seriously.

The other three converts to the Nazi cause were more substantial
figures. Carl Schmitt was the most widely read and respected political scientist of his day, a position he owed to his talent for making
striking formulations (it is from him that we have acquired, among
other things, the overworked term 'pluralism') and to the grace and
clarity of his literary style, which made his brand of cheerful
bloody-mindedness seem plausible to people who were worried
about the delinquencies of the democratic system. A modern
Machiavellian, Schmitt wasted no time on moral considerations and
argued that the prerequisite for sound politics was the jettisoning of
the faded rhetoric and the mealy-mouthedness of the liberals. Incapable of accepting force and conflict as the basic realities of the
political process, the liberal theorists had falsified and denatured even
the language of politics, using power as a term of opprobrium and
insisting that conflict could always be avoided by economic concessions or reasoned discussion. They had, moreover, propagated
the pernicious doctrine that the state, seen properly, was nothing but
an association whose life depended upon compromise between
social groups. During the Weimar period this theory had justified the
process that had turned Germany into an incoherent mass of
administrative units, with a Reichstag that was incapable of carrying
out its assigned functions and a government powerless to make
decisions.

Schmitt seems to have sensed that his own unconditionality might
be too strong for the average German; in 1928 he wrote that the
people's need for the appearance of legality was stronger than their
political sense and that they would find it easier to accept the elimination of the constitution if it were effected by means that could be
justified by theory, rather than overthrown by putsch or revolution.
In 1932, as Germany moved into the protracted constitutional crisis
that eventuated in Hitler's accession, Schmitt gave them what he

[3] Hans von Brescius, *Gerhard Hauptmann. Zeitgeschehen und Bewußtsein in unbekannten Selbstzeugnissen* (Bonn, 1976), pp. 295, 327, 329 f., 348.

thought they wanted in an essay entitled *Der Begriff des Politischen*. Here he argued with skilful casuistry that the actual situation creates its own legality, that emergencies obviate normative law, and that 'he is sovereign who makes the decisions regulating the emergency situation'.[4]

This was widely regarded as an indication that Schmitt had been one of the authors of Papen's *coup* in Prussia in July 1932.[5] This was not true, although Schmitt approved of the action and wrote a justification of it in the *Deutsche Juristenzeitung* in August. The fact was that his theory was infinitely adaptable, and he himself was soon using it to explain his immediate support of Hitler, as he did in a speech at the Handelshochschule in January 1933 and again, later in the year, in his inaugural lecture at the University of Cologne. His argument concerning 'the superiority of the existential situation over mere normality' and the legal consequences of that superiority received its final form in another article in the *Deutsche Juristenzeitung* in July 1934 in which he validated Hitler's bloody action against the SA on 30 June by proving to his own satisfaction that the Führer not only made but was his own law.

Martin Heidegger's road to National Socialism is to be accounted for by a tendency toward introspection that he carried to the point of *Weltfremdheit* and a provincialism that lent an archaic, if not a primitive, cast to his general ideas. A philosopher who has been accorded a degree of respect that is possibly excessive (Jean Améry has described him with brisk asperity as 'a thinker in whose family gallery we recognize the portraits of Pascal and Kierkegaard, but who—after all, God was already dead!—succeeded only in bringing off a slick transcendental philosophy of conventional cast'[6]), Heidegger devoted himself to the investigation of the being and existence of the ordinary man and of the basic problems that affect him— Care, Fear, Death. In pursuing this goal, he rejected the conventional language and concepts of philosophy and sought to achieve a kind of existential discourse that would go directly to the heart of the Being of

---

[4] Carl Schmitt, *Der Begriff des Politischen* (Hamburg, 1932). An interesting analysis is to be found in Christian Graf von Krockow, *Die Entscheidung: Eine Untersuchung über Ernst Jünger, Carl Schmitt, Martin Heidegger* (Stuttgart, 1958).

[5] See Heinrich Muth, 'Carl Schmitt in der deutschen Innenpolitik des Sommers 1932', *Historische Zeitschrift*, Beiheft 1 (1971), 75–147.

[6] Jean Améry 'Die Gefahr der Verklärung: Zum Tode Martin Heideggers', *Die Zeit*, 4 June 1976. See also Theodor W. Adorno, *The Jargon of Authenticity*, trans. Knut Tarnowski and Frederick Will (London, 1973), and Robert Minder, *'Hölderlin unter den Deutschen' und andere Aufsätze zur deutschen Literatur* (Frankfurt-on-Main, 1966), pp. 86–153 ('Heidegger und Hebel oder die Sprache von Meßkirch').

Beings (*Das Sein von Seienden*). The result, as shown in his greatest work, *Being and Time*, baffled many readers and led Günter Grass to argue, in his burlesque of Heideggerian jargon in the novel *Hundejahre*, that, between them, Heidegger and the Nazis and the General Staff of the Wehrmacht had debauched the German language and rendered it unintelligible for any useful purpose.[7]

Concerned with the perennial and immutable problems of daily existence, Heidegger repudiated reason and science and technology, which could not, in his view, affect these primal realities, and he ignored history, perhaps because it is concerned as much with change as with continuity. Never breaking out of the narrowness of his native village, Meßkirch, he came to idealize the still life on the land, the diurnal seasonal flow, the fecundity of the fields, the importance of rootedness. He was at once mystic of the soil, irrationalist, and fatalist; and it was, of course, precisely these characteristics that made him respond passionately to National Socialism and, in his notorious inaugural address as Rektor of the University of Freiburg in 1933, to hail Hitler as a leader called by destiny and sanctioned by all the primal forces of the German soul that made the Leader and the led one flesh 'guided by the inexorability of that spiritual mission that the destiny of the German people forcibly impresses upon its history'.[8]

The liaison with the Nazis was not of great duration, but it lasted long enough for Heidegger to be featured prominently at ceremonial gatherings and to make some remarkably effusive declarations of allegiance to the new order, before he fell back on what Adorno has described as his 'defensive technique of withdrawing into eternity'.[9] There is no reason to quarrel with the summary judgement made by Grass's protagonist, Walter Mathern, who, after vainly trying to seize upon the elusive philosopher, says to the dog which had once belonged to Hitler, 'Think it over, dog, but not with reason. . . . He was good for headaches and warded off thought. . . . He and the Other Guy invented each other.'[10]

Between Heidegger's cast of thought and that of Gottfried Benn there were marked similarities, for Benn, a poet whom Edgar Lohner has compared with Eliot in scrupulousness of style, with Pound in scope, with Auden in formal invention and use of the

---

[7] Günter Grass, *Hundejahre* (1963), pp. 414–23.

[8] Martin Heidegger, *Die Selbstbehauptung der deutschen Universität* (Breslau, 1933), p. 5.

[9] Adorno, *Jargon of Authenticity*, p. 93.

[10] Grass, *Hundejahre*, p. 474.

vernacular, and with Wallace Stevens in content,[11] was also given to attacks upon the inadequacy of reason and to a belief that history was meaningless and absurd. But Benn was impelled also by the loneliness and the resentment that characterized many Weimar intellectuals. He insisted on the one hand that the writer could and should do nothing to affect the course of a stupid and criminal world and that his only legitimate activity was to accumulate experience so as to enhance his creativity. On the other hand, he was never as content with the life of aesthetic detachment as he sounded. With the Weimar Republic, to be sure, he wanted no dealings, for he regarded it with loathing, in part because it insisted on collecting taxes from him, although he saw no reason why 'the free professions always have to come forward to finance this beggarly ragamuffin of a state'.[12] Reinforced by a muddle of ideas derived from Nietzche and Spengler, however, he believed that Germany might still be saved, although only by a revolution that would undo that of 1918, by 'a regeneration through the emanation of spontaneous elements'. 'What will save the state', he wrote, 'will be immanent spiritual strength, productive substance from the darkness of the irrational. And this could be the place where art becomes political.'[13]

What this probably meant was that Benn believed that the salvation of Germany would require the coming of a regime that would give appropriate recognition to the intellectual élite. And in 1933 he convinced himself that such a regime had appeared. With an enthusiasm even greater than Heidegger's, Benn called upon his fellow intellectuals to greet this 'historically logical . . . victory of the national idea' and to regard it as 'more than a change of government', indeed 'as a new vision of the birth of man'. Abandoning himself to what he called 'the drunkenness of destiny (Schicksalsrausch)', he detected in the new state an expression of 'the complete identity of power and the spirit, of individuality and collectivity, of freedom and necessity'. The Führer was 'the creative principle'. 'In him are joined responsibility, danger, decision . . . the complete irrationality of the historical will that only now assumes shape through him . . . the terrible menace without which he is not to be conceived, for he comes not as a model but as an exception; he calls himself forth; one can rightly say he is called forth. It is the voice from the burning bush

[11] Cited in J. M. Ritchie, *Gottfried Benn: the Unreconstructed Expressionist* (London, 1972), p. 24.

[12] Gottfried Benn, *Das gezeichnete Ich: Briefe aus den Jahren 1900–1956* (Hamburg, 1962), p. 32.

[13] Gottfried Benn, *Gesammelte Werke* (4 vols., Wiesbaden, 1954), i. 47; iv. 280 ff.

that he follows. . . . [In his victory] we see the elemental, the inevitable, the ever-expanding and comprehending grasp of historical transformation.' 'There seems no doubt to me', Benn added, 'that from this transformation a new man will come forth in Europe, half by mutation, half by breeding: the German man.'[14]

Thomas Mann's son Klaus wrote from Marseilles that those intellectuals who voluntarily supported Hitler were all too often the victims of self-indulgence and lack of intellectual discipline. 'Too strong a sympathy for the irrational', he wrote, 'leads to political reaction if one is not hellishly careful. First, the great gesture against "civilization", a gesture which, as I know, is all too attractive to men of the spirit; then suddenly one has arrived at the cult of violence, and then one is with Adolf Hitler.'[15] This stung Benn, who answered with an angry essay entitled 'To the Literary Emigrés: A Reply'. The substance and language of this tirade—with its grandiloquence about 'a change of direction in history' based on 'a conception of human nature according to which man may or may not be rational but above all is mythical and profound' and its defiant acknowledgement of commitment to the Nazi order 'because it is my people who are making themselves a new destiny'[16]—merely proved that Mann was right. If Schmitt and Heidegger and Benn and others like them had not been so busy repudiating reason and had used it instead, they might have been able to sense what they all discovered with a shock later on: namely, that Hitler had none of the values they imputed to him, that his own cultural horizons were narrow and his respect for writers and artists who transgressed them minimal, and that his objectives in their regard were entirely political. He had not the slightest intention of allowing the development of an élite of intellectuals who would have real influence in the state. Their role was to be purely representative. They were meant to conform and in their conformity to provide the spectacle of a united Nazi intellectual establishment that would impress the German people and perhaps the outside world as well.

II

This was admitted with brutal frankness by the man who became head of the new Ministry of Propaganda and Popular Education in

[14] Ibid. i. 214 ff., 216, 443. See also his radio speech of 24 May 1933, quoted in Manfred Delley, 'Irrtum und Fehltritt Gottfried Benns', in *Die Welt*, 30 May 1963.

[15] Klaus Mann, 'Brief an Gottfried Benn', in his *Prüfungen. Schriften zur Literatur*, ed. Martin Gregor-Dellin, i (Munich, 1968).

[16] Quoted in Ritchie, *Benn*, pp. 92, 94.

March 1933. There could, Josef Goebbels announced, be no dissonance from now on between cultural expression and the political-ideological propaganda of the state; all intellectual life must be put in the same gear. To regulate this cultural *Gleichschaltung*, a law of September 1933 created a Reichskultuskammer, with separate sections for painting and sculpture, literature, music, theatre, film, radio, and Press, to which all 'makers of culture' and all workers in related occupations must belong (with the exception of those with inadequate Aryan credentials, who were specifically excluded). In assuming the presidency of this Chamber of Culture, Goebbels announced sardonically that he was now in a position to give to the intellectuals the protection that they had always said they needed. It was clear from his tone that this service would not be free.

It was characteristic of Hitler's method of operating, however, that he did not give his Propaganda Minister untrammeled control in the cultural field, but balanced the Reich ministry with a new party agency. This was the Office for the Supervision of Ideological Training and Education of the NSDAP, and its chief was Alfred Rosenberg, a man of pronounced views about cultural uniformity, who had since 1929 been waging war against all modern tendencies in art and letters. His Kampfbund für deutsche Kultur, which had been responsible in the years before the *Machtübernahme* for violent disruption of plays and films of which its chief disapproved (the film based on Erich Maria Remarque's novel *Im Westen nichts Neues*, for example), now became the executive arm or cultural SA of the new Party Ideological Office and was the prime source of the book-burnings, and black lists, and 'cleansings' of museums, and destruction of un-German art that were such prominent features of German cultural activity in the years after 1933.

A natural target for both Goebbels and Rosenberg was the prestigious Prussian Academy of Arts, an organization that owed its foundation to Frederick the Great and had since his time been a living pantheon of German intellectual achievement. It was not, however, universally admired, even before 1933. *Völkisch* intellectuals claimed that many of its members represented modernist and internationalist tendencies that were alien to German culture and expressed resentment over the numbers of Jewish members; and after the formation of the Hitler cabinet these antagonists were intent on finding an opportunity to launch a full-scale attack upon it. They found one at the beginning of February when Heinrich Mann, head of the Academy's Literature Section, and Käthe Kollwitz, a member of its Arts Section, signed and published a petition calling upon the Socialist and Communist parties to pool their efforts in the forthcoming March elections for a new Reichstag in order to prevent Germany from 'sinking into barbarism'.[17]

Immediately the Reichskommissar für Kultur in Prussia, Bernhard Rust, informed the Academy's President, Max von Schilling, that unless he took action against the erring members he was prepared to abolish the Academy or, at the very least to close its Literature Section. Schilling seems to have been too intimidated to point out that Mann and Kollwitz were merely exercising rights that were guaranteed by the Weimar constitution, which was still in force. Instead he had a private talk with Kollwitz about the possible consequences to the Academy of her action, and the distinguished artist, without any hesitation, tendered her resignation. He then called a special meeting of the Academy to discuss the matter, during which Mann, who seemed to have an imperfect idea of what it was he had signed and why, followed Kollwitz's example. This did not please all of the members present, however, and the architect Martin Wagner not only objected to what he called unjustified pressure upon Mann but sought a vote by the members to determine whether they approved of the President's tactics. This was blocked by procedural objections raised by Gottfried Benn, and Wagner promptly resigned.

By this time the Kampfbund für deutsche Kultur had entered the affair and was demanding a thorough purge of the Academy's membership. It was in an atmosphere of some tension, therefore, that the Literature Section met on 13 March to choose a new president in succession to Heinrich Mann. The attendance was unusually small, partly because no travel funds had been provided for non-Berlin members, and this may account for the fact that Gottfried Benn was given a majority of the vote. His first action was to propose a resolution placing the Section solidly behind the National Socialist movement. The members were asked to declare their recognition of the changed historical situation, to foreswear all political activity, and to stand ready to fulfil with unwavering loyalty all national tasks assigned to them. After perfunctory discussion this was accepted by voice vote but ran into difficulties when submitted to the full membership for formal approval. To be sure, the majority signed the Benn resolution, but Alfons Paquet, Alfred Döblin, Thomas Mann, and Ricarda Huch resigned their membership rather than do so,

[17] This incident and its consequences for the Academy are described in Hildegard Brenner, *Ende einer bürgerlichen Kunst-Institution: Die politische Formierung der Preussischen Akademie der Künste ab 1933* (Stuttgart, 1972).

while René Schickele, Jakob Wasserman, and Pannwitz refused to accept the resolution, although without resigning.

For Schilling, Benn, and the Secretaries of the Section, Loerke and Amersdorffer, who were actively pushing the resolution, the resignation of Ricarda Huch was particularly embarrassing. Her work as novelist and historian was universally admired, and it was impossible to tar her with either the internationalist or the Jewish brush. Schilling pleaded with her to withdraw her resignation, arguing that the German sentiment and national consciousness that inspired her work required it. Her answer was unequivocal and crushing. 'That a German should feel German,' she wrote,

I should take almost for granted. But there are different opinions about what is German and how German-ness is to be expressed. What the present regime prescribes as national sentiment, is not my German-ness. The centralization, the compulsion, the brutal methods, the defamation of people who think differently, the boastful self-praise I regard as un-German and unhealthy. Possessing a philosophy that varies so radically from that prescribed by the state I find it impossible to remain one of its academicians. You say that the declaration submitted to me by the Academy would not hinder me in the free expression of my opinion. Apart from the fact that 'loyal collaboration in the national cultural tasks assigned in accordance with the Academy's statutes and in the light of the changed historical circumstances' requires an agreement with the government's programme that I do not feel, I would find no journal or newspaper that would print an oppositional view. Therefore, the right to express one's opinions freely remains mired in theory. . . . I herewith declare my resignation from the Academy.[18]

This uncompromising statement had little resonance because it was given no publicity: indeed, Huch's name was not included when the list of those resigning from the Academy was released to the Press. It is possible that the absence of any strong public reaction persuaded the new rulers of Prussia that there was no reason for further restraint. Without waiting any longer for undesirable members to resign, they resorted to dismissal by ministerial decree, so that by the end of the year half of the 1932 membership of the Literature Section had been expelled. In the Academy's other sections (Creative Arts and Music) the results were much the same, although they took somewhat longer to effect. The vacated seats were filled by artists and writers known for their enthusiastic support of the new regime, who soon discovered, however, that the honour was an empty one, since the Academy's prestige had departed with those who had been forced out. The Academy had no real function in the Nazi state in any case. It lived in the shadow of the

[18] Ibid., p. 65.

Reichskultuskammer, justifying its existence by passing resolutions that supported the policy of the regime whenever the government thought that these might impress foreign opinion, as it did when Hitler ended German membership in the League of Nations in October 1933.

Heinrich Heine had once made fun of the German passion for endless debate over the characteristics of true Germanness.[19] He would have found little to laugh at in the years after 1933, when the charge of being un-German was sufficient to end the productive career of hundreds of Germany's writers and artists. The attack upon the Prussian Academy was only one of many 'actions' against supposed enemies of the German spirit and cultural Bolsheviks. These took the form of book-burnings (like the latter-day Wartburg ceremony in front of the Kaiser Wilhelm University in Berlin, during which the works of Marx, Heine, Freud, Remarque, Kästner, Tucholsky, and dozens of other distinguished writers were gleefully committed to the flames), library purges, emasculations of museums and galleries, disruption of exhibitions and concerts, campaigns against publishers and producers, black lists and dismissals. The pictorial arts were singled out for special attention, the National Socialist *Deutsche Korrespondenz* demanding in 1933 that all work showing foreign influence be removed from museums and all directors who were not motivated by a true German spirit be dismissed. The first 'exhibitions of shameful art (*Schandausstellungen*)' were held in the same year, and featured violent attacks upon the work of Liebermann, Slevogt, Corinth, Marées, and Münch as being degenerate and subversive of German values. There was some initial resistance to this sort of action, particularly when it broadened into a comprehensive campaign against all modern tendencies in art; and the Berlin branch of the National Socialist Deutscher Studentenbund came to the defence of the Expressionist artists Schmidt-Rottluff, Barlach, and Nolde, hailing them as representatives of a new and specifically German artistic movement. But Hitler's own views on art were too primitive to tolerate this deviation; he detested Expressionism and, indeed, any form of painting that was not realistic in the most banal sense, and once declared that 'so-called "modern Art" [was] the outcome of an impudent and unashamed arrogance or of a simply shocking lack of skill . . . which might have been produced by untalented children of from eight to ten years old'.[20] Art, he declared

---

[19] 'Heinrich Heine über Ludwig Börne' (1840), Bk. iv, in Heine, *Werke*, ed. Martin Greiner (2 vols., Cologne, 1962), ii. 752 f.

[20] George L. Mosse (ed.), *Nazi Culture* (New York, 1966), p. 16.

in 1935, must be comprehensible to the people, and must appeal to its noblest instincts and make it proud of its country and anxious to serve it.

This left no place for Schmidt-Rottluff's distorted figures and violent pigments or Barlach's enigmatic *Geistkämpfer*; nor did Nolde's *Blut und Boden* philosophy, or even his party membership, win approval for his style of painting. Confident that they were expressing the Führer's will, Goebbels, Rosenberg, and many self-appointed local Nazi censors opened a full-scale attack upon modern art, which they equated with cultural anarchy. Before long a nation-wide purge of museums and galleries was under way, and this had its symbolic culmination in the notorious exhibition of degenerate art that was mounted in Munich in 1937 and later transported to Berlin. This elaborate, if decidedly illogical, attempt to show the German people what National Socialism was supposed to be saving them from was made possible by the plundering of twenty-five museums, the Berlin National Gallery alone suffering the loss of paintings valued at more than a million marks. Throughout Germany thousands of paintings and graphics were confiscated, some of which were sold, some appropriated by party dignitaries (like Hermann Goering, an impassioned collector who had already established the practice of borrowing paintings from museums in order to embellish his dinner-parties but was not always scrupulous about returning them[21]), and some deliberately destroyed. In 1939, 1,004 paintings and 3,825 drawings were burned publicly in Berlin's Main Fire Station.[22]

German musicians received much the same kind of treatment. Rosenberg's Kampfbund and Goebbels's Reichsmusikkammer (a branch of the Reichskultuskammer) vied with each other in efforts to liberate German music from Jewish and foreign influence and to imbue the country's leading musical institutions with National Socialist principles. The Berlin Hochschule für Musik and other prestigious academies were soon under the direction of their agents, as were leading organs of musical criticism, and the climate for modern music became distinctly uncongenial. While Wagner's music was venerated in the Third Reich, his kind of imagination and adventurousness was frowned on, and anything that was more daring than Bruckner or Pfitzner was attacked as 'futuristic depravity', a term of opprobrium that was much used by Paul Graener,

---

[21] *BD* 2nd Ser. xii. 688–90 (Sir Eric Phipps on a dinner-party given by Goering).
[22] Franz Roh, *German Art in the Twentieth Century: Painting, Sculpture, and Architecture* (London, 1968), p. 152.

vice-president of the Reichsmusikkammer after 1933. These self-appointed guardians of German cultural purity tolerated the music of Richard Strauss largely, one supposes, because his world reputation would have made it embarrassing to attack him openly and also because he was a vain man who had no objection to gracing Nazi cultural festivals with his presence. But Strauss was always an object of suspicion to the Nazi censors; his collaboration with Stefan Zweig in the writing of the comic opera *Die schweigsame Frau*, which was produced in 1934, infuriated them; and ten years later, when he attained the age of eighty, Martin Bormann decreed that this event was not to be celebrated in the Nazi Press, since Strauss had 'failed seriously in his duty toward the requirements of the *Volksgemeinschaft*'.[23]

Paul Hindemith, a composer of remarkable originality and scope, received harsher treatment. In 1934 the Reichsmusikkammer refused to allow performances of his new opera *Mathis der Maler*, presumably because of a scene that appeared to be a criticism of the Nazi book-burnings, and he was subsequently attacked for collaborating with Jewish musicians and for having written an immoral comic work (*Neues vom Tag*, 1929) in which the heroine was shown in a bath-tub. The conductor Furtwängler ridiculed these charges in a spirited defence of Hindemith that appeared in the *Deutsche Allgemeine Zeitung*, but, when he was accused of making a demonstration against the regime, he capitulated swiftly and apologized personally to Goebbels. He was, none the less, *pour encourager les autres*, deprived of his leadership of the Philharmonic Orchestra and his post as director of the State Opera. As for Hindemith, despite his services as a teacher of young musicians, he became a pariah in his own country. In 1938, in an 'Exhibition of Degenerate Music', his works were lumped together with those of Mahler, Krenek, and Weill and described, in the Exhibition's catalogue, as 'the reflection of a veritable witches' sabbath and of the most frivolous spiritual-artistic Bolshevism . . . of the triumph of subhumanity, arrogant Jewish insolence, and complete spiritual cretinization. Jewish music and German music are poles apart... Atonality signifies degeneration.'[24]

Most of what the Nazis encouraged as a replacement for all that

[23] Joseph Wulf, *Musik im Dritten Reich: Eine Dokumentation* (Gutersloh, 1963), pp. 180–2.
[24] Ibid., pp. 17, 88, 92, 337 ff. See also Michael Meyer, 'The Nazi Musicologist as Myth Maker in the Third Reich', *Journal of Contemporary History*, x, no. 4 (Oct. 1975), 649–65. Jazz was attacked as 'a barbarian invasion supported by the Jews', but was so popular that it survived, despite the difficulties described in the memoirs of the band-leader Teddy Stauffer.

they had silenced, expelled, or destroyed was of a quality so inferior as to be embarrassing. What passed for Nazi art, when it was not a mere disguise for propaganda, was a reflection of the aesthetic ideals of the culturally retarded lower middle class, full of moral attitudinizing and mock heroics and sentimentality and emphasis upon the German soul and the sacredness of the soil. The educated reading public was forced to fill shelves emptied by the book-burnings with the works of second-rate writers and party hacks like Beumelburg, Blunck, Johst, Kolbenheyer, Grimm, and Borries von Münchhausen—an intellectual deprivation that was serious and protracted, for as late as the 1960s German university students were still ignorant of the works of Heinrich Mann, Alfred Döblin, and Stefan Zweig, to say nothing of the Expressionist activists of the 1920s, a reading of whose works might have given more sensible direction to their own rebelliousness.

There was little that the Nazis could do about the literary legacy of the past, although they did, to be sure, prevent the appearance of new editions of Heinrich Heine. The great satirist was a source of continual exasperation to them, for many of his poems were firmly imbedded in the popular consciousness, and it was almost impossible to go to a concert of *Lieder* without hearing his verse sung. Attempts were made to cope with this by attributing the poem 'Die Lorelei', which could hardly be excluded from anthologies of verse, to *Anon (Dichter unbekannt)*, and by encouraging the writing of new words for the settings made of Heine's lyrics by Schubert and Schumann. This latter enterprise was so idiotic that the poet Borries von Münchhausen wrote an article in 1936 objecting to it, although he ended it prudently with the statement: 'Ich nenne Heinrich Heine einen Schweinehund.'[25] Nazi authorities in Heine's birthplace Düsseldorf avenged themselves on the poet by confiscating funds collected before 1933 for a Heine memorial and building a new town hall with them. (This was not the only example of petty maliciousness against the dead. The tearing-down of the statue of the composer Mendelssohn-Bartholdy in Leipzig led to the resignation of the city's lord mayor, Carl Goerdeler, and may have been the impulse that turned his mind to active resistance to the regime.)

When it was a matter of giving public performances of the works of dead authors, the Nazi censors showed considerable circumspection. Goethe and Shakespeare were regarded as safe authors; Schiller, on the contrary, was always a suspicious commodity,

[25] See Jeffrey L. Sammons, *Heinrich Heine, the Elusive Poet* (New Haven, 1969), p. 372 n.

excessively political and too intent upon the seductions and misuse of power. *Fiesco* and *Don Carlos* were declared to be 'undesirable' and performances of *Wilhelm Tell* were, after some hesitation, forbidden. Hebbel and Kleist escaped this fate, although producers received orders to make revisions in the texts of plays by the latter. The censors were, to be sure, not always consistent. Nazi policy toward the theatre suffered from some incoherence because the authority of Goebbels's Reich Theatre Chamber, while theoretically all-embracing, did not in practice extend to the Prussian State Theatre, where Goering allowed his favourite, the actor-producer Gustav Gründgens, a degree of freedom that others did not possess. Since, moreover, the theatre did not interest Goebbels greatly, plays of which he disapproved often appeared on the boards anyway. After the anschluss Baldur von Schirach for a time exercised considerable influence over production schedules in the Burgtheater and in 1943 he revived Ibsen's *Ghosts*, although it had been removed from the stage in Weimar two years earlier as a decadent play.[26]

Theatre-goers whose tastes ran to the modern theatre had a difficult time, for almost everything written during the Republic was forbidden, and most of what was written after 1933 should have been. Audiences had to choose between glorifications of the Nazi movement, like Johst's *Schlageter* (1933), and comedies of village life that were filled with rustic humour and intimations that the chief business of men should be procreation. The play that was awarded the Critics' Prize in Berlin in 1934 and was still running a year later, was a *Bauernkomödie* called *Krach um Iolanthe* in which the protagonist was a pig. It was said to be Hitler's favourite play, an opinion which in any country with critical standards would have been regarded as an example of lese-majesty. Goebbels was frank enough to regard the state of the theatre in his time with disgust and is reported to have said, 'To have *only* classics on the one hand and harmless trivialities on the other is not enough for our time.'[27]

After the purges that have been described above, the state of the visual arts was as deplorable as that of the theatre. The best that can be said of the kind of painting and sculpture that was honoured by the Nazi movement was that it was no worse than the socialist realism that reigned in the Soviet Union. The approved subjects were hyperactive, and mostly uniformed, young people, a specialty

[26] Heiber, *Goebbels*, pp. 188 f.
[27] Ibid., p. 190 On the literary scene in general, see Horst Denkler and Karl Prümm (eds.), *Die deutsche Literatur im Dritten Reich: Themen, Tradition, Wirkungen* (Stuttgart, 1976).

of the mural painter Jürgen Wegener; idealized SA or SS men; and naked but carefully unaphrodisiac Teutonic women in awkward symbolic poses, like Adolf Ziegler's *The Four Elements* which Hitler placed over his mantel in his room in the Führer's House in Munich, and the same artist's *Judgement of Paris*, in which the contenders look like young matrons visiting a couturier who is too embarrassed to take their measurements. The official sculptors of the regime were Arnold Breker and Josef Thorak, classical realists who addressed themselves to such themes as 'The Party', 'Comradeship', 'Readiness', 'Sacrifice', and 'Labour' and covered the façades and courts of the new public buildings and the bridges crossing the new autobahnen with over-life-sized and heavily muscled heroes engaged in energetic group action.[28]

It was Hitler's fondest hope that the achievements of National Socialism would find expression in masterpieces of architecture that would impress posterity and serve as a lasting memorial, as 'the word in stone'.[29] He fancied himself as an architect and undoubtedly possessed imagination and a sense of spatial relationships, but these gifts were vitiated by his desire to make all his arches taller and his domes larger than any similar structures in existence. It is safe to say that the architectural masterpieces of his regime were those in which his tendency to excess was controlled by the demands of utility (like the autobahn) and those transient combinations of colonnade, light, and human mass that were dramatic high points of the annual party conferences at Nuremberg. The public buildings built after 1933 imitated classical forms without embodying the grace of their models. Indeed, most of the creations of Hitler's architects Paul Ludwig Troost and Albert Speer, and all of those that were planned by Hitler and Speer for the post-war reconstruction of Berlin, convey a sense of power unenlightened by the spirit. They do nothing to lift the heart; on the contrary, they give the impression of a brutal, menacing heaviness, which was, of course, not inappropriate, considering the system that produced them.

In one field of art the Nazi contribution was not inconsiderable, and that was the film. Goebbels was convinced, as he said in 1933, that 'films constitute one of the most modern and scientific means of influencing the masses. Therefore, a government must not neglect them.' He created a Film Office in July 1933, which was later

[28] See the illustrations in Mosse, *Nazi Culture*, esp. Pls. I, IV, VI, VII, and in Hildegard Brenner, *Die Kunstpolitik des Nationalsozialismus* (Hamburg, 1963), after p. 160.
[29] See Robert R. Taylor, *The Word in Stone: The Architecture of National Socialism* (Berkeley, 1974); Speer, *Inside the Third Reich*, Ch. 5.

transformed into a branch of the Reichskultuskammer, and he maintained a special film section in the Propaganda Ministry as well; and the nationalization of four major studios—UFA, Terra, Tobis, and Bavaria—placed the greater part of the German market in his hands and supplied the means for actualizing the ideas generated by his staff.

Goebbels showed remarkable restraint in the use of this power. He was aware that to most people films were a form of escapism, the value of which, to them and to the regime, he recognized; and he sensed that the insertion of too much propaganda into cinema programmes would be counter-productive. He permitted the film companies, therefore, to do pretty much what they had always done, and he made it easier for them to do so, by protecting popular stars from political or racist attacks by zealous party officials. Of the 1,097 feature films made in Germany between 1933 and 1945, only 96 were initiated by the Ministry of Propaganda, and Goebbels was careful to see that these were of such high quality that they would not be shrugged aside by the public as mere propaganda.

He was not unsuccessful in this, and in the best of the films he sponsored students of the cinema find more to admire than the skilfulness of the political argument. The first of his successes was a hymn to youth, martyrdom, and the swastika called *Hitlerjunge Quex* (1933), directed by Hans Steinhoff, the story of a frail youngster from a proletarian family who is involved in the Communist youth movement but longs to become a member of the Hitlerjugend, a dream that comes true but ends in his death, when he is stabbed while distributing pamphlets in a Communist neighbourhood. The strong story-line, the inspired camera work of Konstantin Tschet, and effective use of musical themes, especially the song of the Hitlerjugend—

> Our flag is fluttering before us.
> One after another we march into the future.
> We march for Hitler through night and through need
> With the flag of youth for freedom and bread
> And the flag leads us into eternity
> Yes, the flag means more than death—

made this a film that deserved the popularity it received. Other notable films that Goebbels helped inspire were *Der Herrscher* (1937), directed by Veit Harlan and featuring Emil Jannings as an enlightened industrialist who gives his wealth to the *Volksgemeinschaft*, which will produce the leaders of the future; Harlan's *Jud Süss* (1940) with Werner Krauss and Ferdinand Marian, an anti-

Semitic film that was shown on Himmler's orders to all police and SS units; Wolfgang Liebeneiner's *Ich klage an* (1941), a skilful and moving plea for euthanasia; Gustav Ucicky's *Heimkehr* (1941), with Paula Wessely, a film about supposed Polish atrocities against their German minority; and Goebbels's attempt to make a film that would be compared with Eisenstein's *Battleship Potemkin*, a slashing attack upon the British treatment of the Boer people before and after the war in South Africa entitled *Ohm Krüger* (1941), directed by Hans Steinhoff, and featuring Jannings as Krüger, Hedwig Wangel as Queen Victoria, and Gründgens as Joseph Chamberlain. The films about Frederick the Great starring Otto Gebühr—Johannes Meyer's *Fridericus* (1936) and Harlan's *Der grosse König* (1942)—and Liebeneiner's two films on Bismarck—*Bismarck* (1940) and *Die Entlassung* (1942), with Paul Hartmann as the Chancellor—should also be mentioned, because in addition to being well made and interesting, they were skilful arguments for the principle of leadership and, by extension, for the legitimacy of Adolf Hitler's dictatorship.[30]

Hitler was also the hero of the two Nazi films that are best known outside Germany, and most admired for their technical qualities, and it is interesting to note that he, rather than Goebbels, inspired them. These were *Triumph des Willens* (1935) and *Olympia* (1937), directed by Leni Riefenstahl, a former dancer and actress who, during the twenties, starred in a number of romantic mountain films directed by Arnold Fanck, and who then turned to directing and, in collaboration with Bela Belázs, made a film in 1932 called *Das blaue Licht* which Hitler, an inveterate film-goer, saw and admired. In 1934 he called her to him and asked her to make a film about the Nazi movement, giving her as the title *Triumph des Willens*.[31] With thirty cameras and staff of 120 technicians Riefenstahl went to Nuremberg to film the 1934 Party Convention; but, as Kracauer has pointed out, the film that resulted can hardly be described as a record of something that happened, for the preparations for the convention were co-ordinated with the preparations for the camera work. The product was a transformation of reality, in which the marching columns and the cheering onlookers and the forest of flags and the fanfares of

---

[30] See, *inter alia*, Leif Furhammar and Folke Isaksson, *Politics and Film*, trans. Kersti French (London, 1971); Erwin Leiser, *Deutschland erwache! Propaganda im Film des Dritten Reiches* (Hamburg, 1968); Kracauer, *Caligari to Hitler*, pp. 275 ff. Interesting also is Karsten Witte, 'Die Filmkomödie im Dritten Reich', in Denkler and Prümm (eds.), *Literatur*, pp. 347–65.

[31] Furhammar and Isaksson, *Politics and Film*, p. 110.

trumpets and the elaborate ceremonies and even the spires and gabled roofs of Nuremberg were subordinated to the director's propaganda purpose.[32] But that purpose was achieved in a film of undoubted beauty and force. It is easy to understand why party members whose loyalty to the movement had been shaken by the events of June 1934 would find in this film reassurance and a new faith in the invincible power of National Socialism. Riefenstahl's second film for Hitler showed the same skilful combination of technical, aesthetic, and political gifts. Its subject was the Olympic Games of 1936 which were held in Berlin; and these—transformed by Riefenstahl's directorial vision—became a tribute to youth and to sport and to the competitive instinct but also a documentation of the recovery of Germany's position in the world under the leadership of Adolf Hitler.

III

If, with the exception of the film, the state of the arts in Germany after 1933 was unhappy, there was no likelihood of this being corrected as a result of openly expressed dissatisfaction and criticism. The agencies which in a free society have usually been the most effective sources of criticism and demand for reform—the Press and the universities—acquiesced in the Nazi destruction of German culture.

In the case of the Press, one can believe that this was done reluctantly. But the liberties that had been secured by the Press Law of 1874 and by Article 118 of the Weimar constitution disappeared with the promulgation of the February decrees of 1933, and in the months that followed the party assured itself of a compliant Press by extending three kinds of controls over newspapers and journals. In June 1933 the Union of German Newspaper Publishers, which had existed since 1894, fell victim to the process of *Gleichschaltung*, and Max Amann, the head of the Eher Verlag and director of the Zentralverlag der NSDAP, which published the *Völkischer Beobachter* and other party papers, became chairman of its board and, through his right-hand man Rolf Rienhardt, began to show an alarming interest in the personal correspondence and affairs of its members. Amann also became president of the Reichspressekammer established in September 1933, and two months later, when a decree elaborating the functions of that body made it mandatory for anyone connected with publishing to belong to the Chamber, he received

[32] Kracauer, *Caligari to Hitler*, p. 301.

the authority to define the requirements for membership and to exclude or expel publishers, and close their presses down without compensation, when they did not meet them. He made unabashed use of this power to eliminate competitors of the party Press, expelling or refusing membership to 1,473 publishers in the first year of his office and, by 1936, eliminating four-fifths of the German Press in what has been called 'the largest confiscation of private property that occurred under the Third Reich'.[33]

Meanwhile the passage of the so-called Reichsschriftstellergesetz of October 1933 fastened even more intimate bonds upon the purveyors of news to the German public. This law drew a distinction between publishers, who were responsible for the financial operations of their journals, and the editors and writers who supplied what was printed in them, and made the latter responsible to the state for the opinions they expressed. Even if the 'Aryan Paragraphs' had not simultaneously been silencing the voices of many of the most gifted and outspoken of the country's journalists, the 'Editor's Law' would have been enough to make freedom of expression all but impossible, for the penalties of speaking one's own mind were fearful and immediate.

These two sets of controls were supplemented by a third: the government's monopoly of news and its dictation of the way in which it was presented to the public. One of the first actions of the government after Hitler became Chancellor was to take over the Wolff Telegraph Agency, the official news service, and Alfred Hugenberg's Telegraph Union, and to combine them into the Deutsches Nachrichtenbüro (DNB) which henceforth served as a filter through which all foreign news passed before it reached the Press. Domestic news was, of course, controlled in the same manner, and the Reich Press Chief, Otto Dietrich, decided what and how much was to be released to the Press corps. Reporters had to cope not only with the regulations that Dietrich imposed but with a further set of 'directions' and 'speech regulations' issued by the Government Press Division, which Goebbels had taken over in July 1933. These not only prescribed themes that should receive special attention by the Press but went to extreme and often ludicrous lengths in monitoring the contents of journals, prohibiting any number of miscellaneous topics for reasons that were either obscure or illogical (Scottish jokes, for example), and declaring that certain formulations were undesirable from an ideological point of view.

---

[33] Hale, *Captive Press*, p. 218.

None of Germany's great newspapers was able to survive the impact of these regulations without making concessions that betrayed the principles that had sustained it in the past. The editors of Ullstein's *Vossische Zeitung* realized that this would be so as early as March 1933, and this distinguished journal, which had championed liberal causes since the eighteenth century, shut down its presses. The leading journal in the Mosse newspaper empire, the *Berliner Tageblatt*, which had been as staunch in its defence of the Republic as 'Auntie Voss', had, in contrast, a lingering death. A clairvoyant leading article of 31 January 1933, in which Theodor Wolff predicted that under the new government 'everything possible [would be done] to intimidate opponents and silence them, to satisfy the SA and SS, and to give a deserved award to the faithful ones who have waited for this opportunity' was not forgotten by the Nazi leaders, and six weeks later the *BT* was closed under authority of the decree of 28 February and reopened only after a shake-up which placed editorial control of the paper in the hands of a pro-Nazi staff member named Karl Vetter and an SA man named Ohst. Under their amateurish direction, which was exercised from an office in the Resi Bar, a dance-hall with table telephones in the Hasenheide, the newspaper became an undistinguished party sheet with a demoralized staff. It was restored to a semblance of life because of Josef Goebbels's admiration for what it had been under Theodor Wolff, and because he needed a newspaper that would command some respect abroad. The Propaganda Minister persuaded Paul Scheffer, a distinguished foreign correspondent who had been head of the *BT*'s Moscow bureau, to undertake the direction of the newspaper, and Scheffer accepted in the hope that Goebbels's need would exempt him from the restrictions that had crippled other journals. The experiment was not a success, and after two and a half years Scheffer asked to be released of his duties and returned to foreign reporting, first in the Far East, and later as the *BT*'s correspondent in Washington. The *BT*'s independence—like that of the *Frankfurter Zeitung*, which Goebbels also used as a channel to the outside world—was largely appearance. The measured objectivity of its leading articles could not disguise the fact that it always argued the Nazi Government's case. If it always saw two sides to any given question, it was only, in matters of national concern at least, to make the point that Hitler's was the right one.[34]

---

[34] See Peter de Mendelssohn, *Zeitungsstadt Berlin: Menschen und Mächte in der Geschichte der deutschen Presse* (Berlin, 1959), pp. 337 ff., 356 ff.; Margret Boveri, *Wir lügen alle: Eine Hauptstadtzeitung unter Hitler* (Freiburg im Breisgau, 1965), pp. 66 ff., 105 ff., 160 ff.

It was not to be expected that editorial boards that were aware of the penalties that rewarded the critical stance would invite trouble by attacking artistic theories or standards of which the party or important members of the party approved. A few brave souls tried to do something by indirection. Gert H. Theunissen, for example, the art critic of the *Kölnische Zeitung*, expressed his disgust of the degeneration of standards in the pictorial arts by writing over-enthusiastic reviews of exhibitions sponsored by the Führer in the House of German Art, in which he carefully recorded the number of canvases hung, listed the themes that were most popular, bestowed excessive praise upon those artists who devoted their talents to the German family, the German landscape, the German joy in labour, and so forth, professed awe at the grandiosity of Thorak's sculptures and Elke Eber's superb ability to render the exact appearance of chinstraps in portraits of SA men, and laboriously explained the symbolism of works like Ziegler's *Four Elements*. This method of exposing the banality of Nazi art deserves our attention and admiration; but it was not widely copied, and its practical results were negligible.[35]

The universities were in no better position than the Press to make a stand against the decline of cultural standards. Their normal state after January 1933 was one of demoralization. The euphoria with which the older members of the professoriate had greeted the destruction of the Republic, which they had always detested, was quickly replaced by lively apprehension when it became clear that the new leaders of the Reich did not intend to respect their pretensions and their traditional freedoms. Hitler's ingrained distrust of all trained intellectuals made him indifferent even to the importance of the university as a breeding-place for the technicians that an industrial society needs if it is to function effectively; and for the university's other functions—its promotion of basic research and its work in the humanistic disciplines—he had nothing but contempt. He made no effort, therefore, to give the Reich Minister of Education, Bernhard Rust, the authority to develop a consistent policy toward the universities, which were left to the mercies of the Gauleiter, whose approach to higher education was often even more primitive than that of their Führer.

The universities never recovered from the expulsion of Jews from their faculties and from the many voluntary resignations of scholars who realized in 1933 that serious work would be impossible under

---

[35] For two of Theunissen's reviews from 1937 and 1938, see 'Ein Kunsthistoriker stellt sich', *Die Zeit* (10 May 1963), 12–13.

the new dispensation. Virtually all of the scientists of the Max Planck institutes left their positions, an immeasurable loss to German science, and other disciplines suffered in proportion. In the field of history, for instance, the most promising of those scholars in mid-career—Hajo Holborn, Hans Rothfels, Dietrich Gerhard, Theodor Ernst Mommsen, Felix Gilbert, Hans Kohn—were to give American university students the benefit of their intellectual energy and imagination, while the chairs that they might have filled with distinction in their own country fell to second-raters like K. A. von Müller, whose talent was limited to brilliantly crafted biographical essays but who commended himself to the Nazis by his idealization of youth and his conviction that 1933 was a turning-point in history that marked the victory of young Germany over the forces of decadence and dissolution. Goering and Hess had sat in Müller's seminars in 1919, and Walter Frank, head of the new Reichsinstitut für die Geschichte des Neuen Deutschlands, was his doctoral student. Thanks to these connections Müller became Meinecke's successor as editor of the *Historische Zeitschrift* in 1935 and celebrated his elevation with a gush of that inflated prose, always richer in quotation than in meaning, that became the approved Nazi ceremonial style: 'German historical scholarship does not come with empty hands to the new German state and its youth. . . . The legacy that the new younger generation inherits from it is one that bears an obligation, and it inherits it, in this new and profoundly transformed time, in order by winning it to possess it.'[36]

Less gifted men than Müller made their way to secure university positions by a combination of byzantinism and intrigue, denouncing their older colleagues for lack of political orthodoxy or zeal for the new political order. How important a role this played in transforming respected academic institutions into 'brown universities' is shown by the fact that a ministerial survey conducted in 1938 revealed that 45 per cent of the established positions in German universities had changed hands within the past five years.[37]

Universities that were being systematically deprived of their most gifted scholars could neither protest against, nor offer solutions for, the decline of cultural standards under the Nazis, for they were themselves part of that problem. This was doubly true because, in the years after 1933, they lost control of the policy of admissions,

[36] Heinz Gollwitzer, 'Karl Alexander von Müller 1882–1964: Ein Nachruf', *Historische Zeitschrift*, 205 (1967), 295 ff.

[37] See *Universitätstage 1966. Nationalsozialismus und die deutsche Universität*, Veröffentlichung der Freien Universität Berlin (Berlin, 1966).

which more and more came to be dominated by the Nazi youth organization, the Hitlerjugend. The leader of the HJ, Baldur von Schirach, a socially prominent youth who had himself failed to win a university degree, and who perhaps enjoyed Hitler's confidence for that very reason, had a deep resentment against the educational establishment and aspired to revolutionize both the universities and the secondary schools by taking education out of the hands of conservative teachers and placing it in those of vigorous young Nazi pedagogues who would emphasize character and physical prowess rather than book-learning. To promote these ideas he encouraged members of the HJ to rebel against their teachers' methods and to be watchdogs over their loyalty to the goals of the Nazi movement, while at the same time absorbing so much of their time in marches and exercises and week-end excursions that they never had the time to do their school work efficiently. In 1934 the Rektor of the Karls-gymnasium in Stuttgart complained to the Minister of Education that the HJ had caused a 33 per cent loss of competence in Latin, Greek, modern languages, and mathematics among his students, and, by making it impossible for students to do any reading at home, had caused equivalent harm to their competence in literature.

Although complaints like this received the support of the Minister of Education, Schirach's activities were not curtailed. A law of December 1936 made membership in the HJ compulsory for all youth between the ages of ten and eighteen, and Schirach was appointed Reich Youth Leader and his former subordination to the Ministries of Education and the Interior ended. He not only continued his campaign against teaching methods in schools, with resultant demoralization of teaching staffs, but succeeded in having service in the HJ weighed in students' records in such a way as to offset deficiencies in academic subjects. This tended to render the Abitur certificate meaningless and to make political reliability rather than intellectual competence the principal requirement for admission to the university.

The results of this process were as shattering as the purge of the faculties had been. By 1939 a large percentage of German university students, because of the anti-intellectual nature of their indoctrination and their failure to acquire basic skills and working habits, were incapable of doing seminar and laboratory work. A series of embarrassingly frank reports by the Security Service of the SS revealed alarmingly high failure rates, exceeding 40 per cent in medicine, and recorded bitter complaints from university authorities to the effect that first-year seminars had now to be largely remedial in character, that new students had neither scientific preparation nor any competence in foreign languages, and that, unless the Abitur were abandoned as a standard of admission, the university could not be expected to produce a new generation of teachers and scholars. Evidence was accumulating, it was reported that foreign students were showing marked superiority to the graduates of German secondary schools, who were so ill prepared and so incapable of sustained concentration that one teacher had asked in despair, 'How can such people become the intellectual leaders of the new Reich?'[38]

IV

The kind of German who was always loudest in his insistence that his country was the land of *Dichter* and *Denker* was probably wholly unaware of the extent to which this description was becoming a bad joke under National Socialism. Josef Goebbels had long been aware that the aesthetic sense of the average citizen was not so highly developed as to enable him to distinguish between the literary quality of a Blunck or a Behrens-Totenohl and that of a Thomas Mann and the Reichskultuskammer had developed great skill in presenting dross as gold. But there were many other Germans who were ashamed and alarmed by the systematic degradation of cultural values that had taken place since 1933, and there is no doubt that their concern was one of the factors contributing to the growth of resistance to the National Socialist regime.

It was probably more important in that negative form of resistance that came to be called 'innere Emigration' than in the movement that led to the attempt on Hitler's life on 20 July 1944. It was not easy to contemplate, let alone plan, active resistance against a government that had a monopoly of power, had demonstrated repeatedly that it was willing to use it ruthlessly, and without concern for law or moral considerations, against real or supposed enemies, and, despite its excesses, enjoyed the support of large sections of the public; and it is understandable that the majority of those people who opposed Hitler in their hearts preferred to express their feelings by means of mental reservation rather than by any form of positive action. The 'inner emigration' occasionally produced a book that could be read as an oblique attack upon the regime, like Werner Bergengruen's *Der Grosstyrann und sein Gericht* (1935), an involved tale of murder and court intrigue in Renaissance Italy, and Ernst Jünger's *Auf den Mar-*

---

[38] Daniel Horn, 'The Hitler Youth and Educational Decline in the Third Reich', *History of Education Quarterly* (winter 1976).

morklippen (1939).[39] But Erich Kästner, who had refused to leave Germany, despite the burning of his books in 1933, in the hope that he might use his pen against the regime, was forced to conclude in the end that the most a mere writer could do was to 'remain as an eyewitness and one day give literary testimony to what he has seen';[40] and this attitude was adopted by many other Germans in many walks of life.

The first attempts to organize more active resistance to the regime came within the German labour organizations, although these were vitiated in the first instance by a failure of leadership in January 1933 and in the subsequent period by the fragmentation of the left. It is possible that a vigorous call for action by the leaders of the Social Democratic party and the trade unions might have elicited a response that would have frustrated Hitler's ambitions at the very moment when he was about to realize them. In several of Germany's cities there were mass demonstrations at the end of January 1933 that might have been effectively co-ordinated, and some units of the SPD's fighting organization, the Reichsbanner, were armed and eager for action, But the party leaders were hesitant to forsake the ways of constitutional legality until Hitler had done so; they were unwilling to assume responsibility for beginning what might end as a blood-bath;[41] and they were all too ready to rationalize their inactivity by arguing that the new government would not be of long duration in any case. The opportunity that they let slip did not recur; and by June 1933 the trade unions, after a futile attempt to appease the new regime, had been absorbed by the Nazi Labour Front, and the party declared illegal. The will to resist was still strong, particularly among the younger members of the labour movement, and in all of the principal urban centres underground groups were formed—like the Sozialistische Arbeiterpartei and the Roter Stosstrupp, which was first organized in the University of Berlin and which, after Hitler's take-over, attracted former Reichsbanner members. These groups were badly co-ordinated; they had varying

[39] In his wartime diaries Jünger said that his novel really showed the ineffectuality of *attentats* against dictators. *Strahlungen* (2 vols., Munich, 1964), ii. 282.

[40] John Winkelman, 'Social Criticism in the Early Work of Erich Kästner' (Dissertation, Univ. of Missouri, 1953), p. 25. See also Erich Kästner, *Gesammelte Schriften für Erwachsene* (8 vols., Zurich, 1969), vii. 92.

[41] This is how Carl Severing justified his failure to act after the war, in a conversation in Kurt Schumacher's house with Stefan Thomas, who in 1933 was a Reichsbanner officer. On the Reichbanner's attitude in 1933, see Allen, *Seizure of Power*, p. 180 and Rohe, *Reichsbanner*, pp. 461 ff. The latter casts doubt on the organization's readiness to resist.

ideas about aims and tactics; and they spent a good deal of time in ideological debates and quarrels with the party executive, which had moved in 1933 to Prague. This is understandable. The problems of Socialist opposition were infinitely more difficult than in the days of Bismarck's Socialist Law. At that time the effectiveness of underground activity was reflected in the growing number of Socialists elected to the Reichstag and the ways in which that political power could be used to frustrate government policy. With the disappearance of parliamentary government there was no way of telling whether anyone was reading the pamphlets that the members of the Socialist underground distributed at the risk of their lives.

The clandestine operations of the Socialist party might have been more extensive and profitable if there had been any basis for co-operation with the Communist underground movement, which had been organized with great difficulty after the mass arrests of February 1933 had all but exterminated the KPD. But the Socialist leaders remembered all too bitterly the way in which the KPD had co-operated with the Nazis in undermining the Republic in 1932, and they had little confidence in their ability to work in harness with people whose tactics conformed strictly to whatever policy was current in the Moscow Politburo. There were intermittent negotiations between the Socialist and Communist underground organizations, and the idea of convergence was actively promoted by the Neu Beginnen group, which was led by a clever tactician and analyst named Walter Loewenheim, who used the pen-name Miles and hoped to create a German equivalent of the French Popular Front. This was made impossible by KPD intrigues against the Prague Executive and by the secession of the KPD from the resistance movement as a consequence of the Nazi–Soviet Pact of August 1939.

After the outbreak of the war Socialist leaders like Wilhelm Leuschner, Julius Leber, and Carlo Mierendorff became convinced that effective resistance against the regime would be impossible unless contact were established with middle-class resistance groups and with oppositional elements within the ministerial bureaucracy and the army. Attempts to co-ordinate activities with the Communists, who had become active again after June 1941, were not wholly discontinued but had negative and, in one case, unfortunate results. Communist resistance cells showed a high degree of vulnerability to Gestapo penetration. In 1942 the Rote Kapelle group, which had been successful in placing agents in several government ministries, was smashed by the secret police and its members hanged; two years later a Communist cell that had been established in Berlin by Anton

Saefgow and Franz Jakob met the same fate, the arrests being made during a meeting to which Julius Leber and Adolf Reichwein had come in an attempt to learn more about Communist aims. Leber, who had been regarded as a strong candidate for the chancellorship once Hitler had been overthrown, died in detention.[42]

If the resistance activities of the political left were barren of impressive result, it must be said that they compared favourably with those of the established Churches, whose organizations had, unlike those of the left, survived the process of *Gleichschaltung*. Their attitude towards National Socialism was highly ambivalent, although both confessions proved capable of taking a firm oppositional stand against policies that violated essential articles of the Christian faith or threatened parochial interests. Spirited opposition by the Evangelical Church, culminating in a formal denunciation of the government's church policy from the pulpits, persuaded Hitler in 1935 to abandon the experiment of establishing a new 'German' religion under a Reich bishop, Ludwig Müller, of his own choosing. Similarly, the Roman Catholic Church courageously opposed the state's euthanasia policy and succeeded in forcing its moderation. But neither Church showed any inclination to take a stand against other crimes of the regime and, while the Catholics, for example, were showing considerable skill in frustrating attempts by the Hitlerjugend to subvert their own youth organizations,[43] they were showing no similar energy in opposing Nazi infringements of basic human rights or their subversion of intellectual and artistic freedom. The authoritarian tradition of both Churches blunted their critical capacities and their collective conscience. It is notable, for instance, that when war came in 1939, the Churches urged their members to be mindful of their patriotic duty and to be ready to sacrifice themselves for their country, an injunction that became more insistent after the attack on Russia in 1941. Members of the Catholic Peace League who refused to do so were liquidated without any attempt of the Church to interfere; indeed, there are documented cases of prison chaplains refusing the sacraments to conscientious objectors to Hitler's war.[44]

[42] See esp. Hans-Joachim Reichhardt, 'Resistance in the Labour Movement', in Hermann Graml, Hans Mommsen, Hans-Joachim Reichhardt, and Ernst Wolf, *The German Resistance to Hitler* (Berkeley, 1970), pp. 151 ff.

[43] See Daniel Horn's forthcoming article, 'The Struggle for Catholic Youth in Hitler's Germany'.

[44] See Gordon C. Zahn, *German Catholics and Hitler's Wars* (London, 1962); Hans Müller (ed.), *Katholische Kirche und Nationalsozialismus: Dokumente* (Munich, 1966).

This is a subject, to be sure, on which it is dangerous to generalize, and one must not forget that from the very beginning of the Nazi regime there were individual churchmen—the Berlin pastor Martin Niemöller, for example, his friend and associate Dietrich Bonhoeffer, and Friedrich Weissler of the Confessional Church —who openly resisted church support of the racial and judicial policies of the regime.[45] Even before the dreadful pogroms of November 1938 men like these had stopped listening to the warnings of their more cautious brethren or superiors and had begun to move from a parochial form of resistance to a more direct one. Some of them used their pulpits for direct attacks upon the regime and suffered for it—like the Berlin Domprobst Lichtenberg, who received a two-year jail sentence for offering public prayers for the Jews, was not released at the end of that time, and died in transit to Dachau. Others—like Bonhoeffer, who also paid for his activities with his life—embarked upon the road of conspiracy, seeking contact with groups of like-minded persons who wished to oppose the government's policies more effectively than mere words could do. Some of these found their way to Socialist cells of resistance; this was true of a number of Catholic churchmen who had earlier been active in the Catholic trade union movement. Others became active in middle-class groups to which they were led by family connection or university acquaintance or other ties.

The German resistance movement, in contrast to the French, had a narrow social base. Despite its Socialist and trade union component, it never extended, as the French movement did, to the masses of the working class or even to the *Mittelstand*. It was, in a real sense, a movement of officers without soldiers, or—to see it in another light—a large and uncoordinated collection of individual groups of intellectuals, civil servants, diplomats, and soldiers, which were rarely fully informed about what other groups were doing. Prominent in these knots of subversion were representatives of Germany's most illustrious families (Helmuth Graf von Moltke, for example, and Peter Graf York von Wartenburg), ambassadors like Ulrich von Hassell, who had served most recently in Rome, and Graf Werner von der Schulenburg, who, as envoy to Moscow, helped negotiate the Nazi–Soviet Pact, functionaries of municipal government, like Carl Goerdeler, formerly lord mayor of Leipzig, and scientists like Erwin Planck. Some of these conspirators tried to do things that were misguided or ill timed and ended up as prisoners of the Ge-

[45] See the account of the activities of the Confessional Church and related groups in *German Dictatorship*, pp. 379 ff.

stapo, like Dr. Arvid Harnack and Oberleutnant Harro Schulze-Boysen and their colleagues of the Rote Kapelle, who died for their espionage activities on behalf of the Soviet Union. Some lost their way in abstract speculation and debates over the orientation of German foreign policy after National Socialism had been overcome. But there were others, particularly those that formed around Carl Goerdeler, who followed practical ends in as systematic a manner as was possible in the circumstances.[46]

In the last years before 1939 their objective was to save their country from the disaster that they became convinced Hitler would bring upon it; and, recognizing their own weakness to effect this end, they tried to induce the Western Powers to adopt the kind of policy that would check Hitler's course and perhaps, by weakening his prestige, bring him down. Through emissaries sent to London and Paris—Goerdeler himself, masquerading as an agent for the Robert Bosch optical firm,[47] and Adam von Trott zu Solz, who, as a former Rhodes Scholar, was well connected in England—and through fellow conspirators who were members of the Diplomatic Service, like Theodor Kordt in the London Embassy, they endeavoured to bring home to the Western governments the inevitability of war unless they were prepared to take a stand against Hitler's demands, and they put forward the additional argument that, if the Western resistance were unequivocal and if Hitler sought to defy it, they would manufacture a putsch against him which could hardly fail to succeed. For reasons that will become clear in the following chapter, the Western governments were not prepared to follow the course suggested to them, and the war that the resistance had hoped to prevent came remorselessly on. The outbreak of hostilities forced a fundamental change in the tactics of the movement. Realism now required that they make plans to assassinate Hitler as the only means of forcing a return to peace before Germany was destroyed.

They were, of course, incapable of executing these plans themselves, nor could they expect an appeal to the German people to be effective in promoting mass action against the regime. If they were to eliminate Hitler, they would have to have effective power at their disposal, and it was clear to them that only the officer corps of the army could provide it. It was true that it was not the homogeneous

---

[46] The authoritative work on all aspects and groups of the German resistance is Peter Hoffmann, *Widerstand, Staatsstreich, Attentat: Der Kampf der Opposition gegen Hitler* (Munich, 1969). On Goerdeler, see Gerhard Ritter, *Carl Goerdeler und die deutsche Widerstandsbewegung* (Stuttgart, 1956).

[47] On Goerdeler's foreign missions, see *DDF* 2nd Ser. vi. 309–13, 442–6.

body that it had once been. The breakneck rearmament programme that had begun in 1935 had forced the commissioning of young men from social strata that had not in the past provided officers for the armed forces, and many of them had had years of National Socialist indoctrination that made them unresponsive to other loyalties. The opportunities for promotion provided by the army's rapid expansion also had divisive effects, ambition, jealousy and willingness to seek outside influence in order to get ahead permeating all ranks. Many officers who detested Hitler in their hearts were unwilling to jeopardize their careers by letting this be known, and these would be as much opposed to resistance to the regime as the large number of 'party soldiers'. On the other hand, the top ranks were still filled with officers who remained true to the ideals of Hans von Seeckt and to the conception of the army as an autonomous force, free from party control, and having as its *raison d'être* the protection of the vital interests of the state.

The leading spirit among those who felt this way was General Ludwig Beck, Army Chief of Staff until 1938. It was his view that, precisely because the German people had always had a kind of *pietas* toward the army, the officer corps had to repay the confidence that the people placed in them by protecting them from disaster. There was no honourable way of avoiding that responsibility. If it became clear that Hitler was embarked on a fatal course, they had a moral obligation to stop him by whatever means were required for that purpose. 'History', he wrote, 'will burden the highest commanders of the army with blood guilt if they do not act in accordance with their professional and political knowledge and conscience . . . Any soldier who holds a leading position and at the same time limits his duty . . . to his military assignment, without being conscious of his supreme responsibility to the nation, shows lack of greatness and understanding of his task.'[48]

Beck could not expect to win all, or even the majority, of the officer corps over to this point of view; but it was persuasive and inspiring enough to bring a remarkable number of officers in key positions to his side. In 1938 they planned a putsch against Hitler that might have succeeded if the Western Powers had not undercut it by capitulating to Hitler's demands; and during the war years they co-ordinated their activities with those of the people around Goerdeler and made the elaborate plans that eventuated in the attempt of 20 July 1944, when Colonel Claus Schenk von Stauffenberg tried to kill Hitler

---

[48] Wolfgang Förster, *Ein General kämpft gegen den Krieg: Aus nachgelassnenen Papiere des Generalstabschefs Ludwig Beck* (Munich, 1949), p. 103.

with a bomb during a staff briefing at his headquarters in Rastenburg in East Prussia.

That event and the collapse of the conspiracy in its muddled aftermath are too well known to require any detailed description here. One may ask, however, why plans so laboriously laid ended in failure, and one cannot help laying the responsibility at the feet of the soldiers. In May 1944 Ernst Jünger, who, as a staff officer in Paris, was aware that a military putsch of some kind was pending, wrote in his diary: 'Generals are, for the most part, energetic and stupid. . . . Or they are cultivated, and that is at the expense of the brutality that belongs to their trade. So there is always something lacking either in will or in vision. Most infrequent is the union of energy and cultivation, such as one found in Caesar and Sulla or, in modern times, in Scharnhorst and Prince Eugene.'[49] Certainly there were no Sullas among those who directed the conspiracy against Hitler, except perhaps Stauffenberg, who was shattered to discover, when he had returned to the Bendlerstraße in Berlin, hours after the explosion in Rastenburg, that his fellow conspirators had done nothing to seize power in the city because they were not sure that Hitler was really dead. Such doubts and hesitations had lamed the resolution of the military conspirators ever since 1938, and in July 1944 they proved critical.

This indecisiveness was rooted in part in the moral dilemma caused by the oath that all officers had taken to Hitler in 1934 and which seemed to many of them to make an act of opposition dishonourable. But it seems safe to say that their political dilemma was even more difficult.[50] Those who were convinced that their obligation to their country and to the German people was more important than their oath to Hitler, and who repeated Beck's argument that the *militärfrommes Volk* would not only expect them to stop Hitler's disastrous course but would support their attempts to do so, did not, in their hearts, believe that this was so. They were aware that their institutional prestige had suffered from their long collaboration with the dictator and from their failure on many critical occasions to protest against his actions. They had been associated too long with Hitler to expect that a break with him now would be understood by the mass of the people. This was particularly true in wartime. In June 1940 Fritz Lehmann wrote in his diary that, if people had been thoughtful and worried in September 1939, 'the fanfares of victory

[49] Jünger, *Strahlungen*, ii. 267.
[50] George K. Romoser, 'The Politics of Uncertainty', *Social Research*, xxxi (1964), 73 ff.

are now drowning out every word of criticism and any thought of concern over the future'.[51] As long as that mood continued, resistance by the army could not hope for popular backing.

Nor was there any indication that this mood would change significantly as the war continued, even when the first victories were followed by defeats in Africa and Russia; and, in any event, the increasingly effective control of the Gauleiter over the civil sector prevented any real communication between the military and the masses. On those rare occasions when differences between the soldiers and the Führer became public property, the Propaganda Ministry was skilful in intimating to the public that these signs of opposition were the result of defeatistm, aristocratic reaction, and inability on the part of the military leaders to understand the revolutionary dynamism of the National Socialist movement. Goebbels succeeded to a surprising extent in turning military doubts into party assets.

The vacillations and doubts that affected the military conspirators in 1944 were attributable in large part to the realization that they had so far lost contact with the German people that they could not hope for popular understanding and must expect to be regarded as traitors and defeatists. That this was not far short of the mark was shown by the readiness with which official explanations of the July Putsch were accepted by the common people. 'Hitler is all of a sudden the man of the people again,' wrote a contemporary observer, 'for whom even former . . . Marxists discovered some sympathy at the moment when he was on the point of being liquidated by "generals and monarchists", by "aristocrats" as they are now called. "An attack on the Führer is a scoundrelly act . . . naturally, the aristocrats . . . they want to have the monarchy back again!" '[52]

This was not far from the truth either. One may admire the moral impulse behind the attempt against Hitler, while at the same time being conscious of the archaic character of the politics of the leaders of the conspiracy. It is not too much to say that Beck and Goerdeler were political romantics who possessed only the haziest notion of the social and mental changes that had occurred in Germany during the last two generations and who seemed to believe that the country would be better off if all the clocks were turned back firmly to 1913. It is clear from two long memorandums found in the Goerdeler papers that the whole cast of their thinking was illiberal and anti-

[51] Fritz Lehmann, *1939–1945: Beobachtungen und Bekenntnisse* (Hamburg, 1946), p. 40.

[52] Joachim Günther, *Das letzte Jahr: Mein Tagebuch 1944/45* (Hamburg, 1948), p. 203.

democratic and that they wanted to establish a society that would be characterized by order rather than by change. The state of the future, as they envisaged it, was to be based on a corporative rather than a parliamentary model, with a complicated electoral system that placed restrictions upon direct voting, with supervisory functions vested in the army, and with a monarchical head of state. It would be a kind of authoritarian welfare state in which the citizen would no longer have to fear the arbitrary lawlessness and terror of totalitarianism but would be denied full freedom of political choice.[53]

A month before the attempt on Hitler's life Major-General Henning von Tresckow, inspired perhaps by the intimations of failure that affected the conspirators, said to Count Stauffenberg, 'The *attentat* must succeed, *coûte que coûte*. . . . It is no longer a matter of its practicality, but a matter of demonstrating to the world and before history that the resistance movement dared the decisive gamble. Beside that, everything else is a matter of indifference.'[54] In these words, perhaps, is to be found the true importance of the German resistance movement: it was to serve as a reminder to future generations of Germans that there had been men who had fought against Hitler's regime of crime and terror and risked their lives in order to put an end to his corruption of the moral and cultural substance of their nation. But it would be difficult to disagree with Ralf Dahrendorf's judgement that, although the resistance was 'a leaf of fame in German history', it was hardly a step on Germany's road to freedom and democracy. Despite the idealism that drove them forward, the resistance leaders were acting in the name of a social tradition that could provide a basis only for authoritarian rule.[55]

[53] See *Beck und Goerdeler: Gemeinschaftsdokumente für den Frieden 1941–1944*, ed. Wilhelm Ritter von Schramm (Munich, 1966); Hans Mommsen, 'Social Views and Constitutional Plans of the Resistance', in *The German Resistance to Hitler*, pp. 57 ff.; W. Scharlau, 'Goerdeler und Beck waren Romantiker', *Die Zeit* (14 June 1966), 12.
[54] Ritter, *Goerdeler*, p. 390.
[55] Dahrendorf, *Society and Democracy in Germany*, p. 412.

XIX
Hitler and Europe:
Foreign Policy
1933–1939

Si le Führer a pu triompher . . . au cours de son aventureuse carrière, des obstacles innombrables que le hasard et ses adversaires ont semés sur ses pas, ce n'est pas seulement grâce à son acharnement et à son opiniâtreté, mais encore grâce à une habilité politique qui n'a fait que croître avec le temps. Il ignore tout respect de la parole donnée. . . . Cette rouerie, cette roublardise, ont trompé plus d'un cerveau subtil . . .

ANDRÉ FRANÇOIS-PONCET (8 February 1933)[1]

Die Vorsehung hat mir das letzte Wort gesprochen und mir den Erfolg gebracht.

ADOLF HITLER (November 1939)[2]

T HE first assessments by the Western governments of Hitler's likely course in foreign policy were characterized by an extraordinary amount of wishful thinking. Despite the clear evidence provided by events inside Germany that the country's new rulers were contemptuous of law and morality and standards of common decency in the treatment of those who disagreed with them, politicians in London and Paris showed no alarm about what this might portend for Germany's future behaviour as a member of the international community. They professed to see no implications for foreign policy in the brutalities of *Gleichschaltung*, which were, in their view, probably transitory in any case; and they inclined to the belief that, when he had time to address himself to foreign problems, Hitler would reveal himself to be a revisionist, like his predecessors, intent on modifying those clauses of the Versailles Treaty that still imposed restrictions upon his country's freedom of action and that, like them, he would be content with carefully measured doses of appeasement.

---

[1] *DDF* 1st Ser. ii. 582.
[2] Jacobsen and Jochmann, *Zur Geschichte des Nationalsozialismus*, Dok. 23 xi 1939, p. 1.

Making due allowance for the fact that governments that are themselves beset with pressing political and economic problems are reluctant to examine too closely new areas of potential trouble, this attitude can only be described as obtuse. Hitler himself had told them in innumerable speeches and in a very long book that their estimate of his foreign intentions was inaccurate, and more recently their own diplomatic representatives in Germany had been doing the same. On 8 February 1933, for instance, André François-Poncet, French ambassador in Berlin since 1931, in his first extensive report on the new Chancellor and his ideas, warned his government that Hitler was a man of action rather than of words, or rather that he was a man of action because he was a man of words and had made so many promises to his followers that 'the eternal agitator will not escape the necessity of acting'. His foreign goals were perhaps not defined very precisely yet, but the West, François-Poncet emphasized, would be well advised to ponder two things: that in pursuing his goals Hitler had never allowed himself to be deterred by verbal professions to others; and, more important, that 'this is not a man of the past, and his objective is not, like that of M. Hugenberg, to restore, purely and simply, the state of things in 1914'.[3]

Even more pointed in his warnings was the British ambassador, Sir Horace Rumbold.[4] An envoy of long experience, who had entered the diplomatic corps in 1891, served in ministerial posts in Switzerland, Poland, Turkey, and Spain, and come to Berlin as ambassador in 1928, he was fascinated by Hitler and was perhaps the first foreign observer to perceive that the Führer was no mere fantast but a serious threat to his neighbours and to the peace of the world. It was no accident that Hitler detested this incisive analyst of his intentions and, during the Second World War, described him as 'the perpetually drunk Sir Rumbold' and said that, when he had told him in 1933 that he considered every German obligation stipulated in the Versailles Treaty as having been assumed under duress and hence invalid, the British ambassador had hiccuped, 'Magnificent! I'll tell my government immediately!'[5] What Rumbold actually told London, in a series of reports that culminated in a remarkable analysis of Hitler's thinking on 26 April 1939, was that somebody had better begin to study *Mein Kampf* seriously, since that work would not only

[3] *DDF* 1st Ser. ii. 580–5.

[4] On Rumbold, and on François-Poncet and the U.S. ambassador William E. Dodd, see Franklin Ford, 'Three Observers in Berlin', in *The Diplomats*, pp. 437 ff.

[5] Henry Picker, *Hitler's Tischgespräche im Führerhauptquartier 1941–42*, ed. Percy Ernst Schramm (Stuttgart, 1963), p. 158.

explain the vital connection between what was currently happening in Germany and what would sooner or later start happening in the foreign sphere, but would also make clear why Hitler's future policy would almost certainly be one of expansion and war. Rumbold suggested that Hitler 'would probably be glad to suppress every copy [of *Mein Kampf*] extant today', and added gravely, 'I fear it would be misleading to base any hopes on a return to sanity or a serious modification of the views of the Chancellor and his entourage. . . . I . . . feel that Germany's neighbours have reason to be vigilant, and that it may be necessary for them to determine their attitude towards coming developments in this country sooner than they may have contemplated.'[6]

The French Government was sufficiently impressed by its ambassador's reports to adopt a highly suspicious attitude towards Berlin, which in 1934 hardened temporarily into an attempt to devise a policy of containment of Germany. But the MacDonald–Baldwin government in England, beset with domestic problems, turned a deaf ear to the warnings from Berlin (and, in time, to French proposals for the adoption of a hard line). To the people in Whitehall, Rumbold was an alarmist, and so were those who agreed with him, like his Third Secretary, Duncan Sandys, who predicted in 1933 that Hitler was already planning to remilitarize the Rhineland,[7] and the Permanent Under-Secretary for Foreign Affairs, Sir Robert Vansittart, who, in a memorandum of 28 August 1933, foresaw German anschluss with Austria as soon as an opportunity presented itself, followed by a move against the Polish Corridor.[8] They preferred to believe that the experience of power would tame Hitler and make him a respectable international citizen, and they saw no reason to worry themselves unnecessarily by brooding over extravagant statements that Hitler had put down on paper in 1924.

This was a mistake, for the basic principles of foreign policy formulated in *Mein Kampf*—that a dynamic policy was the only possible one for a country in Germany's position, that the elimination of potential dissidents was the prerequisite of such a policy, that a mere return, either to the objectives of Wilhelmine policy or to the frontiers of 1914, was incompatible with Germany's economic and security needs, that the acquisition of new living space in Eastern Europe was essential to the future of the German race and must motivate German policy, and that such a course entailed a high risk of war, particularly with France, that must be accepted and prepared

[6] *BD* 2nd Ser. v. 47–55   [7] Gilbert and Gott, *The Appeasers*, p. 33.
[8] *BD* 2nd Ser. v. 547–50.

for by means of diplomatic alliance, military recovery, and preparation of the home front[9]—were things that Hitler took very seriously indeed. That they were not merely a jumble of idle thoughts written down under the impact of the French occupation of the Ruhr[10] was shown by the fact that in 1928 Hitler wrote another book, which was never released to the public and was not discovered until after the Second World War, in which he repeated them, somewhat more succinctly and categorically. In this work he sketched four possible foreign policies for Germany, the first three of which—complete passivity, a search for well-being by purely economic means, and revision of the Versailles Treaty to restore the boundaries of 1914—he rejected out of hand, insisting that the only possible course for Germany was 'a clear, far-seeing territorial policy'. He added:

Thereby, she abandons all attempts at world-industry and world-trade and instead concentrates all her strength in order, through the allotment of sufficent living space for the next hundred years to our people, also to prescribe a path of life. Since this territory can only be in the East, the obligation to be a naval power also recedes into the background. Germany tries anew to champion her interests through the formation of a decisive power on land.

This aim is equally in keeping with the highest national as well as folkish requirements. It likewise presupposes great military power means for its execution, but does not necessarily bring Germany into conflict with all European great powers. As surely as France here will remain Germany's enemy, just as little does the nature of such a political aim contain a reason for England, and especially for Italy, to maintain the enmity of the World War.[11]

Nor is this the only evidence that we possess of the consistency of Hitler's thinking about foreign policy. The basic arguments advanced in his two books are to be found also in such programmatic statements as his address to the industrialists in Düsseldorf in January 1932, in which he proclaimed that Germany would never be able to assert itself before foreign nations until the welter of parties and the clamour of dissident voices had been replaced, through a process of internal consolidation, by 'one iron-hard *Volkskörper*',[12] and his speech to the generals in February 1933, in which he spoke plainly of *Gleichschaltung* and rearmament as the necessary prerequisites of a

[9] See *Mein Kampf*, pt. II, Ch. XIV. For an analysis, see Jäckel, *Hitler's Weltanschauung*, pp. 27–46.

[10] This, essentially, is the argument of A. J. P. Taylor in *The Origins of the Second World War* (New York, 1962), pp. 68–9, in which he holds that *Mein Kampf* has little or no value as a guide to Hitler's policy.

[11] *Hitler's Secret Book*, pp. 142–5.

[12] Domarus, *Hitler: Reden* i. 68 ff., esp. 88.

policy of acquiring living space for the German people.[13] Moreover, the idea of the war with France that would precede the attainment of this ultimate goal—an idea that had run like a red thread through all his statements concerning foreign policy ever since 1919, when he had declared, 'German misery must be broken by German steel! That time must come!'[14]—showed no signs of fading either. In his first interview with a foreign statesman after assuming power, in June 1933, Hitler told his visitor, the Hungarian Prime Minister, Julius Gömbös, 'I will grind France to powder!'[15]

In the first months of his chancellorship, Hitler no longer found it expedient to proclaim his true intentions from the house-tops. He recognized his vulnerability and his need for time and therefore encouraged the democratic governments in their illusions lest they undertake to baulk his plans before he could do anything to prevent that. Indeed, he strengthened the impression that no fundamental change in German policy need be expected by retaining the Foreign Ministry staff and diplomatic personnel that had served his predecessors, keeping Baron von Neurath and Bernhard von Bülow in the posts of Foreign Minister and Secretary of State respectively and leaving the ambassadorial posts untouched, except in the case of Washington, where ambassador von Prittwitz resigned on his own initiative.[16] At the same time, his own public references to foreign affairs were mild and conciliatory, admirably designed to disarm foreign critics and to comfort the hearts of those who wanted to believe that National Socialism was not a danger to the peace. In his first months of power Hitler showed that he possessed unmistakable diplomatic abilities, particularly in the use of the public statement as a means of ingratiation. His speech of 17 May 1933 on disarmament was so filled with intimations of willingness to postpone demands for equality in armament for five years, to renounce the use of offensive weapons, and to accept external inspection of his own paramilitary formations that it produced a notable relaxation of tension—and, incidentally, put an effective end to talk of a general boycott of German trade.[17]

[13] Thilo Vogelsang, 'Hitlers Rede an die Generäle vom 5. Februar 1933', *Vierteljahrshefte für Zeitgeschichte*, ii (1954), 434 f.

[14] Günter Schubert, *Anfänge nationalsozialistischer Außenpolitik* (Cologne, 1963), p. 83.

[15] C. A. Macartney, *October Fifteenth: A History of Modern Hungary* (2 vols., Edinburgh, 1956), i. 139 n.6.

[16] See Karl Dietrich Bracher, 'Das Anfangsstadium der Hitlerischen Außenpolitik', *Vierteljahrshefte für Zeitgeschichte*, v (1957), 69–70.

[17] Domarus, *Hitler: Reden* i. 270 ff. See Walters, *League of Nations*, ii. 547.

Hermann Rauschning, who was for some years close to Hitler and was an admirer of his diplomatic gifts, once wrote that, despite the over-all consistency of the Führer's foreign policy, he did not allow it to hamper his freedom of manœuvre and that, in following his goals, he 'carried to a pitch of virtuosity the pursuit of tactical elasticity'.[18] This was the hallmark of his policy in his first years. While seeking to allay the suspicions of his neighbours, he was using the respite gained to carry out the process of *Gleichschaltung* and to make the first preparations for the all-out rearmament effort that was to come later. Simultaneously, he was looking for an opportunity to withdraw from engagements entered into by Stresemann and Brüning, which promised to be onerous. Finally, he was making his assessment of the attitude that the various Powers would be likely to adopt when he began to move toward his real objectives. This was a process that involved a series of graduated probes intended to test their ability to collaborate effectively to preserve the *status quo* and their willingness to resort to force in order to frustrate his designs.

I

The obligation that was for the moment the most restrictive was Germany's participation in the Disarmament Conference that had begun its meetings in Geneva in 1932; and for a newcomer to foreign affairs Hitler showed a quite remarkable skill in terminating this obligation. This was not entirely pleasing to the diplomats on the spot, and Germany's chief negotiator, Rudolf Nadolny, felt with some justification that the fact that the other Powers had at long last granted Germany equality of status in armaments represented a not inconsiderable victory and one that should be built on. But Hitler was neither impressed by this nor interested in winning new concessions that could only deprive Germany of a grievance that he wanted to exploit. In his eyes, the possibility that the other Powers might agree upon an arms control scheme that was so generous to Germany that he would have no plausible grounds for refusing it was a danger that had to be avoided at all cost. Germany had to make the break, not because, as he later told Rauschning, the German people demanded it, because they wanted 'to see something done', because they were 'tired of being led by the nose',[19] but because any form of control would interfere with Germany's rearmament, which, Hitler told his cabinet on 8 February, must now be given first priority.[20] But it was necessary to avoid appearing to be the villain of

[18] Hermann Rauschning, *The Revolution of Nihilism* (New York, 1939), p. 185.
[19] Rauschning, *Hitler Speaks*, p. 111.   [20] *GD* Ser. C i, no. 16.

the piece. When the rupture came, his Foreign Minister told Nadolny later in the month, 'the lack of an intention to disarm on France's part must seem to be the cause'.[21]

In the end, Hitler effected his purpose by using tactics that fore-shadowed those he would employ in the Sudeten affair five years later: he made demands at Geneva that he was reasonably sure the other Powers would not accept. He insisted that equality of status was not enough and that, since the other Powers were reluctant to reduce their forces to Germany's level, all controls must be lifted so that it could seek actual equality in its own way. To this kind of intransigence the French, supported by the British Government, refused to yield, insisting upon a waiting period in which Germany could prove its good faith and give some indication of what its intentions were. This gave Hitler the excuse he needed and, brushing aside an Italian attempt to find a compromise, he announced on 14 October 1933 that Germany was ending both its participation in the conference and its membership in the League of Nations, an institution that he had always regarded as a symbol of Germany's second-class status and for whose members, including the German ones, he privately felt contempt.[22]

Hitler was later to tell his generals that his action in 1933 was 'a hard decision. The number of prophets who predicted that it would lead to the occupation of the Rhineland was large; the number of believers was very small.'[23] But this proved to be the first of a long series of occasions on which his judgement proved sounder than that of his professional advisers. He sensed correctly that none of the other governments was willing to seek reprisals against Germany for an action that was well within its rights: and he played skilfully upon that reluctance, first, by demonstrating by means of a plebiscite held on 12 November that the German people supported his action overwhelmingly, and second, by insisting loudly and repeatedly in speeches before that plebiscite was held, that Germany was fully prepared, as long as it was treated as an equal, to adhere to mutually advantageous agreements on arms control or anything else. This left the other governments feeling that if they treated Hitler adroitly and did not make the mistake of threatening him, he would return of his

[21] Ibid., no. 20.

[22] See Picker, *Tischgespräche*, pp. 349 f. On the circumstances leading up to the break, see *GD* Ser. C i, nos. 484, 489, 494, 495, 499. See also Christine Fraser, 'Der Austritt Deutschlands aus dem Völkerbund, seine Vorgeschichte und seine Nachwir-kungen' (Dissertation, Friedrich-Wilhelms-Universität zu Bonn, 1969), esp. Ch. 3; and Christoph M. Kimmich, *Germany and the League of Nations* (Chicago, 1967), Ch. 9.

[23] *GD* Ser. D viii, no. 384, p. 440.

own accord to the League and the arms talks. This belief was remarkably stubborn, particularly in England; as late as the spring of 1939 Neville Chamberlain professed to believe it and told reporters that he thought there was a good chance of reopening disarmament talks, with German participation, before the end of the year.

In reality, the Führer had broken once and for all with any kind of collective security arrangement. He continued to affirm his faith in international collaboration, but, whenever a concrete proposal for realizing it was placed before him, he side-stepped it or refused it by indirection, sometimes maintaining that, while he was prepared to accept any agreements that would serve the cause of peace, he preferred them to be bilateral in nature. The other Powers were so anxious to believe that his intentions were peaceful that they made the mistake, on more than one occasion, of dropping their more comprehensive projects and making the kind of agreement he preferred, forgetting in doing so that bilateral agreements are the easiest kind to break.

Hitler's first notable success in this respect came in January 1934 when, to the general stupefaction of the diplomatic community, he concluded a non-aggression pact with Poland. To many German diplomats and soldiers this seemed a deplorable departure from principle, a repudiation of the policy inaugurated by Brockdorff-Rantzau and Seeckt. Planning for a conflict with Poland was a tradition of both the Defence Ministry and the Foreign Ministry; and popular hatred of the Poles was kept alive by frequent incidents in the Corridor and Danzig. But this made Hitler nervous in 1933, particularly in view of the uncertain temperament of the Polish dictator, Pilsudski. He was afraid that too provocative action by the National Socialist party in Danzig might lead to a Polish intervention that might widen into a war for which he was not yet prepared. Throughout 1933, therefore, he not only kept the Danzig party under close control but took the initiative in putting out feelers to the Poles. He was undeterred by the fears expressed by his new ambassador in Moscow, Nadolny, that a Polish agreement would drive the Soviet Union into the arms of the West, agreeing with Bülow's view that 'the trees of the Franco-Russian afforestation (*Anforstung*) will not reach the sky. . . . Russia swinging or swerving into the French camp . . . alignment of the Soviet Union with the front of our opponents . . . are slogans with no actual reality behind them'.[24] Germany's diplomatic isolation after its withdrawal from

[24] *GD* Ser. C ii, no. 251. See also nos. 163, 171, 190, 210. On Nadolny's fight to push his case, see Rudolf Rahn, *Ruheloses Leben* (Düsseldorf, 1950), pp. 83–4.

the League[25] made it seem expedient to seek an agreement with its eastern neighbour in order to obviate the possibility of an unwanted incident. Hitler explained his position to the party leaders on 18 October and told Rauschning, who was President of the Danzig Senate, that he wanted a treaty with Warsaw, which could be broken off later when such termination seemed desirable. 'All our agreements with Poland', he said, 'have a purely temporary significance. I have no intention of maintaining a serious friendship with Poland.'[26]

It is easier to understand Hitler's motives than those of the Polish Government. Perhaps the answer is to be found in Polish nationalism and its not infrequent tendency to produce illusions about Poland's capabilities. The rising man in Warsaw was Colonel Jozef Beck, an elegant saturnine figure who had been active in Pilsudski's *coup d'état* in 1926 and had been his close collaborator ever since. Beck was as much an opponent of collective diplomatic arrangements as Hitler himself and believed that Poland's interests were best served by bilateral agreements. He not only welcomed the pact with Germany but, after it had been consummated by the joint declaration of 26 January 1934,[27] regarded it as an outstanding achievement of Polish foreign policy. He convinced himself that the Third Reich would be a better ally than a republican Germany, which would return to the Rapallo policy, or a nationalist one, which would constantly be trying to pressure the Polish Government to give up territory won in 1919. He had no illusions about Hitler's desire for expansion but thought that it would be directed primarily against Austria and Czechoslovakia, and that Poland would profit from the resultant redrawing of the map. He had no thought of becoming a German satellite or even of orienting his policy exclusively towards Germany. He seems to have believed that the pact would strengthen his hand in his dealings with the Russians and enable him to maintain a balance between Germany and the Soviet Union in the interest of Polish security.[28] This was unrealistic and ended tragically.

To Hitler the pact brought other advantages besides a relaxation of tension on his eastern frontiers. It ended any possibility of a *rapprochement* between Poland and Czechoslovakia, which would have seriously interfered with his long-range plans. More immediately, it helped him to escape from the most dangerous of the attempts made

[25] That this was causing concern to the professional diplomats is illustrated in *GD* Ser. C ii, no. 145.

[26] Rauschning, *Hitler Speaks*, pp. 115, 123.

[27] See *GD* Ser. C ii, no. 219.

[28] See Henry L. Roberts, 'The Diplomacy of Colonel Beck', in *The Diplomats*, esp. pp. 598 ff.

by the other Powers to force him back into a collective system in which he would have been under some restraint. This was the plan of the French Foreign Minister, Jean-Louis Barthou, for a comprehensive eastern security pact. A realist who saw in Hitler's first steps in foreign policy the preparations for a major assault on the *status quo*,[29] Barthou intended to contain the Führer by means of a network of mutual defence treaties, supplemented by a regional security pact that would be signed by Poland, the Danubian and Balkan states, France, the Soviet Union, and Germany. The Soviet Union would simultaneously enter the League of Nations and become a co-guarantor of the Locarno treaties. Barthou was aware that the Soviet Government, preoccupied with a situation in the Far East that was assuming the dimensions of an undeclared war with Japan, was worried about Hitler's intentions, particularly in view of the Polish pact and the simultaneous severance of the ties that had existed between the Reichswehr and the Red Army; and he had actually elaborated the details of his plan in talks with Maxim Litvinov, the Soviet Commissar for Foreign Affairs. This was not lost on Hitler, and he felt compelled to resist the consummation of Barthou's plan, regardless of the cost. He was spared the necessity of being a lonely objector by the Polish Government's utter rejection of the plan, despite all of Barthou's efforts to persuade Beck to go along and, after the French Foreign Minister's death by assassination at Marseilles in October 1934, despite renewed pleas by his successor, Pierre Laval.[30]

The year 1934 was a dangerous one for Hitler. The SA crisis of June threatened his authority within his party, and his method of dealing with it further blackened his reputation abroad for brutality and disrespect for law. The evolution of the Austrian question had even more serious effects. The encouragement and assistance that the NSDAP headquarters in Munich gave to the Austrian National Socialists in the months that followed Dollfuss's take-over in February 1934 not only brought a series of angry protests from the Austrian Government but caused a perceptible deterioration of Italo-German relations.[31] A visit by Hitler to Venice in June that was intended to alleviate the tension by persuading Mussolini that the anschluss question was not acute was only temporarily successful.[32] Mistakenly assuming that the Duce was prepared to withdraw his

[29] His suspicions were expressed in a speech before the Disarmament Conference on 30 May 1934 and led to German protests. See *GD* Ser. C iii, nos. 4, 31, and enc.
[30] See e.g. ibid. ii, nos. 423, 465; iii, nos. 4, 77, 397.
[31] See ibid. ii, nos. 282, 286, 394.   [32] Ibid. iii, nos. 5, 7, 26.

protection from Dollfuss and allow matters in Austria to take their course, Hitler continued the support of the Austrian party at a heightened pace; and the result of this was the abortive Nazi putsch in Vienna in July, which led to Dollfuss's death and the hurried appearance of Italian divisions in battledress at the Brenner Pass.[33] Few responsible statesmen in Europe had any doubts about Hitler's complicity in these events, despite his elaborate disclaimers after the revolt had failed; and there was a quickening of interest in schemes to strengthen collective security.

It was, however, as we have seen, only momentary. The congenital incoherence of Mussolini's foreign policy made it impossible for the Italian Government to give a lead or even to second the efforts of other Powers. The prolonged internal crisis in France that followed the street fighting in Paris in February and the fall of the Daladier government left that country divided and gradually drained away the energy of its foreign policy,[34] although the talks with the Soviet Union continued in a rather desultory way and had the result of bringing the Soviets into the League of Nations in July.[35] The British were not prepared to take any initiative. On the contrary, important figures in the Conservative party, like Lord Allen of Hurtwood and Lord Lothian, were alarmed by the tendencies of French policy and were actively working for closer relations with Germany,[36] and the Foreign Secretary, Sir John Simon, had set his face sternly against arrangements like the Barthou plan that threatened to involve Britain in Eastern Europe. Since Hitler himself was wise enough to avoid any more provocative actions for the remainder of the year, the tension of July was soon forgotten.

In the last months of 1934 the Führer concentrated his attention on the preparations for the plebiscite in the Saar, which was held in January and resulted in an overwhelming pro-German vote and the return of the area to the Reich. This success, with which the other Powers made no attempt to interfere, marked the beginning of a new phase in his policy. He had survived his period of extreme vulnerability unscathed, and, thanks to the distractions and differences of the other Powers, his own tactical skill, and a good deal of luck,

[33] A careful account of the background of the putsch and an assessment of Hitler's complicity is to be found in Gerhard L. Weinberg, *The Foreign Policy of Hitler's Germany: Diplomatic Revolution in Europe, 1933–36* (Chicago, 1970), pp. 87–107.

[34] For an interesting report on the German reaction to these events, see *DDF* 1st Ser. iii, no. 368.

[35] See William E. Scott, *Alliance against Hitler: The Origins of the Franco-Soviet Pact* (Durham, N. C., 1962).

[36] J. R. M. Butler, *Lord Lothian, 1882–1940* (London, 1960), Chs. 11–12.

had been able in the course of two years to free himself from the restraints of the European security system, while at the same time proceeding with the policy of *Gleichschaltung* and the arms build-up that were the necessary prerequisites for his future plans. Now he was ready to test the resistance of the Western Powers to those extensive designs.

II

In doing so, he showed effrontery and abruptness. In February 1935 the British and French governments, still seeking to save something from the abortive disarmament talks, pieced together a new plan that promised Germany equality in armaments in return for adherence to conventions controlling air warfare and certain types of weapons, co-operation in new mutual assistance plans designed to give security to Eastern and Central Europe, and a return to the League. Sir John Simon and his representative for League affairs, Anthony Eden, arranged to go to Berlin to discuss details of the scheme with Hitler. The Chancellor, however, suddenly caught a bad cold—induced, it was said, by the publication of a British White Paper on defence requirements that spoke frankly and critically of German rearmament efforts—and the trip was postponed until he should recover. He proved to be a restless invalid. On 8 March 1935, in the first of what came to be called Hitler's Saturday Surprises, he revealed that Germany had a new military air force; and, a week later, he destroyed what was left of the Anglo-French plan by announcing that he no longer intended to abide by the military clauses of the Versailles Treaty and was expanding the army from its treaty strength of 100,000 to a force of 36 divisions approximating 550,000 men.

It was clear that, if Hitler were allowed to get away with this unilateral repudiation of the treaty, all existing power relations in Europe would be altered. It was questionable whether France would be able to match the new German army in size without changing its conscription law in ways that would cause serious political difficulties. It was therefore in a concerned mood that the governments of Great Britain, France, and Italy sent representatives to Stresa on 11 April to consider the German announcements. Given the domestic problems of the Western Powers and Mussolini's preoccupation with the situation in Abyssinia, where the armed clash at Wal-Wal in December had set in train the events that would soon lead to Italian intervention, it was clear from the outset that there was no desire for joint military or economic action against Germany. Instead the three

Powers issued a ringing declaration of solidarity, jointly condemned the German announcement, and intimated that they would stand firm against further treaty violations. A week later, the League of Nations issued a sterner condemnation of German policy.

With his usual strain of irony, Sir Eric Phipps, Rumbold's successor in Berlin, described Hitler's reaction to these declarations.

Stresa made Hitler scratch his head, Geneva made him lose it. . . . Blame from three strong adversaries . . . is one thing. Blame from the institution containing Bolsheviks, Czechs, and Latvians, not to mention other racially impure weaklings, is quite another and was unbearable for the fair Nordic man, and seemed, moreover, in his blue eyes to be the height of hypocrisy. Baron von Neurath told me in confidence that Herr Hitler, directly he heard of the Geneva resolution, had summoned him by telephone to Munich and had raved at him for five hours without, I hear, stopping to eat or drink. General Göring and Dr. Goebbels urged the Chancellor to double the Air Force at the earliest possible moment.[37]

But the Führer was not so angry as to be injudicious. Before the Stresa meeting he had received the previously postponed visit of Simon and Eden and had been struck by Simon's almost pathetic readiness to believe in his professions of peaceful intent,[38] and he decided now to resort to his old technique of defusing potentially dangerous situations by saying all of the things that peaceful people want to hear. In a major foreign policy address on 21 May, therefore, he offered to conclude bilateral agreements with his neighbours, to recognize the independence of Austria and refrain from interfering in its internal affairs, and to observe the Locarno treaties, including the demilitarization of the Rhineland.[39] How reassuring the effect of this was is shown by the usually sceptical Phipps's advice to his government.

His Majesty's Government may decide that it is now undesirable to conclude any convention with this country. . . . I earnestly hope that they will not allow themselves to be deterred by the mere contemplation of Herr Hitler's past misdeeds or breaches of faith. After all, he now leads nearly 70 millions of industrious, efficient and courageous, not to say pugnacious people. He is, like most men, an amalgam, and he may, like many men, have evolved since the old, somewhat gangster-like days at Munich. His signature, once given, will bind his people as no other could. It need not bind Great Britain to any state of undue weakness: it need not blind her to the undoubted dangers lying ahead. And if the worst befall, and Hitler decide to

[37] BD 2nd Ser. xiii, no. 327.
[38] See the German record of the talks in GD Ser. C iii, no. 555, esp. pp. 1078–80. See also Anthony Eden, Memoirs: Facing the Dictators (Boston, 1962), pp. 153 ff.
[39] Domarus, Hitler: Reden i. 505 ff.

break his freely-given solemn pledge, surely our battle-ground would be all the firmer for having put him to the test?[40]

That Phipps was preaching to the converted became evident a month later, when his government, without consulting its allies, concluded a naval pact with Germany.

The possibility of such a treaty had been raised for the first time, almost incidentally, by Hitler himself in the course of a general discussion of arms agreements with the British ambassador in November 1934[41] and reiterated more firmly during the Führer's conversations with Simon and Eden in March 1935.[42] On both occasions, the ratio of 35:100 was mentioned, the implication being that this would represent no threat to British naval supremacy and that the primary German objective was to secure the Baltic coast against Russian or French aggression. Official and newspaper reaction in Britain was cool, the *Manchester Guardian* urging that, in view of Hitler's repudiation of the Versailles arms clauses, a 'courteous rebuff' was the only appropriate answer to any naval proposals on his part, and *The Times* pointing out that a ratio agreement with Germany would 'upset proportionate strengths elsewhere' and increase the difficulties confronting the forthcoming general naval conference that was scheduled to meet later in the year. Despite these initial doubts, and despite the fact that, when a German delegation arrived in London for talks on 4 June, the peremptory presentation of the German case by its spokesman, Joachim von Ribbentrop, almost caused an abrupt termination of the proceedings, the British not only accepted the 35 per cent ratio but also agreed that Germany should be allowed a 45 per cent ratio in submarine strength and, in principle, parity in U-boats.[43]

The official explanation for this capitulation to German demands, which Sir Robert Vansittart gave to the angry French ambassador on 19 June, was that

it was surely clear that no Government in this country could have rejected the unilateral offer of Germany without incurring the disfavour of public opinion, weakening its internal position and, therefore, its prospects. It was no longer possible to stand on a purely legalistic basis, and it was mere

---

[40] *BD* 2nd Ser. xiii, no. 327.   [41] *GD* Ser. C iii, no. 358.

[42] Ibid., no. 555, pp. 1072–3.

[43] Ibid. iv, nos. 131, 132, 135–7, 141, 148, 154, 156, 165. See D. C. Watt, 'The Anglo-German Naval Agreement of 1935: An Interim Judgement', *Journal of Modern History*, xxviii, no. 2 (June 1956), 155–75; Viscount Templewood, *Nine Troubled Years* (London, 1954); Paul Schmidt, *Statist auf diplomatischer Bühne, 1923–45* (Bonn, 1949), pp. 303–17; Erich Kordt, *Nicht aus den Akten* (Stuttgart, 1950), pp. 98–113; Weinberg, *Foreign Policy of Hitler's Germany*, pp. 210–16.

common sense to seize the opportunity to tie the Germans down to a maximum level before they raised their demands to unreasonable and disquieting heights.[44]

That sensitivity to public opinion was an important factor in the British decision is doubtless true. It was precisely in the days when the talks were being held that Stanley Baldwin replaced MacDonald as Prime Minister. Facing an election in October and conscious of the strength of pacifism in the country and the potential effect of Labour charges that Conservatism and expensive armaments programmes were synonymous, Baldwin was inclined to accept any agreement that might provide a counter-argument.[45] This does not explain why the British Government bolted into the pact without consulting the French, and the most likely explanation is that it did so under the pressure of the Admiralty whose Naval Staff had come to the conclusion that it was beyond the capacity of the fleet to fight Japan and the strongest European naval Power at the same time and was eager, therefore, until it had reached an accommodation with the Japanese, to obtain an agreement with Germany that would prevent a runaway arms race like that before 1914.[46] The strong anti-French feeling in the Admiralty, caused by pronounced differences during the 1930 Naval Conference and reciprocated in the French navy, probably influenced the decision to go ahead without consulting the French beforehand.[47]

Thanks to the Anglo-German naval accord, the short-lived common front against Hitler dissolved into exchanges of bitter recriminations between London and Paris which continued until the third partner of the Stresa discussions decided to take advantage of the disunity of Europe by sending his armies into Abyssinia. From the diplomatic complications that followed upon Mussolini's adventure, Hitler was able to profit without any great effort on his part. There was no question now of interference with the scope or pace of his armament efforts; he no longer had to pretend an interest in new security pacts and could reject all proposals brutally and definitively without fear of the consequences;[48] the diversion of Italy's energies

[44] *BD* 2nd Ser. xiii, no. 357. See also nos. 352, 355, 356.

[45] See Winston Churchill, *The Second World War*, i: *The Gathering Storm* (Boston, 1948), pp. 89, 221; and Keith Middlemas and John Barnes, *Baldwin: A Biography* (London, 1969), pp. 826 ff., 864 ff.

[46] See Sir Warren Fisher's memorandum on defence requirements and naval strategy, 19 Apr. 1934, in *BD* 2nd Ser. xiii, App. I.

[47] See Gregory Perett, 'French Naval Policy and Foreign Policy, 1930–39' (Dissertation, Stanford Univ. 1977).

[48] *GD* Ser. C iv, nos. 460–2.

to Africa gave Germany the opportunity to begin an economic and political penetration of the Danubian and Balkan areas; and by refusing to join in any measures that might have embarrassed Mussolini during his involvement in Abyssinia, Hitler won the Duce's gratitude and laid the basis for the Rome–Berlin Axis of 1936.[49] More important, the divisions that the war brought between the signatories of the Locarno Treaty gave him an opportunity to repudiate that document and to accomplish his next objective, the remilitarization of the Rhineland.

In a conversation with his ambassador in Rome, Ulrich von Hassell, in February 1936 Hitler said that he had originally intended to postpone this step until the spring of 1937. But, despite his recognition of the fact that 'militarily Germany was not yet ready', political developments had convinced him that the psychological conditions for action were now so good as to offset that weakness.[50] The embroilment of the Powers in the Mediterranean had reached a peak of intensity, and the British were now pushing for the imposition of oil sanctions against Italy. In addition, both the British and French governments had reason to doubt their public support, and the difficulties of the latter had been exacerbated by the bitter debate over the Franco-Soviet Pact, which the Chamber of Deputies was to approve at the end of February. Neither country would be prepared to meet a challenge in a different quarter, provided it were made firmly enough and with plausible diplomatic justification, and the Franco-Soviet Pact, which could be represented as a violation of Locarno, would supply that.

This proved to be a correct reading of the situation. Both of the Western governments were aware that Hitler regarded the recovery of full sovereignty in the Rhineland as a major policy objective;[51] and the French had been warned repeatedly by their agents in the Rhineland and their military attachés in Berlin and Berne that a German initiative could be expected soon.[52] After a conversation with Hitler on 21 November 1935 François Poncet had suggested that the Führer might well confront France, as he had done in March 1935, with a *fait accompli*, 'occupying the garrisons and barracks that are already waiting and counting on the fact that we, prisoners of our internal

---

[49] Weinberg, *Foreign Policy of Hitler's Germany*, pp. 218 ff.

[50] *GD* Ser. C iv, no. 564.

[51] The British could be under no illusions about this after Phipps's conversation with Hitler on 13 December 1935. See ibid., nos. 460, 462.

[52] See Commission d'enquête parlementaire sur les événements survenus en France de 1933 à 1945 (Paris, 1951): Rapport, pp. 86–7; and the testimony of Jean Dobler in ibid., Témoignages et documents recueillis, ii. Also *DDF* 2nd Ser. i, nos. 27, 36.

discords and dominated by our love of peace, will not budge'; and a month later members of the Swiss General Staff were warning their French friends to be prepared for German action as early as 30 January, the anniversary of the *Machtübernahme*.[53] But, despite all these signals, the French Government neither challenged the German intentions nor saw to it that its armed forces were ready to resist a *coup*. Instead, in late February, when the German Press began a campaign against the Franco-Soviet Pact that gave urgent weight to the long-neglected warnings, the Foreign Minister, Pierre-Étienne Flandin, panicked and pressed his colleague Eden, who was now Foreign Secretary, to refrain from calling for action by the League on oil sanctions in the hope of making possible a united Anglo-French-Italian-Belgian front to block German action in the Rhineland and asked further whether the British Government would back France if it were forced to take preliminary action by itself. When Eden placed this matter before the British cabinet on 5 March, there was consternation and a muddled discussion at the end of which it was decided to support France provided no military action were envisaged, to postpone the call for oil sanctions, and to explore the possibility of general discussions among all the Locarno Powers in an effort to avert a crisis.[54]

It was too late for that. On 2 March Hitler had issued orders to the armed forces for an advance into the Rhineland on the seventh,[55] and, although there was a not inconsiderable amount of vacillating by the army staff, which was aware of its limited resources in manpower and weapons and lacked the Führer's confidence,[56] these were carried out promptly. As the troops moved in, German ambassadors read to the foreign ministers of the governments to which they were accredited a note accusing the French Government of having destroyed the Locarno Treaty by signing a pact with the Soviet Union that was clearly directed against Germany and was made doubly menacing by the fact that it was supplemented by a Soviet–Czech alliance that was exactly parallel in form. In self-defence, the note continued, Germany had been forced to reclaim full and unrestricted sovereignty in the Rhineland. In order, however, to avoid any misinterpretation of its motives, the German Government wished to make it clear that it

[53] Ibid., no. 37.

[54] Ibid., no. 170; Pierre-Étienne Flandin, *Politique française, 1919–1940* (Paris, 1947), pp. 195–6; Eden, *Facing the Dictators*, pp. 373–9; Middlemas and Barnes, *Baldwin*, pp. 913 f.

[55] *Trial of the Major Criminals before the International Military Tribunal* (Nuremberg, 1947–9), xxxiv. 644–7.

[56] See Craig, *Prussian Army*, p. 486 and notes.

was ready to negotiate with the French and Belgian governments for the delineation of demilitarized zones on both sides of their common boundaries, to conclude non-aggression pacts with those governments, which could be guaranteed by Great Britain and Italy, to enter into similar pacts with the states of Eastern Europe, to negotiate mutual guarantees against attacks from the air, and to return to the League of Nations as soon as appropriate reforms had been effected in that organization.[57]

This note in itself was enough to disarm the British Government;[58] and, as the German ambassador Hoesch pointed out a little later, it not only persuaded a number of prominent politicians to come out openly in defence of the German action but probably influenced the strong popular feeling that Germany had only done what other nations normally did, namely strengthened its borders against possible attack.[59] Winston Churchill was, nevertheless, probably correct when he wrote later that, if the French had taken military action immediately, the British could not have refused to support them.[60] This the French Government decided not to do, despite the pleas of Paul-Boncour, Mandel, and other cabinet members,[61] because of the attitude of the soldiers.

In his book on the collapse of France General André Beaufre wrote that, when he first joined the General Staff, his immediate superior took him aside and said, 'By the way, the general [Gamelin, the Chief of Staff] has no guts.'[62] On 8 March 1936, when the French Government asked whether the armed forces were capable of expelling the German intruders from the Rhineland, Gamelin showed how he acquired that reputation, by pointing out that he had warned the government that the Franco-Soviet Pact would lead to the German action and that to oppose the latter would require general mobilization. Since even that might not persuade the Germans to withdraw and since a major military effort might become necessary, every effort would have to be made in addition to bring British and Italian troops into action immediately and to secure from the Belgian Government permission for a French advance through its territory.[63] About the strength of the German forces presently and potentially engaged, Gamelin seems to have entertained the most unrealistic

---

[57] GD Ser. C v, no. 3 and enc.
[58] See Eden, *Facing the Dictators*, pp. 382, 412.   [59] GD Ser. C v, no. 178.
[60] Churchill, *Gathering Storm*, pp. 197–8.
[61] GD Ser. C v, no. 178; R. A. C. Parker, 'The First Capitulation: France and the Rhineland Crisis of 1936', *World Politics* (1951), 355–73.
[62] André Beaufre, *1940: The Fall of France* (New York, 1968), p. 43.
[63] DDF 2nd Ser. i, no. 334.

fears; and he was so successful in communicating these to the government that it gave up the thought of independent action and allowed itself to be persuaded by the British to take the road of negotiation. The result, after some months of fruitless chasing after the will-o'-the-wisps released by Hitler's note of 7 March, was completely negative.

With the investment of 19 battalions of infantry and 13 artillery groups, plus two anti-aircraft battalions and two groups of 27 single-seater fighter planes without reserves, a total strength of 22,000 men plus 14,000 local police[64] (a far cry from the 265,000 troops that Gamelin maintained were under German command in the Rhineland[65]), Hitler had effectively destroyed the post-First World War security system. The German remilitarization of the Rhineland was a victory not merely in the sense that it enhanced German prestige. Its psychological effect was to reveal the exclusively defensive nature of French strategical thinking, and this had devastating consequences among France's allies. Before the year was out, the King of the Belgians was seeking release from the obligations incurred by the treaties of 1920 and 1925, and his government had abandoned the intention of extending the Maginot Line into Belgium and had set a course back towards strict neutrality.[66] There were tremors in the Little Entente as well, where politicians with an eye to the main chance began to weigh the advantages of getting on to Hitler's bandwagon. All in all, the Führer had good reason to exult, as he viewed the disarray of French fortunes, 'The world belongs to the man with guts! God helps him.'[67]

It was natural now that his mind should turn to his long-term objectives in Eastern Europe, if only to weigh more systematically the preparations that would be necessary to effect them. The increasing urgency of his demands for an acceleration of the rearmament programme, which culminated in his memorandum of August 1936, has already been discussed.[68] It was accompanied by a new effort to acquire associates who would in time either support his eastward drive actively or prevent attempts to interfere with it.

When he wrote *Mein Kampf*, Hitler had described the 'strong man south of the Alps' as a natural ally in Germany's foreign endeavours but had attributed more importance to securing the alliance of Great

---

[64] GD Ser. C v, nos. 23, 189.
[65] Général Gamelin, *Servir* (3 vols., Paris, 1946–7), i. 209–10.
[66] Weinberg, *Foreign Policy of Hitler's Germany*, pp. 282–3.
[67] Fest, *Hitler*, p. 683.
[68] See above, Ch. XVII, pp. 612–13.

Britain, the most valuable of allies, he had written, 'as long as its leaders and the spirit of its masses permit us to expect that brutality and toughness' that had been the historical hallmark of British policy.[69] British conduct during the Rhineland affair had not disillusioned him about the advantages of such an alliance (on the contrary, it seems to have strengthened his belief that, under its new king, Edward VIII, Britain was turning from France to Germany), and in May he decided to test its feasibility, using as his agent the man who had brought home the Naval Pact. On 15 May Joachim von Ribbentrop had a long conversation with a close friend of Stanley Baldwin, the Prime Minister, named Tom Jones, who had come to Germany at his bidding, and urged him to persuade Baldwin to agree to a special meeting with Hitler, at which 'the issues we are to discuss will decide the fate of generations'. He then passed Jones on to Hitler, who expressed his keen desire to talk with the Prime Minister and indicated, apparently, that their discussions would treat not only the future of the League of Nations but also potential trouble-spots in Eastern Europe, including Austria and Czechoslovakia, as well as the need of improving Anglo–German understanding, perhaps by a change of British representation in Berlin. Jones, one of the most ardent and naïve of those who came to be called the appeasers, was overwhelmed by these attentions and returned to England resolved to persuade Baldwin to accept the invitation. The Prime Minister was intrigued by what Jones told him and strongly inclined to a meeting, until his Foreign Secretary intervened. Eden had been trying, with French assistance, to pressure the Germans into accepting some substitute for Locarno, and he pointed out to his chief that the invitation was an attempt to becloud the issue and divide London from Paris. This alarmed Baldwin and, to the dismay of his Germanophile associates, he let the suggested summit meeting die a-borning.[70]

If Hitler was, as one of his entourage said, 'deeply disappointed' by this, he persisted a while longer. When the German ambassador in London, Leopold von Hoesch, died during the summer, he appointed Ribbentrop in his place, and that self-confident amateur, whose painstaking efforts to cultivate a uniquely National Socialist diplomatic style had resulted in a tactlessness that was self-defeating, undertook to bully the British into an alliance, in accordance with which they would give Germany a free hand in the East, by hinting

---

[69] *Mein Kampf*, i, Ch. IV; ii, Chs. XIII, XIV.
[70] Thomas Jones, *A Diary with Letters* (Oxford, 1954), pp. 197 ff., 218 ff.; Eden, *Facing the Dictators*, p. 374.

at dreadful consequences unless they went along. This merely perplexed his hosts, who had difficulty in taking Ribbentrop seriously in any case, and they refused politely to discuss the matter.[71] This rebuff and the coldness shown towards him by British society permanently embittered the ambassador, who wrote in a secret memorandum in 1937, 'Every day in the future in which our political considerations are not determined fundamentally by the assumption that England is our deadliest enemy would be an advantage to our enemies.'[72]

In contrast, the *rapprochement* with Italy was effected without great difficulty and brought some unforeseen advantages.[73] Hitler's success in the Rhineland contributed to this by diverting the Powers from their intention of imposing oil sanctions on Italy, thus enabling Mussolini's forces to complete their conquest of Ethiopia in the late spring of 1936. This might have been followed by a resumption on the Duce's part of his former relations with Britain and France had it not been for the fact that Western public opinion had been outraged by Italian atrocities in the last stages of the war and prevented their governments, unlike Hitler's, from recognizing Mussolini's new empire. His victory in Africa had, moreover, inflated Mussolini's ambitions; he desired now to demonstrate that Italy was the dominant Power in the Mediterranean area; and the outbreak of the Civil War in Spain offered him an opportunity of strengthening that claim. He was eager to intervene and was gratified to discover that National Socialist Germany was prepared to support him by intervening itself.

For this new venture, which alarmed the professionals in the Foreign Ministry and the Wehrmacht Command, because of the political risk and economic cost involved, Hitler had several reasons. By supporting the rebel cause he could pose as the defender of Western civilization against the menace of Bolshevism, represented by the Spanish Republican Government and those who sympathized with it, like the Popular Front Government in France, which his Propaganda Ministry portrayed as tools of the Politburo in Moscow. This promised to lend weight to his continuing campaign against the Franco-Soviet Pact and to contribute to the growing divisions and

---

[71] Jones, *Diary*, p. 251; Churchill, *Gathering Storm*, pp. 222–4.

[72] Joachim von Ribbentrop, *Zwischen London und Moskau. Erinnerungen und letzte Aufzeichnungen* (Leoni, 1953), pp. 122–3.

[73] See, *inter alia*, Elizabeth Wiskemann, *The Rome–Berlin Axis* (New York, 1949), pp. 53–70; and Ivone Kirkpatrick, *Mussolini: A Study in Power* (New York, 1964), pp. 339 ff.

demoralization of his Western neighbour. It seemed likely, moreover, that his intervention would yield economic advantages in the form of concessions from General Franco in return for services rendered and that these would outweigh the cost of intervention while promoting German rearmament. In addition, Spain would serve as a laboratory for testing German weapons and military techniques, as well as for demonstrating their frightfulness to the world. The unconditional use of terror had served Hitler well during his rise to power, impressing and even attracting as many, if not more, people than it repelled. The ruthless employment of German bombers against civilian targets might have a similar effect on a larger scale.[74]

Finally, the association with Mussolini in Spain promised to bring advantages, not only because of the psychological effect it would have on other countries, but because it would divert Mussolini's attention from areas in which Germany had vital interests. It was not a coincidence that in the same month that saw the beginning of the Duce's Spanish involvement, Dollfuss's successor in Austria, Kurt von Schuschnigg, concluded a new agreement with the German Government that was ostensibly designed to end the tension that had existed between Austria and its northern neighbour since the Vienna Putsch of 1934. In return for a pledge that Germany would not interfere in Austria's internal affairs, the Austrian Chancellor engaged to follow a policy that would be 'based always on the principle that Austria acknowledges herself to be a German state' and made an oral commitment to allow German cultural and social organizations to operate in his country and to give a greater share of political responsibility to members of the 'National Opposition,' which really meant advocates of closer union with Germany.[75] Such a decided supplanting of Italian by German predominance in Austrian affairs would have been impossible without Mussolini's acquiescence. In fact, as early as March 1936 the Duce had urged Schuschnigg to reach an accommodation with Germany;[76] later, when he had made up his mind to intervene in Spain, he used this as an earnest

---

[74] Klaus Hildebrand, *The Foreign Policy of the Third Reich*, trans. from German (Berkeley, 1973), p. 46 says that Hitler's chief motivation was 'probably' the hope of extending Germany's strategical and logistical base into Spain after Franco had won the war. He does not present any evidence to support this hypothesis. On concern in the army and Foreign Ministry over Hitler's intervention, see Gordon A. Craig, 'The German Foreign Office from Neurath to Ribbentrop', in *The Diplomats*, pp. 428–9.

[75] See *GD* Ser. C v, editorial note, pp. 755–60.

[76] Ibid. Ser D i, no. 155. See Jürgen Gehl, *Austria, Germany, and the Anschluß, 1931–38* (London, 1963), p. 126.

of his own desire for German friendship and collaboration; and, in November 1936, when extended Italo-German talks had eventuated in a formalization of relations and the birth of the Axis, he was to praise the Austro-German agreement of July for having removed 'an element of dissension between Berlin and Rome'. This was not exactly a green light to Hitler to proceed with anschluss, but it was at least an intimation that Austrian independence was no longer regarded in Rome as a prime requirement of Italian policy.

The Axis collaboration encouraged Italy to make a major investment of strength in Spain and drew it away from South-Eastern Europe, where German diplomats began to lay the basis for their country's later dominance in the area. In contrast, Hitler placed careful limits upon German involvement in the Iberian peninsula. He was unresponsive to the enthusiastic proposals of his ambassador to the Burgos government, a retired general and ardent party member named Faupel, who believed that the war could be won immediately if German infantry divisions were sent to Spain and the direction of the war taken over by a German staff, presumably under his own command.[77] As he was to tell his chief advisers in 1937, 'a hundred percent victory for Franco [was] not desirable', Germany having a greater interest in a continuation of the conflict and the maintenance of tension in the Mediterranean.[78] The support that he sent to Franco was crucial to rightist fortunes—particularly at the outset of the war, when Germany's new Junker-52 transport planes ferried African troops to Seville, and again in the spring of 1937, when rightist morale began to sag—but there were probably never more than 16,000 Germans in Spain, many of these civilian technicians and advisers, and German military formations amounted only to four fighter-bomber, four fighter, one reconnaissance, and two seaplane squadrons (the notorious Condor Legion), and one tank battalion, which was used to train Franco's armoured force, plus thirty anti-tank companies and some transport planes and civilian cargo ships.[79] The Economic Policy Department of the Foreign Ministry calculated in 1939 that Germany's total expenditures in Spain amounted to about 500 million R.M.[80] This was not an excessive price to pay for the political and psychological advantages that Hitler derived

[77] GD Ser. D iii, nos. 125, 144, 145, 148, 187. On Faupel's role in the free corps operations of 1919–20, see above, Ch. XI, pp. 412, 431.

[78] Ibid. i, no. 19, p. 37.

[79] See Hugh Thomas, The Spanish Civil War (London, 1961), pp. 218, 219, 227–31, 634; B. H. Liddell Hart, The Other Side of the Hill (rev. edn., London, 1951), pp. 122–3.

[80] GD Ser. D iii, no. 783.

from the war, to say nothing of the shipments of raw materials that went to Germany.[81]

In the same month in which Mussolini proclaimed the formation of the Axis, Germany acquired another associate. A year earlier, fresh from his triumph with the Naval Pact, Joachim von Ribbentrop had conceived the idea of establishing a special relationship with Japan and had begun conversations with the Japanese military attaché in Berlin about the possibility of a political treaty between the two countries that would be anti-Soviet in orientation although disguised as a mere common front against Communism. These negotiations were kept largely secret from the Foreign Ministry, whose tradition had generally been pro-Chinese,[82] but they seem to have been encouraged by Hitler, and in November 1936 they eventuated in a formal agreement, the Anti-Comintern Pact.[83] For the time being, this was important primarily for its propaganda value, in helping to demonstrate Germany's earnest and consistent opposition to the Communist menace, although it became a more serious instrument after the China Incident of July 1937, when Japan requested a cessation of German aid to China. When Hitler acceded to that wish, and when the Italians were persuaded to join the Pact in November 1937, it assumed a militant character that was consonant with the beginning of the openly aggressive phase of Hitler's foreign policy. But even in its original innocuous form, it brought Hitler satisfaction, for it symbolized to him the growing international stature of the Third Reich. The days of isolation, the days when Germany had had to speak the language of the League Powers and pretend to believe in their principles and norms, were now behind it. It was now respected and courted, a change that filled him with a heady excitement. On 24 February 1937, when he addressed the old guard of the party in the Hofbräuhaus in Munich on the eighteenth anniversary of the founding of the NSDAP, he cried out proudly, 'Today we are once more a world Power!'[84]

---

[81] On shipments of raw materials to Germany, see above, Ch. XVII, p. 615.

[82] See Herbert von Dirksen, *Moskau, Tokyo, London: Erinnerungen und Betrachtungen* (Stuttgart, 1950), p. 184; *GD* Ser. C iv, no. 479.

[83] On the background and course of the talks, see Theo Sommer, *Deutschland und Japan zwischen den Mächten 1935–40* (Tübingen, 1962), pp. 23–42; Weinberg, *Foreign Policy of Hitler's Germany*, pp. 342–8; *GD* Ser. C v, nos. 509, 625, 637, and editorial note, pp. 1138–40.

[84] Hildegard von Kotze and Helmut Krausnick (eds.), *Es spricht der Fuehrer. Sieben exemplarische Hitler-Reden* (Gütersloh, 1966), p. 90.

III

The year in which he made that boast was a bad one for the old Foreign Ministry staff and diplomatic personnel.

Since about 1924 the permanent officials in the Foreign Ministry and the Defence Ministry had been in fundamental agreement about the nature and goals of German foreign policy.[85] Throughout the Stresemann years, they advocated a generally revisionist line that included among its objectives the freeing of the Saar and the end of the demilitarization of the Rhineland, anschluss with Austria, the elimination of the Polish Corridor, the recovery of those parts of Upper Silesia that had been lost to the Poles, and the achievement of military equality with the other Powers. During the Brüning period, there were differences concerning the tactics best designed to accomplish the last of these objectives, but these were soon overcome; and the alliance was in good repair when the Hitler–Papen government was formed in January 1933. Konstantin von Neurath and Bernhard von Bülow in the Foreign Ministry and Ludwig Beck in the Army General Staff, who survived the change of regime, were conservatives who believed in the traditional comity of Great Powers and who wanted their country to regain the authority that it had exercised within that system before 1914. They were not adventurers, nor did they have dreams of world conquest; they were conscious of the mistakes of Wilhelmine policy and determined to avoid them. They were equally bent on preventing the new Chancellor from launching dangerous initiatives of his own, although reasonably confident that his inexperience would lead him to follow their expert advice.

Until the end of 1937 Hitler gave them no reason to disapprove of his policy, which was, at least superficially, congruent with their own. The repudiation of the Disarmament Conference and the arms clauses and the remilitarization of the Rhineland aroused the enthusiasm of the soldiers and were recognized by Foreign Ministry officials as logical extensions of Stresemann's policy. If the partners were startled by Hitler's talent for doing the unexpected—as in the case of the Polish Pact—they came to admire his tactical skill; if his readiness to take risks worried them—as it did in the Rhineland case—they had to admit that his calculations proved to be accurate. Moreover, he seemed capable of profiting from advice. He had, they thought, listened to their warnings about involving himself too

---

[85] This is discussed in detail in Post, *Civil-Military Fabric*, pp. 87 ff.

deeply in Spain or making too many commitments to the Japanese too soon.

This was all illusion. Hitler had allowed the old diplomatic establishment to remain in power in order to mask his intentions from the rest of the world. He had little respect for its talents and no intention of being bound by its counsels, which, he said contemptuously at a later date, were 'miserable. They always had the same quintessence that we ought to do nothing.'[86] The soldiers were no better. Fritsch and Beck, the Wehrmacht Commander and the Chief of Staff, not only failed to make the most of the opportunities he had created for them in 1935, by building a modern mechanized army as fast as possible, but they were as timorous as the diplomats in situations like the Rhineland operation, when daring and cool nerves were required, always overestimating the resources and the will of the other Powers.[87] They were incapable of understanding, let alone carrying out, the policy he had projected, which far exceeded in its scope the limits of their narrow revisionism.

Hitler's feelings on this score were certainly reinforced when he called Neurath and his military chiefs Blomberg, Fritsch, Raeder, and Goering together on 5 November 1937 and for the first time gave them a clear idea of his next objectives in foreign policy. In a long and somewhat disorganized harangue he reiterated the basic premiss of his two books, namely that the only logical and effective foreign policy for Germany was one of acquiring living space (*Lebensraum*) in Eastern Europe, and supported this by arguing that neither participation in world trade nor a policy of economic autarchy could satisfy the nation's needs and maintain the living standards of its people. The acquisition of the space needed would be made possible only by the use of force, which was always accompanied by risk, and in this case 'German policy [would] have to reckon with the two hateful antagonists England and France'. Yet the problem had to be solved at the latest by 1943–5, because at that time the law of obsolescence would begin to blunt the efficiency of Germany's armed forces, and economic problems would begin to be intolerable. Germany must watch, therefore, for the opportunity to launch its eastward drive, the first stages of which would be the absorption of Austria and the destruction of Czechoslovakia, the eastern state most capable of inflicting serious damage on Germany in the event of a war with France. The most favourable opportunities for a blow

[86] Picker, *Tischgespräche*, p. 396.
[87] See e.g. the doubts expressed in Beck's 1934 memorandum, in Förster, *Ein General kämpft*, pp. 26–7; and, in general, Craig, *Prussian Army*, pp. 484–7 and notes.

against these countries would occur if France's energies were paralysed by internal disorders or if a war broke out between France and
another major Power (perhaps as a consequence of the Spanish
conflict). Hitler did not exclude other possibilities. In any event,
Germany must be prepared when the right moment came to strike
out at the Czechs with lightning swiftness (*blitzartig schnell*).[88]

These remarks seem to have shaken Hitler's auditors, even the
usually sanguine Goering expressing some reservations about the
feasibility of the projected operations. Fritsch had good reason for
alarm, for earlier in the year his Chief of Staff, Ludwig Beck, had sent
him a frightening memorandum on Germany's current state of
readiness, in which he pointed out that, despite the government's
success in stimulating industrial production, reserves of raw materials and food supplies were being consumed as fast as they were
accumulated and dependence upon foreign supply was as great as
ever. Beck warned that 'if it should come to developments of a
warlike nature . . . our position would be inconceivable', the more so
because 'an anxious disquietude affects the masses; they fear war; . . .
they see no justifiable grounds for war'. This may have been in the
army commander's mind as he protested that Germany must avoid
any situation that would bring Britain and France into war against it.
Blomberg supported him and pointed out that, even if France were
simultaneously at war with Italy, it would have the capability of
taking offensive action in the west, where Germany's fortifications
were still in a rudimentary state of readiness.[89] Even without such
complications, he continued, an operation against Czechoslovakia
would be difficult, for the Czech defences had assumed the character
of a Maginot complex and would present the attacker with formidable problems.

Hitler must have been nettled by these doubts, although it is
impossible to get a very accurate impression of his feelings from the
colourless prose of the memorandum on the meeting compiled by

---

[88] *GD* Ser. D i. no. 19. A sensible brief discussion is to be found in Norman Rich,
Hitler's War Aims: Ideology, the Nazi State, and the Course of Expansion (2 vols., New
York, 1973). i. 97, 287–8. Taylor (*Origins of the Second World War*, pp. 131–4) seeks
to prove that the meeting was without significance but his interpretation is forced and
unpersuasive. Hildebrand (*Foreign Policy*, pp. 51–3) is chiefly interested in looking for
clues to the policy that Hitler intended to follow *after* he had won the desired
Lebenstraum in the east.

[89] Beck's memorandum is in Förster, *Ein General kämpft*, pp. 44–7. Its effect upon
Fritsch, and perhaps upon Blomberg, was reflected in the attack made on Goering by
the two generals at the end of the meeting, for mismanagement of the Four Year Plan.
See Friedrich Hossbach, *Zwischen Wehrmacht und Hitler 1934–1938* (rev. edn., Göttingen, 1965), p. 120.

his adjutant Hossbach. When Neurath observed that the war in the Mediterranean, upon which a good deal seemed to depend, showed no signs of materializing, Hitler said shortly that things might be different in the summer of 1938 (as, indeed, they were, although not because of a change in Spain). When Blomberg and Fritsch continued to fret about what Britain and France might do, he said flatly that he was convinced that the British would do nothing for Czechoslovakia and that he could not conceive of France taking military action against Germany.[90]

The meeting ended with no sense of urgency. Indeed, when Fritsch, who said that he had already ordered a winter war game on Czechoslovakia to investigate means of penetrating its fortifications, suggested that it might be wise for him to cancel a planned leave, Hitler said that this would not be necessary, since the operation was not imminent. Yet the new year was not far advanced before he had changed his mind and had decided to proceed against Austria and Czechoslovakia without delay; and, as a preliminary step, he effected a thorough purge of his military and diplomatic staffs, getting rid of the doubters.

The unedifying story of how a *mésalliance* on the part of Field-Marshal von Blomberg and an SS plot against Generaloberst von Fritsch, which led to that officer's being falsely arraigned on morals charges, gave him an opportunity to do this has often been told and need not be rehearsed.[91] It is enough to note that Hitler's action in February was designed to bring the command of the armed forces and the administration of foreign affairs directly into his own hands. Blomberg and Fritsch were allowed to retire, the latter being replaced by General Walter von Brauchitsch, whom one knowledgeable observer described as being a man who was 'ready to agree to everything'. Blomberg's post of War Minister was simply abolished, Hitler decreeing that henceforth he would 'exercise immediate command over the whole armed forces', through a staff, the Oberkommando der Wehrmacht (OKW), that was headed by General Wilhelm Keitel, a thoroughgoing admirer of the Führer who was sometimes called 'the rubber lion'. Along with these changes went the retirement of 16 high-ranking generals and the transfer of 44 more, changes motivated by the desire to remove potentially unreliable elements from the higher ranks. All of this represented, in

[90] *GD* Ser. D i, no. 19, p. 38.
[91] On the Blomberg–Fritsch affair, see the authorities cited in Craig, *Prussian Army*, pp. 489 ff. See also Fest, *Hitler*, pp. 745–7, and Robert J. O'Neill, *The German Army, and the Nazi Party, 1933–39* (London, 1966).

effect, the completion of the army's *Gleichschaltung*, which had begun with its complicity in the killings of the Night of the Long Knives and its acceptance of the oath to Hitler in August 1934.

A similar reorganization took place in the Foreign Ministry, where Neurath was eased out and his position, to the dismay of the professionals, given to Joachim von Ribbentrop. There was no question of this true believer's taking an independent line or adopting a critical stance or speaking in any tone save that of his master. After Ribbentrop had been in office for more than a year, François-Poncet wrote of the difficulty of carrying on any useful dialogue with him.

He does not listen to his interlocutor. He only listens to himself. He does not respond to what is said to him. He just goes on singing the same song interminably. He is very poorly informed about the details of problems and tries to cover this up by throwing out ringing declarations of a general nature, in which pacific protestations alternate with menacing affirmations of Germany's power and her readiness to resist all attempts at intimidation. Out of this verbal and verbose abundance, nothing clear or positive emerges; instead something louche and suspicious. I have sometimes had the impression of a man taking evasive action, either because he is trying to hide his ideas or because they lack precision or because in reality it is not M. von Ribbentrop who is doing the thinking but M. Hitler.[92]

These changes, and the speeding-up of Hitler's timetable that they forecast, had been caused by a reassessment of the situation in the countries to the west. As he had shown during his rise to power, Hitler had a talent for detecting and exploiting weakness in others, and a series of events in the winter of 1937–8 convinced him that his earlier assumption of Anglo-French resistance to his eastern plans was exaggerated. The new British Prime Minister, Neville Chamberlain, who had replaced Baldwin after the abdication crisis of December 1936, took pride in his preference for fact rather than theory, and the word 'realism' was often in the mouths of his agents:[93]but it did not take long for Hitler to detect that this was merely a formulation meant to differentiate the Prime Minister's position from the anti-German stance of Eden, Vansittart, and the Foreign Office in general. In November 1937 Chamberlain's close friend Lord Halifax visited the Führer and carried realism to the point of admitting that certain changes in Eastern Europe, notably in Austria, Czechoslovakia, and Danzig, 'could probably not be

[92] *DDF* 2nd Ser. x, no. 79.

[93] See *BD* 3rd Ser. i, pp. 22, 28, 49, 109, 257, 273, 307, 345; *GD* Ser. D i, pp. 221, 264, 1168.

avoided in the long run', and that 'England was only interested in seeing that such changes were brought about by peaceful develop- ment'.[94] This was a signal that Hitler could hardly have disregarded, particularly when it was followed in February by changes in the British Foreign Office that were as dramatic as those that took place almost simultaneously in the Wilhelmstraße, with Eden being forced out to make way for Halifax and Vansittart being kicked upstairs to a position of no importance. With respect to France, the auguries were equally encouraging, the German ambassador reporting at the end of the year that Delbos, the Foreign Minister, was expressing a gratify- ing complacency about the possibility of changes in Austria's status and was so disinclined to consult his Soviet ally that he had not included Moscow in his itinerary for a planned tour of Eastern Europe.[95]

Hitler does not seem, therefore, to have expected Western resis- tance when he decided to move against Austria and, if he was a little nervous about the Italian attitude, this fear was soon demonstrated to be groundless. Indeed, the other governments looked elaborately in another direction while Hitler, in late February, summoned Kurt von Schuschnigg to Berchtesgaden, upbraided him hysterically for breaches of the 1936 agreement, and browbeat him into legalizing the Austrian Nazi party and permitting his government to be honey-combed with pro-German elements; and they remained abstracted in the second week of March, when Hitler, reacting furiously to Schuschnigg's efforts to prove his country's desire for independence by means of a plebiscite, came down over the mountains 'like a storm in the spring', as he had earlier warned the Austrian Chancellor he might do, and effected the anschluss by *force majeure*.

Between the liquidation of the Austrian problem and the begin- ning of the campaign against Czechoslovakia, there was no appreci- able pause. Hitler laid his plans for the ultimate destruction of the country that he called 'a French aircraft-carrier in the middle of Europe' with great confidence, paying no attention to the warnings of professional diplomats who felt that it would be wiser to seek his objectives by diplomacy than by his chosen combination of sub- version and threats of force. When Ernst von Weizsäcker, the Sec- retary of State, argued that a too belligerent policy would elicit a strong Western response, Ribbentrop warned him that 'it was neces- sary to believe in . . . [Hitler's] genius' and that if he 'had not yet

---

[94] *GD* Ser. D i, pp. 69–70.   [95] Ibid., pp. 83, 122, 150.

reached the stage of blind belief . . . then he desired of [him], in a friendly manner, and urgently too, that [he] should do so'.[96]

In fact, Hitler's action against Czechoslovakia was a virtuoso performance, diminished only by the fact that his antagonists made things easier for him than he deserved. He built his case against the country upon the grievances of its German minority in the western fringe area called the Sudetenland. The satisfaction of their complaints was a difficult process because they kept increasing in scope and number; and this, in turn, was because Hitler had ordered the leader of the Sudeten German party, Konrad Henlein, who visited him in March and placed his party at his command, to be inventive in this respect and to make his demands for autonomy and special rights so extreme that no self-respecting government could yield to them.[97] The gap between the earnest efforts of the Czech Government to appease the German minority and Henlein's stubborn refusal to be satisfied was described by Goebbels's Propaganda Ministry as intolerable injustice and 'brutal treatment of mothers and children of German blood'. As the skilfully orchestrated combination of incident and protest heightened the tension between Prague and Berlin, the Powers that were pledged by treaty to protect Czechoslovakia from attack, France and the Soviet Union, failed to stand by their ally, the latter because the Soviet treaty stipulated that it would not come into effect until the French Government carried out its obligations under the Franco-Czech treaty, the former because it was unwilling to invoke that treaty unless the British promised to support it. This the Chamberlain government flatly refused to do, the Prime Minister telling Daladier, the French Premier, in April 1938 that he did not believe that Hitler wanted to destroy Czechoslovakia but that, if he did, he 'did not see how that could be prevented'.[98]

The British attitude towards the Czechs is by all odds the most intriguing feature of the Sudeten crisis of 1938. The country of Masaryk and Benes had never been popular with the Conservative Government, partly, no doubt, because even in Salisbury's days Conservatives regarded lesser states that sought to play a role in European politics as nuisances, more particularly because of Benes's efforts to prevent the League of Nations, another object of their detestation, from being dominated by the Great Powers. But the

[96] Ibid. ii, p. 593.
[97] Ibid., p. 198.
[98] This was the culminating statement of the Anglo-French talks of April. See *BD* 3rd Ser. i. 198–235.

often virulent anti-Czech feeling that can be found in the dispatches of the British ambassador in Berlin, Sir Nevile Henderson, in the leading articles in *The Times* that were inspired by the associate editor Barrington-Ward, and in the table-talk of Chamberlain's inner circle[99] makes one suspect that there is some truth in the saying that the person who has an opportunity to prevent a crime and deliberately fails to do so ends up by being resentful of its victim. When Hitler, who remembered Halifax's assurance that Britain was not opposed to change in Eastern Europe provided it was peaceful, took the line that it was the Czechs who were preventing peaceful change by resisting the fulfilment of his wishes, Chamberlain and his associates did not seem to regard this as illogical. Indeed, the argument gained in plausibility for them after May 1938, when rumours of German troop movements on their borders, especially by General von Reichenau's Army Group IV, led the Czech Government to call up reserves and induced the British and French governments to intervene in Berlin and to warn the German Government against taking any action that might lead to war. The German professions of innocence appeared, in this instance, to be entirely sincere, and the two Western governments, shaken by the experience of finding themselves so close to the brink, ended by accepting the German argument that the crisis had been deliberately contrived by the Czechs, that they, in fact, were the people who were endangering the peace. In England the reaction was sharp, the government henceforth inclining to the view that the best way to promote a solution of the Central European problem was, as Henderson put it inelegantly, 'for Prague to get a real twist of the screw', that would compel the Benes government to end its 'tergiversations' and accede to the demands of its minority.[100]

When, however, the Prague Government did precisely that, by fulfilling every item on Henlein's so-called Karlsbad Programme, they got no credit for it. On 12 September Hitler abandoned the pretence of being interested only in justice for the Sudeten Germans and showed that he was bent on conquest. In a violent and vituperative attack upon the Czech Government, whose hate-filled accents will not easily be forgotten by anyone who heard the broadcast from Nuremberg, he lashed himself into a fury and shouted, 'This is a question of German folk-comrades! I have no intention of

[99] See Ian Colvin, *The Chamberlain Cabinet* (London, 1971), pp. 127–34; *History of The Times*, iv (New York, 1952), pp. 881–950; Gilbert and Gott, *The Appeasers*, pp. 123, 127, 138 ff.; *DDF* 2nd Ser. x, no. 512.
[100] *BD* 3rd Ser. i. 590; ii. 85; *DDF* 2nd Ser. x, no. 519.

allowing a second Palestine to be formed here in the heart of Germany by the labours of other statesmen. . . . The Germans in Czechoslovakia are neither defenceless nor abandoned. Of that you can rest assured!'[101] On the following day Henlein demanded the complete separation of the Sudetenland from Czechoslovakia and fled across the border. But, with Hitler's menaces ringing in their ears, the Western Powers did not find this demand unreasonable. Indeed, on 15 September Neville Chamberlain flew to Berchtesgaden and promised Hitler that he would try to persuade the French and Czech governments to agree to a cession of the disputed area to Germany.

Although it is difficult to define Hitler's intentions at this point with any precision, he seemed to be determined to force the issue to the utmost. He had been infuriated by the events of May, which the Western Press had portrayed as a forced retreat on his part, and in a meeting with his chief military and political advisers on 28 May had announced, with visible emotion, that he intended to wipe Benes's country off the map. A modified version of Plan Green, the directive for operations against Czechoslovakia, began with the words, 'It is my unalterable intention to destroy Czechoslovakia by military action in the foreseeable future' and named 1 October as the operative date.[102] Chamberlain's visit to Berchtesgaden did not alter his objective. On the contrary, as soon as the Prime Minister had gone off to consult the French and the Czechs, the Führer took action designed to vitiate the settlement that Chamberlain had in mind. He urged the Polish and Hungarian governments to make territorial demands of Prague, dispatched agents to Slovakia to stimulate the movement for autonomy there, and authorized the formation of a Sudeten Free Corps which immediately began to plan attacks upon Eger and Asch.[103] When Chamberlain came to Godesberg on 22 September to announce that he had been successful in his talks with the French and the Czechs and that the three governments were prepared to agree to the cession of Sudetenland and to the replacement of Czechoslovakia's treaties with France and the Soviet Union by an international guarantee of the country's remaining borders, Hitler informed him that he was 'very sorry' but that 'after the developments of the last days that solution [would not] work'.

With some asperity Chamberlain pointed out that he had 'risked his whole political career' by forcing the Czechs to accept cession,

[101] Domarus, *Hitler: Reden* i. 904 f.
[102] *GD* Ser. D ii, no. 221.
[103] Ibid., pp. 819, 849, 852, 863–4.

and that Hitler's new terms were nothing short of an ultimatum. Hitler retorted blandly that 'it bore the word "Memorandum" on top'; but the Prime Minister was right. Hitler insisted that the bulk of the Sudeten territory be occupied by German military forces by 1 October, with all of its installations intact, and that the claims of all of Czechoslovakia's minorities and neighbours be settled immediately by plebiscites in the areas affected.[104]

At this point, Hitler was probably hoping that the Czechs would refuse the terms and be abandoned by the Western Powers, in which case he could turn his army against the isolated country. If so, he was disappointed, for the French Government decided to dig its heels in and to demand a return to the terms that Chamberlain had taken to Godesberg on 22 September. Despite considerable British pressure, Daladier said that he would not agree 'to the strangulation of a people', and the British reluctantly pledged their support if war should come. Hitler's surprise was violent and defiant. In a stormy interview with Chamberlain's man of confidence, Sir Horace Wilson, who had been sent to tell him of the Anglo-French decision and to urge him to prevent the worst from occurring, he shouted, 'On the first of October I shall have Czechoslovakia where I want her!, If France and England wanted to attack, let them do it! It was a matter of complete indifference to him. He was ready for any eventuality![105]

If Hitler had tried to make that threat good, it is hard to believe that he could have sustained a war for very long, burdened as he was with an inadequately mobilized war economy, an insufficiency of strategic stockpiles, an incomplete western line of fortifications, and an officer corps whose upper ranks lacked confidence in the chances of success, and faced as he was on both flanks with strong armies, which might in time have been supported by the Soviet Union, the Poles, and others. Perhaps he realized this himself, or was impressed by the manifest lack of popular enthusiasm for a military gamble, and decided that it would be best to take the cherry in two bites. For whatever reason, on the evening of 27 September he lowered the temperature by sending a surprisingly conciliatory letter to the British Prime Minister; and the relief in London and Paris was so great that the resistance in those capitals to the Godesberg terms vanished in a trice, despite the fact that the Czechs still opposed them.[106] Reverting to an idea already discussed in the Inner Cabinet

[104] Ibid. 870–911; *BD* 3rd Ser. ii. 463–73, 499–508.
[105] Bullock, *Hitler*, pp. 460–3; *GD* Ser. D ii. 965; *BD* 3rd Ser. ii. 554–7, 564–7.
[106] *GD* Ser. D ii. 988–9; *BD* 3rd Ser. ii. 576, 587.

on 13 September,[107] Chamberlain invoked the aid of Mussolini in proposing a four-Power conference to settle the Sudeten question; Hitler agreed when the Duce put the plan before him on the twenty-eighth; and, on the following day, Hitler, Mussolini, Chamberlain, and Daladier met at Munich and immediately gave the Führer everything he had demanded at Godesberg, depriving Czechoslovakia of a third of its population, its most important industrial areas, and its only effective means of self-defence.

When the terms of the Munich settlement were made public, the leader of the British Labour party, Clement Attlee, summed them up in words which Chamberlain's supporters found it difficult to refute:

The events of the last few days constitute one of the greatest diplomatic defeats that this country and France have ever sustained. There can be no doubt that it is a tremendous victory for Herr Hitler. Without firing a shot, by the mere display of military force, he has achieved a dominating position in Europe which Germany failed to win after four years of war. He has destroyed the last fortress of democracy in eastern Europe that stood in the way of his ambition. He has opened the way to the food, the oil and the resources that he requires in order to consolidate his military power, and he has successfully defeated and reduced to impotence the forces that might have stood against the rule of violence.[108]

At Munich Chamberlain and Daladier deluded themselves into thinking that they had saved, not destroyed, Czechoslovakia, and that the rump state, healthier because of the operation it had resisted, would enjoy the protection of an international guarantee. But this never materialized and soon became a topic that the Germans refused to discuss and the mere mention of which irritated them.[109] The German interpretation of the Munich settlement was that, in return for the maintenance of peace, the Western Powers had agreed to be 'disinterested in the eastern European question',[110] and had resigned themselves to the fact that the future of Czechoslovakia must depend entirely on Germany's wishes. Hitler himself made this point clear to Chvalkovsky, the Czech Foreign Minister, in January. His country must in all things be allied with Germany, he said, and it was time that the Czechs realized this. At present, they reminded him of a speech in which Bismarck had warned the Liberals that they were following a disastrous course. When they had protested, the Chancellor had compared them, said Hitler, with

---

[107] Colvin, *Chamberlain Cabinet*, p. 166.

[108] Parliamentary Debates, 5th Ser., vol. 339. House of Commons (12th vol. of Session 1937–8), p. 52.

[109] *GD* Ser. D iv, nos. 154, 163, 164, 175.

[110] Ibid., no. 233.

people who wanted to go to Nowawes but boarded the train for Grünau. They asked when the train would arrive at Potsdam and demanded that it should stop at Nowawes. They could not be made to understand that this was quite impossible, because the train did not go there. In Czechoslovakia, they were also on the wrong train. They did not want to go in this direction, but they had to because the points were set that way.[111]

There were other ways of making the Czechs understand their position besides words. Hitler had continued to encourage those disruptive forces within the country that he had let loose before Munich, and, as their effects began to be felt, he was quick to describe the lack of internal order as a threat to Germany. As early as 21 October he had ordered the Wehrmacht to prepare for the liquidation of the remainder of the Czech state;[112] and on 17 December he supplemented this by defining the kinds of units to be used and by stating that 'the case is to be prepared on the assumption that no appreciable resistance is to be expected'.[113] Nothing that happened in the weeks that followed cast serious doubt on this assumption. When his troops were ready and the demoralization of the country at its most extreme point, the Führer, on 15 March 1939, summoned the President of Czechoslovakia, Emil Hácha, to the Reich Chancellery in Berlin and, with Keitel and Goering standing by to give urgency to his threats, bullied the old and infirm man and his Foreign Minister Chvalkovsky into placing the fate of the Czech people and their country into his hands.[114] On the following day German troops marched into Prague.

IV

On the day of the Munich Conference General Alfred Jodl, Keitel's chief aide in the OKW, wrote in his diary: 'The hope remains that the incredulous, the weak, and the doubtful people have been converted and will remain that way.' This hope was to a large extent fulfilled. One of the most ominous by-products of the Munich settlement was that it reinforced the Führer's reputation for infallibility. The possibility of a generals' strike to check his heedless course now collapsed completely; the fears that had affected the public mind in mid-September were dissipated. The lithographs on the walls of public houses, which showed the superimposed profiles of Frederick the Great, Bismarck, and Hitler, now seemed to assume a profound authenticity. History appeared to be working through and for the

---

[111] Ibid., no. 158, p. 191.   [112] Ibid., no. 81.
[113] Ibid., no. 152.   [114] Ibid., nos. 228, 229.

Führer, as it had in the case of his predecessors. And if that were so, who could stand against him?[115]

Munich seemed to convince Hitler too that he could do no wrong, and his policy now betrayed an impatience that had not characterized it earlier. In his search for new triumphs, economic factors no longer had the power to restrain him, for it was clear that the country's readiness for war was as good as it could be without measures of domestic discipline that he was disinclined to take; and it seemed possible, in any case, that conquests might repair deficiencies.[116] Moreover, the acceleration of Hitler's campaign against the Jews at the end of 1938 contributed to the mounting pace of his external policy. One of the complaints that he made against the government of Czechoslovakia was that 'the Jews in Czechoslovakia were still poisoning the nation' against Germany and would have to be dealt with.[117] As he turned to new objectives, it is clear that the conquest of space and the destruction of Jewry were inextricably connected in his thoughts.

Even before the final liquidation of Czechoslovakia his mind had turned to the two former German cities that were still, from his point of view, *in partibus infidelium*, Memel and Danzig, and he may have considered seizing them simultaneously with Prague. On 13 March Weizsäcker, the Secretary of State, warned Dr. Carl Burckhardt, the High Commissioner in Danzig, that it might not be wise to return to the Free City; and, when Burckhardt nevertheless did so, the President of the Danzig Senate, Arthur Greiser, told him that Hitler had said to him that the timing of the joint operation would depend on whether 'the Poles behave[d] nicely'. If they did not, they would 'learn who [was] the master'.[118] On reflection, Hitler decided to separate the two questions. The government of Lithuania received a peremptory request on 19 March to hand over Memel without causing difficulties, and did so four days later.[119] The Danzig question became part of a more elaborate proposal that Ribbentrop handed to the Polish ambassador Lipski on 21 March. It was not the first time that the issue had been raised between the two men, and in

[115] On the mood after Munich, see Marlis G. Steinert, *Hitlers Krieg und die Deutschen: Stimmung und Haltung der deutschen Bevölkerung im Zweiten Weltkrieg* (Düsseldorf and Vienna, 1970), pp. 77–80, and O'Neill, *Army and Party*, p. 65. Jodl's diary is in *International Military Tribunal* xxviii. 345–90.

[116] See above, Ch. XVII, p. 626.

[117] *GD* Ser. D iv, no. 158, p. 193.

[118] *BD* 3rd Ser. iv, no. 419; Carl J. Burckhardt, *Meine Danziger Mission 1937–1939* (Munich, 1962), pp. 219–20.

[119] *BD* 3rd Ser. iv, no. 441.

October Lipski had conveyed to the German Foreign Minister Colonel Beck's insistence that it was unnegotiable.[120] Now Ribbentrop posed the issue with unwonted energy and, after lecturing the ambassador on his government's failure to understand that Poland's future as a national state depended on a 'reasonable relationship' with Germany, he demanded the return of Danzig to the Reich and the construction of an extraterritorial highway across the Corridor, and raised the question of Polish adherence to the Anti-Comintern Pact. In return, he offered a German guarantee of Poland's western frontier and the possibility of territorial compensation in the Ukraine.[121]

These blunt demands destroyed any illusions Colonel Beck had about building a Third Europe under Polish leadership to control the balance between Germany and the Soviet Union. To give in to the Germans would be to invite new demands; a refusal would be more impressive if he could demonstrate that he had powerful friends. He was unwilling to enter into any combination that included the Soviet Union, but he was quick to accept the British offer of an Anglo-French guarantee against aggression, which the British Prime Minister made in the House of Commons on 31 March.[122]

If this was intended as a deterrent, it failed of its purpose. The British action infuriated Hitler ('I'll brew a devil's drink for them!' he swore when he learned of it[123]), and, with respect to Poland, made him defiant. On 3 April he ordered the Wehrmacht, which had been preparing plans for the occupation of Danzig since late November,[124] to make a contingency plan in case it were necessary to destroy the Polish armed forces;[125] and on 28 April, in a speech that was marked by a bravura demolition of a recent suggestion of President Franklin D. Roosevelt that Germany might contribute to the harmony of the globe by giving guarantees to thirty-one states, which he named, the Führer made a slashing attack upon provocateurs and enemies of the peace and abrogated both the Anglo-German naval accord of 1935 and the Nazi-Polish Pact of January 1934.[126]

The course was now set for war with Poland, although five

---

[120] See Anna M. Cienciala, *Poland and the Western Powers, 1938–1939* (London, 1968), pp. 162 ff, 180–3.

[121] *GD* Ser. D vi, no. 61.

[122] See Colvin, *Chamberlain Cabinet*, pp. 187 ff.; Cienciala, *Poland and the Western Powers*, pp. 210 ff.

[123] H. G. Gisevius, *Bis zum bitteren Ende* (2 vols., Zurich, 1946), ii. 124.

[124] *GD* Ser. D iv. 185 n.

[125] *International Military Tribunal* xxxiv. 380 ff.

[126] Domarus, *Hitler: Reden* ii. 1148 ff.

months were to pass before it broke out. This interval was filled with accelerated military preparations—on 14 June the commander of Army Group III, General Blaskowitz, ordered his staff to have plans for the attack on Poland ready by 20 August[127]—and a series of politico-military manœuvres that culminated in Hitler's last stunning diplomatic *coup*. On the one hand, in collaboration with his Axis partner, Hitler sought to distract and weaken the will of the Western Powers. Mussolini's invasion of Albania in April, the conclusion of the Italo-Germany military alliance, the so-called Pact of Steel, in May, and the opening of the Duce's noisy campaign to force France to return Tunis, Savoy, and Djibuti were part of this elaborate but unsuccessful game. At the same time, the Führer delayed any new action in Eastern Europe until he was sure of the position of the Soviet Union.

Even though he professed to believe that the Western Powers did not mean their pledge to Poland seriously, Hitler was unwilling to risk an attack eastwards that might embroil him with the Soviet Union and hearten the British and French to push through Holland and Belgium into the Ruhr, which he once described as 'our Achilles heel'.[128] He was reluctant, for ideological reasons, to make the obvious move to free himself from this dilemma, namely to seek an agreement with the Soviet Union, despite the fact that, at least from March onwards, the Soviet Government seemed interested in investigating that possibility. Partnership with the great Communist state, he was to tell Mussolini in 1941, 'seemed to me to be a break with my whole origin, my concepts, and my former obligations';[129] and in 1939, despite obvious hints from Moscow, he was generally unresponsive, not even pushing the negotiations for a new agreement on trade and payments that began in December 1938[130] with any energy. It was Western obduracy with respect to the pledge to Poland and the belated attempt of the British and French governments, after years of cold-shouldering the Soviets, to make a last-minute agreement with them to contain Germany that finally galvanized him into action. On 11 August 1939 he talked with Burckhardt, the High Commissioner of Danzig, and said with revealing candour, 'Everything I undertake is directed against Russia. If the West is too stupid and too blind to comprehend that, I will be

---

[127] Fest, *Hitler*, p. 803. See also the account of Hitler's meeting with his commanders on 23 May 1939 in *GD* Ser. D vi, no. 433.

[128] *GD* Ser. D viii, no. 384, p. 444.

[129] *Les Lettres secrètes échangées par Hitler et Mussolini*, introduction by André François-Poncet (Paris, 1946), pp. 130 f.

[130] *GD* Ser. D iv, nos. 478, 482, 483.

forced to come to an understanding with the Russians, to smash the West, and then, after its defeat, to turn against the Soviet Union with my assembled forces.'[131] Three days later Ribbentrop proposed to the Soviet Government by telegram that he fly to Moscow 'to set forth the Führer's views to Herr Stalin [and] . . . to lay the foundations for a final settlement of German–Russian relations'. Although they were already engaged in talks with the Anglo-French delegation that had arrived in Moscow on the eleventh, the Russians accepted, suggesting that the talks be concrete and that they centre on the feasibility of a non-aggression pact. It took a week to settle the details, but on 21 August the German radio was able to announce that agreement had been reached.[132]

With the conclusion of the Nazi–Soviet Pact, which struck the Western capitals with the force of a thunderbolt, Hitler's preparations for the next phase of his eastern drive were complete. Had he wanted to do so, he could probably have accomplished his stated objectives in Poland by diplomacy, for the Poles were now sobered by reality and eager for an arrangement. But Hitler did not want another Munich and seemed concerned lest the Poles try to accept the terms they had rejected in March or submit counter-proposals that might compel him to negotiate. To prevent this, he not only declined the good offices of third Powers,[133] but refused to allow his ambassadors to Poland and Great Britain, who were on leave in Germany, to return to their posts.[134] On 22 August he said to his generals, 'Now Poland is in the position in which I wanted her. . . . I am only afraid that at the last moment some swine or other will submit to me a plan for mediation.'[135]

This reference to the intercession that had led to Munich might have pained his friend Mussolini had he heard it. The Italians were bewildered and worried by the course of German policy. In mid-August Ciano, the Foreign Minister, had visited Ribbentrop in Salzburg and, as they walked in the garden after dinner, had asked, 'Ribbentrop, what is it that you want? Danzig? The Corridor?'

[131] Burckhardt, *Meine Danziger Mission*, p. 272.

[132] On the acceleration of the talks with the Russians, see *GD* Ser. D vi, esp. nos. 441, 490, 579, 607, 757, 760, 772; and on their culmination, vii, nos. 51, 56, 70, 75, 143, 157, 213, 228, 229. In general, see James E. McSherry, *Stalin, Hitler and Europe, 1933–39: The Origins of World War II* (Cleveland, Toronto, 1968), esp. pp. 197 ff.

[133] Arnold and Veronica Toynbee (eds.), *Survey of International Affairs, 1939–1946: The Eve of War, 1939* (London, 1958), pp. 342 ff., 377.

[134] *GD* Ser. D vi, no. 674; vii, nos. 2, 32, 82; Carl W. Schorske, 'Two German Ambassadors', in *The Diplomats*, pp. 509–10.

[135] *GD* Ser. D vii, no. 192.

Ribbentrop had fixed him with his arrogant eyes and answered coldly, 'We want war!'[136] To the visitor from the birthplace of diplomacy this was an incredible answer. After all, to insist on battering down an open door was an act of irrationality. But Ribbentrop was merely reflecting the thought of his master. At this point in his career—perhaps because megalomania was beginning to take over—no triumph seemed satisfactory to Hitler if it did not demonstrate the triumphant use of the grey-clad columns that had been poised and waiting for so long, the heavy artillery and the armour, and the new Stuka dive-bombers. He wanted war. As he said to his military chiefs at the meeting at Obersalzburg in November 1939, 'Basically I did not organize the armed forces in order not to strike. The decision to strike was always in me.'[137]

He would doubtless have preferred a local war without Anglo-French intervention, but not so much as to make him willing to stay his hand until he was sure of Western neutrality. As he said in May 1939, 'The idea of getting out cheaply is dangerous. There is no such possibility. We must burn our boats.'[138] Besides, if the Western states came in, this might expedite their destruction and clear the way for the greater war against Russia that would fulfil the German destiny. Thus, when his armies invaded Poland on 1 September 1939 and the British and French governments responded by declaring war, the Führer was only momentarily daunted.

---

[136] Ciano diary for 23 Dec. 1943, cited in Kirkpatrick, *Mussolini*, p. 414. See also Galeazzo Ciano, *Diario* (2 vols., Verona, 1946), i. 140; and *L'Europa verso la catastrofe* (Bari, 1948), pp. 449 ff. Also *GD* Ser. D vii, no. 438.

[137] *GD* Ser. D viii. 441.

[138] Ibid. vi, no. 433.

XX
Hitler's War
1939–1945

Vor dem Marschtritt der deutschen Soldaten
hielt die Erde den Atem und schwieg.
Aus verströmenden Herzblutes Saaten
steigt der Dom der geheiligten Taten:
Der Sieg.

GERHARD SCHUMANN (1940)[1]

Kahlgefegt und ohne Flitter
liegt die Welt, die einst gelacht;
durch entlaubter Äste Gitter
blickt der Winter todesbitter,
und es greift nach uns die Nacht.

HERMANN HESSE (1944)[2]

BEFORE it was over, his commanding generals were referring to him bitterly as *Gröfaz*, a name ugly enough to have served some monster of mythology, some twisted kobold or goblin embodying and spreading evil. In actuality, it was a contraction of the title that General Keitel bestowed upon the Führer in June 1940, Größter Feldherr aller Zeiten, Greatest War Lord of All Times, and it was used cynically by professionals who denied the validity of the claim. Yet the title was not entirely inappropriate. What other commander in history, from the days of Alexander and Tamerlaine to those of Napoleon and Ludendorff, had presided over battlefields so far flung and carnage so universal?

The war that Hitler unleashed with his declaration of 2 September 1939 circled the globe, killing 17 million soldiers and 18 million non-combatants before its fires burned out. No conflict in history had ever been so destructive, and none in the end ever avenged itself so completely upon its authors. *Gröfaz* was one of the last, and surely the least mourned, of its victims, his triumphs proved to be insubstantial, his Thousand Year Reich reduced to dust and rubble in its twelfth year.

---

[1] *Deutschland, Deutschland: Politische Gedichte*, ed. Lamprecht, p. 457.
[2] 'Die letzten Tage', in *Die Gedichte von Hermann Hesse* (Berlin, 1953).

When it became inescapably clear that this was to be the case, Hitler lashed out at those whom he had led to disaster. 'If the war is lost,' he declared in the spring of 1945, 'the people will be lost also. It is not necessary to worry about what the German people will need for elemental survival. On the contrary, it is best for us to destroy even these things.'[3]

He did not quite succeed in doing that. The German people survived, but only after they had been stripped of everything that had obscured their vision of reality during the drunken years of destiny and had been brought to *Stunde Null*, the cold grey dawn in which they were challenged at long last to come to terms with their history.

I

To have predicted such a catastrophic ending in September 1939 would have required powers of divination not granted to ordinary persons. The ruthless efficiency with which the German armies battered the Poles into surrender within three weeks astonished the rest of the world; and the revelation during the brief campaign of weapons that they did not possess (the Stuka dive-bombers that filled the skies over Warsaw, for example) and techniques that were new to them—the use of swiftly moved mechanized columns, like those that burst through the Corridor under Guderian's command, leaving thousands of broken guns and the rags and tatters of a cavalry brigade and half a dozen infantry divisions in its wake; the effective employment of well-articulated infantry assault teams; and the highly developed system of air–ground co-ordination—sobered and depressed foreign military establishments. The psychological effect might have been less profound if they had known of the German weaknesses that the campaign revealed: the not infrequent break-downs in the communications network, the serious deficiencies of supply, the frequency of mechanized failures because of the lack of spare parts, the cases of confusion and panic normal to any force being engaged for the first time.[4] Since they were not aware of these things, they had a tendency to regard the German army as unbeatable; and this had the effect, not only of discouraging the British and French from starting a serious offensive in the west, where they

[3] Speer, *Inside the Third Reich*, p. 557.

[4] Telford Taylor, *Sword and Swastika: Generals and Nazis in the Third Reich* (New York, 1952), p. 328. On the campaign in general, see Robert M. Kennedy, *The German Campaign in Poland* (Washington, 1956) and Nicholas Bethell, *The War Hitler Won: The Fall of Poland, September 1939* (New York, 1972), esp. Ch. 4.

outnumbered the Germans by 76 divisions to 32, while the fighting in Poland was still going on, but of laming their will for action in the months that followed. The eager support that the French Government gave to suggestions of operations in theatres far from the Rhine (Finland, for example, after the outbreak of the Russo-Finnish war in November 1939) and their resistance to British bombing of industrial targets in the Ruhr[5] were manifestations of a reluctance to become seriously engaged with a Power that had demonstrated such frightening destructive capabilities against the Poles.

If Hitler had had his way, he would have exploited this moral weakness without delay. Although he issued an appeal to the Western governments on 6 October, urging them to accept what had happened in Poland and to sit down with him to discuss the resolution of other European problems, it is probable that he never expected, and perhaps did not desire, a positive response. He had informed his military leaders on 27 September that he intended to strike westwards, and, on 9 October, without waiting for a reply from London and Paris, he sent a long memorandum to the chief of the OKW, Keitel, and the commanders of the army, navy, and air force, announcing the necessity, at the earliest possible date, of action to effect 'the destruction of the strength of the Western Powers and their capability of resisting still further the political consolidation and continued expansion of the German people in Europe',[6] supplementing this with a directive of the same date that forecast an offensive in strength through Luxemburg, the Low Countries, and Belgium.[7] This caused consternation among the higher commanders, Generaloberst Ritter von Leeb protesting to Brauchitsch, the Commander-in-Chief of the army, that the projected line of attack was precisely what the French expected and would lead to certain catastrophe; and, when Hitler persisted and set mid-November as the time for the beginning of the offensive, there was a recrudescence of conspiratorial activity, in which Halder, Chief of Staff of the army, his deputy Stülpnagel, and Wagner, the Quartermaster General, were active. But Halder gave this up when he discovered that he could expect no support from Brauchitsch and the

[5] That the British Government was no more eager is shown in Gilbert and Gott, *The Appeasers*, pp. 318–31.

[6] Hans-Adolf Jacobsen, *Dokumente zur Vorgeschichte des Westfeldzugs 1939–1940* (Göttingen, 1956), p. 6.

[7] H. R. Trevor-Roper (ed.), *Blitzkrieg to Defeat: Hitler's War Directives, 1939–1945* (New York, 1964), pp. 13–14.

Commander of the reserve army, Fromm;[8] and, when Hitler's schedule was abandoned and the western drive postponed until the spring, it was not because of the resistance of the soldiers but rather because of the time needed to repair equipment disabled in Poland and to replenish stores of ammunition.[9]

The Western Powers did not profit from this enforced delay. They might possibly have changed the complexion of the war had they taken advantage of the Soviet Union's attack upon Finland to send aid to the defenders and, in the course of doing so, to occupy the Norwegian port of Narvik and the Swedish ore fields that supplied Germany with iron ore through that outlet. This was seriously considered, but British reluctance to violate the rights of neutral states, or to help Finland without a formal request for such assistance, prevented its being tried, and in March it was abandoned completely when the Finns appealed to Moscow for an armistice. The Western Allies fell back on an earlier plan of Winston Churchill for the mining of Norwegian waters, but succeeded only in signalling their intentions so clearly that they were anticipated.

Since October Grand Admiral Raeder had been urging Hitler to occupy Norway, arguing that the British would almost certainly do so themselves sooner or later, and pointing to the advantages Norway possessed for U-boat operations. Hitler had resisted this diversion of effort until British preparations convinced him that there was a serious threat to his flank; he then gave another impressive demonstration of energy.[10] On the morning of 9 April—the day after the Western governments had informed the Norwegians that they were going to begin the sowing of mines—German columns crossed the undefended frontier of Denmark and seized the capital, German planes dropped paratroopers into the Norwegian towns of Oslo, Bergen, Trondheim, Stavanger, and Narvik, and German ships landed infantry at key points on the Norwegian coast. Within forty-eight hours Norway was under effective German control, with a puppet government installed in the capital, headed by Vidkun Quisling, whose name was soon to be used as a synonym of treason in other occupied lands. A belated British attempt to undo this disastrous blow to their plans, by landing troops at Andalsnes and

---

[8] Leeb's *Tagebuch*, cited in Hans-Adolf Jacobsen, *Der Zweite Weltkrieg: Grundzüge der Politik und Strategie in Dokumenten* (Frankfurt-on-Main, 1965), p. 67; Wagner, *Generalquartiermeister*, pp. 140 ff.; Ritter, *Goerdeler*, pp. 240 ff.; and, in general, Harold C. Deutsch, *The Conspiracy against Hitler in the Twilight War* (Minneapolis, 1968).

[9] See above, Ch. XVII, p. 619.

[10] Earl K. Ziemke, *The German Northern Theater of Operations, 1940–1945* (Washington, 1959), pp. 7–10; F. H. Hinsley, *Hitler's Strategy* (Cambridge, 1951), p. 51.

Namsos, resulted only in the decimation and, after a month's hard fighting, the withdrawal, of the units involved.

The brilliance of this 'Weser Exercise' was flawed by losses that were impossible to replace quickly. Although there was only token opposition by the Danish army (13 killed and 23 wounded) and none at all from the Danish navy, the Norwegians fought back bravely, and their shore batteries and units of the British and Norwegian navies had wrought havoc among the naval vessels that Hitler had used to transport his troops. Germany's new heavy cruiser *Blücher* was holed and sunk by coastal batteries in the Oslo fjord, and the battle-cruiser *Lützow* met the same fate and went down with the staff of the 163rd Division, part of the staff of XXI Brigade, and 800 men.[11] The light cruisers *Königsberg* and *Karlsruhe* were lost, as were 10 destroyers, 6 submarines, 1 torpedo boat, and 15 naval aircraft. In addition, a British destroyer torpedoed and badly damaged the heavy cruiser *Scharnhorst*, and another torpedoed her sister ship *Gneisenau* as she tried to make her way back to Germany from Trondheim in June. Other ships, notably *Hipper* and *Emden*, suffered damages, and at the end of the fighting Germany had only one heavy cruiser and two light cruisers fit for action. The effect of these losses was to be felt in imminent operations in which the incapacitated vessels might have played an important role.[12] Even so, there is no doubt that the German demonstration of effective combined operations reinforced the psychological impact of the Polish campaign and contributed to the growing defeatism of the French and Belgian governments. The British, with their characteristic lack of logic, refused to be daunted and reacted to the defeat by forcing the appeasers from office and rallying behind Winston Churchill, who promised more spirited leadership. But this change had no effect in staying the German momentum, and, on the very day of Churchill's appointment, 10 May, the Wehrmacht struck the Low Countries with its full force.

The *Blitzkrieg* in the west was even more spectacular than that in Poland, and for this Hitler himself deserves some credit, although less than he claimed and was claimed for him. Although his original directive for the western offensive had suggested an advance based on the Schlieffen Plan of 1914, with German armies pivoting once more on the Grand Duchy of Luxemburg and wheeling down

[11] Generaloberst Halder, *Kriegstagebuch*, ed. Hans-Adolf Jacobsen (3 vols., Stuttgart, 1962), i. 252.

[12] Richard Petrow, *The Bitter Years: The Invasion and Occupation of Denmark and Norway* (New York, 1974), p. 97.

through Holland and Belgium, he had a sudden inspiration a few weeks later and, on 25 October, asked his staff whether it might not be possible to strike below the line Liège–Namur, making the *Schwerpunkt* of the offensive the supposedly impassable Ardennes. This idea—for it was, as Halder insisted later, no more than that—had also occurred independently to Lieutenant-General Erich von Manstein, Chief of Staff of Army Group A, and he and Halder elaborated it and gave it operational form.[13] When their Plan Yellow was implemented on 9–10 May, it was an unqualified success. A co-ordinated assault across the Meuse by paratroopers and armoured columns and a merciless aerial bombardment of Rotterdam broke Dutch resistance and compelled the government to capitulate in five days. A simultaneous drive across the Albert Canal turned the Belgian flank and forced the first of a series of retirements. The Belgians were supported by the British Second Corps on the River Dyle, the French Seventh Army in the north, and the French Cavalry Corps on the Meuse. Their manœuvrability evaporated on 13–14 May, when General Ewald von Kleist's Panzer Group smashed through the Ardennes, spearheaded by the armoured corps of Guderian and Reinhardt, which crossed the Meuse north of Sedan. Guderian overwhelmed the French Ninth Army and raced for the coast, followed closely by motorized infantry; and, when he reached Abbéville on 23 May, he had the Belgians and their allies in a trap.

On 27 May the King of the Belgians ordered his troops to lay down their arms. The British and French units fought a dogged rearguard action until they reached the beaches of Dunkirk, from where 338,000 of them managed to escape, thanks to the intrepidity of the British small craft that took them off and to certain fortuitous circumstances: the exhaustion of fuel supplies that led to General von Rundstedt's decision to halt the German armour short of Dunkirk; the faulty target selection of the Luftwaffe, which bombed the beaches instead of the shipping; and the absence of German naval units to impede the withdrawal.[14] This was a disappointment for the Germans, but they had no time to dwell upon it. Without a perceptible pause, their columns rolled on into France, pierced the crumbling French front on the Somme, bypassed the Maginot Line, and broke the spirit of a brave army whose high command had

[13] See particularly Hans-Adolf Jacobsen, *Fall Gelb: Der Kampf um den deutschen Operationsplan zur Westoffensive 1940* (Wiesbaden, 1957), esp. pp. 147 ff.

[14] Hans-Adolf Jacobsen, *Dünkirchen: Ein Beitrag zur Geschichte des Westfeldzugs 1940* (Neckargemünd, 1958), esp. pp. 201–10; David Divine, *The Nine Days of Dunkirk* (New York, 1959).

devoted its energies, not to the urgent tasks of national defence, but to recriminations against its allies and shrill attempts to blame its own incompetence upon the political failures of the French Republic. On 17 June a reconstituted government that had rid itself of all those who, like Paul Reynaud and Georges Mandel, wanted to go on fighting, sued for armistice; and Hitler had won what his Propaganda Ministry was soon calling 'the greatest victory of all times'.[15]

It was a dangerous victory in two respects. In the first place, it increased Hitler's already over-inflated self-esteem. His contribution to the strategical plan, while important, had not been decisive, and the success of the operation had been due largely to Halder's meticulous staff work, his success in preventing his supreme commander from panicking at critical moments and insisting upon destructive modifications of the plan, and the *élan* of the front-line officers and men.[16] Nevertheless, Hitler was now convinced that he was the sole author of the triumph. When he addressed the Reichstag on 19 July and reviewed the events of the past ten months, he appeared before it as the Feldherr, whose inspired vision had detected the enemy's weaknesses and known best how to exploit them, whose imagination had inspired the Scandinavian campaign, which he modestly described as 'the most daring undertaking in German military history', and whose strategical flair had brought the victory that had eluded the great Schlieffen. Halder received perfunctory credit, with no indication that he was anything but a useful assistant to Brauchitsch in matters of command; Manstein was not mentioned at all.[17] This augured ill for effective relationships between command and staff in future campaigns.

In the second place, the victory was incomplete, and Hitler had no plan for resolving the problem that this posed. Manstein once said of him that he was always so confident that his force of will would be able to surmount any difficulty that he encountered that he forgot that the enemy always possesses a will too.[18] Now, for the first time, he encountered that awkward truth. The western campaign had been

---

[15] Colonel A. Goutard, *The Battle of France, 1940*, trans. from the French (New York, 1959); Jacques Benoist-Méchin, *Sixty Days That Shook the World*, trans. from the French (London, 1963); Sir Edward Spears, *Assignment to Catastrophe* (2 vols., London, 1954); Heinz Guderian, *Panzer Leaders*, trans. from the German (London, 1952); Telford Taylor, *The March of Conquest: The German Victories in Western Europe, 1940* (New York, 1958).

[16] Halder, *Kriegstagebuch*, i. 302; Jacobsen, *Fall Gelb*, p. 153.

[17] Domarus, *Hitler: Reden* ii. 1545, 1547–8.

[18] Erich von Manstein, *Verlorene Siege* (Bonn, 1955), pp. 305 ff.; Gerd Buchheit, *Hitler der Feldherr* (Rastatt, 1958), pp. 500 f.

intended to free his rear so that he could accomplish his mission in the east. The British refusal to give in when the French did disrupted the Führer's schedule. It also added a dimension to the war that he did not understand and could not master. The effect upon his strategy was disturbing and permanent. From now on it was marked increasingly by impatience, by plans that were ill conceived, implemented without conviction, and then abandoned, by profligacy in the use of human and material resources, and by an impulsive wilfulness that had disastrous results.

It is impossible to believe that Hitler would have been so reckless with his naval forces in the Oslo fjord or that, after Dunkirk, he would have committed 136 divisions to the pursuit of a demoralized foe, if he had had any intimation that he might have to consider invading the British Isles.[19] Yet, when the exasperating British refused to do what he expected them to do—to dismiss the bankrupt warmonger Churchill, to give authority to men well disposed to Germany (among whom he numbered Lloyd George and the Duke of Windsor[20]), and to sue for peace—that was the prospect that confronted him, unless he could find other means of forcing the islanders to leave the war or was willing simply to ignore them and turn eastwards in the expectation that they would, sooner or later, see the light.[21]

It was indicative of Hitler's own indecisiveness that, at this juncture, he was readier than usual to listen to the ideas of his service chiefs. He discovered that they were as unprepared to deal with the new problems of grand strategy as he was himself and were incapable of uniting on a plan of action. The army chiefs were, on the whole, confident that an invasion of Great Britain was feasible, but Admiral Raeder had strong doubts and favoured attempts to sever Britain's lines of supply and its links with the Empire by shrewd blows at Gibraltar and Malta and Suez, landings in North Africa, and naval blockade in the Atlantic. Rather surprisingly, Brauchitsch also leaned to a Mediterranean strategy and seemed to feel that the loss of

---

[19] There are many statements of his that indicate that he believed that this would be unnecessary. See Hillgruber, *Hitlers Strategie*, p. 44; Barry A. Leach, *German Strategy against Russia, 1939–1941* (Oxford, 1973), p. 48.

[20] The hope of using the Duke of Windsor to effect a change in British policy took some bizarre forms, including a plan for kidnapping him during a visit to Spain. See W. Schellenberg, *The Labyrinth*, trans. from the German (New York, 1956), pp. 107 ff.; and *GD* Ser. D x, nos. 152, 159, 175, 211, 216, 224, 235, 257, 264, 265, 276, 277, 285.

[21] See Jodl's description of alternatives in July 1940, in *International Military Tribunal* xxviii. 301 ff.

Gibraltar would bring Britain to its knees. Goering insisted that the Luftwaffe would be able to break British resistance all by itself, although studies in his own ministry in 1938 and 1939 had concluded that this was an impossibility.[22]

Where Hitler's own preference lay was indicated by his insistence in a conference with his chiefs in mid-July that the key to Britain's resistance was its hope of winning the support of the Soviet Union, a theme to which he reverted in a second meeting on 31 July, in which he said:

Britain's hope is in Russia and the United States. If the hope in Russia disappears, America is also lost, because elimination of Russia would tremendously increase Japan's power in the Far East. . . .

If Russia is destroyed, Britain's last hope will be shattered. Germany will then be master of Europe and the Balkans. . . .

The sooner Russia is crushed the better.[23]

General Alfred Jodl was surely expressing Hitler's views when he told the section chiefs of the National Defence Department of the OKW on 29 July that a decision had been taken to 'launch a surprise attack on Russia . . . at the earliest possible moment, i.e. in May 1941' and described this as 'the best method of forcing England to make peace if this had not proved possible by other means'.[24] But the other means remained to be tried, for Hitler did not want to find himself in the two-front war that he had always resolved to avoid. On 16 July he had issued a directive declaring his intention 'to prepare a landing operation against England and, if necessary, to carry it out';[25] and on 31 July, at the same meeting in which he discoursed upon Britain's dependence on Russia, he decided, with the concurrence of Brauchitsch, Halder, Raeder, and Keitel, to launch an all-out air offensive against England in August, to be followed by a cross-Channel assault in September, 'if we have the impression that the English are smashed'.[26] Goering was not present to express his views on this decision, which was confirmed by a directive of 1 August, which ordered him to begin intensified air warfare against Great Britain but left him considerable latitude with respect to time and selection of targets and made no provision for co-ordination of effort

[22] Hillgruber, *Hitlers Strategie*, pp. 39 n. 54, 173.

[23] Halder, *Kriegstagebuch*, ii. 49.

[24] Walter Warliment, *Inside Hitler's Headquarters, 1939–1945*, trans. from the German (New York, 1964), pp. 111–12.

[25] Trevor-Roper, *Blitzkrieg*, pp. 34–7.

[26] Halder, *Kriegstagebuch*, ii. 48.

with other arms.[27] After reading the accounts of these discussions, one is not inclined to disagree with Telford Taylor's comment that 'one would have to search far for a more striking example of shoddy and superficial decision-making on crucial strategic issues'.[28]

Goering had predicted that four days of intensive bombing would knock out the air defences of southern England and that four weeks of more generalized attacks would destroy communications and morale and open the way for a triumphant and bloodless crossing of the Channel. Like many of the Reichsmarschall's wartime judgements, this was based upon a profound ignorance of facts that might have been gleaned from intelligence reports. The British were not so heavily outnumbered in aircraft as he believed, and they enjoyed some important advantages. They had an effective warning system; their Spitfire and Hurricane fighters were faster and more heavily armed than any Luftwaffe aircraft except the Messerschmidt-109s; and they were fighting over their own soil and native waters, which gave both pilots and planes a higher survival rate than the attackers. In contrast, the Germans suffered from the fact that their air force had been designed not for strategic aerial bombardment but for tactical support of ground forces and found it difficult to change its operational mode. In addition, the higher commanders lacked the experience and training of their R.A.F. counterparts (here the Versailles Treaty cost the Germans dearly) and their bombers (Dornier-17s, Heinkel-111s, and Junker-88s) had no means of eluding radar beams and, even more serious, had no effective long-range fighter protection, the Me-109s having only a 125-mile radius of operations and the Me-110s being too clumsy and slow.

Finally, and perhaps most important, Goering's direction of *Adlerangriff*, as the Germans called the Battle of Britain, was amateurish in the extreme and, with a sublime indifference to the unsuitability of his force for the accomplishment of its assigned mission and to its inadequate capacity for replacement, he squandered his aircraft and crews over a variety of targets, repeating the mistake of Dunkirk by failing to concentrate on the vital one, in this case the R.A.F. bases. Nor was he the only culprit. In the directive of 1 August Hitler had written, 'I reserve to myself the right to decide on terror attacks as measures of reprisal.'[29] A British raid on Berlin late in August led him to act upon that paragraph and to order exterminatory raids on

[27] Trevor-Roper, *Blitzkrieg*, pp. 37–8.

[28] Telford Taylor, *The Breaking Wave: The Second World War in the Summer of 1940* (New York, 1967), pp. 72, 96–102.

[29] Trevor-Roper, *Blitzkrieg*, p. 38.

London and other cities. These may have satisfied his desire for revenge, but they saved the bases, and, because of the heavy losses of German aircraft over London (60 planes lost on 15 September alone), they forced the postponement and, ultimately, the abandonment of Operation Sea-Lion, the projected Channel crossing, and the dispersion of the invasion fleet that Raeder had laboriously assembled.[30]

This fiasco aggravated Hitler's problems. He now had increasing reason to be concerned about the attitude of the United States, a country that he had been led to believe, by reports from his embassy in Washington, was profoundly isolationist in sentiment.[31] The spirit with which the British people withstood the German bombing awakened lively sympathy in America, even in traditionally isolationist sections of the country; there was a growing feeling of solidarity with Great Britain; and the government's decision in September to send fifty destroyers that had been decommissioned to the Royal Navy was a commitment that indicated that American intervention in the European war might be only a matter of time.[32] In a clumsy attempt to discourage this, Hitler authorized von Ribbentrop to pursue the negotiations that eventuated, on 27 September 1940, in the Tripartite Pact between Germany, Italy, and Japan. This treaty, in which Japan recognized the legitimacy of Axis efforts to establish a new order in Europe in return for recognition of its similar effort in Asia, included in its third paragraph an unmistakable threat to the United States, for the three signatories undertook 'to assist one another with all political, economic and military means if one of the three Contracting Powers is attacked by a Power at present not involved in the European war or in the Chinese-Japanese conflict'.[33] The effects of this were the opposite of what had been expected, and the pact played an important part not only in spreading the conviction that international Fascism had become a serious threat to American security but also in electing Franklin D. Roosevelt to a third term as president, an event that must have seemed to Hitler to bring American intervention closer. It became

[30] B. Collier, The Battle of Britain (London, 1962); D. Wood and D. Dempster, The Narrow Margin (London, 1961); Peter Fleming, Operation Sea Lion (London, 1957); Walter Ansell, Hitler Confronts England (Durham, N. C., 1960).

[31] See Craig, From Bismarck to Adenauer, pp. 91–4 and notes; James V. Compton, The Swastika and the Eagle: Hitler, the United States, and the Origins of World War II (Boston, 1967), Ch. 7.

[32] GD Ser. D x, nos. 312, 322, 362.

[33] William L. Langer and S. Everett Gleason, The Undeclared War, 1940–41 (New York, 1953), pp. 21–32; Compton, Swastika and Eagle, pp. 195 ff.; GD Ser. D xi, nos. 123, 141, 164.

apparent to him now that the only sure way of preventing this was to knock Britain out of the war quickly, which would also allow him to proceed with his eastern plans.

Since the direct attack upon Great Britain had failed, Hitler allowed himself to be persuaded by Admiral Raeder to try the peripheral approach; and in October he went on a diplomatic tour to see whether he might not enlist the governments of Italy, Vichy France, and Franco Spain in a common effort to destroy Britain's Mediterranean position. In conversations with Mussolini at the Brenner Pass on 4 October and with Pierre Laval and Marshal Pétain at Montoire on 22 and 24 October, he promised Stukas and long-range fighters and heavy artillery and Panzer support of attacks by their forces and Franco's on Gibraltar, the Suez Canal, and Alexandria harbour and painted exciting pictures of their armies driving the British from the Mediterranean, liberating Egypt, and advancing with German backing through Palestine and Syria to Turkey. The French and Italian statesmen seemed interested in the prospect of 'the encirclement of England on all seas and all countries facing her shores', which, they were assured, would lead to British collapse, 'if the community, which the Fuehrer had spoken of, was achieved';[34] but when Hitler moved on to the Spanish frontier, to meet with General Franco at Hendaye, the Spanish dictator proved to be more resistant and, at the end of a wearying discussion, of which Hitler said he would rather have several teeth drawn than repeat it, made it clear that he would refuse to enter any anti-British war unless he were promised Gibraltar, the whole of French Morocco, and part of Algeria.[35]

The disarray of Hitler's plans caused by this intelligence was compounded when Mussolini, who was still waiting for some tangible reward for his belated and inglorious participation in the last days of the war against France, wrote to say that he felt that France should not be a member of the coalition and that Spain would be a doubtful quantity. A few days later, when Hitler met him in Florence and persuaded him to modify these views, the Duce suggested that active participation in the coalition by the Soviet Union would be desirable.[36] This can be seen as an indication of how much in the dark Mussolini was concerning his ally's real intentions; but in point of fact Hitler himself seems to have considered trying to talk the

---

[34] GD Ser. D xi, no. 227. See also nos. 149, 207, 208, 212; and Geoffrey Warner, *Pierre Laval and the Eclipse of France* (London, 1968), pp. 232 ff.

[35] GD Ser. D xi, nos. 220, 221.

[36] Ibid., no. 246.

Russians into attacking British holdings in the Middle East, an enterprise that would serve the double purpose of helping to drive the British out of the war and deceiving the Russians about his real purpose in their regard. For the same reason, Hitler did not attempt to argue Mussolini out of his intention, communicated to him at Hendaye, of attacking Greece. This too might serve as a diversion.

Viewing these manœuvres, one is struck by the high degree of lability and improvisation in Hitler's strategical thinking in these months, an impression that must have been strongly felt in the General Staff of the army. Since July, the Oberkommando des Heeres (OKH) had been ordered to draw up plans for Sea-Lion, the capture of Gibraltar, the Azores, and the Canaries, the defence of the Finnish nickel mines, the defence of the Romanian oil fields, the support of the Italians in North Africa, and the invasion of Russia. They were understandably bewildered concerning Hitler's intentions.[37]

Clarity came at the end of the year, and it came as a result of a perceptible chill in Soviet–German relations. This had been developing for some time, for the Soviet Government had been dismayed by the speed and completeness of the German victory in France and by the subsequent expansion of German influence in South-Eastern Europe. Since 1939 the Soviets had been working furiously to build a glacis around their borders in case Hitler should decide to break the treaty of 23 August. Their hard-won success in Finland and the extension of their military control over the eastern half of Poland and the Baltic countries, in accordance with a secret protocol to the Nazi–Soviet Pact, gave them reasonable security in the north and north-west, but further to the south, where Romania extended in an unbroken belt from the eastern frontier of Hungary to the west coast of the Black Sea, they had no similar protection. In late June 1940, again availing themselves of the terms of the secret protocol, they sought to correct this by occupying those parts of Bessarabia and Bukovina that lay on the north bank of the northernmost arm of the Danube delta, after first informing the German Government of their intention. This availed them nothing, for in August, when the Bulgarians and Hungarians seemed on the point of following the Russian example and seizing Romanian territories to which they had some historical claim, Hitler forced an adjudication of these disputes and, with his ally Mussolini, presided over it. As a result, he not only won an ascendancy in Hungarian and Bulgarian affairs that proved

---

[37] Leach, *Strategy against Russia*, pp. 78 f.

of military importance at a later date but struck a shrewd blow at his Soviet ally. On 31 August Ribbentrop instructed his ambassador in Moscow, Count Friedrich Werner von der Schulenburg, to inform Molotov, the Foreign Minister, that, now that all claims against Romania had been settled, the Axis Powers had been impelled by their close ties with the Romanian economy to guarantee the rump state, 'in order to forestall once and for all a repetition of differences that might easily arise in areas of such territorial and ethnological complexity'.[38] These bland words did not conceal from the men in Moscow that the key position in South-Eastern Europe now lay in Hitler's hands.

When Molotov came to Berlin for talks in mid-November, therefore, he had no desire to commit himself on what Ribbentrop called 'the decisive question . . . whether the Soviet Union was prepared and in a position to cooperate with us in the great liquidation of the British Empire'.[39] Instead he irritated his hosts, who were edgy in any case because of the necessity of twice having to interrupt the talks because of air-raid warnings, by a barrage of complaints about the Romanian guarantee, movement of German troops to Finland, and other German actions, and by insisting that collaboration in any effort against Britain would depend upon concrete assurances ('paper agreements would not suffice for the Soviet Union') that its interests in Finland, South-Eastern Europe, and Turkey would be protected.[40] When the morose Russian had gone his way, Hitler knew that the war against Britain could not be ended before the attack on Russia came.[41] The price would be too high. He told his intimates on 15 November, 'Molotov had let the cat out of the bag. This would not even remain a marriage of convenience. To let the Russians into Europe would be the end of *Mitteleuropa*. And the Balkans and Finland were endangered flanks.' On the same day, he ordered his adjutants to consult the Minister for Armaments and Munitions, Fritz Todt, about the best location for wartime Führer Headquarters in the east, and to get him to start building the necessary installations in the north, the centre, and the south 'with the greatest dispatch'. His permanent headquarters would be in East Prussia.[42]

In Hitler's mind, the decision to attack Russia in the spring was now made. In a *tour d'horizon* with his generals on 5 December he

---

[38] *GD* Ser. D x, no. 415; xi, nos. 1, 4, 7.   [39] Ibid., xi, no. 329, p. 569.
[40] Ibid., nos. 325, 326, 328, 329.
[41] Leach, *Strategy against Russia*, p. 78.
[42] Hillgruber, *Hitlers Strategie*, p. 358 and n. 33.

assumed that this was generally understood. He talked about the Red Army's lack of modern field artillery, the inadequate armouring of its tanks, its lack of trained leaders, and the inferior quality of other ranks (all erroneous judgements that were the result of faulty intelligence, overestimation of the effects of Stalin's purges, and racist assumptions[43]) and made the confident prediction: 'In the spring we shall be at a visible peak in leadership, material, and troops; the Russians will be at an unmistakable nadir. When this Russian army is once hit, disaster will be uncontrollable.'[44] Two weeks later the directive for what was called Operation Barbarossa ordered the armed forces to prepare 'even before the conclusion of the war against England, to crush Soviet Russia in a rapid campaign'.[45]

Mussolini's adventure in Greece had by now, however, become a dangerous liability, for the Italian attack on 28 October had led the British to send troops from Egypt to aid the defenders (who were proving, to the Duce's dismay, that they were perfectly capable of defending themselves), so that by the end of March 1941 almost 30,000 well-trained Australians and New Zealanders were on the mainland and more were on the way. Hitler remembered the British roll-out from Salonika in 1918 too clearly to tolerate this potential danger to his flank, and the diplomatic success that he had won in August provided the key to eliminating it. At the beginning of 1941 he asked the Romanian and Bulgarian governments to allow him to garrison troops in their countries. The Romanians had no option, and the Bulgarians signed an alliance on 1 March and permitted German units to move into Sofia and Varna. The government of Yugoslavia, which was next on the line of march towards Greece, also acquiesced but was deposed on 27 March by pro-Greek elements strongly supported by public opinion. Hitler reacted with fury. On 6 April 1941 the Luftwaffe began a three-day bombardment of Belgrade, while the German 12th Army, advancing from Bulgaria, beat down organized resistance, left the country dazed and divided under German satraps, and rolled on into Greece. The weary Greek armies fought bravely but hopelessly against a relentless enemy who commanded the skies and outmatched them in numbers and equipment. Their British allies tried to find a line that could be defended but, after losing 15,000 men, were forced to

---

[43] Cf. John Erickson, *The Soviet High Command: A Military-Political History, 1918–1941* (London, 1962), pp. 548 ff., 565 ff.

[44] Halder, *Kriegstagebuch*, ii. 214.

[45] Trevor-Roper, *Blitzkrieg*, p. 49.

retreat by sea to Crete, from where they were expelled by bombing attacks and parachute drops in May.[46]

These German victories were matched by others in Africa, where Mussolini had also met with disaster, his commanders managing, in December and January, to lose Somaliland, Eritrea, and most of Libya to the outnumbered but tough desert troopers of General Sir Archibald Wavell. So desperate did the plight of his Axis partner seem and so obvious the dangers of an increasingly strong British presence on the southern Mediterranean shore, that Hitler felt compelled to intervene and in February dispatched General Erwin Rommel, with a reinforced Panzer division, to Libya to check the British drive towards Tunis.[47] Rommel laid his plans cunningly, although in such an unconventional manner that Halder complained that he was conducting 'a war that can no longer be judged by European standards';[48] and in April he struck at the over-extended British lines, bypassed Tobruk, stormed into Bardia, and forced Wavell to retreat into Egypt. These spectacular successes, combined with the seizure of Crete, reawakened the hopes of people like Raeder that the Mediterranean strategy might yet be given priority. Doubts about a Russian campaign while the British were still in the war were pervasive, even among the Führer's closest associates. Goering shared them, and they certainly inspired Rudolf Hess's impulsive flight to Scotland in May, for the deputy leader hoped somehow to persuade the British to stop being so stubborn.[49] Within the army general staff, where methodical planning for Operation Barbarossa had been proceeding since January,[50] there was growing disquiet. Halder had difficulty in understanding what the strategic goals of a Russian war were,[51] and his diary indicates an increasing awareness that they were to be subordinated to ideological ones. To a man who revered Frederick the Great so deeply that he gave books about him to his associates on Frederick's birthday,[52] it must have been appalling to listen to Hitler explaining, as he did on 17 March and again on the thirtieth, that the Russian war must be one of

[46] J. M. G. Stewart, *The Struggle for Crete* (London, 1967); D. M. Davin, *Crete* (London, 1953).

[47] See Hitler's statement of 16 January 1941 on why Germany must intervene. Halder, *Kriegstagebuch*, ii. 244.

[48] Ibid. 400. See also his expression of doubt about Rommel's ability, and his description of him as 'a soldier who has gone mad'. Ibid. 377.

[49] On this, see James Maxwell-Hamilton, *Motive for a Mission* (London, 1971).

[50] Halder, *Kriegstagebuch*, ii. 251, 253, 257 ff., 313 ff.

[51] See the entry in his diary for 28 January: 'Barbarossa: Sinn nicht klar.' Ibid. 261.

[52] Ibid. 252.

extermination, in which not only the leadership cadres of the Soviet state must be destroyed, but the whole Russian intelligentsia, and that the creation of a new one in the conquered state was to be prevented.[53]

It was precisely because Hitler's aim was not solely strategical and because his quest for *Lebensraum* was accompanied by racist objectives (the words 'Bolshevists' and 'Jews' being synonymous in his thinking) that he did not allow himself to be diverted from the purpose that had guided his course for more than twenty years. In what went on in Africa he had no compelling interest. His eyes were fixed myopically upon the Russian steppes. During the spring months he assembled his armies in East Prussia, Poland, and Romania, and, once the operations in Greece and Crete were secured, he loosed them upon Russia. D-Day was 22 June, and within two weeks the Luftwaffe had won almost uncontested mastery of the skies, General von Leeb's northern army group had passed Riga and was on its way to Leningrad, General von Bock's forces had passed Minsk and were rolling towards Smolensk, and Rundstedt's southern army group had taken Kiev and was headed for the line Kharkhov–Taganrog–Kursk.[54]

Despite the momentum of the initial drive, which took 150,000 prisoners, 1,200 tanks, and 600 big guns in the first ten days, the *Blitz* did not work this time. The greatest penetration was made in the south, where Rundstedt had gained Kharkhov by late September, and Kleist was in Rostov-on-Don and Manstein invading the Crimea a month later. But Leeb never got to the Newa, and Bock's armies encountered the most stubborn kind of resistance at Smolensk and were held up for three months before they could resume their advance towards Moscow. By then it was too late, for, when they were within sight of their goal, an early winter immobilized their armour and mechanized transport and inflicted dreadful suffering upon troops unequipped to withstand temperatures that dropped to thirty degrees below zero. As Marshall Zhukhov mounted counter-attacks north and south of the capital, the German army staff urged a general withdrawal to permit a regrouping for the spring campaign. Hitler flatly refused. Sensing that the war would have to be won soon if it were to be won at all, he feared the loss of

[53] Ibid. 320, 336 f.

[54] See *Kriegstagebuch des Oberkommandos der Wehrmacht 1940–1945*, i: *1940–1941*, ed. Hans-Adolf Jacobsen (Frankfurt-on-Main, 1965), p. 417; and for details of the fighting, Trumbull Higgins, *Hitler and Russia* (New York, 1966); Alan Clark, *Barbarossa* (London, 1965); Paul Carell, *Hitler's War on Russia*, trans. from the German (London, 1964).

time that a withdrawal would cause, as well as the possibility of a general disintegration of the battle-line once it was started. He brooked no opposition. He intimated that the failure to take Moscow was the fault of the professionals, and on 19 December, when he accepted the resignation of the ailing Brauchitsch, he took operational command of the army into his own hands.[55] Thereafter officers who ordered withdrawals on their own initiative or who argued for a general retreat too strenuously did so at the risk of losing their commands, as Panzer General Erich Hoepner and General Heinz Guderian soon discovered.[56] Along the thousand-mile front the German armies dug in and waited for the spring thaws.

During this critical debate at the gates of Moscow Hitler had made another decision. Ever since July 1940 he had assured his generals that the destruction of Russia would also mean the end of the British war effort. But he was aware that the British were sustained also by the hope of American assistance. To keep the United States out of the war had been the principal goal of the Tripartite Pact of September 1940, and it had also motivated the directive that Hitler issued on 5 March 1941 'for cooperation with Japan', in which the purpose of this was described as being 'to induce Japan to take action in the Far East as soon as possible', since this would 'tie down strong English forces and . . . divert the main effort of the United States to the Pacific'.[57] On 7 December 1941, when the Japanese demonstrated that they had needed no such persuasion by making their fateful strike against Pearl Harbor, Hitler did not, therefore, hesitate to make what appeared to him to be the logical response.

On the afternoon of 11 December General Jodl put a call through to the chief of the Plans Section of the OKW operations staff, General Warlimont, and informed him that the Führer had just declared war on the United States and that the staff had better make a study of where the Americans were likely to employ the bulk of their forces initially. Warlimont protested, 'So far we have never considered a war against the United States. . . . We can hardly undertake this job just like that.' Jodl answered, 'Well, see what you can do.'[58] There was a ring of despair in the exchange, and that feeling was shared by many who listened to the Führer's speech to the Reichstag on the morning of the eleventh. Hitler might feel that his declaration of war

---

[55] Halder, *Kriegstagebuch*, iii. 354, 356–9. See also David Irving, *Hitler's War* (New York, 1977), pp. 355 ff.

[56] Halder, *Kriegstagebuch*, iii. 376 f.; *Kriegstagebuch des OKW* i. 1084 f.; Liddell Hart, *Other Side of the Hill*, pp. 310 ff.; Guderian, *Panzer Leader*, pp. 263–70.

[57] Trevor-Roper, *Blitzkrieg*, p. 58.

[58] Warlimont, *Inside Hitler's Headquarters*, p. 208.

was the least he could do to thank his Japanese ally for his action and that he need fear no reprisals, since American energies would be completely absorbed by the Pacific conflict until he had disposed of the Russians and become too strong to be challenged by any nation on earth. But the German people remembered the First World War, and the only part of the Führer's speech that registered upon the consciousness of many of them was the passage in which he admitted that, by his own action, he had brought the Americans into war against Germany once more.[59]

II

Eighteen months earlier, when he appeared before the Reichstag after his victory over France, Hitler had interrupted the recital of his triumphs to speak about the attitude of the German people. 'Thanks to National Socialist education', he said,

the German people went into this war, not with a superficial *Hurra-patriotismus*, but with the fanatical earnestness of a race that knows the fate that awaits it in the event that it is conquered. The attempts of enemy propaganda to weaken this tight unity were just as stupid as they were ineffective. Ten months of war have deepened this fanaticism. But it is a misfortune that world opinion is not formed by people who want to see things as they are, but only by people who see what they want to see.[60]

It was a curious passage, the more so because Hitler could not leave it alone, but went on working himself up into a passion over British statesmen who, in order to give their people a little hope, had the effrontery to say that German morale would be dissolved by 'General Hunger' or destroyed by revolution. It seems all too apparent that Hitler himself had doubts about the unity he was celebrating. Else why, at the height of his triumph, should he be thinking—as he obviously was thinking—of the decline of public morale and the slump in confidence in the government that had taken place in the years 1917 and 1918?

Hitler was convinced that it was the home front's collapse that had defeated the German army in 1918, and he was resolved to prevent a repitition of that. To someone as arrogant and self-centred as Ribbentrop, public opinion might seem to be of negligible importance but Hitler had made his way by riding on the tides of public feeling, and he was aware that they could turn. To prevent them from doing so, to sustain the morale of the home front, to search out and eliminate elements of weakness in the national consensus were prin-

---

[59] Domarus, *Hitler: Reden* ii. 1793 ff.   [60] Ibid. 1555 f.

cipal objectives of National Socialist wartime domestic policy. It can be argued, however, that they were pursued in ways that were self-defeating.

In the field of economics, for example, a reluctance to ask the public to bear sacrifices continued to be a basic determinant of policy, as it had been in peacetime. For the first two years of the war the degree of economic regulation was no more rigorous than it had been since the inception of the Four Year Plan in 1936. The production of armaments did not increase significantly, nor did that of consumer goods decline. Indeed, both sectors benefited from the spoils seized in areas occupied by German troops. Food supplies improved, not least of all because of heavy shipments of Soviet grain and soy beans to Germany during the period of the Nazi–Soviet Pact. Effective wage and price controls maintained financial stability. The rationing system was efficient but not yet onerous. Peacetime projects like the construction of the highway network and the historical renovation and beautification of cities, in which Hitler took particular interest, proceeded at a somewhat diminished pace.[61] All of this was a far cry from total war, but, in view of the fact that the Polish, Scandinavian, and French campaigns virtually paid for themselves, this was understandable.

Albert Speer, who was to become Minister of Armaments and Munitions in 1942 and to make fundamental changes in economic mobilization, maintained that 'the war had in a sense been lost by the victories of 1940' and that it would have been better for Germany to have had a Dunkirk at the outset to spur its energies.[62] It would certainly appear that Hitler was so pleased with the effectiveness of his policy of waging war on the cheap that he saw no reason to change it when he began to plan his invasion of Russia. He showed some initial awareness that the new conflict might impose greater demands, and on 31 July 1940 he outlined an economic programme, not put into writing until 28 September, that called for armaments for 180 field divisions and an undefined number of occupation divisions by the spring of 1941, as well as continuation of the U-boat construction programme at its present rate and the speediest possible acceleration of production of anti-aircraft guns. On 14 August Goering told General Thomas that 'only now was real rearmament beginning'. Some days later, however, when General Keitel expressed doubts whether the new demands could be met without

[61] See Gordon Wright, *The Ordeal of Total War, 1939–1945* (New York, 1968), pp. 43–7, 57.
[62] Albert Speer, *Spandau: The Secret Diaries* (New York, 1977), p. 55.

ruthless cuts in consumer goods, the employment of women and increased numbers of foreign workers, and other measures of total war, Hitler flatly refused to listen to him. The forced employment of women he opposed on ideological grounds; reduction of civilian comforts he regarded as politically dangerous. He preferred to gamble on a short war, and to do so without allocating enough labour resources to war production to meet the objectives of the programme he had just announced. Aircraft production actually declined during the second half of 1940, and the doubling of the number of armoured divisions was achieved by reducing their number of tanks and using captured French cars and trucks. Once the attack on Russia began, there was a diversion of effort from munitions for the army to anti-aircraft equipment, so that the production of army weapons declined by 38 per cent in the first six months of the Russian war.[63]

Even after the *Blitz* had failed, and it had become apparent that, while the conflict in the east continued, it was likely that other fronts would become active and demanding, the government did not change its ways significantly. It is true that, at the beginning of 1942, when Hitler ordered massive increases in war material of every kind, he took the first step towards effective co-ordination of the war production effort by giving new powers, first, to Fritz Todt, the Minister of Armaments and Munitions, and then, when Todt was killed in an air crash in February, to the young architect Albert Speer. Within the next three years, sometimes using techniques invented by Walther Rathenau during the First World War, Speer improved procedures and eliminated duplication and waste; he defeated attempts by the navy and the air force to cling to their prerogatives in the matter of the design of weapons, absorbed the army's War Economy Branch, and reduced the organization of the Four Year Plan to a shadow of its former self; and, as a result, he managed to increased production threefold.[64] But he was denied the right to go beyond the limits of what rationalization could accomplish. Attempts to move in the direction of total mobilization of resources, as Great Britain had already done, met immediate opposition, both at the local level and in the highest reaches of the party, where decisions on important questions were often made not on the basis of logic but as a result of inter-agency or personal rivalries.

In April 1943, for example, Speer raised the question of mobilizing

[63] Leach, *Strategy against Russia*, pp. 72, 133–5; Alan S. Milward, *The German Economy at War* (London, 1965), pp. 12, 28–30, 34–5, 42, 45–6.

[64] Wright, *Total War*, pp. 61–5; Speer, *Inside the Third Reich*, pp. 278–86.

women once more, arguing that they would be better workers than foreign labourers, whose quality and competence depended upon the often capricious selection techniques of occupation authorities, who could often not speak German, and who posed certain awkward security problems. Because he had no authority in the field of labour allocation, Speer had to negotiate with Fritz Sauckel, a former Gauleiter whom Hitler had made Commissioner of Manpower at the urging of the powerful Martin Bormann, Reichsleiter and head of the party Chancellery. Sauckel refused to consider Speer's proposal, insisting that factory work would inflict both physical and moral harm upon German women and damage their psychic and emotional life and possibly their potential as mothers. Bormann supported and Hitler confirmed the refusal.[65]

Similarly, in October 1943, after Allied air raids had begun to cause serious disruption of war production and labour shortages were becoming troublesome, Speer went before the assembled Gauleiter and told them that the initiative had shifted to the side of Germany's antagonists and that, unless there was a major change in national priorities, the war would be lost. One and a half of the 6 million Germans currently employed in production of consumer goods would therefore have to be transferred to armaments plants, the deficit in articles of consumption being made up by French factories. He warned his audience that the kind of local obstructionism that had in the past prevented the closing of nonessential plants would no longer be tolerated, and that he would himself order the shut-downs in case of recalcitrance and bring charges against the foot-draggers. This brave show was ineffective, even though Speer had won a promise of support from Heinrich Himmler, the new Minister of the Interior, before he attempted it. The Gauleiter protested in a body to Hitler, who listened sympathetically and referred the matter to Bormann, who in turn convinced Himmler that Speer's views were unsound. Once again, nothing was done.[66]

It is worth asking whether the measures advocated by Speer would have changed the course of the war in any significant way. By his own calculations (and his achievements lend them weight), Germany in June 1941 could easily have had an army that was twice as heavily armed as it was. Moreover, the mobilization of the 5 million women who were performing no useful war service (including 1·4 million who did domestic work, to say nothing of the thousands of

---

[65] Speer, *Inside the Third Reich*, pp. 292 ff.   [66] Ibid., pp. 404–7.

Ukrainian girls who were imported as servants for party functionaries) would have released up to 3 million men for military service.[67] These accretions of strength might have made a difference at Smolensk and, consequently, at Moscow in 1941; they would have permitted vastly greater shipments of equipment and manpower to Rommel in 1942; they might have changed the result at Stalingrad. It is idle to rewrite the history of the war on the basis of conjecture; but it is entirely possible that the shape of the conflict would have been profoundly changed if Hitler had been more willing to demand sacrifices of the home front in the first years of the war.

The regime's sensitivity to public mood—to the *Stimmung* of the people—was illustrated both by the care with which it collected information about it and the effort it made to influence and guide it by propaganda. Before the outbreak of the war the Führer's deputy, Rudolf Hess, had assigned to the Sicherheitsdienst of the SS the task of making 'political situation reports' on the basis of information collected by agents or *Vertrauensmänner* who kept their ears open in markets and public houses, factories and cinemas, grocery stores and barber shops, newspaper kiosks and queues waiting for trams and who collated what postmen, HJ leaders, and local SA-men told them. The directive to the SD emphasized the necessity of completeness, objectivity, and unvarnished truth in the preparation of these reports—they were not to be retouched or have their colours softened by ideological brushes—and this was taken seriously, so much so that, as the war went on, the reports began to worry and annoy the party leadership. In March 1942 Hitler said that, if one judged the state of the country from the complaints included in the reports, the war would have been long lost. He was confident, he added, that the true attitude (the *Haltung*) of the people was in strong contrast to these superficial manifestations. Subsequently, the various reporting agencies received orders to emphasize *Haltung* rather than *Stimmung* from now on (the cynical Goebbels remarking that one does not talk of *Stimmung* when houses are being burned and cities laid waste). The change did not make the reports more cheerful reading and, although they had originally been designed for wide distribution in the party, they were restricted to an increasingly small circle of readers after the middle of 1943.[68]

[67] Ibid., pp. 294–5; *Spandau*, pp. 54–5.
[68] On the origins and history of this information service, see the editor's introduction to *Meldungen aus dem Reich: Auswahl aus den geheimen Lageberichten des Sicherheitsdienstes der SS 1939–1944*, ed. Heinz Boberach (Neuwied and Berlin, 1965). See also Steinert, *Hitler's Krieg*, pp. 40–8.

To counteract the criticisms and correct the signs of weakness revealed by the reports, and to sustain public morale in general, was the task of the propaganda agencies, and principally of the Reich Ministry of Propaganda, headed by Josef Goebbels. As was customary in the National Socialist state, Goebbels's authority was less than complete, for both Alfred Rosenberg, the Führer's plenipotentiary for the supervision of ideological training and education, and Robert Ley, the leader of the Labour Front, claimed rights of control over the dissemination of certain types of information and caused difficulties until their competence was sharply reduced in October 1942; and both the Reich Press Bureau of Otto Dietrich and the War Propaganda Section of the OKW imposed restrictions upon his activities throughout the war.[69] But Goebbels was the most important force in shaping the information that reached the general public; and, in his daily ministerial conferences, which were attended by his department heads, the officials responsible for radio, film, and Press, and representatives from party headquarters and from the Wehrmacht and interested ministries, he showered upon his audience instructions about how issues should be handled, linguistic formulations that were to be used or avoided, reflections upon the purpose and technique of propaganda in the New Order, and warnings to editors who had dared to deviate from his decrees.[70]

Goebbels was well aware that the German people had gone to war without enthusiasm and that from that time on their mood varied—*himmelhochjauchzend, zum Tode betrübt*—between brief periods of exultation when victories were announced and relapses into depression when they were not followed by a return to peace. His approach was to blame both the coming and the prolongation of the war upon the enemy. Although the British Prime Minister had announced, in a broadcast to Germany on 3 September 1939, that England was waging war not against the German people but against Hitlerism, the German Press and radio, at Goebbel's direction, obscured this in a chorus of vituperation against England as a plutocratic land, led by corrupt and degenerate statesmen who had long plotted to destroy Germany as a nation and to restore the conditions of 1648. This campaign was accompanied by a relentless exaltation of the Führer as 'a historic personality, utterly great and utterly lonely', as 'the one man who, as a pioneer, has given meaning,

---

[69] Steinert, *Hitler's Krieg*, pp. 32–3; Jay W. Baird, *The Mythical World of Nazi War Propaganda, 1939–1945* (Minneapolis, 1974), pp. 28–40.

[70] A fine collection of these extraordinary performances is to be found in Boelcke, *Secret Conferences*.

content, and direction to the overall trend of this age', as 'a genius . . . building a new world', in short, as infallible and invulnerable and hence deserving of unquestioning and unlimited loyalty and obedience.[71] The two themes were skilfully combined to overcome uncertainty in the public mood during the *drôle de guerre*, and the attempt on Hitler's life in the Bürgerbräukeller in Munich on 8 November 1939, which took the lives of 7 Nazis and wounded 60 others, provided the ideal opportunity for this. Goebbels immediately directed the Press to make it clear that the plot had been prepared by the British Secret Service and the Jews, while giving maximum coverage to the elaborate ceremonies attendant upon the funeral of the victims, which featured an address by Rudolf Hess. In this curious rhetorical exercise Hess informed the audience that two of the widows had told him that they felt it more important that Hitler should live than that their husbands should. This improving sentiment Goebbels spread in every corner of Germany, along with Hess's peroration:

The miracle of his rescue has enhanced our belief in him. Providence has spared our Fuehrer in the past, and Providence will spare our Fuehrer in the future because he has been sent on a great mission. . . . To our enemies we call out: You wanted to take the Fuehrer from us, and you have only drawn us closer to him. You wanted to weaken us, and you have only made us stronger.[72]

This propaganda and Germany's naval successes (notably the sinking of *Royal Oak* in Scapa Flow as a result of a daring submarine assault commanded by Lieutenant Prien) sustained the war spirit throughout the months of inactivity in Europe, and the victories that followed in Scandinavia, the Low Countries, and France inflamed it further. The SD situation reports at the end of June 1940 agreed that the unity of spirit and will had never been more marked and that, even in circles where Communism had once been strong, it was impossible to detect any organized opposition.[73]

This was the last time that the reports were ever so reassuring. The salient concern in the public mind was apparent within a matter of weeks: the British were still in the war, and apparently nothing was being done to make them give up. Goebbels instructed the Press to undertake a campaign to convince the public that this was no 'saure Gurkenzeit' but a mere pause before the definitive victory.[74] When

---

[71] See the chapter 'The Projection of the Hitler Image', in Ernest K. Bramsted, *Goebbels and National Socialist Propaganda, 1925–1945* (East Lansing, Mich., 1965), esp. pp. 220–1.

[72] Baird, *War Propaganda*, pp. 65–7.

[73] *Meldungen aus dem Reich*, pp. 77 ff.   [74] Steinert, *Hitlers Krieg*, p. 143.

that did not come, despite Goering's strenuous labours, dissatisfaction grew and was reinforced by other discontents. These
included growing fear of shortages now that a second war winter
was inevitable (concern over coal and shoes was particularly strong);
the rising prices of textiles and some foodstuffs while wages
remained generally fixed; concern, particularly on the part of the
established Churches, over the government's secret, but inadequately concealed, euthanasia programme, which was to cause the
deaths of more than 70,000 mentally ill Germans between January
1940 and August of the following year; and the first heavy bombing
of Berlin in August 1940, an event that Berliners had believed, and
had been encouraged to believe, could never happen, and which left
them unhappily aware that it would not be unique.[75] Goebbels
described the German mood at the end of the year as one of 'light
depression'.[76] It did not become any lighter in the six months that
followed, and the sudden announcement on 22 June 1941 that Germany was at war with Russia deepened it and made it permanent.
The dedicated Nazis and the optimists convinced themselves that the
victory over Russia would be quick and that it would discourage the
British from fighting further. But there were many now who saw a
long war ahead, and some, like the historian Friedrich Meinecke,
who were beginning to feel that 'the enemy's real weapon [was]
time, hunger, and America'.[77]

Goebbels himself had few illusions about the magnitude of the
task that lay ahead. In interpreting the course of the war to the
German people, he had generally, even in its first phase, taken the
cautious line and had expected his associates to remember Talleyrand's warning, 'Pas trop de zêle'. Fanfares, he insisted, were to be
reserved for campaigns that had actually been won. When dealing
with current operations, editors were expected not to get ahead of
the facts; and in May 1940 Goebbels reprimanded one of them for
suggesting in print that the fighting in Belgium would be over in a
matter of hours. The task of the Press, he said, was 'merely to report
about what *has* happened, and . . . under no circumstances are
predictions permissible'. After the outbreak of the war in Russia he
became increasingly vigilant in this respect, and he was bitterly
critical of Dietrich's announcement to the Press on 9 October 1941

---

[75] Ibid., pp. 144, 152 ff., 164; on the effects of the bombing of Berlin, William L.
Shirer, *Berlin Diary: The Journal of a Foreign Correspondent, 1934–1941* (New York,
1941), p. 486; and *Meldungen aus dem Reich*, p. 180.

[76] Steinert, *Hitlers Krieg*, p. 172.

[77] To Siegfried Kaehler, 28 Apr. 1941. Meinecke, *Briefwechsel*, p. 370.

that 'the annihilation of Army Group Timoshenko [had] decided the campaign in Russia' and that the Soviet Union was 'done for militarily as a result of this last powerful blow'.[78] Facile optimism of this kind, he was convinced, would gradually sap the people's confidence in the government; in the meantime it prevented them from facing up to the actualities of their situation. 'The people', he once said, 'must always be firmly supported by the corset of realism.'[79]

As the tide of battle began to turn in 1942, with the Allied landings in North Africa and the critical battles of El Alamein and Stalingrad, Goebbels became ever more insistent that, while it was legitimate to go on lying to the foreigner about Germany's condition, a practice that he developed into a fine art, it was necessary to be pitilessly frank in telling the German people what their situation really was. There was an interesting convergence between his views and those of Albert Speer. Like the Minister of Munitions, he believed that salvation lay in a radicalization of the war effort, a total war that would galvanize all of the energies of the people, and that this would be possible only when their illusions were dispelled. But Hitler distrusted these views and did not make him his own, and, as the conflict moved remorselessly towards its end, his Propaganda Minister had occasion to reflect that Joseph Stalin showed a rather better appreciation of the necessities of the situation than the Führer.

III

In his speech in the Sportpalast on 3 October 1941 Hitler for the first time identified the war against Russia as a European effort under German leadership. 'In the ranks of our German soldiers,' he said, 'making common cause with them, march the Italians, the Finns, the Hungarians, the Romanians, the Slovaks, and the Croats; the Spaniards now move into the battle; the Belgians, the Dutch, the Danes, the Norwegians, yes, even the French, have joined this great front.'[80] Out of this joint effort against Communism, he appeared to suggest, a new and better Europe would emerge.

The idea of a New Order in Europe was much in vogue in the first years of the crusade against Russia and was popular both with the ideologues of the NSDAP and with Nazi sympathizers in Western Europe, like Pierre Laval in France and Anton Mussert in the Nether-

---

[78] Hitler authorized the announcement and had himself announced in his address in the Sportpalast on 3 October that 'the enemy is broken and will never rise again'. Domarus, *Hitler: Reden* ii. 1763.

[79] Boelcke, *Secret Conferences*, p. 31.

[80] Domarus, *Hitler: Reden* ii. 1763.

lands, who saw in it both a justification and a promise of preferment. The amount of rhetoric lavished upon it was impressive. The Press chief Otto Dietrich told an audience in Prague in 1941 that the New Order would be based 'not on the principle of a privileged position for individual nations but on the principle of equal chances for all' in a 'racially constituted but organically combined ordering of the nations'.[81] This movement's leading jurist, the brutal Governor-General of Poland, Hans Frank, during a lecture in the Aula of the University of Heidelberg in July 1942, sketched the outlines of a 'united and reciprocal comradeship of the peoples of Europe . . . a kind of useful accommodation of the interests, strengths, and needs of the individual peoples', freed from their previous domination by the Anglo-Saxon world Powers, and pursuing an independent autarchic development under the protection of the Greater German Reich of Adolf Hitler, which would 'promote Europe's culture in every way and give its peoples comradely support'. The Reich Commissioner for Occupied Holland, Arthur Seyß-Inquart, spoke of a *Staatenbund* in which subjects of member states might be granted a confederate citizenship as well, which would give them the right to be economically and politically active in all parts of the community.[82] There were even voices that echoed Hitler's speech by proclaiming that 'the SS is being transformed today into one indissoluble community of European youth'.[83]

There is not the slightest indication that Hitler himself had any intention of lending substance to these cloudy formulations. On the one occasion on which he spoke with any clarity on the subject, in a meeting with the Reichsleiter and Gauleiter in 1943, he had a dusty answer for the communitarians. According to Goebbels, he declared that 'all the rubbish of small nations must be liquidated as fast as possible. The aim of our struggle must be to create a united Europe. The Germans alone can really organize Europe. . . . Today we are practically the only power on the European mainland with a capacity for leadership. . . . The Fuehrer gave expression to his unshakeable

---

[81] Wright, *Total War*, p. 140.

[82] Jacobsen, *Der Zweite Weltkrieg*, pp. 189–93.

[83] The Waffen-SS, which originated as Hitler's private guard and was supplemented after 1933 by the creation of Political Action Squads, to deal with dissidents, and Death's Head Detachments, to run concentration camps, grew swiftly after 1940, until it became, contrary to the Führer's earlier concept, a fourth branch of the Wehrmacht. As it did, the rules of racial homogeneity that had determined its membership were progressively relaxed so that, by 1945, none of its 38 divisions was exclusively German and at least half consisted largely of foreigners. See Stein, *Waffen-SS*, pp. 138 ff., 168 ff.

conviction that the Reich will be the master of all Europe.'[84] This offered little comfort for collaborators like Laval, who believed that France, 'always the country of intelligence', would have a preferred position in the new dispensation,[85] or Erik Scavenius, who brought Denmark into the Anti-Comintern Pact and appeared to believe that Nordic affinity with the master race would count for something.[86] In a Europe reorganized by a triumphant Hitler, Germany would have no peers. Even the other member of the Axis could expect nothing but a satellite status.

Until the victory should be won, Hitler made no attempt to give rational order to the continent that he had all but overrun; and the nature of German control varied from country to country. It was most indirect in those countries that were still neutral, Spain, Portugal, Switzerland, Sweden, and Turkey, although it was not inconsiderable there. Until the fortunes of war had turned definitively against Germany, the governments of these nations had to walk delicately and avoid arousing the Führer's displeasure, and this robbed them of complete control over their policies. It was clearly inexpedient for them, for example, wherever their sympathies might lie, to yield to Allied demands for restriction of their shipments of materials like wolfram and chrome to Germany.

Italy, the three Danubian states Hungary, Romania, and Bulgaria, and Finland were all, in 1941, independent states that were allied with Germany, although, in the case of the first two of them, independence proved to be a fragile thing. In December 1940, when Mussolini pleaded for assistance in overcoming his difficulties in Greece and Africa, Hitler granted it on condition that German officials should henceforth have a voice in determining Italy's needs. The year 1941 saw the progressive penetration of the country by German technicians, military advisers, economic experts, and Gestapo agents; and, before long, the arrival of a Luftwaffe detachment in Sicily laid the foundations for what, after Mussolini's fall in September 1943, became a military occupation.[87] Hungary's fate was much the same. Territorial greed had overcome the government's

---

[84] *The Goebbels Diaries, 1942–1943*, ed. and trans. Louis P. Lochner (New York, 1948), p. 357.

[85] See his radio address of 20 April 1942 in Jacobsen, *Der Zweite Weltkrieg*, pp. 187 ff. In September 1942 he said: 'I defy anyone—and I've said this to the Germans—to build a solid, articulated, and viable Europe without France's consent.' Warner, *Laval*, p. 295.

[86] On the Danish people's repudiation of Scavenius's collaborationist policy, see Petrow, *Bitter Years*, pp. 190–6.

[87] Wiskemann, *Rome–Berlin Axis*, pp. 284 ff.

original hesitation to become too dependent upon the Germans, and Hungary had participated profitably in the destruction of Czechoslovakia and the reduction of Romania in 1940. Hungarian troops also marched with the Germans against Yugoslavia and joined in the attack on Russia in June 1941. Admiral Horthy's enthusiasm for this last adventure faded, however, as the prospect of a quick victory receded, and he began to cast about for some means of returning to non-belligerence. German agents became aware in 1942 that he was treating with the Western Powers, and Hitler might have taken violent action had he not been otherwise occupied. As it was, he kept Budapest under strict observation, came close to ordering military occupation in mid-1943, and finally sent in troops in March 1944. Horthy remained in office as a figure-head in a regime that was henceforth under German direction.[88]

No attempt was made to interfere with the governments of the other allies. Hitler admired and trusted the Romanian leader, General Ion Antonescu, and was grateful for his country's strong military contribution; and, although Germany became heavily dependent upon Romanian oil after the first months of the Russian campaign had almost exhausted its reserves, Hitler did not consider it necessary to seize control of the fields. In Bulgaria, whose role in Hitler's eyes was to guard his flank against an attack from Turkey, if the Allies succeeded in persuading that country to break its neutrality, Germany worked through normal diplomatic channels when it had anything to communicate, and the country's sovereignty was not diminished in any way. As for Finland, another country that Hitler admired, it was, after the first phase of the Russian campaign, in which it participated, permitted to reduce its war effort and devote its efforts to pressing tasks of domestic reconstruction, with Hitler's promise of territorial gains around Leningrad and on the Karelian peninsula.[89]

All the rest of Europe was under Germany's direct or thinly disguised control. In the west, Eupen and Malmédy, which had been lost to Belgium in 1919, were annexed outright, and the Grand Duchy of Luxemburg, Alsace, and part of Lorraine were annexed *de facto*. Belgium, Holland, and the northern industrial areas of France, plus all of its coastal areas, were placed under direct German civil administration, which was also true of Norway, after the flight of King Haakon to England, although the Germans installed Vidkun Quisling as Minister President and gave him limited powers in

---

[88] Rich, *Hitler's War Aims* ii. 241–5. [89] Ibid. 251 ff., 258 ff., 400 f.

domestic matters. This was the privilege also of the government of
Marshal Pétain, which ruled the southern third of France, the area
that became known as Vichy France, until November 1942, when
the Allied landings in North Africa induced the Germans to occupy
this area as well. In Denmark, where King Christian X had resolved
not to leave his country, the government continued to run its affairs
with a minimum of interference until 1943, not entirely to Hitler's
satisfaction, for he would have preferred to see the sovereign
replaced by the head of the Danish Nazi party, an ineffectual politician named Dr. Frits Clausen.

In Eastern Europe, Bohemia and Moravia had formed a German
protectorate and Slovakia had been a satellite since March 1939. The
spring campaigns of 1941 led to the annexation of two-thirds of
Slovenia, the division of Yugoslavia into three states (Croatia, Serbia, and Montenegro) under local strong men who were nominally
responsible to the Italian Government, and the installation of a
collaborationist government in Greece, with an Italian army of
occupation and a formidable German military presence at Salonika,
commanded by Field-Marshal Wilhelm List, who had the mission of
watching over the whole area from Serbia to Skyros. Finally, the
attack upon Russia brought the German annexation of that part of
Poland that had not previously been annexed, and the creation of
two huge Reich Commissariats under German civil administration:
the Ostland, which included the former Baltic states and Byelo-
russia, and the Ukraine.

The conquerors regarded these lands, without exception, as
legitimate objects of economic exploitation. The methods varied,
and there was a decided difference between the style of the bland
representatives of the Deutsche Bank who cheated French and Belgian industrialists out of their holdings by quasi-legal methods and
that of Hermann Goering greedily egging his associates on 'to plunder and plunder copiously';[90] but the result was much the same. To
feed the inordinate appetite of their war machine, the Germans
might have encouraged heightened agricultural and industrial production in the conquered areas according to a rational plan of quotas
and specialization, and intelligent men like Albert Speer saw that,
over the long term, that promised to be the most effective means of
bringing to Germany the materials its armies required. Instead the
government elected to follow the easier and more wasteful way of
shipping back to Germany whatever they could lay their hands on in

[90] *International Military Tribunal* xxxix. 390 f.

the way of material, machinery, and manpower, without regard for the consequences in the despoiled areas. These included inflation, shortages of vital commodities, black markets, and growing resistance.[91]

No country was exempt from these exactions. Although Germany's allies were treated with more circumspection than former enemies, the Hungarian Government was unable to evade German demands for currency adjustments in their favour or to withstand insistence that Germany be given the right to purchase a controlling interest in the country's largest oil company;[92] and the Romanian Government found it politic to sign a ten-year agreement granting German companies a preferred position in technical assistance programmes and corporate investment. With the defeated governments in Western Europe the Germans negotiated occupation agreements that generally called for payments that were so outrageously high that they created excess credit, which was then used to buy up all available stocks of raw materials and manufactured goods, a sophisticated form of seizure. In areas that they occupied in Southern and Eastern Europe the Nazis were more blatant, resorting to confiscations of industrial and financial properties without regard for legal forms. Seizures were often motivated more by ideological than economic purpose. In the General Government of Poland, the area east of the Corridor, Posen and Silesia that had not been incorporated into the Reich in 1939 and was destined as a dumping-ground for Poles expelled from other areas, the Germans systematically removed all resources except those needed to maintain the life of the inhabitants at a bare subsistence level;[93] and in Russia, of which Hitler had said, 'Russia is our Africa, and the Russians are our negroes',[94] the SS deliberately removed or destroyed all forms of industrial production and operated large state farms with forced labour to produce grain for Germany.

Increasingly, the resource most coveted by the conquerors was manpower, for military conscription had greatly aggravated the labour shortage from which Germany had been suffering even before the war, and Hitler stubbornly refused to consider com-

[91] Wright, *Total War*, pp. 116 f.

[92] Rich, *Hitler's War Aims* ii. 243.

[93] At Nuremberg, Hans Frank said that Hitler's orders to him when he was appointed General Governor were 'to reduce the area, as a war zone and a land of booty, to complete poverty, to make it, so to speak, in its economic, social, cultural, and political structure, a shambles'. *International Military Tribunal* xxix. 368.

[94] Gerald Reitlinger, *The House Built on Sand: The Conflicts of German Policy in Russia, 1939–1945* (New York, 1960), p. 176.

pulsory national service for women. At the end of the Polish war, therefore, Nazi occupation authorities began to ship able-bodied prisoners of war and civilians to the Reich as labourers, and after the victory in the west an intensive recruiting campaign began in France and the Low Countries. By December 1941 4 million foreigners were working in German fields and factories. It was soon clear, however, that even this impressive addition to the labour force was inadequate; and in March 1942 Hitler established the office of Plenipotentiary General for Labour Allocation, as a subsidiary of the Four Year Plan, to centralize the procurement, transportation, allocation, and exploitation of foreign labour. The chief of this agency, Fritz Sauckel, was a man of great energy that was unrestrained by humane considerations. To meet the quotas he set, his agents in the east used the most brutal forms of compulsion, rounding people up in the market place or during church services or in cinemas, burning down villages that did not meet the demands made on them, inflicting merciless punishment on recruits who tried to escape, subjecting the convoys of prisoners of war to the most primitive conditions during the journey to Germany. In the last three years of the war, Sauckel's methods succeeded in raising 2·8 million labourers in the occupied lands of the east, not counting the prisoners of war transported to Germany, but the wastage was great and the political damage done to the German cause incalculable.[95] It has been estimated that in 1944 there were as many as 7 million foreign workers in Germany, about 20 per cent of the labour force, and another 7 million labouring for Germany in their own countries, primarily in state farms, in military construction work, and in menial jobs in German military camps and installations.[96]

These forms of economic exploitation coincided with an ambitious programme of colonization and resettlement that originated in October 1939, after the defeat of Poland, when Hitler authorized Heinrich Himmler, the Reichsführer of the SS and the Chief of German Police in the Ministry of the Interior, to formulate a programme for the organization and settlement of the *Lebensraum* which he had long promised the German people and which was now being conquered by German arms. In particular, Himmler was to devise means 'to eliminate the harmful influence of such alien parts of the population, especially in the newly acquired territory, which in their present position constitute a danger to the Reich and the German

---

[95] Alexander Dallin, *German Rule in Russia, 1941–1945: A Study of Occupation Policies* (London, 1957), pp. 429 ff.

[96] Wright, *Total War*, p. 121.

community', and to create new colonies by resettlement of Germans and ethnic Germans coming back to the Reich.[97]

This was a task that could not but be congenial to Himmler, the bloodless unconditional policeman, whose private fantasies belied his impassive exterior, and whose brain teemed with muddled longings for a return to the values of a primitive, if not mythical, German past and dreams of creating a new order of Teutonic Knights. He used his authority to establish a Reich Commission for the Strengthening of Germandom, whose chief was Ulrich Greifelt, a member of the SS since 1933; and this body addressed itself to the problems of screening ethnic Germans who wanted to go back to Germany, of deporting non-collaborators from those areas in the west that had been annexed, and of evacuating non-desirables from the annexed areas of Poland. Originally, it was planned to sequester the deportees—or at least those among them who were useless as labourers—in the General Government of Poland, which was to become a 'German Siberia'. In 1941, however, as German troops advanced into Russia, Himmler's plans became more expansive. The General Government was now to be reserved for German settlement too, and the frontiers of the Reich were to be pushed eastward, where a new *Ordenland* would-be built in the quadrilateral Lublin–Zhitomir–Vinnitsa–Lwow, which would be to the SS what East Prussia had been to the Teutonic Knights, at once a bastion and a jumping-off place for the creation of other SS strong-points further east. Once peace returned, these would serve to control the Slav lands that lay beyond the area of German annexation and colonization and to perform civilizing and Germanizing functions. Like the American frontier in the nineteenth century, the new German borders would be flexible and expanding; the Indians, in this case, would be the original Slavic population, augmented by all those persons who had been resettled, that is to say expelled, from the German lands.[98]

This grandiose scheme of social engineering, which offered the German people the prospect of great economic well-being, as well as the psychic satisfactions provided by the evocation of Germany's ancient mission in the east, was bound to be attractive to anyone who did not stop to inquire how it was to be achieved. Himmler had already answered that question in January 1941, when he told a gathering of SS officials that the destruction of 30 million Slavs was a

---

[97] Robert L. Koehl, *RKFDV: German Resettlement and Population Policy, 1939–1945* (Cambridge, Mass., 1957), pp. 51 f.
[98] Ibid., pp. 147 ff., 226 f.

prerequisite for German planning in the east.[99] These dreadful words might have palsied the tongue of a normal man. Himmler pronounced them as matter-of-factly as he talked of kidnapping Nordic children from non-German areas and training them in special SS schools to be a new race of praetorians. And his personal contribution to the achievement of this ghastly total was far from negligible, for it should be remembered that, in addition to the deaths caused by the forcible eviction of millions of Poles from areas reserved for German settlers and by the excessive work-loads imposed upon those who were impressed into virtual slavery to serve the economic needs of their new masters, he was also responsible for the indiscriminate killing indulged in by the special SS 'action teams' (*Einsatzgruppen*) that moved into Russia behind the advancing armies,[100] as well as for the atrocious treatment accorded Russian prisoners of war, of whom the incredible number of 3,700,000 died in captivity.[101]

A feature of the resettlement plan in its early stages was the creation of a Jewish Pale in the General Government of Poland, and in 1940 Himmler had authorized an Austrian SS official named Odilo Globocnick to make plans for this and to maintain liaison with Adolf Eichmann, head of the Reichssicherheitsamt Section IV D, which handled the deportation of Jews from Germany.[102] But these plans suffered a radical change in the middle of 1941, when Himmler informed Rudolf Hoess, the commandant of the large new concentration camp at Auschwitz, near Cracow, that the Führer had given orders for a final solution of the Jewish question and was going to entrust its execution to the SS.[103] In July 1941 an order from Hermann Goering, Plenipotentiary for the Four Year Plan, to Reinhard Heydrich, head of the Secret Police and the SD, and Eichmann's superior officer, signified the full involvement of the state apparatus in this scheme. That the object was mass murder was obscured in the clotted bureaucratic style that characterized all National Socialist directives. The order read:

As supplement to the task that was entrusted to you in the decree dated 24 January 1939, to solve the Jewish question by emigration and evacuation in the most favourable way possible, I herewith commission you to carry out all necessary preparations with regard to organizational, substantive, and financial viewpoints for a total solution of the Jewish question in the German sphere of influence in Europe.

---

[99] Ibid., p. 146.
[100] Dallin, *German Rule*, p. 73.
[101] Reitlinger, *House Built on Sand*, p. 446.
[102] See above, Ch. XVII, p. 637.
[103] Rudolf Hoess, *Commandant of Auschwitz*, trans. from the German (Cleveland, 1960), pp. 160, 205.

Insofar as the competencies of other central organizations are hereby affected, these are to be involved.[104]

At the end of the year Heydrich presided over a meeting of SS officials and representatives of the ministries and the civil occupation authorities in the General Government and the Ostland at Wannsee in Berlin to discuss administrative procedures and such technical matters as the most efficient means of exterminating and disposing of large numbers of people. The meeting gave some consideration to recent experience in Riga where mass killings of Jews had already started and talked about routes by which prisoners could be transported from west to east and types and locations of camps. Hitler's euthanasia programme had provided opportunities for testing lethal gases, the most effective of which appeared to be a cyanide called Zyklon B; and, after some experiments in Auschwitz, in September 1941, gassing facilities were installed in Chelmno near Lodz and Belzec near Lublin. The Wannsee Conference approved the steps already taken and ordered their acceleration. The first half of 1942 saw the construction of a new death camp at Sobibor and the transformation of the labour concentration camps at Majdanek, near Lublin, and Treblinka, fifty miles from Warsaw, into centres of extermination. Simultaneously, *Einsatzgruppen* in the Ukraine began to use mobile gassing units to facilitate their work. The killing now began in earnest.[105]

The extermination of the Jews is the most dreadful chapter in German history, doubly so because the men who effected it closed their senses to the reality of what they were doing by taking pride in the technical efficiency of their actions and, at moments when conscience threatened to break in, telling themselves that they were doing their duty and serving their country. There were some, to be sure, who had no compunction about admitting that they were engaged in the wholesale slaughter of defenceless people. Hitler never sought to conceal this, and in Poland Hans Frank could actually make jokes about it, telling a group of soldiers that his task was to rid the General Government of lice and Jews, and interrupting a public speech to ask in mock bewilderment, 'How can this be? There used to be thousands and thousands of flat-footed Indians in this city, and now there are none to be seen. You didn't decide to treat them badly, did you?'[106] But others took refuge in the enormous magnitude of the operation, which lent it a convenient depersonalization.

[104] *International Military Tribunal* xxvi. 266–7.
[105] Dawidowicz, *War against the Jews*, pp. 129–39.
[106] Fest, *Gesicht des Dritten Reiches*, pp. 288, 295.

When they ordered a hundred Jews to get on a train in Paris or Amsterdam, they considered their job accomplished and carefully closed their minds to the thought that eventually those passengers would arrive in front of the ovens of Treblinka. A man like Hoess, a lover of children and dogs, buried himself in administrative detail and worried about quotas and norms, without stopping to think that they were made up of human beings. In self-exculpation, he wrote later that whether what he had been doing was necessary and right was a question upon which he had no right to express an opinion, 'for I lacked the necessary breadth of view. If the Fuehrer himself had given the order . . . there could be no question of considering its merits'.[107]

As for Himmler, whose recognition of the enormity of his actions expressed itself, his doctor tells us, in agonizing intestinal pains,[108] he sought justification by romanticizing murder and ennobling it, as in that speech to the SS Gruppenleiter in Posen in October 1943, which dishonoured and perverted the very language in which it was delivered.

I want to speak here before you in all openness about a very delicate subject. Among us it should be talked about quite openly, but despite this we shall never talk about it in public. . . . I mean the evacuation of the Jews, the extermination of the Jewish people. This is one of those things that one says easily enough. 'The Jewish people will be exterminated,' says many a party comrade. 'OK—stands in the programme—elimination of Jews— extermination—we'll do it.' And then they come, the 80 million worthy Germans, and every one has has good Jew. It's clear; the rest are all swine; but this one is a first-class Jew. Of all the people that talk that way, none has seen it happen, none has been through it. The most of you know what it means when a hundred corpses are lying together, when five hundred are lying there, or when a thousand are lying there. To have seen that through and while doing so—leaving aside exceptions owing to human weakness—to have maintained our integrity, that has made us hard. This is an unwritten and never-to-be-written page of glory in our history.[109]

Almost 6 million people died in the camps, most of them Jews, but thousands of non-Jews as well, and almost all of the gypsies in Europe; and uncounted numbers died in transit to the ovens. When the war ended, there were only a million Jews left in Europe west of the Russian border. This was a holocaust unequalled in European history.

[107] Hoess, *Commandant*, p. 160.
[108] See Felix Kersten, *The Kersten Memoirs*, trans. from the German (New York, 1957).
[109] *International Military Tribunal* xxix. 122 f., 145. See also the speech to the Reichs- and Gauleiter two days later in Himmler, *Geheimreden*, p. 170.

Against the persecution of their Jewish fellow citizens, as against the brutalities of Nazi domination and exploitation, Europeans fought back. The cause of collaboration could not hope to make headway against the hatred that the Germans created by their behaviour, and in every country that they occupied resistance movements arose and, as the war continued, grew in strength and, thanks to the weapons and equipment sent to them by the Anglo-Saxon Powers, in ability to harry and inflict losses upon occupation troops. In France there was sporadic, in Yugoslavia continuous, guerilla warfare after 1943. There were active partisan movements in Bohemia and Slovakia, and an underground resistance army in Poland that numbered about 300,000 in 1943–4.

More formidable than any of these was the partisan movement in the Soviet Union. Here the Germans had had a rare opportunity to win large parts of the population to their side by offering to free them from the oppressiveness of the Stalin regime. They failed to take advantage of this. The mistreatment of prisoners of war, who might have been turned against their former masters, the bloody crimes of the *Einsatzgruppen*, and the maladministration and exploitation of civilian populations by addle-pates like Alfred Rosenberg, the ineffectual Minister for the East, and sadists like Erich Koch, the Commissioner for the Ukraine, deprived the Germans of local support, of economic reserves, and of trained soldiers who might have fought on their side and gave them instead the problem of coping with an aggressive and massive partisan movement that was co-ordinated by the Soviet high command and operated effectively behind their lines.

IV

In Hitler's headquarters there was no intimation of these future troubles in the first seven months of 1942, for it looked as if Germany's two most important opponents would be unable to keep on fighting much longer. In the spring the Afrika Korps, whose first thrust towards Cairo had been stopped by the British Eighth Army in December, started to move again, and in May Rommel captured the important base at Tobruk, causing consternation in England and raising a degree of enthusiasm in Germany that had not been reached since the fall of France. The German troopers celebrated their victory with British beer and tinned South African pineapple and pressed on, crossing the Egyptian border on 23 June, bypassing Sidi Barrani, dispersing the British 13th Corps at Mersa Matruh, and coming to a halt only when they had reached El Alamein, sixty miles west of Alexandria, in July. Here they stopped to regroup and await supplies and new weapons. It did not seem unlikely that they would be in Cairo in the autumn and that the whole British position in the Middle East would be a shambles.[110]

This did not represent the full extent of British troubles. In the course of 1942 it began to look as if the British Isles might be starved into submission because of the effectiveness of German submarine attacks. Although Hitler had started the war with only 56 U-boats (a circumstance that indicates that he had not expected to have to fight an all-out war with Great Britain), he started to correct this in July 1940 with a programme of rapid construction; and by January 1942 249 German submarines were operating in the northern seas against British convoys carrying indispensable materials to Murmansk, and, from well-protected bases on the French and Norwegian coasts, were sallying forth to intercept ships carrying munitions, raw materials, and food from America. When the Japanese attack on Pearl Harbor forced the United States Navy to divert to the Pacific vessels that had helped to protect the Atlantic convoys, sinkings mounted sharply. In the first six months of 1942 the Allies lost 4·5 million tons of shipping and, since bombing attacks upon the U-boat bases proved largely ineffective, it appeared that the losses might soon be insupportable.

The Russians too seemed to be in a desperate state, despite the respite given them by the long winter. By the end of 1941 they had already suffered 4,500,000 casualties, and the blood-letting continued in the spring of 1942, when Marshal Timoshenko made an ill-considered thrust toward Kharkhov and found that he had run into the main German striking force. By the end of May, when his badly mangled forces extricated themselves, the Germans had taken 240,000 prisoners, and the offensive capability of the Red Army seemed on the point of extinction. Meanwhile German forces in the south had overrun the Crimea, and on 21 July Hitler was predicting that his armies would soon deprive the enemy of the Caucasus, his most important source of oil, as well as the whole of the Donets industrial basin. Two days later Army Group A took Rostov, and its Sixth and Fourth Panzer Armies closed in on Stalingrad.[111]

In August, when Albert Speer visited Hitler in his headquarters at Vinnitsa in the Ukraine, he found the Führer in a triumphant and expansive mood. 'For a long time', he told Speer,

---

[110] In Washington, the African Section of the Office of Strategic Services was desperately preparing a study of available trans-African supply routes and equipment in case the British should be forced to fall back to Khartoum.

[111] Peter Young, *A Short History of World War II* (New York, 1966), pp. 235–7.

I have had everything prepared. As the next step, we are going to advance south of the Caucasus and then help the rebels in Iran and Iraq against the English. Another thrust will be directed along the Caspian Sea toward Afghanistan and India. Then the English will run out of oil. In two years we'll be on the borders of India. Twenty to thirty elite German divisions will do. Then the British Empire will collapse. They've already lost Singapore to the Japanese. The English will have to look on impotently as their colonial empire falls to pieces.[112]

This may have been Hitler's last moment of real optimism, for troubles now came upon him, and they came not single spies but in battalions. On 23 October 1942 the British Eighth Army, rested and refitted and with an energetic new commander, Lieutenant-General Bernard Law Montgomery, opened a massive attack upon Rommel's lines at El Alamein and threw the Afrika Korps into headlong retreat. On 8 November an Allied invasion fleet bore down upon the coast of Morocco and landed British and American troops at Casablanca, Oran, and Algiers. On 19–20 November the Russians mounted attacks north and south of Stalingrad, which had since August been under attack by the German Sixth Army and supporting Romanian units; within two days, in a brilliant Cannae-like operation, they had closed the pincers and encircled the German forces.

These were fatal blows. Forbidden by Hitler to attempt a break-out, the Sixth Army fought bravely against the rigours of winter and incessant enemy bombardment and finally capitulated in February 1943.[113] In the same month the Russians recaptured Rostov, Kursk, and Kharkhov and, before their momentum slowed, had won back 185,000 square miles of territory. In May Rommel's weary troopers laid down their arms in Tunis, and the victorious British and American armies prepared to cross the Mediterranean. In the same month Admiral Doenitz, who had replaced Raeder as commander of the navy in February and whose energetic direction of the U-boat offensive had cost the Allies half a million tons of shipping within a month, told Hitler that he could no longer press the attack; new Allied detection devices and the use of escort carriers and Liberator bombers had sunk 41 U-boats in May. In July the British and Americans were in Sicily and their planes were bombing the mainland; and, before the month was over, Hitler's fellow dictator had been deposed and arrested. July also saw the failure of the offensive in

---

[112] Speer, *Spandau*, p. 50.
[113] On the sufferings of the Sixth Army before its surrender, see Heinz Schröter, *Stalingrad* (Osnabrück, 1952) and Theodor Plievier's novel *Stalingrad* (1945).

the Kursk salient upon which the German high command had placed high hopes, and, at home, a week of fire-raids by British bombers destroyed much of Hamburg, killing 40,000 people, damaging the harbour and ship-building yards, and forcing a million people to evacuate the city. As Albert Speer wrote later in his Spandau diary, a second front had been opened before the invasion of Europe, and from now on the combined bombing offensive was to prove itself 'the greatest lost battle on the German side'.[114]

Hitler's reaction to these reverses throws light upon his qualities in the role in which he took much satisfaction, that of Feldherr, lord of the battles, Commander-in-Chief of the armed forces. That he possessed undeniable military talents is attested to even by those who resented his having assumed personal command in December 1941. He had an astonishing grasp of detail and a creative fantasy in technical questions and matters of armament; indeed, his personal contributions to weaponry—his suggestion that the Stuka dive-bombers be fitted out with sirens for psychological effect, and his selection of the anti-tank gun used on the Russian front—were highly successful.[115] Manstein, one of his sternest critics, has even admitted that he had 'a certain vision for operative possibilities',[116] an opinion that Alfred Jodl expressed more positively in an assessment written at Nuremberg after the war, in which he did not hesitate to call him 'a great military leader', citing, as evidence of his strategic gifts, his plan for the Scandinavian campaign, his concept for the offensive against France, and his order in the winter of 1941–2 that there should be no retreat from the positions won. Yet Jodl adds that, at the end of 1942—after the Russian breakthrough at Stalingrad and the beginning of the retreat of the Afrika Korps, when 'it was clear, not only to the responsible soldiers, but to Hitler also, that the god of war had now turned from Germany and gone over to the other camp'—'Hitler's activity as a strategist was essentially over', and that, from that point on, he began to interfere with operational matters in a disruptive and eventually disastrous manner.[117]

Hitler had always had a tendency to over-emphasize the power of the will to master difficult situations, and this made him disinclined to admit that space and time and the strength and morale of the enemy impose limits upon one's military capabilities. In the grim

[114] Speer, *Spandau*, pp. 375 f.

[115] See Picker, *Tischgespräche*, p. 96. Speer (*Spandau*, p. 208) argues that he over-valued the psychological aspect of weapons.

[116] Manstein, *Verlorene Siege*, p. 305.

[117] *Kriegstagebuch des OKW*, iv: *1944–45*, ed. Percy Ernst Schramm (Frankfurt-on-Main, 1961), pt. 2, p. 1721.

winter of 1941–2 Halder, Chief of Staff of the army, complained, 'The ever-present under-estimation of enemy capabilities is gradually assuming grotesque forms. One cannot any longer speak of serious work. Cranky reactions to the impression of the moment and complete lack of appreciation of the judgements of the command organization and its capacities give this "leadership" its characteristic stamp.'[118] When the war turned, these tendencies became more pronounced, and Hitler began to demand exertions of his troops that they were incapable of making and should not have been asked to make. In his mind, the moral factor now became the key to victory, and he expected his armies to demonstrate their unbroken will by refusing to yield ground to the enemy even if he appeared to possess overwhelming superiority in strength. Hitler was eventually to devise a theoretical defence of this view, his 'wave-breaking doctrine', which held that positions that refuse to yield serve, even when they have been encircled and bypassed by the enemy, as a means of distracting his energy and slowing his momentum;[119] But essentially his attitude was irrational at base, resting on the belief that one could overcome reality by refusing to admit its existence.

The counter-arguments of the army staff officers, who had been trained to base their decisions upon a weighing of finite data, he rejected impatiently with contemptuous remarks about 'high-nosed *Junker* empty-heads full of intellectual sterility and cowardice' and 'intellectual acrobats and spiritual athletes'. He said once late in the war:

Originality is something like a will-o'-the-wisp if it isn't based on steadfastness and fanatical tenacity. That's the most important thing in all human existence. People who only get fancies and ideas and that sort of thing but have no firmness of character and don't possess tenacity and steadfastness won't accomplish anything, despite all that. They are adventurers. . . . One can make world history only when, in addition to a good head, an active conscience, and an eternal watchfulness, one has a fanatical steadfastness, a power of belief that makes a person a warrior to the very marrow.[120]

A principle that had justified itself on the strategical level in the winter of 1941–2 could not do so in tactical situations in the last years of the war, but merely imposed upon individual units in critical situations an operational rigidity that was self-defeating and fright-

---

[118] Halder, *Kriegstagebuch*, iii. 489.

[119] See Schramm's discussion in *Kriegstagebuch des OKW*, iv, pt. 1, pp. 53 ff.

[120] Ibid., pp. 46 f. Cf. Theodor Mommsen's statement, cited by Schramm, that 'insight into what is possible and what is impossible distinguishes the hero from the adventurer'. Ibid., p. 52.

fully costly in human life. Hitler's refusal to permit the Sixth Army
to break out of the ring that held it at Stalingrad was not based on any
belief that it was still capable of fulfilling its mission (Hitler surely
never put any stock in Goering's confident boast that the Luftwaffe
could keep the army supplied) but rather on a conviction that the
psychological effects of a retreat upon friend and foe alike would be
intolerable. One of General von Paulus's subordinates wrote at this
time, 'To remain where we are deliberately is not only a crime from a
military point of view but a criminal act as regards our responsibility
to the German nation.' This was true, for Hitler's decision condemned 300,000 officers and men to death, or would have done
had not Paulus, when more than half of his command had been
destroyed, decided—to Hitler's considerable consternation and
rage[121]—to surrender. Casualties, which any responsible commander worries about all the time, never seem to have concerned Hitler
for a moment. When he was told of extremely high losses among
junior officers in an operation just concluded, his only comment
was: 'But that's what the young people are there for.'[122]

In 1944 and 1945 Hitler's insistence upon steadfastness took
increasingly extreme forms, and the army commanders' authority to
make local decisions or to dispose of their resources as they saw fit
sank progressively. This reached its most bizarre expression in the
first stages of the Normandy campaign when Rundstedt, the commanding general in the west, had no control over his armoured
support but had to negotiate for it with the OKW. Hitler seemed to
want to fight all of the battles from his own bunker and to make
tactical decisions for all units on all fronts, reducing his commanding
generals, as one of them said bitterly, to the status of 'highly paid
N.C.O.s'. The penalties suffered by commanders who surrendered
or ordered withdrawals on their own initiative in order to save their
troops from certain annihilation were barbarous. The commandant
of Königsberg, General Lasch, capitulated in April 1945 when his
position had become untenable and most of his garrison were dead
or wounded. He was immediately condemned *in absentia* to death by
hanging; his culpability was extended to his family; and his daughter, who was serving in the army as a staff assistant, was arrested.[123]

It is worth asking whether this demand for unyielding determination was sustained by any real confidence on Hitler's part that

---

[121] See the record of Hitler's military conference of 1 February 1943 in Felix Gilbert
(ed.), *Hitler Directs His War* (New York, 1950), pp. 17–22.

[122] Fest, *Gesicht des Dritten Reiches*, p. 87.

[123] *Kriegstagebuch des OKW*, iv. pt. 1, pp. 53 f.

the war could still be won after the reverses of 1942 and 1943. Certainly there was little in the reports from the fighting fronts to justify such a feeling. By January 1944 the Red Army was pressing forward along a line that ran through the recaptured cities of Smolensk and Kiev with a strength that now exceeded that of the Germans opposing them by 5,700,000 to 3,000,000 as well as a strong superiority in tanks and guns, while in the west the Allies had established their first European beachheads at Salerno and Reggio and were about to make another landing at Anzio. Hitler had admitted the gravity of the situation in an order of 27 November 1943, supplementing his Directive no. 51 of 3 November, in which he focused attention on the possibility that a more critical front might soon open in France. 'The struggle for the existence of the German people and the future of Europe,' he now wrote, 'is reaching its culminating point. To throw all the reserves of strength that the Great German Reich can muster into this final struggle is the demand of the hour. The striking force of our Wehrmacht has suffered greatly in the battles of this summer, especially in the east.'[124]

In a meeting with his staff on 20 December the Führer intimated that, if an Anglo-Saxon invasion attempt were repulsed, the situation in the east would improve; if not, Germany would have lost the war.[125] But the prospect was not sufficiently daunting to make him listen to those among his ministers who wanted him to anticipate the inevitable by seeking a separate peace with the Russians;[126] and, when the Normandy landings came in June 1944, and all the arts of Rundstedt and Rommel failed to contain them, he made no attempt to draw the logical consequences of this. He seems to have gone on hoping that the tide of war might still be reversed by the introduction of new weapons—the rocket bombs that had been developed in the laboratories in Peenemünde[127] and the jet plane that Messerschmidt was developing—and, when the speed of the Allied advance frustrated these expectations, he convinced himself that a repetition of the blow that he had struck through the Ardennes in 1940 would return the initiative to his hands and restore the German army's prestige and reputation for invulnerability. 'I haven't the slightest intention of surrendering,' he told Speer as plans for this offensive reached completion, 'Besides, November has always been

[124] Ibid., p. 56. Directive no. 51 is in Trevor-Roper, Blitzkrieg, pp. 149–53.

[125] Gilbert, Hitler Directs His War, p. 77.

[126] The Goebbels Diaries, pp. 509, 510; H. Fraenkel and R. Manvell, Goebbels: Eine Biographie (Cologne and Berlin, 1960), pp. 287 f., 304.

[127] See Walter Dornberger, V–2, trans. from the German (New York, 1954) which tells how rocket development was hampered by inter-departmental rivalries.

my lucky month, and we're in November now.'[128] Despite the fact that he could muster only 32 divisions, a force that, by any rational calculation, was inadequate to attain the objectives he set, it was characteristic of him that he should have rejected the more modest goals suggested by his staff and insisted on an all-out drive to Antwerp, the fall of which, he believed, would have a kind of avalanche effect and spread mounting panic through the opposing host.

Even the failure of that gambler's throw (which was launched, not in his lucky month after all, but in December) did not deprive him completely of hope. There was always the possibility that the enemy coalition, in which signs of internal friction were unmistakable, would disintegrate before it accomplished its purpose. In January, when the Russians had reached Warsaw and were headed for Tilsit, with its uncomfortable memories of a historic capitulation and partition, Hitler asked his circle, 'Do you think that deep down inside the English are enthusiastic about all the Russian developments?', and he seemed to agree when Goering answered, 'They certainly didn't plan that we should hold them off while the Russians conquer all Germany. If this goes on, we will get a telegram in a few days.'[129] But the telegram never came, and Hitler was forced at long last to admit that the game was played out. On 22 April 1945, when he told Jodl that he was resolved to remain and die in Berlin, he added: 'I should have made this decision, the most important of my life, in November 1944 and should never have left the headquarters in East Prussia.'[130]

V

In May 1943, as the Allied combined bombing offensive began to move to a round-the-clock schedule, SD agents in the industrial areas of western Germany reported with some alarm that a subversive song was going around.

> Lieber Tommy, fliege weiter.
> Wir sind alle Bergarbeiter.
> Fliege weiter nach Berlin,
> die haben alle 'ja' geschrien.[131]

The reporters feared that this was evidence of growing disenchantment with the war, as it doubtless was. But this and other

---

[128] Speer, *Spandau*, p. 221. A curious remark, considering the fact that both the collapse of 1918 and the failure of the putsch of 1923 occurred in November.

[129] Gilbert, *Hitler Directs His War*, pp. 117–18.

[130] *Kriegstagebuch des OKW*, iv. pt. 2, p. 1721.

[131] *Meldungen aus dem Reich*, p. 390.

signs of dissatisfaction that found their way into the SD situation reports never became serious enough to justify the kind of apprehension about public opinion that Hitler had expressed at the beginning of the war.[132] Under pounding from the air that was more protracted and periodically of much greater intensity (the fire-raids in Hamburg in 1943, the destruction of Dresden in 1945)[133] than the German bombardment during the Battle of Britain, German morale remained remarkably steadfast.

It is notable that, in the last years of the war, Hitler himself did little to support it. In July 1943 Gottlob Berger, chief of the SS Hauptamt, wrote to Himmler with concern about the infrequency of Hitler's public appearances and said: 'We cannot go on much longer through thick and thin the way things are going now. The German people must be spoken to. . . . In my opinion, the Fuehrer must go before the nation, so that the common man who is doing his duty faithfully and bravely right along, and has remained loyal to him, can see a way out of our problems.'[134] Hitler did not respond until 8 November, when he made a speech to the party leaders in the Löwenbräukeller in Munich which was broadcast publicly that evening. The occasion was the anniversary of the putsch of 1923, and Hitler spoke at some length of the new spirit that had been born then and had blossomed into the Great German Reich; but the greater part of his remarks dealt with the Allied bombing campaign, which, he said, had made 'the hundreds of thousands of people bombed out of their homes the *avant-garde* of revenge'. He promised to rebuild the German cities and make them 'more beautiful than ever before' and said that, within two or three years of the war's end, the government would construct two or three million private homes, no matter how destructive the enemy bombing might be. The Allies were mistaken if they thought that their terror tactics would break the will of the German people. 'No matter how long this war lasts, Germany will never capitulate. Never will we repeat the mistake of 1918, of laying down our arms at a quarter to twelve.' He thanked God for having sustained Germany in its struggle against a world of enemies and said that he was proud of being able to say, 'German people! Be fully reassured! No matter what may come, we shall master it! At the end stands Victory!'[135]

[132] See above, p. 732.
[133] See Noble Frankland, *The Bombing Offensive against Germany* (London, 1965); David Irving, *The Destruction of Dresden* (London, 1963); Hans Rumpf, *The Bombing of Germany*, trans. from the German (London, 1963).
[134] Baird, *War Propaganda*, p. 218.
[135] Domarus, *Hitler: Reden* ii. 2050 ff., esp. 2055–8.

Apart from its note of defiant optimism and its absence of any explanation of how the victory was to be achieved, the notable feature of this speech was that it was the last speech by Hitler to be broadcast, except for an arid and uninspired New Year's Speech,[136] until 20 July 1944, when the Führer felt compelled to reassure the public that he was sound and unwounded after the bomb plot.[137] As far as possible, he distanced himself from the sufferings of the German people, which did not, indeed, move him deeply or he would have been incapable of his jocular remark to Speer in November 1944 about bomb damage in Berlin: 'What does it all signify? Speer, in Berlin alone you would have had to tear down eighty thousand buildings to complete our new building plan. Unfortunately, the English haven't carried out this work exactly in accordance with your plans. But at least they have launched the project.'[138]

Hitler left it to Goebbels to minister to the psychological needs of the German people, a task to which the Propaganda Minister brought his considerable resources of energy and imagination. He fed the people a carefully blended mixture of hopes and fears and threats and promises, cleverly seizing upon Allied declarations, like the Casablanca statement on unconditional surrender and the clumsy revelation of the abortive Morgenthau Plan, to prove that a future of slavery lay ahead for them unless the war was won. He portrayed the Red Army as a horde of barbarians who would burn and rape and loot their way across Germany unless they were thrown back at the borders; he hinted at wonder weapons that would astonish and dismay the enemy; he said darkly, in his much-publicized 'Thirty War Articles for the German Nation' of 1943 and in later broadcasts, that anyone who even thought of 'a cowardly betrayal of the nation's right to live . . . must be expelled with ignominy and outrage from the German community'; and he constantly extolled Adolf Hitler as the leader destined by history to save his people and to liberate all of Europe.[139] In 1944, particularly after his appointment as Reich Plenipotentiary for Total War Deployment, this remarkable man was the dynamo in a National Socialist machine that was beginning to show signs of collapse, visiting bombed-out areas, spurring the Gauleiter on to more effective forms of local relief, introducing at long last a sixty-hour working week, rounding up idlers and making them help with the clearing of rubble, the building of new shelters,

[136] Ibid. 2071–4.   [137] Ibid. 2127–9.
[138] Speer, *Spandau*, p. 220.   [139] See esp. Bramsted, *Goebbels*, Ch. 9.

and the maintenance of public services, and exhorting and bullying the public in dozens of speeches and articles.

To what extent Goebbels's efforts were responsible for maintaining morale it is impossible to judge with any accuracy, but they probably helped convince people to go on doing what they were doing—that is, digging themselves out of the wreckage wrought by the bombers and doing their jobs (so effectively that even in 1944 Allied bombing reduced German production by only 14 per cent and armaments by less than half of that)—rather than to try to do something to alleviate their situation. Late in the war a German writer wrote in his diary:

You, my readers, who will have these lines before your eyes only at some later time, can you grasp it, that such a thing was possible? That our German people in all calmness—yes, in all calmness, that is, without the majority even doing any serious grumbling about it—looked on, while a pack of fools, against whom destiny had long since decided, let the whole wonderful Reich be transformed into one single garbage heap? In the end, even jewels like Freiburg, Würzburg, Heilbronn, Dresden, and all the others![140]

At no time during the war was there any indication that mass anger might force the government to stop the killing and sue for peace. The resistance movements that history will remember—the brave and doomed attempt by Hans and Sophie Scholl and Professor Kurt Huber of Munich to arouse a university movement against the regime in 1942, and the larger conspiracy that tried to kill Hitler in July 1944—had no roots in the mass of the people, and the latter was repudiated by the majority of Germans. Two weeks after the failure of the *coup*, Hans-Georg von Studnitz wrote: 'The repercussions of the *attentat* among the people are less than one might have expected. Although the people were made aware on 20 July of the seriousness of the crisis in leadership, the readiness of the masses to follow that leadership was not broken. Since no one has an overview of the situation or knows a way out of it, since everybody is afraid of making developments even worse by disloyal behaviour, the regime can go on counting on the people's support. In many respects the situation today is different than in 1918. The morale of the homeland has, despite the burdens inflicted by the air attacks, remained intact.'[141] Hitler put it more crudely in his talk with Speer in November. 'Even the worst idiot realizes that his house will never be rebuilt unless we win. For that reason alone, we'll have no revolution

---

[140] Lehmann, *1939–1945*, p. 139.

[141] Hans-Georg von Studnitz, *Als Berlin brannte: Diarium der Jahre 1943–1945* (2nd ed., Stuttgart, 1963), p. 192.

this time. The rabble aren't going to have the chance to cover up their cowardice with a so-called revolution. I'll guarantee that! No city will be left in the enemy's hands until it's a heap of ruins!'[142]

The German people waited, then, fatalistically, until the machine ran down. The last phase of the history of the Great German Reich opened in March, when the Americans captured the Rhine bridge at Remagen and the Red Army took Danzig; and the two months that followed were filled with the nightmarish scenes that have found their proper painters in Curzio Malaparte and Ernst von Salomon and Günter Grass. There is little point in describing here the fruitless experiments with local militia, as if old men and children could be expected to hold back the Russian tanks; or the frantic attempts of Nazi *Honoratioren*, like Himmler, to scuttle to safety by making bargains with Western governments; or the violent ends chosen by other Nazi hierarchs, like the drunken commissioner for Norway, who blew himself up with a cask of gunpowder; or Goebbels's busy efforts to turn the collapse of National Socialism into a myth for the future, telling his staff that they were all actors in a film that would be shown a hundred years hence and must comport themselves so that the audience did not hoot and whistle when they appeared on the scene;[143] or the OKW Führungsstab continuing, like a mad computer, to send out orders to non-existent units and lists of promotions and decorations for men dead or in captivity;[144] or the remorseless operation of the gas ovens, which continued until the camps were overrun by the advancing Allies; or the last macabre events in Hitler's bunker in Berlin. There is nothing edifying about the death throes of any organism, even when, as was true in this case, it is essential that it be destroyed for the general good.

VI

In March 1948 Friedrich Meinecke wrote to his friend, the Göttingen historian Siegfried Kaehler, about an article in which Kaehler had stoutly defended Bismarck against criticisms made by Karl Barth and other writers who were searching for an explanation of the underlying causes of the German catastrophe. Meinecke suggested that perhaps Kaehler had protested too much: Bismarck's achievement had had its 'night side' as well as its 'day side' for the German

---

[142] Speer, *Spandau*, p. 221.

[143] David Stewart Hull, *Film in the Third Reich: Art and Propaganda in Nazi Germany* (New York, 1973), pp. 261–5, which tell the story of Goebbels's last film, *Kolberg*, which was intended to inspire the German people to make a last-ditch stand.

[144] *Kriegstagebuch des OKW*, iv, pt. 1, p. 44.

people, and it might be well to remember what Burckhardt had said of it or, for that matter, what had been the view of Gervinus, who parted company with Bismarck in 1871.

'It would be a grievous perversion,' [Gervinus] wrote in 1871, 'if Germany gave up the activities of a people of culture (*Kulturvolk*) for those of a people of power (*Machtvolk*) and should become involved in one war after another.' For forty-three years, as you say, it did indeed keep the peace, but, all the same, then came the age of the wars. Neither the day-side nor the night-side of the Bismarckian accomplishment ought to be forgotten. It always seems to me now that Schiller's Demetrius is a symbol of our fate: pure and noble when he begins, but in the end a criminal! Puzzling—but, in any case, very tragic. I can't get it out of my head.[145]

If Meinecke was correct in sensing that the roots of Germany's recent experience lay in the inadequacies of Bismarck's work when he created the national state, and that, throughout the short history of united Germany, the emphasis on power at the expense of the spirit had corrupted the values and stunted the political growth of the German people, so that they would tolerate both the irresponsible absolutism of William II and the crimes of the Nationalist Socialist regime, he might have taken some comfort in the thought that the opportunity to correct the mistakes of the past was better now than it ever had been since Bismarck's time, and that this, paradoxically, was due to Adolf Hitler.

In his biography of the Führer, Alan Bullock has written that Hitler's career 'did not exalt but debased the human condition, and his twelve years dictatorship was barren of all ideas save one—the further extension of his own power and that of the nation with which he had identified himself'.[146] It would be difficult to quarrel with that judgement. At the same time, however, it should be added that, in his career of self-aggrandizement, while destroying much that was good in Germany and many thousands of people who might have made that good better, Hitler also eliminated much that was bad. And this included the conservative-militaristic concern that had ‑dominated politics in the Wilhelmine period, done everything possible to shorten the life of the Weimar Republic, and elevated him to power in 1933. The members of that consortium whom he had not liquidated during the Night of the Long Knives in 1934, in his reorganization of the army command and the Foreign Service in 1938, or in the purge that followed the failure of the attempt of 20 July 1944 disappeared in the general shambles of May 1945, and,

---

[145] Meinecke, *Briefwechsel*, pp. 520 f.
[146] Bullock, *Hitler*, p. 806.

since their values and traditions had already perished in the course of the brutal intellectual *Gleichschaltung* of the Nazi period, the most important of the obstacles that had stood in the way of progress towards a free political system had been removed.

Adolf Hitler was nothing if not thorough. He destroyed the basis of the traditional resistance to modernity and liberalism just as completely as he had destroyed the structure of the *Rechtsstaat* and democracy.[147] Because his work of demolition was so complete, he left the German people nothing that could be repaired or built upon. They had to begin all over again, a hard task perhaps, but a challenging one, in the facing of which they were not entirely bereft of guidance. For Hitler had not only restored to them the options that they had had a century earlier but had also bequeathed to them the memory of horror to help them with their choice.

[147] Broszat, *Der Staat Hitlers*, p. 441.

APPENDIX

Translations of the Epigraphs
and other Quotations
in the Text

PREFACE

p. v

Germany is Hamlet! Grave and mute,
There passes through its gates, night after night,
The entombed freedom
And beckons to the men upon the watch.

FERDINAND FREILIGRATH

He picked too much of learning's oakum.
At best he did nothing but think.
He stayed too long in Wittenberg,
In the lecture hall and the pubs.

And therefore he lacks determination.

p. v

And Fortinbras
Comes clanking in and inherits the realm.

p. vii

For all of that and all of that,
Stupidity, guile, and all of that,
We know still that humanity
Will win the fight for all of that.

CHAPTER I

p. 1

Hi! That sounded like thunder.
But it wasn't thunder, it was cannon.
Missunde, Düppel. Hurrah! Further, further!
Boats like nutshells on the Alsen sound.
Up over Lipa storm the squadrons.
A tangle of friend and foe. Look! There he is himself!
The one with the helmet and the brimstone collar.
And Spicheren, Wörth, and Sedan! Further, further!
And through the gate of triumph triumphantly he leads
All Germany into teeth-gnashing Paris.

THEODOR FONTANE

Black, white, and red! Around *one* flag
United stand the south and the north.
You have in fame-crowned murder
Become the leading nation in the world.
Germany, I shudder to look upon you!

GEORG HERWEGH

CHAPTER II

p. 38   Constitution. That means separation of powers. The King does what *he* wants, and, on the other hand, the people do what the *King* wants. The Ministers are responsible for seeing that nothing happens.

ADOLF GLASSBRENNER

CHAPTER III

p. 61   I am a promoter happy and gay
And sit down at the table every day
As if I had no further cares
But to pay the interest on the shares.

Thank God! I am my own best counsellor
And let neither city nor state worry me.
Loyally devoted to the promoter's life,
I fashion a worthy existence for myself.

HEINRICH HOFFMANN VON FALLERSLEBEN

In black frockcoat and white vest,
Kautz decapitated Hödel—
And you too, O Reichstag, come dressed in your best
To the task that has been secretly assigned.

The axe, sharpened for you by the Bundesrat,
Lies before you quite clean,
And the scaffold is erected,
And the block stands firm and unmoved.

But the freedom that you kill
Will not halt its progress.
Even tomorrow, scoffing at its executioners,
It will arise triumphantly from its graves.

MAX KEGEL

CHAPTER V

p. 140   If I don't *putsch*,
I don't get anything accomplished.

OTTO VON BISMARCK

When one day we enter his life in the books,
After he has sunk into his last sleep,
We shall not bless, we shall not curse him.
We shall write as his epitaph:
'To the common weal he arrogantly
Opposed his defiant ego.
It was not ideals, but merely interests
That he served, another Metternich.

'In order to conquer freedom more easily,
He, acting in the service of reaction,
Mounted freedom's own charger,
As Napoleon the Petty had done before him.
But this steed is no Rosinante.
It is a fiery Bucephalus.
What threw him off and cast him on the sand
Was the universal right of suffrage!'

JAKOB STERN

CHAPTER VI

p. 180   A moss-covered senior student, I depart. Adieu!
God guard you, house of philistines. Adieu!
I go back to my old home
To become a philistine myself.
Adieu! Adieu! Adieu!
Yes, parting and departing is sad.

G. SCHWAB

And we: spectators, always, everywhere,
Turned toward the all and never outward!
We are surfeited. We put things in order. They decay.
We put them in order again and decay ourselves.

RAINER MARIA RILKE

p. 211   'Then know that woman
Has grown to maturity in the nineteenth
    century,'
She said with eye dilated, and shot him down.

p. 214   I have a loge in the theater
And also an opera-glass.
I keep a carriage and horses.
My means permit it.

I smoke the finest Havanas
For digestion's sake after eating.
I love the whole *corps de ballet.*
My means permit it.

At ragamuffins like Kepler and Schiller
I just wrinkle my nose in scorn.
I am the most complete boor.
My means permit it.

p. 218   The writer no longer day-dreams in blue coves.
          He sees the shining troops riding out of
              the courtyards.
          His foot treads on the corpses of the wicked.
          His head becomes erect, to accompany the peoples.

          He wants to be their leader.

                                    WALTER HASENCLEVER

p. 219   Scarcely anything
          Hides such poesy
          As an abandoned,
          Half run wild,
          Linden-overgrown,
          Birdsong-filled summer garden.

                                    DETLEV VON LILIENCRON

p. 219   Reach out bravely for sin.
          From sin enjoyment grows.
          Ah, you are like a child
          That has to be shown everything.

          Don't eschew the worldly treasures.
          Wherever they may lie, take them with you.
          The world only has laws
          So that people may trample on them.

          Happy is he who, artfully and gaily,
          Hops over fresh graves.
          Dancing on the steps to the gallows
          Has never yet bored anyone.

                                    FRANK WEDEKIND

p. 221   He has arisen who was long asleep.

                                    GEORG HEYM

          The hat flies from the *Bürger's* pointed head.
          In every breeze there is an echo like a scream.
          Roofers fall from their roofs and are broken
              in pieces,
          And along the coasts, one reads, the flood
              is rising.

The tempest has come. The wild seas leap
Upon the land to destroy thick dams.
Most people have head-colds.
Railway trains are falling from the bridges.

JAKOB VAN HODDIS

CHAPTER VII

p. 224   Surprisingly, contradictorily,
        Headache-makingly, zigzag-suddenly,
    Bombastically, superabundantly,
        Zigzag-suddenly, headache-makingly.

ALFRED KERR

p. 225   What one clearly recognized in him
        Was the absence of intelligence.
    Otherwise, he possessed all the talents
        Needed for the conduct of affairs.

ALFRED KERR

CHAPTER VIII

p. 251   Scarron: Horrible! No interest in politics?
    Theobald: I was intent upon everything Bismarck did.
    Scarron: He's long dead.
    Theobald: Afterwards, not much ever happened.

CARL STERNHEIM

CHAPTER IX

p. 302   I see the earthly globe rolling through the blue night
    And see the bright patches of the planets:
    Those are the lands, which should made us flourish.

    And closer! On the oceans I see hosts
    Of small grey points that fly like gulls.
    Those are the ships that journey through the
        world's seas.

    And closer still: a heavily populated country
    I see, and much unrest in the cities,
    But all too mute the long, long coast.

    Oh, that there was strength and breath and light
        in Germany!
    Oh, that—like a hundred swans,
    Like beams of our strength, like eagles flying—
    A hundred dreadnoughts might ride upon the
        dominated sea!

FRIEDRICH LIENHARD

All roads empty out into black putrefaction.

GEORG TRAKL

p. 324   Straight across Europe from the west to the east
            Rattles and rollicks the song of the train.
            Is it a question of tasting blessedness sooner?
            Is it going to arrive too late in heaven's station?
                On on on! on on on! the wheels are turning,
                Raging along on the network of rails.
                Smoke is the beast's disappearing tail.
                And the conductor's piping and the locomotive's
                    whistle.

DETLEV VON LILIENCRON

CHAPTER X

p. 339   Rejoice, friends, that we are alive
            And that we're young and nimble!
            Never was there a year like this,
            And never such a gift for youth!

            It is given to us to take our stand or to strike out
            Eastwards or westwards.
            The greatest of all of earth's ages
            Sets its brand upon our young hearts.

BRUNO FRANK

p. 340   And our young life, the most beautiful of all, Hurrah!
            Lies in the war, stretched out upon the battlefield.

CHAPTER XII

p. 434   We are drinking up grandma's little house,
                her little house,
            We are drinking up grandma's little house,
                and the first and second mortgage.

POPULAR SONG

CHAPTER XIII

p. 469   . . . our remarkable times, this period
            since the war, troubled and confused,
            but yet so fertile.

HERMANN HESSE

            Germany is not a social and humane enterprise, it is a poetical
            and demoniacal conspiracy.

JEAN GIRAUDOUX

p. 471   Eucharistic and Thomistic,
But at the same time Marxistic,
Theosophic, communistic,
Gothic-smalltown-cathedralbuilding-mystic,
Activistic, arch-Buddhistic,
Excessively-eastern taoistic,
Seeking salvation from the contemporary predic-
ament in Afric plastic,
Language and barricades up-ending,
God and the foxtrot trendily blending.

FRANZ WERFEL

p. 496   The boxing memorial, ceremoniously dedicated,
The poet's grave, which the wind has covered
   with snow,
The ship that was the booty of the waves,
The essence of everything upon the earth that we
Regard as a sensation, the *dernier cri*,
We see—quick! quick!—race by, catching up
   on itself.

HANS HARBECK

CHAPTER XV

p. 534   Through the pages of the latest newspapers
Rustles dried-out politics.
Old men peer out to see what the weather is like.
Will there be a *coup*?
Done for is done for,
   You German Republic!

WALTER MEHRING

CHAPTER XVI

p. 569   We who are becoming a people, we are the raw stone.
You, our Leader, should be the stonemason,

The stonemason who, with creative power,
Frees the stone from its formlessness.

Only strike home! We stand patient and silent
For your stern hand wants to give us shape.

HEINRICH ANACKER

p. 577   Always practise loyalty and honesty
   Until you come to the cold grave

And stray not a finger's breadth
From the grace of God.

CHAPTER XVII

p. 613   Ornaments on the right—ornaments on the left—
              And his belly gets ever fatter.
              In the air he is the master.
              Hermann's his name! Hermann's his name!

CLAIRE WALDOFF

CHAPTER XVIII

p. 638   A country is not only what it does—it is also what it puts up
              with, what it tolerates.

KURT TUCHOLSKY

CHAPTER XIX

p. 673   If the Führer has been able to triumph . . . in the course of his
              adventurous career over innumerable obstacles that chance and
              his enemies have sown in his path, it has not been solely because
              of his tenacity and his obstinacy but also because of a political
              skill that has gone on increasing with time. He ignores any
              respect for the pledged word. . . . This trickery, this cunning,
              has fooled more than one subtle brain.

ANDRÉ FRANÇOIS-PONCET

Providence spoke the last word to me and gave me the victory.

ADOLF HITLER

CHAPTER XX

p. 714   Before the marching step of the German soldier,
              The earth held its breath and was silent.
              From the seeds that streamed from the heart's blood
              Rose the cathedral of sanctified deeds:
              Victory.

GERHARD SCHUMANN

Swept bare and free of tinsel,
Lies the world that once laughed.
Through the grillwork of denuded boughs,
Winter peers, bitter as death,
And Night reaches out for us.

HERMANN HESSE

p. 758   Dear Tommy, fly farther!
              We are all workers in the mines.
              Fly farther to Berlin.
              They are the ones who all shouted 'Ja!'

List of Books and
Articles Cited

AANDAHL, FREDERICK, 'The Rise of German Free Conservatism' (Dissertation, Princeton Univ. 1955).

ADORNO, THEODOR W., *The Jargon of Authenticity*, trans. Knut Tarnowski and Frederick Will (London, 1973).

Akten der Reichskanzlei. Das Kabinett Cuno, ed. Karl-Heinz Harbech (Boppard, 1968).

———, *Die Kabinette Wirth*, ed. Ingrid Schulze Bidlingmaier (2 vols., Boppard, 1973).

Akten zur deutschen auswärtigen Politik, Ser. B. 1925–33 (Bonn, 1966 ff.).

ALBERTI, CONRAD, *Die Alten und Jungen* (Berlin, 1889).

ALBERTI, LUIGI, *Le origini della guerra del 1914* (3 vols., Milan, 1942 ff.).

ALDINGTON, RICHARD, *Death of a Hero* (London, 1929).

ALLEN, WILLIAM SHERIDAN, *The Nazi Seizure of Power: The Experience of a Single German Town, 1930–1935* (Chicago, 1965).

Allgemeiner Kongress der Arbeiter- und Soldatenräte Deutschlands, *Stenographische Berichte* (Berlin, 1918).

ANDERSON, EUGENE N., *The Social and Political Conflict in Prussia, 1858–1864* (Berkeley, 1954).

ANDREAS, W., 'Kiderlen-Wächter: Randglossen zu seinem Nachlass', *Historische Zeitschrift*, 132 (1925).

ANDREW, CHRISTOPHER, 'German World Policy and the Re-shaping of the Dual Alliance', *Journal of Contemporary History*, i, no. 3 (1966).

ANGRESS, WERNER T., *Stillborn Revolution: The Communist Bid for Power in Germany, 1921–1923* (Princeton, 1963).

———, 'Pegasus and Insurrection: *Die Linkskurve* and Its Heritage', *Central European History*, i (1968), 35–55.

ANSCHÜTZ, GERHARD, *Die Verfassung des Deutschen Reiches vom 11. August 1919* (11th edn., Berlin, 1929).

ANSELL, WALTER, *Hitler Confronts England* (Durham, N.C., 1960).

ARENDT, HANNAH, *Men in Dark Times* (New York, 1968).

ARETIN, ERWEIN VON, *Krone und Ketten* (Munich, 1955).

Die auswärtige Politik Preußens 1858–71: Diplomatische Akten, hrsg. von der Historischen Reichskommission (Oldenburg, 1931 ff.).

AYDELOTTE, WILLIAM O., 'The First German Colony and its Diplomatic Consequences', *Cambridge Historical Journal*, v (1937).

BADEN, PRINCE MAX VON, *Erinnerungen und Dokumente* (Stuttgart, 1927).

BADER, OTTILIE, *Ein steiniger Weg: Lebenserinnerungen* (Berlin, 1931).

BAER, HENRY M., 'Carl Peters and German Colonialism: A Study in the Ideas and Actions of Imperialism' (Dissertation, Stanford Univ. 1968).

BAIRD, JAY W., *The Mythical World of Nazi War Propaganda, 1939–45* (Minneapolis, 1974).

BALLHAUSEN, R. S. LUCIUS VON, *Bismarck-Erinnerungen* (Stuttgart and Berlin, 1921).

BARCLAY, DAVID EDWARD, 'Social Politics and Social Reform in Germany, 1890–1933: Rudolf Wissel and the Free Trade Union Movement' (Dissertation, Stanford Univ. 1974).

BARKIN, KENNETH, 'Adolf Wagner and German Industrial Development', *Journal of Modern History*, xli (1969).

——, 'Conflict and Concord in Wilhelmian Social Thought', *Central European History*, v (1972), 55 ff.

BAUMONT, MAURICE, *The Fall of the Kaiser* (New York, 1931).

BAYERN, KRONPRINZ RUPPRECHT VON, *Mein Kriegstagebuch*, ed. W. Frauendienst (2 vols., Berlin, 1929).

BEAUFRE, ANDRÉ, *1940: The Fall of France* (New York, 1968).

BEBEL, AUGUST, *Gewerkschaftsbewegung und politische Parteien* (Stuttgart, 1900).

——, *Aus meinem Leben* (3 vols., Stuttgart, 1914).

BECK, LUDWIG, *Studien*, ed. Hans Speidel (Stuttgart, 1955).

BECKER, CARL HEINRICH, *Kulturpolitische Aufgaben des Reiches* (Berlin, 1919).

BECKER, OTTO, *Bismarcks Ringen um Deutschlands Gestaltung* (Heidelberg, 1958).

BENN, GOTTFRIED, *Gesammelte Werke* (4 vols., Weisbaden, 1954).

——, *Das gezeichnete Ich: Briefe aus den Jahren 1900–1956* (Hamburg, 1962).

BENNETT, EDWARD W., *Germany and the Diplomacy of the Financial Crisis, 1931* (Cambridge, Mass., 1962).

BENOIST-MÉCHIN, JACQUES, *Sixty Days That Shook the World*, trans. from the French (London, 1963).

BERDAHL, ROBERT M., 'Conservative Politics and Aristocratic Landholders in Bismarckian Germany', *Journal of Modern History*, xliv, no. 1 (1972), 1–20.

BERG, GUNTER, *Leopold von Ranke als akademischer Lehrer* (Göttingen, 1968).

BERGHAHN, VOLKER R., *Der Tirpitz-Plan: Genesis und Verfall der innenpolitischen Krisenstrategie unter Wilhelm II* (Düsseldorf, 1971).

BERGSTRÄSSER, LUDWIG, *Geschichte der politischen Parteien in Deutschland* (11th edn., Munich, 1965).

BERLEPSCH, FREIHERR VON, *Sozialpolitische Erfahrungen und Erinnerungen* (Mönchengladbach, 1925).

BETHELL, NICHOLAS, *The War Hitler Won: The Fall of Poland, September 1939* (New York, 1972).

BETHMANN HOLLWEG, THEOBALD VON, *Betrachtungen zum Weltkrieg* (2 vols., Berlin, 1919–21).

BEUST, FRIEDRICH FERDINAND COUNT VON, *Memoirs of Friedrich Ferdinand Count von Beust* (2nd edn., 2 vols., London, 1887).

BING, RUDOLF, *Five Thousand Nights at the Opera* (New York, 1972).

BIRKE, ADOLF M., *Bischoff Ketteler und der deutsche Liberalismus* (Mainz, 1971).

BISMARCK, HERBERT VON, *Aus seiner politischen Privatkorrespondenz*, ed. Walter Bußmann (Göttingen, 1964).

BISMARCK, OTTO VON, *Die politischen Reden des Fürsten Bismarcks*, ed. Horst Kohl (12 vols., Stuttgart, 1892–4).

——, *Briefe an seine Braut und Gattin*, ed. Fürst Herbert Bismarck (Stuttgart, 1900).

——, *Die gesammelten Werke* (1st edn., 15 vols., Berlin 1924 ff.).

——, *Bismarck Gespräche*, ed. Willi Andreas and K. F. Reinking (3 vols., Bremen, 1965).

Bismarcks großes Spiel. Die geheimen Tagebücher Ludwig Bambergers, ed. Ernst Feder (Frankfurt-on-Main, 1932).

BLEUEL, H. P. with A. KLINERT, *Deutsche Studenten auf dem Weg ins Dritte Reich* (Gütersloh, 1967).

BOEHLICH, W. (ed.), *Der Berliner Antisemitismusstreit* (Sammlung Insel, 1965).

BÖHME, HELMUT, *Deutschlands Weg zur Großmacht: Studien zum Verhältnis von Wirtschaft und Staat während der Reichsgründungszeit 1848–1881* (Cologne, 1966).

——, (ed.), *Probleme der Reichsgründungszeit 1848–79* (Cologne and Berlin, 1968).

BONN, MORITZ J., *Wandering Scholar* (New York, 1948).

BONNIN, GEORGES (ed.), *Bismarck and the Hohenzollern Candidature for the Spanish Throne: Documents in the German Diplomatic Archives* (London, 1957).

BOURGEOIS, ÉMILE, *Rome et Napoleon III, 1848–70* (Paris, 1907).

BOVERI, MARGRET, *Wir lügen alle: Eine Haupstadtzeitung unter Hitler* (Freiburg im Breisgau, 1965).

BRACHER, KARL DIETRICH, 'Das Anfangsstadium der Hitlerischen Aussenpolitik', *Vierteljahrshefte für Zeitgeschichte*, v (1957).

——, *Die Auflösung der Weimarer Republik: Eine Studie zum Problem des Machtverfalls in der Demokratie* (2nd edn., Stuttgart, 1957).

——, *The German Dictatorship: The Origins, Structure and Effects of National Socialism* (New York, 1970).

——, WOLFGANG SAUER, and KNUT SCHULZ, *Die nationalsozialistische Machtergreifung. Studien zur Errichtung des totalitären Herrschaftssystems in Deutschland 1933–34* (Cologne and Opladen, 1960).

BRAMSTED, ERNEST K., *Goebbels and National Socialist Propaganda, 1925–45* (East Lansing, Mich., 1965).

BRANDENBURG, ERICH, *From Bismarck to the World War* (Oxford, 1933).

BRAUN, LILY, *Memoiren einer Sozialistin* (2 vols., Berlin, n.d.).

BRAUER, ARTHUR VON, *Im Dienste Bismarcks: Persönliche Erinnerungen*, ed. H. Rogge (Berlin, 1936).

BRECHT, ARNOLD, *Prelude to Silence* (New York, 1944).

——, *Aus nächster Nähe: Erinnerungen 1884–1927* (Stuttgart, 1966).

——, *Mit der Kraft des Geistes: Lebenserinnerungen 1927–1967* (Stuttgart, 1967).

BRENNER, HILDEGARD, *Die Kunstpolitik des Nationalsozialismus* (Hamburg, 1963).

——, *Ende einer bürgerlichen Kunstinstitution: Die politische Formierung der Preußischen Akademie der Künste ab 1933* (Stuttgart, 1972).

BRENTANO, LUJO, *Mein Leben im Kampf um die soziale Entwicklung Deutschlands* (Jena, 1931).

BRESCIANI-TURRONI, CONSTANTINO, *The Economics of Inflation: A Study of Currency Depreciation in Post-War Germany* (London, 1937).

BRESCIUS, HANS VON, *Gerhard Hauptmann. Zeitgeschehen und Bewußtsein in unbekannten Selbstzeugnissen* (Bonn, 1976).

BRETTON, HENRY L., *Stresemann and the Revision of Versailles: A Fight for Reason* (Stanford, 1953).

BRIGGS, MITCHELL P., *George D. Herron and the European Settlement* (Stanford, 1932).

BRÜNING, HEINRICH, *Memoiren 1918–1934* (Stuttgart, 1970).

BRY, GERHARD, *Wages In Germany* (Princeton, 1960).

BUCHHEIM, HANS, with MARTIN BROSZAT, HANS-ADOLF JACOBSEN, and HELMUT KRAUSNICK, *Anatomie des SS-Staates* (Otten and Freiburg im Breisgau, 1965).

BUCHHEIT, GERD, *Hitler der Feldherr* (Rastatt, 1958).

BÜLOW, BERNHARD FÜRST VON, *Denkwürdigkeiten* (4 vols., Berlin, 1930).

BULLOCK, ALAN, *Hitler: A Study in Tyranny* (rev. edn., New York, 1964).

BURCKHARDT, CARL J., *Meine Danziger Mission 1937–1939* (Munich, 1962).

BUSCH, MORITZ, *Tagebuchblätter* (2 vols., Leipzig, 1899).

BUSE, D. K., 'Ebert and the German Crisis, 1917–1920', *Central European History*, v, no. 3 (Sept. 1972).

BUßMANN, WALTER, *Treitschke, sein Welt- und Geschichtsbild* (Göttingen, 1952).

BUTLER, J. R. M., *Lord Lothian, 1882–1940* (London, 1960).

CALLIÈRES, FRANÇOIS, *On the Manner of Negotiating with Princes*, trans. A. F. Whyte (Notre Dame, 1963).

CAMPBELL, F. GREGORY, *Confrontation in Central Europe: Weimar Germany and Czechoslovakia* (Chicago, 1975).

CARELL, PAUL, *Hitler's War on Russia* (London, 1964).

CARSTEN, F. L., *The Reichswehr and Politics, 1918–1933* (Oxford, 1966).

——, *Revolution in Central Europe, 1918–1919* (London, 1972).

CASPAR, GUSTAV ADOLF, *Die Sozialdemokratische Partei und das deutsche Wehrproblem in den Jahren der Weimarer Republik* (Frankfurt-on-Main, 1959).

CASSAU, THEODOR, 'Die Gewerkschaftsbewegung, Ihre Soziologie und ihr Kampf', in *Soziale Organisation der Gegenwart, Forschungen und Beiträge*, ed. Ernst Grünfeld, viii (Halberstadt, 1925).

CECIL, LADY GWENDOLEN, *Life of Robert Marquis of Salisbury* (4 vols., London, 1921–32).

CECIL, LAMAR, *Albert Ballin: Business and Politics in Imperial Germany, 1888–1918* (Princeton, 1967).

——, *The German Diplomatic Service, 1871–1914* (Princeton, 1976).

CHABOD, FEDERICO, *Storia della politica estera italiana dal 1870 al 1896, i: Le premesse* (Bari, 1951).

CHANADY, ATTILA, 'Anton Erkelenz and Erich Koch-Weser: A Portrait of Two German Democrats', *Historical Studies: Australia and New Zealand*, xii (1967).

——, 'The Disintegration of the German National People's Party, 1924–1930', *Journal of Modern History*, xxxix, no. 1 (Mar. 1967).

——, 'The Dissolution of the German Democratic Party', *American Historical Review*, lxxiii no. 5 (1968).

CHICKERING, ROGER, *Imperial Germany and a World Without War: The Peace Movement and German Society, 1892–1914* (Princeton, 1975).

CHURCHILL, RANDOLPH S., *Winston S. Churchill* (2 vols., Boston, 1966–).

CHURCHILL, WINSTON S., *The Second World War* (5 vols., Boston, 1948 ff).

CIANO, GALEZZO, *Diario* (2 vols., Verona, 1946).

——, *L'Europa verso la catastrofe* (Bari, 1948).

CIENCIALA, ANNA M., *Poland and the Western Powers, 1938–1939* (London, 1968).

CLAPHAM, J. H., *The Economic Development of France and Germany, 1815–1914* (4th edn., London, 1936).

CLARK, ALAN, *Barbarossa* (London, 1965).

CLASS, HEINRICH, *Wider den Strom* (Leipzig, 1922).

COLE, G. D. H., *A History of Socialist Thought* (3 vols., London, 1953).

COLLIER, B., *The Battle of Britain* (London, 1962).

COLVIN, IAN, *The Chamberlain Cabinet* (London, 1971).

COMFORT, RICHARD A., *Revolutionary Hamburg: Labor Politics in the Early Weimar Republic* (Stanford, 1966).

Commission d'enquête parlementaire sur les événements survenus en France de 1933 à 1945. Rapport (Paris, 1951).

COMPTON, JAMES V., *The Swastika and the Eagle: Hitler, the United States, and the Origins of World War II* (Boston, 1967).

CONRAD VON HÖTZENDORF, FELDMARSCHALL, *Aus meiner Dienstzeit* (4 vols., Vienna and Berlin, 1921).

CONZE, WERNER, 'Friedrich Naumann. Grundlagen und Ansatz seiner Politik in der nationalsozialen Zeit 1895 bis 1903', in *Schicksalswege deutscher Vergangenheit*, ed. W. Hubatsch (Düsseldorf, 1950).

——, (ed.), *Das Ende der Monarchie 9.11.18* (Berlin, 1952).

——, *Polnische Nation und deutsche Politik im Ersten Weltkriege* (Cologne and Graz, 1958).

COWLEY, MALCOLM, *Exile's Return: A Literary Odyssey of the 1920s* (new edn., New York, 1951).

CRAIG, GORDON A., 'Great Britain and the Belgian Railways Dispute of 1869', *American Historical Review*, l, no. 4 (July 1945).

——, *The Politics of the Prussian Army, 1640–1945* (Oxford, 1955).

——, 'Bismarck and his Ambassadors: The Problem of Discipline', *Foreign Service Journal*, xxxiii (Washington D. C., June 1956).

——, *From Bismarck to Adenauer: Aspects of German Statecraft* (rev. edn., New York, 1965).

——, 'The German Army and the Home Front during the Second World War', in *Comité international des sciences historiques: XIeme Congrès international: Rapports*, iv: *Méthodologie et historie contemporaine* (1965).

——, *War, Politics and Diplomacy: Selected Essays* (New York, 1966).

——, 'Engagement and Neutrality in Weimar Germany', *Journal of Contemporary History*, ii, no. 2 (1967), 49–63.

CRAIG, JOHN ELDON, 'A Mission for German Learning: The University of Strassburg and Alsatian Society, 1870–1918' (Dissertation, Stanford Univ. 1973).

CRAMON, AUGUST VON, *Unser Österreich-Ungarischer Bundesgenosse im Weltkriege* (Berlin, 1920).

CRISPI, FRANCESCO, *Questioni internationali* (Milan, 1913).

CROTHERS, GEORGE D., *The German Elections of 1907* (New York, 1941).

CROWE, S. E., *The Berlin West African Conference, 1884–85* (New York, 1942).

CRUTTWELL, C. R. F. M., *A History of the Great War, 1914–1918* (2nd edn., Oxford, 1936).

CURTIUS, JULIUS, *Sechs Jahre Minister der deutschen Republik* (Heidelberg, 1948).

D'ABERNON, VISCOUNT, *An Ambassador of Peace* (3 vols., London, 1929).

DAHRENDORF, RALF, *Society and Democracy in Germany* (New York, 1967).

DALLIN, ALEXANDER, *German Rule in Russia, 1941–45: A Study of Occupation Policies* (London, 1957).

DANILOV, J. N., *Rußland im Weltkrieg* (Jena, 1925).

DANNER, LOTHAR, *Ordnungspolizei Hamburg: Betrachtungen zu ihrer Geschichte 1918 bis 1933* (Hamburg, 1958).

DAWIDOWICZ, LUCY S., *The War against the Jews, 1933–1945* (New York, 1975).

DEAK, ISTVAN, *Weimar Germany's Left-Wing Intellectuals. A Political History of the Weltbühne and its Circle* (Berkeley, 1968).

DEMETER, KARL, *Das deutsche Heer und seine Offiziere* (Berlin, 1930).

——, *Das deutsche Offizierkorps in Gesellschaft und Staat 1650–1945* (Frankfurt-on-Main, 1962).

DEMPSTER, D. and D. WOOD, *The Narrow Margin* (London, 1961).

DENKLER, HORST and KARL PRUEMM (eds.), *Die deutsche Literatur im Dritten Reich: Themen, Tradition, Wirkungen* (Stuttgart, 1976).

DEUERLEIN, ERNST, *Der Reichstag: Aufsätze, Protokolle und Darstellungen zur Geschichte der parlamentarischen Vertretung des deutschen Volkes 1871–1933* (Bonn, 1963).

——, and THEODOR SCHIEDER (eds.), *Reichsgründung 1870/71: Tatsachen, Kontroversen, Interpretationen* (Stuttgart, 1970).

DEUTSCH, HAROLD C., *The Conspiracy against Hitler in the Twilight War* (Minneapolis, 1968).

Deutschland, Deutschland. Politische Gedichte vom Vormärz bis zur Gegenwart, ed. Helmut Lamprecht (Bremen, 1969).

DIELS, RUDOLF, *Lucifer ante portas* (Stuttgart, 1956).

DIETRICH, OTTO, *Zwölf Jahre mit Hitler* (Munich, 1955).

DIÓSZEGI, ISTVÁN, *Österreich-Ungarn und der französisch-preußische Krieg 1870–1871* (Budapest, 1974).

The Diplomats, 1919–1939, ed. Gordon A. Craig and Felix Gilbert (Princeton, 1953).

DIRKSEN, HERBERT VON, *Moskau, Tokyo, London: Erinnerungen und Betrachtungen* (Stuttgart, 1950).

DITTRICH, JOCHEN, 'Ursachen und Ausbruch des Krieges 1870/71', in *Reichsgründung 1870/71: Tatsachen, Kontroversen, Interpretatien*, ed. Deuerlein and Schieder (Stuttgart, 1970).

DIVINE, DAVID, *The Nine Days of Dunkirk* (New York, 1959).

DÖBLIN, ALFRED, 'Republik', *Die neue Rundschau* (1920), i.

——, *Schicksalsreise* (Frankfurt-on-Main, 1949).

Documents diplomatiques français, 1932–1939 (Paris, 1949 ff.).

Documents on British Foreign Policy, 1919–1939, ed. E. L. Woodward and Rohan Butler (London, 1949 ff.).

Documents on German Foreign Policy, 1918–1945: From the Archives of the German Foreign Ministry (Washington, D.C., 1949 ff.), Ser. C (1933–7), Ser. D (1937–41).

DOMARUS, MAX, *Hitler, Reden und Proklamationen 1932–45, kommentiert von einem deutschen Zeitgenossen* (2 vols., Neustadt a.d. Aisch, 1962–3).

DORNBERGER, WALTER, *V-2* (New York, 1954).

DORPALEN, ANDREAS, *Heinrich von Treitschke* (New Haven, 1957).

——, *Hindenburg and the Weimar Republic* (Princeton, 1964).

DORST, TANKRED with PETER ZADEK and HARTMUT GEHRKE, *Rotmord oder I was a German* (Munich, 1969).

DRACHKOVITCH, MILORAD M., *Les Socialismes français et allemand et le problème de la guerre, 1870–1914* (Geneva, 1953).

DRUCKER, PETER, *The End of Economic Man: A Study in the New Totalitarianism* (New York, 1939).

DRUMMOND, GORDON DOUGLAS, 'The Military Policy of the German Social Democratic Party, 1949–1960' (Dissertation, Stanford Univ. 1968).

DÜWELL, KURT, 'Staat und Wissenschaft in der Weimarer Epoche: Zur Kulturpolitik des Ministers C. H. Becker', *Historische Zeitschrift*, Beihefte (1971).

EARLE, EDWARD MEAD, *Turkey, the Great Powers and the Baghdad Railway* (New York, 1923).

EBERT, FRIEDRICH, *Schriften, Aufzeichnungen, Reden* (2 vols., Dresden, 1926).

ECKARDSTEIN, HERMANN VON, *Lebenserinnerungen und politische Denkwürdigkeiten* (2 vols., Leipzig, 1919–20).

ECKARDT, WOLF VON, 'Bauhaus', *Horizon* (Nov. 1961).

EDEN, ANTHONY, *Memoirs: Facing the Dictators* (Boston, 1962).

EDWARDS, MARVIN L., *Stresemann and the Greater Germany, 1914–1918* (New York, 1963).

EGBERT, DONALD DREW, *Social Radicalism and the Arts: Western Europe* (New York, 1970).

EINEM, GENERALOBERST VON, *Erinnerungen eines Soldaten 1853–1933* (Leipzig, 1933).

EINZIG, PAUL, *Appeasement before, during and after the War* (London, 1941).

——, *In the Centre of Things* (London, 1960).

EPSTEIN, KLAUS, *Matthias Erzberger and the Dilemma of German Democracy* (Princeton, 1959).

ERBE, RENÉ, *Die nationalsozialistische Wirtschaftspolitik 1933–1939 im Lichte der modernen Theorie* (Zurich, 1958).

ERDMANN, KARL DIETRICH, 'Zur Beurteilung Bethmann Hollwegs', *Geschichte in Wissenschaft und Unterricht*, xv (1964).

——, *Adenauer in der Rheinlandpolitik nach dem Ersten Weltkrieg* (Stuttgart, 1966).

ERDMANN, LOTHAR, *Die Gewerkschaften im Ruhrkampf* (Berlin, 1924).

ERGER, JOHANNES, *Der Kapp–Lüttwitz Putsch. Ein Beitrag zur deutschen Innenpolitik 1919–1920* (Düsseldorf, 1967).

ERICKSON, JOHN, *The Soviet High Command: A Military-Political History, 1918–1941* (London, 1962).

ERKELENZ, ANTON (ed.), *Zehn Jahre Deutsche Republik* (Berlin, 1928).

ERNST II, HERZOG VON SACHSEN-KOBURG-GOTHA, *Aus meinem Leben und aus meiner Zeit* (Stuttgart, 1889).

ERNST, FRITZ, 'Walther Reinhardt (1872 bis 1930)', *Zeitschrift für Württembergische Landesgeschichte*, xvi (1957).

ERZBERGER, MATTHIAS, *Erlebnisse im Weltkrieg* (Stuttgart, 1920).

ESCHENBURG, THEODOR, *Das Kaiserreich am Scheideweg: Bassermann, Bülow und der Block* (Berlin, 1929).

——, *Die improvisierte Demokratie: Gesammelte Aufsätze zur Weimarer Republik* (Munich, 1963).

EYCK, ERICH, *Bismarck: Leben und Werk* (3 vols., Zurich, 1941–4).

——, *Das persönliche Regiment Wilhelms II: Politische Geschichte des deutschen Kaiserreiches von 1890 bis 1914* (Zurich, 1948).

——, *A History of the Weimar Republic* (2 vols., Cambridge, Mass., 1962).

FALKENHAYN, ERICH VON, *Die Oberste Heeresleitung, 1914–1916* (Berlin, 1920).

FALLS, CYRIL, *The Great War, 1914–1918* (London, 1959).

FELDMAN, GERALD D., *Army, Industry and Labour, 1914–1918* (Princeton, 1966).

——, 'Big Business and the Kapp Putsch', *Central European History*, iv, no. 2 (June 1971).

——, *Iron and Steel in the German Inflation, 1916—1923* (Princeton, 1977).

FELIX, DAVID, 'Reparations Re-considered with a Vengeance', *Central European History*, iv, no. 2 (June 1971).

——, *Walter Rathenau and the Weimar Republic: The Politics of Reparations* (Baltimore, 1971).

FEST, JOACHIM C., 'Rede Hitlers vor der deutschen Presse 10. Nov. 1938', *Vierteljahrshefte für Zeitgeschichte*, vi, Heft 2 (1958).

——, *Das Gesicht des Dritten Reiches: Profile einer totalitären Herrschaft* (Munich 1963).

——, *Hitler. Eine Biographie* (Frankfurt-on-Main, 1973).

FISCHER, FRITZ, *Griff nach der Weltmacht: Die Kriegszielpolitik des Kaiserlichen Deutschland 1914–1918* (Düsseldorf, 1961; 3rd edn., 1964).

——, 'Der deutsche Protestantismus und die Politik im 19. Jahrhundert', in *Probleme der Reichsgründungszeit 1848–79*, ed. Helmut Böhme (Cologne and Berlin, 1968).

——, *Krieg der Illusionen: Die deutsche Politik von 1911 bis 1914* (Düsseldorf, 1969).

FISCHER, RUTH, *Stalin and German Communism. A Study in the Origins of the State Party* (Cambridge, Mass., 1948).

FISCHER-FRAUENDIENST, IRENE, *Bismarcks Pressepolitik* (Münster, 1963).

FLANDIN, PIERRE-ÉTIENNE, *Politique française, 1919–40* (Paris, 1947).

FLEINER, FRITZ, *Reden und Schriften* (Zurich, 1941).

FLEMING, PETER, *Operation Sea Lion* (London, 1957).

FLETCHER, WILLARD ALLEN, *The Mission of Vincent Benedetti to Berlin, 1864–1870* (The Hague, 1965).

FLECHTHEIM, OSSIP K., *Die Kommunistische Partei Deutschlands in der Weimarer Republik* (Offenbach, 1948).

FÖRSTER, ERICH, *Bismarck* (1927).

FÖRSTER, WOLFGANG, *Ein General kämpft gegen den Krieg: Aus nachgelassenen Papieren des Generalstabschefs Ludwig Beck* (Munich, 1949).

FONTANE, THEODOR, *Fontanes Briefe in zwei Bänden*, ed. Gotthard Erler (Berlin and Weimar, 1968).

FRAENKEL, ERNST, 'Die Krise des Rechtsstaates und die Justiz', *Die Gesellschaft*, viii (1931).

FRAENKEL, H. and R. MANVELL, *Goebbels: Eine Biographie* (Cologne and Berlin, 1960).

FRANK, WALTER, *Hofprediger Adolf Stoecker und die christlichsoziale Bewegung* (2nd edn., Hamburg, 1935).

——, 'Der Geheime Rat Paul Kayser', *Historische Zeitschrift*, 168 (1943).

FRANKLAND, NOBLE, *The Bombing Offensive against Germany* (London, 1965).

FRANTZ, KONSTANTIN, *Der Föderalismus als das leitende Prinzip für die soziale, staatliche und internationale Organisation unter besonderer Bezugnahme auf Deutschland* (Mainz, 1879).

FRASER, CHRISTINE, 'Der Austritt Deutschlands aus dem Völkerbund, seine Vorgeschichte und seine Nachwirkungen' (Dissertation, Friedrich-Wilhelms-Universität zu Bonn, 1969).

FREDERICK, EMPRESS, *Letters of the Empress Frederick*, ed. Sir Frederick Ponsonby (London, 1929).

FREYTAG, GUSTAV, *Gustav Freytags Briefe an Albrecht von Stosch* (Leipzig, 1913).

FRICKE, DIETER, 'Die Affäre Leckart–Lützow–Tausch und die Regierungskrise von 1897 in Deutschland', *Zeitschrift für Geschichtswissenschaft*, no. 7 (1960).

——, 'Der deutsche Imperialismus und die Reichstagswahlen von 1907', *Zeitschrift für Geschichtswissenschaft*, ix (1961).

——, *Bismarcks Praetorianer. Die Berliner politische Polizei gegen die deutsche Arbeiterbewegung 1871–1898* (Berlin, 1962).

FRIEDRICH III, KAISER, *Das Kriegstagebuch von 1870–71*, ed. H. O. Meisner (Berlin, 1926).

——, *Tagebücher von 1848–1866*, ed. H. O. Meisner (Leipzig, 1929).

FRYE, BRUCE B., 'The German Democratic Party, 1918–1930', *Western Political Quarterly*, xvi (1968).

FURHAMMER, LEIF and FOLKE ISAKSSON, *Politics and Film*, trans. Kersti French (London, 1971).

FURTWÄNGLER, FRANZ JOSEF, *Die Gewerkschaften: Ihre Geschichte und internationale Auswirkung* (Hamburg, 1956).

GACKENHOLZ, HERMANN, 'Der Kriegsrat von Czernahora', *Historische Vierteljahrsschrift*, xxvi (1931).

GASIOROWSKI, ZIGMUNT J., 'Stresemann and Poland before Locarno', *Journal of Central European Affairs*, xviii (1958).

GALL, LOTHAR, 'Zur Frage der Annexion von Elsaß und Lothringen 1870', *Historische Zeitschrift*, 206 (1968).

——, 'Staat und Wirtschaft in der Reichsgründungzeit', *Historische Zeitschrift*, 209 (1969).

——, 'Das Problem Elsaß-Lothringen', in *Reichsgründung 1870/71: Tatsachen, Kontroversen, Interpretationen*, ed. Deuerlein and Schieder (Stuttgart, 1970).

GAMELIN, GENERAL, *Servir* (3 vols., Paris, 1946–7).

GATZKE, HANS W., *Germany's Drive to the West* (Baltimore, 1950).

——, *Stresemann and the Rearmament of Germany* (Baltimore, 1954).

——, 'Von Rapallo nach Berlin: Stresemann und die deutsche Rußlandpolitik', *Vierteljahrshefte für Zeitgeschichte*, iv (1956).

——, 'Russo-German Military Collaboration during the Weimar Republic', *American Historical Review*, lxiii (1958).

GAY, PETER, *The Dilemma of Democratic Socialism: Eduard Bernstein's Challenge to Marx* (rev. edn., New York, 1962).

——, *Weimar Culture: The Outsider as Insider* (New York, 1968).

GEIGER, W., *Miquel und die preußische Steuerreform 1890–93* (Groppingen, 1934).

GEISS, IMANUEL (ed.), *Julikrise und Kriegsausbruch 1914* (2 vols., Hanover, 1964).

GÉLINET, L., *Le Grand-Duché de Luxembourg vis-à-vis de la France et de l'Allemagne. Étude militaire* (Paris 1887).

GERLACH, HELLMUTH VON, *Von rechts nach links*, ed. Emil Ludwig (Zurich, 1937).

GESSLER, OTTO, *Reichswehrpolitik in der Weimarerzeit*, ed. Kurt Sendtner (Stuttgart, 1958).

GEUSS, HERBERT, *Bismarck und Napoleon III: Ein Beitrag zur Geschichte der preußisch-französisischen Beziehungen 1851–1871* (Cologne 1959).

GEHL, JÜRGEN, *Austria, Germany, and the Anschluss, 1931–38* (London, 1963).

GIELS, HORST, 'NSDAP und landwirtschaftliche Organisationen in der Endphase der Weimarer Republik', in *Vierteljahrshefte für Zeitgeschichte*, v (1967).

GILBERT, MARTIN, *Winston S. Churchill* (5 vols., London, 1968 ff.).

——, and RICHARD GOTT, *The Appeasers* (London, 1963).

GILLIS, JOHN, *Youth and History: Tradition and Change in European Age Relations, 1770–Present* (New York, 1974).

GISEVIUS, H. G., *Bis zum bitteren Ende* (2 vols., Zurich, 1946).

GOEBBELS, JOSEF, *My Part in Germany's Fight* (London, 1935).

——, *The Goebbels Diaries, 1942–1943*, ed. and trans. Louis P. Lochner (New York, 1948).

——, *The Secret Conferences of Dr. Goebbels: The Nazi Propaganda War 1939–43*, sel. and ed. Willi A. Boelcke; trans. from the German (East Lansing, Mich., 1965).

GÖHRING, MARTIN, *Stresemann, Mensch, Staatsmamm, Europäer: Gedenkrede gehalten am 8. Juli 1956* (Mainz, 1956).

GÖRLITZ, WALTER, *Hindenburg: Ein Lebensbild* (Bonn, 1953).

——, *History of the German General Staff* (New York, 1953).

GOETZ, W. (ed.), 'Der Briefwechsel Gustav Schmollers mit Lujo Brentano', *Archiv fur Kulturgeschichte*, xxx.

GOLDSCHMIDT, H., *Das Reich und Preußen* (Berlin, n.d.).

GOLLWITZER, H., 'Der Cäsarismus Napoleons III. im Widerhall der öffentlichen Meinung Deutschlands', *Historische Zeitschrift*, 173 (1952).

——, 'Karl Alexander von Müller 1882–1964: Ein Nachruf', *Historische Zeitschrift*, 205 (1967).

GOLTZ, RUDIGER GRAF VON DER, *Meine Sendung in Finland und im Baltikum* (Leipzig, 1920).

——, *Als Politischer General im Osten 1918–1919* (Leipzig, 1936).

GOOCH, GEORGE PEABODY, *Before the War: Studies in Diplomacy* (2 vols., London, 1936).

GORDON, HAROLD J., JUN., *The Reichswehr and the German Republic, 1919–1926* (Princeton, 1957).

——, *Hitler and the Beer Hall Putsch* (Princeton, 1972).

GOUTARD, COLONEL A., *The Battle of France, 1940*, trans. from the French (New York, 1959).

GRAML, HERMANN, 'Die Rapallo-Politik im Urteil der westdeutschen Forschung', *Vierteljahrshefte für Zeitgeschichte*, xviii (1970).

——, HANS MOMMSEN, HANS-JOACHIM REICHHARDT, and ERNST WOLF, *The German Resistance to Hitler* (Berkeley, 1970).

GRASS, GÜNTER, *Hundejahre* (Berlin, 1963).

GRATHWOHL, ROBERT, 'Gustav Stresemann: Reflections on his Foreign Policy', *Journal of Modern History*, xlv, no. 1 (Mar. 1973).

GRAY, RONALD, *The German Tradition of Literature, 1871–1945* (Cambridge, 1965).

GRIEWANK, KARL, *Das Problem des christlichen Staatsmannes bei Bismarck* (Berlin, 1953).

GRITZBACK, ERICH, *Hermann Goering, Werk und Mensch* (2nd edn., Munich, 1938).

GROENER, WILHELM, *Lebenserinnerungen*, ed. F. Freiherr Hitler von Gärtringen (Göttingen, 1957).

GROENER-GEYER, DOROTHEA, *General Groener, Soldat und Staatsmann* (Frankfurt-on-Main, 1955).

GROH, DIETER, *Negative Integration und revolutionärer Attentismus: Die deutsche Sozialdemokratie am Vorabend des Ersten Weltkrieges* (Frankfurt-on-Main, 1973).

Die Große Politik der Europäischen Kabinette 1871–1914: Sammlung der diplomatischen Akten des Auswärtigen Amtes (40 vols., Berlin, 1921 ff.).

GUDERIAN, HEINZ, *Panzer Leader*, trans. from the German (London, 1952).

GÜNTHER, JOACHIM, *Das letzte Jahr: Mein Tagebuch 1944/45* (Hamburg, 1948).

GUILLEBAUD, C. W., *The Economic Recovery of Germany* (London, 1939).

GUMBEL, E. I., *Verschwörer: Beiträge zur Geschichte und Soziologie der deutschen nationalistischen Geheimbünde seit 1918* (Vienna, 1924).

HALDER, GENERALOBERST, *Kriegstagebuch*, ed. Hans-Adolf Jacobsen (3 vols., Stuttgart, 1962).

HALE, OREN J., *The Captive Press in the Third Reich* (Princeton, 1964).

HALLE, ERNST VON, *Die Seemacht in der deutschen Geschichte* (Leipzig, 1907).

HALLER, JOHANNES, *Aus dem Leben des Fürsten Philipp zu Eulenburg-Hertefeld* (Berlin, 1924).

HALLGARTEN, GEORGE W. F., *Imperialismus vor 1914* (rev. edn., 2 vols., Munich, 1963).

HALPERIN, S. WILLIAM, 'The Origins of the Franco-Prussian War Re-Visited; Bismarck and the Hohenzollern Candidature for the Spanish Crown', *Journal of Modern History*, xlv, no. 1 (1973).

HAMANN, RICHARD and JOST HERMAND, *Impressionismus* (2nd edn., Berlin, 1966).

——, *Naturalismus* (2nd edn., Berlin, 1968).

——, *Gründerzeit* (Munich, 1971).

HAMEROW, THEODORE S., *The Social Foundations of German Unification, 1858–1871: Struggles and Accomplishments* (Princeton, 1972).

HAMMANN, OTTO, *Bilder aus der letzten Kaiserzeit* (Berlin, 1922).

HANTSCH, HUGO, *Leopold Graf Berchtold: Grandseigneur und Staatsmann* (2 vols., Graz and Vienna, 1963).

HART, HEINRICH, 'Fürst Bismarck und sein Verhältnis zur deutschen Literature', *Gesammelte Werke*, iii (Berlin, 1907).

HARTSHORNE, EDWARD YARNELL, JUN., *The German Universities and National Socialism* (Cambridge, Mass., 1937).

HARTUNG, FRITZ, *Deutsche Verfassungsgeschichte* (2nd rev. edn., Leipzig and Berlin, 1922).

——, 'Verantwortliche Regierung, Kabinette, und Nebenregierungen im konstitutionellen Preußen 1848–1918', *Forschungen zur brandenburgischen und preußischen Geschichte*, xliv (1932).

——, 'Bismarck und Arnim', *Historische Zeitschrift*, 171 (1951).

HATCH, WILLIAM M., 'Württemberg and the November 1918 Revolution' (Dissertation, Stanford Univ. 1973).

HATZFELDT, PAUL GRAF VON, *Nachgelassene Papiere 1838–1901*, ed. Gerhard Ebel and Michael Behnen (2 vols., Boppard, 1976).

HAUPTMANN, GERHARD, *Gesammelte Werke in sechs Bänden* (Berlin, n.d.).

HAUSEN, HORST, *Das Präsidialkabinett. Eine staatsrechtliche Betrachtung der Kabinette von Brüning bis Hitler* (Erlangen, 1933).

HAUSER, ARNOLD, *The Social History of Art* (4 vols., New York, 1958).

HAUSER, OSWALD, 'Der Plan einer Deutsch-Österreichischen Zollunion von 1931 und die europäische Föderation', in *Historische Zeitschrift*, 179 (1955), 45–92.

HAYES, CARLETON J., *A Generation of Materialism, 1871–1900* (New York, 1944).

HEBERLE, RUDOLF, *From Democracy to Nazism: A Regional Case Study on Political Parties in Germany* (Baton Rouge, La., 1945).

HEIBER, HELMUT, *Josef Goebbels* (Berlin, 1962).

——, *Die Republik von Weimar* (Munich, 1966).

——, *Adolf Hitler* (Berlin, 1960).

HEIDEGGER, MARTIN, *Die Selbstbehauptung der deutschen Universität* (Breslau, 1933).

HEIDEN, KONRAD, *The Fuehrer* (Boston, 1944).

HEINE, HEINRICH, *Werke*, ed. Martin Greiner (2 vols., Cologne and Berlin, n.d.).

HELBICH, WOLFGANG J., 'Between Stresemann and Hitler: The Foreign Policy of the Brüning Government', in *World Politics*, xii (1959).

——, *Die Reparationen in der Ära Brüning* (Berlin, 1962).

HELFFERICH, KARL, *Der Weltkrieg* (3 vols., Berlin, 1919).

HELLWIG, FRITZ, *Carl Freiherr von Stumm-Halberg* (Heidelberg, 1936).

HELMREICH, J. E., 'Belgium and the Decision to Occupy the Ruhr: Diplomacy from a Middle Position', *Revue belge de philologie et d'histoire*, li (1973).

HERTZMAN, LEWIS, *DNVP. Right-Wing Opposition in the Weimar Republic, 1918–1924* (Lincoln, Nebr., 1963).

HERWEGH, GEORG, *Morgenruf: Ausgewählte Gedichte* (Leipzig, 1969).

HERWIG, HOLGER H., 'The First German Congress of Workers and Soldiers Councils and the Problem of Military Reforms', *Central European History*, i, no. 2 (June 1968).

HERZFELD, HANS, *Die deutsche Rüstungspolitik vor dem Weltkriege* (Bonn and Leipzig, 1923).

——, *Deutschland und das verschlagene Frankreich* (Berlin, 1924).

——, *Johannes von Miquel* (2 vols., Detmold, 1938).

——, *Ausgewählte Aufsätze* (Berlin, 1962).

HEUß, ALFRED, *Theodor Mommsen und das 19. Jahrhundert* (Kiel, 1956).

HEUß, THEODOR, *Friedrich Naumann, der Mann, das Werk, die Zeit* (Stuttgart and Berlin, 1937).

——, *Vorspiele des Lebens: Jugenderinnerungen* (Tübingen, 1953).

Hier schreibt Berlin: Ein Dokument der 20er Jahre, ed. Herbert Günther (Munich, 1963).

HIGGINS, TRUMBULL, *Hitler and Russia* (New York, 1966).

——, *Winston Churchill and the Dardanelles* (New York, 1963).

HIGHAM, JOHN, with LEONARD KRIEGER and FELIX GILBERT, *History* (Englewood, N.J., 1965).

HILDEBRAND, KLAUS, *The Foreign Policy of the Third Reich*, trans. from the German (Berkeley, 1973).

HILLER VON GÄRTRINGEN, F. FREIHERR, *Fürst Bülows Denkwürdigkeiten: Untersuchungen zu ihrer Entstehungsgeschichte und ihrer Kritik* (Tübingen, 1956).

HILLGRUBER, ANDREAS, *Hitlers Strategie 1940–1941* (Frankfurt-on-Main, 1965).

——, *Kontinuität und Diskontinuität in der deutschen Außenpolitik von Bismarck bis Hitler* (Düsseldorf, 1969).

HIMMLER, HEINRICH, *Heinrich Himmler: Geheimreden 1933 bis 1945*, ed. Bradley F. Smith and Agnes F. Peterson (Frankfurt-on-Main, 1974).

HINSLEY, F. H., *Hitler's Strategy* (Cambridge, 1951).

HINTZE, OTTO, 'Das monarchische Prinzip', *Preußische Jahrbücher* (1911).

HIRSCH, FELIX, *Gustav Stresemann, Patriot und Europäer* (Göttingen, 1964).

HITLER, ADOLF, *Hitler's Secret Book*, trans. Salvator Attanasio, intro. by Telford Taylor (New York, 1961).

——, *Mein Kampf*, trans. Ralph Mannheim (Boston, 1962).

——, *Reden und Proklamationen 1932–45*, ed. Max Domarus (2 vols., Neustadt a. d. Aisch, 1962–3).

——, *Es spricht der Führer. Sieben exemplarische Hitler-Reden*, ed. Hildegard von Kotze and Helmut Krausnick (Gütersloh, 1966).

Hitler Directs His War, ed. Felix Gilbert (New York, 1950).

Hitler's Secret Conversations, with an introduction by H. R. Trevor-Roper (New York, 1953).

Hitlers Tischgespräche im Führerhauptquartier 1941–42, collected by Henry Picker, ed. Percy Ernst Schramm (Stuttgart, 1963).

HÖFELE, KARL HEINRICH, *Geist und Gesellschaft der Bismarckzeit* (Göttingen, 1967).

HÖHNE, HEINS, *The Order of the Death's Head* (New York, 1970).

HOESS, RUDOLF, *Commandant of Auschwitz*, trans. from the German (Cleveland, 1960).

HOFER, WALTHER and CHRISTOPH GRAF, 'Neue Quellen zum Reichstagsbrand', in *Geschichte in Wissenschaft und Unterricht*, 27, Heft 2 (1976).

HOFFMANN, PETER, *Widerstand, Staatsstreich, Attentat: Der Kampf der Opposition gegen Hitler* (Munich, 1969).

HOFSTADTER, RICHARD and WALTER P. METZGER, *The Development of Academic Freedom in the United States* (New York, 1955).

HOHENLOHE-SCHILLINGSFÜRST, CHLODWIG, FÜRST ZU, *Memoirs* (2 vols., London, 1906).

——, *Denkwürdigkeiten der Reichskanzlerzeit*, ed. K. A. von Müller (Stuttgart, 1931).

HOHOFF, CURT and ALBERT SOERGEL, *Dichtung und Dichter der Zeit: Vom Naturalismus bis zur Gegenwart* (2 vols., rev. edn., Düsseldorf, 1961).

HOLBORN, HAJO, 'Bismarck und Werthern', *Archiv für Politik und Geschichte*, v (1925–6).

HOLLYDAY, FREDERICK B., *Bismarck's Rival: A Political Biography of Albrecht von Stosch* (Durham, N. C., 1960).

——, ' "Love Your Enemies! Otherwise Bite Them!" Bismarck, Herbert, and the Morier Affair, 1888–1889', *Central European History* (Mar. 1968).

HOLSTEIN, FRIEDRICH VON, *The Holstein Papers. The Memoirs, Diaries, and Correspondence of Friedrich von Holstein, 1837–1909*, ed. Norman Rich and M. H. Fisher (4 vols., Cambridge, 1955–63).

HOLT, JOHN B., *German Agricultural Policy, 1918–34* (Chapel Hill, N.C., 1936)

HORN, DANIEL, *The German Naval Mutinies of World War I* (New Brunswick, 1969).

——, 'The Hitler Youth and Educational Decline in the Third Reich', *History of Education Quarterly* (winter 1976).

——, (ed.), *War, Mutiny, and Revolution in the German Navy: The World War I Diary of Seaman Richard Stumpf* (New Brunswick, 1967).

HOSSBACH, FRIEDRICH, *Zwischen Wehrmacht und Hitler 1934–38* (rev. edn., Göttingen, 1965).

HOWARD, MICHAEL, *The Franco-Prussian War: The German Invasion of France, 1870–71* (New York, 1961).

HUBATSCH, WALTHER, *Die Ära Tirpitz: Studien zur deutschen Marinepolitik*

——, Die Bismarcksche Reichsverfassung im Zusammenhang der deut-

——, *Der Admiralstab und die obersten Marinebehörden in Deutschland 1848–1945* (Frankfurt-on-Main, 1958).

HUBER, E. R., *Heer und Staat in der deutschen Geschichte* (Hamburg, 1938).

——, *Verfassungsrecht des Großdeutschen Reiches* (2nd edn., Berlin, 1939).

——, 'Die Bismarcksche Reichsverfassung im Zusammenhang der deutschen Verfassungsgeschichte', in *Reichsgründung 1870/71: Tatsachen, Kontroversen, Interpretationen*, ed. Deuerlein and Schieder (Stuttgart, 1970).

HUGHES, H. STUART, *Oswald Spengler: A Critical Estimate* (New York, 1952).

——, *Consciousness and Society: The Reorientation of European Social Thought, 1890–1930* (New York, 1958).

HULL, DAVID STEWART, *Film in the Third Reich: Art and Propaganda in Nazi Germany* (New York, 1973).

HUMBOLDT, WILHELM VON, *Wilhelm und Caroline von Humboldt in ihren Briefen*, ed. Anna von Sydow (7 vols., Berlin, 1906–16).

——, *Werke in fünf Bänden* (Darmstadt, 1964 ff.).

HUNT, RICHARD N., *German Social Democracy, 1918–1933* (New Haven, 1964).

HUTTEN-CZAPSKI, BOGDAN GRAF, *Sechzig Jahre Politik und Gesellschaft* (2 vols., Berlin, 1935–6).

International Military Tribunal, *Trial of the Major War Criminals before the International Military Tribunal* (Nuremberg, 1947–9).

IRVING, DAVID, *The Destruction of Dresden* (London, 1963).

——, *Hitler's War* (New York, 1977).

JACOBSEN, HANS-ADOLF, *Dokumente zur Vorgeschichte des Westfeldzugs 1939–40* (Göttingen, 1956).

——, *Fall Gelb: Der Kampf um den deutschen Operationsplan zur Westoffensive 1940* (Wiesbaden, 1957).

——, *Dünkirchen. Ein Beitrag zur Geschichte des Westfeldzugs 1940* (Neckargemund, 1958).

——, *Der Zweite Weltkrieg: Grundzüge der Politik und Strategie in Dokumenten* (Frankfurt-on-Main, 1965).

——, and WERNER JOCHMANN (eds.), *Zur Geschichte des Nationalsozialismus: Ausgewählte Dokumente* (Bielefeld, 1961).

JACOBSON, JON, *Locarno Diplomacy: Germany and the West, 1925–1929* (Princeton, 1972).

JÄCKEL, EBERHARD, *Hitler's Weltanschauung*, trans. Herbert Arnold (Middletown, Conn., 1972).

JÄCKH, ERNST, *Kiderlen-Wächter: Der Staatsmann und der Mensch* (2 vols., Berlin and Leipzig, 1925).

JÄHNS, MAX, *Feldmarschall Moltke* (new edn., Berlin, 1894).

JANSSEN, KARL-HEINZ, *Macht und Verblendung: Kriegszielpolitik der deutschen Bundesstaaten 1914–1918* (Göttingen, 1963).

——, *Der Kanzler und der General: Die Führungskrise um Bethmann Hollweg und Falkenhayn 1914–1916* (Göttingen, 1967).

JARAUSCH, KONRAD H., *The Enigmatic Chancellor: Bethmann Hollweg and the Hubris of Imperial Germany* (New Haven, 1973).

JERUSSALINSKI, A. S., *Die Außenpolitik und die Diplomatie des deutschen Imperialismus* (2nd edn., Berlin, 1954).

JOLL, JAMES, *Three Intellectuals in Politics* (new edn., New York, 1965).

JONES, THOMAS, *A Diary with Letters* (Oxford, 1954).

JORDAN, W. M., *Great Britain, France, and the German Problem, 1918–1939* (London, 1943).

JÜNGER, ERNST, *Der Kampf als inneres Erlebnis* (new edn., Berlin, 1925).

——, *Der Arbeiter* (1932), in *Werke*, vi (Stuttgart, 1964).

——, *Strahlungen* (2 vols., Munich, 1964).

KAEBER, ERICH, *Berlin 1848* (Berlin, 1948).

KAMINSKI, KURT, *Verfassung und Verfassungskonflikt in Preußen 1862–66* (Königsberg and Berlin, 1938).

KARDORFF, S. VON, *Wilhelm von Kardorff* (Berlin, 1936).

KATER, MICHAEL H., 'Zur Soziographie der frühen NSDAP', *Vierteljahrshefte für Zeitgeschichte*, xix (1971).

——, 'Der NS-Studentenbund von 1926 bis 1928', *Vierteljahrshefte für Zeitgeschichte*, xxii (1974).

KEHR, ECKART, *Schlachtflottenbau und Parteipolitik 1894–1901* (Berlin, 1930).

——, *Economic Interest, Militarism and Foreign Policy: Essays*, ed. Gordon A. Craig (Berkeley, 1977).

KEIM, JEANETTE, *Forty Years of German-American Political Relations* (Philadelphia, 1919).

KENNEDY, PAUL M., 'German Colonial Expansion: Has the "Manipulated Social Imperialism" been Antedated?', *Past and Present*, 54 (1972).

——, *The Samoan Tangle: A Study in Anglo-German-American Relations, 1878–1900* (New York, 1974).

KENNEDY, ROBERT M., *The German Campaign in Poland* (Washington, 1956).

KENT, GEORGE O., *Arnim and Bismarck* (Oxford, 1968).

KERR, ALFRED, *Die Welt im Drama*, ed. Gerhard F. Hering (2nd edn., Cologne and Berlin, 1964).

KERSTEN, FELIX, *The Kersten Memoirs*, trans. from the German (New York, 1957).

KESSEL, EBERHARD, 'Seeckts politisches Programm von 1923', in Konrad Repgen and Stephen Skalweit (eds.), *Spiegel der Geschichte: Festgabe für Max Braubach* (Münster, 1964).

KESTEN, HERMANN, 'Brutstätte allen Unheils', *Die Zeit*, 22 Sept. 1961.

KESSLER, COUNT HARRY, *Walther Rathenau: His Life and Work* (New York, 1930).

——, *Tagebücher 1918–1937* (Frankfurt-on-Main, 1961).

KETTELER, BISCHOF, *Die Arbeiterfrage und das Christentum* (1864).

KEUDELL, R. VON, *Fürst und Fürstin Bismarck* (Leipzig, 1901).

KIAULEHN, WALTHER, *Berlin: Schicksal einer Weltstadt* (Munich and Berlin, 1958).

KILLY, WALTHER, 'Leichenrede auf eine Fakultät', *Die Zeit* (Hamburg), 28 June 1976.

KIMMICH, CHRISTOPH, *Germany and the League of Nations* (Chicago, 1976).

KIRKPATRICK, CLIFFORD, *Nazi Germany: Its Women and Family Life* (Indianapolis, 1938).

KIRKPATRICK, IVONE, *Mussolini: A Study in Power* (New York, 1964).

KITCHEN, MARTIN, *The German Officer Corps, 1890–1914* (Oxford, 1968).

——, 'Militarism and the Development of Fascist Ideology: The Political Ideas of Colonel Max Bauer, 1916–1918', *Central European History*, vii, no. 3 (Sept. 1975).

KLASS, GERT VON, *Stinnes* (Tübingen, 1958).

KLEE, PAUL, *Paul Klee in Selbstzeugnissen und Bilddokumenten*, ed. Carola Giedion-Welcker (Reinbeck bei Hamburg, 1961).

KLEIN, F. (ed.), *Politik im Krieg 1914–1918* (Berlin, 1964).

KLEIN-WUTTIG, ANNELIESE, *Politik und Kriegführung in den deutschen Einigungskriegen* (Berlin, 1934).

KLEMPERER, KLEMENS VON, *Germany's New Conservatism: Its History and Dilemma in the Twentieth Century* (Princeton, 1957).

KLIMERT, A. and H. P. BLEUEL, *Deutsche Studenten auf dem Weg ins Dritte Reich* (Gütersloh, 1967).

KLOSTER, W., *Der deutsche Generalstab und der Präventivkriegsgedanke* (Stuttgart, 1932).

KNESEBECK, G. VON DEM, *Die Wahrheit über den Propagandafeldzug und Deutschlands Zusammenbruch* (Munich, 1927).

KOCKA, JÜRGEN, 'The First World War and the *Mittelstand*: German Artisans and White Collar Workers', *Journal of Contemporary History*, viii, no. 1 (Jan. 1973).

KOEHL, ROBERT L., *RKFDV: German Resettlement and Population Policy, 1939–45* (Cambridge, Mass., 1957).

KÖHLER, HENNING, *Anatomiebewegung oder Separatismus: Die Politik der Kölnischen Volkszeitung, 1918–19* (Berlin, 1974).

KOGON, EUGEN, *The Theory and Practice of Hell: The German Concentration Camps and the System Behind Them* (New York, 1950).

KOHN-BRAMSTEDT, ERNST, *Aristocracy and the Middle Classes in Germany: Social Types in German Literature, 1830–1900* (London, 1937).

KOLB, EBERHARD, 'Bismarck und das Aufkommen der Annexionsforderung 1870', *Historische Zeitschrift*, 290 (Oct. 1969).

——, *Der Kriegsausbruch 1870: Politische Entscheidungsprozesse und Verantwortlichkeiten in der Julikrise 1870* (Göttingen, 1970).

KOLLMAN, ERIC C., 'Walther Rathenau and German Foreign Policy: Thoughts and Actions', *Journal of Modern History*, xxiv (1952).

KOPLIN, RAIMUND, *Carl von Ossietzky als politischer Publizist* (Berlin, 1964).

KORDT, ERICH, *Nicht aus den Akten* (Stuttgart, 1950).

KORTNER, FRITZ, *Aller Tage Abend* (Munich, 1959).

KRACAUER, SIEGFRIED, *From Caligari to Hitler: A Psychological History of the German Film* (Princeton, 1947).

KRAUS, KARL, *Die letzten Tage der Menschheit* (Zurich, 1945).

KRAUSNICK, HELMUT, *Holsteins Geheimpolitik in der Aera Bismarck* (2nd edn., Hamburg, 1942).

——, 'Holsteins großes Spiel im Frühjahr 1887', in *Geschichte und Gegenwartsbewußtsein: Festschrift für Hans Rothfels*, ed. W. Besson and F. Freiherr Hiller von Gärtringen (Göttingen, 1963).

KREUTZBERGER, WOLFGANG, *Studenten und Politik 1918–33: Der Fall Freiburg im Breisgau* (Göttingen, 1972).

Kriegstagebuch des Oberkommandos der Wehrmacht 1940–1945, i: *1940–1941*, ed. Hans-Adolf Jacobsen (Frankfurt-on-Main, 1965).

Kriegstagebuch des OKW, iv: *1944–1945*, ed. Percy Ernst Schramm (Frankfurt-on-Main, 1961).

KROCKOW, CHRISTIAN GRAF VON, *Die Entscheidung: Eine Untersuchung über Ernst Jünger, Carl Schmitt, Martin Heidegger* (Stuttgart, 1958).

KROSIGK, LUTZ GRAF SCHWERIN VON, *Es geschah in Deutschland: Menschenbilder unseres Jahrhunderts* (Tübingen, 1951).

KRUCK, ALFRED, *Geschichte des Alldeutschen Verbandes 1890–1939* (Wiesbaden, 1954).

KRÜGER, PETER, *Deutschland und die Reparationen 1918/1919. Die Genesis des Reparationsproblems in Deutschland zwischen Waffenstillstand und Versailler Friedensschluß (Stuttgart, 1973)*.

KUCZYNSKI, JÜRGEN, *Der Ausbruch des Ersten Weltkrieges und die deutsche Sozialdemokratie* (Berlin, 1957).

KÜHLMANN, RICHARD VON, *Erinnerungen* (Heidelberg, 1948).

KUHN, AUGUST, *Zeit zum Aufstehen: Eine Familienchronik* (Frankfurt-on-Main, 1975).

LABAND, PAUL, *Das Staatsrecht des Deutschen Reiches* (3rd rev. edn., 2 vols., Freiburg im Breisgau and Leipzig, 1895).

LAMBI, IVON N., *Free Trade and Protection in Germany, 1868–1879* (Wiesbaden, 1963).

LANCKEN-WACKENITZ, OSKAR VON DER, *Meine dreißig Dienstjahre 1888–1918* (Berlin, 1931).

LANE, BARBARA MILLER, *Architecture and Politics in Germany, 1918–1945* (Cambridge, 1968).

LANGE, ANNEMARIE, *Das Wilhelminische Berlin* (Berlin, 1967).

——, *Berlin zur Zeit Bebels und Bismarcks* (Berlin, 1972).

LANGE, HELENA, *Lebenserinnerungen* (Berlin, 1922).

LANGE, VICTOR, 'Ausdruck und Erkenntnis: Zur politischen Problematik der deutschen Literatur seit dem Expressionismus', *Die neue Rundschau* (1963).

LANGER, WILLIAM L., *The Franco-Russian Alliance, 1890–1894* (Cambridge, Mass., 1929).

——, *European Alliances and Alignments* (rev. edn., New York, 1950).

——, *The Dipomacy of Imperialism* (rev. edn., New York, 1951).

——, and S. Everett Gleason, *The Undeclared War, 1940–41* (New York, 1953).

Laqueur, Walter, *Young Germany: A History of the Youth Movement* (New York, 1962).

——, *Weimar: A Cultural History* (New York, 1975).

Laubach, Ernst, *Die Politik der Kabinette Wirth 1921/22* (Lübeck, 1968).

Leach, Barry A., *German Strategy against Russia, 1939–41* (Oxford, 1973).

Leber, Annedore (ed.), *Das Gewissen steht auf* (Berlin, 1954).

Leber, Julius, *Ein Mann geht seinen Weg: Schriften, Reden und Briefe von Julius Leber, herausgegeben von seinen Freunden* (Berlin-Schöneburg, 1952).

Lebovics, Hermann, *Social Conservatism and the Middle Classes in Germany, 1914–1933* (Princeton, 1969).

Lehmann, Fritz, *1933–1945: Beobachtungen und Bekenntnisse* (Hamburg, 1946).

Lehmann, Hartmut, 'Bodelschwingh und Bismarck: Christlich-Konservative Sozialpolitik im Kaiserreich', *Historische Zeitschrift*, 208 (1969).

Lehmann, K., 'Die Vorgeschichte der Krügerdepesche', *Archiv für Politik und Geschichte*, v (1925).

Leipart, Theodor, *Carl Legien, Ein Gedenkbuch* (Berlin, 1929).

——, *Zehn Jahre deutscher Geschichte, 1918–1928* (Berlin, 1928).

Leiser, Erwin, *Deutschland erwache! Propaganda im Film des Dritten Reiches* (Hamburg, 1968).

Lerchenfeld–Koefering, Hugo Graf, *Erinnerungen und Denkwürdigkeiten* (2nd edn., Berlin, 1935).

Lethen, Helmuth, *Die neue Sachlichkeit: Studien zur Literatur des 'Weißen Sozialismus'* (Stuttgart, 1970).

Les Lettres secrètes échangées par Hitler et Mussolini, intro. by André François-Poncet (Paris, 1946).

Liang, Hsi-Huey, *The Berlin Police Force in the Weimar Republic* (Berkeley, 1970).

Lichtheim, George, *Marxism: An Historical and Critical Study* (New York, 1961).

Liddell Hart, B. H., *The Other Side of the Hill* (rev. edn., London, 1951).

Lidtke, Vernon L., *The Outlawed Party: Social Democracy in Germany, 1878–1890* (Princeton, 1966).

Liebe, Werner, *Die Deutschnationale Volkspartei 1918–1924* (Düsseldorf, 1956).

Lipgens, Walter, 'Bismarck, die öffentliche Meinung, und die Annexion von Elsaß und Lothringen 1870', *Historische Zeitschrift*, 199 (1964).

Löwenthal, F., *Der preußische Verfassungsstreit 1862–66* (Altenburg, 1914).

Löwith, Karl, 'Max Weber und Carl Schmitt', *Frankfurter Allgemeine Zeitung*, 27 June 1964.

Löwy, Günther, *Die katholische Kirche und das Dritte Reich* (Munich, 1965).

Loftus, Lord Augustus, *Diplomatic Reminiscences* (2nd Ser., 2 vols., London, 1894).

LOHMEYER, H., *Die Politik des zweiten Reiches* (Berlin, 1939).

LORD, ROBERT H., *The Origins of the War of 1870* (Cambridge, 1924).

LOREY, HERMANN, *Der Krieg zur See 1914–1918: Der Krieg in den türkischen Gewässern* (2 vols., Berlin, 1928–38).

LOUGEE, ROBERT W., *Paul de Lagarde, 1827–1891: A Study of Radical Conservatives in Germany* (Cambridge, Mass., 1962).

LUDENDORFF, ERICH, *Meine Kriegserinnerungen* (Berlin, 1920).

——, *Urkunden der Obersten Heeresleitung* (2nd edn., Berlin, 1921).

——, *Mein militärischer Werdegang* (Munich, 1933).

LUKÁCS, GEORG, *Deutsche Literatur im Zeitalter des Imperialismus* (Berlin, 1946).

——, *Skizze einer Geschichte der neuen deutschen Literatur* (Berlin, 1953).

——, *Probleme des Realismus* (Berlin, 1955).

LUTHER, HANS, *Politiker ohne Partei: Erinnerungen* (Stuttgart, 1960).

LUTZ, R. H. (ed.), *The Fall of the German Empire* (2 vols., Stanford, 1932).

MACARTNEY, C. A., *October Fifteenth: A History of Modern Hungary* (2 vols., Edinburgh, 1956).

McSHERRY, JAMES E., *Stalin, Hitler and Europe, 1933–39: The Origins of World War II* (Cleveland and Toronto, 1968).

MAIER, CHARLES J., *Recasting Bourgeois Europe: Stabilization in France, Germany and Italy in the Decade after World War I* (Princeton, 1975).

Makers of Modern Strategy: Military Thought from Machiavelli to Hitler, ed. Edward Mead Earle in collaboration with Gordon A. Craig and Felix Gilbert (Princeton, 1943).

MANN, HEINRICH, *Essays* (Berlin, 1960).

MANN, KLAUS, *Heute und Morgen* (Hamburg, 1927).

——, *Prüfungen, Schriften zur Literatur*, ed Martin Gregor-Dellin, i (Munich, 1968).

MANN, THOMAS, *Betrachtungen eines Unpolitischen* (1918; new edn., Frankfurt-on-Main, 1956).

——, *Reden und Aufsätze* (2 vols., Oldenburg, 1965).

MANSERGH, NICHOLAS, *The Coming of the First World War: A Study in the European Balance* (London, 1949).

MANSTEIN, ERICH VON, *Verlorene Siege* (Bonn, 1955).

MARKS, SALLY, 'Reparations Re-Considered: A Rejoinder', *Central European History*, v, no. 4 (Dec. 1972).

MARX, WILHELM, *Der Nachlass des Reichskanzlers Wilhelm Marx*, ed. Hugo Stehkämper (4 vols., Cologne, 1968).

MASON, TIMOTHY W., *Arbeiterklasse und Volksgemeinschaft: Dokumente und Materialien zur deutschen Arbeiterpolitik 1936–1939* (Opladen, 1975).

——, 'Women in Germany, 1925–1940: Family, Welfare and Work', *History Workshop*, Issue 1 (spring 1976).

MASSING, PAUL W., *Rehearsal for Destruction: A Study of Political Anti-Semitism in Imperial Germany* (New York, 1949).

MATTHIAS, ERIC, 'Der Untergang der alten Sozialdemokratie', *Vierteljahrshefte für Zeitgeschichte*, iv, Hefte 2, 3 (1956).

MAXWELL-HAMILTON, JAMES, *Motive for a Mission* (London, 1971).

MAY, ARTHUR J., *The Passing of the Habsburg Monarchy* (2 vols., New York, 1966).

MAYER, ARNO J., *Politics and Diplomacy of Peacemaking. Containment and Counterrevolution at Versailles, 1918–1919* (New York, 1968).

MAYER, MICHAEL, 'The Nazi Musicologist as Myth Maker in the Third Reich', *Journal of Contemporary History*, x, no. 4 (Oct. 1975).

MEDLICOTT, W. N., *The Congress of Berlin and After* (London, 1938).

——, *Bismarck and Modern Germany* (London, 1965).

MEHRING, FRANZ, *Briefe an Freunde* (Zurich, 1950).

——, *Aufsätze zur deutschen Literaturgeschichte*, ed. Hans Koch (2nd edn., Leipzig, 1961).

——, *Gesammelte Schriften*, ed. Thomas Höhle, Hans Koch, and Josef Schleifstein (15 vols., Berlin, 1960–7).

MEIER-WELCKER, HANS, *Seeckt* (Frankfurt-on-Main, 1967).

MEINECKE, FRIEDRICH, *Erlebtes 1862–1901* (Leipzig, 1941).

——, *Die deutsche Katastrophe: Betrachtungen und Erinnerungen* (3rd edn., Wiesbaden, 1947).

——, *Straßburg, Freiburg, Berlin 1901–1919: Erinnerungen* (Stuttgart, 1949).

——, *Ausgewählter Briefwechsel*, ed. Ludwig Dehio and Peter Classen (Stuttgart, 1962).

——, *Die Idee der Staatsraison* (3rd edn., Munich, 1963).

MEISNER, H. O., 'Militärkabinett, Kriegsminister und Reichskanzler zur Zeit Wilhelms I', *Forschungen zur brandenburgischen und preußischen Geschichte,* I (1935).

——, *Der Kriegsminister 1814–1914, ein Beitrag zur militärischen Verfassungsgeschichte* (Berlin, 1940).

——, 'Der Reichskanzler Caprivi', *Zeitschrift für die gesamte Staatswissenschaft*, iii (1955).

MEISSNER, HANS OTTO and HARRY WILDE, *Die Machtergreifung: Ein Bericht über die Technik des nationalsozialistischen Staatsstreichs* (Stuttgart, 1958).

MEISSNER, OTTO, *Staatssekretär unter Ebert–Hindenburg–Hitler: Der Schicksalsweg des deutschen Volkes von 1918–1945, wie ich ihn erlebte* (Hamburg, 1951).

Meldungen aus dem Reich: Auswahl aus den geheimen Lageberichten des Sicherheitsdienstes der SS 1931–1944, ed. Heinz Boberach (Neuwied and Berlin, 1965).

MENDELSSOHN, PETER DE, *Zeitungsstadt Berlin: Menschen und Mächte in der Geschichte der deutschen Presse* (Berlin, 1959).

MENDELSSOHN-BARTHOLDY, ALBRECHT, *The War and German Society. The Testament of a Liberal* (New Haven, 1937).

MEYER, ARNOLD OSKAR, *Bismarck. Der Mensch und der Staatsmann* (Stuttgart, 1949).

MEYER, HENRY CORD, *Mitteleuropa in German Thought and Action, 1815–1945* (The Hague, 1955).

MICHAELIS, GEORG, *Für Staat und Volk* (Berlin, 1922).

MIDDLEMAS, KEITH and JOHN BARNES, *Baldwin: A Biography* (London, 1969).

MILLER, MAX, *Eugen Bolz, Staatsmann und Erkenner* (Stuttgart, 1951).

MILLMAN, RICHARD, *British Foreign Policy and the Coming of the Franco-Prussian War* (Oxford, 1965).

MILWARD, ALAN S., *The German Economy at War* (London, 1965).

MINDER, ROBERT, *Kultur und Literatur in Deutschland und Frankreich* (Frankfurt-on-Main, 1962).

——, *Dichter in der Gesellschaft. Erfahrungen mit deutscher und französischer Literatur* (Frankfurt-on-Main, 1966).

——, *'Hölderlin unter den Deutschen' und andere Aufsätze* (Frankfurt-on-Main, 1966).

MITCHELL, ALLAN, *Revolution in Bavaria, 1918–1919: The Eisner Regime and the Soviet Republic* (Princeton, 1965).

——, *Bismarck and the French Nation, 1848–1890* (New York, 1971).

MITTIG, HANS-ERNST, 'Zu Joseph Ernst von Bandels Hermannsdenkmal im Teutoburger Wald', *Lippische Mitteilungen aus Geschichte und Landeskunde*, xxvii (1968).

MITTNACHT, FREIHERR VON, *Erinnerungen an Bismarck* (Leipzig, 1904).

——, *Erinnerungen an Bismarck. Neue Folge* (Berlin, 1905).

MITZMAN, ARTHUR, *The Iron Cage: An Historical Interpretation of Max Weber* (New York, 1970).

MOELLER VAN DEN BRUCK, ARTHUR, *Das Dritte Reich* (3rd edn., Hamburg, 1931).

MOHLER, ARMIN, *Die konservative Revolution in Deutschland 1918–1932: Grundriss ihrer Weltanschauungen* (Stuttgart, 1950).

MOLTKE, FELDMARSCHALL HELMUTH, GRAF VON, *Militärische Werke* (Berlin, 1892–1912).

——, *Die deutschen Aufmarschpläne*, ed. Ferdinand von Schmerfeld (Forschungen und Darstellungen aus dem Reichsarchiv, Heft 7, Berlin, 1929.

MOLTKE, FELDMARSCHALL H. J. L. GRAF, *Erinnerungen, Briefe, Dokumente* (Stuttgart, 1922).

MOMMSEN, HANS, *Beamtentum im Dritten Reich* (Stuttgart, 1966).

——, 'Der Reichstagsbrand und seine politischen Folgen', *Vierteljahrshefte für Zeitgeschichte*, xii, Heft 4 (1904).

MOMMSEN, WOLFGANG, *Deutsche Parteiprogramme* (Munich, 1960).

MOMMSEN, WOLFGANG J., 'The Debate on German War Aims', *Journal of Contemporary History*, i. no. 3 (1966).

——, *Max Weber und die deutsche Politik 1890–1920* (Tübingen, 1969).

——, 'Die deutsche "Weltpolitik" und der Erste Weltkrieg', *Neue politische Literatur*, xvi (1971).

——, 'Domestic Factors in German Foreign Policy before 1914', *Central European History*, vi, no. 1 (Mar. 1973).

MONTS, A. GRAF VON, *Erinnerungen und Gedanken*, ed. K. Nowak and F. Thimm (Berlin, 1932).

MOOREHEAD, ALAN, *Gallipoli* (New York, 1956).

MORGAN, DAVID W., *The Socialist Left and the German Revolution: A History of the German Independent Social Democratic Party, 1917–1922* (Ithaca and New York, 1975).

MORGAN, J. H., *Assize of Arms: The Disarmament of Germany and her Rearmament, 1919–1939* (New York, 1946).

MORGAN, R. F., *The German Social Democrats and the First International, 1864–1872* (Cambridge, 1965).

MORK, GORDON R., 'The Prussian Railway Scandal of 1873: Economics and Politics in the German Empire', *European Studies Review*, i (1971).

MORSEY, RUDOLF, *Die deutsche Zentrumspartei 1917–1923* (Düsseldorf, 1966).

MORSEY, R. and E. MATTHIAS (eds.), *Das Ende der Parteien 1933* (Düsseldorf, 1960).

MOSSE, GEORGE L., *The Crisis of German Ideology: Intellectual Origins of the Third Reich* (New York, 1964).

——, *Germans and Jews* (New York, 1970).

——, *The Nationalization of the Masses: Political Symbolism and Mass Movements in Germany from the Napoleonic Wars through the Third Reich* (New York, 1975).

——, (ed.), *Nazi Culture* (New York, 1966).

MOULTON, HAROLD G., *The Reparation Plan. An Interpretation of the Reports of the Expert Committees Appointed by the Reparations Commission* (new edn., Westport, 1970).

MÜLLER, GEORG ALEXANDER VON, *Regierte der Kaiser? Kriegstagebücher, Aufzeichnungen und Briefe des Chefs des Marine-Kabinetts Admiral Georg Alexander von Müller 1914–1918*, ed. Walter Görlitz (Göttingen, 1959).

——, *Der Kaiser . . . Aufzeichungen des Chefs des Marinekabinetts Admiral Georg Alexander von Müller über die Ära Wilhelms II*, ed. W. Görlitz (Göttingen, 1965).

MÜLLER, HANS (ed.), *Katholische Kirche und Nationalsozialismus: Dokumente* (Munich, 1966).

MÜLLER, KLAUS-JÜRGEN, 'Reichswehr und Röhm-Affäre', in *Militargeschichtliche Mitteilungen*, xix, no. 8 (25 Aug. 1934).

MÜLLER-BRANDENBURG, H., *Von Schlieffen bis Ludendorff* (Leipzig, 1925).

MÜLLER-HILLEBRAND, B., *Das Heer 1935–45*, i (Darmstadt, 1954).

MURALT, LEONHARD VON, *Bismarcks Verantwortlichkeit* (Göttingen, 1955).

MUSCHG, WALTER, *Die Zerstörung der deutschen Literatur* (3rd edn., Berne and Munich, n.d.).

MUTH, HEINRICH, 'Carl Schmitt in der deutschen Innenpolitik des Sommers 1932', *Historische Zeitschrift*, Beiheft I (1971).

MYERS, BERNARD S., *The German Expressionists: A Generation in Revolt* (concise edn., New York, 1966).

Nationalism and Internationalism: Essays Inscribed to Carleton J. H. Hayes, ed. Edward Mead Earle (New York, 1950).

NAUJOKS, EBERHARD, 'Bismarck und die Organisation der Regierungspresse', *Historische Zeitschrift*, 205 (1967).

NAUMANN, FRIEDRICH, *Demokratie und Kaisertum* (Berlin, 1900).

NETTL, J. P., *Rosa Luxemburg* (2 vols., London, 1966).

NEUMANN, FRANZ, *Behemoth: The Structure and Practice of National Socialism* (2nd edn., New York, 1944).

NEUMANN, SIGMUND, *Die Parteien der Weimarer Republik* (new edn., Stuttgart, 1965).

NICHOLS, J. ALDEN, *Germany after Bismarck: The Caprivi Era, 1890–1894* (Cambridge, 1958).

NICOLSON, HAROLD, *Portrait of a Diplomatist* (New York, 1930).

——, *Curzon: The Last Phase, 1919–1925* (new edn., New York, 1939).

NIETZSCHE, FRIEDRICH, *Götzendämmerung* (Kröner edn., Stuttgart, 1964).

——, *Unzeitgemäße Betrachtungen* (Kröner edn., Stuttgart, 1964).

NIPPERDEY, THOMAS, 'Nationalidee und Nationaldenkmal in Deutschland', *Historische Zeitschrift*, 206 (1968).

NOAKES, JEREMY, 'Conflict and Development in the NSDAP, 1924–1927', *Journal of Contemporary History*, i, no. 4 (1966).

NOSKE, GUSTAV, *Aufstieg und Niedergang der deutschen Sozialdemokratie. Erlebtes* (Zurich and Offenbach, 1947).

NURENBERGER, R., 'Imperialismus, Sozialismus und Christentum bei Friedrich Naumann', *Historische Zeitschrift*, 170 (1950).

NUSCHKE, OTTO, 'Wie die Demokratische Partei wurde', *Zehn Jahre Deutscher Republik*, ed. Anton Erkelenz (Berlin, 1928).

Österreich-Ungarns letzter Krieg 1914–1918, bearbeitet im Österreichischen Bundesministerium für Heereswesen und Kriegsarchiv (Vienna, 1931).

OLDEN, RUDOLF, *Stresemann* (Berlin, 1929).

——, *History of Liberty in Germany* (London, 1946).

ONCKEN, HERMANN, *Rudolf von Bennigsen* (2 vols., Stuttgart, 1910).

——, *Die Rheinpolitik Kaiser Napoleons III von 1863 bis 1870 und der Ursprung des Krieges von 1870/71* (3 vols., Stuttgart, 1926).

O'NEILL, ROBERT J., *The German Army and the Nazi Party 1933–39* (London, 1966).

Les Origines diplomatiques de la guerre de 1870/71. Recueil de documents publié par le Ministre des affaires étrangères (29 vols., Paris, 1910–32).

ORLOW, DIETRICH, *History of the Nazi Party, 1919–1933* (Pittsburgh, 1969).

OSTWALD, HANS, *Sittengeschichte der Inflation: Ein Kulturdokument aus den Jahren des Marksturzes* (Berlin, 1931).

PAPEN, FRANZ VON, *Memoirs*, trans. Brian Connell (London, 1952).

PARKER, R. A. C., 'The First Capitulation: France and the Rhineland Crisis of 1936', *World Politics* (1951).

PASTENACI, KURT, 'Der Jungdeutsche Orden und die deutsche Jugendbewegung', *Süddeutsche Monatshefte*, xxxv (1926).

PAULSEN, FRIEDRICH, *The German Universities and University Study*, trans. from the German, (New York, 1906).

——, *An Autobiography*, trans. from the German (New York, 1938).

PERETT, GREGORY, 'French Naval Policy and Foreign Policy, 1930–39' (Dissertation, Stanford Univ. 1977).

PERLMAN, SELIG, *A Theory of the Labor Movement* (New York, 1928).

PETERSON, EDWARD N., *The Limits of Hitler's Power* (Princeton, 1969).

PETROW, RICHARD, *The Bitter Years: The Invasion and Occupation of Denmark and Norway* (New York, 1974).

PETZINA, DIETER, *Autarkiepolitik im Dritten Reich: Der nationalsozialistische Vierjahrsplan* (Stuttgart, 1968).

PFLANZE, OTTO, *Bismarck and the Development of Germany: The Period of Unification, 1815–1871* (Princeton, 1963).

PHELPS, REGINALD H., 'Aus den Seeckt-Dokumenten: Die Verabschiedung Seeckts 1926', *Deutsche Rundschau* (Sept. 1952).

PHILIPPI, HANS, 'Zur Geschichte des Welfenfonds', *Niedersächsiche Jahrbücher für Landesgeschichte*, 31 (1959).

PICKER, HENRY, *Hitlers Tischgespräche im Führerhauptquartier 1941–42*, ed. Percy Ernst Schramm (Stuttgart, 1963).

PÖLS, WERNER, *Sozialistenfrage und Revolutionsfurcht in ihrem Zusammenhang mit der angeblichen Staatsstreichplänen Bismarcks* (Lübeck and Hamburg, 1960).

POIS, ROBERT A., 'The Bourgeois Democrats of Weimar Germany', *Transactions of the American Philosophical Society*, N.S. 66, pt. 4 (1976).

POST, GAINES, JUN., *The Civil-Military Fabric of Weimar Foreign Policy* (Princeton, 1973).

PROSS, HARRY, *Vor und nach Hitler* (Olten and Freiburg im Breisgau, 1962).

——, *Jugend, Eros, Politik* (Berne and Munich, 1964).

——, (ed.), *Die Zerstörung der deutschen Politik: Dokumente 1871–1933* (Frankfurt-on-Main, 1959).

PUHLE, HANS-JÜRGEN, *Agrarische Interessenpolitik und Preussischer Konservatismus im Wilhelminischen Reich: Ein Beitrag zur Analyse des Nationalismus in Deutschland am Beispiel des Bundes der Landwirte und der Deutsch-Konservativen Partei* (Hanover, 1966).

PULZER, PETER G. J., *The Rise of Political Anti-Semitism in Germany and Austria* (New York, 1964).

PUTTKAMMER, ELLINOR VON (ed.), *Föderative Elemente im deutschen Staatsrecht seit 1648* (Göttingen, 1955).

RABINBACH, ANSON G., 'The Aesthetics of Production in the Third Reich', *Journal of Contemporary History*, xi, no. 4 (Oct. 1976).

RADBRUCH, GUSTAV, *Der innere Weg* (Stuttgart, 1951).

RADOWITZ, J. M. VON, *Aufzeichungen und Erinnerungen aus dem Leben des Botschafters J. M. von Radowitz*, ed. Hajo Holborn (2 vols., Stuttgart, 1925).

RAHN, RUDOLF, *Ruheloses Leben* (Düsseldorf, 1950).

RASCHDAU, LUDWIG, *Unter Bismarck und Caprivi, Erinnerungen eines deutschen Diplomaten aus den Jahren 1885–1894* (2nd edn., Berlin, 1939).

RASSOW, PETER, 'Schlieffen und Holstein', *Historische Zeitschrift*, 173 (1952).

RATHENAU, WALTHER, *Gesammelte Reden* (Berlin, 1924).

RATHMANN, LOTHAR, *Berlin–Baghdad* (Berlin, 1962).

RAUSCHNING, HERMANN, *The Revolution of Nihilism* (New York, 1939).

REGELE, OSKAR, *Feldmarschall Conrad, Auftrag und Erfüllung 1906–1918* (Vienna and Munich, 1955).

REICHSARCHIV, *Der Weltkrieg 1914–1918* (12 vols., Berlin, 1925–39).

——, *Kriegsrüstung und Kriegswirtschaft* (Berlin, 1930).

REIN, G. A., *Die Revolution in der Politik Bismarcks* (Göttingen, 1957).

REINHARDT, WALTHER, *Aus dem Nachlass des Generals Walther Reinhardt*, ed. Fritz Ernst (Stuttgart, 1958).

REITLINGER, GERALD, *SS: Alibi of a Nation, 1922–45* (New York, 1957).

——, *The House Built on Sand: The Conflicts of German Policy on Russia, 1939–45* (New York, 1960).

REMAK, JOACHIM, '1914—The Third Balkan War: Origins Reconsidered', *Journal of Modern History*, xliii (Sept. 1971).

RENOUVIN, PIERRE, *Histoire des relations internationales*, v: *Le XIXe siècle* 1: *De 1815 à 1871* (Paris, 1954).

RIBBENTROP, JOACHIM VON, *Zwischen London und Moskau. Erinnerungen und letzte Aufzeichnungen* (Leoni, 1953).

RICH, NORMAN, 'Holstein and the Arnim Affair', *Journal of Modern History*, xxviii (1956).

——, *Friedrich von Holstein: Politics and Diplomacy in the Era of Bismarck and William II* (2 vols., Cambridge, 1965).

——, *Hitler's War Aims: Ideology, the Nazi State, and the Course of Expansion* (2 vols., New York, 1973).

RICHTER, WERNER, *Bismarck* (Frankfurt-on-Main, 1962).

RIEZLER, KURT, *Tagebücher, Aufsätze, Dokumente*, ed. Karl Dietrich Erdmann (Göttingen, 1972).

RINGER, FRITZ, K., 'Higher Education in Germany in the Nineteenth Century', *Journal of Contemporary History*, ii (1967).

——, *The Decline of the German Mandarins: The German Academic Community, 1890–1933* (Cambridge, Mass., 1969).

——, (ed.), *The German Inflation of 1923* (New York, 1969).

RITCHIE, J. M., *Gottfried Benn: The Unreconstructed Expressionist* (London, 1972).

RITTER, GERHARD, 'Die Entstehung der Indemnitätsvorlage von 1866', *Historische Zeitschrift*, 114 (1915), 17–64.

——, *Staatskunst und Kriegshandwerk: Das Problem des 'Militarismus' im Deutschland* (4 vols., Munich, 1954 ff.).

——, *Carl Goerdeler und die deutsche Widerstandsbewegung* (Stuttgart, 1956).

——, *Der Schlieffenplan: Kritik eines Mythos* (Munich, 1956).

RITTER, GERHARD A., *Die Arbeiterbewegung im Wilhelminischen Reich: Die Sozialdemokratische Partei und die Freien Gewerkschaften 1890–1900* (Berlin, 1959).

——, and SUSAN MILLER (eds.), *Die deutsche Revolution 1918–1919* (Frankfurt-on-Main, 1968).

RITTER, GERHARD A., and JÜRGEN KOCKA (eds.), *Deutsche Sozialgeschichte: Dokumente und Skizzen. Bild II: 1870–1914* (Munich, 1974).

RITTER, GERHARD A., GEORG KOTOWSKI, and WERNER PÖLS (eds.), *Das Wilhelminische Deutschland: Stimmen der Zeitgenossen* (Frankfurt-on-Main and Hamburg, 1965).

ROCHS, HUGO, *Schlieffen. Ein Lebens-und Charakterbild für das deutsche Volk* (5th edn., Berlin, 1940).

RÖHL, JOHN C. G., 'Admiral von Mueller and the Approach to War', *Historical Journal*, xii (1966).

——, *Germany without Bismarck: The Crisis of Government in the Second Reich, 1890–1900* (Berkeley, 1967).

——, 'Staatsstreichplan oder Staatsstreichbereitschaft? Bismarcks Politik in der Entlassungskrise', *Historische Zeitschrift*, 203 (1966).

ROGGE, HELMUTH, *Holstein und Hohenlohe* (Stuttgart, 1957).

ROGGENBACH, FRANZ VON, *Im Ring der Gegner Bismarcks: Politische Briefe*

Franz von Roggenbachs 1865–96, ed. Julius Heyderhoff (2nd edn., Leipzig, 1943).

ROHE, FRANZ, *German Art in the Twentieth Century* (London, 1968).

ROHE, KARL, *Das Reichsbanner Schwarz-Rot-Gold* (Düsseldorf, 1966).

ROLOFF, GUSTAV, 'Bismarcks Friedensschlusse mit den Süddeutschen 1866', *Historische Zeitschrift*, 146 (1932), 1–70.

ROMOSER, GEORGE K., 'The Politics of Uncertainty', *Social Research*, xxxi (1964).

ROON, ALBRECHT GRAF VON, *Denkwürdigkeiten* (3rd edn., 3 vols., Berlin, 1905).

ROSENBERG, ARTHUR, *Geschichte der Weimarer Republik*, ed. Kurt Kersten (Frankfurt-on-Main, 1961).

ROSENBERG, HANS, *Grosse Depression und Bismarckzeit: Wirtschaftsablauf. Gesellschaft und Politik in Mitteleuropa* (Berlin, 1967).

ROTH, GÜNTHER, *The Social Democrats in Imperial Germany: A Study in Working Class Isolation and National Integration* (Totowa, N.J., 1963).

ROTHENBURG, GUNTHER E., *The Army of Francis Joseph* (West Lafayette, Ind. 1976).

ROTHFELS, HANS, *Theodor Lohmann und die Kampfjahre der staatlichen Sozialpolitik* (Berlin, 1927).

——, *Bismarck und der Staat: Ausgewählte Dokumente* (2nd edn., Stuttgart, 1954).

ROTHFRITZ, HERBERT, *Die Politik des preußischen Botschafters Grafen Robert von der Goltz in Paris 1863–69* (Berlin, 1934).

RÜDT VON COLLENBERG, L. K. G. W., *Die deutsche Armee von 1871 bis 1914* (Forschungen und Darstellungen aus dem Reichsarchiv, Heft 4, Berlin, 1922).

RÜHLE, JÜRGEN, *Literatur und Revolution: Schriftsteller und Kommunismus* (Cologne and Berlin, 1960).

——, *Theater und Revolution* (Munich, 1963).

RUMPF, HANS, *The Bombing of Germany*, trans. from the German (London, 1963).

RUPIEPER, HERMANN-JOSEF, 'Politics and Economics: The Cuno Government and Reparations, 1922–1923' (Dissertation, Stanford Univ. 1974).

SACHSE, ARNOLD, *Althoff und sein Werk* (Berlin, 1928).

SAGAVE, PIERRE-PAUL, *1871: Berlin–Paris, Reichshauptstadt und Haupstadt der Welt* (Frankfurt-on-Main, 1971).

SALANDRA, A., *Italy and the Great War: From Neutrality to Intervention* (London, 1932).

SALEWSKI, MICHAEL, *Entwaffnung und Militärkontrolle in Deutschland 1919–1927* (Munich, 1966).

——, 'Zur deutschen Sicherheitspolitik in der Spätzeit der Weimarer Republik', *Vierteljahrshefte für Zeitgeschichte*, xxii (1974).

SAMMONS, JEFFREY L., *Heinrich Heine, the Elusive Poet* (New Haven, 1969).

SAMUEL, R. H., and R. HINTON THOMAS, *Education and Society in Modern Germany* (London, 1949).

SAUER, WOLFGANG, 'Das Problem des deutschen Nationalstaates', in *Moderne deutsche Sozialgeschichte*, ed. Hans-Ulrich Wehler (Cologne and Berlin, 1966).

SCHACHT, HJALMAR GREELEY, *Das Ende der Reparationen* (Oldenburg, 1931).

——, *Confessions of 'The Old Wizard'* (Boston, 1956).

SCHÄFER, WOLFGANG, *NSDAP, Entwicklung und Struktur der Staatspartei des Dritten Reiches* (Morburg, 1957).

SCHARLAU, W., 'Goerdeler und Beck waren Romantiker', *Die Zeit*, 14 June 1966.

SCHEELE, GODFREY, *The Weimar Republik: Overture to the Third Reich* (London, 1946).

SCHEIDEMANN, PHILIPP, *Memoiren* (2 vols., Dresden, 1928).

SCHELLENBERG, W., *The Labyrinth*, trans. from the German (New York, 1956).

SCHENK, ERWIN, *Der Fall Zabern* (Stuttgart, 1927).

SCHIEDER, THEODOR, *Das deutsche Kaiserreich von 1871 als Nationalstaat* (Cologne, 1961).

——, 'Die Enstehungsgeschichte des Rapallo Vertrages', *Historische Zeitschrift*, 204 (1967).

——, (ed.), *Erster Weltkrieg. Ursachen, Entstehung und Kriegsziele* (Cologne and Berlin, 1969).

SCHIFFER, EUGEN, *Die deutsche Justiz* (Berlin, 1928).

SCHLIEFFEN, GENERALFELDMARSCHALL GRAF ALFRED, *Briefe* (Göttingen, 1958).

SCHLÖZER, KURD VON, *Petersburger Briefe*, ed. Leopold von Schlözer (Stuttgart, 1921).

——, *Letzte römische Briefe*, ed. L. von Schlözer (Stuttgart, 1924).

SCHMIDT, PAUL, *Statist auf diplomatischer Bühne 1923–45* (Bonn, 1949).

SCHMIDT-BÜCKEBURG, R., *Das Militärkabinett der preußischen Könige und deutschen Kaiser* (Berlin, 1933).

SCHMITT, BERNADOTTE, *The Coming of the War 1914* (2 vols., New York, 1930).

SCHMITT, CARL, *Der Begriff des Politischen* (Hamburg, 1932).

SCHOENBAUM, DAVID, *Hitler's Social Revolution: Class and Status in Nazi Germany, 1933–39* (New York, 1967).

SCHORSKE, CARL W., *German Social Democracy, 1905–1917* (Cambridge, 1955).

SCHRAMM, WILHELM RITTER VON, *Beck und Goedeler: Gemeinschaftsdokumente für den Frieden 1941–1944* (Munich, 1966).

SCHROEDER, PAUL W., 'World War I as Galloping Gertie: A Reply to Joachin Remak', *Journal of Modern History*, xliv, no. 3 (Sept. 1972).

SCHRÖTER, HEINZ, *Stalingrad* (Osnabrück, 1952).

SCHUBERT, GÜNTHER. *Anfänge nationalsozialistischer Aussenpolitik* (Cologne, 1963).

SCHÜDDEKOPF, OTTO-ERNST, *Das Heer und die Republik: Quellen zur Politik der Reichswehrführung 1918 bis 1933* (Hanover and Frankfurt-on-Main, 1955).

——, *Linke Leute von Rechts: Die nationalrevolutionären Minderheiten und die Weimarer Republik* (Stuttgart, 1960).

SCHÜSSLER, WILHELM, *Die Daily-Telegraph-Affaire: Fürst Bülow, Kaiser Wilhelm und die Krise des zweiten Reiches 1908* (Göttingen, 1952).

SCHUMANN, HANS-GERD, *Nationalsozialismus und Gewerkschaftsbewegung* (Hanover, 1958).

SCHWABE, KLAUS, 'Die deutschen Professoren und die politischen Grundfragen des Ersten Weltkrieges' (Dissertation, Philosophische Fakultät, Albert Ludwigs Universität, Freiburg im Breisgau, 1958).

——, 'Zur politischen Haltung der deutschen Professoren im Ersten Weltkrieg', *Historische Zeitschrift*, 193 (1961).

SCHWARZ, HANS-PETER, *Der konservative Anarchist: Politik und Zeitchronik Ernst Jüngers* (Freiburg im Breisgau, 1962).

SCHWEINITZ, H. L. VON, *Denkwürdigkeiten*, ed. W. von Schweinitz (2 vols., Berlin, 1927).

——, *Briefwechsel*, ed. W. von Schweinitz (Berlin, 1928).

SCHWEND, KARL, *Bayern zwischen Monarchie und Diktatur* (Munich, 1954).

SCOTT, WILLIAM E., *Alliance against Hitler: The Origins of the Franco-Soviet Pact* (Durham, N.C., 1962).

SEABURY, PAUL, *The Wilhelmstraße* (Berkeley, 1954).

SEVERING, CARL, *Mein Lebensweg* (2 vols., Cologne, 1950).

——, 'Zur innenpolitischen Lage in Deutschland im Herbst 1929', *Vierteljahrshefte für Zeitgeschichte*, viii (1960).

SHANAHAN, W. O. 'Friedrich Naumann: A German View of Power and Nationalism', *Nationalism and Internationalism: Essays Inscribed to Carlton J. H. Hayes*, ed. Edward Mead Earle (New York, 1950).

SHEEHAN, JAMES J., *The Career of Lujo Brentano: A Study of Liberalism and Social Reform in Imperial Germany* (Chicago, 1966).

——, 'Leadership in the German Reichstag, 1871–1918', *American Historical Review*, lxxiv (1968).

SHIRER, WILLIAM L., *Berlin Diary: The Journal of a Foreign Correspondent, 1934–41* (New York, 1941).

SIMON, W. M., *Germany in the Age of Bismarck* (New York, 1968).

SKIDELSKY, ROBERT, *Politicians and the Slump: the Labour Government of 1929–1931* (London, 1967).

SNOWDEN, PHILIP, *An Autobiography* (2 vols., London, 1934).

SNYDER, LOUIS L., 'Bismarck and the Lasker Revolution, 1884', *Review of Politics*, xxix, no. 1 (Jan. 1967).

SOERGEL, ALBERT and CURT HOHOFF, *Dichtung und Dichter der Zeit: Vom Naturalismus bis zur Gegenwart* (rev. edn., 2 vols., Düsseldorf, 1961).

SOMMER, THEO, *Deutschland und Japan zwischen den Mächten 1935–40* (Tübingen, 1962).

SONTAG, RAYMOND J., *Germany and England: The Background of Conflict, 1848–1894* (New York, 1939).

SONTHEIMER, KURT, *Anti-Demokratisches Denken in der Weimarer Republik* (Munich, 1962).

——, 'Anti-Demokratisches Denken in der Weimarer Republik', in Christian Gneuss (ed.), *Der Weg in die Diktatur* (Munich, 1962).

SPAHN, M., *Die päpstliche Friedensvermittlung* (Berlin, 1919).

SPEARS, SIR EDWARD, *Assignment to Catastrophe* (2 vols., London, 1954).

SPEER, ALBERT, *Inside the Third Reich: Memoirs* (New York, 1971).
——, *Spandau: The Secret Diaries*, trans. from the German (New York, 1977).
SPEIER, HANS, *Social Order and the Risks of War: Papers in Political Sociology* (New York, 1952).
SPENGLER, OSWALD, *The Decline of the West*, trans. Charles Francis Atkinson (2 vols., New York, 1926).
——, *Preußenthum und Sozialismus* (new edn., Munich, 1934).
——, *Briefe 1913–1936*, ed. Anton M. Koktanek and Manfred Schröter (Munich, 1963).
SPETHMANN, HANS, *Zwölf Jahre Ruhrbergbau 1914–1925* (4 vols., Berlin, 1930).
SPENZ, JÜRGEN, *Die diplomatische Vorgeschichte des Beitritts Deutschlands zum Völkerbund 1924–1926: Ein Beitrag zur Außenpolitik der Weimarer Republik* (Göttingen, 1966).
SPIDLE, JAKE WILTON, JUN., 'The German Colonial Service: Organization, Selection, and Training' (Dissertation, Stanford Univ. 1972).
SRBIK, H. RITTER VON, *Deutsche Einheit* (4 vols., Munich, 1935–42).
STAFF, ILSA, *Justiz im Dritten Reich* (Frankfurt-on-Main, 1964).
STAMBROOK, F. G., 'The German–Austrian Customs Union Project of 1931: A Study of German Methods and Motives', *Journal of Central European Affairs*, xxi (1961).
——, ' "Das Kind"—Lord d'Abernon and the Origins of the Locarno Pact', *Central European History*, i (1968).
STAMPFER, FRIEDRICH, *Die vierzehn Jahre der ersten deutschen Republik* (Karlsbad, 1936).
STEEFEL, LAWRENCE D., *Bismarck, the Hohenzollern Candidacy, and the Origins of the Franco-Prussian War of 1870* (Cambridge, Mass., 1962).
STEGMANN, DIRK, *Die Erben Bismarcks. Parteien und Verbände in der Spätphase des Wilhelminischen Deutschlands. Sammlungspolitik 1897–1918* (Cologne, 1970).
STEIN, GEORGE, *The Waffen-SS* (Ithaca, N.Y., 1966).
STEINBERG, JONATHAN, *Yesterday's Deterrent: Tirpitz and the Birth of the German Battle Fleet* (New York, 1965).
——, 'The Copenhagen Complex', *Journal of Contemporary History*, i, no. 3 (1966).
——, 'Germany and the Russo-Japanese War', *American Historical Review*, 74, no. 7 (Dec. 1970).
STEINER, ZARA, *The Foreign Office and Foreign Policy, 1898–1914* (Cambridge, 1969).
STEINERT, MARTIN G., *Hitlers Krieg und die Deutschen: Stimmung und Haltung der deutschen Bevölkerung im Zweiten Weltkrieg* (Düsseldorf and Vienna, 1970).
STERN, FRITZ, *The Politics of Cultural Despair: A Study in the Rise of the Germanic Ideology* (Berkeley, 1961).
——, 'Bethmann Hollweg and the War: The Limits of Responsibility', in Fritz Stern and Leonard Krieger (eds.), *The Responsibility of Power: Historical Essays in Honor of Hajo Holborn* (New York, 1967).

——, *The Failure of Illiberalism: Essays on the Political Culture of Modern Germany* (New York, 1972).

——, *Gold and Iron: Bismarck, Bleichröder and the Building of the German Empire* (New York, 1977).

STERN, J. P., *Re-Interpretations. Seven Studies in Nineteenth Century German Literature* (London, 1964).

STIEBER, DR., *Denkwürdigkeiten des Geheimen Regierungsrathes Dr. Stieber*, ed. L. Auerbach (Berlin, 1884).

STIMSON, HENRY L., *The Politics of Integrity: The Diaries of Henry L. Stimson, 1931–1945*, ed. Francis Loewenheim and Harold Langley (New York, 1978).

STEWART, J. M. G., *The Struggle for Crete* (London, 1967).

STOLFI, RUSSEL HENRY, 'Reality and Myth: French and German Preparations for War 1933–1940' (Dissertation, Stanford Univ. 1966).

——, 'Equipment for Victory in France 1940', *History*, i, no. 183 (1970).

STOLPER, GUSTAV, *German Economy, 1870–1940* (New York, 1940).

STONE, NORMAN, *The Eastern Front, 1914–1917* (New York, 1975).

——, 'Moltke–Conrad: Relations between the Austro-Hungarian and German General Staffs, 1909–1914', *The Historical Journal*, ix (1966).

STOSCH, ULRICH VON (ed.), *Denkwürdigkeiten des Generals und Admirals Albrecht von Stosch* (Stuttgart, 1904).

STRANDMANN, H. POGGE VON, 'Großindustrie und Rapallopolitik', *Historische Zeitschrift*, 222 (1976).

STRAUß, D. F., *Der alte und der neue Glaube* (5th edn., Bonn, 1873).

STRESEMANN, GUSTAV, *Vermächtnis*, ed. H. Bernhard (3 vols., Berlin, 1932–3).

STRUVE, WALTER, *Elites against Democracy: Leadership Ideals in Bourgeois Political Thought in Germany, 1890–1933* (Princeton, 1973).

STUDNITZ, HANS-GEORG VON, *Als Berlin brannte: Diarium der Jahre 1943–45* (2nd edn., Stuttgart, 1963).

STÜRMER, MICHAEL, *Koalition und Opposition in der Weimarer Republik 1924–1928* (Düsseldorf, 1967).

——, 'Staatsstreichgedanken im Bismarckreich', *Historische Zeitschrift*, 209 (1969).

——, *Bismarck und die preußisch-deutsche Politik* (Munich, 1970).

STURMTHAL, ADOLF, *The Tragedy of European Labor, 1918–1939* (New York, 1943).

SUMNER, B. H., *Russia and the Balkans, 1870–80* (Oxford, 1937).

SYLVESTER, A. J., *The Real Lloyd George* (London, 1947).

TAFFS, WINIFRED, *Lord Odo Russell* (London, 1938).

TAYLOR, A. J. P., *The Struggle for the Mastery of Europe, 1848–1918* (Oxford, 1954).

——, *The Origins of the Second World War* (New York, 1962).

TAYLOR, ROBERT R., *The Word in Stone: The Architecture of National Socialism* (Berkeley, 1974).

TAYLOR, TELFORD, *Sword and Swastika: Generals and Nazis in the Third Reich* (New York, 1952).

——, *The March of Conquest: The German Victories in Western Europe, 1940* (New York, 1958).

——, *The Breaking Wave: The Second World War in the Summer of 1940* (New York, 1967).

TEMPLEWOOD, VISCOUNT, *Nine Troubled Years* (London, 1954).

THIMME, ANNELIESE, 'Gustav Stresemann, Legende und Wirklichkeit', *Historische Zeitschrift*, 181 (1956).

——, *Gustav Stresemann, eine politische Biographie zur Geschichte der Weimarer Republik* (Hanover and Frankfurt-on-Main, 1957).

THIMME, FRIEDRICH, 'Die Krüger-Depesche', *Europäische Gespräche* (May–June 1924).

——, 'Botschafter und Militärattaché', *Europäische Gespräche*, viii (1930).

THIMME, H., *Weltkrieg ohne Waffen* (Stuttgart, 1932).

THOMAS, GEORG, *Georg Thomas, Geschichte der deutschen Wehr- und Rüstungswirtschaft 1918–1943–1945*, ed. Wolfgang Birkenfeld (Boppard, 1967).

THOMAS, HUGH, *The Spanish Civil War* (London, 1961).

THOMAS, R. HINTON and R. H. SAMUEL, *Education and Society in Germany* (London, 1949).

TIMES, THE, *History of The Times* (4 vols., New York, 1952).

TIMM, HELGA, *Die Deutsche Sozialpolitik und der Bruch der Grossen Koalition im März 1930* (Düsseldorf, 1952).

TIMS, R. W., *Germanizing the Poles: The H-K-T Society of the Eastern Marches, 1894–1914* (New York, 1941).

TIRPITZ, ADMIRAL VON, *Lebenserinnerungen* (Leipzig, 1920).

TOBIAS, F., *Der Reichstagsbrand. Legende und Wirklichkeit* (Rastatt, 1962).

TORMIN, WALTER, *Geschichte der deutschen Parteien seit 1848* (Stuttgart, 1966).

TOYNBEE, ARNOLD and VERONICA, *Survey of International Affairs, 1939–46: The Eve of War 1939* (London, 1958).

TREITSCHKE, HEINRICH VON, *Politik. Vorlesungen gehalten an der Universität zu Berlin*, ed. Max Cornicelius (2nd edn., 2 vols., Leipzig, 1899).

——, *Briefe*, ed. Max Cornicelius (3 vols., Leipzig, 1913–20).

——, *Aufsätze, Reden, Briefe* (4 vols., Berlin, 1929).

——, *History of Germany in the Nineteenth Century*, ed. Gordon A. Craig (Chicago, 1975).

TREUE, WILHELM, 'Ein General im Zwielicht', *Die Zeit*, 24 Jan. 1967.

TREVIRANUS, REINHOLD, *Das Ende von Weimar: Heinrich Brüning und seine Zeit* (Düsseldorf and Vienna, 1968).

TREVOR-ROPER, H. R. (ed.), *Blitzkrieg to Defeat: Hitler's War Directives, 1939–45* (New York, 1964).

TROELTSCH, ERNST, *Spektator-Briefe. Aufsätze über die deutsche Revolution und die Weltpolitik 1918–1922* (Tübingen, 1924).

TRUMPENER, ULRICH, *Germany and the Ottoman Empire, 1914–1918* (Princeton, 1968).

TUCHMAN, BARBARA W., *The Zimmermann Telegram* (New York, 1958).

TUCHOLSKY, KURT, *Ausgewählte Werke*, ed. Fritz J. Raddatz (2 vols., Hamburg, 1965).

TURNER, HENRY ASHBY, JUN., *Stresemann and the Politics of the Weimar Republic* (Princeton, 1963).
——, 'Bismarck's Imperialist Venture: Anti-British in Origin?', in *Britain and Germany in Africa: Imperial Rivalry and Colonial Rule*, ed. Prosser Gifford and William Roger Lewis (New Haven, 1967).
——, 'Big Business and the Rise of Hitler', *American Historical Review*, lxxv (1969).
——, 'Grossunternehmertum und Nationalsozialismus 1930–1933', *Historische Zeitschrift*, 221 (1975).
——, 'Stresemann und das Problem der Kontinuität in der deutschen Außenpolitik', in *Grundfragen der deutschen Außenpolitik seit 1871*, ed. Gilbert Ziebura (Darmstadt, 1975).

ULBRICHT, WALTER, *Zur Geschichte der deutschen Arbeiterbewegung* (Berlin, 1953).
Universitätstage 1966. Nationalsozialismus und die deutsche Universität, Veröffentlichung der Freien Universität Berlin (Berlin, 1966).
Die Ursachen des deutschen Zusammenbruches im Jahre 1918, das Werk des Untersuchungsausschusses der deutschen verfassunggebenden Nationalversammlung und des deutschen Reichtages 1919 bis 1928 (Berlin, 1920–9).

VAGTS, ALFRED, *A History of Militarism* (New York, 1939).
——, *The Military Attaché* (Princeton, 1967).
VALLENTIN, ANTONINA, *Stresemann. Vom Werden einer Staatsidee* (Leipzig, 1930).
VALTIN, JAN, *Out of the Night* (New York, 1941).
VANDREY, MAX, *Der politische Witz im Dritten Reich* (Munich, 1967).
VICTORIA, QUEEN, *Letters of Queen Victoria*, ed. G. E. Buckle (3rd Ser., London, 1930–2).
VIGENER, FRITZ, *Ketteler: Ein deutsches Bischofsleben im 19. Jahrhundert* (Munich and Berlin, 1924).
VOGELSANG, THILO, 'Hitlers Rede an die Generale vom 5. Februar 1933', *Vierteljahrshefte für Zeitgeschichte*, ii (1954).
——, *Reichswehr, Staat und NSDAP* (Stuttgart, 1962).
VOLKMANN, E. O., *Revolution über Deutschland* (Oldenburg, 1930).
VOLLMAR, GEORG, *Über die nächsten Aufgaben der Sozialdemokratie* (Munich, 1891).
VOSSLER, OTTO, 'Bismarcks Ethos', *Historische Zeitschrift*, 171 (1951).
——, 'Bismarcks Sozialpolitik', *Historische Zeitschrift*, 167 (1953).

WAGNER, EDUARD, *Der Generalquartiermeister. Briefe und Tagebuchaufzeichnungen des Generalquartiermeisters des Heeres, General der Artillerie Eduard Wagner*, ed. Elisabeth Wagner (Munich, 1963).
WAHL, ADALBERT, *Deutsche Geschichte von der Reichsgründung bis zum Ausbruch des Weltkrieges* (4 vols., Stuttgart, 1926–36).
WAITE, ROBERT G. L., *Vanguard of Nazism: The Free Corps Movement in Germany, 1918–1923* (Cambridge, Mass., 1952).

WALDERSEE, ALFRED GRAF VON, *Denkwürdigkeiten des Generalfeldmarschalls Alfred Grafen von Waldersee*, ed. H. O. Meisner (3 vols., Stuttgart, 1923–5).
——, *Aus dem Briefwechsel des Generalfeldmarschalls Alfred Grafen von Waldersee 1886–91*, ed. H. O. Meisner (Berlin, 1928).

WALTERS, F. P., *A History of the League of Nations* (2 vols., London, 1952).

WAMPACH, G., *Le Luxembourg neutre. Étude d'histoire diplomatique* (Paris, 1900).

WANDRUSZKA, ADAM, 'Zwischen Nikolsburg und Bad Ems', in *Reichsgründung 1870/71: Tatsachen, Kontroversen, Interpretationon*, ed. Ernst Deuerlein and Theodor Schieder (Stuttgart, 1970).

WARLIMONT, WALTER, *Inside Hitler's Headquarters 1939–45*, trans. from the German (New York, 1964).

WARNER, GEOFFREY, *Pierre Laval and the Eclipse of France* (London, 1968).

WATT, D. C., 'The Anglo-German Naval Agreement of 1935: An Interim Judgement', *Journal of Modern History*, xxviii. no. 2 (June 1956).

WEBER, MAX, *Grundriß der Sozialpolitik* (Tübingen, 1922).
——, *Gesammelte Politische Schriften* (3rd edn., Tübingen, 1971).

WEDEL, GRAF VON, *Zwischen Kaiser und Kanzler* (Leipzig, 1943).

WEHLER, HANS-ULRICH, 'Der Fall Zabern. Rückblick auf eine Verfassungskrise des Wilhelminischen Kaiserreiches', *Die Welt als Geschichte*, xxiii (1963).
——, *Bismarck und der Imperialismus* (Cologne and Berlin, 1969).
——, *Krisenherde des Kaiserreiches 1871–1918* (Göttingen, 1970).

WEINBERG, GERHARD L., *The Foreign Policy of Hitler's Germany: Diplomatic Revolution in Europe 1933–36* (Chicago, 1970).

WERMUTH, ADOLF, 'Das Reichsfinanzprogramm', *Deutsche Revue*, xxxvii (July 1912).
——, *Ein Beamtenleben* (Berlin, 1922).

WERNER, BRUNO, *Die Zwanziger Jahre von Morgens bis Mitternachts* (Munich, 1962).

WERTHEIMER, E. VON, 'Der Prozeß Arnim', *Preußische Jahrbücher*, ccxxii (1930).

WESTARP, GRAF, *Konservative Politik im letzten Jahrzehnt des Kaiserreiches* (2 vols., Berlin, 1935).

WHEELER-BENNETT, JOHN W., *Information on the Reparation Settlement, Being the Background and History of the Young Plan and the Hague Agreements, 1929–1930* (London, 1930).
——, *The Forgotten Peace: Brest Litovsk* (London, 1938).
——, *The Nemesis of Power: The Army in Politics, 1918–1945* (London, 1953).

WHITE, ANDREW D., *Selected Chapters from his Autobiography* (Ithaca, N.Y., 1939).

WICHERT, L., 'Theodor Mommsen und Jacob Bernays', *Historische Zeitschrift*, 205 (1969).

WIDENMANN, WILHELM, *Marine-Attaché in London 1907–1912* (Göttingen, 1952).

WIESE, BENNO VON, *Der deutsche Roman* (2 vols., Düsseldorf, 1963).

WILDE, HARRY and HANS OTTO MEISSNER, *Die Machtergreifung: Ein Bericht über die Technik des nationalsozialistischen Staatsstreichs* (Stuttgart, 1958).

WILHELM II, KAISER, *Die Reden in den Jahren von 1888 bis 1905*, ed. Johannes Penzler (Leipzig, n. d.).

WILLIAMS, ROGER L., *The Mortal Napoleon III* (Princeton, 1971).

WILLIAMSON, JOHN G., *Karl Helfferich, 1872–1924: Economist, Financier, Politician* (Princeton, 1971).

WILSON, EDMUND, *To the Finland Station* (New York, 1948).

WINDELBAND, W., *Bismarck und die europäischen Großmächte 1879–85* (2nd edn., Essen, 1942).

WINDTHORST, LUDWIG, *Ausgewählte Reden* (Osnabrück, 1903).

WINGLER, HANS M., *The Bauhaus* (New York, 1969).

WINKELMANN, JOHN, 'Social Criticism in the Early Work of Erich Kästner' (Dissertation, Univ. of Missouri, 1953).

WINKLER, HEINRICH AUGUST, *Mittelstand, Demokratie, und Nationalsozialismus: Die politische Entwicklung von Handwerk und Kleinhandel in der Weimarer Republik* (Cologne, 1972).

WISKEMANN, ELIZABETH, *The Rome–Berlin Axis* (New York, 1949).

WITT, PETER-CHRISTIAN, *Die Finanzpolitik des Deutschen Reiches von 1903 bis 1913: Eine Studie zur Innenpolitik des Wilhelminischen Deutschland* (Lübeck, 1970).

WOLF, EUGEN, *Vom Fürsten Bismarck* (Leipzig, 1904).

WOLF, JOHN B., *The Diplomatic History of the Baghdad Railway* (Columbus, Mo., 1936).

WOLFE, BERTRAM D., *Marxism: 100 Years in the Life of a Doctrine* (New York, 1965).

WOOD, D. and D. DEMPSTER, *The Narrow Margin* (London, 1961).

WOODWARD, E. L., *Great Britain and the German Navy* (Oxford, 1935).

WRIGHT, GORDON, *The Ordeal of Total War 1939–45* (New York, 1968).

WRISBERG, ERNST VON, *Heer und Heimat 1914–1918* (Leipzig, 1921).

——, *Wehr und Waffen 1914–1918* (Leipzig, 1922).

WULF, JOSEPH, *Musik in Dritten Reich: Eine Dokumentation* (Gütersloh, 1963).

YARNELL, HOWARD E., *The Great Powers and the Congo Conference* (Göttingen, 1934).

YOUNG, PETER, *A Short History of World War II* (New York, 1966).

ZAHN, GORDON C., *German Catholics and Hitler's Wars* (London, 1962).

ZECHLIN, EGMONT, *Bismarck und die Grundlegung der deutschen Großmacht* (Stuttgart, 1930).

——, 'Bethmann Hollweg, Kriegsrisiko und SPD 1914', *Der Monat* (1966).

——, 'Friedensbestrebungen und Revolutionierungsversuche', in *Aus Politik und Geschichte* (Beilage, *Das Parlament*).

——, *Staatsstreichpläne Bismarcks und Wilhelms II 1890–1894* (Stuttgart, 1929).

ZEDLITZ-TRÜTZSCHLER, GRAF, *Zwölf Jahre am deutschen Kaiserhof* (Berlin, 1924).

ZEENDER, JOHN K., 'The German Center Party, 1890–1906', *Transactions of the American Philosophical Society*, lxvi, pt. 1 (Philadelphia, 1976).

ZEILER, ULRICH, *Schlaglichter* (Frankfurt-on-Main, 1924).

ZEMAN, Z. A. B., *Nazi Propaganda* (2nd edn., London, 1973).

ZIEBURA, GILBERT (ed.), *Grundfragen der deutschen Außenpolitik seit 1971* (Darmstadt, 1975).

ZEIGLER, WILHELM, *Die deutsche Nationalversammlung 1919–20 und ihr Verfassungswerk*, (Berlin, 1932).

ZIEKURSCH, JOHANNES, *Politische Geschichte des neuen deutschen Kaiserreiches* (3 vols., Frankfurt-on-Main, 1925 ff.).

ZIEMKE, EARL K., *The German Northern Theater of Operations, 1940–45* (Washington, 1959).

ZIMMERMANN, A., *Front wider Bülow*, ed. F. Thimme (Munich, 1931).

ZIMMERMAN, LUDWIG, *Studien zur Geschichte der Weimarer Republik* (Erlangen, 1956).

ZMARZLIK. HANS-GÜNTER, 'Der Antisemitismus im Zweiten Reich', *Geschichte in Wissenschaft und Unterricht*, xiv (1963).

——, *Bethmann Hollweg als Reichskanzler 1909–1914. Studien zu Möglichkeiten und Grenzen seiner innenpolitischen Machtstellung* (Düsseldorf, 1957).

ZORN, WOLFGANG, 'Student Politics in the Weimar Republic', *Journal of Contemporary History*, v (1970).

ZUCKMAYER, CARL, *Als wär's ein Stück von mir* (Vienna, 1966).

ZWEHL, H. VON, *Erich von Falkenhayn, General der Infanterie: Eine biographische Studie* (Berlin, 1926).

ZWEIG, STEFAN, *Die Welt von Gestern: Erinnerungen* (Frankfurt-on-Main, 1970).

INDEX

Adenauer, Konrad, 445, 509

Agriculture, 88, 357–8; politics of grain producers, 98–100, 173, 203, 238, 239, 259, 276, 277, 278, 507, 558, 560; pressure groups, 88–9, 253, 301, 360, 584; small farmers, 500–1, 551–2, 584; in Third Reich, 604, 609–10; *see also* Bund der Landwirte

Albedyll, General E. L. von, Chief of the Military Cabinet (1871–87), 134, 161, 162, 163, 165 n.

Alberti, Conrad, 214, 216

Alexander II, Emperor of Russia, 6, 104, 109, 113, 149

Alexander III, Emperor of Russia, 119

Alexander of Battenberg, Prince, 124–5, 127, 128, 170

Alliances and ententes: Three Emperors' League (1873), 104, 108, 109, 112; Dual Alliance (1879), 102, 114–16, 134; Three Emperors' League (1881), 115, 125, 131; Triple Alliance (1882), 115, 116, 124, 130, 131, 134, 135, 236, 239, 241, 243, 246, 248, 268, 333; Franco-Russian Alliance (1891), 237–9, 248; Anglo-Japanese Alliance (1902), 313; Entente Cordiale (1904), 314–15; Triple Entente (1907), 325, 333; *see also* Axis, Treaties

Alsace-Lorraine, 39, 62, 85, 119, 128, 129, 262, 290, 359, 519, 743; annexation (1871), 29, 33, 79, 94, 366; Zabern incident (1913), 297–301

Alst, Schorlemer, 88

Altenstein, Friedrich von, 73, 188

Althoff, Friedrich, 200–2

Amann, Max, 596, 657 f.

Andrássy, Count Julius, 104, 114

Anschluss, *see* Austria

Anti-Semitism, 84 f., 153–5, 184 n., 203, 204, 206, 254, 261 and n., 422, 507; Anti-Semite party, 280, 298; and National Socialism, 542, 546, 551, 552, 575 f., 579, 612, 632–6, 640, 646, 648, 650, 651, 660, 738; Final Solution, 600, 636–7, 709, 748–51

Antonelli, papal secretary, 71

Antonescu, General Ion, 743

Anzengruber, Ludwig, 69–70

Architecture, 469, 473, 474; in Third Reich, 654

Army: adjutants, 229–30; administrative reform of (1883), 53, 133, 163, 230; arrangements with south German states (1866–70), 6–7, 15, 18, 27–8; budget, 18, 46, 47, 50–3, 68; civil–military disputes, 3–6, 31–3, 270–2, 297–301, 368–86, 386–95, 523;

constitutional powers, 50–3, 54; General Staff, 28, 31, 53, 107, 133, 161, 163, 178, 229, 294–5, 316, 345–6, 367, 378; military attachés, 277, 315; Military Cabinet, 51, 53, 161, 178, 229; military justice, 246, 270–2; and National Socialism, 567–8, 571, 578, 585–90, 591, 595, 600–1, 612, 614, 625, 668–71, 689, 693, 698–701, 706, 708, 710–11, 713; operations in World War I, 342–51, 371–3, 393–5; operations in World War II, 714–32, 751–8, 762; and preventive war, 107–8, 133–4, 319–20, 332, 336; reserve officers, 159–60, 289; royal power of command, 39–40, 50; war of 1870, 28–9, 36; War Ministry, 53, 161, 162, 163, 164, 229, 294–5, 354–7, 378; and Weimar Republic, 404–12, 426–32, 459–60, 463–7, 513, 521, 523, 534 ff., 558 ff., 565–8

Army laws: Iron Budget (1867), 51; Septennat (1874), 51–3, 107; law of 1887, 128–9, 169; law of 1892, 237; law of 1905, 279; law of 1912, 293–5; law of 1913, 295–6, 300; law of 1933, 585

Arnim, Harry Count, 104–6, 137

Arons, Leo, 201, 202

Arts: alienation of the artist, 58, 214, 217–18; *see also* Expressionism, Film, Impressionism, Literature, Music, Naturalism, Painting, Theatre

Attlee, Clement, 707

Auer, Erich, 400, 410

Auer, Ignaz, 147

Austria (and Austria-Hungary), 10, 11, 14, 23, 28, 29, 30, 44, 65, 90, 92, 103, 104, 110 ff., 125 f., 241; peace settlement (1866), 3, 4, 5–7; Dual Alliance (1879), 102, 114–16, 232, 323; Bosnian crisis (1908), 321–2; crisis of 1914, 335–7; in World War I, 345–6, 349, 352, 353, 372, 374–5, 384, 392, 395; republic, 400, 439, 682–3; Customs Union (1930), 555–6; anschluss, 512, 555, 616, 635, 675, 692, 694–5, 697, 698, 700, 701, 702

Axis, 592, 688, 693–6, 711, 727

Baden, Grand Duchy of, 6, 14, 18, 19, 21, 24, 27, 33, 176, 269, 576

Bäumer, Gertrud, 212, 503, 628

Baghdad railway, 314, 334, 337 n.

Baldwin, Stanley, 458, 675, 687, 692, 701

Balfour, Arthur Lord, 311, 313

Ballin, Albert, 274, 286 n., 330, 348 n., 445

Bamberger, Ludwig, 71, 84, 151, 156, 165

Banking, 81, 83, 84, 446, 447, 633; Reichsbank,

Banking—*contd.*
65, 132, 467, 530; Darmstädter Bank, 248;
Deutsche Bank, 123, 245, 248, 744;
Diskonto-Gesellschaft, 120, 123, 248; Dres-
dener Bank, 123, 248; Rothschild, 15
Barth, Karl, 762
Barthou, Jean-Louis, 682, 683
Baruch, Bernard, 437
Bassermann, Albert, 285 n., 292, 299
Bassermann, Ernst, 471
Bauer, Gustav, Reich Chancellor (1919), 427
Bauer, Colonel Max, 355, 377, 378, 383, 384,
386, 387, 429
Bauhaus, 469, 473–4, 639
Baum, Vicki, 478–9, 484
Bavaria, 6, 14, 18, 19, 21, 27, 34, 41, 42, 92, 94,
176, 256, 271, 282, 283, 400–1, 410–12, 418,
420–1, 429, 432, 439, 441, 462–7, 476, 560,
576, 599
Bavarian People's party (BVP), 432, 524, 532,
542, 578, 582
Bazaine, Maréchal, 28, 31, 32
Bebel, August, 12, 69 n., 94, 147, 148, 151, 152,
155, 156, 168 n., 210, 266, 268, 403, 525
Beck, Colonel Jozef, 681, 682, 710
Beck, Lieutenant-General Ludwig, 589,
669–71, 697, 698, 699 and n.
Beer Hall Putsch (1923), 421, 466, 759
Begas, Reinhold, 58
Belgium, 16, 17, 23, 62, 186, 316, 317, 436, 443,
447, 448; in World War I, 341, 343, 359, 360,
363, 365, 366, 376, 377, 382, 388, 393, 394;
and Third Reich, 689, 690, 691, 711; in
World War II, 716, 719, 739, 743
Benedek, Feldzeugmeister Ludwig August
von, 2, 3
Benedetti, Vincent, 16, 26, 27
Benes, Eduard, 703, 704, 705
Benn, Gottfried, 469, 643–5, 647
Bennigsen, Rudolf von, 10, 63, 91, 92, 95, 96,
97
Berchem, Count von, 127, 135, 232
Berchtold, Leopold Count, 333, 334
Bergengruen, Werner, 663
Berlepsch, Freiherr von, 262, 263, 265
Berlin, 216 n., 475–6, 483–4, 496
Berliner Post, 68, 108, 129
Berliner Tageblatt, 503, 659
Bernhardi, Friedrich von, 204
Bernstein, Eduard, 147, 148, 152
Beseler, General von, 375, 376, 391
Bethmann Hollweg, Theobald von, Reich
Chancellor (1909–17), 287–301, 317, 343;
character and temperament, 287–8; and
Reichstag, 292, 299; and foreign policy,
325–8; and crisis of 1914, 335–8; in World
War I, 347, 348, 353, 364–5, 366–7, 368–86
Bethusy-Huc, Eduard Count von, 11
Beust, Friedrich Ferdinand Count von, 23, 72,
104

Bismarck, Herbert von, 120, 121, 125, 126,
127, 135, 172, 230, 256
Bismarck, Johanna von, 2
Bismarck-Schönhausen, Otto von, 50, 100,
140, 165, 202, 213, 230, 231, 232–4, 236, 248,
254, 256, 269, 271, 275, 285, 303, 304, 315,
323, 327, 351, 367, 369, 498, 512, 513, 517,
538, 540, 543, 554, 656, 707, 708, 762, 763;
and anti-Semitism, 155 n.; and army, 3–4,
31–3, 108, 133–4, 163, 172, 178; and colonies,
116–17, 123; constitutional theory, 13–15,
38–43, 44, 66, 158, 171, 174; as culture hero,
58–9; diplomatic gifts, 21, 112; dismissal,
140–2, 171–9; and Foreign Ministry and
Diplomatic Service, 41, 134–9; foreign policy, 101–39; economic views, 64 n., 89,
90–2, 93; and national unity, 14 ff., 20–1, 24,
33–4; and North German Confederation,
12–13; and parties, 63, 64, 71 ff., 89 ff., 97;
political style, 55, 59–60, 143, 144, 168,
174–5; and Press, 29, 68–9; principles of foreign policy, 101–2, 104, 112, 115, 125–6; and
Prussian constitutional conflict (1861–6), 2,
3, 7– 11, 142–3, 168, 174; Reich Chancellor
(1871–90), 61–179; and Reichstag, 144 n.,
157; and religion, 71–2, 108; and social
insurance, 150–2; and socialism, 94 n., 95–6,
101–2; and Spanish affairs (1868–70), 22–7;
views of chancellorship, 45–6, 54
Bleichröder, Gerson von, 68 n., 79, 80, 84,
105 n., 118, 121 n., 123, 132 n., 155, 178 n.
Blomberg, Field-Marshal Werner von,
Wehrmacht Minister (1933–8), 567, 568,
569, 589, 591, 606, 611, 612, 614, 698, 699,
700
Blowitz, Henri de, 109
Blücher, Field-Marshal G. L. von, 140–1
Bock, Field-Marshal Fedor von, 730
Böcklin, Arnold, 59, 70, 215
Börne, Ludwig, 60, 215, 216
Boetticher, Heinrich von, 174, 177, 271, 272,
273
Bonhoeffer, Dietrich, 667
Bonn, M. J., 438, 445
Bormann, Martin, 592–3, 594, 651, 735
Bosch, Robert, 355, 393
Bosnia, 110, 113, 321–2
Boulanger, Général Georges, 124, 128, 129
Bourbaki, Général, 32
Bracher, Karl Dietrich, 553
Brandler, Heinrich, 461, 464, 465
Brauchitsch, General Walter von, 700, 717,
720, 721, 722, 731
Brauer, Arthur von, 21, 127, 135, 138, 252–
3
Braun, Lily, 208, 210
Braun, Otto, 448
Brecht, Arnold, 539, 574
Brecht, Bertolt, 473, 475, 484
Bredt, J. V., 537

Breitscheid, Hugo, 538, 566
Brentano, Lujo, 96, 197, 202, 203, 361
Briand, Aristide, 443, 512, 518, 521, 522, 527
Broch, Hermann, 228 and n.
Brockdorff-Rantzau, Ulrich Count von, 425, 513, 517, 519, 520, 680
Bronsart von Schellendorf, General Paul, War Minister (1883–9), 163, 246
Bronsart von Schellendorf, General Walter, War Minister (1893–6), 265, 270, 271
Brüning, Heinrich, 504, 530, 531, 532, 533, 561, 575, 578, 582, 678; Reich Chancellor (1930–2), 535–43, 547, 551, 553–60
Bucher, Lothar, 21, 25, 135, 138
Buchrucker, Major Bruno, 459–60
Bueck, H. A., 86
Bülow, Bernhard von, Secretary of State for Foreign Affairs (1873–9), 21
Bülow, Bernhard Prince von, 234, 249, 251, 252, 287, 298, 308, 312, 322, 323, 324, 352–3, 385; Reich Chancellor (1900–9), 272–86, 303, 317, 318–20, 321; Sammlungspolitik, 274–5; Weltpolitik, 275, 314, 321
Bülow, Bernhard W. von, Secretary of State for Foreign Affairs (1929–36), 677, 680, 697
Bulgaria, 113, 239, 331, 333, 353, 395, 726, 728, 743; crises (1885–8), 124–34, 141, 168
Bullock, Alan Lord, 763
Bund der Landwirte, 239, 253, 259, 261, 269, 277, 282, 360, 552
Bundesrat, 39, 42, 43, 45, 66, 73, 144 n., 284, 296, 301, 328, 367, 379, 381, 383; abolition of Federal Council (1934), 583
Burckhardt, Dr. Carl, 709, 711
Burckhardt, Jakob, 195, 763
Bureaucracy, 46, 48, 77, 287, 292 n., 419–20; Puttkamer's reforms, 99, 157–9, 420; Beamtenerlass (1882), 158; Gleichschaltung (1933–4), 578; Civil Service Law (1937), 593
Busch, Clemens von, 135, 138, 165
Busch, Wilhelm, 70, 74

Camphausen, Ludwig, 84, 87, 90, 92
Caprivi, General Leo Count von, Reich Chancellor (1890–4), 230–3, 235–6, 241, 244, 248, 249, 251, 252, 254, 256, 260, 287, 304, 305, 315; army bill of 1893, 257–9; trade treaties, 238, 239, 242, 253, 259, 277; resignation, 260–1
Cassell, Sir Ernest, 330
Centre party, 12, 19, 63, 70–1, 89, 92–3, 96, 97, 156 f., 161, 168, 169, 174, 175, 177, 183, 253, 254, 269, 271, 278, 279, 282–6, 287, 289, 290, 292, 359, 380, 384; Kulturkampf, 71–7; elections of 1907, 280–1; and Weimar Republic, 413, 414, 432, 441, 504, 509, 510, 513, 524, 533, 542; after 1933, 573, 575, 578, 581–2
Chabod, Federico, 302
Chamberlain, Austen, 512, 515, 516, 518, 521
Chamberlain, Joseph, 311–14

Chamberlain, Neville, 548, 680, 701, 703, 704–7, 710
Charles, Emperor of Austria, 384
Christian Social movement, 153, 155, 156, 185, 254, 506
Churchill, Winston Spencer, 330, 350–1, 640, 690, 717, 718, 721, 737
Chvalkovsky, Czech Foreign Minister, 637, 707, 708
Ciano, Count Galeazzo, 712–13
Civil Service, see Bureaucracy
Class, Heinrich, 205, 360, 363, 527
Clemenceau, Georges, 107, 437
Coal mining industry, 413, 414; strikes (1889), 172
Colonial Union (Kolonialverein), 119, 247, 288, 307, 325
Commercial policy: free trade, 64, 65–6, 85, 86, 87, 88; shift to protectionism (1879), 88 ff., 97–9; National Socialist policy, 608, 610, 613, 614–16; see also Reparations
Commune, Paris, 94, 105, 152
Communist party (KPD) and communism, 403, 407, 409, 411, 431, 433, 458, 460–2, 463–5, 466, 479, 485, 500, 510, 511, 512, 514, 525, 534, 539, 540, 542, 563, 564, 567, 573, 574, 575, 577, 580; after 1933, 665–6; see also Spartacus Union
Conferences and congresses: London (1867), 17; Reichstadt (1876), 110, 112; Berlin (1878), 111–13, 115, 272; Berlin Congo Conference (1885), 122; Algeciras (1906), 137, 320, 321, 327, 328; The Hague (1899, 1907), 324 n., 326; Spa (1920), 438, 439; Cannes (1922), 443; Genoa (1922), 443–4; London (1924), 514; Locarno (1925), 517–18; Thoiry (1926), 522; The Hague (1929), 526–7, 528; Lausanne (1932), 561; World Economic (1933), 569, 581; Disarmament (1932–4), 559, 562, 586, 605, 678–80, 684, 697; Stresa (1935), 684–5; Munich (1938), 707, 709
Congo dispute (1894), 244
Conrad, Michael Georg, 216
Conrad von Hötzendorf, Field-Marshal, 322, 323, 324, 331, 332, 336, 345–6, 349
Conservatism, 7, 8, 9, 10–11, 14, 19
Conservative party, 62–3, 73, 91, 93, 96, 156, 157, 167, 168, 169, 173, 174, 175, 253, 269, 277, 278, 279, 280, 281–6, 287, 289, 290–1, 293, 296, 298, 301, 359, 372, 379, 394, 506; Tivoli Programme (1892), 254, 261 n.
Council of People's Representatives, 404, 413
Courland, 359, 391
Courths-Mahler, Hedwig, 211
Crash of 1873, 82–5, 101, 106, 204
Crispi, Francesco, 123–4, 351
Cuno, Wilhelm, Reich Chancellor (1922–3), 445–9, 456, 457, 458, 459, 462, 514, 516
Currie, Sir Philip, 241
Curtius, E. R., 491

Curtius, Julius, 505, 524, 528, 554, 556
Czechoslovakia, 518, 556, 616, 681, 689, 692, 698, 699, 700, 701, 709; Sudeten question (1938), 679, 702–7; occupation (1939), 626, 708
Czernahora Council (1866), 4
Czernin, Ottokar Count, 384, 389

D'Abernon, Viscount, 442, 515, 516, 520, 521
Dahlmann, F. C., 57, 195
Dahn, Felix, 84 and n.
Dahrendorf, Ralf, 48, 49, 191, 672
Daladier, Eduard, 683, 703, 706, 707
Daluege, Kurt, 572, 573–4
D'Annunzio, Gabriele, 352
Darré, Walther, 581, 584, 599, 609, 619, 625
David, Eduard, 341 n.
Davis, Norman H., 436
Dawes Plan, 514–15, 516, 522, 523, 526
Dawidowicz, Lucy, 632
Déak, Francis, 23
Decazes, duc de, 106, 109
Dehmel, Richard, 218
Deines, Major Adolf von, 134
De Lagarde, Paul, 188, 487
Delbrück, Hans, 196, 201, 361
Delbrück, Rudolf, 54, 64–6, 73, 89, 90
Delcassé, Theophile, 320
Democratic party (DDP), 413, 414, 432, 502–4, 506, 509, 524, 532, 541, 581
Denmark, 717, 718, 742, 744
Dernburg, Bernhard, 280 n., 361
Dietrich, Otto, 596, 658, 737, 739, 741
Dietrich, Sepp, 600
Dilthey, Wilhelm, 196
Diplomatic Service: under Bismarck, 136–9; under William II, 233–4; under Hitler, 677, 698
Disarmament, 324 n., 326, 607, 677; Conference (1932–4), 559, 562, 586, 605, 678–80, 684, 697
Disraeli, Benjamin, 103, 110, 113
Döblin, Alfred, 338, 469, 483, 484, 498, 647, 652
Doenitz, Admiral Karl, 753
Dohnanyi, Hans von, 591
Dollfuss, Engelbert, 682, 683, 694
Duisberg, Carl, 387
Duncker, Max, 12

Ebert, Friedrich, 401, 402, 403–7, 412, 413; Reich President (1919–25), 415, 426, 427, 430, 431, 433, 445, 448, 457, 458, 463, 467, 485, 510, 574, 592
Eckardstein, Hermann Baron von, 313
Eckhardt, Julius von, 30
Eden, Anthony, 684, 685, 686, 689, 692, 701, 702
Education, 40, 73, 158; academic freedom, 198–207; anti-Semitism in higher education,

204, 660–1; elementary schools, 186–92, 423, 524; historical instruction, 189, 661; secondary education, 190–1, 423–4, 662–3; and social mobility, 190–2, 423; student organizations, 205–6, 422, 649; universities, 192–8, 421–3, 660–3; women's education, 207–8, 212, 422, 423, 478, 628; see also Intelligentsia
Edward VIII, King of Britain, 692; Duke of Windsor, 721 and n.
Egypt, 116, 121, 122
Ehrhardt, Captain Hermann, 430, 431, 432, 462
Eichmann, Adolf, 637, 748
Eicke, Theodor, 600
Einem, General Karl von, War Minister (1903–9), 294
Einstein, Albert, 362, 470
Eisner, Kurt, 400–1, 410, 421
Engels, Friedrich, 152, 168 n.
Epp, Franz Ritter von, 412, 431, 576
Erzberger, Matthias, 279, 281, 283, 352–3, 359–60, 372, 384–6, 387, 391 n., 425, 441, 445, 457
Eschenburg, Theodor, 284
Escherich, Georg, 429, 432
Esthonia, 382, 391
Eugénie, Empress of the French, 23
Eulenburg, August Count von, 286
Eulenburg, Botho Count von, 255, 259, 260, 261, 286
Eulenburg, Friedrich Count von, 67, 91
Eulenburg, Philipp Count von, 176 n., 230, 234, 260, 261, 272, 273, 274, 283 n., 318 n.
Evangelical Church, 181; Evangelical Workers' Union, 262–3; Inner Mission, 172, 183, 185; social conservatism, 184; and Third Reich, 181, 666–7
Expressionism, 221–2, 469, 470, 472–3, 476, 480, 481, 482, 483, 494, 495
Eyck, Erich, 77, 150

Fabri, Friedrich, 119
Falk, Adalbert, 73, 75, 76, 158, 189
Falkenhayn, General Erich von, War Minister (1913–15), 298, 299, 335; Chief of General Staff (1914–16), 346–9, 353, 354, 363, 368–75
Fatherland party (Vaterlandspartei), 388, 389, 390, 391, 394, 508
Faupel, Wilhelm, 412, 431; Lieutenant-General (ret.), 695
Favre, Jules, 31, 33
Fehrenbach, Konstantin, Reich Chancellor (1920–1), 438, 441
Feilitzsch, Freiherr von, 94
Ferdinand of Coburg, 132
Ferry, Jules, 119, 124
Feuchtwanger, Lion, 420, 463 n., 472
Feuerbach, Anselm, 49, 215
Film, 477, 495–6, 654–7, 762 and n.
Finland, 391, 716, 717, 726, 742, 743

Fischer, Ruth, 461, 465
Flandin, Pierre-Étienne, 689
Fontane, Theodor, 1, 141, 171, 179, 208–9, 217, 269
Forckenbeck, Max von, 9, 92, 156, 165
Foreign Ministry: under Bismarck, 134–6; under William II, 232–3; under Hitler, 595, 693, 696, 697–701
Four Year Plan (1936), 594, 604, 607, 611, 613–18, 621, 635
France, 3, 4, 5, 6, 11, 14, 15, 17, 18, 22–7, 34, 36, 62, 72, 79, 90, 102, 104–6, 116, 122, 127, 186, 232, 245, 291, 318; war with Prussia, 27 ff.; revanchisme, 30, 115, 124, 129; crisis of 1875, 90, 107–10; rapprochement with Russia (1890–3), 237–8; Moroccan crises, 318–21, 327–9; in World War I, 371–3, 389; and Weimar Republic, 429, 436, 442–3, 447–8, 458, 459, 513, 514–19, 526–7, 554, 556; and Third Reich, 605, 675, 679, 680, 682, 683, 684–5, 688–91, 698–9, 700, 701, 702–7, 710–13; in World War II, 717–20, 725, 751
Francis Joseph, Emperor of Austria, 5, 104, 134, 226, 256, 335, 352 n.
Franco, General Francisco, 694, 695, 725
François-Poncet, André, 616, 673, 674, 688, 701
Frank, Hans, 580, 741, 745 n., 749
Frank, Leonhard, 370, 477, 481, 484
Frank, Walter, 661
Frantz, Konstantin, 55–6, 153
Frederick II, King of Prussia, 20, 50, 97, 227, 273, 543, 646, 656, 708, 729
Frederick III, King and Emperor, 170; as Crown Prince, 3, 6, 7, 9, 12, 28, 32, 34, 62, 119, 120, 159, 162, 163, 164, 165, 166, 167, 168, 228
Frederick Charles, Prince of Prussia, 3, 31, 228
Frederick William, the Great Elector, 227, 273
Frederick William I, King of Prussia, 97, 205, 226, 227, 247
Frederick William III, King of Prussia, 141, 187
Frederick William IV, King of Prussia, i, 44, 188, 227
Free Conservative party, 11, 63, 64, 65, 96, 157, 169, 175, 253, 277, 292, 506
Free corps, 407–12, 431
Freiligrath, Ferdinand, i, iii, 59
Freisinnige party, 166, 167, 169, 174, 175
Freisler, Roland, 580
Freud, Sigmund, 470
Freytag, Gustav, 34, 36, 59, 60, 84, 99, 145 n., 198
Frick, Wilhelm, 568, 571, 593, 596, 597, 599, 600
Fritsch, Colonel-General Werner Freiherr von, 569, 586, 698, 699 and n., 700
Fritzsche, Friedrich Wilhelm, 147, 148
Fromm, General Erich, 717
Furtwängler, Wilhelm, 475, 651

Gablenz, Field-Marshal Ludwig von der, 82
Gambetta, Léon, 105
Gamelin, Général, 690, 691
Gartenlaube, Die, 83, 213
Gayl, Freiherr von, 563, 564
Geffcken, Heinrich, 165, 170 n.
George, Stefan, 218, 469
Gerhard, Dietrich, 661
Gerlach, Hellmuth von, 205
Gerlach, Leopold von, 10
Germany: Germanic Confederation, 55; Frankfurt Parliament and constitution of 1849, 41, 55, 57; North German Confederation, 4, 7, 10, 11–14, 18, 20, 21, 24, 38, 41, 42, 45, 49; proclamation of Empire, 33, 44, 49–50; constitution and institutional structure of Empire, 13, 38–60; economic development, 15, 17, 19, 20, 64–6, 78–85, 98, 100, 118, 248–9; financial reform and tax policy, 90–1, 97–8, 277–9, 282–6, 290–1, 292, 293–4, 296; see also Weimar Republic, Third Reich
Gervinus, Georg Gottfried, 763
Gessler, Otto, Minister of Defence (1920–8), 438, 444
Gilbert, Felix, 661
Gladstone, William Ewart, 61–2, 103, 116, 130, 166, 237, 239, 245
Gläser, Ernst, 339
Glagau, Otto, 83
Globocnick, Odilo, 748
Gneist, Rudolf von, 9
Goebbels, Josef, 543, 545, 547, 550, 573, 577, 592, 596, 625, 631, 638, 640, 646, 651, 653, 654–6, 659, 663, 671, 703, 737–40, 741, 762; and total war, 760–2
Gömbös, Julius, 677
Goerdeler, Carl, 652, 667, 668, 669, 671
Goering, Hermann, 568, 572, 573, 574, 585, 588, 594, 599, 600, 610, 611, 635, 636, 637, 650, 661, 698, 708, 722, 723, 729, 733, 739, 744, 748, 756; and Four Year Plan, 612–18, 699 and n.
Goethe, Johann Wolfgang, 60, 216, 217, 218, 415, 640, 652
Goldschmidt, Jakob, 560
Goltz, General Colmar von der, 286
Goltz, Robert Count von der, 5, 139
Goltz, General Rüdiger Count von der, 428
Gorchakov, Prince, 108, 109, 111, 112, 113
Gossler, General Heinrich von, War Minister (1896–1903), 294
Gramont, duc de, 23, 25, 26, 27
Grant, Ulysses S., President of the United States, 38, 39
Granville, Lord, 122
Grass, Günter, 643, 762
Gray, Ronald, 218
Great Britain, 15, 23, 46, 62, 103, 109, 110–13, 115, 127, 130–2, 134, 186, 275, 291; anti-

Great Britain—*contd.*
English feeling in Germany, 205; anti-German feeling in England, 247; colonial disputes with Germany, 120–2, 124, 167, 235, 240, 242–8; deterioration of Anglo-German relations (1897–1914), 303–38; in World War I, 342–3, 350, 369, 393–5; and Weimar Republic, 436–7, 447, 449, 458, 513, 514–19, 526–7, 554–5; and Third Reich, 616–17, 675, 679, 683, 684–5, 686–7, 688–91, 692, 700, 701, 702, 703–7, 710–13; in World War II, 717–30, 751–2

Greece, 331, 351, 726, 728, 744
Gregorovius, Ferdinand, 29
Greiser, Arthur, 709
Grenzboten, 8, 36
Grey of Falloden, Earl, 330 n., 331
Griesbach, Eduard, 70
Groener, General Wilhelm, 319 n., 320 n., 368, 378, 379, 386–7, 404–7, 426, 427, 428; Minister of Defence (1928–32), 525, 535–7, 553, 554, 557–9
Gropius, Walter, 471, 473, 474
Grosz, Georg, 551
Gründerzeit, 61, 78–85
Guderian, Colonel-General Heinz, 715, 719, 731
Guertner, Franz von, 591

Haber, Fritz, 355, 357
Hácha, Emil, President of Czechoslovakia, 708
Haeckel, Ernst, 181, 182
Haeften, Colonel Hans von, 394
Hahnke, General von, Chief of the Military Cabinet (1888—1901), 178, 271
Haldane, Lord, 330, 331
Halder, Colonel-General Franz, 716, 719, 720, 722, 729, 755
Halifax, Sir Edward Frederick Lindley Wood, Earl of, 701, 702
Hamburg, 11, 147, 155, 157 n., 249, 264, 399; rising (1923), 465
Hammann, Otto, 282, 378
Hammerstein, Wilhelm von, 254, 259, 260 n.
Hammerstein-Equord, Colonel-General Kurt Freiherr von, 571, 586
Hanover, Kingdom of, 5, 6, 19, 63
Harden, Maximilian, 202, 216, 234, 283 n.
Harnack, Adolf von, 182, 186, 195, 362
Hart, Heinrich, 56, 213, 216, 222 n.
Hartmann, Eduard von, 82, 194 and n.
Hasenclever, Walter, 218, 476, 482
Hassell, Ulrich von, 667, 688
Hasselmann, Wilhelm, 149
Hatzfeldt, Paul von, 21, 135, 137, 138, 139, 234, 235, 236, 237, 239, 244, 245, 247 n., 311, 312, 313
Hatzfeldt, Sopie Countess von, 209
Hauptmann, Gerhard, 217, 472, 640–1
Hauser, Arnold, 218

Haussmann, Conrad, 399
Heeringen, General von, War Minister (1909–13), 294, 296
Hegel, Georg Friedrich, 35, 47, 48, 49, 64, 186, 192, 194, 218
Heidegger, Martin, 642–3, 645
Heiden, Konrad, 571
Heine, Heinrich, 215, 216, 485, 504, 649, 652
Held, Heinrich, 467, 576
Helfferich, Karl, 356–7, 371, 378, 379, 380 n., 384, 441, 507
Helldorf-Bedra, Count von, 174, 177, 254
Henckel-Donnersmarck, Guido Count von, 79, 256
Henderson, Sir Nevile, 704, 705
Henlein, Konrad, 703, 704, 705
Hermes, Andreas, 609
Herriot, Eduard, 515
Hertling, Georg Count von, Reich Chancellor (1917–18), 390, 393, 397
Herwegh, Georg, 1
Hess, Rudolf, 549, 566, 592, 625, 661, 729, 736, 738
Hesse, Electoral, 5, 6
Hesse-Darmstadt, 6, 11, 13, 18, 19, 33
Hesse, Hermann, 469, 482–3, 714
Heuß, Theodor, 152, 197
Heydrich, Reinhard, 573, 598, 599, 636, 637, 748, 749
Heym, Georg, 221, 222
Heyse, Paul, 59, 70, 215
Hilferding, Rudolf, 413, 467, 498, 510, 529, 530, 532
Himmler, Heinrich, 188, 588, 594, 595, 598–601, 602; Reichsführer-SS (1936–45), 600, 636, 656, 735, 746–50, 762
Hindemith, Paul, 474, 475, 651
Hindenburg, Oskar von, 560
Hindenburg, Field-Marshal Paul von Beneckendorff und, 344–5, 348, 349, 363, 368, 369 n., 373–86, 389, 390, 393, 397, 405, 407, 426, 427; Reich President (1925–34), 510–11, 519, 522, 531, 532, 535–6, 538, 541, 542, 558, 559–60, 562–5, 574, 575, 576, 577, 578, 586, 588, 589, 590, 592
Hintze, Otto, 196, 197, 285, 341 n., 360, 361 n., 534
Hitler, Adolf, 392, 409, 412, 417, 421, 462, 466, 469, 474, 483, 493, 500, 508, 527, 542, 556, 558, 560, 561, 562, 565–8, 640, 642, 644–5; Reich Chancellor (1933–4), 568–89; Führer and Reich Chancellor (1934–45), 590–764; on art, 649–50, 653, 654, 656; *attentat* on (1944), 669–71, 761; character and political gifts, 543–53; economic policy, 603–37; and Europe, 741–2; as Feldherr, 720–1, 730–1, 754–8; foreign policy, 611, 612, 626, 634, 672–713; and German people, 715, 759–60, 761–2; and industry, 556, 558; and intel-

lectuals, 638–9, 645; and Jews, 632, 634, 635, 637
Hödel, 61, 95
Hoepner, General Erich, 731
Hoesch, Leopold von, 690, 692
Hoess, Rudolf, 748, 750
Hoffmann, Johannes, 410–11, 418, 432
Hoffmann, General Max, 373, 389
Hoffmann von Fallersleben, Heinrich, 61
Hofmannsthal, Hugo von, 219, 472
Hohenlohe-Schillingsfürst, Prince Chlodwig zu, 21, 42, 136; Reich Chancellor (1894–1900), 242, 246, 249, 261–2, 263, 265, 270–2, 273, 308, 311, 312
Hohenzollern dynasty, 23, 227, 230, 373, 398, 401, 402, 507
Hohenzollern-Sigmaringen, Charles Anthony Prince von, 22, 26
Hohenzollern-Sigmaringen, Leopold von, 22, 23, 24, 25, 26
Holborn, Hajo, 661
Holland, 17, 366, 402, 711, 716, 719, 743
Hollmann, Admiral Friedrich von, 272 n., 305, 306, 307
Holstein, Friedrich von, 21, 119, 126–8, 132–3, 134, 135, 136, 138, 139, 178, 224, 226, 233–4, 236–8, 239, 246, 256 and n., 263, 265, 274, 311, 317, 327; and break with Russia (1890), 231–2; and Moroccan crisis (1905), 318–20
Holz, Arno, 217
Hoover, Herbert Clark, President of the United States, 553, 556
Horthy, Admiral, 743
Hossbach, Friedrich, 700
Hubbe-Schleiden, Wilhelm, 119
Huber, Ernst R., 590
Huber, Kurt, 761
Huber, V. A., 183
Huch, Ricarda, 207–8, 647–8
Hugenberg, Alfred, 348, 360, 361, 362, 364, 508–9, 526, 527–8, 529, 531, 541, 542, 568, 569, 571, 581, 609, 658, 674
Hughes, Charles Evans, 514
Humanistic disciplines: historical studies, 195–7; German studies, 194–5; philology, 194; philosophy, 194
Humboldt, Wilhelm von, 59, 193, 200, 215
Hungary, 677, 705, 726, 742–3, 745
Husserl, Edmund, 194
Hutten-Czapski, Bogdan Count von, 317

I. G. Farben, 606, 617–18
Immermann, Karl, 99
Imperialism and colonies, 30, 116–24, 134, 167, 205, 242–7, 248, 279–80, 364, 403; Colonial Union, 119, 247, 288, 307; Weltpolitik, 249, 275, 306
Impressionism, 218–19
Indemnity Act (1866), 9–10, 143
Independent Socialist party (USPD), 384, 386,

391 n., 401, 404, 406, 409, 432–3, 460, 500
Industrialism, 144, 146, 187, 203, 215 n., 276, 505; industrial pressure groups, 86, 203, 269, 277, 301, 360, 506, 529; industry and Hitler, 556, 558, 584–5, 606–7, 676
Inflation (1919–23), 450–6, 467, 468
Intelligentsia: artists and writers, 214–23, 480–6; Communist, 479; of the right, 486–95; university professors, 193–8, 198–205, 360–2, 422, 479–80
Iron and steel industry, 85, 97, 203, 378, 379, 413, 446, 525; and Fatherland party, 388; and Third Reich, 636
Isabella II, Queen of Spain, 22
Italy, 23, 28, 71, 103, 237, 329, 349, 351–3, 389, 443, 448; Triple Alliance (1882–1914), 115, 130, 232, 236, 321; and Third Reich, 679, 682–3, 684–5, 687–8, 693–6, 702; in World War II, 724, 725, 742; see also Axis
Izvolsky, Alexander, 322, 327

Jacoby, Johann, 9
Jäckh, Ernst, 249, 362 n.
Jagow, F. L. von, 317, 332 n., 378
Japan, 244, 321, 351, 696, 698, 724, 731, 732, 752
Jessner, Leopold, 471
Jesuits, 73–4, 77, 84, 125, 178 n.
Jodl, Colonel-General Alfred, 708, 722, 731, 754, 758
Jörg, Edmund, 18, 21
Jones, Tom, 692
Jünger, Ernst, 492, 493, 494, 565, 663–4, 670
Justice, 66, 158, 420–1, 579–80

Kaas, Monsignor, 504, 533, 578, 581
Kaehler, Siegfried, 762
Kästner, Erich, 483–4, 649, 664
Kahr, Gustav von, 432, 462, 463, 466–7, 589
Kaiser, Georg, 473, 481, 482, 497
Kálnoky, Gustav Count von, 241
Kaltenborn-Stachau, General Hans von, War Minister (1890–3), 258
Kameke, General A. K. G. von, War Minister (1873–83), 162, 163
Kapp, Wolfgang, Generallandschaftsdirektor, 364, 429, 432
Kapp Putsch (1920), 421, 430–1, 432, 438, 454, 507, 562
Kardorff, Wilhelm von, 87, 90
Kayser, Paul, 136, 138, 240, 246 n.
Kegel, Max, 61
Kehr, Eckart, 160, 422
Keim, General August, 258 n., 295
Keitel, Field-Marshal Wilhelm, 700, 708, 714, 716, 722, 733
Kerr, Alfred, 219, 224, 225
Kessler, Harry Count, 396, 490, 510, 542, 561
Ketteler, Bishop Wilhelm Emmanuel von, 63, 71, 88, 152, 183

Keudell, Robert von, 30
Kiaochow, 277, 305, 310, 314
Kiderlen-Wächter, Alfred von, 136, 138, 226, 234, 327–9
Kirdorff, Emil, 348
Kleist, General Ewald von, 719
Kleist-Retzow, Hans von, 9
Knies, Karl, 87, 197
Knilling, Eugen von, 462
Knorr, Admiral von, 306, 307
Koch, Erich, 751
Koch-Weser, Erich, 503
Köller, E. M. von, 271, 272
Kölnische Zeitung, 8, 68, 108, 332, 660
Königgrätz, Battle of (1866), 2, 4, 8, 14, 23, 30, 31, 51, 103, 164, 189, 215 n., 228, 255 n., 581
Kohn, Hans, 661
Kollwitz, Käthe, 217, 646–7
Kolping, Adolf, 63, 183
Kordt, Theo von, 668
Kortner, Fritz, 471
Kracauer, Siegfried, 495, 656
Kreisordnung of 1872, 66–7
Kreuzzeitung, 9, 72, 84, 89, 173, 254, 328, 507
Kruger, Paul, President of the Transvaal, 243, 246, 247
Krupp of Essen, 308, 360
Kühlmann, Richard von, 333, 388, 389, 390, 394
Küstrin Putsch (1923), 459–60
Kulturkampf, see Religion

Laband, Paul, 40, 49
Labour Front (DAF) (1933–45), 583, 594, 605, 623, 624, 625, 664
Lambach, Walter, 507–8
Lammers, Heinrich, 592
Lamprecht, Karl, 196
Lancken, Oskar Count von der, 319–20
Landauer, Gustav, 411, 412, 421
Langbehn, Julius, 188, 202, 487
Lange, Helene, 210, 212
Lansdowne, Lord, 313, 389
Laqueur, Walter, 479
Lasker, Eduard, 21, 68, 69, 77, 82, 83, 84, 96, 166, 171
Lassalle, Ferdinand, 47, 94, 149, 209, 267, 501
Laube, Heinrich, 69
Laval, Pierre, 682, 725, 740, 742 and n.
League of Nations, 516–18, 519, 520, 521, 522, 523, 546, 556, 605, 649, 679–80, 682, 683, 690, 703
Leber, Julius, 420, 500, 501, 665, 666
Leeb, Colonel-General Wilhelm Ritter von, 586, 717, 730
Legien, Carl, 268, 393, 454
Lenau, Nicholas, 59
Lenbach, Franz von, 59
Leo XIII, Pope, 76, 92, 181, 183, 185
Leopold II, King of Belgium, 122

Leuschner, Wilhelm, 665
Levi, Paul, 460
Leviné, Eugen, 411, 412
Ley, Robert, 583, 594, 624, 625, 737
Liberalism, 3, 7, 8, 9, 10, 20, 43, 51, 58, 62, 66, 68, 70–1, 75, 77–8, 87, 89, 99, 102, 143, 162, 166, 167, 179, 487, 488, 505, 506, 541, 641; see also Democratic, Freisinnige, National Liberal, People's, and Progressive parties
Lichtenberg, Dromprobst Bernhard, 667
Liebknecht, Karl, iii n., 403, 409
Liebknecht, Wilhelm, 10, 94, 147, 148, 151, 155, 268
Liliencron, Detlev von, 218–19, 324
Liman von Sanders, General, 337 n.
Lindau, Paul, 217
Lindau, Rudolf, 136
Lipski, Jozef, 709–10
Literature: Gründerzeit, 59, 70; Naturalism, 217, 220–1; Impressionism, 218–19; Expressionism, 221–2, 469, 470, 476; New Objectivity, 483–6; on war, 493; in Third Reich, 646–8
Lithuania, 359, 376, 382, 391, 428, 459, 709
Litvinov, Maxim, 682
Lloyd George, David, 328, 329, 425, 428, 436–7, 438, 443, 721
Locarno, see Treaties
Lohmann, Theodor, 185, 262, 265
Lombardverbot (1887), 132
Lossow, General Otto von, 462, 463
Lothian, Philip Kerr, Marquess of, 683
Ludendorff, General Erich, 294–5, 344–5, 346 n., 348, 363, 368, 369 n., 373–86, 387, 388, 389, 390, 392, 393, 394, 395, 396, 421, 429, 514
Lüderitz, Bremen mercantile firm, 120, 121, 123
Lüders, Else, 212
Lüttwitz, General Walther Freiherr von, 408, 409, 427, 428, 429, 430, 431
Luftwaffe, 606, 610, 684, 722–4, 728, 730
Lukács, Georg, 481
Luthardt, Ernst, 75
Luther, Hans, 467; Reich Chancellor (1925–6), 509, 519, 520
Luxemburg, Grand Duchy of, 16, 17, 23, 46, 316, 382, 403, 716, 718, 743
Luxemburg, Rosa, 403, 409, 460
Lyncker, General Moritz von, Chief of the Military Cabinet (1908–18), 335, 369 n., 373

MacDonald, Ramsay, 515, 675, 687
MacMahon, Maréchal, 28, 106
Maercker, General Ludwig, 407–8, 409, 410, 427
Mahan, Alfred Thayer, 307, 369
Makart, Hans, 82
Malaparte, Curzio, 762

Mann, Heinrich, 100, 220–1, 222, 223, 469, 639, 646–7, 652

Mann, Klaus, 477, 478, 645

Mann, Thomas, 222 n., 415, 469, 472, 482, 484, 490, 491, 573, 639, 640, 647, 663

Manstein, Field-Marshal Friedrich Erich von, 719, 720, 730, 754

Manteuffel, Edwin von, 7, 51, 142, 144, 161

Marlitt, Eugenie, 211

Marschall von Bieberstein, Adolf Freiherr, 231, 233, 242 n., 245, 246 and n., 247, 271 and n., 272

Marx, Karl, 94, 152, 267, 403

Marx, Wilhelm, Reich Chancellor (1926–8), 504, 510, 524

Mason, Tim, 630

Materialism, 78, 81–2, 203, 204, 214, 219–20, 325, 337, 338

Max von Baden, Prince, Reich Chancellor (1918), 397, 399–401, 402

Mayer, Oskar, 532

Mecklenburg, 11, 13, 58, 66

Mehring, Franz, 65, 78, 95, 153 f., 167, 215 n., 403

Mehring, Walter, 534, 627

Meidner, Ludwig, 220–1

Mein Kampf, 546–7, 674–6, 691

Meinecke, Friedrich, 180, 196, 341, 362, 395, 398, 408, 661, 739, 762–3

Meissner, Otto, 556, 576, 592

Memel question, 459, 709

Menzel, Adolf, 215 n.

Metternich, Clemens Prince, 22

Mevissen, Gustav, 8

Meyer, Conrad Ferdinand, 59, 70, 215

Michaelis, Georg, Reich Chancellor (1917), 385, 388

Michels, Robert, 202

Middle class: feudalization of upper, 99–100, 160, 220; *Mittelstand* organizations, 360, 455–6, 550–2, 557, 581, 584; patriotism, 288, 291 n.

Mierendorff, Carlo, 665

Minoux, Friedrich, 462

Miquel, Johannes, 10, 70, 107, 167, 171, 176, 255 and n., 260, 264, 267, 274, 277, 308

Mittnacht, Freiherr von, 157

Moellendorff, Wichard von, 413

Moeller van den Bruck, Arthur, 487–9, 490, 493, 494

Moldenhauer, Paul, 530, 532, 537

Molotov, Vyacheslav, 727

Moltke, General Field-Marshal Helmuth Count von, Chief of the General Staff (1857–88), 3, 4, 31, 32, 33, 50, 51, 95, 107, 108, 133, 134, 161, 315, 316, 365

Moltke, Field-Marshal Helmuth J. L. Count von, Chief of the General Staff (1906–14), 294, 295, 315, 323, 324, 329, 332, 336, 343–4, 350

Moltke, Helmuth Count von, resistance leader, 667

Mommsen, Theodor, 193, 195, 201, 203, 204

Mommsen, Theodor Ernst, 661

Mommsen, Wolfgang J., 292

Montenegro, 113, 331

Montgomery, Lieutenant-General Bernard Law, 753

Monts, Alfred Count, 286 and n., 287

Morier, Sir Robert, 170

Moroccan crises: (1905), 318–21; (1911), 291, 293, 327–9

Mosse, George L., 84

Most, Johannes, 147, 148, 149

Motteler, Julius, 148 n.

Mühsam, Erich, 411, 412, 481, 574

Müller, Admiral Georg Alexander von, Chief of the Naval Cabinet (1913–18), 368, 383

Müller, Hermann, 433, 509; Reich Chancellor (1928–30), 524–33, 536

Münster, Georg Herbert Prince of Derneburg, 120, 121 and n., 137, 139, 234, 315, 327

Munich, 216, 219

Munich Conference (1938), *see* Conferences

Music, 222 and n., 474–5, 650–1

Mussert, Anton, 740

Mussolini, Benito, 351, 682–3, 684, 687–8, 691, 693–4, 696, 707, 711, 712, 725, 726, 728, 753

Nachtigal, Gustav, 121

Nadolny, Rudolf, 678, 680

Napoleon Bonaparte, 26, 187, 192

Napoleon III, Emperor of the French, 4, 5, 6, 14, 16, 17, 24, 25, 27, 28, 29, 31

National Assembly (1919), 403, 405, 412–13, 414, 415–19, 502

National Liberal party, 10, 21, 47, 63–9, 83, 84, 85, 91, 92, 95, 96, 97, 98, 156, 166, 167, 168, 169, 173, 175, 189, 253, 254, 269, 277, 278, 279, 280, 289, 292, 359, 372, 384, 385, 394, 413, 503, 506; and *Daily Telegraph* affair, 285 n.

National People's party (DNVP), 413, 433, 466, 469, 487, 506–9, 510, 511, 513, 514, 517, 519, 528, 531, 539, 542, 552, 574, 581, 584

National Socialism, 423, 456, 466, 482, 501, 572, 597, 610, 625, 657, 762; intellectuals and, 639–45

National Socialist Workers' party (NSDAP), 456, 510, 511, 513, 519, 534, 539, 540, 542, 548, 549–53, 556–7, 562, 563, 564, 566, 567, 568, 581, 582, 622, 625, 696; Hitlerjugend, 655, 662, 666; Schutzstaffel (SS), 556, 559–60, 561, 572, 573, 576, 583, 588, 589, 590, 597–601, 625, 736, 741, 745, 747–8, 750–1; Sturmabteilung (SA), 556, 559–60, 561, 563, 572, 573, 576, 583, 585, 586–90, 597, 598, 632, 633, 682; and women, 627 ff.

Nationalism, 18, 24, 27, 29–30, 33, 43–4,

Nationalism—*contd.*
55–60, 206, 288, 421, 423–4; national symbols, 58; as tool against socialism, 205
Natural and experimental sciences, 193
Naturalism, 210, 216–18, 222 n.
Naumann, Friedrich, 185, 205, 206, 212, 249, 262, 265, 276, 281 n., 285 n., 288, 393, 398, 503
Navalism, 205, 276, 296; Naval League (Flottenverein), 280, 288, 295, 308; propaganda, 307, 312
Navy, 229, 231, 246; early history, 303, 304 n.; Executive Command (Oberkommando), 305; Imperial Naval Office (Reichsmarineamt), 305, 309; naval attachés, 330; Naval Cabinet, 304, 309; risk theory (Risikogedanke), 309–10; in World War I, 342–3, 350, 369–70; Kiel mutiny (1918), 398–400; and Weimar Republic, 524–5; and Third Reich, 618, 686–7; in World War II, 717–18, 738, 752, 753
Navy laws: (1898), 282 n., 308, 309; (1900), 276, 282 n., 308, 311, 312; (1906), 282 n., 326; (1908), 326
Near Eastern crisis (1875), 90, 110–13
Neumann, Franz, 602
Neurath, Konstantin Baron von, 677, 697, 701
New Objectivity, *see* Literature
Niemöller, Martin, 667
Nietzsche, Friedrich, 35, 36, 59, 182, 187, 188, 192, 214, 487, 490, 644
Nobiling, Dr. Karl, 95, 145
Norddeutsche Allgemeine Zeitung, 68, 106
Norway, 717, 743
Noske, Gustav, 399, 405, 532; Minister of Defence (1919–20), 407–10, 412, 413, 427, 428, 430, 431

Ollivier, Émile, 24, 27
Oppenheimer, H. B., 84, 123
Ossietzky, Carl von, 485, 574
Ott, Colonel Eugen, 564
Otto-Peters, Louise, 210

Pabst, Captain Waldemar, 410, 412, 429
Pacelli, Cardinal Eugenio, 581
Painting: Naturalism and Impressionism, 216–17; Sezession, 216–17; Expressionism, 221–2, 470, 649–50; in Third Reich, 649–50, 653–4, 660
Pan-German League, 205, 206, 247, 249, 280, 288, 290 n., 301, 307, 325, 336, 358, 360–2, 363, 364, 365, 395, 508, 527
Pan-Slavism, 102, 103, 111, 112, 113, 114, 115, 124, 134, 334, 348
Papal infallibility, doctrine of (1870), 70
Papen, Franz von, 505, 567, 568, 569, 570, 572, 589, 642; Reich Chancellor (1932), 560–5
Paquet, Alfons, 647

Particularism, 34, 42, 43, 46, 253, 255, 418, 421, 432, 467, 596–7
Paulsen, Friedrich, 190 n., 193, 200, 201, 202, 205 n.
Paulus, Field-Marshal Friedrich von, 756
Payer, Friedrich, 285
Penitentiary Bill (1899), 265
People's party (DVP), 413, 433, 439, 444, 505–6, 509, 511, 524, 525, 526, 528, 529, 531, 532, 533, 539, 540, 581
Pétain, Maréchal, 725, 744
Peters, Carl, 119, 122, 123, 204
Pflanze, Otto, 43
Philippi, Felix, 81
Phipps, Sir Eric, 685–6
Pilsudski, Marshal Jozef, 680, 681
Pius IX, Pope, 70, 76
Planck, Erwin, 667
Planck, Max, 362
Plessen, Colonel-General Hans von, 335, 347, 369 n.
Pöhner, Ernst, 432
Poincaré, Raymond, 334, 443, 444, 447, 448, 458, 516, 519, 522
Poland, 80, 316, 348, 359, 363, 365, 375–6, 382, 391, 407, 408, 512, 513, 518, 519, 520, 522, 564, 586, 675, 687; Nazi–Polish Pact (1934), 680–2; Danzig question, 701, 709–12; in World War II, 619, 713, 715–16, 726, 744, 745, 747, 751
Popitz, Johannes von, 530
Posadowsky-Wehner, Count von, 264, 272 n.
Press Law (1874), 68–9
Preußische Jahrbücher, 8, 118, 154, 201, 204, 361, 489
Prim, Marshal, 22
Prittwitz und Gafron, Friedrich Wilhem Baron von, 677
Progressive party, 8, 9, 10, 12, 64, 96, 124, 156, 160, 167, 212, 253, 254, 259, 271, 280, 290, 295, 367, 384, 502
Prussia, 2, 4, 5, 6, 11, 12, 13, 14, 18, 23, 24, 33, 63, 406; Academy of Arts, 639, 646–9; constitution of 1850, 142, 143; constitutional conflict (1862–6), 3, 7–10, 47, 51, 64, 68, 78, 142–3; education, 254, 279, 281; local self-government, 66–7; Polish districts, 12, 19, 62, 63, 72, 289, 290, 299 n.; and Reich, 42–3, 255, 278, 419, 529, 561–2, 572, 574, 599; suffrage, 43, 281, 289, 381–2, 385, 393
Puttkamer, Robert von, 99, 148, 157–9

Quidde, Ludwig, 362
Quisling, Vidkun, 717, 743

Raabe, Wilhelm, 78, 84, 215 n.
Radbruch, Gustav, 420
Radio, 496
Radolin-Radolinski, H. L. von, 233

Radowitz, J. M. von, 21, 108, 109, 126, 137, 232, 233, 237
Raeder, Grand Admiral Erich, 698, 717, 721, 722, 725, 729, 753
Railways, 80, 85, 98, 125
Ranke, Leopold von, 195–6
Rantzau, Kuno von, 135, 138
Raschdau, Ludwig von, 135, 232, 233
Rathenau, Walther, 354, 357, 413, 441–4, 445, 457, 493, 517, 607, 734
Rauschning, Hermann, 588, 678, 681
Reichenau, General Walter von, 567, 586, 589, 704
Reichensperger, August, 77
Reichsbanner, 465 n., 559, 561, 576, 580, 664
Reichspartei, see Free Conservative party
Reichstag, 39, 40, 43, 45–9, 51–3, 64–6, 73, 86, 88, 91, 92, 95, 97, 119, 124, 129, 134, 144, 145, 146 n., 147, 149, 163, 171, 251–2, 271, 339; coup d'état against?, 144, 174–5; Daily Telegraph affair, 283–5; Kartell (1887–90), 169, 170, 173, 253, 275; and naval appropriations, 306–9, 327; stalemate of party system (1912–14), 292; Zabern debate (1913), 298–301; in World War I, 339, 367, 379, 380, 381, 382, 384, 385, 387, 393, 394; in Weimar Republic, 416–17, 459, 511, 515, 519, 527–8, 538–9, 540; after 1933, 571, 577, 582, 613, 637, 732
Reichstag elections: (1881), 156–7; (1884), 164, 166–8; (1887), 169; (1890), 175; (1893), 259; (1898), 278; (1903), 278; (1907), 280–1; (1912), 291–2; (1920), 432–3; (1930), 540–3
Reichwein, Adolf, 666
Reinhard, Colonel Wilhelm, 408, 412, 415
Reinhardt, Max, 403, 472
Reinhardt, General Walther, Chief of the Army Command (1919–20), 426, 428, 430, 461
Religion, 325; Kulturkampf, 69–78; Modernism and doctrinal criticism, 181–2; strength of established churches, 181, 476
Remarque, Erich Maria, 451, 453, 493, 646, 649
Reparations, 425, 436–48, 449, 459, 514, 526–8, 530, 539, 554, 555, 561
Reuß, Prince Henry VII, 126, 134, 136, 138
Reuter, Ernst, 460
Reuter, Gabriele, 211
Rhineland, 63, 426, 437, 447, 459, 465, 515, 517–19, 521, 522, 523, 526, 528, 555, 679, 685; remilitarization (1936), 611, 675, 688–91, 697, 699
Ribbentrop, Joachim von, 595, 596, 686, 692–3, 696; Foreign Minister (1938–45), 595, 701, 702–3, 709–10, 712–13, 724, 727, 732
Richter, Eugen, 156, 161, 162 n.
Riefenstahl, Leni, 545, 623, 630, 656–7
Riezler, Kurt, 335, 337, 348 n., 352 n., 365–6, 369 n., 381
Rilke, Rainer Maria, 180, 219, 469, 475

Ringer, Fritz, 191
Ritschl, Albrecht, 182, 185, 186
Roehm, Ernst, 462, 587–8, 589, 595, 597, 599, 600
Rößler, Konstantin, 108
Roggenbach, Franz von, 165, 175
Rohrbach, Paul, 249, 362 n.
Roman Catholic Church, 181; anti-Catholic feeling, 69–72; and education, 72, 254, 279; Kulturkampf, 74–8, 90, 106, 254; and National Socialism, 577, 581–2, 666–7; Social Catholicism, 63, 183; Vatican Council (1869–70), 70
Romania, 80, 113, 125, 232, 239, 351, 353, 371, 374, 383, 391, 610, 726, 727, 728, 743, 745
Rommel, General Erwin, 729, 736, 751, 753, 757
Roon, Albrecht von, War Minister (1859–73), 5, 51, 52, 55
Roosevelt, Franklin D., President of the United States, 538, 569, 604, 710, 724
Roscher, Wilhelm, 87, 197
Rosebery, Lord, 237, 241, 243
Rosenberg, Alfred, 595, 596, 646, 737, 751
Rosenberg, Hans, 98
Rote Kapelle, 665, 668
Roth, Guenther, 270
Rothfels, Hans, 661
Rouher, Eugène, 23
Ruge, Arnold, 27
Rumbold, Sir Horace, 537, 674–5
Rumelin, Gustav, 35, 48
Rundstedt, Field-Marshal Gerd von, 586, 719, 730, 756, 757
Russell, Lord Odo, 125
Russia, 15, 23, 24, 29, 31, 90, 102, 103, 110–16, 124–34, 170, 178, 242, 275, 277, 310; Reinsurance Treaty (1887), 131–2, 139, 231–2; rapprochement with France (1890–3), 237–9; alienation from Germany (1902–14), 314, 321, 329; in World War I, 344–5, 348–9, 372, 375–6, 389, 391; see also Soviet Union
Rust, Bernhard, 647, 660

SA, see National Socialist Workers' party
Saar, 522, 684, 697; plebiscite (1935), 683–4
Saburov, Petr Alexandrovich, 115
Sackett, Frederic M., 537, 554
Salandra, Antonio, 351, 352
Salazar, Eusebio, 22
Salisbury, Robert Cecil, 3rd Marquis of, 113, 130, 131, 139, 235, 243
Salomon, Ernst von, 444 n., 762
Sammlungspolitik, 255 n., 274–6, 302, 308
Samoa, 118, 242, 244, 311
Sarajevo, 334, 336
Sauckel, Fritz, 594, 597, 735, 746
Sauer, Wolfgang, 143
Savigny, Karl Friedrich von, 12
Saxe-Weimar, 11, 13

Saxony, 5, 6, 11, 13, 34, 41, 94, 205, 256, 278, 359, 455, 458, 460–2, 463–4

Scavenius, Erik, 742

Schacht, Hjalmar Greeley, 467, 530, 531, 585, 591, 602, 603, 608, 610, 611, 614, 615, 632, 633, 634

Schäfer, Dietrich, 362, 363

Scheffer, Paul, 659

Scheidemann, Philip, 299, 300, 401; Reich Chancellor (1919), 425, 426, 509

Scherer, Wilhelm, 195

Schickele, René, 648

Schieder, Theodor, 58

Schiele, Martin, 519, 537

Schiller, Friedrich, 57, 214, 216, 403, 415, 471, 472, 652–3, 763

Schirach, Baldur von, 653, 662

Schleicher, General Kurt von, 406, 535, 554, 559–65, 589; Reich Chancellor (1932), 565–7

Schlieffen, Alfred Count von, Chief of the General Staff (1891–1906), 228, 257, 258, 294, 316, 319, 337, 354, 720; Schlieffen Plan, 310 n., 315, 316–17, 323, 332, 336, 343, 719

Schlözer, Kurd von, 138, 233

Schmitt, Carl, 494, 641–2, 645

Schmoller, Gustav, 87, 96, 97, 119, 197

Schoenbaum, David, 621

Schönberg, Arnold, 469, 475

Scholl, Hans and Sophie, 761

Scholz, Ernst, 506, 509, 530, 531

Schücking, Levin, 362

Schulenburg, Werner Count von der, 667, 727

Schuschnigg, Kurt von, 694, 702

Schwabach, Paul, 123

Schwarzenberg, Felix Prince zu, 168

Schwarzkoppen, Colonel, 315

Schweinitz, Lothar von, 120, 136, 159, 174, 232, 233 and n.

Schweitzer, J. B., 94

Schwerin von Krosigk, Count Lutz, 591, 592, 595

Secessionist party (1881–4), 156, 161, 166, 167

Sedan, Battle of (1870), 28–9, 31, 51, 124, 214

Seeckt, Colonel-General Hans von, 363, 430, 567, 586, 669, 680; Chief of the Army Command (1920–6), 431, 438, 448, 460, 463, 485, 490, 513, 519, 520, 521, 523

Seeley, Sir John, 119

Seisser, Hans Ritter von, 462, 463

Seldte, Franz, 508, 527, 568, 581, 594, 625

Senden-Bibran, Admiral Freiherr von, 304, 305 n., 306, 307

Serbia, 113, 125, 322, 323, 331, 333, 334–6, 345–6, 350, 351, 353, 382, 395; see also Yugoslavia

Severing, Carl, 532, 664 n.

Seyß-Inquart, Artur, 741

Shimoneseki (1895), 244

Shuvalov, Peter Andreievich, 111, 112, 113, 127, 230

Sichler, Richard, 356, 357

Siemens corporation, 463

Siemens, Georg von, 99

Simmel, Georg, 198

Simon, Sir John, 683, 684, 685, 686

Singer, Paul, 147

Snowden, Philip, 526

Social Democratic party (SPD), 64, 93–4, 95, 96, 118, 151, 152, 161, 169, 212, 254, 259, 264, 271, 278, 290, 292, 300; conferences, 94, 149–50, 266, 499, 500, 501, 510; patriotism, 267, 288, 296; Press, 95, 146, 148, 266, 268; revisionism, 266–9, 292, 403; Socialist Law (1878–90), 96, 144–50, 155–6, 166–7, 168, 173–8; and World War I, 340–1, 357, 359, 367, 379, 382, 383, 384, 391; and revolution of 1918, 400, 402, 403, 404, 405; and Weimar Republic, 412, 418, 426, 432–3, 444, 445, 457, 459, 460, 461, 466, 467, 476, 485, 499–502, 503, 513, 519, 521, 524, 525, 531, 532, 533, 539, 542, 559, 561; after 1933, 573, 575, 577–8, 580–1, 664–6; see also Independent Socialist party, Socialism

Social insurance legislation, 150–2, 153, 166, 167, 288

Social Policy Association (Verein für Sozialpolitik), 87, 197, 263, 362

Social sciences: economics, 197; psychology, 198; sociology, 198

Socialism, 49, 93, 94, 102, 145, 202, 263, 275

Socialization Commission (1918–19), 413

Soldiers' and workers' councils, 401, 402, 404, 405, 406, 411, 500

Sombart, Werner, 360

Soviet Union, 444, 512, 513, 516–17, 520, 521, 523, 586, 610, 668, 680, 681, 682, 683, 688, 689, 703, 705, 706, 710, 717, 725–6; Nazi–Soviet Pact (1939), 711–13, 726; in World War II, 727–8, 739–40, 745, 751, 752

Spahn, Martin, 200, 201, 281

Spain, 312, 520, 615; succession question (1868–70), 22–7; Civil War (1936–9), 693–6; in World War II, 725, 742

Spartacus Union, 402, 403, 404, 405, 406, 407, 408, 409, 412

Speer, Albert, 594, 612 n., 631, 654, 733–5, 740, 744, 752–3, 754, 757, 760, 761

Spengler, Oswald, 396, 402, 487, 489–92, 565, 644

Spielhagen, Friedrich, 57, 80–1, 82, 215 n.

Sports, 496–7

Springer, Anton, 199

SS, see National Socialist Workers' party

Stahlhelm, 485, 508, 522, 526, 527, 572, 576, 581, 586

Stalin, Josef, 464, 465, 712, 728, 740

Stampfer, Friedrich, 403, 427

States' rights, 34, 40–3, 54, 55, 66, 97, 419; end of (1933), 576, 578, 582–3

Stauffenberg, Colonel Claus Schenk von, 669–70, 672
Stauffenberg, Freiherr von, 92, 156
Stegerwald, Adam, 445, 575
Sternheim, Carl, 220, 221, 222, 251, 402, 472
Stimson, Henry L., 537
Stinnes, Hugo, 348, 375, 387, 438, 439, 442, 443, 451–2, 453, 454, 462, 466, 489, 505
Stoecker, Adolf, 152–6, 171, 172, 184, 185, 254, 276
Stöpel, Friedrich, 87
Stolper, Gustav, 439
Storm, Theodor, 82
Stosch, General Albrecht von, Chief of the Admiralty (1827–83), 59, 162, 165, 231 n., 275, 304, 306 and n.
Strasser, Gregor, 550, 565, 566, 589
Strasser, Otto, 489, 546, 584
Strauß, David Friedrich, 181, 182
Strauß, Richard, 650–1
Stresa Front (1935), 684–5, 687
Stresemann, Gustav, 384, 385, 413, 445, 447, 454 n., 468, 481, 505–6, 529, 537, 541, 543, 547, 556, 595, 678, 697; Reich Chancellor (1923), 457–67; Foreign Minister (1924–9), 498, 511–28, 544
Strousberg, Bethel, 80, 82
Stürmer, Michael, 55
Stumm, Ferdinand von, 233
Stumm-Halberg, Carl Freiherr von, 185, 202, 203, 256, 263, 266
Subversion Bill (1894–5), 202, 259, 260, 263–4
Sudermann, Hermann, 200, 217
Sweden, 742
Switzerland, 742
Sybel, Heinrich von, 69 n., 119, 195, 196 n.
Syllabus Errorum (1864), 70

Tariffs: (1879), 97, 98, 102, 113; (1888), 173; (1902), 276–8, 314
Taylor, Telford, 723
Textile industry, 86–7
Thälmann, Ernst, 510, 558, 561
Theatre, 70, 216, 217, 219–20, 471–2; Expressionist, 469, 471–3; in Third Reich, 652–3
Thiers, Adolphe, 32, 33, 106
Third Reich: administration, 591–7; arts and letters, 639–57; concentration and extermination camps, 600, 748–51, 762; constitutional theory, 590–1; education, 660–3; Enabling Act (1933), 577–8; and European New Order, 740–51; euthanasia programme, 739, 749; February Decrees (1933), 574–5; Gauleiter, 597, 611, 625, 626, 671, 735, 741, 760; Gleichschaltung, 578–90, 676, 678, 684; labour policy, 621–7; local government, 596; Press, 634, 657–60, 737–9; Propaganda Ministry, 573, 596, 655, 671, 703, 737–40; rearmament, 605, 608, 610, 611,

614, 616, 618–19, 669, 676, 678, 684, 691; Reichskultuskammer, 646, 647, 649, 650, 655, 663; resistance movement, 663–72, 761; security forces, 597–601; and women, 627–31; see also Anti-Semitism, National Socialism, National Socialist Workers' party
Thomas, General Georg, 606, 619, 621, 625, 626, 733
Thuringia, 11, 458, 461–2, 463, 476
Thyssen, Fritz, 348, 527, 585
Tiedemann, Christoph von, 69 n.
Tirpitz, Grand Admiral Alfred von, 204, 249, 272 n., 275, 293, 332, 337, 343, 364, 369–72, 388, 426; early career, 303–7; at the Naval Office, 307–14, 325, 327; Haldane mission, 330
Tisza, Count Stefan, 353
Todt, Fritz, 594, 727, 734
Todt, Rudolf, 152
Tönnies, Friedrich, 198, 201 and n., 362
Toller, Ernst, 411, 412, 473, 481
Trade unions, 146, 147 n., 183, 267, 268, 379, 386, 387, 414, 445, 446, 453–4, 460, 502, 509, 524, 529, 532, 533, 561–2, 565, 576, 583, 622, 664
Transvaal, 243, 245–7
Treaties: Paris (1856), 23, 31; Prague (1866), 6, 8, 11, 14; Frankfurt (1871), 33, 103, 104, 106; Mediterranean Agreements (1887), 131, 132, 235; Reinsurance (1887), 131–2, 139, 231–2; London (1915), 353; Brest-Litovsk (1918), 389–92; Bucharest (1918), 391; Versailles (1919), 424–32, 436, 512, 515, 525, 527, 546, 608, 634, 672, 676, 684, 686; Rapallo (1922), 444, 517, 520; Locarno (1925), 510, 511, 513, 516–19, 520, 521, 526, 685, 688, 689, 692; Berlin (1926), 520; Polish–German (1934), 680–2, 697, 710; Anglo–German Naval Accord (1935), 686–7, 710; Franco-Soviet Pact (1935), 683, 688, 689, 690, 693; Anti-Comintern Pact (1937), 696, 710; Pact of Steel (1939), 711; Nazi–Soviet Pact (1939), 712; Tripartite Pact (1940), 724, 731
Treitschke, Heinrich, 30, 42, 48–9, 57, 58, 59, 66, 70, 71, 72, 95, 97, 119, 145, 154, 195, 204–5, 422
Tresckow, Major-General Henning von, 672
Treviranus, Gottfried, 536, 542, 555
Trochu, Général, 31
Troeltsch, Ernst, 196, 362, 433 n.
Trott zu Solz, Adam von, 668
Tucholsky, Kurt, 434, 485–6, 499, 627, 638, 649
Turkey, 110–13, 131, 239, 242, 286, 314, 321–2, 329, 333, 337, 349–51, 395, 725, 727, 742
Twesten, Karl, 10

United States of America, 38, 44, 46, 88, 166,

United States of America—*contd.*
303, 312, 370, 376, 377, 381, 443, 447, 554, 608, 724, 731–2, 739, 752
Urbanization, 83, 181

Valentini, Rudolf von, Chief of the Civil Cabinet (1908–18), 286, 378 n., 381, 383, 390
Van Hoddis, Jakob, 221
Vansittart, Sir Robert, 555, 675, 686–7, 701, 702
Vaterlandspartei, *see* Fatherland party
Vatican, 70, 106, 108, 352, 578
Verein deutscher Studenten, 154 n., 206
Verein für Sozialpolitik, *see* Social Policy Association
Versailles Treaty, *see* Treaties
Versen, Major von, 25
Victoria, Empress of Germany, 170; as Crown Princess, 130, 164, 165, 224
Victoria, Queen of Great Britain, 109, 130, 164, 170, 224, 304
Virchow, Rudolf, 9, 74, 193, 202, 203
Vögler, A., 505
Vollmar, Georg, 148, 266–7, 501
Vorwärts, 95, 146, 268, 400, 403, 407
Vossler, Otto, 93

Wächter, Theodor von, 185
Wagener, Hermann, 12, 82
Wagner, Adolf, economist, 87, 89, 119, 197, 202, 203, 361
Wagner, Adolf, Gauleiter, 599
Wagner, General Eduard, 716
Wagner, Richard, 215 and n., 476, 650
Wahl, Adalbert, 422
Waldersee, Field-Marshal Alfred Count von, 133, 134, 161, 162, 318; Chief of the General Staff (1888–91), 171, 172, 176 n., 228, 315, 316; Commanding General 9th Army Corps, 256, 263, 264, 265, 266, 272, 274
Wandel, General von, War Minister (1915), 157
Warlimont, General Walter, 731
Wars: Danish (1864), 8, 88; Austro-Prussian (1866), 1–6, 14, 16; Franco-Prussian (1870–1), 14, 27–34, 94; Russo-Turkish (1877–8), 90, 110–11; Spanish-American (1898), 308; Boer (1899–1901), 276, 283 n., 302, 312, 319; Russo-Japanese (1905), 319; Balkan (1912–13), 329, 331, 333, 334; Abyssinian (1935–6), 684, 687–8, 693; Spanish Civil (1936–9), 615, 693–5, 698; Russo-Finnish (1939), 716, 717; *see also* World War I, World War II
Wavell, Field-Marshal Sir Archibald, 729
Weber, Ernst von, 118
Weber, Max, 198, 202, 249, 251, 275, 276 n., 362 n., 494, 503
Wedekind, Frank, 219–20, 221, 222
Wedel, General Karl von, 234, 297, 299, 300

Wehrverein, 295, 363
Weidfeldt, Otto von, 462
Weill, Kurt, 475, 651
Weimar Republic: Civil Service, 419–20; constitution, 416–19; cultural activities, 469–76, 495–7; economic problems, 435–50, 453–4, 456–7, 528–33; education, 421–4; intellectual opposition, 479–95; judiciary, 420; manners and morals, 476–9; party system, 416, 417–18, 499–511, 524–33; social problems, 454–5; taxes, 419, 449–50, 453, 458; unemployment, 448, 457, 528–30, 538, 553, 566
Weissler, Friedrich, 667
Weizsäcker, Ernst von, 702, 708
Wellhausen, Julius, 182
Wels, Otto, 577, 580
Weltbühne, Die, 485
Werder, General Bernhard von, 233
Werfel, Franz, 470, 476, 480, 482, 639
Wermuth, Adolf, 290–1, 293, 294
Werner, Anton von, 50, 215 n.
Werthern, Georg Freiherr von, 20, 21, 137
Westarp, Count, 507, 508, 519, 542
Wichern, J. H., 183
Widenmann, Captain Wilhelm, 331
William I, King and Emperor, 5, 6, 9, 16, 17, 19, 22, 24, 25, 26, 27, 30, 31, 32–3, 34, 44, 45, 52, 53, 62, 71, 92, 93, 95, 105, 109, 119, 134, 145, 155 n., 162, 164, 168, 170, 184, 228, 264
William II, King and Emperor, 49, 136, 160, 171–4, 176–8, 184, 185, 189, 254, 256, 261, 270, 273–4, 286–7, 293, 297–301, 314, 324, 328, 330, 331–2, 337, 340, 343, 422, 426, 470, 543, 763; abdication, 398–402; and army, 228–30, 258–9, 270–2, 298; character and temperament, 224–30; *Daily Telegraph* affair, 283–4, 367, 390; and foreign policy, 230–50, 303, 318; Kruger telegram, 246–7; and navy, 304, 305, 309, 310; as Prince, 127, 171, 304; and Reichstag, 259, 260, 292, 300–1; and Social Democratic party, 263–4; in World War I, 367–8, 369 n., 371, 372, 373–5, 377, 380, 381, 383, 385, 388, 389, 390, 393, 398
William, Crown Prince of Prussia, 297 n., 301, 336, 362 n., 385, 517
Wilson, Sir Horace, 706
Wilson, Woodrow, President of the United States, 370, 377, 392, 398, 410, 424
Windthorst, Ludwig, 50, 69 n., 73, 76, 78, 88, 89, 177, 178
Wirth, Josef, Reich Chancellor (1921–2), 433, 438, 441–6, 504
Wirtschaftspartei, 537, 541
Wissell, Rudolf, 413–14, 529, 530, 532
Wittelsbach dynasty, 22, 359
Woermann, Adolf, 123, 279
Wolff, Theodor, 361, 503, 658, 659
Wolff-Metternich, Count, 329
Wolzogen, Ernst von, 206

Women: Baum's *Helene Willfüer*, 478–9; education, 207–8, 212, 422, 423, 478; Fontane's
Effi Briest, 208–9; rights' associations, 210,
212; workers, 478, 627–31, 734–6
Working class, 58, 191, 203, 265, 269, 338, 430,
481; foreign workers in Third Reich, 746;
and higher education, 189–92, 423; laws
governing working conditions, 173, 253,
262; salaried employees, 506, 507; in Third
Reich, 620–7, 734–6; white-collar workers,
456, 551–2; women workers, 210, 627–31,
734–6; *see also* Social insurance legislation
World War I, 339–42; economic mobilization,
354–5; food supplies, 367, 386, 387, 393;
manpower allocation, 355–6, 378, 386; naval
operations, 342–3, 350, 369–71, 380, 384;
negotiated peace, 348, 375, 376–7, 382, 383,
384, 389, 394, 395; operations in Eastern
Europe, 344–5, 349, 372; operations in Near
East, 350, 395; operations in Western
Europe, 343–4, 347, 372–3, 393–4, 394–5;
strikes, 382, 386, 387, 397–8; taxes, 356–7;
war aims, 348, 358–9, 360–2, 363–5, 366–7,
377, 382–3
World War II, 714–62; Polish campaign, 619,
715; Norwegian campaign, 717–18; Low
Countries and France (1940), 718–20; Battle
of Britain, 722–5; Yugoslavia and Greece
(1941), 728–9; North Africa, 779, 751–2,
753; Russian campaigns, 730–1, 752, 753–4,
757–8, 762; Italian campaign (1943–5), 757;
Western Europe (1944–5), 751, 762; Allied
bombing offensive, 758–9, 761; economic
mobilization, 733–6, 760; home front,
732–40, 758–62
Württemberg, 6, 15, 18, 19, 27, 30, 33–4, 41,
359, 398, 576

York von Wartenburg, Peter Count, 667
Young German Order (Jungdo), 504, 541
Young Germany, 59, 60, 209, 216, 222 n.
Young Plan (1929), 417, 508, 526–8, 530, 539,
546, 554, 555, 561
Youth, problem of, 477–8, 494–5
Yugoslavia, 728, 744, 751

Zedlitz-Trützschler, Robert Count von, 254
Zehrer, Hans, 463, 494, 565
Zeigner, Erich, 461–2, 464, 465, 466
Zetkin, Clara, 210, 628
Zhukhov, Marshal Georgi Konstantinovich,
730
Zille, Heinrich, 217
Zimmermann, Arthur, 335, 348, 373, 378 n.,
381, 383
Zollverein and Zollparlament, 15, 17, 19, 65,
157 n.
Zweig, Stefan, 651, 652